Geometry

(A = area, B = area of base, C = circumference, S = lateral area or surface area, V = volume)

1. Triangle

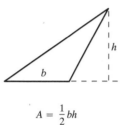

$$A = \frac{1}{2}bh$$

2. Similar Triangles

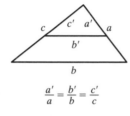

$$\frac{a'}{a} = \frac{b'}{b} = \frac{c'}{c}$$

3. Pythagorean Theorem

$$a^2 + b^2 = c^2$$

4. Parallelogram

$$A = bh$$

5. Trapezoid

$$A = \frac{1}{2}(a + b)h$$

6. Circle

$$A = \pi r^2, \quad C = 2\pi r$$

7. Any Cylinder or Prism with Parallel Bases

$$V = Bh$$

8. Right Circular Cylinder

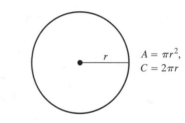

$$V = \pi r^2 h, \; S = 2\pi rh$$

9. Any Cone or Pyramid

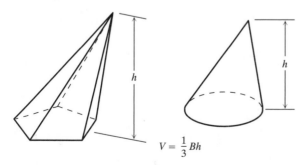

$$V = \frac{1}{3}Bh$$

10. Right Circular Cone

$$V = \frac{1}{3}\pi r^2 h, \; S = \pi rs$$

11. Sphere

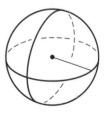

$$V = \frac{4}{3}\pi r^3, \; S = 4\pi r^2$$

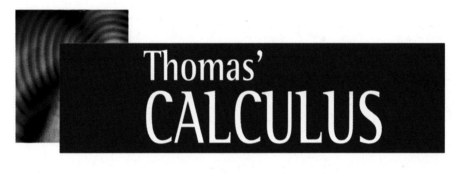

Thomas'
CALCULUS

TENTH EDITION

PART II

Thomas' CALCULUS

TENTH EDITION
PART II

Based on the original work by
George B. Thomas, Jr.
Massachusetts Institute of Technology

As revised by
Ross L. Finney
Maurice D. Weir
Naval Postgraduate School
and
Frank R. Giordano

Addison
Wesley

Boston San Francisco New York
London Toronto Sydney Tokyo Singapore Madrid
Mexico City Munich Paris Cape Town Hong Kong Montreal

Publisher	Greg Tobin
Senior Editor	Laurie Rosatone
Associate Project Editor	Ellen Keohane
Editorial Assistant	Susan Laferriere
Managing Editor	Karen Guardino
Senior Production Supervisor	Becky Malone
Editorial and Production Services	UG / GGS Information Services, Inc.
Art Editor	Geri Davis/The Davis Group, Inc.
Marketing Manager	Carter Fenton
Illustrators	Tech Graphics\cs
Technical Art Consultants	Scott Silva and Joe Vetere
Senior Prepress Supervisor	Caroline Fell
Compositor	UG / GGS Information Services, Inc.
Text Designer	Geri Davis/The Davis Group, Inc.
Cover Designer	Barbara T. Atkinson
Print Buyer	Evelyn Beaton

Photo Credits: 47, Courtesy of Agilent Technologies, Inc. **124,** John Elk III/Bruce Coleman, Inc. **139,** NASA/JPL **171, 272, 440, 631, 759, 864,** PSSC Physics 2/e, 1965; D.C. Heath & Co. with Educational Development Center, Inc., Newton, MA **220,** "Differentiation" by W.U. Walton et. Al., Project CALC, Educational Development Center, Inc., Newton, MA **222,** AP/Wide World Photos **302,** Scott Burns, Urbana, IL., www.designbyalgorithm.com **304,** COMAP, Inc. **433, 754,** Corbis **854,** Richard F. Voss/IBM Research **877,** Appalachian Mountain Club **911,** Department of History, US Military Academy, West Point, New York **929,** ND Roger-Viollet **1060, 1061,** Adapted from "NCFMF Book of Film Notes", 1974, MIT Press with Educational Development Center, Inc., Newton, MA **1061,** InterNetwork Media, Inc. and NASA/JPL

Library of Congress Cataloging-in-Publication Data
Finney, Ross L.
   Thomas' calculus.—10th ed. / based on the original work by George B. Thomas, Jr., as revised by Ross L. Finney, Maurice D. Weir, and Frank R. Giordano.
     p. cm.
   Rev. ed. of Calculus and analytic geometry / George B. Thomas, Jr., Ross L. Finney, 9th ed. c1996.
   Includes bibliographical references and index.
   ISBN 0-201-44143-8
   1. Calculus.   2. Geometry, Analytic.   I. Title: Calculus.   II. Weir, Maurice D.   III. Giordano, Frank R.   IV. Thomas, George Brinton, 1914– Calculus and analytic geometry.   V. Title.
   QA303.F47 2000
   515'.15—dc21   00-032786

Contents

8 Infinite Series   607

9 Vectors in the Plane and Polar Functions   717

13 Integration in Vector Fields 1053

Appendices 1143

Computer Algebra System (CAS) Exercises

To the Instructor

Throughout its illustrious history, *Thomas' Calculus* has been used to support a variety of courses and teaching methods, from traditional to experimental. This tenth edition is a substantial revision, yet it retains the traditional strengths of the text: sound mathematics, relevant and important applications to the sciences and engineering, and excellent exercises. This flexible and modern text contains all the elements needed to teach the many different kinds of courses that exist today.

A book does not make a course; the instructor and the students do. This text is a resource to support your course. With this in mind, we have added a number of features to the tenth edition making it even more flexible and useful, both for teaching and learning calculus.

Features of the Tenth Edition

- For the first time, this classic text is available in *both* standard and Early Transcendentals versions.

- The new *Annotated Instructor's Edition* contains suggestions for the incorporation of technology, highlighting how the Web site and CD-ROM can be used to enhance the presentation of chapter topics.

- As always, this text continues to be easy to read, conversational, and mathematically rich. Each new topic is motivated by clear, easy-to-understand examples and is then reinforced by its application to real-world problems of immediate interest to students.

- Each section now begins with a list of subsection headings, making key concepts readily apparent.

- Within the tenth edition is an increased emphasis on modeling and applications using real data. As a result, there is an improved balance of graphical, numerical, and analytic methods and techniques, accomplished without compromising the mathematical integrity of the book.

- Vectors and projectile motion in the plane are now covered separately in one chapter, concluding the treatment of single-variable calculus. Three-dimensional vectors are then treated in conjunction with multivariable calculus.

- Exercise sets continue to be grouped within appropriate headings. Titles that indicate the content or application have been added for most word problems, and those requiring the use of a graphing utility are identified throughout the text by the icon $\boxed{\text{T}}$. Computer Algebra System (CAS) exercises also appear in every chapter and are grouped in special subsections labeled "Computer Explorations."

- Together, the CD-ROM and Web site provide students and instructors with even more support:
  - A collection of Maple® and *Mathematica*® modules, videos, and Java applets are available to help students visualize key calculus concepts.
  - Interactive online tutorials help students review precalculus and textbook-specific material, take practice tests, and receive diagnostic feedback on their performance.
  - Chapter-by-chapter quizzes are also provided. These quizzes can be administered and graded online for skills-based mastery assessment.
  - Downloadable technology resources are provided for specific computer algebra systems and graphing calculators.
  - Expanded historical biographies are now on the Web site and CD-ROM, leaving more room in the margin of the text for notes, observations, and annotations and giving the book a more open look.

With all these changes, we have not compromised our belief that the fundamental goal of calculus is helping prepare students to enter the worlds of mathematics, science, and engineering.

Mastering Skills and Concepts

As always, this text continues to maintain a strong skill-building emphasis. Throughout this edition, we have included examples and discussions encouraging students to think visually, analytically, and numerically. Almost every exercise set contains problems requiring students to generate and interpret graphs as a tool for understanding mathematical or real-world relationships. Many sections also contain problems to extend the range of applications, mathematical ideas, and rigor.

Students are asked to explore and explain a variety of calculus concepts and applications in writing exercises placed throughout the text. In addition, each chapter ends with a list of questions to help students review and summarize what they have learned. Many of these review questions make great writing assignments.

Problem-Solving Strategies

We believe students learn best when procedural techniques are laid out as clearly and simply as possible. To this end, stepwise problem-solving summaries are included as appropriate, especially for the more difficult or complicated procedures. As always, we are especially careful that examples in the text illustrate the steps outlined by the summaries.

Exercises

Exercise sets have been carefully reviewed and revised in this new edition. They are grouped by topic, with special sections for computer explorations. These sections contain CAS explorations and projects.

Within exercise sets are practice and applied problems, critical thinking and challenging exercises (in subsections marked "Applications and Theory"), and exercises requiring students to write about important calculus concepts. Writing exercises appear throughout exercise sets. Exercises generally follow the order of presentation in the text, and those requiring a graphing utility (such as a graphing calculator) are identified throughout the text by the icon $\boxed{\text{T}}$.

Chapter-End Support Material

At the end of each chapter are three features summarizing the chapter contents:

"Questions to Guide Your Review" ask students to think about key chapter concepts and then verbalize their understanding of them and include illustrative examples. These are questions suitable for writing exercises.

"Practice Exercises" provide a review of the techniques, computational and numerical skills, and key applications.

"Additional Exercises: Theory, Examples, and Applications" provide students with more theoretical or challenging applications and problems to further deepen their understanding of the mathematical ideas.

Applications and Examples

A hallmark of this book has been the application of calculus to science and engineering. These applied problems have been updated, improved, and extended continually over the last several editions. With this edition, we include more problems based on real data requiring graphical and numerical techniques for their solution. Throughout the text, we cite sources for the data or articles from which these applications are drawn, helping students understand that calculus is a current, dynamic field requiring a multiplicity of different techniques and approaches. Most of these applications are directed toward the physical sciences and engineering, but there are many from biology and the social sciences as well.

Technology: Graphing Utility and Computer Explorations

Virtually every section of the text contains exercises to explore numerical patterns or graphing utility exercises that ask students to generate and interpret graphs as a tool to understanding mathematical and real-world relationships. Many of the graphing utility exercises are suitable for classroom demonstration or for group work by students in or out of class. These exercises are identified throughout the text by the icon $\boxed{\text{T}}$ or the heading "Computer Explorations."

Computer Explorations

CD-ROM
WEBsite

Numbering more than 200, the computer explorations exercises have been solved using both *Mathematica* and Maple. In addition, *Mathematica* and Maple modules are available on the Web site and CD-ROM. These modules have been carefully designed to help students develop a geometric intuition and a deeper understanding and appreciation of calculus concepts, methodologies, and applications. CD/Web site icons mark the locations in the text where material related to these modules is covered.

Notes also appear throughout the text that encourage students to explore with graphing utilities and help them assess when the use of technology is helpful and when it may be misleading.

CD-ROM
WEBsite

Historical Biography

Expanded History and Biographies

Any student is enriched by seeing the human side of mathematics through its historical development. In previous editions, we featured history boxes describing the origins of ideas, conflicts concerning ownership of these ideas, and interesting sidelights into modern topics such as fractals and chaos. For the tenth edition, we have expanded and written more biographies and historical essays. These essays are now available on the CD-ROM and Web site; they are referenced by icons throughout the text, leaving more room in the margins for student notes, observations, and annotations.

The Many Faces of This Book

Mathematics Is a Formal and Beautiful Language

Calculus is one of the most powerful of human intellectual achievements. One goal of this book is to give students an appreciation of the beauty of calculus. As in previous editions, we have been careful to say only what is true and mathematically sound. Every definition, theorem, corollary, and proof has been reviewed for clarity and mathematical correctness.

Whether calculus is taught in a traditional lecture format or entirely in labs with individual and group learning focusing on numerical and graphical experimentation, its ideas and techniques need to be articulated clearly and accurately.

Students Will Learn from This Book for Many Years to Come

We intentionally provide far more material than any one instructor would want to teach. Students can continue to learn calculus from this book long after the class has ended. It provides an accessible review of the calculus a student has already studied and is a resource for the working engineer or scientist.

Highlights of New Content Features, by Chapter

Preliminaries

- All the familiar precalculus functions are covered completely.
- Parametric equations are introduced.
- Inverses of familiar functions, including inverse trigonometric functions, are also covered.
- Mathematical modeling, with modeling exercises, is introduced.
- New examples and exercises employ real data and regression analysis using a calculator.

Chapter 1   Limits and Continuity

- Limits are introduced by way of rates of change, with a concluding section on tangent lines to connect and complete the initial discussion.
- All the fundamental ideas on limits are now together in a single chapter, including finite limits, infinite limits, asymptotes, limit rules, and $\lim_{\theta \to 0}((\sin \theta)/\theta)$.
- Both informal and precise definitions of the limit concept are given, but there is less emphasis on using the precise definition to prove theorems.

Chapter 2   Derivatives

- The derivative as a rate of change is presented earlier to stress its importance in studying motion along a line in modeling real-world phenomena.
- Differentiation rules are presented in two sections to enhance the clarity and flow of the presentation.
- First and second derivatives for parametric equations are included as an application of the Chain Rule.

Chapter 3   Applications of Derivatives

- The treatment of using the first and second derivatives to determine the shape of a graph is more focused and streamlined.
- A new section on using the first and second derivative to produce graphical solutions to autonomous first-order differential equations acts as a graphical prelude to Chapters 4 and 6.
- The new section includes an introduction to population modeling.

Chapter 4   Integration

- As before, indefinite integrals are presented first, stressing their importance for solving elementary differential equations. The rules for antiderivatives and the substitution method follow next.
- As in the previous edition, estimating with finite sums in a variety of application settings motivates the ideas of Riemann sums and definite integrals. Students see the definite integral early as more than just a tool for finding area.
- The section defining the definite integral as a limit of Riemann sums has been streamlined and now focuses on continuous functions. Piecewise-continuous functions are treated in the Additional Exercises at the end of the chapter.
- All the material on single integral area calculations (including areas between curves) is now treated in this chapter.

Chapter 5   Applications of Integrals

- The treatment of volumes has been combined from three into two sections.
- Arc length formulas are developed for both explicit function and parametric curves in the plane.
- Surface area has been moved to Chapter 13, where it is needed for surface integrals. There, it is treated in a unified fashion rather than as a special case of surfaces of revolution.
- The important applications to springs, pumping and lifting, fluid forces, and moments have all been retained from the previous edition.

Chapter 6   Transcendental Functions and Differential Equations

- This chapter has been reorganized to present the calculus of logarithmic, exponential, and inverse trigonometric functions immediately. (The differential calculus of these functions is presented in Chapters 2 and 3 in the Early Transcendentals version.) The treatment includes integrals leading to inverse trigonometric functions.
- Separable variable and linear first-order differential equations follow, modeling growth and decay, heat transfer, a falling body with resisting forces, and mixture problems.
- Euler's method and the improved Euler's method are combined with additional material on population models, illustrating graphical, numerical, and analytic solution methods.

Chapter 7   Integration Techniques, L'Hôpital's Rule, and Improper Integrals

- Monte Carlo integration is now included with the use of integral tables or computer algebra systems (CAS) to find integrals.
- L'Hôpital's Rule is covered in this chapter just prior to its use for calculating some improper integrals and limits of sequences (in Chapter 8).

Chapter 8   Infinite Series

- The basic ideas concerning sequences of numbers and their limits are covered in the first section. The next section, which is optional, treats the more theoretical ideas involving subsequences and bounded monotonic sequences.

- Most of the important series convergence tests are presented together in a single, streamlined section.
- Two new optional sections at the end of the chapter cover the basics of Fourier series. This inclusion allows for an earlier introduction to these important concepts for students requiring their use right away in their applied science and engineering courses. Completing the elementary introduction to series, these sections illustrate important representations of functions by series other than power series.

Chapter 9   Vectors in the Plane and Polar Functions

- This is a new chapter on vectors and projectile motion in the plane, with two sections at the end covering polar coordinates and graphs and the calculus of polar curves to prepare students for their use in multivariable calculus. It permits an earlier self-contained treatment of planar vectors, if desired. The chapter can be covered any time after the coverage of the integral and the calculus of exponential and logarithmic functions.
- Chapters P through 9 now form a complete package treating the ideas of single variable calculus. Three-dimensional vectors are presented independently along with multivariable calculus, beginning in Chapter 10.
- Vector ideas are motivated by their application to studying paths, velocities, accelerations, and forces associated with bodies moving along planar paths.
- The detailed analytic geometry of conic sections and quadratic equations has been eliminated. These ideas are thoroughly covered in high school and precalculus courses, but we nevertheless review many of the basics throughout the text as needed.
- Parametrizations of plane curves has been moved to earlier chapters.

Chapter 10   Vectors and Motion in Space

- Three-dimensional vectors, the geometry of space, and vector-valued functions defining space curves are now organized together in this single chapter with fresh introductions and examples. This chapter now constitutes, and clearly delineates, the entry point for the multivariable calculus.
- Letters representing vectors have been changed from uppercase letters to the now more standard lowercase letters.
- Vectors in the plane are reviewed along with the development of the algebra and geometry of three-dimensional vectors to help students bridge any possible gap between Calculus II and Calculus III courses.
- The logical treatment and organization of motion along space curves and the **TNB** frame has been retained from the previous edition.

Chapter 11   Multivariable Functions and Their Derivatives

- The chapter has been reorganized to improve efficiency and flow. The treatment of partial derivatives with constrained variables has been moved toward the end of the chapter to follow the introduction to Lagrange multipliers. The treatment of linearization and differentials now follows the treatment of directional derivatives, gradient vectors, and tangent planes.
- The treatment of gradients and tangent planes is shorter and more direct.
- A new introduction to extreme values and saddle points compares and contrasts the multivariable case with the single-variable case.
- The exercise sets have been streamlined and all applications exercises labeled for quick identification.

Chapter 12   Multiple Integrals

- The treatment of the calculation of masses, moments, and centers of mass with multiple integrals is now self-contained. It no longer assumes previous exposure to the single-integral calculations in Chapter 5, which may now be bypassed entirely.
- Again, the practice of titling exercises makes them noticeably easier to select than before.

Chapter 13   Integration in Vector Fields

- In the treatment of Green's Theorem in the plane, circulation density at a point is introduced as the **k**-component of a more general circulation vector called the curl, which is treated in detail in the later section on Stokes' Theorem. This arrangement resolves the apparent inconsistency of having circulation in the plane represented by a scalar while circulation in space is represented by a vector.

Supplements for the Instructor

TestGen-EQ with QuizMaster-EQ

Windows and Macintosh CD (dual platform)
ISBN 0-201-70287-8
TestGen-EQ's friendly graphical interface enables instructors to view, edit, and add questions, transfer questions to tests, and print tests in a variety of fonts and forms easily. Search and sort features let the instructor quickly locate questions and arrange them in a preferred order. Six question formats are available, including short answer, true–false, multiple choice, essay, matching, and bimodal formats. A built-in question editor gives the user power to create graphs, import graphics, insert mathematical symbols and templates, and insert variable numbers or text. Computerized test banks include algorithmically defined problems organized according to each version of the textbook (standard and Early Transcendentals). An "Export to HTML" feature allows instructors to create practice tests for the Web.

QuizMaster-EQ enables instructors to create and save tests using *TestGen-EQ* so that students can take them for either practice or a grade on a computer network. Instructors can set preferences for how and when tests are administered. *QuizMaster-EQ* automatically grades exams, stores results on disk, and allows the instructor to view or print a variety of reports for individual students, classes, or courses.

This software is free to adopters of the text. Consult your Addison-Wesley representative for details.

Instructor's Solutions Manual

Volume I (Chapters P–9), ISBN 0-201-50403-0
Volume II (Chapters 8–13), ISBN 0-201-50404-9
The *Instructor's Solutions Manual* by Maurice D. Weir and John L. Scharf contains complete worked-out solutions to all the exercises in the text.

Answer Book

ISBN 0-201-44144-6
The *Answer Book* by Maurice D. Weir and John L. Scharf contains short answers to most of the exercises in the text.

Technology Resource Manuals for Computer Algebra Systems and Graphing Calculators

TI-Graphing Calculator Manual ISBN 0-201-72198-8
Maple Manual ISBN 0-201-72197-X
Mathematica Manual ISBN 0-201-72196-1
Each manual provides detailed guidance for integrating a specific software package or graphing calculator throughout the course, including syntax and commands.

Transparency Masters

Instructors may download from the CD-ROM a full set of color PowerPoint art transparencies featuring a number of the more complex figures from the text for use in the classroom.

Supplements for the Student

Student's Study Guide

Volume I (Chapters P–9), ISBN 0-201-50405-7
Volume II (Chapters 8–13), ISBN 0-201-50406-5
Organized to correspond with the text, the *Student's Study Guide* reinforces important concepts and provides study tips and additional practice problems.

Student's Solutions Manual

Volume I (Chapters P–9), ISBN 0-201-50381-6
Volume II (Chapters 8–13), ISBN 0-201-50402-2
The *Student's Solutions Manual* by Maurice D. Weir and John L. Scharf is designed for the student and contains carefully worked-out solutions to all the odd-numbered exercises in the text.

Just-in-Time Algebra and Trigonometry for Students of Calculus, Second Edition

ISBN 0-201-66974-9
Sharp algebra and trigonometry skills are critical to mastering calculus, and *Just-in-Time Algebra and Trigonometry for Students of Calculus, Second Edition* by Guntram Mueller and Ronald I. Brent is designed to bolster these skills while students study calculus. As students make their way through calculus, this text is with them every step of the way, showing them the necessary algebra or trigonometry topics and pointing out potential problem spots. The easy-to-use contents has algebra and trigonometry topics arranged in the order in which students will need them as they study calculus.

AWL Math Tutor Center

The AWL Math Tutor Center (www.awl.com/tutorcenter) provides assistance to students who take calculus and purchase a mathematics textbook published by Addison Wesley Longman. Help is provided via phone, fax, and e-mail. Students who use the service will be helped by tutors who are qualified mathematics instructors.

CD-ROM and Web Site

Maple and Mathematica Modules

Over 35 modules have been written by John L. Scharf and Marie M. Vanisko of Carroll College in Montana and Colonel D. Chris Arney of the U.S. Military Academy. These modules have been carefully designed to help students develop their geometric intuition and deepen their understanding of calculus concepts and methods. Based on real-world applications, they encourage students to visualize calculus and to discover its importance in everyday life. Users will need *Mathematica* or Maple to access these modules. Icons reference these modules throughout the text.

CD-ROM
WEBsite

Interactive Calculus (Java Applets)

These unique interactive calculus Java applets are easy to use, with no syntax or special languages to learn. Students can manipulate equations and graphs in "real time." Topics span limits, projectile motion, slopes, tangents, derivatives, integrals, **TNB** frames, and the concept of curl. By bringing these applets into classroom demonstration and discussion, laboratory and homework assignments, or independent study, teachers and students can explore the mathematics of time and motion. These applets are designed to build a clear understanding of concepts when they are first encountered and to help students over the hurdles of abstraction that have often confused them in the past.

Video Clips

Video clips of real-world situations provide motivation for learning and applying calculus. These videos have been developed specifically to accompany several of the calculus modules described above.

CD-ROM
WEBsite
Historical Biography

Expanded History and Biographies

Icons throughout the book refer to expanded historical biographies and notes on the Web site and CD-ROM. These materials have been written by Colonel D. Chris Arney of the U.S. Military Academy in collaboration with Joe B. Albree of Auburn University.

Just-in-Time Online Algebra and Trigonometry

Compiled by Ronald I. Brent and Guntram Mueller of the University of Massachusetts, Lowell, this interactive Web-based testing and tutorial system allows students to practice the algebra and trigonometry skills critical to mastering calculus. *Just-in-Time Online* tracks student progress and provides personalized study plans to help students succeed. The registration coupon at the back of this text provides access to this feature of the Web site.

Interactive Calculus Tutorial

Written by G. Donald Allen, Michael Stecher, and Philip B. Yasskin of Texas A&M University, this interactive online calculus tutorial lets students review textbook-specific material by chapter via practice quizzes and receive diagnostic feedback on their performance.

Skill Mastery Quizzes

A collection of chapter-by-chapter quizzes is also provided on the Web site. These quizzes can be administered and graded online for skills-based mastery assessment.

Transparency Masters

Instructors may download from the CD-ROM a full set of color PowerPoint art transparencies featuring a number of the more complex figures from the text for use in the classroom.

Downloadable Technology Resources for Specific Computer Algebra Systems and Graphing Calculators

Each manual provides detailed guidance for integrating a specific software package or graphing calculator throughout the course, including syntax and commands. These manuals are available on the Web site for downloading in PDF form.

Collaborative Network

The Collaborative Network is a suite of online communication tools, which includes message boards and i-chat. These tools can be used to deliver courses in a distance learning environment. Message boards allow users to post messages and check back periodically for responses. Students can also use message boards to obtain peer support for study guide activities, freeing up instructor time. I-chat is a perfect arena for instructor-led live discussions with groups of students. The i-chat auditorium allows instructors to post a series of slides in the upper part of the screen while fielding questions (text only) from students in the bottom portion. This feature is particularly useful either as a review of lectures or for class meetings of geographically dispersed students.

Syllabus Manager™

Syllabus Manager™ is a free online syllabus creation and management tool for instructors and students who use this text. It can be used by a nontechnical person to build and maintain one or more syllabi on the Web. Students may "turn on" an instructor's syllabus from the Web site.

Acknowledgments

We would like to express our thanks for the many valuable contributions of the people who reviewed this edition as it developed through its various stages:

Manuscript Reviewers

Tuncay Aktosun, North Dakota State University
Andrew G. Bennett, Kansas State University
Terri A. Bourdon, Virginia Polytechnic Institute and State University

Mark Brittenham, University of Nebraska, Lincoln
Bob Brown, Essex Community College
David A. Edwards, University of Delaware
Mark Farris, Midwestern State University
Kim Jongerius, Northwestern College
Jeff Knisley, East Tennessee State University
Slawomir Kwasik, Tulane University
Jeuel LaTorre, Clemson University
Daniel G. Martinez, California State University, Long Beach
Sandra E. McLaurin, University of North Carolina, Wilmington
Stephen J. Merrill, Marquette University
Shai Neumann, Brevard Community College
Linda Powers, Virginia Polytechnic Institute and State University
William L. Siegmann, Rensselaer Polytechnic Institute
Rick L. Smith, University of Florida
James W. Thomas, Colorado State University
Abraham Ungar, North Dakota State University
Harvey E. Wolff, University of Toledo

Technology Reviewers

Mark Brittenham, University of Nebraska, Lincoln
Warren J. Burch, Brevard Community College, Cocoa
Lyle Cochran, Whitworth College
Philip S. Crooke III, Vanderbilt University
Linda Powers, Virginia Polytechnic Institute and State University
David Ruch, Metropolitan State College of Denver
Paul Talaga, Weber State University
James W. Thomas, Colorado State University
Robert L. Wheeler, Virginia Polytechnic Institute and State University

Other Contributors

We especially thank Colonel D. Chris Arney, John L. Scharf, and Marie M. Vanisko for sharing their insights in using technology to help make calculus come alive for the student, and Colonel D. Chris Arney and Joe B. Albree for their contributions on the history of calculus. Their dedication, encouragement, and team efforts in working with us to conceive and create the technology modules and historical biographies and essays is deeply appreciated. Further thanks to John L. Scharf for his contributions to the solutions manuals.

To the Student

What Is Calculus?

Calculus is the mathematics of motion and change. Where there is motion or growth, where variable forces are at work producing acceleration, calculus is the mathematics to apply. This was true in the beginnings of the subject, and it is true today.

Calculus was first invented to meet the mathematical needs of the scientists of the sixteenth and seventeenth centuries, needs that were mainly mechanical in nature. Differential calculus dealt with the problem of calculating rates of change. It enabled people to define slopes of curves, to calculate velocities and accelerations of moving bodies, to find firing angles that would give cannons their greatest range, and to predict the times when planets would be closest together or farthest apart. Integral calculus dealt with the problem of determining a function from information about its rate of change. It enabled people to calculate the future location of a body from its present position and a knowledge of the forces acting on it, to find the areas of irregular regions in the plane, to measure the lengths of curves, and to find the volumes and masses of arbitrary solids.

Today, calculus and its extensions in mathematical analysis are far-reaching indeed, and the physicists, mathematicians, and astronomers who first invented the subject would surely be amazed and delighted, as we hope you will be, to see what a profusion of problems it solves and what a range of fields now use it in the mathematical models that bring understanding about the universe and the world around us. The goal of this edition is to present a modern view of calculus enhanced by the use of technology.

How to Learn Calculus

Learning calculus is not the same as learning arithmetic, algebra, and geometry. In those subjects, you learn primarily how to calculate with numbers; how to simplify algebraic expressions and calculate with variables; and how to reason about points, lines, and figures in the plane. Calculus involves those techniques and skills but develops others as well, with greater precision and at a deeper level. Calculus introduces so many new concepts and computational operations, in fact, that you will no longer be able to learn everything you need in class. You will have to learn a fair amount on your own or by working with other students. What should you do to learn?

1. *Read the text.* You will not be able to learn all the meanings and connections you need just by attempting the exercises. You will need to read relevant passages in

the book and work through examples step by step. Speed reading will not work here. You are reading and searching for detail in a step-by-step, logical fashion. This kind of reading, required by any deep and technical content, takes attention, patience, and practice.

2. *Do the homework*, keeping the following principles in mind.
   (a) *Sketch diagrams* whenever possible.
   (b) *Write your solutions in a connected step-by-step, logical fashion*, as if you were explaining it to someone else.
   (c) *Think about why* each exercise is there. Why was it assigned? How is it related to the other assigned exercises?

3. *Use your graphing calculator and computer* whenever possible. Complete as many grapher and Computer Exploration exercises as you can, even if they are not assigned. Graphs provide insight and visual representation of important concepts and relationships. Numbers can reveal important patterns. A graphing calculator or computer gives you the freedom to explore realistic problems and examples that involve calculations too difficult or lengthy to do by hand.

4. Try on your own to *write short descriptions of the key points* each time you complete a section of the text. If you succeed, you probably understand the material. If you do not, you will know where there is a gap in your understanding.

Learning calculus is a process; it does not come all at once. Be patient, persevere, ask questions, discuss ideas and work with classmates, and seek help when you need it, right away. The rewards of learning calculus will be very satisfying, both intellectually and professionally.

8 Infinite Series

OVERVIEW   One infinite process that had puzzled mathematicians for centuries was the summing of infinite series. Sometimes an infinite series of terms added to a number, as in

$$\frac{1}{2} + \frac{1}{4} + \frac{1}{8} + \frac{1}{16} + \cdots = 1.$$

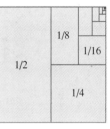

(You can see this by adding the areas in the "infinitely halved" unit square at the right.) Sometimes the infinite sum was infinite, however, as in

$$\frac{1}{1} + \frac{1}{2} + \frac{1}{3} + \frac{1}{4} + \frac{1}{5} + \cdots = \infty$$

(although this is far from obvious), and sometimes the infinite sum was impossible to pin down, as in

$$1 - 1 + 1 - 1 + 1 - 1 + \cdots .$$

(Is it 0? Is it 1? Is it neither?)

Nonetheless, mathematicians like Gauss and Euler successfully used infinite series to derive previously inaccessible results. Laplace used infinite series to prove the stability of the solar system (although that does not stop some people from worrying about it today when they feel that "too many" planets have swung to the same side of the sun). It was years later that careful analysts like Cauchy developed the theoretical foundation for series computations, sending many mathematicians (including Laplace) back to their desks to verify their results.

Infinite series form the basis for a remarkable formula that enables us to express many functions as "infinite polynomials" and at the same time tells how much error we incur if we truncate those polynomials to make them finite. In addition to providing effective polynomial approximations of differentiable functions, these infinite polynomials (called power series) have many other uses. We also see how to use infinite sums of trigonometric terms, called Fourier series, to represent important functions used in science and engineering applications. Infinite series provide an efficient way to evaluate nonelementary integrals, and they solve differential equations that give insight into heat flow, vibration, chemical diffusion, and signal transmission. What you learn here sets the stage for the roles played by series of functions of all kinds in science and mathematics.

8.1   Limits of Sequences of Numbers

Definitions and Notation   •   Convergence and Divergence   •
Calculating Limits of Sequences   •   Using L'Hôpital's Rule   •   Limits That
Arise Frequently

Informally, a sequence is an ordered list of things, but in this chapter, the things will usually be numbers. We have seen sequences before, such as the sequence $x_0, x_1, \ldots, x_n, \ldots$ of numbers generated by Newton's method. Later we consider sequences involving powers of x and others involving trigonometric terms like $\sin x, \cos x, \sin 2x, \cos 2x, \ldots, \sin nx, \cos nx, \ldots$. A central question is whether a sequence has a limit or not.

Definitions and Notation

We can list the integer multiples of 3 by assigning each multiple a position:

$$\begin{array}{cccccc}
\text{Domain:} & 1 & 2 & 3 & \ldots\, n & \ldots \\
 & \downarrow & \downarrow & \downarrow & \downarrow & \\
\text{Range:} & 3 & 6 & 9 & 3n &
\end{array}$$

The first number is 3, the second 6, the third 9, and so on. The assignment is a function that assigns $3n$ to the nth place. That is the basic idea for constructing sequences. There is a function placing each number in the range in its correct ordered position.

> **Definition**   Sequence
>
> An infinite **sequence** of numbers is a function whose domain is the set of integers greater than or equal to some integer n_0.

Usually, n_0 is 1 and the domain of the sequence is the set of positive integers. Sometimes, however, we want to start sequences elsewhere. We take $n_0 = 0$ when we begin Newton's method. We might take $n_0 = 3$ if we were defining a sequence of n-sided polygons.

Sequences are defined the same way as other functions, some typical rules being

$$a(n) = \sqrt{n}, \qquad a(n) = (-1)^{n+1}\frac{1}{n}, \qquad a(n) = \frac{n-1}{n}$$

(Example 1 and Figure 8.1). To indicate that the domains are sets of integers, we use a letter like n from the middle of the alphabet for the independent variable, instead of the x, y, z, and t used widely in other contexts. The formulas in the defining rules, however, like those above, are often valid for domains larger than the set of positive integers. This can be an advantage, as we will see. The number

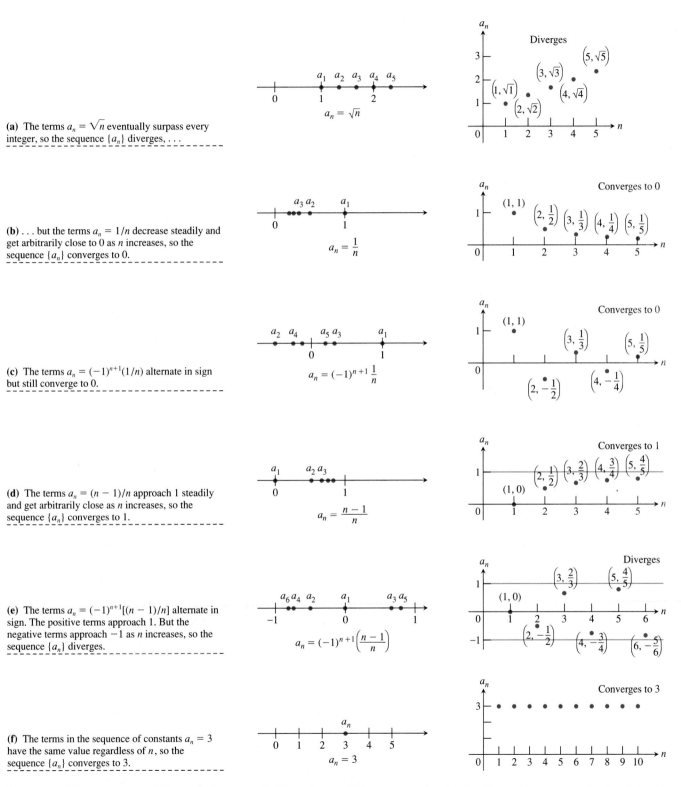

(a) The terms $a_n = \sqrt{n}$ eventually surpass every integer, so the sequence $\{a_n\}$ diverges, . . .

(b) . . . but the terms $a_n = 1/n$ decrease steadily and get arbitrarily close to 0 as n increases, so the sequence $\{a_n\}$ converges to 0.

(c) The terms $a_n = (-1)^{n+1}(1/n)$ alternate in sign but still converge to 0.

(d) The terms $a_n = (n-1)/n$ approach 1 steadily and get arbitrarily close as n increases, so the sequence $\{a_n\}$ converges to 1.

(e) The terms $a_n = (-1)^{n+1}[(n-1)/n]$ alternate in sign. The positive terms approach 1. But the negative terms approach -1 as n increases, so the sequence $\{a_n\}$ diverges.

(f) The terms in the sequence of constants $a_n = 3$ have the same value regardless of n, so the sequence $\{a_n\}$ converges to 3.

FIGURE 8.1 The sequences of Example 1 are graphed here in two different ways: by plotting the numbers a_n on a horizontal axis and by plotting the points (n, a_n) in the coordinate plane.

$a(n)$ is the **nth term** of the sequence, or the **term with index n**. If $a(n) = (n - 1)/n$, we have

First term	Second term	Third term		nth term
$a(1) = 0$	$a(2) = \dfrac{1}{2},$	$a(3) = \dfrac{2}{3},$	$\dots,$	$a(n) = \dfrac{n - 1}{n}.$

When we use the subscript notation a_n for $a(n)$, the sequence is written

$$a_1 = 0, \qquad a_2 = \frac{1}{2}, \qquad a_3 = \frac{2}{3}, \qquad \dots, \qquad a_n = \frac{n - 1}{n}.$$

To describe sequences, we often write the first few terms as well as a formula for the nth term.

Example 1   Describing Sequences

We write	For the sequence whose defining rule is
(a) $1, \sqrt{2}, \sqrt{3}, \sqrt{4}, \dots, \sqrt{n}, \dots$	$a_n = \sqrt{n}$
(b) $1, \dfrac{1}{2}, \dfrac{1}{3}, \dots, \dfrac{1}{n}, \dots$	$a_n = \dfrac{1}{n}$
(c) $1, -\dfrac{1}{2}, \dfrac{1}{3}, -\dfrac{1}{4}, \dots, (-1)^{n+1}\dfrac{1}{n}, \dots$	$a_n = (-1)^{n+1}\dfrac{1}{n}$
(d) $0, \dfrac{1}{2}, \dfrac{2}{3}, \dfrac{3}{4}, \dots, \dfrac{n-1}{n}, \dots$	$a_n = \dfrac{n-1}{n}$
(e) $0, -\dfrac{1}{2}, \dfrac{2}{3}, -\dfrac{3}{4}, \dots, (-1)^{n+1}\left(\dfrac{n-1}{n}\right), \dots$	$a_n = (-1)^{n+1}\left(\dfrac{n-1}{n}\right)$
(f) $3, 3, 3, \dots, 3, \dots$	$a_n = 3$

Notation   We refer to the sequence whose nth term is a_n with the notation $\{a_n\}$ ("the sequence a sub n"). The second sequence in Example 1 is $\{1/n\}$ ("the sequence 1 over n"); the last sequence is $\{3\}$ ("the constant sequence 3").

Convergence and Divergence

As Figure 8.1 shows, the sequences of Example 1 do not behave the same way. The sequences $\{1/n\}$, $\{(-1)^{n+1}(1/n)\}$, and $\{(n - 1)/n\}$ each seem to approach a single limiting value as n increases, and $\{3\}$ is at a limiting value from the very first. On the other hand, terms of $\{(-1)^{n+1}(n - 1)/n\}$ seem to accumulate near two different values, -1 and 1, whereas the terms of $\{\sqrt{n}\}$ become increasingly large and do not accumulate anywhere.

The following definition distinguishes those sequences that approach a unique limiting value L, as n increases, from those that do not.

Definitions   Converges, Diverges, Limit

The sequence $\{a_n\}$ **converges** to the number L if to every positive number ϵ there corresponds an integer N such that for all n,

$$n > N \;\Rightarrow\; |a_n - L| < \epsilon.$$

If no such number L exists, we say that $\{a_n\}$ **diverges.**

If $\{a_n\}$ converges to L, we write $\lim_{n\to\infty} a_n = L$, or simply $a_n \to L$, and call L the **limit** of the sequence (Figure 8.2).

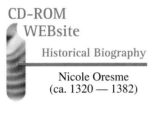

CD-ROM
WEBsite

Historical Biography

Nicole Oresme
(ca. 1320 — 1382)

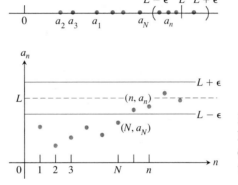

FIGURE 8.2 $a_n \to L$ if $y = L$ is a horizontal asymptote of the sequence of points $\{(n, a_n)\}$. In this figure, all the a_n's after a_N lie within ϵ of L.

Example 2   Testing the Definition

Show that

(a) $\displaystyle \lim_{n\to\infty} \frac{1}{n} = 0$

(b) $\displaystyle \lim_{n\to\infty} k = k$ (any constant k).

Solution

(a) Let $\epsilon > 0$ be given. We must show that there exists an integer N such that for all n,

$$n > N \;\Rightarrow\; \left|\frac{1}{n} - 0\right| < \epsilon.$$

This implication will hold if $(1/n) < \epsilon$ or $n > 1/\epsilon$. If N is any integer greater than $1/\epsilon$, the implication will hold for all $n > N$. This proves $\lim_{n\to\infty} (1/n) = 0$.

(b) Let $\epsilon > 0$ be given. We must show that there exists an integer N such that for all n,

$$n > N \;\Rightarrow\; |k - k| < \epsilon.$$

Since $k - k = 0$, we can use any positive integer for N and the implication will hold. This proves that $\lim_{n\to\infty} k = k$ for any constant k.

Example 3   A Divergent Sequence

Show that $\{(-1)^{n+1}[(n-1)/n]\}$ diverges.

Solution   Take a positive ϵ smaller than 1 so that the bands shown in Figure 8.3 about the lines $y = 1$ and $y = -1$ do not overlap. Any $\epsilon < 1$ will do. Convergence to 1 would require every point of the graph beyond a certain index N to lie inside the upper band, but this will never happen. As soon as a point (n, a_n) lies in the upper band, every alternate point starting with $(n + 1, a_{n+1})$ will lie in the lower band. Hence, the sequence cannot converge to 1. Likewise, it cannot converge to -1. On the other hand, because the terms of the sequence get alternately closer to 1 and -1, they never accumulate near any other value. Therefore, the sequence diverges.

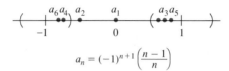

$$a_n = (-1)^{n+1}\left(\frac{n-1}{n}\right)$$

Neither the ϵ-interval about 1 nor the ϵ-interval about -1 contains all a_n satisfying $n \geq N$ for some N.

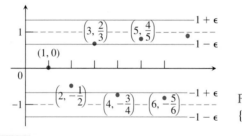

FIGURE 8.3 The sequence $\{(-1)^{n+1}[(n-1)/n]\}$ diverges.

The behavior of $\{(-1)^{n+1}[(n-1)/n]\}$ is qualitatively different from that of $\{\sqrt{n}\}$, which diverges because it outgrows every real number L. To describe the behavior of $\{\sqrt{n}\}$, we write

$$\lim_{n \to \infty} (\sqrt{n}) = \infty.$$

In speaking of infinity as a limit of a sequence $\{a_n\}$, we do not mean that the difference between a_n and infinity becomes small as n increases. We mean that a_n becomes numerically large as n increases.

Calculating Limits of Sequences

The study of limits would be cumbersome if we had to answer every question about convergence by applying the definition. Fortunately, three theorems make this largely unnecessary. The first theorem is not surprising, based on our previous work with limits. We omit the proofs.

Theorem 1   Limit Laws for Sequences

Let $\{a_n\}$ and $\{b_n\}$ be sequences of real numbers and let A and B be real numbers. The following rules hold if $\lim_{n\to\infty} a_n = A$ and $\lim_{n\to\infty} b_n = B$.

1. *Sum Rule*: $\lim_{n\to\infty} (a_n + b_n) = A + B$

2. *Difference Rule*: $\lim_{n\to\infty} (a_n - b_n) = A - B$

3. *Product Rule*: $\lim_{n\to\infty} (a_n \cdot b_n) = A \cdot B$

4. *Constant Multiple Rule*: $\lim_{n\to\infty} (k \cdot b_n) = k \cdot B$ (any number k)

5. *Quotient Rule*: $\lim_{n\to\infty} \dfrac{a_n}{b_n} = \dfrac{A}{B}$ if $B \neq 0$

Example 4   Applying the Limit Laws

By combining Theorem 1 with the limit results in Example 2, we have

(a) $\displaystyle\lim_{n\to\infty} \left(-\frac{1}{n} \right) = -1 \cdot \lim_{n\to\infty} \frac{1}{n} = -1 \cdot 0 = 0$

(b) $\displaystyle\lim_{n\to\infty} \left(\frac{n-1}{n} \right) = \lim_{n\to\infty} \left(1 - \frac{1}{n} \right) = \lim_{n\to\infty} 1 - \lim_{n\to\infty} \frac{1}{n} = 1 - 0 = 1$

(c) $\displaystyle\lim_{n\to\infty} \frac{5}{n^2} = 5 \cdot \lim_{n\to\infty} \frac{1}{n} \cdot \lim_{n\to\infty} \frac{1}{n} = 5 \cdot 0 \cdot 0 = 0$

(d) $\displaystyle\lim_{n\to\infty} \frac{4 - 7n^6}{n^6 + 3} = \lim_{n\to\infty} \frac{(4/n^6) - 7}{1 + (3/n^6)} = \frac{0 - 7}{1 + 0} = -7.$

Example 5   Constant Multiples of Divergent Sequences Diverge

Every nonzero multiple of a divergent sequence $\{a_n\}$ diverges. Suppose, to the contrary, that $\{ca_n\}$ converges for some number $c \neq 0$. Then, by taking $k = 1/c$ in the Constant Multiple Rule in Theorem 1, we see that the sequence

$$\left\{ \frac{1}{c} \cdot ca_n \right\} = \{a_n\}$$

converges. Thus, $\{ca_n\}$ cannot converge unless $\{a_n\}$ also converges. If $\{a_n\}$ does not converge, then $\{ca_n\}$ does not converge.

You are asked to prove the next Theorem in Exercise 69.

Theorem 2   The Sandwich Theorem for Sequences

Let $\{a_n\}$, $\{b_n\}$, and $\{c_n\}$ be sequences of real numbers. If $a_n \leq b_n \leq c_n$ holds for all n beyond some index N and if $\lim_{n\to\infty} a_n = \lim_{n\to\infty} c_n = L$, then $\lim_{n\to\infty} b_n = L$ also.

An immediate consequence of Theorem 2 is that if $|b_n| \leq c_n$ and $c_n \to 0$, then $b_n \to 0$ because $-c_n \leq b_n \leq c_n$. We use this fact in the next example.

Example 6 Using the Sandwich Theorem

Since $1/n \to 0$, we know that

(a) $\dfrac{\cos n}{n} \to 0$ because $\left| \dfrac{\cos n}{n} \right| = \dfrac{|\cos n|}{n} \leq \dfrac{1}{n}$

(b) $\dfrac{1}{2^n} \to 0$ because $\dfrac{1}{2^n} \leq \dfrac{1}{n}$

(c) $(-1)^n \dfrac{1}{n} \to 0$ because $\left| (-1)^n \dfrac{1}{n} \right| \leq \dfrac{1}{n}$.

The application of Theorems 1 and 2 is broadened by a theorem stating that applying a continuous function to a convergent sequence produces a convergent sequence. We state the theorem without proof (Exercise 70).

Theorem 3 The Continuous Function Theorem for Sequences

Let $\{a_n\}$ be a sequence of real numbers. If $a_n \to L$ and if f is a function that is continuous at L and defined at all a_n, then $f(a_n) \to f(L)$.

Example 7 Applying Theorem 3

Show that $\sqrt{(n+1)/n} \to 1$.

Solution We know that $(n+1)/n \to 1$. Taking $f(x) = \sqrt{x}$ and $L = 1$ in Theorem 3 gives $\sqrt{(n+1)/n} \to \sqrt{1} = 1$.

Example 8 The Sequence $\{2^{1/n}\}$

The sequence $\{1/n\}$ converges to 0. By taking $a_n = 1/n$, $f(x) = 2^x$, and $L = 0$ in Theorem 3, we see that $2^{1/n} = f(1/n) \to f(L) = 2^0 = 1$. The sequence $\{2^{1/n}\}$ converges to 1 (Figure 8.4).

Using L'Hôpital's Rule

The next theorem enables us to use l'Hôpital's Rule to find the limits of some sequences. It matches values of a (usually differentiable) function with the values of a given sequence.

Theorem 4

Suppose that $f(x)$ is a function defined for all $x \geq n_0$ and that $\{a_n\}$ is a sequence of real numbers such that $a_n = f(n)$ for $n \geq n_0$. Then

$$\lim_{x \to \infty} f(x) = L \implies \lim_{n \to \infty} a_n = L.$$

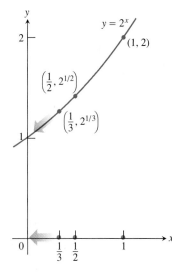

FIGURE 8.4 As $n \to \infty$, $1/n \to 0$ and $2^{1/n} \to 2^0$.

Example 9   Applying L'Hôpital's Rule

Show that

$$\lim_{n \to \infty} \frac{\ln n}{n} = 0.$$

Solution   The function $(\ln x)/x$ is defined for all $x \geq 1$ and agrees with the given sequence at positive integers. Therefore, by Theorem 4, $\lim_{n \to \infty} (\ln n)/n$ will equal $\lim_{x \to \infty} (\ln x)/x$ if the latter exists. A single application of l'Hôpital's Rule shows that

$$\lim_{x \to \infty} \frac{\ln x}{x} = \lim_{x \to \infty} \frac{1/x}{1} = \frac{0}{1} = 0.$$

We conclude that $\lim_{n \to \infty} (\ln n)/n = 0$.

When we use l'Hôpital's Rule to find the limit of a sequence, we often treat n as a continuous real variable and differentiate directly with respect to n. This saves us from having to rewrite the formula for a_n as we did in Example 9.

Example 10   Applying L'Hôpital's Rule

Find

$$\lim_{n \to \infty} \frac{2^n}{5n}.$$

Solution   By l'Hôpital's Rule (differentiating with respect to n),

$$\lim_{n \to \infty} \frac{2^n}{5n} = \lim_{n \to \infty} \frac{2^n \cdot \ln 2}{5}$$

$$= \infty.$$

Proof of Theorem 4   Suppose that $\lim_{x \to \infty} f(x) = L$. Then for each positive number ϵ there is a number M such that for all x,

$$x > M \implies |f(x) - L| < \epsilon.$$

Let N be an integer greater than M and greater than or equal to n_0. Then

$$n > N \implies a_n = f(n) \quad \text{and} \quad |a_n - L| = |f(n) - L| < \epsilon. \qquad \rule{1em}{0.4pt}$$

Example 11   Applying L'Hôpital's Rule to Determine Convergence

Does the sequence whose nth term is

$$a_n = \left(\frac{n+1}{n-1}\right)^n$$

converge? If so, find $\lim_{n \to \infty} a_n$.

Solution The limit leads to the indeterminate form 1^∞. We can apply l'Hôpital's Rule if we first change the form to $\infty \cdot 0$ by taking the natural logarithm of a_n:

$$\ln a_n = \ln \left(\frac{n+1}{n-1}\right)^n$$

$$= n \ln \left(\frac{n+1}{n-1}\right).$$

Then,

$$\lim_{n\to\infty} \ln a_n = \lim_{n\to\infty} n \ln \left(\frac{n+1}{n-1}\right) \qquad \infty \cdot 0$$

$$= \lim_{n\to\infty} \frac{\ln \left(\frac{n+1}{n-1}\right)}{1/n} \qquad \frac{0}{0}$$

$$= \lim_{n\to\infty} \frac{-2/(n^2-1)}{-1/n^2} \qquad \text{l'Hôpital's Rule}$$

$$= \lim_{n\to\infty} \frac{2n^2}{n^2-1} = 2.$$

Since $\ln a_n \to 2$ and $f(x) = e^x$ is continuous, Theorem 3 tells us that

$$a_n = e^{\ln a_n} \to e^2.$$

The sequence $\{a_n\}$ converges to e^2.

Limits That Arise Frequently

The limits in Table 8.1 arise frequently. The first limit is from Example 9. The next two can be proved by taking logarithms and applying Theorem 3 (Exercises 67 and 68). The remaining proofs can be found in Appendix 7.

Table 8.1

1. $\lim_{n\to\infty} \dfrac{\ln n}{n} = 0$

2. $\lim_{n\to\infty} \sqrt[n]{n} = 1$

3. $\lim_{n\to\infty} x^{1/n} = 1 \qquad (x > 0)$

4. $\lim_{n\to\infty} x^n = 0 \qquad (|x| < 1)$

5. $\lim_{n\to\infty} \left(1 + \dfrac{x}{n}\right)^n = e^x \qquad (\text{any } x)$

6. $\lim_{n\to\infty} \dfrac{x^n}{n!} = 0 \qquad (\text{any } x)$

In formulas (3) through (6), x remains fixed as $n \to \infty$.

Example 12 Limits from Table 8.1

(a) $\dfrac{\ln (n^2)}{n} = \dfrac{2 \ln n}{n} \to 2 \cdot 0 = 0$ Formula 1

(b) $\sqrt[n]{n^2} = n^{2/n} = (n^{1/n})^2 \to (1)^2 = 1$ Formula 2

(c) $\sqrt[n]{3n} = 3^{1/n}(n^{1/n}) \to 1 \cdot 1 = 1$ Formula 3 with $x = 3$ and Formula 2

(d) $\left(-\dfrac{1}{2}\right)^n \to 0$ Formula 4 with $x = -\dfrac{1}{2}$

(e) $\left(\dfrac{n-2}{n}\right)^n = \left(1 + \dfrac{-2}{n}\right)^n \to e^{-2}$ Formula 5 with $x = -2$

(f) $\dfrac{100^n}{n!} \to 0$ Formula 6 with $x = 100$

EXERCISES 8.1

Finding Terms of a Sequence

Each of Exercises 1–4 gives a formula for the nth term a_n of a sequence $\{a_n\}$. Find the values of $a_1, a_2, a_3,$ and a_4.

1. $a_n = \dfrac{1-n}{n^2}$

2. $a_n = \dfrac{1}{n!}$

3. $a_n = \dfrac{(-1)^{n+1}}{2n-1}$

4. $a_n = \dfrac{2^n}{2^{n+1}}$

Finding Formulas for Sequences

In Exercises 5–12, find a formula for the nth term of the sequence.

5. The sequence $1, -1, 1, -1, 1, \ldots$ 1's with alternating signs

6. The sequence $1, -4, 9, -16, 25, \ldots$ Squares of the positive integers, with alternating signs

7. The sequence $0, 3, 8, 15, 24, \ldots$ Squares of the positive integers diminished by 1

8. The sequence $-3, -2, -1, 0, 1, \ldots$ Integers beginning with -3

9. The sequence $1, 5, 9, 13, 17, \ldots$ Every other odd positive integer

10. The sequence $2, 6, 10, 14, 18, \ldots$ Every other even positive integer

11. The sequence $1, 0, 1, 0, 1, \ldots$ Alternating 1's and 0's

12. The sequence $0, 1, 1, 2, 2, 3, 3, 4, \ldots$ Each positive integer repeated

Finding Limits

Which of the sequences $\{a_n\}$ in Exercises 13–56 converge, and which diverge? Find the limit of each convergent sequence.

13. $a_n = 2 + (0.1)^n$

14. $a_n = \dfrac{n + (-1)^n}{n}$

15. $a_n = \dfrac{1 - 2n}{1 + 2n}$

16. $a_n = \dfrac{1 - 5n^4}{n^4 + 8n^3}$

17. $a_n = \dfrac{n^2 - 2n + 1}{n - 1}$

18. $a_n = \dfrac{n + 3}{n^2 + 5n + 6}$

19. $a_n = 1 + (-1)^n$

20. $a_n = (-1)^n \left(1 - \dfrac{1}{n}\right)$

21. $a_n = \left(\dfrac{n+1}{2n}\right)\left(1 - \dfrac{1}{n}\right)$

22. $a_n = \dfrac{(-1)^{n+1}}{2n - 1}$

23. $a_n = \sqrt{\dfrac{2n}{n+1}}$

24. $a_n = \sin\left(\dfrac{\pi}{2} + \dfrac{1}{n}\right)$

25. $a_n = \dfrac{\sin n}{n}$

26. $a_n = \dfrac{\sin^2 n}{2^n}$

27. $a_n = \dfrac{n}{2^n}$

28. $a_n = \dfrac{\ln(n+1)}{\sqrt{n}}$

29. $a_n = \dfrac{\ln n}{n^{1/n}}$

30. $a_n = \ln n - \ln(n+1)$

31. $a_n = \left(1 + \dfrac{7}{n}\right)^n$

32. $a_n = \left(1 - \dfrac{1}{n}\right)^n$

33. $a_n = \sqrt[n]{10n}$

34. $a_n = \sqrt[n]{n^2}$

35. $a_n = \left(\dfrac{3}{n}\right)^{1/n}$

36. $a_n = (n+4)^{1/(n+4)}$

37. $a_n = \sqrt[n]{4^n\, n}$

38. $a_n = \sqrt[n]{3^{2n+1}}$

39. $a_n = \dfrac{n!}{n^n}$ (*Hint:* Compare with $1/n$.)

40. $a_n = \dfrac{(-4)^n}{n!}$

41. $a_n = \dfrac{n!}{10^{6n}}$

42. $a_n = \dfrac{n!}{2^n \cdot 3^n}$

43. $a_n = \left(\dfrac{1}{n}\right)^{1/(\ln n)}$

44. $a_n = \ln\left(1 + \dfrac{1}{n}\right)^n$

45. $a_n = \left(\dfrac{3n+1}{3n-1}\right)^n$

46. $a_n = \left(\dfrac{n}{n+1}\right)^n$

47. $a_n = \left(\dfrac{x^n}{2n+1}\right)^{1/n}$, $x > 0$

48. $a_n = \left(1 - \dfrac{1}{n^2}\right)^n$

49. $a_n = \dfrac{3^n \cdot 6^n}{2^{-n} \cdot n!}$

50. $a_n = \dfrac{n^2}{2n - 1} \sin \dfrac{1}{n}$

51. $a_n = \tan^{-1} n$

52. $a_n = \dfrac{1}{\sqrt{n}} \tan^{-1} n$

53. $a_n = \left(\dfrac{1}{3}\right)^n + \dfrac{1}{\sqrt{2^n}}$

54. $a_n = \sqrt[n]{n^2 + n}$

55. $a_n = \dfrac{(\ln n)^5}{\sqrt{n}}$

56. $a_n = n - \sqrt{n^2 - n}$

Calculator Explorations of Limits

In Exercises 57–60, experiment with a calculator to find a value of N that will make the inequality hold for all $n > N$. Assuming that the inequality is the one from the formal definition of the limit of a sequence, what sequence is being considered in each case, and what is its limit?

57. $|\sqrt[n]{0.5} - 1| < 10^{-3}$

58. $|\sqrt[n]{n} - 1| < 10^{-3}$

59. $(0.9)^n < 10^{-3}$

60. $(2^n/n!) < 10^{-7}$

Theory and Examples

61. A sequence of rational numbers is described as follows:

$$\frac{1}{1}, \frac{3}{2}, \frac{7}{5}, \frac{17}{12}, \ldots, \frac{a}{b}, \frac{a + 2b}{a + b}, \ldots.$$

Here the numerators form one sequence, the denominators form a second sequence, and their ratios form a third sequence. Let x_n and y_n be, respectively, the numerator and the denominator of the nth fraction $r_n = x_n/y_n$.

(a) Verify that $x_1^2 - 2y_1^2 = -1$, $x_2^2 - 2y_2^2 = +1$, and, more generally, that if $a^2 - 2b^2 = -1$ or $+1$, then

$$(a + 2b)^2 - 2(a + b)^2 = +1 \quad \text{or} \quad -1,$$

respectively.

(b) The fractions $r_n = x_n/y_n$ approach a limit as n increases. What is that limit? (*Hint*: Use part (a) to show that $r_n^2 - 2 = \pm(1/y_n)^2$ and that y_n is not less than n.)

62. (a) Suppose that $f(x)$ is differentiable for all x in [0, 1] and that $f(0) = 0$. Define the sequence $\{a_n\}$ by the rule $a_n = nf(1/n)$. Show that $\lim_{n\to\infty} a_n = f'(0)$.

Use the result in part (a) to find the limits of the following sequences $\{a_n\}$.

(b) $a_n = n \tan^{-1} \dfrac{1}{n}$

(c) $a_n = n(e^{1/n} - 1)$

(d) $a_n = n \ln\left(1 + \dfrac{2}{n}\right)$

63. *Pythagorean triples* A triple of positive integers a, b, and c is called a **Pythagorean triple** if $a^2 + b^2 = c^2$. Let a be an odd positive integer and let

$$b = \left\lfloor \frac{a^2}{2} \right\rfloor \quad \text{and} \quad c = \left\lceil \frac{a^2}{2} \right\rceil$$

be, respectively, the integer floor and ceiling for $a^2/2$.

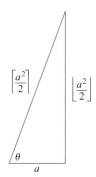

(a) Show that $a^2 + b^2 = c^2$. (*Hint*: Let $a = 2n + 1$ and express b and c in terms of n.)

(b) By direct calculation, or by appealing to the figure, find

$$\lim_{a\to\infty} \frac{\left\lfloor \dfrac{a^2}{2} \right\rfloor}{\left\lceil \dfrac{a^2}{2} \right\rceil}.$$

64. *The nth root of $n!$*

(a) Show that $\lim_{n\to\infty} (2n\pi)^{1/(2n)} = 1$ and hence, using Stirling's approximation (Chapter 7, Additional Exercise 50, part (a), that

$$\sqrt[n]{n!} \approx \frac{n}{e} \quad \text{for large values of } n.$$

(b) Test the approximation in part (a) for $n = 40, 50, 60, \ldots$ as far as your calculator will allow.

65. (a) Assuming that $\lim_{n\to\infty} (1/n^c) = 0$ if c is any positive constant, show that

$$\lim_{n\to\infty} \frac{\ln n}{n^c} = 0$$

if c is any positive constant.

(b) Prove that $\lim_{n\to\infty} (1/n^c) = 0$ if c is any positive constant. (*Hint*: If $\epsilon = 0.001$ and $c = 0.04$, how large should N be to ensure that $|1/n^c - 0| < \epsilon$ if $n > N$?)

66. *The Zipper Theorem* Prove the "Zipper Theorem" for sequences: If $\{a_n\}$ and $\{b_n\}$ both converge to L, then the sequence

$$a_1, b_1, a_2, b_2, \ldots, a_n, b_n, \ldots$$

converges to L.

67. Prove that $\lim_{n\to\infty} \sqrt[n]{n} = 1$.

68. Prove that $\lim_{n\to\infty} x^{1/n} = 1 \ (x > 0)$.

69. Prove Theorem 2.

70. Prove Theorem 3.

71. *Terms become arbitrarily close in convergent sequences* Prove that if $\{a_n\}$ is a convergent sequence, then to every positive number ϵ there corresponds an integer N such that for all m and n,

$$m > N \quad \text{and} \quad n > N \implies |a_m - a_n| < \epsilon.$$

72. *Uniqueness of limits* Prove that limits of sequences are unique. That is, show that if L_1 and L_2 are numbers such that $a_n \to L_1$ and $a_n \to L_2$, then $L_1 = L_2$.

73. *Convergence and absolute value* Prove that a sequence $\{a_n\}$ converges to 0 if and only if the sequence of absolute values $\{|a_n|\}$ converges to 0.

74. *Improving automobile production* According to a front-page article in the December 15, 1992 issue of the *Wall Street Journal*, Ford Motor Company now uses about $7\frac{1}{4}$ h of labor to produce stampings for the average vehicle, down from an estimated 15 h in 1980. The Japanese need only about $3\frac{1}{2}$ h.

Ford's improvement since 1980 represents an average decrease of 6% per year. If that rate continues, then n years from now Ford will use about

$$S_n = 7.25(0.94)^n$$

hours of labor to produce stampings for the average vehicle. Assuming that the Japanese continue to spend $3\frac{1}{2}$ h per vehicle, how many more years will it take Ford to catch up? Find out two ways:

(a) Find the first term of the sequence $\{S_n\}$ that is less than or equal to 3.5.

T (b) Graph $f(x) = 7.25(0.94)^x$ and use Trace to find where the graph crosses the line $y = 3.5$.

COMPUTER EXPLORATIONS

Looking for Signs of Convergence and Divergence

Use a CAS to perform the following steps for the sequences in Exercises 75–84.

(a) Calculate and then plot the first 25 terms of the sequence. Does the sequence appear to converge or diverge? If it does converge, what is the limit L?

(b) If the sequence converges, find an integer N such that $|a_n - L| \le 0.01$ for $n \ge N$. How far in the sequence do you have to get for the terms to lie within 0.0001 of L?

75. $a_n = \sqrt[n]{n}$

76. $a_n = \left(1 + \dfrac{0.5}{n}\right)^n$

77. $a_n = \sin n$

78. $a_n = n \sin \dfrac{1}{n}$

79. $a_n = \dfrac{\sin n}{n}$

80. $a_n = \dfrac{\ln n}{n}$

81. $a_n = (0.9999)^n$

82. $a_n = 123456^{1/n}$

83. $a_n = \dfrac{8^n}{n!}$

84. $a_n = \dfrac{n^{41}}{19^n}$

8.2 Subsequences, Bounded Sequences, and Picard's Method

Subsequences • Monotonic and Bounded Sequences • Recursively Defined Sequences • Picard's Method for Finding Roots

This section continues our study of the convergence or divergence of a sequence.

Subsequences

If the terms of one sequence appear in another sequence in their given order, we call the first sequence a **subsequence** of the second.

> **Example 1** Subsequences of the Sequence of Positive Integers
>
> (a) The subsequence of even integers: $2, 4, 6, \ldots, 2n, \ldots$
>
> (b) The subsequence of odd integers: $1, 3, 5, \ldots, 2n - 1, \ldots$
>
> (c) The subsequence of primes: $2, 3, 5, 7, 11, \ldots$

Subsequences are important for two reasons:

1. If a sequence $\{a_n\}$ converges to L, then all its subsequences converge to L. If we know that a sequence converges, it may be quicker to find or estimate its limit by examining a particular subsequence.

2. If any subsequence of a sequence $\{a_n\}$ diverges or if two subsequences have different limits, then $\{a_n\}$ diverges. For example, the sequence $\{(-1)^n\}$ diverges because the subsequence $-1, -1, -1, \ldots$ of odd-numbered terms converge to -1, whereas the subsequence $1, 1, 1, \ldots$ of even-numbered terms converges to 1, a different limit.

The convergence or divergence of a sequence has nothing to do with how the sequence begins. It depends only on how the tails behave.

Subsequences also provide a new way to view convergence. A **tail** of a sequence is a subsequence that consists of all terms of the sequence from some index N on. In other words, a tail is one of the sets $\{a_n \mid n \geq N\}$. Another way to say that $a_n \to L$ is to say that every ϵ-interval about L contains a tail of the sequence.

Monotonic and Bounded Sequences

> **Definition**   Nondecreasing, Nonincreasing, Monotonic Sequence
>
> A sequence $\{a_n\}$ with the property that $a_n \leq a_{n+1}$ for all n is called a **nondecreasing sequence**; that is, $a_1 \leq a_2 \leq a_3 \leq \dots$.
>
> It is called **nonincreasing** if $a_n \geq a_{n+1}$ for all n. A sequence is **monotonic** if it is either nondecreasing or nonincreasing.

CD-ROM
WEBsite

Historical Biography

Fibonacci
(1170 — 1240)

Example 2   Monotonic Sequences

(a) The sequence $1, 2, 3, \dots, n, \dots$ of natural numbers is nondecreasing.

(b) The sequence $\dfrac{1}{2}, \dfrac{2}{3}, \dfrac{3}{4}, \dots, \dfrac{n}{n+1}, \dots$ is nondecreasing.

(c) The sequence $\dfrac{3}{8}, \dfrac{3}{9}, \dfrac{3}{10}, \dots, \dfrac{3}{n+7}, \dots$ is nonincreasing.

(d) The constant sequence $\{3\}$ is both nondecreasing and nonincreasing.

Example 3   A Nondecreasing Sequence

Show that the sequence

$$a_n = \frac{n-1}{n+1}$$

is nondecreasing.

Solution

(a) We show that for all $n \geq 1$, $a_n \leq a_{n+1}$; that is,

$$\frac{n-1}{n+1} \leq \frac{(n+1)-1}{(n+1)+1}.$$

The inequality is equivalent to the one we get by cross multiplication:

$$\frac{n-1}{n+1} \leq \frac{(n+1)-1}{(n+1)+1} \Leftrightarrow \frac{n-1}{n+1} \leq \frac{n}{n+2}$$

$$\Leftrightarrow (n-1)(n+2) \leq n(n+1)$$

$$\Leftrightarrow n^2 + n - 2 \leq n^2 + n$$

$$\Leftrightarrow -2 \leq 0.$$

Since $-2 \leq 0$ is true, $a_n \leq a_{n+1}$ and the sequence $\{a_n\}$ is nondecreasing.

(b) Another way to show that $\{a_n\}$ is nondecreasing is by defining $f(n) = a_n$ and establishing that $f'(x) \geq 0$. In this example, $f(n) = (n - 1)/(n + 1)$ and

$$f'(x) = \frac{d}{dx}\left(\frac{x - 1}{x + 1}\right)$$

$$= \frac{(x + 1)(1) - (x - 1)(1)}{(x + 1)^2} \qquad \text{Quotient Rule}$$

$$= \frac{2}{(x + 1)^2} > 0.$$

Therefore, f is an increasing function, so $f(n + 1) \geq f(n)$, or $a_{n+1} \geq a_n$.

Definition Bounded from Above, Upper Bound, Bounded from Below, Lower Bound, Bounded Sequence

A sequence $\{a_n\}$ is **bounded from above** if there exists a number M such that $a_n \leq M$ for all n. The number M is an **upper bound** for $\{a_n\}$. The sequence is **bounded from below** if there exists a number m such that $m \leq a_n$ for all n. The number m is a **lower bound** for $\{a_n\}$. If it is bounded from above and below, then $\{a_n\}$ is a **bounded sequence.**

Example 4 Applying The Definition For Boundedness

(a) The sequence $1, 2, 3, \ldots, n, \ldots$ has no upper bound, but it is bounded below by $m = 1$.

(b) The sequence $\frac{1}{2}, \frac{2}{3}, \frac{3}{4}, \ldots, \frac{n}{n + 1}, \ldots$ is bounded above by $M = 1$ and below by $m = \frac{1}{2}$.

(c) The sequence $-1, 2, -3, 4, \ldots, (-1)^n n, \ldots$ is neither bounded from above nor from below.

We know that not every bounded sequence converges because the sequence $a_n = (-1)^n$ is bounded ($-1 \leq a_n \leq 1$) but is divergent. Also, not every monotonic sequence converges because the sequence $1, 2, 3, \ldots, n, \ldots$ of natural numbers is monotonic but diverges. If a sequence is *both* bounded and monotonic, however, then it must converge. This fact is summarized in the following theorem.

Theorem 5 Monotonic Sequence Theorem

Every bounded, monotonic sequence is convergent.

Although we do not prove Theorem 5, Figure 8.5 helps us understand why it is true for a nondecreasing sequence that is bounded from above. Since the sequence is nondecreasing and cannot go above M, the terms are forced to bunch together around some number $L \leq M$.

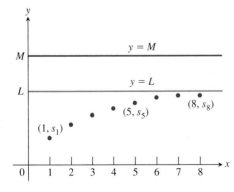

FIGURE 8.5 If the terms of a nondecreasing sequence have an upper bound M, they have a limit $L \leq M$.

Example 5 Applying Theorem 5

(a) The nondecreasing sequence $\left\{\dfrac{n}{n+1}\right\}$ is convergent because it is bounded above by $M = 1$. In fact,

$$\lim_{n\to\infty} \frac{n}{n+1} = \lim_{n\to\infty} \frac{1}{1 + (1/n)}$$

$$= \frac{1}{1+0}$$

$$= 1,$$

and the sequence converges to $L = 1$.

(b) The nonincreasing sequence $\left\{\dfrac{1}{n+1}\right\}$ is bounded below by $m = 0$ and is therefore convergent. It converges to $L = 0$.

Recursively Defined Sequences

Recursion formulas arise regularly in computer programs and numerical routines for solving differential equations, such as Euler's method.

So far, the sequences we have studied calculated each a_n directly from the value of n. Sequences, however, are often defined **recursively** by giving

1. The value(s) of the initial term or terms and

2. A rule, called a **recursion formula,** for calculating any later term from terms that precede it.

Factorial Notation

The notation $n!$ ("n factorial") means the product $1 \cdot 2 \cdot 3 \cdots n$ of the integers from 1 to n. Notice that $(n + 1)! = (n + 1) \cdot n!$. Thus, $4! = 1 \cdot 2 \cdot 3 \cdot 4 = 24$ and $5! = 1 \cdot 2 \cdot 3 \cdot 4 \cdot 5 = 5 \cdot 4! = 120$. We define $0!$ to be 1. Factorials grow even faster than exponentials, as the following table suggests.

n	e^n (rounded)	$n!$
1	3	1
5	148	120
10	22,026	3,628,800
20	4.9×10^8	2.4×10^{18}

Example 6 Sequences Constructed Recursively

(a) The statements $a_1 = 1$ and $a_n = a_{n-1} + 1$ define the sequence $1, 2, 3, \ldots,$ $n, \ldots$ of positive integers. With $a_1 = 1$, we have $a_2 = a_1 + 1 = 2$, $a_3 = a_2 + 1 = 3$, and so on.

(b) The statements $a_1 = 1$ and $a_n = n \cdot a_{n-1}$ define the sequence $1, 2, 6, 24, \ldots,$ $n!, \ldots$ of factorials. With $a_1 = 1$, we have $a_2 = 2 \cdot a_1 = 2$, $a_3 = 3 \cdot a_2 = 6$, $a_4 = 4 \cdot a_3 = 24$, and so on.

(c) The statements $a_1 = 1$, $a_2 = 1$, and $a_{n+1} = a_n + a_{n-1}$ define the sequence $1, 1, 2, 3, 5, \ldots$ of **Fibonacci numbers.** With $a_1 = 1$ and $a_2 = 1$, we have $a_3 = 1 + 1 = 2$, $a_4 = 2 + 1 = 3$, $a_5 = 3 + 2 = 5$, and so on.

(d) As we can see by applying Newton's method, the statements $x_0 = 1$ and $x_{n+1} = x_n - [(\sin x_n - x_n^2)/(\cos x_n - 2x_n)]$ define a sequence that converges to a solution of the equation $\sin x - x^2 = 0$.

Picard's Method for Finding Roots

The problem of solving the equation

$$f(x) = 0 \tag{1}$$

is equivalent to that of solving the equation

$$g(x) = f(x) + x = x,$$

obtained by adding x to both sides of Equation (1). By this simple change, we cast Equation (1) into a form that may render it solvable on a computer by a powerful method called **Picard's method.**

If the domain of g contains the range of g, we can start with a point x_0 in the domain and apply g repeatedly to get

$$x_1 = g(x_0), \qquad x_2 = g(x_1), \qquad x_3 = g(x_2), \ldots.$$

Under simple restrictions that we describe shortly, the sequence generated by the recursion formula $x_{n+1} = g(x_n)$ will converge to a point x for which $g(x) = x$. This point solves the equation $f(x) = 0$ because

$$f(x) = g(x) - x = x - x = 0.$$

A point x for which $g(x) = x$ is a **fixed point** of g. We see from the last equation that the fixed points of g are precisely the roots of f.

Example 7   Testing Picard's Method

Solve the equation

$$\frac{1}{4}x + 3 = x.$$

Solution   By algebra, we know that the solution is $x = 4$. To apply Picard's method, we take

$$g(x) = \frac{1}{4}x + 3,$$

choose a starting point, say $x_0 = 1$, and calculate the initial terms of the sequence $x_{n+1} = g(x_n)$. Table 8.2 lists the results. In 10 steps, the solution of the original equation is found with an error of magnitude less than 3×10^{-6}.

Table 8.2 Successive iterates of $g(x) = (1/4)x + 3$, starting with $x_0 = 1$	
x_n	$x_{n+1} = g(x_n) = (1/4)\, x_n + 3$
$x_0 = 1$	$x_1 = g(x_0) = (1/4)(1) + 3 = 3.25$
$x_1 = 3.25$	$x_2 = g(x_1) = (1/4)(3.25) + 3 = 3.8125$
$x_2 = 3.8125$	$x_3 = g(x_2) = 3.9531\,25$
$x_3 = 3.9531\,25$	$x_4 = 3.9882\,8125$
$\cdot$	$x_5 = 3.9970\,70313$
$\cdot$	$x_6 = 3.9992\,67578$
$\cdot$	$x_7 = 3.9998\,16895$
	$x_8 = 3.9999\,54224$
	$x_9 = 3.9999\,88556$
	$x_{10} = 3.9999\,97139$
	$\vdots$

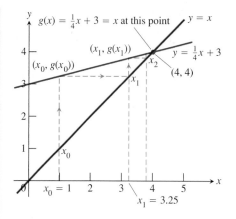

FIGURE 8.6 The Picard solution of the equation $g(x) = (1/4)x + 3 = x$. (Example 7)

Figure 8.6 shows the geometry of the solution. We start with $x_0 = 1$ and calculate the first value $g(x_0)$. This becomes the second x-value x_1. The second y-value $g(x_1)$ becomes the third x-value x_2, and so on. The process is shown as a path (called the *iteration path*) that starts at $x_0 = 1$, moves up to $(x_0, g(x_0)) = (x_0, x_1)$, over to (x_1, x_1), up to $(x_1, g(x_1))$, and so on. The path converges to the point where the graph of g meets the line $y = x$. This is the point where $g(x) = x$.

Example 8   Using Picard's Method

Solve the equation $\cos x = x$.

Solution   We take $g(x) = \cos x$, choose $x_0 = 1$ as a starting value, and use the recursion formula $x_{n+1} = g(x_n)$ to find

$$x_0 = 1, \qquad x_1 = \cos 1, \qquad x_2 = \cos (x_1), \ldots.$$

We can approximate the first 50 terms or so on a calculator in radian mode by entering 1 and taking the cosine repeatedly. The display stops changing when $\cos x = x$ to the number of decimal places in the display.

Try it for yourself. As you continue to take the cosine, the successive approximations lie alternately above and below the fixed point $x = 0.739085133\ldots$.

Figure 8.7 shows that the values oscillate this way because the path of the procedure spirals around the fixed point.

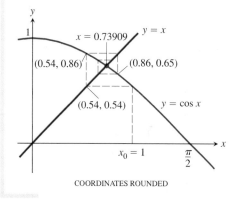

COORDINATES ROUNDED

FIGURE 8.7 The solution of $\cos x = x$ by Picard's method starting at $x_0 = 1$. (Example 8)

Example 9   Picard's Method May Fail to Solve an Equation

Picard's method will not solve the equation

$$g(x) = 4x - 12 = x.$$

As Figure 8.8 shows, any choice of x_0 except $x_0 = 4$, the solution itself, generates a divergent sequence that moves away from the solution.

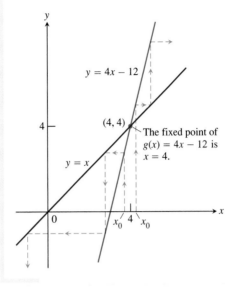

FIGURE 8.8 Applying the Picard method to $g(x) = 4x - 12$ will not find the fixed point unless x_0 is the fixed point 4 itself. (Example 9)

The difficulty in Example 9 can be traced to the slope of the line $y = 4x - 12$ exceeding 1, the slope of the line $y = x$. Conversely, the process worked in Example 7 because the slope of the line $y = (1/4)x + 3$ was numerically less than 1. A theorem from advanced calculus tells us that if $g'(x)$ is continuous on a closed interval I whose interior contains a solution of the equation $g(x) = x$ and if $|g'(x)| < 1$ on I, then any choice of x_0 in the interior of I will lead to the solution.

EXERCISES 8.2

Finding Terms of a Recursively Defined Sequence

Each of Exercises 1–6 gives the first term or two of a sequence along with a recursion formula for the remaining terms. Write out the first ten terms of the sequence.

1. $a_1 = 1, \quad a_{n+1} = a_n + (1/2^n)$

2. $a_1 = 1, \quad a_{n+1} = a_n/(n + 1)$

3. $a_1 = 2, \quad a_{n+1} = (-1)^{n+1} a_n/2$

4. $a_1 = -2, \quad a_{n+1} = na_n/(n + 1)$

5. $a_1 = a_2 = 1, \quad a_{n+2} = a_{n+1} + a_n$

6. $a_1 = 2, \quad a_2 = -1, \quad a_{n+2} = a_{n+1}/a_n$

T **7.** *Sequences generated by Newton's method* Newton's method, applied to a differentiable function $f(x)$, begins with a starting value x_0 and constructs from it a sequence of numbers $\{x_n\}$ that under favorable circumstances converges to a zero of f. The recursion formula for the sequence is

$$x_{n+1} = x_n - \frac{f(x_n)}{f'(x_n)}.$$

(a) Show that the recursion formula for $f(x) = x^2 - a$, $a > 0$, can be written as $x_{n+1} = (x_n + a/x_n)/2$.

(b) *Writing to Learn* Starting with $x_0 = 1$ and $a = 3$, calculate successive terms of the sequence until the display begins to repeat. What number is being approximated? Explain.

T **8.** (*Continuation of Exercise 7*) Repeat part (b) of Exercise 7 with $a = 2$ in place of $a = 3$.

T **9.** *Newton's method* The following sequences come from the recursion formula for Newton's method (see Exercise 7).

Do the sequences converge? If so, to what value? In each case, begin by identifying the function f that generates the sequence.

(a) $x_0 = 1$, $x_{n+1} = x_n - \dfrac{x_n^2 - 2}{2x_n} = \dfrac{x_n}{2} + \dfrac{1}{x_n}$

(b) $x_0 = 1$, $x_{n+1} = x_n - \dfrac{\tan x_n - 1}{\sec^2 x_n}$

(c) $x_0 = 1$, $x_{n+1} = x_n - 1$

T **10.** *A recursive definition of $\pi/2$* If you start with $x_1 = 1$ and define the subsequent terms of $\{x_n\}$ by the rule $x_n = x_{n-1} + \cos x_{n-1}$, you generate a sequence that converges rapidly to $\pi/2$.

(a) Try it.

(b) Use the accompanying figure to explain why the convergence is so rapid.

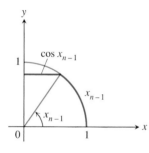

Theory and Examples

In Exercises 11–14, determine if the sequence is nondecreasing and if it is bounded from above.

11. $a_n = \dfrac{3n + 1}{n + 1}$

12. $a_n = \dfrac{(2n + 3)!}{(n + 1)!}$

13. $a_n = \dfrac{2^n 3^n}{n!}$

14. $a_n = 2 - \dfrac{2}{n} - \dfrac{1}{2^n}$

Which of the sequences in Exercises 15–24 converge, and which diverge? Give reasons for your answers.

15. $a_n = 1 - \dfrac{1}{n}$

16. $a_n = n - \dfrac{1}{n}$

17. $a_n = \dfrac{2^n - 1}{2^n}$

18. $a_n = \dfrac{2^n - 1}{3^n}$

19. $a_n = ((-1)^n + 1)\left(\dfrac{n + 1}{n}\right)$

20. The first term of a sequence is $x_1 = \cos(1)$. The next terms are $x_2 = x_1$ or $\cos(2)$, whichever is larger, and $x_3 = x_2$ or $\cos(3)$, whichever is larger (farther to the right). In general,

$$x_{n+1} = \max\{x_n, \cos(n + 1)\}.$$

21. $a_n = \dfrac{n + 1}{n}$

22. $a_n = \dfrac{1 + \sqrt{2n}}{\sqrt{n}}$

23. $a_n = \dfrac{1 - 4^n}{2^n}$

24. $a_n = \dfrac{4^{n+1} + 3^n}{4^n}$

25. *Limits and subsequences* Prove that if two subsequences of a sequence $\{a_n\}$ have different limits $L_1 \neq L_2$, then $\{a_n\}$ diverges.

26. *Even and odd indices* For a sequence $\{a_n\}$, the terms of even index are denoted by a_{2k} and the terms of odd index by a_{2k+1}. Prove that if $a_{2k} \to L$ and $a_{2k+1} \to L$, then $a_n \to L$.

Picard's Method

Use Picard's method to solve the equations in Exercises 27–32.

27. $\sqrt{x} = x$

28. $x^2 = x$

29. $\cos x + x = 0$

30. $\cos x = x + 1$

31. $x - \sin x = 0.1$

32. $\sqrt{x} = 4 - \sqrt{1 + x}$ (*Hint:* Square both sides first.)

33. Solving the equation $\sqrt{x} = x$ by Picard's method finds the solution $x = 1$ but not the solution $x = 0$. Why? (*Hint:* Graph $y = x$ and $y = \sqrt{x}$ together.)

34. Solving the equation $x^2 = x$ by Picard's method with $|x_0| \neq 1$ can find the solution $x = 0$ but not the solution $x = 1$. Why? (*Hint:* Graph $y = x^2$ and $y = x$ together.)

COMPUTER EXPLORATIONS

Looking for Convergence of Recursively Defined Sequences

Use a CAS to perform the following steps for the sequences in Exercises 35 and 36.

(a) Calculate and then plot the first 25 terms of the sequence. Does the sequence appear to be bounded from above or below? Does it appear to converge or diverge? If it does converge, what is the limit L?

(b) If the sequence converges, find an integer N such that $|a_n - L| \leq 0.01$ for $n \geq N$. How far in the sequence do you have to get for the terms to lie within 0.0001 of L?

35. $a_1 = 1$, $a_{n+1} = a_n + \dfrac{1}{5^n}$

36. $a_1 = 1$, $a_{n+1} = a_n + (-2)^n$

37. *Compound interest, deposits, and withdrawals* If you invest an amount of money A_0 at a fixed annual interest rate r compounded m times per year and if the constant amount b is added to the account at the end of each compounding period (or taken from the account if $b < 0$), then the amount you have after $n + 1$ compounding periods is

$$A_{n+1} = \left(1 + \dfrac{r}{m}\right)A_n + b. \tag{2}$$

(a) If $A_0 = 1000$, $r = 0.02015$, $m = 12$, and $b = 50$, calculate and plot the first 100 points (n, A_n). How much money is in your account at the end of 5 years? Does $\{A_n\}$ converge? Is $\{A_n\}$ bounded?

(b) Repeat part (a) with $A_0 = 5000$, $r = 0.0589$, $m = 12$, and $b = -50$.

(c) If you invest 5000 dollars in a certificate of deposit (CD) that pays 4.5% annually, compounded quarterly, and you make no further investments in the CD, approximately how many years will it take before you have 20,000 dollars? What if the CD earns 6.25%?

(d) It can be shown that for any $k \geq 0$, the sequence defined recursively by Equation (2) satisfies the relation

$$A_k = \left(1 + \frac{r}{m}\right)^k \left(A_0 + \frac{mb}{r}\right) - \frac{mb}{r}. \tag{3}$$

For the values of the constants A_0, r, m, and b given in part (a), validate this assertion by comparing the values of the first 50 terms of both sequences. Then show by direct substitution that the terms in Equation (3) satisfy the recursion formula (2).

38. *Logistic difference equation and bifurcation* The recursive relation

$$a_{n+1} = ra_n(1 - a_n)$$

is called the **logistic difference equation,** and when the initial value a_0 is given, the equation defines the **logistic sequence** $\{a_n\}$. Throughout this exercise, we choose a_0 in the interval $0 < a_0 < 1$, say $a_0 = 0.3$.

(a) Choose $r = 3/4$. Calculate and plot the points (n, a_n) for the first 100 terms in the sequence. Does it appear to converge? What do you guess is the limit? Does the limit seem to depend on your choice of a_0?

(b) Choose several values of r in the interval $1 < r < 3$ and repeat the procedures in part (a). Be sure to choose some points near the endpoints of the interval. Describe the behavior of the sequences you observe in your plots.

(c) Now examine the behavior of the sequence for values of r near the endpoints of the interval $3 < r < 3.45$. The transition value $r = 3$ is called a **bifurcation value,** and the new behavior of the sequence in the interval is called an **attracting 2-cycle.** Explain why this reasonably describes the behavior.

(d) Next explore the behavior for r values near the endpoints of each of the intervals $3.45 < r < 3.54$ and $3.54 < r < 3.55$. Plot the first 200 terms of the sequences. Describe in your own words the behavior observed in your plots for each interval. Among how many values does the sequence appear to oscillate for each interval? The values $r = 3.45$ and $r = 3.54$ (rounded to 2 decimal places) are also called bifurcation values because the behavior of the sequence changes as r crosses over those values.

(e) The situation gets even more interesting. There is actually an increasing sequence of bifurcation values $3 < 3.45 < 3.54 < \ldots < c_n < c_{n+1} \ldots$ such that for $c_n < r < c_{n+1}$, the logistic sequence $\{a_n\}$ eventually oscillates steadily among 2^n values, called an **attracting 2^n-cycle.** Moreover, the bifurcation sequence $\{c_n\}$ is bounded above by 3.57 (so it converges). If you choose a value of $r < 3.57$, you will observe a 2^n-cycle of some sort. Choose $r = 3.5695$ and plot 300 points.

(f) Let us see what happens when $r > 3.57$. Choose $r = 3.65$ and calculate and plot the first 300 terms of $\{a_n\}$. Observe how the terms wander around in an unpredictable, chaotic fashion. You cannot predict the value of a_{n+1} from the value of a_n.

(g) For $r = 3.65$, choose two starting values of a_0 that are close together, say $a_0 = 0.3$ and $a_0 = 0.301$. Calculate and plot the first 300 values of the sequences determined by each starting value. Compare the behaviors observed in your plots. How far out do you go before the corresponding terms of your two sequences appear to depart from each other? Repeat the exploration for $r = 3.75$. Can you see how the plots look different depending on your choice of a_0? We say that the logistic sequence is **sensitive to the initial condition a_0.**

8.3 Infinite Series

Series and Partial Sums • Geometric Series • Divergent Series • nth-Term Test for Divergence • Adding or Deleting Terms • Reindexing • Combining Series

In mathematics and science, we often write functions as infinite polynomials, such as

$$\frac{1}{1 - x} = 1 + x + x^2 + x^3 + \cdots + x^n + \cdots, \qquad |x| < 1$$

(we see the importance of doing so as the chapter continues). For any allowable value of x, we evaluate the polynomial as an infinite sum of constants, a sum we call an *infinite series*. The goal of this section is to familiarize ourselves with infinite series.

Series and Partial Sums

The first thing to get straight about an infinite series is that it is not simply an example of addition. Addition of real numbers is a *binary* operation, meaning that we really add numbers two at a time. The only reason that $1 + 2 + 3$ makes sense as "addition" is that we can *group* the numbers and then add them two at a time. The associative property of addition guarantees that we get the same sum no matter how we group them:

$$1 + (2 + 3) = 1 + 5 = 6 \quad \text{and} \quad (1 + 2) + 3 = 3 + 3 = 6.$$

In short, a *finite sum* of real numbers always produces a real number (the result of a finite number of binary additions), but an *infinite sum* of real numbers is something else entirely. That is why we need a careful definition of infinite series.

We begin by asking how to assign meaning to an expression like

$$1 + \frac{1}{2} + \frac{1}{4} + \frac{1}{8} + \frac{1}{16} + \cdots.$$

The way to do so is not to try to add all the terms at once (we cannot) but rather to add the terms one at a time from the beginning and look for a pattern in how these "partial sums" grow.

Partial sum		Value
First:	$s_1 = 1$	$2 - 1$
Second:	$s_2 = 1 + \frac{1}{2}$	$2 - \frac{1}{2}$
Third:	$s_3 = 1 + \frac{1}{2} + \frac{1}{4}$	$2 - \frac{1}{4}$
$\vdots$	$\vdots$	$\vdots$
nth	$s_n = 1 + \frac{1}{2} + \frac{1}{4} + \cdots + \frac{1}{2^{n-1}}$	$2 - \frac{1}{2^{n-1}}$

Indeed there is a pattern. The partial sums form a sequence whose nth term is

$$s_n = 2 - \frac{1}{2^{n-1}}.$$

(We see why momentarily.) This sequence converges to 2 because $\lim_{n \to \infty} (1/2^n) = 0$. We say,

"The sum of the infinite series $1 + \frac{1}{2} + \frac{1}{4} + \cdots + \frac{1}{2^{n-1}} + \cdots$ is 2."

Is the sum of any finite number of terms in this series equal to 2? No. Can we actually add an infinite number of terms one by one? No. We can, however, still define their sum by defining it to be the limit of the sequence of partial sums as $n \to \infty$, in this case 2 (Figure 8.9). Our knowledge of sequences and limits enables us to break away from the confines of finite sums to define this entirely new concept.

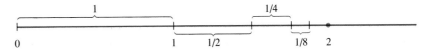

FIGURE 8.9 As the lengths $1, \frac{1}{2}, \frac{1}{4}, \frac{1}{8}, \ldots$ are added one by one, the sum approaches 2.

CD-ROM
WEBsite

Historical Biography

Blaise Pascal
(1623 — 1662)

Definition Infinite Series

Given a sequence of numbers $\{a_n\}$, an expression of the form

$$a_1 + a_2 + a_3 + \cdots + a_n + \cdots$$

is an **infinite series.** The number a_n is the **nth term** of the series.

The **partial sums** of the series form a sequence

$$s_1 = a_1$$
$$s_2 = a_1 + a_2$$
$$s_3 = a_1 + a_2 + a_3$$
$$\vdots$$
$$s_n = \sum_{k=1}^{n} a_k$$
$$\vdots$$

of real numbers, each defined as a finite sum. If the sequence of partial sums has a limit S as $n \to \infty$, we say that the series **converges** to the sum S, and we write

$$a_1 + a_2 + a_3 + \cdots + a_n + \cdots = \sum_{k=1}^{\infty} a_k = S.$$

Otherwise, we say that the series **diverges.**

Example 1 Identifying a Convergent Series

Does the series

$$\frac{3}{10} + \frac{3}{100} + \frac{3}{1000} + \cdots + \frac{3}{10^n} + \cdots$$

converge?

Solution   Here is the sequence of partial sums, written in decimal form.

$$0.3, 0.33, 0.333, 0.3333, \ldots$$

This sequence has a limit $0.\overline{3}$, which we recognize as the fraction $1/3$. The series converges to the sum $1/3$.

When we begin to study a given series $a_1 + a_2 + \cdots + a_n + \cdots$, we might not know whether it converges or diverges. In either case, it is convenient to use sigma notation to write the series as

$$\sum_{n=1}^{\infty} a_n, \qquad \sum_{k=1}^{\infty} a_k, \qquad \text{or} \qquad \sum a_n.$$

A useful shorthand when summation from 1 to ∞ is understood

Geometric Series

The series in Example 1 is a **geometric series** because each term is obtained from its preceding term by multiplying by the same number r, in this case, $r = 1/10$. (The series of areas for the infinitely halved square at the beginning of this chapter is also geometric.) The convergence of geometric series is one of the few infinite processes with which mathematicians were reasonably comfortable prior to calculus. Let's see why.

Geometric series are series of the form

$$a + ar + ar^2 + \cdots + ar^{n-1} + \cdots = \sum_{n=1}^{\infty} ar^{n-1}$$

in which a and r are fixed real numbers and $a \neq 0$. The **ratio** r can be positive, as in

$$1 + \frac{1}{2} + \frac{1}{4} + \cdots + \left(\frac{1}{2}\right)^{n-1} + \cdots,$$

or negative, as in

$$1 - \frac{1}{3} + \frac{1}{9} - \cdots + \left(-\frac{1}{3}\right)^{n-1} + \cdots.$$

If $|r| \neq 1$, we can determine the convergence or divergence of the series in the following way, starting with the nth partial sum:

$$s_n = a + ar + ar^2 + \cdots + ar^{n-1}$$
$$rs_n = ar + ar^2 + \cdots + ar^{n-1} + ar^n \qquad \text{Multiply } s_n \text{ by } r.$$
$$s_n - rs_n = a - ar^n \qquad \text{Subtract } rs_n \text{ from } s_n. \text{ Most of the terms on the right cancel.}$$
$$s_n(1 - r) = a(1 - r^n) \qquad \text{Factor.}$$
$$s_n = \frac{a(1 - r^n)}{1 - r}, \qquad (r \neq 1). \qquad \text{We can solve for } s_n \text{ if } r \neq 1.$$

If $|r| < 1$, then $r^n \to 0$ as $n \to \infty$ (Table 8.1, Formula 4) and $s_n \to a/(1 - r)$. If $|r| > 1$, then $|r^n| \to \infty$ and the series diverges.

If $r = 1$, the nth partial sum of the geometric series is

$$s_n = a + a(1) + a(1)^2 + \cdots + a(1)^{n-1} = na,$$

and the series diverges because $\lim_{n \to \infty} s_n = \pm\infty$, depending on the sign of a. If $r = -1$, the series diverges because the nth partial sums alternate between a and 0. Let's summarize our results.

The equation

$$\sum_{n=1}^{\infty} ar^{n-1} = \frac{a}{1 - r}, \qquad |r| < 1$$

holds only if the summation begins with $n = 1$.

The geometric series

$$a + ar + ar^2 + ar^3 + \cdots + ar^{n-1} + \cdots = \sum_{n=1}^{\infty} ar^{n-1}$$

converges to the sum $a/(1 - r)$ if $|r| < 1$ and diverges if $|r| \geq 1$.

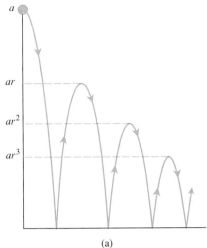

a

ar

ar^2

ar^3

(a)

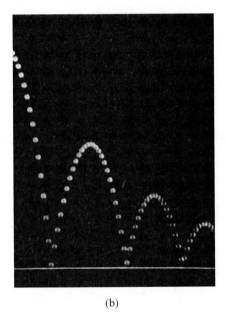

(b)

FIGURE 8.10 (a) Example 3 shows how to use a geometric series to calculate the total vertical distance traveled by a bouncing ball if the height of each rebound is reduced by the factor r. (b) A stroboscopic photo of a bouncing ball.

CD-ROM
WEBsite

This completely settles the issue for geometric series. We know which ones converge and which ones diverge, and for the convergent ones, we know what the sums must be. The interval $-1 < r < 1$ is the **interval of convergence.**

Example 2   Analyzing Geometric Series

Tell whether each series converges or diverges. If it converges, give its sum.

(a) $\displaystyle\sum_{n=1}^{\infty} 3\left(\frac{1}{2}\right)^{n-1}$

(b) $1 - \dfrac{1}{2} + \dfrac{1}{4} - \dfrac{1}{8} + \cdots + \left(-\dfrac{1}{2}\right)^{n-1} + \cdots$

(c) $\displaystyle\sum_{k=0}^{\infty} \left(\frac{3}{5}\right)^{k} = \sum_{k=1}^{\infty} \left(\frac{3}{5}\right)^{k-1}$

(d) $\dfrac{\pi}{2} + \dfrac{\pi^2}{4} + \dfrac{\pi^3}{8} + \cdots$

Solution

(a) First term is $a = 3$ and $r = 1/2$. The series converges to

$$\frac{3}{1 - (1/2)} = 6.$$

(b) First term is $a = 1$ and $r = -1/2$. The series converges to

$$\frac{1}{1 - (-1/2)} = \frac{2}{3}.$$

(c) First term is $a = (3/5)^0 = 1$ and $r = 3/5$. The series converges to

$$\frac{1}{1 - (3/5)} = \frac{5}{2}.$$

(d) In this series, $r = \pi/2 > 1$. The series diverges.

Example 3   A Bouncing Ball

You drop a ball from a meters above a flat surface. Each time the ball hits the surface after falling a distance h, it rebounds a distance rh, where r is positive but less than 1. Find the total distance the ball travels up and down (Figure 8.10).

Solution   The total distance is

$$s = a + \underbrace{2ar + 2ar^2 + 2ar^3 + \cdots}_{\text{This sum is } 2ar/(1 - r).} = a + \frac{2ar}{1 - r} = a\,\frac{1 + r}{1 - r}.$$

If $a = 6$ m and $r = 2/3$, for instance, the distance is

$$s = 6\,\frac{1 + (2/3)}{1 - (2/3)} = 6\left(\frac{5/3}{1/3}\right) = 30 \text{ m}.$$

Example 4   Repeating Decimals

Express the repeating decimal 5.23 23 23 . . . as the ratio of two integers.

Solution

$$5.23\ 23\ 23\ldots = 5 + \frac{23}{100} + \frac{23}{(100)^2} + \frac{23}{(100)^3} + \cdots$$

$$= 5 + \frac{23}{100}\underbrace{\left(1 + \frac{1}{100} + \left(\frac{1}{100}\right)^2 + \cdots\right)}_{1/(1-0.01)} \qquad \begin{array}{l} a = 1, \\ r = 1/100 \end{array}$$

$$= 5 + \frac{23}{100}\left(\frac{1}{0.99}\right) = 5 + \frac{23}{99} = \frac{518}{99}$$

We have hardly begun our study of infinite series, but knowing everything there is to know about the convergence and divergence of an *entire class* of series (geometric) is an impressive start. Like the Renaissance mathematicians, we are ready to explore where this might lead.

Unfortunately, formulas like the one for the sum of a convergent geometric series are rare, and we usually have to settle for an estimate of a series' sum (more about this later). The next example, however, is another case in which we can find the sum exactly.

Example 5   A Nongeometric but Telescoping Series

Find the sum of the series

$$\sum_{n=1}^{\infty} \frac{1}{n(n+1)}.$$

Solution   We look for a pattern in the sequence of partial sums that might lead to a formula for s_k. The key is partial fractions. The observation that

$$\frac{1}{k(k+1)} = \frac{1}{k} - \frac{1}{k+1}$$

permits us to write the partial sum

$$\sum_{n=1}^{k} \frac{1}{n(n+1)} = \frac{1}{1 \cdot 2} + \frac{1}{2 \cdot 3} + \cdots + \frac{1}{k \cdot (k+1)}$$

as

$$s_k = \left(\frac{1}{1} - \frac{1}{2}\right) + \left(\frac{1}{2} - \frac{1}{3}\right) + \cdots + \left(\frac{1}{k} - \frac{1}{k+1}\right).$$

Removing parentheses and canceling the terms of opposite sign collapses the sum to

$$s_k = 1 - \frac{1}{k+1}.$$

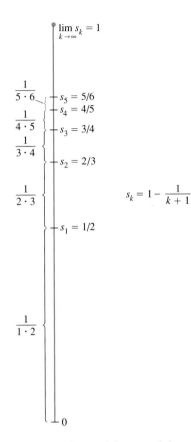

FIGURE 8.11 **The partial sums of the series in Example 5.**

We now see that $s_k \to 1$ as $k \to \infty$. The series converges, and its sum is 1 (Figure 8.11).

$$\sum_{n=1}^{\infty} \frac{1}{n(n+1)} = 1.$$

Divergent Series

Geometric series with $|r| \geq 1$ are not the only series to diverge.

Example 6   Identifying a Divergent Series

Does the series $1 - 1 + 1 - 1 + 1 - 1 + \cdots$ converge?

Solution   You might be tempted to pair the terms as

$$(1 - 1) + (1 - 1) + (1 - 1) + \cdots.$$

That strategy, however, requires an *infinite* number of pairings, so it cannot be justified by the associative property of addition. This is an infinite series, not a finite sum, so if it has a sum it *has to be* the limit of its sequence of partial sums,

$$1, 0, 1, 0, 1, 0, 1, \ldots.$$

Since this sequence has no limit, the series has no sum. It diverges.

Example 7   Partial Sums Outgrowing Any Bound

(a) The series

$$\sum_{n=1}^{\infty} n^2 = 1 + 4 + 9 + \cdots + n^2 + \cdots$$

diverges because the partial sums grow beyond every number L. After $n = 1$, the partial sum $s_n = 1 + 4 + 9 + \cdots + n^2$ is greater than n^2.

(b) The series

$$\sum_{n=1}^{\infty} \frac{n+1}{n} = \frac{2}{1} + \frac{3}{2} + \frac{4}{3} + \cdots + \frac{n+1}{n} + \cdots$$

diverges because the partial sums eventually outgrow every preassigned number. Each term is greater than 1, so the sum of n terms is greater than n.

nth-Term Test for Divergence

Observe that $\lim_{n \to \infty} a_n$ must equal zero if the series $\sum_{n=1}^{\infty} a_n$ converges. To see why, let S represent the series' sum and $s_n = a_1 + a_2 + \cdots + a_n$ the nth partial sum. When n is large, both s_n and s_{n-1} are close to S, so their difference, a_n, is close to zero. More formally,

$$a_n = s_n - s_{n-1} \to S - S = 0. \qquad \text{Difference Rule for sequences}$$

CAUTION Theorem 6 *does not say* that $\sum_{n=1}^{\infty} a_n$ converges if $a_n \to 0$. It is possible for a series to diverge when $a_n \to 0$.

Theorem 6 Limit of the nth Term of a Convergent Series

If $\sum_{n=1}^{\infty} a_n$ converges, then $a_n \to 0$.

Theorem 6 leads to a test for detecting the kind of divergence that occurred in Examples 6 and 7.

nth-Term Test for Divergence

$\sum_{n=1}^{\infty} a_n$ diverges if $\lim_{n \to \infty} a_n$ fails to exist or is different from zero.

Example 8 Applying the *nth*-Term Test

(a) $\sum_{n=1}^{\infty} n^2$ diverges because $n^2 \to \infty$.

(b) $\sum_{n=1}^{\infty} \frac{n+1}{n}$ diverges because $\frac{n+1}{n} \to 1$.

(c) $\sum_{n=1}^{\infty} (-1)^{n+1}$ diverges because $\lim_{n \to \infty} (-1)^{n+1}$ does not exist.

(d) $\sum_{n=1}^{\infty} \frac{-n}{2n+5}$ diverges because $\lim_{n \to \infty} \left(\frac{-n}{2n+5} \right) = -\frac{1}{2} \neq 0$.

Example 9 $a_n \to 0$, but the Series Diverges

The series

$$1 + \underbrace{\frac{1}{2} + \frac{1}{2}}_{2 \text{ terms}} + \underbrace{\frac{1}{4} + \frac{1}{4} + \frac{1}{4} + \frac{1}{4}}_{4 \text{ terms}} + \cdots + \underbrace{\frac{1}{2^n} + \frac{1}{2^n} + \cdots + \frac{1}{2^n}}_{2^n \text{ terms}} + \cdots$$

$$= 1 + 1 + 1 + \cdots + 1 + \cdots$$

diverges even though its terms form a sequence that converges to 0.

Adding or Deleting Terms

We can always add a finite number of terms to a series or delete a finite number of terms without altering the series' convergence or divergence, although in the case of convergence, this will usually change the sum. If $\sum_{n=1}^{\infty} a_n$ converges, then $\sum_{n=k}^{\infty} a_n$ converges for any $k > 1$, and

$$\sum_{n=1}^{\infty} a_n = a_1 + a_2 + \cdots + a_{k-1} + \sum_{n=k}^{\infty} a_n.$$

Conversely, if $\sum_{n=k}^{\infty} a_n$ converges for any $k > 1$, then $\sum_{n=1}^{\infty} a_n$ converges. Thus,

$$\sum_{n=1}^{\infty} \frac{1}{5^n} = \frac{1}{5} + \frac{1}{25} + \frac{1}{125} + \sum_{n=4}^{\infty} \frac{1}{5^n}$$

and

$$\sum_{n=4}^{\infty} \frac{1}{5^n} = \left(\sum_{n=1}^{\infty} \frac{1}{5^n} \right) - \frac{1}{5} - \frac{1}{25} - \frac{1}{125}.$$

CD-ROM
WEBsite

Historical Biography

Richard Dedekind
(1831 — 1916)

Reindexing

As long as we preserve the order of its terms, we can reindex any series without altering its convergence (see Example 2c). To raise the starting value of the index h units, replace the n in the formula for a_n by $n - h$:

$$\sum_{n=1}^{\infty} a_n = \sum_{n=1+h}^{\infty} a_{n-h} = a_1 + a_2 + a_3 + \cdots.$$

To lower the starting value of the index h units, replace the n in the formula for a_n by $n + h$:

$$\sum_{n=1}^{\infty} a_n = \sum_{n=1-h}^{\infty} a_{n+h} = a_1 + a_2 + a_3 + \cdots.$$

It works like a horizontal shift.

Example 10 Reindexing A Geometric Series

We can write the geometric series that starts with

$$1 + \frac{1}{2} + \frac{1}{4} + \cdots$$

as

$$\sum_{n=0}^{\infty} \frac{1}{2^n}, \qquad \sum_{n=5}^{\infty} \frac{1}{2^{n-5}}, \qquad \text{or even} \qquad \sum_{n=-4}^{\infty} \frac{1}{2^{n+4}}.$$

The partial sums remain the same no matter what indexing we choose.

We usually give preference to indexings that lead to simple expressions.

Combining Series

Whenever we have two convergent series, we can add them term by term, subtract them term by term, or multiply them by constants to make new convergent series.

Theorem 7 Properties of Convergent Series

If $\Sigma a_n = A$ and $\Sigma b_n = B$ are convergent series, then

1. *Sum Rule:* $\Sigma (a_n + b_n) = \Sigma a_n + \Sigma b_n = A + B$

2. *Difference Rule:* $\Sigma (a_n - b_n) = \Sigma a_n - \Sigma b_n = A - B$

3. *Constant Multiple Rule:* $\Sigma ka_n = k \Sigma a_n = kA$ (any number k).

Example 11   Applying Theorem 7

Find the sums of the following series.

(a) $\displaystyle\sum_{n=1}^{\infty} \frac{3^{n-1} - 1}{6^{n-1}} = \sum_{n=1}^{\infty} \left(\frac{1}{2^{n-1}} - \frac{1}{6^{n-1}} \right)$

$\displaystyle \qquad = \sum_{n=1}^{\infty} \frac{1}{2^{n-1}} - \sum_{n=1}^{\infty} \frac{1}{6^{n-1}}$ Difference Rule

$\displaystyle \qquad = \frac{1}{1 - (1/2)} - \frac{1}{1 - (1/6)}$ Geometric series with $a = 1$ and $r = 1/2, 1/6$

$\displaystyle \qquad = 2 - \frac{6}{5}$

$\displaystyle \qquad = \frac{4}{5}$

(b) $\displaystyle\sum_{n=1}^{\infty} \frac{4}{2^{n-1}} = 4 \sum_{n=1}^{\infty} \frac{1}{2^{n-1}}$ Constant Multiple Rule

$\displaystyle \qquad = 4 \left(\frac{1}{1 - (1/2)} \right)$ Geometric series with $a = 1, r = 1/2$

$\displaystyle \qquad = 8$

Proof of Theorem 7   The three rules for series follow from the analogous rules for sequences in Theorem 1, Section 8.1. To prove the Sum Rule for series, let

$$A_n = a_1 + a_2 + \cdots + a_n, \qquad B_n = b_1 + b_2 + \cdots + b_n.$$

Then the partial sums of $\Sigma\,(a_n + b_n)$ are

$$\begin{aligned} S_n &= (a_1 + b_1) + (a_2 + b_2) + \cdots + (a_n + b_n) \\ &= (a_1 + \cdots + a_n) + (b_1 + \cdots + b_n) \\ &= A_n + B_n. \end{aligned}$$

Since $A_n \to A$ and $B_n \to B$, we have $S_n \to A + B$ by the Sum Rule for sequences. The proof of the Difference Rule is similar.

To prove the Constant Multiple Rule for series, observe that the partial sums of $\Sigma\,ka_n$ form the sequence

$$S_n = ka_1 + ka_2 + \cdots + ka_n = k(a_1 + a_2 + \cdots + a_n) = kA_n,$$

which converges to kA by the Constant Multiple Rule for sequences.   ▬

Interpreting Theorem 7 for Divergence

1.   Every nonzero constant multiple of a divergent series diverges.

2.   If $\Sigma\,a_n$ converges and $\Sigma\,b_n$ diverges, then $\Sigma\,(a_n + b_n)$ and $\Sigma\,(a_n - b_n)$ both diverge.

We omit the proofs.

EXERCISES 8.3

Finding nth Partial Sums

In Exercises 1–6, find a formula for the nth partial sum of each series and use it to find the series' sum if the series converges.

1. $2 + \dfrac{2}{3} + \dfrac{2}{9} + \dfrac{2}{27} + \cdots + \dfrac{2}{3^{n-1}} + \cdots$

2. $\dfrac{9}{100} + \dfrac{9}{100^2} + \dfrac{9}{100^3} + \cdots + \dfrac{9}{100^n} + \cdots$

3. $1 - \dfrac{1}{2} + \dfrac{1}{4} - \dfrac{1}{8} + \cdots + (-1)^{n-1}\dfrac{1}{2^{n-1}} + \cdots$

4. $1 - 2 + 4 - 8 + \cdots + (-1)^{n-1} 2^{n-1} + \cdots$

5. $\dfrac{1}{2 \cdot 3} + \dfrac{1}{3 \cdot 4} + \dfrac{1}{4 \cdot 5} + \cdots + \dfrac{1}{(n+1)(n+2)} + \cdots$

6. $\dfrac{5}{1 \cdot 2} + \dfrac{5}{2 \cdot 3} + \dfrac{5}{3 \cdot 4} + \cdots + \dfrac{5}{n(n+1)} + \cdots$

Series with Geometric Terms

In Exercises 7–12, write out the first few terms of each series to show how the series starts. Then find the sum of the series.

7. $\displaystyle\sum_{n=0}^{\infty} \dfrac{(-1)^n}{4^n}$

8. $\displaystyle\sum_{n=1}^{\infty} \dfrac{7}{4^n}$

9. $\displaystyle\sum_{n=0}^{\infty} \left(\dfrac{5}{2^n} + \dfrac{1}{3^n}\right)$

10. $\displaystyle\sum_{n=0}^{\infty} \left(\dfrac{5}{2^n} - \dfrac{1}{3^n}\right)$

11. $\displaystyle\sum_{n=0}^{\infty} \left(\dfrac{1}{2^n} + \dfrac{(-1)^n}{5^n}\right)$

12. $\displaystyle\sum_{n=0}^{\infty} \left(\dfrac{2^{n+1}}{5^n}\right)$

Telescoping Series

Use partial fractions to find the sum of each series in Exercises 13–16.

13. $\displaystyle\sum_{n=1}^{\infty} \dfrac{4}{(4n-3)(4n+1)}$

14. $\displaystyle\sum_{n=1}^{\infty} \dfrac{6}{(2n-1)(2n+1)}$

15. $\displaystyle\sum_{n=1}^{\infty} \dfrac{40n}{(2n-1)^2(2n+1)^2}$

16. $\displaystyle\sum_{n=1}^{\infty} \dfrac{2n+1}{n^2(n+1)^2}$

Find the sums of the series in Exercises 17 and 18.

17. $\displaystyle\sum_{n=1}^{\infty} \left(\dfrac{1}{\sqrt{n}} - \dfrac{1}{\sqrt{n+1}}\right)$

18. $\displaystyle\sum_{n=1}^{\infty} \left(\dfrac{1}{\ln(n+2)} - \dfrac{1}{\ln(n+1)}\right)$

Convergence or Divergence

Which series in Exercises 19–32 converge, and which diverge? Give reasons for your answers. If a series converges, find its sum.

19. $\displaystyle\sum_{n=0}^{\infty} \left(\dfrac{1}{\sqrt{2}}\right)^n$

20. $\displaystyle\sum_{n=0}^{\infty} (\sqrt{2})^n$

21. $\displaystyle\sum_{n=1}^{\infty} (-1)^{n+1} \dfrac{3}{2^n}$

22. $\displaystyle\sum_{n=0}^{\infty} \dfrac{\cos n\pi}{5^n}$

23. $\displaystyle\sum_{n=0}^{\infty} e^{-2n}$

24. $\displaystyle\sum_{n=1}^{\infty} \ln \dfrac{1}{n}$

25. $\displaystyle\sum_{n=0}^{\infty} \dfrac{1}{x^n}, \quad |x| > 1$

26. $\displaystyle\sum_{n=0}^{\infty} \dfrac{2^n - 1}{3^n}$

27. $\displaystyle\sum_{n=1}^{\infty} \left(1 - \dfrac{1}{n}\right)^n$

28. $\displaystyle\sum_{n=0}^{\infty} \left(\dfrac{e}{\pi}\right)^n$

29. $\displaystyle\sum_{n=1}^{\infty} \ln \left(\dfrac{n}{n+1}\right)$

30. $\displaystyle\sum_{n=0}^{\infty} \dfrac{e^{n\pi}}{\pi^{ne}}$

31. $\displaystyle\sum_{n=0}^{\infty} \dfrac{n!}{1000^n}$

32. $\displaystyle\sum_{n=1}^{\infty} \dfrac{n^n}{n!}$

Geometric Series

In each of the geometric series in Exercises 33–36, write out the first few terms of the series to find a and r and find the sum of the series. Then express the inequality $|r| < 1$ in terms of x and find the values of x for which the inequality holds and the series converges.

33. $\displaystyle\sum_{n=0}^{\infty} (-1)^n x^n$

34. $\displaystyle\sum_{n=0}^{\infty} (-1)^n x^{2n}$

35. $\displaystyle\sum_{n=0}^{\infty} 3\left(\dfrac{x-1}{2}\right)^n$

36. $\displaystyle\sum_{n=0}^{\infty} \dfrac{(-1)^n}{2} \left(\dfrac{1}{3 + \sin x}\right)^n$

In Exercises 37–40, find the values of x for which the given geometric series converges. Also, find the sum of the series (as a function of x) for those values of x.

37. $\displaystyle\sum_{n=0}^{\infty} 2^n x^n$

38. $\displaystyle\sum_{n=0}^{\infty} (-1)^n x^{-2n}$

39. $\displaystyle\sum_{n=0}^{\infty} \left(-\dfrac{1}{2}\right)^n (x-3)^n$

40. $\displaystyle\sum_{n=0}^{\infty} (\ln x)^n$

Repeating Decimals

Express each of the numbers in Exercises 41–46 as the ratio of two integers.

41. $0.\overline{23} = 0.23\ 23\ 23 \ldots$

42. $0.\overline{234} = 0.234\ 234\ 234 \ldots$

43. $0.\overline{7} = 0.7777 \ldots$

44. $1.\overline{414} = 1.414\ 414\ 414 \ldots$

45. $1.24\overline{123} = 1.24\ 123\ 123\ 123 \ldots$

46. $3.\overline{142857} = 3.142857\ 142857 \ldots$

Theory and Examples

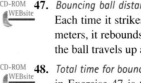 **47.** *Bouncing ball distance* A ball is dropped from a height of 4 m. Each time it strikes the pavement after falling from a height of h meters, it rebounds to a height of $0.75h$ m. Find the total distance the ball travels up and down.

48. *Total time for bouncing* Find the total number of seconds the ball in Exercise 47 is traveling. (*Hint:* The formula $s = 4.9t^2$ gives $t = \sqrt{s/4.9}$.)

49. *Summing areas* The accompanying figure shows the first five of a sequence of squares. The outermost square has an area of 4 m^2. Each of the other squares is obtained by joining the midpoints of the sides of the squares before it. Find the sum of the areas of all the squares.

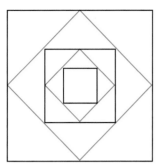

50. *Summing areas* The accompanying figure shows the first three rows and part of the fourth row of a sequence of rows of semicircles. There are 2^n semicircles in the nth row, each of radius $1/2^n$. Find the sum of the areas of all the semicircles.

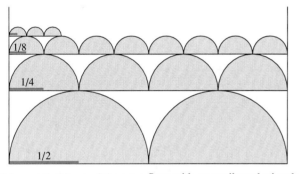

51. *Helge von Koch's snowflake curve* Start with an equilateral triangle whose sides have length 1, calling it Curve 1. On the middle third of each side, build an equilateral triangle pointing outward. Then erase the interiors of the old middle thirds. Call the expanded curve Curve 2. Now put equilateral triangles, again pointing outward, on the middle thirds of the sides of Curve 2. Erase the interiors of the old middle thirds to make Curve 3. Repeat the process, as shown, to define an infinite sequence of plane curves. The limit curve of the sequence is Koch's snowflake curve.

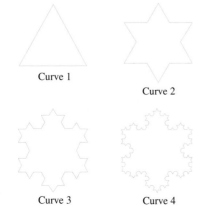

Here's how to show that the snowflake is a curve of infinite length enclosing a region of finite area.

(a) Find the length L_n of the nth curve C_n and show that $\lim_{n\to\infty} L_n = \infty$.

(b) Find the area A_n of the region enclosed by C_n and calculate $\lim_{n\to\infty} A_n$.

52. *Writing to Learn* The accompanying figure provides an informal proof that $\sum_{n=1}^{\infty} (1/n^2)$ is less than 2. Explain what is going on. (*Source*: "Convergence with Pictures" by P. J. Rippon, *American Mathematical Monthly*, Vol. 93, No. 6 (1986), pp. 476—478.)

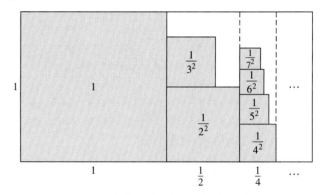

53. *Reindexing* The series in Exercise 5 can also be written as

$$\sum_{n=1}^{\infty} \frac{1}{(n+1)(n+2)} \quad \text{and} \quad \sum_{n=-1}^{\infty} \frac{1}{(n+3)(n+4)}.$$

Write it as a sum beginning with

(a) $n = -2$

(b) $n = 0$

(c) $n = 5$.

54. *Writing to Learn* Make up an infinite series of nonzero terms whose sum is

(a) 1

(b) -3

(c) 0.

Can you make an infinite series of nonzero terms that converges to any number you want? Explain.

55. *Geometric series* Find the value of b for which

$$1 + e^b + e^{2b} + e^{3b} + \cdots = 9.$$

56. *Modified geometric series* For what values of r does the infinite series

$$1 + 2r + r^2 + 2r^3 + r^4 + 2r^5 + r^6 + \cdots$$

converge? Find the sum of the series when it converges.

57. *Error using a partial sum* Show that the error $(L - s_n)$ obtained by replacing a convergent geometric series with one of its partial sums s_n is $ar^n/(1 - r)$.

58. *Term-by-term product* Find convergent geometric series $A = \Sigma\, a_n$ and $B = \Sigma\, b_n$ that illustrate that $\Sigma\, a_n b_n$ may converge without being equal to AB.

59. *Term-by-term quotient* Show by example that $\Sigma\, (a_n/b_n)$ may converge to something other than A/B even when $A = \Sigma\, a_n$, $B = \Sigma\, b_n \neq 0$, and no b_n equals 0.

60. *Term-by-term quotient* Show by example that $\Sigma\, (a_n/b_n)$ may diverge even though $\Sigma\, a_n$ and $\Sigma\, b_n$ converge and no b_n equals 0.

61. *Term-by-term reciprocals* If $\Sigma\, a_n$ converges and $a_n > 0$ for all n, can anything be said about $\Sigma\, (1/a_n)$? Give reasons for your answer.

62. *Adding or deleting terms* What happens if you add a finite number of terms to a divergent series or delete a finite number of terms from a divergent series? Give reasons for your answer.

63. *Summing convergent and divergent series* If $\Sigma\, a_n$ converges and $\Sigma\, b_n$ diverges, can anything be said about their term-by-term sum $\Sigma\, (a_n + b_n)$? Give reasons for your answer.

8.4 Series of Nonnegative Terms

Integral Test • Harmonic Series and *p*-Series • Comparison Tests • Ratio and Root Tests

Given a series $\Sigma\, a_n$, we have two questions.

1. Does the series converge?

2. If it converges, what is its sum?

In this section, we study series that do not have negative terms. The reason for this restriction is that the partial sums of these series form nondecreasing sequences, and nondecreasing sequences that are bounded from above always converge. The partial sums are nondecreasing because $s_{n+1} = s_n + a_n$ and $a_n \geq 0$:

$$s_1 \leq s_2 \leq s_3 \leq \cdots \leq s_n \leq s_{n+1} \leq \cdots .$$

From the Monotonic Sequence Theorem (Theorem 5, Section 8.2), the series will converge if $\{s_n\}$ is bounded from above.

Corollary of Theorem 5

A series $\sum_{n=1}^{\infty} a_n$ of nonnegative terms converges if its partial sums are bounded from above.

This result is the basis for the tests to establish convergence we study in this section.

Integral Test

We introduce the Integral Test with an example.

Example 1 Applying Corollary of Theorem 5

Show that the series

$$\sum_{n=1}^{\infty} \frac{1}{n^2} = 1 + \frac{1}{4} + \frac{1}{9} + \frac{1}{16} + \cdots + \frac{1}{n^2} + \cdots$$

converges.

Solution We determine the convergence of $\sum_{n=1}^{\infty} (1/n^2)$ by comparing it with $\int_1^{\infty} (1/x^2)\,dx$. To carry out the comparison, we think of the terms of the series as values of the function $f(x) = 1/x^2$ and interpret these values as the areas of rectangles under the curve $y = 1/x^2$.

As Figure 8.12 shows,

$$s_n = \frac{1}{1^2} + \frac{1}{2^2} + \frac{1}{3^2} + \cdots + \frac{1}{n^2}$$
$$= f(1) + f(2) + f(3) + \cdots + f(n)$$
$$< f(1) + \int_1^n \frac{1}{x^2}\,dx$$
$$< 1 + \int_1^{\infty} \frac{1}{x^2}\,dx \qquad \text{As in Section 7.7. Example 3, with } p = 2,$$
$$< 1 + 1 = 2. \qquad\qquad \int_1^{\infty} (1/x^2)\,dx = 1.$$

Thus, the partial sums of $\sum_{n=1}^{\infty} (1/n^2)$ are bounded from above (by 2) and the series converges. The sum of the series is known to be $\pi^2/6 \approx 1.64493$.

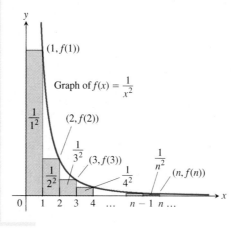

FIGURE 8.12 Figure for the area comparisons in Example 1.

The Integral Test

Let $\{a_n\}$ be a sequence of positive terms. Suppose that $a_n = f(n)$, where f is a continuous, positive, decreasing function of x for all $x \geq N$ (N a positive integer). Then the series $\sum_{n=N}^{\infty} a_n$ and the integral $\int_N^{\infty} f(x)\,dx$ both converge or both diverge.

CAUTION The series and integral need not have the same value in the convergent case. In Example 1, $\sum_{n=1}^{\infty} (1/n^2) = \pi^2/6$, whereas $\int_1^{\infty} (1/x^2)\,dx = 1$.

Proof We establish the test for the case $N = 1$. The proof for general N is similar.

We start with the assumption that f is a decreasing function with $f(n) = a_n$ for every n. This leads us to observe that the rectangles in Figure 8.13a, which have areas $a_1, a_2, \ldots, a_n$, collectively enclose more area than that under the curve $y = f(x)$ from $x = 1$ to $x = n + 1$. That is,

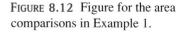

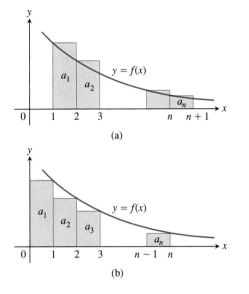

FIGURE 8.13 Subject to the conditions of the Integral Test, the series $\sum_{n=1}^{\infty} a_n$ and the integral $\int_1^{\infty} f(x)\, dx$ both converge or both diverge.

In Figure 8.13b the rectangles have been faced to the left instead of to the right. If we momentarily disregard the first rectangle, of area a_1, we see that

$$a_2 + a_3 + \cdots + a_n \leq \int_1^n f(x)\, dx.$$

If we include a_1, we have

$$a_1 + a_2 + \cdots + a_n \leq a_1 + \int_1^n f(x)\, dx.$$

Combining these results gives

$$\int_1^{n+1} f(x)\, dx \leq a_1 + a_2 + \cdots + a_n \leq a_1 + \int_1^n f(x)\, dx.$$

If $\int_1^{\infty} f(x)\, dx$ is finite, the right-hand inequality shows that $\sum a_n$ is finite. If $\int_1^{\infty} f(x)\, dx$ is infinite, the left-hand inequality shows that $\sum a_n$ is infinite.

Hence, the series and the integral are both finite or both infinite.

Example 2   Applying the Integral Test

Does $\displaystyle\sum_{n=1}^{\infty} \frac{1}{n\sqrt{n}}$ converge?

Solution   The Integral Test applies because

$$f(x) = \frac{1}{x\sqrt{x}}$$

is a continuous, positive, decreasing function of x for $x > 1$.

We have

$$\int_1^{\infty} \frac{1}{x\sqrt{x}}\, dx = \lim_{k\to\infty} \int_1^k x^{-3/2}\, dx$$

$$= \lim_{k\to\infty} \left[-2x^{-1/2} \right]_1^k$$

$$= \lim_{k\to\infty} \left(-\frac{2}{\sqrt{k}} + 2 \right)$$

$$= 2.$$

Since the integral converges, so must the series.

Harmonic Series and p-Series

The Integral Test can be used to settle the question of convergence for any series of the form $\sum_{n=1}^{\infty} (1/n^p)$, p a real constant. (The series in Example 2 had this form, with $p = 3/2$.) Such series are called **p-series**.

The p-Series

$$\sum_{n=1}^{\infty} \frac{1}{n^p} = \frac{1}{1^p} + \frac{1}{2^p} + \frac{1}{3^p} + \cdots + \frac{1}{n^p} + \cdots$$

(p a real constant) converges if $p > 1$ and diverges if $p \leq 1$.

Proof From Example 3 in Section 7.7, the integral $\int_1^\infty dx/x^p$ converges if $p > 1$ and diverges if $p \le 1$. From the Integral Test, the same holds true of the p-series $\sum_{n=1}^\infty (1/n^p)$: It converges if $p > 1$ and diverges if $p \le 1$. ▬

The p-series with $p = 1$ is the **harmonic series**, and it is probably the most famous divergent series in mathematics. The p-Series Test shows that the harmonic series is just *barely* divergent; if we increase p to 1.000000001, for instance, the series converges!

The slowness with which the partial sums of the harmonic series approaches infinity is most impressive. Consider the following example.

Example 3   The Slow Divergence of the Harmonic Series

Approximately how many terms of the harmonic series are required to form a partial sum larger than 20?

Solution   The graphs tell the story (Figure 8.14).

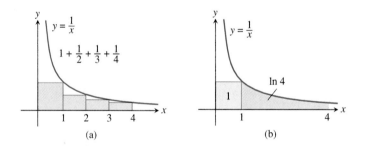

(a)   (b)

FIGURE 8.14 Finding an upper bound for one of the partial sums of the harmonic series. (Example 3)

Let H_n denote the nth partial sum of the harmonic series. Comparing the two graphs, we see that $H_4 < (1 + \ln 4)$ and (in general) that $H_n \le (1 + \ln n)$. If we wish H_n to be greater than 20, then

$$1 + \ln\ n > H_n > 20$$
$$1 + \ln\ n > 20$$
$$\ln\ n > 19$$
$$n > e^{19}.$$

The exact value of e^{19} rounds up to 178,482,301. It will take *at least* that many terms of the harmonic series to move the partial sums beyond 20. It would take your calculator several weeks to compute a sum with this many terms. Nonetheless, the harmonic series really does diverge!

Comparison Tests

The p-Series Test tells everything there is to know about the convergence or divergence of series of the form $\sum (1/n^p)$. This is admittedly a rather narrow class of se-

---

What Is Harmonic About the Harmonic Series?

The terms in the harmonic series correspond to the nodes on a vibrating string that produce multiples of the fundamental frequency. For example, 1/2 produces the harmonic that is twice the fundamental frequency, 1/3 produces a frequency that is three times the fundamental frequency, and so on. The fundamental frequency is the lowest note or pitch we hear when a string is plucked.

ries, but we can test many other kinds (including those in which the nth term is any rational function of n) by *comparing* them with p-series.

The Direct Comparison Test

Let $\Sigma \, a_n$ be a series with no negative terms.

(a) $\Sigma \, a_n$ converges if there is a convergent series $\Sigma \, c_n$ with $a_n \leq c_n$ for all $n > N$, for some integer N.

(b) $\Sigma \, a_n$ diverges if there is a divergent series of nonnegative terms $\Sigma \, d_n$ with $a_n \geq d_n$ for all $n > N$, for some integer N.

Proof   In part (a), the partial sums of $\Sigma \, a_n$ are bounded above by

$$M = a_1 + a_2 + \cdots + a_n + \sum_{n=N+1}^{\infty} c_n.$$

They therefore form a nondecreasing sequence with a limit $L \leq M$.

In part (b), the partial sums of $\Sigma \, a_n$ are not bounded from above. If they were, the partial sums for $\Sigma \, d_n$ would be bounded by

$$M^* = d_1 + d_2 + \cdots + d_N + \sum_{n=N+1}^{\infty} a_n$$

and $\Sigma \, d_n$ would have to converge instead of diverge. ▬

To apply the Direct Comparison Test to a series, we need not include the early terms of the series. We can start the test with any index N provided that we include all the terms of the series being tested from there on.

Example 4   Applying the Direct Comparison Test

Does the following series converge?

$$5 + \frac{2}{3} + 1 + \frac{1}{7} + \frac{1}{2} + \frac{1}{3!} + \frac{1}{4!} + \cdots + \frac{1}{k!} + \cdots$$

Solution   We ignore the first four terms and compare the remaining terms with those of the convergent geometric series $\sum_{n=1}^{\infty} (1/2^n)$. We see that

$$\frac{1}{2} + \frac{1}{3!} + \frac{1}{4!} + \cdots \leq \frac{1}{2} + \frac{1}{4} + \frac{1}{8} + \cdots.$$

Therefore, the original series converges by the Direct Comparison Test.

To apply the Direct Comparison Test, we need to have on hand a list of series whose convergence or divergence we know. Here is what we know so far:

Convergent series	Divergent series
Geometric series with $\lvert r \rvert < 1$	Geometric series with $\lvert r \rvert \geq 1$
Telescoping series like $\displaystyle\sum_{n=1}^{\infty} \frac{1}{n(n+1)}$	The harmonic series $\displaystyle\sum_{n=1}^{\infty} \frac{1}{n}$
The series $\displaystyle\sum_{n=0}^{\infty} \frac{1}{n!}$	Any series $\sum a_n$ for which $\lim_{n\to\infty} a_n$ does not exist or $\lim_{n\to\infty} a_n \neq 0$
Any p-series $\displaystyle\sum_{n=1}^{\infty} \frac{1}{n^p}$ with $p > 1$	Any p-series $\displaystyle\sum_{n=1}^{\infty} \frac{1}{n^p}$ with $p \leq 1$

The Direct Comparison Test is one method of comparison; the *Limit Comparison Test* is another.

The Limit Comparison Test

Suppose that $a_n > 0$ and $b_n > 0$ for all $n \geq N$ (N a positive integer).

1. If $\displaystyle\lim_{n\to\infty} \frac{a_n}{b_n} = c, 0 < c < \infty$, then $\Sigma \, a_n$ and $\Sigma \, b_n$ both converge or both diverge.

2. If $\displaystyle\lim_{n\to\infty} \frac{a_n}{b_n} = 0$ and $\Sigma \, b_n$ converges, then $\Sigma \, a_n$ converges.

3. If $\displaystyle\lim_{n\to\infty} \frac{a_n}{b_n} = \infty$ and $\Sigma \, b_n$ diverges, then $\Sigma \, a_n$ diverges.

Proof   We will prove part (1). Parts (2) and (3) are left as Exercise 67.
Since $c/2 > 0$, there exists an integer N such that for all n,

$$n > N \implies \left\lvert \frac{a_n}{b_n} - c \right\rvert < \frac{c}{2}. \qquad \text{Limit definition with } \epsilon = c/2,$$
$$\text{$L = c$, and a_n replaced by a_n/b_n.}$$

Thus, for $n > N$,

$$-\frac{c}{2} < \frac{a_n}{b_n} - c < \frac{c}{2},$$

$$\frac{c}{2} < \frac{a_n}{b_n} < \frac{3c}{2},$$

$$\left(\frac{c}{2}\right) b_n < a_n < \left(\frac{3c}{2}\right) b_n.$$

If $\Sigma \, b_n$ converges then $\Sigma \, (3c/2)b_n$ converges and $\Sigma \, a_n$ converges by the Direct Comparison Test. If $\Sigma \, b_n$ diverges, then $\Sigma \, (c/2)b_n$ diverges and $\Sigma \, a_n$ diverges by the Direct Comparison Test.

Example 5   Using the Limit Comparison Test

Determine whether the series converge or diverge.

(a) $\dfrac{3}{4} + \dfrac{5}{9} + \dfrac{7}{16} + \dfrac{9}{25} + \cdots = \displaystyle\sum_{n=1}^{\infty} \dfrac{2n+1}{(n+1)^2} = \displaystyle\sum_{n=1}^{\infty} \dfrac{2n+1}{n^2+2n+1}$

(b) $\dfrac{1}{1} + \dfrac{1}{3} + \dfrac{1}{7} + \dfrac{1}{15} + \cdots = \displaystyle\sum_{n=1}^{\infty} \dfrac{1}{2^n-1}$

(c) $\dfrac{1+2\ln 2}{9} + \dfrac{1+3\ln 3}{14} + \dfrac{1+4\ln 4}{21} + \cdots = \displaystyle\sum_{n=2}^{\infty} \dfrac{1+n\ln n}{n^2+5}$

Solution

We could just as well have taken $b_n = 2/n$, but $1/n$ is simpler.

(a) Let $a_n = (2n+1)/(n^2+2n+1)$. For n large, we expect a_n to behave like $2n/n^2 = 2/n$, so we let $b_n = 1/n$. Since

$$\sum_{n=1}^{\infty} b_n = \sum_{n=1}^{\infty} \frac{1}{n}$$

diverges and

$$\lim_{n\to\infty} \frac{a_n}{b_n} = \lim_{n\to\infty} \frac{2n^2+n}{n^2+2n+1} = 2,$$

$\Sigma\, a_n$ diverges by part 1 of the Limit Comparison Test.

(b) Let $a_n = 1/(2^n-1)$. For n large, we expect a_n to behave like $1/2^n$, so we let $b_n = 1/2^n$. Since

$$\sum_{n=1}^{\infty} b_n = \sum_{n=1}^{\infty} \frac{1}{2^n}$$

converges and

$$\lim_{n\to\infty} \frac{a_n}{b_n} = \lim_{n\to\infty} \frac{2^n}{2^n-1}$$

$$= \lim_{n\to\infty} \frac{1}{1-(1/2^n)}$$

$$= 1,$$

$\Sigma\, a_n$ converges by part 1 of the Limit Comparison Test.

(c) Let $a_n = (1+n\ln n)/(n^2+5)$. For n large, we expect a_n to behave like $(n\ln n)/n^2 = (\ln n)/n$, which is greater than $1/n$ for $n \geq 3$, so we take $b_n = 1/n$. Since

$$\sum_{n=2}^{\infty} b_n = \sum_{n=2}^{\infty} \frac{1}{n}$$

diverges and

$$\lim_{n\to\infty} \frac{a_n}{b_n} = \lim_{n\to\infty} \frac{n+n^2\ln n}{n^2+5}$$

$$= \infty,$$

$\Sigma\, a_n$ diverges by part 3 of the Limit Comparison Test.

Ratio and Root Tests

The Ratio Test measures the rate of growth (or decline) of a series by examining the ratio a_{n+1}/a_n. For a geometric series $\Sigma \, ar^n$, this rate is a constant $((ar^{n+1})/(ar^n) = r)$, and the series converges if and only if its ratio is less than 1 in absolute value. The Ratio Test is a powerful rule extending that result.

The Ratio Test

Let $\Sigma \, a_n$ be a series with positive terms and suppose that

$$\lim_{n \to \infty} \frac{a_{n+1}}{a_n} = \rho.$$

Then

(a) the series *converges* if $\rho < 1$
(b) the series *diverges* if $\rho > 1$ or ρ is infinite
(c) the test is *inconclusive* if $\rho = 1$.

Proof

(a) $\rho < 1$. Let r be a number between ρ and 1. Then the number $\epsilon = r - \rho$ is positive. Since

$$\frac{a_{n+1}}{a_n} \to \rho,$$

a_{n+1}/a_n must lie within ϵ of ρ when n is large enough, say for all $n \geq N$. In particular

$$\frac{a_{n+1}}{a_n} < \rho + \epsilon = r, \qquad \text{when } n \geq N.$$

That is,

$$a_{N+1} < r \, a_N,$$
$$a_{N+2} < r \, a_{N+1} < r^2 a_N,$$
$$a_{N+3} < r \, a_{N+2} < r^3 a_N,$$
$$\vdots$$
$$a_{N+m} < r \, a_{N+m-1} < r^m a_N.$$

These inequalities show that the terms of our series, after the Nth term, approach zero more rapidly than the terms in a geometric series with ratio $r < 1$. More precisely, consider the series $\Sigma \, c_n$, where $c_n = a_n$ for $n = 1, 2, \ldots, N$ and $c_{N+1} = ra_N, c_{N+2} = r^2 a_N, \ldots, c_{N+m} = r^m a_N, \ldots$. Now $a_n \leq c_n$ for all n, and

$$\sum_{n=1}^{\infty} c_n = a_1 + a_2 + \cdots + a_{N-1} + a_N + ra_N + r^2 a_N + \cdots$$

$$= a_1 + a_2 + \cdots + a_{N-1} + a_N (1 + r + r^2 + \cdots).$$

The geometric series $1 + r + r^2 + \cdots$ converges because $|r| < 1$, so $\Sigma \, c_n$ converges. Since $a_n \le c_n$, $\Sigma \, a_n$ also converges.

(b) $1 < \rho \le \infty$. From some index M on,

$$\frac{a_{n+1}}{a_n} > 1 \quad \text{and} \quad a_M < a_{M+1} < a_{M+2} < \cdots .$$

The terms of the series do not approach zero as n becomes infinite, and the series diverges by the nth-Term Test.

(c) $\rho = 1$. The two series

$$\sum_{n=1}^{\infty} \frac{1}{n} \quad \text{and} \quad \sum_{n=1}^{\infty} \frac{1}{n^2}$$

show that some other test for convergence must be used when $\rho = 1$.

For $\displaystyle\sum_{n=1}^{\infty} \frac{1}{n}$: $\quad \dfrac{a_{n+1}}{a_n} = \dfrac{1/(n+1)}{1/n} = \dfrac{n}{n+1} \to 1.$

For $\displaystyle\sum_{n=1}^{\infty} \frac{1}{n^2}$: $\quad \dfrac{a_{n+1}}{a_n} = \dfrac{1/(n+1)^2}{1/n^2} = \left(\dfrac{n}{n+1}\right)^2 \to 1^2 = 1.$

In both cases, $\rho = 1$, yet the first series diverges, whereas the second converges. ▬

Example 6 Applying the Ratio Test

Investigate the convergence of the following series.

(a) $\displaystyle\sum_{n=0}^{\infty} \frac{2^n + 5}{3^n}$ **(b)** $\displaystyle\sum_{n=1}^{\infty} \frac{(2n)!}{n!n!}$ **(c)** $\displaystyle\sum_{n=1}^{\infty} \frac{4^n n! n!}{(2n)!}$

The Ratio Test is often effective when the terms of a series contain factorials of expressions involving n or expressions raised to the nth power.

Solution

(a) For the series $\sum_{n=0}^{\infty} (2^n + 5)/3^n$,

$$\frac{a_{n+1}}{a_n} = \frac{(2^{n+1} + 5)/3^{n+1}}{(2^n + 5)/3^n} = \frac{1}{3} \cdot \frac{2^{n+1} + 5}{2^n + 5} = \frac{1}{3} \cdot \left(\frac{2 + 5 \cdot 2^{-n}}{1 + 5 \cdot 2^{-n}}\right) \to \frac{1}{3} \cdot \frac{2}{1} = \frac{2}{3}.$$

The series converges because $\rho = 2/3$ is less than 1. This does *not* mean that $2/3$ is the sum of the series. In fact,

$$\sum_{n=0}^{\infty} \frac{2^n + 5}{3^n} = \sum_{n=0}^{\infty} \left(\frac{2}{3}\right)^n + \sum_{n=0}^{\infty} \frac{5}{3^n} = \frac{1}{1 - (2/3)} + \frac{5}{1 - (1/3)} = \frac{21}{2}.$$

(b) If $a_n = \dfrac{(2n)!}{n!n!}$, then $a_{n+1} = \dfrac{(2n+2)!}{(n+1)!(n+1)!}$ and

$$\frac{a_{n+1}}{a_n} = \frac{n!n!(2n+2)(2n+1)(2n)!}{(n+1)!(n+1)!(2n)!}$$

$$= \frac{(2n+2)(2n+1)}{(n+1)(n+1)} = \frac{4n+2}{n+1} \to 4.$$

The series diverges because $\rho = 4$ is greater than 1.

(c) If $a_n = 4^n n! n! / (2n)!$, then

$$\frac{a_{n+1}}{a_n} = \frac{4^{n+1}(n+1)!(n+1)!}{(2n+2)(2n+1)(2n)!} \cdot \frac{(2n)!}{4^n n! n!}$$

$$= \frac{4(n+1)(n+1)}{(2n+2)(2n+1)} = \frac{2(n+1)}{2n+1} \to 1.$$

Because the limit is $\rho = 1$, we cannot decide from the Ratio Test whether the series converges. When we notice that $a_{n+1}/a_n = (2n+2)/(2n+1)$, we conclude that a_{n+1} is always greater than a_n because $(2n+2)/(2n+1)$ is always greater than 1. Therefore, all terms are greater than or equal to $a_1 = 2$, and the nth term does not approach zero as $n \to \infty$. The series diverges.

The nth-Root Test is another useful tool for answering the question of convergence for series with nonnegative terms. We state the result here without proof.

The nth-Root Test

Let $\Sigma\, a_n$ be a series with $a_n \geq 0$ for $n \geq N$ and suppose that

$$\lim_{n \to \infty} \sqrt[n]{a_n} = \rho.$$

Then

(a) the series *converges* if $\rho < 1$
(b) the series *diverges* if $\rho > 1$ or ρ is infinite
(c) the test is *inconclusive* if $\rho = 1$.

Example 7   Applying the nth-Root Test

Let

$$a_n = \begin{cases} n/2^n, & n \text{ odd} \\ 1/2^n, & n \text{ even.} \end{cases}$$

Does $\Sigma\, a_n$ converge?

Solution   We apply the nth-Root Test, finding that

$$\sqrt[n]{a_n} = \begin{cases} \sqrt[n]{n}/2, & n \text{ odd} \\ 1/2, & n \text{ even.} \end{cases}$$

Therefore,

$$\frac{1}{2} \leq \sqrt[n]{a_n} \leq \frac{\sqrt[n]{n}}{2}.$$

Since $\sqrt[n]{n} \to 1$ (Section 8.1, Table 8.1), we have $\lim_{n \to \infty} \sqrt[n]{a_n} = 1/2$ by the Sandwich Theorem. The limit is less than 1, so the series converges by the nth-Root Test.

Example 8   Applying the nth-Root Test

Which of the following series converge, and which diverge?

(a) $\displaystyle\sum_{n=1}^{\infty} \frac{n^2}{2^n}$ (b) $\displaystyle\sum_{n=1}^{\infty} \frac{2^n}{n^2}$

Solution

(a) $\displaystyle\sum_{n=1}^{\infty} \frac{n^2}{2^n}$ converges because $\displaystyle\sqrt[n]{\frac{n^2}{2^n}} = \frac{\sqrt[n]{n^2}}{\sqrt[n]{2^n}} = \frac{(\sqrt[n]{n})^2}{2} \to \frac{1}{2} < 1.$

(b) $\displaystyle\sum_{n=1}^{\infty} \frac{2^n}{n^2}$ diverges because $\displaystyle\sqrt[n]{\frac{2^n}{n^2}} = \frac{2}{(\sqrt[n]{n})^2} \to \frac{2}{1} > 1.$

EXERCISES 8.4

Integral Test

Use the Integral Test to determine which of the series in Exercises 1–8 converge and which diverge.

1. $\displaystyle\sum_{n=1}^{\infty} \frac{5}{n+1}$

2. $\displaystyle\sum_{n=1}^{\infty} \frac{1}{2n-1}$

3. $\displaystyle\sum_{n=2}^{\infty} \frac{\ln n}{n}$

4. $\displaystyle\sum_{n=2}^{\infty} \frac{\ln n}{\sqrt{n}}$

5. $\displaystyle\sum_{n=1}^{\infty} \frac{e^n}{1+e^{2n}}$

6. $\displaystyle\sum_{n=1}^{\infty} \frac{1}{\sqrt{n}(\sqrt{n}+1)}$

7. $\displaystyle\sum_{n=3}^{\infty} \frac{(1/n)}{(\ln n)\sqrt{\ln^2 n - 1}}$

8. $\displaystyle\sum_{n=1}^{\infty} \frac{1}{n(1+\ln^2 n)}$

Direct Comparison Test

Use the Direct Comparison Test to determine which of the series in Exercises 9–14 converge and which diverge.

9. $\displaystyle\sum_{n=1}^{\infty} \frac{1}{2\sqrt{n}+\sqrt[3]{n}}$

10. $\displaystyle\sum_{n=1}^{\infty} \frac{3}{n+\sqrt{n}}$

11. $\displaystyle\sum_{n=1}^{\infty} \frac{\sin^2 n}{2^n}$

12. $\displaystyle\sum_{n=1}^{\infty} \frac{1+\cos n}{n^2}$

13. $\displaystyle\sum_{n=1}^{\infty} \left(\frac{n}{3n+1}\right)^n$

14. $\displaystyle\sum_{n=3}^{\infty} \frac{1}{\ln(\ln n)}$

Limit Comparison Test

Use the Limit Comparison Test to determine which of the series in Exercises 15–20 converge and which diverge.

15. $\displaystyle\sum_{n=2}^{\infty} \frac{1}{(\ln n)^2}$

16. $\displaystyle\sum_{n=1}^{\infty} \frac{(\ln n)^2}{n^3}$

17. $\displaystyle\sum_{n=1}^{\infty} \frac{(\ln n)^3}{n^3}$

18. $\displaystyle\sum_{n=2}^{\infty} \frac{1}{\sqrt{n}\ln n}$

19. $\displaystyle\sum_{n=1}^{\infty} \frac{(\ln n)^2}{n^{3/2}}$

20. $\displaystyle\sum_{n=1}^{\infty} \frac{1}{1+\ln n}$

Ratio Test

Use the Ratio Test to determine which of the series in Exercises 21–28 converge and which diverge.

21. $\displaystyle\sum_{n=1}^{\infty} \frac{n^{\sqrt{2}}}{2^n}$

22. $\displaystyle\sum_{n=1}^{\infty} n^2 e^{-n}$

23. $\displaystyle\sum_{n=1}^{\infty} n! e^{-n}$

24. $\displaystyle\sum_{n=1}^{\infty} \frac{n!}{10^n}$

25. $\displaystyle\sum_{n=1}^{\infty} \frac{n^{10}}{10^n}$

26. $\displaystyle\sum_{n=1}^{\infty} \frac{n\ln n}{2^n}$

27. $\displaystyle\sum_{n=1}^{\infty} \frac{(n+1)(n+2)}{n!}$

28. $\displaystyle\sum_{n=1}^{\infty} e^{-n}(n^3)$

Root Test

Use the nth-Root Test to determine which of the series in Exercises 29–34 converge and which diverge.

29. $\displaystyle\sum_{n=1}^{\infty} \frac{(\ln n)^n}{n^n}$

30. $\displaystyle\sum_{n=1}^{\infty} \left(\frac{1}{n} - \frac{1}{n^2}\right)^n$

31. $\displaystyle\sum_{n=2}^{\infty} \frac{n}{(\ln n)^n}$

32. $\displaystyle\sum_{n=2}^{\infty} \frac{n}{(\ln n)^{(n/2)}}$

33. $\displaystyle\sum_{n=1}^{\infty} \frac{(n!)^n}{(n^n)^2}$

34. $\displaystyle\sum_{n=1}^{\infty} \frac{n^n}{(2^n)^2}$

Determining Convergence or Divergence

Which of the series in Exercises 35–60 converge, and which diverge? Give reasons for your answers. (When checking your answers, remember that there may be more than one way to determine a series' convergence or divergence.)

35. $\sum_{n=1}^{\infty} e^{-n}$

36. $\sum_{n=1}^{\infty} \dfrac{n}{n+1}$

37. $\sum_{n=1}^{\infty} \dfrac{3}{\sqrt{n}}$

38. $\sum_{n=1}^{\infty} \dfrac{-2}{n\sqrt{n}}$

39. $\sum_{n=1}^{\infty} \dfrac{1}{(1+\ln n)^2}$

40. $\sum_{n=2}^{\infty} \dfrac{\ln(n+1)}{n+1}$

41. $\sum_{n=2}^{\infty} \dfrac{1}{n\sqrt{n^2-1}}$

42. $\sum_{n=1}^{\infty} \left(\dfrac{n-2}{n}\right)^n$

43. $\sum_{n=1}^{\infty} \dfrac{(n+3)!}{3!n!3^n}$

44. $\sum_{n=1}^{\infty} \dfrac{n2^n(n+1)!}{3^n n!}$

45. $\sum_{n=1}^{\infty} \dfrac{n!}{(2n+1)!}$

46. $\sum_{n=1}^{\infty} \dfrac{n!}{n^n}$

47. $\sum_{n=1}^{\infty} \dfrac{8\tan^{-1} n}{1+n^2}$

48. $\sum_{n=1}^{\infty} \dfrac{n}{n^2+1}$

49. $\sum_{n=1}^{\infty} \operatorname{sech} n$

50. $\sum_{n=1}^{\infty} \operatorname{sech}^2 n$

51. $\sum_{n=1}^{\infty} \dfrac{2+(-1)^n}{1.25^n}$

52. $\sum_{n=1}^{\infty} \left(1-\dfrac{1}{3n}\right)^n$

53. $\sum_{n=1}^{\infty} \dfrac{\ln n}{n^3}$

54. $\sum_{n=1}^{\infty} \dfrac{\ln n}{n}$

55. $\sum_{n=1}^{\infty} \dfrac{10n+1}{n(n+1)(n+2)}$

56. $\sum_{n=3}^{\infty} \dfrac{5n^3-3n}{n^2(n-2)(n^2+5)}$

57. $\sum_{n=1}^{\infty} \dfrac{\tan^{-1} n}{n^{1.1}}$

58. $\sum_{n=1}^{\infty} \dfrac{\sec^{-1} n}{n^{1.3}}$

59. $\sum_{n=1}^{\infty} n\sin\dfrac{1}{n}$

60. $\sum_{n=1}^{\infty} \dfrac{2}{1+e^n}$

Terms Defined Recursively

Which of the series $\sum_{n=1}^{\infty} a_n$ defined by the formulas in Exercises 61–66 converge, and which diverge? Give reasons for your answers.

61. $a_1 = 2, \quad a_{n+1} = \dfrac{1+\sin n}{n} a_n$

62. $a_1 = 1, \quad a_{n+1} = \dfrac{1+\tan^{-1} n}{n} a_n$

63. $a_1 = \dfrac{1}{3}, \quad a_{n+1} = \dfrac{3n-1}{2n+5} a_n$

64. $a_1 = 3, \quad a_{n+1} = \dfrac{n}{n+1} a_n$

65. $a_1 = \dfrac{1}{3}, \quad a_{n+1} = \sqrt[n]{a_n}$

66. $a_1 = \dfrac{1}{2}, \quad a_{n+1} = (a_n)^{n+1}$

Theory and Examples

67. Prove

  (a) Part 2 of the Limit Comparison Test

  (b) Part 3 of the Limit Comparison Test.

68. *Writing to Learn* If $\sum_{n=1}^{\infty} a_n$ is a convergent series of nonnegative numbers, can anything be said about $\sum_{n=1}^{\infty} (a_n/n)$? Explain.

69. *Writing to Learn* Suppose that $a_n > 0$ and $b_n > 0$ for $n \ge N$ (N an integer). If $\lim_{n\to\infty} (a_n/b_n) = \infty$ and Σa_n converges, can anything be said about Σb_n? Give reasons for your answer.

70. *Term-by-term squaring* Prove that if Σa_n is a convergent series of nonnegative terms, then Σa_n^2 converges.

For what values of a, if any, do the series in Exercises 71 and 72 converge?

71. $\sum_{n=1}^{\infty} \left(\dfrac{a}{n+2} - \dfrac{1}{n+4}\right)$

72. $\sum_{n=3}^{\infty} \left(\dfrac{1}{n-1} - \dfrac{2a}{n+1}\right)$

73. *The Cauchy Condensation Test* The Cauchy Condensation Test says: Let $\{a_n\}$ be a nonincreasing sequence ($a_n \ge a_{n+1}$ for all n) of positive terms that converges to 0. Then Σa_n converges if and only if $\Sigma 2^n a_{2^n}$ converges. For example, $\Sigma (1/n)$ diverges because $\Sigma 2^n \cdot (1/2^n) = \Sigma 1$ diverges. Show why the test works.

74. Use the Cauchy Condensation Test from Exercise 73 to show that

  (a) $\sum_{n=2}^{\infty} \dfrac{1}{n\ln n}$ diverges

  (b) $\sum_{n=1}^{\infty} \dfrac{1}{n^p}$ converges if $p > 1$ and diverges if $p \le 1$.

75. *Logarithmic p-series*

  (a) Show that

$$\int_2^{\infty} \dfrac{dx}{x(\ln x)^p} \qquad (p \text{ a positive constant})$$

  converges if and only if $p > 1$.

  (b) What implications does the fact in part (a) have for the convergence of the series

$$\sum_{n=2}^{\infty} \dfrac{1}{n(\ln n)^p}?$$

  Give reasons for your answer.

76. (Continuation of Exercise 75) Use the result in Exercise 75 to determine which of the following series converge and which diverge. Support your answer in each case.

  (a) $\sum_{n=2}^{\infty} \dfrac{1}{n(\ln n)}$

  (b) $\sum_{n=2}^{\infty} \dfrac{1}{n(\ln n)^{1.01}}$

  (c) $\sum_{n=2}^{\infty} \dfrac{1}{n\ln(n^3)}$

  (d) $\sum_{n=2}^{\infty} \dfrac{1}{n(\ln n)^3}$

77. *Another logarithmic* p-*series* Show that neither the Ratio Test nor the nth-Root Test provides information about the convergence of

$$\sum_{n=2}^{\infty} \frac{1}{(\ln n)^p} \quad (p \text{ constant}).$$

78. Let

$$a_n = \begin{cases} n/2^n & \text{if } n \text{ is a prime number} \\ 1/2^n & \text{otherwise.} \end{cases}$$

Does $\Sigma\, a_n$ converge? Give reasons for your answer.

79. p-*Series* Neither the Ratio Test nor the nth-Root Test helps with p-series. Try these tests on

$$\sum_{n=1}^{\infty} \frac{1}{n^p}$$

and show that both fail to provide information about convergence.

COMPUTER EXPLORATION

A Current Mystery

80. It is not yet known whether the series

$$\sum_{n=1}^{\infty} \frac{1}{n^3 \sin^2 n}$$

converges or diverges. Use a CAS to explore the behavior of the series by performing the following steps.

(a) Define the sequence of partial sums

$$s_k = \sum_{n=1}^{k} \frac{1}{n^3 \sin^2 n}.$$

What happens when you try to find the limit of s_k as $k \to \infty$? Does your CAS find a closed-form answer for this limit?

(b) Plot the first 100 points (k, s_k) for the sequence of partial sums. Do they appear to converge? What would you estimate the limit to be?

(c) Next plot the first 200 points (k, s_k). Discuss the behavior in your own words.

(d) Plot the first 400 points (k, s_k). What happens when $k = 355$? Calculate the number $355/113$. Explain from your calculation what happened at $k = 355$. For what values of k would you guess this behavior might occur again?

You will find an interesting discussion of this series in Chapter 72 of *Mazes for the Mind* by Clifford A. Pickover (New York: St. Martin's Press, 1992).

8.5 Alternating Series, Absolute and Conditional Convergence

Alternating Series • Absolute Convergence • Rearranging Series • Procedure for Determining Convergence

The convergence tests investigated so far apply only to series with nonnegative terms. In this section, we learn how to deal with series that may have negative terms. An important example is the *alternating series,* whose terms alternate in sign. We also learn which convergent series can have their terms rearranged (that is, changing the order in which they appear) without changing their sum.

Alternating Series

A series in which the terms are alternately positive and negative is an **alternating series.**

Here are three examples.

$$1 - \frac{1}{2} + \frac{1}{3} - \frac{1}{4} + \frac{1}{5} - \cdots + \frac{(-1)^{n+1}}{n} + \cdots \tag{1}$$

$$-2 + 1 - \frac{1}{2} + \frac{1}{4} - \frac{1}{8} + \cdots + \frac{(-1)^n 4}{2^n} + \cdots \tag{2}$$

$$1 - 2 + 3 - 4 + 5 - 6 + \cdots + (-1)^{n+1} n + \cdots \tag{3}$$

Series (1), called the **alternating harmonic series,** converges, as we see shortly. Series (2), a geometric series with $a = -2$ and $r = -1/2$, converges to $-2/[1 + (1/2)] = -4/3$. Series (3) diverges by the nth-Term Test.

We prove the convergence of the alternating harmonic series by applying the following test.

Theorem 8   The Alternating Series Test (Leibniz's Theorem)

The series

$$\sum_{n=1}^{\infty} (-1)^{n+1} u_n = u_1 - u_2 + u_3 - u_4 + \cdots$$

converges if all three of the following conditions are satisfied.

1. The u_n's are all positive.

2. $u_n \geq u_{n+1}$ for all $n \geq N$, for some integer N.

3. $u_n \to 0$.

Proof   If n is an even integer, say $n = 2m$, then the sum of the first n term is

$$s_{2m} = (u_1 - u_2) + (u_3 - u_4) + \cdots + (u_{2m-1} - u_{2m})$$
$$= u_1 - (u_2 - u_3) - (u_4 - u_5) - \cdots - (u_{2m-2} - u_{2m-1}) - u_{2m}.$$

The first equality shows that s_{2m} is the sum of m nonnegative terms, since each term in parentheses is positive or zero. Hence, $s_{2m+2} \geq s_{2m}$, and the sequence $\{s_{2m}\}$ is nondecreasing. The second equality shows that $s_{2m} \leq u_1$. Since $\{s_{2m}\}$ is nondecreasing and bounded from above, it has a limit, say

$$\lim_{m \to \infty} s_{2m} = L. \tag{4}$$

If n is an odd integer, say $n = 2m + 1$, then the sum of the first n terms is $s_{2m+1} = s_{2m} + u_{2m+1}$. Since $u_n \to 0$,

$$\lim_{m \to \infty} u_{2m+1} = 0$$

and, as $m \to \infty$,

$$s_{2m+1} = s_{2m} + u_{2m+1} \to L + 0 = L. \tag{5}$$

Combining the results of Equations (4) and (5) gives $\lim_{n \to \infty} s_n = L$ (Section 8.2, Exercise 26). Figure 8.15 illustrates the convergence of the partial sums to their limit L.   ▬

Figure 8.15 actually shows more than the *fact* of convergence; it also shows the *way* that an alternating series converges when it satisfies the conditions of the test. The partial sums keep "overshooting" the limit as they go back and forth on the number line, gradually closing in as the terms tend to zero. If we stop at the nth partial sum, we know that the next term ($\pm u_{n+1}$) will again cause us to overshoot the limit in the positive direction or negative direction, depending on the sign carried by u_{n+1}. This gives us a convenient bound for the **truncation error,** which we state as another theorem.

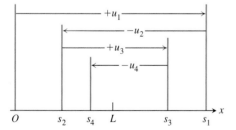

FIGURE 8.15 The partial sums of an alternating series that satisfies the hypotheses of Theorem 8 for $N = 1$ straddle the limit from the beginning.

Theorem 9   The Alternating Series Estimation Theorem

If the alternating series $\sum_{n=1}^{\infty} (-1)^{n+1} u_n$ satisfies the conditions of Theorem 8, then the truncation error for the nth partial sum is less than u_{n+1} and has the same sign as the unused term.

Example 1   The Alternating Harmonic Series

Prove that the alternating harmonic series is convergent, but that the corresponding series of absolute values is not convergent. Find a bound for the truncation error after 99 terms.

Solution   The terms are strictly alternating in sign and decrease in absolute value from the start:

$$1 > \frac{1}{2} > \frac{1}{3} > \cdots.$$

Also,

$$\frac{1}{n} \to 0.$$

By the Alternating Series Test,

$$\sum_{n=1}^{\infty} \frac{(-1)^{n+1}}{n}$$

converges.

On the other hand, the series $\sum_{n=1}^{\infty} (1/n)$ of absolute values is the harmonic series, which diverges.

The Alternating Series Estimation Theorem guarantees that the truncation error after 99 terms is less than $u_{99+1} = 1/(99 + 1) = 1/100$.

A Note on the Error Bound

Theorem 9 does not give a *formula* for the truncation error but a *bound* for the truncation error. The bound might be fairly conservative. For example, the first 99 terms of the alternating harmonic series add to about 0.6981721793, whereas the series itself has a sum of ln 2 ≈ 0.6931471806. That makes the actual truncation error very close to 0.005, about half the size of the bound of 0.01 given by Theorem 9.

Example 2   Applying The Estimation Theorem

We try Theorem 9 on a series whose sum we know:

$$\sum_{n=0}^{\infty} (-1)^n \frac{1}{2^n} = 1 - \frac{1}{2} + \frac{1}{4} - \frac{1}{8} + \frac{1}{16} - \frac{1}{32} + \frac{1}{64} - \frac{1}{128} \; \bigg| \; + \frac{1}{256} - \cdots.$$

The theorem says that if we truncate the series after the eighth term, we throw away a total that is positive and less than $1/256$. The sum of the first eight terms is 0.6640 625. The sum of the series is

$$\frac{1}{1 - (-1/2)} = \frac{1}{3/2} = \frac{2}{3}.$$

The difference, $(2/3) - 0.6640\,625 = 0.0026\,0416\,6\ldots$, is positive and less than $(1/256) = 0.0039\,0625$.

Absolute Convergence

> **Definition**   Absolute Convergence
>
> A series $\Sigma\, a_n$ **converges absolutely** (is **absolutely convergent**) if the corresponding series of absolute values, $\Sigma\, |a_n|$, converges.

CD-ROM
WEBsite

Historical Biography

Niccolo Tartaglia
(1499 — 1557)

The geometric series

$$1 - \frac{1}{2} + \frac{1}{4} - \frac{1}{8} + \cdots$$

converges absolutely because the corresponding series of absolute values

$$1 + \frac{1}{2} + \frac{1}{4} + \frac{1}{8} + \cdots$$

converges. The alternating harmonic series (Example 1) does not converge absolutely. The corresponding series of absolute values is the (divergent) harmonic series.

> **Definition**   Conditional Convergence
>
> A series that converges but does not converge absolutely **converges conditionally.**

The alternating harmonic series converges conditionally.

Example 3   Absolute and Conditional Convergence

Determine which of the following series is absolutely or conditionally convergent, or divergent.

(a) $\displaystyle\sum_{n=1}^{\infty} (-1)^{n+1}\frac{1}{\sqrt{n}} = 1 - \frac{1}{\sqrt{2}} + \frac{1}{\sqrt{3}} - \frac{1}{\sqrt{4}} + \cdots$

(b) $\displaystyle\sum_{n=2}^{\infty} (-1)^{n}\left(1 - \frac{1}{n}\right)^{n} = \frac{1}{2} - \left(\frac{2}{3}\right)^{3} + \left(\frac{3}{4}\right)^{4} - \cdots$

(c) $\displaystyle\sum_{n=1}^{\infty} (-1)^{n(n+1)/2}\frac{1}{2^{n}} = -\frac{1}{2} - \frac{1}{4} + \frac{1}{8} + \frac{1}{16} - \cdots$

Solution

(a) The series converges by the Alternating Series Test since $(1/\sqrt{n}) > (1/\sqrt{n+1})$ and $(1/\sqrt{n}) \to 0$. The series $\sum_{n=1}^{\infty} (1/\sqrt{n})$ of absolute values diverges, however, because it is a p-series with $p = (1/2) < 1$. Therefore, the given series is *conditionally convergent*.

(b) The series *diverges* by the *n*th-Term Test since $\lim_{n \to \infty} (1 - (1/n))^n = e^{-1} \neq 0$ (Table 8.1, Formula 5).

(c) This is *not* an alternating series. However,

$$\sum_{n=1}^{\infty} \left| (-1)^{n(n+1)/2} \frac{1}{2^n} \right| = \sum_{n=1}^{\infty} \frac{1}{2^n}$$

is a convergent geometric series, and we conclude that the given series is *absolutely convergent*.

Absolute convergence is important for two reasons. First, we have good tests for convergence of series of positive terms. Second, if a series converges absolutely, then it converges. That is the thrust of the next theorem.

CAUTION   We can rephrase Theorem 10 to say that *every absolutely convergent series converges*. The converse statement is false, however: Many convergent series do not converge absolutely.

Theorem 10   The Absolute Convergence Test

If $\sum_{n=1}^{\infty} |a_n|$ converges, then $\sum_{n=1}^{\infty} a_n$ converges.

Proof   For each *n*,

$$-|a_n| \leq a_n \leq |a_n|, \qquad \text{so} \qquad 0 \leq a_n + |a_n| \leq 2|a_n|.$$

If $\sum_{n=1}^{\infty} |a_n|$ converges, then $\sum_{n=1}^{\infty} 2|a_n|$ converges and, by the Direct Comparison Test, the nonnegative series $\sum_{n=1}^{\infty} (a_n + |a_n|)$ converges. The equality $a_n = (a_n + |a_n|) - |a_n|$ now lets us express $\sum_{n=1}^{\infty} a_n$ as the difference of two convergent series:

$$\sum_{n=1}^{\infty} a_n = \sum_{n=1}^{\infty} (a_n + |a_n| - |a_n|) = \sum_{n=1}^{\infty} (a_n + |a_n|) - \sum_{n=1}^{\infty} |a_n|.$$

Therefore, $\sum_{n=1}^{\infty} a_n$ converges.   ▬

Example 4   Applying the Absolute Convergence Test

For

$$\sum_{n=1}^{\infty} (-1)^{n+1} \frac{1}{n^2} = 1 - \frac{1}{4} + \frac{1}{9} - \frac{1}{16} + \cdots,$$

the corresponding series of absolute values is the convergent series

$$\sum_{n=1}^{\infty} \frac{1}{n^2} = 1 + \frac{1}{4} + \frac{1}{9} + \frac{1}{16} + \cdots.$$

The original alternating series converges because it converges absolutely.

Example 5   Applying the Absolute Convergence Test

For

$$\sum_{n=1}^{\infty} \frac{\sin n}{n^2} = \frac{\sin 1}{1} + \frac{\sin 2}{4} + \frac{\sin 3}{9} + \cdots,$$

the corresponding series of absolute values is

$$\sum_{n=1}^{\infty} \left| \frac{\sin n}{n^2} \right| = \frac{|\sin 1|}{1} + \frac{|\sin 2|}{4} + \cdots,$$

which converges by comparison with $\sum_{n=1}^{\infty} (1/n^2)$ because $|\sin n| \le 1$ for every n. The original series converges absolutely; therefore, it converges.

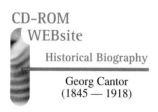

CD-ROM
WEBsite

Historical Biography

Georg Cantor
(1845 — 1918)

Example 6   Alternating p-Series

If p is a positive constant, the sequence $\{1/n^p\}$ is a decreasing sequence with limit zero. Therefore, the alternating p-series

$$\sum_{n=1}^{\infty} \frac{(-1)^{n-1}}{n^p} = 1 - \frac{1}{2^p} + \frac{1}{3^p} - \frac{1}{4^p} + \cdots, \qquad p > 0,$$

converges.

If $p > 1$, the series converges absolutely. If $0 < p \le 1$, the series converges conditionally.

Conditional convergence: $1 - \dfrac{1}{\sqrt{2}} + \dfrac{1}{\sqrt{3}} - \dfrac{1}{\sqrt{4}} + \cdots$

Absolute convergence: $1 - \dfrac{1}{2^{3/2}} + \dfrac{1}{3^{3/2}} - \dfrac{1}{4^{3/2}} + \cdots$

Rearranging Series

> **Theorem 11**   The Rearrangement Theorem for Absolutely Convergent Series
>
> If $\sum_{n=1}^{\infty} a_n$ converges absolutely and $b_1, b_2, \ldots, b_n, \ldots$, is any arrangement of the sequence $\{a_n\}$, then $\sum b_n$ converges absolutely and
>
> $$\sum_{n=1}^{\infty} b_n = \sum_{n=1}^{\infty} a_n.$$

(For an outline of the proof, see Exercise 60.)

Example 7   Applying the Rearrangement Theorem

As we saw in Example 4, the series

$$1 - \frac{1}{4} + \frac{1}{9} - \frac{1}{16} + \cdots + (-1)^{n-1} \frac{1}{n^2} + \cdots$$

converges absolutely. A possible rearrangement of the terms of the series might start with a positive term, then two negative terms, then three positive terms, then four negative terms, and so on: After k terms of one sign, take $k + 1$ terms of the opposite sign. The first 10 terms of such a series look like this:

$$1 - \frac{1}{4} - \frac{1}{16} + \frac{1}{9} + \frac{1}{25} + \frac{1}{49} - \frac{1}{36} - \frac{1}{64} - \frac{1}{100} - \frac{1}{144} + \cdots.$$

The Rearrangement Theorem says that both series converge to the same value. In this example, if we had the second series to begin with, we would probably be glad to exchange it for the first, if we knew that we could. We can do even better: The sum of either series is also equal to

$$\sum_{n=1}^{\infty} \frac{1}{(2n-1)^2} - \sum_{n=1}^{\infty} \frac{1}{(2n)^2}.$$

(See Exercise 61.)

CAUTION   If we rearrange infinitely many terms of a conditionally convergent series, we can get results that are far different from the sum of the original series.

The kind of behavior illustrated by this example is typical of what can happen with any conditionally convergent series. Moral: Add the terms of a conditionally convergent series in the order given.

Example 8   Rearranging the Alternating Harmonic Series

The alternating harmonic series

$$\frac{1}{1} - \frac{1}{2} + \frac{1}{3} - \frac{1}{4} + \frac{1}{5} - \frac{1}{6} + \frac{1}{7} - \frac{1}{8} + \frac{1}{9} - \frac{1}{10} + \frac{1}{11} - \cdots$$

can be rearranged to diverge or to reach any preassigned sum.

(a) *Rearranging* $\sum_{n=1}^{\infty} (-1)^{n+1}/n$ *to diverge.* The series of terms $\sum [1/(2n-1)]$ diverges to $+\infty$, and the series of terms $\sum (-1/2n)$ diverges to $-\infty$. No matter how far out in the sequence of odd-numbered terms we begin, we can always add enough positive terms to get an arbitrarily large sum. Similarly, with the negative terms, no matter how far out we start, we can add enough consecutive even-numbered terms to get a negative sum of arbitrarily large absolute value. If we wished to do so, we could start adding odd-numbered terms until we had a sum greater than $+3$, say, and then follow that with enough consecutive negative terms to make the new total less than -4. We could then add enough positive terms to make the total greater than $+5$ and follow with consecutive unused negative terms to make a new total less than -6, and so on. In this way, we could make the swings arbitrarily large in either direction.

(b) *Rearranging* $\sum_{n=1}^{\infty} (-1)^{n+1}/n$ *to converge to 1.* Another possibility is to focus on a particular limit. Suppose that we try to get sums that converge to 1. We start with the first term, $1/1$, and then subtract $1/2$. Next we add $1/3$ and $1/5$, which brings the total back to 1 or above. Then we add consecutive negative terms until the total is less than 1. We continue in this manner: When the sum is less than 1, add positive terms until the total is 1 or more, then subtract (add negative) terms until the total is again less than 1. This process can be continued indefinitely. Because both the odd-numbered terms and the even-numbered terms of the original series approach zero as $n \to \infty$, the amount by which our partial sums exceed 1 or fall below it approaches zero. So the new series converges to 1. The rearranged series starts like this:

$$\frac{1}{1} - \frac{1}{2} + \frac{1}{3} + \frac{1}{5} - \frac{1}{4} + \frac{1}{7} + \frac{1}{9} - \frac{1}{6} + \frac{1}{11} + \frac{1}{13} - \frac{1}{8} + \frac{1}{15} + \frac{1}{17} - \frac{1}{10}$$

$$+ \frac{1}{19} + \frac{1}{21} - \frac{1}{12} + \frac{1}{23} + \frac{1}{25} - \frac{1}{14} + \frac{1}{27} - \frac{1}{16} + \cdots.$$

Procedure For Determining Convergence

The following flowchart is often useful for deciding whether a given infinite series converges or diverges.

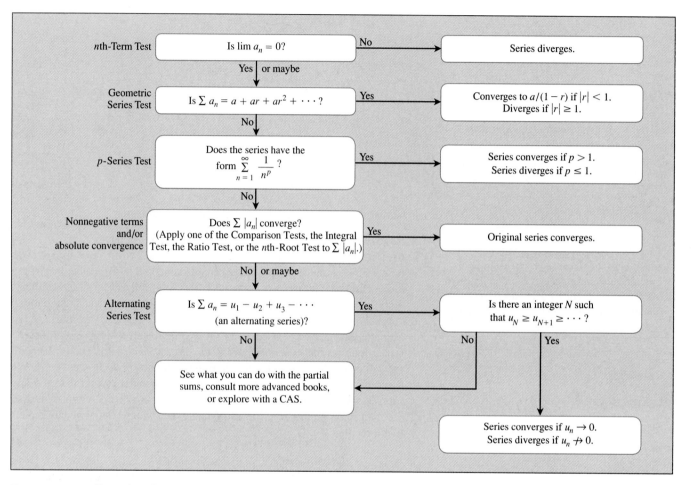

FLOWCHART 8.1 Procedure for determining convergence.

EXERCISES 8.5

Determining Convergence or Divergence

Which of the alternating series in Exercises 1–10 converge, and which diverge? Give reasons for your answers.

1. $\displaystyle\sum_{n=1}^{\infty} (-1)^{n+1} \frac{1}{n^2}$

2. $\displaystyle\sum_{n=1}^{\infty} (-1)^{n+1} \frac{1}{n^{3/2}}$

3. $\displaystyle\sum_{n=1}^{\infty} (-1)^{n+1} \left(\frac{n}{10}\right)^n$

4. $\displaystyle\sum_{n=1}^{\infty} (-1)^{n+1} \frac{10^n}{n^{10}}$

5. $\displaystyle\sum_{n=2}^{\infty} (-1)^{n+1} \frac{1}{\ln n}$

6. $\displaystyle\sum_{n=1}^{\infty} (-1)^{n+1} \frac{\ln n}{n}$

7. $\displaystyle\sum_{n=2}^{\infty} (-1)^{n+1} \frac{\ln n}{\ln n^2}$

8. $\displaystyle\sum_{n=1}^{\infty} (-1)^n \ln\left(1 + \frac{1}{n}\right)$

9. $\displaystyle\sum_{n=1}^{\infty} (-1)^{n+1} \frac{\sqrt{n}+1}{n+1}$

10. $\displaystyle\sum_{n=1}^{\infty} (-1)^{n+1} \frac{3\sqrt{n}+1}{\sqrt{n}+1}$

Absolute Versus Conditional Convergence

Which of the series in Exercises 11–44 converge absolutely, which converge conditionally, and which diverge? Give reasons for your answers.

11. $\displaystyle\sum_{n=1}^{\infty} (-1)^{n+1} (0.1)^n$

12. $\displaystyle\sum_{n=1}^{\infty} (-1)^{n+1} \frac{(0.1)^n}{n}$

13. $\displaystyle\sum_{n=1}^{\infty} (-1)^n \frac{1}{\sqrt{n+1}}$

14. $\displaystyle\sum_{n=1}^{\infty} \frac{(-1)^n}{1 + \sqrt{n}}$

15. $\displaystyle\sum_{n=1}^{\infty} (-1)^{n+1} \frac{n}{n^3 + 1}$

16. $\displaystyle\sum_{n=1}^{\infty} (-1)^{n+1} \frac{n!}{2^n}$

17. $\displaystyle\sum_{n=1}^{\infty} (-1)^n \frac{1}{n+3}$

18. $\displaystyle\sum_{n=1}^{\infty} (-1)^n \frac{\sin n}{n^2}$

19. $\displaystyle\sum_{n=1}^{\infty} (-1)^{n+1} \frac{3+n}{5+n}$

20. $\displaystyle\sum_{n=2}^{\infty} (-1)^n \frac{1}{\ln (n^3)}$

21. $\displaystyle\sum_{n=1}^{\infty} (-1)^{n+1} \frac{1+n}{n^2}$

22. $\displaystyle\sum_{n=1}^{\infty} \frac{(-2)^{n+1}}{n + 5^n}$

23. $\displaystyle\sum_{n=1}^{\infty} (-1)^n n^2(2/3)^n$

24. $\displaystyle\sum_{n=1}^{\infty} (-1)^{n+1} (\sqrt[n]{10})$

25. $\displaystyle\sum_{n=1}^{\infty} (-1)^n \frac{\tan^{-1} n}{n^2 + 1}$

26. $\displaystyle\sum_{n=2}^{\infty} (-1)^{n+1} \frac{1}{n \ln n}$

27. $\displaystyle\sum_{n=1}^{\infty} (-1)^n \frac{n}{n+1}$

28. $\displaystyle\sum_{n=1}^{\infty} (-1)^n \frac{\ln n}{n - \ln n}$

29. $\displaystyle\sum_{n=1}^{\infty} \frac{(-100)^n}{n!}$

30. $\displaystyle\sum_{n=1}^{\infty} (-5)^{-n}$

31. $\displaystyle\sum_{n=1}^{\infty} \frac{(-1)^{n-1}}{n^2 + 2n + 1}$

32. $\displaystyle\sum_{n=2}^{\infty} (-1)^n \left(\frac{\ln n}{\ln n^2}\right)^n$

33. $\displaystyle\sum_{n=1}^{\infty} \frac{\cos n\pi}{n\sqrt{n}}$

34. $\displaystyle\sum_{n=1}^{\infty} \frac{\cos n\pi}{n}$

35. $\displaystyle\sum_{n=1}^{\infty} \frac{(-1)^n (n+1)^n}{(2n)^n}$

36. $\displaystyle\sum_{n=1}^{\infty} \frac{(-1)^{n+1}(n!)^2}{(2n)!}$

37. $\displaystyle\sum_{n=1}^{\infty} (-1)^n \frac{(2n)!}{2^n n! \, n}$

38. $\displaystyle\sum_{n=1}^{\infty} (-1)^n \frac{(n!)^2 3^n}{(2n+1)!}$

39. $\displaystyle\sum_{n=1}^{\infty} (-1)^n (\sqrt{n+1} - \sqrt{n})$

40. $\displaystyle\sum_{n=1}^{\infty} (-1)^n (\sqrt{n^2 + n} - n)$

41. $\displaystyle\sum_{n=1}^{\infty} (-1)^n (\sqrt{n + \sqrt{n}} - \sqrt{n})$

42. $\displaystyle\sum_{n=1}^{\infty} \frac{(-1)^n}{\sqrt{n} + \sqrt{n+1}}$

43. $\displaystyle\sum_{n=1}^{\infty} (-1)^n \operatorname{sech} n$

44. $\displaystyle\sum_{n=1}^{\infty} (-1)^n \operatorname{csch} n$

Error Estimation

In Exercises 45–48, estimate the magnitude of the error involved in using the sum of the first four terms to approximate the sum of the entire series.

45. $\displaystyle\sum_{n=1}^{\infty} (-1)^{n+1} \frac{1}{n}$ It can be shown that the sum is $\ln 2$.

46. $\displaystyle\sum_{n=1}^{\infty} (-1)^{n+1} \frac{1}{10^n}$

47. $\displaystyle\sum_{n=1}^{\infty} (-1)^{n+1} \frac{(0.01)^n}{n}$ As you will see in Section 8.6 the sum is $\ln (1.01)$.

48. $\displaystyle\frac{1}{1+t} = \sum_{n=0}^{\infty} (-1)^n t^n$, $\quad 0 < t < 1$

Approximate the sums in Exercises 49 and 50 with an error of magnitude less than 5×10^{-6}.

49. $\displaystyle\sum_{n=0}^{\infty} (-1)^n \frac{1}{(2n)!}$ As you will see in Section 8.7, the sum is $\cos 1$, the cosine of 1 radian.

50. $\displaystyle\sum_{n=0}^{\infty} (-1)^n \frac{1}{n!}$ As you will see in Section 8.7, the sum is e^{-1}.

Theory and Examples

51. (a) *Writing to Learn* The series

$$\frac{1}{3} - \frac{1}{2} + \frac{1}{9} - \frac{1}{4} + \frac{1}{27} - \frac{1}{8} + \cdots + \frac{1}{3^n} - \frac{1}{2^n} + \cdots$$

does not meet one of the conditions of Theorem 8. Which one?

(b) Find the sum of the series in part (a).

52. The limit L of an alternating series that satisfies the conditions of Theorem 8 lies between the values of any two consecutive partial sums. This suggests using the average

$$\frac{s_n + s_{n+1}}{2} = s_n + \frac{1}{2}(-1)^{n+2}a_{n+1}$$

to estimate L. Compute

$$s_{20} + \frac{1}{2} \cdot \frac{1}{21}$$

as an approximation to the sum of the alternating harmonic series. The exact sum is $\ln 2 = 0.6931 \ldots$.

53. *The sign of the remainder of an alternating series that satisfies the conditions of Theorem 8* Prove the assertion in Theorem 9 that whenever an alternating series satisfying the conditions of Theorem 8 is approximated with one of its partial sums, then the remainder (sum of the unused terms) has the same sign as the first unused term. (*Hint:* Group the remainder's terms in consecutive pairs.)

54. *Writing to Learn* Show that the sum of the first $2n$ terms of the series

$$1 - \frac{1}{2} + \frac{1}{2} - \frac{1}{3} + \frac{1}{3} - \frac{1}{4} + \frac{1}{4} - \frac{1}{5} + \frac{1}{5} - \frac{1}{6} + \cdots$$

is the same as the sum of the first n terms of the series

$$\frac{1}{1 \cdot 2} + \frac{1}{2 \cdot 3} + \frac{1}{3 \cdot 4} + \frac{1}{4 \cdot 5} + \frac{1}{5 \cdot 6} + \cdots.$$

Do these series converge? What is the sum of the first $2n + 1$ terms of the first series? If the series converge, what is their sum?

55. *Divergence* Show that if $\sum_{n=1}^{\infty} a_n$ diverges, then $\sum_{n=1}^{\infty} |a_n|$ diverges.

56. Show that if $\sum_{n=1}^{\infty} a_n$ converges absolutely, then

$$\left| \sum_{n=1}^{\infty} a_n \right| \le \sum_{n=1}^{\infty} |a_n|.$$

57. *Rules of absolute convergence* Show that if $\sum_{n=1}^{\infty} a_n$ and $\sum_{n=1}^{\infty} b_n$ both converge absolutely, then so does

(a) $\displaystyle\sum_{n=1}^{\infty} (a_n + b_n)$ **(b)** $\displaystyle\sum_{n=1}^{\infty} (a_n - b_n)$

(c) $\displaystyle\sum_{n=1}^{\infty} ka_n$ (*k* any number)

58. *Term-by-term products* Show by example that $\sum_{n=1}^{\infty} a_n b_n$ may diverge even if $\sum_{n=1}^{\infty} a_n$ and $\sum_{n=1}^{\infty} b_n$ both converge.

59. *Rearrangement* In Example 8, suppose that the goal is to arrange the terms to get a new series that converges to $-1/2$. Start the new arrangement with the first negative term, which is $-1/2$. Whenever you have a sum that is less than or equal to $-1/2$, start introducing positive terms, taken in order, until the new total is greater than $-1/2$. Then add negative terms until the total is less than or equal to $-1/2$ again. Continue this process until your partial sums have been above the target at least three times and finish at or below it. If s_n is the sum of the first n terms of your new series, plot the points (n, s_n) to illustrate how the sums are behaving.

60. *Outline of the proof of the Rearrangement Theorem (Theorem 11)*
(a) Let ϵ be a positive real number, let $L = \sum_{n=1}^{\infty} a_n$, and let $s_k = \sum_{n=1}^{k} a_n$. Show that for some index N_1 and for some index $N_2 \geq N_1$,

$$\sum_{n=N_1}^{\infty} |a_n| < \frac{\epsilon}{2} \quad \text{and} \quad |s_{N_2} - L| < \frac{\epsilon}{2}.$$

Since all the terms $a_1, a_2, \ldots, a_{N_2}$ appear somewhere in the sequence $\{b_n\}$, there is an index $N_3 \geq N_2$ such that if $n \geq N_3$, then $\left(\sum_{k=1}^{k} b_k\right) - s_{N_2}$ is at most a sum of terms a_m with $m \geq N_1$. Therefore, if $n \geq N_3$,

$$\left| \sum_{k=1}^{n} b_k - L \right| \leq \left| \sum_{k=1}^{n} b_k - s_{N_2} \right| + |s_{N_2} - L|$$

$$\leq \sum_{k=N_1}^{\infty} |a_k| + |s_{N_2} - L| < \epsilon.$$

(b) The argument in part (a) shows that if $\sum_{n=1}^{\infty} a_n$ converges absolutely, then $\sum_{n=1}^{\infty} b_n$ converges and $\sum_{n=1}^{\infty} b_n = \sum_{n=1}^{\infty} a_n$. Now show that because $\sum_{n=1}^{\infty} |a_n|$ converges, $\sum_{n=1}^{\infty} |b_n|$ converges to $\sum_{n=1}^{\infty} |a_n|$.

61. *Unzipping absolutely convergent series*
(a) Show that if $\sum_{n=1}^{\infty} |a_n|$ converges and

$$b_n = \begin{cases} a_n & \text{if } a_n \geq 0 \\ 0 & \text{if } a_n < 0, \end{cases}$$

then $\sum_{n=1}^{\infty} b_n$ converges.

(b) Use the results in part (a) to show likewise that if $\sum_{n=1}^{\infty} |a_n|$ converges and

$$c_n = \begin{cases} 0 & \text{if } a_n \geq 0 \\ a_n & \text{if } a_n < 0, \end{cases}$$

then $\sum_{n=1}^{\infty} c_n$ converges.

In other words, if a series converges absolutely, its positive terms form a convergent series, and so do its negative terms. Furthermore,

$$\sum_{n=1}^{\infty} a_n = \sum_{n=1}^{\infty} b_n + \sum_{n=1}^{\infty} c_n$$

because $b_n = (a_n + |a_n|)/2$ and $c_n = (a_n - |a_n|)/2$.

62. *Alternating harmonic series revisited* What is wrong here: Multiply both sides of the alternating harmonic series.

$$S = 1 - \frac{1}{2} + \frac{1}{3} - \frac{1}{4} + \frac{1}{5} - \frac{1}{6} + \frac{1}{7} - \frac{1}{8} + \frac{1}{9} - \frac{1}{10} + \frac{1}{11} - \frac{1}{12} + \cdots$$

by 2 to get

$$2S = 2 - 1 + \frac{2}{3} - \frac{1}{2} + \frac{2}{5} - \frac{1}{3} + \frac{2}{7} - \frac{1}{4} + \frac{2}{9} - \frac{1}{5} + \frac{2}{11} - \frac{1}{6} + \cdots.$$

Collect terms with the same denominator, as the arrows indicate, to arrive at

$$2S = 1 - \frac{1}{2} + \frac{1}{3} - \frac{1}{4} + \frac{1}{5} - \frac{1}{6} + \cdots.$$

The series on the right-hand side of this equation is the series we started with. Therefore, $2S = S$, and dividing by S gives $2 = 1$. (*Source*: "Riemann's Rearrangement Theorem" by Stewart Galanor, *Mathematics Teacher*, Vol. 80, No. 8 (1987), pp. 675–681.)

63. Draw a figure similar to Figure 8.15 to illustrate the convergence of the series in Theorem 8 when $N > 1$.

8.6 Power Series

Power Series and Convergence • The Radius and Interval of Convergence • Term-by Term Differentiation • Term-by-Term Integration • Multiplication of Power Series

If $|x| < 1$, then the geometric series formula assures us that

$$1 + x + x^2 + x^3 + \cdots + x^n + \cdots = \frac{1}{1-x}.$$

Consider this statement for a moment. The expression on the right defines a function whose domain is the set of all numbers $x \neq 1$. The expression on the left defines a function whose domain is the interval of convergence, $|x| < 1$. The equality is understood to hold only on this latter domain, where both sides of the equation are defined. On this domain, the series *represents* the function $1/(1 - x)$.

In this section, we study the "infinite polynomials" like $\sum_{n=0}^{\infty} x^n$, and in the next section, we take up the question of representing a particular function with such an infinite polynomial (called a power series).

Power Series and Convergence

The expression $\sum_{n=0}^{\infty} c_n x^n$ is like a polynomial in that it is a sum of coefficients times powers of x, but polynomials have *finite* degrees and do not suffer from divergence for the wrong values of x. Just as an infinite series of numbers is not a mere sum, this series of powers of x is not a mere polynomial.

When we set $x = 0$ in the expression

$$\sum_{n=0}^{\infty} c_n x^n = c_0 + c_1 x + c_2 x^2$$
$$+ \cdots + c_n x^n + \cdots,$$

we get c_0 on the right but $c_0 \cdot 0^0$ on the left. Since 0^0 is not a number, this is a slight flaw in the notation, which we agree to overlook. The same situation arises when we set

$$x = a \quad \text{in} \quad \sum_{n=0}^{\infty} c_n (x - a)^n.$$

In either case, we agree that the expression will equal c_0. (It really *should* equal c_0, so we are not compromising the mathematics; we are clarifying the notation we use to convey the mathematics.)

> **Definition**   Power Series
>
> An expression of the form
>
> $$\sum_{n=0}^{\infty} c_n x^n = c_0 + c_1 x + c_2 x^2 + \cdots + c_n x^n + \cdots$$
>
> is a **power series centered at $x = 0$.** An expression of the form
>
> $$\sum_{n=0}^{\infty} c_n (x - a)^n = c_0 + c_1 (x - a) + c_2 (x - a)^2 + \cdots + c_n (x - a)^n + \cdots$$
>
> is a **power series centered at $x = a$.** The term $c_n (x - a)^n$ is the **nth term;** the number a is the **center.**

Example 1   The Geometric Series

The geometric series

$$\sum_{n=0}^{\infty} x^n = 1 + x + x^2 + \cdots + x^n + \cdots$$

is a power series centered at $x = 0$. It converges to $1/(1 - x)$ on the interval $-1 < x < 1$, also centered at $x = 0$. (Figure 8.16). This is typical behavior, as we soon see. A power series converges for all x, converges on a finite interval with the same center as the series, or converges only at the center itself.

Up to now, we have used the equation

$$\frac{1}{1 - x} = 1 + x + x^2 + \cdots + x^n + \cdots, \qquad -1 < x < 1$$

as a formula for the sum of the series on the right.

We now change the focus: We think of the partial sums of the series on the right as polynomials $P_n(x)$ that approximate the function on the left. For values of x near zero, we need take only a few terms of the series to get a good approximation. As

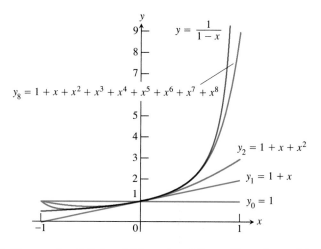

FIGURE 8.16 The graphs of $f(x) = 1/(1 - x)$ and four of its polynomial approximations. (Example 1)

we move toward $x = 1$, or -1, we must take more terms. Figure 8.16 shows the graphs of $f(x) = 1/(1 - x)$ and the approximating polynomials $y_n = P_n(x)$ for $n = 0, 1, 2,$ and 8.

Example 2 Applying the Definition

The power series

$$1 - \frac{1}{2}(x - 2) + \frac{1}{4}(x - 2)^2 + \cdots + \left(-\frac{1}{2}\right)^n (x - 2)^n + \cdots \tag{1}$$

is centered at $a = 2$ with coefficients $c_0 = 1$, $c_1 = -1/2$, $c_2 = 1/4, \ldots, c_n = (-1/2)^n$. This is a geometric series with first term 1 and ratio $r = -\dfrac{x - 2}{2}$. The series converges for $\left| \dfrac{x - 2}{2} \right| < 1$ or $0 < x < 4$. The sum is

$$\frac{1}{1 - r} = \frac{1}{1 + \dfrac{x - 2}{2}} = \frac{2}{x},$$

so

$$\frac{2}{x} = 1 - \frac{(x - 2)}{2} + \frac{(x - 2)^2}{4} - \cdots + \left(-\frac{1}{2}\right)^n (x - 2)^n + \cdots, \qquad 0 < x < 4.$$

Series (1) generates useful polynomial approximations of $f(x) = 2/x$ for values of x near 2:

$$P_0(x) = 1$$

$$P_1(x) = 1 - \frac{1}{2}(x - 2) = 2 - \frac{x}{2}$$

$$P_2(x) = 1 - \frac{1}{2}(x - 2) + \frac{1}{4}(x - 2)^2 = 3 - \frac{3x}{2} + \frac{x^2}{4},$$

and so on (Figure 8.17).

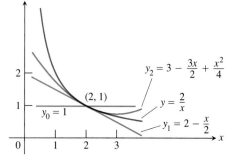

FIGURE 8.17 The graphs of $f(x) = 2/x$ and its first three polynomial approximations. (Example 2)

The Radius and Interval of Convergence

The power series in Examples 1 and 2 happen to be geometric, so we could find the intervals for which they converge. For nongeometric series, we begin by noting that any power series of the form $\sum_{n=0}^{\infty} c_n(x - a)^n$ always converges at $x = a$, thus assuring us of at least one coordinate on the real number line where the series must converge. We have encountered power series like the series in Examples 1 and 2 that converge only on a finite interval centered at a. Some power series converge for all real numbers. A useful fact about power series is that those are the only possibilities, as the following theorem attests.

Theorem 12 The Convergence Theorem for Power Series

There are three possibilities for $\sum_{n=0}^{\infty} c_n(x - a)^n$ with respect to convergence.

1. There is a positive number R such that the series diverges for $|x - a| > R$ but converges for $|x - a| < R$. The series may or may not converge at either of the endpoints $x = a - R$ and $x = a + R$.

2. The series converges for every x $(R = \infty)$.

3. The series converges at $x = a$ and diverges elsewhere $(R = 0)$.

The number R is the **radius of convergence,** and the set of all values of x for which the series converges is the **interval of convergence.** The radius of convergence completely determines the interval of convergence if R is either zero or infinite. For $0 < R < \infty$, however, there remains the question of what happens at the endpoints of the interval. The next example illustrates how to find the interval of convergence.

Example 3 Finding the Interval of Convergence Using the Ratio Test

For what values of x do the following power series converge?

(a) $\displaystyle\sum_{n=1}^{\infty} (-1)^{n-1} \frac{x^n}{n} = x - \frac{x^2}{2} + \frac{x^3}{3} - \cdots$

(b) $\displaystyle\sum_{n=1}^{\infty} (-1)^{n-1} \frac{x^{2n-1}}{2n - 1} = x - \frac{x^3}{3} + \frac{x^5}{5} - \cdots$

(c) $\displaystyle\sum_{n=0}^{\infty} \frac{x^n}{n!} = 1 + x + \frac{x^2}{2!} + \frac{x^3}{3!} + \cdots$

(d) $\displaystyle\sum_{n=0}^{\infty} n!\, x^n = 1 + x + 2!\, x^2 + 3!\, x^3 + \cdots$

Solution Apply the Ratio Test to the series $\Sigma |u_n|$, where u_n is the nth term of the series in question.

(a) $\left| \dfrac{u_{n+1}}{u_n} \right| = \dfrac{n}{n + 1} |x| \rightarrow |x|.$

The series converges absolutely for $|x| < 1$. It diverges if $|x| > 1$ because the nth term does not converge to zero. At $x = 1$, we get the alternating harmonic series $1 - 1/2 + 1/3 - 1/4 + \cdots$, which converges. At $x = -1$, we get $-1 - 1/2 - 1/3 - 1/4 - \cdots$, the negative of the harmonic series; it diverges. Series (a) converges for $-1 < x \le 1$ and diverges elsewhere.

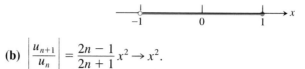

(b) $\left| \dfrac{u_{n+1}}{u_n} \right| = \dfrac{2n - 1}{2n + 1} x^2 \to x^2$.

The series converges absolutely for $x^2 < 1$. It diverges for $x^2 > 1$ because the nth term does not converge to zero. At $x = 1$, the series becomes $1 - 1/3 + 1/5 - 1/7 + \cdots$, which converges by the Alternating Series Theorem. It also converges at $x = -1$ because it is again an alternating series that satisfies the conditions for convergence. The value at $x = -1$ is the negative of the value at $x = 1$. Series (b) converges for $-1 \le x \le 1$ and diverges elsewhere.

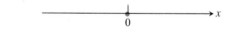

(c) $\left| \dfrac{u_{n+1}}{u_n} \right| = \left| \dfrac{x^{n+1}}{(n + 1)!} \cdot \dfrac{n!}{x^n} \right| = \dfrac{|x|}{n + 1} \to 0$ for every x.

The series converges absolutely for all x.

(d) $\left| \dfrac{u_{n+1}}{u_n} \right| = \left| \dfrac{(n + 1)! x^{n+1}}{n! x^n} \right| = (n + 1) |x| \to \infty$ unless $x = 0$.

The series diverges for all values of x except $x = 0$.

Here's a summary of steps for finding the interval of convergence of a power series.

Finding the Interval of Convergence

Step 1: Use the Ratio Test (or nth-Root Test) to find the interval where the series converges absolutely. Ordinarily, this is an open interval

$$|x - a| < R \qquad \text{or} \qquad a - R < x < a + R.$$

Step 2: If the interval of absolute convergence is finite, test for convergence or divergence at each endpoint, as in Examples 3(a) and (b). Use a Comparison Test, the Integral Test, or the Alternating Series Test.

Step 3: If the interval of absolute convergence is $a - R < x < a + R$, the series diverges for $|x - a| > R$ (it does not even converge conditionally), because the nth term does not approach zero for those values of x.

The convergence of a power series is absolute at every point in the interior of the interval. If a power series converges absolutely for all values of x, we say that its **radius of convergence is infinite.** If it converges only at $x = a$, the **radius of convergence is zero.**

Term-by-Term Differentiation

A theorem from advanced calculus says that a power series can be differentiated term by term at each interior point of its interval of convergence.

A WORD OF CAUTION   Term-by-term differentiation might not work for other kinds of series. For example, the trigonometric series

$$\sum_{n=1}^{\infty} \frac{\sin(n!x)}{n^2}$$

converges for all x. But if we differentiate term by term, we get the series

$$\sum_{n=1}^{\infty} \frac{n! \cos(n!x)}{n^2}$$

which diverges for all x.

Theorem 13   The Term-by-Term Differentiation Theorem

If $\Sigma\, c_n(x - a)^n$ converges for $a - R < x < a + R$ for some $R > 0$, it defines a function f:

$$f(x) = \sum_{n=0}^{\infty} c_n (x - a)^n, \qquad a - R < x < a + R.$$

Such a function f has derivatives of all orders inside the interval of convergence. We can obtain the derivatives by differentiating the original series term by term:

$$f'(x) = \sum_{n=1}^{\infty} nc_n(x - a)^{n-1}$$

$$f''(x) = \sum_{n=2}^{\infty} n(n - 1)c_n(x - a)^{n-2},$$

and so on. Each of these derived series converges at every interior point of the interval of convergence of the original series.

Example 4   Applying Term-by-Term Differentiation

Find series for $f'(x)$ and $f''(x)$ if

$$f(x) = \frac{1}{1 - x} = 1 + x + x^2 + x^3 + x^4 + \cdots + x^n + \cdots$$

$$= \sum_{n=0}^{\infty} x^n, \qquad -1 < x < 1.$$

Solution

$$f'(x) = \frac{1}{(1 - x)^2} = 1 + 2x + 3x^2 + 4x^3 + \cdots + nx^{n-1} + \cdots$$

$$= \sum_{n=1}^{\infty} nx^{n-1}, \qquad -1 < x < 1$$

$$f''(x) = \frac{2}{(1 - x)^3} = 2 + 6x + 12x^2 + \cdots + n(n - 1)x^{n-2} + \cdots$$

$$= \sum_{n=2}^{\infty} n(n - 1) x^{n-2}, \qquad -1 < x < 1$$

Term-by-Term Integration

Another advanced theorem states that a power series can be integrated term by term throughout its interval of convergence.

Theorem 14   The Term-by-Term Integration Theorem

Suppose that

$$f(x) = \sum_{n=0}^{\infty} c_n(x - a)^n$$

converges for $a - R < x < a + R$ $(R > 0)$. Then

$$\sum_{n=0}^{\infty} c_n \frac{(x - a)^{n+1}}{n + 1}$$

converges for $a - R < x < a + R$ and

$$\int f(x)\, dx = \sum_{n=0}^{\infty} c_n \frac{(x - a)^{n+1}}{n + 1} + C$$

for $a - R < x < a + R$.

Example 5   A Series for $\tan^{-1} x$, $-1 \le x \le 1$

Identify the function

$$f(x) = x - \frac{x^3}{3} + \frac{x^5}{5} - \cdots, \qquad -1 \le x \le 1.$$

Solution   We differentiate the original series term by term and get

$$f'(x) = 1 - x^2 + x^4 - x^6 + \cdots, \qquad -1 < x < 1.$$

This is a geometric series with first term 1 and ratio $-x^2$, so

$$f'(x) = \frac{1}{1 - (-x^2)} = \frac{1}{1 + x^2}.$$

We can now integrate $f'(x) = 1/(1 + x^2)$ to get

$$\int f'(x)\, dx = \int \frac{dx}{1 + x^2} = \tan^{-1} x + C.$$

The series for $f(x)$ is zero when $x = 0$, so $C = 0$. Hence,

$$f(x) = x - \frac{x^3}{3} + \frac{x^5}{5} - \frac{x^7}{7} + \cdots = \tan^{-1} x, \qquad -1 < x < 1.$$

In Section 8.8, we see that the series also converges to $\tan^{-1} x$ at $x = \pm 1$.

Notice that the original series in Example 5 converges at both endpoints of the original interval of convergence, but Theorem 13 can guarantee the convergence of the differentiated series only inside the interval.

Example 6   A Series for $\ln (1 + x)$, $-1 < x \le 1$

The series

$$\frac{1}{1 + t} = 1 - t + t^2 - t^3 + \cdots$$

converges on the open interval $-1 < t < 1$. Therefore,

$$\ln(1 + x) = \int_0^x \frac{1}{1+t}\, dt = t - \frac{t^2}{2} + \frac{t^3}{3} - \frac{t^4}{4} + \cdots \Big]_0^x$$

$$= x - \frac{x^2}{2} + \frac{x^3}{3} - \frac{x^4}{4} + \cdots, \qquad -1 < x < 1.$$

It can also be shown that the series converges at $x = 1$ to the number $\ln 2$, but that was not guaranteed by the theorem.

Multiplication of Power Series

Still another advanced theorem states that absolutely converging power series can be multiplied the way we multiply polynomials to produce new absolutely convergent series.

Theorem 15   The Series Multiplication Theorem for Power Series

If $A(x) = \sum_{n=0}^{\infty} a_n x^n$ and $B(x) = \sum_{n=0}^{\infty} b_n x^n$ converge absolutely for $|x| < R$ and if

$$c_n = a_0 b_n + a_1 b_{n-1} + a_2 b_{n-2} + \cdots + a_{n-1} b_1 + a_n b_0 = \sum_{k=0}^{n} a_k b_{n-k},$$

then $\sum_{n=0}^{\infty} c_n x^n$ converges absolutely to $A(x)\, B(x)$ for $|x| < R$:

$$\left(\sum_{n=0}^{\infty} a_n x^n \right) \cdot \left(\sum_{n=0}^{\infty} b_n x^n \right) = \sum_{n=0}^{\infty} c_n x^n.$$

Example 7   Applying the Multiplication Theorem

Multiply the geometric series

$$\sum_{n=0}^{\infty} x^n = 1 + x + x^2 + \cdots + x^n + \cdots = \frac{1}{1-x} \qquad \text{for } |x| < 1,$$

by itself to get a power series for $1/(1-x)^2$, for $|x| < 1$.

Solution   Let

$$A(x) = \sum_{n=0}^{\infty} a_n x^n = 1 + x + x^2 + \cdots + x^n + \cdots = 1/(1-x)$$

$$B(x) = \sum_{n=0}^{\infty} b_n x^n = 1 + x + x^2 + \cdots + x^n + \cdots = 1/(1-x)$$

and

$$c_n = \underbrace{a_0 b_n + a_1 b_{n-1} + \cdots + a_k b_{n-k} + \cdots + a_n b_0}_{n+1 \text{ terms}}$$

$$= \underbrace{1 + 1 + \cdots + 1}_{n+1 \text{ ones}} = n + 1.$$

Then, by the Series Multiplication Theorem,

$$A(x) \cdot B(x) = \sum_{n=0}^{\infty} c_n x^n = \sum_{n=0}^{\infty} (n + 1)x^n$$

$$= 1 + 2x + 3x^2 + 4x^3 + \cdots + (n + 1)x^n + \cdots$$

is the series for $1/(1 - x)^2$. The series all converge absolutely for $|x| < 1$. Example 4 gives the same answer because

$$\frac{d}{dx}\left(\frac{1}{1 - x}\right) = \frac{1}{(1 - x)^2}.$$

EXERCISES 8.6

Intervals of Convergence

In Exercises 1–32, (a) find the series' radius and interval of convergence. For what values of x does the series converge (b) absolutely and (c) conditionally?

1. $\displaystyle\sum_{n=0}^{\infty} x^n$

2. $\displaystyle\sum_{n=0}^{\infty} (x + 5)^n$

3. $\displaystyle\sum_{n=0}^{\infty} (-1)^n (4x + 1)^n$

4. $\displaystyle\sum_{n=1}^{\infty} \frac{(3x - 2)^n}{n}$

5. $\displaystyle\sum_{n=0}^{\infty} \frac{(x - 2)^n}{10^n}$

6. $\displaystyle\sum_{n=0}^{\infty} (2x)^n$

7. $\displaystyle\sum_{n=0}^{\infty} \frac{nx^n}{n + 2}$

8. $\displaystyle\sum_{n=1}^{\infty} \frac{(-1)^n (x + 2)^n}{n}$

9. $\displaystyle\sum_{n=1}^{\infty} \frac{x^n}{n\sqrt{n}3^n}$

10. $\displaystyle\sum_{n=1}^{\infty} \frac{(x - 1)^n}{\sqrt{n}}$

11. $\displaystyle\sum_{n=0}^{\infty} \frac{(-1)^n x^n}{n!}$

12. $\displaystyle\sum_{n=0}^{\infty} \frac{3^n x^n}{n!}$

13. $\displaystyle\sum_{n=0}^{\infty} \frac{x^{2n+1}}{n!}$

14. $\displaystyle\sum_{n=0}^{\infty} \frac{(2x + 3)^{2n+1}}{n!}$

15. $\displaystyle\sum_{n=0}^{\infty} \frac{x^n}{\sqrt{n^2 + 3}}$

16. $\displaystyle\sum_{n=0}^{\infty} \frac{(-1)^n x^n}{\sqrt{n^2 + 3}}$

17. $\displaystyle\sum_{n=0}^{\infty} \frac{n(x + 3)^n}{5^n}$

18. $\displaystyle\sum_{n=0}^{\infty} \frac{nx^n}{4^n(n^2 + 1)}$

19. $\displaystyle\sum_{n=0}^{\infty} \frac{\sqrt{n}\, x^n}{3^n}$

20. $\displaystyle\sum_{n=1}^{\infty} \sqrt[n]{n}(2x + 5)^n$

21. $\displaystyle\sum_{n=1}^{\infty} \left(1 + \frac{1}{n}\right)^n x^n$

22. $\displaystyle\sum_{n=1}^{\infty} (\ln n) x^n$

23. $\displaystyle\sum_{n=1}^{\infty} n^n x^n$

24. $\displaystyle\sum_{n=0}^{\infty} n!\,(x - 4)^n$

25. $\displaystyle\sum_{n=1}^{\infty} \frac{(-1)^{n+1}(x + 2)^n}{n2^n}$

26. $\displaystyle\sum_{n=0}^{\infty} (-2)^n (n + 1)(x - 1)^n$

27. $\displaystyle\sum_{n=2}^{\infty} \frac{x^n}{n\,(\ln n)^2}$ (Get the information you need about $\sum 1/(n(\ln n)2)$ from Section 8.4, Exercise 75).

28. $\displaystyle\sum_{n=2}^{\infty} \frac{x^n}{n \ln n}$ (Get the information you need about $\sum 1/(n(\ln n)2)$ from Section 8.4, Exercise 75).

29. $\displaystyle\sum_{n=1}^{\infty} \frac{(4x - 5)^{2n+1}}{n^{3/2}}$

30. $\displaystyle\sum_{n=1}^{\infty} \frac{(3x + 1)^{n+1}}{2n + 2}$

31. $\displaystyle\sum_{n=1}^{\infty} \frac{(x + \pi)^n}{\sqrt{n}}$

32. $\displaystyle\sum_{n=0}^{\infty} \frac{(x - \sqrt{2})^{2n+1}}{2^n}$

Geometric Series in x

In Exercises 33–38, find the series' interval of convergence and, within this interval, the sum of the series as a function of x.

33. $\displaystyle\sum_{n=0}^{\infty} \frac{(x - 1)^{2n}}{4^n}$

34. $\displaystyle\sum_{n=0}^{\infty} \frac{(x + 1)^{2n}}{9^n}$

35. $\displaystyle\sum_{n=0}^{\infty} \left(\frac{\sqrt{x}}{2} - 1\right)^n$

36. $\displaystyle\sum_{n=0}^{\infty} (\ln x)^n$

37. $\displaystyle\sum_{n=0}^{\infty} \left(\frac{x^2 + 1}{3}\right)^n$

38. $\displaystyle\sum_{n=0}^{\infty} \left(\frac{x^2 - 1}{2}\right)^n$

Theory and Examples

39. *Term-by-term differentiation* For what values of x does the series

$$1 - \frac{1}{2}(x - 3) + \frac{1}{4}(x - 3)^2 + \cdots + \left(-\frac{1}{2}\right)^n (x - 3)^n + \cdots$$

converge? What is its sum? What series do you get if you differentiate the given series term by term? For what values of x does the new series converge? What is its sum?

40. *Term-by-term integration* If you integrate the series in Exercise 39 term by term, what new series do you get? For what values of x does the new series converge, and what is another name for its sum?

41. *Power series for* sin *x* The series

$$\sin x = x - \frac{x^3}{3!} + \frac{x^5}{5!} - \frac{x^7}{7!} + \frac{x^9}{9!} - \frac{x^{11}}{11!} + \cdots$$

converges to sin *x* for all *x*.

(a) Find the first six terms of a series for cos *x*. For what values of *x* should the series converge?

(b) By replacing *x* by 2*x* in the series for sin *x*, find a series that converges to sin 2*x* for all *x*.

(c) Using the result in part (a) and series multiplication, calculate the first six terms of a series for 2 sin *x* cos *x*. Compare your answer with the answer in part (b).

42. *Power series for* e^x The series

$$e^x = 1 + x + \frac{x^2}{2!} + \frac{x^3}{3!} + \frac{x^4}{4!} + \frac{x^5}{5!} + \cdots$$

converges to e^x for all *x*.

(a) Find a series for $(d/dx)e^x$. Do you get the series for e^x? Explain your answer.

(b) Find a series for $\int e^x \, dx$. Do you get the series for e^x? Explain your answer.

(c) Replace *x* by $-x$ in the series for e^x to find a series that converges to e^{-x} for all *x*. Then multiply the series for e^x and e^{-x} to find the first six terms of a series for $e^{-x} \cdot e^x$.

43. *Power series for* tan *x* The series

$$\tan x = x + \frac{x^3}{3} + \frac{2x^5}{15} + \frac{17x^7}{315} + \frac{62x^9}{2835} + \cdots$$

converges to tan *x* for $-\pi/2 < x < \pi/2$.

(a) Find the first five terms of the series for $\ln |\sec x|$. For what values of *x* should the series converge?

(b) Find the first five terms of the series for $\sec^2 x$. For what values of *x* should this series converge?

(c) Check your result in part (b) by squaring the series given for sec *x* in Exercise 44.

44. *Power series for* sec *x* The series for

$$\sec x = 1 + \frac{x^2}{2} + \frac{5}{24}x^4 + \frac{61}{720}x^6 + \frac{277}{8064}x^8 + \cdots$$

converges to sec *x* for $-\pi/2 < x < \pi/2$.

(a) Find the first five terms of a power series for the function $\ln |\sec x + \tan x|$. For what values of *x* should the series converge?

(b) Find the first four terms of a series for sec *x* tan *x*. For what values of *x* should the series converge?

(c) Check your result in part (b) by multiplying the series for sec *x* by the series given for tan *x* in Exercise 43.

45. *Uniqueness of convergent power series*

(a) Show that if two power series $\sum_{n=0}^{\infty} a_n x^n$ and $\sum_{n=0}^{\infty} b_n x^n$ are convergent and equal for all values of *x* in an open interval $(-c, c)$, then $a_n = b_n$ for every *n*. (*Hint:* Let $f(x) = \sum_{n=0}^{\infty} a_n x^n = \sum_{n=0}^{\infty} b_n x^n$. Differentiate term by term to show that a_n and b_n both equal $f^{(n)}(0)/(n!)$.)

(b) Show that if $\sum_{n=0}^{\infty} a_n x^n = 0$ for all *x* in an open interval $(-c, c)$, then $a_n = 0$ for every *n*.

46. *The sum of the series* $\sum_{n=0}^{\infty} (n^2/2^n)$ To find the sum of this series, express $1/(1 - x)$ as a geometric series, differentiate both sides of the resulting equation with respect to *x*, multiply both sides of the result by *x*, differentiate again, multiply by *x* again, and set *x* equal to 1/2. What do you get? (*Source:* David E. Dobbs's letter to the editor, *Illinois Mathematics Teacher*, Vol. 33, Issue 4 (1982), p. 27.)

47. *Convergence at endpoints* Show by examples that the convergence of a power series at an endpoint of its interval of convergence may be either conditional or absolute.

48. *Intervals of convergence* Make up a power series whose interval of convergence is

(a) $(-3, 3)$ **(b)** $(-2, 0)$ **(c)** $(1, 5)$.

Taylor and Maclaurin Series

Constructing a Series • Taylor and Maclaurin Series • Taylor Polynomials • Remainder of a Taylor Polynomial • Estimating the Remainder • Truncation Error • Table of Maclaurin Series • Combining Taylor Series

A comprehensive understanding of geometric series served us well in the last section, enabling us to find power series to represent certain functions and functions that are equivalent to certain power series (all these equivalencies being subject to the condition of convergence). In this section, we learn a more general technique for constructing power series, one that makes good use of the tools of calculus. In many cases, these series can provide useful polynomial approximations of the generating functions.

Constructing a Series

We know that within its interval of convergence, the sum of a power series is a continuous function with derivatives of all orders, but what about the other way around? If a function $f(x)$ has derivatives of all orders on an interval I, can it be expressed as a power series on I? If it can, what will its coefficients be?

We can answer the last question readily if we assume that $f(x)$ is the sum of a power series

$$f(x) = \sum_{n=0}^{\infty} a_n(x - a)^n$$
$$= a_0 + a_1(x - a) + a_2(x - a)^2 + \cdots + a_n(x - a)^n + \cdots$$

with a positive radius of convergence. By repeated term-by-term differentiation within the interval of convergence I, we obtain

$$f'(x) = a_1 + 2a_2(x - a) + 3a_3(x - a)^2 + \cdots + na_n(x - a)^{n-1} + \cdots$$
$$f''(x) = 1 \cdot 2a_2 + 2 \cdot 3a_3(x - a) + 3 \cdot 4a_4(x - a)^2 + \cdots$$
$$f'''(x) = 1 \cdot 2 \cdot 3a_3 + 2 \cdot 3 \cdot 4a_4(x - a) + 3 \cdot 4 \cdot 5a_5(x - a)^2 + \cdots,$$

with the nth derivative, for all n, being

$$f^{(n)}(x) = n!a_n + \text{a sum of terms with } (x - a) \text{ as a factor.}$$

Since these equations all hold at $x = a$, we have

$$f'(a) = a_1,$$
$$f''(a) = 1 \cdot 2a_2,$$
$$f'''(a) = 1 \cdot 2 \cdot 3a_3,$$

and, in general,

$$f^{(n)}(a) = n!a_n.$$

These formulas reveal a marvelous pattern in the coefficients of any power series $\sum_{n=0}^{\infty} a_n(x - a)^n$ that converges to the values of f on I ("represents f on I," we say). If there *is* such a series (still an open question), then there is only one such series and its nth coefficient is

$$a_n = \frac{f^{(n)}(a)}{n!}.$$

If f has a series representation, then the series must be

$$f(x) = f(a) + f'(a)(x - a) + \frac{f''(a)}{2!}(x - a)^2 + \cdots + \frac{f^{(n)}(a)}{n!}(x - a)^n + \cdots. \quad (1)$$

If we start with an arbitrary function f that is infinitely differentiable on an interval I centered at $x = a$ and use it to generate the series in Equation (1), however, will the series then converge to $f(x)$ at each x in the interior of I? The answer is maybe; for some functions it will, but for other functions it will not, as we will see.

Taylor and Maclaurin Series

Definitions   Taylor Series, Maclaurin Series

Let f be a function with derivatives of all orders throughout some interval containing a as an interior point. Then the **Taylor series generated by f at $x = a$ is**

$$\sum_{k=0}^{\infty} \frac{f^{(k)}(a)}{k!} (x - a)^k = f(a) + f'(a)(x - a) + \frac{f''(a)}{2!} (x - a)^2 + \cdots +$$

$$\frac{f^{(n)}(a)}{n!} (x - a)^n + \cdots.$$

The **Maclaurin series generated by f** is

$$\sum_{k=0}^{\infty} \frac{f^{(k)}(0)}{k!} x^k = f(0) + f'(0)x + \frac{f''(0)}{2!} x^2 + \cdots + \frac{f^{(n)}(0)}{n!} x^n + \cdots,$$

the Taylor series generated by f at $x = 0$.

Example 1   Finding a Taylor Series

Find the Taylor series generated by $f(x) = 1/x$ at $a = 2$. Where, if anywhere, does the series converge to $1/x$?

Solution   We need to find $f(2), f'(2), f''(2), \ldots$. Taking derivatives, we get

$$f(x) = x^{-1}, \qquad\qquad f(2) = 2^{-1} = \frac{1}{2},$$

$$f'(x) = -x^{-2}, \qquad\qquad f'(2) = -\frac{1}{2^2},$$

$$f''(x) = 2! x^{-3}, \qquad\qquad \frac{f''(2)}{2!} = 2^{-3} = \frac{1}{2^3},$$

$$f'''(x) = -3! \, x^{-4}, \qquad\qquad \frac{f'''(2)}{3!} = -\frac{1}{2^4},$$

$$\vdots \qquad\qquad\qquad \vdots$$

$$f^{(n)}(x) = (-1)^n n! x^{-(n+1)}, \qquad \frac{f^{(n)}(2)}{n!} = \frac{(-1)^n}{2^{n+1}}.$$

The Taylor series is

$$f(2) + f'(2)(x - 2) + \frac{f''(2)}{2!} (x - 2)^2 + \cdots + \frac{f^{(n)}}{n!} (x - 2)^n + \cdots$$

$$= \frac{1}{2} - \frac{(x - 2)}{2^2} + \frac{(x - 2)^2}{2^3} - \cdots + (-1)^n \frac{(x - 2)^n}{2^{n+1}} + \cdots.$$

This is a geometric series with first term $1/2$ and ratio $r = -(x - 2)/2$. It converges absolutely for $|x - 2| < 2$, and its sum is

$$\frac{1/2}{1 + (x - 2)/2} = \frac{1}{2 + (x - 2)} = \frac{1}{x}.$$

In this example, the Taylor series generated by $f(x) = 1/x$ at $a = 2$ converges to $1/x$ for $|x - 2| < 2$ or $0 < x < 4$.

Taylor Polynomials

The linearization of a differentiable function f at a point a is the polynomial

$$P_1(x) = f(a) + f'(a)(x - a).$$

If f has derivatives of higher order at a, then it has higher-order polynomial approximations as well, one for each available derivative. These polynomials are called the Taylor polynomials of f.

We speak of a Taylor polynomial of *order n* rather than *degree n* because $f^{(n)}(a)$ may be zero. The first two Taylor polynomials of $\cos x$ at $x = 0$, for example, are $P_0(x) = 1$ and $P_1(x) = 1$. The first-order polynomial has degree zero, not one.

Definition   Taylor Polynomial of Order n

Let f be a function with derivatives of order k for $k = 1, 2, \ldots, N$ in some interval containing a as an interior point. Then for any integer n from 0 through N, the **Taylor polynomial of order n** generated by f at $x = a$ is the polynomial

$$P_n(x) = f(a) + f'(a)(x - a) + \frac{f''(a)}{2!}(x - a)^2 + \cdots$$

$$+ \frac{f^{(k)}(a)}{k!}(x - a)^k + \cdots + \frac{f^{(n)}(a)}{n!}(x - a)^n.$$

Just as the linearization of f at $x = a$ provides the best linear approximation of f in the neighborhood of a, the higher-order Taylor polynomials provide the best polynomial approximations of their respective degrees. (See Exercise 58.)

CD-ROM
WEBsite

Example 2   Finding Taylor Polynomials for e^x

Find the Taylor series and the Taylor polynomials generated by $f(x) = e^x$ at $x = 0$.

Solution   Since

$$f(x) = e^x, \qquad f'(x) = e^x, \qquad \ldots, \qquad f^{(n)}(x) = e^x, \ldots,$$

we have

$$f(0) = e^0 = 1, \qquad f'(0) = 1, \qquad \ldots, \qquad f^{(n)}(0) = 1, \ldots.$$

The Taylor series generated by f at $x = 0$ is

$$f(0) + f'(0)x + \frac{f''(0)}{2!}x^2 + \cdots + \frac{f^{(n)}(0)}{n!}x^n + \cdots = 1 + x + \frac{x^2}{2} + \cdots + \frac{x^n}{n!} + \cdots$$

$$= \sum_{k=0}^{\infty} \frac{x^k}{k!}.$$

By definition, this is also the Maclaurin series for e^x. We soon see that the series converges to e^x at every x.

The Taylor polynomial of order n at $x = 0$ is

$$P_n(x) = 1 + x + \frac{x^2}{2} + \cdots + \frac{x^n}{n!}.$$

See Figure 8.18.

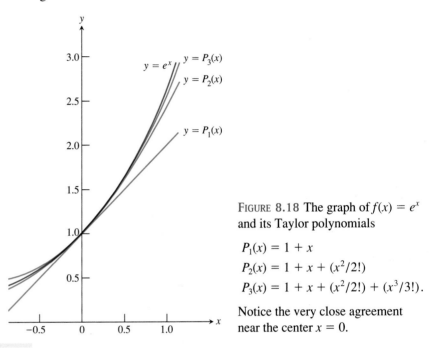

FIGURE 8.18 The graph of $f(x) = e^x$ and its Taylor polynomials

$$P_1(x) = 1 + x$$
$$P_2(x) = 1 + x + (x^2/2!)$$
$$P_3(x) = 1 + x + (x^2/2!) + (x^3/3!).$$

Notice the very close agreement near the center $x = 0$.

CD-ROM
WEBsite

Example 3   Finding Taylor Polynomials For cos x

Find the Taylor series and Taylor polynomials generated by $f(x) = \cos x$ at $x = 0$.

Solution   The cosine and its derivatives are

$$f(x) = \cos x, \qquad f'(x) = -\sin x,$$
$$f''(x) = -\cos x, \qquad f^{(3)}(x) = \sin x,$$
$$\vdots \qquad\qquad \vdots$$
$$f^{(2n)}(x) = (-1)^n \cos x, \qquad f^{(2n+1)}(x) = (-1)^{n+1} \sin x.$$

At $x = 0$, the cosines are 1 and the sines are 0, so

$$f^{(2n)}(0) = (-1)^n, \qquad f^{(2n+1)}(0) = 0.$$

The Taylor series generated by f at 0 is

$$f(0) + f'(0)x + \frac{f''(0)}{2!}x^2 + \frac{f'''(0)}{3!}x^3 + \cdots + \frac{f^{(n)}(0)}{n!}x^n + \cdots$$

$$= 1 + 0 \cdot x - \frac{x^2}{2!} + 0 \cdot x^3 + \frac{x^4}{4!} + \cdots + (-1)^n \frac{x^{2n}}{(2n)!} + \cdots = \sum_{n=0}^{\infty} \frac{(-1)^n x^{2n}}{(2n)!}.$$

By definition, this is also the Maclaurin series for $\cos x$. We see later that the series converges to $\cos x$ at every x.

Because $f^{(2n+1)}(0) = 0$, the Taylor polynomials of orders $2n$ and $2n + 1$ are identical:

$$P_{2n}(x) = P_{2n+1}(x) = 1 - \frac{x^2}{2!} + \frac{x^4}{4!} - \cdots + (-1)^n \frac{x^{2n}}{(2n)!}.$$

Figure 8.19 shows how well these polynomials approximate $f(x) = \cos x$ near $x = 0$. Only the right-hand portions of the graphs are given because the graphs are symmetric about the y-axis.

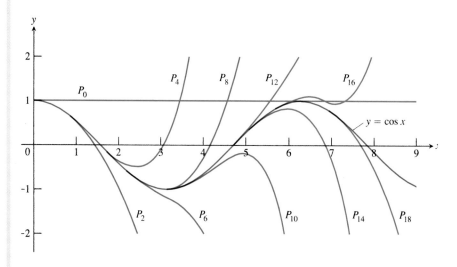

FIGURE 8.19 The polynomials

$$P_{2n}(x) = \sum_{k=0}^{n} \frac{(-1)^k x^{2k}}{(2k)!}$$

converge to $\cos x$ as $n \to \infty$. We can deduce the behavior of $\cos x$ arbitrarily far away solely from knowing the values of the cosine and its derivatives at $x = 0$.

Infinitely differentiable functions that are represented by their Taylor series only at isolated points are, in practice, quite rare.

Example 4 A Function f Whose Taylor Series Converges at Every x But Converges to $f(x)$ Only at $x = 0$

It can be shown (although not easily) that

$$f(x) = \begin{cases} 0, & x = 0 \\ e^{-1/x^2}, & x \neq 0 \end{cases}$$

(Figure 8.20) has derivatives of all orders at $x = 0$ and that $f^{(n)}(0) = 0$ for all n. Hence, the Taylor series generated by f at $x = 0$ is

$$f(0) + f'(0)x + \frac{f''(0)}{2!}x^2 + \cdots + \frac{f^{(n)}(0)}{n!}x^n + \cdots$$

$$= 0 + 0 \cdot x + 0 \cdot x^2 + \cdots + 0 \cdot x^n + \cdots$$

$$= 0 + 0 + \cdots + 0 + \cdots.$$

The series converges for every x (its sum is 0) but converges to $f(x)$ only at $x = 0$.

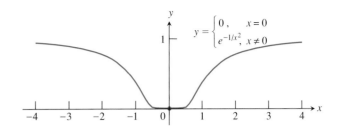

FIGURE 8.20 The graph of the continuous extension of $y = e^{-1/x^2}$ is so flat at the origin that all of its derivatives there are zero. (Example 4)

Two questions still remain.

1. For what values of x can we normally expect a Taylor series to converge to its generating function?

2. How accurately do a function's Taylor polynomials approximate the function on a given interval?

We answer these questions next.

Remainder of a Taylor Polynomial

We need a measure of the accuracy in approximating a function value $f(x)$ by its Taylor polynomial $P_n(x)$. We can use the idea of a **remainder** $R_n(x)$ defined by

$$f(x) = P_n(x) + R_n(x).$$

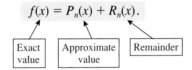

The absolute value $|R_n(x)| = |f(x) - P_n(x)|$ is called the **error** associated with the approximation.

The next theorem gives a way to estimate the remainder associated with a Taylor polynomial.

Theorem 16   Taylor's Theorem

If f is differentiable through order $n + 1$ in an open interval I containing a, then for each x in I, there exists a number c between x and a such that

$$f(x) = f(a) + f'(a)(x - a) + \frac{f''(a)}{2!}(x - a)^2 + \cdots + \frac{f^{(n)}(a)}{n!}(x - a)^n + R_n(x),$$

where

$$R_n(x) = \frac{f^{(n+1)}(c)}{(n+1)!}(x - a)^{n+1}.$$

Taylor's Theorem is a generalization of the Mean Value Theorem (Exercise 49). The proof is lengthy and given in Appendix 8.

If $R_n(x) \to 0$ as $n \to \infty$ for all x in I, we say that the Taylor series generated by f at $x = a$ **converges** to f on I, and we write

$$f(x) = \sum_{k=0}^{\infty} \frac{f^{(k)}(a)}{k!} (x - a)^k.$$

Example 5 The Maclaurin Series for e^x Revisited

Show that the Taylor series generated by $f(x) = e^x$ at $x = 0$ converges to $f(x)$ for every real value of x.

Solution   The function has derivatives of all orders throughout the interval $I = (-\infty, \infty)$, and from Example 2,

$$e^x = 1 + x + \frac{x^2}{2!} + \cdots + \frac{x^n}{n!} + R_n(x),$$

where

$$R_n(x) = \frac{e^c}{(n + 1)!} x^{n+1} \qquad \text{for some } c \text{ between } 0 \text{ and } x.$$

Since e^x is an increasing function of x, e^c lies between $e^0 = 1$ and e^x. When x is negative, so is c, and $e^c < 1$. When x is zero, $e^x = 1$ and $R_n(x) = 0$. When x is positive, so is c, and $e^c < e^x$. Thus,

$$|R_n(x)| \le \frac{|x|^{n+1}}{(n + 1)!} \qquad \text{when } x \le 0,$$

and

$$|R_n(x)| < e^x \frac{x^{n+1}}{(n + 1)!} \qquad \text{when } x > 0.$$

Finally, because

$$\lim_{n \to \infty} \frac{x^{n+1}}{(n + 1)!} = 0 \qquad \text{for every } x, \qquad \text{Table 8.1, Formula 6}$$

$\lim_{n \to \infty} R_n(x) = 0$, and the series converges to e^x for every x.

Estimating the Remainder

It is often possible to estimate $R_n(x)$ as we did in Example 5. This method of estimation is so convenient that we state it as a theorem for future reference.

Theorem 17   The Remainder Estimation Theorem

If there are positive constants M and r such that $|f^{(n+1)}(t)| \le Mr^{n+1}$ for all t between a and x, inclusive, then the remainder term $R_n(x)$ in Taylor's Theorem satisfies the inequality

$$|R_n(x)| \le M \frac{r^{n+1}|x - a|^{n+1}}{(n + 1)!}.$$

If these conditions hold for every n and all the other conditions of Taylor's Theorem are satisfied by f, then the series converges to $f(x)$.

In the simplest examples, we can take $r = 1$ provided f and all its derivatives are bounded in magnitude by some constant M. In other cases, we may need to consider r. For example, if $f(x) = 2 \cos (3x)$, each time we differentiate we get a factor of 3 and r needs to be greater than 1. In this particular case, we can take $r = 3$ along with $M = 2$.

We are now ready to look at some examples of how the Remainder Estimation Theorem and Taylor's Theorem can be used together to settle questions of convergence. As you will see, they can also be used to determine the accuracy with which a function is approximated by one of its Taylor polynomials.

Example 6   The Maclaurin Series for sin *x*

Show that the Maclaurin series for $\sin x$ converges to $\sin x$ for all x.

Solution   The function and its derivatives are

$$
\begin{aligned}
f(x) &= \sin x, & f'(x) &= \cos x, \\
f''(x) &= -\sin x, & f'''(x) &= -\cos x, \\
&\;\;\vdots & &\;\;\vdots \\
f^{(2k)}(x) &= (-1)^k \sin x, & f^{(2k+1)}(x) &= (-1)^k \cos x,
\end{aligned}
$$

so

$$
f^{(2k)}(0) = 0 \quad \text{and} \quad f^{(2k+1)}(0) = (-1)^k.
$$

The series has only odd-powered terms and, for $n = 2k + 1$, Taylor's Theorem gives

$$
\sin x = x - \frac{x^3}{3!} + \frac{x^5}{5!} - \cdots + \frac{(-1)^k x^{2k+1}}{(2k+1)!} + R_{2k+1}(x).
$$

All the derivatives of $\sin x$ have absolute values less than or equal to 1, so we can apply the Remainder Estimation Theorem with $M = 1$ and $r = 1$ to obtain

$$
|R_{2k+1}(x)| \le 1 \cdot \frac{|x|^{2k+2}}{(2k+2)!}.
$$

Since $(|x|^{2k+2}/(2k+2)!) \to 0$ as $k \to \infty$, whatever the value of x, $R_{2k+1}(x) \to 0$, and the Maclaurin series for $\sin x$ converges to $\sin x$ for every x.

Example 7   The Maclaurin Series for cos *x* Revisited

Show that the Maclaurin series for $\cos x$ converges to $\cos x$ for every value of x.

Solution   We add the remainder term to the Taylor polynomial for $\cos x$ in Example 3 to obtain Taylor's formula for $\cos x$ with $n = 2k$:

$$
\cos x = 1 - \frac{x^2}{2!} + \frac{x^4}{4!} - \cdots + (-1)^k \frac{x^{2k}}{(2k)!} + R_{2k}(x).
$$

Because the derivatives of the cosine have absolute value less than or equal to 1, the Remainder Estimation Theorem with $M = 1$ and $r = 1$ gives

$$
|R_{2k}(x)| \le 1 \cdot \frac{|x|^{2k+1}}{(2k+1)!}.
$$

For every value of x, $R_{2k} \to 0$ as $k \to \infty$. Therefore, the series converges to $\cos x$ for every value of x.

Truncation Error

The Maclaurin series for e^x converges to e^x for all x, but we still need to decide how many terms to use to approximate e^x to a given degree of accuracy. We get this information from the Remainder Estimation Theorem.

Example 8   Calculating the Number e

Calculate e with an error of less than 10^{-6}.

Solution   We can use the result of Example 2 with $x = 1$ to write

$$e = 1 + 1 + \frac{1}{2!} + \cdots + \frac{1}{n!} + R_n(1),$$

with

$$R_n(1) = e^c \frac{1}{(n+1)!} \qquad \text{for some } c \text{ between 0 and 1.}$$

For the purposes of this example, we assume that we know that $e < 3$. Hence, we are certain that

$$\frac{1}{(n+1)!} < R_n(1) < \frac{3}{(n+1)!}$$

because $1 < e^c < 3$ for $0 < c < 1$.

By experiment, we find that $1/9! > 10^{-6}$, whereas $3/10! < 10^{-6}$. Thus, we should take $(n+1)$ to be at least 10 or n to be at least 9. With an error of less than 10^{-6},

$$e = 1 + 1 + \frac{1}{2} + \frac{1}{3!} + \cdots + \frac{1}{9!} \approx 2.7182\,82.$$

Example 9   Sine Function as a Polynomial of Degree 3

For what values of x can we replace $\sin x$ by $x - (x^3/3!)$ with an error of magnitude no greater than 3×10^{-4}?

Solution   Using the result of Example 6, $x - (x^2/3!) = 0 + x + 0x^2 - (x^3/3!) + 0x^4$ is the Taylor polynomial of order 4 as well as of order 3 for $\sin x$. Then,

$$\sin x = x - \frac{x^3}{3!} + 0 + R_4,$$

and the Remainder Estimation Theorem with $M = r = 1$ gives

$$|R_4| \le 1 \cdot \frac{|x|^5}{5!} = \frac{|x|^5}{120}.$$

Therefore, the error will be less than or equal to 3×10^{-4} if

$$\frac{|x|^5}{120} < 3 \times 10^{-4} \qquad \text{or} \qquad |x| < \sqrt[5]{360 \times 10^{-4}} \approx 0.514. \qquad \text{Rounded down, to be safe}$$

The Alternating Series Estimation Theorem tells us something that the Remainder Estimation Theorem does not: namely, that the estimate $x - (x^3/3!)$ for $\sin x$ is an underestimate when x is positive because then $x^5/120$ is positive.

Figure 8.21 shows the graph of $\sin x$, along with the graphs of a number of its approximating Taylor polynomials. The graph of $P_3(x) = x - (x^3/3!)$ is almost indistinguishable from the sine curve when $-1 \le x \le 1$.

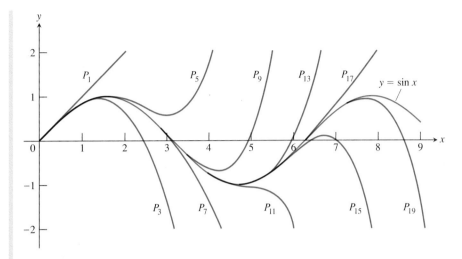

FIGURE 8.21 The polynomials

$$P_{2n+1}(x) = \sum_{k=0}^{n} \frac{(-1)^k x^{2k+1}}{(2k+1)!}$$

converge to $\sin x$ as $n \to \infty$.

Table of Maclaurin Series

Here we list some of the most useful Maclaurin series, which have all been derived in one way or another in this chapter. The exercises will ask you to use these series as basic building blocks for constructing other series (e.g., $\tan^{-1} x^2$ or $7xe^x$). We also list the intervals of convergence.

Maclaurin series

1. $\dfrac{1}{1-x} = 1 + x + x^2 + \cdots + x^n + \cdots = \displaystyle\sum_{n=0}^{\infty} x^n \qquad (|x| < 1)$

2. $\dfrac{1}{1+x} = 1 - x + x^2 - \cdots + (-x)^n + \cdots = \displaystyle\sum_{n=0}^{\infty} (-1)^n x^n \qquad (|x| < 1)$

3. $e^x = 1 + x + \dfrac{x^2}{2!} + \cdots + \dfrac{x^n}{n!} + \cdots = \displaystyle\sum_{n=0}^{\infty} \dfrac{x^n}{n!} \qquad$ (all real x)

4. $\sin x = x - \dfrac{x^3}{3!} + \dfrac{x^5}{5!} - \cdots + (-1)^n \dfrac{x^{2n+1}}{(2n+1)!} + \cdots \quad = \displaystyle\sum_{n=0}^{\infty} (-1)^n \dfrac{x^{2n+1}}{(2n+1)!}$ (all real x)

5. $\cos x = 1 - \dfrac{x^2}{2!} + \dfrac{x^4}{4!} - \cdots + (-1)^n \dfrac{x^{2n}}{(2n)!} + \cdots \quad = \displaystyle\sum_{n=0}^{\infty} (-1)^n \dfrac{x^{2n}}{(2n)!} \qquad$ (all real x)

6. $\ln(1+x) = x - \dfrac{x^2}{2} + \dfrac{x^3}{3} - \cdots + (-1)^{n-1} \dfrac{x^n}{n} + \cdots \quad = \displaystyle\sum_{n=1}^{\infty} (-1)^{n-1} \dfrac{x^n}{n} \quad (-1 < x \le 1)$

7. $\tan^{-1} x = x - \dfrac{x^3}{3} + \dfrac{x^5}{5} - \cdots + (-1)^n \dfrac{x^{2n+1}}{2n+1} + \cdots \quad = \displaystyle\sum_{n=0}^{\infty} (-1)^n \dfrac{x^{2n+1}}{2n+1} \quad (|x| \le 1)$

Combining Taylor Series

On the intersection of their intervals of convergence, Taylor series can be added, subtracted, and multiplied by constants and powers of x, and the results are once again Taylor series. The Taylor series for $f(x) + g(x)$ is the sum of the Taylor series for $f(x)$ and the Taylor series for $g(x)$ because the nth derivative of $f + g$ is $f^{(n)} + g^{(n)}$, and so on. We can obtain the Maclaurin series for $(1 + \cos 2x)/2$ by substituting $2x$ in the Maclaurin series for $\cos x$, adding 1, and dividing the result by 2. The Maclaurin series for $\sin x + \cos x$ is the term-by-term sum of the series for $\sin x$ and $\cos x$. We obtain the Maclaurin series for $x \sin x$ by multiplying all the terms of the Maclaurin series for $\sin x$ by x.

Example 10   Finding a Maclaurin Series by Substitution

Find the Maclaurin series for $\cos 2x$.

Solution   We can find the Maclaurin series for $\cos 2x$ by substituting $2x$ for x in the Maclaurin series for $\cos x$:

$$\cos 2x = \sum_{k=0}^{\infty} \frac{(-1)^k (2x)^{2k}}{(2k)!} = 1 - \frac{(2x)^2}{2!} + \frac{(2x)^4}{4!} - \frac{(2x)^6}{6!} + \cdots \qquad \text{Eq. (5) with } 2x \text{ for } x$$

$$= 1 - \frac{2^2 x^2}{2!} + \frac{2^4 x^4}{4!} - \frac{2^6 x^6}{6!} + \cdots$$

$$= \sum_{k=0}^{\infty} (-1)^k \frac{2^{2k} x^{2k}}{(2k)!}.$$

Equation (5) holds for $-\infty < x < \infty$, implying that it holds for $-\infty < 2x < \infty$, so the newly created series converges for all x. Exercise 54 explains why the series is in fact the Maclaurin series for $\cos 2x$.

Example 11   Finding a Maclaurin Series by Multiplication

Find the Maclaurin series for $x \sin x$.

Solution   We can find the Maclaurin series for $x \sin x$ by multiplying the Maclaurin series for $\sin x$ (Equation 4) by x:

$$x \sin x = x \left(x - \frac{x^3}{3!} + \frac{x^5}{5!} - \frac{x^7}{7!} + \cdots \right)$$

$$= x^2 - \frac{x^4}{3!} + \frac{x^6}{5!} - \frac{x^8}{7!} + \cdots .$$

The new series converges for all x because the series for $\sin x$ converges for all x. Exercise 54 explains why the series is the Maclaurin series for $x \sin x$.

EXERCISES 8.7

Finding Taylor Polynomials

CD-ROM
WEBsite

In Exercises 1–6 find the Taylor polynomials of orders 0, 1, 2, and 3 generated by f at a.

1. $f(x) = \ln x, \quad a = 1$

2. $f(x) = \ln (1 + x), \quad a = 0$

3. $f(x) = \dfrac{1}{(x + 2)}, \quad a = 0$

4. $f(x) = \sin x, \quad a = \pi/4$

5. $f(x) = \cos x, \quad a = \pi/4$

6. $f(x) = \sqrt{x}, \quad a = 4$

Finding Maclaurin Series

Find the Maclaurin series for the functions in Exercises 7–14.

7. e^{-x}

8. $\dfrac{1}{1 + x}$

9. $\sin 3x$

10. $7 \cos (-x)$

11. $\cosh x = \dfrac{e^x + e^{-x}}{2}$

12. $\sinh x = \dfrac{e^x - e^{-x}}{2}$

13. $x^4 - 2x^3 - 5x + 4$

14. $(x + 1)^2$

Finding Taylor Series

In Exercises 15–20, find the Taylor series generated by f at $x = a$.

15. $f(x) = x^3 - 2x + 4, \quad a = 2$

16. $f(x) = 3x^5 - x^4 + 2x^3 + x^2 - 2, \quad a = -1$

17. $f(x) = 1/x^2, \quad a = 1$

18. $f(x) = x/(1 - x), \quad a = 0$

19. $f(x) = e^x, \quad a = 2$

20. $f(x) = 2^x, \quad a = 1$

Maclaurin Series by Substitution

Use substitution as in Example 10 to find the Maclaurin series of the functions in Exercises 21–24.

21. e^{-5x}

22. $e^{-x/2}$

23. $\sin\left(\dfrac{\pi x}{2}\right)$

24. $\cos \sqrt{x}$

More Maclaurin Series

Using the series in the Maclaurin series table as basic building blocks, combine series expressions to find Maclaurin series for the functions in Exercises 25–34.

25. xe^x

26. $x^2 \sin x$

27. $\dfrac{x^2}{2} - 1 + \cos x$

28. $\sin x - x + \dfrac{x^3}{3!}$

29. $x \cos \pi x$

30. $\cos^2 x$ (*Hint:* $\cos^2 x = (1 + \cos 2x)/2$.)

31. $\sin^2 x$

32. $\dfrac{x^2}{1 - 2x}$

33. $x \ln (1 + 2x)$

34. $\dfrac{1}{(1 - x)^2}$

Error Estimates

35. *Writing to Learn* For approximately what values of x can you replace $\sin x$ by $x - (x^3/6)$ with an error of magnitude no greater than 5×10^{-4}? Give reasons for your answer.

36. *Writing to Learn* If $\cos x$ is replaced by $1 - (x^2/2)$ and $|x| < 0.5$, what estimate can be made of the error? Does $1 - (x^2/2)$ tend to be too large or too small? Give reasons for your answer.

37. *Linear approximation for* $\sin x$ How close is the approximation $\sin x = x$ when $|x| < 10^{-3}$? For which of these values of x is $x < \sin x$?

38. *Linear approximation for* $\sqrt{1 + x}$ The estimate $\sqrt{1 + x} = 1 + (x/2)$ is used when x is small. Estimate the error when $|x| < 0.01$.

39. *Quadratic approximation for* e^x

   (a) The approximation $e^x = 1 + x + (x^2/2)$ is used when x is small. Use the Remainder Estimation Theorem to estimate the error when $|x| < 0.1$.

   (b) When $x < 0$, the series for e^x is an alternating series. Use the Alternating Series Estimation Theorem to estimate the error that results from replacing e^x by $1 + x + (x^2/2)$ when $-0.1 < x < 0$. Compare your estimate with the one you obtained in part (a).

40. *Cubic approximation for* $\sinh x$ Estimate the error in the approximation $\sinh x = x + (x^3/3!)$ when $|x| < 0.5$. (*Hint:* Use R_4, not R_3.)

41. *Linear approximation for* e^h When $0 \le h \le 0.01$, show that e^h may be replaced by $1 + h$ with an error of magnitude no greater than 0.6% of h. Use $e^{0.01} = 1.01$.

42. *Approximating* $\ln (1 + x)$ *by* x For what positive values of x can you replace $\ln (1 + x)$ by x with an error of magnitude no greater than 1% of the value of x?

43. *Estimating $\pi/4$* You plan to estimate $\pi/4$ by evaluating the Maclaurin series for $\tan^{-1} x$ at $x = 1$. Use the Alternating Series Estimation Theorem to determine how many terms of the series you would have to add to be sure the estimate is good to 2 decimal places.

44. *Bounding* $y = (\sin x)/x$

(a) Use the Maclaurin series for $\sin x$ and the Alternating Series Estimation Theorem to show that

$$1 - \frac{x^2}{6} < \frac{\sin x}{x} < 1, \qquad x \neq 0.$$

T (b) *Writing to Learn* Graph $f(x) = (\sin x)/x$ together with the functions $y = 1 - (x^2/6)$ and $y = 1$ for $-5 \leq x \leq 5$. Comment on the relationships among the graphs.

Quadratic Approximations

CD-ROM
WEBsite The Taylor polynomial of order 2 generated by a twice-differentiable function $f(x)$ at $x = a$ is called the **quadratic approximation** of f at $x = a$. In Exercises 45–48, find the

(a) linearization (Taylor polynomial of order 1) at $x = 0$

(b) quadratic approximation of f at $x = 0$.

45. $f(x) = \ln (\cos x)$ **46.** $f(x) = e^{\sin x}$

47. $f(x) = 1/\sqrt{1 - x^2}$ **48.** $f(x) = \cosh x$

Theory and Examples

49. *Taylor's Theorem and the Mean Value Theorem* Explain how the Mean Value Theorem (Section 3.2, Theorem 4) is a special case of Taylor's Theorem.

50. *Linearizations at inflection points* (*Continuation of Section 3.6, Exercise 49*) Show that if the graph of a twice-differentiable function $f(x)$ has an inflection point at $x = a$, then the linearization of f at $x = a$ is also the quadratic approximation of f at $x = a$. This explains why tangent lines fit so well at inflection points.

51. *The (Second) Second Derivative Test* Use the equation

$$f(x) = f(a) + f'(a)(x - a) + \frac{f''(c_2)}{2}(x - a)^2$$

to establish the following test.

Let f have continuous first and second derivatives and suppose that $f'(a) = 0$. Then

(a) f has a local maximum at a if $f'' \leq 0$ throughout an interval whose interior contains a

(b) f has a local minimum at a if $f'' \geq 0$ throughout an interval whose interior contains a.

52. *A cubic approximation* Use Taylor's formula with $a = 0$ and $n = 3$ to find the standard cubic approximation of $f(x) = 1/(1 - x)$ at $x = 0$. Give an upper bound for the magnitude of the error in the approximation when $|x| \leq 0.1$.

53. *Improving approximations to π*

(a) Let P be an approximation of π accurate to n decimals. Show that $P + \sin P$ gives an approximation correct to $3n$ decimals. (*Hint*: Let $P = \pi + x$.)

(b) Try it with a calculator.

54. *The Maclaurin series generated by* $f(x) = \sum_{n=0}^{\infty} a_n x^n$ *is* $\sum_{n=0}^{\infty} a_n x^n$ A function defined by a power series $\sum_{n=0}^{\infty} a_n x^n$ with a radius of convergence $c > 0$ has a Maclaurin series that converges to the function at every point of $(-c, c)$. Show this by showing that the Maclaurin series generated by $f(x) = \sum_{n=0}^{\infty} a_n x^n$ is the series $\sum_{n=0}^{\infty} a_n x^n$ itself.

An immediate consequence of this is that series like

$$x \sin x = x^2 - \frac{x^4}{3!} + \frac{x^6}{5!} - \frac{x^8}{7!} + \cdots$$

and

$$x^2 e^x = x^2 + x^3 + \frac{x^4}{2!} + \frac{x^5}{3!} + \cdots,$$

obtained by multiplying Maclaurin series by powers of x, as well as series obtained by integration and differentiation of convergent power series are themselves the Maclaurin series generated by the functions they represent.

55. *Maclaurin series for even functions and odd functions* Suppose that $f(x) = \sum_{n=0}^{\infty} a_n x^n$ converges for all x in an open interval $(-c, c)$.

(a) Show that if f is even, then $a_1 = a_3 = a_5 = \cdots = 0$; that is, the series for f contains only even powers of x.

(b) Show that if f is odd, then $a_0 = a_2 = a_4 = \cdots = 0$; that is, the series for f contains only odd powers of x.

56. *Taylor polynomials of periodic functions*

(a) Show that every continuous periodic function $f(x)$, $-\infty < x < \infty$, is bounded in magnitude by showing that there exists a positive constant M such that $|f(x)| \leq M$ for all x.

(b) Show that the graph of every Taylor polynomial of positive degree generated by $f(x) = \cos x$ must eventually move away from the graph of $\cos x$ as $|x|$ increases. You can see this in Figure 8.19. The Taylor polynomials of $\sin x$ behave in a similar way (Figure 8.21).

T 57. (a) *Two graphs* Graph the curves $y = (1/3) - (x^2)/5$ and $y = (x - \tan^{-1} x)/x^3$ together with the line $y = 1/3$.

(b) Use a Maclaurin series to explain what you see. What is

$$\lim_{x \to 0} \frac{x - \tan^{-1} x}{x^3}?$$

58. *Of all polynomials of degree $\leq n$, the Taylor polynomial of n gives the best approximation* Suppose that $f(x)$ is differentiable on an interval centered at $x = a$ and that $g(x) = b_0 + b_1(x - a) + \cdots + b_n(x - a)^n$ is a polynomial of degree n with constant coefficients $b_0, \ldots, b_n$. Let $E(x) = f(x) - g(x)$. Show that if we impose on g the conditions

(a) $E(a) = 0$ The approximation error is zero at $x = a$.

(b) $\lim\limits_{x \to a} \dfrac{E(x)}{(x - a)^n} = 0$,   The error is negligible when compared to $(x - a)^n$.

then

$$g(x) = f(a) + f'(a)(x - a) + \frac{f''(a)}{2!}(x - a)^2 + \cdots + \frac{f^{(n)}(a)}{n!}(x - a)^n.$$

Thus, the Taylor polynomial $P_n(x)$ is the only polynomial of degree less than or equal to n whose error is both zero at $x = a$ and negligible when compared with $(x - a)^n$.

COMPUTER EXPLORATIONS

Linear, Quadratic, and Cubic Approximations

Taylor's formula with $n = 1$ and $a = 0$ gives the linearization of a function at $x = 0$. With $n = 2$ and $n = 3$, we obtain the standard quadratic and cubic approximations. In these exercises, we explore the errors associated with these approximations. We seek answers to two questions:

    (a) For what values of x can the function be replaced by each approximation with an error less than 10^{-2}?

    (b) What is the maximum error we could expect if we replace the function by each approximation over the specified interval?

Using a CAS, perform the following steps to aid in answering questions (a) and (b) for the functions and intervals in Exercises 59–64.

Step 1: Plot the function over the specified interval.

Step 2: Find the Taylor polynomials $P_1(x)$, $P_2(x)$, and $P_3(x)$ at $x = 0$.

Step 3: Calculate the $(n + 1)$st derivative $f^{(n+1)}(c)$ associated with the remainder term for each Taylor polynomial. Plot the derivative as a function of c over the specified interval and estimate its maximum absolute value, M.

Step 4: Calculate the remainder $R_n(x)$ for each polynomial. Using the estimate M from step 3 in place of $f^{(n+1)}(c)$, plot $R_n(x)$ over the specified interval. Then estimate the values of x that answer question (a).

Step 5: Compare your estimated error with the actual error $E_n(x) = |f(x) - P_n(x)|$ by plotting $E_n(x)$ over the specified interval. This will help answer question (b).

Step 6: Graph the function and its three Taylor approximations together. Discuss the graphs in relation to the information discovered in steps 4 and 5.

59. $f(x) = \dfrac{1}{\sqrt{1 + x}}, \quad |x| \le \dfrac{3}{4}$

60. $f(x) = (1 + x)^{3/2}, \quad -\dfrac{1}{2} \le x \le 2$

61. $f(x) = \dfrac{x}{x^2 + 1}, \quad |x| \le 2$

62. $f(x) = (\cos x)(\sin 2x), \quad |x| \le 2$

63. $f(x) = e^{-x} \cos 2x, \quad |x| \le 1$

64. $f(x) = e^{x/3} \sin 2x, \quad |x| \le 2$

8.8 Applications of Power Series

Binomial Series for Powers and Roots   •   Series Solutions of Differential Equations   •   Evaluating Indeterminate Forms   •   Arctangents

This section shows how power series are used by scientists and engineers in a variety of applications.

Binomial Series for Powers and Roots

The Maclaurin series generated by $f(x) = (1 + x)^m$, when m is constant, is

$$1 + mx + \frac{m(m - 1)}{2!}x^2 + \frac{m(m - 1)(m - 2)}{3!}x^3 + \cdots$$

$$+ \frac{m(m - 1)(m - 2) \cdots (m - k + 1)}{k!}x^k + \cdots.$$

This series, called the **binomial series,** converges absolutely for $|x| < 1$. To derive the series, we first list the function and its derivatives:

$$f(x) = (1 + x)^m$$
$$f'(x) = m(1 + x)^{m-1}$$
$$f''(x) = m(m - 1)(1 + x)^{m-2}$$
$$f'''(x) = m(m - 1)(m - 2)(1 + x)^{m-3}$$

$$\vdots$$

$$f^{(k)}(x) = m(m - 1)(m - 2) \cdots (m - k + 1)(1 + x)^{m-k}.$$

We then evaluate these at $x = 0$ and substitute into the Maclaurin series formula to obtain the binomial series.

If m is an integer greater than or equal to zero, the series stops after $(m + 1)$ terms because the coefficients from $k = m + 1$ on are zero.

If m is not a positive integer or zero, the series is infinite and converges for $|x| < 1$. To see why, let u_k be the term involving x^k. Then apply the Ratio Test for absolute convergence to see that

$$\left| \frac{u_{k+1}}{u_k} \right| = \left| \frac{m - k}{k + 1} x \right| \to |x| \qquad \text{as } k \to \infty.$$

Our derivation of the binomial series shows only that it is generated by $(1 + x)^m$ and converges for $|x| < 1$. The derivation does not show that the series converges to $(1 + x)^m$. It does, but we assume that part without proof.

Binomial Series

For $-1 < x < 1$,

$$(1 + x)^m = 1 + \sum_{k=1}^{\infty} \binom{m}{k} x^k,$$

where we define

$$\binom{m}{1} = m, \qquad \binom{m}{2} = \frac{m(m - 1)}{2!},$$

and

$$\binom{m}{k} = \frac{m(m - 1)(m - 2) \cdots (m - k + 1)}{k!} \qquad \text{for } k \geq 3.$$

Example 1   Using the Binomial Series

If $m = -1$,

$$\binom{-1}{1} = -1, \qquad \binom{-1}{2} = \frac{-1(-2)}{2!} = 1,$$

and

$$\binom{-1}{k} = \frac{-1(-2)(-3) \cdots (-1 - k + 1)}{k!} = (-1)^k \left(\frac{k!}{k!} \right) = (-1)^k.$$

With these coefficient values, the binomial series formula gives the familiar geometric series

$$(1 + x)^{-1} = 1 + \sum_{k=1}^{\infty} (-1)^k x^k = 1 - x + x^2 - x^3 + \cdots + (-1)^k x^k + \cdots.$$

Example 2   Using the Binomial Series

We know from Section 3.6, Example 1, that $\sqrt{1 + x} \approx 1 + (x/2)$ for $|x|$ small. With $m = 1/2$, the binomial series gives quadratic and higher-order approximations as well, along with error estimates that come from the Alternating Series Estimation Theorem:

$$(1 + x)^{1/2} = 1 + \frac{x}{2} + \frac{\left(\frac{1}{2}\right)\left(-\frac{1}{2}\right)}{2!} x^2 + \frac{\left(\frac{1}{2}\right)\left(-\frac{1}{2}\right)\left(-\frac{3}{2}\right)}{3!} x^3$$

$$+ \frac{\left(\frac{1}{2}\right)\left(-\frac{1}{2}\right)\left(-\frac{3}{2}\right)\left(-\frac{5}{2}\right)}{4!} x^4 + \cdots$$

$$= 1 + \frac{x}{2} - \frac{x^2}{8} + \frac{x^3}{16} - \frac{5x^4}{128} + \cdots.$$

Substitution for x gives still other approximations. For example,

$$\sqrt{1 - x^2} \approx 1 - \frac{x^2}{2} - \frac{x^4}{8} \qquad \text{for } |x^2| \text{ small}$$

$$\sqrt{1 - \frac{1}{x}} \approx 1 - \frac{1}{2x} - \frac{1}{8x^2} \qquad \text{for } \left|\frac{1}{x}\right| \text{ small, that is, } |x| \text{ large.}$$

Series Solutions of Differential Equations

When we cannot find a relatively simple expression for the solution of an initial value problem or differential equation, we try to get information about the solution in other ways. One way is to try to find a power series representation for the solution. If we can do so, we immediately have a source of polynomial approximations of the solution, which may be all that we really need. The first example (Example 3) deals with a first-order linear differential equation that could be solved as a linear equation using the method studied earlier. The example shows how, not knowing this, we can solve the equation with power series. The second example (Example 4) deals with an equation that cannot be solved by previous methods.

Example 3   Series Solution of an Initial Value Problem

Solve the initial value problem

$$y' - y = x, \qquad y(0) = 1.$$

Solution   We assume that there is a solution of the form

$$y = a_0 + a_1 x + a_2 x^2 + \cdots + a_{n-1} x^{n-1} + a_n x^n + \cdots. \tag{1}$$

Our goal is to find values for the coefficients a_k that make the series and its first derivative

$$y' = a_1 + 2a_2x + 3a_3x^2 + \cdots + na_nx^{n-1} + \cdots \tag{2}$$

satisfy the given differential equation and initial condition. The series $y' - y$ is the difference of the series in Equations (1) and (2):

$$y' - y = (a_1 + a_0) + (2a_2 - a_1)x + (3a_3 - a_2)x^2 + \cdots$$
$$+ (na_n - a_{n-1})x^{n-1} + \cdots. \tag{3}$$

CD-ROM
WEBsite

Historical Biography

John Van Neumann
(1903 — 1957)

If y is to satisfy the equation $y' - y = x$, the series in Equation (3) must equal x. Since power series representations are unique, as you saw if you did Exercise 45 in Section 8.6, the coefficients in Equation (3) must satisfy the equations

$$
\begin{aligned}
a_1 - a_0 &= 0 \qquad \text{Constant terms} \\
2a_2 - a_1 &= 1 \qquad \text{Coefficients of } x \\
3a_3 - a_2 &= 0 \qquad \text{Coefficients of } x^2 \\
&\ \ \vdots \\
na_n - a_{n-1} &= 0 \qquad \text{Coefficients of } x^{n-1} \\
&\ \ \vdots
\end{aligned}
$$

We can also see from Equation (1) that $y = a_0$ when $x = 0$, so that $a_0 = 1$ (this being the initial condition). Putting it all together, we have

$$a_0 = 1, \qquad a_1 = a_0 = 1, \qquad a_2 = \frac{1 + a_1}{2} = \frac{1 + 1}{2} = \frac{2}{2},$$

$$a_3 = \frac{a_2}{3} = \frac{2}{3 \cdot 2} = \frac{2}{3!}, \qquad \cdots, \qquad a_n = \frac{a_{n-1}}{n} = \frac{2}{n!}, \cdots.$$

Substituting these coefficient values into the equation for y (Equation (1)) gives

$$y = 1 + x + 2 \cdot \frac{x^2}{2!} + 2 \cdot \frac{x^3}{3!} + \cdots + 2 \cdot \frac{x^n}{n!} + \cdots$$

$$= 1 + x + 2 \underbrace{\left(\frac{x^2}{2!} + \frac{x^3}{3!} + \cdots + \frac{x^n}{n!} + \cdots \right)}_{\text{The Maclaurin series for } e^x - 1 - x}$$

$$= 1 + x + 2(e^x - 1 - x) = 2e^x - 1 - x.$$

The solution of the initial value problem is $y = 2e^x - 1 - x$.

As a check, we see that

$$y(0) = 2e^0 - 1 - 0 = 2 - 1 = 1$$

and

$$y' - y = (2e^x - 1) - (2e^x - 1 - x) = x.$$

Example 4   Solving a Differential Equation

Find a power series solution for

$$y'' + x^2 y = 0. \tag{4}$$

Solution   We assume that there is a solution of the form

$$y = a_0 + a_1 x + a_2 x^2 + \cdots + a_n x^n + \cdots \tag{5}$$

and find what the coefficients a_k have to be to make the series and its second derivative

$$y'' = 2a_2 + 3 \cdot 2a_3 x + \cdots + n(n-1)a_n x^{n-2} + \cdots \tag{6}$$

satisfy Equation (4). The series for $x^2 y$ is x^2 times the right-hand side of Equation (5):

$$x^2 y = a_0 x^2 + a_1 x^3 + a_2 x^4 + \cdots + a_n x^{n+2} + \cdots . \tag{7}$$

The series for $y'' + x^2 y$ is the sum of the series in Equations (6) and (7):

$$y'' + x^2 y = 2a_2 + 6a_3 x + (12a_4 + a_0)x^2 + (20a_5 + a_1)x^3$$
$$+ \cdots + (n(n-1)a_n + a_{n-4})x^{n-2} + \cdots . \tag{8}$$

Notice that the coefficient of x^{n-2} in Equation (7) is a_{n-4}. If y and its second derivative y'' are to satisfy Equation (4), the coefficients of the individual powers of x on the right-hand side of Equation (8) must all be zero:

$$2a_2 = 0, \quad 6a_3 = 0, \qquad 12a_4 + a_0 = 0, \qquad 20a_5 + a_1 = 0, \tag{9}$$

and for all $n \geq 4$,

$$n(n-1)a_n + a_{n-4} = 0. \tag{10}$$

We can see from Equation (5) that

$$a_0 = y(0), \qquad a_1 = y'(0).$$

In other words, the first two coefficients of the series are the values of y and y' at $x = 0$. The equations in Equation (9) and the recursion formula in Equation (10) enable us to evaluate all the other coefficients in terms of a_0 and a_1.

The first two of Equations (9) give

$$a_2 = 0, \qquad a_3 = 0.$$

Equation (10) shows that if $a_{n-4} = 0$, then $a_n = 0$, so we conclude that

$$a_6 = 0, \qquad a_7 = 0, \qquad a_{10} = 0, \qquad a_{11} = 0,$$

and whenever $n = 4k + 2$ or $4k + 3$, a_n is zero. For the other coefficients, we have

$$a_n = \frac{-a_{n-4}}{n(n-1)}$$

so that

$$a_4 = \frac{-a_0}{4 \cdot 3}, \qquad a_8 = \frac{-a_4}{8 \cdot 7} = \frac{a_0}{3 \cdot 4 \cdot 7 \cdot 8},$$

$$a_{12} = \frac{-a_8}{11 \cdot 12} = \frac{-a_0}{3 \cdot 4 \cdot 7 \cdot 8 \cdot 11 \cdot 12}$$

and

$$a_5 = \frac{-a_1}{5 \cdot 4}, \qquad a_9 = \frac{-a_5}{9 \cdot 8} = \frac{a_1}{4 \cdot 5 \cdot 8 \cdot 9},$$

$$a_{13} = \frac{-a_9}{12 \cdot 13} = \frac{-a_1}{4 \cdot 5 \cdot 8 \cdot 9 \cdot 12 \cdot 13}.$$

The answer is best expressed as the sum of two separate series, one multiplied by a_0, the other by a_1:

$$y = a_0 \left(1 - \frac{x^4}{3 \cdot 4} + \frac{x^8}{3 \cdot 4 \cdot 7 \cdot 8} - \frac{x^{12}}{3 \cdot 4 \cdot 7 \cdot 8 \cdot 11 \cdot 12} + \cdots \right)$$

$$+ a_1 \left(x - \frac{x^5}{4 \cdot 5} + \frac{x^9}{4 \cdot 5 \cdot 8 \cdot 9} - \frac{x^{13}}{4 \cdot 5 \cdot 8 \cdot 9 \cdot 12 \cdot 13} + \cdots \right).$$

Both series converge absolutely for all x, as is readily seen by the Ratio Test.

Evaluating Indeterminate Forms

We can sometimes evaluate indeterminate forms by expressing the functions involved as Taylor series.

Example 5   Limits Using Power Series

Evaluate

$$\lim_{x \to 0} \frac{\sin x - \tan x}{x^3}.$$

Solution   The Maclaurin series for $\sin x$ and $\tan x$, to terms in x^5, are

$$\sin x = x - \frac{x^3}{3!} + \frac{x^5}{5!} - \cdots, \qquad \tan x = x + \frac{x^3}{3} + \frac{2x^5}{15} + \cdots.$$

Hence,

$$\sin x - \tan x = -\frac{x^3}{2} - \frac{x^5}{8} - \cdots = x^3 \left(-\frac{1}{2} - \frac{x^2}{8} - \cdots \right)$$

and

$$\lim_{x \to 0} \frac{\sin x - \tan x}{x^3} = \lim_{x \to 0} \left(-\frac{1}{2} - \frac{x^2}{8} - \cdots \right)$$

$$= -\frac{1}{2}.$$

If we apply series to calculate $\lim_{n \to 0} ((1/\sin x) - (1/x))$, we not only find the limit successfully but also discover an approximation formula for $\csc x$.

Example 6   Limits Using Power Series

Find

$$\lim_{x \to 0} \left(\frac{1}{\sin x} - \frac{1}{x} \right).$$

Solution

$$\frac{1}{\sin x} - \frac{1}{x} = \frac{x - \sin x}{x \sin x} = \frac{x - \left(x - \dfrac{x^3}{3!} + \dfrac{x^5}{5!} - \cdots\right)}{x \cdot \left(x - \dfrac{x^3}{3!} + \dfrac{x^5}{5!} - \cdots\right)}$$

$$= \frac{x^3\left(\dfrac{1}{3!} - \dfrac{x^2}{5!} + \cdots\right)}{x^2\left(1 - \dfrac{x^2}{3!} + \cdots\right)} = x \frac{\dfrac{1}{3!} - \dfrac{x^2}{5!} + \cdots}{1 - \dfrac{x^2}{3!} + \cdots}.$$

Therefore,

$$\lim_{x \to 0}\left(\frac{1}{\sin x} - \frac{1}{x}\right) = \lim_{x \to 0}\left(x \frac{\dfrac{1}{3!} - \dfrac{x^2}{5!} + \cdots}{1 - \dfrac{x^2}{3!} + \cdots}\right) = 0.$$

From the quotient on the right, we can see that if $|x|$ is small, then

$$\frac{1}{\sin x} - \frac{1}{x} \approx x \cdot \frac{1}{3!} = \frac{x}{6} \qquad \text{or} \qquad \csc x \approx \frac{1}{x} + \frac{x}{6}.$$

Arctangents

In Section 8.6, Example 5, we found a series for $\tan^{-1} x$ by differentiating to get

$$\frac{d}{dx} \tan^{-1} x = \frac{1}{1 + x^2} = 1 - x^2 + x^4 - x^6 + \cdots$$

and integrating to get

$$\tan^{-1} x = x - \frac{x^3}{3} + \frac{x^5}{5} - \frac{x^7}{7} + \cdots.$$

We did not, however, prove the term-by-term integration theorem on which this conclusion depended. We now derive the series again by integrating both sides of the finite formula

$$\frac{1}{1 + t^2} = 1 - t^2 + t^4 - t^6 + \cdots + (-1)^n t^{2n} + \frac{(-1)^{n+1} t^{2n+2}}{1 + t^2},$$

in which the last term comes from adding the remaining terms as a geometric series with first term $a = (-1)^{n+1} t^{2n+2}$ and ratio $r = -t^2$. Integrating both sides of the last equation from $t = 0$ to $t = x$ gives

$$\tan^{-1} x = x - \frac{x^3}{3} + \frac{x^5}{5} - \frac{x^7}{7} + \cdots + (-1)^n \frac{x^{2n+1}}{2n + 1} + R(n, x),$$

where

$$R(n, x) = \int_0^x \frac{(-1)^{n+1} t^{2n+2}}{1 + t^2} \, dt.$$

The denominator of the integrand is greater than or equal to 1; hence,

$$|R(n, x)| \le \int_0^{|x|} t^{2n+2} \, dt = \frac{|x|^{2n+3}}{2n + 3}.$$

We take this route instead of finding the Maclaurin series directly because the formulas for the higher-order derivatives of $\tan^{-1} x$ are unmanageable.

If $|x| \le 1$, the right side of this inequality approaches zero as $n \to \infty$. Therefore, $\lim_{n \to \infty} R(n, x) = 0$ if $|x| \le 1$ and

$$\tan^{-1} x = \sum_{n=0}^{\infty} \frac{(-1)^n x^{2n+1}}{2n + 1}, \qquad |x| \le 1.$$

When we put $x = 1$ in the series for $\tan^{-1} x$ we get **Leibniz's formula:**

$$\frac{\pi}{4} = 1 - \frac{1}{3} + \frac{1}{5} - \frac{1}{7} + \frac{1}{9} - \cdots + \frac{(-1)^n}{2n + 1} + \cdots .$$

This series converges too slowly to be a useful source of decimal approximations of π. It is better to use a formula like

$$\pi = 48 \, \tan^{-1} \frac{1}{18} + 32 \, \tan^{-1} \frac{1}{57} - 20 \, \tan^{-1} \frac{1}{239},$$

which uses values of x closer to zero.

EXERCISES 8.8

Binomial Series

Find the first four terms of the binomial series for the functions in Exercises 1–10.

1. $(1 + x)^{1/2}$

2. $(1 + x)^{1/3}$

3. $(1 - x)^{-1/2}$

4. $(1 - 2x)^{1/2}$

5. $\left(1 + \frac{x}{2}\right)^{-2}$

6. $\left(1 - \frac{x}{2}\right)^{-2}$

7. $(1 + x^3)^{-1/2}$

8. $(1 + x^2)^{-1/3}$

9. $\left(1 + \frac{1}{x}\right)^{1/2}$

10. $\left(1 - \frac{2}{x}\right)^{1/3}$

Find the binomial series for the functions in Exercises 11–14.

11. $(1 + x)^4$

12. $(1 + x^2)^3$

13. $(1 - 2x)^3$

14. $\left(1 - \frac{x}{2}\right)^4$

Initial Value Problems

Find series solutions for the initial value problems in Exercises 15–32.

15. $y' + y = 0, \quad y(0) = 1$

16. $y' - 2y = 0, \quad y(0) = 1$

17. $y' - y = 1, \quad y(0) = 0$

18. $y' + y = 1, \quad y(0) = 2$

19. $y' - y = x, \quad y(0) = 0$

20. $y' + y = 2x, \quad y(0) = -1$

21. $y' - xy = 0, \quad y(0) = 1$

22. $y' - x^2y = 0, \quad y(0) = 1$

23. $(1 - x)y' - y = 0, \quad y(0) = 2$

24. $(1 + x^2)y' + 2xy = 0, \quad y(0) = 3$

25. $y'' - y = 0, \quad y'(0) = 1$ and $y(0) = 0$

26. $y'' + y = 0, \quad y'(0) = 0$ and $y(0) = 1$

27. $y'' + y = x, \quad y'(0) = 1$ and $y(0) = 2$

28. $y'' - y = x, \quad y'(0) = 2$ and $y(0) = -1$

29. $y'' - y = -x, \quad y'(2) = -2$ and $y(2) = 0$

30. $y'' - x^2y = 0, \quad y'(0) = b$ and $y(0) = a$

31. $y'' + x^2y = x, \quad y'(0) = b$ and $y(0) = a$

32. $y'' - 2y' + y = 0, \quad y'(0) = 1$ and $y(0) = 0$

Approximating Integral Functions by Polynomials

In Exercises 33–36, find a polynomial that will approximate $F(x)$ throughout the given interval with an error of magnitude less than 10^{-3}.

33. $F(x) = \int_0^x \sin t^2 \, dt, \quad [0, 1]$

34. $F(x) = \int_0^x t^2 e^{-t^2} \, dt, \quad [0, 1]$

35. $F(x) = \int_0^x \tan^{-1} t \, dt, \quad$ (a) $[0, 0.5]$ (b) $[0, 1]$

36. $F(x) = \int_0^x \frac{\ln (1 + t)}{t} \, dt, \quad$ (a) $[0, 0.5]$ (b) $[0, 1]$

Indeterminate Forms

Use series to evaluate the limits in Exercises 37–42.

37. $\lim\limits_{x\to 0} \dfrac{e^x - (1 + x)}{x^2}$

38. $\lim\limits_{t\to 0} \dfrac{1 - \cos t - (t^2/2)}{t^4}$

39. $\lim\limits_{x\to\infty} x^2(e^{-1/x^2} - 1)$

40. $\lim\limits_{y\to 0} \dfrac{\tan^{-1} y - \sin y}{y^3 \cos y}$

41. $\lim\limits_{x\to 0} \dfrac{\ln (1 + x^2)}{1 - \cos x}$

42. $\lim\limits_{x\to\infty} (x + 1) \sin \dfrac{1}{x + 1}$

Theory and Examples

43. *Series for* $\ln (1 - x),\, |x| < 1$ Replace x by $-x$ in the Maclaurin series for $\ln (1 + x)$ to obtain a series for $\ln (1 - x)$. Then subtract this from the Maclaurin series for $\ln (1 + x)$ to show that for $|x| < 1$,

$$\ln \frac{1 + x}{1 - x} = 2\left(x + \frac{x^3}{3} + \frac{x^5}{5} + \cdots\right).$$

44. *Writing to Learn* How many terms of the Maclaurin series for $\ln (1 + x)$ should you add to be sure of calculating $\ln (1.1)$ with an error of magnitude less than 10^{-8}? Give reasons for your answer.

45. *Writing to Learn* According to the Alternating Series Estimation Theorem, how many terms of the Maclaurin series for $\tan^{-1} 1$ would you have to add to be sure of finding $\pi/4$ with an error of magnitude less than 10^{-3}? Give reasons for your answer.

46. *Maclaurin series for* $\tan^{-1} x$ Show that the Maclaurin series for $f(x) = \tan^{-1} x$ diverges for $|x| > 1$.

47. *Taylor polynomial for* $\sin^{-1} x$

(a) Use the binomial series and that

$$\frac{d}{dx} \sin^{-1} x = (1 - x^2)^{-1/2}$$

to generate the first four nonzero terms of the Maclaurin series for $\sin^{-1} x$. What is the radius of convergence?

(b) *Taylor polynomial for* $\cos^{-1} x$ Use your result in part (a) to find the first five nonzero terms of the Maclaurin series for $\cos^{-1} x$.

48. *Maclaurin series for* $\sin^{-1} x$ Integrate the binomial series for the function $(1 - x^2)^{-1/2}$ to show that for $|x| < 1$,

$$\sin^{-1} x = x + \sum_{n=1}^{\infty} \frac{1 \cdot 3 \cdot 5 \cdot \cdots \cdot (2n - 1)}{2 \cdot 4 \cdot 6 \cdot \cdots \cdot (2n)} \frac{x^{2n+1}}{2n + 1}.$$

49. *Series for* $\tan^{-1} x$ *for* $|x| > 1$ Derive the series

$$\tan^{-1} x = \frac{\pi}{2} - \frac{1}{x} + \frac{1}{3x^3} - \frac{1}{5x^5} + \cdots, \quad x > 1$$

$$\tan^{-1} x = -\frac{\pi}{2} - \frac{1}{x} + \frac{1}{3x^3} - \frac{1}{5x^5} + \cdots, \quad x < -1$$

by integrating the series

$$\frac{1}{1 + t^2} = \frac{1}{t^2} \cdot \frac{1}{1 + (1/t^2)} = \frac{1}{t^2} - \frac{1}{t^4} + \frac{1}{t^6} - \frac{1}{t^8} + \cdots$$

in the first case from x to ∞ and in the second case from $-\infty$ to x.

50. *The value of* $\sum_{n=0}^{\infty} \tan^{-1} (2/n^2)$

(a) Use the formula for the tangent of the difference of two angles to show that

$$\tan (\tan^{-1} (n + 1) - \tan^{-1} (n - 1)) = \frac{2}{n^2}$$

and hence that

$$\tan^{-1} \frac{2}{n^2} = \tan^{-1} (n + 1) - \tan^{-1} (n - 1).$$

(b) Show that

$$\sum_{n=1}^{N} \tan^{-1} \frac{2}{n^2} = \tan^{-1} (N + 1) + \tan^{-1} N - \frac{\pi}{4}.$$

(c) Find the value of $\sum_{n=1}^{\infty} \tan^{-1} (2/n^2)$.

8.9 Fourier Series

Coefficients in the Fourier Series Expansion • Convergence of the Fourier Series • Periodic Extension

CD-ROM
WEBsite
Historical Biography

Jean-Baptiste
Joseph Fourier
(1766 — 1830)

When investigating the problem of heat conduction in a long thin insulated rod, French mathematician Jean-Baptiste Joseph Fourier needed to express a function $f(x)$ as a trigonometric series. Generally, if $f(x)$ is defined on the interval $-L < x < L$, we need to know the coefficients a_0, a_n, and b_n ($n \geq 1$) for which

$$f(x) = \frac{a_0}{2} + \sum_{n=1}^{\infty} \left(a_n \cos \frac{n\pi x}{L} + b_n \sin \frac{n\pi x}{L}\right). \tag{1}$$

Notice that the interval $-L < x < L$ is *symmetric* about the origin. Equation (1) is called a **Fourier series** for f on the interval $(-L, L)$. These series have a wide range of science and engineering applications in the study of heat conduction, wave phenomena, concentrations of chemicals and pollutants, and other models of the physical world. In this section, we introduce these important trigonometric series representations of a given function f.

Coefficients in the Fourier Series Expansion

Suppose that f is a function defined over the *symmetric* interval $-L < x < L$. Assume that f is expressible as the trigonometric series given by Equation (1). We want to find a way to calculate the coefficients $a_0, a_1, a_2, \ldots, b_1, b_2, \ldots$. The key to the calculations is the definite integral, based on the results in Table 8.3.

Table 8.3 Trigonometric Integrals

If m and n are positive integers, then

1. $\displaystyle\int_{-L}^{L} \cos \frac{n\pi x}{L} \, dx = 0$

2. $\displaystyle\int_{-L}^{L} \sin \frac{n\pi x}{L} \, dx = 0$

3. $\displaystyle\int_{-L}^{L} \cos \frac{n\pi x}{L} \cos \frac{m\pi x}{L} \, dx = \begin{cases} 0, & m \neq n, \\ L, & m = n \end{cases}$

4. $\displaystyle\int_{-L}^{L} \sin \frac{n\pi x}{L} \cos \frac{m\pi x}{L} \, dx = 0$

5. $\displaystyle\int_{-L}^{L} \sin \frac{n\pi x}{L} \sin \frac{m\pi x}{L} \, dx = \begin{cases} 0, & m \neq n, \\ L, & m = n. \end{cases}$

(We ask you to evaluate these trigonometric integrals in Exercises 17 through 21.)

Calculation of a_0   We integrate both sides of Equation (1) from $-L$ to L and assume that the operations for integration and summation can be interchanged to obtain

$$\int_{-L}^{L} f(x) \, dx = \frac{a_0}{2} \int_{-L}^{L} dx + \sum_{n=1}^{\infty} a_n \int_{-L}^{L} \cos \frac{n\pi x}{L} \, dx$$

$$+ \sum_{n=1}^{\infty} b_n \int_{-L}^{L} \sin \frac{n\pi x}{L} \, dx. \tag{2}$$

The term $a_0/2$ in Equation (1) keeps consistency with the formulas calculating the Fourier coefficients.

For every positive integer n, the last two integrals on the right-hand side of Equation (2) are zero (Formulas 1 and 2 in Table 8.3). Therefore,

$$\int_{-L}^{L} f(x) \, dx = \frac{a_0}{2} \int_{-L}^{L} dx = \frac{a_0 x}{2} \Big]_{-L}^{L} = L a_0.$$

Solving for a_0 yields

$$a_0 = \frac{1}{L} \int_{-L}^{L} f(x) \, dx. \tag{3}$$

Calculation of a_m We multiply both sides of Equation (1) by $\cos(m\pi x/L)$, $m > 0$, and integrate the result from $-L$ to L:

$$\int_{-L}^{L} f(x) \cos \frac{m\pi x}{L}\, dx = \frac{a_0}{2} \int_{-L}^{L} \cos \frac{m\pi x}{L}\, dx$$

$$+ \sum_{n=1}^{\infty} a_n \int_{-L}^{L} \cos \frac{n\pi x}{L} \cos \frac{m\pi x}{L}\, dx \tag{4}$$

$$+ \sum_{n=1}^{\infty} b_n \int_{-L}^{L} \sin \frac{n\pi x}{L} \cos \frac{m\pi x}{L}\, dx.$$

The first integral on the right-hand side of Equation (4) is zero (Formula 1 in Table 8.3). Formulas 3 and 4 in Table 8.3, further reduce the equation to

$$\int_{-L}^{L} f(x) \cos \frac{m\pi x}{L}\, dx = a_m \int_{-L}^{L} \cos \frac{m\pi x}{L} \cos \frac{m\pi x}{L}\, dx = La_m.$$

Therefore,

$$a_m = \frac{1}{L} \int_{-L}^{L} f(x) \cos \frac{m\pi x}{L}\, dx. \tag{5}$$

Calculation of b_m We multiply both sides of Equation (1) by $\sin(m\pi x/L)$, $m > 0$, and integrate the result from $-L$ to L:

$$\int_{-L}^{L} f(x) \sin \frac{m\pi x}{L}\, dx = \frac{a_0}{2} \int_{-L}^{L} \sin \frac{m\pi x}{L}\, dx$$

$$+ \sum_{n=1}^{\infty} a_n \int_{-L}^{L} \cos \frac{n\pi x}{L} \sin \frac{m\pi x}{L}\, dx$$

$$+ \sum_{n=1}^{\infty} b_n \int_{-L}^{L} \sin \frac{n\pi x}{L} \sin \frac{m\pi x}{L}\, dx.$$

From Formulas 2, 4, and 5 in Table 8.3, we obtain

$$\int_{-L}^{L} f(x) \sin \frac{m\pi x}{L}\, dx = b_m \int_{-L}^{L} \sin \frac{m\pi x}{L} \sin \frac{m\pi x}{L}\, dx = Lb_m.$$

Therefore,

$$b_m = \frac{1}{L} \int_{-L}^{L} f(x) \sin \frac{m\pi x}{L}\, dx. \tag{6}$$

The trigonometric series (1), whose coefficients a_0, a_n, b_n are determined by Equations (3), (5), and (6), respectively (with m replaced by n), is called the **Fourier series expansion** of the function f over the interval $-L < x < L$. The constants a_0, a_n, and b_n are the **Fourier coefficients** of f.

CD-ROM
WEBsite

Example 1   Finding a Fourier Series Expansion

Find the Fourier series expansion of the function

$$f(x) = \begin{cases} 1, & -\pi < x < 0, \\ x, & 0 < x < \pi, \end{cases}$$

(Figure 8.22).

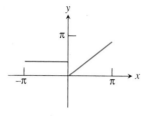

FIGURE 8.22 The piecewise continuous function in Example 1.

Solution Notice from Figure 8.22 that $L = \pi$. Thus, from Equation (3) we have

$$a_0 = \frac{1}{\pi} \int_{-\pi}^{\pi} f(x)\,dx$$

$$= \frac{1}{\pi} \int_{-\pi}^{0} dx + \frac{1}{\pi} \int_{0}^{\pi} x\,dx$$

$$= 1 + \frac{\pi}{2}.$$

To find a_n, we use Equation (5) with m replaced by n:

$$a_n = \frac{1}{\pi} \int_{-\pi}^{\pi} f(x)\, \cos\, nx\,dx$$

$$= \frac{1}{\pi} \int_{-\pi}^{0} \cos\, nx\,dx + \frac{1}{\pi} \int_{0}^{\pi} x\, \cos\, nx\,dx$$

$$= \frac{1}{n\pi} \sin\, nx \bigg]_{-\pi}^{0} + \frac{1}{\pi} \left[\frac{x}{n} \sin\, nx \right]_{0}^{\pi} - \frac{1}{\pi n} \int_{0}^{\pi} \sin\, nx\,dx$$

$$= \frac{1}{\pi n^2} \cos\, nx \bigg]_{0}^{\pi}$$

$$= \frac{1}{\pi n^2} (\cos\, n\pi - 1)$$

$$= \frac{(-1)^n - 1}{\pi n^2}. \qquad \cos n\pi = (-1)^n$$

In a similar manner, from Equation (6) with m replaced by n:

$$b_n = \frac{1}{\pi} \int_{-\pi}^{\pi} f(x)\, \sin\, nx\,dx$$

$$= \frac{1}{\pi} \int_{-\pi}^{0} \sin\, nx\,dx + \frac{1}{\pi} \int_{0}^{\pi} x\, \sin\, nx\,dx$$

$$= \frac{(-1)^n(1 - \pi) - 1}{n\pi}.$$

Therefore, the Fourier expansion is

$$f(x) = \frac{1}{2} + \frac{\pi}{4} + \sum_{n=1}^{\infty} \frac{(-1)^n - 1}{\pi n^2} \cos\, nx + \sum_{n=1}^{\infty} \frac{(-1)^n(1 - \pi) - 1}{\pi n} \sin\, nx.$$

A graph of the Fourier series approximations as n varies up to 1, 5, and 20 terms is given in Figure 8.23. Notice how the approximations get closer and closer to the graph of the function at all points of continuity as n increases. At the point $x = 0$, where f is discontinuous, the Fourier approximations approach the value

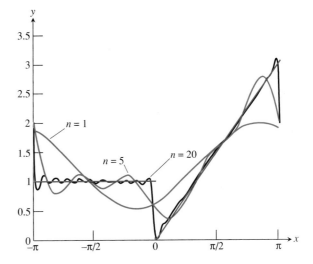

FIGURE 8.23 Fourier series approximations of the function in Example 1 as n varies up to 1, 5, and 20 terms in the infinite series. As n increases, the Fourier approximations approach the actual $f(x)$ values.

0.5 halfway between the jump. These results are consistent with the theorem on Fourier convergence stated below.

In calculating the coefficients a_0, a_n, and b_n, we assumed that f was integrable on the interval $(-L, L)$. We also assumed that the trigonometric series on the right side of Equation (1), as well as the series obtained when we multiply it by $\cos (m\pi x/L)$ or $\sin (m\pi x/L)$, converge in a way to permit term-by-term integration. These convergence issues are studied in advanced calculus, as is the question of when the Fourier series actually equals $f(x)$ for $-L < x < L$. Most of the functions you will encounter in applications guarantee both convergence of the series and its equality with f. We say a little more about this in a moment, but first we summarize our results.

Definition   Fourier Series
The **Fourier series** of a function $f(x)$ defined on the interval $-L < x < L$ is

$$f(x) = \frac{a_0}{2} + \sum_{n=1}^{\infty} \left[a_n \cos \frac{n\pi x}{L} + b_n \sin \frac{n\pi x}{L} \right], \tag{7}$$

where

$$a_0 = \frac{1}{L} \int_{-L}^{L} f(x)\, dx, \tag{8}$$

$$a_n = \frac{1}{L} \int_{-L}^{L} f(x) \cos \frac{n\pi x}{L}\, dx, \tag{9}$$

$$b_n = \frac{1}{L} \int_{-L}^{L} f(x) \sin \frac{n\pi x}{L}\, dx. \tag{10}$$

Convergence of the Fourier Series

We now state without proof the result concerning the convergence of the Fourier series expansion for a wide class of functions commonly encountered in simplified models of several physical behaviors. Recall that a function f is *piecewise continuous* over an interval I if both limits

$$\lim_{x \to c^+} f(x) = f(c^+) \qquad \text{and} \qquad \lim_{x \to c^-} f(x) = f(c^-)$$

exist at every interior point c in I and, moreover, the appropriate one-sided limits exist at the endpoints of I, and f has at most finitely many discontinuities in I. Notice that a piecewise continuous function over a closed interval must be bounded (so it cannot tend toward infinity).

Theorem 18 Convergence of Fourier Series

If the function f and its derivative f' are piecewise continuous over the interval $-L < x < L$, then f equals its Fourier series at all points of continuity. At a point c where a jump discontinuity occurs in f, the Fourier series converges to the average

$$\frac{f(c^+) + f(c^-)}{2},$$

where $f(c^+)$ and $f(c^-)$ denote the right and left limits of f at c, respectively.

Example 2   Convergence Values

The function in Example 1 satisfies the conditions of Theorem 18. For every $x \neq 0$ in the interval $-\pi < x < \pi$, the Fourier series converges to $f(x)$. At $x = 0$, the function has a jump discontinuity and the Fourier series converges to the average value

$$\frac{f(0^+) + f(0^-)}{2} = \frac{0 + 1}{2} = \frac{1}{2}$$

(Figure 8.23).

Periodic Extension

The trigonometric terms $\sin\,(n\pi x/L)$ and $\cos\,(n\pi x/L)$ in the Fourier series are periodic with period $2L$:

$$\sin \frac{n\pi(x + 2L)}{L} = \sin \frac{n\pi x}{L} \cos 2n\pi + \cos \frac{n\pi x}{L} \sin 2n\pi$$

$$= \sin \frac{n\pi x}{L}$$

and

$$\cos \frac{n\pi(x + 2L)}{L} = \cos \frac{n\pi x}{L} \cos 2n\pi - \sin \frac{n\pi x}{L} \sin 2n\pi$$

$$= \cos \frac{n\pi x}{L}.$$

It follows that the Fourier series is also periodic with period $2L$. Thus, the Fourier series not only represents the function f over the interval $-L < x < L$, but it also produces the **periodic extension** of f over the entire real-number line. From Theorem 18, the series converges to the average value $[f(L^-) + f(-L^+)]/2$ at the endpoints of the interval, as well as to this value extended periodically to $\pm 3L, \pm 5L, \pm 7L$, and so forth.

Example 3   Convergence and Periodic Extension

The Fourier series for $f(x) = x$ on $-\pi < x < \pi$ is

$$f(x) = \sum_{n=1}^{\infty} \frac{2(-1)^{n+1}}{n} \sin\ nx.$$

(You are asked to find this series in Exercise 3.) The series converges to the periodic extension of $f(x) = x$ on the entire x-axis. The solid dots in Figure 8.24 represent the value

$$\frac{f(\pi^+) + f(\pi^-)}{2} = \frac{\pi + (-\pi)}{2} = 0.$$

The series converges to 0 at the interval endpoints $\pm\pi, \pm 3\pi, \pm 5\pi, \ldots$.

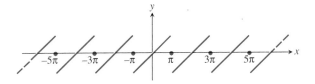

FIGURE **8.24** The Fourier series of $f(x) = x$ converges to f over the interval $-\pi < x < \pi$ and to its periodic extension along the real axis (Theorem 18).

EXERCISES 8.9

Finding Fourier Series

In Exercises 1–14, find the Fourier series expansion for the functions over the specified intervals.

1. $f(x) = 1, \quad -\pi < x < \pi$

2. $f(x) = \begin{cases} -1, & -\pi < x < 0 \\ 1, & 0 < x < \pi \end{cases}$

3. $f(x) = x, \quad -\pi < x < \pi$

4. $f(x) = 1 - x, \quad -\pi < x < \pi$

CD-ROM
WEBsite

5. $f(x) = \dfrac{x^2}{4}, \quad -\pi < x < \pi$

6. $f(x) = \begin{cases} 0, & -\pi < x < 0 \\ x^2, & 0 < x < \pi \end{cases}$

7. $f(x) = e^x, \quad -\pi < x < \pi$

8. $f(x) = \begin{cases} 0, & -\pi < x < 0 \\ e^x, & 0 < x < \pi \end{cases}$

9. $f(x) = \begin{cases} 0, & -\pi < x < 0 \\ \cos\ x, & 0 < x < \pi \end{cases}$

10. $f(x) = \begin{cases} -x, & -2 < x < 0 \\ 2, & 0 < x < 2 \end{cases}$

11. $f(x) = \begin{cases} 0, & -\pi < x < -\dfrac{\pi}{2} \\ 1, & -\dfrac{\pi}{2} < x < \dfrac{\pi}{2} \\ 0, & \dfrac{\pi}{2} < x < \pi \end{cases}$

12. $f(x) = |x|, \quad -1 < x < 1$

13. $f(x) = |2x - 1|, \quad -1 < x < 1$

14. $f(x) = x|x|, \quad -\pi < x < \pi$

Theory and Examples

15. Use the Fourier series in Exercise 5 to show that

CD-ROM
WEBsite

$$1 + \frac{1}{4} + \frac{1}{9} + \frac{1}{16} + \frac{1}{25} + \cdots = \frac{\pi^2}{6}.$$

16. Use the Fourier series in Exercise 6 to show that

$$1 - \frac{1}{4} + \frac{1}{9} - \frac{1}{16} + \cdots = \frac{\pi^2}{12}.$$

Establish the results in Exercises 17–21, where m and n are positive integers.

17. $\int_{-L}^{L} \cos \frac{m\pi x}{L} \, dx = 0 \quad$ for all m.

18. $\int_{-L}^{L} \sin \frac{m\pi x}{L} \, dx = 0 \quad$ for all m.

19. $\int_{-L}^{L} \cos \frac{n\pi x}{L} \cos \frac{m\pi x}{L} \, dx = \begin{cases} 0, & m \neq n \\ L, & m = n \end{cases}$

(*Hint*: $\cos A \cos B = (1/2) [\cos (A + B) + \cos (A - B)]$.)

20. $\int_{-L}^{L} \sin \frac{n\pi x}{L} \sin \frac{m\pi x}{L} \, dx = \begin{cases} 0, & m \neq n \\ L, & m = n \end{cases}$

(*Hint*: $\sin A \sin B = (1/2) [\cos (A - B) - \cos (A + B)]$.)

21. $\int_{-L}^{L} \sin \frac{n\pi x}{L} \cos \frac{m\pi x}{L} \, dx = 0 \quad$ for all m and n.

(*Hint*: $\sin A \cos B = (1/2) [\sin (A + B) + \sin (A - B)]$.)

22. *Writing to Learn: Fourier series of sums of functions* If $f(x)$ and $g(x)$ both satisfy the conditions of Theorem 18, is the Fourier series of $f(x) + g(x)$ on $(-L, L)$ the sum of the Fourier series of $f(x)$ and $g(x)$ on the interval? Give reasons for your answers.

23. *Term-by-term differentiation*

(a) Use Theorem 18 to verify that the Fourier series for $f(x) = x$ in Exercise 3 converges to $f(x)$ for $-\pi < x < \pi$.

(b) Although $f'(x) = 1$, show that the series obtained from term-by-term differentiation of the Fourier series in part (a) diverges.

(c) *Writing to Learn* What do you conclude from part (b)? Give reasons for your answer.

24. *Term-by-term integration* In advanced calculus, it is proved that the Fourier series of a piecewise continuous function on $[-L, L]$ can be integrated term by term. Use this fact to show that if $f(x)$ is piecewise continuous on $-\pi < x < \pi$, then

$$\int_{-\pi}^{\pi} f(s) \, ds = \frac{1}{2} a_0 (x + \pi)$$

$$+ \sum_{n=1}^{\infty} \frac{1}{n} (a_n \sin nx - b_n (\cos nx - \cos n\pi)) \quad \text{for } -\pi \leq x \leq \pi,$$

where a_0, a_n, and b_n are the Fourier coefficients of f.

8.10   Fourier Cosine and Sine Series

CD-ROM
WEBsite

Integrals of Even and Odd Functions • Even Extension: Fourier Cosine Series • Odd Extension: Fourier Sine Series • Gibbs Phenomenon

In modeling heat conduction in a long, thin insulated rod or wire, we assume that the x-axis is aligned with the length L of the rod and that $0 < x < L$. The temperature $u(x, t)$ along the length of the rod generally varies with both position x and time t. (In Chapter 12, you will study functions like this, which depend on two or more independent variables for their values.) The problem is to determine $u(x, t)$ given the initial temperature $u(x, 0) = f(x)$ along the rod. For example, it might be hot at one end and cooler at the other end, so heat will flow from the hot to the cool end and we might want to know what the temperature distribution will look like in an hour's time. One method used to solve this problem requires the expansion

$$f(x) = \sum_{n=1}^{\infty} b_n \sin \frac{n\pi x}{L}$$

over the *nonsymmetric* interval $0 < x < L$. How then can we calculate a Fourier series expansion for f? To do so, we extend the function so that it is defined over the symmetric interval $-L < x < L$. How, though, do we define the extension of f for $-L < x < 0$? The answer is that we can define the extension to be *any function* over $-L < x < 0$ we choose as long as the extension and its derivative are piecewise continuous (in order to satisfy the hypothesis of Theorem 18). No matter what piecewise continuous function we define as the extension over $-L < x < 0$, the resulting Fourier series is guaranteed to equal $f(x)$ at all points of continuity over the original domain $0 < x < L$. Of course, the Fourier series also converges to whatever extension function we have chosen for $-L < x < 0$. Nevertheless, there are two special extensions that are particularly useful and whose Fourier coefficients are especially easy to calculate; these are the even and odd extensions of f.

Integrals of Even and Odd Functions

Recall (Preliminaries Chapter, Section 2) that a function $g(x)$ is an even function of x if $g(-x) = g(x)$ for all x in the domain of g. If $g(-x) = -g(x)$ instead, g is said to be an odd function of x. The function $\cos x$ is even, the function $\sin x$ is odd. The graph of an even function is symmetric about the y-axis, whereas the graph of an odd function is symmetric about the origin (Figure 8.25).

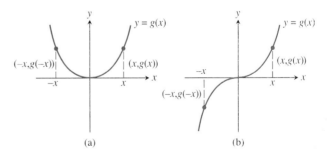

FIGURE 8.25 (a) The graph of an even function is symmetric about the y-axis. (b) The graph of an odd function is symmetric about the origin.

This observation can make the integrals of even and odd functions over intervals symmetric about the origin relatively easy to calculate. For instance, if we consider the "appropriately signed" portions of the graphs in Figure 8.25, we obtain the following:

Odd function:

$$\int_{-L}^{L} g(x)\,dx = 0. \tag{1}$$

Even function:

$$\int_{-L}^{L} g(x)\,dx = 2\int_{0}^{L} g(x)\,dx. \tag{2}$$

Because of rules (1) and (2), even and odd extensions of a function are convenient to use. The following results also hold for even and odd functions.

---

1. The product of two even functions is even.

2. The product of an even function with an odd function is odd.

3. The product of two odd functions is even.

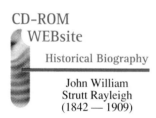

Even Extension: Fourier Cosine Series

Suppose that the function $y = f(x)$ is specified for the interval $0 < x < L$. We define the **even extension of** f by requiring that

$$f(-x) = f(x), \qquad -L < x < L.$$

Graphically, we obtain the even extension by reflecting $y = f(x)$ about the y-axis. The even extension of a function is illustrated in Figure 8.26. Therefore, if we use the even extension for a function f, we obtain the Fourier coefficients

$$a_0 = \frac{1}{L}\int_{-L}^{L} f(x)\,dx = \frac{2}{L}\int_{0}^{L} f(x)\,dx,$$

$$a_n = \frac{1}{L}\int_{-L}^{L} \underbrace{f(x)\,\cos\frac{n\pi x}{L}}_{\text{even}}\,dx = \frac{2}{L}\int_{0}^{L} f(x)\,\cos\frac{n\pi x}{L}\,dx,$$

$$b_n = \frac{1}{L}\int_{-L}^{L} \underbrace{f(x)\,\sin\frac{n\pi x}{L}}_{\text{odd}}\,dx = 0.$$

The Fourier series of f is

$$f(x) = \frac{a_0}{2} + \sum_{n=1}^{\infty} a_n\,\cos\frac{n\pi x}{L}.$$

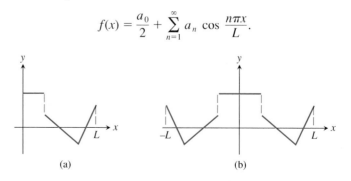

(a)   (b)

FIGURE 8.26 (a) The original piecewise continuous function f defined over nonsymmetric interval $0 < x < L$. (b) The even extension of f over $-L < x < L$.

Because the Fourier coefficients b_n are all zero, no sine terms appear in the Fourier series expansion, and the series is called the **Fourier cosine series** of the function f. It converges to the original function f over the interval $0 < x < L$ and to the even extension over the interval $-L < x < 0$ (assuming the piecewise continuity of f and f'). We summarize this result.

CD-ROM
WEBsite

Fourier Cosine Series

The Fourier series of an even function on the interval $-L < x < L$ is the **cosine series**

$$f(x) = \frac{a_0}{2} + \sum_{n=1}^{\infty} a_n \cos \frac{n\pi x}{L}, \tag{3}$$

where

$$a_0 = \frac{2}{L} \int_0^L f(x)\, dx, \tag{4}$$

$$a_n = \frac{2}{L} \int_0^L f(x) \cos \frac{n\pi x}{L}\, dx. \tag{5}$$

Example 1   Finding a Fourier Cosine Series

Find the Fourier cosine series for the function

$$f(x) = \begin{cases} 1, & 0 < x < \dfrac{\pi}{2}, \\[2mm] 0, & \dfrac{\pi}{2} < x < \pi, \end{cases}$$

depicted in Figure 8.27.

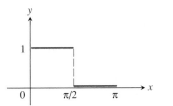

FIGURE 8.27 The function given in Example 1.

Solution   For the Fourier cosine series, we select the even extension of the function over $-\pi < x < \pi$ as shown in Figure 8.28. The Fourier coefficients are

$$a_0 = \frac{2}{\pi} \int_0^{\pi} f(x)\, dx \qquad \text{Eq. (4) with } L = \pi$$

$$= \frac{2}{\pi} \int_0^{\pi/2} dx \qquad \begin{array}{l} f(x) = 0 \text{ for} \\ \pi/2 < x < \pi \end{array}$$

$$= \frac{2x}{\pi} \Big]_0^{\pi/2} = 1$$

$$a_n = \frac{2}{\pi} \int_0^{\pi} f(x) \cos \frac{n\pi x}{\pi}\, dx \qquad \text{Eq. (5) with } L = \pi$$

$$= \frac{2}{\pi} \int_0^{\pi/2} \cos nx\, dx$$

$$= \frac{2}{n\pi} \sin \frac{n\pi}{2}.$$

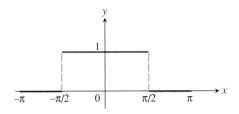

FIGURE 8.28 The even extension of the function in Example 1.

Therefore, we have the Fourier cosine expansion

$$f(x) = \frac{1}{2} + \sum_{n=1}^{\infty} \frac{2}{n\pi} \sin \frac{n\pi}{2} \cos nx.$$

The Fourier cosine series equals exactly the values of $f(x)$ for $x \neq \pi/2$; at the point $x = \pi/2$, the value of the Fourier cosine series is $1/2$. Plots of Fourier cosine approximations for $f(x)$ as n varies up to 1, 5, and 20 terms are given in Figure 8.29.

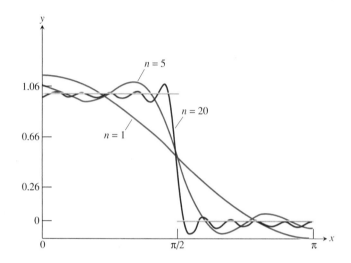

FIGURE 8.29 Fourier cosine series approximations of the function in Example 1 as n varies up to 1, 5, and 20 terms in the infinite series. As n increases, the Fourier cosine approximations approach the actual values of function $f(x)$. Each Fourier cosine approximation passes through the value $y = 0.5$, the midvalue of the jump, at the point of discontinuity $x = \pi/2$.

Odd Extension: Fourier Sine Series

Consider again a function $y = f(x)$ specified for the interval $0 < x < L$. We define the **odd extension of f** by requiring that

$$f(-x) = -f(x), \qquad -L < x < L.$$

Graphically, we obtain the odd extension by reflecting $y = f(x)$ about the origin. The odd extension of a function is illustrated in Figure 8.30. For the odd extension of f, we obtain

$$a_0 = \frac{1}{L} \int_{-L}^{L} f(x)\, dx = 0$$

$$a_n = \frac{1}{L} \int_{-L}^{L} \underbrace{f(x) \cos \frac{n\pi x}{L}}_{\text{Odd}}\, dx = 0$$

$$b_n = \frac{1}{L} \int_{-L}^{L} \underbrace{f(x) \sin \frac{n\pi x}{L}}_{\text{Even}}\, dx = \frac{2}{L} \int_{0}^{L} f(x) \sin \frac{n\pi x}{L}\, dx.$$

The Fourier series of f is

$$f(x) = \sum_{n=1}^{\infty} b_n \sin \frac{n\pi x}{L}.$$

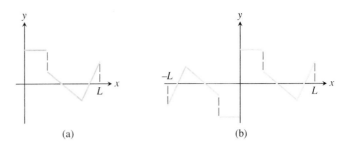

(a)   (b)

FIGURE 8.30 (a) The original piecewise continuous function f defined over nonsymmetric interval $0 < x < L$. (b) The odd extension of f over $-L < x < L$.

Because the Fourier coefficients a_0 and a_n are all zero, no cosine terms appear in the Fourier series expansion, and the series is called the **Fourier sine series** of the function f. This series converges to the original function f over the interval $0 < x < L$, and to the *odd* extension over the interval $-L < x < 0$ (assuming the piecewise continuity of f and f'). We summarize this result.

CD-ROM
WEBsite

Fourier Sine Series

The Fourier series of an odd function on the interval $-L < x < L$ is the **sine series**

$$f(x) = \sum_{n=1}^{\infty} b_n \sin \frac{n\pi x}{L},\tag{6}$$

where

$$b_n = \frac{2}{L} \int_0^L f(x) \sin \frac{n\pi x}{L}\, dx.\tag{7}$$

Example 2   Finding a Fourier Sine Series

Find the Fourier sine series for the function

$$f(x) = \begin{cases} 1, & 0 < x < \dfrac{\pi}{2}, \\ 0, & \dfrac{\pi}{2} < x < \pi, \end{cases}$$

in Example 1.

Solution   We select the *odd* extension of the function $f(x)$. The Fourier coefficients are

$$b_n = \frac{2}{\pi} \int_0^\pi f(x) \sin \frac{n\pi x}{\pi}\, dx$$

$$= \frac{2}{\pi} \int_0^{\pi/2} \sin nx\, dx$$

$$= -\frac{2}{n\pi} \cos nx \Big]_0^{\pi/2} = \frac{2}{n\pi}\left(1 - \cos \frac{n\pi}{2}\right).$$

Therefore, we have the Fourier sine expansion

$$f(x) = \sum_{n=1}^{\infty} \frac{2}{n\pi} \left(1 - \cos \frac{n\pi}{2}\right) \sin nx.$$

A graph of the Fourier sine approximations for $f(x)$ for $n = 1, 5,$ and 20 terms is shown in Figure 8.31.

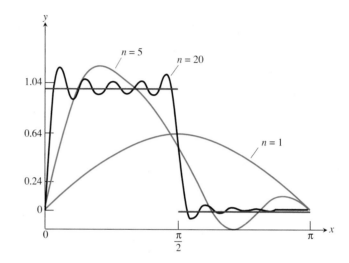

FIGURE 8.31 Fourier sine approximations of the function in Example 2 for $n = 1, 5,$ and 20 terms in the infinite series. As n increases, the Fourier sine approximations approach the values of $f(x)$. The approximations converge to the midpoint of the jump at the point of discontinuity, $x = \pi/2$.

Gibbs Phenomenon

In Figures 8.29 and 8.31, the **overshoot** at $x = \pi/2^-$ and the **undershoot** at $x = \pi/2^+$ are characteristic of Fourier series expansions near points of discontinuity. Known as the **Gibbs phenomenon,** after American mathematical physicist Josiah Willard Gibbs, this characteristic persists even when a large number of terms are summed. The combined overshoot and undershoot amount to about 18% of the difference between the function's values at the point of discontinuity. Figure 8.32 reveals the phenomenon for

$$f(x) = \begin{cases} 1, & 0 \le x < 1 \\ 0, & x = 1 \end{cases}$$

with $n = 2, 4, 8, 16, 32,$ and 64 terms. With more terms, the highest peak moves closer to the discontinuity at $x = 1$, but the overshoot remains approximately 1.09.

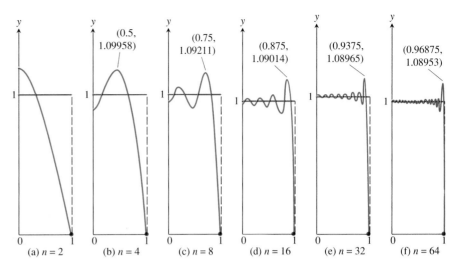

FIGURE 8.32   The Gibbs phenomenon for $n = 2, 4, 8, 16, 32,$ and 64 terms. The highest peak moves from 0.5 to 0.75, then to 0.875, and so forth, getting closer to the discontinuity at $x = 1$. The overshoot is always close to 1.09, or about 9% of the distance between $y = 0$ and $y = 1$ at the discontinuity, $x = 1$.

EXERCISES 8.10

Finding Fourier Cosine Series

Each of Exercises 1–8 gives a function $f(x)$ defined on an interval $(0, L)$. Graph f and its even extension to $(-L, L)$. Then find the Fourier cosine series expansion for f.

1. $f(x) = x,   0 < x < \pi$

2. $f(x) = \sin x,   0 < x < \pi$

3. $f(x) = e^x,   0 < x < 1$

4. $f(x) = \cos x,   0 < x < \pi$

5. $f(x) = \begin{cases} 1, & 0 < x < 1 \\ -x, & 1 < x < 2 \end{cases}$

6. $f(x) = \begin{cases} -1, & 0 < x < 0.5 \\ 1, & 0.5 < x < 1 \end{cases}$

7. $f(x) = |2x - 1|,   0 < x < 1$

8. $f(x) = |2x - \pi|,   0 < x < \pi$

Finding Fourier Sine Series

Each of Exercises 9–16 gives a function $f(x)$ defined on an interval $(0, L)$. Graph f and its odd extension to $(-L, L)$. Then find the Fourier sine series expansion for f.

9. $f(x) = -x,   0 < x < 1$

10. $f(x) = x^2,   0 < x < \pi$

11. $f(x) = \cos x,   0 < x < \pi$

12. $f(x) = e^x,   0 < x < 1$

13. $f(x) = \sin x,   0 < x < \pi$

14. $f(x) = \begin{cases} x, & 0 < x < 1 \\ 1, & 1 < x < 2 \end{cases}$

15. $f(x) = \begin{cases} 1 - x, & 0 < x < 1 \\ 0, & 1 < x < 2 \end{cases}$

16. $f(x) = |2x - \pi|,   0 < x < \pi$

Theory and Examples

17. *A series for $\pi/4$*

(a) Find the Fourier sine series for

$$f(x) = \begin{cases} 1, & 0 < x < \pi \\ 0, & x = 0 \text{ and } x = \pi. \end{cases}$$

(b) Use the result of part (a) to show that

$$\frac{\pi}{4} = 1 - \frac{1}{3} + \frac{1}{5} - \frac{1}{7} + \cdots.$$

18. *A function with a triangular graph*

(a) Graph the triangular function

$$f(x) = \begin{cases} 1 - x, & 0 < x < 1 \\ x - 1, & 1 < x < 2 \end{cases}$$

(b) Find a Fourier series expansion for $f(x)$.

(c) Find a Fourier cosine series expansion for $f(x)$.

19. *Evaluating a series* Use the result of Exercise 2 to find the value of

$$\sum_{n=1}^{\infty} \frac{(-1)^n}{4n^2 - 1}.$$

20. *Fourier sine series* Given the function

$$f(x) = 2 - x, \qquad 0 < x < 2,$$

define a function whose Fourier sine series representation will converge to $f(x)$ for all values of x. (*Note*: The answer is not unique.)

Questions to Guide Your Review

1. What is an infinite sequence? What does it mean for such a sequence to converge? To diverge? Give examples.

2. What theorems are available for calculating limits of sequences? Give examples.

3. What theorem sometimes enables us to use l'Hôpital's Rule to calculate the limit of a sequence? Give an example.

4. What six sequence limits are likely to arise when you work with sequences and series?

5. What is a subsequence? Why are subsequences important? What uses can be found for subsequences? Give examples.

6. What is a nondecreasing sequence? A nonincreasing sequence? A monotonic sequence? Under what circumstances do these sequences have a limit? Give examples.

7. What is Picard's method for solving the equation $f(x) = 0$? Give an example.

8. What is an infinite series? What does it mean for such a series to converge? To diverge? Give examples.

9. What is a geometric series? When does such a series converge? Diverge? When it does converge, what is its sum? Give examples.

10. Besides geometric series, what other convergent and divergent series do you know?

11. What is the nth-Term Test for Divergence? What is the idea behind the test?

12. What can be said about term-by-term sums and differences of convergent series? About constant multiples of convergent and divergent series?

13. What happens if you add a finite number of terms to a convergent series? A divergent series? What happens if you delete a finite number of terms from a convergent series? A divergent series?

14. Under what circumstances will an infinite series of nonnegative terms converge? Diverge? Why study series of nonnegative terms?

15. What is the Integral Test? What is the reasoning behind it? Give an example of its use.

16. When do p-series converge? Diverge? How do you know? Give examples of convergent and divergent p-series.

17. What are the Direct Comparison Test and the Limit Comparison Test? What is the reasoning behind these tests? Give examples of their use.

18. What are the Ratio and Root Tests? Do they always give you the information you need to determine convergence or divergence? Give examples.

19. What is an alternating series? What theorem is available for determining the convergence of such a series?

20. How can you estimate the error involved in approximating the sum of an alternating series with one of the series' partial sums? What is the reasoning behind the estimate?

21. What is absolute convergence? Conditional convergence? How are the two related?

22. What do you know about rearranging the terms of an absolutely convergent series? Of a conditionally convergent series? Give examples.

23. What is a power series? How do you test a power series for convergence? What are the possible outcomes?

24. What are the basic facts about

    (a) term-by-term differentiation of power series?

    (b) term-by-term integration of power series?

    (c) multiplication of power series?

    Give examples.

25. What is the Taylor series generated by a function $f(x)$ at a point $x = a$? What information do you need about f to construct the series? Give an example.

26. What is a Maclaurin series?

27. Does a Taylor series always converge to its generating function? Explain.

28. What are Taylor polynomials? Of what use are they?

29. What is Taylor's Theorem? What does it say about the errors involved in using Taylor polynomials to approximate functions? In particular, what does the Remainder Estimation Theorem say about the error in a linearization? A quadratic approximation?

30. What is the binomial series? On what interval does it converge? How is it used?

31. What are the Maclaurin series for $1/(1 - x)$, $1/(1 + x)$, e^x, $\sin x$, $\cos x$, $\ln (1 + x)$, and $\tan^{-1} x$?

32. What is a Fourier series? How do you calculate the Fourier coefficients for a function $f(x)$ defined over the interval $-L < x < L$? Under what conditions does a Fourier series converge to its generating function? What happens at a point of discontinuity?

33. What is the periodic extension to the entire real line of a function $f(x)$ defined on $-L < x < L$?

34. What is the even extension to $-L < x < 0$ of a function $f(x)$ defined on $0 < x < L$? What is a Fourier cosine series? How do you calculate its coefficients?

35. What is the odd extension to $-L < x < 0$ of a function $f(x)$ defined on $0 < x < L$? What is a Fourier sine series? How do you calculate its coefficients?

36. What is the Gibbs phenomenon? How is it affected when you sum more and more terms in the Fourier series?

Practice Exercises

Convergent or Divergent Sequences

Which of the sequences whose nth terms appear in Exercises 1–18 converge, and which diverge? Find the limit of each convergent sequence.

1. $a_n = 1 + \dfrac{(-1)^n}{n}$

2. $a_n = \dfrac{1 - (-1)^n}{\sqrt{n}}$

3. $a_n = \dfrac{1 - 2^n}{2^n}$

4. $a_n = 1 + (0.9)^n$

5. $a_n = \sin \dfrac{n\pi}{2}$

6. $a_n = \sin n\pi$

7. $a_n = \dfrac{\ln (n^2)}{n}$

8. $a_n = \dfrac{\ln (2n + 1)}{n}$

9. $a_n = \dfrac{n + \ln n}{n}$

10. $a_n = \dfrac{\ln (2n^3 + 1)}{n}$

11. $a_n = \left(\dfrac{n - 5}{n}\right)^n$

12. $a_n = \left(1 + \dfrac{1}{n}\right)^{-n}$

13. $a_n = \sqrt[n]{\dfrac{3^n}{n}}$

14. $a_n = \left(\dfrac{3}{n}\right)^{1/n}$

15. $a_n = n(2^{1/n} - 1)$

16. $a_n = \sqrt[n]{2n + 1}$

17. $a_n = \dfrac{(n + 1)!}{n!}$

18. $a_n = \dfrac{(-4)^n}{n!}$

Convergent Series

Find the sums of the series in Exercises 19–24.

19. $\displaystyle\sum_{n=3}^{\infty} \dfrac{1}{(2n - 3)(2n - 1)}$

20. $\displaystyle\sum_{n=2}^{\infty} \dfrac{-2}{n(n + 1)}$

21. $\displaystyle\sum_{n=1}^{\infty} \dfrac{9}{(3n - 1)(3n + 2)}$

22. $\displaystyle\sum_{n=3}^{\infty} \dfrac{-8}{(4n - 3)(4n + 1)}$

23. $\displaystyle\sum_{n=0}^{\infty} e^{-n}$

24. $\displaystyle\sum_{n=1}^{\infty} (-1)^n \dfrac{3}{4^n}$

Convergent or Divergent Series

Which of the series in Exercises 25–40 converge absolutely, which converge conditionally, and which diverge? Give reasons for your answers.

25. $\displaystyle\sum_{n=1}^{\infty} \dfrac{1}{\sqrt{n}}$

26. $\displaystyle\sum_{n=1}^{\infty} \dfrac{-5}{n}$

27. $\displaystyle\sum_{n=1}^{\infty} \dfrac{(-1)^n}{\sqrt{n}}$

28. $\displaystyle\sum_{n=1}^{\infty} \dfrac{1}{2n^3}$

29. $\displaystyle\sum_{n=1}^{\infty} \dfrac{(-1)^n}{\ln (n + 1)}$

30. $\displaystyle\sum_{n=2}^{\infty} \dfrac{1}{n(\ln n)^2}$

31. $\displaystyle\sum_{n=1}^{\infty} \dfrac{\ln n}{n^3}$

32. $\displaystyle\sum_{n=3}^{\infty} \dfrac{\ln n}{\ln (\ln n)}$

33. $\displaystyle\sum_{n=1}^{\infty} \dfrac{(-1)^n}{n\sqrt{n^2 + 1}}$

34. $\displaystyle\sum_{n=1}^{\infty} \dfrac{(-1)^n 3n^2}{n^3 + 1}$

35. $\displaystyle\sum_{n=1}^{\infty} \dfrac{n + 1}{n!}$

36. $\displaystyle\sum_{n=1}^{\infty} \dfrac{(-1)^n(n^2 + 1)}{2n^2 + n - 1}$

37. $\displaystyle\sum_{n=1}^{\infty} \dfrac{(-3)^n}{n!}$

38. $\displaystyle\sum_{n=1}^{\infty} \dfrac{2^n 3^n}{n^n}$

39. $\displaystyle\sum_{n=1}^{\infty} \dfrac{1}{\sqrt{n(n + 1)(n + 2)}}$

40. $\displaystyle\sum_{n=2}^{\infty} \dfrac{1}{n\sqrt{n^2 - 1}}$

Power Series

In Exercises 41–50, (a) find the series' radius and interval of convergence. Then identify the values of x for which the series converges (b) absolutely and (c) conditionally.

41. $\displaystyle\sum_{n=1}^{\infty} \dfrac{(x + 4)^n}{n3^n}$

42. $\displaystyle\sum_{n=1}^{\infty} \dfrac{(x - 1)^{2n-2}}{(2n - 1)!}$

43. $\displaystyle\sum_{n=1}^{\infty} \dfrac{(-1)^{n-1}(3x - 1)^n}{n^2}$

44. $\displaystyle\sum_{n=0}^{\infty} \dfrac{(n + 1)(2x + 1)^n}{(2n + 1)2^n}$

45. $\displaystyle\sum_{n=1}^{\infty} \dfrac{x^n}{n^n}$

46. $\displaystyle\sum_{n=1}^{\infty} \dfrac{x^n}{\sqrt{n}}$

47. $\displaystyle\sum_{n=0}^{\infty} \dfrac{(n + 1) x^{2n-1}}{3^n}$

48. $\displaystyle\sum_{n=0}^{\infty} \dfrac{(-1)^n(x - 1)^{2n+1}}{2n + 1}$

49. $\displaystyle\sum_{n=1}^{\infty} (\operatorname{csch} n) x^n$

50. $\displaystyle\sum_{n=1}^{\infty} (\coth n) x^n$

Maclaurin Series

Each of the series in Exercises 51–56 is the value of the Maclaurin series of a function $f(x)$ at a particular point. What function and what point? What is the sum of the series?

51. $1 - \dfrac{1}{4} + \dfrac{1}{16} - \cdots + (-1)^n \dfrac{1}{4^n} + \cdots$

52. $\dfrac{2}{3} - \dfrac{4}{18} + \dfrac{8}{81} - \cdots + (-1)^{n-1} \dfrac{2^n}{n3^n} + \cdots$

53. $\pi - \dfrac{\pi^3}{3!} + \dfrac{\pi^5}{5!} - \cdots + (-1)^n \dfrac{\pi^{2n+1}}{(2n + 1)!} + \cdots$

54. $1 - \dfrac{\pi^2}{9 \cdot 2!} + \dfrac{\pi^4}{81 \cdot 4!} - \cdots + (-1)^n \dfrac{\pi^{2n}}{3^{2n}(2n)!} + \cdots$

55. $1 + \ln 2 + \dfrac{(\ln 2)^2}{2!} + \cdots + \dfrac{(\ln 2)^n}{n!} + \cdots$

56. $\dfrac{1}{\sqrt{3}} - \dfrac{1}{9\sqrt{3}} + \dfrac{1}{45\sqrt{3}} - \cdots + (-1)^{n-1} \dfrac{1}{(2n - 1)(\sqrt{3})^{2n-1}} + \cdots$

Find Maclaurin series for the functions in Exercises 57–64.

57. $\dfrac{1}{1-2x}$

58. $\dfrac{1}{1+x^3}$

59. $\sin \pi x$

60. $\sin \dfrac{2x}{3}$

61. $\cos (x^{5/2})$

62. $\cos \sqrt{5x}$

63. $e^{(\pi x/2)}$

64. e^{-x^2}

Taylor Series

In Exercises 65–68, find the first four nonzero terms of the Taylor series generated by f at $x = a$.

65. $f(x) = \sqrt{3 + x^2}$ at $x = -1$

66. $f(x) = 1/(1 - x)$ at $x = 2$

67. $f(x) = 1/(x + 1)$ at $x = 3$

68. $f(x) = 1/x$ at $x = a > 0$

Initial Value Problems

Use power series to solve the initial value problems in Exercises 69–76.

69. $y' + y = 0, \quad y(0) = -1$

70. $y' - y = 0, \quad y(0) = -3$

71. $y' + 2y = 0, \quad y(0) = 3$

72. $y' + y = 1, \quad y(0) = 0$

73. $y' - y = 3x, \quad y(0) = -1$

74. $y' + y = x, \quad y(0) = 0$

75. $y' - y = x, \quad y(0) = 1$

76. $y' - y = -x, \quad y(0) = 2$

Indeterminate Forms

In Exercises 77–82:

   (a) Use power series to evaluate the limit.

   T (b) Then use a grapher to support your calculation.

77. $\displaystyle\lim_{x \to 0} \dfrac{7 \sin x}{e^{2x} - 1}$

78. $\displaystyle\lim_{\theta \to 0} \dfrac{e^{\theta} - e^{-\theta} - 2\theta}{\theta - \sin \theta}$

79. $\displaystyle\lim_{t \to 0} \left(\dfrac{1}{2 - 2 \cos t} - \dfrac{1}{t^2} \right)$

80. $\displaystyle\lim_{h \to 0} \dfrac{(\sin h)/h - \cos h}{h^2}$

81. $\displaystyle\lim_{z \to 0} \dfrac{1 - \cos^2 z}{\ln (1 - z) + \sin z}$

82. $\displaystyle\lim_{y \to 0} \dfrac{y^2}{\cos y - \cosh y}$

83. Use a series representation of $\sin 3x$ to find values of r and s for which

$$\lim_{x \to 0} \left(\dfrac{\sin 3x}{x^3} + \dfrac{r}{x^2} + s \right) = 0.$$

84. (a) Show that the approximation $\csc x \approx 1/x + x/6$ in Section 8.8, Example 6, leads to the approximation $\sin x \approx 6x/(6 + x^2)$.

   T (b) *Writing to Learn* Compare the accuracies of the approximations $\sin x \approx x$ and $\sin x \approx 6x/(6 + x^2)$ by comparing the graphs of $f(x) = \sin x - x$ and $g(x) = \sin x - (6x/(6 + x^2))$. Describe what you find.

Fourier Series

In Exercises 85–90, find the Fourier series of f on the given interval.

85. $f(x) = \begin{cases} -1, & -\pi < x < 0 \\ 2, & 0 < x < \pi \end{cases}$

86. $f(x) = \begin{cases} 0, & -1 < x < 0 \\ x, & 0 < x < 1 \end{cases}$

87. $f(x) = x + \pi, \quad -\pi < x < \pi$

88. $f(x) = \begin{cases} 0, & -\pi < x < 0 \\ \sin x, & 0 < x < \pi \end{cases}$

89. $f(x) = \begin{cases} 1, & -2 < x < 0 \\ 1 + x, & 0 < x < 2 \end{cases}$

90. $f(x) = \begin{cases} 0, & -2 < x < 0 \\ x, & 0 < x < 1 \\ 1, & 1 < x < 2 \end{cases}$

Fourier Cosine and Sine Series

In Exercises 91–96, find

   (a) the Fourier cosine series

   (b) the Fourier sine series of f on the given interval.

91. $f(x) = \begin{cases} 1, & 0 < x < 1/2 \\ 0, & 1/2 < x < 1 \end{cases}$

92. $f(x) = \begin{cases} 0, & 0 < x < 1 \\ x, & 1 < x < 2 \end{cases}$

93. $f(x) = \sin \pi x, \quad 0 < x < 1$

94. $f(x) = \cos x, \quad 0 < x < \pi/2$

95. $f(x) = 2x + x^2, \quad 0 < x < 3$

96. $f(x) = e^{-x}, \quad 0 < x < 2$

Theory and Examples

97. *A convergent series*

   (a) Show that the series

$$\sum_{n=1}^{\infty} \left(\sin \dfrac{1}{2n} - \sin \dfrac{1}{2n + 1} \right)$$

   converges.

   (b) *Writing to Learn* Estimate the magnitude of the error involved in using the sum of the sines through $n = 20$ to approximate the sum of the series. Is the approximation too large, or too small? Give reasons for your answer.

98. (a) *A convergent series* Show that the series

$$\sum_{n=1}^{\infty} \left(\tan \frac{1}{2n} - \tan \frac{1}{2n+1} \right)$$

converges.

(b) *Writing to Learn* Estimate the magnitude of the error in using the sum of the tangents through $-\tan (1/41)$ to approximate the sum of the series. Is the approximation too large or too small? Give reasons for your answer.

99. *Radius of convergence* Find the radius of convergence of the series

$$\sum_{n=1}^{\infty} \frac{2 \cdot 5 \cdot 8 \cdot \cdots \cdot (3n-1)}{2 \cdot 4 \cdot 6 \cdot \cdots \cdot (2n)} x^n.$$

100. *Radius of convergence* Find the radius of convergence of the series

$$\sum_{n=1}^{\infty} \frac{3 \cdot 5 \cdot 7 \cdot \cdots \cdot (2n-1)}{4 \cdot 9 \cdot 14 \cdot \cdots \cdot (5n-1)} (x-1)^n.$$

101. *nth partial sum* Find a closed-form formula for the nth partial sum of the series $\sum_{n=2}^{\infty} \ln (1 - (1/n^2))$ and use it to determine the convergence or divergence of the series.

102. *nth partial sum* Evaluate $\sum_{k=2}^{\infty} (1/(k^2-1))$ by finding the limit as $n \to \infty$ of the series' nth partial sum.

103. (a) *Interval of convergence* Find the interval of convergence of the series

$$y = 1 + \frac{1}{6} x^3 + \frac{4}{720} x^6 + \cdots + \frac{1 \cdot 4 \cdot 7 \cdot \cdots \cdot (3n-2)}{(3n)!} x^{3n} + \cdots.$$

(b) *Differential equation* Show that the function defined by the series satisfies a differential equation of the form

$$\frac{d^2 y}{dx^2} = x^a y + b$$

and find the values of the constants a and b.

104. (a) *Maclaurin series* Find the Maclaurin series for the function $x^2/(1+x)$.

(b) Does the series converge at $x = 1$? Explain.

105. *Writing to Learn* If $\sum_{n=1}^{\infty} a_n$ and $\sum_{n=1}^{\infty} b_n$ are convergent series of nonnegative numbers, can anything be said about $\sum_{n=1}^{\infty} a_n b_n$? Give reasons for your answer.

106. *Writing to Learn* If $\sum_{n=1}^{\infty} a_n$ and $\sum_{n=1}^{\infty} b_n$ are divergent series of nonnegative numbers, can anything be said about $\sum_{n=1}^{\infty} a_n b_n$? Give reasons for your answer.

107. *Sequence and series* Prove that the sequence $\{x_n\}$ and the series $\sum_{k=1}^{\infty} (x_{k+1} - x_k)$ both converge or both diverge.

108. *Convergence* Prove that $\sum_{n=1}^{\infty} (a_n/(1+a_n))$ converges if $a_n > 0$ for all n and $\sum_{n=1}^{\infty} a_n$ converges.

109. (a) *Divergence* Suppose that $a_1, a_2, a_3, \ldots, a_n$ are positive numbers satisfying the following conditions:

i. $a_1 \geq a_2 \geq a_3 \geq \cdots$

ii. the series $a_2 + a_4 + a_8 + a_{16} + \cdots$ diverges.

Show that the series

$$\frac{a_1}{1} + \frac{a_2}{2} + \frac{a_3}{3} + \cdots$$

diverges.

(b) Use the result in part (a) to show that

$$1 + \sum_{n=2}^{\infty} \frac{1}{n \ln n}$$

diverges.

110. *Estimating an integral* Suppose that you wish to obtain a quick estimate for the value of $\int_0^1 x^2 e^x \, dx$. There are several ways to do this.

(a) Use the Trapezoidal Rule with $n = 2$ to estimate $\int_0^1 x^2 e^x \, dx$.

(b) Write out the first three nonzero terms of the Maclaurin series for $x^2 e^x$ to obtain the fourth Maclaurin polynomial $P(x)$ for $x^2 e^x$. Use $\int_0^1 P(x) \, dx$ to obtain another estimate for $\int_0^1 x^2 e^x \, dx$.

(c) *Writing to Learn* The second derivative of $f(x) = x^2 e^x$ is positive for all $x > 0$. Explain why this enables you to conclude that the trapezoidal rule estimate obtained in part (a) is too large.

(d) *Writing to Learn* All the derivatives of $f(x) = x^2 e^x$ are positive for $x > 0$. Explain why this enables you to conclude that all Maclaurin polynomial approximations to $f(x)$ for x in $[0, 1]$ will be too small. (*Hint:* $f(x) = P_n(x) + R_n(x)$.)

(e) Use integration by parts to evaluate $\int_0^1 x^2 e^x \, dx$.

111. *Series for* $\tan^{-1} x$

(a) Integrate from $t = 0$ to $t = x$ both sides of the equation

$$\frac{1}{1+t^2} = 1 - t^2 + t^4 - t^6 + \cdots + (-1)^n t^{2n} + \frac{(-1)^{n+1} t^{2n+2}}{1+t^2}$$

in which the last term comes from adding the remaining terms as a geometric series with first term $a = (-1)^{n+1} t^{2n+2}$ and ratio $r = -t^2$.

(b) Show that the remainder term from part (a) is

$$R_n(x) = \int_0^x \frac{(-1)^{n+1} t^{2n+2}}{1+t^2} \, dt$$

and find $\lim_{n \to \infty} R_n(x)$ if $|x| \leq 1$.

(c) Find a power series for $\tan^{-1} x$ based on the result in part (b).

(d) Set $x = 1$ in the series for $\tan^{-1} x$ to obtain **Leibniz's formula**

$$\frac{\pi}{4} = 1 - \frac{1}{3} + \frac{1}{5} - \frac{1}{7} + \frac{1}{9} - \cdots + \frac{(-1)^n}{2n + 1} + \cdots.$$

112. *Evaluating nonelementary integrals* As you know, Maclaurin series can be used to express nonelementary integrals in terms of series.

  (a) Express $\int_0^x \sin t^2 \, dt$ as a power series.

  (b) According to the Alternating Series Estimation Theorem, how many terms of the series in part (a) should you use to estimate $\int_0^1 \sin x^2 \, dx$ with an error of less than 0.001?

113. *Picard's method for slope greater than 1* Example 9 in Section 8.2 showed that we cannot apply Picard's method to find a fixed point of $g(x) = 4x - 12$, but we can apply the method to find a fixed point of $g^{-1}(x) = (1/4)x + 3$ because the derivative of g^{-1} is $1/4$, whose value is less than 1 in magnitude on any interval.

In Example 7 of Section 8.2, we found the fixed point of g^{-1} to be $x = 4$. Now notice that 4 is also a fixed point of g, since

$$g(4) = 4(4) - 12 = 4.$$

In finding the fixed point of g^{-1}, we found the fixed point of g.

A function and its inverse always have the same fixed points. The graphs of the functions are symmetric about the line $y = x$ and therefore intersect the line at the same points.

We now see that the application of Picard's method is quite broad. Suppose g is one-to-one, with a continuous first derivative whose magnitude is greater than 1 on a closed interval I whose interior contains a fixed point of g. Then the derivative of g^{-1}, being the reciprocal of g', has magnitude less than 1 on I. Picard's method applied to g^{-1} on I will find the fixed point of g. As cases in point, find the fixed points of the following functions.

  (a) $g(x) = 2x + 3$

  (b) $g(x) = 1 - 4x$

Additional Exercises: Theory, Examples, Applications

Convergence or Divergence

Which of the series $\sum_{n=1}^{\infty} a_n$ defined by the formulas in Exercises 1–4 converge, and which diverge? Give reasons for your answers.

1. $\displaystyle\sum_{n=1}^{\infty} \frac{1}{(3n - 2)^{n+(1/2)}}$

2. $\displaystyle\sum_{n=1}^{\infty} \frac{(\tan^{-1} n)^2}{n^2 + 1}$

3. $\displaystyle\sum_{n=1}^{\infty} (-1)^n \tanh n$

4. $\displaystyle\sum_{n=2}^{\infty} \frac{\log_n (n!)}{n^3}$

Which of the series $\sum_{n=1}^{\infty} a_n$ defined by the formulas in Exercises 5–8 converge, and which diverge? Give reasons for your answers.

5. $a_1 = 1, \quad a_{n+1} = \dfrac{n(n + 1)}{(n + 2)(n + 3)} a_n$ (*Hint:* Write out several terms, see which factors cancel, and then generalize.)

6. $a_1 = a_2 = 7, \quad a_{n+1} = \dfrac{n}{(n - 1)(n + 1)} a_n$ if $n \geq 2$

7. $a_1 = a_2 = 1, \quad a_{n+1} = \dfrac{1}{1 + a_n}$ if $n \geq 2$

8. $a_n = 1/3^n$ if n is odd, $\quad a_n = n/3^n$ if n is even

Choosing Centers for Taylor Series

Taylor's formula

$$f(x) = f(a) + f'(a)(x - a) + \frac{f''(a)}{2!} (x - a)^2$$

$$+ \cdots + \frac{f^{(n)}(a)}{n!} (x - a)^n + \frac{f^{(n+1)}(c)}{(n + 1)!} (x - a)^{n+1}$$

expresses the value of f at x in terms of the values of f and its derivatives at $x = a$. In numerical computations, we therefore need a to be a point where we know the values of f and its derivatives. We also need a to be close enough to the values of f we are interested in to make $(x - a)^{n+1}$ so small we can neglect the remainder.

In Exercises 9–14, what Taylor series would you choose to represent the function near the given value of x? (There may be more than one good answer.) Write out the first four nonzero terms of the series you choose.

9. $\cos x \quad$ near $\quad x = 1$

10. $\sin x \quad$ near $\quad x = 6.3$

11. $e^x \quad$ near $\quad x = 0.4$

12. $\ln x \quad$ near $\quad x = 1.3$

13. $\cos x \quad$ near $\quad x = 69$

14. $\tan^{-1} x \quad$ near $\quad x = 2$

Theory and Examples

15. *nth root of* $a^n + b^n$ Let a and b be constants with $0 < a < b$. Does the sequence $\{(a^n + b^n)^{1/n}\}$ converge? If it does converge, what is the limit?

16. *Repeating decimal* Find the sum of the infinite series

$$1 + \frac{2}{10} + \frac{3}{10^2} + \frac{7}{10^3} + \frac{2}{10^4} + \frac{3}{10^5} + \frac{7}{10^6} + \frac{2}{10^7} + \frac{3}{10^8} + \frac{7}{10^9} + \cdots .$$

17. *Summing integrals* Evaluate

$$\sum_{n=0}^{\infty} \int_n^{n+1} \frac{1}{1+x^2}\, dx.$$

18. *Absolute convergence* Find all values of x for which

$$\sum_{n=1}^{\infty} \frac{nx^n}{(n+1)(2x+1)^n}$$

converges absolutely.

19. *Euler's constant* Graphs like those in Figure 8.13, suggest that as n increases, there is little change in the difference between the sum

$$1 + \frac{1}{2} + \cdots + \frac{1}{n}$$

and the integral

$$\ln n = \int_1^n \frac{1}{x}\, dx .$$

To explore this idea, carry out the following steps.

(a) By taking $f(x) = 1/x$ in Figure 8.13, show that

$$\ln (n+1) \le 1 + \frac{1}{2} + \cdots + \frac{1}{n} \le 1 + \ln n$$

or

$$0 < \ln (n+1) - \ln n \le 1 + \frac{1}{2} + \cdots + \frac{1}{n} - \ln n \le 1.$$

Thus, the sequence

$$a_n = 1 + \frac{1}{2} + \cdots + \frac{1}{n} - \ln n$$

is bounded from below and from above.

(b) Show that

$$\frac{1}{n+1} < \int_n^{n+1} \frac{1}{x}\, dx = \ln (n+1) - \ln n$$

and use this result to show that the sequence $\{a_n\}$ in part (a) is nonincreasing.

Since a nonincreasing sequence that is bounded from below converges, the numbers a_n defined in part (a) converge:

$$1 + \frac{1}{2} + \cdots + \frac{1}{n} - \ln n \to \gamma.$$

The number γ, whose value is $0.5772\ldots$, is called *Euler's constant*. In contrast to other special numbers like π and e, no other expression with a simple law of formulation has ever been found for γ.

20. *Generalizing Euler's constant* The figure below shows the graph of a positive twice-differentiable decreasing functizon f whose second derivative is positive on $(0, \infty)$. For each n, the number A_n is the area of the lunar region between the curve and the line segment joining the points $(n, f(n))$ and $(n+1, f(n+1))$.

(a) Use the figure to show that $\sum_{n=1}^{\infty} A_n < (1/2)(f(1) - f(2))$.

(b) Next show the existence of

$$\lim_{n\to\infty} \left[\sum_{k=1}^{n} f(k) - \frac{1}{2}(f(1) + f(n)) - \int_1^n f(x)\, dx \right].$$

(c) Then show the existence of

$$\lim_{n\to\infty} \left[\sum_{k=1}^{n} f(k) - \int_1^n f(x)\, dx \right].$$

If $f(x) = 1/x$, the limit in part (c) is Euler's constant. (*Source:* "Convergence with Pictures" by P. J. Rippon, *American Mathematical Monthly*, Vol. 93, No. 6 (1986), pp. 476–478.)

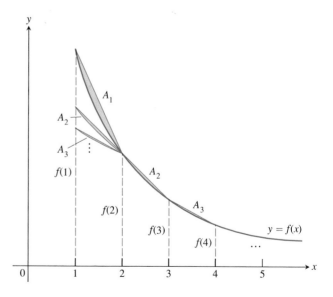

21. *Punching out triangles* This exercise refers to the "right side up" equilateral triangle with sides of length $2b$ in the accompanying figure. "Upside down" equilateral triangles are removed from the original triangle as the sequence of pictures suggests. The sum of the areas removed from the original triangle forms an infinite series.

(a) Find this infinite series.

(b) Find the sum of this infinite series and hence find the total area removed from the original triangle.

(c) Is every point on the original triangle removed? Explain why or why not.

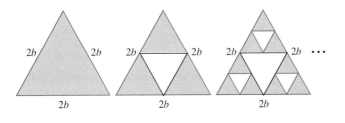

22. *A fast estimate of $\pi/2$* As you saw if you did Exercise 10 in Section 8.2, the sequence generated by starting with $x_0 = 1$ and applying the recursion formula $x_{n+1} = x_n + \cos x_n$ converges rapidly to $\pi/2$. To explain the speed of the convergence, let $\epsilon_n = (\pi/2) - x_n$. (See the accompanying figure.) Then

$$\epsilon_{n+1} = \frac{\pi}{2} - x_n - \cos x_n$$

$$= \epsilon_n - \cos \left(\frac{\pi}{2} - \epsilon_n \right)$$

$$= \epsilon_n - \sin \epsilon_n$$

$$= \frac{1}{3!} (\epsilon_n)^3 - \frac{1}{5!} (\epsilon_n)^5 + \cdots.$$

Use this equality to show that

$$0 < \epsilon_{n+1} < \frac{1}{6} (\epsilon_n)^3.$$

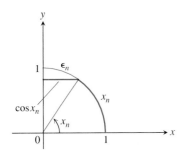

23. *Computer exploration*

(a) *Writing to Learn* Does the value of

$$\lim_{n \to \infty} \left(1 - \frac{\cos (a/n)}{n} \right)^n, \qquad a \text{ constant},$$

appear to depend on the value of a? If so, how?

(b) *Writing to Learn* Does the value of

$$\lim_{n \to \infty} \left(1 - \frac{\cos (a/n)}{bn} \right)^n, \qquad a \text{ and } b \text{ constant}, b \neq 0,$$

appear to depend on the value of b? If so, how?

(c) Use calculus to confirm your findings in parts (a) and (b).

24. Show that if $\sum_{n=1}^{\infty} a_n$ converges, then

$$\sum_{n=1}^{\infty} \left(\frac{1 + \sin (a_n)}{2} \right)^n$$

converges.

25. *Radius of convergence* Find a value for the constant b that will make the radius of convergence of the power series

$$\sum_{n=2}^{\infty} \frac{b^n x^n}{\ln n}$$

equal to 5.

26. *Writing to Learn: Transcendental functions* How do you know that the functions $\sin x$, $\ln x$, and e^x are not polynomials? Give reasons for your answer.

27. *Raabe's (or Gauss's) Test* The following test, which we state without proof, is an extension of the Ratio Test.

Raabe's Test: If $\sum_{n=1}^{\infty} u_n$ is a series of positive constants and there exist constants C, K, and N such that

$$\frac{u_n}{u_{n+1}} = 1 + \frac{C}{n} + \frac{f(n)}{n^2},$$

where $|f(n)| < K$ for $n \geq N$, then $\sum_{n=1}^{\infty} u_n$ converges if $C > 1$ and diverges if $C \leq 1$.

Show that the results of Raabe's Test agree with what you know about the series $\sum_{n=1}^{\infty} (1/n^2)$ and $\sum_{n=1}^{\infty} (1/n)$.

28. *Using Raabe's Test* Suppose that the terms of $\sum_{n=1}^{\infty} u_n$ are defined recursively by the formulas

$$u_1 = 1, \qquad u_{n+1} = \frac{(2n - 1)^2}{(2n)(2n + 1)} u_n.$$

Apply Raabe's Test to determine whether the series converges.

29. Assume that $\sum_{n=1}^{\infty} a_n$ converges, $a_n \neq 1$, and $a_n > 0$ for all n.

(a) *Squaring terms* Show that $\sum_{n=1}^{\infty} a_n^2$ converges.

(b) *Writing to Learn* Does $\sum_{n=1}^{\infty} a_n/(1 - a_n)$ converge? Explain.

30. (*Continuation of Exercise 29*) If $\sum_{n=1}^{\infty} a_n$ converges and if $1 > a_n > 0$ for all n, show that $\sum_{n=1}^{\infty} \ln (1 - a_n)$ converges. (*Hint:* First show that $|\ln (1 - a_n)| \leq a_n/(1 - a_n)$.)

31. *Nicole Oresme's Theorem* Prove Nicole Oresme's Theorem that

$$1 + \frac{1}{2} \cdot 2 + \frac{1}{4} \cdot 3 + \cdots + \frac{n}{2^{n-1}} + \cdots = 4.$$

(*Hint:* differentiate both sides of the equation $1/(1 - x) = 1 + \sum_{n=1}^{\infty} x^n$.)

32. (a) *Term-by-term differentiation* Show that

$$\sum_{n=1}^{\infty} \frac{n(n + 1)}{x^n} = \frac{2x^2}{(x - 1)^3}$$

for $|x| > 1$ by differentiating the identity

$$\sum_{n=1}^{\infty} x^{n+1} = \frac{x^2}{1 - x}$$

twice, multiplying the result by x, and then replacing x by $1/x$.

(b) Use part (a) to find the real solution greater than 1 of the equation

$$x = \sum_{n=1}^{\infty} \frac{n(n + 1)}{x^n}.$$

33. *Summing exponential powers* Use the integral test to show that

$$\sum_{n=0}^{\infty} e^{-n^2}$$

converges.

34. *Writing to Learn* If $\sum_{n=1}^{\infty} a_n$ is a convergent series of positive numbers, can anything be said about the convergence of $\sum_{n=1}^{\infty} \ln (1 + a_n)$? Give reasons for your answer.

35. *Quality control*

(a) Differentiate the series

$$\frac{1}{1 - x} = 1 + x + x^2 + \cdots + x^n + \cdots$$

to obtain a series for $1/(1 - x)^2$.

(b) *Rolling dice* In one throw of two dice, the probability of getting a roll of 7 is $p = 1/6$. If you throw the dice repeatedly, the probability that a 7 will appear for the first time at the nth throw is $q^{n-1}p$, where $q = 1 - p = 5/6$. The expected number of throws until a 7 first appears is $\sum_{n=1}^{\infty} nq^{n-1}p$. Find the sum of this series.

(c) As an engineer applying statistical control to an industrial operation, you inspect items taken at random from the assembly line. You classify each sampled item as either "good" or "bad." If the probability of an item's being good is p and of an item's being bad is $q = 1 - p$, the probability that the first bad item found is the nth one inspected is $p^{n-1}q$.

The average number inspected up to and including the first bad item found is $\sum_{n=1}^{\infty} np^{n-1}q$. Evaluate this sum, assuming $0 < p < 1$.

36. *Expected value* Suppose that a random variable X may assume the values 1, 2, 3, ..., with probabilities $p_1, p_2, p_3, \ldots$, where p_k is the probability that X equals k ($k = 1, 2, 3, \ldots$). Suppose also that $p_k \geq 0$ and $\sum_{k=1}^{\infty} p_k = 1$. The **expected value** of X, denoted by $E(X)$, is the number $\sum_{k=1}^{\infty} kp_k$, provided the series converges. In each of the following cases, show that $\sum_{k=1}^{\infty} p_k = 1$ and find $E(X)$ if it exists. (*Hint:* See Exercise 35.)

(a) $p_k = 2^{-k}$ **(b)** $p_k = \dfrac{5^{k-1}}{6^k}$

(c) $p_k = \dfrac{1}{k(k + 1)} = \dfrac{1}{k} - \dfrac{1}{k + 1}$

37. *Safe and effective dosage* The concentration in the blood resulting from a single dose of a drug normally decreases with time as the drug is eliminated from the body. Doses may therefore need to be repeated periodically to keep the concentration from dropping below some particular level. One model for the effect of repeated doses gives the residual concentration just before the $(n + 1)$st dose as

$$R_n = C_0 e^{-kt_0} + C_0 e^{-2kt_0} + \cdots + C_0 e^{-nkt_0},$$

where C_0 = the change in concentration achievable by a single dose (milligrams per milliliter), k = the *elimination constant* (per hour), and t_0 = time between doses (hours). See the accompanying figure.

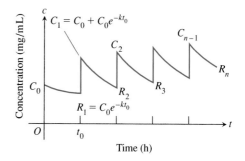

(a) Write R_n in closed form as a single fraction and find $R = \lim_{n \to \infty} R_n$.

(b) Calculate R_1 and R_{10} for $C_0 = 1$ mg/mL, $k = 0.1$ h^{-1}, and $t_0 = 10$ h. How good an estimate of R is R_{10}?

(c) If $k = 0.01$ h^{-1} and $t_0 = 10$ h, find the smallest n such that $R_n > (1/2)R$.

(*Source: Prescribing Safe and Effective Dosage* by B. Horelick and S. Koont (Lexington, MA: COMAP, Inc., 1979).)

38. *Time between drug doses (continuation of Exercise 37)* If a drug is known to be ineffective below a concentration C_L and harmful above some higher concentration C_H, one needs to find values of

C_0 and t_0 that will produce a concentration that is safe (not above C_H) but effective (not below C_L). See the accompanying figure.

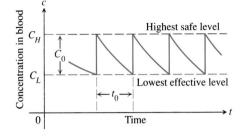

We therefore want to find values for C_0 and t_0 for which

$$R = C_L \quad \text{and} \quad C_0 + R = C_H.$$

Thus, $C_0 = C_H - C_L$. When these values are substituted in the equation for R obtained in part (a) of Exercise 37, the resulting equation simplifies to

$$t_0 = \frac{1}{k} \ln \frac{C_H}{C_L}.$$

To reach an effective level rapidly, one might administer a "loading" dose that would produce a concentration of C_H milligrams per milliliter. This could be followed every t_0 hours by a dose that raises the concentration by $C_0 = C_H - C_L$ milligrams per milliliter.

(a) Verify the preceding equation for t_0.

(b) If $k = 0.05 \text{ h}^{-1}$ and the highest safe concentration is e times the lowest effective concentration, find the length of time between doses that will assure safe and effective concentrations.

(c) *Writing to Learn* Given $C_H = 2 \text{ mg/mL}$, $C_L = 0.5 \text{ mg/mL}$, and $k = 0.02 \text{ h}^{-1}$, determine a scheme for administering the drug.

(d) Suppose that $k = 0.2 \text{ h}^{-1}$ and that the smallest effective concentration is 0.03 mg/mL. A single dose that produces a concentration of 0.1 mg/mL is administered. About how long will the drug remain effective?

39. *An infinite product* The infinite product

$$\prod_{n=1}^{\infty} (1 + a_n) = (1 + a_1)(1 + a_2)(1 + a_3) \cdots$$

is said to converge if the series

$$\sum_{n=1}^{\infty} \ln (1 + a_n),$$

obtained by taking the natural logarithm of the product, converges. Prove that the product converges if $a_n > -1$ for every n and if $\sum_{n=1}^{\infty} |a_n|$ converges. (*Hint:* Show that

$$|\ln (1 + a_n)| \le \frac{|a_n|}{1 - |a_n|} \le 2 |a_n|$$

when $|a_n| < 1/2$.)

40. *Extended logarithmic p-series* If p is a constant, show that the series

$$1 + \sum_{n=3}^{\infty} \frac{1}{n \cdot \ln n \cdot [\ln (\ln n)]^p}$$

(a) converges if $p > 1$

(b) diverges if $p \le 1$.

In general, if $f_1(x) = x$, $f_{n+1}(x) = \ln (f_n(x))$ and n takes on the values $1, 2, 3, \ldots$, we find that $f_2(x) = \ln x$, $f_3(x) = \ln (\ln x)$, and so on. If $f_n(a) > 1$, then

$$\int_a^{\infty} \frac{dx}{f_1(x) f_2(x) \cdots f_n(x) (f_{n+1}(x))^p}$$

converges if $p > 1$ and diverges if $p \le 1$.

9

Vectors in the Plane and Polar Functions

OVERVIEW When a body travels in the xy-plane, the parametric equations $x = f(t)$ and $y = g(t)$ can be used to model the body's motion and path. In this chapter, we introduce the *vector* form of parametric equations, which allows us to track the positions of moving bodies with vectors, calculate the directions and magnitudes of their velocities and accelerations, and predict the effects of the forces we see working on them.

One of the principal applications of vector functions is the analysis of motion in space. Planetary motion is best described with polar coordinates (another of Newton's inventions, although Jakob Bernoulli usually gets the credit because he published first), so we investigate curves, derivatives, and integrals in this new coordinate system.

9.1 Vectors in the Plane

Component Form • Zero Vector and Unit Vectors • Vector Algebra
Operations • Standard Unit Vectors • Length and Direction •
Tangents and Normals

Some of the things we measure are determined by their magnitudes. To record mass, length, or time, for example, we need only write down a number and name an appropriate unit of measure. These are *scalar quantities*, and the associated real numbers are **scalars.** We need more information to describe a force, displacement, or velocity. To describe a force, we need to record the direction in which it acts as well as how large it is. To describe a body's displacement, we have to say in what direction it moved as well as how far. To describe a body's velocity, we have to know where the body is headed as well as how fast it is going.

Component Form

A quantity such as force, displacement, or velocity is represented by a **directed line segment** (Figure 9.1). The arrow points in the direction of the action and its length gives the magnitude of the action in terms of a suitably chosen unit. For example, a force vector points in the direction in which it is applied and its length is a measure of its strength; a velocity vector points in the direction of motion and its length is the speed of the moving object. (We say more about force and velocity in Sections 9.3 and 9.4.)

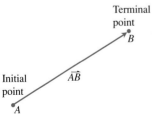

FIGURE 9.1 The directed line segment $\overrightarrow{AB}$.

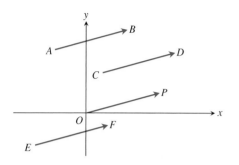

FIGURE 9.2 The four arrows (directed line segments) shown here have the same length and direction. They therefore represent the same vector, and we write $\overrightarrow{AB} = \overrightarrow{CD} = \overrightarrow{OP} = \overrightarrow{EF}$.

The directed line segment $\overrightarrow{AB}$ has **initial point** A and **terminal point** B; its **length** is denoted by $|\overrightarrow{AB}|$. Directed line segments that have the same length and direction are **equivalent.**

Definitions   Vector, Equal Vectors

A **vector** in the plane is a directed line segment. Two vectors are **equal** (or **the same**) if they have the same length and direction.

Thus, the arrows we use when we draw vectors are understood to represent the same vector if they have the same length, are parallel, and point in the same direction (Figure 9.2).

In textbooks, vectors are usually written in lowercase, boldface letters, for example **u**, **v**, and **w**. Sometimes we use uppercase boldface letters, such as **F**, to denote a force vector. In handwritten form, it is customary to draw small arrows above the letters, for example $\overrightarrow{u}$, $\overrightarrow{v}$, $\overrightarrow{w}$, and $\overrightarrow{F}$.

Example 1   Showing Vectors are Equal

Let $A = (0, 0)$, $B = (3, 4)$, $C = (-4, 2)$, and $D = (-1, 6)$. Show that the vectors $\mathbf{u} = \overrightarrow{AB}$ and $\mathbf{v} = \overrightarrow{CD}$ are equal.

Solution   We need to show that **u** and **v** have the same length and direction (Figure 9.3). We use the distance formula to find their lengths.

$$|\mathbf{u}| = |\overrightarrow{AB}| = \sqrt{(3 - 0)^2 + (4 - 0)^2} = 5$$
$$|\mathbf{v}| = |\overrightarrow{CD}| = \sqrt{(-1 - (-4))^2 + (6 - 2)^2} = 5$$

Next we calculate the slopes of the two line segments.

$$\text{Slope of } \overrightarrow{AB} = \frac{4 - 0}{3 - 0} = \frac{4}{3}, \qquad \text{slope of } \overrightarrow{CD} = \frac{6 - 2}{-1 - (-4)} = \frac{4}{3}$$

The line segments have the same direction because they are parallel and directed toward the upper right. Therefore, $\mathbf{u} = \mathbf{v}$ because they have the same length and direction.

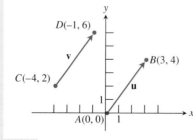

FIGURE 9.3 Two equal vectors. They have the same length and direction. (Example 1)

Let $\mathbf{v} = \overrightarrow{PQ}$. There is one directed line segment equivalent to $\overrightarrow{PQ}$ whose initial point is the origin (Figure 9.4). It is the representative of **v** in **standard position** and is the vector we normally use to represent **v.**

CD-ROM
WEBsite

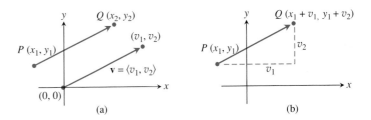

FIGURE 9.4 (a) The standard position of a vector is where the initial point is the origin. (b) The coordinates of Q satisfy $x_2 = x_1 + v_1$ and $y_2 = y_1 + v_2$.

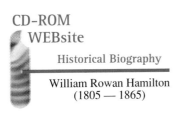

CD-ROM
WEBsite

Historical Biography

William Rowan Hamilton
(1805 — 1865)

Definition Component Form of a Vector

If **v** is a vector in the plane equal to the vector with initial point $(0, 0)$ and terminal point (v_1, v_2), then the **component form** of **v** is

$$\mathbf{v} = \langle v_1, v_2 \rangle.$$

Thus, a vector in the plane is also an ordered pair $\langle v_1, v_2 \rangle$ of real numbers. The numbers v_1 and v_2 are the **components** of **v**. The vector $\langle v_1, v_2 \rangle$ is called the **position vector** of the point (v_1, v_2).

Observe that if $\mathbf{v} = \langle v_1, v_2 \rangle$ is represented by the directed line segment $\overrightarrow{PQ}$, where the initial point is $P(x_1, y_1)$ and the terminal point is $Q(x_2, y_2)$, then $x_1 + v_1 = x_2$ and $y_1 + v_2 = y_2$ (Figure 9.4) so that $v_1 = x_2 - x_1$ and $v_2 = y_2 - y_1$ are the components of $\overrightarrow{PQ}$. In summary,

---

Given the points $P(x_1, y_1)$ and $Q(x_2, y_2)$, the position vector $\mathbf{v} = \langle v_1, v_2 \rangle$ equivalent to $\overrightarrow{PQ}$ is

$$\mathbf{v} = \langle x_2 - x_1, y_2 - y_1 \rangle.$$

Two vectors $\langle a, b \rangle$ and $\langle c, d \rangle$ are equal if and only if $a = c$ and $b = d$, so that $\langle v_1, v_2 \rangle = \langle x_2 - x_1, y_2 - y_1 \rangle$.

The **magnitude** or **length** of the vector $\overrightarrow{PQ}$ is the length of any of its equivalent directed line segment representations. In particular, if $\mathbf{v} = \langle x_2 - x_1, y_2 - y_1 \rangle$ is the position vector for $\overrightarrow{PQ}$ (Figure 9.4), then the distance formula gives the magnitude or length of **v**, denoted by the symbol $|\mathbf{v}|$ or $\|\mathbf{v}\|$.

The **magnitude** or **length** of the vector $\mathbf{v} = \overrightarrow{PQ}$ is

$$|\mathbf{v}| = \sqrt{v_1^2 + v_2^2} = \sqrt{(x_2 - x_1)^2 + (y_2 - y_1)^2}$$

(Figure 9.4).

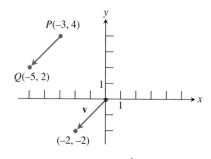

FIGURE 9.5 The vector $\overrightarrow{PQ}$ equals the position vector $v = \langle -2, -2 \rangle$. (Example 2)

Example 2   Finding the Component Form and Length of a Vector

Find the **(a)** component form and **(b)** length of the vector with initial point $P = (-3, 4)$ and terminal point $Q = (-5, 2)$.

Solution

(a) The position vector **v** representing $\overrightarrow{PQ}$ has components $v_1 = x_2 - x_1 = (-5) - (-3) = -2$ and $v_2 = y_2 - y_1 = 2 - 4 = -2$ (Figure 9.5). The component form of $\overrightarrow{PQ}$ is

$$v = \langle -2, -2 \rangle.$$

(b) The length of $v = \overrightarrow{PQ}$ is

$$|v| = \sqrt{(-2)^2 + (-2)^2} = 2\sqrt{2}.$$

Example 3   Force Moving a Cart

A small cart is being pulled along a smooth horizontal floor with a 20 lb force **F** making a 45° angle to the floor (Figure 9.6). What is the effective force moving the cart forward?

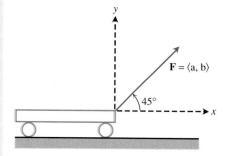

FIGURE 9.6 The force pulling the cart forward is represented by the vector **F** of length 20 (pounds) making an angle of 45° with the horizontal ground (positive *x*-axis). (Example 3)

Solution   The effective force is the horizontal component of $\mathbf{F} = \langle a, b \rangle$, given by

$$a = |\mathbf{F}| \cos 45° = (20) \left(\frac{\sqrt{2}}{2} \right) \approx 14.14 \text{ lb}.$$

Zero Vector and Unit Vectors

The only vector with length 0 is the **zero vector**

$$\mathbf{0} = \langle 0, 0 \rangle.$$

The zero vector is also the only vector with no specific direction.

Any vector **v** of length 1 is a **unit vector.** If $\mathbf{v} = \langle v_1, v_2 \rangle$ makes an angle θ with the positive *x*-axis, then

$$v_1 = |\mathbf{v}| \cos \theta = \cos \theta \qquad |\mathbf{v}| = 1$$
$$v_2 = |\mathbf{v}| \sin \theta = \sin \theta$$

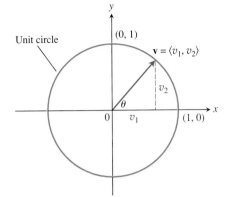

FIGURE 9.7 The unit vector $\mathbf{v} = \langle v_1, v_2 \rangle$ has length 1, so $v_1 = \cos \theta$ and $v_2 = \sin \theta$, where θ is the angle $\mathbf{v}$ makes with the positive x-axis. As θ varies from 0 to 2π, the terminal point of $\mathbf{v}$ traces the unit circle.

(Figure 9.7). In summary,

A unit vector $\mathbf{v}$ in the plane having angle θ with the positive x-axis is represented by

$$\mathbf{v} = \langle \cos \theta, \sin \theta \rangle.$$

As θ varies from 0 to 2π, the terminal point of a unit vector $\mathbf{v}$ traces the unit circle counterclockwise, taking into account all possible directions.

Vector Algebra Operations

Two principal operations involving vectors are *vector addition* and *scalar multiplication*.

Definitions Vector Addition and Multiplication of a Vector by a Scalar

Let $\mathbf{u} = \langle u_1, u_2 \rangle$, $\mathbf{v} = \langle v_1, v_2 \rangle$ be vectors with k a scalar (real number).

Addition: $\mathbf{u} + \mathbf{v} = \langle u_1, u_2 \rangle + \langle v_1, v_2 \rangle = \langle u_1 + v_1, u_2 + v_2 \rangle$

Scalar multiplication: $k\mathbf{u} = \langle ku_1, ku_2 \rangle$

The definition of vector addition is illustrated geometrically in Figure 9.8a, where the initial point of one vector is placed at the terminal point of the other. Another interpretation is shown in Figure 9.8b (called the **parallelogram law** of addition), where the sum, called the **resultant vector,** is the diagonal of the parallelogram. In physics, forces add vectorially as do velocities, accelerations, and so on.

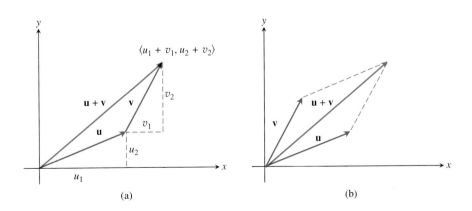

FIGURE 9.8 (a) Geometric interpretation of the vector sum. (b) The parallelogram law of vector addition.

A geometric interpretation of the product $k\mathbf{u}$ of the scalar k and vector $\mathbf{u}$ is displayed in Figure 9.9. First, if $k > 0$, then $k\mathbf{u}$ has the same direction as $\mathbf{u}$; if $k < 0$, then the direction of $k\mathbf{u}$ is opposite to that of $\mathbf{u}$. Comparing the lengths of $\mathbf{u} = \langle u_1, u_2 \rangle$ and $k\mathbf{u}$, we see that

$$|k\mathbf{u}| = \sqrt{(ku_1)^2 + (ku_2)^2} = \sqrt{k^2(u_1{}^2 + u_2{}^2)}$$
$$= \sqrt{k^2}\sqrt{u_1{}^2 + u_2{}^2} = |k|\,|\mathbf{u}|.$$

That is, the length of $k\mathbf{u}$ is the absolute value of the scalar k times the length of $\mathbf{u}$. In particular, the vector $(-1)\,\mathbf{u} = -\mathbf{u}$ has the same length as $\mathbf{u}$ but points in the opposite direction.

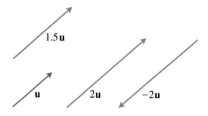

FIGURE 9.9 Scalar multiples of $\mathbf{u}$.

By the **difference** $\mathbf{u} - \mathbf{v}$ of two vectors, we mean

$$\mathbf{u} - \mathbf{v} = \mathbf{u} + (-\mathbf{v}).$$

If $\mathbf{u} = \langle u_1, u_2 \rangle$ and $\mathbf{v} = \langle v_1, v_2 \rangle$, then

$$\mathbf{u} - \mathbf{v} = \langle u_1 - v_1, u_2 - v_2 \rangle.$$

Note that $(\mathbf{u} - \mathbf{v}) + \mathbf{v} = \mathbf{u}$, so adding the vector $(\mathbf{u} - \mathbf{v})$ to $\mathbf{v}$ gives $\mathbf{u}$ (Figure 9.10a). Figure 9.10b shows the difference $\mathbf{u} - \mathbf{v}$ as the sum $\mathbf{u} + (-\mathbf{v})$.

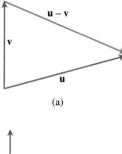

(a)

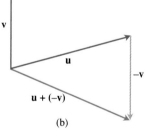

(b)

FIGURE 9.10 (a) The vector $\mathbf{u} - \mathbf{v}$, when added to $\mathbf{v}$, gives $\mathbf{u}$. (b) $\mathbf{u} - \mathbf{v} = \mathbf{u} + (-\mathbf{v})$.

Example 4   Performing Operations on Vectors

Let $\mathbf{u} = \langle -1, 3 \rangle$ and $\mathbf{v} = \langle 4, 7 \rangle$. Find

(a) $2\mathbf{u} + 3\mathbf{v}$ (b) $\mathbf{u} - \mathbf{v}$ (c) $\left| \dfrac{1}{2}\mathbf{u} \right|$.

Solution

(a) $2\mathbf{u} + 3\mathbf{v} = 2\langle -1, 3 \rangle + 3\langle 4, 7 \rangle$
$$= \langle 2(-1) + 3(4),\ 2(3) + 3(7) \rangle = \langle 10, 27 \rangle$$

(b) $\mathbf{u} - \mathbf{v} = \langle -1, 3 \rangle - \langle 4, 7 \rangle$
$$= \langle -1 - 4,\ 3 - 7 \rangle = \langle -5, -4 \rangle$$

(c) $\left| \dfrac{1}{2}\mathbf{u} \right| = \left| \left\langle -\dfrac{1}{2}, \dfrac{3}{2} \right\rangle \right| = \sqrt{\left(-\dfrac{1}{2} \right)^2 + \left(\dfrac{3}{2} \right)^2} = \dfrac{1}{2}\sqrt{10}$

Vector operations have many of the properties of ordinary arithmetic. These properties are readily verified using the definitions of vector addition and multiplication by a scalar.

Properties of Vector Operations
Let **u**, **v**, **w** be vectors and a, b be scalars.

1. $\mathbf{u} + \mathbf{v} = \mathbf{v} + \mathbf{u}$ 2. $(\mathbf{u} + \mathbf{v}) + \mathbf{w} = \mathbf{u} + (\mathbf{v} + \mathbf{w})$

3. $\mathbf{u} + \mathbf{0} = \mathbf{u}$ 4. $\mathbf{u} + (-\mathbf{u}) = \mathbf{0}$

5. $0\mathbf{u} = \mathbf{0}$ 6. $1\mathbf{u} = \mathbf{u}$

7. $a(b\mathbf{u}) = (ab)\mathbf{u}$ 8. $a(\mathbf{u} + \mathbf{v}) = a\mathbf{u} + a\mathbf{v}$

9. $(a + b)\mathbf{u} = a\mathbf{u} + b\mathbf{u}$

An important application of vectors occurs in navigation.

Example 5 Finding Ground Speed and Direction

A Boeing® 727® airplane, flying due east at 500 mph in still air, encounters a 70 mph tailwind acting in the direction 60° north of east. The airplane holds its compass heading due east but, because of the wind, acquires a new ground speed and direction. What are they?

Solution   If **u** = the velocity of the airplane alone and **v** = the velocity of the tailwind, then $|\mathbf{u}| = 500$ and $|\mathbf{v}| = 70$ (Figure 9.11). We need to find the magnitude and direction of the *resultant vector* **u** + **v**. If we let the positive x-axis represent east and the positive y-axis represent north, then the component forms of **u** and **v** are

$$\mathbf{u} = \langle 500, 0 \rangle \qquad \text{and} \qquad \mathbf{v} = \langle 70 \cos 60°, 70 \sin 60° \rangle = \langle 35, 35\sqrt{3} \rangle.$$

Therefore,

$$\mathbf{u} + \mathbf{v} = \langle 535, 35\sqrt{3} \rangle$$

$$|\mathbf{u} + \mathbf{v}| = \sqrt{535^2 + (35\sqrt{3})^2} \approx 538.4$$

and

$$\theta = \tan^{-1} \frac{35\sqrt{3}}{535} \approx 6.5°. \qquad \text{Fig. 9.11}$$

Interpret
The new ground speed of the airplane is about 538.4 mph, and its new direction is about 6.5° north of east.

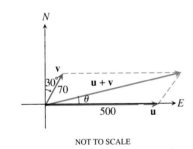

FIGURE 9.11 Vectors representing the velocities of the airplane and tailwind in Example 5.

Standard Unit Vectors

Any vector $\mathbf{v} = \langle a, b \rangle$ in the plane can be written as a *linear combination* of the two **standard unit vectors**

$$\mathbf{i} = \langle 1, 0 \rangle \qquad \text{and} \qquad \mathbf{j} = \langle 0, 1 \rangle$$

as follows:

$$\mathbf{v} = \langle a, b \rangle = \langle a, 0 \rangle + \langle 0, b \rangle = a\langle 1, 0 \rangle + b\langle 0, 1 \rangle$$

$$= a\mathbf{i} + b\mathbf{j}.$$

The vector **v** is a **linear combination** of the vectors **i** and **j**; the scalar a is the **horizontal** or **i-component** of **v** and the scalar b is the **vertical** or **j-component** of **v**. The **slope** of a nonvertical vector $\mathbf{v} = \langle a, b \rangle$ is the slope shared by the lines parallel to it. Thus, if $a \neq 0$, the vector **v** has slope b/a (Figure 9.12).

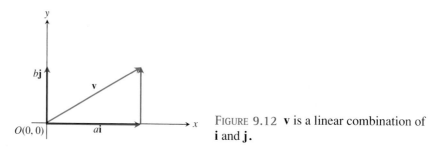

FIGURE 9.12 **v** is a linear combination of **i** and **j**.

Example 6   Expressing Vectors as Linear Combinations of i and j

Let $P = (-1, 5)$ and $Q = (3, 2)$. Write the vector $\mathbf{v} = \overrightarrow{PQ}$ as a linear combination of **i** and **j** and find its slope.

Solution   The component form of **v** is $\langle 3 - (-1), 2 - 5 \rangle = \langle 4, -3 \rangle$. Thus,

$$\mathbf{v} = \langle 4, -3 \rangle = 4\mathbf{i} + (-3)\mathbf{j} = 4\mathbf{i} - 3\mathbf{j}.$$

The slope of **v** is $-3/4$.

Length and Direction

In studying motion, we often want to know the direction an object is headed and how fast it is going.

Example 7   Expressing Velocity as Speed Times Direction

If $\mathbf{v} = 3\mathbf{i} - 4\mathbf{j}$ is a velocity vector, express **v** as a product of its speed times a unit vector in the direction of motion.

Solution   Speed is the magnitude (length) of **v**:

$$|\mathbf{v}| = \sqrt{(3)^2 + (-4)^2} = \sqrt{9 + 16} = 5.$$

The vector $\mathbf{v}/|\mathbf{v}|$ has the same direction as **v**:

$$\frac{\mathbf{v}}{|\mathbf{v}|} = \frac{3\mathbf{i} - 4\mathbf{j}}{5} = \frac{3}{5}\mathbf{i} - \frac{4}{5}\mathbf{j}.$$

Moreover, $\mathbf{v}/|\mathbf{v}|$ is a unit vector:

$$\left| \frac{\mathbf{v}}{|\mathbf{v}|} \right| = \sqrt{\left(\frac{3}{5} \right)^2 + \left(-\frac{4}{5} \right)^2} = \sqrt{\frac{9}{25} + \frac{6}{25}} = 1.$$

Thus,

$$\mathbf{v} = 3\mathbf{i} - 4\mathbf{j} = 5\left(\frac{3}{5}\mathbf{i} - \frac{4}{5}\mathbf{j} \right).$$

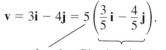

Length   Direction of motion
(speed)

Generally, if $\mathbf{v} \neq \mathbf{0}$, then its length $|\mathbf{v}|$ is not zero and

$$\left| \frac{1}{|\mathbf{v}|} \mathbf{v} \right| = \frac{1}{|\mathbf{v}|} |\mathbf{v}| = 1.$$

That is, $\mathbf{v}/|\mathbf{v}|$ is a unit vector in the direction of $\mathbf{v}$. We can therefore express $\mathbf{v}$ in terms of its two important features, length and direction, by writing $\mathbf{v} = |\mathbf{v}|(\mathbf{v}/|\mathbf{v}|)$.

If $\mathbf{v} \neq \mathbf{0}$, then

1. $\dfrac{\mathbf{v}}{|\mathbf{v}|}$ is a unit vector in the direction of $\mathbf{v}$;

2. the equation $\mathbf{v} = |\mathbf{v}| \dfrac{\mathbf{v}}{|\mathbf{v}|}$ expresses $\mathbf{v}$ in terms of its length and direction.

The unit vector $\mathbf{v}/|\mathbf{v}|$ is called the **direction** of $\mathbf{v}$. Thus, $\mathbf{v} = 5((3/5)\mathbf{i} - (4/5)\mathbf{j})$ expresses the velocity vector in Example 7 as a *product* of its length and direction.

Tangents and Normals

When an object is moving along a path in the plane (or in space), its velocity is a vector tangent to the path. Moreover, if the object is speeding up or slowing down, forces are acting in the tangent direction and perpendicular (or normal) to it. (We investigate motion along a path in the plane in Section 9.3.)

A vector is **tangent** or **normal** to a curve at a point P if it is parallel or normal, respectively, to the line that is tangent to the curve at P. Example 8 shows how to find such vectors for a differentiable curve $y = f(x)$ in the plane.

Example 8 Finding Vectors Tangent and Normal to a Curve

An object is moving along the curve

$$y = \frac{x^3}{2} + \frac{1}{2}.$$

Find unit vectors tangent and normal to the curve at the point $(1, 1)$.

Solution   We find the unit vectors that are parallel and normal to the curve's tangent line at $(1, 1)$ (Figure 9.13).

The slope of the line tangent to the curve at $(1, 1)$ is

$$y' = \frac{3x^2}{2} \bigg|_{x=1} = \frac{3}{2}.$$

We look for a unit vector with this slope. The vector $\mathbf{v} = 2\mathbf{i} + 3\mathbf{j}$ has slope $3/2$, as does every nonzero multiple of $\mathbf{v}$. To find a multiple of $\mathbf{v}$ that is a unit vector, we divide $\mathbf{v}$ by

$$|\mathbf{v}| = \sqrt{2^2 + 3^2} = \sqrt{13},$$

obtaining

$$\mathbf{u} = \frac{\mathbf{v}}{|\mathbf{v}|} = \frac{2}{\sqrt{13}}\mathbf{i} + \frac{3}{\sqrt{13}}\mathbf{j}.$$

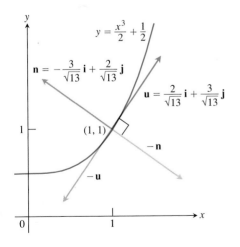

FIGURE 9.13 The unit tangent and normal vectors at the point $(1, 1)$ on the curve $y = (x^3/2) + 1/2$. (Example 8)

The vector **u** is tangent to the curve at $(1, 1)$ because it has the same direction as **v**. Of course,

$$-\mathbf{u} = -\frac{2}{\sqrt{13}}\mathbf{i} - \frac{3}{\sqrt{13}}\mathbf{j},$$

which points in the opposite direction, is also tangent to the curve at $(1, 1)$. Without some additional requirement (such as specifying the direction of motion), there is no reason to prefer one of these vectors to the other.

To find unit vectors normal to the curve at $(1, 1)$, we look for unit vectors whose slopes are the negative reciprocal of the slope of **u**. This is quickly done by interchanging the scalar components of **u** and changing the sign of one of them. We obtain

$$\mathbf{n} = -\frac{3}{\sqrt{13}}\mathbf{i} + \frac{2}{\sqrt{13}}\mathbf{j} \quad \text{and} \quad -\mathbf{n} = \frac{3}{\sqrt{13}}\mathbf{i} - \frac{2}{\sqrt{13}}\mathbf{j}.$$

Again, either one will do. The vectors have opposite directions but both are normal to the curve at $(1, 1)$. (See Figure 9.13.)

EXERCISES 9.1

Component Form

In Exercises 1–8, let $\mathbf{u} = \langle 3, -2 \rangle$ and $\mathbf{v} = \langle -2, 5 \rangle$. Find the **(a)** component form and **(b)** magnitude (length) of the vector.

1. $3\mathbf{u}$

2. $-2\mathbf{v}$

3. $\mathbf{u} + \mathbf{v}$

4. $\mathbf{u} - \mathbf{v}$

5. $2\mathbf{u} - 3\mathbf{v}$

6. $-2\mathbf{u} + 5\mathbf{v}$

7. $\dfrac{3}{5}\mathbf{u} + \dfrac{4}{5}\mathbf{v}$

8. $-\dfrac{5}{13}\mathbf{u} + \dfrac{12}{13}\mathbf{v}$

In Exercises 9–16, find the component form of the vector.

9. The vector $\overrightarrow{PQ}$, where $P = (1, 3)$ and $Q = (2, -1)$

10. The vector $\overrightarrow{OP}$ where O is the origin and P is the midpoint of segment RS, where $R = (2, -1)$ and $S = (-4, 3)$

11. The vector from the point $A = (2, 3)$ to the origin

12. The sum of $\overrightarrow{AB}$ and $\overrightarrow{CD}$, where $A = (1, -1)$, $B = (2, 0)$, $C = (-1, 3)$, and $D = (-2, 2)$

13. The unit vector that makes an angle $\theta = 2\pi/3$ with the positive x-axis

14. The unit vector that makes an angle $\theta = -3\pi/4$ with the positive x-axis

15. The unit vector obtained by rotating the vector $\langle 0, 1 \rangle$ 120° counterclockwise about the origin

16. The unit vector obtained by rotating the vector $\langle 1, 0 \rangle$ 135° counterclockwise about the origin

Geometry and Calculation

In Exercises 17 and 18, copy vectors **u**, **v**, and **w** head to tail as needed to sketch the indicated vector.

17.

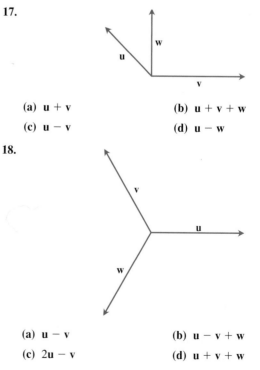

(a) $\mathbf{u} + \mathbf{v}$

(b) $\mathbf{u} + \mathbf{v} + \mathbf{w}$

(c) $\mathbf{u} - \mathbf{v}$

(d) $\mathbf{u} - \mathbf{w}$

18.

(a) $\mathbf{u} - \mathbf{v}$

(b) $\mathbf{u} - \mathbf{v} + \mathbf{w}$

(c) $2\mathbf{u} - \mathbf{v}$

(d) $\mathbf{u} + \mathbf{v} + \mathbf{w}$

Using Linear Combinations

Express the vectors in Exercises 19–24 in the form $a\mathbf{i} + b\mathbf{j}$ and sketch them as arrows in the coordinate plane beginning at the origin.

19. $\overrightarrow{P_1P_2}$ if P_1 is the point $(5, 7)$ and P_2 is the point $(2, 9)$

20. $\overrightarrow{P_1P_2}$ if P_1 is the point $(1, 2)$ and P_2 is the point $(-3, 5)$

21. $\overrightarrow{AB}$ if A is the point $(-5, 3)$ and B is the point $(-10, 8)$

22. $\overrightarrow{AB}$ if A is the point $(-7, -8)$ and B is the point $(6, 11)$

23. $\overrightarrow{P_1P_2}$ if P_1 is the point $(1, 3)$ and P_2 is the point $(2, -1)$

24. $\overrightarrow{P_3P_4}$ if P_3 is the point $(1, 3)$ and P_4 is the midpoint of the line segment P_1P_2 joining $P_1(2, -1)$ and $P_2(-4, 3)$

Unit Vectors

Sketch the vectors in Exercises 25–28 and express each vector in the form $a\mathbf{i} + b\mathbf{j}$.

25. The unit vectors $\mathbf{u} = (\cos\theta)\mathbf{i} + (\sin\theta)\mathbf{j}$ for $\theta = \pi/6$ and $\theta = 2\pi/3$. Include the circle $x^2 + y^2 = 1$ in your sketch.

26. The unit vectors $\mathbf{u} = (\cos\theta)\mathbf{i} + (\sin\theta)\mathbf{j}$ for $\theta = -\pi/4$ and $\theta = -3\pi/4$. Include the circle $x^2 + y^2 = 1$ in your sketch.

27. The unit vector obtained by rotating $\mathbf{j}$ counterclockwise $3\pi/4$ rad about the origin

28. The unit vector obtained by rotating $\mathbf{j}$ clockwise $2\pi/3$ rad about the origin

In Exercises 29–32, find a unit vector in the direction of the given vector.

29. $\langle 3, 4 \rangle$

30. $\langle 4, -3 \rangle$

31. $\langle -15, 8 \rangle$

32. $\langle -5, -2 \rangle$

For the vectors in Exercises 33 and 34, find unit vectors $\mathbf{u} = (\cos\theta)\mathbf{i} + (\sin\theta)\mathbf{j}$ in the same direction.

33. $6\mathbf{i} - 8\mathbf{j}$

34. $-\mathbf{i} + 3\mathbf{j}$

Length and Direction

In Exercises 35 and 36, express each vector as a product of its length and direction.

35. $5\mathbf{i} + 12\mathbf{j}$

36. $2\mathbf{i} - 3\mathbf{j}$

37. Find the unit vectors that are parallel to the vector $3\mathbf{i} - 4\mathbf{j}$ (two vectors in all).

38. Find a vector of length 2 whose direction is the opposite of the direction of the vector $-\mathbf{i} + 2\mathbf{j}$. How many such vectors are there?

Tangent and Normal Vectors

In Exercises 39–42, find the unit vectors that are tangent and normal to the curve at the given point (four vectors in all). Then sketch the vectors and curve together.

39. $y = x^2$, $(2, 4)$

40. $x^2 + 2y^2 = 6$, $(2, 1)$

41. $y = \tan^{-1} x$, $(1, \pi/4)$

42. $y = \displaystyle\sum_{n=0}^{\infty} \frac{x^n}{n!}$, $(0, 1)$

In Exercises 43–46, find the unit vectors that are tangent and normal to the curve at the given point (four vectors in all).

43. $3x^2 + 8xy + 2y^2 - 3 = 0$, $(1, 0)$

44. $x^2 - 6xy + 8y^2 - 2x - 1 = 0$, $(1, 1)$

45. $y = \int_0^x \sqrt{3 + t^4}\, dt$, $(0, 0)$

46. $y = \int_e^x \ln(\ln t)\, dt$, $(e, 0)$

Theory and Applications

47. *Linear combination* Let $\mathbf{u} = 2\mathbf{i} + \mathbf{j}$, $\mathbf{v} = \mathbf{i} + \mathbf{j}$, and $\mathbf{w} = \mathbf{i} - \mathbf{j}$. Find scalars a and b such that $\mathbf{u} = a\mathbf{v} + b\mathbf{w}$.

48. *Linear combination* Let $\mathbf{u} = \mathbf{i} - 2\mathbf{j}$, $\mathbf{v} = 2\mathbf{i} + 3\mathbf{j}$, and $\mathbf{w} = \mathbf{i} + \mathbf{j}$. Write $\mathbf{u} = \mathbf{u}_1 + \mathbf{u}_2$, where $\mathbf{u}_1$ is parallel to $\mathbf{v}$ and $\mathbf{u}_2$ is parallel to $\mathbf{w}$. (See Exercise 47.)

49. *Force vector* You are pulling on a suitcase with a force $\mathbf{F}$ (pictured here) whose magnitude is $|\mathbf{F}| = 10$ lb. Find the $\mathbf{i}$- and $\mathbf{j}$-components of $\mathbf{F}$.

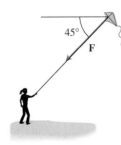

50. *Force vector* A kite string exerts a 12 lb pull ($|\mathbf{F}| = 12$) on a kite and makes a $45°$ angle with the horizontal. Find the horizontal and vertical components of $\mathbf{F}$.

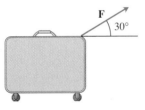

51. *Velocity* An airplane is flying in the direction $25°$ west of north at 800 km/h. Find the component form of the velocity of the airplane, assuming that the positive x-axis represents due east and the positive y-axis represents due north.

52. *Velocity* An airplane is flying in the direction $10°$ east of south at 600 km/h. Find the component form of the velocity of the airplane, assuming that the positive x-axis represents due east and the positive y-axis represents due north.

53. *Location* A bird flies from its nest 5 km in the direction 60° north of east, where it stops to rest on a tree. It then flies 10 km in the direction due southeast and lands atop a telephone pole. Place an *xy*-coordinate system so that the origin is the bird's nest, the *x*-axis points east, and the *y*-axis points north.

  (a) At what point is the tree located?

  (b) At what point is the telephone pole?

54. *Location* A bird flies from its nest 7 km in the direction northeast, where it stops to rest on a tree. It then flies 8 km in the direction 30° south of west and lands atop a telephone pole. Place an *xy*-coordinate system so that the origin is the bird's nest, the *x*-axis points east, and the *y*-axis points north.

  (a) At what point is the tree located?

  (b) At what point is the telephone pole?

9.2   Dot Products

Angle Between Vectors • Laws of the Dot Product • Perpendicular (Orthogonal) Vectors • Vector Projections • Work • Writing a Vector as a Sum of Orthogonal Vectors

If a force $\mathbf{F}$ is applied to a particle moving along a path, we often need to know the magnitude of the force in the direction of motion. If $\mathbf{v}$ is parallel to the tangent line to the path at the point where $\mathbf{F}$ is applied, then we want the magnitude of $\mathbf{F}$ in the direction of $\mathbf{v}$. Figure 9.14 shows that the scalar quantity we seek is the length $|\mathbf{F}|\cos\theta$, where θ is the angle between the two vectors $\mathbf{F}$ and $\mathbf{v}$.

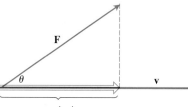

Length $= |\mathbf{F}|\cos\theta$

FIGURE 9.14 The magnitude of the force $\mathbf{F}$ in the direction of vector $\mathbf{v}$ is the length $|\mathbf{F}|\cos\theta$ of the projection of $\mathbf{F}$ onto $\mathbf{v}$.

In this section, you learn how to calculate easily the angle between two vectors directly from their components. A key part of the calculation is an expression called the *dot product*. Dot products are also called *scalar* products because the product results in a scalar, not a vector. After investigating the dot product, we apply it to finding the projection of one vector onto another (as displayed in Figure 9.14) and to finding the work done by a constant force acting through a displacement.

Angle Between Vectors

When two nonzero vectors $\mathbf{u}$ and $\mathbf{v}$ are placed so their initial points coincide, they form an angle θ of measure $0 \le \theta \le \pi$ (Figure 9.15). This angle is the **angle between u and v**.

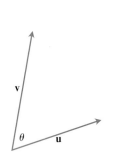

FIGURE 9.15 The angle between $\mathbf{u}$ and $\mathbf{v}$.

Theorem 1 gives a formula we can use to determine the angle between two vectors.

> **Theorem 1** Angle Between Two Vectors
>
> The angle θ between two nonzero vectors $\mathbf{u} = \langle u_1, u_2 \rangle$ and $\mathbf{v} = \langle v_1, v_2 \rangle$ is given by
>
> $$\theta = \cos^{-1} \frac{u_1 v_1 + u_2 v_2}{|\mathbf{u}||\mathbf{v}|}.$$

Before proving Theorem 1 (which is a consequence of the law of cosines), let's focus attention on the expression $u_1 v_1 + u_2 v_2$ in the calculation for θ.

> **Definition** Dot Product (Inner Product)
>
> The **dot product** (or **inner product**) $\mathbf{u} \cdot \mathbf{v}$ ("$\mathbf{u}$ dot $\mathbf{v}$") of vectors $\mathbf{u} = \langle u_1, u_2 \rangle$ and $\mathbf{v} = \langle v_1, v_2 \rangle$ is the number
>
> $$\mathbf{u} \cdot \mathbf{v} = u_1 v_1 + u_2 v_2.$$

Example 1 Finding Dot Products

(a) $\langle 1, -2 \rangle \cdot \langle -6, 2 \rangle = (1)(-6) + (-2)(2)$
$$= -6 - 4 = -10$$

(b) $\left(\frac{1}{2}\mathbf{i} + 3\mathbf{j} \right) \cdot (4\mathbf{i} - \mathbf{j}) = \left(\frac{1}{2} \right)(4) + (3)(-1)$
$$= 2 - 3 = -1$$

We can use the dot product to rewrite the formula in Theorem 1 for finding the angle between two vectors.

> **Corollary** Angle Between Two Vectors
>
> The angle between nonzero vectors $\mathbf{u}$ and $\mathbf{v}$ is
>
> $$\theta = \cos^{-1} \left(\frac{\mathbf{u} \cdot \mathbf{v}}{|\mathbf{u}||\mathbf{v}|} \right).$$

Example 2 Finding an Angle of a Triangle

Find the angle θ in the triangle ABC determined by the vertices $A = (0, 0)$, $B = (3, 5)$, and $C = (5, 2)$ (Figure 9.16).

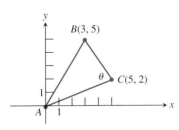

FIGURE 9.16 The triangle in Example 2.

Solution   The angle θ is the angle between the vectors $\overrightarrow{CA}$ and $\overrightarrow{CB}$. The component forms of these two vectors are

$$\overrightarrow{CA} = \langle -5, -2 \rangle \quad \text{and} \quad \overrightarrow{CB} = \langle -2, 3 \rangle.$$

First we calculate the dot product and magnitudes of these two vectors.

$$\overrightarrow{CA} \cdot \overrightarrow{CB} = (-5)(-2) + (-2)(3) = 4$$
$$|\overrightarrow{CA}| = \sqrt{(-5)^2 + (-2)^2} = \sqrt{29}$$
$$|\overrightarrow{CB}| = \sqrt{(-2)^2 + (3)^2} = \sqrt{13}$$

Then applying the corollary to Theorem 1, we have

$$\theta = \cos^{-1}\left(\frac{\overrightarrow{CA} \cdot \overrightarrow{CB}}{|\overrightarrow{CA}||\overrightarrow{CB}|}\right)$$

$$= \cos^{-1}\left(\frac{4}{(\sqrt{29})(\sqrt{13})}\right)$$

$$\approx 78.1° \quad \text{or} \quad 1.36 \text{ radians.}$$

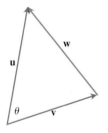

FIGURE 9.17 The parallelogram law of addition of vectors gives $\mathbf{w} = \mathbf{u} - \mathbf{v}$.

Proof of Theorem 1   Applying the law of cosines to the triangle in Figure 9.17, we find that

$$|\mathbf{w}|^2 = |\mathbf{u}|^2 + |\mathbf{v}|^2 - 2|\mathbf{u}||\mathbf{v}|\cos\theta$$
$$2|\mathbf{u}||\mathbf{v}|\cos\theta = |\mathbf{u}|^2 + |\mathbf{v}|^2 - |\mathbf{w}|^2.$$

Because $\mathbf{w} = \mathbf{u} - \mathbf{v}$, the component form of $\mathbf{w}$ is $\langle u_1 - v_1, u_2 - v_2 \rangle$. Thus,

$$|\mathbf{u}|^2 = \left(\sqrt{u_1^2 + u_2^2}\right)^2 = u_1^2 + u_2^2$$
$$|\mathbf{v}|^2 = \left(\sqrt{v_1^2 + v_2^2}\right)^2 = v_1^2 + v_2^2$$
$$|\mathbf{w}|^2 = \left(\sqrt{(u_1 - v_1)^2 + (u_2 - v_2)^2}\right)^2 = (u_1 - v_1)^2 + (u_2 - v_2)^2$$
$$= (u_1^2 - 2u_1v_1 + v_1^2) + (u_2^2 - 2u_2v_2 + v_2^2)$$

and

$$|\mathbf{u}|^2 + |\mathbf{v}|^2 - |\mathbf{w}|^2 = 2(u_1v_1 + u_2v_2).$$

Therefore,

$$2|\mathbf{u}||\mathbf{v}|\cos\theta = |\mathbf{u}|^2 + |\mathbf{v}|^2 - |\mathbf{w}|^2 = 2(u_1v_1 + u_2v_2)$$
$$|\mathbf{u}||\mathbf{v}|\cos\theta = u_1v_1 + u_2v_2$$
$$\cos\theta = \frac{u_1v_1 + u_2v_2}{|\mathbf{u}||\mathbf{v}|}.$$

So

$$\theta = \cos^{-1}\left(\frac{u_1v_1 + u_2v_2}{|\mathbf{u}||\mathbf{v}|}\right).$$

Laws of the Dot Product

The dot product obeys many of the laws that hold for ordinary products of real numbers (scalars).

Properties of the Dot Products
If **u**, **v**, and **w** are any vectors and c is a scalar, then

1. $\mathbf{u} \cdot \mathbf{v} = \mathbf{v} \cdot \mathbf{u}$

2. $(c\mathbf{u}) \cdot \mathbf{v} = \mathbf{u} \cdot (c\mathbf{v}) = c(\mathbf{u} \cdot \mathbf{v})$

3. $\mathbf{u} \cdot (\mathbf{v} + \mathbf{w}) = \mathbf{u} \cdot \mathbf{v} + \mathbf{u} \cdot \mathbf{w}$

4. $\mathbf{u} \cdot \mathbf{u} = |\mathbf{u}|^2$

5. $\mathbf{0} \cdot \mathbf{u} = 0.$

CD-ROM
WEBsite

Historical Biography

Carl Friedrich Gauss
(1777 — 1855)

The properties are easy to prove using the definition. For instance, here are the proofs of Properties 1 and 3.

1. $\mathbf{u} \cdot \mathbf{v} = u_1 v_1 + u_2 v_2 = v_1 u_1 + v_2 u_2 = \mathbf{v} \cdot \mathbf{u}$

3. $\mathbf{u} \cdot (\mathbf{v} + \mathbf{w}) = \langle u_1, u_2 \rangle \cdot \langle v_1 + w_1, v_2 + w_2 \rangle$
$$= u_1(v_1 + w_1) + u_2(v_2 + w_2)$$
$$= u_1 v_1 + u_1 w_1 + u_2 v_2 + u_2 w_2$$
$$= (u_1 v_1 + u_2 v_2) + (u_1 w_1 + u_2 w_2)$$
$$= \mathbf{u} \cdot \mathbf{v} + \mathbf{u} \cdot \mathbf{w}$$

Perpendicular (Orthogonal) Vectors

Two nonzero vectors **u** and **v** are perpendicular or **orthogonal** if the angle between them is $\pi/2$. For such vectors, we automatically have $\mathbf{u} \cdot \mathbf{v} = 0$ because $\cos(\pi/2) = 0$. The converse is also true. If **u** and **v** are nonzero vectors with $\mathbf{u} \cdot \mathbf{v} = |\mathbf{u}||\mathbf{v}| \cos \theta = 0$, then $\cos \theta = 0$ and $\theta = \cos^{-1} 0 = \pi/2$.

Definition   Orthogonal Vectors
Vectors **u** and **v** are **orthogonal (perpendicular)** if and only if $\mathbf{u} \cdot \mathbf{v} = 0$.

Example 3   Applying the Definition of Orthogonality

(a) $\mathbf{u} = \langle 3, -2 \rangle$ and $\mathbf{v} = \langle 4, 6 \rangle$ are orthogonal because $\mathbf{u} \cdot \mathbf{v} = (3)(4) + (-2)(6) = 0.$

(b) $\mathbf{u} = \mathbf{i} + 2\mathbf{j}$ is orthogonal to $\mathbf{v} = -10\mathbf{i} + 5\mathbf{j}$ because $\mathbf{u} \cdot \mathbf{v} = (1)(-10) + (2)(5) = 0.$

(c) **0** is orthogonal to every vector **u** since $\mathbf{0} \cdot \mathbf{u} = 0$ from Property 5.

We now return to the problem of projecting one vector onto another, posed in the opening to this section.

Vector Projections

The **vector projection** of $\mathbf{u} = \overrightarrow{PQ}$ onto a nonzero vector $\mathbf{v} = \overrightarrow{PS}$ (Figure 9.18) is the vector $\overrightarrow{PR}$ determined by dropping a perpendicular from Q to the line PS. The notation for this vector is

$$\text{proj}_\mathbf{v}\ \mathbf{u} \qquad (\text{``the vector projection of } \mathbf{u} \text{ onto } \mathbf{v}\text{''}).$$

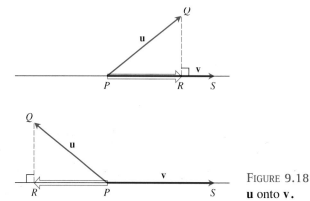

FIGURE 9.18 The vector projection of **u** onto **v**.

If $\mathbf{u}$ represents a force, then $\text{proj}_\mathbf{v}\ \mathbf{u}$ represents the effective force in the direction of $\mathbf{v}$ (Figure 9.19).

If the angle θ between $\mathbf{u}$ and $\mathbf{v}$ is acute, $\text{proj}_\mathbf{v}\ \mathbf{u}$ has length $|\mathbf{u}|\cos\theta$ and direction $\mathbf{v}/|\mathbf{v}|$ (Figure 9.20). If θ is obtuse, $\cos\theta < 0$ and $\text{proj}_\mathbf{v}\ \mathbf{u}$ has length $-|\mathbf{u}|\cos\theta$ and direction $-\mathbf{v}/|\mathbf{v}|$. In any case,

$$\text{proj}_\mathbf{v}\ \mathbf{u} = (|\mathbf{u}|\cos\theta)\frac{\mathbf{v}}{|\mathbf{v}|}$$

$$= \left(\frac{\mathbf{u}\cdot\mathbf{v}}{|\mathbf{v}|}\right)\frac{\mathbf{v}}{|\mathbf{v}|} \qquad |\mathbf{u}|\cos\theta = \frac{|\mathbf{u}||\mathbf{v}|\cos\theta}{|\mathbf{v}|}$$

$$= \left(\frac{\mathbf{u}\cdot\mathbf{v}}{|\mathbf{v}|^2}\right)\mathbf{v}. \qquad\qquad = \frac{\mathbf{u}\cdot\mathbf{v}}{|\mathbf{v}|}$$

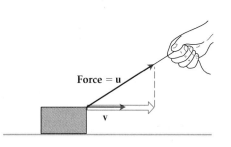

FIGURE 9.19 If we pull on the box with force **u**, the effective force moving the box forward in the direction **v** is the projection of **u** onto **v**.

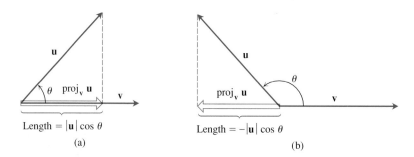

Length $= |\mathbf{u}|\cos\theta$ (a)

Length $= -|\mathbf{u}|\cos\theta$ (b)

FIGURE 9.20 The length of $\text{proj}_\mathbf{v}\ \mathbf{u}$ is (a) $|\mathbf{u}|\cos\theta$ if $\cos\theta \geq 0$ and (b) $-|\mathbf{u}|\cos\theta$ if $\cos\theta < 0$.

The number $|\mathbf{u}|\cos\theta$ is called the **scalar component of u in the direction of v.** To summarize,

---

Vector projection of **u** onto **v**:

$$\text{proj}_{\mathbf{v}}\,\mathbf{u} = \left(\frac{\mathbf{u}\cdot\mathbf{v}}{|\mathbf{v}|^2}\right)\mathbf{v}$$

Scalar component of **u** in the direction of **v**:

$$|\mathbf{u}|\cos\theta = \frac{\mathbf{u}\cdot\mathbf{v}}{|\mathbf{v}|} = \mathbf{u}\cdot\frac{\mathbf{v}}{|\mathbf{v}|}$$

Example 4   Finding Vector Projections and Scalar Components

Find the vector projection of a force $\mathbf{F} = 5\mathbf{i} + 2\mathbf{j}$ onto $\mathbf{v} = \mathbf{i} - 3\mathbf{j}$ and the scalar component of **F** in the direction of **v**.

Solution   The vector projection is

$$\text{proj}_{\mathbf{v}}\,\mathbf{F} = \left(\frac{\mathbf{F}\cdot\mathbf{v}}{|\mathbf{v}|^2}\right)\mathbf{v}$$

$$= \frac{5-6}{1+9}(\mathbf{i} - 3\mathbf{j}) = -\frac{1}{10}(\mathbf{i} - 3\mathbf{j})$$

$$= -\frac{1}{10}\mathbf{i} + \frac{3}{10}\mathbf{j}.$$

The scalar component of **F** in the direction of **v** is

$$|\mathbf{F}|\cos\theta = \frac{\mathbf{F}\cdot\mathbf{v}}{|\mathbf{v}|} = \frac{5-6}{\sqrt{1+9}} = -\frac{1}{10}.$$

Work

In Chapter 5, we calculated the work done by a constant force of magnitude F in moving an object through a distance d as $W = Fd$. That formula holds only if the force is directed along the line of motion. If a force **F** moving an object through a displacement $\mathbf{D} = \overrightarrow{PQ}$ has some other direction, the work is performed by the component of **F** in the direction of **D**. If θ is the angle between **F** and **D** (Figure 9.21), then

$$\text{Work} = \begin{pmatrix}\text{scalar component of }\mathbf{F}\\ \text{in the direction of }\mathbf{D}\end{pmatrix}(\text{length of }\mathbf{D})$$

$$= (|\mathbf{F}|\cos\theta)|\mathbf{D}|$$

$$= \mathbf{F}\cdot\mathbf{D}.$$

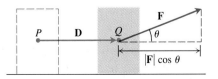

FIGURE 9.21 The work done by a constant force **F** during a displacement **D** is $(|\mathbf{F}|\cos\theta)|\mathbf{D}|$.

> **Definition**   Work Done by a Constant Force
>
> The **work** done by a constant force $\mathbf{F}$ acting through a displacement $\mathbf{D} = \overrightarrow{PQ}$ is
>
> $$W = \mathbf{F} \cdot \mathbf{D} = |\mathbf{F}||\mathbf{D}| \cos \theta,$$
>
> where θ is the angle between $\mathbf{F}$ and $\mathbf{D}$.

Work

The standard units of work are the foot-pound and the newton-meter, both force-distance units. The newton-meter is usually called a *joule*.

Example 5   Applying the Definition of Work

If $|\mathbf{F}| = 40$ N (newtons), $|\mathbf{D}| = 3$ m, and $\theta = 60°$, the work done by $\mathbf{F}$ in acting from P to Q is

$$
\begin{aligned}
\text{Work} &= |\mathbf{F}||\mathbf{D}| \cos \theta & \text{Definition}\\
&= (40)(3) \cos 60° & \text{Given values}\\
&= (120)(1/2)\\
&= 60 \text{ J (joules)}.
\end{aligned}
$$

We encounter more interesting work problems in Chapter 13 when we learn to find the work done by a variable force along a *path* in space.

Writing a Vector as a Sum of Orthogonal Vectors

We know one way to write a vector $\mathbf{u} = \langle a, b \rangle$ as a sum of orthogonal vectors:

$$\mathbf{u} = \langle a, b \rangle = a\mathbf{i} + b\mathbf{j}$$

(since $\mathbf{i} \cdot \mathbf{j} = 0$). Sometimes, however, it is more informative to express $\mathbf{u}$ as a different sum. In mechanics, for instance, we often need to write a vector $\mathbf{u}$ as a sum of a vector parallel to a given vector $\mathbf{v}$ and a vector orthogonal to $\mathbf{v}$. As an example, in studying the motion of a particle moving along a path in the plane (or space), it is desirable to know the components of the acceleration vector in the direction of the tangent to the path (at a point) and of the normal to the path. (These *tangential* and *normal components* of acceleration are investigated in Section 10.6.) The acceleration vector can then be expressed as the sum of its (vector) tangential and normal components (which reflect important geometric properties about the nature of the path itself, such as *curvature*). Velocity and acceleration vectors are studied in the next section.

Generally, for vectors $\mathbf{u}$ and $\mathbf{v}$, it is easy to see from Figure 9.22 that the vector

$$\mathbf{u} - \text{proj}_{\mathbf{v}}\, \mathbf{u}$$

is orthogonal to the projection vector $\text{proj}_{\mathbf{v}}\, \mathbf{u}$ (which has the same direction as $\mathbf{v}$). Thus,

$$\mathbf{u} = \text{proj}_{\mathbf{v}}\, \mathbf{u} + (\mathbf{u} - \text{proj}_{\mathbf{v}}\, \mathbf{u})$$

expresses $\mathbf{u}$ as a sum of orthogonal vectors.

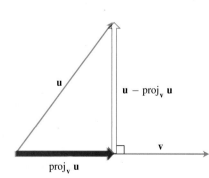

FIGURE 9.22 Writing $\text{proj}_{\mathbf{v}}\, \mathbf{u}$ as the sum of vectors parallel and orthogonal to $\mathbf{v}$.

> **How to Write u as a Vector Parallel to v Plus a Vector Orthogonal to v**
>
> $$\mathbf{u} = \text{proj}_\mathbf{v}\, \mathbf{u} + (\mathbf{u} - \text{proj}_\mathbf{v}\, \mathbf{u})$$
>
>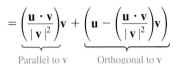
>
> $$= \underbrace{\left(\frac{\mathbf{u} \cdot \mathbf{v}}{|\mathbf{v}|^2}\right)\mathbf{v}}_{\text{Parallel to v}} + \underbrace{\left(\mathbf{u} - \left(\frac{\mathbf{u} \cdot \mathbf{v}}{|\mathbf{v}|^2}\right)\mathbf{v}\right)}_{\text{Orthogonal to v}}$$

Example 6   Sum of Orthogonal Vectors

In Example 8, Section 9.1, we found the vector $\mathbf{v} = 2\mathbf{i} + 3\mathbf{j}$ to be tangent to the path

$$y = \frac{x^3}{2} + \frac{1}{2}$$

at the point $(1, 1)$. If $\mathbf{u} = 4\mathbf{i} - \mathbf{j}$ is the acceleration at the point of a particle moving along the path, express $\mathbf{u}$ as the sum of a vector parallel to $\mathbf{v}$ and a vector orthogonal to $\mathbf{v}$.

Solution   With $\mathbf{u} \cdot \mathbf{v} = 8 - 3 = 5$ and $|\mathbf{v}|^2 = \mathbf{v} \cdot \mathbf{v} = 4 + 9 = 13$, we have

$$\mathbf{u} = \left(\frac{\mathbf{u} \cdot \mathbf{v}}{|\mathbf{v}|^2}\right)\mathbf{v} + \left(\mathbf{u} - \left(\frac{\mathbf{u} \cdot \mathbf{v}}{|\mathbf{v}|^2}\right)\mathbf{v}\right)$$

$$= \frac{5}{13}(2\mathbf{i} + 3\mathbf{j}) + \left(4\mathbf{i} - \mathbf{j} - \frac{5}{13}(2\mathbf{i} + 3\mathbf{j})\right)$$

$$= \left(\frac{10}{13}\mathbf{i} + \frac{15}{13}\mathbf{j}\right) + \left(\frac{42}{13}\mathbf{i} - \frac{28}{13}\mathbf{j}\right).$$

Check: The first vector in the sum is parallel to $\mathbf{v}$ because it is $(5/13)\mathbf{v}$. The second vector is orthogonal to $\mathbf{v}$ because

$$\left(\frac{42}{13}\mathbf{i} - \frac{28}{13}\mathbf{j}\right) \cdot (2\mathbf{i} + 3\mathbf{j}) = \frac{84}{13} - \frac{84}{13} = 0.$$

In the next chapter, we learn how to write velocity and acceleration vectors as linear combinations of other mutually orthogonal vectors.

EXERCISES 9.2

Calculations

In Exercises 1–6, find

   (a) $\mathbf{v} \cdot \mathbf{u}$, $|\mathbf{v}|$, $|\mathbf{u}|$

   (b) the cosine of the angle between $\mathbf{v}$ and $\mathbf{u}$

   (c) the scalar component of $\mathbf{u}$ in the direction of $\mathbf{v}$

   (d) the vector $\text{proj}_\mathbf{v}\, \mathbf{u}$.

1. $\mathbf{v} = 2\mathbf{i} - 4\mathbf{j}$, $\mathbf{u} = 2\mathbf{i} + 4\mathbf{j}$

2. $\mathbf{v} = 2\mathbf{i} + 10\mathbf{j}$, $\mathbf{u} = 2\mathbf{i} + 2\mathbf{j}$

3. $\mathbf{v} = -\mathbf{i} + \mathbf{j}$, $\mathbf{u} = \sqrt{2}\mathbf{i} + \sqrt{3}\mathbf{j}$

4. $\mathbf{v} = 5\mathbf{i} + \mathbf{j}$, $\mathbf{u} = 2\mathbf{i} + \sqrt{17}\mathbf{j}$

5. $v = \left\langle \dfrac{1}{\sqrt{2}}, \dfrac{1}{\sqrt{3}} \right\rangle, \quad u = \left\langle \dfrac{1}{\sqrt{2}}, -\dfrac{1}{\sqrt{3}} \right\rangle$

6. $v = \left\langle \dfrac{1}{\sqrt{2}}, \dfrac{1}{\sqrt{2}} \right\rangle, \quad u = \left\langle -\dfrac{1}{\sqrt{2}}, -\dfrac{1}{\sqrt{2}} \right\rangle$

Angles Between Vectors

Find the angles between the vectors in Exercises 7–10 to the nearest hundredth of a radian.

7. $v = 2i + j, \quad u = i + 2j$

8. $v = 2i - 2j, \quad u = 3i$

9. $v = \sqrt{3}i - 7j, \quad u = \sqrt{3}i + j$

10. $v = i + \sqrt{2}j, \quad u = -i + j$

11. *Triangle* Find the measures of the angles of the triangle whose vertices are $A = (-1, 0)$, $B = (2, 1)$, and $C = (1, -2)$.

12. *Rectangle* Find the measures of the angles between the diagonals of the rectangle whose vertices are $A = (1, 0)$, $B = (0, 3)$, $C = (3, 4)$, and $D = (4, 1)$.

Geometry and Examples

13. *Writing to Learn: Sums and differences* In the accompanying figure, it looks as if $v_1 + v_2$ and $v_1 - v_2$ are orthogonal. Is this mere coincidence, or are there circumstances under which we may expect the sum of two vectors to be orthogonal to their difference? Give reasons for your answer.

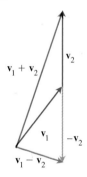

14. *Orthogonality on a circle* Suppose that AB is the diameter of a circle with center O and that C is a point on one of the two arcs joining A and B. Show that $\vec{CA}$ and $\vec{CB}$ are orthogonal.

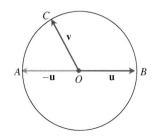

15. *Diagonals of a rhombus* Show that the diagonals of a rhombus (parallelogram with sides of equal length) are perpendicular.

16. *Perpendicular diagonals* Show that squares are the only rectangles with perpendicular diagonals.

17. *When parallelograms are rectangles* Prove that a parallelogram is a rectangle if and only if its diagonals are equal in length. (This fact is often exploited by carpenters.)

18. *Diagonal of parallelogram* Show that the indicated diagonal of the parallelogram determined by vectors u and v bisects the angle between u and v if $|u| = |v|$.

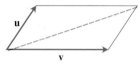

19. *Projectile motion* A gun with muzzle velocity of 1200 ft/sec is fired at an angle of 8° above the horizontal. Find the horizontal and vertical components of the velocity.

20. *Inclined plane* Suppose that a box is being towed up an inclined plane as shown in the figure. Find the force w needed to make the component of the force parallel to the inclined plane equal to 2.5 lb.

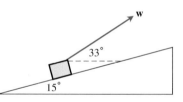

Theory and Examples

21. **(a)** *Cauchy-Schwartz inequality* Use the fact that $u \cdot v = |u||v| \cos \theta$ to show that the inequality $|u \cdot v| \le |u||v|$ holds for any vectors u and v.

   (b) *Writing to Learn* Under what circumstances, if any, does $|u \cdot v|$ equal $|u||v|$? Give reasons for your answer.

22. *Writing to Learn* Copy the axes and vector shown here. Then shade in the points (x, y) for which $(xi + yj) \cdot v \le 0$. Justify your answer.

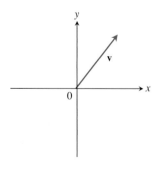

23. *Orthogonal unit vectors* If $\mathbf{u}_1$ and $\mathbf{u}_2$ are orthogonal unit vectors and $\mathbf{v} = a\mathbf{u}_1 + b\mathbf{u}_2$, find $\mathbf{v} \cdot \mathbf{u}_1$.

24. *Writing to Learn: Cancellation in dot products* In real-number multiplication, if $uv_1 = uv_2$ and $u \neq 0$, we can cancel the u and conclude that $v_1 = v_2$. Does the same rule hold for the dot product: If $\mathbf{u} \cdot \mathbf{v}_1 = \mathbf{u} \cdot \mathbf{v}_2$ and $\mathbf{u} \neq \mathbf{0}$, can you conclude that $\mathbf{v}_1 = \mathbf{v}_2$? Give reasons for your answer.

Equations for Lines in the Plane

25. *Line perpendicular to a vector* Show that the vector $\mathbf{v} = a\mathbf{i} + b\mathbf{j}$ is perpendicular to the line $ax + by = c$ by establishing that the slope of $\mathbf{v}$ is the negative reciprocal of the slope of the given line.

26. *Line parallel to a vector* Show that the vector $\mathbf{v} = a\mathbf{i} + b\mathbf{j}$ is parallel to the line $bx - ay = c$ by establishing that the slope of the line segment representing $\mathbf{v}$ is the same as the slope of the given line.

In Exercises 27–30, use the result of Exercise 25 to find an equation for the line through P perpendicular to $\mathbf{v}$. Then sketch the line. Include $\mathbf{v}$ in your sketch *as a vector starting at the origin.*

27. $P(2, 1), \quad \mathbf{v} = \mathbf{i} + 2\mathbf{j}$

28. $P(-1, 2), \quad \mathbf{v} = -2\mathbf{i} - \mathbf{j}$

29. $P(-2, -7), \quad \mathbf{v} = -2\mathbf{i} + \mathbf{j}$

30. $P(11, 10), \quad \mathbf{v} = 2\mathbf{i} - 3\mathbf{j}$

In Exercises 31–34, use the result of Exercise 26 to find an equation for the line through P parallel to $\mathbf{v}$. Then sketch the line. Include $\mathbf{v}$ in your sketch *as a vector starting at the origin.*

31. $P(-2, 1), \quad \mathbf{v} = \mathbf{i} - \mathbf{j}$

32. $P(0, -2), \quad \mathbf{v} = 2\mathbf{i} + 3\mathbf{j}$

33. $P(1, 2), \quad \mathbf{v} = -\mathbf{i} - 2\mathbf{j}$

34. $P(1, 3), \quad \mathbf{v} = 3\mathbf{i} - 2\mathbf{j}$

Work

35. *Work along a line* Find the work done by a force $\mathbf{F} = 5\,\mathbf{i}$ (magnitude 5 N) in moving an object along the line from the origin to the point $(1, 1)$ (distance in meters).

36. *Locomotive* The union Pacific's *Big Boy* locomotive could pull 6000-ton trains with a tractive effort (pull) of 602,148 N (135,375 lb). At this level of effort, about how much work did *Big Boy* do on the (approximately straight) 605 km journey from San Francisco to Los Angeles?

37. *Inclined plane* How much work does it take to slide a crate 20 m along a loading dock by pulling on it with a 200 N force at an angle of 30° from the horizontal?

38. *Sailboat* The wind passing over a boat's sail exerted a 1000 lb magnitude force $\mathbf{F}$ as shown here. How much work did the wind perform in moving the boat forward 1 mi? Answer in foot-pounds.

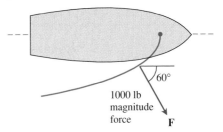

1000 lb
magnitude
force $\mathbf{F}$

Angles Between Lines in the Plane

The acute angle between intersecting lines that do not cross at right angles is the same as the angle determined by vectors normal to the lines or by the vectors parallel to the lines.

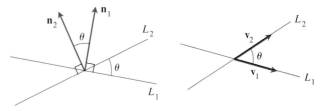

Use this fact and the results of Exercise 25 or 26 to find the acute angles between the lines in Exercises 39–44.

39. $3x + y = 5, \quad 2x - y = 4$

40. $y = \sqrt{3}x - 1, \quad y = -\sqrt{3}x + 2$

41. $\sqrt{3}x - y = -2, \quad x - \sqrt{3}y = 1$

42. $x + \sqrt{3}y = 1, \quad (1 - \sqrt{3})x + (1 + \sqrt{3})y = 8$

43. $3x - 4y = 3, \quad x - y = 7$

44. $12x + 5y = 1, \quad 2x - 2y = 3$

Angles Between Differentiable Curves

The angles between two differentiable curves at a point of intersection are the angles between the curves' tangent lines at these points. Find the angles between the curves in Exercises 45–48.

45. $y = (3/2) - x^2, \quad y = x^2$ (two points of intersection)

46. $x = (3/4) - y^2, \quad x = y^2 - (3/4)$ (two points of intersection)

47. $y = x^3, \quad x = y^2$ (two points of intersection)

48. $y = -x^2, \quad y = \sqrt[3]{x}$ (two points of intersection)

9.3 Vector-Valued Functions

Planar Curves • Limits and Continuity • Derivatives • Motion • Integrals

In this section, we show how to use the calculus of vectors to study the paths, velocities, and accelerations of bodies moving in the plane. This allows us to answer questions later about the motions of projectiles.

Planar Curves

When a particle moves through the plane during a time interval I, we think of the particle's coordinates as functions defined on I:

$$x = f(t), \qquad y = g(t), \qquad t \in I. \tag{1}$$

The points $(x, y) = (f(t), g(t))$, $t \in I$, make up the curve in the plane that is the particle's **path.** The equations and interval in Equation (1) parametrize the curve. The vector

$$\mathbf{r}(t) = \overrightarrow{OP} = \langle f(t), g(t) \rangle = f(t)\mathbf{i} + g(t)\mathbf{j} \tag{2}$$

from the origin to the particle's **position** $P(f(t), g(t))$ at time t is the particle's **position vector.** The functions f and g are the **component functions (components)** of the position vector. We think of the particle's path as the **curve traced by r** during the time interval I (Figure 9.23).

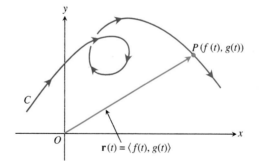

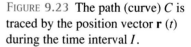

FIGURE 9.23 The path (curve) C is traced by the position vector $\mathbf{r}(t)$ during the time interval I.

Equation (2) defines $\mathbf{r}$ as a *vector function* of the real variable t on the interval I. More generally, a **vector function** or **vector-valued function** on a domain D is a rule that assigns a vector in the plane to each element in D. The curve traced by a vector function is its **graph.**

We refer to real-valued functions as **scalar functions** to distinguish them from vector functions. The components of $\mathbf{r}$ are scalar functions of t. When we define a vector-valued function by giving its component functions, we assume that the vector function's domain to be the common domain of the components.

Example 1   Graphing an Archimedes Spiral

Graph the vector function

$$\mathbf{r}(t) = (t \cos t)\mathbf{i} + (t \sin t)\mathbf{j}, \qquad t \geq 0.$$

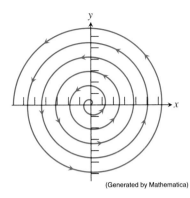

FIGURE 9.24 The graph of $\mathbf{r}(t) = (t \cos t)\mathbf{i} + (t \sin t)\mathbf{j}, t \geq 0$, is the curve $x = t \cos t, y = t \sin t, t \geq 0$. (Example 1)

(Generated by Mathematica)

Solution We can graph the vector function parametrically on a graphing calculator or computer using

$$x = t \cos t, \qquad y = t \sin t, \qquad t \geq 0.$$

As t increases from 0 to 2π, the point (x, y) starts at the origin $(0, 0)$ and then winds once around the origin, getting farther away from the origin as t increases. This spiral continues winding around the origin, getting farther and farther away as t increases beyond 2π. The spiral is shown in Figure 9.24.

Limits and Continuity

We define limits of vector functions in terms of their scalar components.

Definition   Limit

Let $\mathbf{r}(t) = f(t)\mathbf{i} + g(t)\mathbf{j}$. If

$$\lim_{t \to c} f(t) = L_1 \qquad \text{and} \qquad \lim_{t \to c} g(t) = L_2,$$

then the **limit** of $\mathbf{r}(t)$ as t approaches c is

$$\lim_{t \to c} \mathbf{r}(t) = \mathbf{L} = L_1\mathbf{i} + L_2\mathbf{j}.$$

Example 2   Finding a Limit of a Vector Function

If $\mathbf{r}(t) = (\cos t)\mathbf{i} + (\sin t)\mathbf{j}$, then

$$\lim_{t \to \pi/4} \mathbf{r}(t) = \left(\lim_{t \to \pi/4} \cos t \right)\mathbf{i} + \left(\lim_{t \to \pi/4} \sin t \right)\mathbf{j} = \frac{\sqrt{2}}{2}\mathbf{i} + \frac{\sqrt{2}}{2}\mathbf{j}.$$

We define continuity for vector functions in the same way we define continuity for scalar functions.

Definition   Continuity at a Point

A vector function $\mathbf{r}(t)$ is **continuous at a point** $t = c$ in its domain if

$$\lim_{t \to c} \mathbf{r}(t) = \mathbf{r}(c).$$

A vector function $\mathbf{r}(t)$ is **continuous** if it is continuous at every point in its domain. Since limits of vector functions are defined in terms of components, we have the following test for continuity.

Component Test for Continuity at a Point

The vector function $\mathbf{r}(t) = f(t)\mathbf{i} + g(t)\mathbf{j}$ is continuous at $t = c$ if and only if f and g are continuous at $t = c$.

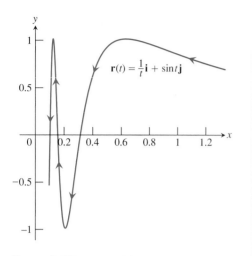

FIGURE 9.25 As $t > 0$ increases, the path of $\mathbf{r}(t)$ oscillates between $y = -1$ and $y = 1$, approaching the y-axis as the i-component approaches 0. As $t \to 0^+$, the i-component approaches ∞ and the j-component approaches 0 through positive values. (The portion of the graph to the left of the y-axis is not shown.)

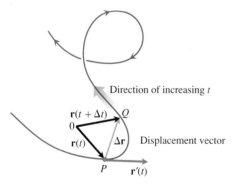

FIGURE 9.26 Between time t and time $t + \Delta t$, the particle moving along the path shown here undergoes the displacement $\overrightarrow{PQ} = \Delta \mathbf{r}$. The vector sum $\mathbf{r}(t) + \Delta \mathbf{r}$ gives the new position, $\mathbf{r}(t + \Delta t)$. As $\Delta t \to 0$, the point Q approaches P along the curve and the vector $\Delta \mathbf{r}/\Delta t$ approaches the limiting tangent position $\mathbf{r}'(t)$.

Example 3   Finding Points of Continuity and Discontinuity

(a) The vector function

$$\mathbf{r}(t) = (t \cos t)\mathbf{i} + (t \sin t)\mathbf{j}$$

is continuous everywhere because the component functions, $t \cos t$, and $t \sin t$ are continuous everywhere.

(b) The vector function

$$\mathbf{r}(t) = \frac{1}{t}\mathbf{i} + (\sin t)\mathbf{j}$$

is not continuous at $t = 0$ because the first component is not continuous at $t = 0$. It is a continuous vector function, however, because it is continuous on its domain, the set of all nonzero real numbers (Figure 9.25).

Derivatives

Suppose that $\mathbf{r}(t) = f(t)\mathbf{i} + g(t)\mathbf{j}$ is the position vector of a particle moving along a curve in the plane and that f and g are differentiable functions of t. Then (see Figure 9.26) the difference between the particle's positions at time $t + \Delta t$ and time t is $\Delta \mathbf{r} = \mathbf{r}(t + \Delta t) - \mathbf{r}(t)$. In terms of components,

$$\Delta \mathbf{r} = \mathbf{r}(t + \Delta t) - \mathbf{r}(t)$$
$$= [f(t + \Delta t)\mathbf{i} + g(t + \Delta t)\mathbf{j}] - [f(t)\mathbf{i} + g(t)\mathbf{j}]$$
$$= [f(t + \Delta t) - f(t)]\mathbf{i} + [g(t + \Delta t) - g(t)]\mathbf{j}.$$

As Δt approaches zero, three things seem to happen simultaneously. First, Q approaches P along the curve. Second, the secant line PQ seems to approach a limiting position tangent to the curve at P. Third, the quotient $\Delta \mathbf{r}/\Delta t$ approaches the limit

$$\lim_{\Delta t \to 0} \frac{\Delta \mathbf{r}}{\Delta t} = \left[\lim_{\Delta t \to 0} \frac{f(t + \Delta t) - f(t)}{\Delta t}\right]\mathbf{i} + \left[\lim_{\Delta t \to 0} \frac{g(t + \Delta t) - g(t)}{\Delta t}\right]\mathbf{j}$$

$$= \left[\frac{df}{dt}\right]\mathbf{i} + \left[\frac{dg}{dt}\right]\mathbf{j}.$$

We are therefore led by past experience to the following definition.

Definition   Derivative at a Point

The vector function $\mathbf{r}(t) = f(t)\mathbf{i} + g(t)\mathbf{j}$ has a **derivative (is differentiable) at t** if f and g have derivatives at t. The derivative is the vector function

$$\mathbf{r}'(t) = \frac{d\mathbf{r}}{dt} = \lim_{\Delta t \to 0} \frac{\mathbf{r}(t + \Delta t) - \mathbf{r}(t)}{\Delta t} = \frac{df}{dt}\mathbf{i} + \frac{dg}{dt}\mathbf{j}.$$

A vector function $\mathbf{r}$ is **differentiable** if it is differentiable at every point of its domain. The curve traced by $\mathbf{r}$ is **smooth** if $d\mathbf{r}/dt$ is continuous and never $\mathbf{0}$, that is,

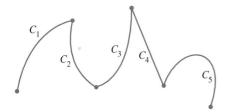

FIGURE 9.27 A piecewise smooth curve made by connecting five smooth curves end to end in continuous fashion.

if f and g have continuous first derivatives that are not simultaneously 0. On a smooth curve, there are no sharp corners or cusps.

The vector $d\mathbf{r}/dt$, when different from $\mathbf{0}$, is also a vector *tangent* to the curve at each point where it exists. The **tangent line** to the curve at a point $P = (f(a), g(a))$ is defined to be the line through P parallel to $d\mathbf{r}/dt$ at $t = a$ (Figure 9.26).

A curve that is made up of a finite number of smooth curves pieced together in a continuous fashion is **piecewise smooth** (Figure 9.27).

Example 4 Finding Derivatives

Find the derivative $d\mathbf{r}/dt$ of the vector function

$$\mathbf{r}(t) = (t \cos t)\mathbf{i} + (t \sin t)\mathbf{j}.$$

Solution

$$\mathbf{r}'(t) = \frac{d\mathbf{r}}{dt} = \frac{d}{dt}(t \cos t)\mathbf{i} + \frac{d}{dt}(t \sin t)\mathbf{j}$$
$$= (\cos t - t \sin t)\mathbf{i} + (\sin t + t \cos t)\mathbf{j}$$

Because the derivatives of vector functions are computed component by component, the rules for differentiating vector functions have the same form as the rules for differentiating scalar functions.

Differentiation Rules for Vector Functions

Let $\mathbf{u}$ and $\mathbf{v}$ be differentiable vector functions of t, $\mathbf{C}$ a constant vector, c any scalar, and f any differentiable scalar function.

1. *Constant Function Rule*: $\quad \dfrac{d}{dt}\mathbf{C} = \mathbf{0}$

2. *Scalar Multiple Rules*: $\quad \dfrac{d}{dt}[c\mathbf{u}(t)] = c\mathbf{u}'(t)$

$$\dfrac{d}{dt}[f(t)\mathbf{u}(t)] = f'(t)\mathbf{u}(t) + f(t)\mathbf{u}'(t)$$

3. *Sum Rule*: $\quad \dfrac{d}{dt}[\mathbf{u}(t) + \mathbf{v}(t)] = \mathbf{u}'(t) + \mathbf{v}'(t)$

4. *Difference Rule*: $\quad \dfrac{d}{dt}[\mathbf{u}(t) - \mathbf{v}(t)] = \mathbf{u}'(t) - \mathbf{v}'(t)$

5. *Dot Product Rule*: $\quad \dfrac{d}{dt}[\mathbf{u}(t) \cdot \mathbf{v}(t)] = \mathbf{u}'(t) \cdot \mathbf{v}(t) + \mathbf{u}(t) \cdot \mathbf{v}'(t)$

6. *Chain Rule*: $\quad \dfrac{d}{dt}[\mathbf{u}(f(t))] = f'(t)\mathbf{u}'(f(t))$

We will prove the Dot Product Rule but leave the rest for Exercises 37–40.

Proof of Rule 5   Suppose that

$$\mathbf{u} = u_1(t)\mathbf{i} + u_2(t)\mathbf{j} \quad \text{and} \quad \mathbf{v} = v_1(t)\mathbf{i} + v_2(t)\mathbf{j}.$$

Then

$$\frac{d}{dt}(\mathbf{u} \cdot \mathbf{v}) = \frac{d}{dt}(u_1 v_1 + u_2 v_2)$$

$$= u_1' v_1 + u_2' v_2 + u_1 v_1' + u_2 v_2'$$

$$= \quad \mathbf{u}' \cdot \mathbf{v} \quad + \quad \mathbf{u} \cdot \mathbf{v}'.$$

___

Example 5   Applying the Differentiation Rules

For the functions given by $\mathbf{u}(t) = 2t^3\mathbf{i} - t^2\mathbf{j}$, $\mathbf{v}(t) = (1/t)\mathbf{i} + (\sin t)\mathbf{j}$, and $f(t) = e^{-t}$, find

(a) $\dfrac{d}{dt}[f(t)\,\mathbf{u}(t)]$ **(b)** $\dfrac{d}{dt}[\mathbf{u}(t) + \mathbf{v}(t)]$

(c) $\dfrac{d}{dt}[\mathbf{u}(t) \cdot \mathbf{v}(t)]$.

Solution

(a) Because $f'(t) = e^{-t}$ and $\mathbf{u}'(t) = 6t^2\mathbf{i} - 2t\mathbf{j}$, we have

$$\frac{d}{dt}[f(t)\,\mathbf{u}(t)] = f'(t)\,\mathbf{u}(t) + f(t)\,\mathbf{u}'(t)$$

$$= (-e^{-t})(2t^3\mathbf{i} - t^2\mathbf{j}) + e^{-t}(6t^2\mathbf{i} - 2t\mathbf{j})$$

$$= e^{-t}(6t^2 - 2t^3)\mathbf{i} + e^{-t}(t^2 - 2t)\mathbf{j}$$

$$= 2t^2 e^{-t}(3 - t)\mathbf{i} + te^{-t}(t - 2)\mathbf{j}.$$

(b) $\mathbf{u}'(t) = 6t^2\mathbf{i} - 2t\mathbf{j}$ and $\mathbf{v}'(t) = -\dfrac{1}{t^2}\mathbf{i} + (\cos t)\mathbf{j}$ so that

$$\frac{d}{dt}[\mathbf{u}(t) + \mathbf{v}(t)] = \mathbf{u}'(t) + \mathbf{v}'(t)$$

$$= (6t^2\mathbf{i} - 2t\mathbf{j}) + \left(-\frac{1}{t^2}\mathbf{i} + (\cos t)\mathbf{j}\right)$$

$$= \left(6t^2 - \frac{1}{t^2}\right)\mathbf{i} + (\cos t - 2t)\mathbf{j}.$$

(c) Using the derivatives in part (b) and the Dot Product Rule, we have

$$\frac{d}{dt}[\mathbf{u}(t) \cdot \mathbf{v}(t)] = \mathbf{u}'(t) \cdot \mathbf{v}(t) + \mathbf{u}(t) \cdot \mathbf{v}'(t)$$

$$= (6t^2\mathbf{i} - 2t\mathbf{j}) \cdot \left(\frac{1}{t}\mathbf{i} + (\sin t)\mathbf{j}\right) + (2t^3\mathbf{i} - t^2\mathbf{j}) \cdot \left(-\frac{1}{t^2}\mathbf{i} + (\cos t)\mathbf{j}\right)$$

$$= (6t^2)\left(\frac{1}{t}\right) + (-2t)(\sin t) + (2t^3)\left(-\frac{1}{t^2}\right) + (-t^2)(\cos t)$$

$$= 6t - 2t \sin t - 2t - t^2 \cos t$$

$$= 4t - 2t \sin t - t^2 \cos t.$$

Observe that the derivative of the dot product of vector functions is a scalar function.

Check:

$$\frac{d}{dt}[\mathbf{u}(t) \cdot \mathbf{v}(t)] = \frac{d}{dt}(2t^2 - t^2 \sin t)$$

$$= 4t - 2t \sin t - t^2 \cos t.$$

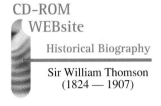

CD-ROM
WEBsite

Historical Biography

Sir William Thomson
(1824 — 1907)

Motion

Look once again at Figure 9.26. We drew the figure for Δt positive, so $\Delta \mathbf{r}$ points forward, in the direction of the motion. The vector $\Delta \mathbf{r}/\Delta t$ (not shown), having the same direction as $\Delta \mathbf{r}$, points forward also. Had Δt been negative, $\Delta \mathbf{r}$ would have pointed backwards, against the direction of motion. The quotient $\Delta \mathbf{r}/\Delta t$, however, being a negative scalar multiple of $\Delta \mathbf{r}$, would have once again pointed forward. No matter how $\Delta \mathbf{r}$ points, $\Delta \mathbf{r}/\Delta t$ points forward and we expect the vector $d\mathbf{r}/dt = \lim_{\Delta t \to 0} \Delta \mathbf{r}/\Delta t$, when different from $\mathbf{0}$, to do the same. This means that the derivative $d\mathbf{r}/dt$ is just what we want for modeling a particle's velocity. It points in the direction of motion and gives the rate of change of position with respect to time. For a smooth curve, the velocity is never zero; the particle does not stop or reverse direction.

CD-ROM
WEBsite

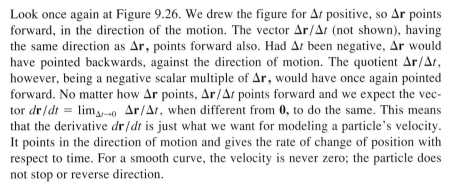

Definitions   Velocity, Speed, Acceleration, Direction of Motion

If $\mathbf{r}$ is the position vector of a particle moving along a smooth curve in the plane, then at any time t,

1. $\mathbf{v}(t) = \dfrac{d\mathbf{r}}{dt}$ is the particle's **velocity vector** and is tangent to the curve

2. $|\mathbf{v}(t)|$, the magnitude of $\mathbf{v}$, is the particle's **speed**

3. $\mathbf{a}(t) = \dfrac{d\mathbf{v}}{dt} = \dfrac{d^2\mathbf{r}}{dt^2}$, the derivative of velocity and the second derivative of position, is the particle's **acceleration vector**

4. $\dfrac{\mathbf{v}}{|\mathbf{v}|}$, a unit vector, is the **direction of motion.**

We can express the velocity of a moving particle as the product of its speed and direction (Example 7, Section 9.1).

$$\text{Velocity} = |\mathbf{v}|\left(\frac{\mathbf{v}}{|\mathbf{v}|}\right) = (\text{speed})(\text{direction})$$

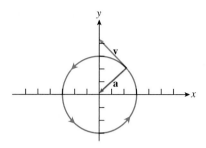

FIGURE 9.28 At $t = \pi/4$, the velocity vector $-(3/\sqrt{2})\mathbf{i} + (3/\sqrt{2})\mathbf{j}$ is tangent to the circle and the acceleration vector $-(3/\sqrt{2})\mathbf{i} - (3/\sqrt{2})\mathbf{j}$ is perpendicular to the tangent, pointing toward the center of the circle. (Example 6)

Example 6   Studying Motion on a Circle

The vector $\mathbf{r}(t) = (3\cos t)\mathbf{i} + (3\sin t)\mathbf{j}$ gives the position of a particle at time t moving counterclockwise on the circle of radius 3 centered at the origin (Figure 9.28). Find

(a) the velocity and acceleration vectors

(b) the velocity, acceleration, speed, and direction of motion at $t = \pi/4$

(c) $\mathbf{v} \cdot \mathbf{a}$. Interpret this result geometrically.

Solution

(a) $\mathbf{v} = \dfrac{d\mathbf{r}}{dt} = (-3\sin t)\mathbf{i} + (3\cos t)\mathbf{j}$

$\mathbf{a} = \dfrac{d\mathbf{v}}{dt} = (-3\cos t)\mathbf{i} - (3\sin t)\mathbf{j}$

(b) At $t = \pi/4$, the particle's velocity and acceleration are

Velocity: $\mathbf{v}\!\left(\dfrac{\pi}{4}\right) = \left(-3\sin\dfrac{\pi}{4}\right)\mathbf{i} + \left(3\cos\dfrac{\pi}{4}\right)\mathbf{j} = -\dfrac{3}{\sqrt{2}}\mathbf{i} + \dfrac{3}{\sqrt{2}}\mathbf{j}$

Acceleration: $\mathbf{a}\!\left(\dfrac{\pi}{4}\right) = \left(-3\cos\dfrac{\pi}{4}\right)\mathbf{i} - \left(3\sin\dfrac{\pi}{4}\right)\mathbf{j} = -\dfrac{3}{\sqrt{2}}\mathbf{i} - \dfrac{3}{\sqrt{2}}\mathbf{j}.$

Its speed and direction are

Speed: $\left|\mathbf{v}\!\left(\dfrac{\pi}{4}\right)\right| = \sqrt{\left(\dfrac{-3}{\sqrt{2}}\right)^2 + \left(\dfrac{3}{\sqrt{2}}\right)^2} = 3$

Direction: $\dfrac{\mathbf{v}(\pi/4)}{|\mathbf{v}(\pi/4)|} = \dfrac{-3/\sqrt{2}}{3}\mathbf{i} + \dfrac{3/\sqrt{2}}{3}\mathbf{j} = -\dfrac{1}{\sqrt{2}}\mathbf{i} + \dfrac{1}{\sqrt{2}}\mathbf{j}.$

(c) $\mathbf{v} \cdot \mathbf{a} = 9\sin t\cos t - 9\sin t\cos t = 0$

Thus, in this example, $\mathbf{v}$ and $\mathbf{a}$ are perpendicular for all values of t.

Figure 9.28 shows the path and the velocity and acceleration vectors at $t = \pi/4$.

Example 7   Studying Motion

The vector $\mathbf{r}(t) = (2t^3 - 3t^2)\mathbf{i} + (t^3 - 12t)\mathbf{j}$ gives the position of a moving particle at time t.

(a) Write an equation for the line tangent to the path of the particle at the point where $t = -1$.

(b) Find the coordinates of each point on the path where the horizontal component of the velocity is 0.

Solution

(a) $\mathbf{v}(t) = \dfrac{d\mathbf{r}}{dt} = (6t^2 - 6t)\mathbf{i} + (3t^2 - 12)\mathbf{j}$

At $t = -1$, $\mathbf{r}(-1) = -5\mathbf{i} + 11\mathbf{j}$ and $\mathbf{v}(-1) = 12\mathbf{i} - 9\mathbf{j}$. Thus, we want the equation of the line through $(-5, 11)$ with slope $-9/12 = -3/4$.

$$y - 11 = -\frac{3}{4}(x + 5) \qquad \text{or} \qquad y = -\frac{3}{4}x + \frac{29}{4}$$

(b) The horizontal component of the velocity is $6t^2 - 6t$. It equals 0 when $t = 0$ and $t = 1$. The point corresponding to $t = 0$ is the origin $(0, 0)$; the point corresponding to $t = 1$ is $(-1, -11)$.

Integrals

A differentiable vector function $\mathbf{R}(t)$ is an **antiderivative** of a vector function $\mathbf{r}(t)$ on an interval I if $d\mathbf{R}/dt = \mathbf{r}$ at each point t of I. If $\mathbf{R}$ is an antiderivative of $\mathbf{r}$ on I, it can be shown, working one component at a time, that every antiderivative of $\mathbf{r}$ on I has the form $\mathbf{R} + \mathbf{C}$ for some constant vector $\mathbf{C}$ (Exercise 35).

> **Definition** Indefinite Integral
>
> The **indefinite integral** of $\mathbf{r}$ with respect to t is the set of all antiderivatives of $\mathbf{r}$, denoted by $\int \mathbf{r}(t)\, dt$. If $\mathbf{R}$ is any antiderivative of $\mathbf{r}$, then
>
> $$\int \mathbf{r}(t)\, dt = \mathbf{R}(t) + \mathbf{C}.$$

The usual arithmetic rules for indefinite integrals apply.

Example 8 Finding Antiderivatives

$$\int ((\cos t)\mathbf{i} - 2t\mathbf{j})\, dt = \left(\int \cos t\, dt\right)\mathbf{i} - \left(\int 2t\, dt\right)\mathbf{j} \qquad (3)$$

$$= (\sin t + C_1)\mathbf{i} - (t^2 + C_2)\mathbf{j} \qquad (4)$$

$$= (\sin t)\mathbf{i} - t^2\mathbf{j} + \mathbf{C} \qquad \mathbf{C} = C_1\mathbf{i} + C_2\mathbf{j}$$

As with integration of scalar functions, we recommend that you skip the steps in Equations 3 and 4 and go directly to the final form. Find an antiderivative for each component and add a constant vector at the end.

As with derivatives and indefinite integrals, definite integrals of vector functions are calculated component by component.

> **Definition** Definite Integral
>
> If the components of $\mathbf{r}(t) = f(t)\mathbf{i} + g(t)\mathbf{j}$ are integrable on $[a, b]$, then so is $\mathbf{r}$, and the **definite integral** of $\mathbf{r}$ from a to b is
>
> $$\int_a^b \mathbf{r}(t)\, dt = \left(\int_a^b f(t)\, dt\right)\mathbf{i} + \left(\int_a^b g(t)\, dt\right)\mathbf{j}.$$

Example 9 Evaluating Definite Integrals

$$\int_0^\pi ((\cos t)\mathbf{i} - 2t\mathbf{j})\, dt = \left(\int_0^\pi \cos t\, dt\right)\mathbf{i} - \left(\int_0^\pi 2t\, dt\right)\mathbf{j}$$

$$= \left(\sin t\Big]_0^\pi\right)\mathbf{i} - \left(t^2\Big]_0^\pi\right)\mathbf{j} = 0\mathbf{i} - \pi^2\mathbf{j} = -\pi^2\mathbf{j}$$

Example 10 Finding a Path

The velocity vector of a particle moving in the plane (scaled in meters) is

$$\frac{d\mathbf{r}}{dt} = \frac{1}{t+1}\mathbf{i} + 2t\mathbf{j}, \qquad t \ge 0.$$

(a) Find the particle's position as a vector function of t if $\mathbf{r} = (\ln 2)\mathbf{i}$ when $t = 1$.

(b) Find the distance the particle travels from $t = 0$ to $t = 2$.

Solution

(a) $\mathbf{r} = \left(\int \dfrac{dt}{t+1}\right)\mathbf{i} + \left(\int 2t\, dt\right)\mathbf{j} = (\ln (t+1))\mathbf{i} + t^2\mathbf{j} + \mathbf{C}$

$\mathbf{r}(1) = (\ln 2)\mathbf{i} + \mathbf{j} + \mathbf{C} = (\ln 2)\mathbf{i}$

Thus, $\mathbf{C} = -\mathbf{j}$ and

$$\mathbf{r} = (\ln (t+1))\mathbf{i} + (t^2 - 1)\mathbf{j}.$$

(b) The parametrization

$$x = \ln (t+1), \qquad y = t^2 - 1, \qquad 0 \le t \le 2$$

is smooth, and because x and y are increasing functions of t, the path is traversed exactly once as t increases from 0 to 2 (Figure 9.29). The length is

$$L = \int_0^2 \sqrt{\left(\frac{dx}{dt}\right)^2 + \left(\frac{dy}{dt}\right)^2}\, dt = \int_0^2 \sqrt{\left(\frac{1}{t+1}\right)^2 + (2t)^2}\, dt \approx 4.34 \text{ m}.$$

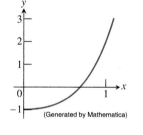

(Generated by Mathematica)

FIGURE 9.29 The path of the particle in Example 10 for $0 \le t \le 2$.

EXERCISES 9.3

Studying Motion

In Exercises 1–4, $\mathbf{r}(t)$ is the position vector of a particle in the plane at time t.

T **(a)** Draw the graph of the path of the particle.

(b) Find the velocity and acceleration vectors.

(c) Find the particle's speed and direction of motion at the given value of t.

(d) Write the particle's velocity at that time as the product of its speed and direction.

1. $\mathbf{r}(t) = (2 \cos t)\mathbf{i} + (3 \sin t)\mathbf{j}, \quad t = \pi/2$

2. $\mathbf{r}(t) = (\cos 2t)\mathbf{i} + (2 \sin t)\mathbf{j}, \quad t = 0$

3. $\mathbf{r}(t) = (\sec t)\mathbf{i} + (\tan t)\mathbf{j}, \quad t = \pi/6$

4. $\mathbf{r}(t) = (2 \ln (t+1))\mathbf{i} + (t^2)\mathbf{j}, \quad t = 1$

In Exercises 5–8, $\mathbf{r}(t)$ is the position vector of a particle in the plane at time t. Find the time, or times, in the given time interval when the velocity and acceleration vectors are perpendicular.

5. $\mathbf{r}(t) = (t - \sin t)\mathbf{i} + (1 - \cos t)\mathbf{j}, \quad 0 \le t \le 2\pi$

6. $\mathbf{r}(t) = (\sin t)\mathbf{i} + t\mathbf{j}, \quad t \ge 0$

7. $r(t) = (3 \cos t)i + (4 \sin t)j, \quad t \geq 0$

8. $r(t) = (5 \cos t)i + (5 \sin t)j, \quad t \geq 0$

In Exercises 9 and 10, $r(t)$ is the position vector of a particle in the plane at time t. Find the angle between the velocity and acceleration vectors at the given value of t.

9. $r(t) = (2 \cos t)i + (\sin t)j, \quad t = \pi/4$

10. $r(t) = (3t + 1)i + (t^2)j, \quad t = 0$

Limits and Continuity

In Exercises 11 and 12, (a) evaluate the limit, and (b) find the values of t for which the vector function is continuous and (c) discontinuous.

11. $\lim\limits_{t \to 3} \left[ti + \dfrac{t^2 - 9}{t^2 + 3t} j \right]$

12. $\lim\limits_{t \to 0} \left[\dfrac{\sin 2t}{t} i + (\ln (t + 1))j \right]$

Tangents and Normals

In Exercises 13 and 14, find an equation for the line that is (a) tangent and (b) normal to the curve $r(t)$ at the point determined by the given value of t.

13. $r(t) = (\sin t)i + (t^2 - \cos t)j, \quad t = 0$

14. $r(t) = (2 \cos t - 3)i + (3 \sin t + 1)j, \quad t = \pi/4$

Integration

In Exercises 15–18, evaluate the integral.

15. $\displaystyle\int_1^2 [(6 - 6t)i + 3\sqrt{t}\,j]\, dt$

16. $\displaystyle\int_{-\pi/4}^{\pi/4} [(\sin t)i + (1 + \cos t)j]\, dt$

17. $\displaystyle\int [(\sec t \tan t)i + (\tan t)j]\, dt$

18. $\displaystyle\int \left[\dfrac{1}{t} i + \dfrac{1}{5 - t} j \right] dt$

Initial Value Problems

In Exercises 19–22, solve the initial value problem for r as a vector function of t.

19. $\dfrac{dr}{dt} = \dfrac{3}{2}(t + 1)^{1/2} i + e^{-t}j, \quad r(0) = 0$

20. $\dfrac{dr}{dt} = (t^3 + 4t)i + tj, \quad r(0) = i + j$

21. $\dfrac{d^2r}{dt^2} = -32j, \quad r(0) = 100i, \quad \dfrac{dr}{dt}\Big|_{t=0} = 8i + 8j$

22. $\dfrac{d^2r}{dt^2} = -i - j, \quad r(0) = 10i + 10j, \quad \dfrac{dr}{dt}\Big|_{t=0} = 0$

Paths and Motion

23. *Finding distance traveled* The position of a particle in the plane at time t is given by

$$r(t) = (1 - \cos t)i + (t - \sin t)j.$$

Find the distance the particle travels along the path from $t = 0$ to $t = 2\pi/3$.

24. *Length of a path* Let C be the path traced by

$$r(t) = \left(\frac{1}{4} e^{4t} - t \right)i + (e^{2t})j, \qquad 0 \leq t \leq 2.$$

(a) Find the initial and terminal points of C.

(b) Find the length of C.

25. *Velocity on a path* The position of a particle is given by

$$r(t) = (\sin t)i + (\cos 2t)j.$$

(a) Find the velocity vector for the particle.

(b) For what values of t in the interval $0 \leq t \leq 2\pi$ is dr/dt equal to 0?

(c) *Writing to Learn* Find a Cartesian equation for a curve that contains the particle's path. What portion of the graph of the Cartesian equation is traced by the particle? Describe the motion as t increases from 0 to 2π.

26. *Revisiting Example 7* The position of a particle is given by $r(t) = (2t^3 - 3t^2)i + (t^3 - 12t)j$.

(a) Find dy/dx in terms of t.

(b) *Writing to Learn* Find the x- and y-coordinates for each critical point of the path (point where dy/dx is zero or does not exist). Does the path have a vertical or horizontal tangent at the critical point? Explain.

27. *Finding a position vector* At time $t = 0$, a particle is located at the point $(1, 2)$. It travels in a straight line to the point $(4, 1)$, has speed 2 at $(1, 2)$, and constant acceleration $3i - j$. Find an equation for the position vector $r(t)$ of the particle at time t.

28. *Studying a motion* The path of a particle for $t > 0$ is given by

$$r(t) = \left(t + \frac{2}{t} \right)i + (3t^2)j.$$

(a) Find the coordinates of each point on the path where the horizontal component of the velocity of the particle is zero.

(b) Find dy/dx when $t = 1$.

(c) Find d^2y/dx^2 when $y = 12$.

29. *Motion on circular paths* Each of equations (a) through (e) describes the motion of a particle having the same path, namely, the unit circle $x^2 + y^2 = 1$. Although the path of each particle in (a) through (e) is the same, the behavior, or "dynamics," of each particle is different. For each particle, answer the following questions.

i. Does the particle have constant speed? If so, what is its constant speed?

ii. Is the particle's acceleration vector always orthogonal to its velocity vector?

iii. Does the particle move clockwise or counterclockwise around the circle?

iv. Does the particle begin at the point $(1, 0)$?

(a) $\mathbf{r}(t) = (\cos t)\mathbf{i} + (\sin t)\mathbf{j}, \quad t \geq 0$

(b) $\mathbf{r}(t) = (\cos 2t)\mathbf{i} + (\sin 2t)\mathbf{j}, \quad t \geq 0$

(c) $\mathbf{r}(t) = \cos(t - \pi/2)\mathbf{i} + \sin(t - \pi/2)\mathbf{j}, \quad t \geq 0$

(d) $\mathbf{r}(t) = (\cos t)\mathbf{i} - (\sin t)\mathbf{j}, \quad t \geq 0$

(e) $\mathbf{r}(t) = \cos(t^2)\mathbf{i} + \sin(t^2)\mathbf{j}, \quad t \geq 0$

30. *Motion on a parabola* A particle moves along the top of the parabola $y^2 = 2x$ from left to right at a constant speed of 5 units per second. Find the velocity of the particle as it moves through the point $(2, 2)$.

Applications

31. *Flying a kite* The position of a kite is given by

$$\mathbf{r}(t) = \frac{t}{8}\mathbf{i} - \frac{3}{64}t(t - 160)\mathbf{j},$$

where $t \geq 0$ is measured in seconds and distance is measured in meters.

(a) How long is the kite above ground?

(b) How high is the kite at $t = 40$ sec?

(c) At what rate is the kite's altitude increasing at $t = 40$ sec?

(d) At what time does the kite start to lose altitude?

32. *Colliding particles* The paths of two particles for $t \geq 0$ are given by

$$\mathbf{r}_1(t) = (t - 3)\mathbf{i} + (t - 3)^2\mathbf{j},$$

$$\mathbf{r}_2(t) = \left(\frac{3t}{2} - 4\right)\mathbf{i} + \left(\frac{3t}{2} - 2\right)\mathbf{j}.$$

(a) Determine the exact time(s) at which the particles collide.

(b) Find the direction of motion of each particle at the time(s) of collision.

33. *A satellite in circular orbit* A satellite of mass m is moving at a constant speed v around a planet of mass M in a circular orbit of radius r_0, as measured from the planet's center of mass. Determine the satellite's orbital period T (the time to complete one full orbit), as follows.

(a) Coordinatize the orbital plane by placing the origin at the planet's center of mass, with the satellite on the x-axis at $t = 0$ and moving counterclockwise, as in the accompanying figure.

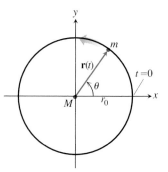

Let $\mathbf{r}(t)$ be the satellite's position vector at time t. Show that $\theta = vt/r_0$ and hence that

$$\mathbf{r}(t) = \left(r_0 \cos \frac{vt}{r_0}\right)\mathbf{i} + \left(r_0 \sin \frac{vt}{r_0}\right)\mathbf{j}.$$

(b) Find the acceleration of the satellite.

(c) According to Newton's law of gravitation, the gravitational force exerted on the satellite by the planet is directed toward the origin and is given by

$$\mathbf{F} = \left(-\frac{GmM}{r_0^2}\right)\frac{\mathbf{r}}{r_0},$$

where G is the universal constant of gravitation. Using Newton's second law, $\mathbf{F} = m\mathbf{a}$, show that $v^2 = GM/r_0$.

(d) Show that the orbital period T satisfies $vT = 2\pi r_0$.

(e) From parts (c) and (d), deduce that

$$T^2 = \frac{4\pi^2}{GM}r_0^3;$$

that is, the square of the period of a satellite in circular orbit is proportional to the cube of the radius from the orbital center.

34. *Rowing across a river* A straight river is 100 m wide. A rowboat leaves the far shore at time $t = 0$. The person in the boat rows at a rate of 20 m/min always toward the near shore. The velocity of the river at (x, y) is

$$\mathbf{v} = \left(-\frac{1}{250}(y - 50)^2 + 10\right)\mathbf{i} \quad \text{m/min}, \qquad 0 < y < 100.$$

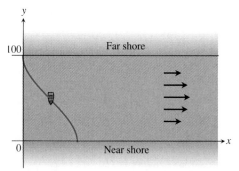

(a) Given that $\mathbf{r}(0) = 0\mathbf{i} + 100\mathbf{j}$, what is the position of the boat at time t?

(b) How far downstream will the boat land on the near shore?

Theory and Examples

35. *Antiderivatives of vector functions*

(a) Use Corollary 2 in Section 3.2 (a consequence of the Mean Value Theorem for scalar functions) to show that two vector functions $\mathbf{R}_1(t)$ and $\mathbf{R}_2(t)$ that have identical derivatives on an interval I differ by a constant vector value throughout I.

(b) Use the result in part (a) to show that if $\mathbf{R}(t)$ is any antiderivative of $\mathbf{r}(t)$ on I, then every other antiderivative of $\mathbf{r}(t)$ on I equals $\mathbf{R}(t) + \mathbf{C}$ for some constant vector $\mathbf{C}$.

36. *Constant-length vector functions* Let $\mathbf{v}$ be a differentiable vector function of t. Show that if $\mathbf{v} \cdot (d\mathbf{v}/dt) = 0$ for all t, then $|\mathbf{v}|$ is constant.

37. *Constant function rule* Prove that if $\mathbf{u}$ is the vector function with the constant value $\mathbf{C}$, then $d\mathbf{u}/dt = \mathbf{0}$.

38. *Scalar multiple rules*

(a) Prove that if $\mathbf{u}$ is a differentiable function of t and c is any real number, then

$$\frac{d(c\mathbf{u})}{dt} = c\frac{d\mathbf{u}}{dt}.$$

(b) Prove that if $\mathbf{u}$ is a differentiable function of t and f is a differentiable scalar function of t, then

$$\frac{d(f\mathbf{u})}{dt} = \frac{df}{dt}\mathbf{u} + f\frac{d\mathbf{u}}{dt}.$$

39. *Sum and difference rules* Prove that if $\mathbf{u}$ and $\mathbf{v}$ are differentiable functions of t, then

(a) $\dfrac{d}{dt}(\mathbf{u} + \mathbf{v}) = \dfrac{d\mathbf{u}}{dt} + \dfrac{d\mathbf{v}}{dt}.$

(b) $\dfrac{d}{dt}(\mathbf{u} - \mathbf{v}) = \dfrac{d\mathbf{u}}{dt} - \dfrac{d\mathbf{v}}{dt}.$

40. *Chain rule* Prove that if $\mathbf{u}$ is a differentiable vector function of s and $s = f(t)$ is a differentiable scalar function of t, then

$$\frac{d}{dt}[\mathbf{u}(f(t))] = f'(t)\mathbf{u}'(f(t)).$$

41. *Differentiable vector functions are continuous* Show that if $\mathbf{r}(t) = f(t)\mathbf{i} + g(t)\mathbf{j}$ is differentiable at $t = c$, then $\mathbf{r}$ is continuous at c as well.

42. *Integration properties* Establish the following properties of integrable vector functions.

(a) *Constant Scalar Multiple Rule:*

$$\int_a^b k\mathbf{r}(t)\,dt = k\int_a^b \mathbf{r}(t)\,dt$$

for any scalar constant k.

(b) *Sum and Difference Rules:*

$$\int_a^b (\mathbf{r}_1(t) \pm \mathbf{r}_2(t))\,dt = \int_a^b \mathbf{r}_1(t)\,dt \pm \int_a^b \mathbf{r}_2(t)\,dt$$

(c) *Constant Vector Multiple Rule:*

$$\int_a^b \mathbf{C} \cdot \mathbf{r}(t)\,dt = \mathbf{C} \cdot \int_a^b \mathbf{r}(t)\,dt$$

for any constant vector $\mathbf{C}$.

43. *Fundamental theorem of calculus* The Fundamental Theorem of Calculus for scalar functions of a real variable holds for vector functions of a real variable as well.

(a) Prove this by using the theorem for scalar functions to show that if a vector function $\mathbf{r}(t)$ is continuous for $a \le t \le b$, then

$$\frac{d}{dt}\int_a^t \mathbf{r}(q)\,dq = \mathbf{r}(t)$$

at every point t of $[a, b]$.

(b) Use the conclusion in part (b) of Exercise 35 to show that if $\mathbf{R}$ is any antiderivative of $\mathbf{r}$ on $[a, b]$, then

$$\int_a^b \mathbf{r}(t)\,dt = \mathbf{R}(b) - \mathbf{R}(a).$$

9.4 Modeling Projectile Motion

CD-ROM
WEBsite

Ideal Projectile Motion • Height, Flight Time, and Range • Ideal Trajectories Are Parabolic • Firing from (x_0, y_0) • Projectile Motion with Wind Gusts

When we shoot a projectile into the air, we usually want to know beforehand how far it will go (will it reach the target?), how high it will rise (will it clear the hill?), and when it will land (when do we get results?) We get this information from the di-

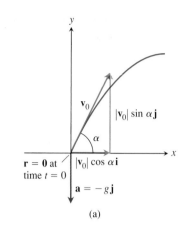

(a)

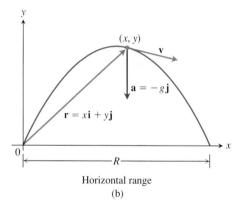

Horizontal range
(b)

FIGURE 9.30 (a) Position, velocity, acceleration, and launch angle at $t = 0$. (b) Position, velocity, and acceleration at a later time t

rection and magnitude of the projectile's initial velocity vector, using Newton's second law of motion.

Ideal Projectile Motion

We are going to model *ideal* projectile motion. This assumes that the projectile behaves like a particle moving in a vertical coordinate plane and that the only force acting on the projectile during its flight (close to Earth's surface) is the constant force of gravity, always pointing straight down.

We assume that the projectile is launched from the origin at time $t = 0$ into the first quadrant with an initial velocity $\mathbf{v}_0$ (Figure 9.30). If $\mathbf{v}_0$ makes an angle α with the horizontal, then

$$\mathbf{v}_0 = (|\mathbf{v}_0| \cos \alpha)\mathbf{i} + (|\mathbf{v}_0| \sin \alpha)\mathbf{j}.$$

If we use the simpler notation v_0 for the initial speed $|\mathbf{v}_0|$, then

$$\mathbf{v}_0 = (v_0 \cos \alpha)\mathbf{i} + (v_0 \sin \alpha)\mathbf{j}. \tag{1}$$

The projectile's initial position is

$$\mathbf{r}_0 = 0\mathbf{i} + 0\mathbf{j} = \mathbf{0}. \tag{2}$$

Newton's second law of motion says that the force acting on the projectile is equal to the projectile's mass m times its acceleration, or $m(d^2\mathbf{r}/dt^2)$ if $\mathbf{r}$ is the projectile's position vector and t is time. If the force is solely the gravitational force $-mg\mathbf{j}$, then

$$m\frac{d^2\mathbf{r}}{dt^2} = -mg\mathbf{j} \qquad \text{and} \qquad \frac{d^2\mathbf{r}}{dt^2} = -g\mathbf{j}.$$

We find $\mathbf{r}$ as a function of t by solving the following initial value problem.

Differential equation: $\dfrac{d^2\mathbf{r}}{dt^2} = -g\mathbf{j}$

Initial conditions: $\mathbf{r} = \mathbf{r}_0$ and $\dfrac{d\mathbf{r}}{dt} = \mathbf{v}_0$ when $t = 0$

The first integration gives

$$\frac{d\mathbf{r}}{dt} = -(gt)\mathbf{j} + \mathbf{v}_0.$$

A second integration gives

$$\mathbf{r} = -\frac{1}{2} gt^2\mathbf{j} + \mathbf{v}_0 t + \mathbf{r}_0.$$

Substituting the values of $\mathbf{v}_0$ and $\mathbf{r}_0$ from Equations 1 and 2 gives

$$\mathbf{r} = -\frac{1}{2} gt^2\mathbf{j} + \underbrace{(v_0 \cos \alpha)t\mathbf{i} + (v_0 \sin \alpha)t\mathbf{j}}_{\mathbf{v}_0 t} + \mathbf{0}$$

or

$$\mathbf{r} = (v_0 \cos \alpha)\, t\, \mathbf{i} + \left((v_0 \sin \alpha)\, t - \frac{1}{2} gt^2 \right) \mathbf{j}. \tag{3}$$

Equation (3) is the **vector equation** for ideal projectile motion. The angle α is the projectile's **launch angle (firing angle, angle of elevation),** and v_0, as we said before, is the projectile's **initial speed.**

The components of $\mathbf{r}$ give

$$x = (v_0 \cos \alpha)t \qquad \text{and} \qquad y = (v_0 \sin \alpha)t - \frac{1}{2}gt^2, \tag{4}$$

where x is the distance downrange and y is the height of the projectile at time $t \geq 0$.

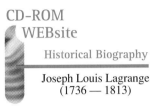

CD-ROM
WEBsite

Historical Biography

Joseph Louis Lagrange
(1736 — 1813)

Example 1 Firing an Ideal Projectile

A projectile is fired from the origin over horizontal ground at an initial speed of 500 m/sec and a launch angle of 60°. Where will the projectile be 10 sec later?

Solution We use Equation (3) with $v_0 = 500$, $\alpha = 60°$, $g = 9.8$, and $t = 10$ to find the projectile's components 10 sec after firing.

$$\mathbf{r} = (v_0 \cos \alpha)t\,\mathbf{i} + \left((v_0 \sin \alpha)t - \frac{1}{2}gt^2\right)\mathbf{j}$$

$$= (500)\left(\frac{1}{2}\right)(10)\mathbf{i} + \left((500)\left(\frac{\sqrt{3}}{2}\right)10 - \left(\frac{1}{2}\right)(9.8)(100)\right)\mathbf{j}$$

$$\approx 2500\mathbf{i} + 3840\mathbf{j}.$$

Interpret

Ten seconds after firing, the projectile is about 3840 m in the air and 2500 m downrange.

Height, Flight Time, and Range

Equation (3) enables us to answer most questions about the ideal motion for a projectile fired from the origin.

The projectile reaches its highest point when its vertical velocity component is zero, that is, when

$$\frac{dy}{dt} = v_0 \sin \alpha - gt = 0, \qquad \text{or} \qquad t = \frac{v_0 \sin \alpha}{g}.$$

For this value of t, the value of y is

$$y_{\max} = (v_0 \sin \alpha)\left(\frac{v_0 \sin \alpha}{g}\right) - \frac{1}{2}g\left(\frac{v_0 \sin \alpha}{g}\right)^2 = \frac{(v_0 \sin \alpha)^2}{2g}.$$

To find when the projectile lands when fired over horizontal ground, we set the vertical component equal to zero in Equation (3) and solve for t.

$$(v_0 \sin \alpha)t - \frac{1}{2}gt^2 = 0$$

$$t\left(v_0 \sin \alpha - \frac{1}{2}gt\right) = 0$$

$$t = 0, \qquad t = \frac{2v_0 \sin \alpha}{g}$$

Since 0 is the time the projectile is fired, $(2v_0 \sin \alpha)/g$ must be the time when the projectile strikes the ground.

To find the projectile's **range** R, the distance from the origin to the point of impact on horizontal ground, we find the value of the horizontal component when $t = (2v_0 \sin \alpha)/g$.

$$x = (v_0 \cos \alpha)t$$

$$R = (v_0 \cos \alpha)\left(\frac{2v_0 \sin \alpha}{g}\right) = \frac{v_0^2}{g}(2 \sin \alpha \cos \alpha) = \frac{v_0^2}{g} \sin 2\alpha$$

The range is largest when $\sin 2\alpha = 1$ or $\alpha = 45°$.

Height, Flight Time, and Range for Ideal Projectile Motion
For ideal projectile motion when an object is launched from the origin over a horizontal surface with initial speed v_0 and launch angle α:

$$\textit{Maximum height:} \qquad y_{\max} = \frac{(v_0 \sin \alpha)^2}{2g}$$

$$\textit{Flight time:} \qquad t = \frac{2v_0 \sin \alpha}{g}$$

$$\textit{Range:} \qquad R = \frac{v_0^2}{g} \sin 2\alpha.$$

Example 2   Investigating Ideal Projectile Motion

Find the maximum height, flight time, and range of a projectile fired from the origin over horizontal ground at an initial speed of 500 m/sec and a launch angle of 60° (same projectile as Example 1).

Solution

$$\text{Maximum height: } y_{\max} = \frac{(v_0 \sin \alpha)^2}{2g}$$

$$= \frac{(500 \sin 60°)^2}{2(9.8)} \approx 9566.33 \text{ m}$$

$$\text{Flight time: } \qquad t = \frac{2v_0 \sin \alpha}{g}$$

$$= \frac{2(500) \sin 60°}{9.8} \approx 88.37 \text{ sec}$$

$$\text{Range: } \qquad R = \frac{v_0^2}{g} \sin 2\alpha$$

$$= \frac{(500)^2 \sin 120°}{9.8} \approx 22{,}092.48 \text{ m}$$

From Equation (3), the position vector of the projectile is

$$\mathbf{r} = (v_0 \cos \alpha)t\,\mathbf{i} + \left((v_0 \sin \alpha)t - \frac{1}{2}gt^2\right)\mathbf{j}$$

$$= (500 \cos 60°)t\,\mathbf{i} + \left((500 \sin 60°)t - \frac{1}{2}(9.8)t^2\right)\mathbf{j}$$

$$= 250t\,\mathbf{i} + \left((250\sqrt{3})t - 4.9t^2\right)\mathbf{j}.$$

A graph of the projectile's path is shown in Figure 9.31.

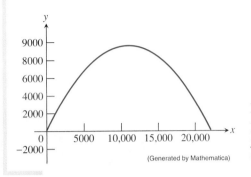

FIGURE 9.31 The graph of the parametric equations $x = 250t$, $y = (250\sqrt{3})t - 4.9t^2$ for $0 \leq t \leq 88.4$. (Example 2)

(Generated by Mathematica)

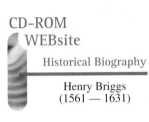

Ideal Trajectories Are Parabolic

It is often claimed that water from a hose traces a parabola in the air, but any one who looks closely enough will see this is not so. The air slows the water down, and its forward progress is too slow at the end to keep pace with the rate at which it falls.

What is really being claimed is that ideal projectiles move along parabolas, and this we can see from Equation (4). If we substitute $t = x/(v_0 \cos \alpha)$ from the first equation into the second, we obtain the Cartesian-coordinate equation

$$y = -\left(\frac{g}{2v_0{}^2 \cos^2 \alpha}\right)x^2 + (\tan \alpha)\,x.$$

This equation has the form $y = ax^2 + bx$, so its graph is a parabola.

Firing from (x_0, y_0)

If we fire our ideal projectile from the point (x_0, y_0) instead of the origin (Figure 9.32), the position vector for the path of motion is

$$\mathbf{v} = (x_0 + (v_0 \cos \alpha)\,t)\mathbf{i} + \left(y_0 + (v_0 \sin \alpha)\,t - \frac{1}{2}\,gt^2\right)\mathbf{j}, \qquad (5)$$

as you are asked to show in Exercise 19.

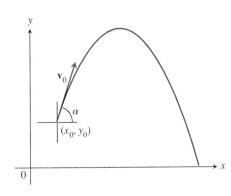

FIGURE 9.32 The path of a projectile fired from (x_0, y_0) with an initial velocity $\mathbf{v}_0$ at an angle of α degrees with the horizontal.

Example 3   Firing a Flaming Arrow

To open the 1992 Summer Olympics in Barcelona, bronze medalist archer Antonio Rebollo lit the Olympic torch with a flaming arrow (Figure 9.33). Suppose that Rebollo shot the arrow at a height of 6 ft above ground level 90 ft from the 70-ft-high cauldron, and he wanted the arrow to reach maximum height exactly 4 ft above the center of the cauldron (Figure 9.34).

FIGURE 9.33 Spanish archer Antonio Rebollo lights the Olympic torch in Barcelona with a flaming arrow.

(a) Express y_{max} in terms of the initial speed v_0 and firing angle α.

(b) Use $y_{max} = 74$ ft (Figure 9.34) and the result from part (a) to find the value of $v_0 \sin \alpha$.

(c) Find the value of $v_0 \cos \alpha$.

(d) Find the initial firing angle of the arrow.

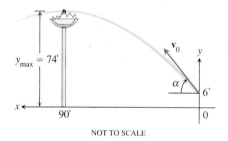

FIGURE 9.34 Ideal path of the arrow that lit the Olympic torch.

Solution

(a) We use a coordinate system in which the positive x-axis lies along the ground toward the left (to match the second photograph in Figure 9.33) and the coordinates of the flaming arrow at $t = 0$ are $x_0 = 0$ and $y_0 = 6$ (Figure 9.34). We have

$$y = y_0 + (v_0 \sin \alpha)t - \frac{1}{2}gt^2 \qquad \text{Equation (5), j-component}$$

$$= 6 + (v_0 \sin \alpha)t - \frac{1}{2}gt^2. \qquad y_0 = 6$$

We find the time when the arrow reaches its highest point by setting $dy/dt = 0$ and solving for t, obtaining

$$t = \frac{v_0 \sin \alpha}{g}.$$

For this value of t, the value of y is

$$y_{\max} = 6 + (v_0 \sin \alpha)\left(\frac{v_0 \sin \alpha}{g}\right) - \frac{1}{2}g\left(\frac{v_0 \sin \alpha}{g}\right)^2$$

$$= 6 + \frac{(v_0 \sin \alpha)^2}{2g}.$$

(b) Using $y_{\max} = 74$ and $g = 32$, we see from the preceeding equation in part (a) that

$$74 = 6 + \frac{(v_0 \sin \alpha)^2}{2(32)}$$

or

$$v_0 \sin \alpha = \sqrt{(68)(64)}.$$

(c) When the arrow reaches $y_{\max}$, the horizontal distance traveled to the center of the cauldron is $x = 90$ ft. We substitute the time to reach $y_{\max}$ from part (a) and the horizontal distance $x = 90$ ft into the **i**-component of Equation (5) to obtain

$$x = x_0 + (v_0 \cos \alpha)t \qquad \text{Equation (5), i-component}$$
$$90 = 0 + (v_0 \cos \alpha)t \qquad x = 90, x_0 = 0$$
$$= (v_0 \cos \alpha)\left(\frac{v_0 \sin \alpha}{g}\right). \qquad t = (v_0 \sin \alpha)/g$$

Solving this equation for $v_0 \cos \alpha$ and using $g = 32$ and the result from part (b), we have

$$v_0 \cos \alpha = \frac{90g}{v_0 \sin \alpha} = \frac{(90)(32)}{\sqrt{(68)(64)}}.$$

(d) Parts (b) and (c) together tell us that

$$\tan \alpha = \frac{v_0 \sin \alpha}{v_0 \cos \alpha} = \frac{(\sqrt{(68)(64)}\,)^2}{(90)(32)} = \frac{68}{45}$$

or

$$\alpha = \tan^{-1}\left(\frac{68}{45}\right) \approx 56.5°.$$

This is Rebollo's firing angle.

Projectile Motion with Wind Gusts

The next example shows how to account for another force acting on a projectile. We also assume that the path of the baseball in Example 4 lies in a vertical plane.

Example 4   Hitting a Baseball

A baseball is hit when it is 3 ft above the ground. It leaves the bat with initial speed of 152 ft/sec, making an angle of 20° with the horizontal. At the instant the ball is hit, an instantaneous gust of wind blows in the horizontal direction directly opposite the direction the ball is taking toward the out-field, adding a component of $-8.8\mathbf{i}$ (ft/sec) to the ball's initial velocity (8.8 ft/sec = 6 mph).

(a) Find a vector equation (position vector) for the path of the baseball.

(b) How high does the baseball go, and when does it reach maximum height?

(c) Assuming that the ball is not caught, find its range and flight time.

Solution

(a) Using Equation (1) and accounting for the gust of wind, the initial velocity of the baseball is

$$\mathbf{v}_0 = (v_0 \cos \alpha)\mathbf{i} + (v_0 \sin \alpha)\mathbf{j} - 8.8\mathbf{i}$$
$$= (152 \cos 20°)\mathbf{i} + (152 \sin 20°)\mathbf{j} - (8.8)\mathbf{i}$$
$$= (152 \cos 20° - 8.8)\mathbf{i} + (152 \sin 20°)\mathbf{j}.$$

The initial position is $\mathbf{r}_0 = 0\mathbf{i} + 3\mathbf{j}$. Integration of $d^2\mathbf{r}/dt^2 = -g\mathbf{j}$ gives

$$\frac{d\mathbf{r}}{dt} = (gt)\mathbf{j} + \mathbf{v}_0.$$

A second integration gives

$$\mathbf{r} = -\frac{1}{2} gt^2\mathbf{j} + \mathbf{v}_0 t + \mathbf{r}_0.$$

Substituting the values of $\mathbf{v}_0$ and $\mathbf{r}_0$ into the last equation gives the position vector of the baseball.

$$\mathbf{r} = -\frac{1}{2} gt^2\mathbf{j} + \mathbf{v}_0 t + \mathbf{r}_0$$
$$= -16t^2\mathbf{j} + (152 \cos 20° - 8.8)t\mathbf{i} + (152 \sin 20°)t\mathbf{j} + 3\mathbf{j}$$
$$= (152 \cos 20° - 8.8)t\mathbf{i} + (3 + (152 \sin 20°)t - 16t^2)\mathbf{j}.$$

(b) The baseball reaches its highest point when the vertical component of velocity is zero, or

$$\frac{dy}{dt} = 152 \sin 20° - 32t = 0.$$

Solving for t we find

$$t = \frac{152 \sin 20°}{32} \approx 1.62 \text{ sec.}$$

Substituting this time into the vertical component for $\mathbf{r}$ gives the maximum height

$$y_{max} = 3 + (152 \sin 20°)(1.62) - 16(1.62)^2$$
$$\approx 45.2 \text{ ft.}$$

That is, the maximum height of the baseball is about 45.2 ft, reached about 1.6 sec after leaving the bat.

(c) To find when the baseball lands, we set the vertical component for **r** equal to 0 and solve for t:

$$3 + (152 \sin 20°)t - 16t^2 = 0$$
$$3 + (51.99)t - 16t^2 = 0.$$

The solution values are about $t = 3.3$ sec and $t = -0.06$ sec. Substituting the positive time into the horizontal component for **r**, we find the range

$$R = (152 \cos 20° - 8.8)(3.3)$$
$$\approx 442.3 \text{ ft}.$$

Thus, the horizontal range is about 442.3 ft, and the flight time is about 3.3 sec.

In Exercises 29 through 31, we consider projectile motion when there is air resistance slowing down the flight.

EXERCISES 9.4

Projectile flights in the following exercises are to be treated as ideal unless stated otherwise. All launch angles are assumed to be measured from the horizontal. All projectiles are assumed to be launched from the origin over a horizontal surface unless stated otherwise.

1. *Travel time* A projectile is fired at a speed of 840 m/sec at an angle of 60°. How long will it take to get 21 km downrange?

2. *Finding muzzle speed* Find the muzzle speed of a gun whose maximum range is 24.5 km.

3. *Flight time and height* A projectile is fired with an initial speed of 500 m/sec at an angle of elevation of 45°.

   (a) When and how far away will the projectile strike?

   (b) How high overhead will the projectile be when it is 5 km downrange?

   (c) What is the greatest height reached by the projectile?

4. *Throwing a baseball* A baseball is thrown from the stands 32 ft above the field at an angle of 30° up from the horizontal. When and how far away will the ball strike the ground if its initial speed is 32 ft/sec?

5. *Shot put* An athlete puts a 16 lb shot at an angle of 45° to the horizontal from 6.5 ft above the ground at an initial speed of 44 ft/sec as suggested in the accompanying figure. How long after launch and how far from the inner edge of the stopboard does the shot land?

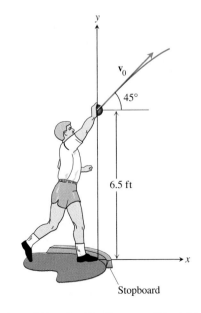

6. *(Continuation of Exercise 5)* Because of its initial elevation, the shot in Exercise 5 would have gone slightly farther if it had been launched at a 40° angle. How much farther? Answer in inches.

7. *Firing golf balls* A spring gun at ground level fires a golf ball at an angle of 45°. The ball lands 10 m away.

   (a) What was the ball's initial speed?

   (b) For the same initial speed, find the two firing angles that make the range 6 m.

8. *Beaming electrons* An electron in a TV tube is beamed horizontally at a speed of 5×10^6 m/sec toward the face of the tube 40 cm away. About how far will the electron drop before it hits?

9. *Finding golf ball speed* Laboratory tests designed to find how far golf balls of different hardness go when hit with a driver showed that a 100-compression ball hit with a club-head speed of 100 mph at a launch angle of 9° carried 248.8 yd. What was the launch speed of the ball? (It was more than 100 mph. At the same time the club head was moving forward, the compressed ball was kicking away from the club face, adding to the ball's forward speed.)

10. *Writing to Learn:* A *human cannonball* is to be fired with an initial speed of $v_0 = 80\sqrt{10}/3$ ft/sec. The circus performer (of the right caliber, naturally) hopes to land on a special cushion located 200 ft downrange at the same height as the muzzle of the cannon. The circus is being held in a large room with a flat ceiling 75 ft higher than the muzzle. Can the performer be fired to the cushion without striking the ceiling? If so, what should the cannon's angle of elevation be?

11. *Writing to Learn* A golf ball leaves the ground at a 30° angle at a speed of 90 ft/sec. Will it clear the top of a 30 ft tree that is in the way, 135 ft down the fairway? Explain.

12. *Elevated green* A golf ball is hit with an initial speed of 116 ft/sec at an angle of elevation of 45° from the tee to a green that is elevated 45 ft above the tee as shown in the diagram. Assuming that the pin, 369 ft downrange, does not get in the way, where will the ball land in relation to the pin?

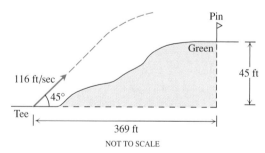

Pin

Green

116 ft/sec

45°

Tee

45 ft

369 ft

NOT TO SCALE

13. *The Green Monster* A baseball hit by a Boston Red Sox player at a 20° angle from 3 ft above the ground just cleared the left end of the "Green Monster," the left-field wall in Fenway Park (retired after the 2002 season). This wall is 37 ft high and 315 ft from home plate (see the accompanying figure).

   (a) What was the initial speed of the ball?

   (b) How long did it take the ball to reach the wall?

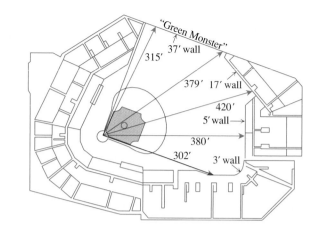

"Green Monster"

37′ wall

315′

379′   17′ wall

420′

5′ wall →

380′

302′   3′ wall

14. *Equal-range firing angles* Show that a projectile fired at an angle of α degrees, $0 < \alpha < 90$, has the same range as a projectile fired at the same speed at an angle of $(90 - \alpha)$ degrees. (In models that take air resistance into account, this symmetry is lost.)

15. *Equal-range firing angles* What two angles of elevation will enable a projectile to reach a target 16 km downrange on the same level as the gun if the projectile's initial speed is 400 m/sec?

16. *Range and height versus speed*

   (a) Show that doubling a projectile's initial speed at a given launch angle multiplies its range by 4.

   (b) By about what percentage should you increase the initial speed to double the height and range?

17. *Shot put* In Moscow in 1987, Natalya Lisouskaya set a women's world record by putting an 8 lb 13 oz shot 73 ft 10 in. Assuming that she launched the shot at a 40° angle to the horizontal from 6.5 ft above the ground, what was the shot's initial speed?

18. *Height versus time* Show that a projectile attains three-quarters of its maximum height in half the time it takes to reach the maximum height.

19. *Firing from* (x_0, y_0) Derive the equations

$$x = x_0 + (v_0 \cos \alpha)t,$$

$$y = y_0 + (v_0 \sin \alpha)t - \frac{1}{2} gt^2,$$

(see Equation 5 in the text) by solving the following initial value problem for a vector **r** in the plane.

Differential equation:	$\dfrac{d^2\mathbf{r}}{dt^2} = -g\mathbf{j}$
Initial conditions:	$\mathbf{r}(0) = x_0\mathbf{i} + y_0\mathbf{j}$
	$\dfrac{d\mathbf{r}}{dt}(0) = (v_0 \cos \alpha)\mathbf{i} + (v_0 \sin \alpha)\mathbf{j}$

20. *Flaming arrow* Using the firing angle found in Example 3, find the speed at which the flaming arrow left Rebollo's bow. See Figure 9.34.

21. *Flaming arrow* The cauldron in Example 3 is 12 ft in diameter. Using Equation 5 and Example 3c, find how long it takes the flaming arrow to cover the horizontal distance to the rim. How high is the arrow at this time?

22. *Writing to Learn* Describe the path of a projectile given by Equations 4 when $\alpha = 90°$.

23. *Model train* The accompanying multiflash photograph shows a model train engine moving at a constant speed on a straight horizontal track. As the engine moved along, a marble was fired into the air by a spring in the engine's smokestack. The marble, which continued to move with the same forward speed as the engine, rejoined the engine 1 sec after it was fired. Measure the angle the marble's path made with the horizontal and use the information to find how high the marble went and how fast the engine was moving.

24. *Writing to Learn: Colliding marbles* The figure shows an experiment with two marbles. Marble A was launched toward marble B with launch angle α and initial speed v_0. At the same instant, marble B was released to fall from rest at $R \tan \alpha$ units directly above a spot R units downrange from A. The marbles were found to collide regardless of the value of v_0. Was this mere coincidence, or must this happen? Give reasons for your answer.

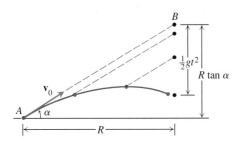

25. *Launching downhill* An ideal projectile is launched straight down an inclined plane as shown in the accompanying figure.

(a) Show that the greatest downhill range is achieved when the initial velocity vector bisects angle AOR.

(b) *Writing to Learn* If the projectile were fired uphill instead of down, what launch angle would maximize its range? Give reasons for your answer.

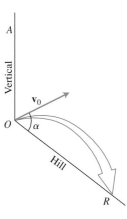

26. *Hitting a baseball under a wind gust* A baseball is hit when it is 2.5 ft above the ground. It leaves the bat with an initial velocity of 145 ft/sec at a launch angle of 23°. At the instant the ball is hit, an instantaneous gust of wind blows against the ball, adding a component of $-14\mathbf{i}$ (ft/sec) to the ball's initial velocity. A 15-ft-high fence lies 300 ft from home plate in the direction of the flight.

(a) Find a vector equation for the path of the baseball.

(b) How high does the baseball go, and when does it reach maximum height?

(c) Find the range and flight time of the baseball, assuming that the ball is not caught.

(d) When is the baseball 20 ft high? How far (ground distance) is the baseball from home plate at that height?

(e) *Writing to Learn* Has the batter hit a home run? Explain.

27. *Volleyball* A volleyball is hit when it is 4 ft above the ground and 12 ft from a 6-ft-high net. It leaves the point of impact with an initial velocity of 35 ft/sec at an angle of 27° and slips by the opposing team untouched.

(a) Find a vector equation for the path of the volleyball.

(b) How high does the volleyball go, and when does it reach maximum height?

(c) Find its range and flight time.

(d) When is the volleyball 7 ft above the ground? How far (ground distance) is the volleyball from where it will land?

(e) *Writing to Learn* Suppose that the net is raised to 8 ft. Does this change things? Explain.

28. *Where trajectories crest* For a projectile fired from the ground at launch angle α with initial speed v_0, consider α as a variable and v_0 as a fixed constant. For each α, $0 < \alpha < \pi/2$, we obtain a parabolic trajectory as shown in the accompanying figure. Show that the points in the plane that give the maximum heights of these parabolic trajectories all lie on the ellipse

$$x^2 + 4\left(y - \frac{v_0^2}{4g}\right)^2 = \frac{v_0^4}{4g^2},$$

where $x \geq 0$.

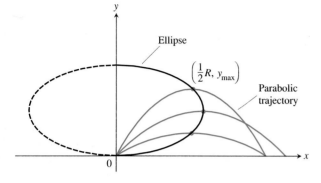

Projectile Motion with Linear Drag

The main force affecting the motion of a projectile, other than gravity, is air resistance. This slowing down force is **drag force,** and it acts in a direction *opposite* to the velocity of the projectile (see accompanying figure). For projectiles moving through the air at relatively low speeds, however, the drag force is (very nearly) proportional to the speed (to the first power) and so is called **linear.**

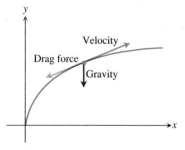

29. *Linear drag* Derive the equations

$$x = \frac{v_0}{k}(1 - e^{-kt})\cos\alpha$$

$$y = \frac{v_0}{k}(1 - e^{-kt})(\sin\alpha) + \frac{g}{k^2}(1 - kt - e^{-kt})$$

by solving the following initial value problem for a vector **r** in the plane.

Differential equation: $\dfrac{d^2\mathbf{r}}{dt^2} = -g\mathbf{j} - k\mathbf{v} = -g\mathbf{j} - k\dfrac{d\mathbf{r}}{dt}$

Initial conditions: $\mathbf{r}(0) = \mathbf{0}$

$$\frac{d\mathbf{r}}{dt}\bigg|_{t=0} = \mathbf{v}_0 = (v_0\cos\alpha)\mathbf{i} + (v_0\sin\alpha)\mathbf{j}$$

The **drag coefficient** k is a positive constant representing resistance due to air density, v_0 and α are the projectile's initial speed and launch angle, and g is the acceleration of gravity.

30. *Hitting a baseball with linear drag* Consider the baseball problem in Example 4 when there is linear drag (see Exercise 29). Assume a drag coefficient $k = 0.12$, but no gust of wind.

   (a) From Exercise 29, find a vector form for the path of the baseball.

   (b) How high does the baseball go, and when does it reach maximum height?

   (c) Find the range and flight time of the baseball.

   (d) When is the baseball 30 ft high? How far (ground distance) is the baseball from home plate at that height?

   (e) *Writing to Learn* A 10-ft-high outfield fence is 340 ft from home plate in the direction of the flight of the baseball. The outfielder can jump and catch any ball up to 11 ft off the ground to stop it from going over the fence. Has the batter hit a home run?

31. *Hitting a baseball with linear drag under a wind gust* Consider again the baseball problem in Example 4. This time assume a drag coefficient of 0.08 *and* an instantaneous gust of wind that adds a component of $-17.6\mathbf{i}$ (ft/sec) to the initial velocity at the instant the baseball is hit.

   (a) Find a vector equation for the path of the baseball.

   (b) How high does the baseball go, and when does it reach maximum height?

   (c) Find the range and flight time of the baseball?

   (d) When is the baseball 35 ft high? How far (ground distance) is the baseball from home plate at that height?

   (e) *Writing to Learn* A 20-ft-high outfield fence is 380 ft from home plate in the direction of the flight of the baseball. Has the batter hit a home run? If "yes," what change in the horizontal component of the ball's initial velocity would have kept the ball in the park? If "no," what change would have allowed it to be a home run?

9.5   Polar Coordinates and Graphs

Polar Coordinates   •   Polar Graphing   •   Symmetry   •   Relating Polar and Cartesian Coordinates   •   Finding Points Where Polar Graphs Intersect

In radar tracking, an operator is interested in the bearing or angle the tracked object makes with some fixed ray (e.g., a directed line pointing due east) and how far away the object is currently located. In this section, we study a coordinate system devised by Newton, called the **polar coordinate system,** which is practical to use for such purposes.

CD-ROM
WEBsite

Historical Biography
Maria Gaetana Agnesi
(1718 — 1799)

Polar Coordinates

To define polar coordinates, we first choose a point in the plane called the **pole** (or **origin**) and labeled O. Then we draw an **initial ray** (or **polar axis**) starting at O. This ray is usually drawn horizontally and pointing to the right, corresponding to the positive x-axis in Cartesian coordinates (Figure 9.35). Then each point P can be located by assigning to it a **polar coordinate pair** (r, θ) in which r gives the directed distance from O to P and θ gives the directed angle from the initial ray to ray OP.

FIGURE 9.35 To define polar coordinates for the plane, we start with an origin, called the pole, and an initial ray.

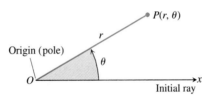

Polar Coordinates

$P(r, \theta)$

Directed distance from O to P Directed angle from initial ray to ray OP

As in trigonometry, θ is positive when measured counterclockwise and negative when measured clockwise. The angle associated with a given point is not unique. For instance, the point 2 units from the origin along the ray $\theta = \pi/6$ has polar coordinates $r = 2$, $\theta = \pi/6$. It also has coordinates $r = 2$, $\theta = -11\pi/6$ (Figure 9.36).

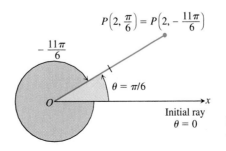

FIGURE 9.36 Polar coordinates are not unique.

There are also occasions when we wish to allow r to be negative. This is why we use *directed* distance in defining $P(r, \theta)$. The point $P(2, 7\pi/6)$ can be reached by turning $7\pi/6$ radians counterclockwise from the initial ray and going forward 2 units (Figure 9.37). It can also be reached by turning $\pi/6$ radians counterclockwise from the initial ray and going *backwards* 2 units. So the point also has polar coordinates $r = -2$, $\theta = \pi/6$.

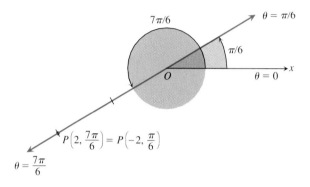

FIGURE 9.37 Polar coordinates can have negative r-values.

Polar Graphing

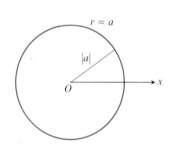

FIGURE 9.38 The polar equation for this circle is $r = a$.

If we hold r fixed at a constant value $a \neq 0$, the point $P(r, \theta)$ will lie $|a|$ units from the origin O. As θ varies over any interval of length 2π, P traces a circle of radius $|a|$ centered at O (Figure 9.38).

If we hold θ fixed at a constant value $\theta = \alpha$ and let r vary between $-\infty$ and ∞, the point $P(r, \theta)$ traces the line through O that makes an angle of measure α with the initial ray.

Equation	Polar Graph
$r = a$	Circle of radius $|a|$ centered at O
$\theta = \alpha$	Line through O making an angle α with the initial ray

Example 1 Finding Polar Equations for Graphs

(a) $r = 1$ and $r = -1$ are equations for the circle of radius 1 centered at O.

(b) $\theta = \pi/6$, $\theta = 7\pi/6$, and $\theta = -5\pi/6$ are equations for the line in Figure 9.37.

Equations of the form $r = a$ and $\theta = \alpha$ can be combined to define regions, segments, and rays.

Example 2 Graphing Equations and Inequalities

Graph the set of points whose polar coordinates satisfy the given conditions.

(a) $1 \leq r \leq 2$ and $0 \leq \theta \leq \dfrac{\pi}{2}$

(b) $-3 \leq r \leq 2$ and $\theta = \dfrac{\pi}{4}$

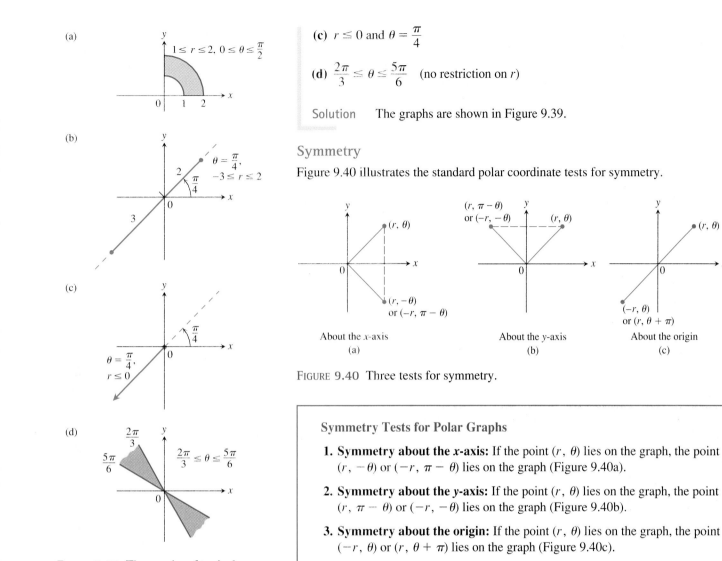

(c) $r \le 0$ and $\theta = \dfrac{\pi}{4}$

(d) $\dfrac{2\pi}{3} \le \theta \le \dfrac{5\pi}{6}$ (no restriction on r)

Solution   The graphs are shown in Figure 9.39.

Symmetry

Figure 9.40 illustrates the standard polar coordinate tests for symmetry.

About the x-axis
(a)

About the y-axis
(b)

About the origin
(c)

FIGURE 9.40 Three tests for symmetry.

FIGURE 9.39 The graphs of typical inequalities in r and θ. (Example 2)

Symmetry Tests for Polar Graphs

1. **Symmetry about the x-axis:** If the point (r, θ) lies on the graph, the point $(r, -\theta)$ or $(-r, \pi - \theta)$ lies on the graph (Figure 9.40a).

2. **Symmetry about the y-axis:** If the point (r, θ) lies on the graph, the point $(r, \pi - \theta)$ or $(-r, -\theta)$ lies on the graph (Figure 9.40b).

3. **Symmetry about the origin:** If the point (r, θ) lies on the graph, the point $(-r, \theta)$ or $(r, \theta + \pi)$ lies on the graph (Figure 9.40c).

Example 3   A cardioid

Graph the curve $r = 1 - \cos \theta$.

Solution   The curve is symmetric about the x-axis because

$$(r, \theta) \text{ on the graph} \Rightarrow r = 1 - \cos \theta$$
$$\Rightarrow r = 1 - \cos (-\theta) \qquad \cos \theta = \cos (-\theta)$$
$$\Rightarrow (r, -\theta) \text{ on the graph.}$$

As θ increases from 0 to π, $\cos \theta$ decreases from 1 to -1 and $r = 1 - \cos \theta$ increases from a minimum value of 0 to a maximum value of 2. As θ continues on from π to 2π, $\cos \theta$ increases from -1 back to 1 and r decreases from 2 back to 0. The curve starts to repeat when $\theta = 2\pi$ because the cosine has period 2π.

   The curve leaves the origin with slope $\tan (0) = 0$ and returns to the origin with slope $\tan (2\pi) = 0$.

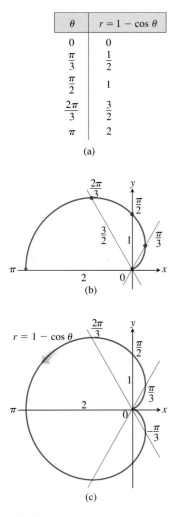

θ	$r = 1 - \cos \theta$
0	0
$\dfrac{\pi}{3}$	$\dfrac{1}{2}$
$\dfrac{\pi}{2}$	1
$\dfrac{2\pi}{3}$	$\dfrac{3}{2}$
π	2

(a)

(b)

(c)

FIGURE 9.41 The steps in graphing the cardioid $r = 1 - \cos \theta$ (Example 3). The arrow shows the direction of increasing θ.

We make a table of values from $\theta = 0$ to $\theta = \pi$, plot the points, draw a smooth curve through them with a horizontal tangent at the origin, and reflect the curve across the x-axis to complete the graph (Figure 9.41). The curve is called a *cardioid* because of its heart shape. Cardioid shapes appear in the cams that direct the even layering of thread on bobbins and reels, and in the signal-strength patterns of certain radio antennae.

Example 4   Polar Graphing

Graph the curve $r^2 = 4 \cos \theta$.

Solution   The equation $r^2 = 4 \cos \theta$ requires $\cos \theta \geq 0$, so we get the entire graph by running θ from $-\pi/2$ to $\pi/2$. The curve is symmetric about the x-axis because

$$(r, \theta) \text{ on the graph} \Rightarrow r^2 = 4 \cos \theta$$
$$\Rightarrow r^2 = 4 \cos (-\theta) \qquad \cos \theta = \cos (-\theta)$$
$$\Rightarrow (r, -\theta) \text{ on the graph.}$$

The curve is also symmetric about the origin because

$$(r, \theta) \text{ on the graph} \Rightarrow r^2 = 4 \cos \theta$$
$$\Rightarrow (-r)^2 = 4 \cos \theta$$
$$\Rightarrow (-r, \theta) \text{ on the graph.}$$

Together, these two symmetries imply symmetry about the y-axis.
    The curve passes through the origin when $\theta = -\pi/2$ and $\theta = \pi/2$. It has a vertical tangent both times because $\tan \theta$ is infinite.
    For each value of θ in the interval between $-\pi/2$ and $\pi/2$, the formula $r^2 = 4 \cos \theta$ gives two values of r:

$$r = \pm 2\sqrt{\cos \theta}.$$

We make a short table of values, plot the corresponding points, and use information about symmetry and tangents to guide us in connecting the points with a smooth curve (Figure 9.42).

θ	$\cos \theta$	$r = \pm 2\sqrt{\cos \theta}$
0	1	± 2
$\pm \dfrac{\pi}{6}$	$\dfrac{\sqrt{3}}{2}$	± 1.9
$\pm \dfrac{\pi}{4}$	$\dfrac{1}{\sqrt{2}}$	± 1.7
$\pm \dfrac{\pi}{3}$	$\dfrac{1}{2}$	± 1.4
$\pm \dfrac{\pi}{2}$	0	0

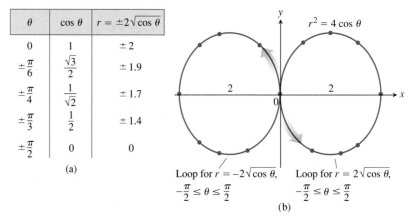

(a)

(b)

FIGURE 9.42 The graph of $r^2 = 4 \cos \theta$. The arrows show the direction of increasing θ. The values of r in the table are rounded. (Example 4)

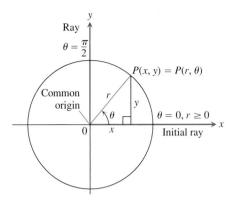

FIGURE 9.43 The usual way to relate polar and Cartesian coordinates.

Relating Polar and Cartesian Coordinates

When we use both polar and Cartesian coordinates in a plane, we place the two origins together and take the polar initial ray as the positive x-axis. The ray $\theta = \pi/2$, $r > 0$, becomes the positive y-axis (Figure 9.43). The two coordinate systems are then related by the following equations.

Equations Relating Polar and Cartesian Coordinates

$$x = r \cos \theta, \qquad y = r \sin \theta, \qquad x^2 + y^2 = r^2, \qquad \frac{y}{x} = \tan \theta$$

We use these equations and algebra (sometimes a lot of it!) to rewrite polar equations in Cartesian form and vice versa.

Example 5   Equivalent Equations

Polar equation	Cartesian equivalent
$r \cos \theta = 2$	$x = 2$
$r^2 \cos \theta \sin \theta = 4$	$xy = 4$
$r^2 \cos^2 \theta - r^2 \sin^2 \theta = 1$	$x^2 - y^2 = 1$
$r = 1 + 2r \cos \theta$	$y^2 - 3x^2 - 4x - 1 = 0$
$r = 1 - \cos \theta$	$x^4 + y^4 + 2x^2y^2 + 2x^3 + 2xy^2 - y^2 = 0$

With some curves, we are better off with polar coordinates; with others, we aren't.

Example 6   Converting Cartesian to Polar

Find a polar equation for the circle $x^2 + (y - 3)^2 = 9$ (Figure 9.44). Support graphically.

Solution

$$x^2 + y^2 - 6y + 9 = 9 \qquad \text{Expand } (y-3)^2.$$
$$x^2 + y^2 - 6y = 0$$
$$r^2 - 6r \sin \theta = 0 \qquad x^2 + y^2 = r^2, \quad y = r \sin \theta$$
$$r = 0 \text{ or } r - 6 \sin \theta = 0$$

The equation $r = 6 \sin \theta$ includes the possibility that $r = 0$.

Example 7   Converting Polar to Cartesian

Find a Cartesian equivalent for the polar equation. Identify the graph.

(a) $r^2 = 4r \cos \theta$ **(b)** $r = \dfrac{4}{2 \cos \theta - \sin \theta}$

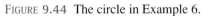

FIGURE 9.44 The circle in Example 6.

Solution

(a)
$$r^2 = 4r \cos \theta$$
$$x^2 + y^2 = 4x \qquad \qquad r^2 = x^2 + y^2, \ r\cos\theta = x$$
$$x^2 - 4x + y^2 = 0$$
$$x^2 - 4x + 4 + y^2 = 4 \qquad \qquad \text{Completing the square}$$
$$(x - 2)^2 + y^2 = 4$$

The graph of the equivalent Cartesian equation $(x - 2)^2 + y^2 = 4$ is a circle with radius 2 and center $(2, 0)$.

(b)
$$r = \frac{4}{2 \cos \theta - \sin \theta}$$
$$r(2 \cos \theta - \sin \theta) = 4$$
$$2r \cos \theta - r \sin \theta = 4$$
$$2x - y = 4 \qquad \qquad r\cos\theta = x, \ r\sin\theta = y$$
$$y = 2x - 4$$

The graph of the equivalent Cartesian equation $y = 2x - 4$ is a line with slope 2 and y-intercept -4.

Finding Points Where Polar Graphs Intersect

That we can represent a point in different ways in polar coordinates makes extra care necessary in deciding when a point lies on the graph of a polar equation and in determining the points in which polar graphs intersect. The problem is that a point of intersection may satisfy the equation of one curve with polar coordinates that are different from the ones with which it satisfies the equation of another curve. Thus, solving the equations of two curves simultaneously may not identify all their points of intersection. The only sure way to identify all the points of intersection is to graph the equations.

Example 8   Deceptive Coordinates

Show that the point $(2, \pi/2)$ lies on the curve $r = 2 \cos 2\theta$.

Solution   It may seem at first that the point $(2, \pi/2)$ does not lie on the curve because substituting the given coordinates into the equation gives

$$2 = 2 \cos 2 \left(\frac{\pi}{2} \right) = 2 \cos \pi = -2,$$

which is not a true equality. The magnitude is right, but the sign is wrong. This suggests looking for a pair of coordinates for the given point in which r is negative, for example, $(-2, -(\pi/2))$. If we try these in the equation $r = 2 \cos 2\theta$, we find

$$-2 = 2 \cos 2 \left(-\frac{\pi}{2} \right) = 2(-1) = -2,$$

and the equation is satisfied. The point $(2, \pi/2)$ does lie on the curve.

Example 9   Elusive Intersection Points

Find the points of intersection of the curves

$$r^2 = 4\cos\theta \qquad \text{and} \qquad r = 1 - \cos\theta.$$

Solution   In Cartesian coordinates, we can always find the points where two curves cross by solving their equations simultaneously. In polar coordinates, the story is different. Simultaneous solution may reveal some intersection points without revealing others. In this example, simultaneous solution reveals only two of the four intersection points. The others are found by graphing. (Also, see Exercise 79.)

If we substitute $\cos\theta = r^2/4$ in the equation $r = 1 - \cos\theta$, we get

$$r = 1 - \cos\theta = 1 - \frac{r^2}{4}$$

$$4r = 4 - r^2$$

$$r^2 + 4r - 4 = 0$$

$$r = -2 \pm 2\sqrt{2}. \qquad \text{Quadratic formula}$$

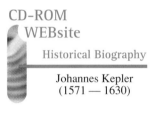

CD-ROM
WEBsite

Historical Biography

Johannes Kepler
(1571 — 1630)

The value $r = -2 - 2\sqrt{2}$ has too large an absolute value to belong to either curve. The values of θ corresponding to $r = -2 + 2\sqrt{2}$ are

$$\begin{aligned}
\theta &= \cos^{-1}(1 - r) & &\text{From } r = 1 - \cos\theta \\
&= \cos^{-1}(1 - (2\sqrt{2} - 2)) & &\text{Set } r = 2\sqrt{2} - 2. \\
&= \cos^{-1}(3 - 2\sqrt{2}) \\
&= \pm 80°. & &\begin{array}{l}\text{Rounded to the nearest}\\\text{degree}\end{array}
\end{aligned}$$

We have thus identified two intersection points: $(r, \theta) = (2\sqrt{2} - 2, \pm 80°)$.

If we graph the equations $r^2 = 4\cos\theta$ and $r = 1 - \cos\theta$ together (Figure 9.45), as we can now do by combining the graphs in Figures 9.41 and 9.42, we see that the curves also intersect at the point $(2, \pi)$ and the origin. Why weren't the r-values of these points revealed by the simultaneous solution? The answer is that the points $(0, 0)$ and $(2, \pi)$ are not on the curves "simultaneously." They are not reached at the same value of θ. On the curve $r = 1 - \cos\theta$, the point $(2, \pi)$ is reached when $\theta = \pi$. On the curve $r^2 = 4\cos\theta$, it is reached when $\theta = 0$, where it is identified not by the coordinates $(2, \pi)$, which do not satisfy the equation, but by the coordinates $(-2, 0)$, which do. Similarly, the cardioid reaches the origin when $\theta = 0$, but the curve $r^2 = 4\cos\theta$ reaches the origin when $\theta = \pi/2$.

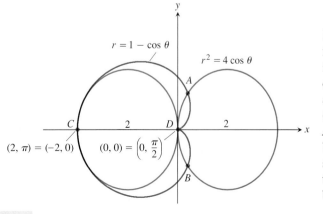

FIGURE 9.45 The four points of intersection of the curves $r = 1 - \cos\theta$ and $r^2 = 4\cos\theta$ (Example 9). Only A and B were found by simultaneous solution. The other two were disclosed by graphing.

USING
TECHNOLOGY

Finding Intersections The *simultaneous mode* of a graphing utility gives new meaning to the *simultaneous solution* of a pair of polar coordinate equations. A simultaneous solution occurs only where the two graphs "collide" while they are being drawn simultaneously and not where one graph intersects the other at a point that had been illuminated earlier. The distinction is particularly important in the areas of traffic control or missile defense. For example, in traffic control, the only issue is whether two aircraft are in the same place at the same time. The question of whether the curves the craft follow intersect is unimportant.

To illustrate, graph the polar equations

$$r = \cos 2\theta \qquad \text{and} \qquad r = \sin 2\theta$$

in simultaneous mode with $0 \leq \theta < 2\pi$, θ Step $= 0.1$ and view dimensions [xmin, xmax] $= [-1, 1]$ by [ymin, ymax] $= [-1, 1]$. *While the graphs are being drawn on the screen*, count the number of times the two graphs illuminate a single pixel simultaneously. Explain why these points of intersection of the two graphs correspond to simultaneous solutions of the equations. (You may find it helpful to slow down the graphing by making θ Step smaller, say 0.05, for example.) In how many points total do the graphs actually intersect?

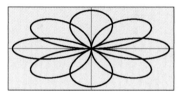

EXERCISES 9.5

Polar Coordinate Pairs

In Exercises 1 and 2, determine which polar coordinate pairs name the same point.

1. (a) $(3, 0)$ (b) $(-3, 0)$ (c) $(2, 2\pi/3)$
   (d) $(2, 7\pi/3)$ (e) $(-3, \pi)$ (f) $(2, \pi/3)$
   (g) $(-3, 2\pi)$ (h) $(-2, -\pi/3)$

2. (a) $(-2, \pi/3)$ (b) $(2, -\pi/3)$ (c) (r, θ)
   (d) $(r, \theta + \pi)$ (e) $(-r, \theta)$ (f) $(2, -2\pi/3)$
   (g) $(-r, \theta + \pi)$ (h) $(-2, 2\pi/3)$

In Exercises 3 and 4, plot the points with the given polar coordinates and find their Cartesian coordinates.

3. (a) $(\sqrt{2}, \pi/4)$ (b) $(1, 0)$
   (c) $(0, \pi/2)$ (d) $(-\sqrt{2}, \pi/4)$

4. (a) $(-3, 5\pi/6)$ (b) $(5, \tan^{-1}(4/3))$
   (c) $(-1, 7\pi)$ (d) $(2\sqrt{3}, 2\pi/3)$

In Exercises 5 and 6, plot the points with the given Cartesian coordinates and find two sets of polar coordinates for each.

5. (a) $(-1, 1)$ (b) $(1, -\sqrt{3})$
   (c) $(0, 3)$ (d) $(-1, 0)$

6. (a) $(-\sqrt{3}, -1)$ (b) $(3, 4)$
   (c) $(0, -2)$ (d) $(2, 0)$

Graphing Polar Equations and Inequalities

In Exercises 7–18, graph the set of points whose polar coordinates satisfy the given equations and inequalities.

7. $r = 2$ 8. $0 \leq r \leq 2$
9. $r \geq 1$ 10. $0 \leq \theta \leq \pi/6, \quad r \geq 0$
11. $\theta = 2\pi/3, \quad r \leq -2$ 12. $\theta = \pi/3, \quad -1 \leq r \leq 3$
13. $0 \leq \theta \leq \pi, \quad r = 1$ 14. $0 \leq \theta \leq \pi, \quad r = -1$
15. $\theta = \pi/2, \quad r \leq 0$

16. $\pi/4 \le \theta \le 3\pi/4, \quad 0 \le r \le 1$

17. $-\pi/4 \le \theta \le \pi/4, \quad -1 \le r \le 1$

18. $0 \le \theta \le \pi/2, \quad 1 \le |r| \le 2$

Polar to Cartesian Equations

In Exercises 19–36, replace the polar equation by an equivalent Cartesian equation. Then identify or describe the graph.

19. $r \sin \theta = 0$

20. $r \cos \theta = 0$

21. $r = 4 \csc \theta$

22. $r = -3 \sec \theta$

23. $r \cos \theta + r \sin \theta = 1$

24. $r^2 = 1$

25. $r^2 = 4r \sin \theta$

26. $r = \dfrac{5}{\sin \theta - 2 \cos \theta}$

27. $r^2 \sin 2\theta = 2$

28. $r = \cot \theta \csc \theta$

29. $r = (\csc \theta) \, e^{r \cos \theta}$

30. $\cos^2 \theta = \sin^2 \theta$

31. $r \sin \theta = \ln r + \ln \cos \theta$

32. $r^2 + 2r^2 \cos \theta \sin \theta = 1$

33. $r^2 = -4r \cos \theta$

34. $r = 8 \sin \theta$

35. $r = 2 \cos \theta + 2 \sin \theta$

36. $r \sin \left(\theta + \dfrac{\pi}{6} \right) = 2$

Cartesian to Polar Equations

In Exercises 37–48, replace the Cartesian equation by an equivalent polar equation.

37. $x = 7$

38. $y = 1$

39. $x = y$

40. $x - y = 3$

41. $x^2 + y^2 = 4$

42. $x^2 - y^2 = 1$

43. $\dfrac{x^2}{9} + \dfrac{y^2}{4} = 1$

44. $xy = 2$

45. $y^2 = 4x$

46. $x^2 + xy + y^2 = 1$

47. $x^2 + (y - 2)^2 = 4$

48. $(x - 3)^2 + (y + 1)^2 = 4$

Symmetries and Polar Graphs

In Exercises 49–58, **(a)** graph the polar curve. **(b)** What is the shortest length a θ-interval can have and still produce the graph?

49. $r = 1 + \cos \theta$

50. $r = 2 - 2 \cos \theta$

51. $r^2 = -\sin 2\theta$

52. $r = 1 - \sin \theta$

53. $r = 1 - 2 \sin 3\theta$

54. $r = \sin (\theta/2)$

55. $r = \theta$

56. $r = 1 + \sin \theta$

57. $r = 2 \cos 3\theta$

58. $r = 1 + 2 \sin \theta$

In Exercises 59–62, determine the symmetries of the curve.

59. $r^2 = 4 \cos 2\theta$

60. $r^2 = 4 \sin 2\theta$

61. $r = 2 + \sin \theta$

62. $r^2 = -\cos 2\theta$

63. *Writing to Learn: Vertical and horizontal lines*

    (a) Explain why every vertical line in the plane has a polar equation of the form $r = a \sec \theta$.

    (b) Find an analogous polar equation for horizontal lines. Give reasons for your answer.

64. *Writing to Learn: Do two symmetries imply three?* If a curve has any two of the symmetries listed at the beginning of the section, can anything be said about its having or not having the third symmetry? Give reasons for your answer.

Intersections

65. Show that the point $(2, 3\pi/4)$ lies on the curve $r = 2 \sin 2\theta$.

66. Show that $(1/2, 3\pi/2)$ lies on the curve $r = -\sin (\theta/3)$.

Find the points of intersection of the pairs of curves in Exercises 67–70.

67. $r = 1 + \cos \theta, \quad r = 1 - \cos \theta$

68. $r = 2 \sin \theta, \quad r = 2 \sin 2\theta$

69. $r = \cos \theta, \quad r = 1 - \cos \theta$

70. $r = 1, \quad r^2 = 2 \sin 2\theta$

T Find the points of intersection of the pairs of curves in Exercises 71–74.

71. $r^2 = \sin 2\theta, \quad r^2 = \cos 2\theta$

72. $r = 1 + \cos \dfrac{\theta}{2}, \quad r = 1 - \sin \dfrac{\theta}{2}$

73. $r = 1, \quad r = 2 \sin 2\theta$

74. $r = 1, \quad r^2 = 2 \sin 2\theta$

T **75.** Which of the following has the same graph as $r = 1 - \cos \theta$?

    (a) $r = -1 - \cos \theta$

    (b) $r = 1 + \cos \theta$

    Confirm your answer with alegbra.

T **76.** *Rose curves* Let $r = 2 \sin n\theta$.

    (a) Graph $r = 2 \sin n\theta$ for $n = \pm 2, \pm 4, \pm 6$. Describe the curves.

    (b) What is the smallest length a θ-interval can have and still produce the graphs in part (a)?

    (c) Based on your observations in part (a), describe the graph of $r = 2 \sin n\theta$ when n is a nonzero even integer.

    (d) Graph $r = 2 \sin n\theta$ for $n = \pm 3, \pm 5, \pm 7$. Describe the curves.

    (e) What is the smallest length a θ-interval can have and still produce the graphs in part (d)?

    (f) Based on your observations in part (d), describe the graph of $r = 2 \sin n\theta$ when n is an odd integer different from ± 1.

T **77.** *A rose within a rose* Graph the equation $r = 1 - 2 \sin 3\theta$.

T 78. *The nephroid of Freeth* Graph the nephroid of Freeth:

$$r = 1 + 2 \sin \frac{\theta}{2}.$$

Theory and Examples

79. (*Continuation of Example 9*) The simultaneous solution of the equations

$$r^2 = 4 \cos \theta \tag{1}$$
$$r = 1 - \cos \theta \tag{2}$$

in the text did not reveal the points $(0, 0)$ and $(2, \pi)$ in which their graphs intersected.

(a) We could have found the point $(2, \pi)$, however, by replacing the (r, θ) in Equation (1) by the equivalent $(-r, \theta + \pi)$ to obtain

$$r^2 = 4 \cos \theta$$
$$(-r)^2 = 4 \cos (\theta + \pi) \tag{3}$$
$$r^2 = -4 \cos \theta.$$

Solve Equations (2) and (3) simultaneously to show that $(2, \pi)$ is a common solution. (This will still not reveal that the graphs intersect at $(0, 0)$.)

(b) The origin is still a special case. (It often is.) Here is one way to handle it: Set $r = 0$ in Equations (1) and (2) and solve each equation for a corresponding value of θ. Since $(0, \theta)$ is the origin for *any* θ, this will show that both curves pass through the origin even if they do so for different θ-values.

80. *Relating polar equations to parametric equations* Let $r = f(\theta)$ be a polar curve.

(a) *Writing to Learn* Explain why

$$x = f(t) \cos t, \qquad y = f(t) \sin t$$

are parametric equations for the curve.

T (b) Use part (a) to write parametric equations for the circle $r = 3$. Support your answer by graphing the parametric equations.

T (c) Repeat part (b) with $r = 1 - \cos \theta$.

T (d) Repeat part (b) with $r = 3 \sin 2\theta$.

81. *Distance formula* Show that the distance between points (r_1, θ_1), and (r_2, θ_2) in polar coordinates is

$$d = \sqrt{r_1{}^2 + r_2{}^2 - 2r_1 r_2 \cos (\theta_1 - \theta_2)}.$$

82. *Height of a cardioid* Find the maximum height above the x-axis of the cardioid $r = 2(1 + \cos \theta)$.

9.6 Calculus of Polar Curves

Slope • Area in the Plane • Length of a Curve

In this section, you will see how to find slopes, areas, and lengths of polar curves $r = f(\theta)$.

Slope

The slope of a polar curve $r = f(\theta)$ is given by dy/dx, not by $r' = df/d\theta$. To see why, think of the graph of f as the graph of the parametric equations

$$x = r \cos \theta = f(\theta) \cos \theta, \qquad y = r \sin \theta = f(\theta) \sin \theta.$$

If f is a differentiable function of θ, then so are x and y, and when $dx/d\theta \neq 0$, we can calculate dy/dx from the parametric formula

$$\frac{dy}{dx} = \frac{dy/d\theta}{dx/d\theta} \qquad \text{Section 2.5, Equation (4) with } t = \theta$$

$$= \frac{\dfrac{d}{d\theta}(f(\theta) \sin \theta)}{\dfrac{d}{d\theta}(f(\theta) \cos \theta)}$$

$$= \frac{\dfrac{df}{d\theta} \sin \theta + f(\theta) \cos \theta}{\dfrac{df}{d\theta} \cos \theta - f(\theta) \sin \theta} \qquad \text{Product Rule for Derivatives}$$

> **Slope of the Polar Curve $r = f(\theta)$**
>
> $$\left. \frac{dy}{dx} \right|_{(r,\theta)} = \frac{f'(\theta)\ \sin\ \theta + f(\theta)\ \cos\ \theta}{f'(\theta)\ \cos\ \theta - f(\theta)\ \sin\ \theta}, \tag{1}$$
>
> provided $dx/d\theta \neq 0$ at (r, θ).

We can see from Equation 1 and its derivation that the curve $r = f(\theta)$ has a

1.   Horizontal tangent at a point where $dy/d\theta = 0$ and $dx/d\theta \neq 0$

2.   Vertical tangent at a point where $dx/d\theta = 0$ and $dy/d\theta \neq 0$.

If both derivatives are zero, no conclusion can be drawn without further investigation, as illustrated in Example 1.

Example 1   Finding Horizontal and Vertical Tangents

Find the horizontal and vertical tangents to the graph of the cardioid $r = 1 - \cos\ \theta$, $0 \leq \theta \leq 2\pi$.

Solution   The graph in Figure 9.46 suggests that there are at least two horizontal and three vertical tangents.

The parametric form of the equation is

$$x = r\ \cos\ \theta = (1 - \cos\ \theta)\ \cos\ \theta = \cos\ \theta - \cos^2\ \theta,$$
$$y = r\ \sin\ \theta = (1 - \cos\ \theta)\ \sin\ \theta = \sin\ \theta - \cos\ \theta\ \sin\ \theta.$$

We need to find the zeros of $dy/d\theta$ and $dx/d\theta$.

(a) Zeros of $dy/d\theta$ in $[0, 2\pi]$:

$$\frac{dy}{d\theta} = \cos\ \theta + \sin^2\ \theta - \cos^2\ \theta = \cos\ \theta + (1 - \cos^2\ \theta) - \cos^2\ \theta$$
$$= 1 + \cos\ \theta - 2\ \cos^2\ \theta = (1 + 2\ \cos\ \theta)(1 - \cos\ \theta).$$

Now,

$$1 - \cos\ \theta = 0 \Rightarrow \theta = 0, 2\pi$$
$$1 + 2\ \cos\ \theta = 0 \Rightarrow \theta = 2\pi/3, 4\pi/3.$$

Thus, $dy/d\theta = 0$ in $0 \leq \theta \leq 2\pi$ if $\theta = 0, 2\pi/3, 4\pi/3$, or 2π.

(b) Zeros of $dx/d\theta$ in $[0, 2\pi]$:

$$\frac{dx}{d\theta} = -\sin\ \theta + 2\ \cos\ \theta\ \sin\ \theta = (2\ \cos\ \theta - 1)\ \sin\ \theta.$$

Now,

$$2\ \cos\ \theta - 1 = 0 \Rightarrow \theta = \pi/3, 5\pi/3$$
$$\sin\ \theta = 0 \Rightarrow \theta = 0, \pi, 2\pi.$$

Thus, $dx/d\theta = 0$ in $0 \leq \theta \leq 2\pi$ if $\theta = 0, \pi/3, \pi, 5\pi/3$, or 2π.

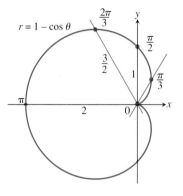

FIGURE 9.46 Where are the horizontal and vertical tangents to this cardioid? (Example 1)

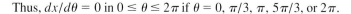

We can now see that there are horizontal tangents ($dy/d\theta = 0$, $dx/d\theta \neq 0$) at the points where $\theta = 2\pi/3$ and $4\pi/3$, and vertical tangents ($dx/d\theta = 0$, $dy/d\theta \neq 0$) at the points where $\theta = \pi/3$, π, and $5\pi/3$.

At the points where $\theta = 0$ or 2π, the right side of Equation (1) takes the form 0/0. We can use l'Hôpital's Rule (Section 7.6) to see that

$$\lim_{\theta \to 0, 2\pi} \frac{dy/d\theta}{dx/d\theta} = \lim_{\theta \to 0, 2\pi} \frac{1 + \cos\theta - 2\cos^2\theta}{2\cos\theta\sin\theta - \sin\theta}$$

$$= \lim_{\theta \to 0, 2\pi} \frac{-\sin\theta + 4\cos\theta\sin\theta}{2\cos^2\theta - 2\sin^2\theta - \cos\theta} = \frac{0}{1} = 0.$$

The curve has a horizontal tangent at the point where $\theta = 0$ or 2π. Summarizing, we have

Horizontal tangents at $(0, 0) = (0, 2\pi), \ (1.5, 2\pi/3), \ (1.5, 4\pi/3)$

Vertical tangents at $(0.5, \pi/3), \ (2, \pi), \ (0.5, 5\pi/3).$

If the curve $r = f(\theta)$ passes through the origin at $\theta = \theta_0$, then $f(\theta_0) = 0$, and Equation (1) gives

$$\left.\frac{dy}{dx}\right|_{(0, \theta_0)} = \frac{f'(\theta_0)\sin\theta_0}{f'(\theta_0)\cos\theta_0} = \tan\theta_0,$$

provided $f'(\theta_0) \neq 0$ (not the case in Example 1). The reason we say "slope at $(0, \theta_0)$" and not just "slope at the origin" is that a polar curve may pass through the origin more than once, with different slopes at different θ-values.

Example 2   Finding Tangent Lines at the Pole (Origin)

Find the lines tangent to the rose curve

$$r = f(\theta) = 2\sin 3\theta, \qquad 0 \leq \theta \leq \pi,$$

at the pole.

Solution $f(\theta)$ is zero when $\theta = 0$, $\pi/3$, $2\pi/3$, and π. The derivative $f'(\theta) = 6\cos 3\theta$ is not zero at these four values of θ. Thus, this curve has tangent lines at the pole (Figure 9.47) with slopes $\tan 0 = \tan \pi = 0$, $\tan(\pi/3) = \sqrt{3}$, and $\tan(2\pi/3) = -\sqrt{3}$. The three corresponding tangent lines are $y = 0$, $y = \sqrt{3}x$, and $y = -\sqrt{3}x$.

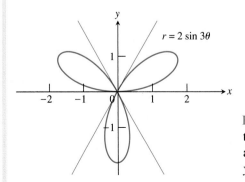

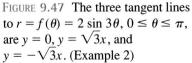

FIGURE 9.47 The three tangent lines to $r = f(\theta) = 2\sin 3\theta$, $0 \leq \theta \leq \pi$, are $y = 0$, $y = \sqrt{3}x$, and $y = -\sqrt{3}x$. (Example 2)

Area in the Plane

The region OTS in Figure 9.48 is bounded by the rays $\theta = \alpha$ and $\theta = \beta$ and the curve $r = f(\theta)$. We approximate the region with n nonoverlapping circular sectors based on a partition P of angle TOS. The typical sector has radius $r_k = f(\theta_k)$ and central angle of radian measure $\Delta\theta_k$. Its area is

$$A_k = \frac{1}{2} r_k^2 \, \Delta\theta_k = \frac{1}{2} (f(\theta_k))^2 \, \Delta\theta_k.$$

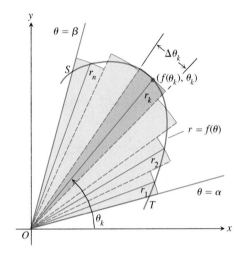

FIGURE 9.48 To derive a formula for the area of region OTS, we approximate the region with fan-shaped circular sectors.

The area of the region OTS is approximately

$$\sum_{k=1}^{n} A_k = \sum_{k=1}^{n} \frac{1}{2} (f(\theta_k))^2 \, \Delta\theta_k .$$

If f is continuous, we expect the approximations to improve as $\| P \| \to 0$, and we are led to the following formula for the region's area:

$$A = \lim_{\| P \| \to 0} \sum_{k=1}^{n} \frac{1}{2} (f(\theta_k))^2 \, \Delta\theta_k$$

$$= \int_{\alpha}^{\beta} \frac{1}{2} (f(\theta))^2 \, d\theta .$$

Area in Polar Coordinates

The **area** of the region **between the origin and the curve** $r = f(\theta)$, $\alpha \le \theta \le \beta$, is

$$A = \int_{\alpha}^{\beta} \frac{1}{2} r^2 \, d\theta .$$

This is the integral of the **area differential** (Figure 9.49),

$$dA = \frac{1}{2} r^2 \, d\theta .$$

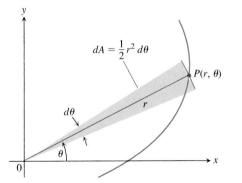

FIGURE 9.49 The area differential dA.

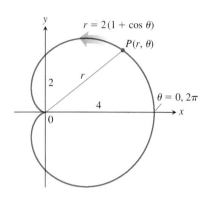

FIGURE 9.50 The cardioid in Example 3.

Example 3   Finding Area

Find the area of the region in the plane enclosed by the cardioid $r = 2(1 + \cos \theta)$.

Solution   We graph the cardioid (Figure 9.50) and determine that the *radius r* sweeps out the region exactly once as θ runs from 0 to 2π. The area is therefore

$$\int_{\theta=0}^{\theta=2\pi} \frac{1}{2} r^2 \, d\theta = \int_0^{2\pi} \frac{1}{2} \cdot 4(1 + \cos \theta)^2 \, d\theta$$

$$= \int_0^{2\pi} 2(1 + 2 \cos \theta + \cos^2 \theta) \, d\theta$$

$$= \int_0^{2\pi} \left(2 + 4 \cos \theta + 2 \frac{1 + \cos 2\theta}{2} \right) d\theta$$

$$= \int_0^{2\pi} (3 + 4 \cos \theta + \cos 2\theta) \, d\theta$$

$$= \left[3\theta + 4 \sin \theta + \frac{\sin 2\theta}{2} \right]_0^{2\pi} = 6\pi - 0 = 6\pi.$$

Example 4   Finding Area

Find the area inside the smaller loop of the limaçon $r = 2 \cos \theta + 1$.

Solution   After sketching the curve (Figure 9.51), we see that the smaller loop is traced out by the point (r, θ) as θ increases from $\theta = 2\pi/3$ to $\theta = 4\pi/3$. Since the curve is symmetric about the x-axis (the equation is unaltered when we replace θ by $-\theta$), we may calculate the area of the shaded half of the inner loop by integrating from $\theta = 2\pi/3$ to $\theta = \pi$. The area we seek will be twice the resulting integral:

$$A = 2 \int_{2\pi/3}^{\pi} \frac{1}{2} r^2 \, d\theta = \int_{2\pi/3}^{\pi} r^2 \, d\theta.$$

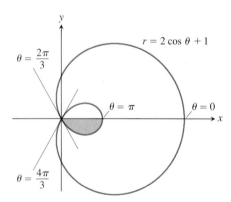

FIGURE 9.51 The limaçon in Example 4. Limaçon (pronounced LEE-ma-sahn) is an old French word for *snail*.

Since

$$r^2 = (2 \cos \theta + 1)^2 = 4 \cos^2 \theta + 4 \cos \theta + 1$$

$$= 4 \cdot \frac{1 + \cos 2\theta}{2} + 4 \cos \theta + 1$$

$$= 2 + 2 \cos 2\theta + 4 \cos \theta + 1$$

$$= 3 + 2 \cos 2\theta + 4 \cos \theta,$$

we have

$$A = \int_{2\pi/3}^{\pi} (3 + 2 \cos 2\theta + 4 \cos \theta) \, d\theta$$

$$= \left[3\theta + \sin 2\theta + 4 \sin \theta \right]_{2\pi/3}^{\pi}$$

$$= (3\pi) - \left(2\pi - \frac{\sqrt{3}}{2} + 4 \cdot \frac{\sqrt{3}}{2} \right)$$

$$= \pi - \frac{3\sqrt{3}}{2}.$$

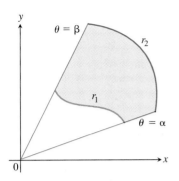

FIGURE 9.52 The area of the shaded region is calculated by subtracting the area of the region between r_1 and the origin from the area of the region between r_2 and the origin.

To find the area of a region like the one in Figure 9.52 which lies between two polar curves $r_1 = r_1(\theta)$ and $r_2 = r_2(\theta)$ from $\theta = \alpha$ to $\theta = \beta$, we subtract the integral of $(1/2)r_1^2$ from the integral of $(1/2)r_2^2$. This leads to the following formula.

> **Area Between Polar Curves**
>
> The area of the region $0 \le r_1(\theta) \le r_2(\theta)$, $\alpha \le \theta \le \beta$, is
>
> $$A = \int_\alpha^\beta \frac{1}{2} r_2^2 \, d\theta - \int_\alpha^\beta \frac{1}{2} r_1^2 \, d\theta = \int_\alpha^\beta \frac{1}{2} (r_2^2 - r_1^2) \, d\theta. \qquad (2)$$

Example 5   Finding Area Between Curves

Find the area of the region that lies inside the circle $r = 1$ and outside the cardioid $r = 1 - \cos \theta$.

Solution   The region is shown in Figure 9.53. The outer curve is $r_2 = 1$, the inner curve is $r_1 = 1 - \cos \theta$, and θ runs from $-\pi/2$ to $\pi/2$. The area, from Equation (2), is

$$A = \int_{-\pi/2}^{\pi/2} \frac{1}{2} (r_2^2 - r_1^2) \, d\theta$$

$$= 2 \int_0^{\pi/2} \frac{1}{2} (r_2^2 - r_1^2) \, d\theta \qquad \text{Symmetry}$$

$$= \int_0^{\pi/2} (1 - (1 - 2 \cos \theta + \cos^2 \theta)) \, d\theta$$

$$= \int_0^{\pi/2} (2 \cos \theta - \cos^2 \theta) \, d\theta = \int_0^{\pi/2} \left(2 \cos \theta - \frac{1 + \cos 2\theta}{2} \right) d\theta$$

$$= \left[2 \sin \theta - \frac{\theta}{2} - \frac{\sin 2\theta}{4} \right]_0^{\pi/2} = 2 - \frac{\pi}{4}.$$

$r_1 = 1 - \cos \theta$

Upper limit $\theta = \pi/2$

$r_2 = 1$

Lower limit $\theta = -\pi/2$

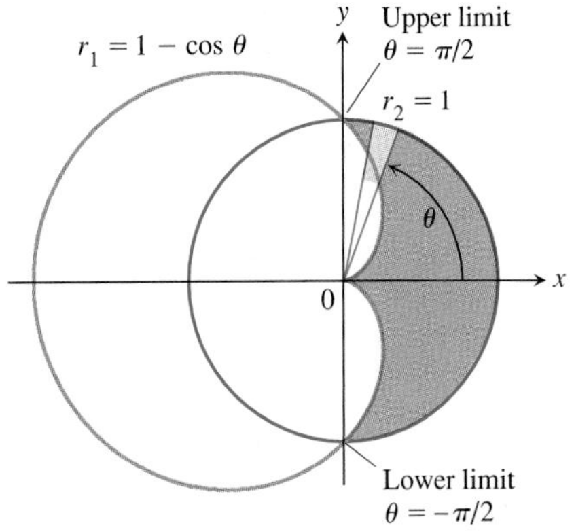

FIGURE 9.53 The region and limits of integration in Example 5.

Length of a Curve

We can obtain a polar coordinate formula for the length of a curve $r = f(\theta)$, $\alpha \le \theta \le \beta$, by parametrizing the curve as

$$x = r \cos \theta = f(\theta) \cos \theta, \qquad y = r \sin \theta = f(\theta) \sin \theta, \qquad \alpha \le \theta \le \beta. \qquad (3)$$

The parametric length formula from Section 5.3 then gives the length as

$$L = \int_{\alpha}^{\beta} \sqrt{\left(\frac{dx}{d\theta}\right)^2 + \left(\frac{dy}{d\theta}\right)^2} \, d\theta.$$

This equation becomes

$$L = \int_{\alpha}^{\beta} \sqrt{r^2 + \left(\frac{dr}{d\theta}\right)^2} \, d\theta$$

when Equations (3) are substituted for x and y (Exercise 41).

Length of a Polar Curve

If $r = f(\theta)$ has a continuous first derivative for $\alpha \le \theta \le \beta$ and if the point $P(r, \theta)$ traces the curve $r = f(\theta)$ exactly once as θ runs from α to β, then the length of the curve is

$$L = \int_{\alpha}^{\beta} \sqrt{r^2 + \left(\frac{dr}{d\theta}\right)^2} \, d\theta. \tag{4}$$

Example 6   Finding the Length of a Cardioid

Find the length of the cardioid $r = 1 - \cos \theta$.

Solution   The graph is shown in Figure 9.54. The point $P(r, \theta)$ traces the curve once counterclockwise as θ runs from 0 to 2π, so these are the values we take for the limits of integration.

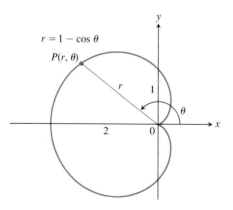

FIGURE 9.54 Example 6 calculates the length of this cardioid.

Since $r = 1 - \cos \theta$, $dr/d\theta = \sin \theta$, and we have

$$r^2 + \left(\frac{dr}{d\theta}\right)^2 = (1 - \cos \theta)^2 + (\sin \theta)^2$$

$$= 1 - 2 \cos \theta + \underbrace{\cos^2 \theta + \sin^2 \theta}_{1} = 2 - 2 \cos \theta.$$

Therefore,

$$L = \int_\alpha^\beta \sqrt{r^2 + \left(\frac{dr}{d\theta}\right)^2}\, d\theta \qquad \text{Equation (4)}$$

$$= \int_0^{2\pi} \sqrt{2 - 2\cos\theta}\, d\theta$$

$$= \int_0^{2\pi} \sqrt{4\sin^2\frac{\theta}{2}}\, d\theta \qquad 1 - \cos\theta = 2\sin^2\frac{\theta}{2}$$

$$= \int_0^{2\pi} \left|2\sin\frac{\theta}{2}\right| d\theta$$

$$= \int_0^{2\pi} 2\sin\frac{\theta}{2}\, d\theta \qquad \sin\frac{\theta}{2} \geq 0 \text{ for } 0 \leq \theta \leq 2\pi$$

$$= \left[-4\cos\frac{\theta}{2}\right]_0^{2\pi} = 4 + 4 = 8.$$

EXERCISES 9.6

Slopes of Polar Curves

In Exercises 1–4, find the slope of the curve at each indicated point.

1. $r = -1 + \sin\theta, \quad \theta = 0, \pi$

2. $r = \cos 2\theta, \quad \theta = 0, \pm\pi/2, \pi$

3. $r = 2 - 3\sin\theta$

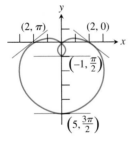

4. $r = 3(1 - \cos\theta)$

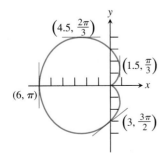

In Exercises 5–8, find the tangent lines at the pole.

5. $r = 3\cos\theta, \quad 0 \leq \theta \leq 2\pi$

6. $r = 2\cos 3\theta, \quad 0 \leq \theta \leq \pi$

7. $r = \sin 5\theta, \quad 0 \leq \theta \leq \pi$

8. $r = 2\sin 2\theta, \quad 0 \leq \theta \leq 2\pi$

In Exercises 9–12, find equations for the horizontal and vertical tangent lines to the curve.

9. $r = -1 + \sin\theta, \quad 0 \leq \theta \leq 2\pi$

10. $r = 1 + \cos\theta, \quad 0 \leq \theta \leq 2\pi$

11. $r = 2\sin\theta, \quad 0 \leq \theta \leq \pi$

12. $r = 3 - 4\cos\theta, \quad 0 \leq \theta \leq 2\pi$

Areas Inside Polar Curves

Find the areas of the regions in Exercises 13–18.

13. Inside the oval limaçon $r = 4 + 2\cos\theta$

14. Inside the cardioid $r = a(1 + \cos\theta), \quad a > 0$

15. Inside one leaf of the four-leaved rose $r = \cos 2\theta$

16. Inside the lemniscate $r^2 = 2a^2\cos 2\theta, \quad a > 0$

17. Inside one loop of the lemniscate $r^2 = 4\sin 2\theta$

18. Inside the six-leaved rose $r^2 = 2\sin 3\theta$

Areas Shared by Polar Regions

Find the areas of the regions in Exercises 19–28.

19. Shared by the circles $r = 2 \cos \theta$ and $r = 2 \sin \theta$

20. Shared by the circles $r = 1$ and $r = 2 \sin \theta$

21. Shared by the circle $r = 2$ and the cardioid $r = 2(1 - \cos \theta)$

22. Shared by the cardioids $r = 2(1 + \cos \theta)$ and $r = 2(1 - \cos \theta)$

23. Inside the lemniscate $r^2 = 6 \cos 2\theta$ and outside the circle $r = \sqrt{3}$

24. Inside the circle $r = 3a \cos \theta$ and outside the cardioid $r = a(1 + \cos \theta), a > 0$

25. Inside the circle $r = -2 \cos \theta$ and outside the circle $r = 1$

26. (a) Inside the outer loop of the limaçon $r = 1 + 2 \cos \theta$ (See Figure 9.51.)

(b) Inside the outer loop and outside the inner loop of the limaçon $r = 1 + 2 \cos \theta$

27. Inside the circle $r = 6$ above the line $r = 3 \csc \theta$

28. Inside the lemniscate $r^2 = 6 \cos 2\theta$ to the right of the line $r = (3/2) \sec \theta$

29. (a) Find the area of the shaded region in the accompanying figure.

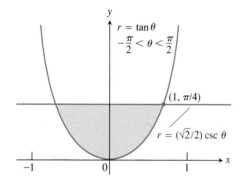

$r = \tan \theta$
$-\dfrac{\pi}{2} < \theta < \dfrac{\pi}{2}$

$(1, \pi/4)$

$r = (\sqrt{2}/2) \csc \theta$

(b) *Writing to Learn* It looks as if the graph of $r = \tan \theta$, $-\pi/2 < \theta < \pi/2$, could be asymptotic to the lines $x = 1$ and $x = -1$. Is it? Give reasons for your answer.

30. *Writing to Learn* The area of the region that lies inside the cardioid curve $r = 1 + \cos \theta$ and outside the circle $r = \cos \theta$ is not

$$\frac{1}{2} \int_0^{2\pi} [(1 + \cos \theta)^2 - \cos^2 \theta] \, d\theta = \pi.$$

Why not? What *is* the area? Give reasons for your answers.

Lengths of Polar Curves

Find the lengths of the curves in Exercises 31–39.

31. The spiral $r = \theta^2$, $0 \le \theta \le \sqrt{5}$

32. The spiral $r = e^\theta/\sqrt{2}$, $0 \le \theta \le \pi$

33. The cardioid $r = 1 + \cos \theta$

34. The curve $r = a \sin^2 (\theta/2)$, $0 \le \theta \le \pi$, $a > 0$

35. The parabolic segment $r = 6/(1 + \cos \theta)$, $0 \le \theta \le \pi/2$

36. The parabolic segment $r = 2/(1 - \cos \theta)$, $\pi/2 \le \theta \le \pi$

37. The curve $r = \cos^3 (\theta/3)$, $0 \le \theta \le \pi/4$

38. The curve $r = \sqrt{1 + \sin 2\theta}$, $0 \le \theta \le \pi\sqrt{2}$

39. The curve $r = \sqrt{1 + \cos 2\theta}$, $0 \le \theta \le \pi\sqrt{2}$

40. *Circumferences of circles* As usual, when faced with a new formula, it is a good idea to try it on familiar objects to be sure it gives results consistent with past experience. Use the length formula in Equation (4) to calculate the circumferences of the following circles $(a > 0)$:

(a) $r = a$ **(b)** $r = a \cos \theta$ **(c)** $r = a \sin \theta$.

Theory and Examples

41. *Length of a polar curve* Assuming that the necessary derivatives are continuous, show how the substitutions

$$x = f(\theta) \cos \theta, \qquad y = f(\theta) \sin \theta$$

(Equations (3) in the text) transform

$$L = \int_\alpha^\beta \sqrt{\left(\frac{dx}{d\theta}\right)^2 + \left(\frac{dy}{d\theta}\right)^2} \, d\theta$$

into

$$L = \int_\alpha^\beta \sqrt{r^2 + \left(\frac{dr}{d\theta}\right)^2} \, d\theta.$$

42. *Average value* If f is continuous, the average value of the polar coordinate r over the curve $r = f(\theta)$, $\alpha \le \theta \le \beta$, with respect to θ is

$$r_{av} = \frac{1}{\beta - \alpha} \int_\alpha^\beta f(\theta) \, d\theta.$$

Use this formula to find the average value of r with respect to θ over the following curves $(a > 0)$.

(a) The cardioid $r = a(1 - \cos \theta)$

(b) The circle $r = a$

(c) The circle $r = a \cos \theta$, $-\pi/2 \le \theta \le \pi/2$

43. *Writing to Learn* Can anything be said about the relative lengths of the curves

$$r = f(\theta), \qquad \alpha \le \theta \le \beta,$$

and

$$r = 2f(\theta), \qquad \alpha \le \theta \le \beta?$$

Give reasons for your answer.

44. *Videocassette tape length* The length of a tape wound onto a take-up reel as shown in the figure is

$$L = \int_0^\alpha \sqrt{r^2 + \left(\frac{b}{2\pi}\right)^2}\, d\theta,$$

where b is the tape thickness and

$$r = r_0 + \left(\frac{\alpha}{2\pi}\right) b$$

is the radius of the tape on the take-up reel. The initial radius of the tape on the take-up reel is r_0 and α is the angle in radians through which the wheel has turned.

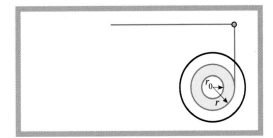

(a) Find a spiral that models the tape accumulating on the take-up reel using polar graphing with $r_0 = 1.75$ cm and $b = 0.06$ cm.

(b) Confirm the formula for L analytically.

(c) Determine the length of tape on the take-up reel if the reel has turned through an angle of 80π with $r_0 = 1.75$ cm and $b = 0.06$ cm.

(d) Assume that b is very small in comparison to r at any time. Show analytically that

$$L_a = \int_0^\alpha r\, d\theta$$

is an excellent approximation to the exact value of L.

(e) For the values given in part (c), compare L_a with L.

45. *(Continuation of Exercise 44)* Let n be the number of complete turns the take-up reel has made.

(a) Find a formula for n in terms of L, the tape length.

(b) When a VCR operates, the tape moves past the heads at a constant speed. Describe the speed of the take-up reel as time progresses.

(c) Suppose that the VCR tape counter is the number n of complete turns of the take-up reel. Describe the counter values as a function of time t.

Questions to Guide Your Review

1. When do directed line segments in the plane represent the same vector?

2. How are vectors added and subtracted geometrically? Algebraically?

3. How do you find a vector's magnitude and direction?

4. If a vector is multiplied by a positive scalar, how is the result related to the original vector? What if the scalar is zero? Negative?

5. Define the *dot product* (*scalar product*) of two vectors. Which algebraic laws are satisfied by dot products? Give examples. When is the dot product of two vectors equal to zero?

6. What geometric interpretation does the dot product have? Give examples.

7. What is the vector projection of a vector **u** onto a vector **v**? How do you write **u** as the sum of a vector parallel to **v** and a vector orthogonal to **v**?

8. State the rules for differentiating and integrating vector functions. Give examples.

9. How do you define and calculate the velocity, speed, direction of motion, and acceleration of a body moving along a sufficiently differentiable plane curve? Give examples.

10. What are the vector and parametric equations for ideal projectile motion? How do you find an ideal projectile's maximum height, flight time, and range? Give examples.

11. What are polar coordinates? What equations relate polar coordinates to Cartesian coordinates? Why might you want to change from one coordinate system to the other?

12. What consequence does the lack of uniqueness of polar coordinates have for graphing? Give an example.

13. How do you graph equations in polar coordinates? Include in your discussion symmetry and slope. Give examples.

14. How do you find the area of a region $0 \leq r_1(\theta) \leq r \leq r_2(\theta)$, $\alpha \leq \theta \leq \beta$, in the polar coordinate plane? Give examples.

15. Under what conditions can you find the length of a curve $r = f(\theta)$, $\alpha \leq \theta \leq \beta$, in the polar coordinate plane? Give an example of a typical calculation.

Practice Exercises

Vector Calculations

In Exercises 1–4, let $\mathbf{u} = \langle -3, 4 \rangle$ and $\mathbf{v} = \langle 2, -5 \rangle$. Find (**a**) the component form of the vector and (**b**) its magnitude.

1. $3\mathbf{u} - 4\mathbf{v}$

2. $\mathbf{u} + \mathbf{v}$

3. $-2\mathbf{u}$

4. $5\mathbf{v}$

In Exercises 5–8, find the component form of the vector.

5. The vector obtained by rotating $\langle 0, 1 \rangle$ through an angle of $2\pi/3$ radians

6. The unit vector that makes an angle of $\pi/6$ radian with the positive x-axis

7. The vector 2 units long in the direction $4\mathbf{i} - \mathbf{j}$

8. The vector 5 units long in the direction opposite to the direction of $(3/5)\mathbf{i} + (4/5)\mathbf{j}$

Length and Direction

Express the vectors in Exercises 9–12 in terms of their lengths and directions.

9. $\sqrt{2}\mathbf{i} + \sqrt{2}\mathbf{j}$

10. $-\mathbf{i} - \mathbf{j}$

11. Velocity vector to $\mathbf{r} = (2\cos t)\mathbf{i} + (2\sin t)\mathbf{j}$ at the point $(0, 2)$.

12. Velocity vector to $\mathbf{r} = (e^t \cos t)\mathbf{i} + (e^t \sin t)\mathbf{j}$ when $t = \ln 2$.

Tangent and Normal Vectors

In Exercises 13 and 14, find the unit vectors that are tangent and normal to the curve at point P.

13. $y = \tan x$, $P(\pi/4, 1)$

14. $x^2 + y^2 = 25$, $P(3, 4)$

Vector Projections

15. Copy the vectors $\mathbf{u}$ and $\mathbf{v}$ and sketch the vector projection of $\mathbf{v}$ onto $\mathbf{u}$.

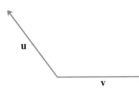

16. Express vectors $\mathbf{a}$, $\mathbf{b}$, and $\mathbf{c}$ in terms of $\mathbf{u}$ and $\mathbf{v}$.

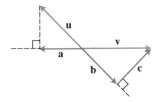

In Exercises 17 and 18, find $|\mathbf{v}|$, $|\mathbf{u}|$, $\mathbf{v} \cdot \mathbf{u}$, $\mathbf{u} \cdot \mathbf{v}$, the angle between $\mathbf{v}$ and $\mathbf{u}$, the scalar component of $\mathbf{u}$ in the direction of $\mathbf{v}$, and the vector projection of $\mathbf{u}$ onto $\mathbf{v}$.

17. $\mathbf{v} = \mathbf{i} + \mathbf{j}$

   $\mathbf{u} = 2\mathbf{i} + \mathbf{j}$

18. $\mathbf{v} = \mathbf{i} + \mathbf{j}$

   $\mathbf{u} = -\mathbf{i} - 3\mathbf{j}$

In Exercises 19 and 20, write $\mathbf{u}$ as the sum of a vector parallel to $\mathbf{v}$ and a vector orthogonal to $\mathbf{v}$.

19. $\mathbf{v} = 2\mathbf{i} - \mathbf{j}$

   $\mathbf{u} = \mathbf{i} + \mathbf{j}$

20. $\mathbf{v} = \mathbf{i} - 2\mathbf{j}$

   $\mathbf{u} = -\mathbf{i} + \mathbf{j}$

Velocity and Acceleration Vectors

In Exercises 21 and 22, $\mathbf{r}(t)$ is the position vector of a particle in the plane at time t.

   (a) Find the velocity and acceleration vectors.

   (b) Find the speed at the given value of t.

   (c) Find the angle between the velocity and acceleration vectors at the given value of t.

21. $\mathbf{r}(t) = (4 \cos t)\mathbf{i} + (\sqrt{2} \sin t)\mathbf{j}$, $t = \pi/4$

22. $\mathbf{r}(t) = (\sqrt{3} \sec t)\mathbf{i} + (\sqrt{3} \tan t)\mathbf{j}$, $t = 0$

23. *Maximum speed* The position of a particle in the plane at time t is

$$\mathbf{r} = \frac{1}{\sqrt{1 + t^2}}\mathbf{i} + \frac{t}{\sqrt{1 + t^2}}\mathbf{j}.$$

Find the particle's greatest speed.

24. *Writing to Learn: Minimum speed* The position of a particle in the plane at time $t \geq 0$ is

$$\mathbf{r}(t) = (e^t \cos t)\mathbf{i} + (e^t \sin t)\mathbf{j}.$$

Find the particle's minimum speed. Does it have a maximum speed? Give reasons for your answer.

Integrals and Initial Value Problems

In Exercises 25 and 26, evaluate the integral.

25. $\displaystyle\int_0^1 [(3 + 6t)\mathbf{i} + (6\pi \cos \pi t)\mathbf{j}] \, dt$

26. $\displaystyle\int_e^{e^2} \left[\left(\frac{2 \ln t}{t}\right)\mathbf{i} + \left(\frac{1}{t \ln t}\right)\mathbf{j}\right] dt$

In Exercises 27–30, solve the initial value problem.

27. $\dfrac{d\mathbf{r}}{dt} = -(\sin t)\mathbf{i} + (\cos t)\mathbf{j}$, $\mathbf{r}(0) = \mathbf{j}$

28. $\dfrac{d\mathbf{r}}{dt} = \dfrac{1}{t^2 + 1}\mathbf{i} + \dfrac{t}{\sqrt{t^2 + 1}}\mathbf{j}$, $\mathbf{r}(0) = \mathbf{i} + \mathbf{j}$

29. $\dfrac{d^2\mathbf{r}}{dt^2} = 2\mathbf{j}$, $\left.\dfrac{d\mathbf{r}}{dt}\right|_{t=0} = \mathbf{0}$, $\mathbf{r}(0) = \mathbf{i}$

30. $\dfrac{d^2\mathbf{r}}{dt^2} = -2\mathbf{i} - 2\mathbf{j}$, $\left.\dfrac{d\mathbf{r}}{dt}\right|_{t=1} = 4\mathbf{i}$, $\mathbf{r}(1) = 3\mathbf{i} + 3\mathbf{j}$

Graphs in the Polar Plane

Sketch the regions defined by the polar coordinate inequalities in Exercises 31 and 32.

31. $0 \leq r \leq 6 \cos \theta$ **32.** $-4 \sin \theta \leq r \leq 0$

Match each graph in Exercises 33–40 with the appropriate equation (a) through (l). There are more equations than graphs, so some equations will not be matched.

(a) $r = \cos 2\theta$ **(b)** $r \cos \theta = 1$

(c) $r = \dfrac{6}{1 - 2 \cos \theta}$ **(d)** $r = \sin 2\theta$

(e) $r = \theta$ **(f)** $r^2 = \cos 2\theta$

(g) $r = 1 + \cos \theta$

(h) $r = 1 - \sin \theta$

(i) $r = \dfrac{2}{1 - \cos \theta}$

(j) $r^2 = \sin 2\theta$

(k) $r = -\sin \theta$

(l) $r = 2 \cos \theta + 1$

33. Four-leaved rose

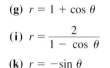

34. Spiral

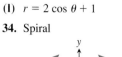

35. Limaçon

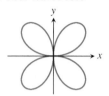

36. Lemniscate

37. Circle

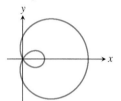

38. Cardioid

39. Parabola

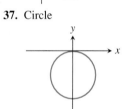

40. Lemniscate

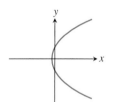

In Exercises 41–44, **(a)** graph the polar curve. **(b)** What is the smallest length θ-interval that will produce the graph?

41. $r = \cos 2\theta$

42. $r \cos \theta = 1$

43. $r^2 = \sin 2\theta$

44. $r = -\sin \theta$

Tangent Lines to Polar Graphs

In Exercises 45 and 46, find the tangent lines at the pole.

45. $r = \cos 2\theta$, $0 \le \theta \le 2\pi$

46. $r = 1 + \cos 2\theta$, $0 \le \theta \le 2\pi$

In Exercises 47 and 48, find equations for the horizontal and vertical tangent lines to the curve.

47. $r = 1 - \cos (\theta/2)$, $0 \le \theta \le 4\pi$

48. $r = 2(1 - \sin \theta)$, $0 \le \theta \le 2\pi$

49. Find equations for the lines that are tangent to the tips of the petals of the four-leaved rose $r = \sin 2\theta$.

50. Find equations for the lines that are tangent to the graph of the cardioid $r = 1 + \sin \theta$ at the points where it crosses the x-axis.

Polar to Cartesian Equations

In Exercises 51–56, replace the polar equation by an equivalent Cartesian equation. Then identify or describe the graph.

51. $r \cos \theta = r \sin \theta$

52. $r = 3 \cos \theta$

53. $r = 4 \tan \theta \sec \theta$

54. $r \cos (\theta + \pi/3) = 2\sqrt{3}$

55. $r = 2 \sec \theta$

56. $r = -(3/2) \csc \theta$

Cartesian to Polar Equations

In Exercises 57–60, replace the Cartesian equation by an equivalent polar equation.

57. $x^2 + y^2 + 5y = 0$

58. $x^2 + y^2 - 2y = 0$

59. $x^2 + 4y^2 = 16$

60. $(x + 2)^2 + (y - 5)^2 = 16$

Area in the Polar Plane

Find the areas of the regions in the polar coordinate plane described in Exercises 61–64.

61. Enclosed by the limaçon $r = 2 - \cos \theta$

62. Enclosed by one leaf of the three-leaved rose $r = \sin 3\theta$

63. Inside the "figure eight" $r = 1 + \cos 2\theta$ and outside the circle $r = 1$

64. Inside the cardioid $r = 2(1 + \sin \theta)$ and outside the circle $r = 2 \sin \theta$

Lengths of Polar Curves

Find the lengths of the curves given by the polar coordinate equations in Exercises 65–68.

65. $r = -1 + \cos \theta$

66. $r = 2 \sin \theta + 2 \cos \theta$, $0 \le \theta \le \pi/2$

67. $r = 8 \sin^3(\theta/3), \quad 0 \le \theta \le \pi/4$

68. $r = \sqrt{1 + \cos 2\theta}, \quad -\pi/2 \le \theta \le \pi/2$

Theory and Examples

69. *Navigation* An airplane, flying in the direction 80° east of north at 540 mph in still air, encounters a 55 mph tailwind acting in the direction 100° east of north. The airplane holds its compass heading but, because of the wind, acquires a different ground speed and direction. What are they?

70. *Combining forces* A force of 120 lb pulls up on an object at an angle of 20° with the horizontal. A second force of 300 lb pulls down on the object at an angle of −5°. Find the direction and length of the resultant force vector.

71. *Shot put* A shot leaves the thrower's hand 6.5 ft above the ground at a 45° angle at 44 ft/sec. Where is it 3 sec later?

72. *Javelin* A javelin leaves the thrower's hand 7 ft above the ground at a 45° angle at 80 ft/sec. How high does it go?

73. *Rolling wheel* A circular wheel with radius 1 ft and center C rolls to the right along the x-axis at a half-turn per second (see figure). At time t seconds, the position vector of the point P on the wheel's circumference is

$$\mathbf{r}(t) = (\pi t - \sin \pi t)\mathbf{i} + (1 - \cos \pi t)\mathbf{j}.$$

☐**T** **(a)** Graph the curve traced by P during the interval $0 \le t \le 3$.

(b) Find velocity and acceleration vectors $\mathbf{v}$ and $\mathbf{a}$ at $t = 0, 1, 2,$ and 3.

(c) *Writing to Learn* At any given time, what is the forward speed of the topmost point of the wheel? Of C? Give reasons for your answers.

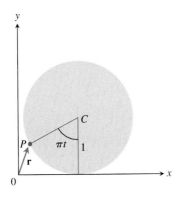

74. *The dictator* The Civil War mortar Dictator weighed so much (17,120 lb) that it had to be mounted on a railroad car. It had a 13 in. bore and used a 20 lb powder charge to fire a 200 lb shell. The mortar was made by Mr. Charles Knapp in his ironworks in Pittsburgh, Pennsylvania, and was used by the Union army in 1864 in

the siege of Petersburg, Virginia. How far did it shoot? Here we have a difference of opinion. The ordnance manual claimed 4325 yd, whereas field officers claimed 4752 yd. Assuming a 45° firing angle, what muzzle speeds are involved here?

75. *World's record for popping a champagne cork*

(a) Until 1988, the world's record for popping a champagne cork, 109 ft 6 in., was held by Captain Michael Hill of the British Royal Artillery. Assuming that Captain Hill held the bottle at ground level at a 45° angle and the cork behaved like an ideal projectile, how fast was the cork going as it left the bottle?

(b) A new world record, 177 ft 9 in., was set on June 5, 1988, by Prof. Emeritus Heinrich of Rensselaer Polytechnic Institute, firing from 4 ft above ground level at a 45° angle at the Woodbury Vineyards Winery, New York. Assuming an ideal trajectory, what was the cork's initial speed?

76. *Javelin* In Potsdam in 1988, Petra Felke of (then) East Germany set a women's world record by throwing a javelin 262 ft 5 in.

(a) Assuming that Felke launched the javelin at a 40° angle to the horizontal from 6.5 ft above the ground, what was the javelin's initial speed?

(b) How high did the javelin go?

77. *Synchronous curves* By eliminating α from the ideal projectile equations

$$x = (v_0 \cos \alpha)t, \qquad y = (v_0 \sin \alpha)t - \frac{1}{2}gt^2,$$

show that $x^2 + (y + gt^2/2)^2 = v_0^2 t^2$. This shows that projectiles launched simultaneously from the origin at the same initial speed will, at any given instant, all lie on the circle of radius $v_0 t$ centered at $(0, -gt^2/2)$, regardless of their launch angle. These circles are the *synchronous curves* of the launching.

78. *Hitting a baseball under a wind gust* A baseball is hit when it is 4 ft above the ground. It leaves the bat with an intial velocity of 155 ft/sec, making an angle of 18° with the horizontal. At the instant the ball is hit, an instantaneous 11.7 ft/sec gust of wind blows in the horizontal direction against the ball, adding a component of

$-11.7\mathbf{i}$ to the ball's initial velocity. A 10-foot-high fence is 380 ft from home plate in the direction of the flight.

(a) Find vector and parametric equations for the path of the baseball.

(b) How high does the baseball go, and when does it reach maximum height?

(c) Find the range and flight time of the baseball.

(d) When is the baseball 25 ft high? How far (ground distance) is the baseball from home plate at that height?

(e) *Writing to Learn* Has the batter hit a home run? Explain.

79. *Linear drag* (*Continuation of Exercise 78*) Consider the baseball problem of Exercise 78 again. This time, assume a linear drag model with a drag coefficient of 0.09.

(a) Find vector and parametric equations for the path of the baseball.

(b) How high does the baseball go, and when does it reach maximum height?

(c) Find the range and flight time of the baseball.

(d) When is the baseball 30 ft high? How far (ground distance) is the baseball from home plate at that height?

(e) Has the batter hit a home run? If "yes," find a drag coefficient that would have prevented a home run. If "no," find a drag coefficient that would have allowed the hit to be a home run.

80. *Parallelogram* The accompanying figure shows parallelogram $ABCD$ and the midpoint P of diagonal BD.

(a) Express $\overrightarrow{BD}$ in terms of $\overrightarrow{AB}$ and $\overrightarrow{AD}$.

(b) Express $\overrightarrow{AP}$ in terms of $\overrightarrow{AB}$ and $\overrightarrow{AD}$.

(c) Prove that P is also the midpoint of diagonal AC.

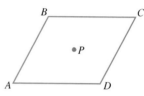

81. *Archimedes spirals* The graph of an equation of the form $r = a\theta$, where a is a nonzero constant, is called an Archimedes spiral. Is there anything special about the widths between the successive turns of such a spiral?

Additional Exercises: Theory, Examples, Applications

1. *Rowing across a river* A straight river is 20 m wide. The velocity of the river at (x, y) is

$$\mathbf{v} = -\frac{3x(20 - x)}{100}\mathbf{j} \quad \text{m/min}, \qquad 0 \le x \le 20.$$

A boat leaves the shore at $(0, 0)$ and travels through the water with a constant velocity. It arrives at the opposite shore at $(20, 0)$. The speed of the boat is always $\sqrt{20}$ m/min.

(a) Find the velocity of the boat.

(b) Find the location of the boat at time t.

(c) Sketch the path of the boat.

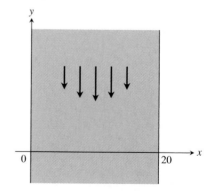

2. *Motion on a circle* A particle moves in the plane so that its velocity and position vectors are always orthogonal. Show that the particle moves in a circle centered at the origin.

3. *Angle between position and acceleration vectors* Suppose that $\mathbf{r}(t) = (e^t \cos t)\mathbf{i} + (e^t \sin t)\mathbf{j}$. Show that the angle between $\mathbf{r}$ and $\mathbf{a}$ never changes. What *is* the angle?

4. *Motion on a circle* A particle moves around the unit circle in the xy-plane. Its position at time t is $\mathbf{r} = x\mathbf{i} + y\mathbf{j}$, where x and y are differentiable functions of t. Find dy/dt if $\mathbf{v} \cdot \mathbf{i} = y$. Is the motion clockwise, or counterclockwise?

5. *Motion on a cubic* You send a message through a pneumatic tube that follows the curve $9y = x^3$ (distance in meters). At the point $(3, 3)$, $\mathbf{v} \cdot \mathbf{i} = 4$ and $\mathbf{a} \cdot \mathbf{i} = -2$. Find the values of $\mathbf{v} \cdot \mathbf{j}$ and $\mathbf{a} \cdot \mathbf{j}$ at $(3, 3)$.

6. *Angle bisection* Show that $\mathbf{w} = |\mathbf{v}|\mathbf{u} + |\mathbf{u}|\mathbf{v}$ bisects the angle between $\mathbf{u}$ and $\mathbf{v}$.

Polar Coordinates

7. **(a)** *Finding a polar equation* Find an equation in polar coordinates for the curve

$$x = e^{2t} \cos t, \qquad y = e^{2t} \sin t, \qquad -\infty < t < \infty.$$

     (b) *Length of curve* Find the length of the curve from $t = 0$ to $t = 2\pi$.

8. *Length of curve* Find the length of the curve $r = 2 \sin^3 (\theta/3)$, $0 \le \theta \le 3\pi$, in the polar coordinate plane.

9. *Polar area* Sketch the regions enclosed by the curves $r = 2a \cos^2 (\theta/2)$ and $r = 2a \sin^2 (\theta/2)$, $a > 0$, in the polar coordinate plane and find the area of the portion of the plane they have in common.

T **10.** Graph the curve $r = \cos 5\theta + n \cos \theta$, $0 \le \theta \le \pi$ for integers $n = -5$ (heart) to $n = 5$ (bell). (*Source: The College Mathematics Journal*, Vol. 25, No. 1 (Jan. 1994).)

10 Vectors and Motion in Space

OVERVIEW   This chapter introduces vectors within a three-dimensional coordinate system. Just as the coordinate plane is the natural place to study functions of a single variable, coordinate space is the place to study functions of two variables (or more). We establish coordinates in space by adding a third axis that measures distance above and below the xy-plane. This axis is designated the z-axis, and the standard unit vector parallel to it pointing in the positive direction is denoted by **k**.

When a body travels through space, the equations $x = f(t)$, $y = g(t)$, and $z = h(t)$ that give the body's coordinates as functions of time serve as parametric equations for the body's motion and path. With vector notation, we can condense these into a single equation $\mathbf{r}(t) = f(t)\mathbf{i} + g(t)\mathbf{j} + h(t)\mathbf{k}$ that gives the body's position as a vector function of time.

In this chapter, we show how to use calculus to study the paths, velocities, and accelerations of moving bodies. As we go along, we see how our work answers the standard questions about the paths and motions of planets and satellites. In the final section, we use our new vector calculus to derive Kepler's laws of planetary motion from Newton's laws of motion and gravitation.

10.1   Cartesian (Rectangular) Coordinates and Vectors in Space

Cartesian Coordinates • Vectors in Space • Magnitude • The Zero Vector • Unit Vectors • Length and Direction • Distance and Spheres in Space • Midpoints

Our goal now is to describe the three-dimensional Cartesian coordinate system. Then we can define and study vectors in space.

Cartesian Coordinates

To locate points in space, we use three mutually perpendicular coordinate axes, arranged as in Figure 10.1. The axes shown there make a *right-handed* coordinate frame. When you hold your right hand so that the fingers curl from the positive x-axis toward the positive y-axis, your thumb points along the positive z-axis.

The Cartesian coordinates (x, y, z) of a point P in space are the numbers at which the planes through P perpendicular to the axes cut the axes. Cartesian

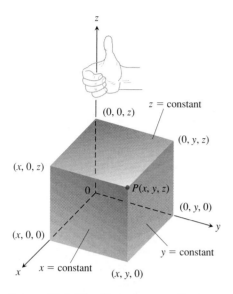

FIGURE 10.1 The Cartesian coordinate system is right-handed.

coordinates for space are also called **rectangular coordinates** because the axes that define them meet at right angles.

Points on the x-axis have y- and z-coordinates equal to zero. That is, they have coordinates of the form $(x, 0, 0)$. Similarly, points on the y-axis have coordinates of the form $(0, y, 0)$. Points on the z-axis have coordinates of the form $(0, 0, z)$.

The planes determined by the coordinates axes are the **xy-plane**, whose standard equation is $z = 0$; the **yz-plane**, whose standard equation is $x = 0$; and the **xz-plane**, whose standard equation is $y = 0$. They meet at the **origin** $(0, 0, 0)$ (Figure 10.2).

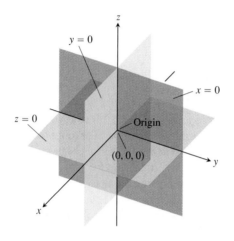

FIGURE 10.2 The planes $x = 0$, $y = 0$, and $z = 0$ divide space into eight octants.

The three **coordinate planes** $x = 0$, $y = 0$, and $z = 0$ divide space into eight cells called **octants**. The octant in which the point coordinates are all positive is called the **first octant;** there is no conventional numbering for the other seven octants.

In the following examples, we match coordinate equations and inequalities with the sets of points they define in space.

Example 1   Interpreting Equations and Inequalities Geometrically

(a) $z \geq 0$ — The half-space consisting of the points on and above the xy-plane.

(b) $x = -3$ — The plane perpendicular to the x-axis at $x = -3$. This plane lies parallel to the yz-plane and 3 units behind it.

(c) $z = 0$, $x \leq 0$, $y \geq 0$ — The second quadrant of the xy-plane.

(d) $x \geq 0$, $y \geq 0$, $z \geq 0$ — The first octant.

(e) $-1 \leq y \leq 1$ — The slab between the planes $y = -1$ and $y = 1$ (planes included).

(f) $y = -2$, $z = 2$ — The line in which the planes $y = -2$ and $z = 2$ intersect. Alternatively, the line through the point $(0, -2, 2)$ parallel to the x-axis.

Example 2 Graphing Equations

What points $P(x, y, z)$ satisfy the equations

$$x^2 + y^2 = 4 \quad \text{and} \quad z = 3?$$

Solution   The points lie in the horizontal plane $z = 3$ and, in this plane, make up the circle $x^2 + y^2 = 4$. We call this set of points "the circle $x^2 + y^2 = 4$ in the plane $z = 3$" or, more simply, "the circle $x^2 + y^2 = 4$, $z = 3$" (Figure 10.3).

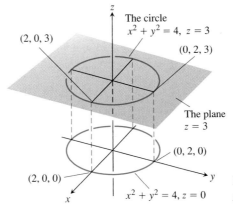

FIGURE 10.3 The circle $x^2 + y^2 = 4$, $z = 3$.

Vectors in Space

Vectors in space are like vectors in the plane except there is a third component. Just as in the plane (Section 9.1), **vectors** in space are directed line segments. Two such vectors are **equal** if they have the same length and direction. Vectors are used to represent forces, displacements, velocities, and accelerations in space. In this section, we summarize the properties of vectors in space (which are identical to the properties studied in Section 9.1 for planar vectors).

If $\mathbf{v}$ is a vector in space equal to a vector with initial point $(0, 0, 0)$ and terminal point (v_1, v_2, v_3), then the **component form** of $\mathbf{v}$ is $\mathbf{v} = \langle v_1, v_2, v_3 \rangle$. As in the plane, this is also the **position vector** of the point (v_1, v_2, v_3). The vector from the initial point $P_1(x_1, y_1, z_1)$ to the terminal point $P_2(x_2, y_2, z_2)$ is $\mathbf{v} = \overrightarrow{P_1 P_2} = \langle x_2 - x_1, y_2 - y_1, z_2 - z_1 \rangle$.

The vectors represented by the directed line segments from the origin to the points $(1, 0, 0)$, $(0, 1, 0)$, and $(0, 0, 1)$ are the **standard unit vectors** and are denoted by $\mathbf{i}$, $\mathbf{j}$, and $\mathbf{k}$ (Figure 10.4). The position vector $\mathbf{r}$ from the origin to the typical point $P(x, y, z)$ can then be written as

$$\mathbf{r} = \overrightarrow{OP} = x\mathbf{i} + y\mathbf{j} + z\mathbf{k}.$$

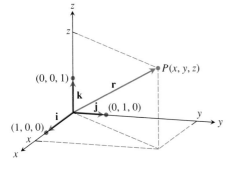

FIGURE 10.4 The position vector of a point in space.

Thus, the vector $\overrightarrow{P_1 P_2} = \langle x_2 - x_1, y_2 - y_1, z_2 - z_1 \rangle$ can be expressed as

$$\overrightarrow{P_1 P_2} = (x_2 - x_1)\mathbf{i} + (y_2 - y_1)\mathbf{j} + (z_2 - z_1)\mathbf{k}.$$

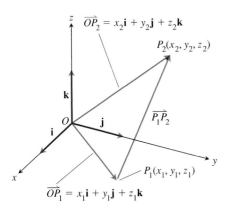

FIGURE 10.5 The vector from P_1 to P_2 is $\overrightarrow{P_1 P_2} = (x_2 - x_1)\mathbf{i} + (y_2 - y_1)\mathbf{j} + (z_2 - z_1)\mathbf{k}.$

(See Figure 10.5.) We use this as our primary notation for vectors in space.

The definitions of addition, subtraction, and scalar multiplication are the same as in the plane. They also satisfy the same properties and interpretations.

> **Definitions**   Vector Operations
>
> Let $\mathbf{u} = u_1\mathbf{i} + u_2\mathbf{j} + u_3\mathbf{k}$ and $\mathbf{v} = v_1\mathbf{i} + v_2\mathbf{j} + v_3\mathbf{k}$ be vectors with k a scalar (real number).
>
> **Addition:** $\mathbf{u} + \mathbf{v} = (u_1 + v_1)\mathbf{i} + (u_2 + v_2)\mathbf{j} + (u_3 + v_3)\mathbf{k}$
>
> **Subtraction:** $\mathbf{u} - \mathbf{v} = (u_1 - v_1)\mathbf{i} + (u_2 - v_2)\mathbf{j} + (u_3 - v_3)\mathbf{k}$
>
> **Scalar Multiplication:** $k\mathbf{u} = (ku_1)\mathbf{i} + (ku_2)\mathbf{j} + (ku_3)\mathbf{k}$

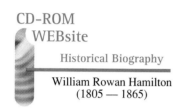

CD-ROM
WEBsite

Historical Biography

William Rowan Hamilton
(1805 — 1865)

Magnitude

As for planar vectors, magnitude and direction are important features of a vector in space. We find a formula for the magnitude (length) of $\mathbf{v} = v_1\mathbf{i} + v_2\mathbf{j} + v_3\mathbf{k}$ by applying the Pythagorean Theorem to the right triangles in Figure 10.6. From triangle ABC,

$$|\overrightarrow{AC}| = \sqrt{v_1^2 + v_2^2},$$

and from triangle ACD,

$$|\mathbf{v}| = |v_1\mathbf{i} + v_2\mathbf{j} + v_3\mathbf{k}| = |\overrightarrow{AD}| = \sqrt{|\overrightarrow{AC}|^2 + |\overrightarrow{CD}|^2}$$
$$= \sqrt{v_1^2 + v_2^2 + v_3^2}.$$

FIGURE 10.6 We find the length of $\mathbf{v} = \overrightarrow{AD}$ by applying the Pythagorean Theorem to the right triangles ABC and ACD.

> **Definition**   Magnitude (Length) of a Space Vector
> The **magnitude (length)** of $\mathbf{v} = v_1\mathbf{i} + v_2\mathbf{j} + v_3\mathbf{k}$ is
> $$|\mathbf{v}| = |v_1\mathbf{i} + v_2\mathbf{j} + v_3\mathbf{k}| = \sqrt{v_1^2 + v_2^2 + v_3^2}.$$

The Zero Vector

The **zero vector** in space is the vector $\mathbf{0} = \langle 0, 0, 0 \rangle = 0\mathbf{i} + 0\mathbf{j} + 0\mathbf{k}$. As in the plane, $\mathbf{0}$ has zero length and no direction.

Unit Vectors

A **unit vector** in space is a vector of length 1. The lengths of the standard unit vectors are

$$|\mathbf{i}| = |1\mathbf{i} + 0\mathbf{j} + 0\mathbf{k}| = \sqrt{1^2 + 0^2 + 0^2} = 1$$
$$|\mathbf{j}| = |0\mathbf{i} + 1\mathbf{j} + 0\mathbf{k}| = \sqrt{0^2 + 1^2 + 0^2} = 1$$
$$|\mathbf{k}| = |0\mathbf{i} + 0\mathbf{j} + 1\mathbf{k}| = \sqrt{0^2 + 0^2 + 1^2} = 1$$

confirming that the standard unit vectors are indeed unit vectors.

If $\mathbf{v} \neq \mathbf{0}$, then $\mathbf{v}/|\mathbf{v}|$ is a unit vector in the direction of $\mathbf{v}$.

Example 3   Finding a Unit Vector

Find a unit vector $\mathbf{u}$ in the direction of the vector from $P_1(1, 0, 1)$ to $P_2(3, 2, 0)$.

Solution   We divide $\overrightarrow{P_1P_2}$ by its length:

$$\overrightarrow{P_1P_2} = (3 - 1)\mathbf{i} + (2 - 0)\mathbf{j} + (0 - 1)\mathbf{k} = 2\mathbf{i} + 2\mathbf{j} - \mathbf{k}$$

$$|\overrightarrow{P_1P_2}| = \sqrt{(2)^2 + (2)^2 + (-1)^2} = \sqrt{4 + 4 + 1} = \sqrt{9} = 3$$

$$\mathbf{u} = \frac{\overrightarrow{P_1P_2}}{|\overrightarrow{P_1P_2}|} = \frac{2\mathbf{i} + 2\mathbf{j} - \mathbf{k}}{3} = \frac{2}{3}\mathbf{i} + \frac{2}{3}\mathbf{j} - \frac{1}{3}\mathbf{k}.$$

Length and Direction

As in the plane, if $\mathbf{v} \neq \mathbf{0}$ is a nonzero vector in space, then $\mathbf{v}/|\mathbf{v}|$ is a unit vector in the direction of $\mathbf{v}$. The equation

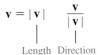

$$\mathbf{v} = |\mathbf{v}| \quad \frac{\mathbf{v}}{|\mathbf{v}|}$$

Length Direction

expresses $\mathbf{v}$ as a product of its length and direction.

Example 4   Velocity as Speed Times Direction

Express the velocity vector $\mathbf{v} = \mathbf{i} - 2\mathbf{j} + 3\mathbf{k}$ of a projectile as a product of its speed and direction.

Solution   As in the plane, speed is the magnitude of the velocity vector, and we have

$$|\mathbf{v}| = \sqrt{1^2 + (-2)^2 + 3^2} = \sqrt{14}.$$

Then,

$$\mathbf{v} = |\mathbf{v}|\frac{\mathbf{v}}{|\mathbf{v}|}$$

$$= \sqrt{14} \cdot \frac{\mathbf{i} - 2\mathbf{j} + 3\mathbf{k}}{\sqrt{14}}$$

$$= \sqrt{14}\left(\frac{1}{\sqrt{14}}\mathbf{i} - \frac{2}{\sqrt{14}}\mathbf{j} + \frac{3}{\sqrt{14}}\mathbf{k}\right) = (\text{length of } \mathbf{v}) \cdot (\text{direction of } \mathbf{v}).$$

Interpret   If distance is measured in feet and time in seconds, then the speed of the object is $\sqrt{14}$ ft/sec and it is moving in the direction of the unit vector $(1/\sqrt{14})\mathbf{i} - (2/\sqrt{14})\mathbf{j} + (3/\sqrt{14})\mathbf{k}$.

Example 5   A Force Vector

A force of 6 N is applied in the direction of the vector $\mathbf{v} = 2\mathbf{i} + 2\mathbf{j} - \mathbf{k}$. Express the force $\mathbf{F}$ as a product of its length and direction.

Solution   The force vector is

$$\mathbf{F} = 6 \frac{\mathbf{v}}{|\mathbf{v}|} = 6 \frac{2\mathbf{i} + 2\mathbf{j} - \mathbf{k}}{\sqrt{2^2 + 2^2 + (-1)^2}} = 6 \frac{2\mathbf{i} + 2\mathbf{j} - \mathbf{k}}{3}$$

$$= 6 \left(\frac{2}{3}\mathbf{i} + \frac{2}{3}\mathbf{j} - \frac{1}{3}\mathbf{k} \right).$$

Distance and Spheres in Space

The distance between two points P_1 and P_2 in space is the length of $\overrightarrow{P_1P_2}$.

The Distance Between $P_1(x_1, y_1, z_1)$ and $P_2(x_2, y_2, z_2)$

$$|\overrightarrow{P_1P_2}| = \sqrt{(x_2 - x_1)^2 + (y_2 - y_1)^2 + (z_2 - z_1)^2}$$

Example 6   Finding the Distance Between Two Points

The distance between $P_1(2, 1, 5)$ and $P_2(-2, 3, 0)$ is

$$|\overrightarrow{P_1P_2}| = \sqrt{(-2 - 2)^2 + (3 - 1)^2 + (0 - 5)^2}$$

$$= \sqrt{16 + 4 + 25}$$

$$= \sqrt{45} \approx 6.708.$$

We use the distance formula to write equations for spheres in space (Figure 10.7). A point $P(x, y, z)$ lies on the sphere of radius a centered at $P_0(x_0, y_0, z_0)$ precisely when $|\overrightarrow{P_0P}| = a$ or

$$(x - x_0)^2 + (y - y_0)^2 + (z - z_0)^2 = a^2.$$

The Standard Equation for the Sphere of Radius a and Center (x_0, y_0, z_0)

$$(x - x_0)^2 + (y - y_0)^2 + (z - z_0)^2 = a^2$$

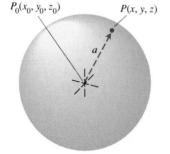

$P_0(x_0, y_0, z_0)$ $P(x, y, z)$

FIGURE 10.7 The sphere

$$(x - x_0)^2 + (y - y_0)^2 + (z - z_0)^2 = a^2.$$

Example 7   Finding the Center and Radius of a Sphere

Find the center and radius of the sphere

$$x^2 + y^2 + z^2 + 3x - 4z + 1 = 0.$$

Solution   We find the center and radius of a sphere the way we find the center and radius of a circle: Complete the squares on the x-, y-, and z-terms as necessary and write each quadratic as a squared linear expression. Then, from the equation in standard form, read off the center and radius. For the sphere here, we have

$$x^2 + y^2 + z^2 + 3x - 4z + 1 = 0$$

$$(x^2 + 3x) + y^2 + (z^2 - 4z) = -1$$

$$\left(x^2 + 3x + \left(\frac{3}{2}\right)^2\right) + y^2 + \left(z^2 - 4z + \left(\frac{-4}{2}\right)^2\right) = -1 + \left(\frac{3}{2}\right)^2 + \left(\frac{-4}{2}\right)^2$$

$$\left(x + \frac{3}{2}\right)^2 + y^2 + (z - 2)^2 = -1 + \frac{9}{4} + 4 = \frac{21}{4}.$$

From this standard form, we read that $x_0 = -3/2$, $y_0 = 0$, $z_0 = 2$, and $a = \sqrt{21}/2$. The center is $(-3/2, 0, 2)$. The radius is $\sqrt{21}/2$.

Example 8   Interpreting Equations and Inequalities

(a) $x^2 + y^2 + z^2 < 4$ The interior of the sphere $x^2 + y^2 + z^2 = 4$.

(b) $x^2 + y^2 + z^2 \le 4$ The solid ball bounded by the sphere $x^2 + y^2 + z^2 = 4$. Alternatively, the sphere $x^2 + y^2 + z^2 = 4$ together with its interior.

(c) $x^2 + y^2 + z^2 > 4$ The exterior of the sphere $x^2 + y^2 + z^2 = 4$.

(d) $x^2 + y^2 + z^2 = 4$,   The lower hemisphere cut from the sphere $x^2 + y^2 + z^2 = 4$ by the xy-plane (the plane $z = 0$).
    $z \le 0$

Midpoints

The coordinates of the midpoint of a line segment are found by averaging.

The **midpoint** M of the line segment joining points $P_1(x_1, y_1, z_1)$ and $P_2(x_2, y_2, z_2)$ is the point

$$\left(\frac{x_1 + x_2}{2}, \frac{y_1 + y_2}{2}, \frac{z_1 + z_2}{2}\right).$$

To see why, observe (Figure 10.8) that

$$\overrightarrow{OM} = \overrightarrow{OP_1} + \frac{1}{2}(\overrightarrow{P_1P_2}) = \overrightarrow{OP_1} + \frac{1}{2}(\overrightarrow{OP_2} - \overrightarrow{OP_1})$$

$$= \frac{1}{2}(\overrightarrow{OP_1} + \overrightarrow{OP_2})$$

$$= \frac{x_1 + x_2}{2}\mathbf{i} + \frac{y_1 + y_2}{2}\mathbf{j} + \frac{z_1 + z_2}{2}\mathbf{k}.$$

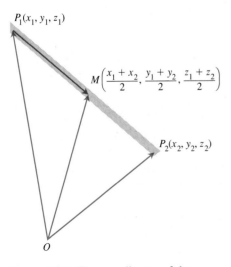

$P_1(x_1, y_1, z_1)$

$M\left(\frac{x_1 + x_2}{2}, \frac{y_1 + y_2}{2}, \frac{z_1 + z_2}{2}\right)$

$P_2(x_2, y_2, z_2)$

O

FIGURE 10.8 The coordinates of the midpoint are the averages of the coordinates of P_1 and P_2.

Example 9   Finding Midpoints

The midpoint of the segment joining $P_1(3, -2, 0)$ and $P_2(7, 4, 4)$

$$\left(\frac{3+7}{2}, \frac{-2+4}{2}, \frac{0+4}{2}\right) = (5, 1, 2).$$

EXERCISES 10.1

Sets, Equations, and Inequalities

In Exercises 1–10, give a geometric description of the set of points in space whose coordinates satisfy the given pairs of equations.

1. $x = 2, \quad y = 3$

2. $x = -1, \quad z = 0$

3. $y = 0, \quad z = 0$

4. $x = 1, \quad y = 0$

5. $x^2 + y^2 = 4, \quad z = -2$

6. $x^2 + z^2 = 4, \quad y = 0$

7. $x^2 + y^2 + z^2 = 1, \quad x = 0$

8. $x^2 + y^2 + z^2 = 25, \quad y = -4$

9. $x^2 + y^2 + (z + 3)^2 = 25, \quad z = 0$

10. $x^2 + (y - 1)^2 + z^2 = 4, \quad y = 0$

In Exercises 11–16, describe the sets of points in space whose coordinates satisfy the given inequalities or combinations of equations and inequalities.

11. (a) $x \geq 0, \quad y \geq 0, \quad z = 0$

(b) $x \geq 0, \quad y \leq 0, \quad z = 0$

12. (a) $0 \leq x \leq 1$

(b) $0 \leq x \leq 1, \quad 0 \leq y \leq 1$

(c) $0 \leq x \leq 1, \quad 0 \leq y \leq 1, \quad 0 \leq z \leq 1$

13. (a) $x^2 + y^2 + z^2 \leq 1$

(b) $x^2 + y^2 + z^2 > 1$

14. (a) $x^2 + y^2 \leq 1, \quad z = 0$

(b) $x^2 + y^2 \leq 1, \quad z = 3$

(c) $x^2 + y^2 \leq 1, \quad$ no restriction on z

15. (a) $x^2 + y^2 + z^2 = 1, \quad z \geq 0$

(b) $x^2 + y^2 + z^2 \leq 1, \quad z \geq 0$

16. (a) $x = y, \quad z = 0$

(b) $x = y, \quad$ no restriction on z

In Exercises 17–26, describe the given set with a single equation or with a pair of equations.

17. The plane perpendicular to the

(a) x-axis at $(3, 0, 0)$

(b) y-axis at $(0, -1, 0)$

(c) z-axis at $(0, 0, -2)$

18. The plane through the point $(3, -1, 2)$ perpendicular to the

(a) x-axis   **(b)** y-axis   **(c)** z-axis

19. The plane through the point $(3, -1, 1)$ parallel to the

(a) xy-plane   **(b)** yz-plane   **(c)** xz-plane

20. The circle of radius 2 centered at $(0, 0, 0)$ and lying in the

(a) xy-plane   **(b)** yz-plane   **(c)** xz-plane

21. The circle of radius 2 centered at $(0, 2, 0)$ and lying in the

(a) xy-plane   **(b)** yz-plane   **(c)** plane $y = 2$

22. The circle of radius 1 centered at $(-3, 4, 1)$ and lying in a plane parallel to the

(a) xy-plane   **(b)** yz-plane   **(c)** xz-plane

23. The line through the point $(1, 3, -1)$ parallel to the

(a) x-axis   **(b)** y-axis   **(c)** z-axis

24. The set of points in space equidistant from the origin and the point $(0, 2, 0)$

25. The circle in which the plane through the point $(1, 1, 3)$ perpendicular to the z-axis meets the sphere of radius 5 centered at the origin

26. The set of points in space that lie 2 units from the point $(0, 0, 1)$ and, at the same time, 2 units from the point $(0, 0, -1)$

Write inequalities to describe the sets in Exercises 27–32.

27. The slab bounded by the planes $z = 0$ and $z = 1$ (planes included)

28. The solid cube in the first octant bounded by the coordinate planes and the planes $x = 2$, $y = 2$, and $z = 2$

29. The half-space consisting of the points on and below the xy-plane

30. The upper hemisphere of the sphere of radius 1 centered at the origin

31. The **(a)** interior and **(b)** exterior of the sphere of radius 1 centered at the point $(1, 1, 1)$

32. The closed region bounded by the spheres of radius 1 and radius 2 centered at the origin. (*Closed* means the spheres are to be included. Had we wanted the spheres left out, we would have asked for the *open* region bounded by the spheres. This is analogous to the way we use *closed* and *open* to describe intervals: *closed* means endpoints included, *open* means endpoints left out. Closed sets include boundaries; open sets leave them out.)

Length and Direction

In Exercises 33–38, express each vector as a product of its length and direction.

33. $2\mathbf{i} + \mathbf{j} - 2\mathbf{k}$

34. $9\mathbf{i} - 2\mathbf{j} + 6\mathbf{k}$

35. $5\mathbf{k}$

36. $\dfrac{3}{5}\mathbf{i} + \dfrac{4}{5}\mathbf{k}$

37. $\dfrac{1}{\sqrt{6}}\mathbf{i} - \dfrac{1}{\sqrt{6}}\mathbf{j} - \dfrac{1}{\sqrt{6}}\mathbf{k}$

38. $\dfrac{\mathbf{i}}{\sqrt{3}} + \dfrac{\mathbf{j}}{\sqrt{3}} + \dfrac{\mathbf{k}}{\sqrt{3}}$

39. Find the vectors whose lengths and directions are given. Try to do the calculations without writing.

Length	Direction
(a) 2	$\mathbf{i}$
(b) $\sqrt{3}$	$-\mathbf{k}$
(c) $\dfrac{1}{2}$	$\dfrac{3}{5}\mathbf{j} + \dfrac{4}{5}\mathbf{k}$
(d) 7	$\dfrac{6}{7}\mathbf{i} - \dfrac{2}{7}\mathbf{j} + \dfrac{3}{7}\mathbf{k}$

40. Find the vectors whose lengths and directions are given. Try to do the calculations without writing.

Length	Direction
(a) 7	$-\mathbf{j}$
(b) $\sqrt{2}$	$-\dfrac{3}{5}\mathbf{i} - \dfrac{4}{5}\mathbf{k}$
(c) $\dfrac{13}{12}$	$\dfrac{3}{13}\mathbf{i} - \dfrac{4}{13}\mathbf{j} - \dfrac{12}{13}\mathbf{k}$
(d) $a > 0$	$\dfrac{1}{\sqrt{2}}\mathbf{i} + \dfrac{1}{\sqrt{3}}\mathbf{j} - \dfrac{1}{\sqrt{6}}\mathbf{k}$

41. Find a vector of magnitude 7 in the direction of $\mathbf{v} = 12\mathbf{i} - 5\mathbf{k}$.

42. Find a vector of magnitude 3 in the direction opposite to the direction of $\mathbf{v} = (1/2)\mathbf{i} - (1/2)\mathbf{j} - (1/2)\mathbf{k}$.

Vectors Determined by Points; Midpoints and Distance

In Exercises 43–46, find

    (a) the distance between points P_1 and P_2

    (b) the direction of $\overrightarrow{P_1P_2}$

    (c) the midpoint of line segment P_1P_2.

43. $P_1(-1, 1, 5)$, $P_2(2, 5, 0)$

44. $P_1(1, 4, 5)$, $P_2(4, -2, 7)$

45. $P_1(3, 4, 5)$, $P_2(2, 3, 4)$

46. $P_1(0, 0, 0)$, $P_2(2, -2, -2)$

47. If $\overrightarrow{AB} = \mathbf{i} + 4\mathbf{j} - 2\mathbf{k}$ and B is the point $(5, 1, 3)$, find A.

48. If $\overrightarrow{AB} = -7\mathbf{i} + 3\mathbf{j} + 8\mathbf{k}$ and A is the point $(-2, -3, 6)$, find B.

Spheres

In Exercises 49 and 50, find equations for the spheres with given center and radius.

49. Center: $(1, 2, 3)$,   radius: $\sqrt{14}$

50. Center: $(0, -1, 5)$,   radius: 2

Find the centers and radii of the spheres in Exercises 51–56.

51. $(x + 2)^2 + y^2 + (z - 2)^2 = 8$

52. $\left(x + \dfrac{1}{2}\right)^2 + \left(y + \dfrac{1}{2}\right)^2 + \left(z + \dfrac{1}{2}\right)^2 = \dfrac{21}{4}$

53. $x^2 + y^2 + z^2 + 4x - 4z = 0$

54. $x^2 + y^2 + z^2 - 6y + 8z = 0$

55. $2x^2 + 2y^2 + 2z^2 + x + y + z = 9$

56. $3x^2 + 3y^2 + 3z^2 + 2y - 2z = 9$

Theory and Examples

57. *Distance to coordinate axes* Find a formula for the distance from the point $P(x, y, z)$ to the

    (a) x-axis   **(b)** y-axis   **(c)** z-axis.

58. *Distance to coordinate planes* Find a formula for the distance from the point $P(x, y, z)$ to the

    (a) xy-plane   **(b)** yz-plane   **(c)** xz-plane.

59. *Medians of a triangle* Suppose that A, B, and C are the corner points of the thin triangular plate of constant density shown in the accompanying figure.

    (a) Find the vector from C to the midpoint M of side AB.

    (b) Find the vector from C to the point that lies two-thirds of the way from C to M on the median CM.

(c) Find the coordinates of the point in which the medians of $\triangle ABC$ intersect. According to Exercise 29, Section 5.6, this point is the plate's center of mass.

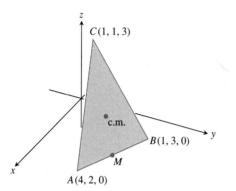

60. *Geometry and vectors* Find the vector from the origin to the point of intersection of the medians of the triangle whose vertices are

$$A(1, -1, 2), \qquad B(2, 1, 3), \qquad \text{and} \qquad C(-1, 2, -1).$$

61. *Quadrilateral* Let *ABCD* be a general, not necessarily planar, quadrilateral in space. Show that the two segments joining the midpoints of opposite sides of *ABCD* bisect each other. (*Hint:* Show that the segments have the same midpoint.)

62. *Writing to Learn* Vectors are drawn from the center of a regular *n*-sided polygon in the plane to the vertices of the polygon. Show that the sum of the vectors is zero. (*Hint:* What happens to the sum if you rotate the polygon about its center?)

63. *Triangle* Suppose that *A*, *B*, and *C* are vertices of a triangle and that *a*, *b*, and *c* are, respectively, the midpoints of the opposite sides. Show that $\overrightarrow{Aa} + \overrightarrow{Bb} + \overrightarrow{Cc} = 0$.

10.2   Dot and Cross Products

Dot Products • Properties of the Dot Product • Perpendicular (Orthogonal) Vectors and Projections • The Cross Product of Two Vectors in Space • Properties of the Cross Product • Determinant Formula for $\mathbf{u} \times \mathbf{v}$ • Torque • Triple Scalar or Box Product

In this section, we extend the definition of the dot product studied in Section 9.2 to vectors in space. Then we introduce a new product, the *cross product*, for vectors in space. The cross product is useful for the geometry of space such as describing how a plane is tilting by identifying a vector that is perpendicular to the plane. The direction of this vector tells us the "inclination" of the plane, just as the slope or angle of inclination describes how lines in the plane are tilting.

Dot Products

The dot product (or inner product) of two vectors in space is defined in the same way as for vectors in the plane (see Section 9.2). When two nonzero vectors $\mathbf{u}$ and $\mathbf{v}$ are placed so their initial points coincide, they form an angle θ of measure $0 \le \theta \le \pi$.

> **Definition**   Dot Product (Inner Product)
>
> The **dot product (inner product) $\mathbf{u} \cdot \mathbf{v}$** ("$\mathbf{u}$ dot $\mathbf{v}$") of vectors $\mathbf{u}$ and $\mathbf{v}$ is the number
>
> $$\mathbf{u} \cdot \mathbf{v} = |\mathbf{u}||\mathbf{v}| \cos \theta,$$
>
> where θ is the angle between $\mathbf{u}$ and $\mathbf{v}$.

In Section 9.2, we proved (see Theorem 1) that the dot product can be expressed using the components of the vectors. The same proof yields the following formula.

CD-ROM
WEBsite

Historical Biography

Carl Friedrich Gauss
(1777 — 1855)

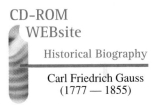

Computing the Dot Product

If $\mathbf{u} = u_1\mathbf{i} + u_2\mathbf{j} + u_3\mathbf{k}$ and $\mathbf{v} = v_1\mathbf{i} + v_2\mathbf{j} + v_3\mathbf{k}$, then

$$\mathbf{u} \cdot \mathbf{v} = u_1v_1 + u_2v_2 + u_3v_3.$$

Thus, to find the dot product of two given vectors, we multiply their corresponding $\mathbf{i}$-, $\mathbf{j}$-, and $\mathbf{k}$-components and add the results. This is the same procedure we used for planar vectors except there were only two components.

Solving for θ in the definition of dot product gives a formula for finding angles between vectors in space.

Angle Between Nonzero Vectors
The angle between two nonzero vectors $\mathbf{u}$ and $\mathbf{v}$ is

$$\theta = \cos^{-1}\left(\frac{\mathbf{u} \cdot \mathbf{v}}{|\mathbf{u}||\mathbf{v}|}\right).$$

Example 1   Finding the Angle Between Two Vectors in Space

Find the angle between $\mathbf{u} = \mathbf{i} - 2\mathbf{j} - 2\mathbf{k}$ and $\mathbf{v} = 6\mathbf{i} + 3\mathbf{j} + 2\mathbf{k}$.

Solution   We use the formula above:

$$\mathbf{u} \cdot \mathbf{v} = (1)(6) + (-2)(3) + (-2)(2) = 6 - 6 - 4 = -4$$
$$|\mathbf{u}| = \sqrt{(1)^2 + (-2)^2 + (-2)^2} = \sqrt{9} = 3$$
$$|\mathbf{v}| = \sqrt{(6)^2 + (3)^2 + (2)^2} = \sqrt{49} = 7$$
$$\theta = \cos^{-1}\left(\frac{\mathbf{u} \cdot \mathbf{v}}{|\mathbf{u}||\mathbf{v}|}\right)$$
$$= \cos^{-1}\left(\frac{-4}{(3)(7)}\right) \approx 1.76 \text{ rad.}$$

Properties of the Dot Product

We can use the component form of the dot product to establish the following properties (which are the same as for vectors in the plane studied in Section 9.2).

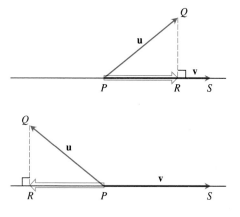

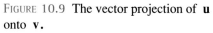

FIGURE 10.9 The vector projection of **u** onto **v**.

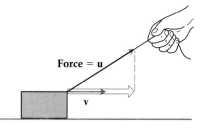

FIGURE 10.10 If we pull on a box with force **v**, the effective force in the direction of **u** is the vector projection of **v** onto **u**.

Properties of Dot Products

If **u**, **v**, and **w** are any vectors and c is a scalar, then

1. $\mathbf{u} \cdot \mathbf{v} = \mathbf{v} \cdot \mathbf{u}$

2. $(c\mathbf{u}) \cdot \mathbf{v} = \mathbf{u} \cdot (c\mathbf{v}) = c(\mathbf{u} \cdot \mathbf{v})$

3. $\mathbf{u} \cdot (\mathbf{v} + \mathbf{w}) = \mathbf{u} \cdot \mathbf{v} + \mathbf{u} \cdot \mathbf{w}$

4. $\mathbf{u} \cdot \mathbf{u} = |\mathbf{u}|^2$

5. $\mathbf{0} \cdot \mathbf{u} = 0$

Perpendicular (Orthogonal) Vectors and Projections

Just as for vectors in the plane, two nonzero vectors **u** and **v** are perpendicular or **orthogonal** if and only if $\mathbf{u} \cdot \mathbf{v} = 0$. The **vector projection** of $\mathbf{u} = \overrightarrow{PQ}$ onto a nonzero vector $\mathbf{v} = \overrightarrow{PS}$ (Figure 10.9) is the vector $\overrightarrow{PR}$ determined by dropping a perpendicular from Q to the line PS. This is exactly the same definition as for vectors in the plane (Section 9.2). The notation for this vector is

$$\text{proj}_{\mathbf{v}} \mathbf{u} \qquad (\text{``the vector projection of } \mathbf{u} \text{ onto } \mathbf{v}\text{''}).$$

If **u** represents a force, then $\text{proj}_{\mathbf{v}} \mathbf{u}$ represents the effective force in the direction of **v** (Figure 10.10).

Calculation of $\text{proj}_{\mathbf{v}} \mathbf{u}$ is the same as before.

Vector projection of u onto v:

$$\text{proj}_{\mathbf{v}} \mathbf{u} = \left(\frac{\mathbf{u} \cdot \mathbf{v}}{|\mathbf{v}|^2} \right) \mathbf{v} \tag{1}$$

The number $|\mathbf{u}| \cos \theta$ is called the **scalar component of u in the direction of v**. Since

$$|\mathbf{u}| \cos \theta = \frac{\mathbf{u} \cdot \mathbf{v}}{|\mathbf{v}|} = \mathbf{u} \cdot \frac{\mathbf{v}}{|\mathbf{v}|}, \tag{2}$$

we can find the scalar component by "dotting" **u** with the direction of **v**.

Example 2   Finding the Vector Projection

Find the vector projection of $\mathbf{u} = 6\mathbf{i} + 3\mathbf{j} + 2\mathbf{k}$ onto $\mathbf{v} = \mathbf{i} - 2\mathbf{j} - 2\mathbf{k}$ and the scalar component of **u** in the direction of **v**.

Solution   We find $\text{proj}_{\mathbf{v}} \mathbf{u}$ from Equation (1):

$$\text{proj}_{\mathbf{v}} \mathbf{u} = \frac{\mathbf{u} \cdot \mathbf{v}}{\mathbf{v} \cdot \mathbf{v}} \mathbf{v} = \frac{6 - 6 - 4}{1 + 4 + 4} (\mathbf{i} - 2\mathbf{j} - 2\mathbf{k})$$

$$= -\frac{4}{9} (\mathbf{i} - 2\mathbf{j} - 2\mathbf{k}) = -\frac{4}{9}\mathbf{i} + \frac{8}{9}\mathbf{j} + \frac{8}{9}\mathbf{k}.$$

We find the scalar component of **u** in the direction of **v** from Equation (2):

$$|\mathbf{u}|\cos\theta = \mathbf{u}\cdot\frac{\mathbf{v}}{|\mathbf{v}|} = (6\mathbf{i} + 3\mathbf{j} + 2\mathbf{k})\cdot\left(\frac{1}{3}\mathbf{i} - \frac{2}{3}\mathbf{j} - \frac{2}{3}\mathbf{k}\right)$$

$$= 2 - 2 - \frac{4}{3} = -\frac{4}{3}.$$

As with vectors in the plane, we can express a vector **u** as a sum of a vector parallel to a vector **v** and a vector orthogonal to **v**. We accomplish this with the equation

$$\mathbf{u} = \mathrm{proj}_\mathbf{v}\,\mathbf{u} + (\mathbf{u} - \mathrm{proj}_\mathbf{v}\,\mathbf{u}),$$

shown in Figure 10.11.

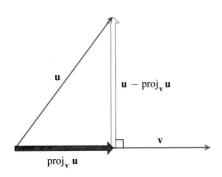

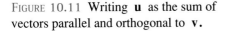

FIGURE 10.11 Writing **u** as the sum of vectors parallel and orthogonal to **v**.

Example 3   Force on a Spacecraft

A force $\mathbf{F} = 2\mathbf{i} + \mathbf{j} - 3\mathbf{k}$ N is applied to a spacecraft with velocity vector $\mathbf{v} = 3\mathbf{i} - \mathbf{j}$. Express **F** as a sum of a vector parallel to **v** and a vector orthogonal to **v**.

Solution

$$\mathbf{F} = \mathrm{proj}_\mathbf{v}\,\mathbf{F} + (\mathbf{F} - \mathrm{proj}_\mathbf{v}\,\mathbf{F})$$

$$= \frac{\mathbf{F}\cdot\mathbf{v}}{\mathbf{v}\cdot\mathbf{v}}\,\mathbf{v} + \left(\mathbf{F} - \frac{\mathbf{F}\cdot\mathbf{v}}{\mathbf{v}\cdot\mathbf{v}}\,\mathbf{v}\right)$$

$$= \left(\frac{6-1}{9+1}\right)\mathbf{v} + \left(\mathbf{F} - \left(\frac{6-1}{9+1}\right)\mathbf{v}\right)$$

$$= \frac{5}{10}(3\mathbf{i} - \mathbf{j}) + \left(2\mathbf{i} + \mathbf{j} - 3\mathbf{k} - \frac{5}{10}(3\mathbf{i} - \mathbf{j})\right)$$

$$= \left(\frac{3}{2}\mathbf{i} - \frac{1}{2}\mathbf{j}\right) + \left(\frac{1}{2}\mathbf{i} + \frac{3}{2}\mathbf{j} - 3\mathbf{k}\right).$$

Interpret The force $(3/2)\mathbf{i} - (1/2)\mathbf{j}$ is the effective force parallel to the velocity **v**. The force $(1/2)\mathbf{i} + (3/2)\mathbf{j} - 3\mathbf{k}$ is orthogonal to **v**. To check that this vector is orthogonal to **v**, we find the dot product:

$$\left(\frac{1}{2}\mathbf{i} + \frac{3}{2}\mathbf{j} - 3\mathbf{k}\right)\cdot(3\mathbf{i} - \mathbf{j}) = \frac{3}{2} - \frac{3}{2} = 0.$$

The Cross Product of Two Vectors in Space

We start with two nonzero vectors **u** and **v** in space. If **u** and **v** are not parallel, they determine a plane. We select a unit vector **n** perpendicular to the plane by the **right-hand rule.** This means that we choose **n** to be the unit (normal) vector that points the way your right thumb points when your fingers curl through the angle

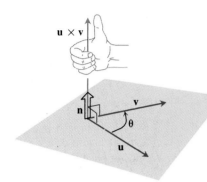

FIGURE 10.12 **The construction of u × v.**

θ from **u** to **v** (Figure 10.12). Then the **vector product u × v** ("u cross v") is the *vector* defined as follows.

Definition   Vector (Cross) Product

$$\mathbf{u} \times \mathbf{v} = (|\,\mathbf{u}\,\|\,\mathbf{v}\,|\ \sin\ \theta)\,\mathbf{n}$$

The vector **u × v** is orthogonal to both **u** and **v** because it is a scalar multiple of **n**. The vector product of **u** and **v** is often called the **cross product** of **u** and **v** because of the cross in the notation **u × v**.

Since the sines of 0 and π are both zero, it makes sense to define the cross product of two parallel nonzero vectors to be **0**.

If one or both of **u** and **v** are zero, we also define **u × v** to be zero. This way, the cross product of two vectors **u** and **v** is zero if and only if **u** and **v** are parallel or one or both of them are zero.

Parallel Vectors
Nonzero vectors **u** and **v** are parallel if and only if **u × v = 0.**

Properties of the Cross Product

The cross product obeys the following laws.

Properties of the Cross Product
If **u**, **v,** and **w** are any vectors and r, s are scalars, then

1. $(r\mathbf{u}) \times (s\mathbf{v}) = (rs)(\mathbf{u} \times \mathbf{v})$

2. $\mathbf{u} \times (\mathbf{v} + \mathbf{w}) = \mathbf{u} \times \mathbf{v} + \mathbf{u} \times \mathbf{w}$

3. $(\mathbf{v} + \mathbf{w}) \times \mathbf{u} = \mathbf{v} \times \mathbf{u} + \mathbf{w} \times \mathbf{u}$

4. $\mathbf{v} \times \mathbf{u} = -(\mathbf{u} \times \mathbf{v})$

5. $\mathbf{0} \times \mathbf{u} = \mathbf{0}$

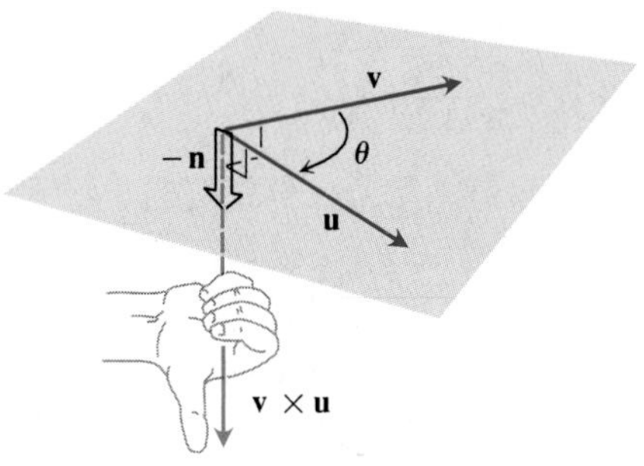

FIGURE 10.13 **The construction of v × u.**

To visualize Property 4, for example, we notice that when the fingers of our right hand curl through the angle θ from **v** to **u,** our thumb points the opposite way and the unit vector we choose in forming **v × u** is the negative of the one we choose in forming **u × v** (Figure 10.13).

Property 1 can be verified by applying the definition of cross product to both sides of the equation and comparing the results. Property 2 is proved in Appendix 9. Property 3 follows by multiplying both sides of the equation in Property 2 by -1 and reversing the order of the products using Property 4. Property 5 is by definition. As a rule, cross-product multiplication is *not associative* because $(\mathbf{u} \times \mathbf{v}) \times \mathbf{w}$ lies in the plane of **u** and **v** whereas $\mathbf{u} \times (\mathbf{v} \times \mathbf{w})$ lies in the plane of **v** and **w.**

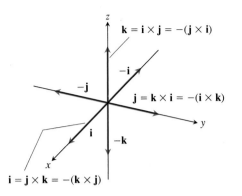

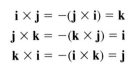

When we apply the definition to calculate the pairwise cross products of $\mathbf{i}$, $\mathbf{j}$, and $\mathbf{k}$, we find (Figure 10.14)

$$\mathbf{i} \times \mathbf{j} = -(\mathbf{j} \times \mathbf{i}) = \mathbf{k}$$
$$\mathbf{j} \times \mathbf{k} = -(\mathbf{k} \times \mathbf{j}) = \mathbf{i}$$
$$\mathbf{k} \times \mathbf{i} = -(\mathbf{i} \times \mathbf{k}) = \mathbf{j}$$

Diagram for recalling these products

and

$$\mathbf{i} \times \mathbf{i} = \mathbf{j} \times \mathbf{j} = \mathbf{k} \times \mathbf{k} = \mathbf{0}.$$

FIGURE 10.14 The pairwise cross products of $\mathbf{i}$, $\mathbf{j}$, and $\mathbf{k}$.

$|\mathbf{u} \times \mathbf{v}|$ Is the Area of a Parallelogram

Because $\mathbf{n}$ is a unit vector, the magnitude of $\mathbf{u} \times \mathbf{v}$ is

$$|\mathbf{u} \times \mathbf{v}| = |\mathbf{u}| |\mathbf{v}| |\sin \theta| |\mathbf{n}| = |\mathbf{u}| |\mathbf{v}| \sin \theta.$$

This is the area of the parallelogram determined by $\mathbf{u}$ and $\mathbf{v}$ (Figure 10.15), $|\mathbf{u}|$ being the base of the parallelogram and $|\mathbf{v}| \sin \theta|$ the height.

Determinants

(For more information, see Appendix 10.)

$$\begin{vmatrix} a & b \\ c & d \end{vmatrix} = ad - bc$$

EXAMPLE

$$\begin{vmatrix} 2 & 1 \\ -4 & 3 \end{vmatrix} = (2)(3) - (1)(-4)$$
$$= 6 + 4 = 10$$

$$\begin{vmatrix} a_1 & a_2 & a_3 \\ b_1 & b_2 & b_3 \\ c_1 & c_2 & c_3 \end{vmatrix}$$

$$= a_1 \begin{vmatrix} b_2 & b_3 \\ c_2 & c_3 \end{vmatrix} - a_2 \begin{vmatrix} b_1 & b_3 \\ c_1 & c_3 \end{vmatrix} + a_3 \begin{vmatrix} b_1 & b_2 \\ c_1 & c_2 \end{vmatrix}$$

EXAMPLE

$$\begin{vmatrix} -5 & 3 & 1 \\ 2 & 1 & 1 \\ -4 & 3 & 1 \end{vmatrix}$$

$$= (-5) \begin{vmatrix} 1 & 1 \\ 3 & 1 \end{vmatrix} - (3) \begin{vmatrix} 2 & 1 \\ -4 & 1 \end{vmatrix}$$

$$+ (1) \begin{vmatrix} 2 & 1 \\ -4 & 3 \end{vmatrix}$$

$$= -5(1 - 3) - 3(2 + 4) + 1(6 + 4)$$
$$= 10 - 18 + 10 = 2$$

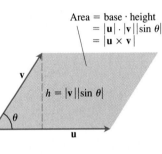

Area = base · height
$= |\mathbf{u}| \cdot |\mathbf{v}| |\sin \theta|$
$= |\mathbf{u} \times \mathbf{v}|$

$h = |\mathbf{v}| |\sin \theta|$

FIGURE 10.15 The parallelogram determined by $\mathbf{u}$ and $\mathbf{v}$.

Determinant Formula for $\mathbf{u} \times \mathbf{v}$

Our next objective is to calculate $\mathbf{u} \times \mathbf{v}$ from the components of $\mathbf{u}$ and $\mathbf{v}$ relative to a Cartesian coordinate system.

Suppose that

$$\mathbf{u} = u_1\mathbf{i} + u_2\mathbf{j} + u_3\mathbf{k}, \qquad \mathbf{v} = v_1\mathbf{i} + v_2\mathbf{j} + v_3\mathbf{k}.$$

Then the distributive laws and the rules for multiplying $\mathbf{i}$, $\mathbf{j}$, and $\mathbf{k}$ tell us that

$$\begin{aligned}
\mathbf{u} \times \mathbf{v} &= (u_1\mathbf{i} + u_2\mathbf{j} + u_3\mathbf{k}) \times (v_1\mathbf{i} + v_2\mathbf{j} + v_3\mathbf{k}) \\
&= u_1v_1\mathbf{i} \times \mathbf{i} + u_1v_2\mathbf{i} \times \mathbf{j} + u_1v_3\mathbf{i} \times \mathbf{k} \\
&\quad + u_2v_1\mathbf{j} \times \mathbf{i} + u_2v_2\mathbf{j} \times \mathbf{j} + u_2v_3\mathbf{j} \times \mathbf{k} \\
&\quad + u_3v_1\mathbf{k} \times \mathbf{i} + u_3v_2\mathbf{k} \times \mathbf{j} + u_3v_3\mathbf{k} \times \mathbf{k} \\
&= (u_2v_3 - u_3v_2)\mathbf{i} - (u_1v_3 - u_3v_1)\mathbf{j} + (u_1v_2 - u_2v_1)\mathbf{k}.
\end{aligned}$$

The terms in the last line are the same as the terms in the expansion of the symbolic determinant

$$\begin{vmatrix} \mathbf{i} & \mathbf{j} & \mathbf{k} \\ u_1 & u_2 & u_3 \\ v_1 & v_2 & v_3 \end{vmatrix}.$$

We therefore have the following rule.

Calculating Cross Products Using Determinants

If $\mathbf{u} = u_1\mathbf{i} + u_2\mathbf{j} + u_3\mathbf{k}$ and $\mathbf{v} = v_1\mathbf{i} + v_2\mathbf{j} + v_3\mathbf{k}$, then

$$\mathbf{u} \times \mathbf{v} = \begin{vmatrix} \mathbf{i} & \mathbf{j} & \mathbf{k} \\ u_1 & u_2 & u_3 \\ v_1 & v_2 & v_3 \end{vmatrix}.$$

Example 4   Calculating Cross Products with Determinants

Find $\mathbf{u} \times \mathbf{v}$ and $\mathbf{v} \times \mathbf{u}$ if $\mathbf{u} = 2\mathbf{i} + \mathbf{j} + \mathbf{k}$ and $\mathbf{v} = -4\mathbf{i} + 3\mathbf{j} + \mathbf{k}$.

Solution

$$\mathbf{u} \times \mathbf{v} = \begin{vmatrix} \mathbf{i} & \mathbf{j} & \mathbf{k} \\ 2 & 1 & 1 \\ -4 & 3 & 1 \end{vmatrix} = \begin{vmatrix} 1 & 1 \\ 3 & 1 \end{vmatrix}\mathbf{i} - \begin{vmatrix} 2 & 1 \\ -4 & 1 \end{vmatrix}\mathbf{j} + \begin{vmatrix} 2 & 1 \\ -4 & 3 \end{vmatrix}\mathbf{k}$$

$$= -2\mathbf{i} - 6\mathbf{j} + 10\mathbf{k}$$

$$\mathbf{v} \times \mathbf{u} = -(\mathbf{u} \times \mathbf{v}) = 2\mathbf{i} + 6\mathbf{j} - 10\mathbf{k}$$

Example 5   Finding Vectors Perpendicular to a Plane

Find a vector perpendicular to the plane of $P(1, -1, 0)$, $Q(2, 1, -1)$, and $R(-1, 1, 2)$ (Figure 10.16).

Solution   The vector $\overrightarrow{PQ} \times \overrightarrow{PR}$ is perpendicular to the plane because it is perpendicular to both vectors. In terms of components,

$$\overrightarrow{PQ} = (2 - 1)\mathbf{i} + (1 + 1)\mathbf{j} + (-1 - 0)\mathbf{k} = \mathbf{i} + 2\mathbf{j} - \mathbf{k}$$

$$\overrightarrow{PR} = (-1 - 1)\mathbf{i} + (1 + 1)\mathbf{j} + (2 - 0)\mathbf{k} = -2\mathbf{i} + 2\mathbf{j} + 2\mathbf{k}$$

$$\overrightarrow{PQ} \times \overrightarrow{PR} = \begin{vmatrix} \mathbf{i} & \mathbf{j} & \mathbf{k} \\ 1 & 2 & -1 \\ -2 & 2 & 2 \end{vmatrix} = \begin{vmatrix} 2 & -1 \\ 2 & 2 \end{vmatrix}\mathbf{i} - \begin{vmatrix} 1 & -1 \\ -2 & 2 \end{vmatrix}\mathbf{j} + \begin{vmatrix} 1 & 2 \\ -2 & 2 \end{vmatrix}\mathbf{k}$$

$$= 6\mathbf{i} + 6\mathbf{k}.$$

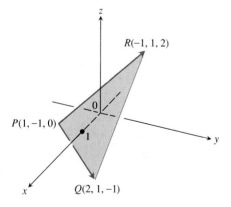

FIGURE 10.16 The area of triangle PQR is half of $|\overrightarrow{PQ} \times \overrightarrow{PR}|$. (Example 6)

Example 6   Finding the Area of a Triangle

Find the area of the triangle with vertices $P(1, -1, 0)$, $Q(2, 1, -1)$, and $R(-1, 1, 2)$ (Figure 10.16).

Solution   The area of the parallelogram determined by P, Q, and R is

$$|\overrightarrow{PQ} \times \overrightarrow{PR}| = |6\mathbf{i} + 6\mathbf{k}| \quad \text{Values from Example 5.}$$

$$= \sqrt{(6)^2 + (6)^2} = \sqrt{2 \cdot 36} = 6\sqrt{2}.$$

The triangle's area is half of this, or $3\sqrt{2}$.

Example 7 Finding a Unit Normal to a Plane

Find a unit vector perpendicular to the plane of $P(1, -1, 0)$, $Q(2, 1, -1)$, and $R(-1, 1, 2)$.

Solution   Since $\vec{PQ} \times \vec{PR}$ is perpendicular to the plane, its direction $\mathbf{n}$ is a unit vector perpendicular to the plane. Taking values from Examples 5 and 6, we have

$$\mathbf{n} = \frac{\vec{PQ} \times \vec{PR}}{|\vec{PQ} \times \vec{PR}|} = \frac{6\mathbf{i} + 6\mathbf{k}}{6\sqrt{2}} = \frac{1}{\sqrt{2}}\mathbf{i} + \frac{1}{\sqrt{2}}\mathbf{k}.$$

Torque

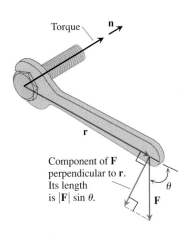

Torque

Component of $\mathbf{F}$ perpendicular to $\mathbf{r}$. Its length is $|\mathbf{F}| \sin \theta$.

FIGURE 10.17 The torque vector describes the tendency of the force $\mathbf{F}$ to drive the bolt forward.

When we turn a bolt by applying a force $\mathbf{F}$ to a wrench (Figure 10.17), the torque we produce acts along the axis of the bolt to drive the bolt forward. The magnitude of the torque depends on how far out on the wrench the force is applied and on how much of the force is perpendicular to the wrench at the point of application. The number we use to measure the torque's magnitude is the product of the length of the lever arm $\mathbf{r}$ and the scalar component of $\mathbf{F}$ perpendicular to $\mathbf{r}$. In the notation of Figure 10.17,

$$\text{Magnitude of torque vector} = |\mathbf{r}||\mathbf{F}| \sin \theta,$$

or $|\mathbf{r} \times \mathbf{F}|$. If we let $\mathbf{n}$ be a unit vector along the axis of the bolt in the direction of the torque, then a complete description of the torque vector is $\mathbf{r} \times \mathbf{F}$, or

$$\text{Torque vector} = (|\mathbf{r}||\mathbf{F}| \sin \theta)\, \mathbf{n}.$$

Recall that we defined $\mathbf{u} \times \mathbf{v}$ to be $\mathbf{0}$ when $\mathbf{u}$ and $\mathbf{v}$ are parallel. This is consistent with the torque interpretation as well. If the force $\mathbf{F}$ in Figure 10.17 is parallel to the wrench, meaning that we are trying to turn the bolt by pushing or pulling along the line of the wrench's handle, the torque produced is zero.

Example 8 Finding the Magnitude of a Torque

The magnitude of the torque generated by force $\mathbf{F}$ at the pivot point P in Figure 10.18 is

$$|\vec{PQ} \times \mathbf{F}| = |\vec{PQ}||\mathbf{F}| \sin 70°$$
$$\approx (3)(20)(0.94)$$
$$\approx 56.4 \text{ ft-lb.}$$

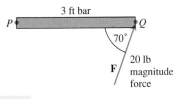

3 ft bar

P Q

70°

$\mathbf{F}$ 20 lb magnitude force

FIGURE 10.18 The magnitude of the torque exerted by $\mathbf{F}$ at P is about 56.4 ft-lb. (Example 8)

Triple Scalar or Box Product

The product $(\mathbf{u} \times \mathbf{v}) \cdot \mathbf{w}$ is called the **triple scalar product** of $\mathbf{u}, \mathbf{v}$, and $\mathbf{w}$ (in that order) . As you can see from the formula

$$|(\mathbf{u} \times \mathbf{v}) \cdot \mathbf{w}| = |\mathbf{u} \times \mathbf{v}||\mathbf{w}| |\cos \theta|,$$

the absolute value of the product is the volume of the parallelepiped (parallelogram-sided box) determined by **u**, **v**, and **w** (Figure 10.19). The number $|\mathbf{u} \times \mathbf{v}|$ is the area of the base parallelogram. The number $|\mathbf{w}||\cos\theta|$ is the parallelepiped's height. Because of this geometry, $(\mathbf{u} \times \mathbf{v}) \cdot \mathbf{w}$ is also called the **box product** of **u**, **v**, and **w**.

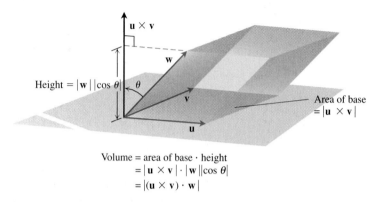

Volume = area of base · height
$$= |\mathbf{u} \times \mathbf{v}| \cdot |\mathbf{w}||\cos\theta|$$
$$= |(\mathbf{u} \times \mathbf{v}) \cdot \mathbf{w}|$$

FIGURE 10.19 The number $|(\mathbf{u} \times \mathbf{v}) \cdot \mathbf{w}|$ is the volume of a parallelepiped.

By treating the planes of **v** and **w** and of **w** and **u** as the base planes of the parallelepiped determined by **u**, **v**, and **w**, we see that

$$(\mathbf{u} \times \mathbf{v}) \cdot \mathbf{w} = (\mathbf{v} \times \mathbf{w}) \cdot \mathbf{u} = (\mathbf{w} \times \mathbf{u}) \cdot \mathbf{v}.$$

Since the dot product is commutative, we also have

$$(\mathbf{u} \times \mathbf{v}) \cdot \mathbf{w} = \mathbf{u} \cdot (\mathbf{v} \times \mathbf{w}).$$

The triple scalar product can be evaluated as a determinant:

$$(\mathbf{u} \times \mathbf{v}) \cdot \mathbf{w} = \left[\begin{vmatrix} u_2 & u_3 \\ v_2 & v_3 \end{vmatrix} \mathbf{i} - \begin{vmatrix} u_1 & u_3 \\ v_1 & v_3 \end{vmatrix} \mathbf{j} + \begin{vmatrix} u_1 & u_2 \\ v_1 & v_2 \end{vmatrix} \mathbf{k} \right] \cdot \mathbf{w}$$

$$= w_1 \begin{vmatrix} u_2 & u_3 \\ v_2 & v_3 \end{vmatrix} - w_2 \begin{vmatrix} u_1 & u_3 \\ v_1 & v_3 \end{vmatrix} + w_3 \begin{vmatrix} u_1 & u_2 \\ v_1 & v_2 \end{vmatrix}$$

$$= \begin{vmatrix} u_1 & u_2 & u_3 \\ v_1 & v_2 & v_3 \\ w_1 & w_2 & w_3 \end{vmatrix}.$$

The dot and cross may be interchanged in a triple scalar product without altering its value.

CD-ROM
WEBsite

Historical Biography

Hermann Grassmann
(1809 — 1877)

Triple Scalar Product

$$(\mathbf{u} \times \mathbf{v}) \cdot \mathbf{w} = \begin{vmatrix} u_1 & u_2 & u_3 \\ v_1 & v_2 & v_3 \\ w_1 & w_2 & w_3 \end{vmatrix}$$

Example 9   Finding the Volume of a Parallelepiped

Find the volume of the box (parallelepiped) determined by $\mathbf{u} = \mathbf{i} + 2\mathbf{j} - \mathbf{k}$, $\mathbf{v} = -2\mathbf{i} + 3\mathbf{k}$, and $\mathbf{w} = 7\mathbf{j} - 4\mathbf{k}$.

Solution   Using a calculator, we find

$$(\mathbf{u} \times \mathbf{v}) \cdot \mathbf{w} = \begin{vmatrix} 1 & 2 & -1 \\ -2 & 0 & 3 \\ 0 & 7 & -4 \end{vmatrix} = -23.$$

The volume is $|(\mathbf{u} \times \mathbf{v}) \cdot \mathbf{w}| = 23$ units cubed.

EXERCISES 10.2

Dot Product and Projections

In Exercises 1–6, find

(a) $\mathbf{v} \cdot \mathbf{u}, |\mathbf{v}|, |\mathbf{u}|$

(b) the cosine of the angle between $\mathbf{v}$ and $\mathbf{u}$

(c) the scalar component of $\mathbf{v}$ in the direction of $\mathbf{u}$

(d) the vector $\text{proj}_\mathbf{v}\, \mathbf{u}$.

1. $\mathbf{v} = 2\mathbf{i} - 4\mathbf{j} + \sqrt{5}\mathbf{k}, \quad \mathbf{u} = -2\mathbf{i} + 4\mathbf{j} - \sqrt{5}\mathbf{k}$

2. $\mathbf{v} = (3/5)\mathbf{i} + (4/5)\mathbf{k}, \quad \mathbf{u} = 5\mathbf{i} + 12\mathbf{j}$

3. $\mathbf{v} = 10\mathbf{i} + 11\mathbf{j} - 2\mathbf{k}, \quad \mathbf{u} = 3\mathbf{j} + 4\mathbf{k}$

4. $\mathbf{v} = 2\mathbf{i} + 10\mathbf{j} - 11\mathbf{k}, \quad \mathbf{u} = 2\mathbf{i} + 2\mathbf{j} + \mathbf{k}$

5. $\mathbf{v} = 5\mathbf{j} - 3\mathbf{k}, \quad \mathbf{u} = \mathbf{i} + \mathbf{j} + \mathbf{k}$

6. $\mathbf{v} = -\mathbf{i} + \mathbf{j}, \quad \mathbf{u} = \sqrt{2}\mathbf{i} + \sqrt{3}\mathbf{j} + 2\mathbf{k}$

Decomposing Vectors

In Exercises 7–9, write $\mathbf{v}$ as the sum of a vector parallel to $\mathbf{u}$ and a vector orthogonal to $\mathbf{u}$.

7. $\mathbf{u} = 3\mathbf{j} + 4\mathbf{k}, \quad \mathbf{v} = \mathbf{i} + \mathbf{j}$

8. $\mathbf{u} = \mathbf{j} + \mathbf{k}, \quad \mathbf{v} = \mathbf{i} + \mathbf{j}$

9. $\mathbf{u} = 8\mathbf{i} + 4\mathbf{j} - 12\mathbf{k}, \quad \mathbf{v} = \mathbf{i} + 2\mathbf{j} - \mathbf{k}$

10. *Sum of vectors* $\mathbf{u} = \mathbf{i} + (\mathbf{j} + \mathbf{k})$ is already the sum of a vector parallel to $\mathbf{i}$ and a vector orthogonal to $\mathbf{i}$. If you use $\mathbf{v} = \mathbf{i}$, in the decomposition $\mathbf{u} = \text{proj}_\mathbf{v}\, \mathbf{u} + (\mathbf{u} - \text{proj}_\mathbf{v}\, \mathbf{u})$, do you get $\text{proj}_\mathbf{v}\, \mathbf{u} = \mathbf{i}$ and $(\mathbf{u} - \text{proj}_\mathbf{v}\, \mathbf{u}) = \mathbf{j} + \mathbf{k}$? Try it and find out.

Angles Between Vectors

Find the angles between the vectors in Exercises 11–14 to the nearest hundredth of a radian.

11. $\mathbf{u} = 2\mathbf{i} + \mathbf{j}, \quad \mathbf{v} = \mathbf{i} + 2\mathbf{j} - \mathbf{k}$

12. $\mathbf{u} = 2\mathbf{i} - 2\mathbf{j} + \mathbf{k}, \quad \mathbf{v} = 3\mathbf{i} + 4\mathbf{k}$

13. $\mathbf{u} = \sqrt{3}\mathbf{i} - 7\mathbf{j}, \quad \mathbf{v} = \sqrt{3}\mathbf{i} + \mathbf{j} - 2\mathbf{k}$

14. $\mathbf{u} = \mathbf{i} + \sqrt{2}\mathbf{j} - \sqrt{2}\mathbf{k}, \quad \mathbf{v} = -\mathbf{i} + \mathbf{j} + \mathbf{k}$

15. *Direction angles and direction cosines* The **direction angles** α, β, and γ of a vector $\mathbf{v} = a\mathbf{i} + b\mathbf{j} + c\mathbf{k}$ are defined as follows:

α is the angle between $\mathbf{v}$ and the positive x-axis ($0 \le \alpha \le \pi$)

β is the angle between $\mathbf{v}$ and the positive y-axis ($0 \le \beta \le \pi$)

γ is the angle between $\mathbf{v}$ and the positive z-axis ($0 \le \gamma \le \pi$).

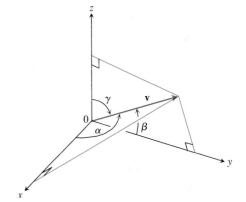

(a) Show that

$$\cos \alpha = \frac{a}{|\mathbf{v}|}, \qquad \cos \beta = \frac{b}{|\mathbf{v}|}, \qquad \cos \gamma = \frac{c}{|\mathbf{v}|},$$

and $\cos^2 \alpha + \cos^2 \beta + \cos^2 \gamma = 1$. These cosines are called the **direction cosines** of $\mathbf{v}$.

(b) *Unit vectors are built from direction cosines* Show that if $\mathbf{v} = a\mathbf{i} + b\mathbf{j} + c\mathbf{k}$ is a unit vector, then a, b, and c *are* the direction cosines of $\mathbf{v}$.

16. *Water main construction* A water main is to be constructed with a 20% grade in the north direction and a 10% grade in the east direction. Determine the angle θ required in the water main for the turn from north to east.

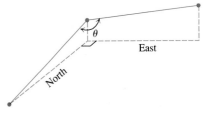

Cross-Product Calculations

In Exercises 17–24, find the length and direction (when defined) of $\mathbf{u} \times \mathbf{v}$ and $\mathbf{v} \times \mathbf{u}$.

17. $\mathbf{u} = 2\mathbf{i} - 2\mathbf{j} - \mathbf{k}, \quad \mathbf{v} = \mathbf{i} - \mathbf{k}$

18. $\mathbf{u} = 2\mathbf{i} + 3\mathbf{j}, \quad \mathbf{v} = -\mathbf{i} + \mathbf{j}$

19. $\mathbf{u} = 2\mathbf{i} - 2\mathbf{j} + 4\mathbf{k}, \quad \mathbf{v} = -\mathbf{i} + \mathbf{j} - 2\mathbf{k}$

20. $\mathbf{u} = \mathbf{i} + \mathbf{j} - \mathbf{k}, \quad \mathbf{v} = 0$

21. $\mathbf{u} = 2\mathbf{i}, \quad \mathbf{v} = -3\mathbf{j}$

22. $\mathbf{u} = \mathbf{i} \times \mathbf{j}, \quad \mathbf{v} = \mathbf{j} \times \mathbf{k}$

23. $\mathbf{u} = -8\mathbf{i} - 2\mathbf{j} - 4\mathbf{k}, \quad \mathbf{v} = 2\mathbf{i} + 2\mathbf{j} + \mathbf{k}$

24. $\mathbf{u} = \dfrac{3}{2}\mathbf{i} - \dfrac{1}{2}\mathbf{j} + \mathbf{k}, \quad \mathbf{v} = \mathbf{i} + \mathbf{j} + 2\mathbf{k}$

In Exercises 25–28, sketch the coordinate axes and then include the vectors $\mathbf{u}$, $\mathbf{v}$, and $\mathbf{u} \times \mathbf{v}$ as vectors starting at the origin.

25. $\mathbf{u} = \mathbf{i} - \mathbf{k}, \quad \mathbf{v} = \mathbf{j}$

26. $\mathbf{u} = \mathbf{i} - \mathbf{k}, \quad \mathbf{v} = \mathbf{j} + \mathbf{k}$

27. $\mathbf{u} = \mathbf{i} + \mathbf{j}, \quad \mathbf{v} = \mathbf{i} - \mathbf{j}$

28. $\mathbf{u} = \mathbf{j} + 2\mathbf{k}, \quad \mathbf{v} = \mathbf{i}$

Triangles in Space

In Exercises 29–32:

(a) Find the area of the triangle determined by the points P, Q, and R.

(b) Find a unit vector perpendicular to plane PQR.

29. $P(1, -1, 2), \quad Q(2, 0, -1), \quad R(0, 2, 1)$

30. $P(1, 1, 1), \quad Q(2, 1, 3), \quad R(3, -1, 1)$

31. $P(2, -2, 1), \quad Q(3, -1, 2), \quad R(3, -1, 1)$

32. $P(-2, 2, 0), \quad Q(0, 1, -1), \quad R(-1, 2, -2)$

Triple Scalar Products

In Exercises 33–36, verify that $(\mathbf{u} \times \mathbf{v}) \cdot \mathbf{w} = (\mathbf{v} \times \mathbf{w}) \cdot \mathbf{u} = (\mathbf{w} \times \mathbf{u}) \cdot \mathbf{v}$ and find the volume of the parallelepiped (box) determined by $\mathbf{u}, \mathbf{v},$ and $\mathbf{w}$.

u	v	w
33. $2\mathbf{i}$	$2\mathbf{j}$	$2\mathbf{k}$
34. $\mathbf{i} - \mathbf{j} + \mathbf{k}$	$2\mathbf{i} + \mathbf{j} - 2\mathbf{k}$	$-\mathbf{i} + 2\mathbf{j} - \mathbf{k}$
35. $2\mathbf{i} + \mathbf{j}$	$2\mathbf{i} - \mathbf{j} + \mathbf{k}$	$\mathbf{i} + 2\mathbf{k}$
36. $\mathbf{i} + \mathbf{j} - 2\mathbf{k}$	$-\mathbf{i} - \mathbf{k}$	$2\mathbf{i} + 4\mathbf{j} - 2\mathbf{k}$

Theory and Examples

37. *Writing to Learn: Parallel and perpendicular vectors* Let $\mathbf{u} = 5\mathbf{i} - \mathbf{j} + \mathbf{k}$, $\mathbf{v} = \mathbf{j} - 5\mathbf{k}, \mathbf{w} = -15\mathbf{i} + 3\mathbf{j} - 3\mathbf{k}$. Which vectors, if any, are (a) perpendicular? (b) Parallel? Give reasons for your answers.

38. *Writing to Learn: Parallel and perpendicular vectors* Let $\mathbf{u} = \mathbf{i} + 2\mathbf{j} - \mathbf{k}$, $\mathbf{v} = -\mathbf{i} + \mathbf{j} + \mathbf{k}, \mathbf{w} = \mathbf{i} + \mathbf{k}, \mathbf{r} = -(\pi/2)\mathbf{i} - \pi\mathbf{j} + (\pi/2)\mathbf{k}$. Which vectors, if any, are (a) perpendicular? (b) Parallel? Give reasons for your answers.

In Exercises 39 and 40, find the magnitude of the torque exerted by $\mathbf{F}$ on the bolt at P if $|\overrightarrow{PQ}| = 8$ in. and $|\mathbf{F}| = 30$ lb. Answer in foot-pounds.

39.   **40.**

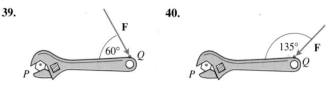

41. Which of the following are *always true*, and which are *not always true*? Give reasons for your answers.

(a) $|\mathbf{u}| = \sqrt{\mathbf{u} \cdot \mathbf{u}}$ (b) $\mathbf{u} \cdot \mathbf{u} = |\mathbf{u}|$

(c) $\mathbf{u} \times \mathbf{0} = \mathbf{0} \times \mathbf{u} = \mathbf{0}$ (d) $\mathbf{u} \times (-\mathbf{u}) = \mathbf{0}$

(e) $\mathbf{u} \times \mathbf{v} = \mathbf{v} \times \mathbf{u}$

(f) $\mathbf{u} \times (\mathbf{v} + \mathbf{w}) = \mathbf{u} \times \mathbf{v} + \mathbf{u} \times \mathbf{w}$

(g) $(\mathbf{u} \times \mathbf{v}) \cdot \mathbf{v} = 0$

(h) $(\mathbf{u} \times \mathbf{v}) \cdot \mathbf{w} = \mathbf{u} \cdot (\mathbf{v} \times \mathbf{w})$

42. Which of the following are *always true*, and which are *not always true*? Give reasons for your answers.

(a) $\mathbf{u} \cdot \mathbf{v} = \mathbf{v} \cdot \mathbf{u}$ (b) $\mathbf{u} \times \mathbf{v} = -(\mathbf{v} \times \mathbf{u})$

(c) $(-\mathbf{u}) \times \mathbf{v} = -(\mathbf{u} \times \mathbf{v})$

(d) $(c\mathbf{u}) \cdot \mathbf{v} = \mathbf{u} \cdot (c\mathbf{v}) = c(\mathbf{u} \cdot \mathbf{v})$ (any number c)

(e) $c(\mathbf{u} \times \mathbf{v}) = (c\mathbf{u}) \times \mathbf{v} = \mathbf{u} \times (c\mathbf{v})$ (any number c)

(f) $\mathbf{u} \cdot \mathbf{u} = |\mathbf{u}|^2$ (g) $(\mathbf{u} \times \mathbf{u}) \cdot \mathbf{u} = 0$

(h) $(\mathbf{u} \times \mathbf{v}) \cdot \mathbf{u} = \mathbf{v} \cdot (\mathbf{u} \times \mathbf{v})$

43. Given nonzero vectors $\mathbf{u}, \mathbf{v},$ and $\mathbf{w}$, use dot-product and cross-product notation, as appropriate, to describe the following.

(a) The vector projection of $\mathbf{u}$ onto $\mathbf{v}$

(b) A vector orthogonal to $\mathbf{u}$ and $\mathbf{v}$

(c) A vector orthogonal to $\mathbf{u} \times \mathbf{v}$ and $\mathbf{w}$

(d) The volume of the parallelepiped determined by $\mathbf{u}, \mathbf{v},$ and $\mathbf{w}$

44. Given nonzero vectors $\mathbf{u}, \mathbf{v},$ and $\mathbf{w}$, use dot-product and cross-product notation to describe the following.

(a) A vector orthogonal to $\mathbf{u} \times \mathbf{v}$ and $\mathbf{u} \times \mathbf{w}$

(b) A vector orthogonal to $\mathbf{u} + \mathbf{v}$ and $\mathbf{u} - \mathbf{v}$

(c) A vector of length $|\mathbf{u}|$ in the direction of $\mathbf{v}$

(d) The area of the parallelogram determined by $\mathbf{u}$ and $\mathbf{w}$

45. *Writing to Learn* Let $\mathbf{u}, \mathbf{v},$ and $\mathbf{w}$ be vectors. Which of the following make sense, and which do not? Give reasons for your answers.

(a) $(\mathbf{u} \times \mathbf{v}) \cdot \mathbf{w}$

(b) $\mathbf{u} \times (\mathbf{v} \cdot \mathbf{w})$

(c) $\mathbf{u} \times (\mathbf{v} \times \mathbf{w})$

(d) $\mathbf{u} \cdot (\mathbf{v} \cdot \mathbf{w})$

46. *Writing to Learn: Cross products of three vectors* Show that except in degenerate cases, $(\mathbf{u} \times \mathbf{v}) \times \mathbf{w}$ lies in the plane of $\mathbf{u}$ and $\mathbf{v}$, whereas $\mathbf{u} \times (\mathbf{v} \times \mathbf{w})$ lies in the plane of $\mathbf{v}$ and $\mathbf{w}$. What *are* the degenerate cases?

47. *Cancellation in cross products* If $\mathbf{u} \times \mathbf{v} = \mathbf{u} \times \mathbf{w}$ and $\mathbf{u} \neq \mathbf{0}$, then does $\mathbf{v} = \mathbf{w}$? Give reasons for your answer.

48. *Double cancellation* If $\mathbf{u} \neq \mathbf{0}$ and if $\mathbf{u} \times \mathbf{v} = \mathbf{u} \times \mathbf{w}$ and $\mathbf{u} \cdot \mathbf{v} = \mathbf{u} \cdot \mathbf{w}$, then does $\mathbf{v} = \mathbf{w}$? Give reasons for your answer.

Area in the Plane

Find the areas of the parallelograms whose vertices are given in Exercises 49–52.

49. $A(1, 0)$, $B(0, 1)$, $C(-1, 0)$, $D(0, -1)$

50. $A(0, 0)$, $B(7, 3)$, $C(9, 8)$, $D(2, 5)$

51. $A(-1, 2)$, $B(2, 0)$, $C(7, 1)$, $D(4, 3)$

52. $A(-6, 0)$, $B(1, -4)$, $C(3, 1)$, $D(-4, 5)$

Find the areas of the triangles whose vertices are given in Exercises 53–56.

53. $A(0, 0)$, $B(-2, 3)$, $C(3, 1)$

54. $A(-1, -1)$, $B(3, 3)$, $C(2, 1)$

55. $A(-5, 3)$, $B(1, -2)$, $C(6, -2)$

56. $A(-6, 0)$, $B(10, -5)$, $C(-2, 4)$

57. *Writing to Learn: Triangle area* Find a formula for the area of the triangle in the xy-plane with vertices at $(0, 0)$, (a_1, a_2), and (b_1, b_2). Explain your work.

58. *Triangle area* Find a concise formula for the area of a triangle with vertices (a_1, a_2), (b_1, b_2), and (c_1, c_2).

10.3 Lines and Planes in Space

Lines and Line Segments in Space • Equations for Planes in Space • Lines of Intersection

In the calculus of functions of a single variable, we began with lines and used our knowledge of lines to study curves in the plane. We investigated tangents and found that, when highly magnified, differentiable curves were effectively linear.

To study the calculus of functions of more than one variable in the next chapter, we begin much the same way. We start with planes and use our knowledge of planes to study the surfaces that are the graphs of functions in space.

This section shows how to use scalar and vector products to write equations for lines, line segments, and planes in space.

Lines and Line Segments in Space

In the plane, a line is determined by a point and a number giving the slope of the line. Analogously, in space a line is determined by a point and a *vector* giving the direction of the line.

Suppose that L is a line in space passing through a point $P_0(x_0, y_0, z_0)$ parallel to a vector $\mathbf{v} = v_1\mathbf{i} + v_2\mathbf{j} + v_3\mathbf{k}$. Then L is the set of all points $P(x, y, z)$ for which $\overrightarrow{P_0P}$ is parallel to $\mathbf{v}$ (Figure 10.20). Thus, $\overrightarrow{P_0P} = t\mathbf{v}$ for some scalar parameter t. The value of t depends on the location of the point P along the line, and the domain of t is $(-\infty, \infty)$. The expanded form of the equation $\overrightarrow{P_0P} = t\mathbf{v}$ is

$$(x - x_0)\mathbf{i} + (y - y_0)\mathbf{j} + (z - z_0)\mathbf{k} = t(v_1\mathbf{i} + v_2\mathbf{j} + v_3\mathbf{k}),$$

and this last equation can be rewritten as

$$x\mathbf{i} + y\mathbf{j} + z\mathbf{k} = x_0\mathbf{i} + y_0\mathbf{j} + z_0\mathbf{k} + t(v_1\mathbf{i} + v_2\mathbf{j} + v_3\mathbf{k}). \tag{1}$$

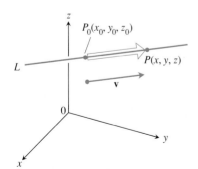

FIGURE 10.20 A point P lies on L through P_0 parallel to $\mathbf{v}$ if and only if $\overrightarrow{P_0P}$ is a scalar multiple of $\mathbf{v}$.

If $\mathbf{r}(t)$ is the position vector of a point $P(x, y, z)$ on the line and $\mathbf{r}_0$ is the position vector of the point $P_0(x_0, y_0, z_0)$, then Equation (1) gives the following vector form for the equation of a line in space.

Vector Equation for a Line
A **vector equation for the line** L **through** $P_0(x_0, y_0, z_0)$ **parallel to** $\mathbf{v}$ is

$$\mathbf{r}(t) = \mathbf{r}_0 + t\mathbf{v}, \qquad -\infty < t < \infty, \tag{2}$$

where $\mathbf{r}$ is the position vector of a point $P(x, y, z)$ on L and $\mathbf{r}_0$ is the position vector of $P_0(x_0, y_0, z_0)$.

Equating the corresponding components of the two sides of Equation (1) gives three scalar equations involving the parameter t:

$$x = x_0 + tv_1, \qquad y = y_0 + tv_2, \qquad z = z_0 + tv_3.$$

These equations give us the standard parametrization of the line for the parameter interval $-\infty < t < \infty$.

Parametric Equations for a Line
The standard parametrization of the line through $P_0(x_0, y_0, z_0)$ **parallel to** $\mathbf{v} = v_1\mathbf{i} + v_2\mathbf{j} + v_3\mathbf{k}$ is

$$x = x_0 + tv_1, \qquad y = y_0 + tv_2, \qquad z = z_0 + tv_3, \qquad -\infty < t < \infty \tag{3}$$

CD-ROM
WEBsite

Example 1   Parametrizing a Line Through a Point Parallel to a Vector

Find parametric equations for the line through $(-2, 0, 4)$ parallel to $\mathbf{v} = 2\mathbf{i} + 4\mathbf{j} - 2\mathbf{k}$ (Figure 10.21).

Solution   With $P_0(x_0, y_0, z_0)$ equal to $(-2, 0, 4)$ and $v_1\mathbf{i} + v_2\mathbf{j} + v_3\mathbf{k}$ equal to $2\mathbf{i} + 4\mathbf{j} - 2\mathbf{k}$, Equations (3) become

$$x = -2 + 2t, \qquad y = 4t, \qquad z = 4 - 2t.$$

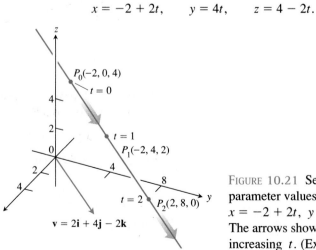

FIGURE 10.21 Selected points and parameter values on the line $x = -2 + 2t$, $y = 4t$, $z = 4 - 2t$. The arrows show the direction of increasing t. (Example 1)

Example 2   Parametrizing a Line Through Two Points

Find parametric equations for the line through $P(-3, 2, -3)$ and $Q(1, -1, 4)$.

Solution   The vector

$$\vec{PQ} = (1 - (-3))\mathbf{i} + (-1 - 2)\mathbf{j} + (4 - (-3))\mathbf{k}$$
$$= 4\mathbf{i} - 3\mathbf{j} + 7\mathbf{k}$$

is parallel to the line, and Equations (3) with $(x_0, y_0, z_0) = (-3, 2, -3)$ give

$$x = -3 + 4t, \qquad y = 2 - 3t, \qquad z = -3 + 7t.$$

We could have chosen $Q(1, -1, 4)$ as the "base point" and written

$$x = 1 + 4t, \qquad y = -1 - 3t, \qquad z = 4 + 7t.$$

These equations serve as well as the first; they simply place you at a different point on the line for a given value of t.

Notice that parametrizations are not unique. Not only can the "base point" change, but so can the parameter. The equations $x = -3 + 4t^3$, $y = 2 - 3t^3$, and $z = -3 + 7t^3$ also parametrize the line in Example 2.

To parametrize a line segment joining two points, we first parametrize the line through the points. We then find the t-values for the endpoints and restrict t to lie in the closed interval bounded by these values. The line equations together with this added restriction parametrize the segment.

Example 3   Parametrizing a Line Segment

Parametrize the line segment joining the points $P(-3, 2, -3)$ and $Q(1, -1, 4)$ (Figure 10.22).

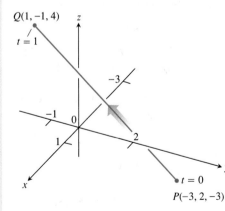

FIGURE 10.22 Example 3 derives a parametrization of line segment PQ. The arrow shows the direction of increasing t.

Solution   We begin with equations for the line through P and Q, taking them, in this case, from Example 2:

$$x = -3 + 4t, \qquad y = 2 - 3t, \qquad z = -3 + 7t.$$

We observe that the point

$$(x, y, z) = (-3 + 4t, 2 - 3t, -3 + 7t)$$

passes through $P(-3, 2, -3)$ at $t = 0$ and $Q(1, -1, 4)$ at $t = 1$. We add the restriction $0 \le t \le 1$ to parametrize the segment:

$$x = -3 + 4t, \qquad y = 2 - 3t, \qquad z = -3 + 7t, \qquad 0 \le t \le 1.$$

The vector form (Equation (2)) for a line in space is more revealing if we think of a line as the path of a particle starting at position $P_0(x_0, y_0, z_0)$ and moving in the direction of vector $\mathbf{v}$. Rewriting Equation (2), we have

$$\mathbf{r}(t) = \mathbf{r}_0 + t\mathbf{v}$$
$$= \mathbf{r}_0 + t\,|\mathbf{v}|\,\frac{\mathbf{v}}{|\mathbf{v}|}. \tag{4}$$

Initial position   Time   Speed   Direction

In other words, the position of the particle at time t is its initial position plus its rate × time (distance moved) in the direction $\mathbf{v}/|\mathbf{v}|$ of its straight-line motion.

Example 4 Flight of a Helicopter

A helicopter is to fly directly from a helipad at the origin toward the point $(1, 1, 1)$ at a speed of 60 ft/sec. What is the position of the helicopter after 10 sec?

Solution We place the origin at the starting position (helipad) of the helicopter. Then the unit vector

$$\mathbf{u} = \frac{1}{\sqrt{3}}\mathbf{i} + \frac{1}{\sqrt{3}}\mathbf{j} + \frac{1}{\sqrt{3}}\mathbf{k}$$

gives the flight direction of the helicopter. From Equation (4), the position of the helicopter at any time t is

$$\mathbf{r}(t) = \mathbf{r}_0 + t\,(\text{speed})\mathbf{u}$$
$$= \mathbf{0} + t(60)\left(\frac{1}{\sqrt{3}}\mathbf{i} + \frac{1}{\sqrt{3}}\mathbf{j} + \frac{1}{\sqrt{3}}\mathbf{k}\right)$$
$$= 20\sqrt{3}\,t\,(\mathbf{i} + \mathbf{j} + \mathbf{k}).$$

When $t = 10$ sec,

$$\mathbf{r}(10) = 200\sqrt{3}(\mathbf{i} + \mathbf{j} + \mathbf{k})$$
$$= \langle 200\sqrt{3}, 200\sqrt{3}, 200\sqrt{3}\rangle.$$

Interpret After 10 sec of flight from the origin toward $(1, 1, 1)$, the helicopter is located at the point $(200\sqrt{3}, 200\sqrt{3}, 200\sqrt{3})$ in space. It has traveled a distance of $(60 \text{ ft/sec})(10 \text{ sec}) = 600$ ft, which is the length of the vector $\mathbf{r}(10)$.

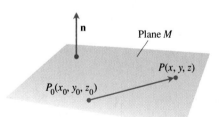

FIGURE 10.23 The standard equation for a plane in space is defined in terms of a vector normal to the plane: A point P lies in the plane through P_0 normal to $\mathbf{n}$ if and only if $\mathbf{n} \cdot \overrightarrow{P_0P} = 0$.

Equations for Planes in Space

A plane in space is determined by knowing a point on the plane and its "tilt" or orientation. This "tilt" is defined by specifying a vector that is perpendicular or normal to the plane.

Suppose that plane M passes through a point $P_0(x_0, y_0, z_0)$ and is normal (perpendicular) to the nonzero vector $\mathbf{n} = A\mathbf{i} + B\mathbf{j} + C\mathbf{k}$. Then M is the set of all points $P(x, y, z)$ for which $\overrightarrow{P_0P}$ is orthogonal to $\mathbf{n}$ (Figure 10.23). Thus, the dot product $\mathbf{n} \cdot \overrightarrow{P_0P} = 0$. This equation is equivalent to

$$(A\mathbf{i} + B\mathbf{j} + C\mathbf{k}) \cdot [(x - x_0)\mathbf{i} + (y - y_0)\mathbf{j} + (z - z_0)\mathbf{k}] = 0$$

or

$$A(x - x_0) + B(y - y_0) + C(z - z_0) = 0.$$

Equation for a Plane

The **plane through** $P_0(x_0, y_0, z_0)$ **normal to** $\mathbf{n} = A\mathbf{i} + B\mathbf{j} + C\mathbf{k}$ has

Vector equation:	$\mathbf{n} \cdot \overrightarrow{P_0P} = 0$
Component equation:	$A(x - x_0) + B(y - y_0) + C(z - z_0) = 0$
Component equation simplified:	$Ax + By + Cz = D,$ where $D = Ax_0 + By_0 + Cz_0$

Example 5 Finding an Equation for a Plane

Find an equation for the plane through $P_0(-3, 0, 7)$ perpendicular to $\mathbf{n} = 5\mathbf{i} + 2\mathbf{j} - \mathbf{k}$.

Solution The component equation is

$$5(x - (-3)) + 2(y - 0) + (-1)(z - 7) = 0.$$

Simplifying, we obtain

$$5x + 15 + 2y - z + 7 = 0$$
$$5x + 2y - z = -22.$$

$A\mathbf{i} + B\mathbf{j} + C\mathbf{k}$ is normal to the plane
$Ax + By + Cz = D$.

Notice in Example 5 how the components of $\mathbf{n} = 5\mathbf{i} + 2\mathbf{j} - \mathbf{k}$ became the coefficients of x, y, and z in the equation $5x + 2y - z = -22$.

Example 6 Finding an Equation for a Plane Through Three Points

Find an equation for the plane through $A(0, 0, 1)$, $B(2, 0, 0)$, and $C(0, 3, 0)$.

Solution We find a vector normal to the plane and use it with one of the points (it does not matter which) to write an equation for the plane.
The cross product

$$\overrightarrow{AB} \times \overrightarrow{AC} = \begin{vmatrix} \mathbf{i} & \mathbf{j} & \mathbf{k} \\ 2 & 0 & -1 \\ 0 & 3 & -1 \end{vmatrix} = 3\mathbf{i} + 2\mathbf{j} + 6\mathbf{k}$$

is normal to the plane. We substitute the components of this vector and the coordinates of $A(0, 0, 1)$ into the component form of the equation to obtain

$$3(x - 0) + 2(y - 0) + 6(z - 1) = 0$$
$$3x + 2y + 6z = 6.$$

Just as lines are parallel if and only if they have the same direction, two planes are **parallel** if and only if their normals are parallel, or $\mathbf{n}_1 = k\mathbf{n}_2$ for some scalar k.

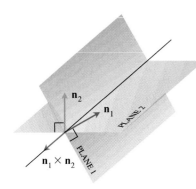

FIGURE 10.24 How the line of intersection of two planes is related to the planes' normal vectors. (Example 7)

Lines of Intersection

Two planes that are not parallel intersect in a line.

Example 7 Finding a Vector Parallel to the Line of Intersection of Two Planes

Find a vector parallel to the line of intersection of the planes $3x - 6y - 2z = 15$ and $2x + y - 2z = 5$.

Solution The line of intersection of two planes is perpendicular to the planes' normal vectors $\mathbf{n}_1$ and $\mathbf{n}_2$ (Figure 10.24) and therefore parallel to $\mathbf{n}_1 \times \mathbf{n}_2$. Turning this around, $\mathbf{n}_1 \times \mathbf{n}_2$ is a vector parallel to the planes' line of intersection. In our case,

$$\mathbf{n}_1 \times \mathbf{n}_2 = \begin{vmatrix} \mathbf{i} & \mathbf{j} & \mathbf{k} \\ 3 & -6 & -2 \\ 2 & 1 & -2 \end{vmatrix} = 14\mathbf{i} + 2\mathbf{j} + 15\mathbf{k}.$$

Any nonzero scalar multiple of $\mathbf{n}_1 \times \mathbf{n}_2$ will do as well.

Example 8 Parametrizing the Line of Intersection of Two Planes

Find parametric equations for the line in which the planes $3x - 6y - 2z = 15$ and $2x + y - 2z = 5$ intersect.

Solution We find a vector parallel to the line and a point on the line and use Equations (3).

Example 7 identifies $\mathbf{v} = 14\mathbf{i} + 2\mathbf{j} + 15\mathbf{k}$ as a vector parallel to the line. To find a point on the line, we can take any point common to the two planes. Substituting $z = 0$ in the plane equations and solving for x and y simultaneously identifies one of these points as $(3, -1, 0)$. The line is

$$x = 3 + 14t, \qquad y = -1 + 2t, \qquad z = 15t.$$

Sometimes we want to know where a line and a plane intersect. For example, if we are looking at a flat plate and a line segment passes through it, we may be interested in knowing what portion of the line segment is hidden from our view by the plate. This application is used in computer graphics (Exercise 62).

Example 9 Finding the Intersection of a Line and a Plane

Find the point where the line

$$x = \frac{8}{3} + 2t, \qquad y = -2t, \qquad z = 1 + t$$

intersects the plane $3x + 2y + 6z = 6$.

Solution The point

$$\left(\frac{8}{3} + 2t, -2t, 1 + t \right)$$

lies in the plane if its coordinates satisfy the equation of the plane, that is, if

$$3\left(\frac{8}{3} + 2t\right) + 2(-2t) + 6(1 + t) = 6$$
$$8 + 6t - 4t + 6 + 6t = 6$$
$$8t = -8$$
$$t = -1.$$

The point of intersection is

$$(x, y, z)\big|_{t=-1} = \left(\frac{8}{3} - 2, 2, 1 - 1\right) = \left(\frac{2}{3}, 2, 0\right).$$

EXERCISES 10.3

Lines and Line Segments

Find vector and parametric equations for the lines in Exercises 1–10.

1. The line through the point $P(3, -4, -1)$ parallel to the vector $\mathbf{i} + \mathbf{j} + \mathbf{k}$

2. The line through $P(1, 2, -1)$ and $Q(-1, 0, 1)$

3. The line through $P(-2, 0, 3)$ and $Q(3, 5, -2)$

4. The line through the origin parallel to the vector $2\mathbf{j} + \mathbf{k}$

5. The line through the point $(3, -2, 1)$ parallel to the line $x = 1 + 2t, y = 2 - t, z = 3t$

6. The line through $(1, 1, 1)$ parallel to the z-axis

7. The line through $(2, 4, 5)$ perpendicular to the plane $3x + 7y - 5z = 21$

8. The line through $(0, -7, 0)$ perpendicular to the plane $x + 2y + 2z = 13$

9. The line through $(2, 3, 0)$ perpendicular to the vectors $\mathbf{u} = \mathbf{i} + 2\mathbf{j} + 3\mathbf{k}$ and $\mathbf{v} = 3\mathbf{i} + 4\mathbf{j} + 5\mathbf{k}$

10. The x-axis

Find parametrizations for the line segments joining the points in Exercises 11–14. Draw coordinate axes and sketch each segment, indicating the direction of increasing t for your parametrization.

11. $(0, 0, 0), \quad (1, 1, 3/2)$

12. $(1, 0, 0), \quad (1, 1, 0)$

13. $(0, 1, 1), \quad (0, -1, 1)$

14. $(1, 0, -1), \quad (0, 3, 0)$

Planes

Find equations for the planes in Exercises 15–20.

15. The plane through $P_0(0, 2, -1)$ normal to $\mathbf{n} = 3\mathbf{i} - 2\mathbf{j} - \mathbf{k}$

16. The plane through $(1, -1, 3)$ parallel to the plane $3x + y + z = 7$

17. The plane through $(1, 1, -1), (2, 0, 2)$, and $(0, -2, 1)$

18. The plane through $(2, 4, 5), (1, 5, 7)$, and $(-1, 6, 8)$

19. The plane through $P_0(2, 4, 5)$ perpendicular to the line
$$x = 5 + t, \qquad y = 1 + 3t, \qquad z = 4t$$

20. The plane through $A(1, -2, 1)$ perpendicular to the vector from the origin to A

21. Find the point of intersection of the lines $x = 2t + 1, y = 3t + 2, z = 4t + 3$, and $x = s + 2, y = 2s + 4, z = -4s - 1$, and then find the plane determined by these lines.

22. Find the point of intersection of the lines $x = t, y = -t + 2, z = t + 1$, and $x = 2s + 2, y = s + 3, z = 5s + 6$, and then find the plane determined by these lines.

In Exercises 23 and 24, find the plane determined by the intersecting lines.

23. $L1$: $x = -1 + t, y = 2 + t, z = 1 - t, -\infty < t < \infty$
   $L2$: $x = 1 - 4s, y = 1 + 2s, z = 2 - 2s, -\infty < s < \infty$

24. $L1$: $x = t, y = 3 - 3t, z = -2 - t, -\infty < t < \infty$
   $L2$: $x = 1 + s, y = 4 + s, z = -1 + s, -\infty < s < \infty$

25. Find a plane through $P_0(2, 1, -1)$ and perpendicular to the line of intersection of the planes $2x + y - z = 3, x + 2y + z = 2$.

26. Find a plane through the points $P_1(1, 2, 3), P_2(3, 2, 1)$ and perpendicular to the plane $4x - y + 2z = 7$.

Distance from a Point to a Line

27. Follow these steps to find the distance from a point S to a line that passes through a point P parallel to a vector $\mathbf{v}$ as shown in the figure.

   (a) Show that the length of the component of $\overrightarrow{PS}$ normal to the line is $|\overrightarrow{PS}| \sin \theta$.

(b) *Distance formula* Show that the distance d from S to the line through P parallel to $\mathbf{v}$ is

$$d = \frac{|\overrightarrow{PS} \times \mathbf{v}|}{|\mathbf{v}|}.$$

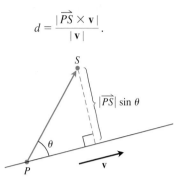

In Exercises 28–30, use the result of Exercise 27 to find the distance from the point to the line.

28. $(0, 0, 0)$; $\quad x = 5 + 3t, \quad y = 5 + 4t, \quad z = -3 - 5t$

29. $(2, 1, 3)$; $\quad x = 2 + 2t, \quad y = 1 + 6t, \quad z = 3$

30. $(3, -1, 4)$; $\quad x = 4 - t, \quad y = 3 + 2t, \quad z = -5 + 3t$

Distance from a Point to a Plane

31. Follow these steps to find the distance d from a point S to a plane $Ax + By + Cz = D$.

(a) Find a point P on the plane.

(b) Find $\overrightarrow{PS}$.

(c) *Distance formula* Show that the distance is

$$d = \left| \overrightarrow{PS} \cdot \frac{\mathbf{n}}{|\mathbf{n}|} \right|,$$

where $\mathbf{n} = A\mathbf{i} + B\mathbf{j} + C\mathbf{k}$.

The accompanying figure shows the situation for finding the distance from $S(1, 1, 3)$ to the plane $3x + 2y + 6z = 6$. In Exercises 32–34, use the result of Exercise 31 to find the distance from the point to the plane.

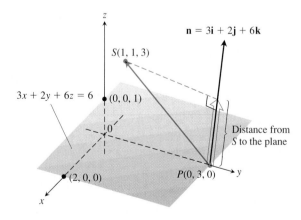

32. $(2, -3, 4)$, $\quad x + 2y + 2z = 13$

33. $(0, 1, 1)$, $\quad 4y + 3z = -12$

34. $(0, -1, 0)$, $\quad 2x + y + z = 4$

35. Find the distance from the plane $x + 2y + 6z = 1$ to the plane $x + 2y + 6z = 10$.

36. Find the distance from the line $x = 2 + t$, $y = 1 + t$, $z = -1/2 - (1/2)t$ to the plane $x + 2y + 6z = 10$.

Angle Between Planes

37. The **angle between two intersecting planes** is defined to be the (acute) angle determined by the normal vectors as shown in the figure.

(a) *Angle formula* If $\mathbf{n}_1$ and $\mathbf{n}_2$ are the normals to two planes, show that the angle between the planes is

$$\theta = \cos^{-1} \left(\frac{\mathbf{n}_1 \cdot \mathbf{n}_2}{|\mathbf{n}_1 \| \mathbf{n}_2|} \right).$$

(b) *Finding an angle* Show that the angle between the planes $3x - 6y - 2z = 15$ and $2x + y - 2z = 5$ is about 1.38 radians.

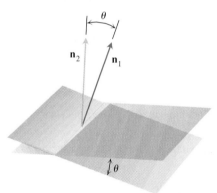

In Exercises 38–40, use the result of Exercise 37 to find the acute angle between the planes.

38. $x + y + z = 1, \quad z = 0$

39. $2x + 2y - z = 3, \quad x + 2y + z = 2$

40. $4y + 3z = -12, \quad 3x + 2y + 6z = 6$

Intersecting Lines and Planes

In Exercises 41–44, find the point in which the line meets the plane.

41. $x = 1 - t, \quad y = 3t, \quad z = 1 + t; \quad 2x - y + 3z = 6$

42. $x = 2, \quad y = 3 + 2t, \quad z = -2 - 2t; \quad 6x + 3y - 4z = -12$

43. $x = 1 + 2t, \quad y = 1 + 5t, \quad z = 3t; \quad x + y + z = 2$

44. $x = -1 + 3t, \quad y = -2, \quad z = 5t; \quad 2x - 3z = 7$

Find parametrizations for the lines in which the planes in Exercises 45–48 intersect.

45. $x + y + z = 1$, $x + y = 2$

46. $3x - 6y - 2z = 3$, $2x + y - 2z = 2$

47. $x - 2y + 4z = 2$, $x + y - 2z = 5$

48. $5x - 2y = 11$, $4y - 5z = -17$

Given two lines in space, they are parallel, or they intersect, or they are skew (imagine, for example, the flight paths of two planes in the sky). Exercises 49 and 50 each give three lines. In each exercise, determine whether the lines, taken two at a time, are parallel, intersect, or are skew. If they intersect, find the point of intersection.

49. $L1$: $x = 3 + 2t$, $y = -1 + 4t$, $z = 2 - t$, $-\infty < t < \infty$

   $L2$: $x = 1 + 4s$, $y = 1 + 2s$, $z = -3 + 4s$, $-\infty < s < \infty$

   $L3$: $x = 3 + 2r$, $y = 2 + r$, $z = -2 + 2r$, $-\infty < r < \infty$

50. $L1$: $x = 1 + 2t$, $y = -1 - t$, $z = 3t$, $-\infty < t < \infty$

   $L2$: $x = 2 - s$, $y = 3s$, $z = 1 + s$, $-\infty < s < \infty$

   $L3$: $x = 5 + 2r$, $y = 1 - r$, $z = 8 + 3r$, $-\infty < r < \infty$

Theory and Examples

51. *Finding a line* Use Equations (3) to generate a parametrization of the line through $P(2, -4, 7)$ parallel to $\mathbf{v}_1 = 2\mathbf{i} - \mathbf{j} + 3\mathbf{k}$. Then generate another parametrization of the line using the point $P_2(-2, -2, 1)$ and the vector $\mathbf{v}_2 = -\mathbf{i} + (1/2)\mathbf{j} - (3/2)\mathbf{k}$.

52. *Finding a plane* Use the component form to generate an equation for the plane through $P_1(4, 1, 5)$ normal to $\mathbf{n}_1 = \mathbf{i} - 2\mathbf{j} + \mathbf{k}$. Then generate another equation for the same plane using the point $P_2(3, -2, 0)$ and the normal vector

$$\mathbf{n}_2 = \sqrt{2}\mathbf{i} + 2\sqrt{2}\mathbf{j} - \sqrt{2}\mathbf{k}.$$

53. *Writing to Learn* Find the points in which the line $x = 1 + 2t$, $y = -1 - t$, $z = 3t$ meets the coordinate planes. Describe the reasoning behind your answer.

54. *Writing to Learn* Find equations for the line in the plane $z = 3$ that makes an angle of $\pi/6$ rad with $\mathbf{i}$ and an angle of $\pi/3$ rad with $\mathbf{j}$. Describe the reasoning behind your answer.

55. *Writing to Learn* Is the line $x = 1 - 2t$, $y = 2 + 5t$, $z = -3t$ parallel to the plane $2x + y - z = 8$? Give reasons for your answer.

56. *Writing to Learn* How can you tell when two planes $A_1x + B_1y + C_1z = D_1$ and $A_2x + B_2y + C_2z = D_2$ are parallel? Perpendicular? Give reasons for your answer.

57. *Writing to Learn: Planes intersecting in a given line* Find two different planes whose intersection is the line $x = 1 + t$, $y = 2 - t$, $z = 3 + 2t$. Write an equation for each plane in the form $Ax + By + Cz = D$. Explain how you found your planes.

58. *Writing to Learn* Find a plane through the origin that meets the plane M: $2x + 3y + z = 12$ in a right angle. How do you know that your plane is perpendicular to M?

59. *Writing to Learn* For any nonzero numbers a, b, and c, the graph of $(x/a) + (y/b) + (z/c) = 1$ is a plane. Which planes have an equation of this form? Give reasons for your answer.

60. *Writing to learn* Suppose that L_1 and L_2 are disjoint (nonintersecting) nonparallel lines. Is it possible for a nonzero vector to be perpendicular to both L_1 and L_2? Give reasons for your answer.

Computer Graphics

61. *Perspective in computer graphics* In computer graphics and perspective drawing, we need to represent objects seen by the eye in space as images on a two-dimensional plane. Suppose that the eye is at $E(x_0, 0, 0)$ as shown here and that we want to represent a point $P_1(x_1, y_1, z_1)$ as a point on the yz-plane. We do this by projecting P_1 onto the plane with a ray from E. The point P_1 will be portrayed as the point $P(0, y, z)$. The problem for us as graphics designers is to find y and z given E and P_1.

(a) Write a vector equation that holds between $\overrightarrow{EP}$ and $\overrightarrow{EP_1}$. Use the equation to express y and z in terms of x_0, x_1, y_1, and z_1.

(b) Test the formulas obtained for y and z in part (a) by investigating their behavior at $x_1 = 0$ and $x_1 = x_0$ and by seeing what happens as $x_0 \to \infty$. What do you find?

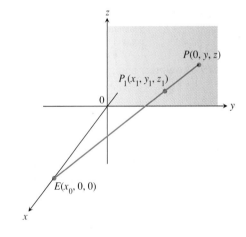

62. *Hidden lines* Here is another typical problem in computer graphics. Your eye is at $(4, 0, 0)$. You are looking at a triangular plate whose vertices are at $(1, 0, 1)$, $(1, 1, 0)$, and $(-2, 2, 2)$. The line segment from $(1, 0, 0)$ to $(0, 2, 2)$ passes through the plate. What portion of the line segment is hidden from your view by the plate? (This is an exercise in finding intersections of lines and planes.)

10.4   Cylinders and Quadric Surfaces

Cylinders   •   Quadric Surfaces

Up to now, we have studied two special types of surfaces necessary to understanding vector calculus and the calculus of space, namely spheres and planes in space. In this section, we extend our inventory to include a variety of cylinders and quadric surfaces. Quadric surfaces are surfaces defined by second-degree equations in x, y, and z. Spheres are quadric surfaces, but there are others of equal interest.

Cylinders

A **cylinder** is the surface composed of all the lines that (1) lie parallel to a given line in space and (2) pass through a given plane curve. The curve is a **generating curve** for the cylinder (Figure 10.25). In solid geometry, where *cylinder* means *circular cylinder*, the generating curves are circles, but now we allow generating curves of any kind. The cylinder in our first example is generated by a parabola.

When graphing a cylinder or other surface by hand or analyzing one generated by a computer, it helps to look at the curves formed by intersecting the surface with planes parallel to the coordinate planes. These curves are called **cross sections** or **traces**.

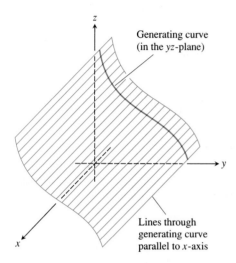

FIGURE 10.25 **A cylinder and generating curve.**

Example 1   The Parabolic Cylinder $y = x^2$

Find an equation for the cylinder made by the lines parallel to the z-axis that pass through the parabola $y = x^2$, $z = 0$ (Figure 10.26).

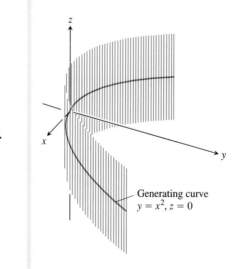

FIGURE 10.26 **The cylinder of lines passing through the parabola $y = x^2$ in the xy-plane parallel to the z-axis. (Example 1)**

Generating curve
$y = x^2, z = 0$

Solution   Suppose that the point $P_0(x_0, x_0^2, 0)$ lies on the parabola $y = x^2$ in the xy-plane. Then, for any value of z, the point $Q(x_0, x_0^2, z)$ will lie on the cylinder because it lies on the line $x = x_0$, $y = x_0^2$ through P_0 parallel to the z-axis. Conversely, any point $Q(x_0, x_0^2, z)$ whose y-coordinate is the square of its x-coordinate lies on the cylinder because it lies on the line $x = x_0$, $y = x_0^2$ through P_0 parallel to the z-axis (Figure 10.27).

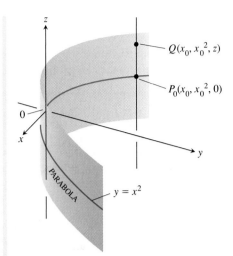

FIGURE 10.27 Every point of the cylinder in Figure 10.26 has coordinates of the form (x_0, x_0^2, z). We call the cylinder "the cylinder $y = x^2$."

Regardless of the value of z, therefore, the points on the surface are the points whose coordinates satisfy the equation $y = x^2$. This makes $y = x^2$ an equation for the cylinder. Because of this, we call the cylinder "the cylinder $y = x^2$."

As Example 1 suggests, any curve $f(x, y) = c$ in the xy-plane defines a cylinder parallel to the z-axis whose equation is also $f(x, y) = c$. The equation $x^2 + y^2 = 1$ defines the circular cylinder made by the lines parallel to the z-axis that pass through the circle $x^2 + y^2 = 1$ in the xy-plane. The equation $x^2 + 4y^2 = 9$ defines the elliptical cylinder made by the lines parallel to the z-axis that pass through the ellipse $x^2 + 4y^2 = 9$ in the xy-plane.

In a similar way, any curve $g(x, z) = c$ in the xz-plane defines a cylinder parallel to the y-axis whose space equation is also $g(x, z) = c$ (Figure 10.28). Any curve $h(y, z) = c$ defines a cylinder parallel to the x-axis whose space equation is also $h(y, z) = c$ (Figure 10.29).

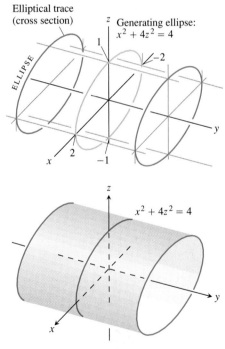

FIGURE 10.28 The elliptic cylinder $x^2 + 4z^2 = 4$ is made of lines parallel to the y-axis and passing through the ellipse $x^2 + 4z^2 = 4$ in the xz-plane. The cross sections or "traces" of the cylinder in planes perpendicular to the y-axis are ellipses congruent to the generating ellipse. The cylinder extends along the entire y-axis.

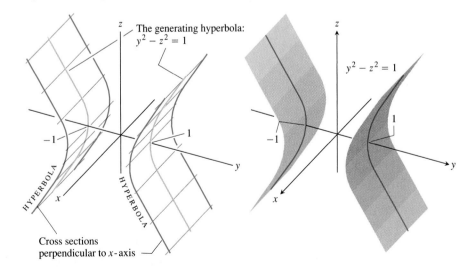

FIGURE 10.29 The hyperbolic cylinder $y^2 - z^2 = 1$ is made of lines parallel to the x-axis and passing through the hyperbola $y^2 - z^2 = 1$ in the yz-plane. The cross sections of the cylinder in planes perpendicular to the x-axis are hyperbolas congruent to the generating hyperbola.

> **Equation of a Cylinder**
> An equation in any two of the three Cartesian coordinates defines a cylinder parallel to the axis of the third coordinate.

The axis of a cylinder need not be parallel to a coordinate axis, however.

Quadric Surfaces

The next type of surface we study is a *quadric* surface. These surfaces are the three-dimensional analogues of ellipses, parabolas, and hyperbolas.

A **quadric surface** is the graph in space of a second-degree equation in x, y, and z. The most general form is

$$Ax^2 + By^2 + Cz^2 + Dxy + Eyz + Fxz + Gx + Hy + Jz + K = 0,$$

where A, B, C, and so on are constants, but the equation can be simplified by translation and rotation, as in the two-dimensional case. We will study only the simpler equations. Although the definition did not require it, the cylinders in Figures 10.27 through 10.29 were also examples of quadric surfaces. The basic quadric surfaces are **ellipsoids, paraboloids, elliptic cones,** and **hyperboloids.** (We can think of spheres as special ellipsoids.) We now present examples of each type.

Example 2   Graphing Ellipsoids

The **ellipsoid**

$$\frac{x^2}{a^2} + \frac{y^2}{b^2} + \frac{z^2}{c^2} = 1 \tag{1}$$

(Figure 10.30) cuts the coordinate axes at $(\pm a, 0, 0)$, $(0, \pm b, 0)$, and $(0, 0, \pm c)$. It lies within the rectangular box defined by the inequalities $|x| \le a, |y| \le b,$ and $|z| \le c$. The surface is symmetric with respect to each of the coordinate planes because the variables in the defining equation are squared.

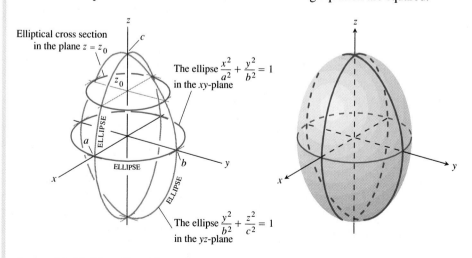

FIGURE 10.30 The ellipsoid

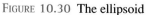

in Example 2.

The curves in which the three coordinate planes cut the surface are ellipses. For example,

$$\frac{x^2}{a^2} + \frac{y^2}{b^2} = 1 \qquad \text{when} \qquad z = 0.$$

The section cut from the surface by the plane $z = z_0, |z_0| < c$, is the ellipse

$$\frac{x^2}{a^2(1 - (z_0/c)^2)} + \frac{y^2}{b^2(1 - (z_0/c)^2)} = 1.$$

If any two of the semiaxes a, b, and c are equal, the surface is an **ellipsoid of revolution.** If all three are equal, the surface is a sphere.

Example 3   Graphing Paraboloids

The **elliptic paraboloid**

$$\frac{x^2}{a^2} + \frac{y^2}{b^2} = \frac{z}{c} \tag{2}$$

is symmetric with respect to the planes $x = 0$ and $y = 0$ (Figure 10.31). The only intercept on the axes is the origin. Except for this point, the surface lies above (if $c > 0$) or entirely below (if $c < 0$) the xy-plane, depending on the sign of c. The sections cut by the coordinate planes are

$$x = 0: \quad \text{the parabola } z = \frac{c}{b^2} y^2$$

$$y = 0: \quad \text{the parabola } z = \frac{c}{a^2} x^2$$

$$z = 0: \quad \text{the point } (0, 0, 0).$$

Each plane $z = z_0$ above the xy-plane cuts the surface in the ellipse

$$\frac{x^2}{a^2} + \frac{y^2}{b^2} = \frac{z_0}{c}.$$

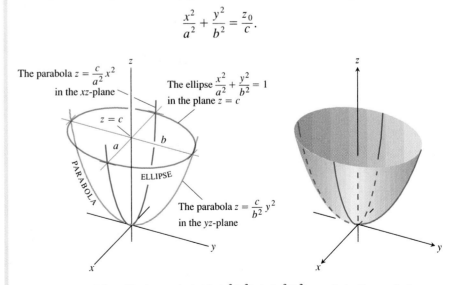

FIGURE 10.31 The elliptic paraboloid $(x^2/a^2) + (y^2/b^2) = z/c$ in Example 3, shown for $c > 0$. The cross sections perpendicular to the z-axis above the xy-plane are ellipses. The cross sections in the planes that contain the z-axis are parabolas.

Example 4   Graphing Cones

The **elliptic cone**

$$\frac{x^2}{a^2} + \frac{y^2}{b^2} = \frac{z^2}{c^2} \tag{3}$$

is symmetric with respect to the three coordinate planes (Figure 10.32). The sections cut by the coordinate planes are

$$x = 0: \quad \text{the lines } z = \pm\frac{c}{b}y$$

$$y = 0: \quad \text{the lines } z = \pm\frac{c}{a}x$$

$$z = 0: \quad \text{the point } (0, 0, 0).$$

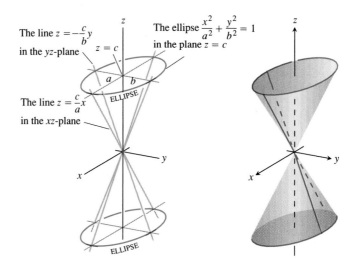

FIGURE 10.32 The elliptic cone $(x^2/a^2) + (y^2/b^2) = (z^2/c^2)$ in Example 4. Planes perpendicular to the z-axis cut the cone in ellipses above and below the xy-plane. Vertical planes that contain the z-axis cut it in pairs of intersecting lines.

The sections cut by planes $z = z_0$ above and below the xy-plane are ellipses whose centers lie on the z-axis and whose vertices lie on the lines given above.

If $a = b$, the cone is a right circular cone.

Example 5   Graphing Hyperboloids

The **hyperboloid of one sheet**

$$\frac{x^2}{a^2} + \frac{y^2}{b^2} - \frac{z^2}{c^2} = 1 \tag{4}$$

is symmetric with respect to each of the three coordinate planes (Figure 10.33).

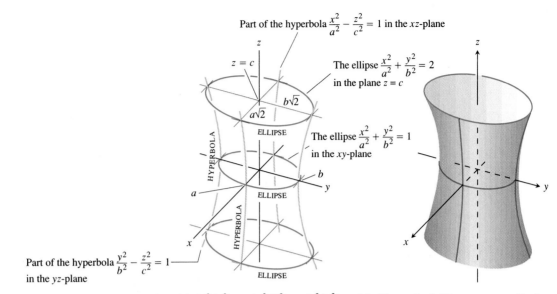

Part of the hyperbola $\dfrac{x^2}{a^2} - \dfrac{z^2}{c^2} = 1$ in the xz-plane

The ellipse $\dfrac{x^2}{a^2} + \dfrac{y^2}{b^2} = 2$ in the plane $z = c$

The ellipse $\dfrac{x^2}{a^2} + \dfrac{y^2}{b^2} = 1$ in the xy-plane

Part of the hyperbola $\dfrac{y^2}{b^2} - \dfrac{z^2}{c^2} = 1$ in the yz-plane

FIGURE 10.33 The hyperboloid $(x^2/a^2) + (y^2/b^2) - (z^2/c^2) = 1$ in Example 5. Planes perpendicular to the z-axis cut it in ellipses. Vertical planes containing the z-axis cut it in hyperbolas.

The sections cut out by the coordinate planes are

$$x = 0: \quad \text{the hyperbola } \dfrac{y^2}{b^2} - \dfrac{z^2}{c^2} = 1$$

$$y = 0: \quad \text{the hyperbola } \dfrac{x^2}{a^2} - \dfrac{z^2}{c^2} = 1$$

$$z = 0: \quad \text{the ellipse } \dfrac{x^2}{a^2} + \dfrac{y^2}{b^2} = 1.$$

The plane $z = z_0$ cuts the surface in an ellipse with center on the z-axis and vertices on one of the hyperbolic sections above.

The surface is connected, meaning that it is possible to travel from one point on it to any other without leaving the surface. For this reason, it is said to have *one* sheet, in contrast to the hyperboloid in the next example, which has two sheets.

If $a = b$, the hyperboloid is a surface of revolution.

Example 6   Graphing Hyperboloids

The **hyperboloid of two sheets**

$$\dfrac{z^2}{c^2} - \dfrac{x^2}{a^2} - \dfrac{y^2}{b^2} = 1 \tag{5}$$

is symmetric with respect to the three coordinate planes (Figure 10.34). The plane $z = 0$ does not intersect the surface; in fact, for a horizontal plane to intersect the surface, we must have $|z| \geq c$. The hyperbolic sections

$$x = 0: \quad \dfrac{z^2}{c^2} - \dfrac{y^2}{b^2} = 1$$

$$y = 0: \quad \dfrac{z^2}{c^2} - \dfrac{x^2}{a^2} = 1$$

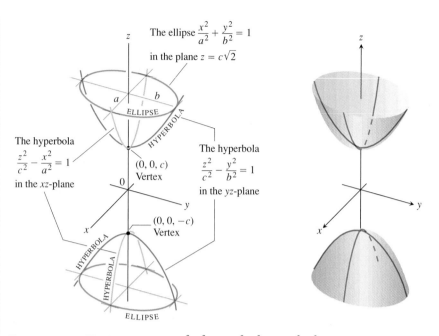

The ellipse $\dfrac{x^2}{a^2} + \dfrac{y^2}{b^2} = 1$

in the plane $z = c\sqrt{2}$

ELLIPSE

The hyperbola

$\dfrac{z^2}{c^2} - \dfrac{x^2}{a^2} = 1$

in the xz-plane

HYPERBOLA

$(0, 0, c)$
Vertex

The hyperbola

$\dfrac{z^2}{c^2} - \dfrac{y^2}{b^2} = 1$

in the yz-plane

$(0, 0, -c)$
Vertex

HYPERBOLA

HYPERBOLA

ELLIPSE

FIGURE 10.34 The hyperboloid $(z^2/c^2) - (x^2/a^2) - (y^2/b^2) = 1$ in Example 6. Planes perpendicular to the z-axis above and below the vertices cut it in ellipses. Vertical planes containing the z-axis cut it in hyperbolas.

have their vertices and foci on the z-axis. The surface is separated into two portions, one above the plane $z = c$ and the other below the plane $z = -c$. This accounts for its name.

Equations (4) and (5) have different numbers of negative terms. The number in each case is the same as the number of sheets of the hyperboloid. If we replace the 1 on the right side of either Equation (4) or Equation (5) by 0, we obtain the equation

$$\frac{x^2}{a^2} + \frac{y^2}{b^2} = \frac{z^2}{c^2}$$

for an elliptic cone (Equation (3)). The hyperboloids are asymptotic to this cone (Figure 10.35) in the same way that the hyperbolas

$$\frac{x^2}{a^2} - \frac{y^2}{b^2} = \pm 1$$

are asymptotic to the lines

$$\frac{x^2}{a^2} - \frac{y^2}{b^2} = 0$$

in the xy-plane.

Example 7   Graphing a Saddle

The **hyperbolic paraboloid**

$$\frac{y^2}{b^2} - \frac{x^2}{a^2} = \frac{z}{c}, \qquad c > 0 \tag{6}$$

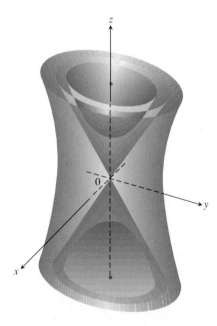

FIGURE 10.35 Both hyperboloids are asymptotic to the cone. (Example 6)

has symmetry with respect to the planes $x = 0$ and $y = 0$ (Figure 10.36). The sections in these planes are

$$x = 0: \quad \text{the parabola } z = \frac{c}{b^2} y^2 \tag{7}$$

$$y = 0: \quad \text{the parabola } z = -\frac{c}{a^2} x^2. \tag{8}$$

In the plane $x = 0$, the parabola opens upward from the origin. The parabola in the plane $y = 0$ opens downward.

If we cut the surface by a plane $z = z_0 > 0$, the section is a hyperbola,

$$\frac{y^2}{b^2} - \frac{x^2}{a^2} = \frac{z_0}{c},$$

with its focal axis parallel to the y-axis and its vertices on the parabola in Equation (7). If z_0 is negative, the focal axis is parallel to the x-axis and the vertices lie on the parabola in Equation (8).

Near the origin, the surface is shaped like a saddle. To a person traveling along the surface in the yz-plane, the origin looks like a minimum. To a person traveling in the xz-plane, the origin looks like a maximum. Such a point is called a **minimax** or **saddle point** of a surface.

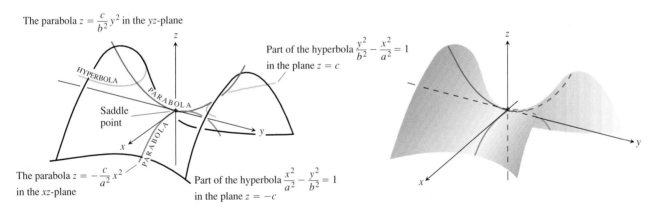

FIGURE 10.36 The hyperbolic paraboloid $(y^2/b^2) - (x^2/a^2) = z/c$, $c > 0$. The cross sections in planes perpendicular to the z-axis above and below the xy-plane are hyperbolas. The cross sections in planes perpendicular to the other axes are parabolas.

USING TECHNOLOGY

Visualizing in space A computer algebra system (CAS) or other computer graphing utility can help in visualizing surfaces in space. It can draw traces in different planes with far more patience than most people can muster. Many computer graphing systems can rotate a figure so you can see it as if it were a physical model you could turn in your hand. Hidden-line algorithms (see Exercise 62, Section 10.3) are used to block out portions of the surface that you would not see from your current viewing angle. Often a CAS will require surfaces to be entered in parametric form, as discussed in Section 13.6 (see also CAS Exercises 57 through 60 in Section 11.1). Sometimes you may have to manipulate the grid mesh to see all portions of a surface.

EXERCISES 10.4

Matching Equations with Surfaces

In Exercises 1–12, match the equation with the surface it defines. Also, identify each surface by type (paraboloid, ellipsoid, etc.). The surfaces are labeled (a) through (l).

1. $x^2 + y^2 + 4z^2 = 10$

2. $z^2 + 4y^2 - 4x^2 = 4$

3. $9y^2 + z^2 = 16$

4. $y^2 + z^2 = x^2$

5. $x = y^2 - z^2$

6. $x = -y^2 - z^2$

7. $x^2 + 2z^2 = 8$

8. $z^2 + x^2 - y^2 = 1$

9. $x = z^2 - y^2$

10. $z = -4x^2 - y^2$

11. $x^2 + 4z^2 = y^2$

12. $9x^2 + 4y^2 + 2z^2 = 36$

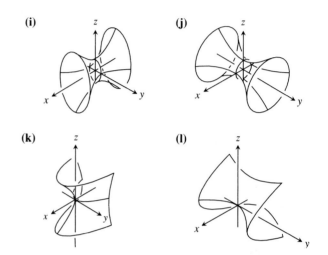

(a)

(b)

(c)

(d)

(e)

(f)

(g)

(h)

(i)

(j)

(k)

(l)

Theory and Examples

13. *Area and volume* Express the area A of the cross section cut from the ellipsoid

$$x^2 + \frac{y^2}{4} + \frac{z^2}{9} = 1$$

by the plane $z = c$ as a function of c. (The area of an ellipse with semiaxes a and b is πab.)

(b) Use slices perpendicular to the z-axis to find the volume of the ellipsoid in part (a).

(c) Now find the volume of the ellipsoid

$$\frac{x^2}{a^2} + \frac{y^2}{b^2} + \frac{z^2}{c^2} = 1.$$

Does your formula give the volume of a sphere of radius a if $a = b = c$?

14. *Volume of a barrel* The barrel shown here is shaped like an ellipsoid with equal pieces cut from the ends by planes perpendicular to the z-axis. The cross sections perpendicular to the z-axis are circular. The barrel is $2h$ units high, its midsection radius is R, and its end radii are both r. Find a formula for the barrel's volume. Then check two things. First, suppose that the sides of the barrel are straightened to turn the barrel into a cylinder of radius R and height $2h$. Does your formula give the cylinder's volume? Second, suppose that $r = 0$ and $h = R$

so the barrel is a sphere. Does your formula give the sphere's volume?

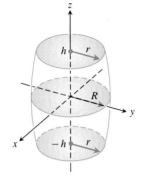

15. *Volume of paraboloid* Show that the volume of the segment cut from the paraboloid

$$\frac{x^2}{a^2} + \frac{y^2}{b^2} = \frac{z}{c}$$

by the plane $z = h$ equals half the segment's base times its altitude. (Figure 10.31 shows the segment for the special case $h = c$.)

16. *Volume of hyperboloid*

(a) Find the volume of the solid bounded by the hyperboloid

$$\frac{x^2}{a^2} + \frac{y^2}{b^2} - \frac{z^2}{c^2} = 1$$

and the planes $z = 0$ and $z = h$, $h > 0$.

(b) Express your answer in part (a) in terms of h and the areas A_0 and A_h of the regions cut by the hyperboloid from the planes $z = 0$ and $z = h$.

(c) Show that the volume in part (a) is also given by the formula

$$V = \frac{h}{6}(A_0 + 4A_m + A_h),$$

where A_m is the area of the region cut by the hyperboloid from the plane $z = h/2$.

Graphing Surfaces

T Plot the surfaces in Exercises 17–20 over the indicated domains. If you can, rotate the surface into different viewing positions.

17. $z = y^2$, $\quad -2 \le x \le 2$, $\quad -0.5 \le y \le 2$

18. $z = 1 - y^2$, $\quad -2 \le x \le 2$, $\quad -2 \le y \le 2$

19. $z = x^2 + y^2$, $\quad -3 \le x \le 3$, $\quad -3 \le y \le 3$

20. $z = x^2 + 2y^2$ over

(a) $-3 \le x \le 3$, $\quad -3 \le y \le 3$

(b) $-1 \le x \le 1$, $\quad -2 \le y \le 3$

(c) $-2 \le x \le 2$, $\quad -2 \le y \le 2$

(d) $-2 \le x \le 2$, $\quad -1 \le y \le 1$

COMPUTER EXPLORATIONS

Surface Plots

CD-ROM
WEBsite Use a CAS to plot the surfaces in Exercises 21–26. Identify the type of quadric surface from your graph.

21. $\dfrac{x^2}{9} + \dfrac{y^2}{36} = 1 - \dfrac{z^2}{25}$

22. $\dfrac{x^2}{9} - \dfrac{z^2}{9} = 1 - \dfrac{y^2}{16}$

23. $5x^2 = z^2 - 3y^2$

24. $\dfrac{y^2}{16} = 1 - \dfrac{x^2}{9} + z$

25. $\dfrac{x^2}{9} - 1 = \dfrac{y^2}{16} + \dfrac{z^2}{2}$

26. $y - \sqrt{4 - z^2} = 0$

10.5 Vector-Valued Functions and Space Curves

Space Curves • Limits and Continuity • Derivatives and Motion • Differentiation Rules • Vector Functions of Constant Length • Integrals of Vector Functions

Just as we did for planar curves in Section 9.3, to track a particle moving in space, we run a vector **r** from the origin to the particle (Figure 10.37) and study the

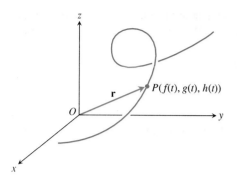

FIGURE 10.37 The position vector $\mathbf{r} = \overrightarrow{OP}$ of a particle moving through space is a function of time.

changes in **r.** If the particle's position coordinates are twice-differentiable functions of time, then so is **r,** and we can find the particle's velocity and acceleration vectors at any time by differentiating **r.** Conversely, if we know either the particle's velocity vector or acceleration vector as a continuous function of time and if we have enough information about the particle's initial velocity and position, we can find **r** as a function of time by integration. We study space curves in the remainder of this chapter.

Space Curves

When a particle moves through space during a time interval I, we think of the particle's coordinates as functions defined on I:

$$x = f(t), \qquad y = g(t), \qquad z = h(t), \qquad t \in I. \tag{1}$$

The points $(x, y, z) = (f(t), g(t), h(t))$, $t \in I$, make up the **curve** in space that we call the particle's **path.** The equations and interval in Equation (1) **parametrize** the curve. A curve in space can also be represented in vector form. The vector

$$\mathbf{r}(t) = \overrightarrow{OP} = f(t)\mathbf{i} + g(t)\mathbf{j} + h(t)\mathbf{k} \tag{2}$$

from the origin to the particle's **position** $P(f(t), g(t), h(t))$ at time t is the particle's **position vector.** The functions f, g, and h are the **component functions (components)** of the position vector. We think of the particle's path as the **curve traced by r** during the time interval I. Figure 10.38 displays several space curves generated by a computer graphing program. It would not be easy to plot these curves by hand.

CD-ROM
WEBsite

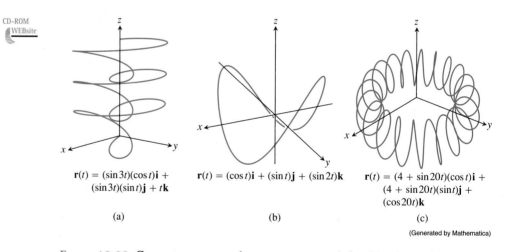

$\mathbf{r}(t) = (\sin 3t)(\cos t)\mathbf{i} + (\sin 3t)(\sin t)\mathbf{j} + t\mathbf{k}$

(a)

$\mathbf{r}(t) = (\cos t)\mathbf{i} + (\sin t)\mathbf{j} + (\sin 2t)\mathbf{k}$

(b)

$\mathbf{r}(t) = (4 + \sin 20t)(\cos t)\mathbf{i} + (4 + \sin 20t)(\sin t)\mathbf{j} + (\cos 20t)\mathbf{k}$

(c)

(Generated by Mathematica)

FIGURE 10.38 Computer-generated space curves are defined by the position vectors $\mathbf{r}(t)$.

Equation (2) defines **r** as a vector function of the real variable t on the interval I. More generally, a **vector function** or **vector-valued function** on a domain set D is a rule that assigns a vector in space to each element in D. For now, the domains will be intervals of real numbers resulting in a space curve. Later, in Chapter 13, the domains will be regions in the plane. Vector functions will then represent surfaces in space. Vector functions on a domain in the plane or space also give rise to "vector fields," which are important to the study of the flow of a fluid, gravitational fields, and electromagnetic phenomena. We investigate vector fields and their applications in Chapter 13.

As in Chapter 9, we refer to real-valued functions as **scalar functions** to distinguish them from vector functions. The components of **r** are scalar functions of t. When we define a vector-valued function by giving its component functions, we assume the vector function's domain to be the common domain of the components. You should find this material to be very similar to the material on planar curves in Section 9.3.

Example 1   Graphing a Helix

Graph the vector function

$$\mathbf{r}(t) = (\cos t)\mathbf{i} + (\sin t)\mathbf{j} + t\mathbf{k}.$$

Solution

The vector function

$$\mathbf{r}(t) = (\cos t)\mathbf{i} + (\sin t)\mathbf{j} + t\mathbf{k}$$

is defined for all real values of t. The curve traced by **r** is a helix (from an old Greek word for "spiral") that winds around the circular cylinder $x^2 + y^2 = 1$ (Figure 10.39). The curve lies on the cylinder because the **i**- and **j**-components of **r**, being the x- and y-coordinates of the tip of **r**, satisfy the cylinder's equation:

$$x^2 + y^2 = (\cos t)^2 + (\sin t)^2 = 1.$$

The curve rises as the **k**-component $z = t$ increases. Each time t increases by 2π, the curve completes one turn around the cylinder. The equations

$$x = \cos t, \qquad y = \sin t, \qquad z = t$$

parametrize the helix, the interval $-\infty < t < \infty$ being understood. You will find more helices in Figure 10.40.

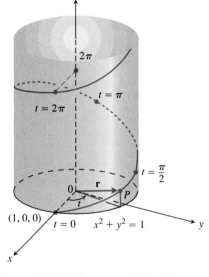

FIGURE 10.39 The upper half of the helix $\mathbf{r}(t) = (\cos t)\mathbf{i} + (\sin t)\mathbf{j} + t\mathbf{k}$. (Example 1)

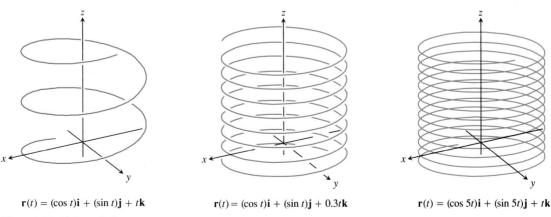

$\mathbf{r}(t) = (\cos t)\mathbf{i} + (\sin t)\mathbf{j} + t\mathbf{k}$

(Generated by Mathematica)

$\mathbf{r}(t) = (\cos t)\mathbf{i} + (\sin t)\mathbf{j} + 0.3t\mathbf{k}$

$\mathbf{r}(t) = (\cos 5t)\mathbf{i} + (\sin 5t)\mathbf{j} + t\mathbf{k}$

FIGURE 10.40 Helices drawn by computer.

Limits and Continuity

We define limits and continuity of vector-valued functions for space the same way we define limits of vector-valued functions for the plane.

Definition   Limit and Continuity

If $\mathbf{r}(t) = f(t)\mathbf{i} + g(t)\mathbf{j} + h(t)\mathbf{k}$, then

$$\lim_{t \to t_0} \mathbf{r}(t) = \left(\lim_{t \to t_0} f(t) \right)\mathbf{i} + \left(\lim_{t \to t_0} g(t) \right)\mathbf{j} + \left(\lim_{t \to t_0} h(t) \right)\mathbf{k}. \qquad (3)$$

A vector function $\mathbf{r}(t)$ is **continuous at a point** $t = t_0$ in its domain if $\lim_{t \to t_0} \mathbf{r}(t) = \mathbf{r}(t_0)$. The function is **continuous** if it is continuous at every point in its domain.

From Equation (3), we see that $\mathbf{r}(t)$ is continuous at $t = t_0$ if and only if each component function is continuous there.

Example 2   Continuity of Space Curves

All the space curves shown in Figures 10.38 and 10.40 are continuous because their component functions are continuous at every value of t in $(-\infty, \infty)$.

Example 3   Finding Limits of Vector Functions

If $\mathbf{r}(t) = (\cos t)\mathbf{i} + (\sin t)\mathbf{j} + t\mathbf{k}$, then

$$\lim_{t \to \pi/4} \mathbf{r}(t) = \left(\lim_{t \to \pi/4} \cos t \right)\mathbf{i} + \left(\lim_{t \to \pi/4} \sin t \right)\mathbf{j} + \left(\lim_{t \to \pi/4} t \right)\mathbf{k}$$

$$= \frac{\sqrt{2}}{2}\mathbf{i} + \frac{\sqrt{2}}{2}\mathbf{j} + \frac{\pi}{4}\mathbf{k}.$$

Derivatives and Motion

The derivative of a vector function in space is defined in the same way as for planar functions, but with one more component.

Definition   Derivative at a Point

The vector function $\mathbf{r}(t) = f(t)\mathbf{i} + g(t)\mathbf{j} + h(t)\mathbf{k}$ is **differentiable at** $t = t_0$ if f, g, and h are differentiable at t_0. The **derivative** is the vector

$$\mathbf{r}'(t) = \frac{d\mathbf{r}}{dt} = \lim_{\Delta t \to 0} \frac{\mathbf{r}(t + \Delta t) - \mathbf{r}(t)}{\Delta t} = \frac{df}{dt}\mathbf{i} + \frac{dg}{dt}\mathbf{j} + \frac{dh}{dt}\mathbf{k}.$$

A vector function $\mathbf{r}$ is **differentiable** if it is differentiable at every point of its domain. The curve traced by $\mathbf{r}$ is **smooth** if $\mathbf{r}'(t)$ is continuous and never $\mathbf{0}$, that is, if f, g, and h have continuous first derivatives that are not simultaneously 0.

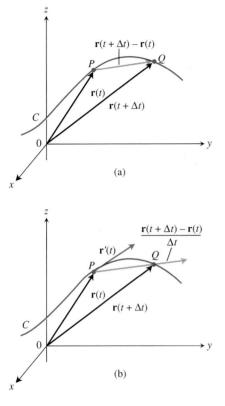

(a)

(b)

FIGURE 10.41 As $\Delta t \to 0$, the point Q approaches the point P along the curve C, and the vector $\overrightarrow{PQ}/\Delta t$ becomes the tangent vector $\mathbf{r}'(t)$ in the limit.

CD-ROM
WEBsite

The geometric significance of the definition of derivative is the same as for planar curves and is shown in Figure 10.41. The points P and Q have position vectors $\mathbf{r}(t)$ and $\mathbf{r}(t + \Delta t)$, and the vector $\overrightarrow{PQ}$ is represented by $\mathbf{r}(t + \Delta t) - \mathbf{r}(t)$. For $\Delta t > 0$, the scalar multiple $(1/\Delta t)(\mathbf{r}(t + \Delta t) - \mathbf{r}(t))$ points in the same direction as the vector $\overrightarrow{PQ}$. As $\Delta t \to 0$, this vector approaches a vector that is tangent to the curve at P (Figure 10.41b). We define $\mathbf{r}'(t)$, when different from $\mathbf{0}$, to be the vector **tangent** to the curve at P. The **tangent line** to the curve at a point $(f(t_0), g(t_0), h(t_0))$ is defined to be the line through the point parallel to $\mathbf{r}'(t_0)$. We require $d\mathbf{r}/dt \neq \mathbf{0}$ for a smooth curve to make sure the curve has a continuously turning tangent at each point. On a smooth curve, there are no sharp corners or cusps.

A curve that is made up of a finite number of smooth curves pieced together in a continuous fashion is called **piecewise smooth** (Figure 10.42).

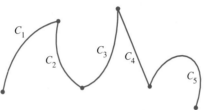

FIGURE 10.42 A piecewise smooth curve made up of five smooth curves connected end to end in continuous fashion.

As we found for vector functions in the plane, when $d\mathbf{r}/dt$ is different from $\mathbf{0}$, the derivative models a particle's velocity as it moves along the space curve defined by $\mathbf{r}$. The derivative points in the direction of motion and gives the rate of change of position with respect to time. For a smooth curve, the velocity is never zero; the particle does not stop or reverse direction.

Definitions   Velocity, Speed, Acceleration, Direction of Motion

If $\mathbf{r}$ is the position vector of a particle moving along a smooth curve in space, then at any time t, the following definitions apply.

1. $\mathbf{v}(t) = \dfrac{d\mathbf{r}}{dt}$, the derivative of position, is the particle's **velocity vector** and is tangent to the curve.

2. $|\mathbf{v}(t)|$, the magnitude of $\mathbf{v}$, is the particle's **speed.**

3. $\mathbf{a}(t) = \dfrac{d\mathbf{v}}{dt} = \dfrac{d^2\mathbf{r}}{dt^2}$, the derivative of velocity and the second derivative of position, is the particle's **acceleration vector.**

4. $\dfrac{\mathbf{v}}{|\mathbf{v}|}$, a unit vector, is the **direction of motion.**

As for plane curves, we can express the velocity of a moving particle as the product of its speed and direction:

$$\text{Velocity} = |\mathbf{v}|\left(\frac{\mathbf{v}}{|\mathbf{v}|}\right) = (\text{speed})(\text{direction}).$$

In Section 10.3, we found this expression for velocity useful in locating, for example, the position of a helicopter moving along a straight line in space. Now let's look at an example of an object moving along a (nonlinear) space curve.

Example 4   Flight of a Hang Glider

A person on a hang glider is spiraling upward due to rapidly rising air on a path having position vector $\mathbf{r}(t) = (3 \cos t)\mathbf{i} + (3 \sin t)\mathbf{j} + t^2\mathbf{k}$. The path is similar to that of a helix (although it's *not* a helix, as you will see in Section 10.7) and is shown in Figure 10.43 for $0 \leq t \leq 4\pi$. Find

(a) the velocity and acceleration vectors

(b) the glider's speed at any time t

(c) the times, if any, when the glider's acceleration is orthogonal to its velocity.

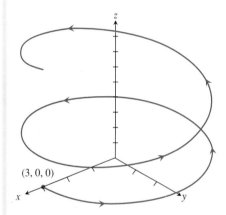

FIGURE 10.43 The path of a hang glider with position vector $\mathbf{r}(t) = (3 \cos t)\mathbf{i} + (3 \sin t)\mathbf{j} + t^2\mathbf{k}$.
(Example 4)

Solution

(a) $\mathbf{r} = (3 \cos t)\mathbf{i} + (3 \sin t)\mathbf{j} + t^2\mathbf{k}$

$$\mathbf{v} = \frac{d\mathbf{r}}{dt} = -(3 \sin t)\mathbf{i} + (3 \cos t)\mathbf{j} + 2t\mathbf{k}$$

$$\mathbf{a} = \frac{d^2\mathbf{r}}{dt^2} = -(3 \cos t)\mathbf{i} - (3 \sin t)\mathbf{j} + 2\mathbf{k}$$

(b) Speed is the magnitude of $\mathbf{v}$:

$$|\mathbf{v}(t)| = \sqrt{(-3 \sin t)^2 + (3 \cos t)^2 + (2t)^2}$$
$$= \sqrt{9 \sin^2 t + 9 \cos^2 t + 4t^2}$$
$$= \sqrt{9 + 4t^2}.$$

The glider is moving faster and faster as it rises along its path.

(c) To find the times when $\mathbf{v}$ and $\mathbf{a}$ are orthogonal, we look for values of t for which

$$\mathbf{v} \cdot \mathbf{a} = 9 \sin t \cos t - 9 \cos t \sin t + 4t = 4t = 0.$$

Thus, the only time the acceleration vector is orthogonal to **v** is when $t = 0$. We study acceleration for motions along paths in more detail in Section 10.7. There we discover how the acceleration vector reveals the curving nature and tendency of the path to "twist" out of a plane containing the velocity vector.

Differentiation Rules

Because the derivatives of vector functions may be computed component by component, the rules for differentiating vector functions have the same form as the rules for differentiating scalar functions.

Differentiation Rules for Vector Functions

Let **u** and **v** be differentiable vector functions of t, **C** a constant vector, c any scalar, and f any differentiable scalar function.

1. *Constant Function Rule:* $\dfrac{d}{dt}\mathbf{C} = \mathbf{0}$

2. *Scalar Multiple Rules:* $\dfrac{d}{dt}[c\mathbf{u}(t)] = c\mathbf{u}'(t)$

  $\dfrac{d}{dt}[f(t)\mathbf{u}(t)] = f'(t)\mathbf{u}(t) + f(t)\mathbf{u}'(t)$

3. *Sum Rule:* $\dfrac{d}{dt}[\mathbf{u}(t) + \mathbf{v}(t)] = \mathbf{u}'(t) + \mathbf{v}'(t)$

4. *Difference Rule:* $\dfrac{d}{dt}[\mathbf{u}(t) - \mathbf{v}(t)] = \mathbf{u}'(t) - \mathbf{v}'(t)$

5. *Dot Product Rule:* $\dfrac{d}{dt}[\mathbf{u}(t) \cdot \mathbf{v}(t)] = \mathbf{u}'(t) \cdot \mathbf{v}(t) + \mathbf{u}(t) \cdot \mathbf{v}'(t)$

6. *Cross Product Rule:* $\dfrac{d}{dt}[\mathbf{u}(t) \times \mathbf{v}(t)] = \mathbf{u}'(t) \times \mathbf{v}(t) + \mathbf{u}(t) \times \mathbf{v}'(t)$

7. *Chain Rule:* $\dfrac{d}{dt}[\mathbf{u}(f(t))] = f'(t)\mathbf{u}'(f(t))$

When you use the Cross Product Rule, remember to preserve the order of the factors. If **u** comes first on the left side of the equation, it must also come first on the right or the signs will be wrong.

Applying the differentiation rules is the same as for planar vector functions (Example 5, Section 9.3) except that now we have a third component. As before, the rules can be proved by applying the definition or the corresponding differentiation formulas for scalar functions to the components of the vector functions. For example, here's how to prove the Cross Product and Chain Rules.

Proof of the Cross Product Rule   We model the proof after the proof of the product rule for scalar functions. According to the definition of derivative,

$$\frac{d}{dt}(\mathbf{u} \times \mathbf{v}) = \lim_{h \to 0} \frac{\mathbf{u}(t + h) \times \mathbf{v}(t + h) - \mathbf{u}(t) \times \mathbf{v}(t)}{h}.$$

To change this fraction into an equivalent one that contains the difference quotients for the derivatives of **u** and **v,** we subtract and add $\mathbf{u}(t) \times \mathbf{v}(t + h)$ in the numerator.

Then

$$\frac{d}{dt}(\mathbf{u} \times \mathbf{v}) = \lim_{h \to 0} \frac{\mathbf{u}(t+h) \times \mathbf{v}(t+h) - \mathbf{u}(t) \times \mathbf{v}(t+h) + \mathbf{u}(t) \times \mathbf{v}(t+h) - \mathbf{u}(t) \times \mathbf{v}(t)}{h}$$

$$= \lim_{h \to 0} \left[\frac{\mathbf{u}(t+h) - \mathbf{u}(t)}{h} \times \mathbf{v}(t+h) + \mathbf{u}(t) \times \frac{\mathbf{v}(t+h) - \mathbf{v}(t)}{h} \right]$$

$$= \lim_{h \to 0} \frac{\mathbf{u}(t+h) - \mathbf{u}(t)}{h} \times \lim_{h \to 0} \mathbf{v}(t+h) + \lim_{h \to 0} \mathbf{u}(t) \times \lim_{h \to 0} \frac{\mathbf{v}(t+h) - \mathbf{v}(t)}{h}.$$

The last of these equalities holds because the limit of the cross product of two vector functions is the cross product of their limits if the latter exist (Exercise 39). As h approaches zero, $\mathbf{v}(t+h)$ approaches $\mathbf{v}(t)$ because $\mathbf{v}$, being differentiable at t, is continuous at t (Exercise 40). The two fractions approach the values of $d\mathbf{u}/dt$ and $d\mathbf{v}/dt$ at t. In short,

$$\frac{d}{dt}(\mathbf{u} \times \mathbf{v}) = \frac{d\mathbf{u}}{dt} \times \mathbf{v} + \mathbf{u} \times \frac{d\mathbf{v}}{dt}.$$

As an algebraic convenience, we sometimes write the product of a scalar c and a vector $\mathbf{v}$ as $\mathbf{v}c$ instead of $c\mathbf{v}$. This permits us, for instance, to write the Chain Rule in a familiar form:

$$\frac{du}{dt} = \frac{d\mathbf{u}}{ds}\frac{ds}{dt},$$

where $s = f(t)$.

Proof of the Chain Rule   Suppose that $\mathbf{u}(s) = a(s)\mathbf{i} + b(s)\mathbf{j} + c(s)\mathbf{k}$ is a differentiable vector function of s and that $s = f(t)$ is a differentiable scalar function of t. Then a, b, and c are differentiable functions of t, and the Chain Rule for differentiable real-valued functions gives

$$\frac{d}{dt}[\mathbf{u}(s)] = \frac{da}{dt}\mathbf{i} + \frac{db}{dt}\mathbf{j} + \frac{dc}{dt}\mathbf{k}$$

$$= \frac{da}{ds}\frac{ds}{dt}\mathbf{i} + \frac{db}{ds}\frac{ds}{dt}\mathbf{j} + \frac{dc}{ds}\frac{ds}{dt}\mathbf{k}$$

$$= \frac{ds}{dt}\left(\frac{da}{ds}\mathbf{i} + \frac{db}{ds}\mathbf{j} + \frac{dc}{ds}\mathbf{k}\right)$$

$$= \frac{ds}{dt}\frac{d\mathbf{u}}{ds}$$

$$= f'(t)\mathbf{u}'(f(t)). \qquad {\scriptstyle s = f(t)}$$

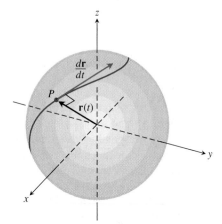

FIGURE 10.44 If a particle moves on a sphere in such a way that its position $\mathbf{r}$ is a differentiable function of time, then $\mathbf{r} \cdot (d\mathbf{r}/dt) = 0$.

Vector Functions of Constant Length

When we track a particle moving on a sphere centered at the origin (Figure 10.44), the position vector has a constant length equal to the radius of the sphere. The velocity vector $d\mathbf{r}/dt$, tangent to the path of motion, is tangent to the sphere and hence perpendicular to $\mathbf{r}$. This is always the case for a differentiable vector function of constant length: The vector and its first derivative are orthogonal. With the length constant, the change in the function is a change in direction only, and direction changes take place at right angles. We can also obtain this result by direct calculation:

$$\mathbf{r}(t) \cdot \mathbf{r}(t) = c^2 \qquad {\scriptstyle |\mathbf{r}(t)| = c \ \text{is constant.}}$$

$$\frac{d}{dt}[\mathbf{r}(t) \cdot \mathbf{r}(t)] = 0 \qquad {\scriptstyle \text{Differentiate both sides.}}$$

$$\mathbf{r}'(t) \cdot \mathbf{r}(t) + \mathbf{r}(t) \cdot \mathbf{r}'(t) = 0 \qquad {\scriptstyle \text{Rule 5 with } \mathbf{r}(t) = \mathbf{u}(t) = \mathbf{v}(t)}$$

$$2\mathbf{r}'(t) \cdot \mathbf{r}(t) = 0.$$

The vectors $\mathbf{r}'(t)$ and $\mathbf{r}(t)$ are orthogonal because their dot product is 0. In summary,

We will use this observation repeatedly in Section 10.7.

> If $\mathbf{r}$ is a differentiable vector function of t of constant length, then
>
> $$\mathbf{r} \cdot \frac{d\mathbf{r}}{dt} = 0. \tag{4}$$

Example 5   Supporting Equation (4)

Show that $\mathbf{r}(t) = (\sin t)\mathbf{i} + (\cos t)\mathbf{j} + \sqrt{3}\mathbf{k}$ has constant length and is orthogonal to its derivative.

Solution

$$\mathbf{r}(t) = (\sin t)\mathbf{i} + (\cos t)\mathbf{j} + \sqrt{3}\mathbf{k}$$

$$|\mathbf{r}(t)| = \sqrt{(\sin t)^2 + (\cos t)^2 + (\sqrt{3})^2} = \sqrt{1 + 3} = 2$$

$$\frac{d\mathbf{r}}{dt} = (\cos t)\mathbf{i} - (\sin t)\mathbf{j}$$

$$\mathbf{r} \cdot \frac{d\mathbf{r}}{dt} = \sin t \cos t - \sin t \cos t = 0$$

Integrals of Vector Functions

A differentiable vector function $\mathbf{R}(t)$ is an **antiderivative** of a vector function $\mathbf{r}(t)$ on an interval I if $d\mathbf{R}/dt = \mathbf{r}$ at each point of I. If $\mathbf{R}$ is an antiderivative of $\mathbf{r}$ on I, it can be shown, working one component at a time, that every antiderivative of $\mathbf{r}$ on I has the form $\mathbf{R} + \mathbf{C}$ for some constant vector $\mathbf{C}$ (Exercise 45). The set of all antiderivatives of $\mathbf{r}$ on I is the **indefinite integral** of $\mathbf{r}$ on I.

> **Definition**   Indefinite Integral
> The **indefinite integral** of $\mathbf{r}$ with respect to t is the set of all antiderivatives of $\mathbf{r}$, denoted by $\int \mathbf{r}(t)\, dt$. If $\mathbf{R}$ is any antiderivative of $\mathbf{r}$, then
>
> $$\int \mathbf{r}(t)\, dt = \mathbf{R}(t) + \mathbf{C}.$$

The usual arithmetic rules for indefinite integrals apply.

Example 6   Finding Antiderivatives

$$\int ((\cos t)\mathbf{i} + \mathbf{j} - 2t\mathbf{k})\, dt = \left(\int \cos t\, dt\right)\mathbf{i} + \left(\int dt\right)\mathbf{j} - \left(\int 2t\, dt\right)\mathbf{k} \tag{5}$$

$$= (\sin t + C_1)\mathbf{i} + (t + C_2)\mathbf{j} - (t^2 + C_3)\mathbf{k} \tag{6}$$

$$= (\sin t)\mathbf{i} + t\mathbf{j} - t^2\mathbf{k} + \mathbf{C} \qquad \mathbf{C} = C_1\mathbf{i} + C_2\mathbf{j} - C_3\mathbf{k}$$

As in the integration of scalar functions, we recommend that you skip the steps in Equations (5) and (6) and go directly to the final form. Find an antiderivative for each component and add a constant vector at the end.

Definite integrals of vector functions are defined in terms of components.

Definition   Definite Integral

If the components of $\mathbf{r}(t) = f(t)\mathbf{i} + g(t)\mathbf{j} + h(t)\mathbf{k}$ are integrable over $[a, b]$, then so is $\mathbf{r}$, and the **definite integral** of $\mathbf{r}$ from a to b is

$$\int_a^b \mathbf{r}(t)\, dt = \left(\int_a^b f(t)\, dt\right)\mathbf{i} + \left(\int_a^b g(t)\, dt\right)\mathbf{j} + \left(\int_a^b h(t)\, dt\right)\mathbf{k}.$$

Example 7   Evaluating Definite Integrals

$$\int_0^\pi ((\cos t)\mathbf{i} + \mathbf{j} - 2t\mathbf{k})\, dt = \left(\int_0^\pi \cos t\, dt\right)\mathbf{i} + \left(\int_0^\pi dt\right)\mathbf{j} - \left(\int_0^\pi 2t\, dt\right)\mathbf{k}$$

$$= [\sin t]_0^\pi\, \mathbf{i} + [t]_0^\pi\, \mathbf{j} - [t^2]_0^\pi\, \mathbf{k}$$

$$= [0 - 0]\mathbf{i} + [\pi - 0]\mathbf{j} - [\pi^2 - 0^2]\mathbf{k}$$

$$= \pi\mathbf{j} - \pi^2\mathbf{k}$$

Example 8   Revisiting the Flight of a Glider

Suppose that we did not know the path of the glider in Example 4, but only its acceleration vector $\mathbf{a}(t) = -(3 \cos t)\mathbf{i} - (3 \sin t)\mathbf{j} + 2\mathbf{k}$. We also know that initially (at time $t = 0$), the glider departed from the point $(3, 0, 0)$ with velocity $\mathbf{v}(0) = 3\mathbf{j}$. Find the glider's position as a function of t.

Solution   Our goal is to find $\mathbf{r}(t)$ knowing

The differential equation: $\mathbf{a} = \dfrac{d^2\mathbf{r}}{dt^2} = -(3 \cos t)\mathbf{i} - (3 \sin t)\mathbf{j} + 2\mathbf{k}$

The initial conditions: $\mathbf{v}(0) = 3\mathbf{j}$ and $\mathbf{r}(0) = 3\mathbf{i} + 0\mathbf{j} + 0\mathbf{k}.$

Integrating both sides of the differential equation with respect to t gives

$$\mathbf{v}(t) = -(3 \sin t)\mathbf{i} + (3 \cos t)\mathbf{j} + 2t\mathbf{k} + \mathbf{C}_1.$$

We use $\mathbf{v}(0) = 3\mathbf{j}$ to find $\mathbf{C}_1$:

$$3\mathbf{j} = -(3 \sin 0)\mathbf{i} + (3 \cos 0)\mathbf{j} + (0)\mathbf{k} + \mathbf{C}_1$$

$$3\mathbf{j} = 3\mathbf{j} + \mathbf{C}_1$$

$$\mathbf{C}_1 = \mathbf{0}.$$

The glider's velocity as a function of time is

$$\frac{d\mathbf{r}}{dt} = \mathbf{v}(t) = -(3 \sin t)\mathbf{i} + (3 \cos t)\mathbf{j} + 2t\mathbf{k}.$$

Integrating both sides of this last differential equation gives

$$\mathbf{r}(t) = (3 \cos t)\mathbf{i} + (3 \sin t)\mathbf{j} + t^2\mathbf{k} + \mathbf{C}_2.$$

We then use the initial condition $\mathbf{r}(0) = 3\mathbf{i}$ to find $\mathbf{C}_2$:

$$3\mathbf{i} = (3 \cos 0)\mathbf{i} + (3 \sin 0)\mathbf{j} + (0^2)\mathbf{k} + \mathbf{C}_2$$
$$3\mathbf{i} = 3\mathbf{i} + (0)\mathbf{j} + (0)\mathbf{k} + \mathbf{C}_2$$
$$\mathbf{C}_2 = \mathbf{0}.$$

The glider's position as a function of t is

$$\mathbf{r}(t) = (3 \cos t)\mathbf{i} + (3 \sin t)\mathbf{j} + t^2\mathbf{k}.$$

This is the path of the glider we know from Example 4 and is shown in Figure 10.43.

Note: It was peculiar to this example that both of the constant vectors of integration, $\mathbf{C}_1$ and $\mathbf{C}_2$, turned out to be $\mathbf{0}$. Exercises 23 and 24 give different results.

EXERCISES 10.5

Velocity and Acceleration in Space

In Exercises 1–6, $\mathbf{r}(t)$ is the position of a particle in space at time t. Find the particle's velocity and acceleration vectors. Then find the particle's speed and direction of motion at the given value of t. Write the particle's velocity at that time as the product of its speed and direction.

1. $\mathbf{r}(t) = (t + 1)\mathbf{i} + (t^2 - 1)\mathbf{j} + 2t\mathbf{k}, \quad t = 1$

2. $\mathbf{r}(t) = (1 + t)\mathbf{i} + \dfrac{t^2}{\sqrt{2}}\mathbf{j} + \dfrac{t^3}{3}\mathbf{k}, \quad t = 1$

3. $\mathbf{r}(t) = (2 \cos t)\mathbf{i} + (3 \sin t)\mathbf{j} + 4t\mathbf{k}, \quad t = \pi/2$

4. $\mathbf{r}(t) = (\sec t)\mathbf{i} + (\tan t)\mathbf{j} + \dfrac{4}{3}t\mathbf{k}, \quad t = \pi/6$

5. $\mathbf{r}(t) = (2 \ln (t + 1))\mathbf{i} + t^2\mathbf{j} + \dfrac{t^2}{2}\mathbf{k}, \quad t = 1$

6. $\mathbf{r}(t) = (e^{-t})\mathbf{i} + (2 \cos 3t)\mathbf{j} + (2 \sin 3t)\mathbf{k}, \quad t = 0$

In Exercises 7–10, $\mathbf{r}(t)$ is the position of a particle in space at time t. Find the angle between the velocity and acceleration vectors at time $t = 0$.

7. $\mathbf{r}(t) = (3t + 1)\mathbf{i} + \sqrt{3}t\mathbf{j} + t^2\mathbf{k}$

8. $\mathbf{r}(t) = \left(\dfrac{\sqrt{2}}{2}t\right)\mathbf{i} + \left(\dfrac{\sqrt{2}}{2}t - 16t^2\right)\mathbf{j}$

9. $\mathbf{r}(t) = (\ln (t^2 + 1))\mathbf{i} + (\tan^{-1} t)\mathbf{j} + \sqrt{t^2 + 1}\,\mathbf{k}$

10. $\mathbf{r}(t) = \dfrac{4}{9}(1 + t)^{3/2}\mathbf{i} + \dfrac{4}{9}(1 - t)^{3/2}\mathbf{j} + \dfrac{1}{3}t\mathbf{k}$

In Exercises 11 and 12, $\mathbf{r}(t)$ is the position vector of a particle in space at time t. Find the time or times in the given time interval when the velocity and acceleration vectors are orthogonal.

11. $\mathbf{r}(t) = (t - \sin t)\mathbf{i} + (1 - \cos t)\mathbf{j}, \quad 0 \le t \le 2\pi$

12. $\mathbf{r}(t) = (\sin t)\mathbf{i} + t\mathbf{j} + (\cos t)\mathbf{k}, \quad t \ge 0$

Integrating Vector-Valued Functions

Evaluate the integrals in Exercises 13–18.

13. $\displaystyle\int_0^1 [t^3\mathbf{i} + 7\mathbf{j} + (t + 1)\mathbf{k}]\, dt$

14. $\displaystyle\int_1^2 \left[(6 - 6t)\mathbf{i} + 3\sqrt{t}\mathbf{j} + \left(\dfrac{4}{t^2}\right)\mathbf{k}\right] dt$

15. $\displaystyle\int_{-\pi/4}^{\pi/4} [(\sin t)\mathbf{i} + (1 + \cos t)\mathbf{j} + (\sec^2 t)\mathbf{k}]\, dt$

16. $\displaystyle\int_0^{\pi/3} [(\sec t \tan t)\mathbf{i} + (\tan t)\mathbf{j} + (2 \sin t \cos t)\mathbf{k}]\, dt$

17. $\displaystyle\int_1^4 \left[\dfrac{1}{t}\mathbf{i} + \dfrac{1}{5 - t}\mathbf{j} + \dfrac{1}{2t}\mathbf{k}\right] dt$

18. $\displaystyle\int_0^1 \left[\dfrac{2}{\sqrt{1 - t^2}}\mathbf{i} + \dfrac{\sqrt{3}}{1 + t^2}\mathbf{k}\right] dt$

Initial Value Problems for Vector-Valued Functions

Solve the initial value problems in Exercises 19–24 for $\mathbf{r}$ as a vector function of t.

19. Differential equation: $\dfrac{d\mathbf{r}}{dt} = -t\mathbf{i} - t\mathbf{j} - t\mathbf{k}$

   Initial condition: $\mathbf{r}(0) = \mathbf{i} + 2\mathbf{j} + 3\mathbf{k}$

20. Differential equation: $\dfrac{d\mathbf{r}}{dt} = (180t)\mathbf{i} + (180t - 16t^2)\mathbf{j}$

   Initial condition: $\mathbf{r}(0) = 100\mathbf{j}$

21. Differential equation: $\dfrac{d\mathbf{r}}{dt} = \dfrac{3}{2}(t + 1)^{1/2}\mathbf{i} + e^{-t}\mathbf{j} + \dfrac{1}{t + 1}\mathbf{k}$

   Initial condition: $\mathbf{r}(0) = \mathbf{k}$

22. Differential equation: $\dfrac{d\mathbf{r}}{dt} = (t^3 + 4t)\mathbf{i} + t\mathbf{j} + 2t^2\mathbf{k}$

Initial condition: $\mathbf{r}(0) = \mathbf{i} + \mathbf{j}$

23. Differential equation: $\dfrac{d^2\mathbf{r}}{dt^2} = -32\mathbf{k}$

Initial conditions: $\mathbf{r}(0) = 100\mathbf{k}$ and

$$\dfrac{d\mathbf{r}}{dt}\bigg|_{t=0} = 8\mathbf{i} + 8\mathbf{j}$$

24. Differential equation: $\dfrac{d^2\mathbf{r}}{dt^2} = -(\mathbf{i} + \mathbf{j} + \mathbf{k})$

Initial conditions: $\mathbf{r}(0) = 10\mathbf{i} + 10\mathbf{j} + 10\mathbf{k}$ and

$$\dfrac{d\mathbf{r}}{dt}\bigg|_{t=0} = \mathbf{0}$$

Tangent Lines to Smooth Curves

As mentioned in the text, the tangent line to a smooth curve $\mathbf{r}(t) = f(t)\mathbf{i} + g(t)\mathbf{j} + h(t)\mathbf{k}$ at $t = t_0$ is the line that passes through the point $(f(t_0), g(t_0), h(t_0))$ parallel to $\mathbf{v}(t_0)$, the curve's velocity vector at t_0. In Exercises 25–28, find parametric equations for the line that is tangent to the given curve at the given parameter value $t = t_0$.

25. $\mathbf{r}(t) = (\sin t)\mathbf{i} + (t^2 - \cos t)\mathbf{j} + e^t\mathbf{k}, \quad t_0 = 0$

26. $\mathbf{r}(t) = (2 \sin t)\mathbf{i} + (2 \cos t)\mathbf{j} + 5t\mathbf{k}, \quad t_0 = 4\pi$

27. $\mathbf{r}(t) = (a \sin t)\mathbf{i} + (a \cos t)\mathbf{j} + bt\mathbf{k}, \quad t_0 = 2\pi$

28. $\mathbf{r}(t) = (\cos t)\mathbf{i} + (\sin t)\mathbf{j} + (\sin 2t)\mathbf{k}, \quad t_0 = \dfrac{\pi}{2}$

Motion Along a Straight Line

29. At time $t = 0$, a particle is located at the point $(1, 2, 3)$. It travels in a straight line to the point $(4, 1, 4)$, has speed 2 at $(1, 2, 3)$ and constant acceleration $3\mathbf{i} - \mathbf{j} + \mathbf{k}$. Find an equation for the position vector $\mathbf{r}(t)$ of the particle at time t.

30. A particle traveling in a straight line is located at the point $(1, -1, 2)$ and has speed 2 at time $t = 0$. The particle moves toward the point $(3, 0, 3)$ with constant acceleration $2\mathbf{i} + \mathbf{j} + \mathbf{k}$. Find its position vector $\mathbf{r}(t)$ at time t.

Theory and Examples

31. *Motion along a cycloid* A particle moves in the xy-plane in such a way that its position at time t is

$$\mathbf{r}(t) = (t - \sin t)\mathbf{i} + (1 - \cos t)\mathbf{j}.$$

T **(a)** Graph $\mathbf{r}(t)$. The resulting curve is called a cycloid.

(b) Find the maximum and minimum values of $|\mathbf{v}|$ and $|\mathbf{a}|$. (*Hint:* Find the extreme values of $|\mathbf{v}|^2$ and $|\mathbf{a}|^2$ first and take square roots later.)

32. *Motion along a circle* Show that the vector-valued function

$$\mathbf{r}(t) = (2\mathbf{i} + 2\mathbf{j} + \mathbf{k}) + (\cos t)\left(\dfrac{1}{\sqrt{2}}\mathbf{i} - \dfrac{1}{\sqrt{2}}\mathbf{j}\right)$$

$$+ (\sin t)\left(\dfrac{1}{\sqrt{3}}\mathbf{i} + \dfrac{1}{\sqrt{3}}\mathbf{j} + \dfrac{1}{\sqrt{3}}\mathbf{k}\right)$$

describes the motion of a particle moving on the circle of radius 1 centered at the point $(2, 2, 1)$ and lying in the plane $x + y - 2z = 2$.

33. *Motion along an ellipse* A particle moves around the ellipse $(y/3)^2 + (z/2)^2 = 1$ in the yz-plane in such a way that its position at time t is

$$\mathbf{r}(t) = (3 \cos t)\mathbf{j} + (2 \sin t)\mathbf{k}.$$

Find the maximum and minimum values of $|\mathbf{v}|$ and $|\mathbf{a}|$. (*Hint:* Find the extreme values of $|\mathbf{v}|^2$ and $|\mathbf{a}|^2$ first and take square roots later.)

34. *Constant magnitude* Let $\mathbf{v}$ be a differentiable vector function of t. Show that if $\mathbf{v} \cdot (d\mathbf{v}/dt) = 0$ for all t, then $|\mathbf{v}|$ is constant.

35. *Constant function rule* Prove that if $\mathbf{u}$ is the vector function with the constant value $\mathbf{C}$, then $d\mathbf{u}/dt = \mathbf{0}$.

36. *Scalar multiple rules*

(a) Prove that if $\mathbf{u}$ is a differentiable function of t and c is any real number, then

$$\dfrac{d(c\mathbf{u})}{dt} = c\dfrac{d\mathbf{u}}{dt}.$$

(b) Prove that if $\mathbf{u}$ is a differentiable function of t and f is a differentiable scalar function of t, then

$$\dfrac{d}{dt}(f\mathbf{u}) = \dfrac{df}{dt}\mathbf{u} + f\dfrac{d\mathbf{u}}{dt}.$$

37. *Sum and difference rules* Prove that if $\mathbf{u}$ and $\mathbf{v}$ are differentiable functions of t, then

$$\dfrac{d}{dt}(\mathbf{u} + \mathbf{v}) = \dfrac{d\mathbf{u}}{dt} + \dfrac{d\mathbf{v}}{dt}.$$

and

$$\dfrac{d}{dt}(\mathbf{u} - \mathbf{v}) = \dfrac{d\mathbf{u}}{dt} - \dfrac{d\mathbf{v}}{dt}.$$

38. *Component test for continuity at a point* Show that the vector function $\mathbf{r}$ defined by the rule $\mathbf{r}(t) = f(t)\mathbf{i} + g(t)\mathbf{j} + h(t)\mathbf{k}$ is continuous at $t = t_0$ if and only if f, g, and h are continuous at t_0.

39. *Limits of cross products of vector functions* Suppose that $\mathbf{r}_1(t) = f_1(t)\mathbf{i} + f_2(t)\mathbf{j} + f_3(t)\mathbf{k}$, $\mathbf{r}_2(t) = g_1(t)\mathbf{i} + g_2(t)\mathbf{j} + g_3(t)\mathbf{k}$, $\lim_{t \to t_0} \mathbf{r}_1(t) = \mathbf{u}$, and $\lim_{t \to t_0} \mathbf{r}_2(t) = \mathbf{v}$. Use the determinant formula for cross products and the Limit Product Rule for scalar functions to show that

$$\lim_{t \to t_0} (\mathbf{r}_1(t) \times \mathbf{r}_2(t)) = \mathbf{u} \times \mathbf{v}.$$

40. *Differentiable vector functions are continuous* Show that if $\mathbf{r}(t) = f(t)\mathbf{i} + g(t)\mathbf{j} + h(t)\mathbf{k}$ is differentiable at $t = t_0$, then it is continuous at t_0 as well.

41. *Derivatives of triple scalar products*

(a) Show that if **u**, **v**, and **w** are differentiable vector functions of t, then

$$\frac{d}{dt}(\mathbf{u} \cdot \mathbf{v} \times \mathbf{w}) = \frac{d\mathbf{u}}{dt} \cdot \mathbf{v} \times \mathbf{w} + \mathbf{u} \cdot \frac{d\mathbf{v}}{dt} \times \mathbf{w} + \mathbf{u} \cdot \mathbf{v} \times \frac{d\mathbf{w}}{dt}. \quad (7)$$

(b) Show that Equation (7) is equivalent to

$$\frac{d}{dt}\begin{vmatrix} u_1 & u_2 & u_3 \\ v_1 & v_2 & v_3 \\ w_1 & w_2 & w_3 \end{vmatrix} = \begin{vmatrix} \frac{du_1}{dt} & \frac{du_2}{dt} & \frac{du_3}{dt} \\ v_1 & v_2 & v_3 \\ w_1 & w_2 & w_3 \end{vmatrix} + \begin{vmatrix} u_1 & u_2 & u_3 \\ \frac{dv_1}{dt} & \frac{dv_2}{dt} & \frac{dv_3}{dt} \\ w_1 & w_2 & w_3 \end{vmatrix}$$

$$+ \begin{vmatrix} u_1 & u_2 & u_3 \\ v_1 & v_2 & v_3 \\ \frac{dw_1}{dt} & \frac{dw_2}{dt} & \frac{dw_3}{dt} \end{vmatrix}. \quad (8)$$

Equation (8) says that the derivative of a 3 by 3 determinant of differentiable functions is the sum of the three determinants obtained from the original by differentiating one row at a time. The result extends to determinants of any order.

42. *(Continuation of Exercise 41.)* Suppose that $\mathbf{r}(t) = f(t)\mathbf{i} + g(t)\mathbf{j} + h(t)\mathbf{k}$ and that f, g, and h have derivatives through order three. Use Equation (7) or (8) to show that

$$\frac{d}{dt}\left(\mathbf{r} \cdot \frac{d\mathbf{r}}{dt} \times \frac{d^2\mathbf{r}}{dt^2}\right) = \mathbf{r} \cdot \left(\frac{d\mathbf{r}}{dt} \times \frac{d^3\mathbf{r}}{dt^3}\right). \quad (9)$$

(*Hint:* Differentiate on the left and look for vectors whose products are zero.)

43. *Properties of integrable vector functions* Establish the following properties of integrable vector functions.

(a) The *Constant Scalar Multiple Rule:*

$$\int_a^b k\mathbf{r}(t)\,dt = k \int_a^b \mathbf{r}(t)\,dt \qquad \text{(any scalar } k\text{)}$$

The *Rule for Negatives,*

$$\int_a^b (-\mathbf{r}(t))\,dt = -\int_a^b \mathbf{r}(t)\,dt,$$

is obtained by taking $k = -1$.

(b) The *Sum and Difference Rules:*

$$\int_a^b (\mathbf{r}_1(t) \pm \mathbf{r}_2(t))\,dt = \int_a^b \mathbf{r}_1(t)\,dt \pm \int_a^b \mathbf{r}_2(t)\,dt$$

(c) The *Constant Vector Multiple Rules:*

$$\int_a^b \mathbf{C} \cdot \mathbf{r}(t)\,dt = \mathbf{C} \cdot \int_a^b \mathbf{r}(t)\,dt \qquad \text{(any constant vector } \mathbf{C}\text{)}$$

and

$$\int_a^b \mathbf{C} \times \mathbf{r}(t)\,dt = \mathbf{C} \times \int_a^b \mathbf{r}(t)\,dt \qquad \text{(any constant vector } \mathbf{C}\text{)}$$

44. *Products of scalar and vector functions* Suppose that the scalar function $u(t)$ and the vector function $\mathbf{r}(t)$ are both defined for $a \le t \le b$.

(a) Show that $u\mathbf{r}$ is continuous on $[a, b]$ if u and $\mathbf{r}$ are continuous on $[a, b]$.

(b) If u and $\mathbf{r}$ are both differentiable on $[a, b]$, show that $u\mathbf{r}$ is differentiable on $[a, b]$ and that

$$\frac{d}{dt}(u\mathbf{r}) = u\frac{d\mathbf{r}}{dt} + \mathbf{r}\frac{du}{dt}.$$

45. *Antiderivatives of vector functions*

(a) Use Corollary 2 of the Mean Value Theorem for scalar functions to show that if two vector functions $\mathbf{R}_1(t)$ and $\mathbf{R}_2(t)$ have identical derivatives on an interval I, then the functions differ by a constant vector value throughout I.

(b) Use the result in part (a) to show that if $\mathbf{R}(t)$ is any antiderivative of $\mathbf{r}(t)$ on I, then every other antiderivative of $\mathbf{r}$ on I equals $\mathbf{R}(t) + \mathbf{C}$ for some constant vector $\mathbf{C}$.

46. *The Fundamental Theorem of Calculus* The Fundamental Theorem of Calculus for scalar functions of a real variable holds for vector functions of a real variable as well. Prove this by using the theorem for scalar functions to show first that if a vector function $\mathbf{r}(t)$ is continuous for $a \le t \le b$, then

$$\frac{d}{dt}\int_a^t \mathbf{r}(\tau)\,d\tau = \mathbf{r}(t)$$

at every point t of $[a, b]$. Then use the conclusion in part (b) of Exercise 45 to show that if $\mathbf{R}$ is any antiderivative of $\mathbf{r}$ on $[a, b]$, then

$$\int_a^b \mathbf{r}(t)\,dt = \mathbf{R}(b) - \mathbf{R}(a).$$

COMPUTER EXPLORATIONS

Drawing Tangents to Space Curves

Use a CAS to perform the following steps in Exercises 47–50.

(a) Plot the space curve traced out by the position vector **r**.

(b) Find the components of the velocity vector $d\mathbf{r}/dt$.

(c) Evaluate $d\mathbf{r}/dt$ at the given point t_0 and find an equation for the tangent line to the curve at $\mathbf{r}(t_0)$.

(d) Plot the tangent line together with the curve over the given interval.

47. $\mathbf{r}(t) = (\sin t - t \cos t)\mathbf{i} + (\cos t + t \sin t)\mathbf{j} + t^2\mathbf{k}, \quad 0 \le t \le 6\pi, \quad t_0 = 3\pi/2$

48. $\mathbf{r}(t) = \sqrt{2}t\mathbf{i} + e^t\mathbf{j} + e^{-t}\mathbf{k}, \quad -2 \le t \le 3, \quad t_0 = 1$

49. $\mathbf{r}(t) = (\sin 2t)\mathbf{i} + (\ln(1 + t))\mathbf{j} + t\mathbf{k}, \quad 0 \le t \le 4\pi, \quad t_0 = \pi/4$

50. $\mathbf{r}(t) = (\ln(t^2 + 2))\mathbf{i} + (\tan^{-1} 3t)\mathbf{j} + \sqrt{t^2 + 1}\mathbf{k}, \quad -3 \le t \le 5, \quad t_0 = 3$

Exploring Helices

In Exercises 51 and 52, you will explore graphically the behavior of the helix

$$\mathbf{r}(t) = (\cos at)\mathbf{i} + (\sin at)\mathbf{j} + bt\mathbf{k}$$

as you change the values of the constants a and b. Use a CAS to perform the steps in each exercise.

51. Set $b = 1$. Plot the helix $\mathbf{r}(t)$ together with the tangent line to the curve at $t = 3\pi/2$ for $a = 1, 2, 4,$ and 6 over the interval $0 \le t \le 4\pi$. Describe in your own words what happens to the graph of the helix and the position of the tangent line as a increases through these positive values.

52. Set $a = 1$. Plot the helix $\mathbf{r}(t)$ together with the tangent line to the curve at $t = 3\pi/2$ for $b = 1/4, 1/2, 2,$ and 4 over the interval $0 \le t \le 4\pi$. Describe in your own words what happens to the graph of the helix and the position of the tangent line as b increases through these positive values.

10.6 Arc Length and the Unit Tangent Vector T

Arc Length Along a Curve • Speed on a Smooth Curve • Unit Tangent Vector **T** • Curvature and the Principal Unit Normal for Plane Curves • Circle of Curvature and Radius of Curvature

Imagine the motions you might experience traveling at high speeds along a path through the air or space. Specifically, imagine the motions of turning to your left or right and the up-and-down motions tending to lift you from, or pin you down to, your seat. Pilots flying through the atmosphere, turning and twisting in flight acrobatics, certainly experience these motions. Modern roller-coaster rides try to capture them for thrill seekers who are more earthbound. The intensity of the experience is heightened by the "tightness" of the turning, the strength of the "lift" perpendicular to your seat, and the overall speed along the path. Turns that are too tight, descents or climbs that are too steep, or either one coupled with high and increasing speed can cause an aircraft to spin out of control, possibly even to break up in midair, and crash to Earth.

In this section and the next, we study the features of the curve's shape that describe mathematically the sharpness of turning and the twisting perpendicular to the forward motion. We further see how this geometry of the curve is actually carried numerically in the velocity and acceleration vectors defining the motion (just as speed is intrinsic to the velocity vector itself).

Arc Length Along a Curve

Early in our calculus studies, we learned that speed is the derivative of distance with respect to time. Up to now, we considered motion occurring primarily along a straight line (although we have also looked at projectile motion along a parabolic arc). To study motion along other smooth space curves, we need to have a measurable length along the curve. This enables us to locate points along these curves by giving their directed distance s along the curve from some **base point,** the way we locate points on coordinate axes by giving their directed distance from the origin (Figure 10.45). Time is the natural parameter for describing a moving body's velocity and acceleration, but s is the natural parameter for studying a curve's shape. Both parameters are useful in studying space curves, as we soon see.

The following formula defines how to measure distance along a smooth curve in space. It is the three-dimensional form of the parametric formula we obtained for planar curves in Section 5.3, and it should come as no surprise.

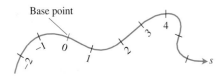

FIGURE 10.45 Smooth curves can be scaled like number lines, the coordinate of each point being its directed distance from a preselected base point.

Definition Arc Length: Length of a Smooth Curve

The **length** of a smooth curve $\mathbf{r}(t) = f(t)\mathbf{i} + g(t)\mathbf{j} + h(t)\mathbf{k}, a \le t \le b$, that is traced exactly once as t increases from $t = a$ to $t = b$ is

$$L = \int_a^b \sqrt{\left(\frac{df}{dt}\right)^2 + \left(\frac{dg}{dt}\right)^2 + \left(\frac{dh}{dt}\right)^2}\, dt$$

$$= \int_a^b \sqrt{\left(\frac{dx}{dt}\right)^2 + \left(\frac{dy}{dt}\right)^2 + \left(\frac{dz}{dt}\right)^2}\, dt. \qquad (1)$$

Just as for plane curves, we can calculate the length of a curve in space from any convenient parametrization that meets the stated conditions. We omit the proof.

The square root in Equation (1) is $|\mathbf{v}|$, the length of a velocity vector $d\mathbf{r}/dt$. This enables us to write the formula for length a shorter way.

Arc **Length Formula (Short Form)**

$$L = \int_a^b |\mathbf{v}|\, dt \qquad (2)$$

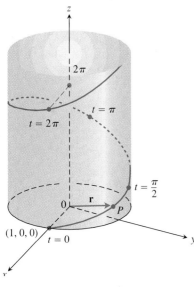

FIGURE 10.46 The helix $\mathbf{r}(t) = (\cos t)\mathbf{i} + (\sin t)\mathbf{j} + t\mathbf{k}$ in Example 1.

Example 1 Distance Traveled by a Glider

A glider is soaring upward along the helix $\mathbf{r}(t) = (\cos t)\mathbf{i} + (\sin t)\mathbf{j} + t\mathbf{k}$. How far does the glider travel along its path from $t = 0$ to $t = 2\pi \approx 6.28$ sec?

Solution The path segment during this time corresponds to one full turn of the helix (Figure 10.46). The length of this portion of the curve is

$$L = \int_a^b |\mathbf{v}|\, dt = \int_0^{2\pi} \sqrt{(-\sin t)^2 + (\cos t)^2 + (1)^2}\, dt$$

$$= \int_0^{2\pi} \sqrt{2}\, dt = 2\pi\sqrt{2} \text{ units of length.}$$

This is $\sqrt{2}$ times the length of the circle in the xy-plane over which the helix stands.

If we choose a base point $P(t_0)$ on a smooth curve C parametrized by t, each value of t determines a point $P(t) = (x(t), y(t), z(t))$ on C and a "directed distance"

$$s(t) = \int_{t_0}^t |\mathbf{v}(\tau)|\, d\tau,$$

measured along C from the base point (Figure 10.47). If $t > t_0$, $s(t)$ is the distance from $P(t_0)$ to $P(t)$. If $t < t_0$, $s(t)$ is the negative of the distance. Each value of s determines a point on C and this parametrizes C with respect to s. We call s an **arc length parameter** for the curve. The parameter's value increases in the direction of increasing t. The arc length parameter is particularly effective for investigating the turning and twisting nature of a space curve.

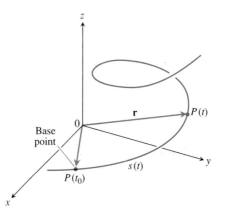

FIGURE 10.47 The directed distance along the curve from $P(t_0)$ to any point $P(t)$ is
$$s(t) = \int_{t_0}^{t} |\mathbf{v}(\tau)| \, d\tau.$$

We use the Greek letter τ ("tau") as the variable of integration in Equation (3) because the letter t is already in use as the upper limit.

Arc Length Parameter with Base Point $P(t_0)$

$$s(t) = \int_{t_0}^{t} \sqrt{[x'(\tau)]^2 + [y'(\tau)]^2 + [z'(\tau)]^2} \, d\tau = \int_{t_0}^{t} |\mathbf{v}(\tau)| \, d\tau \qquad (3)$$

If a curve $\mathbf{r}(t)$ is already given in terms of some parameter t and $s(t)$ is the arc length function given by Equation (3), then we may be able to solve for t as a function of s: $t = t(s)$. Then the curve can be reparameterized in terms of s by substituting for t: $\mathbf{r} = \mathbf{r}(t(s))$. Here's a simple example.

Example 2   Finding an Arc Length Parametrization

If $t_0 = 0$, the arc length parameter along the helix

$$\mathbf{r}(t) = (\cos t)\mathbf{i} + (\sin t)\mathbf{j} + t\mathbf{k}$$

from t_0 to t is

$$s(t) = \int_{t_0}^{t} |\mathbf{v}(\tau)| \, d\tau \qquad \text{Eq. (3)}$$

$$= \int_{0}^{t} \sqrt{2} \, d\tau \qquad \text{Value from Example 1}$$

$$= \sqrt{2}\, t.$$

Solving this equation for t gives $t = s/\sqrt{2}$. Substituting into the position vector $\mathbf{r}$ gives the following arc length parametrization for the helix:

$$\mathbf{r}(t(s)) = \left(\cos \frac{s}{\sqrt{2}} \right)\mathbf{i} + \left(\sin \frac{s}{\sqrt{2}} \right)\mathbf{j} + \frac{s}{\sqrt{2}}\mathbf{k}.$$

Unlike Example 2, the arc length parametrization is generally difficult to find analytically for a curve already given in terms of some other parameter t. Fortunately, however, we rarely need an exact formula for $s(t)$ or its inverse $t(s)$.

Speed on a Smooth Curve

Since the derivatives beneath the radical in Equation (3) are continuous (the curve is smooth), the Fundamental Theorem of Calculus tells us that s is a differentiable function of t with derivative

$$\frac{ds}{dt} = |\mathbf{v}(t)|. \tag{4}$$

As we already knew, the speed with which a particle moves along its path is the magnitude of $\mathbf{v}$.

Notice that although the base point $P(t_0)$ plays a role in defining s in Equation (3), it plays no role in Equation (4). The rate at which a moving particle covers distance along its path has nothing to do with how far away the base point is.

Notice also that $ds/dt > 0$ since, by definition, $|\mathbf{v}|$ is never zero for a smooth curve. We see once again that s is an increasing function of t.

Unit Tangent Vector T

We already know the velocity vector $\mathbf{v} = d\mathbf{r}/dt$ is tangent to the curve and that the vector

$$\mathbf{T} = \frac{\mathbf{v}}{|\mathbf{v}|}$$

is therefore a unit vector tangent to the (smooth) curve. There is more to the story, however, when we consider the arc length parameter. Since $ds/dt > 0$ for the curves we are considering, s is one-to-one and has an inverse that gives t as a differentiable function of s (Section 6.2). The derivative of the inverse is

$$\frac{dt}{ds} = \frac{1}{ds/dt} = \frac{1}{|\mathbf{v}|}.$$

This makes $\mathbf{r}$ a differentiable function of s whose derivative can be calculated with the Chain Rule to be

$$\frac{d\mathbf{r}}{ds} = \frac{d\mathbf{r}}{dt}\frac{dt}{ds} = \mathbf{v}\frac{1}{|\mathbf{v}|} = \frac{\mathbf{v}}{|\mathbf{v}|} = \mathbf{T}.$$

This equation says that $d\mathbf{r}/ds$ is the unit tangent vector in the direction of the velocity vector $\mathbf{v}$ (Figure 10.48).

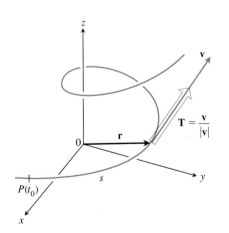

FIGURE 10.48 We find the unit tangent vector $\mathbf{T}$ by dividing $\mathbf{v}$ by $|\mathbf{v}|$.

Definition   Unit Tangent Vector
The **unit tangent vector** of a differentiable curve $\mathbf{r}(t)$ is

$$\mathbf{T} = \frac{d\mathbf{r}}{ds} = \frac{d\mathbf{r}/dt}{ds/dt} = \frac{\mathbf{v}}{|\mathbf{v}|}. \tag{5}$$

The unit tangent vector **T** is a differentiable function of t whenever **v** is a differentiable function of t. As we see in the next section, **T** is one of three unit vectors in a traveling reference frame that is used to describe the motion of space vehicles and other bodies moving in three dimensions.

Example 3   Finding the Unit Tangent Vector T

Find the unit tangent vector of the curve

$$\mathbf{r}(t) = (3 \cos t)\mathbf{i} + (3 \sin t)\mathbf{j} + t^2\mathbf{k}$$

representing the path of the glider in Example 4, Section 10.5.

Solution   In that example, we found

$$\mathbf{v} = \frac{d\mathbf{r}}{dt} = -(3 \sin t)\mathbf{i} + (3 \cos t)\mathbf{j} + 2t\mathbf{k}$$

and

$$\sin^2 t + \cos^2 t = 1$$

$$|\mathbf{v}| = \sqrt{9 + 4t^2}.$$

Thus,

$$\mathbf{T} = \frac{\mathbf{v}}{|\mathbf{v}|} = -\frac{3 \sin t}{\sqrt{9 + 4t^2}}\mathbf{i} + \frac{3 \cos t}{\sqrt{9 + 4t^2}}\mathbf{j} + \frac{2t}{\sqrt{9 + 4t^2}}\mathbf{k}.$$

Curvature and the Principal Unit Normal Vector for Plane Curves

To understand how a curve is "turning" as opposed to "twisting," it is easiest to begin with curves in the plane (turning, but no twisting out of the plane). Based on that understanding, we will take the next step and study space curves in Section 10.7.

As a particle moves along a smooth curve in the plane, $\mathbf{T} = d\mathbf{r}/ds$ turns as the curve bends. Since **T** is a unit vector, its length remains constant and only its direction changes as the particle moves along the curve. The rate at which **T** turns per unit of length along the curve is called the *curvature* (Figure 10.49). The traditional symbol for the curvature function is the Greek letter κ ("kappa").

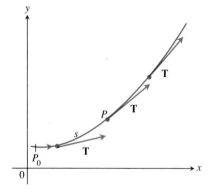

FIGURE 10.49 As P moves along the curve in the direction of increasing arc length, the unit tangent vector turns. The value of $|d\mathbf{T}/ds|$ at P is called the *curvature* of the curve at P.

Definition   Curvature

If **T** is the unit vector of a smooth curve, the **curvature** function of the curve is

$$\kappa = \left|\frac{d\mathbf{T}}{ds}\right|.$$

If $|d\mathbf{T}/ds|$ is large, **T** turns sharply as the particle passes through P, and the curvature at P is large. If $|d\mathbf{T}/ds|$ is close to zero, **T** turns more slowly and the curvature at P is smaller.

If a smooth curve $\mathbf{r}(t)$ is already given in terms of some parameter t other than the arc length parameter s, we can calculate the curvature as

$$\kappa = \left|\frac{d\mathbf{T}}{ds}\right| = \left|\frac{d\mathbf{T}}{dt}\frac{dt}{ds}\right|$$

$$= \frac{1}{|ds/dt|}\left|\frac{d\mathbf{T}}{dt}\right|$$

$$= \frac{1}{|\mathbf{v}|}\left|\frac{d\mathbf{T}}{dt}\right|. \qquad \frac{ds}{dt} = |\mathbf{v}|$$

Formula for Calculating Curvature

If $\mathbf{r}(t)$ is a smooth curve, then the curvature is

$$\kappa = \frac{1}{|\mathbf{v}|}\left|\frac{d\mathbf{T}}{dt}\right|, \qquad (6)$$

where $\mathbf{T} = \mathbf{v}/|\mathbf{v}|$ is the unit tangent vector.

Testing the definition, we see in Examples 4 and 5 that the curvature is constant for straight lines and circles.

Example 4   The Curvature of a Straight Line is Zero

On a straight line, the unit tangent vector $\mathbf{T}$ always points in the same direction, so its components are constants. Therefore, $|d\mathbf{T}/ds| = |\mathbf{0}| = 0$ (Figure 10.50).

Example 5   The Curvature of a Circle of Radius a is $1/a$

To see why, we begin with the parametrization

$$\mathbf{r}(t) = (a\cos t)\mathbf{i} + (a\sin t)\mathbf{j}$$

of a circle of radius a. Then,

$$\mathbf{v} = \frac{d\mathbf{r}}{dt} = -(a\sin t)\mathbf{i} + (a\cos t)\mathbf{j}$$

$$|\mathbf{v}| = \sqrt{(-a\sin t)^2 + (a\cos t)^2} = \sqrt{a^2} = |a| = a. \qquad \text{Since } a > 0, \ |a| = a.$$

From this we find

$$\mathbf{T} = \frac{\mathbf{v}}{|\mathbf{v}|} = -(\sin t)\mathbf{i} + (\cos t)\mathbf{j}$$

$$\frac{d\mathbf{T}}{dt} = -(\cos t)\mathbf{i} - (\sin t)\mathbf{j}$$

$$\left|\frac{d\mathbf{T}}{dt}\right| = \sqrt{\cos^2 t + \sin^2 t} = 1.$$

Hence, for any value of the parameter t,

$$\kappa = \frac{1}{|\mathbf{v}|}\left|\frac{d\mathbf{T}}{dt}\right| = \frac{1}{a}(1) = \frac{1}{a}.$$

FIGURE 10.50 Along a straight line, $\mathbf{T}$ always points in the same direction. The curvature, $|d\mathbf{T}/ds|$, is zero. (Example 4)

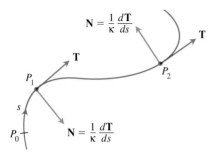

FIGURE 10.51 The vector $d\mathbf{T}/ds$, normal to the curve, always points in the direction in which $\mathbf{T}$ is turning. The vector $\mathbf{N}$ is the direction of $d\mathbf{T}/ds$.

Although the formula for calculating κ in Equation (6) is also valid for space curves, in the next section we find a computational formula that is usually more convenient to apply.

Among the vectors orthogonal to the unit tangent vector $\mathbf{T}$ is one of particular significance because it points in the direction in which the curve is turning. Since $\mathbf{T}$ has constant length (namely, 1), the derivative $d\mathbf{T}/ds$ is orthogonal to $\mathbf{T}$ (Section 10.5). Therefore, if we divide $d\mathbf{T}/ds$ by its length κ, we obtain a *unit* vector $\mathbf{N}$ orthogonal to $\mathbf{T}$ (Figure 10.51).

Definition   Principal Unit Normal

At a point where $\kappa \neq 0$, the **principal unit normal** vector for a curve in the plane is

$$\mathbf{N} = \frac{1}{\kappa}\frac{d\mathbf{T}}{ds}.$$

The vector $d\mathbf{T}/ds$ points in the direction in which $\mathbf{T}$ turns as the curve bends. Therefore, if we face in the direction of increasing arc length, the vector $d\mathbf{T}/ds$ points toward the right if $\mathbf{T}$ turns clockwise and toward the left if $\mathbf{T}$ turns counterclockwise. In other words, the principal normal vector $\mathbf{N}$ will point toward the concave side of the curve (Figure 10.51).

If a smooth curve $\mathbf{r}(t)$ is already given in terms of some parameter t other than the arc length parameter s, we can use the Chain Rule to calculate $\mathbf{N}$ directly:

$$\mathbf{N} = \frac{d\mathbf{T}/ds}{|d\mathbf{T}/ds|}$$

$$= \frac{(d\mathbf{T}/dt)(dt/ds)}{|d\mathbf{T}/dt\,\|\,dt/ds|}$$

$$= \frac{d\mathbf{T}/dt}{|d\mathbf{T}/dt|}.$$

This formula enables us to find $\mathbf{N}$ without having to find κ and s first.

Formula for Calculating N

If $\mathbf{r}(t)$ is a smooth curve, then the principal unit normal is

$$\mathbf{N} = \frac{d\mathbf{T}/dt}{|d\mathbf{T}/dt|}, \qquad (7)$$

where $\mathbf{T} = \mathbf{v}/|\mathbf{v}|$ is the unit tangent vector.

Example 6   Finding T and N

Find $\mathbf{T}$ and $\mathbf{N}$ for the circular motion

$$\mathbf{r}(t) = (\cos 2t)\mathbf{i} + (\sin 2t)\mathbf{j}.$$

Solution　We first find **T**:

$$\mathbf{v} = -(2 \sin 2t)\mathbf{i} + (2 \cos 2t)\mathbf{j}$$

$$|\mathbf{v}| = \sqrt{4 \sin^2 2t + 4 \cos^2 2t} = 2$$

$$\mathbf{T} = \frac{\mathbf{v}}{|\mathbf{v}|} = -(\sin 2t)\mathbf{i} + (\cos 2t)\mathbf{j}.$$

From this we find

$$\frac{d\mathbf{T}}{dt} = -(2 \cos 2t)\mathbf{i} - (2 \sin 2t)\mathbf{j}$$

$$\left|\frac{d\mathbf{T}}{dt}\right| = \sqrt{4 \cos^2 2t + 4 \sin^2 2t} = 2$$

and

$$\mathbf{N} = \frac{d\mathbf{T}/dt}{|d\mathbf{T}/dt|}$$

$$= -(\cos 2t)\mathbf{i} - (\sin 2t)\mathbf{j}. \qquad \text{Eq. (7)}$$

Notice that $\mathbf{T} \cdot \mathbf{N} = 0$, verifying that **N** is orthogonal to **T**.

Circle of Curvature and Radius of Curvature

The **circle of curvature** or **osculating circle** at a point P on a plane curve where $\kappa \neq 0$ is the circle in the plane of the curve that

1.　is tangent to the curve at P (has the same tangent line the curve has)

2.　has the same curvature the curve has at P

3.　lies toward the concave or inner side of the curve (as in Figure 10.52).

　　The **radius of curvature** of the curve at P is the radius of the circle of curvature, which, according to Example 5, is

$$\text{Radius of curvature} = \rho = \frac{1}{\kappa}.$$

To find ρ, we find κ and take the reciprocal. The **center of curvature** of the curve at P is the center of the circle of curvature.

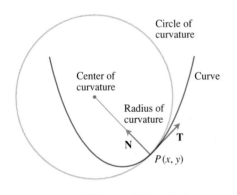

FIGURE 10.52　The osculating circle at $P(x, y)$ lies toward the inner side of the curve.

Example 7　Finding the Osculating Circle for a Parabola

Find and graph the osculating circle of the parabola $y = x^2$ at the origin.

Solution　We parametrize the parabola using the parameter $t = x$ (Preliminary Section 6),

$$\mathbf{r}(t) = t\mathbf{i} + t^2\mathbf{j}.$$

First we find the curvature of the parabola at the origin, using Equation (6):

$$\mathbf{v} = \frac{d\mathbf{r}}{dt} = \mathbf{i} + 2t\mathbf{j}$$

$$|\mathbf{v}| = \sqrt{1 + 4t^2}$$

so that

$$\mathbf{T} = \frac{\mathbf{v}}{|\mathbf{v}|} = (1 + 4t^2)^{-1/2}\mathbf{i} + 2t(1 + 4t^2)^{-1/2}\mathbf{j}.$$

From this we find

$$\frac{d\mathbf{T}}{dt} = -4t(1 + 4t^2)^{-3/2}\mathbf{i} + [2(1 + 4t^2)^{-1/2} - 8t^2(1 + 4t^2)^{-3/2}]\mathbf{j}.$$

At the origin, $t = 0$, so the curvature is

$$\kappa(0) = \frac{1}{|\mathbf{v}(0)|}\left|\frac{d\mathbf{T}}{dt}(0)\right| \qquad \text{Eq. (6)}$$

$$= \frac{1}{\sqrt{1}}|0\mathbf{i} + 2\mathbf{j}|$$

$$= (1)\sqrt{0^2 + 2^2} = 2.$$

Therefore, the radius of curvature is $1/\kappa = \dfrac{1}{2}$ and the center of the circle is $\left(0, \dfrac{1}{2}\right)$ (see Figure 10.53). The equation of the osculating circle is

$$(x - 0)^2 + \left(y - \frac{1}{2}\right)^2 = \left(\frac{1}{2}\right)^2$$

or

$$x^2 + \left(y - \frac{1}{2}\right)^2 = \frac{1}{4}.$$

You can see from Figure 10.53 that the osculating circle is a better approximation to the parabola at the origin than is the tangent line approximation $y = 0$.

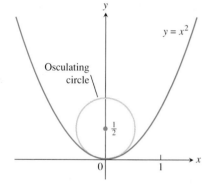

FIGURE 10.53 The osculating circle for the parabola $y = x^2$ at the origin is $x^2 + \left(y - \dfrac{1}{2}\right)^2 = \dfrac{1}{4}$. (Example 7)

EXERCISES 10.6

Finding Unit Tangent Vectors and Lengths of Curves in Space

In Exercises 1–8, find the curve's unit tangent vector. Also, find the length of the indicated portion of the curve.

1. $\mathbf{r}(t) = (2\cos t)\mathbf{i} + (2\sin t)\mathbf{j} + \sqrt{5}t\mathbf{k}, \quad 0 \le t \le \pi$

2. $\mathbf{r}(t) = (6\sin 2t)\mathbf{i} + (6\cos 2t)\mathbf{j} + 5t\mathbf{k}, \quad 0 \le t \le \pi$

3. $\mathbf{r}(t) = t\mathbf{i} + (2/3)t^{3/2}\mathbf{k}, \quad 0 \le t \le 8$

4. $\mathbf{r}(t) = (2 + t)\mathbf{i} - (t + 1)\mathbf{j} + t\mathbf{k}, \quad 0 \le t \le 3$

5. $\mathbf{r}(t) = (\cos^3 t)\mathbf{j} + (\sin^3 t)\mathbf{k}, \quad 0 \le t \le \pi/2$

6. $\mathbf{r}(t) = 6t^3\mathbf{i} - 2t^3\mathbf{j} - 3t^3\mathbf{k}, \quad 1 \le t \le 2$

7. $\mathbf{r}(t) = (t\cos t)\mathbf{i} + (t\sin t)\mathbf{j} + (2\sqrt{2}/3)t^{3/2}\mathbf{k}, \quad 0 \le t \le \pi$

8. $\mathbf{r}(t) = (t\sin t + \cos t)\mathbf{i} + (t\cos t - \sin t)\mathbf{j}, \quad \sqrt{2} \le t \le 2$

9. Find the point on the curve

$$\mathbf{r}(t) = (5\sin t)\mathbf{i} + (5\cos t)\mathbf{j} + 12t\mathbf{k}$$

at a distance 26π units along the curve from the point $(0, 5, 0)$ when $t = 0$ in the direction of increasing arc length.

10. Find the point on the curve

$$\mathbf{r}(t) = (12\sin t)\mathbf{i} - (12\cos t)\mathbf{j} + 5t\mathbf{k}$$

at a distance 13π units along the curve from the point $(0, -12, 0)$ when $t = 0$ in the direction opposite to the direction of increasing arc length.

Arc Length Parameter

In Exercises 11–14, find the arc length parameter along the curve from the point where $t = 0$ by evaluating the integral

$$s = \int_0^t |\mathbf{v}(\tau)| \, d\tau$$

from Equation (3). Then find the length of the indicated portion of the curve.

11. $\mathbf{r}(t) = (4 \cos t)\mathbf{i} + (4 \sin t)\mathbf{j} + 3t\mathbf{k}, \quad 0 \le t \le \pi/2$

12. $\mathbf{r}(t) = (\cos t + t \sin t)\mathbf{i} + (\sin t - t \cos t)\mathbf{j}, \quad \pi/2 \le t \le \pi$

13. $\mathbf{r}(t) = (e^t \cos t)\mathbf{i} + (e^t \sin t)\mathbf{j} + e^t\mathbf{k}, \quad -\ln 4 \le t \le 0$

14. $\mathbf{r}(t) = (1 + 2t)\mathbf{i} + (1 + 3t)\mathbf{j} + (6 - 6t)\mathbf{k}, \quad -1 \le t \le 0$

Plane Curves

Find $\mathbf{T}, \mathbf{N}$, and κ for the plane curves in Exercises 15–18.

15. $\mathbf{r}(t) = t\mathbf{i} + (\ln \cos t)\mathbf{j}, \quad -\pi/2 < t < \pi/2$

16. $\mathbf{r}(t) = (\ln \sec t)\mathbf{i} + t\mathbf{j}, \quad -\pi/2 < t < \pi/2$

17. $\mathbf{r}(t) = (2t + 3)\mathbf{i} + (5 - t^2)\mathbf{j}$

18. $\mathbf{r}(t) = (\cos t + t \sin t)\mathbf{i} + (\sin t - t \cos t)\mathbf{j}, \quad t > 0$

Theory and Examples

19. *Arc length* Find the length of the curve

$$\mathbf{r}(t) = (\sqrt{2}t)\mathbf{i} + (\sqrt{2}t)\mathbf{j} + (1 - t^2)\mathbf{k}$$

from $(0, 0, 1)$ to $(\sqrt{2}, \sqrt{2}, 0)$.

20. *Length of helix* The length $2\pi\sqrt{2}$ of the turn of the helix in Example 1 is also the length of the diagonal of a square 2π units on a side. Show how to obtain this square by cutting away and flattening a portion of the cylinder around which the helix winds.

21. *Ellipse*

   (a) Show that the curve $\mathbf{r}(t) = (\cos t)\mathbf{i} + (\sin t)\mathbf{j} + (1 - \cos t)\mathbf{k}$, $0 \le t \le 2\pi$, is an ellipse by showing that it is the intersection of a right circular cylinder and a plane. Find equations for the cylinder and plane.

   (b) Sketch the ellipse on the cylinder. Add to your sketch the unit tangent vectors at $t = 0, \pi/2, \pi$, and $3\pi/2$.

   (c) Show that the acceleration vector always lies parallel to the plane (orthogonal to a vector normal to the plane). Thus, if you draw the acceleration as a vector attached to the ellipse, it will lie in the plane of the ellipse. Add the acceleration vectors for $t = 0, \pi/2, \pi$, and $3\pi/2$ to your sketch.

   (d) Write an integral for the length of the ellipse. Do not try to evaluate the integral; it is nonelementary.

    (e) *Numerical integrator* Estimate the length of the ellipse to two decimal places.

22. *Length is independent of parametrization* To illustrate that the length of a smooth space curve does not depend on the parametrization you use to compute it, calculate the length of one turn of the helix in Example 1 with the following parametrizations.

   (a) $\mathbf{r}(t) = (\cos 4t)\mathbf{i} + (\sin 4t)\mathbf{j} + 4t\mathbf{k}, \quad 0 \le t \le \pi/2$

   (b) $\mathbf{r}(t) = [\cos (t/2)]\mathbf{i} + [\sin (t/2)]\mathbf{j} + (t/2)\mathbf{k}, \quad 0 \le t \le 4\pi$

   (c) $\mathbf{r}(t) = (\cos t)\mathbf{i} - (\sin t)\mathbf{j} - t\mathbf{k}, \quad -2\pi \le t \le 0$

23. *Circle of curvature* Find an equation for the circle of curvature of the curve $\mathbf{r}(t) = t\mathbf{i} + (\sin t)\mathbf{j}$ at the point $(\pi/2, 1)$. (The curve parametrizes the graph of $y = \sin x$ in the xy-plane.)

24. *Circle of curvature* Find an equation for the circle of curvature of the curve $\mathbf{r}(t) = (2 \ln t)\mathbf{i} - [t + (1/t)]\mathbf{j}, \ e^{-2} \le t \le e^2$, at the point $(0, -2)$, where $t = 1$.

10.7 The TNB Frame; Tangential and Normal Components of Acceleration

Curvature and Normal Vectors for Space Curves • Torsion and the Binormal Vector • Tangential and Normal Components of Acceleration • Formulas for Computing Curvature and Torsion

---

If you are traveling along a space curve, the Cartesian $\mathbf{i}, \mathbf{j}$, and $\mathbf{k}$ coordinate system for representing the vectors describing your motion are not truly relevant to you. What is meaningful instead are the vectors representative of your forward direction (the unit tangent vector $\mathbf{T}$), the direction in which your path is turning (the unit normal vector $\mathbf{N}$), and the tendency of your motion to "twist" out of the plane created by these vectors in the direction perpendicular to this plane (defined by the *unit binormal vector* $\mathbf{B} = \mathbf{T} \times \mathbf{N}$). Expressing the acceleration vector along the curve as a linear combination of this **TNB** frame of mutually orthogonal unit vectors traveling with the motion (Figure 10.54) is particularly revealing of the nature of the path and motion along it.

CD-ROM
WEBsite

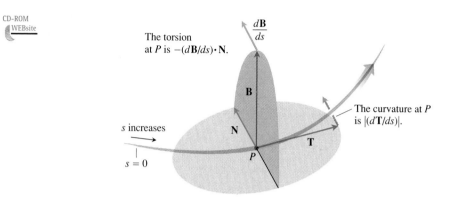

The torsion at P is $-(d\mathbf{B}/ds) \cdot \mathbf{N}$.

The curvature at P is $|(d\mathbf{T}/ds)|$.

s increases

$s = 0$

FIGURE 10.54 Every moving body travels with a **TNB** frame that characterizes the geometry of its path of motion.

For example, $|d\mathbf{T}/ds|$ tells how much a vehicle's path turns to the left or right as it moves along; it is called the *curvature* of the vehicle's path. The number $-(d\mathbf{B}/ds) \cdot \mathbf{N}$ tells how much a vehicle's path rotates or twists out of its plane of motion as the vehicle moves along; it is called the *torsion* of the vehicle's path. Look at Figure 10.54 again. If P is a train climbing up a curved track, the rate at which the headlight turns from side to side per unit distance is the curvature of the track. The rate at which the engine tends to twist out of the plane formed by $\mathbf{T}$ and $\mathbf{N}$ is the torsion.

Curvature and Normal Vectors for Space Curves

The unit tangent vector $\mathbf{T}$ for space curves is defined the same way as for planar curves. If the smooth curve is specified by the position vector $\mathbf{r}(t)$ as a function of some parameter t, and if s is the arc length parameter of the curve, then $\mathbf{T} = d\mathbf{r}/ds = \mathbf{v}/|\mathbf{v}|$. The **curvature** in space is then defined to be

$$\kappa = \left| \frac{d\mathbf{T}}{ds} \right| = \frac{1}{|\mathbf{v}|} \left| \frac{d\mathbf{T}}{dt} \right| \qquad (1)$$

just as for plane curves (Section 10.6, Equation 6). The vector $d\mathbf{T}/ds$ is orthogonal to $\mathbf{T}$, and we define the **principal unit normal** to be

$$\mathbf{N} = \frac{1}{\kappa} \frac{d\mathbf{T}}{ds} = \frac{d\mathbf{T}/dt}{|d\mathbf{T}/dt|}. \qquad (2)$$

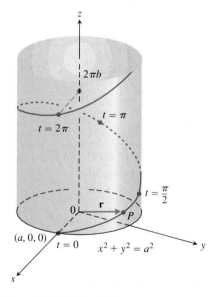

FIGURE 10.55 The helix

$$\mathbf{r}(t) = (a \cos t)\mathbf{i} + (a \sin t)\mathbf{j} + bt\mathbf{k},$$

drawn with a and b positive and $t \ge 0$. (Example 1)

Example 1   Finding Curvature

Find the curvature for the helix (Figure 10.55)

$$\mathbf{r}(t) = (a \cos t)\mathbf{i} + (a \sin t)\mathbf{j} + bt\mathbf{k}, \qquad a, b \ge 0, \qquad a^2 + b^2 \ne 0.$$

Solution   We calculate $\mathbf{T}$ from the velocity vector $\mathbf{v}$:

$$\mathbf{v} = -(a \sin t)\mathbf{i} + (a \cos t)\mathbf{j} + b\mathbf{k}$$

$$|\mathbf{v}| = \sqrt{a^2 \sin^2 t + a^2 \cos^2 t + b^2} = \sqrt{a^2 + b^2}$$

$$\mathbf{T} = \frac{\mathbf{v}}{|\mathbf{v}|} = \frac{1}{\sqrt{a^2 + b^2}} [-(a \sin t)\mathbf{i} + (a \cos t)\mathbf{j} + b\mathbf{k}].$$

Then using Equation (1),

$$\kappa = \frac{1}{|\mathbf{v}|} \left| \frac{d\mathbf{T}}{dt} \right|$$

$$= \frac{1}{\sqrt{a^2 + b^2}} \left| \frac{1}{\sqrt{a^2 + b^2}} [-(a \cos t)\mathbf{i} - (a \sin t)\mathbf{j}] \right|$$

$$= \frac{a}{a^2 + b^2} |-(\cos t)\mathbf{i} - (\sin t)\mathbf{j}|$$

$$= \frac{a}{a^2 + b^2} \sqrt{(\cos t)^2 + (\sin t)^2} = \frac{a}{a^2 + b^2}.$$

From this equation, we see that increasing b for a fixed a decreases the curvature. Decreasing a for a fixed b eventually decreases the curvature as well. Stretching a spring tends to straighten it.

If $b = 0$, the helix reduces to a circle of radius a and its curvature reduces to $1/a$, as it should. If $a = 0$, the helix becomes the z-axis, and its curvature reduces to 0, again as it should.

Example 2 Finding the Principal Unit Normal Vector **N**

Find **N** for the helix in Example 1.

Solution We have

$$\frac{d\mathbf{T}}{dt} = -\frac{1}{\sqrt{a^2 + b^2}} [(a \cos t)\mathbf{i} + (a \sin t)\mathbf{j}] \qquad \text{Example 1}$$

$$\left| \frac{d\mathbf{T}}{dt} \right| = \frac{1}{\sqrt{a^2 + b^2}} \sqrt{a^2 \cos^2 t + a^2 \sin^2 t} = \frac{a}{\sqrt{a^2 + b^2}}$$

$$\mathbf{N} = \frac{d\mathbf{T}/dt}{|d\mathbf{T}/dt|} \qquad \text{Eq. (2)}$$

$$= -\frac{\sqrt{a^2 + b^2}}{a} \cdot \frac{1}{\sqrt{a^2 + b^2}} [(a \cos t)\mathbf{i} + (a \sin t)\mathbf{j}]$$

$$= -(\cos t)\mathbf{i} - (\sin t)\mathbf{j}.$$

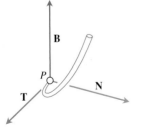

FIGURE 10.56 The vectors **T**, **N**, and **B** (in that order) make a right-handed frame of mutually orthogonal unit vectors in space. You can call it the **Frenet** ("fre-*nay*") **frame** (after Jean-Frédéric Frenet, 1816–1900), or you can call it the **TNB frame.**

Torsion and the Binormal Vector

The **binormal vector** of a curve in space is $\mathbf{B} = \mathbf{T} \times \mathbf{N}$, a unit vector orthogonal to both **T** and **N** (Figure 10.56). Together **T**, **N**, and **B** define a moving right-handed vector frame that plays a significant role in calculating the paths of particles moving through space.

How does $d\mathbf{B}/ds$ behave in relation to **T**, **N**, and **B**? From the rule for differentiating a cross product, we have

$$\frac{d\mathbf{B}}{ds} = \frac{d\mathbf{T}}{ds} \times \mathbf{N} + \mathbf{T} \times \frac{d\mathbf{N}}{ds}.$$

Since **N** is the direction of $d\mathbf{T}/ds$, $(d\mathbf{T}/ds) \times \mathbf{N} = \mathbf{0}$ and

$$\frac{d\mathbf{B}}{ds} = \mathbf{0} + \mathbf{T} \times \frac{d\mathbf{N}}{ds} = \mathbf{T} \times \frac{d\mathbf{N}}{ds}.$$

From this we see that $d\mathbf{B}/ds$ is orthogonal to $\mathbf{T}$ since a cross product is orthogonal to its factors.

Since $d\mathbf{B}/ds$ is also orthogonal to $\mathbf{B}$ (the latter has constant length), it follows that $d\mathbf{B}/ds$ is orthogonal to the plane of $\mathbf{B}$ and $\mathbf{T}$. In other words, $d\mathbf{B}/ds$ is parallel to $\mathbf{N}$, so $d\mathbf{B}/ds$ is a scalar multiple of $\mathbf{N}$. In symbols,

$$\frac{d\mathbf{B}}{ds} = -\tau\mathbf{N}.$$

The minus sign in this equation is traditional. The scalar τ is called the **torsion** along the curve. Notice that

$$\frac{d\mathbf{B}}{ds} \cdot \mathbf{N} = -\tau\mathbf{N} \cdot \mathbf{N} = -\tau(1) = -\tau,$$

so that

$$\tau = -\frac{d\mathbf{B}}{ds} \cdot \mathbf{N}.$$

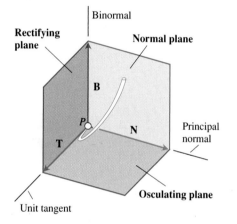

Binormal

Rectifying plane

Normal plane

$\mathbf{B}$

P

$\mathbf{N}$

$\mathbf{T}$

Principal normal

Osculating plane

Unit tangent

FIGURE 10.57 The names of the three planes determined by $\mathbf{T}$, $\mathbf{N}$, and $\mathbf{B}$.

> **Definition**   Torsion
> Let $\mathbf{B} = \mathbf{T} \times \mathbf{N}$. The **torsion** function of a smooth curve is
> $$\tau = -\frac{d\mathbf{B}}{ds} \cdot \mathbf{N}.$$

Unlike the curvature κ, which is never negative, the torsion τ may be positive, negative, or zero.

The three planes determined by $\mathbf{T}$, $\mathbf{N}$, and $\mathbf{B}$ are shown in Figure 10.57. The curvature $\kappa = |d\mathbf{T}/ds|$ can be thought of as the rate at which the normal plane turns as the point P moves along its path. Similarly, the torsion $\tau = -(d\mathbf{B}/ds) \cdot \mathbf{N}$ is the rate at which the osculating plane turns about $\mathbf{T}$ as P moves along the curve. Torsion measures how the curve twists.

Tangential and Normal Components of Acceleration

When a body is accelerated by gravity, brakes, a combination of rocket motors, or whatever, we usually want to know how much of the acceleration acts in the direction of motion, in the tangential direction $\mathbf{T}$. We can find out if we use the Chain Rule to rewrite $\mathbf{v}$ as

$$\mathbf{v} = \frac{d\mathbf{r}}{dt} = \frac{d\mathbf{r}}{ds}\frac{ds}{dt} = \mathbf{T}\frac{ds}{dt}$$

and differentiate both ends of this string of equalities to get

$$\mathbf{a} = \frac{d\mathbf{v}}{dt} = \frac{d}{dt}\left(\mathbf{T}\frac{ds}{dt}\right) = \frac{d^2s}{dt^2}\mathbf{T} + \frac{ds}{dt}\frac{d\mathbf{T}}{dt}$$

$$= \frac{d^2s}{dt^2}\mathbf{T} + \frac{ds}{dt}\left(\frac{d\mathbf{T}}{ds}\frac{ds}{dt}\right) = \frac{d^2s}{dt^2}\mathbf{T} + \frac{ds}{dt}\left(\kappa\mathbf{N}\frac{ds}{dt}\right) \quad \begin{array}{l} \frac{d\mathbf{T}}{ds} = \kappa\mathbf{N} \text{ from} \\ \text{Eq. (2)} \end{array}$$

$$= \frac{d^2s}{dt^2}\mathbf{T} + \kappa\left(\frac{ds}{dt}\right)^2\mathbf{N}.$$

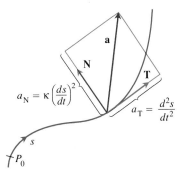

Definition Tangential and Normal Components of Acceleration

$$\mathbf{a} = a_\mathrm{T}\mathbf{T} + a_\mathrm{N}\mathbf{N}, \tag{3}$$

where

$$a_\mathrm{T} = \frac{d^2 s}{dt^2} = \frac{d}{dt}|\mathbf{v}| \qquad \text{and} \qquad a_\mathrm{N} = \kappa \left(\frac{ds}{dt}\right)^2 = \kappa|\mathbf{v}|^2 \tag{4}$$

are the **tangential** and **normal** scalar components of acceleration.

Equation (3) is remarkable in that **B** does not appear. No matter how the path of the moving body we are watching may appear to twist and turn in space, the acceleration **a** *always lies in the plane of* **T** and **N** orthogonal to **B**. The equation also tells us exactly how much of the acceleration takes place tangent to the motion $(d^2 s/dt^2)$ and how much takes place normal to the motion $[\kappa(ds/dt)^2]$ (Figure 10.58).

FIGURE 10.58 The tangential and normal components of acceleration. The acceleration **a** always lies in the plane of **T** and **N**, orthogonal to **B**.

What information can we read from Equations (4)? By definition, acceleration **a** is the rate of change of velocity **v**, and in general, both the length and direction of **v** change as a body moves along its path. The tangential component of acceleration a_T measures the rate of change of the *length* of **v** (that is, the change in the speed). The normal component of acceleration a_N measures the rate of change of the *direction* of **v**.

Notice that the normal scalar component of the acceleration is the curvature times the *square* of the speed. This explains why you have to hold on when your car makes a sharp (large κ), high-speed (large $|\mathbf{v}|$) turn. If you double the speed of your car, you will experience four times the normal component of acceleration for the same curvature.

If a body moves in a circle at a constant speed, $d^2 s/dt^2$ is zero and all the acceleration points along **N** toward the circle's center. If the body is speeding up or slowing down, **a** has a nonzero tangential component (Figure 10.59).

To calculate a_N, we usually use the formula $a_\mathrm{N} = \sqrt{|\mathbf{a}|^2 - a_\mathrm{T}^2}$, which comes from solving the equation $|\mathbf{a}|^2 = \mathbf{a} \cdot \mathbf{a} = a_\mathrm{T}^2 + a_\mathrm{N}^2$ for a_N. With this formula, we can find a_N without having to calculate κ first.

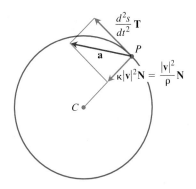

FIGURE 10.59 The tangential and normal components of the acceleration of a body that is speeding up as it moves counterclockwise around a circle of radius ρ.

Formula for Calculating the Normal Component of Acceleration

$$a_\mathrm{N} = \sqrt{|\mathbf{a}|^2 - a_\mathrm{T}^2} \tag{5}$$

CD-ROM
WEBsite

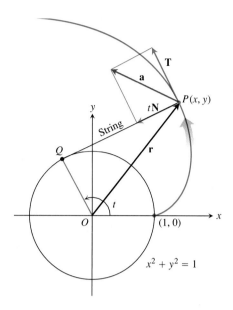

FIGURE 10.60 The tangential and normal components of the acceleration of the motion $\mathbf{r}(t) = (\cos t + t \sin t)\mathbf{i} + (\sin t - t \cos t)\mathbf{j}$, for $t > 0$. If a string wound around a fixed circle is unwound while held taught in the plane of the circle, its end P traces an involute of the circle. (Example 3)

Example 3   Finding the Acceleration Scalar Components a_T, a_N

Without finding $\mathbf{T}$ and $\mathbf{N}$, write the acceleration of the motion

$$\mathbf{r}(t) = (\cos t + t \sin t)\mathbf{i} + (\sin t - t \cos t)\mathbf{j}, \qquad t > 0$$

in the form $\mathbf{a} = a_T\mathbf{T} + a_N\mathbf{N}$. (The path of the motion is the involute of the circle in Figure 10.60.

Solution   We use the first of Equations (4) to find a_T:

$$\mathbf{v} = \frac{d\mathbf{r}}{dt} = (-\sin\ t + \ \sin\ t + t\ \cos\ t)\mathbf{i} + (\cos\ t - \ \cos\ t + t\ \sin\ t)\mathbf{j}$$

$$= (t \cos t)\mathbf{i} + (t \sin t)\mathbf{j}$$

$$|\mathbf{v}| = \sqrt{t^2\ \cos^2 t + t^2\ \sin^2 t} = \sqrt{t^2} = |t| = t \qquad t > 0$$

$$a_T = \frac{d}{dt}|\mathbf{v}| = \frac{d}{dt}(t) = 1. \qquad\qquad \text{Eq. (4)}$$

Knowing a_T, we use Equation (5) to find a_N:

$$\mathbf{a} = (\cos\ t - t \sin\ t)\mathbf{i} + (\sin\ t + t \cos\ t)\mathbf{j}$$

$$|\mathbf{a}|^2 = t^2 + 1 \qquad\qquad \textit{After some algebra}$$

$$a_N = \sqrt{|\mathbf{a}|^2 - a_T^2}$$

$$= \sqrt{(t^2 + 1) - (1)} = \sqrt{t^2} = t.$$

We then use Equation (3) to find $\mathbf{a}$:

$$a = a_T\mathbf{T} + a_N\mathbf{N} = (1)\mathbf{T} + (t)\,\mathbf{N} = \mathbf{T} + t\mathbf{N}.$$

See Figure 10.60.

Formulas for Computing Curvature and Torsion

We now give some easy-to-use formulas for computing the curvature and torsion of a smooth curve. From Equation (3), we have

$$\mathbf{v} \times \mathbf{a} = \left(\frac{ds}{dt}\mathbf{T}\right) \times \left[\frac{d^2s}{dt^2}\mathbf{T} + \kappa\left(\frac{ds}{dt}\right)^2\mathbf{N}\right] \qquad \begin{array}{l}\text{From Section 10.6, Eq.}\\ \text{(5), } \mathbf{v} = d\mathbf{r}/dt = \\ (ds/dt)\mathbf{T}\end{array}$$

$$= \left(\frac{ds}{dt}\frac{d^2s}{dt^2}\right)(\mathbf{T} \times \mathbf{T}) + \kappa\left(\frac{ds}{dt}\right)^3(\mathbf{T} \times \mathbf{N})$$

$$= \kappa\left(\frac{ds}{dt}\right)^3\mathbf{B}. \qquad\qquad \begin{array}{l}\mathbf{T} \times \mathbf{T} = \mathbf{0} \text{ and}\\ \mathbf{T} \times \mathbf{N} = \mathbf{B}\end{array}$$

It follows that

$$|\mathbf{v} \times \mathbf{a}| = \kappa\left|\frac{ds}{dt}\right|^3|\mathbf{B}| = \kappa|\mathbf{v}|^3. \qquad \frac{ds}{dt} = |\mathbf{v}| \text{ and } |\mathbf{B}| = 1$$

Solving for κ gives the following formula.

Vector Formula for Curvature

$$\kappa = \frac{|\mathbf{v} \times \mathbf{a}|}{|\mathbf{v}|^3} \qquad\qquad (6)$$

Newton's Dot Notation for Derivatives

The dots in Equation (7) denote differentiation with respect to t, one derivative for each dot. Thus, $\dot{x}$ ("x dot") means dx/dt, $\ddot{x}$ ("x double dot") means d^2x/dt^2, and $\dddot{x}$ ("x triple dot") means d^3x/dt^3. Similarly, $\dot{y} = dy/dt$ and so on.

Equation (6) calculates the curvature, a geometric property of the curve, from the velocity and acceleration of any vector representation of the curve in which $|\mathbf{v}|$ is different from zero. Take a moment to think about how remarkable this really is: From any formula for motion along a curve, no matter how variable the motion may be (as long as $\mathbf{v}$ is never zero), we can calculate a physical property of the curve that seems to have nothing to do with the way the curve is traversed.

The most widely used formula for torsion, derived in more advanced texts, is

$$\tau = \frac{\begin{vmatrix} \dot{x} & \dot{y} & \dot{z} \\ \ddot{x} & \ddot{y} & \ddot{z} \\ \dddot{x} & \dddot{y} & \dddot{z} \end{vmatrix}}{|\mathbf{v} \times \mathbf{a}|^2} \qquad (\text{if } \mathbf{v} \times \mathbf{a} \neq \mathbf{0}). \tag{7}$$

This formula calculates the torsion directly from the derivatives of the component functions $x = f(t)$, $y = g(t)$, $z = h(t)$ that make up $\mathbf{r}$. The determinant's first row comes from $\mathbf{v}$, the second row comes from $\mathbf{a}$, and the third row comes from $\dot{\mathbf{a}} = d\mathbf{a}/dt$.

Example 4   Finding Curvature and Torsion

Use Equations (6) and (7) to find κ and τ for the helix

$$\mathbf{r}(t) = (a \cos t)\mathbf{i} + (a \sin t)\mathbf{j} + bt\mathbf{k}, \qquad a, b \geq 0, \qquad a^2 + b^2 \neq 0.$$

Solution   We calculate the curvature with Equation (6):

$$\mathbf{v} = -(a \sin t)\mathbf{i} + (a \cos t)\mathbf{j} + b\mathbf{k}$$

$$\mathbf{a} = -(a \cos t)\mathbf{i} - (a \sin t)\mathbf{j}$$

$$\mathbf{v} \times \mathbf{a} = \begin{vmatrix} \mathbf{i} & \mathbf{j} & \mathbf{k} \\ -a \sin t & a \cos t & b \\ -a \cos t & -a \sin t & 0 \end{vmatrix}$$

$$= (ab \sin t)\mathbf{i} - (ab \cos t)\mathbf{j} + a^2\mathbf{k}$$

$$\kappa = \frac{|\mathbf{v} \times \mathbf{a}|}{|\mathbf{v}|^3} = \frac{\sqrt{a^2b^2 + a^4}}{(a^2 + b^2)^{3/2}} = \frac{a\sqrt{a^2 + b^2}}{(a^2 + b^2)^{3/2}} = \frac{a}{a^2 + b^2}. \tag{8}$$

Notice that Equation (8) agrees with the result in Example 1, where we calculated the curvature directly from its definition.

To evaluate Equation (7) for the torsion, we find the entries in the determinant by differentiating $\mathbf{r}$ with respect to t. We already have $\mathbf{v}$ and $\mathbf{a}$, and

$$\dot{\mathbf{a}} = \frac{d\mathbf{a}}{dt} = (a \sin t)\mathbf{i} - (a \cos t)\mathbf{j}.$$

Hence,

$$\tau = \frac{\begin{vmatrix} \dot{x} & \dot{y} & \dot{z} \\ \ddot{x} & \ddot{y} & \ddot{z} \\ \dddot{x} & \dddot{y} & \dddot{z} \end{vmatrix}}{|\mathbf{v} \times \mathbf{a}|^2} = \frac{\begin{vmatrix} -a \sin t & a \cos t & b \\ -a \cos t & -a \sin t & 0 \\ a \sin t & -a \cos t & 0 \end{vmatrix}}{\left(a\sqrt{a^2 + b^2}\right)^2} \qquad \text{Value of } |\mathbf{v} \times \mathbf{a}| \text{ from Eq. (8)}$$

$$= \frac{b(a^2 \cos^2 t + a^2 \sin^2 t)}{a^2(a^2 + b^2)}$$

$$= \frac{b}{a^2 + b^2}. \tag{9}$$

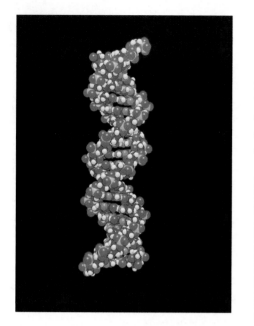

FIGURE 10.61 The helical shape of a DNA molecule is characterized by its constant curvature and torsion.

CD-ROM
WEBsite

From Equation (9), we see that the torsion of a helix about a circular cylinder is constant. In fact, constant curvature and constant torsion characterize the helix among all curves in space.

The DNA molecule, the basic building block of life forms, is designed in the form of two helices winding around each other, a little like the rungs and sides of a twisted rope ladder (Figure 10.61). Not only is the space occupied by the DNA molecule very much smaller than it would be if it were unraveled, but when the molecule is damaged, the imperfect piece can be snipped out by a kind of molecular scissors (because the curvature and torsion functions are constant) and the DNA made right again.

Formulas for Curves in Space

Unit tangent vector:

$$\mathbf{T} = \frac{\mathbf{v}}{|\mathbf{v}|}$$

Principal unit normal vector:

$$\mathbf{N} = \frac{d\mathbf{T}/dt}{|d\mathbf{T}/dt|}$$

Binormal vector:

$$\mathbf{B} = \mathbf{T} \times \mathbf{N}$$

Curvature:

$$\kappa = \left|\frac{d\mathbf{T}}{ds}\right| = \frac{|\mathbf{v} \times \mathbf{a}|}{|\mathbf{v}|^3}$$

Torsion:

$$\tau = -\frac{d\mathbf{B}}{ds} \cdot \mathbf{N} = \frac{\begin{vmatrix} \dot{x} & \dot{y} & \dot{z} \\ \ddot{x} & \ddot{y} & \ddot{z} \\ \dddot{x} & \dddot{y} & \dddot{z} \end{vmatrix}}{|\mathbf{v} \times \mathbf{a}|^2}$$

Tangential and normal scalar components of acceleration:

$$\mathbf{a} = a_T\mathbf{T} + a_N\mathbf{N}$$

$$a_T = \frac{d}{dt}|\mathbf{v}|$$

$$a_N = \kappa|\mathbf{v}|^2 = \sqrt{|\mathbf{a}|^2 - a_T^2}$$

EXERCISES 10.7

Space Curves

Find $\mathbf{T}, \mathbf{N}, \mathbf{B}, \kappa$, and τ for the space curves in Exercises 1–8.

1. $\mathbf{r}(t) = (3\sin t)\mathbf{i} + (3\cos t)\mathbf{j} + 4t\mathbf{k}$

2. $\mathbf{r}(t) = (\cos t + t\sin t)\mathbf{i} + (\sin t - t\cos t)\mathbf{j} + 3\mathbf{k}$

3. $\mathbf{r}(t) = (e^t\cos t)\mathbf{i} + (e^t\sin t)\mathbf{j} + 2\mathbf{k}$

4. $\mathbf{r}(t) = (6\sin 2t)\mathbf{i} + (6\cos 2t)\mathbf{j} + 5t\mathbf{k}$

5. $\mathbf{r}(t) = (t^3/3)\mathbf{i} + (t^2/2)\mathbf{j}, \quad t > 0$

6. $\mathbf{r}(t) = (\cos^3 t)\mathbf{i} + (\sin^3 t)\mathbf{j}, \quad 0 < t < \pi/2$

7. $\mathbf{r}(t) = t\mathbf{i} + (a\cosh(t/a))\mathbf{j}, \quad a > 0$

8. $\mathbf{r}(t) = (\cosh t)\mathbf{i} - (\sinh t)\mathbf{j} + t\mathbf{k}$

In Exercises 9 and 10, write $\mathbf{a}$ in the form $a_T\mathbf{T} + a_N\mathbf{N}$ without finding $\mathbf{T}$ and $\mathbf{N}$.

9. $\mathbf{r}(t) = (a\cos t)\mathbf{i} + (a\sin t)\mathbf{j} + bt\mathbf{k}$

10. $\mathbf{r}(t) = (1 + 3t)\mathbf{i} + (t - 2)\mathbf{j} - 3t\mathbf{k}$

In Exercises 11–14, write $\mathbf{a}$ in the form $\mathbf{a} = a_T\mathbf{T} + a_N\mathbf{N}$ at the given value of t without finding $\mathbf{T}$ and $\mathbf{N}$.

11. $\mathbf{r}(t) = (t + 1)\mathbf{i} + 2t\mathbf{j} + t^2\mathbf{k}, \quad t = 1$

12. $\mathbf{r}(t) = (t\cos t)\mathbf{i} + (t\sin t)\mathbf{j} + t^2\mathbf{k}, \quad t = 0$

13. $\mathbf{r}(t) = t^2\mathbf{i} + (t + (1/3)t^3)\mathbf{j} + (t - (1/3)t^3)\mathbf{k}, \quad t = 0$

14. $\mathbf{r}(t) = (e^t\cos t)\mathbf{i} + (e^t\sin t)\mathbf{j} + \sqrt{2}e^t\mathbf{k}, \quad t = 0$

In Exercises 15 and 16, find $\mathbf{r}$, $\mathbf{T}$, $\mathbf{N}$, and $\mathbf{B}$ at the given value of t. Then find equations for the osculating, normal, and rectifying planes (Figure 10.57) at that value of t.

15. $\mathbf{r}(t) = (\cos t)\mathbf{i} + (\sin t)\mathbf{j} - \mathbf{k}, \quad t = \pi/4$

16. $\mathbf{r}(t) = (\cos t)\mathbf{i} + (\sin t)\mathbf{j} + t\mathbf{k}, \quad t = 0$

Physical Applications

17. *Writing to Learn* The speedometer on your car reads a steady 35 mph. Could you be accelerating? Explain.

18. *Writing to Learn* Can anything be said about the acceleration of a particle that is moving in space at a constant speed? Give reasons for your answer.

19. *Writing to Learn* Can anything be said about the speed of a particle whose acceleration is always orthogonal to its velocity? Give reasons for your answer.

20. *Motion along a parabola* An object of mass m travels along the parabola $y = x^2$ with a constant speed of 10 units/sec. What is the force on the object due to its acceleration at $(0, 0)$? At $(\sqrt{2}, 2)$? Write your answers in terms of $\mathbf{i}$ and $\mathbf{j}$. (Remember Newton's law, $\mathbf{F} = m\mathbf{a}$.)

21. *Writing to Learn* The following is a quotation from an article in the *American Mathematical Monthly*, titled "Curvature in the Eighties" by Robert Osserman (October 1990, p. 731):

Curvature also plays a key role in physics. The magnitude of a force required to move an object at constant speed along a curved path is, according to Newton's laws, a constant multiple of the curvature of the trajectories.

Explain mathematically why the second sentence of the quotation is true.

22. *What happens if $a_N = 0$?* Show that a moving particle will move in a straight line if the normal component of its acceleration is zero.

Curvature and Torsion   CD-ROM ◀WEBsite

23. *A formula for the curvature of the graph of a function in the xy-plane*

(a) The graph $y = f(x)$ in the xy-plane automatically has the parametrization $x = x$, $y = f(x)$, and the vector formula $\mathbf{r}(x) = x\mathbf{i} + f(x)\mathbf{j}$. Use this formula to show that if f is a twice-differentiable function of x, then

$$\kappa(x) = \frac{|f''(x)|}{[1 + (f'(x))^2]^{3/2}}.$$

(b) Use the formula for κ in part (a) to find the curvature of $y = \ln (\cos x)$, $-\pi/2 < x < \pi/2$.

(c) Show that the curvature is zero at a point of inflection.

24. *A formula for the curvature of a parametrized plane curve*

(a) Show that the curvature of a smooth curve $\mathbf{r}(t) = f(t)\mathbf{i} + g(t)\mathbf{j}$ defined by twice-differentiable functions $x = f(t)$ and $y = g(t)$ is given by the formula

$$\kappa = \frac{|\dot{x}\ddot{y} - \dot{y}\ddot{x}|}{(\dot{x}^2 + \dot{y}^2)^{3/2}}.$$

Apply the formula to find the curvatures of the following curves.

(b) $\mathbf{r}(t) = t\mathbf{i} + (\ln \sin t)\mathbf{j}, \quad 0 < t < \pi$

(c) $\mathbf{r}(t) = [\tan^{-1} (\sinh t)]\mathbf{i} + (\ln \cosh t)\mathbf{j}$

25. *Normals to plane curves*

(a) Show that $\mathbf{n}(t) = -g'(t)\mathbf{i} + f'(t)\mathbf{j}$ and $-\mathbf{n}(t) = g'(t)\mathbf{i} - f'(t)\mathbf{j}$ are both normal to the curve $\mathbf{r}(t) = f(t)\mathbf{i} + g(t)\mathbf{j}$ at the point $(f(t), g(t))$.

To obtain $\mathbf{N}$ for a particular plane curve, we can choose the one of $\mathbf{n}$ or $-\mathbf{n}$ from part (a) that points toward the concave side of the curve, and make it into a unit vector. (See Figure 10.51.) Apply this method to find $\mathbf{N}$ for the following curves.

(b) $\mathbf{r}(t) = t\mathbf{i} + e^{2t}\mathbf{j}$

(c) $\mathbf{r}(t) = \sqrt{4 - t^2}\,\mathbf{i} + t\mathbf{j}, \quad -2 \le t \le 2$

26. *(Continuation of Exercise 25)*

(a) Use the method of Exercise 25 to find $\mathbf{N}$ for the curve $\mathbf{r}(t) = t\mathbf{i} + (1/3)t^3\mathbf{j}$ when $t < 0$ and when $t > 0$.

(b) *Writing to Learn* Calculate

$$\mathbf{N} = \frac{d\mathbf{T}/dt}{|d\mathbf{T}/dt|}, \qquad t \ne 0,$$

for the curve in part (a). Does $\mathbf{N}$ exist at $t = 0$? Graph the curve and explain what is happening to $\mathbf{N}$ as t passes from negative to positive values.

27. *Curvature extremes* Show that the parabola $y = ax^2$, $a \ne 0$, has its largest curvature at its vertex and has no minimum curvature. (*Note:* Since the curvature of a curve remains the same if the curve is translated or rotated, this result is true for any parabola.)

28. *Curvature extremes* Show that the ellipse $x = a \cos t$, $y = b \sin t$, $a > b > 0$, has its largest curvature on its major axis and its smallest curvature on its minor axis. (As in Exercise 27, the same is true for any ellipse.)

29. *Writing to Learn: Maximizing the curvature of a helix* In Example 1, we found the curvature of the helix $\mathbf{r}(t) = (a \cos t)\mathbf{i} + (a \sin t)\mathbf{j} + bt\mathbf{k}$ $(a, b \ge 0)$ to be $\kappa = a/(a^2 + b^2)$. What is the largest value κ can have for a given value of b? Give reasons for your answer.

30. *A sometime shortcut to curvature* If you already know $|a_N|$ and $|\mathbf{v}|$, then the formula $a_N = \kappa |\mathbf{v}|^2$ gives a convenient way to find the curvature. Use it to find the curvature and radius of curvature of the curve

$$\mathbf{r}(t) = (\cos t + t \sin t)\mathbf{i} + (\sin t - t \cos t)\mathbf{j}, \qquad t > 0.$$

(Take a_N and $|\mathbf{v}|$ from Example 3.)

31. *Curvature and torsion for a line* Show that κ and τ are both zero for the line

$$\mathbf{r}(t) = (x_0 + At)\mathbf{i} + (y_0 + Bt)\mathbf{j} + (z_0 + Ct)\mathbf{k}.$$

32. *Total curvature* We find the **total curvature** of the portion of a smooth curve that runs from $s = s_0$ to $s = s_1 > s_0$ by integrating κ from s_0 to s_1. If the curve has some other parameter, say t, then the total curvature is

$$K = \int_{s_0}^{s_1} \kappa \, ds = \int_{t_0}^{t_1} \kappa \frac{ds}{dt} \, dt = \int_{t_0}^{t_1} \kappa |\mathbf{v}| \, dt,$$

where t_0 and t_1 correspond to s_0 and s_1. Find the total curvature of the portion of the helix $\mathbf{r}(t) = (3 \cos t)\mathbf{i} + (3 \sin t)\mathbf{j} + t\mathbf{k}$, $0 \le t \le 4\pi$.

33. (*Continuation of Exercise 32.*) Find the total curvatures of the following curves.

  (a) The involute of the unit circle: $\mathbf{r}(t) = (\cos t + t \sin t)\mathbf{i} + (\sin t - t \cos t)\mathbf{j}$, $a \le t \le b$ $(a > 0)$. (Exercise 30 gives a convenient way to find κ. Use values from Example 3.)

  (b) The parabola $y = x^2$, $-\infty < x < \infty$.

34. *Writing to Learn: The torsion of a helix* In Example 4, we found the torsion of the helix

$$\mathbf{r}(t) = (a \cos t)\mathbf{i} + (a \sin t)\mathbf{j} + bt\mathbf{k}, \qquad a, b \ge 0$$

to be $\tau = b/(a^2 + b^2)$. What is the largest value τ can have for a given value of a? Give reasons for your answer.

35. *Differentiable curves with zero torsion lie in planes* That a sufficiently differentiable curve with zero torsion lies in a plane is a special case of a particle whose velocity remains perpendicular to a fixed vector $\mathbf{C}$ moving in a plane perpendicular to $\mathbf{C}$. This, in turn, can be viewed as the solution of the following problem in calculus.

  Suppose that $\mathbf{r}(t) = f(t)\mathbf{i} + g(t)\mathbf{j} + h(t)\mathbf{k}$ is twice differentiable for all t in an interval $[a, b]$, that $\mathbf{r} = 0$ when $t = a$, and that $\mathbf{v} \cdot \mathbf{k} = 0$ for all t in $[a, b]$. Then $h(t) = 0$ for all t in $[a, b]$.

  Solve this problem. (*Hint:* Start with $\mathbf{a} = d^2\mathbf{r}/dt^2$ and apply the initial conditions in reverse order.)

36. *A formula that calculates τ from $\mathbf{B}$ and $\mathbf{v}$* If we start with the definition $\tau = -(d\mathbf{B}/ds) \cdot \mathbf{N}$ and apply the Chain Rule to rewrite $d\mathbf{B}/ds$ as

$$\frac{d\mathbf{B}}{ds} = \frac{d\mathbf{B}}{dt} \frac{dt}{ds} = \frac{d\mathbf{B}}{dt} \frac{1}{|\mathbf{v}|},$$

we arrive at the formula

$$\tau = -\frac{1}{|\mathbf{v}|} \left(\frac{d\mathbf{B}}{dt} \cdot \mathbf{N} \right).$$

The advantage of this formula over Equation (7) is that it is easier to derive and state. The disadvantage is that it can take a lot of work to evaluate without a computer. Use the new formula to find the torsion of the helix in Example 4.

  The formula

$$\kappa(x) = \frac{|f''(x)|}{[1 + (f'(x))^2]^{3/2}},$$

derived in Exercise 23, expresses the curvature $\kappa(x)$ of a twice-differentiable plane curve $y = f(x)$ as a function of x. Find the curvature function of each of the curves in Exercises 37–40. Then graph $f(x)$ together with $\kappa(x)$ over the given interval. You will find some surprises.

T **37.** $y = x^2$, $-2 \le x \le 2$

T **38.** $y = x^4/4$, $-2 \le x \le 2$

T **39.** $y = \sin x$, $0 \le x \le 2\pi$

T **40.** $y = e^x$, $-1 \le x \le 2$

COMPUTER EXPLORATIONS

Circles of Curvature

In Exercises 41–48, you will use a CAS to explore the osculating circle at a point P on a plane curve where $\kappa \ne 0$. Use a CAS to perform the following steps:

  (a) Plot the plane curve given in parametric or function form over the specified interval to see what it looks like.

  (b) Calculate the curvature κ of the curve at the given value t_0 using the appropriate formula from Exercise 23 or 24. Use the parametrization $x = t$ and $y = f(t)$ if the curve is given as a function $y = f(x)$.

  (c) Find the unit normal vector $\mathbf{N}$ at t_0. Notice that the signs of the components of $\mathbf{N}$ depend on whether the unit tangent vector $\mathbf{T}$ is turning clockwise or counterclockwise at $t = t_0$. (See Exercise 25.)

  (d) If $\mathbf{C} = a\mathbf{i} + b\mathbf{j}$ is the vector from the origin to the center (a, b) of the osculating circle (see Section 10.6), find the center $\mathbf{C}$ from the vector equation

$$\mathbf{C} = \mathbf{r}(t_0) + \frac{1}{\kappa(t_0)} \mathbf{N}(t_0).$$

The point $P(x_0, y_0)$ on the curve is given by the position vector $\mathbf{r}(t_0)$.

  (e) Plot implicitly the equation $(x - a)^2 + (y - b)^2 = 1/\kappa^2$ of the osculating circle. Then plot the curve and osculating circle together. You may need to experiment with the size of the viewing window, but be sure it is square.

41. $\mathbf{r}(t) = (3 \cos t)\mathbf{i} + (5 \sin t)\mathbf{j}$, $0 \le t \le 2\pi$, $t_0 = \pi/4$

42. $\mathbf{r}(t) = (\cos^3 t)\mathbf{i} + (\sin^3 t)\mathbf{j}$, $0 \le t \le 2\pi$, $t_0 = \pi/4$

43. $\mathbf{r}(t) = t^2\mathbf{i} + (t^3 - 3t)\mathbf{j}$, $-4 \le t \le 4$, $t_0 = 3/5$

44. $\mathbf{r}(t) = (t^3 - 2t^2 - t)\mathbf{i} + \dfrac{3t}{\sqrt{1 + t^2}}\mathbf{j}$, $-2 \le t \le 5$, $t_0 = 1$

45. $\mathbf{r}(t) = (2t - \sin t)\mathbf{i} + (2 - 2 \cos t)\mathbf{j}$, $0 \le t \le 3\pi$, $t_0 = 3\pi/2$

46. $\mathbf{r}(t) = (e^{-t} \cos t)\mathbf{i} + (e^{-t} \sin t)\mathbf{j}$, $0 \le t \le 6\pi$, $t_0 = \pi/4$

47. $y = x^2 - x$, $-2 \le x \le 5$, $x_0 = 1$

48. $y = x(1 - x)^{2/5}$, $-1 \le x \le 2$, $x_0 = 1/2$

10.8 Planetary Motion and Satellites

Motion in Polar and Cylindrical Coordinates • Planets Move in Planes • Coordinates and Initial Conditions • Kepler's First Law (The Conic Section Law) • Kepler's Second Law (The Equal Area Law) • Proof of Kepler's First Law • Kepler's Third Law (The Time–Distance Law) • Orbit Data

In this section, we derive Kepler's laws of planetary motion from Newton's laws of motion and gravitation and discuss the orbits of Earth satellites. The derivation of Kepler's laws from Newton's is one of the triumphs of calculus. It draws on almost everything we have studied so far, including the algebra and geometry of vectors in space, the calculus of vector functions, the solutions of differential equations and initial value problems, and polar coordinates.

Motion in Polar and Cylindrical Coordinates

When a particle moves along a curve in the polar coordinate plane, we express its position, velocity, and acceleration in terms of the moving unit vectors

$$\mathbf{u}_r = (\cos \theta)\mathbf{i} + (\sin \theta)\mathbf{j}, \qquad \mathbf{u}_\theta = -(\sin \theta)\mathbf{i} + (\cos \theta)\mathbf{j}, \tag{1}$$

shown in Figure 10.62. The vector $\mathbf{u}_r$ points along the position vector $\overrightarrow{OP}$, so $\mathbf{r} = r\mathbf{u}_r$. The vector $\mathbf{u}_\theta$, orthogonal to $\mathbf{u}_r$, points in the direction of increasing θ.

We find from Equations (1) that

$$\frac{d\mathbf{u}_r}{d\theta} = -(\sin \theta)\mathbf{i} + (\cos \theta)\mathbf{j} = \mathbf{u}_\theta$$

$$\frac{d\mathbf{u}_\theta}{d\theta} = -(\cos \theta)\mathbf{i} - (\sin \theta)\mathbf{j} = -\mathbf{u}_r. \tag{2}$$

When we differentiate $\mathbf{u}_r$ and $\mathbf{u}_\theta$ with respect to t to find how they change with time, the Chain Rule gives

$$\dot{\mathbf{u}}_r = \frac{d\mathbf{u}_r}{d\theta}\dot{\theta} = \dot{\theta}\mathbf{u}_\theta, \qquad \dot{\mathbf{u}}_\theta = \frac{d\mathbf{u}_\theta}{d\theta}\dot{\theta} = -\dot{\theta}\mathbf{u}_r. \tag{3}$$

Hence,

$$\mathbf{v} = \dot{\mathbf{r}} = \frac{d}{dt}(r\mathbf{u}_r) = \dot{r}\mathbf{u}_r + r\dot{\mathbf{u}}_r = \dot{r}\mathbf{u}_r + r\dot{\theta}\mathbf{u}_\theta. \tag{4}$$

See Figure 10.63.

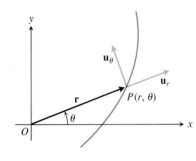

FIGURE 10.62 The length of **r** is the positive polar coordinate r of the point P. Thus, $\mathbf{u}_r$, which is $\mathbf{r}/|\mathbf{r}|$, is also $\mathbf{r}/r$. Equations (1) express $\mathbf{u}_r$ and $\mathbf{u}_\theta$ in terms of **i** and **j**.

As in the previous section, we use Newton's dot notation for time derivatives to keep the formulas as simple as we can: $\dot{\mathbf{u}}_r$ means $d\mathbf{u}_r/dt$, $\dot{\theta}$ means $d\theta/dt$, and so on.

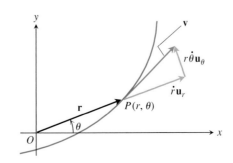

FIGURE 10.63 In polar coordinates, the velocity vector is

The acceleration is

$$\mathbf{a} = \dot{\mathbf{v}} = (\ddot{r}\mathbf{u}_r + \dot{r}\dot{\mathbf{u}}_r) + (\dot{r}\dot{\theta}\mathbf{u}_\theta + r\ddot{\theta}\mathbf{u}_\theta + r\dot{\theta}\dot{\mathbf{u}}_\theta). \qquad (5)$$

When Equations (3) are used to evaluate $\dot{\mathbf{u}}_r$ and $\dot{\mathbf{u}}_\theta$ and the components are separated, the equation for acceleration becomes

$$\mathbf{a} = (\ddot{r} - r\dot{\theta}^2)\mathbf{u}_r + (r\ddot{\theta} + 2\dot{r}\dot{\theta})\mathbf{u}_\theta. \qquad (6)$$

To extend these equations of motion to space, we add $z\mathbf{k}$ to the right-hand side of the equation $\mathbf{r} = r\mathbf{u}_r$. Then, in cylindrical coordinates,

$$\mathbf{r} = r\mathbf{u}_r + z\mathbf{k}$$
$$\mathbf{v} = \dot{r}\mathbf{u}_r + r\dot{\theta}\mathbf{u}_\theta + \dot{z}\mathbf{k} \qquad (7)$$
$$\mathbf{a} = (\ddot{r} - r\dot{\theta}^2)\mathbf{u}_r + (r\ddot{\theta} + 2\dot{r}\dot{\theta})\mathbf{u}_\theta + \ddot{z}\mathbf{k}.$$

The vectors $\mathbf{u}_r$, $\mathbf{u}_\theta$, and $\mathbf{k}$ make a right-handed frame (Figure 10.64) in which

$$\mathbf{u}_r \times \mathbf{u}_\theta = \mathbf{k}, \qquad \mathbf{u}_\theta \times \mathbf{k} = \mathbf{u}_r, \qquad \mathbf{k} \times \mathbf{u}_r = \mathbf{u}_\theta. \qquad (8)$$

Notice that $|\mathbf{r}| \neq r$ if $z \neq 0$.

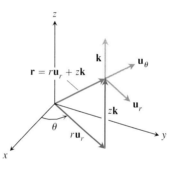

FIGURE 10.64 Position vector and basic unit vectors in cylindrical coordinates.

Planets Move in Planes

Newton's Law of Gravitation says that if $\mathbf{r}$ is the radius vector from the center of a sun of mass M to the center of a planet of mass m, then the force $\mathbf{F}$ of the gravitational attraction between the planet and sun is

$$\mathbf{F} = -\frac{GmM}{|\mathbf{r}|^2}\frac{\mathbf{r}}{|\mathbf{r}|} \qquad (9)$$

(Figure 10.65). The number G is the **universal gravitational constant.** If we measure mass in kilograms, force in newtons, and distance in meters, G is about 6.6726×10^{-11} Nm^{2}kg^{-2}.

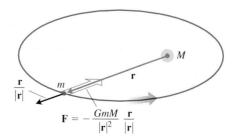

FIGURE 10.65 The force of gravity is directed along the line joining the centers of mass.

Combining Equation (9) with Newton's second law $\mathbf{F} = m\ddot{\mathbf{r}}$ for the force acting on the planet, gives

$$m\ddot{\mathbf{r}} = -\frac{GmM}{|\mathbf{r}|^2}\frac{\mathbf{r}}{|\mathbf{r}|}$$

$$\ddot{\mathbf{r}} = -\frac{GM}{|\mathbf{r}|^2}\frac{\mathbf{r}}{|\mathbf{r}|}. \tag{10}$$

The planet is accelerated toward the sun's center at all times.

Equation (10) says $\ddot{\mathbf{r}}$ is a scalar multiple of $\mathbf{r}$, so that

$$\mathbf{r} \times \ddot{\mathbf{r}} = \mathbf{0}. \tag{11}$$

A routine calculation shows $\mathbf{r} \times \ddot{\mathbf{r}}$ to be the derivative of $\mathbf{r} \times \dot{\mathbf{r}}$:

$$\frac{d}{dt}(\mathbf{r} \times \dot{\mathbf{r}}) = \underbrace{\dot{\mathbf{r}} \times \dot{\mathbf{r}}}_{\mathbf{0}} + \mathbf{r} \times \ddot{\mathbf{r}} = \mathbf{r} \times \ddot{\mathbf{r}}. \tag{12}$$

Hence, Equation (11) is equivalent to

$$\frac{d}{dt}(\mathbf{r} \times \dot{\mathbf{r}}) = \mathbf{0}, \tag{13}$$

which integrates to

$$\mathbf{r} \times \dot{\mathbf{r}} = \mathbf{C} \tag{14}$$

for some constant vector $\mathbf{C}$.

Equation (14) tells us that $\mathbf{r}$ and $\dot{\mathbf{r}}$ always lie in a plane perpendicular to $\mathbf{C}$. Hence, the planet moves in a fixed plane through the center of its sun (Figure 10.66).

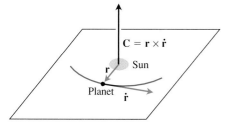

FIGURE 10.66 A planet that obeys Newton's laws of gravitation and motion travels in the plane through the sun's center of mass perpendicular to $\mathbf{C} = \mathbf{r} \times \dot{\mathbf{r}}$.

Coordinates and Initial Conditions

We now introduce coordinates in a way that places the origin at the sun's center of mass and makes the plane of the planet's motion the polar coordinate plane. This makes $\mathbf{r}$ the planet's polar coordinate position vector and makes $|\mathbf{r}|$ equal to r and $\mathbf{r}/|\mathbf{r}|$ equal to $\mathbf{u}_r$. We also position the z-axis in a way that makes $\mathbf{k}$ the direction of $\mathbf{C}$. Thus, $\mathbf{k}$ has the same right-hand relation to $\mathbf{r} \times \dot{\mathbf{r}}$ that $\mathbf{C}$ does, and the planet's motion is counterclockwise when viewed from the positive z-axis. This makes θ increase with t, so that $\dot{\theta} > 0$ for all t. Finally, we rotate the polar coordinate plane about the z-axis, if necessary, to make the initial ray coincide with the direction $\mathbf{r}$ has when the planet is closest to the sun. This runs the ray through the planet's **perihelion** position (Figure 10.67).

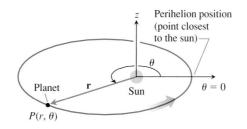

FIGURE 10.67 The coordinate system for planetary motion. The motion is counterclockwise when viewed from above, as it is here, and $\dot{\theta} > 0$.

If we measure time so that $t = 0$ at perihelion, we have the following initial conditions for the planet's motion.

1. $r = r_0$, the minimum radius, when $t = 0$

2. $\dot{r} = 0$ when $t = 0$ (because r has a minimum value then)

3. $\theta = 0$ when $t = 0$

4. $|\mathbf{v}| = v_0$ when $t = 0$

Since

$$v_0 = |\mathbf{v}|_{t=0}$$
$$= |\dot{r}\mathbf{u}_r + r\dot{\theta}\mathbf{u}_\theta|_{t=0} \qquad \text{Eq. (4)}$$
$$= |r\dot{\theta}\mathbf{u}_\theta|_{t=0} \qquad \dot{r} = 0 \text{ when } t = 0$$
$$= (|r\dot{\theta}||\mathbf{u}_\theta|)_{t=0}$$
$$= |r\dot{\theta}|_{t=0} \qquad |\mathbf{u}_\theta| = 1$$
$$= (r\dot{\theta})_{t=0}, \qquad r \text{ and } \dot{\theta} \text{ both positive}$$

we also know that

5. $r\dot{\theta} = v_0$ when $t = 0$.

Kepler's First Law (The Conic Section Law)

Kepler's first law says that a planet's path is a conic section with the sun at one focus. The eccentricity of the conic is

$$e = \frac{r_0 v_0{}^2}{GM} - 1 \tag{15}$$

and the polar equation is

$$r = \frac{(1 + e)r_0}{1 + e \cos \theta}. \tag{16}$$

The derivation uses Kepler's second law, so we will state and prove the second law before proving the first law.

Kepler's Second Law (The Equal Area Law)

Kepler's second law says that the radius vector from the sun to a planet (the vector $\mathbf{r}$ in our model) sweeps out equal areas in equal times (Figure 10.68). To derive the law, we use Equation (4) to evaluate the cross product $\mathbf{C} = \mathbf{r} \times \dot{\mathbf{r}}$ from Equation (14):

$$\mathbf{C} = \mathbf{r} \times \dot{\mathbf{r}} = \mathbf{r} \times \mathbf{v}$$
$$= r\mathbf{u}_r \times (\dot{r}\,\mathbf{u}_r + r\dot{\theta}\mathbf{u}_\theta) \qquad \text{Eq. (4)}$$
$$= r\dot{r}\underbrace{(\mathbf{u}_r \times \mathbf{u}_r)}_{0} + r(r\dot{\theta})\underbrace{(\mathbf{u}_r \times \mathbf{u}_\theta)}_{\mathbf{k}} \tag{17}$$
$$= r(r\dot{\theta})\mathbf{k}.$$

Setting t equal to zero shows that

$$\mathbf{C} = [r(r\dot{\theta})]_{t=0}\mathbf{k} = r_0 v_0 \mathbf{k}. \tag{18}$$

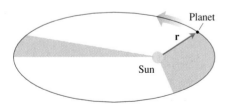

FIGURE 10.68 The line joining a planet to its sun sweeps over equal areas in equal times.

Substituting this value for $\mathbf{C}$ in Equation (17) gives

$$r_0 v_0 \mathbf{k} = r^2 \dot{\theta} \mathbf{k}, \qquad \text{or} \qquad r^2 \dot{\theta} = r_0 v_0. \tag{19}$$

This is where the area comes in. The area differential in polar coordinates is

$$dA = \frac{1}{2} r^2 \, d\theta$$

(Section 9.6). Accordingly, dA/dt has the constant value

$$\frac{dA}{dt} = \frac{1}{2} r^2 \dot{\theta} = \frac{1}{2} r_0 v_0, \tag{20}$$

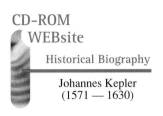

CD-ROM
WEBsite

Historical Biography

Johannes Kepler
(1571 — 1630)

which is Kepler's second law.

For Earth, r_0 is about 150,000,000 km, v_0 is about 30 km/sec, and dA/dt is about 2,250,000,000 km^2/sec. Every time your heart beats, Earth advances 30 km along its orbit, and the radius joining Earth to the sun sweeps out 2,250,000,000 km^2 of area.

Proof of Kepler's First Law

To prove that a planet moves along a conic section with one focus at its sun, we need to express the planet's radius r as a function of θ. This requires a long sequence of calculations and some substitutions that are not altogether obvious.

We begin with the equation that comes from equating the coefficients of $\mathbf{u}_r = \mathbf{r}/|\mathbf{r}|$ in Equations (6) and (10):

$$\ddot{r} - r\dot{\theta}^2 = -\frac{GM}{r^2}. \tag{21}$$

We eliminate $\dot{\theta}$ temporarily by replacing it with $r_0 v_0 / r^2$ from Equation (19) and rearrange the resulting equation to get

$$\ddot{r} = \frac{r_0^2 v_0^2}{r^3} - \frac{GM}{r^2}. \tag{22}$$

We change this into a first order equation by a change of variable. With

$$p = \frac{dr}{dt}, \qquad \frac{d^2 r}{dt^2} = \frac{dp}{dt} = \frac{dp}{dr}\frac{dr}{dt} = p\frac{dp}{dr}, \qquad \text{Chain Rule}$$

Equation (22) becomes

$$p\frac{dp}{dr} = \frac{r_0^2 v_0^2}{r^3} - \frac{GM}{r^2}. \tag{23}$$

Multiplying through by 2 and integrating with respect to r gives

$$p^2 = (\dot{r})^2 = -\frac{r_0^2 v_0^2}{r^2} + \frac{2GM}{r} + C_1. \tag{24}$$

The initial conditions that $r = r_0$ and $\dot{r} = 0$ when $t = 0$ determine the value of C_1 to be

$$C_1 = v_0^2 - \frac{2GM}{r_0}.$$

Accordingly, Equation (24), after a suitable rearrangement, becomes

$$\dot{r}^2 = v_0{}^2\left(1 - \frac{r_0{}^2}{r^2}\right) + 2GM\left(\frac{1}{r} - \frac{1}{r_0}\right). \tag{25}$$

The effect of going from Equation (21) to Equation (25) has been to replace a second-order differential equation in r by a first order differential equation in r. Our goal is still to express r in terms of θ, so we now bring θ back into the picture. To accomplish this, we divide both sides of Equation (25) by the squares of the corresponding sides of the equation $r^2\dot{\theta} = r_0 v_0$ (Equation (19)) and use the equation $\dot{r}/\dot{\theta} = (dr/dt)/(d\theta/dt) = dr/d\theta$ to get

$$\frac{1}{r^4}\left(\frac{dr}{d\theta}\right)^2 = \frac{1}{r_0{}^2} - \frac{1}{r^2} + \frac{2GM}{r_0{}^2 v_0{}^2}\left(\frac{1}{r} - \frac{1}{r_0}\right)$$

$$= \frac{1}{r_0{}^2} - \frac{1}{r^2} + 2h\left(\frac{1}{r} - \frac{1}{r_0}\right). \qquad h = \frac{GM}{r_0{}^2 v_0{}^2} \tag{26}$$

To simplify further, we substitute

$$u = \frac{1}{r}, \qquad u_0 = \frac{1}{r_0}, \qquad \frac{du}{d\theta} = -\frac{1}{r^2}\frac{dr}{d\theta}, \qquad \left(\frac{du}{d\theta}\right)^2 = \frac{1}{r^4}\left(\frac{dr}{d\theta}\right)^2,$$

obtaining

$$\left(\frac{du}{d\theta}\right)^2 = u_0{}^2 - u^2 + 2hu - 2hu_0 = (u_0 - h)^2 - (u - h)^2 \tag{27}$$

$$\frac{du}{d\theta} = \pm\sqrt{(u_0 - h)^2 - (u - h)^2}. \tag{28}$$

Which sign do we take? We know that $\dot{\theta} = r_0 v_0/r^2$ is positive. Also, r starts from a minimum value at $t = 0$, so it cannot immediately decrease, and $\dot{r} \geq 0$, at least for early positive values of t. Therefore,

$$\frac{dr}{d\theta} = \frac{\dot{r}}{\dot{\theta}} \geq 0 \qquad \text{and} \qquad \frac{du}{d\theta} = -\frac{1}{r^2}\frac{dr}{d\theta} \leq 0.$$

The correct sign for Equation (28) is the negative sign. With this determined, we rearrange Equation (28) and integrate both sides with respect to θ:

$$\frac{-1}{\sqrt{(u_0 - h)^2 - (u - h)^2}}\frac{du}{d\theta} = 1$$

$$\cos^{-1}\left(\frac{u - h}{u_0 - h}\right) = \theta + C_2. \tag{29}$$

The constant C_2 is zero because $u = u_0$ when $\theta = 0$ and $\cos^{-1}(1) = 0$. Therefore,

$$\frac{u - h}{u_0 - h} = \cos\theta$$

and

$$\frac{1}{r} = u = h + (u_0 - h)\cos\theta. \tag{30}$$

A few more algebraic maneuvers produce the final equation

$$r = \frac{(1 + e)r_0}{1 + e\cos\theta}, \tag{31}$$

where

$$e = \frac{1}{r_0 h} - 1 = \frac{r_0 v_0^2}{GM} - 1. \tag{32}$$

Together, Equations (31) and (32) say that the path of the planet is a conic section with one focus at the sun and with eccentricity $(r_0 v_0^2 / GM) - 1$. This is the modern formulation of Kepler's first law.

Kepler's Third Law (The Time–Distance Law)

The time T it takes a planet to go around its sun once is the planet's **orbital period.** *Kepler's third law* says that T and the orbit's semimajor axis a are related by the equation

$$\frac{T^2}{a^3} = \frac{4\pi^2}{GM}. \tag{33}$$

Since the right-hand side of this equation is constant within a given solar system, the ratio of T^2 to a^3 *is the same for every planet in the system.*

Kepler's third law is the starting point for working out the size of our solar system. It allows the semimajor axis of each planetary orbit to be expressed in astronomical units, Earth's semimajor axis being one unit. The distance between any two planets at any time can then be predicted in astronomical units and all that remains is to find one of these distances in kilometers. This can be done by bouncing radar waves off Venus, for example. The astronomical unit is now known, after a series of such measurements, to be 149,597,870 km.

We derive Kepler's third law by combining two formulas for the area enclosed by the planet's elliptical orbit:

Formula 1:   Area $= \pi ab$ The geometry formula in which a is the semimajor axis and b is the semiminor axis

Formula 2:   Area $= \displaystyle\int_0^T dA$

$$= \int_0^T \frac{1}{2} r_0 v_0 \, dt \quad \text{Eq. (20)}$$

$$= \frac{1}{2} T r_0 v_0.$$

Equating these gives

$$T = \frac{2\pi ab}{r_0 v_0} = \frac{2\pi a^2}{r_0 v_0} \sqrt{1 - e^2}. \qquad \text{For any ellipse,} \atop b = a\sqrt{1 - e^2} \tag{34}$$

It remains only to express a and e in terms of r_0, v_0, G, and M. Equation (32) does this for e. For a, we observe that setting θ equal to π in Equation (31) gives

$$r_{max} = r_0 \frac{1 + e}{1 - e}.$$

Hence,

$$2a = r_0 + r_{max} = \frac{2r_0}{1 - e} = \frac{2r_0 GM}{2GM - r_0 v_0^2}. \tag{35}$$

Squaring both sides of Equation (34) and substituting the results of Equations (32) and (35) now produces Kepler's third law (Exercise 15).

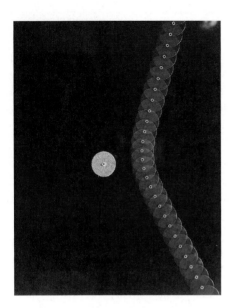

FIGURE 10.69 This multiflash photograph shows an air puck being deflected by an inverse square law force. It moves along a hyperbola.

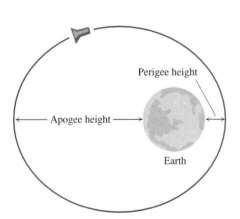

FIGURE 10.70 The orbit of an Earth satellite: $2a$ = diameter of earth + perigee height + apogee height.

Orbit Data

Although Kepler discovered his laws empirically and stated them only for the six planets known at the time, the modern derivations of Kepler's laws show that they apply to any body driven by a force that obeys an inverse square law. They apply to Halley's comet and the asteroid Icarus. They apply to the moon's orbit about Earth, and they applied to the orbit of the spacecraft *Apollo 8* about the moon. They also applied to the air puck shown in Figure 10.69 being deflected by an inverse square law force; its path is a hyperbola. Charged particles fired at the nuclei of atoms scatter along hyperbolic paths.

Tables 10.1 through 10.3 give additional data for planetary orbits and for the orbits of seven of Earth's artificial satellites (Figure 10.70). *Vanguard 1* sent back data that revealed differences between the levels of Earth's oceans and provided the first determination of the precise locations of some of the more isolated Pacific islands. The data also verified that the gravitation of the sun and moon would affect the orbits of Earth's satellites and that solar radiation could exert enough pressure to deform an orbit.

Table 10.1 Values of a, e, and T for the major planets

Planet	Semimajor axis a*	Eccentricity e	Period T
Mercury	57.95	0.2056	87.967 days
Venus	108.11	0.0068	224.71 days
Earth	149.57	0.0167	365.256 days
Mars	227.84	0.0934	1.8808 years
Jupiter	778.14	0.0484	11.8613 years
Saturn	1427.0	0.0543	29.4568 years
Uranus	2870.3	0.0460	84.0081 years
Neptune	4499.9	0.0082	164.784 years
Pluto	5909	0.2481	248.35 years

*Millions of kilometers

Syncom 3 is one of a series of U.S. Department of Defense telecommunications satellites. *Tiros 11* (for "television infrared observation satellite") is one of a series of weather satellites. *GOES 4* (for "geostationary operational environmental satellite") is one of a series of satellites designed to gather information about Earth's atmosphere. Its orbital period, 1436.2 min, is nearly the same as Earth's rotational period of 1436.1 min, and its orbit is nearly circular ($e = 0.0003$). *Intelsat 5* is a heavy-capacity commercial telecommunications satellite.

Table 10.2 Data on Earth's satellites

Name	Launch date	Time or expected time aloft	Mass at launch (kg)	Period (min)	Perigee height (km)	Apogee height (km)	Semimajor axis a (km)	Eccentricity
Sputnik 1	Oct. 1957	57.6 days	83.6	96.2	215	939	6,955	0.052
Vanguard 1	March 1958	300 years	1.47	138.5	649	4,340	8,872	0.208
Syncom 3	Aug. 1964	$>10^6$ years	39	1436.2	35,718	35,903	42,189	0.002
Skylab 4	Nov. 1973	84.06 days	13,980	93.11	422	437	6,808	0.001
Tiros II	Oct. 1978	500 years	734	102.12	850	866	7,236	0.001
GOES 4	Sept. 1980	$>10^6$ years	627	1436.2	35,776	35,800	42,166	0.0003
Intelsat 5	Dec. 1980	$>10^6$ years	1,928	1417.67	35,143	35,707	41,803	0.007

Table 10.3 Numerical data

Universal gravitational constant: $G = 6.6726 \times 10^{-11} \ \mathrm{Nm^2kg^{-2}}$
(When you use this value of G in a calculation, remember to express force in newtons, distance in meters, mass in kilograms, and time in seconds.)

Sun's mass:	1.99×10^{30} kg
Earth's mass:	5.975×10^{24} kg
Equatorial radius of Earth:	6378.533 km
Polar radius of Earth:	6356.912 km
Earth's rotational period:	1436.1 min
Earth's orbital period:	1 year = 365.256 days

EXERCISES 10.8

Reminder: When a calculation involves the gravitational constant G, express force in newtons, distance in meters, mass in kilograms, and time in seconds.

1. *Period of Skylab 4* Since the orbit of *Skylab 4* had a semimajor axis of $a = 6808$ km, Kepler's third law with M equal to Earth's mass should give the period. Calculate it. Compare your result with the value in Table 10.2.

2. *Earth's velocity at perihelion* Earth's distance from the sun at perihelion is approximately 149,577,000 km, and the eccentricity of Earth's orbit about the sun is 0.0167. Find the velocity v_0 of Earth in its orbit at perihelion. (Use Equation (15).)

3. *Semimajor axis of Proton I* In July 1965, the USSR launched *Proton I*, weighing 12,200 kg (at launch), with a perigee height of 183 km, an apogee height of 589 km, and a period of 92.25 min. Using the relevant data for the mass of Earth and the gravitational constant G, find the semimajor axis a of the orbit from Equation (3). Compare your answer with the number you get by adding the perigee and apogee heights to the diameter of the Earth.

4. *Semimajor axis of Viking I* The *Viking I* orbiter, which surveyed Mars from August 1975 to June 1976, had a period of 1639 min. Use this and the mass of Mars, 6.418×10^{23} kg, to find the semimajor axis of the *Viking I* orbit.

5. *Average diameter of Mars (Continuation of Exercise 4)* The *Viking I* orbiter was 1499 km from the surface of Mars at its closest point and 35,800 km from the surface at its farthest point. Use this information together with the value you obtained in Exercise 4 to estimate the average diameter of Mars.

6. *Period of Viking 2* The *Viking 2* orbiter, which surveyed Mars from September 1975 to August 1976, moved in an ellipse whose semimajor axis was 22,030 km. What was the orbital period? (Express your answer in minutes.)

7. *Geosynchronous orbits* Several satellites in Earth's equatorial plane have nearly circular orbits whose periods are the same as the earth's rotational period. Such orbits are **geosynchronous** or **geostationary** because they hold the satellite over the same spot on Earth's surface.

  (a) *Writing to Learn* Approximately what is the semimajor axis of a geosynchronous orbit? Give reasons for your answer.

  (b) About how high is a geosynchronous orbit above the Earth's surface?

  (c) Which of the satellites in Table 10.2 have (nearly) geosynchronous orbits?

8. *Writing to Learn* The mass of Mars is 6.418×10^{23} kg. If a satellite revolving about Mars is to hold a stationary orbit (have the same period as the period of Mar's rotation, which is 1477.4 min), what must the semimajor axis of its orbit be? Give reasons for your answer.

9. *Distance from Earth to the moon* The period of the moon's rotation about Earth is 2.36055×10^6 sec. About how far away is the moon?

10. *Finding satellite speed* A satellite moves around Earth in a circular orbit. Express the satellite's speed as a function of the orbit's radius.

11. *Orbital period* If T is measured in seconds and a in meters, what is the value of T^2/a^3 for planets in our solar system? For satellites orbiting Earth? For satellites orbiting the moon? (The moon's mass is 7.354×10^{22} kg.)

12. *Type of orbit* For what values of v_0 in Equation (15) is the orbit in Equation (16) a circle? An ellipse? A parabola? A hyperbola?

13. *Circular orbits* Show that a planet in a circular orbit moves with a constant speed. (*Hint:* This is a consequence of one of Kepler's laws.)

14. Suppose that **r** is the position vector of a particle moving along a plane curve and dA/dt is the rate at which the vector sweeps out area. Without introducing coordinates, and assuming the necessary derivatives exist, give a geometric argument based on increments and limits for the validity of the equation

$$\frac{dA}{dt} = \frac{1}{2}|\mathbf{r} \times \dot{\mathbf{r}}|.$$

15. *Kepler's third law* Complete the derivation of Kepler's third law (the part following Equation (34)).

In Exercises 16 and 17, two planets, planet A and planet B, are orbiting their sun in circular orbits with A being the inner planet and B being farther away from the sun. Suppose the positions of A and B at time t are

$$\mathbf{r}_A(t) = 2\cos(2\pi t)\mathbf{i} + 2\sin(2\pi t)\mathbf{j}$$

and

$$\mathbf{r}_B(t) = 3\cos(\pi t)\mathbf{i} + 3\sin(\pi t)\mathbf{j},$$

respectively, where the sun is assumed to be located at the origin and distance is measured in astronomical units. (Notice that planet A moves faster than planet B.)

The people on planet A regard their planet, not the sun, as the center of their planetary system (their solar system).

16. Using planet A as the origin of a new coordinate system, give parametric equations for the location of planet B at time t. Write your answer in terms of $\cos(\pi t)$ and $\sin(\pi t)$.

T 17. Using planet A as the origin, graph the path of planet B.

    This exercise illustrates the difficulty that people before Kepler's time, with an earth-centered (planet A) view of our solar system, had in understanding the motions of the planets (i.e., planet B = Mars). See D. G. Saari's article in the *American Monthly*, Vol. 97 (Feb. 1990), pp. 105–119.

18. *Writing to Learn* Kepler discovered that the path of the Earth around the sun is an ellipse with the sun at one of the foci. Let $\mathbf{r}(t)$ be the position vector from the center of the sun to the center of the Earth at time t. Let **w** be the vector from the Earth's South Pole to North Pole. It is known that **w** is constant and not orthogonal to the plane of the ellipse (Earth's axis is tilted). In terms of $\mathbf{r}(t)$ and **w,** give the mathematical meaning of (i) perihelion, (ii) aphelion, (iii) equinox, (iv) summer solstice, (v) winter solstice.

Questions to Guide Your Review

1. When do directed line segments (in space) represent the same vector?

2. How are space vectors added and subtracted geometrically? Algebraically?

3. How do you find a space vector's magnitude and direction?

4. If a vector is multiplied by a positive scalar, how is the result related to the original vector? What if the scalar is zero? Negative?

5. Define the *dot product (scalar product)* of two space vectors. Which algebraic laws (commutative, associative, distributive, cancellation) are satisfied by dot products, and which, if any, are not? Give examples. When is the dot product of two vectors equal to zero?

6. What geometric or physical interpretations do dot products have? Give examples.

7. What is the vector projection of a vector **v** onto a vector **u**? How do you write **v** as the sum of a vector parallel to **u** and a vector orthogonal to **u**?

8. Define the *cross product* (*vector product*) of two vectors. Which algebraic laws (commutative, associative, distributive, cancellation) are satisfied by cross products, and which are not? Give examples. When is the cross product of two vectors equal to zero?

9. What geometric or physical interpretations do cross products have? Give examples.

10. What is the determinant formula for calculating the cross product of two vectors relative to the Cartesian **i, j, k**-coordinate system? Use it in an example.

11. How do you find equations for lines, line segments, and planes in space? Give examples. Can you express a line in space by a single equation? A plane?

12. What are box products? What significance do they have? How are they evaluated? Give an example.

13. How do you find equations for spheres in space? Give examples.

14. How do you find the intersection of two lines in space? A line and a plane? Two planes? Give examples.

15. What is a cylinder? Give examples of equations that define cylinders in Cartesian coordinates.

16. What are quadric surfaces? Give examples of different kinds of ellipsoids, paraboloids, cones, and hyperboloids (equations and sketches).

17. State the rules for differentiating and integrating vector functions. Give examples.

18. How do you define and calculate the velocity, speed, direction of motion, and acceleration of a body moving along a sufficiently differentiable space curve? Give an example.

19. What is special about the derivatives of vector functions of constant length? Give an example.

20. How do you define and calculate the length of a segment of a smooth space curve? Give an example. What mathematical assumptions are involved in the definition?

21. How do you measure distance along a smooth curve in space from a preselected base point? Give an example.

22. What is a smooth curve's unit tangent vector? Give an example.

23. Define curvature, circle of curvature (osculating circle), center of curvature, and radius of curvature for twice-differentiable curves in the plane. Give examples. What curves have zero curvature? constant curvature?

24. What is a plane curve's principal normal vector? When is it defined? Which way does it point? Give an example.

25. How do you define **N** and κ for curves in space? How are these quantities related? Give examples.

26. What is a curve's binormal vector? Give an example. How is this vector related to the curve's torsion? Give an example.

27. What formulas are available for writing a moving body's acceleration as a sum of its tangential and normal components? Give an example. Why might one want to write the acceleration this way? What if the body moves at a constant speed? at a constant speed around a circle?

28. State Kepler's laws. To what do they apply?

Practice Exercises

Vector Calculations

Express the vectors in Exercises 1 and 2 in terms of their lengths and directions.

1. $2\mathbf{i} - 3\mathbf{j} + 6\mathbf{k}$
2. $\mathbf{i} + 2\mathbf{j} - \mathbf{k}$

3. Find a vector 2 units long in the direction of $\mathbf{v} = 4\mathbf{i} - \mathbf{j} + 4\mathbf{k}$.

4. Find a vector 5 units long in the direction opposite to the direction of $\mathbf{v} = (3/5)\mathbf{i} + (4/5)\mathbf{k}$.

In Exercises 5 and 6, find $|\mathbf{v}|, |\mathbf{u}|, \mathbf{v} \cdot \mathbf{u}, \mathbf{u} \cdot \mathbf{v}, \mathbf{v} \times \mathbf{u}, \mathbf{u} \times \mathbf{v}, |\mathbf{v} \times \mathbf{u}|$, the angle between **v** and **u**, the scalar component of **u** in the direction of **v**, and the vector projection of **u** onto **v**.

5. $\mathbf{v} = \mathbf{i} + \mathbf{j}$
   $\mathbf{u} = 2\mathbf{i} + \mathbf{j} - 2\mathbf{k}$

6. $\mathbf{v} = \mathbf{i} + \mathbf{j} + 2\mathbf{k}$
   $\mathbf{u} = -\mathbf{i} - \mathbf{k}$

In Exercises 7 and 8, write **v** as the sum of a vector parallel to **u** and a vector orthogonal to **u**.

7. $\mathbf{v} = 2\mathbf{i} + \mathbf{j} - \mathbf{k}$
   $\mathbf{u} = \mathbf{i} + \mathbf{j} - 5\mathbf{k}$

8. $\mathbf{u} = \mathbf{i} - 2\mathbf{j}$
   $\mathbf{v} = \mathbf{i} + \mathbf{j} + \mathbf{k}$

In Exercises 9 and 10, draw coordinate axes and then sketch **u**, **v**, and $\mathbf{u} \times \mathbf{v}$ as vectors at the origin.

9. $\mathbf{u} = \mathbf{i}, \quad \mathbf{v} = \mathbf{i} + \mathbf{j}$

10. $\mathbf{u} = \mathbf{i} - \mathbf{j}, \quad \mathbf{v} = \mathbf{i} + \mathbf{j}$

11. If $|\mathbf{v}| = 2, |\mathbf{w}| = 3$, and the angle between **v** and **w** is $\pi/3$, find $|\mathbf{v} - 2\mathbf{w}|$.

12. For what value or values of a will the vectors $\mathbf{u} = 2\mathbf{i} + 4\mathbf{j} - 5\mathbf{k}$ and $\mathbf{v} = -4\mathbf{i} - 8\mathbf{j} + a\mathbf{k}$ be parallel?

In Exercises 13 and 14, find **(a)** the area of the parallelogram determined by vectors **u** and **v** and **(b)** the volume of the parallelepiped determined by the vectors **u**, **v**, and **w**.

13. $\mathbf{u} = \mathbf{i} + \mathbf{j} - \mathbf{k}, \quad \mathbf{v} = 2\mathbf{i} + \mathbf{j} + \mathbf{k}, \quad \mathbf{w} = -\mathbf{i} - 2\mathbf{j} + 3\mathbf{k}$

14. $\mathbf{u} = \mathbf{i} + \mathbf{j}, \quad \mathbf{v} = \mathbf{j}, \quad \mathbf{w} = \mathbf{i} + \mathbf{j} + \mathbf{k}$

Lines, Planes, and Distances

15. *Writing to Learn* Suppose that **n** is normal to a plane and **v** is parallel to the plane. Describe how you would find a vector **u** that is both perpendicular to **v** and parallel to the plane.

16. *Vector parallel to plane* Find a vector in the plane parallel to the line $ax + by = c$.

17. *Line parallel to vector* Parametrize the line that passes through the point $(1, 2, 3)$ parallel to the vector $\mathbf{v} = -3\mathbf{i} + 7\mathbf{k}$.

18. *Line segment* Parametrize the line segment joining the points $P(1, 2, 0)$ and $Q(1, 3, -1)$.

19. *Plane normal to vector* Find an equation for the plane that passes through the point $(3, -2, 1)$ normal to the vector $\mathbf{n} = 2\mathbf{i} + \mathbf{j} + \mathbf{k}$.

20. *Plane perpendicular to line* Find an equation for the plane that passes through the point $(-1, 6, 0)$ perpendicular to the line $x = -1 + t, y = 6 - 2t, z = 3t$.

In Exercises 21 and 22, find an equation for the plane through points $P, Q,$ and R.

21. $P(1, -1, 2), \quad Q(2, 1, 3), \quad R(-1, 2, -1)$

22. $P(1, 0, 0), \quad Q(0, 1, 0), \quad R(0, 0, 1)$

23. *Points of intersection* Find the points in which the line $x = 1 + 2t$, $y = -1 - t, z = 3t$ meets the three coordinate planes.

24. *Point of intersection* Find the point in which the line through the origin perpendicular to the plane $2x - y - z = 4$ meets the plane $3x - 5y + 2z = 6$.

25. *Angle between planes* Find the acute angle between the planes $x = 7$ and $x + y + \sqrt{2}z = -3$.

26. *Intersection of planes* Find parametric equations for the line in which the planes $x + 2y + z = 1$ and $x - y + 2z = -8$ intersect.

27. *Intersection of planes* Show that the line in which the planes

$$x + 2y - 2z = 5 \quad \text{and} \quad 5x - 2y - z = 0$$

intersect is parallel to the line

$$x = -3 + 2t, \quad y = 3t, \quad z = 1 + 4t.$$

28. *Intersection of planes* The planes $3x + 6z = 1$ and $2x + 2y - z = 3$ intersect in a line.

(a) Show that the planes are orthogonal.

(b) Find equations for the line of intersection.

29. *Plane parallel to vectors* Find an equation for the plane that passes through the point $(1, 2, 3)$ parallel to $\mathbf{u} = 2\mathbf{i} + 3\mathbf{j} + \mathbf{k}$ and $\mathbf{v} = \mathbf{i} - \mathbf{j} + 2\mathbf{k}$.

30. *Vector parallel to plane* Find a vector parallel to the plane $2x - y - z = 4$ and orthogonal to $\mathbf{i} + \mathbf{j} + \mathbf{k}$.

31. *Vector in a plane* Find a unit vector orthogonal to **u** in the plane of **v** and **w** if $\mathbf{u} = 2\mathbf{i} - \mathbf{j} + \mathbf{k}, \mathbf{v} = \mathbf{i} + 2\mathbf{j} + \mathbf{k},$ and $\mathbf{w} = \mathbf{i} + \mathbf{j} - 2\mathbf{k}$.

32. *Vector parallel to line* Find a vector of magnitude 2 parallel to the line of intersection of the planes $x + 2y + z - 1 = 0$ and $x - y + 2z + 7 = 0$.

33. *Point of intersection* Find the point in which the line through the origin perpendicular to the plane $2x - y - z = 4$ meets the plane $3x - 5y + 2z = 6$.

34. *Point of intersection* Find the point in which the line through $P(3, 2, 1)$ normal to the plane $2x - y + 2z = -2$ meets the plane.

35. *Plane* Which of the following are equations for the plane through the points $P(1, 1, -1), Q(3, 0, 2),$ and $R(-2, 1, 0)$?

(a) $(2\mathbf{i} - 3\mathbf{j} + 3\mathbf{k}) \cdot ((x + 2)\mathbf{i} + (y - 1)\mathbf{j} + z\mathbf{k}) = 0$

(b) $x = 3 - t, \quad y = -11t, \quad z = 2 - 3t$

(c) $(x + 2) + 11(y - 1) = 3z$

(d) $(2\mathbf{i} - 3\mathbf{j} + 3\mathbf{k}) \times ((x + 2)\mathbf{i} + (y - 1)\mathbf{j} + z\mathbf{k}) = \mathbf{0}$

(e) $(2\mathbf{i} - \mathbf{j} + 3\mathbf{k}) \times (-3\mathbf{i} + \mathbf{k}) \cdot ((x + 2)\mathbf{i} + (y - 1)\mathbf{j} + z\mathbf{k}) = 0$

36. *Parallelogram* The parallelogram shown here has vertices at $A(2, -1, 4), B(1, 0, -1), C(1, 2, 3),$ and D. Find

(a) The coordinates of D

(b) The cosine of the interior angle at B

(c) The vector projection of $\overrightarrow{BA}$ onto $\overrightarrow{BC}$

(d) The area of the parallelogram

(e) An equation for the plane of the parallelogram

(f) The areas of the orthogonal projections of the parallelogram on the three coordinate planes.

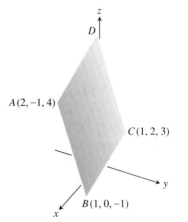

Distances between Points and Lines and Planes

In Exercises 37 and 38, find the distance from the point to the plane.

37. $(2, 2, 0);\quad x = -t,\quad y = t,\quad z = -1 + t$

38. $(0, 4, 1);\quad x = 2 + t,\quad y = 2 + t,\quad z = t$

In Exercises 39 and 40, find the distance from the point to the plane.

39. $(6, 0, -6),\quad x - y = 4$

40. $(3, 0, 10),\quad 2x + 3y + z = 2$

41. Find the distance from the point $P(1, 4, 0)$ to the plane through $A(0, 0, 0)$, $B(2, 0, -1)$ and $C(2, -1, 0)$.

42. Find the distance from the point $(2, 2, 3)$ to the plane $2x + 3y + 5z = 0$.

43. *Distance between lines* Find the distance between the line L_1 through the points $A(1, 0, -1)$ and $B(-1, 1, 0)$ and the line L_2 through the points $C(3, 1, -1)$ and $D(4, 5, -2)$. The distance is to be measured along the line perpendicular to the two lines. First find a vector $\mathbf{n}$ perpendicular to both lines. Then project $\overrightarrow{AC}$ onto $\mathbf{n}$.

44. *(Continuation of Exercise 43)* Find the distance between the line through $A(4, 0, 2)$ and $B(2, 4, 1)$ and the line through $C(1, 3, 2)$ and $D(2, 2, 4)$.

Quadric Surfaces

Identify and sketch the surfaces in Exercises 45–50.

45. $x^2 + y^2 + z^2 = 4$

46. $4x^2 + 4y^2 + z^2 = 4$

47. $z = -(x^2 + y^2)$

48. $x^2 + y^2 = z^2$

49. $x^2 + y^2 - z^2 = 4$

50. $y^2 - x^2 - z^2 = 1$

Motion in Space

Find the lengths of the curves in Exercises 51 and 52.

51. $\mathbf{r}(t) = (2 \cos t)\mathbf{i} + (2 \sin t)\mathbf{j} + t^2\mathbf{k},\quad 0 \le t \le \pi/4$

52. $\mathbf{r}(t) = (3 \cos t)\mathbf{i} + (3 \sin t)\mathbf{j} + 2t^{3/2}\mathbf{k},\quad 0 \le t \le 3$

In Exercises 53–56, find $\mathbf{T}$, $\mathbf{N}$, $\mathbf{B}$, κ, and τ at the given value of t.

53. $\mathbf{r}(t) = \dfrac{4}{9}(1 + t)^{3/2}\mathbf{i} + \dfrac{4}{9}(1 - t)^{3/2}\mathbf{j} + \dfrac{1}{3}t\mathbf{k},\quad t = 0$

54. $\mathbf{r}(t) = (e^t \sin 2t)\mathbf{i} + (e^t \cos 2t)\mathbf{j} + 2e^t\mathbf{k},\quad t = 0$

55. $\mathbf{r}(t) = t\mathbf{i} + \dfrac{1}{2}e^{2t}\mathbf{j},\quad t = \ln 2$

56. $\mathbf{r}(t) = (3 \cosh 2t)\mathbf{i} + (3 \sinh 2t)\mathbf{j} + 6t\mathbf{k},\quad t = \ln 2$

In Exercises 57 and 58, write $\mathbf{a}$ in the form $\mathbf{a} = a_\mathbf{T}\mathbf{T} + a_\mathbf{N}\mathbf{N}$ at $t = 0$ without finding $\mathbf{T}$ and $\mathbf{N}$.

57. $\mathbf{r}(t) = (2 + 3t + 3t^2)\mathbf{i} + (4t + 4t^2)\mathbf{j} - (6 \cos t)\mathbf{k}$

58. $\mathbf{r}(t) = (2 + t)\mathbf{i} + (t + 2t^2)\mathbf{j} + (1 + t^2)\mathbf{k}$

59. Find $\mathbf{T}$, $\mathbf{N}$, $\mathbf{B}$, κ, and τ as functions of t if $\mathbf{r}(t) = (\sin t)\mathbf{i} + (\sqrt{2} \cos t)\mathbf{j} + (\sin t)\mathbf{k}$.

60. *Velocity and acceleration* At what times in the interval $0 \le t \le \pi$ are the velocity and acceleration vectors of the motion $\mathbf{r}(t) = \mathbf{i} + (5 \cos t)\mathbf{j} + (3 \sin t)\mathbf{k}$ orthogonal?

61. *Orthogonality of position vector* The position of a particle moving in space at time $t \ge 0$ is

$$\mathbf{r}(t) = 2\mathbf{i} + \left(4 \sin \frac{t}{2}\right)\mathbf{j} + \left(3 - \frac{t}{\pi}\right)\mathbf{k}.$$

Find the first time $\mathbf{r}$ is orthogonal to the vector $\mathbf{i} - \mathbf{j}$.

62. *Osculating, normal, and rectifying planes* Find equations for the osculating, normal, and rectifying planes of the curve $\mathbf{r}(t) = t\mathbf{i} + t^2\mathbf{j} + t^3\mathbf{k}$ at the point $(1, 1, 1)$.

63. *Tangent line* Find parametric equations for the line that is tangent to the curve $\mathbf{r}(t) = e^t\mathbf{i} + (\sin t)\mathbf{j} + \ln(1 - t)\mathbf{k}$ at $t = 0$.

64. *Tangent line* Find parametric equations for the line tangent to the helix $\mathbf{r}(t) = (\sqrt{2} \cos t)\mathbf{i} + (\sqrt{2} \sin t)\mathbf{j} + t\mathbf{k}$ at the point where $t = \pi/4$.

65. *The view from Skylab 4* What percentage of Earth's surface area could the astronauts see when *Skylab 4* was at its apogee height, 437 km above the surface? To find out, model the visible surface as the surface generated by revolving the circular arc GT, shown here, about the *y*-axis.

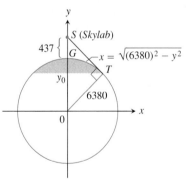

Then carry out these steps.

1. Use similar triangles in the figure to show that $y_0/6380 = 6380/(6380 + 437)$. Solve for y_0.

2. To four significant digits, calculate the visible area as

$$VA = \int_{y_0}^{6380} 2\pi x \sqrt{1 + \left(\frac{dx}{dy}\right)^2}\, dy.$$

3. Express the result as a percentage of Earth's surface area.

66. *Radius of curvature* Show that the radius of curvature of a twice-differentiable plane curve $\mathbf{r}(t) = f(t)\mathbf{i} + g(t)\mathbf{j}$ is given by the formula

$$\rho = \frac{\dot{x}^2 + \dot{y}^2}{\sqrt{\ddot{x}^2 + \ddot{y}^2 - \ddot{s}^2}},\qquad \text{where } \ddot{s} = \frac{d}{dt}\sqrt{\dot{x}^2 + \dot{y}^2}.$$

Additional Exercises: Theory, Examples, Applications

Applications and Examples

1. *Submarine hunting* Two surface ships on maneuvers are trying to determine a submarine's course and speed to prepare for an aircraft intercept. As shown here, ship A is located at $(4, 0, 0)$, whereas ship B is located at $(0, 5, 0)$. All coordinates are given in thousands of feet. Ship A locates the submarine in the direction of the vector $2\mathbf{i} + 3\mathbf{j} - (1/3)\mathbf{k}$, and ship B locates it in the direction of the vector $18\mathbf{i} - 6\mathbf{j} - \mathbf{k}$. Four minutes ago, the submarine was located at $(2, -1, -1/3)$. The aircraft is due in 20 min. Assuming that the submarine moves in a straight line at a constant speed, to what position should the surface ships direct the aircraft?

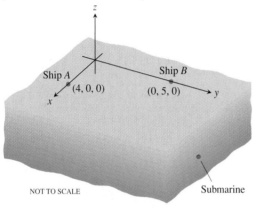

NOT TO SCALE

2. *A helicopter rescue* Two helicopters, H_1 and H_2, are traveling together. At time $t = 0$, they separate and follow different straight-line paths given by

$$H_1: \quad x = 6 + 40t, \quad y = -3 + 10t, \quad z = -3 + 2t$$
$$H_2: \quad x = 6 + 110t, \quad y = -3 + 4t, \quad z = -3 + t.$$

Time t is measured in hours and all coordinates are measured in miles. Due to system malfunctions, H_2 stops its flight at $(446, 13, 1)$ and, in a negligible amount of time, lands at $(446, 13, 0)$. Two hours later, H_1 is advised of this fact and heads toward H_2 at 150 mph. How long will it take H_1 to reach H_2?

3. *Torque* The operator's manual for the Toro® 21 in. lawnmower says "tighten the spark plug to 15 ft-lb (20.4 N · m)." If you are installing the plug with a 10.5 in. socket wrench that places the center of your hand 9 in. from the axis of the spark plug, about how hard should you pull? Answer in pounds.

9 in.

4. *Rotating body* The line through the origin and the point $A(1, 1, 1)$ is the axis of rotation of a rigid body rotating with a constant angular speed of $3/2$ rad/sec. The rotation appears to be clockwise when we look toward the origin from A. Find the velocity $\mathbf{v}$ of the point of the body that is at the position $B(1, 3, 2)$.

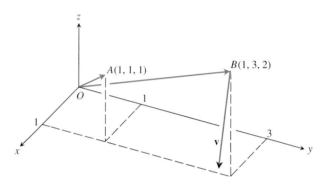

5. *Determinants and planes* Show that

$$\begin{vmatrix} x_1 - x & y_1 - y & z_1 - z \\ x_2 - x & y_2 - y & z_2 - z \\ x_3 - x & y_3 - y & z_3 - z \end{vmatrix} = 0$$

is an equation for the plane through the three noncollinear points $P_1(x_1, y_1, z_1)$, $P_2(x_2, y_2, z_2)$, and $P_3(x_3, y_3, z_3)$.

(b) What set of points in space is described by the equation

$$\begin{vmatrix} x & y & z & 1 \\ x_1 & y_1 & z_1 & 1 \\ x_2 & y_2 & z_2 & 1 \\ x_3 & y_3 & z_3 & 1 \end{vmatrix} = 0?$$

6. *Determinants and lines* Show that the lines

$$x = a_1 s + b_1, y = a_2 s + b_2, z = a_3 s + b_3, -\infty < s < \infty,$$

and

$$x = c_1 t + d_1, y = c_2 t + d_2, z = c_3 t + d_3, -\infty < t < \infty,$$

intersect or are parallel if and only if

$$\begin{vmatrix} a_1 & c_1 & b_1 - d_1 \\ a_2 & c_2 & b_2 - d_2 \\ a_3 & c_3 & b_3 - d_3 \end{vmatrix} = 0.$$

7. *Distance from point to plane* Use vectors to show that the distance from $P_1(x_1, y_1, z_1)$ to the plane $Ax + By + Cz = D$ is

$$d = \frac{|Ax_1 + By_1 + Cz_1 - D|}{\sqrt{A^2 + B^2 + C^2}}.$$

8. *Sphere tangent to plane* Find an equation for the sphere that is tangent to the planes $x + y + z = 3$ and $x + y + z = 9$ if the planes $2x - y = 0$ and $3x - z = 0$ pass through the center of the sphere.

9. *Distance between planes*

    (a) Show that the distance between the parallel planes $Ax + By + Cz = D_1$ and $Ax + By + Cz = D_2$ is

$$d = \frac{|D_1 - D_2|}{|A\mathbf{i} + B\mathbf{j} + C\mathbf{k}|}.$$

    (b) Use the equation in part (a) to find the distance between the planes $2x + 3y - z = 6$ and $2x + 3y - z = 12$.

10. *Parallel planes* Find an equation for the plane parallel to the plane $2x - y + 2z = -4$ if the point $(3, 2, -1)$ is equidistant from the two planes.

11. *Coplanar points* Prove that four points A, B, C, and D are coplanar (lie in a common plane) if and only if $\overrightarrow{AD} \cdot (\overrightarrow{AB} \times \overrightarrow{BC}) = 0$.

12. *Triple vector products* The **triple vector products** $(\mathbf{u} \times \mathbf{v}) \times \mathbf{w}$ and $\mathbf{u} \times (\mathbf{v} \times \mathbf{w})$ are usually not equal, although the formulas for evaluating them from components are similar:

$$(\mathbf{u} \times \mathbf{v}) \times \mathbf{w} = (\mathbf{u} \cdot \mathbf{w})\mathbf{v} - (\mathbf{v} \cdot \mathbf{w})\mathbf{u}.$$
$$\mathbf{u} \times (\mathbf{v} \times \mathbf{w}) = (\mathbf{u} \cdot \mathbf{w})\mathbf{v} - (\mathbf{u} \cdot \mathbf{v})\mathbf{w}.$$

Verify each formula for the following vectors by evaluating its two sides and comparing the results.

$\mathbf{u}$	$\mathbf{v}$	$\mathbf{w}$
(a) $2\mathbf{i}$	$2\mathbf{j}$	$2\mathbf{k}$
(b) $\mathbf{i} - \mathbf{j} + \mathbf{k}$	$2\mathbf{i} + \mathbf{j} - 2\mathbf{k}$	$-\mathbf{i} + 2\mathbf{j} - \mathbf{k}$
(c) $2\mathbf{i} + \mathbf{j}$	$2\mathbf{i} - \mathbf{j} + \mathbf{k}$	$\mathbf{i} + 2\mathbf{k}$
(d) $\mathbf{i} + \mathbf{j} - 2\mathbf{k}$	$-\mathbf{i} - \mathbf{k}$	$2\mathbf{i} + 4\mathbf{j} - 2\mathbf{k}$

13. *Cross and dot products* Show that if $\mathbf{u}, \mathbf{v}, \mathbf{w}$, and $\mathbf{r}$ are any vectors, then

    (a) $\mathbf{u} \times (\mathbf{v} \times \mathbf{w}) + \mathbf{v} \times (\mathbf{w} \times \mathbf{u}) + \mathbf{w} \times (\mathbf{u} \times \mathbf{v}) = \mathbf{0}$

    (b) $\mathbf{u} \times \mathbf{v} = (\mathbf{u} \cdot \mathbf{v} \times \mathbf{i})\mathbf{i} + (\mathbf{u} \cdot \mathbf{v} \times \mathbf{j})\mathbf{j} + (\mathbf{u} \cdot \mathbf{v} \times \mathbf{k})\mathbf{k}$

    (c) $(\mathbf{u} \times \mathbf{v}) \cdot (\mathbf{w} \times \mathbf{r}) = \begin{vmatrix} \mathbf{u} \cdot \mathbf{w} & \mathbf{v} \cdot \mathbf{w} \\ \mathbf{u} \cdot \mathbf{r} & \mathbf{v} \cdot \mathbf{r} \end{vmatrix}$.

14. *Cross and dot products* Prove or disprove the formula

$$\mathbf{u} \times (\mathbf{u} \times (\mathbf{u} \times \mathbf{v})) \cdot \mathbf{w} = -|\mathbf{u}|^2 \mathbf{u} \cdot \mathbf{v} \times \mathbf{w}.$$

15. *The projection of a vector on a plane* Let P be a plane in space and let $\mathbf{v}$ be a vector. The vector projection of $\mathbf{v}$ onto the plane P, $\text{proj}_P \, \mathbf{v}$, can be defined informally as follows. Suppose that the sun is shining so that its rays are normal to the plane P. Then $\text{proj}_P \, \mathbf{v}$ is the "shadow" of $\mathbf{v}$ onto P. If P is the plane $x + 2y + 6z = 6$ and $\mathbf{v} = \mathbf{i} + \mathbf{j} + \mathbf{k}$, find $\text{proj}_P \, \mathbf{v}$.

16. *Trigonometry and vectors* By forming the cross product of two appropriate vectors, derive the trigonometric identity

$$\sin (A - B) = \sin A \cos B - \cos A \sin B.$$

17. *Point masses and gravitation* In physics, the law of gravitation says that if P and Q are (point) masses with mass M and m, respectively, then P is attracted to Q by the force

$$\mathbf{F} = \frac{GMm\mathbf{r}}{|\mathbf{r}|^3},$$

where $\mathbf{r}$ is the vector from P to Q and G is the universal gravitational constant. Moreover, if $Q_1, \ldots, Q_k$ are (point) masses with mass $m_1, \ldots, m_k$, respectively, then the force on P due to all the Q_i's is

$$\mathbf{F} = \sum_{i=1}^{k} \frac{GMm_i}{|\mathbf{r}_i|^3} \mathbf{r}_i,$$

where $\mathbf{r}_i$ is the vector from P to Q_i.

    (a) Let point P with mass M be located at the point $(0, d)$, $d > 0$, in the coordinate plane. For $i = -n, -n + 1, \ldots, -1, 0, 1, \ldots, n$, let Q_i be located at the point $(id, 0)$ and have mass mi. Find the magnitude of the gravitational force on P due to all the Q_i's.

    (b) Is the limit as $n \to \infty$ of the magnitude of the force on P finite? Why, or why not?

18. *Relativistic sums* Einstein's special theory of relativity roughly says that with respect to a reference frame (coordinate system) no material object can travel as fast as c, the speed of light. So, if $\overrightarrow{x}$ and $\overrightarrow{y}$ are two velocities such that $|\overrightarrow{x}| < c$ and $|\overrightarrow{y}| < c$, then the **relativistic sum** $\overrightarrow{x} \oplus \overrightarrow{y}$ of $\overrightarrow{x}$ and $\overrightarrow{y}$ must have length less than c. Einstein's special theory of relativity says that

$$\overrightarrow{x} \oplus \overrightarrow{y} = \frac{\overrightarrow{x} + \overrightarrow{y}}{1 + \dfrac{\overrightarrow{x} \cdot \overrightarrow{y}}{c^2}} + \frac{1}{c^2} \cdot \frac{\gamma_x}{\gamma_x + 1} \cdot \frac{\overrightarrow{x} \times (\overrightarrow{x} \times \overrightarrow{y})}{1 + \dfrac{\overrightarrow{x} \cdot \overrightarrow{y}}{c^2}},$$

where

$$\gamma_x = \frac{1}{\sqrt{1 - \dfrac{\overrightarrow{x} \cdot \overrightarrow{x}}{c^2}}}.$$

It can be shown that if $|\overrightarrow{x}| < c$ and $|\overrightarrow{y}| < c$, then $|\overrightarrow{x} \oplus \overrightarrow{y}| < c$. This exercise deals with two special cases.

    (a) Prove that if $\overrightarrow{x}$ and $\overrightarrow{y}$ are orthogonal, $|\overrightarrow{x}| < c, |\overrightarrow{y}| < c$, then $|\overrightarrow{x} \oplus \overrightarrow{y}| < c$.

    (b) Prove that if $\overrightarrow{x}$ and $\overrightarrow{y}$ are parallel, $|\overrightarrow{x}| < c, |\overrightarrow{y}| < c$, then $|\overrightarrow{x} \oplus \overrightarrow{y}| < c$.

    (c) Compute $\lim_{c \to \infty} \overrightarrow{x} \oplus \overrightarrow{y}$.

Polar Coordinate Systems and Motion in Space

19. *Minimum distance to sun* Deduce from the orbit equation

$$r = \frac{(1 + e)r_0}{1 + e \cos \theta}$$

that a planet is closest to its sun when $\theta = 0$ and show that $r = r_0$ at that time.

20. *A Kepler equation* The problem of locating a planet in its orbit at a given time and date eventually leads to solving "Kepler" equations of the form

$$f(x) = x - 1 - \frac{1}{2} \sin x = 0.$$

(a) Show that this particular equation has a solution between $x = 0$ and $x = 2$.

$\boxed{\text{T}}$ **(b)** With your computer or calculator in radian mode, use Newton's method to find the solution to as many places as you can.

21. In Section 10.8, we found the velocity of a particle moving in the plane to be

$$\mathbf{v} = \dot{x}\mathbf{i} + \dot{y}\mathbf{j} = \dot{r}\mathbf{u}_r + r\dot{\theta}\mathbf{u}_\theta.$$

(a) Express $\dot{x}$ and $\dot{y}$ in terms of $\dot{r}$ and $r\dot{\theta}$ by evaluating the dot products $\mathbf{v} \cdot \mathbf{i}$ and $\mathbf{v} \cdot \mathbf{j}$.

(b) Express $\dot{r}$ and $r\dot{\theta}$ in terms of $\dot{x}$ and $\dot{y}$ by evaluating the dot products $\mathbf{v} \cdot \mathbf{u}_r$ and $\mathbf{v} \cdot \mathbf{u}_\theta$.

22. *Curvature in polar coordinates* Express the curvature of a twice-differentiable curve $r = f(\theta)$ in the polar coordinate plane in terms of f and its derivatives.

23. *Beetle on rotating rod* A slender rod through the origin of the polar coordinate plane rotates (in the plane) about the origin at the rate of 3 rad/min. A beetle starting from the point (2, 0) crawls along the rod toward the origin at the rate of 1 in./min.

(a) Find the beetle's acceleration and velocity in polar form when it is halfway to (1 in. from) the origin.

(b) To the nearest tenth of an inch, what will be the length of the path the beetle has traveled by the time it reaches the origin?

24. *Conservation of angular momentum* Let $\mathbf{r}(t)$ denote the position in space of a moving object at time t. Suppose that the force acting on the object at time t is

$$\mathbf{F}(t) = -\frac{c}{|\mathbf{r}(t)|^3} \mathbf{r}(t),$$

where c is a constant. In physics, the **angular momentum** of an object at time t is defined to be $\mathbf{L}(t) = \mathbf{r}(t) \times m\mathbf{v}(t)$, where m is the mass of the object and $\mathbf{v}(t)$ is the velocity. Prove that angular momentum is a conserved quantity; that is, prove that $\mathbf{L}(t)$ is a constant vector, independent of time. Remember Newton's law $\mathbf{F} = m\mathbf{a}$. (This is a calculus problem, not a physics problem.)

11 Multivariable Functions and their Derivatives

OVERVIEW Functions with two or more independent variables appear more often in science than functions of a single variable, and their calculus is even richer. Their derivatives are more varied and more interesting because of the different ways in which the variables can interact. Their integrals lead to a greater variety of applications. The studies of probability, statistics, fluid dynamics, and electricity, to mention only a few, all lead in natural ways to functions of more than one variable. The mathematics of these functions is one of the finest achievements in science.

As we see in this chapter, the rules of calculus remain essentially the same as we move into higher dimensions. We need to keep track of multiple directions of change at the same time, necessitating some new notation that uses the vector notation of previous chapters, but fortunately we do not need to reinvent the theory. Indeed, the calculus of several variables is really single-variable calculus applied to several variables at once.

 ## Functions of Several Variables

Functions of Two Variables • Domains and Ranges • Graphs and Level Curves of Functions of Two Variables • Contour Curves • Computer Graphing • Functions of Three or More Variables • Level Surfaces of Functions of Three Variables

Many functions depend on more than one independent variable. The function $V = \pi r^2 h$ calculates the volume of a right circular cylinder from its radius and height. The function $f(x, y) = x^2 + y^2$ calculates the height of the paraboloid $z = x^2 + y^2$ above the point $P(x, y)$ from the two coordinates of P. The temperature T of a point on Earth's surface depends on its latitude x and longitude y, expressed by writing $T = f(x, y)$. In this section, we define functions of more than one independent variable and discuss ways to graph them.

Functions of Two Variables

The domains of real-valued functions of two independent real variables are sets of ordered pairs of real numbers, and the ranges are sets of real numbers of the kind we have worked with all along.

CD-ROM
WEBsite

Historical Essay

Multivariable Calculus

Definitions   Functions of Two Variables

Suppose that D is a set of ordered pairs of real numbers (x, y). A **real-valued function** f **of two variables** on D is a rule that assigns a unique real number

$$w = f(x, y)$$

to each ordered pair (x, y) in D. The set D is the **domain** of f, and the set of w-values taken on by f is its **range**. The **independent variables** x and y are the function's **input** variables, and the **dependent variable** w is the function's **output** variable.

In applications, we tend to use letters that remind us of what the variables stand for. To say that the volume of a right circular cylinder is a function of its radius and height, we might write $V = f(r, h)$. To be more specific, we might replace the notation $f(r, h)$ by the formula that calculates the value of V from the values of r and h, and write $V = \pi r^2 h$. In either case, r and h would be the independent variables and V the dependent variable of the function.

As usual, we evaluate functions defined by formulas by substituting the values of the independent variables in the formula and calculating the corresponding value of the dependent variable.

Example 1   Distance Function from the Origin to a Point in the Plane

When we use rectangular coordinates, the distance of a point (x, y) from the origin is given by the function $D(x, y) = \sqrt{x^2 + y^2}$. The value of D at the point $(3, 4)$ is $D(3, 4) = \sqrt{3^2 + 4^2} = \sqrt{25} = 5$.

Domains and Ranges

In defining functions of two variables, we follow the usual practice of excluding inputs that lead to complex numbers or division by zero. If $f(x, y) = \sqrt{y - x^2}$, y cannot be less than x^2. If $f(x, y) = 1/(xy)$, xy cannot be zero. The domains of functions are otherwise assumed to be the largest sets for which the defining rules generate real numbers. The range consists of the set of output values for the dependent variable.

Example 2   Identifying Domains and Ranges

	Function	**Domain**	**Range**
(a)	$w = \sqrt{y - x^2}$	$y \geq x^2$	$[0, \infty)$
(b)	$w = \dfrac{1}{xy}$	$xy \neq 0$	$(-\infty, 0) \cup (0, \infty)$
(c)	$w = \sin xy$	Entire plane	$[-1, 1]$

The domains of functions defined on portions of the plane can have interior points and boundary points just the way the domains of functions defined on intervals of the real line can.

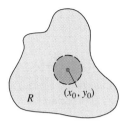

(a) Interior point

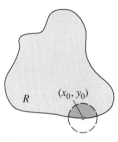

(b) Boundary point

FIGURE 11.1 Interior points and boundary points of a plane region R. An interior point is necessarily a point of R. A boundary point of R need not belong to R.

Definitions   Interior, Boundary, Open, Closed (2-space)

A point (x_0, y_0) in a region (set) R in the xy-plane is an **interior point** of R if it is the center of a disk that lies entirely in R (Figure 11.1). A point (x_0, y_0) is a **boundary point** of R if every disk centered at (x_0, y_0) contains points that lie outside of R as well as points that lie in R. (The boundary point itself need not belong to R.)

The interior points of a region, as a set, make up the **interior** of the region. The region's boundary points make up its **boundary.** A region is **open** if it consists entirely of interior points. A region is **closed** if it contains all its boundary points (Figure 11.2).

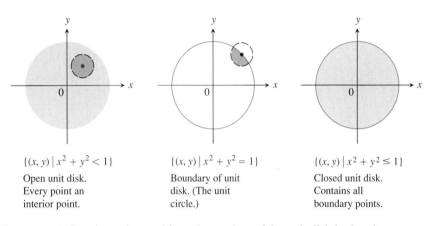

$\{(x, y) \mid x^2 + y^2 < 1\}$
Open unit disk.
Every point an
interior point.

$\{(x, y) \mid x^2 + y^2 = 1\}$
Boundary of unit
disk. (The unit
circle.)

$\{(x, y) \mid x^2 + y^2 \le 1\}$
Closed unit disk.
Contains all
boundary points.

FIGURE 11.2 Interior points and boundary points of the unit disk in the plane.

As with intervals of real numbers, some regions in the plane are neither open nor closed. If you start with the open disk in Figure 11.2 and add to it some of but not all its boundary points, the resulting set is neither open nor closed. The boundary points that *are* there keep the set from being open. The absence of the remaining boundary points keeps the set from being closed.

Definitions   Bounded and Unbounded Regions in the Plane

A region in the plane is **bounded** if it lies inside a disk of fixed radius. A region is **unbounded** if it is not bounded.

Examples of *bounded* sets in the plane include line segments, triangles, interiors of triangles, rectangles, circles, and disks. Examples of *unbounded* sets in the plane include lines, coordinate axes, the graphs of functions defined on infinite intervals, quadrants, half-planes, and the plane itself.

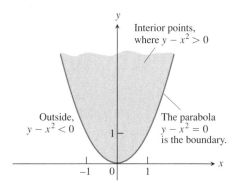

FIGURE 11.3 The domain of $f(x, y) = \sqrt{y - x^2}$ consists of the shaded region and its bounding parabola $y = x^2$. (Example 3)

CD-ROM
WEBsite

Example 3 Describing the Domain of a Function of Two Variables

Describe the domain of the function $f(x, y) = \sqrt{y - x^2}$.

Solution
Since f is defined only where $y - x^2 \geq 0$, the domain is the closed, unbounded region shown in Figure 11.3. The parabola $y = x^2$ is the boundary of the domain. The points above the parabola make up the domain's interior.

Graphs and Level Curves of Functions of Two Variables

There are two standard ways to picture the values of a function $f(x, y)$. One is to draw and label curves in the domain on which f has a constant value. The other is to sketch the surface $z = f(x, y)$ in space.

> **Definitions** Level Curve, Graph, Surface (Functions of Two Variables)
> The set of points in the plane where a function $f(x, y)$ has a constant value $f(x, y) = c$ is called a **level curve** of f. The set of all points $(x, y, f(x, y))$ in space, for (x, y) in the domain of f, is called the **graph** of f. The graph of f is also called the **surface $z = f(x, y)$.**

Example 4 Graphing a Function of Two Variables

Graph $f(x, y) = 100 - x^2 - y^2$ and plot the level curves $f(x, y) = 0$, $f(x, y) = 51$, and $f(x, y) = 75$ in the domain of f in the plane.

Solution
The domain of f is the entire xy-plane, and the range of f is the set of real numbers less than or equal to 100. The graph is the paraboloid $z = 100 - x^2 - y^2$, a portion of which is shown in Figure 11.4.

The level curve $f(x, y) = 0$ is the set of points in the xy-plane at which

$$f(x, y) = 100 - x^2 - y^2 = 0, \quad \text{or} \quad x^2 + y^2 = 100,$$

which is the circle of radius 10 centered at the origin. Similarly, the level curves $f(x, y) = 51$ and $f(x, y) = 75$ (Figure 11.4) are the circles

$$f(x, y) = 100 - x^2 - y^2 = 51, \quad \text{or} \quad x^2 + y^2 = 49$$
$$f(x, y) = 100 - x^2 - y^2 = 75, \quad \text{or} \quad x^2 + y^2 = 25.$$

The level curve $f(x, y) = 100$ consists of the origin alone. (It is still a level curve.)

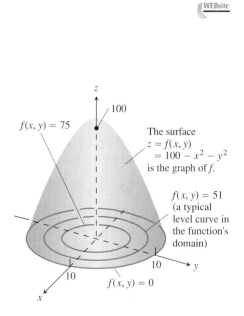

FIGURE 11.4 The graph and selected level curves of the function $f(x, y) = 100 - x^2 - y^2$. (Example 4)

Contour Curves

The curve in space in which the plane $z = c$ cuts a surface $z = f(x, y)$ is made up of the points that represent the function value $f(x, y) = c$. It is called the **contour curve** $f(x, y) = c$ to distinguish it from the level curve $f(x, y) = c$ in the domain of f. Figure 11.5 shows the contour curve $f(x, y) = 75$ on the surface $z = 100 - x^2 - y^2$ defined by the function $f(x, y) = 100 - x^2 - y^2$. The contour curve lies directly above the circle $x^2 + y^2 = 25$, which is the level curve $f(x, y) = 75$ in the function's domain.

The contour curve $f(x, y) = 100 - x^2 - y^2 = 75$ is the circle $x^2 + y^2 = 25$ in the plane $z = 75$.

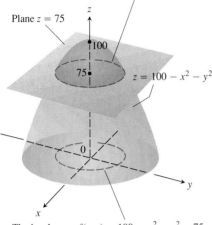

The level curve $f(x, y) = 100 - x^2 - y^2 = 75$ is the circle $x^2 + y^2 = 25$ in the xy-plane.

FIGURE 11.5 The graph of $f(x, y) = 100 - x^2 - y^2$ and its intersection with the plane $z = 75$.

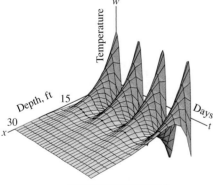

(Generated by Mathematica)

FIGURE 11.7 This computer-generated graph of

$$w = \cos (1.7 \times 10^{-2}t - 0.2x)e^{-0.2x}$$

shows the seasonal variation of the temperature below ground as a fraction of surface temperature. At $x = 15$ ft, the variation is only 5% of the variation at the surface. At $x = 30$ ft, the variation is less than 0.25% of the surface variation. (Example 5) (Adapted from art provided by Norton Starr.)

Not everyone makes this distinction, however, and you may wish to call both kinds of curves by a single name and rely on context to convey which one you have in mind. On most maps, for example, the curves that represent constant elevation (height above sea level) are called contours, not level curves (Figure 11.6).

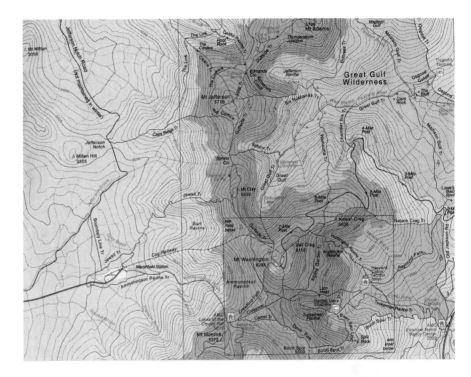

FIGURE 11.6 Contours on Mt. Washington in central New Hampshire.

Computer Graphing

Three-dimensional graphing programs for computers and calculators make it possible to graph functions of two variables with only a few keystrokes. We can often get information more quickly from a graph than from a formula.

Example 5   Modeling Temperature Beneath Earth's Surface

The temperature beneath Earth's surface is a function of the depth x beneath the surface and the time t of the year. If we measure x in feet and t as the number of days elapsed from the average date of the yearly highest surface temperature, we can model the variation in temperature with the function

$$w = \cos (1.7 \times 10^{-2}t - 0.2x) \, e^{-0.2x}.$$

(The temperature at 0 ft is scaled to vary from $+1$ to -1, so that the variation at x feet can be interpreted as a fraction of the variation at the surface.)

Figure 11.7 shows a computer-generated graph of the function. At a depth of 15 ft, the variation (change in vertical amplitude in the figure) is about 5% of the surface variation. At 30 ft, there is almost no variation during the year.

The graph also shows that the temperature 15 ft below the surface is about half a year out of phase with the surface temperature. When the temperature is lowest on the surface (late January, say), it is at its highest 15 ft below. Fifteen feet below the ground, the seasons are reversed.

Functions of Three or More Variables

A **function f of three variables** is a rule that assigns to each ordered triple (x, y, z) in some domain D in space a unique real number $w = f(x, y, z)$. Again the range consists of the output values for w. For instance, similar to Example 1, the function $D(x, y, z) = \sqrt{x^2 + y^2 + z^2}$ gives the distance from the origin to the point (x, y, z) in space for rectangular coordinates.

Example 6   Functions of Three Variables

	Function	Domain	Range
(a)	$w = \sqrt{x^2 + y^2 + z^2}$	Entire space	$[0, \infty)$
(b)	$w = \dfrac{1}{x^2 + y^2 + z^2}$	$(x, y, z) \neq (0, 0, 0)$	$(0, \infty)$
(c)	$w = xy \ln z$	Half-space $z > 0$	$(-\infty, \infty)$

CD-ROM
WEBsite

Level Surfaces of Functions of Three Variables

In the plane, the points where a function of two independent variables has a constant value $f(x, y) = c$ make a curve in the function's domain. In space, the points where a function of three independent variables has a constant value $f(x, y, z) = c$ make a surface in the function's domain.

> **Definition   Level Surface**
> The set of points (x, y, z) in space where a function of three independent variables has a constant value $f(x, y, z) = c$ is called a **level surface** of f.

Since the graphs of functions of three variables consist of points $(x, y, z, f(x, y, z))$ lying in a four-dimensional space, we cannot sketch them effectively in our three-dimensional frame of reference. We can see how the function behaves, however, by looking at its three-dimensional level surfaces.

Example 7   Describing Level Surfaces of a Function of Three Variables

Describe the level surfaces of the function

$$f(x, y, z) = \sqrt{x^2 + y^2 + z^2}.$$

Solution   The value of f is the distance from the origin to the point (x, y, z). Each level surface $\sqrt{x^2 + y^2 + z^2} = c$, $c > 0$, is a sphere of radius c centered at the origin. Figure 11.8 shows a cutaway view of three of these spheres. The level surface $\sqrt{x^2 + y^2 + z^2} = 0$ consists of the origin alone.

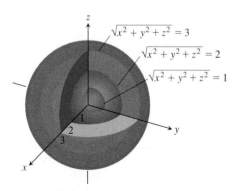

FIGURE 11.8 The level surfaces of $f(x, y, z) = \sqrt{x^2 + y^2 + z^2}$ are concentric spheres.

We are not graphing the function here; we are looking at level surfaces in the function's domain. The level surfaces show how the function's values change as we move through its domain. If we remain on a sphere of radius c centered at the origin, the function maintains a constant value, namely c. If we move from one sphere to another, the function's value changes. It increases if we move away from the origin and decreases if we move toward the origin. The way the values change depends on the direction we take. The dependence of change on direction is important. We return to it in Section 11.5.

The definitions of interior, boundary, open, closed, bounded, and unbounded for regions in space are similar to those for regions in the plane. To accommodate the extra dimension, we use solid spheres instead of disks.

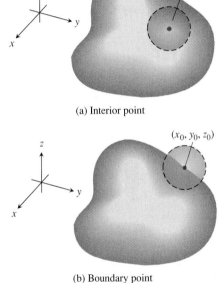

(a) Interior point

(b) Boundary point

FIGURE 11.9 Interior points and boundary points of a region in space.

> **Definitions**   Interior, Boundary, Open, Closed (3–space)
>
> A point (x_0, y_0, z_0) in a region R in space is an **interior point** of R if it is the center of a solid sphere that lies entirely in R (Figure 11.9a). A point (x_0, y_0, z_0) is a **boundary point** of R if every sphere centered at (x_0, y_0, z_0) encloses points that lie outside of R as well as points that lie inside R (Figure 11.9b). The **interior** of R is the set of interior points of R. The **boundary** of R is the set of boundary points of R.
>
> A region is **open** if it consists entirely of interior points. A region is **closed** if it contains its entire boundary.

Examples of *open* sets in space include the interior of a sphere, the open half-space $z > 0$, the first octant (where x, y, and z are all positive), and space itself.

Examples of *closed* sets in space include lines, planes, the closed half-space $z \geq 0$, the first octant together with its bounding planes, and space itself (since it has no boundary points).

A solid sphere with part of its boundary removed or a solid cube with a missing face, edge, or corner point would be *neither open nor closed*.

Functions of more than three independent variables are also important. For example, the temperature on a surface in space may depend not only on the location of the point $P(x, y, z)$ on the surface, but also on time t it is visited, so we would write $T = f(x, y, z, t)$.

In general, a **function f of n variables** is a rule that assigns to each n-tuple $(x_1, x_2, \ldots, x_n)$ of real numbers a unique real number $w = f(x_1, x_2, \ldots, x_n)$. The variables x_1 to x_n are the **independent (input)** variables, and w is the **dependent (output)** variable.

Functions of more than three variables are not easily visualized, but powerful mathematical methods have been developed to analyze them. You may study some of these methodologies in your advanced mathematics or science courses. In this text, we restrict our attention to functions of two or three independent variables, visualized by their graphs, level curves, or level surfaces, as appropriate.

EXERCISES 11.1

Domain, Range, and Level Curves

In Exercises 1–12,

    (a) Find the function's domain

    (b) Find the function's range

    (c) Describe the function's level curves

    (d) Find the boundary of the function's domain

    (e) Determine if the domain is an open region, a closed region, or neither

    (f) Decide if the domain is bounded or unbounded.

1. $f(x, y) = y - x$ **2.** $f(x, y) = \sqrt{y - x}$

3. $f(x, y) = 4x^2 + 9y^2$ **4.** $f(x, y) = x^2 - y^2$

5. $f(x, y) = xy$ **6.** $f(x, y) = y/x^2$

7. $f(x, y) = \dfrac{1}{\sqrt{16 - x^2 - y^2}}$ **8.** $f(x, y) = \sqrt{9 - x^2 - y^2}$

9. $f(x, y) = \ln(x^2 + y^2)$ **10.** $f(x, y) = e^{-(x^2 + y^2)}$

11. $f(x, y) = \sin^{-1}(y - x)$

12. $f(x, y) = \tan^{-1}\left(\dfrac{y}{x}\right)$

Identifying Surfaces and Level Curves

Execises 13–18 show level curves for the functions graphed in (a)–(f). Match each set of curves with the appropriate function.

13.   **14.**

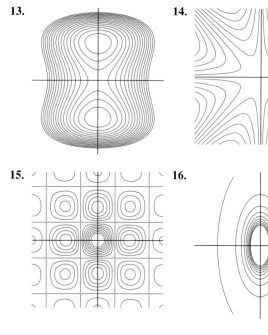

15.   **16.**

17.   **18.**

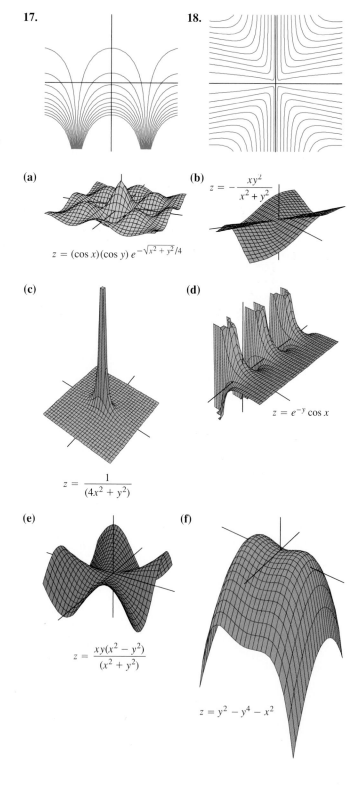

(a)

$z = (\cos x)(\cos y)\, e^{-\sqrt{x^2 + y^2}/4}$

(b) $z = -\dfrac{xy^2}{x^2 + y^2}$

(c)

$z = \dfrac{1}{(4x^2 + y^2)}$

(d) $z = e^{-y}\cos x$

(e)

$z = \dfrac{xy(x^2 - y^2)}{(x^2 + y^2)}$

(f)

$z = y^2 - y^4 - x^2$

Identifying Functions of Two Variables

Display the values of the functions in Exercises 19–28 in two ways: (a) by sketching the surface $z = f(x, y)$ and (b) by drawing an assortment of level curves in the function's domain. Label each level curve with its function value.

19. $f(x, y) = y^2$

20. $f(x, y) = 4 - y^2$

21. $f(x, y) = x^2 + y^2$

22. $f(x, y) = \sqrt{x^2 + y^2}$

23. $f(x, y) = -(x^2 + y^2)$

24. $f(x, y) = 4 - x^2 - y^2$

25. $f(x, y) = 4x^2 + y^2$

26. $f(x, y) = 4x^2 + y^2 + 1$

27. $f(x, y) = 1 - |y|$

28. $f(x, y) = 1 - |x| - |y|$

Finding a Level Curve

In Exercises 29–32, find an equation for the level curve of the function $f(x, y)$ that passes through the given point.

29. $f(x, y) = 16 - x^2 - y^2$, $(2\sqrt{2}, \sqrt{2})$

30. $f(x, y) = \sqrt{x^2 - 1}$, $(1, 0)$

31. $f(x, y) = \int_x^y \dfrac{dt}{1 + t^2}$, $(-\sqrt{2}, \sqrt{2})$

32. $f(x, y) = \sum_{n=0}^{\infty} \left(\dfrac{x}{y}\right)^n$, $(1, 2)$

Sketching Level Surfaces

In Exercises 33–40, sketch a typical level surface for the function.

33. $f(x, y, z) = x^2 + y^2 + z^2$

34. $f(x, y, z) = \ln(x^2 + y^2 + z^2)$

35. $f(x, y, z) = x + z$

36. $f(x, y, z) = z$

37. $f(x, y, z) = x^2 + y^2$

38. $f(x, y, z) = y^2 + z^2$

39. $f(x, y, z) = z - x^2 - y^2$

40. $f(x, y, z) = (x^2/25) + (y^2/16) + (z^2/9)$

Finding a Level Surface

In Exercises 41–44, find an equation for the level surface of the function through the given point.

41. $f(x, y, z) = \sqrt{x - y} - \ln z$, $(3, -1, 1)$

42. $f(x, y, z) = \ln(x^2 + y + z^2)$, $(-1, 2, 1)$

43. $g(x, y, z) = \sum_{n=0}^{\infty} \dfrac{(x + y)^n}{n!\, z^n}$, $(\ln 2, \ln 4, 3)$

44. $g(x, y, z) = \int_x^y \dfrac{d\theta}{\sqrt{1 - \theta^2}} + \int_{\sqrt{2}}^z \dfrac{dt}{t\sqrt{t^2 - 1}}$, $(0, 1/2, 2)$

Theory and Examples

45. *The maximum value of a function on a line in space* Does the function $f(x, y, z) = xyz$ have a maximum value on the line $x = 20 - t$, $y = t$, $z = 20$? If so, what is it? Give reasons for your answer. (*Hint:* Along the line, $w = f(x, y, z)$ is a differentiable function of t.)

46. *The minimum value of a function on a line in space* Does the function $f(x, y, z) = xy - z$ have a minimum value on the line $x = t - 1$, $y = t - 2$, $z = t + 7$? If so, what is it? Give reasons for your answer. (*Hint:* Along the line, $w = f(x, y, z)$ is a differentiable function of t.)

47. *The Concorde's sonic booms* The width w of the region in which people on the ground hear the *Concorde*'s sonic boom directly, not reflected from a layer in the atmosphere, is a function of

T = air temperature at ground level (in degrees Kelvin)

h = the *Concorde*'s altitude (in kilometers)

d = the vertical temperature gradient (temperature drop in degrees Kelvin per kilometer).

The formula for w is

$$w = 4\left(\frac{Th}{d}\right)^{1/2}.$$

See Figure 11.10.

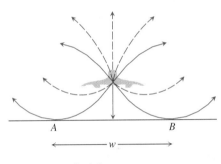

Sonic boom carpet

FIGURE 11.10 Sound waves from the *Concorde* bend as the temperature changes above and below the altitude at which the plane flies. The sonic boom carpet is the region on the ground that receives shock waves directly from the plane, not reflected from the atmosphere or diffracted along the ground. The carpet is determined by the grazing rays striking the ground from the point directly under the plane. (Exercise 47)

The Washington-bound *Concorde* approaches the United States from Europe on a course that takes it south of Nantucket Island at an altitude of 16.8 km. If the surface temperature is 290 K and the vertical temperature gradient is 5 K/km, how many kilometers south of Nantucket must the plane be flown to keep its sonic boom carpet away from the island? (From "Concorde Sonic Booms as an Atmospheric Probe" by N. K. Balachandra, W. L. Donn, and D. H. Rind, *Science*, Vol. 197 (July 1, 1977), pp. 47–49.)

48. *Writing to Learn* As you know, the graph of a real-valued function of a single real variable is a set in a two-coordinate space. The graph of a real-valued function of two independent real variables is a set in a three-coordinate space. The graph of a real-valued function of three independent real variables is a set in a four-coordinate space. How would you define the graph of a real-valued function $f(x_1, x_2, x_3, x_4)$ of four independent real variables? How would you define the graph of a real-valued function $f(x_1, x_2, x_3, \dots, x_n)$ of n independent real variables?

COMPUTER EXPLORATIONS

Explicit Surfaces

Use a CAS to perform the following steps for each of the functions in Exercises 49–52.

(a) Plot the surface over the given rectangle.

(b) Plot several level curves in the rectangle.

(c) Plot the level curve of f through the given point.

49. $f(x, y) = x \sin \dfrac{y}{2} + y \sin 2x, \quad 0 \le x \le 5\pi \quad 0 \le y \le 5\pi,$
$P(3\pi, 3\pi)$

50. $f(x, y) = (\sin x)(\cos y)\, e^{\sqrt{x^2+y^2}/8}, \quad 0 \le x \le 5\pi, \quad 0 \le y \le 5\pi,$
$P(4\pi, 4\pi)$

51. $f(x, y) = \sin(x + 2 \cos y), \quad -2\pi \le x \le 2\pi, \quad -2\pi \le y \le 2\pi,$
$P(\pi, \pi)$

52. $f(x, y) = e^{(x^{0.1}-y)} \sin(x^2 + y^2), \quad 0 \le x \le 2\pi, \quad -2\pi \le y \le \pi,$
$P(\pi, -\pi)$

Implicit Surfaces

CD-ROM
WEBsite

Use a CAS to plot the level surfaces in Exercises 53–56.

53. $4 \ln(x^2 + y^2 + z^2) = 1$

54. $x^2 + z^2 = 1$

55. $x + y^2 - 3z^2 = 1$

56. $\sin\left(\dfrac{x}{2}\right) - (\cos y)\sqrt{x^2 + z^2} = 2$

Parametrized Surfaces

Just as you describe curves in the plane parametrically with a pair of equations $x = f(t), y = g(t)$ defined on some parameter interval I, you can sometimes describe surfaces in space with a triple of equations $x = f(u, v), y = g(u, v), z = h(u, v)$ defined on some parameter rectangle $a \le u \le b, c \le v \le d$. Many computer algebra systems permit you to plot such surfaces in *parametric mode*. (Parametrized surfaces are discussed in detail in Section 13.6.) Use a CAS to plot the surfaces in Exercises 57–60. Also plot several level curves in the *xy*-plane.

57. $x = u \cos v, \quad y = u \sin v, \quad z = u, \quad 0 \le u \le 2, \quad 0 \le v \le 2\pi$

58. $x = u \cos v, \quad y = u \sin v, \quad z = v, \quad 0 \le u \le 2, \quad 0 \le v \le 2\pi$

59. $x = (2 + \cos u) \cos v, \quad y = (2 + \cos u) \sin v, \quad z = \sin u,$
$0 \le u \le 2\pi, \quad 0 \le v \le 2\pi$

60. $x = 2 \cos u \cos v, \quad y = 2 \cos u \sin v, \quad z = 2 \sin u,$
$0 \le u \le 2\pi, \quad 0 \le v \le \pi$

11.2 Limits and Continuity in Higher Dimensions

Limit of a Function of Two Variables • Continuity of a Function of Two Variables • Functions of More Than Two Variables • Extreme Values of Continuous Functions on Closed, Bounded Sets

This section treats limits and continuity for multivariable functions. The definition of the limit of a function of two or three variables is similar to the definition of the limit of a function of a single variable but with a crucial difference, as we now see.

Limit of a Function of Two Variables

If the values of a real-valued function $f(x, y)$ lie close to a fixed real number L for all points (x, y) sufficiently close to the point (x_0, y_0) but not equal to (x_0, y_0), we say that L is the limit of f as (x, y) approaches (x_0, y_0). In symbols, we write

$$\lim_{(x,y)\to(x_0,y_0)} f(x, y) = L,$$

and we say, "The limit of f as (x, y) approaches (x_0, y_0) equals L." This is like the limit of a function of one variable, except that two independent variables are involved instead of one, complicating the issue of "closeness." If (x_0, y_0) is an interior point of f's domain, (x, y) can approach (x_0, y_0) from any direction, whereas in the single-variable case, x only approached x_0 along the x-axis. The direction of approach can be an issue, as in some of the examples that follow.

Definition   Limit of a Function of Two Independent Variables
The function f **has limit** L as (x, y) approaches (x_0, y_0) if, given any positive number ϵ, there is a positive number δ such that for all (x, y) in the domain of f,

$$0 < \sqrt{(x - x_0)^2 + (y - y_0)^2} < \delta \implies |f(x, y) - L| < \epsilon.$$

We write

$$\lim_{(x,y) \to (x_0, y_0)} f(x, y) = L.$$

The δ-ϵ requirement in the definition of limit is equivalent to the requirement that, given $\epsilon > 0$, there exists a corresponding $\delta > 0$ such that for all x,

$$0 < |x - x_0| < \delta \quad \text{and} \quad 0 < |y - y_0| < \delta \implies |f(x, y) - L| < \epsilon$$

(Exercise 43). Thus, in calculating limits, we can think either in terms of distance in the plane or in terms of differences in coordinates.

The definition of limit applies to boundary points (x_0, y_0) as well as interior points of the domain of f. The only requirement is that the point (x, y) remain in the domain at all times.

It can be shown, as for functions of a single variable, that

$$\lim_{(x,y) \to (x_0, y_0)} x = x_0$$

$$\lim_{(x,y) \to (x_0, y_0)} y = y_0$$

$$\lim_{(x,y) \to (x_0, y_0)} k = k \qquad \text{(any number } k\text{)}.$$

It can also be shown that the limit of the sum of two functions is the sum of their limits (when they both exist), with similar results for the limits of the differences, products, constant multiples, quotients, and powers.

Theorem 1   Properties of Limits of Functions of Two Variables
The following rules hold if L, M, and k are real numbers and

$$\lim_{(x,y) \to (x_0, y_0)} f(x, y) = L \qquad \text{and} \qquad \lim_{(x,y) \to (x_0, y_0)} g(x, y) = M.$$

1. *Sum Rule:* $\displaystyle \lim_{(x,y) \to (x_0, y_0)} [f(x, y) + g(x, y)] = L + M$

2. *Difference Rule:* $\displaystyle \lim_{(x,y) \to (x_0, y_0)} [f(x, y) - g(x, y)] = L - M$

3. *Product Rule:* $\displaystyle \lim_{(x,y) \to (x_0, y_0)} f(x, y) \cdot g(x, y) = L \cdot M$

4. *Constant Multiple Rule:* $\displaystyle \lim_{(x,y) \to (x_0, y_0)} k f(x, y) = k L$ (any number k)

5. *Quotient Rule:* $\displaystyle \lim_{(x,y) \to (x_0, y_0)} \frac{f(x, y)}{g(x, y)} = \frac{L}{M}$ if $M \neq 0$.

6. *Power Rule:* If m and n are integers, then

$$\lim_{(x,y) \to (x_0, y_0)} [f(x, y)]^{m/n} = L^{m/n},$$

provided $L^{m/n}$ is a real number.

When we apply Theorem 1 to polynomials and rational functions, we obtain the useful result that the limits of these functions as $(x, y) \to (x_0, y_0)$ can be calculated by evaluating the functions at (x_0, y_0). The only requirement is that the rational functions be defined at (x_0, y_0).

Example 1   Calculating Limits

(a) $\displaystyle \lim_{(x,y)\to(0,1)} \frac{x - xy + 3}{x^2 y + 5xy - y^3} = \frac{0 - (0)(1) + 3}{(0)^2(1) + 5(0)(1) - (1)^3} = -3$

(b) $\displaystyle \lim_{(x,y)\to(3,-4)} \sqrt{x^2 + y^2} = \sqrt{(3)^2 + (-4)^2} = \sqrt{25} = 5$

Example 2   Calculating Limits

Find

$$\lim_{(x,y)\to(0,0)} \frac{x^2 - xy}{\sqrt{x} - \sqrt{y}}.$$

Solution   Since the denominator $\sqrt{x} - \sqrt{y}$ approaches 0 as $(x, y) \to (0, 0)$, we cannot use the Quotient Rule from Theorem 1. If we multiply numerator and denominator by $\sqrt{x} + \sqrt{y}$, however, we produce an equivalent fraction whose limit we *can* find:

We can cancel the factor $(x - y)$ in Example 2 because the path $y = x$ (along which $x - y = 0$) is *not* in the domain of the function

$$\frac{x^2 - xy}{\sqrt{x} - \sqrt{y}}.$$

$$\lim_{(x,y)\to(0,0)} \frac{x^2 - xy}{\sqrt{x} - \sqrt{y}} = \lim_{(x,y)\to(0,0)} \frac{(x^2 - xy)(\sqrt{x} + \sqrt{y})}{(\sqrt{x} - \sqrt{y})(\sqrt{x} + \sqrt{y})}$$

$$= \lim_{(x,y)\to(0,0)} \frac{x(x - y)(\sqrt{x} + \sqrt{y})}{x - y} \qquad \text{Algebra}$$

$$= \lim_{(x,y)\to(0,0)} x(\sqrt{x} + \sqrt{y}) \qquad \begin{array}{l}\text{Cancel the factor}\\ (x - y).\end{array}$$

$$= 0(\sqrt{0} + \sqrt{0}) = 0$$

Continuity of a Function of Two Variables

The definition of continuity for functions of two variables is essentially the same as for functions of a single variable.

Definitions   Continuity at a Point, Continuity

A function $f(x, y)$ is **continuous at the point** (x_0, y_0) if

1. f is defined at (x_0, y_0)

2. $\lim_{(x, y)\to(x_0, y_0)} f(x, y)$ exists

3. $\lim_{(x, y)\to(x_0, y_0)} f(x, y) = f(x_0, y_0)$.

A function is **continuous** if it is continuous at every point of its domain.

As with the definition of limit, the definition of continuity applies at boundary points as well as interior points of the domain of f. The only requirement is that the point (x, y) remain in the domain at all times.

As you may have guessed, one of the consequences of Theorem 1 is that algebraic combinations of continuous functions are continuous at every point at which all the functions involved are defined. Hence, sums, differences, products, constant multiples, quotients, and powers of continuous functions are continuous where defined. In particular, polynomials and rational functions of two variables are continuous at every point at which they are defined.

If $z = f(x, y)$ is a continuous function of x and y, and $w = g(z)$ is a continuous function of z, then the composite $w = g(f(x, y))$ is continuous. Thus,

$$e^{x-y}, \qquad \cos \frac{xy}{x^2 + 1}, \qquad \ln (1 + x^2y^2)$$

are continuous at every point (x, y).

As with functions of a single variable, the general rule is that composites of continuous functions are continuous. The only requirement is that each function be continuous where it is applied.

Example 3 A Function with a Single Point of Discontinuity

Show that

$$f(x, y) = \begin{cases} \dfrac{2xy}{x^2 + y^2}, & (x, y) \neq (0, 0) \\ 0, & (x, y) = (0, 0) \end{cases}$$

is continuous at every point except the origin (Figure 11.11).

Solution   The function f is continuous at any point $(x, y) \neq (0, 0)$ because its values are then given by a rational function of x and y.

At $(0, 0)$, the value of f is defined, but f, we claim, has no limit as $(x, y) \rightarrow (0, 0)$. The reason is that different paths of approach to the origin can lead to different results, as we now see.

For every value of m, the function f has a constant value on the "punctured" line $y = mx$, $x \neq 0$, because

$$f(x, y)\Big|_{y=mx} = \frac{2xy}{x^2 + y^2}\Big|_{y=mx} = \frac{2x(mx)}{x^2 + (mx)^2} = \frac{2mx^2}{x^2 + m^2x^2} = \frac{2m}{1 + m^2}.$$

Therefore, f has this number as its limit as (x, y) approaches $(0, 0)$ along the line:

$$\lim_{\substack{(x,y)\to(0,0) \\ \text{along } y=mx}} f(x, y) = \lim_{(x,y)\to(0,0)} \left[f(x, y)\Big|_{y=mx} \right] = \frac{2m}{1 + m^2}.$$

This limit changes with m. There is therefore no single number we may call the limit of f as (x, y) approaches the origin. The limit fails to exist, and the function is not continuous.

Example 3 illustrates an important point about limits of functions of two variables (or even more variables, for that matter). For a limit to exist at a point, the limit must be the same along every approach path. This result is analogous to the single-variable case where both the left- and right-sided limits had to have the same value therefore, for functions of two or more variables, if we ever find paths with different limits, we know the function has no limit at the point they approach.

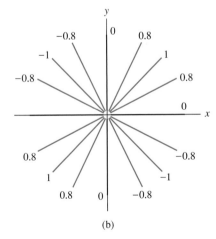

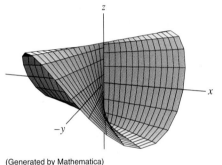

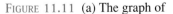

Figure 11.11 (a) The graph of

$$f(x, y) = \begin{cases} \dfrac{2xy}{x^2 + y^2}, & (x, y) \neq (0, 0) \\ 0, & (x, y) = (0, 0). \end{cases}$$

The function is continuous at every point except the origin. (b) The level curves of f. (Example 3)

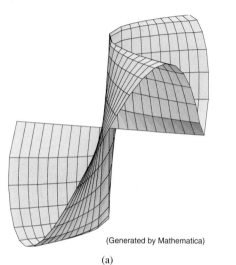

(Generated by Mathematica)

(a)

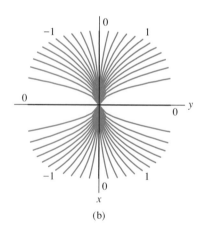

(b)

FIGURE 11.12 (a) The graph of $f(x, y) = 2x^2y/(x^4 + y^2)$. As the graph suggests and the level-curve values in part (b) confirm, $\lim_{(x,y)\to(0,0)} f(x, y)$ does not exist. (Example 4)

> **Two-Path Test for Nonexistence of a Limit**
> If a function $f(x, y)$ has different limits along two different paths as (x, y) approaches (x_0, y_0), then $\lim_{(x,y)\to(x_0,y_0)} f(x, y)$ does not exist.

Example 4 Applying the Two-Path Test

Show that the function

$$f(x, y) = \frac{2x^2y}{x^4 + y^2}$$

(Figure 11.12) has no limit as (x, y) approaches $(0, 0)$.

Solution Along the curve $y = kx^2$, $x \neq 0$, the function has the constant value

$$f(x, y)\Big|_{y=kx^2} = \frac{2x^2y}{x^4 + y^2}\Big|_{y=kx^2} = \frac{2x^2(kx^2)}{x^4 + (kx^2)^2} = \frac{2kx^4}{x^4 + k^2x^4} = \frac{2k}{1 + k^2}.$$

Therefore,

$$\lim_{\substack{(x,y)\to(0,0) \\ \text{along } y=kx^2}} f(x, y) = \lim_{(x,y)\to(0,0)} \left[f(x, y)\Big|_{y=kx^2} \right] = \frac{2k}{1 + k^2}.$$

This limit varies with the path of approach. If (x, y) approaches $(0, 0)$ along the parabola $y = x^2$, for instance, $k = 1$ and the limit is 1. If (x, y) approaches $(0, 0)$ along the x-axis, $k = 0$ and the limit is 0. By the two-path test, f has no limit as (x, y) approaches $(0, 0)$.

The language here may seem contradictory. You might well ask, "What do you mean f has no limit as (x, y) approaches the origin—it has lots of limits." But that is the point. There is no single path-independent limit, and therefore, by the definition, $\lim_{(x,y)\to(0,0)} f(x, y)$ does not exist. It is our translating this formal statement into the more colloquial "has no limit" that creates the apparent contradiction. The mathematics is fine. The problem arises in how we talk about it. We need the formality to keep things straight.

Functions of More Than Two Variables

The definitions of limit and continuity for functions of two variables and the conclusions about limits and continuity for sums, products, quotients, powers, and composites all extend to functions of three or more variables. Functions like

$$\ln (x + y + z) \qquad \text{and} \qquad \frac{y \sin z}{x - 1}$$

are continuous throughout their domains, and limits like

$$\lim_{P\to(1,0,-1)} \frac{e^{x+z}}{z^2 + \cos \sqrt{xy}} = \frac{e^{1-1}}{(-1)^2 + \cos 0} = \frac{1}{2},$$

where P denotes the point (x, y, z), may be found by direct substitution.

Extreme Values of Continuous Functions on Closed, Bounded Sets

We have seen that a function of a single variable that is continuous throughout a closed, bounded interval $[a, b]$ takes on an absolute maximum value and an absolute minimum value at least once in $[a, b]$. The same is true of a function $z = f(x, y)$ that is continuous on a closed, bounded set R in the plane (like a line segment, a disk, or a filled-in triangle). The function takes on an absolute maximum value at some point in R and an absolute minimum value at some point in R.

Theorems similar to these and other theorems of this section hold for functions of three or more variables. A continuous function $w = f(x, y, z)$, for example, must take on absolute maximum and minimum values on any closed, bounded set (solid ball or cube, spherical shell, rectangular solid) on which it is defined.

We learn how to find these extreme values when we get to Section 11.8, but first we need to know about derivatives in higher dimensions. That is the topic of the next section.

EXERCISES 11.2

Limits with Two Variables

Find the limits in Exercises 1–12.

1. $\displaystyle\lim_{(x,y)\to(0,0)} \frac{3x^2 - y^2 + 5}{x^2 + y^2 + 2}$

2. $\displaystyle\lim_{(x,y)\to(0,4)} \frac{x}{\sqrt{y}}$

3. $\displaystyle\lim_{(x,y)\to(3,4)} \sqrt{x^2 + y^2 - 1}$

4. $\displaystyle\lim_{(x,y)\to(2,-3)} \left(\frac{1}{x} + \frac{1}{y}\right)^2$

5. $\displaystyle\lim_{(x,y)\to(0,\pi/4)} \sec x \tan y$

6. $\displaystyle\lim_{(x,y)\to(0,0)} \cos \frac{x^2 + y^3}{x + y + 1}$

7. $\displaystyle\lim_{(x,y)\to(0,\ln2)} e^{x-y}$

8. $\displaystyle\lim_{(x,y)\to(1,1)} \ln |1 + x^2 y^2|$

9. $\displaystyle\lim_{(x,y)\to(0,0)} \frac{e^y \sin x}{x}$

10. $\displaystyle\lim_{(x,y)\to(1,1)} \cos \sqrt[3]{|xy| - 1}$

11. $\displaystyle\lim_{(x,y)\to(1,0)} \frac{x \sin y}{x^2 + 1}$

12. $\displaystyle\lim_{(x,y)\to(\pi/2,0)} \frac{\cos y + 1}{y - \sin x}$

Limits of Quotients

Find the limits in Exercises 13–20 by rewriting the fractions first.

13. $\displaystyle\lim_{\substack{(x,y)\to(1,1) \\ x\neq y}} \frac{x^2 - 2xy + y^2}{x - y}$

14. $\displaystyle\lim_{\substack{(x,y)\to(1,1) \\ x\neq y}} \frac{x^2 - y^2}{x - y}$

15. $\displaystyle\lim_{\substack{(x,y)\to(1,1) \\ x\neq 1}} \frac{xy - y - 2x + 2}{x - 1}$

16. $\displaystyle\lim_{\substack{(x,y)\to(2,-4) \\ y\neq -4, x\neq x^2}} \frac{y + 4}{x^2 y - xy + 4x^2 - 4x}$

17. $\displaystyle\lim_{\substack{(x,y)\to(0,0) \\ x\neq y}} \frac{x - y + 2\sqrt{x} - 2\sqrt{y}}{\sqrt{x} - \sqrt{y}}$

18. $\displaystyle\lim_{\substack{(x,y)\to(2,2) \\ x+y\neq 4}} \frac{x + y - 4}{\sqrt{x + y} - 2}$

19. $\displaystyle\lim_{\substack{(x,y)\to(2,0) \\ 2x-y\neq 4}} \frac{\sqrt{2x - y} - 2}{2x - y - 4}$

20. $\displaystyle\lim_{\substack{(x,y)\to(4,3) \\ x\neq y+1}} \frac{\sqrt{x} - \sqrt{y + 1}}{x - y - 1}$

Limits with Three Variables

Find the limits in Exercises 21–26.

21. $\displaystyle\lim_{P\to(1,3,4)} \left(\frac{1}{x} + \frac{1}{y} + \frac{1}{z}\right)$

22. $\displaystyle\lim_{P\to(1,-1,-1)} \frac{2xy + yz}{x^2 + z^2}$

23. $\displaystyle\lim_{P\to(3,3,0)} (\sin^2 x + \cos^2 y + \sec^2 z)$

24. $\displaystyle\lim_{P\to(-1/4,\pi/2,2)} \tan^{-1} xyz$

25. $\displaystyle\lim_{P\to(\pi,0,3)} ze^{-2y} \cos 2x$

26. $\displaystyle\lim_{P\to(0,-2,0)} \ln \sqrt{x^2 + y^2 + z^2}$

Continuity in the Plane

At what points (x, y) in the plane are the functions in Exercise 27–30 continuous?

27. (a) $f(x, y) = \sin(x + y)$ **(b)** $f(x, y) = \ln(x^2 + y^2)$

28. (a) $f(x, y) = \dfrac{x + y}{x - y}$ **(b)** $f(x, y) = \dfrac{y}{x^2 + 1}$

29. (a) $g(x, y) = \sin \dfrac{1}{xy}$ **(b)** $g(x, y) = \dfrac{x + y}{2 + \cos x}$

30. (a) $g(x, y) = \dfrac{x^2 + y^2}{x^2 - 3x + 2}$ **(b)** $g(x, y) = \dfrac{1}{x^2 - y}$

Continuity in Space

At what points (x, y, z) in space are the functions in Exercises 31–34 continuous?

31. (a) $f(x, y, z) = x^2 + y^2 - 2z^2$

  (b) $f(x, y, z) = \sqrt{x^2 + y^2 - 1}$

32. (a) $f(x, y, z) = \ln xyz$ (b) $f(x, y, z) = e^{x+y} \cos z$

33. (a) $h(x, y, z) = xy \sin \dfrac{1}{z}$ (b) $h(x, y, z) = \dfrac{1}{x^2 + z^2 - 1}$

34. (a) $h(x, y, z) = \dfrac{1}{|y| + |z|}$ (b) $h(x, y, z) = \dfrac{1}{|xy| + |z|}$

Applying the Two-Path Test

By considering different paths of approach, show that the functions in Exercises 35–42 have no limit as $(x, y) \to (0, 0)$.

35. $f(x, y) = -\dfrac{x}{\sqrt{x^2 + y^2}}$ **36.** $f(x, y) = \dfrac{x^4}{x^4 + y^2}$

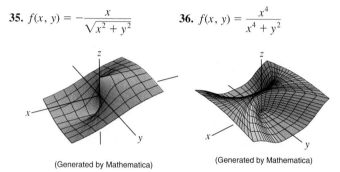

(Generated by Mathematica)   (Generated by Mathematica)

37. $f(x, y) = \dfrac{x^4 - y^2}{x^4 + y^2}$ **38.** $f(x, y) = \dfrac{xy}{|xy|}$

39. $g(x, y) = \dfrac{x - y}{x + y}$ **40.** $g(x, y) = \dfrac{x + y}{x - y}$

41. $h(x, y) = \dfrac{x^2 + y}{y}$ **42.** $h(x, y) = \dfrac{x^2}{x^2 - y}$

Using the δ-ϵ Definition

43. Show that the δ-ϵ requirement in the definition of limit is equivalent to

$$0 < |x - x_0| < \delta \quad \text{and} \quad 0 < |y - y_0| < \delta \Rightarrow |f(x, y) - L| < \epsilon.$$

44. Using the formal δ-ϵ definition of limit of a function $f(x, y)$ as $(x, y) \to (x_0, y_0)$ as a guide, state a formal definition for the limit of a function $g(x, y, z)$ as $(x, y, z) \to (x_0, y_0, z_0)$. What would be the analogous definition for a function $h(x, y, z, t)$ of four independent variables?

Each of Exercises 45–48 gives a function $f(x, y)$ and a positive number ϵ. In each exercise, either show that there exists a $\delta > 0$ such that for all (x, y),

$$\sqrt{x^2 + y^2} < \delta \Rightarrow |f(x, y) - f(0, 0)| < \epsilon$$

or show that there exists a $\delta > 0$ such that for all (x, y),

$$|x| < \delta \quad \text{and} \quad |y| < \delta \Rightarrow |f(x, y) - f(0, 0)| < \epsilon.$$

Do either one or the other, whichever seems more convenient. There is no need to do both.

45. $f(x, y) = x^2 + y^2, \quad \epsilon = 0.01$

46. $f(x, y) = y/(x^2 + 1), \quad \epsilon = 0.05$

47. $f(x, y) = (x + y)/(x^2 + 1), \quad \epsilon = 0.01$

48. $f(x, y) = (x + y)/(2 + \cos x), \quad \epsilon = 0.02$

Each of Exercises 49–52 gives a function $f(x, y, z)$ and a positive number ϵ. In each exercise, either show that there exists a $\delta > 0$ such that for all (x, y, z),

$$\sqrt{x^2 + y^2 + z^2} < \delta \Rightarrow |f(x, y, z) - f(0, 0, 0)| < \epsilon$$

or show that there exists a $\delta > 0$ such that for all (x, y, z),

$$|x| < \delta, \quad |y| < \delta, \quad \text{and} \quad |z| < \delta \Rightarrow |f(x, y, z) - f(0, 0, 0)| < \epsilon.$$

Do either one or the other, whichever seems more convenient. There is no need to do both.

49. $f(x, y, z) = x^2 + y^2 + z^2, \quad \epsilon = 0.015$

50. $f(x, y, z) = xyz, \quad \epsilon = 0.008$

51. $f(x, y, z) = \dfrac{x + y + z}{x^2 + y^2 + z^2 + 1}, \quad \epsilon = 0.015$

52. $f(x, y, z) = \tan^2 x + \tan^2 y + \tan^2 z, \quad \epsilon = 0.03$

53. Show that $f(x, y, z) = x + y - z$ is continuous at every point (x_0, y_0, z_0).

54. Show that $f(x, y, z) = x^2 + y^2 + z^2$ is continuous at the origin.

Changing to Polar Coordinates

If you cannot make any headway with $\lim_{(x,y)\to(0,0)} f(x, y)$ in rectangular coordinates, try changing to polar coordinates. Substitute $x = r \cos \theta$, $y = r \sin \theta$ and investigate the limit of the resulting expression as $r \to 0$. In other words, try to decide whether there exists a number L satisfying the following criterion:

Given $\epsilon > 0$, there exists a $\delta > 0$ such that for all r and θ,

$$|r| < \delta \Rightarrow |f(r, \theta) - L| < \epsilon. \tag{1}$$

If such an L exists, then

$$\lim_{(x,y)\to(0,0)} f(x, y) = \lim_{r\to0} f(r, \theta) = L.$$

For instance,

$$\lim_{(x,y)\to(0,0)} \frac{x^3}{x^2 + y^2} = \lim_{r\to0} \frac{r^3 \cos^3 \theta}{r^2} = \lim_{r\to0} r \cos^3 \theta = 0.$$

To verify the last of these equalities, we need to show that Equation (1) is satisfied with $f(r, \theta) = r \cos^3 \theta$ and $L = 0$. That is, we need to show that given any $\epsilon > 0$ there exists a $\delta > 0$ such that for all r and θ,

$$|r| < \delta \Rightarrow |r \cos^3 \theta - 0| < \epsilon.$$

Since

$$|r \cos^3 \theta| = |r| |\cos^3 \theta| \leq |r| \cdot 1 = |r|,$$

the implication holds for all r and θ if we take $\delta = \epsilon$.

In contrast,

$$\frac{x^2}{x^2 + y^2} = \frac{r^2 \cos^2 \theta}{r^2} = \cos^2 \theta$$

takes on all values from 0 to 1 regardless of how small $|r|$ is, so that $\lim_{(x,y)\to(0,0)} x^2/(x^2 + y^2)$ does not exist.

In each of these instances, the existence or nonexistence of the limit as $r \to 0$ is fairly clear. Shifting to polar coordinates does not always help, however, and may even tempt us to false conclusions. For example, the limit may exist along every straight line (or ray) $\theta = $ constant and yet fail to exist in the broader sense. Example 4 illustrates this point. In polar coordinates, $f(x, y) = (2x^2y)/(x^4 + y^2)$ becomes

$$f(r \cos \theta, r \sin \theta) = \frac{r \cos \theta \sin 2\theta}{r^2 \cos^4 \theta + \sin^2 \theta}$$

for $r \neq 0$. If we hold θ constant and let $r \to 0$, the limit is 0. On the path $y = x^2$, however, we have $r \sin \theta = r^2 \cos^2 \theta$ and

$$f(r \cos \theta, r \sin \theta) = \frac{r \cos \theta \sin 2\theta}{r^2 \cos^4 \theta + (r \cos^2 \theta)^2}$$

$$= \frac{2r \cos^2 \theta \sin \theta}{2r^2 \cos^4 \theta} = \frac{r \sin \theta}{r^2 \cos^2 \theta} = 1.$$

In Exercises 55–60, find the limit of f as $(x, y) \to (0, 0)$ or show that the limit does not exist.

55. $f(x, y) = \dfrac{x^3 - xy^2}{x^2 + y^2}$

56. $f(x, y) = \cos \left(\dfrac{x^3 - y^3}{x^2 + y^2} \right)$

57. $f(x, y) = \dfrac{y^2}{x^2 + y^2}$

58. $f(x, y) = \dfrac{2x}{x^2 + x + y^2}$

59. $f(x, y) = \tan^{-1} \left(\dfrac{|x| + |y|}{x^2 + y^2} \right)$

60. $f(x, y) = \dfrac{x^2 - y^2}{x^2 + y^2}$

In Exercises 61 and 62, define $f(0, 0)$ in a way that extends f to be continuous at the origin.

61. $f(x, y) = \ln \left(\dfrac{3x^2 - x^2y^2 + 3y^2}{x^2 + y^2} \right)$

62. $f(x, y) = \dfrac{2xy^2}{x^2 + y^2}$

Theory and Examples

63. *Writing to Learn* If $\lim_{(x,y)\to(x_0,y_0)} f(x, y) = L$, must f be defined at (x_0, y_0)? Give reasons for your answer.

64. *Writing to Learn* If $f(x_0, y_0) = 3$, what can you say about

$$\lim_{(x,y)\to(x_0,y_0)} f(x, y)$$

if f is continuous at (x_0, y_0)? If f is not continuous at (x_0, y_0)? Give reasons for your answer.

65. *(Continuation of Example 3)*

(a) Reread Example 3. Then substitute $m = \tan \theta$ into the formula

$$f(x, y) \Big|_{y=mx} = \frac{2m}{1 + m^2}$$

and simplify the result to show how the value of f varies with the line's angle of inclination.

(b) Use the formula you obtained in part (a) to show that the limit of f as $(x, y) \to (0, 0)$ along the line $y = mx$ varies from -1 to 1 depending on the angle of approach.

66. *Continuous extension* Define $f(0, 0)$ in a way that extends

$$f(x, y) = xy \frac{x^2 - y^2}{x^2 + y^2}$$

to be continuous at the origin.

The Sandwich Theorem

The Sandwich Theorem for functions of two variables states that if $g(x, y) \leq f(x, y) \leq h(x, y)$ for all $(x, y) \neq (x_0, y_0)$ in a disk centered at (x_0, y_0) and if g and h have the same finite limit L as $(x, y) \to (x_0, y_0)$, then

$$\lim_{(x,y)\to(x_0,y_0)} f(x, y) = L.$$

Use this result to support your answers to the questions in Exercises 67–70.

67. *Writing to Learn* Does knowing that

$$1 - \frac{x^2 y^2}{3} < \frac{\tan^{-1} xy}{xy} < 1$$

tell you anything about

$$\lim_{(x,y)\to(0,0)} \frac{\tan^{-1} xy}{xy}?$$

Give reasons for your answer.

68. *Writing to Learn* Does knowing that

$$2|xy| - \frac{x^2 y^2}{6} < 4 - 4 \cos \sqrt{|xy|} < 2|xy|$$

tell you anything about

$$\lim_{(x,y)\to(0,0)} \frac{4 - 4 \cos \sqrt{|xy|}}{|xy|}?$$

Give reasons for your answer.

69. *Writing to Learn* Does knowing that $|\sin (1/x)| \leq 1$ tell you anything about

$$\lim_{(x,y)\to(0,0)} y \sin \frac{1}{x}?$$

Give reasons for your answer.

70. *Writing to Learn*   Does knowing that $|\cos(1/y)| \le 1$ tell you anything about

$$\lim_{(x,y)\to(0,0)} x \cos \frac{1}{y}?$$

Give reasons for your answer.

COMPUTER EXPLORATIONS

71. Explore the graphs of the four functions whose limits you considered in Exercises 67–70. Try to find a view that supports your results in those exercises.

11.3 Partial Derivatives

Partial Derivatives of a Function of Two Variables   •   Calculations   •
Functions of More than Two Variables   •   Partial Derivatives and
Continuity   •   Second-Order Partial Derivatives   •   The Mixed Derivative
Theorem   •   Partial Derivatives of Still Higher Order   •   Differentiability

When we hold all but one of the independent variables of a function constant and differentiate with respect to that one variable, we get a "partial" derivative. This section shows how partial derivatives arise and how to calculate partial derivatives by applying the rules for differentiating functions of a single variable.

Partial Derivatives of a Function of Two Variables

If (x_0, y_0) is a point in the domain of a function $f(x, y)$, the vertical plane $y = y_0$ will cut the surface $z = f(x, y)$ in the curve $z = f(x, y_0)$ (Figure 11.13). This curve is the graph of the function $z = f(x, y_0)$ in the plane $y = y_0$. The horizontal coordinate in this plane is x; the vertical coordinate is z.

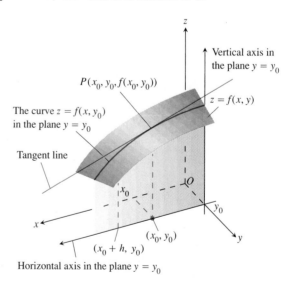

FIGURE 11.13 The intersection of the plane $y = y_0$ with the surface $z = f(x, y)$, viewed from a point above the first quadrant of the xy-plane.

We define the partial derivative of f with respect to x at the point (x_0, y_0) as the ordinary derivative of $f(x, y_0)$ with respect to x at the point $x = x_0$.

Definition Partial Derivative with Respect to x

The **partial derivative of** $f(x, y)$ **with respect to** x at the point (x_0, y_0) is

$$\frac{\partial f}{\partial x}\bigg|_{(x_0, y_0)} = \frac{d}{dx} f(x, y_0)\bigg|_{x = x_0} = \lim_{h \to 0} \frac{f(x_0 + h, y_0) - f(x_0, y_0)}{h},$$

provided the limit exists.

The stylized "∂" (similar to the lowercase Greek letter "δ" used in the limit definition) is just another kind of "d." It is convenient to have this distinguishable way of extending the Leibniz differential notation into a multivariable context.

The slope of the curve $z = f(x, y_0)$ at the point $P(x_0, y_0, f(x_0, y_0))$ in the plane $y = y_0$ is the value of the partial derivative of f with respect to x at (x_0, y_0). The tangent line to the curve at P is the line in the plane $y = y_0$ that passes through P with this slope. The partial derivative $\partial f / \partial x$ at (x_0, y_0) gives the rate of change of f with respect to x when y is held fixed at the value y_0. This is the rate of change of f in the direction of **i** at (x_0, y_0).

The notation for a partial derivative depends on what we want to emphasize:

$\dfrac{\partial f}{\partial x}(x_0, y_0)$ or $f_x(x_0, y_0)$ "Partial derivative of f with respect to x at (x_0, y_0)" or "f sub x at (x_0, y_0)." Convenient for stressing the point (x_0, y_0).

$\dfrac{\partial z}{\partial x}\bigg|_{(x_0, y_0)}$ "Partial derivative of z with respect to x at (x_0, y_0)." Common in science and engineering when you are dealing with variables and do not mention the function explicitly.

$f_x, \dfrac{\partial f}{\partial x}, z_x,$ or $\dfrac{\partial z}{\partial x}$ "Partial derivative of f (or z) with respect to x." Convenient when you regard the partial derivative as a function in its own right.

The definition of the partial derivative of $f(x, y)$ with respect to y at a point (x_0, y_0) is similar to the definition of the partial derivative of f with respect to x. We hold x fixed at the value x_0 and take the ordinary derivative of $f(x_0, y)$ with respect to y at y_0.

Definition Partial Derivative with Respect to y

The **partial derivative of** $f(x, y)$ **with respect to** y at the point (x_0, y_0) is

$$\frac{\partial f}{\partial y}\bigg|_{(x_0, y_0)} = \frac{d}{dy} f(x_0, y)\bigg|_{y = y_0}$$

$$= \lim_{h \to 0} \frac{f(x_0, y_0 + h) - f(x_0, y_0)}{h},$$

provided the limit exists.

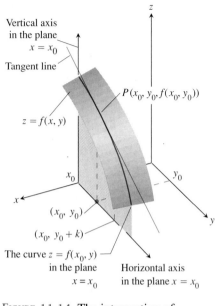

FIGURE 11.14 The intersection of the plane $x = x_0$ with the surface $z = f(x, y)$, viewed from above the first quadrant of the xy-plane.

The slope of the curve $z = f(x_0, y)$ at the point $P(x_0, y_0, f(x_0, y_0))$ in the vertical plane $x = x_0$ (Figure 11.14) is the partial derivative of f with respect to y at (x_0, y_0). The tangent line to the curve at P is the line in the plane $x = x_0$ that passes through P with this slope. The partial derivative gives the rate of change of f with respect to y at (x_0, y_0) when x is held fixed at the value x_0. This is the rate of change of f in the direction of $\mathbf{j}$ at (x_0, y_0).

The partial derivative with respect to y is denoted the same way as the partial derivative with respect to x:

$$\frac{\partial f}{\partial y}(x_0, y_0), \qquad f_y(x_0, y_0), \qquad \frac{\partial f}{\partial y}, \qquad f_y.$$

Notice that we now have two tangent lines associated with the surface $z = f(x, y)$ at the point $P(x_0, y_0, f(x_0, y_0))$ (Figure 11.15). Is the plane they determine tangent to the surface at P? It would be nice if it were, but we have to learn more about partial derivatives before we can find out.

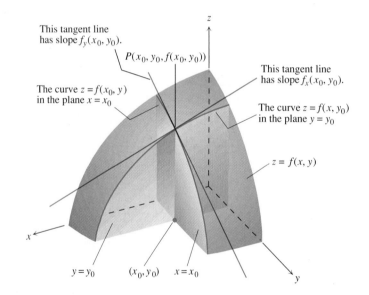

FIGURE 11.15 Figures 11.13 and 11.14 combined. The tangent lines at the point $(x_0, y_0, f(x_0, y_0))$ determine a plane that, in this picture at least, appears to be tangent to the surface.

Calculations

The definitions of $\partial f/\partial x$ and $\partial f/\partial y$ give us two different ways of differentiating f at a point: with respect to x in the usual way while treating y as a constant and with respect to y in the usual way while treating x as constant. As the following examples show, the values of these partial derivatives are usually different at a given point (x_0, y_0).

Example 1   Finding Partial Derivatives at a Point

Find the values of $\partial f/\partial x$ and $\partial f/\partial y$ at the point $(4, -5)$ if

$$f(x, y) = x^2 + 3xy + y - 1.$$

Solution   To find $\partial f / \partial x$, we treat y as a constant and differentiate with respect to x:

$$\frac{\partial f}{\partial x} = \frac{\partial}{\partial x} (x^2 + 3xy + y - 1) = 2x + 3 \cdot 1 \cdot y + 0 - 0 = 2x + 3y.$$

The value of $\partial f / \partial x$ at $(4, -5)$ is $2(4) + 3(-5) = -7$.

To find $\partial f / \partial y$, we treat x as a constant and differentiate with respect to y:

$$\frac{\partial f}{\partial y} = \frac{\partial}{\partial y} (x^2 + 3xy + y - 1) = 0 + 3 \cdot x \cdot 1 + 1 - 0 = 3x + 1.$$

The value of $\partial f / \partial y$ at $(4, -5)$ is $3(4) + 1 = 13$.

Example 2   Finding a Partial Derivative as a Function

Find $\partial f / \partial y$ if $f(x, y) = y \sin xy$.

Solution   We treat x as a constant and f as a product of y and $\sin xy$:

$$\frac{\partial f}{\partial y} = \frac{\partial}{\partial y} (y \sin xy) = y \frac{\partial}{\partial y} \sin xy + (\sin xy) \frac{\partial}{\partial y} (y)$$

$$= (y \cos xy) \frac{\partial}{\partial y} (xy) + \sin xy = xy \cos xy + \sin xy.$$

USING TECHNOLOGY

Partial Differentiation A simple grapher can support your calculations even in multiple dimensions. If you specify the values of all but one independent variable, the grapher can calculate partial derivatives and can plot traces with respect to that remaining variable. Typically, a CAS can compute partial derivatives symbolically and numerically as easily as it can compute simple derivatives. Most systems use the same command to differentiate a function, regardless of the number of variables. (Simply specify the variable with which differentiation is to take place).

Example 3   Partial Derivatives May Be Different Functions

Find f_x and f_y if

$$f(x, y) = \frac{2y}{y + \cos x}.$$

Solution   We treat f as a quotient. With y held constant, we get

$$f_x = \frac{\partial}{\partial x} \left(\frac{2y}{y + \cos x} \right) = \frac{(y + \cos x) \frac{\partial}{\partial x} (2y) - 2y \frac{\partial}{\partial x} (y + \cos x)}{(y + \cos x)^2}$$

$$= \frac{(y + \cos x)(0) - 2y(-\sin x)}{(y + \cos x)^2} = \frac{2y \sin x}{(y + \cos x)^2}.$$

With x held constant, we get

$$f_y = \frac{\partial}{\partial y}\left(\frac{2y}{y + \cos x}\right) = \frac{(y + \cos x)\frac{\partial}{\partial y}(2y) - 2y\frac{\partial}{\partial y}(y + \cos x)}{(y + \cos x)^2}$$

$$= \frac{(y + \cos x)(2) - 2y(1)}{(y + \cos x)^2} = \frac{2 \cos x}{(y + \cos x)^2}.$$

Implicit differentiation works for partial derivatives the way it works for ordinary derivatives, as the next example illustrates.

Example 4   Implicit Partial Differentiation

Find $\partial z/\partial x$ if the equation

$$yz - \ln z = x + y$$

defines z as a function of the two independent variables x and y and the partial derivative exists.

Solution   We differentiate both sides of the equation with respect to x, holding y constant and treating z as a differentiable function of x:

$$\frac{\partial}{\partial x}(yz) - \frac{\partial}{\partial x}\ln z = \frac{\partial x}{\partial x} + \frac{\partial y}{\partial x}$$

$$y\frac{\partial z}{\partial x} - \frac{1}{z}\frac{\partial z}{\partial x} = 1 + 0 \qquad \text{With } y \text{ constant,}$$

$$\left(y - \frac{1}{z}\right)\frac{\partial z}{\partial x} = 1 \qquad \qquad \frac{\partial}{\partial x}(yz) = y\frac{\partial z}{\partial x}.$$

$$\frac{\partial z}{\partial x} = \frac{z}{yz - 1}.$$

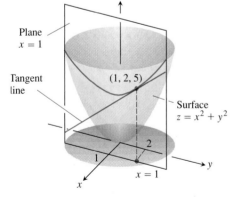

FIGURE 11.16 The tangent to the curve of intersection of the plane $x = 1$ and surface $z = x^2 + y^2$ at the point $(1, 2, 5)$. (Example 5)

Example 5   Finding the Slope of a Surface in the y-Direction

The plane $x = 1$ intersects the paraboloid $z = x^2 + y^2$ in a parabola. Find the slope of the tangent to the parabola at $(1, 2, 5)$ (Figure 11.16).

Solution   The slope is the value of the partial derivative $\partial z/\partial y$ at $(1, 2)$:

$$\left.\frac{\partial z}{\partial y}\right|_{(1,2)} = \left.\frac{\partial}{\partial y}(x^2 + y^2)\right|_{(1,2)} = 2y\bigg|_{(1,2)} = 2(2) = 4.$$

As a check, we can treat the parabola as the graph of the single-variable function $z = (1)^2 + y^2 = 1 + y^2$ in the plane $x = 1$ and ask for the slope at $y = 2$. The slope, calculated now as an ordinary derivative, is

$$\left.\frac{dz}{dy}\right|_{y=2} = \left.\frac{d}{dy}(1 + y^2)\right|_{y=2} = 2y\bigg|_{y=2} = 4.$$

Functions of More Than Two Variables

The definitions of the partial derivatives of functions of more than two independent variables are like the definitions for functions of two variables. They are ordinary derivatives with respect to one variable, taken while the other independent variables are held constant.

Example 6   A Function of Three Variables

If x, y, and z are independent variables and

$$f(x, y, z) = x \sin (y + 3z),$$

then

$$\frac{\partial f}{\partial z} = \frac{\partial}{\partial z} [x \sin (y + 3z)] = x \frac{\partial}{\partial z} \sin (y + 3z)$$

$$= x \cos (y + 3z) \frac{\partial}{\partial z} (y + 3z) = 3x \cos (y + 3z).$$

Example 7   Electrical Resistors in Parallel

If resistors of R_1, R_2, and R_3 ohms are connected in parallel to make an R-ohm resistor, the value of R can be found from the equation

$$\frac{1}{R} = \frac{1}{R_1} + \frac{1}{R_2} + \frac{1}{R_3}$$

(Figure 11.17). Find the value of $\partial R / \partial R_2$ when $R_1 = 30$, $R_2 = 45$, and $R_3 = 90$ ohms.

Solution   To find $\partial R / \partial R_2$, we treat R_1 and R_3 as constants and differentiate both sides of the equation with respect to R_2:

$$\frac{\partial}{\partial R_2} \left(\frac{1}{R} \right) = \frac{\partial}{\partial R_2} \left(\frac{1}{R_1} + \frac{1}{R_2} + \frac{1}{R_3} \right)$$

$$-\frac{1}{R^2} \frac{\partial R}{\partial R_2} = 0 - \frac{1}{R_2^2} + 0$$

$$\frac{\partial R}{\partial R_2} = \frac{R^2}{R_2^2} = \left(\frac{R}{R_2} \right)^2.$$

When $R_1 = 30$, $R_2 = 45$, and $R_3 = 90$,

$$\frac{1}{R} = \frac{1}{30} + \frac{1}{45} + \frac{1}{90} = \frac{3 + 2 + 1}{90} = \frac{6}{90} = \frac{1}{15},$$

so $R = 15$ and

$$\frac{\partial R}{\partial R_2} = \left(\frac{15}{45} \right)^2 = \left(\frac{1}{3} \right)^2 = \frac{1}{9}.$$

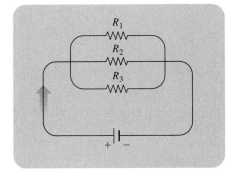

FIGURE 11.17 Resistors arranged this way are said to be connected in parallel (Example 7). Each resistor lets a portion of the current through. Their combined resistance R is calculated with the formula

$$\frac{1}{R} = \frac{1}{R_1} + \frac{1}{R_2} + \frac{1}{R_3}.$$

Partial Derivatives and Continuity

A function $f(x, y)$ can have partial derivatives with respect to both x and y at a point without being continuous there. This is different from functions of a single variable, where the existence of a derivative implies continuity. If the partial derivatives of $f(x, y)$ exist and are continuous throughout a disk centered at (x_0, y_0), however, then f is continuous at (x_0, y_0), as we see in the next section.

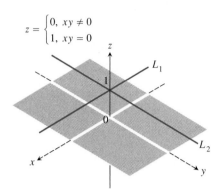

$$z = \begin{cases} 0, & xy \neq 0 \\ 1, & xy = 0 \end{cases}$$

FIGURE 11.18 The graph of

$$f(x, y) = \begin{cases} 0, & xy \neq 0 \\ 1, & xy = 0 \end{cases}$$

consists of the lines L_1 and L_2 and the four open quadrants of the xy-plane. The function has partial derivatives at the origin but is not continuous there.

Example 8 Partials Exist, But f Discontinuous

Let

$$f(x, y) = \begin{cases} 0, & xy \neq 0 \\ 1, & xy = 0 \end{cases}$$

(Figure 11.18).

(a) Find the limit of f as (x, y) approaches $(0, 0)$ along the line $y = x$.

(b) Prove that f is not continuous at the origin.

(c) Show that both partial derivatives $\partial f / \partial x$ and $\partial f / \partial y$ exist at the origin.

Solution

(a) Since $f(x, y)$ is constantly zero along the line $y = x$ (except at the origin), we have

$$\lim_{(x,y) \to (0,0)} f(x, y) \Big|_{y=x} = \lim_{(x,y) \to (0,0)} 0 = 0.$$

(b) Since $f(0, 0) = 1$, the limit in part (a) proves that f is not continuous at $(0, 0)$.

(c) To find $\partial f / \partial x$ at $(0, 0)$, we hold y fixed at $y = 0$. Then $f(x, y) = 1$ for all x, and the graph of f is the line L_1 in Figure 11.18. The slope of this line at any x is $\partial f / \partial x = 0$. In particular, $\partial f / \partial x = 0$ at $(0, 0)$. Similarly, $\partial f / \partial y$ is the slope of line L_2 at any y, so $\partial f / \partial y = 0$ at $(0, 0)$.

Example 8 notwithstanding, it is still true in higher dimensions that *differentiability* at a point implies continuity. What Example 8 suggests is that we need a stronger requirement for differentiability in higher dimensions than the mere existence of the partial derivatives. We define differentiability for functions of two variables at the end of this section and revisit the connection to continuity.

Second-Order Partial Derivatives

When we differentiate a function $f(x, y)$ twice, we produce its second-order derivatives. These derivatives are usually denoted by

$$\frac{\partial^2 f}{\partial x^2} \quad \text{"d squared } f\, d\, x \text{ squared"} \quad \text{or} \quad f_{xx} \quad \text{"f sub } x\, x\text{"}$$

$$\frac{\partial^2 f}{\partial y^2} \quad \text{"d squared } f\, d\, y \text{ squared"} \quad f_{yy} \quad \text{"f sub } y\, y\text{"}$$

$$\frac{\partial^2 f}{\partial x \partial y} \quad \text{"d squared } f\, d\, x\, d\, y\text{"} \quad f_{yx} \quad \text{"f sub } y\, x\text{"}$$

$$\frac{\partial^2 f}{\partial y \partial x} \quad \text{"d squared } f\, d\, y\, d\, x\text{"} \quad f_{xy} \quad \text{"f sub } x\, y\text{"}$$

The defining equations are

$$\frac{\partial^2 f}{\partial x^2} = \frac{\partial}{\partial x}\left(\frac{\partial f}{\partial x}\right), \qquad \frac{\partial^2 f}{\partial x \partial y} = \frac{\partial}{\partial x}\left(\frac{\partial f}{\partial y}\right),$$

and so on. Notice the order in which the derivatives are taken:

$$\frac{\partial^2 f}{\partial x \partial y}$$ Differentiate first with respect to y, then with respect to x.

$$f_{yx} = (f_y)_x$$ Means the same thing.

CD-ROM
WEBsite

Historical Biography

Pierre-Simon Laplace
(1749 — 1827)

Example 9   Finding Second-Order Partial Derivatives

If $f(x, y) = x \cos y + y e^x$, find

$$\frac{\partial^2 f}{\partial x^2}, \qquad \frac{\partial^2 f}{\partial y \partial x}, \qquad \frac{\partial^2 f}{\partial y^2}, \qquad \text{and} \qquad \frac{\partial^2 f}{\partial x \partial y}.$$

Solution

$$\frac{\partial f}{\partial x} = \frac{\partial}{\partial x}(x \cos y + y e^x) \qquad\qquad \frac{\partial f}{\partial y} = \frac{\partial}{\partial y}(x \cos y + y e^x)$$

$$= \cos y + y e^x \qquad\qquad\qquad\qquad = -x \sin y + e^x$$

So   So

$$\frac{\partial^2 f}{\partial y \partial x} = \frac{\partial}{\partial y}\left(\frac{\partial f}{\partial x}\right) = -\sin y + e^x \qquad \frac{\partial^2 f}{\partial x \partial y} = \frac{\partial}{\partial x}\left(\frac{\partial f}{\partial y}\right) = -\sin y + e^x$$

$$\frac{\partial^2 f}{\partial x^2} = \frac{\partial}{\partial x}\left(\frac{\partial f}{\partial x}\right) = y e^x. \qquad\qquad \frac{\partial^2 f}{\partial y^2} = \frac{\partial}{\partial y}\left(\frac{\partial f}{\partial y}\right) = -x \cos y.$$

The Mixed Derivative Theorem

You may have noticed that the "mixed" second-order partial derivatives

$$\frac{\partial^2 f}{\partial y \partial x} \qquad \text{and} \qquad \frac{\partial^2 f}{\partial x \partial y}$$

in Example 9 were equal. This was not a coincidence. They must be equal whenever f, f_x, f_y, f_{xy}, and f_{yx} are continuous, as stated in the following theorem.

Theorem 2   The Mixed Derivative Theorem

If $f(x, y)$ and its partial derivatives f_x, f_y, f_{xy}, and f_{yx} are defined throughout an open region containing a point (a, b) and are all continuous at (a, b), then

$$f_{xy}(a, b) = f_{yx}(a, b).$$

You can find a proof of Theorem 2 in Appendix 11.

Theorem 2 says that to calculate a mixed second-order derivative, we may differentiate in either order. This can work to our advantage.

Example 10   Choosing the Order of Differentiation

Find $\partial^2 w / \partial x \partial y$ if

$$w = xy + \frac{e^y}{y^2 + 1}.$$

Solution   The symbol $\partial^2 w / \partial x \partial y$ tells us to differentiate first with respect to y and then with respect to x. If we postpone the differentiation with respect to y and differentiate first with respect to x, however, we get the answer more quickly. In two steps,

$$\frac{\partial w}{\partial x} = y \qquad \text{and} \qquad \frac{\partial^2 w}{\partial y \partial x} = 1.$$

We are in for more work if we differentiate first with respect to y. (Just try it.)

Partial Derivatives of Still Higher Order

Although we will deal mostly with first- and second-order partial derivatives, because these appear the most frequently in applications, there is no theoretical limit to how many times we can differentiate a function as long as the derivatives involved exist. Thus, we get third- and fourth-order derivatives denoted by symbols like

$$\frac{\partial^3 f}{\partial x \partial y^2} = f_{yyx}$$

$$\frac{\partial^4 f}{\partial x^2 \partial y^2} = f_{yyxx},$$

and so on. As with second-order derivatives, the order of differentiation is immaterial as long as the derivatives through the order in question are continuous.

Differentiability

Surprising as it may seem, the starting point for differentiability is not Fermat's difference quotient but rather the idea of increment. You may recall from our work with functions of a single variable that if $y = f(x)$ is differentiable at $x = x_0$, then the change in the value of f that results from changing x from x_0 to $x_0 + \Delta x$ is given by an equation of the form

$$\Delta y = f'(x_0)\,\Delta x + \epsilon\,\Delta x$$

in which $\epsilon \to 0$ as $\Delta x \to 0$. For functions of two variables, the analogous property becomes the definition of differentiability. The Increment Theorem (from advanced calculus) tells us when to expect the property to hold.

Theorem 3   The Increment Theorem for Functions of Two Variables

Suppose that the first partial derivatives of $f(x, y)$ are defined throughout an open region R containing the point (x_0, y_0) and that f_x and f_y are continuous at (x_0, y_0). Then the change

$$\Delta z = f(x_0 + \Delta x, y_0 + \Delta y) - f(x_0, y_0)$$

in the value of f that results from moving from (x_0, y_0) to another point $(x_0 + \Delta x, y_0 + \Delta y)$ in R satisfies an equation of the form

$$\Delta z = f_x(x_0, y_0)\,\Delta x + f_y(x_0, y_0)\,\Delta y + \epsilon_1\,\Delta x + \epsilon_2\,\Delta y,$$

in which $\epsilon_1, \epsilon_2 \to 0$ as $\Delta x, \Delta y \to 0$.

You will see where the epsilons come from if you read the proof in Appendix 11. You will also see that similar results hold for functions of more than two independent variables.

> **Definition** Differentiability of a Function of Two Variables
>
> A function $z = f(x, y)$ is **differentiable at** (x_0, y_0) if $f_x(x_0, y_0)$ and $f_y(x_0, y_0)$ exist and Δz satisfies an equation of the form
>
> $$\Delta z = f_x(x_0, y_0) \, \Delta x + f_y(x_0, y_0) \, \Delta y + \epsilon_1 \, \Delta x + \epsilon_2 \, \Delta y,$$
>
> in which $\epsilon_1, \epsilon_2 \to 0$ as $\Delta x, \Delta y \to 0$. We call f **differentiable** if it is differentiable at every point in its domain.

In light of this definition, we have the immediate corollary of Theorem 3 that a function is differentiable if its first partial derivatives are *continuous*.

> **Corollary of Theorem 3** Continuity of Partial Derivatives Implies Differentiability
>
> If the partial derivatives f_x and f_y of a function $f(x, y)$ are continuous throughout an open region R, then f is differentiable at every point of R.

If $z = f(x, y)$ is differentiable, then the definition of differentiability assures that $\Delta z = f(x_0 + \Delta x, y_0 + \Delta y) - f(x_0, y_0)$ approaches 0 as Δx and Δy approach 0. This tells us that a function of two variables is continuous at every point where it is differentiable.

As we can see from Theorems 3 and 4, a function $f(x, y)$ must be continuous at a point (x_0, y_0) if f_x and f_y are continuous throughout an open region containing (x_0, y_0). Remember, however, that it is still possible for a function of two variables to be discontinuous at a point where its first partial derivatives exist, as we saw in Example 8. Existence alone is not enough.

> **Theorem 4** Differentiability Implies Continuity
>
> If a function $f(x, y)$ is differentiable at (x_0, y_0), then f is continuous at (x_0, y_0).

EXERCISES 11.3

Calculating First-Order Partial Derivatives

In Exercises 1–22, find $\partial f/\partial x$ and $\partial f/\partial y$.

1. $f(x, y) = 2x^2 - 3y - 4$ **2.** $f(x, y) = x^2 - xy + y^2$

3. $f(x, y) = (x^2 - 1)(y + 2)$

4. $f(x, y) = 5xy - 7x^2 - y^2 + 3x - 6y + 2$

5. $f(x, y) = (xy - 1)^2$ **6.** $f(x, y) = (2x - 3y)^3$

7. $f(x, y) = \sqrt{x^2 + y^2}$ **8.** $f(x, y) = (x^3 + (y/2))^{2/3}$

9. $f(x, y) = 1/(x + y)$ **10.** $f(x, y) = x/(x^2 + y^2)$

11. $f(x, y) = (x + y)/(xy - 1)$ **12.** $f(x, y) = \tan^{-1}(y/x)$

13. $f(x, y) = e^{(x+y+1)}$ **14.** $f(x, y) = e^{-x} \sin(x + y)$

15. $f(x, y) = \ln(x + y)$ **16.** $f(x, y) = e^{xy} \ln y$

17. $f(x, y) = \sin^2(x - 3y)$ **18.** $f(x, y) = \cos^2(3x - y^2)$

19. $f(x, y) = x^y$ **20.** $f(x, y) = \log_y x$

21. $f(x, y) = \int_x^y g(t) \, dt$ (*g* continuous for all *t*)

22. $f(x, y) = \sum_{n=0}^{\infty} (xy)^n$ ($|xy| < 1$)

In Exercises 23–34, find f_x, f_y, and f_z.

23. $f(x, y, z) = 1 + xy^2 - 2z^2$ **24.** $f(x, y, z) = xy + yz + xz$

25. $f(x, y, z) = x - \sqrt{y^2 + z^2}$

26. $f(x, y, z) = (x^2 + y^2 + z^2)^{-1/2}$

27. $f(x, y, z) = \sin^{-1}(xyz)$ **28.** $f(x, y, z) = \sec^{-1}(x + yz)$

29. $f(x, y, z) = \ln(x + 2y + 3z)$

30. $f(x, y, z) = yz \ln(xy)$ **31.** $f(x, y, z) = e^{-(x^2+y^2+z^2)}$

32. $f(x, y, z) = e^{-xyz}$

33. $f(x, y, z) = \tanh(x + 2y + 3z)$

34. $f(x, y, z) = \sinh(xy - z^2)$

In Exercises 35–40, find the partial derivative of the function with respect to each variable.

35. $f(t, \alpha) = \cos(2\pi t - \alpha)$ **36.** $g(u, v) = v^2 e^{(2u/v)}$

37. $h(\rho, \phi, \theta) = \rho \sin \phi \cos \theta$

38. $g(r, \theta, z) = r(1 - \cos \theta) - z$

39. *Work done by the heart* (Section 3.6, Exercise 41)

$$W(P, V, \delta, v, g) = PV + \frac{V\delta v^2}{2g}$$

40. *Wilson lot size formula* (Section 3.5, Exercise 43)

$$A(c, h, k, m, q) = \frac{km}{q} + cm + \frac{hq}{2}$$

Calculating Second-Order Partial Derivatives

Find all the second-order partial derivatives of the functions in Exercises 41–46.

41. $f(x, y) = x + y + xy$ **42.** $f(x, y) = \sin xy$

43. $g(x, y) = x^2 y + \cos y + y \sin x$

44. $h(x, y) = xe^y + y + 1$ **45.** $r(x, y) = \ln(x + y)$

46. $s(x, y) = \tan^{-1}(y/x)$

Mixed Partial Derivatives

In Exercises 47–50, verify that $w_{xy} = w_{yx}$.

47. $w = \ln(2x + 3y)$ **48.** $w = e^x + x \ln y + y \ln x$

49. $w = xy^2 + x^2 y^3 + x^3 y^4$ **50.** $w = x \sin y + y \sin x + xy$

51. *Writing to Learn* Which order of differentiation will calculate f_{xy} faster: x first or y first? Try to answer without writing anything down.

(a) $f(x, y) = x \sin y + e^y$

(b) $f(x, y) = 1/x$

(c) $f(x, y) = y + (x/y)$

(d) $f(x, y) = y + x^2 y + 4y^3 - \ln(y^2 + 1)$

(e) $f(x, y) = x^2 + 5xy + \sin x + 7e^x$

(f) $f(x, y) = x \ln xy$

52. *Writing to Learn* The fifth-order partial derivative $\partial^5 f / \partial x^2 \partial y^3$ is zero for each of the following functions. To show this as quickly as possible, which variable would you differentiate with respect to first: x or y? Try to answer without writing anything down.

(a) $f(x, y) = y^2 x^4 e^x + 2$

(b) $f(x, y) = y^2 + y(\sin x - x^4)$

(c) $f(x, y) = x^2 + 5xy + \sin x + 7e^x$

(d) $f(x, y) = xe^{y^2/2}$

Using the Partial Derivative Definition

In Exercises 53 and 54, use the limit definition of partial derivative to compute the partial derivatives of the functions at the specified points.

53. $f(x, y) = 1 - x + y - 3x^2 y$, $\dfrac{\partial f}{\partial x}$ and $\dfrac{\partial f}{\partial y}$ at $(1, 2)$

54. $f(x, y) = 4 + 2x - 3y - xy^2$, $\dfrac{\partial f}{\partial x}$ and $\dfrac{\partial f}{\partial y}$ at $(-2, 1)$

55. *Three variables* Let $w = f(x, y, z)$ be a function of three independent variables and write the formal definition of the partial derivative $\partial f / \partial z$ at (x_0, y_0, z_0). Use this definition to find $\partial f / \partial z$ at $(1, 2, 3)$ for $f(x, y, z) = x^2 y z^2$.

56. *Three variables* Let $w = f(x, y, z)$ be a function of three independent variables and write the formal definition of the partial derivative $\partial f / \partial y$ at (x_0, y_0, z_0). Use this definition to find $\partial f / \partial y$ at $(-1, 0, 3)$ for $f(x, y, z) = -2xy^2 + yz^2$.

Differentiating Implicitly

57. Find the value of $\partial z / \partial x$ at the point $(1, 1, 1)$ if the equation

$$xy + z^3 x - 2yz = 0$$

defines z as a function of the two independent variables x and y and the partial derivative exists.

58. Find the value of $\partial x / \partial z$ at the point $(1, -1, -3)$ if the equation

$$xz + y \ln x - x^2 + 4 = 0$$

defines x as a function of the two independent variables y and z and the partial derivative exists.

Exercises 59 and 60 are about the triangle shown here.

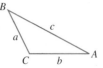

59. Express A implicitly as a function of a, b, and c and calculate $\partial A / \partial a$ and $\partial A / \partial b$.

60. Express a implicitly as a function of A, b, and B and calculate $\partial a / \partial A$ and $\partial a / \partial B$.

61. *Two dependent variables* Express v_x in terms of u and v if the equations $x = v \ln u$ and $y = u \ln v$ define u and v as functions of the independent variables x and y, and if v_x exists. (*Hint:* Differentiate both equations with respect to x and solve for v_x with Cramer's Rule.)

62. *Two dependent variables* Find $\partial x/\partial u$ and $\partial y/\partial u$ if the equations $u = x^2 - y^2$ and $v = x^2 - y$ define x and y as functions of the independent variables u and v, and the partial derivatives exist. (See the hint in Exercise 61.) Then let $s = x^2 + y^2$ and find $\partial s/\partial u$.

Laplace Equations

The **three-dimensional Laplace equation**

$$\frac{\partial^2 f}{\partial x^2} + \frac{\partial^2 f}{\partial y^2} + \frac{\partial^2 f}{\partial z^2} = 0$$

is satisfied by steady-state temperature distributions $T = f(x, y, z)$ in space, by gravitational potentials, and by electrostatic potentials. The **two-dimensional Laplace equation**

$$\frac{\partial^2 f}{\partial x^2} + \frac{\partial^2 f}{\partial y^2} = 0,$$

obtained by dropping the $\partial^2 f/\partial z^2$ term from the previous equation, describes potentials and steady-state temperature distributions in a plane (Figure 11.19).

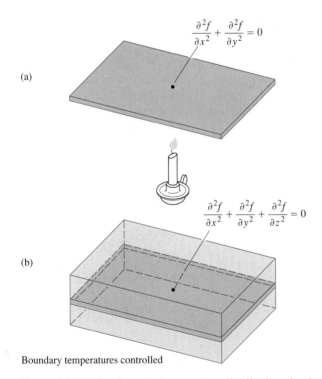

(a)

(b)

Boundary temperatures controlled

FIGURE 11.19 Steady-state temperature distributions in planes and solids satisfy Laplace equations. The plane (a) may be treated as a thin slice of the solid (b) perpendicular to the z-axis.

Show that each function in Exercises 63–68 satisfies a Laplace equation.

63. $f(x, y, z) = x^2 + y^2 - 2z^2$

64. $f(x, y, z) = 2z^3 - 3(x^2 + y^2)z$

65. $f(x, y) = e^{-2y} \cos 2x$

66. $f(x, y) = \ln \sqrt{x^2 + y^2}$

67. $f(x, y, z) = (x^2 + y^2 + z^2)^{-1/2}$

68. $f(x, y, z) = e^{3x+4y} \cos 5z$

The Wave Equation

If we stand on an ocean shore and take a snapshot of the waves, the picture shows a regular pattern of peaks and valleys in an instant of time. We see periodic vertical motion in space, with respect to distance. If we stand in the water, we can feel the rise and fall of the water as the waves go by. We see periodic vertical motion in time. In physics, this beautiful symmetry is expressed by the **one-dimensional wave equation**

$$\frac{\partial^2 w}{\partial t^2} = c^2 \frac{\partial^2 w}{\partial x^2},$$

where w is the wave height, x is the distance variable, t is the time variable, and c is the velocity with which the waves are propagated.

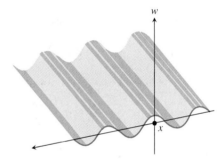

In our example, x is the distance across the ocean's surface, but in other applications, x might be the distance along a vibrating string, distance through air (sound waves), or distance through space (light waves). The number c varies with the medium and type of wave.

Show that the functions in Exercises 69–75 are all solutions of the wave equation.

69. $w = \sin (x + ct)$　　　　**70.** $w = \cos (2x + 2ct)$

71. $w = \sin (x + ct) + \cos (2x + 2ct)$

72. $w = \ln (2x + 2ct)$

73. $w = \tan (2x - 2ct)$

74. $w = 5 \cos (3x + 3ct) + e^{x+ct}$

75. $w = f(u)$, where f is a differentiable function of u, and $u = a(x + ct)$, where a is a constant

Continuous Partial Derivatives

76. *Writing to Learn* Does a function $f(x, y)$ with continuous first partial derivatives throughout an open region R have to be continuous on R? Give reasons for your answer.

77. *Writing to Learn* If a function $f(x, y)$ has continuous second partial derivatives throughout an open region R, must the first-order partial derivatives of f be continuous on R? Give reasons for your answer.

The Chain Rule

Composite Functions in Higher Dimensions • Functions of Two Variables
• Functions of Three Variables • Functions Defined on Surfaces •
Implicit Differentiation Revisited • Functions of Many Variables

We can form composites of multivariable functions over appropriate domains just as we create composites of single-variable functions. This section shows how to find partial derivatives of composites of multivariable functions.

Composite Functions in Higher Dimensions

When we are interested in the temperature $w = f(x, y, z)$ at points along a curve $x = g(t)$, $y = h(t)$, $z = k(t)$ in space or in the pressure or density along a path through a gas or fluid, we may think of f as a function of the single variable t. For each value of t, the temperature at the point $(g(t), h(t), k(t))$ is the value of the composite function $f(g(t), h(t), k(t))$. If we then wish to know the rate at which f changes with respect to t along the path, we have only to differentiate this composite with respect to t, provided, of course, the derivative exists.

Sometimes we can find the derivative by substituting the formulas for g, h, and k into the formula for f and differentiating directly with respect to t, but we often have to work with functions whose formulas are too complicated for convenient substitution or for which formulas are not readily available. To find a function's derivatives under circumstances like these, we use the Chain Rule. The form the Chain Rule takes depends on how many variables are involved but, except for the presence of additional variables, it works just like the Chain Rule in Section 2.5.

Functions of Two Variables

In Section 2.5, when $w = f(x)$ was a differentiable function of x and $x = g(t)$ was a differentiable function of t, w became a differentiable function of t and the Chain Rule said that dw/dt could be calculated with the formula

$$\frac{dw}{dt} = \frac{dw}{dx}\frac{dx}{dt}.$$

The analogous formula for a function $w = f(x, y)$ is given in Theorem 5.

Theorem 5 Chain Rule for Functions of Two Independent Variables

If $w = f(x, y)$ is differentiable and x and y are differentiable functions of t, then w is a differentiable function of t and

$$\frac{dw}{dt} = \frac{\partial f}{\partial x}\frac{dx}{dt} + \frac{\partial f}{\partial y}\frac{dy}{dt}.$$

Proof The proof consists of showing that if x and y are differentiable at $t = t_0$, then w is differentiable at t_0 and

$$\left(\frac{dw}{dt}\right)_{t_0} = \left(\frac{\partial w}{\partial x}\right)_{P_0}\left(\frac{dx}{dt}\right)_{t_0} + \left(\frac{\partial w}{\partial y}\right)_{P_0}\left(\frac{dy}{dt}\right)_{t_0},$$

where $P_0 = (x(t_0), y(t_0))$.

Let Δx, Δy, and Δw be the increments that result from changing t from t_0 to $t_0 + \Delta t$. Since f is differentiable (remember the definition in Section 11.3),

$$\Delta w = \left(\frac{\partial w}{\partial x}\right)_{P_0} \Delta x + \left(\frac{\partial w}{\partial y}\right)_{P_0} \Delta y + \epsilon_1 \Delta x + \epsilon_2 \Delta y,$$

where $\epsilon_1, \epsilon_2 \to 0$ as $\Delta x, \Delta y \to 0$. To find dw/dt, we divide this equation through by Δt and let Δt approach zero. The division gives

$$\frac{\Delta w}{\Delta t} = \left(\frac{\partial w}{\partial x}\right)_{P_0} \frac{\Delta x}{\Delta t} + \left(\frac{\partial w}{\partial y}\right)_{P_0} \frac{\Delta y}{\Delta t} + \epsilon_1 \frac{\Delta x}{\Delta t} + \epsilon_2 \frac{\Delta y}{\Delta t}.$$

Letting Δt approach zero gives

$$\left(\frac{dw}{dt}\right)_{t_0} = \lim_{\Delta t \to 0} \frac{\Delta w}{\Delta t}$$

$$= \left(\frac{\partial w}{\partial x}\right)_{P_0} \left(\frac{dx}{dt}\right)_{t_0} + \left(\frac{\partial w}{\partial y}\right)_{P_0} \left(\frac{dy}{dt}\right)_{t_0} + 0 \cdot \left(\frac{dx}{dt}\right)_{t_0} + 0 \cdot \left(\frac{dy}{dt}\right)_{t_0}. \quad —$$

The **tree diagram** in the margin provides a convenient way to remember the Chain Rule. From the diagram, you see that when $t = t_0$, the derivatives dx/dt and dy/dt are evaluated at t_0. The value of t_0 then determines the value x_0 for the differentiable function x and the value y_0 for the differentiable function y. The partial derivatives $\partial w/\partial x$ and $\partial w/\partial y$ (which are themselves functions of x and y) are evaluated at the point $P_0(x_0, y_0)$ corresponding to t_0. The "true" independent variable is t, whereas x and y are *intermediate variables* (controlled by t) and w is the dependent variable.

A more precise notation for the Chain Rule shows how the various derivatives in Theorem 5 are evaluated:

$$\frac{dw}{dt}(t_0) = \frac{\partial f}{\partial x}(x_0, y_0) \cdot \frac{dx}{dt}(t_0) + \frac{\partial f}{\partial y}(x_0, y_0) \cdot \frac{dy}{dt}(t_0).$$

To remember the Chain Rule picture the diagram below. To find dw/dt, start at w and read down each route to t, multiplying derivatives along the way. Then add the products.

Chain Rule

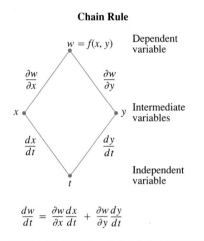

$w = f(x, y)$ — Dependent variable

$\frac{\partial w}{\partial x}$ $\frac{\partial w}{\partial y}$

x y — Intermediate variables

$\frac{dx}{dt}$ $\frac{dy}{dt}$

t — Independent variable

$$\frac{dw}{dt} = \frac{\partial w}{\partial x}\frac{dx}{dt} + \frac{\partial w}{\partial y}\frac{dy}{dt}$$

Example 1   Applying the Chain Rule

Use the Chain Rule to find the derivative of

$$w = xy$$

with respect to t along the path $x = \cos t$, $y = \sin t$. What is the derivative's value at $t = \pi/2$?

Solution   We apply the Chain Rule to find dw/dt as follows:

$$\frac{dw}{dt} = \frac{\partial w}{\partial x}\frac{dx}{dt} + \frac{\partial w}{\partial y}\frac{dy}{dt}$$

$$= \frac{\partial(xy)}{\partial x} \cdot \frac{d}{dt}(\cos t) + \frac{\partial(xy)}{\partial y} \cdot \frac{d}{dt}(\sin t)$$

$$= (y)(-\sin t) + (x)(\cos t)$$

$$= (\sin t)(-\sin t) + (\cos t)(\cos t)$$

$$= -\sin^2 t + \cos^2 t$$

$$= \cos(2t).$$

Here we have three routes from w to t instead of two, but finding dw/dt is still the same. Read down each route, multiplying derivatives along the way; then add.

Chain Rule

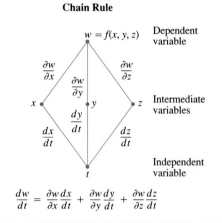

$$\frac{dw}{dt} = \frac{\partial w}{\partial x}\frac{dx}{dt} + \frac{\partial w}{\partial y}\frac{dy}{dt} + \frac{\partial w}{\partial z}\frac{dz}{dt}$$

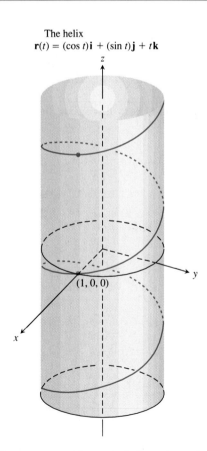

The helix
$$\mathbf{r}(t) = (\cos t)\mathbf{i} + (\sin t)\mathbf{j} + t\mathbf{k}$$

FIGURE 11.20 Example 2 shows how the values of $w = xy + z$ vary with t along this helix.

In this example, we can check the result with a more direct calculation. As a function of t,

$$w = xy = \cos t \, \sin t = \frac{1}{2} \sin 2t,$$

so

$$\frac{dw}{dt} = \frac{d}{dt}\left(\frac{1}{2} \sin 2t\right) = \frac{1}{2} \cdot 2 \cos 2t = \cos 2t.$$

In either case, at the given value of t,

$$\left(\frac{dw}{dt}\right)_{t=\pi/2} = \cos\left(2 \cdot \frac{\pi}{2}\right) = \cos \pi = -1.$$

Functions of Three Variables

You can probably predict the Chain Rule for functions of three variables, as it only involves adding the expected third term to the two-variable formula.

Theorem 6   Chain Rule for Functions of Three Independent Variables

If $w = f(x, y, z)$ is differentiable and x, y, and z are differentiable functions of t, then w is a differentiable function of t and

$$\frac{dw}{dt} = \frac{\partial f}{\partial x}\frac{dx}{dt} + \frac{\partial f}{\partial y}\frac{dy}{dt} + \frac{\partial f}{\partial z}\frac{dz}{dt}.$$

The proof is identical with the proof of Theorem 5 except that there are now three intermediate variables instead of two. The diagram we use for remembering the new equation is similar as well, with three routes from w to t.

Example 2   Changes in a Function's Values Along a Helix

Find dw/dt if

$$w = xy + z, \qquad x = \cos t, \qquad y = \sin t, \qquad z = t$$

(Figure 11.20). What is the derivative's value at $t = 0$?

Solution

$$\frac{dw}{dt} = \frac{\partial w}{\partial x}\frac{dx}{dt} + \frac{\partial w}{\partial y}\frac{dy}{dt} + \frac{\partial w}{\partial z}\frac{dz}{dt}$$
$$= (y)(-\sin t) + (x)(\cos t) + (1)(1)$$
$$= (\sin t)(-\sin t) + (\cos t)(\cos t) + 1 \qquad \text{Substitute for the intermediate variables.}$$
$$= -\sin^2 t + \cos^2 t + 1 = 1 + \cos 2t$$
$$\left(\frac{dw}{dt}\right)_{t=0} = 1 + \cos(0) = 2.$$

Here is a physical interpretation of Theorem 6. If $w = T(x, y, z)$ is the temperature at each point (x, y, z) along a curve C with parametric equations $x = x(t)$, $y = y(t)$, and $z = z(t)$, then the composite function $w = T(x(t), y(t), z(t))$, represents the temperature relative to t along the curve. The derivative dw/dt is then the instantaneous rate of change of temperature along the curve.

Functions Defined on Surfaces

If we are interested in the temperature $w = f(x, y, z)$ at points (x, y, z) on a globe in space, we might prefer to think of x, y, and z as functions of the variables r and s that give the points' longitudes and latitudes. If $x = g(r, s)$, $y = h(r, s)$, and $z = k(r, s)$, we could then express the temperature as a function of r and s with the composite function

$$w = f(g(r, s), h(r, s), k(r, s)).$$

Under the right conditions, w would have partial derivatives with respect to both r and s that could be calculated in the following way.

Theorem 7   Chain Rule for Two Independent Variables and Three Intermediate Variables

Suppose that $w = f(x, y, z)$, $x = g(r, s)$, $y = h(r, s)$, and $z = k(r, s)$. If all four functions are differentiable, then w has partial derivatives with respect to r and s, given by the formulas

$$\frac{\partial w}{\partial r} = \frac{\partial w}{\partial x}\frac{\partial x}{\partial r} + \frac{\partial w}{\partial y}\frac{\partial y}{\partial r} + \frac{\partial w}{\partial z}\frac{\partial z}{\partial r}$$

$$\frac{\partial w}{\partial s} = \frac{\partial w}{\partial x}\frac{\partial x}{\partial s} + \frac{\partial w}{\partial y}\frac{\partial y}{\partial s} + \frac{\partial w}{\partial z}\frac{\partial z}{\partial s}.$$

The first of these equations can be derived from the Chain Rule in Theorem 6 by holding s fixed and treating r as t. The second can be derived in the same way, holding r fixed and treating s as t. The tree diagrams for both equations are shown in Figure 11.21.

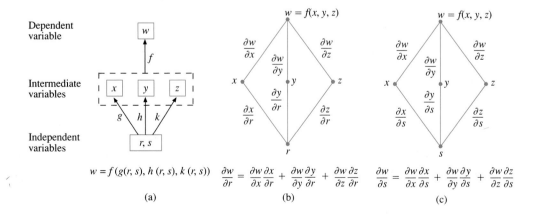

FIGURE 11.21 Composite function and tree diagrams for Theorem 7.

Example 3   Partial Derivatives Using Theorem 7

Express $\partial w / \partial r$ and $\partial w / \partial s$ in terms of r and s if

$$w = x + 2y + z^2, \qquad x = \frac{r}{s}, \qquad y = r^2 + \ln s, \qquad z = 2r.$$

Solution

$$\frac{\partial w}{\partial r} = \frac{\partial w}{\partial x} \frac{\partial x}{\partial r} + \frac{\partial w}{\partial y} \frac{\partial y}{\partial r} + \frac{\partial w}{\partial z} \frac{\partial z}{\partial r}$$

$$= (1)\left(\frac{1}{s}\right) + (2)(2r) + (2z)(2)$$

$$= \frac{1}{s} + 4r + (4r)(2) = \frac{1}{s} + 12r \qquad \text{Substitute for intermediate variable } z.$$

$$\frac{\partial w}{\partial s} = \frac{\partial w}{\partial x} \frac{\partial x}{\partial s} + \frac{\partial w}{\partial y} \frac{\partial y}{\partial s} + \frac{\partial w}{\partial z} \frac{\partial z}{\partial s}$$

$$= (1)\left(-\frac{r}{s^2}\right) + (2)\left(\frac{1}{s}\right) + (2z)(0) = \frac{2}{s} - \frac{r}{s^2}$$

If f is a function of two variables instead of three, each equation in Theorem 7 becomes correspondingly one term shorter.

If $w = f(x, y)$, $x = g(r, s)$, and $y = h(r, s)$, then

$$\frac{\partial w}{\partial r} = \frac{\partial w}{\partial x} \frac{\partial x}{\partial r} + \frac{\partial w}{\partial y} \frac{\partial y}{\partial r} \qquad \text{and} \qquad \frac{\partial w}{\partial s} = \frac{\partial w}{\partial x} \frac{\partial x}{\partial s} + \frac{\partial w}{\partial y} \frac{\partial y}{\partial s}.$$

Figure 11.22 shows the tree diagram for the first of these equations. The diagram for the second equation is similar, just replace r with s.

Example 4   More Partial Derivatives

Express $\partial w / \partial r$ and $\partial w / \partial s$ in terms of r and s if

$$w = x^2 + y^2, \qquad x = r - s, \qquad y = r + s.$$

Solution

$$\frac{\partial w}{\partial r} = \frac{\partial w}{\partial x} \frac{\partial x}{\partial r} + \frac{\partial w}{\partial y} \frac{\partial y}{\partial r} \qquad\qquad \frac{\partial w}{\partial s} = \frac{\partial w}{\partial x} \frac{\partial x}{\partial s} + \frac{\partial w}{\partial y} \frac{\partial y}{\partial s}$$

$$= (2x)(1) + (2y)(1) \qquad\qquad\quad = (2x)(-1) + (2y)(1)$$

$$= 2(r - s) + 2(r + s) \qquad\qquad = -2(r - s) + 2(r + s) \qquad \text{Substitute for the intermediate variables.}$$

$$= 4r \qquad\qquad\qquad\qquad\qquad\quad = 4s$$

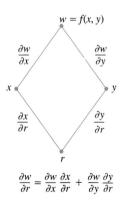

Chain Rule

$$w = f(x, y)$$

$$\frac{\partial w}{\partial x} \qquad \frac{\partial w}{\partial y}$$

$$x \qquad\qquad y$$

$$\frac{\partial x}{\partial r} \qquad \frac{\partial y}{\partial r}$$

$$r$$

$$\frac{\partial w}{\partial r} = \frac{\partial w}{\partial x} \frac{\partial x}{\partial r} + \frac{\partial w}{\partial y} \frac{\partial y}{\partial r}$$

FIGURE 11.22 Tree diagram for the equation

$$\frac{\partial w}{\partial r} = \frac{\partial w}{\partial w} \frac{\partial x}{\partial r} + \frac{\partial w}{\partial y} \frac{\partial y}{\partial r}.$$

$R \, \text{g} \, S \longrightarrow$

Chain Rule

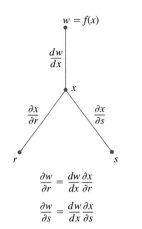

FIGURE 11.23 Tree diagram for differentiating f as a composite function of r and s with one intermediate variable.

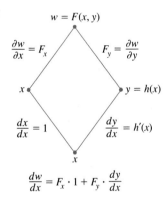

$$\frac{dw}{dx} = F_x \cdot 1 + F_y \cdot \frac{dy}{dx}$$

FIGURE 11.24 Three diagram for differentiating $w = F(x, y)$ with respect to x. Setting $dw/dx = 0$ leads to a simple computational formula for implicit differentiation (Theorem 8).

If f is a function of x alone, our equations become even simpler.

> If $w = f(x)$ and $x = g(r, s)$, then *derivative with respect to 'x' only*
> $$\frac{\partial w}{\partial r} = \frac{dw}{dx}\frac{\partial x}{\partial r} \qquad \text{and} \qquad \frac{\partial w}{\partial s} = \frac{dw}{dx}\frac{\partial x}{\partial s}.$$

In this case, we can use the ordinary (single-variable) derivative, dw/dx. The tree diagram is shown in Figure 11.23.

Implicit Differentiation Revisited

Believe it or not, the two-variable Chain Rule in Theorem 5 leads to a formula that takes most of the work out of implicit differentiation. Suppose that

1. The function $F(x, y)$ is differentiable and

2. The equation $F(x, y) = 0$ defines y implicitly as a differentiable function of x, say $y = h(x)$.

Since $w = F(x, y) = 0$, the derivative dw/dx must be zero. Computing the derivative from the Chain Rule (tree diagram in Figure 11.24), we find

$$0 = \frac{dw}{dx} = F_x\frac{dx}{dx} + F_y\frac{dy}{dx} \qquad \begin{array}{l}\text{Theorem 5 with } t = x \\ \text{and } f = F\end{array}$$

$$= F_x \cdot 1 + F_y \cdot \frac{dy}{dx}.$$

If $F_y = \partial w/\partial y \neq 0$, we can solve this equation for dy/dx to get

$$\frac{dy}{dx} = -\frac{F_x}{F_y}.$$

This relationship gives a surprisingly simple shortcut to finding derivatives of implicitly defined functions, which we state here as a theorem.

> **Theorem 8** A Formula for Implicit Differentiation
> Suppose that $F(x, y)$ is differentiable and that the equation $F(x, y) = 0$ defines y as a differentiable function of x. Then at any point where $F_y \neq 0$,
> $$\frac{dy}{dx} = -\frac{F_x}{F_y}.$$

Example 5 Speedy Implicit Differentiation

Use Theorem 8 to find dy/dx if $y^2 - x^2 - \sin xy = 0$.

Solution Take $F(x, y) = y^2 - x^2 - \sin xy$. Then

$$\frac{dy}{dx} = -\frac{F_x}{F_y} = -\frac{-2x - y\cos xy}{2y - x\cos xy}$$

$$= \frac{2x + y\cos xy}{2y - x\cos xy}.$$

This calculation is significantly shorter than the single-variable calculation with which we found dy/dx in Section 2.6, Example 2.

Functions of Many Variables

We have seen several different forms of the Chain Rule in this section, but you do not have to memorize them all if you can see them as special cases of the same general formula. When solving particular problems, it may help to draw the appropriate tree diagram by placing the dependent variable on top, the intermediate variables in the middle, and the selected independent variable at the bottom. To find the derivative of the dependent variable with respect to the selected independent variable, start at the dependent variable and read down each route of the tree to the independent variable, calculating and multiplying the derivatives along each route. Then add the products you found for the different routes.

In general, suppose that $w = f(x, y, \dots, v)$ is a differentiable function of the variables $x, y, \dots, v$ (a finite set) and the $x, y, \dots, v$ are differentiable functions of $p, q, \dots, t$ (another finite set). Then w is a differentiable function of the variables p through t and the partial derivatives of w with respect to these variables are given by equations of the form

$$\frac{\partial w}{\partial p} = \frac{\partial w}{\partial x}\frac{\partial x}{\partial p} + \frac{\partial w}{\partial y}\frac{\partial y}{\partial p} + \cdots + \frac{\partial w}{\partial v}\frac{\partial v}{\partial p}.$$

The other equations are obtained by replacing p by $q, \dots, t$, one at a time.

One way to remember this equation is to think of the right-hand side as the dot product of two vectors with components

$$\underbrace{\left(\frac{\partial w}{\partial x}, \frac{\partial w}{\partial y}, \dots, \frac{\partial w}{\partial v}\right)}_{\substack{\text{Derivatives of } w \text{ with} \\ \text{respect to the} \\ \text{intermediate variables}}} \quad \text{and} \quad \underbrace{\left(\frac{\partial x}{\partial p}, \frac{\partial y}{\partial p}, \dots, \frac{\partial v}{\partial p}\right)}_{\substack{\text{Derivatives of the intermediate} \\ \text{variables with respect to the} \\ \text{selected independent variable}}}.$$

EXERCISES 11.4

Chain Rule: One Independent Variable

In Exercises 1–6, (a) express dw/dt as a function of t, both by using the Chain Rule and by expressing w in terms of t and differentiating directly with respect to t. Then (b) evaluate dw/dt at the given value of t.

1. $w = x^2 + y^2$, $\quad x = \cos t$, $\quad y = \sin t$; $\quad t = \pi$

2. $w = x^2 + y^2$, $\quad x = \cos t + \sin t$, $\quad y = \cos t - \sin t$; $\quad t = 0$

3. $w = \frac{x}{z} + \frac{y}{z}$, $\quad x = \cos^2 t$, $\quad y = \sin^2 t$, $\quad z = 1/t$; $\quad t = 3$

4. $w = \ln (x^2 + y^2 + z^2)$, $\quad x = \cos t$, $\quad y = \sin t$, $\quad z = 4\sqrt{t}$; $\quad t = 3$

5. $w = 2ye^x - \ln z$, $\quad x = \ln (t^2 + 1)$, $\quad y = \tan^{-1} t$, $\quad z = e^t$; $\quad t = 1$

6. $w = z - \sin xy$, $\quad x = t$, $\quad y = \ln t$, $\quad z = e^{t-1}$; $\quad t = 1$

Chain Rule: Two and Three Independent Variables

In Exercises 7 and 8, (a) express $\partial z/\partial r$ and $\partial z/\partial \theta$ as functions of r and θ both by using the Chain Rule and by expressing z directly in terms of r and θ before differentiating. Then (b) evaluate $\partial z/\partial r$ and $\partial z/\partial \theta$ at the given point (r, θ).

7. $z = 4e^x \ln y$, $\quad x = \ln (u \cos v)$, $\quad y = u \sin v$; $\quad (u, v) = (2, \pi/4)$

8. $z = \tan^{-1}(x/y)$, $\quad x = u \cos v$, $\quad y = u \sin v$; $\quad (u, v) = (1.3, \pi/6)$

In Exercises 9 and 10, (a) express $\partial w/\partial u$ and $\partial w/\partial v$ as functions of u and v both by using the Chain Rule and by expressing w directly in terms of u and v before differentiating. Then (b) evaluate $\partial w/\partial u$ and $\partial w/\partial v$ at the given point (u, v).

9. $w = xy + yz + xz, \quad x = u + v, \quad y = u - v, \quad z = uv;$
$(u, v) = (1/2, 1)$

10. $w = \ln (x^2 + y^2 + z^2), \quad x = ue^v \sin u, \quad y = ue^v \cos u,$
$z = ue^v; \quad (u, v) = (-2, 0)$

In Exercises 11 and 12, (a) express $\partial u/\partial x$, $\partial u/\partial y$, and $\partial u/\partial z$ as functions of x, y, and z both by using the Chain Rule and by expressing u directly in terms of x, y, and z before differentiating. Then (b) evaluate $\partial u/\partial x$, $\partial u/\partial y$, and $\partial u/\partial z$ at the given point (x, y, z).

11. $u = \dfrac{p - q}{q - r}, \quad p = x + y + z, \quad q = x - y + z, \quad r = x + y - z;$
$(x, y, z) = (\sqrt{3}, 2, 1)$

12. $u = e^{qr} \sin^{-1} p, \quad p = \sin x, \quad q = z^2 \ln y, \quad r = 1/z;$
$(x, y, z) = (\pi/4, 1/2, -1/2)$

Using a Tree Diagram

In Exercises 13–24, draw a tree diagram and write a Chain Rule formula for each derivative.

13. $\dfrac{dz}{dt}$ for $z = f(x, y), \quad x = g(t), \quad y = h(t)$

14. $\dfrac{dz}{dt}$ for $z = f(u, v, w), \quad u = g(t), \quad v = h(t), \quad w = k(t)$

15. $\dfrac{\partial w}{\partial u}$ and $\dfrac{\partial w}{\partial v}$ for $w = h(x, y, z), \quad x = f(u, v), \quad y = g(u, v),$
$z = k(u, v)$

16. $\dfrac{\partial w}{\partial x}$ and $\dfrac{\partial w}{\partial y}$ for $w = f(r, s, t), \quad r = g(x, y), \quad s = h(x, y),$
$t = k(x, y)$

17. $\dfrac{\partial w}{\partial u}$ and $\dfrac{\partial w}{\partial v}$ for $w = g(x, y), \quad x = h(u, v), \quad y = k(u, v)$

18. $\dfrac{\partial w}{\partial x}$ and $\dfrac{\partial w}{\partial y}$ for $w = g(u, v), \quad u = h(x, y), \quad v = k(x, y)$

19. $\dfrac{\partial z}{\partial t}$ and $\dfrac{\partial z}{\partial s}$ for $z = f(x, y), \quad x = g(t, s), \quad y = h(t, s)$

20. $\dfrac{\partial y}{\partial r}$ for $y = f(u), \quad u = g(r, s)$

21. $\dfrac{\partial w}{\partial s}$ and $\dfrac{\partial w}{\partial t}$ for $w = g(u), \quad u = h(s, t)$

22. $\dfrac{\partial w}{\partial p}$ for $w = f(x, y, z, v), \quad x = g(p, q), \quad y = h(p, q),$
$z = j(p, q), \quad v = k(p, q)$

23. $\dfrac{\partial w}{\partial r}$ and $\dfrac{\partial w}{\partial s}$ for $w = f(x, y), \quad x = g(r), \quad y = h(s)$

24. $\dfrac{\partial w}{\partial s}$ for $w = g(x, y), \quad x = h(r, s, t), \quad y = k(r, s, t)$

Implicit Differentiation

Assuming that the equations in Exercises 25–28 define y as a differentiable function of x, use Theorem 8 to find the value of dy/dx at the given point.

25. $x^3 - 2y^2 + xy = 0, \quad (1, 1)$

26. $xy + y^2 - 3x - 3 = 0, \quad (-1, 1)$

27. $x^2 + xy + y^2 - 7 = 0, \quad (1, 2)$

28. $xe^y + \sin xy + y - \ln 2 = 0, \quad (0, \ln 2)$

Three-Variable Implicit Differentiation

Theorem 8 can be generalized to functions of three variables and even more. The three-variable version goes like this: If the equation $F(x, y, z) = 0$ determines z as a differentiable function of x and y, then, at points where $F_z \neq 0$,

$$\frac{\partial z}{\partial x} = -\frac{F_x}{F_z} \quad \text{and} \quad \frac{\partial z}{\partial y} = -\frac{F_y}{F_z}.$$

Use these equations to find the values of $\partial z/\partial x$ and $\partial z/\partial y$ at the points in Exercises 29–32.

29. $z^3 - xy + yz + y^3 - 2 = 0, \quad (1, 1, 1)$

30. $\dfrac{1}{x} + \dfrac{1}{y} + \dfrac{1}{z} - 1 = 0, \quad (2, 3, 6)$

31. $\sin (x + y) + \sin (y + z) + \sin (x + z) = 0, \quad (\pi, \pi, \pi)$

32. $xe^y + ye^z + 2 \ln x - 2 - 3 \ln 2 = 0, \quad (1, \ln 2, \ln 3)$

Finding Specified Partial Derivatives

33. Find $\partial w/\partial r$ when $r = 1, s = -1$ if $w = (x + y + z)^2, x = r - s,$
$y = \cos (r + s), z = \sin (r + s).$

34. Find $\partial w/\partial v$ when $u = -1, v = 2$ if $w = xy + \ln z, x = v^2/u,$
$y = u + v, z = \cos u.$

35. Find $\partial w/\partial v$ when $u = 0, v = 0$ if $w = x^2 + (y/x), x = u - 2v + 1,$
$y = 2u + v - 2.$

36. Find $\partial z/\partial u$ when $u = 0, v = 1$ if $z = \sin xy + x \sin y,$
$x = u^2 + v^2, y = uv.$

37. Find $\partial z/\partial u$ and $\partial z/\partial v$ when $u = \ln 2, v = 1$ if $z = 5 \tan^{-1} x$ and
$x = e^u + \ln v.$

38. Find $\partial z/\partial u$ and $\partial z/\partial v$ when $u = 1$ and $v = -2$ if $z = \ln q$ and
$q = \sqrt{v} + 3 \tan^{-1} u.$

Theory and Examples

39. *Changes within an electric circuit* The voltage V in a circuit that satisfies the law $V = IR$ is slowly dropping as the battery wears out. At the same time, the resistance R is increasing as the resistor heats up. Use the equation

$$\frac{dV}{dt} = \frac{\partial V}{\partial I} \frac{dI}{dt} + \frac{\partial V}{\partial R} \frac{dR}{dt}$$

to find how the current is changing at the instant when $R = 600$ ohms, $I = 0.04$ amp, $dR/dt = 0.5$ ohm/sec, and $dV/dt = -0.01$ volt/sec.

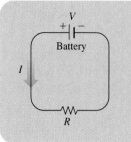

40. *Changing dimensions in a box* The lengths a, b, and c of the edges of a rectangular box are changing with time. At the instant in question, $a = 1$ m, $b = 2$ m, $c = 3$ m, $da/dt = db/dt = 1$ m/sec, and $dc/dt = -3$ m/sec. At what rates are the box's volume V and surface area S changing at that instant? Are the box's interior diagonals increasing in length or decreasing?

41. *Summing partial derivatives* If $f(u, v, w)$ is differentiable and $u = x - y$, $v = y - z$, and $w = z - x$, show that

$$\frac{\partial f}{\partial x} + \frac{\partial f}{\partial y} + \frac{\partial f}{\partial z} = 0.$$

42. *Polar coordinates* Suppose that we substitute polar coordinates $x = r \cos \theta$ and $y = r \sin \theta$ in a differentiable function $w = f(x, y)$.

(a) Show that

$$\frac{\partial w}{\partial r} = f_x \cos \theta + f_y \sin \theta$$

and

$$\frac{1}{r} \frac{\partial w}{\partial \theta} = -f_x \sin \theta + f_y \cos \theta.$$

(b) Solve the equations in part (a) to express f_x and f_y in terms of $\partial w/\partial r$ and $\partial w/\partial \theta$.

(c) Show that

$$(f_x)^2 + (f_y)^2 = \left(\frac{\partial w}{\partial r}\right)^2 + \frac{1}{r^2}\left(\frac{\partial w}{\partial \theta}\right)^2.$$

43. *Laplace equations* Show that if $w = f(u, v)$ satisfies the Laplace equation $f_{uu} + f_{vv} = 0$ and if $u = (x^2 - y^2)/2$ and $v = xy$, then w satisfies the Laplace equation $w_{xx} + w_{yy} = 0$.

44. *Laplace equations* Let $w = f(u) + g(v)$, where $u = x + iy$ and $v = x - iy$ and $i = \sqrt{-1}$. Show that w satisfies the Laplace equation $w_{xx} + w_{yy} = 0$ if all the necessary functions are differentiable.

Changes in Functions Along Curves

45. *Extreme values on a helix* Suppose that the partial derivatives of a function $f(x, y, z)$ at points on the helix $x = \cos t$, $y = \sin t$, $z = t$ are

$$f_x = \cos t, \qquad f_y = \sin t, \qquad f_z = t^2 + t - 2.$$

At what points on the curve, if any, can f take on extreme values?

46. *A space curve* Let $w = x^2 e^{2y} \cos 3z$. Find the value of dw/dt at the point $(1, \ln 2, 0)$ on the curve $x = \cos t$, $y = \ln (t + 2)$, $z = t$.

47. *Temperature on a circle* Let $T = f(x, y)$ be the temperature at the point (x, y) on the circle $x = \cos t$, $y = \sin t$, $0 \le t \le 2\pi$ and suppose that

$$\frac{\partial T}{\partial x} = 8x - 4y, \qquad \frac{\partial T}{\partial y} = 8y - 4x.$$

(a) Find where the maximum and minimum temperatures on the circle occur by examining the derivatives dT/dt and d^2T/dt^2.

(b) Suppose that $T = 4x^2 - 4xy + 4y^2$. Find the maximum and minimum values of T on the circle.

48. *Temperature on an ellipse* Let $T = g(x, y)$ be the temperature at the point (x, y) on the ellipse

$$x = 2\sqrt{2} \cos t, \qquad y = \sqrt{2} \sin t, \qquad 0 \le t \le 2\pi,$$

and suppose that

$$\frac{\partial T}{\partial x} = y, \qquad \frac{\partial T}{\partial y} = x.$$

(a) Locate the maximum and minimum temperatures on the ellipse by examining dT/dt and d^2T/dt^2.

(b) Suppose that $T = xy - 2$. Find the maximum and minimum values of T on the ellipse.

Differentiating Integrals

Under mild continuity restrictions, it is true that if

$$F(x) = \int_a^b g(t, x) \, dt,$$

then $F'(x) = \int_a^b g_x(t, x) \, dt$. Using this fact and the Chain Rule, we can find the derivative of

$$F(x) = \int_a^{f(x)} g(t, x) \, dt$$

by letting

$$G(u, x) = \int_a^u g(t, x) \, dt,$$

Where $u = f(x)$. Find the derivatives of the functions in Exercises 49 and 50.

49. $F(x) = \displaystyle\int_0^{x^2} \sqrt{t^4 + x^3} \, dt$

50. $F(x) = \displaystyle\int_{x^2}^1 \sqrt{t^3 + x^2} \, dt$

Directional Derivatives, Gradient Vectors, and Tangent Planes

Directional Derivatives in the Plane • Interpretation of the Directional Derivative • Calculation • Properties of Directional Derivatives • Gradients and Tangents to Level Curves • Algebra Rules for Gradients • Increments and Distance • Functions of Three Variables • Tangent Planes and Normal Lines • Planes Tangent to a Surface $z = f(x, y)$ • Other Applications

If you look at the map (Figure 11.25) showing contours on the West Point Fortress along the Hudson River in New York, you will notice that the tributary streams flow perpendicular to the contours. The streams are following paths of steepest descent so the waters reach the Hudson as quickly as possible. Therefore, the instantaneous rate of change in a stream's altitude above sea level has a particular direction. In this section, you see why this direction is perpendicular to the contours.

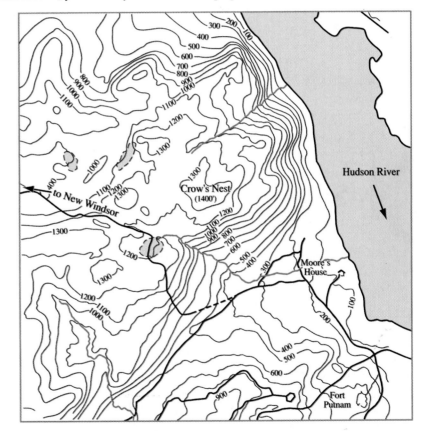

FIGURE 11.25 Contours of the West Point Fortress in New York show streams, which follow paths of steepest descent, running perpendicular to the contours.

We know from Section 11.4 that if $f(x, y)$ is differentiable, then the rate at which f changes with respect to t along a differentiable curve $x = g(t), y = h(t)$ is

$$\frac{df}{dt} = \frac{\partial f}{\partial x}\frac{dx}{dt} + \frac{\partial f}{\partial y}\frac{dy}{dt}.$$

At any point $P_0(x_0, y_0) = P_0(g(t_0), h(t_0))$, this equation gives the rate of change of f with respect to increasing t and therefore depends, among other things, on the direction of motion along the curve. This observation is particularly important when the curve is a straight line and t is the arc length parameter along the line measured from P_0 in the direction of a given unit vector $\mathbf{u}$. For then, df/dt is the rate of change of f with respect to distance in its domain in the direction of $\mathbf{u}$. By varying $\mathbf{u}$, we find the rates at which f changes with respect to distance as we move through P_0 in different directions. These "directional derivatives" have useful interpretations in science and engineering as well as in mathematics. This section develops a formula for calculating them and proceeds from there to find equations for tangent planes and normal lines on surfaces in space.

Directional Derivatives in the Plane

Suppose that the function $f(x, y)$ is defined throughout a region R in the xy-plane, that $P_0(x_0, y_0)$ is a point in R, and that $\mathbf{u} = u_1\mathbf{i} + u_2\mathbf{j}$ is a unit vector. Then the equations

$$x = x_0 + su_1, \qquad y = y_0 + su_2$$

parametrize the line through P_0 parallel to $\mathbf{u}$. If the parameter s measures arc length from P_0 in the direction of $\mathbf{u}$, we find the rate of change of f at P_0 in the direction of $\mathbf{u}$ by calculating df/ds at P_0 (Figure 11.26):

Definition   Directional Derivative

The **derivative of f at $P_0(x_0, y_0)$ in the direction of the unit vector** $\mathbf{u} = u_1\mathbf{i} + u_2\mathbf{j}$ is the number

$$\left(\frac{df}{ds}\right)_{\mathbf{u}, P_0} = \lim_{s \to 0} \frac{f(x_0 + su_1, y_0 + su_2) - f(x_0, y_0)}{s}, \tag{1}$$

provided the limit exists.

The directional derivative is also denoted by

$$(D_{\mathbf{u}}f)_{P_0}. \qquad \text{"The derivative of } f \text{ at } P^0 \text{ in the direction of } \mathbf{u}\text{"}$$

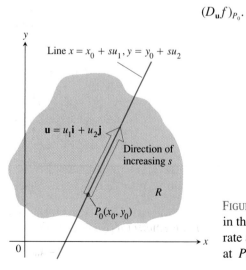

FIGURE 11.26 The rate of change of f in the direction of $\mathbf{u}$ at a point P_0 is the rate at which f changes along this line at P_0.

Example 1 Finding a Directional Derivative Using the Definition

Find the derivative of

$$f(x, y) = x^2 + xy$$

at $P_0(1, 2)$ in the direction of the unit vector $\mathbf{u} = (1/\sqrt{2})\mathbf{i} + (1/\sqrt{2})\mathbf{j}$.

$$u_1 \qquad u_2$$

Solution

$$\left(\frac{df}{ds}\right)_{\mathbf{u}, P_0} = \lim_{s \to 0} \frac{f(x_0 + su_1, y_0 + su_2) - f(x_0, y_0)}{s} \qquad \text{Eq. (1)}$$

$$= \lim_{s \to 0} \frac{f\left(1 + s \cdot \dfrac{1}{\sqrt{2}}, \ 2 + s \cdot \dfrac{1}{\sqrt{2}}\right) - f(1, 2)}{s}$$

$$= \lim_{s \to 0} \frac{\left(1 + \dfrac{s}{\sqrt{2}}\right)^2 + \left(1 + \dfrac{s}{\sqrt{2}}\right)\left(2 + \dfrac{s}{\sqrt{2}}\right) - (1^2 + 1 \cdot 2)}{s}$$

$$= \lim_{s \to 0} \frac{\left(1 + \dfrac{2s}{\sqrt{2}} + \dfrac{s^2}{2}\right) + \left(2 + \dfrac{3s}{\sqrt{2}} + \dfrac{s^2}{2}\right) - 3}{s}$$

$$= \lim_{s \to 0} \frac{\dfrac{5s}{\sqrt{2}} + s^2}{s} = \lim_{s \to 0} \left(\frac{5}{\sqrt{2}} + s\right) = \left(\frac{5}{\sqrt{2}} + 0\right) = \frac{5}{\sqrt{2}}.$$

The rate of change of $f(x, y) = x^2 + xy$ at $P_0(1, 2)$ in the direction $\mathbf{u} = (1/\sqrt{2})\mathbf{i} + (1/\sqrt{2})\mathbf{j}$ is $5/\sqrt{2}$.

Interpretation of the Directional Derivative

The equation $z = f(x, y)$ represents a surface S in space. If $z_0 = f(x_0, y_0)$, then the point $P(x_0, y_0, z_0)$ lies on S. The vertical plane that passes through P and $P_0(x_0, y_0)$ parallel to $\mathbf{u}$ intersects S in a curve C (Figure 11.27). The rate of change of f in the direction of $\mathbf{u}$ is the slope of the tangent to C at P.

When $\mathbf{u} = \mathbf{i}$, the directional derivative at P_0 is $\partial f/\partial x$ evaluated at (x_0, y_0). When $\mathbf{u} = \mathbf{j}$, the directional derivative at P_0 is $\partial f/\partial y$ evaluated at (x_0, y_0). The directional derivative generalizes the two partial derivatives. We can now ask for the rate of change of f in any direction $\mathbf{u}$, not just the directions $\mathbf{i}$ and $\mathbf{j}$.

Here's a physical interpretation of the directional derivative. Suppose that $T = f(x, y)$ is the temperature at each point (x, y) over a region in the plane. Then $f(x_0, y_0)$ is the temperature at the point $P_0(x_0, y_0)$ and $(D_{\mathbf{u}}f)_{P_0}$ is the instantaneous rate of change of the temperature at P_0 stepping off in the direction $\mathbf{u}$.

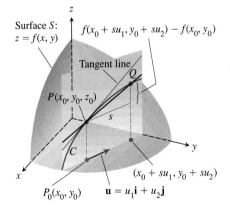

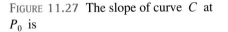

FIGURE 11.27 The slope of curve C at P_0 is

$$\lim_{Q \to P} \text{slope}(PQ)$$

$$= \lim_{s \to 0} \frac{f(x_0 + su_1, y_0 + su_2) - f(x_0, y_0)}{s}$$

$$= \left(\frac{df}{ds}\right)_{\mathbf{u}, P_0} = (D_{\mathbf{u}}f)_{P_0}.$$

Calculation

As you know, it is rarely convenient to calculate a derivative directly from its definition as a limit, and the directional derivative is no exception. We can develop a more efficient formula in the following way. We begin with the line

$$x = x_0 + su_1, \qquad y = y_0 + su_2, \tag{2}$$

through $P_0(x_0, y_0)$, parametrized with the arc length parameter s increasing in the direction of the unit vector $\mathbf{u} = u_1 \mathbf{i} + u_2 \mathbf{j}$. Then

$$
\begin{aligned}
\left(\frac{df}{ds} \right)_{\mathbf{u}, P_0} &= \left(\frac{\partial f}{\partial x} \right)_{P_0} \frac{dx}{ds} + \left(\frac{\partial f}{\partial y} \right)_{P_0} \frac{dy}{ds} \qquad \text{Chain Rule} \\
&= \left(\frac{\partial f}{\partial x} \right)_{P_0} \cdot u_1 + \left(\frac{\partial f}{\partial y} \right)_{P_0} \cdot u_2 \qquad \text{From Eqs. (2), } dx/ds = u_1 \text{ and } dy/ds = u_2 \\
&= \underbrace{\left[\left(\frac{\partial f}{\partial x} \right)_{P_0} \mathbf{i} + \left(\frac{\partial f}{\partial y} \right)_{P_0} \mathbf{j} \right]}_{\text{Gradient of } f \text{ at } P_0} \cdot \underbrace{\left[u_1 \mathbf{i} + u_2 \mathbf{j} \right]}_{\text{Direction } \mathbf{u}} . \qquad (3)
\end{aligned}
$$

The notation ∇f is read "grad f" as well as "gradient of f" and "del f." The symbol ∇ by itself is read "del." Another notation for the gradient is grad f, read the way it is written.

Definition Gradient Vector or Gradient

The **gradient vector (gradient)** of $f(x, y)$ at a point $P_0(x_0, y_0)$ is the vector

$$
\nabla f = \frac{\partial f}{\partial x} \mathbf{i} + \frac{\partial f}{\partial y} \mathbf{j}
$$

obtained by evaluating the partial derivatives of f at P_0.

Equation (3) says that the derivative of f in the direction of $\mathbf{u}$ at P_0 is the dot product of $\mathbf{u}$ with the gradient of f at P_0.

CD-ROM
WEBsite

Theorem 9 The Directional Derivative is a Dot Product

If the partial derivatives of $f(x, y)$ are defined at $P_0(x_0, y_0)$, then

$$
\left(\frac{df}{ds} \right)_{\mathbf{u}, P_0} = (\nabla f)_{P_0} \cdot \mathbf{u}, \qquad (4)
$$

the dot product of the gradient f at P_0 and $\mathbf{u}$.

Example 2 Finding the Directional Derivative Using the Gradient

Find the derivative of $f(x, y) = xe^y + \cos(xy)$ at the point $(2, 0)$ in the direction of $\mathbf{v} = 3\mathbf{i} - 4\mathbf{j}$.

Solution The direction of $\mathbf{v}$ is obtained by dividing $\mathbf{v}$ by its length:

$$
\mathbf{u} = \frac{\mathbf{v}}{|\mathbf{v}|} = \frac{\mathbf{v}}{5} = \frac{3}{5} \mathbf{i} - \frac{4}{5} \mathbf{j}.
$$

The partial derivatives of f at $(2, 0)$ are

$$
\begin{aligned}
f_x(2, 0) &= (e^y - y \sin(xy))_{(2,0)} = e^0 - 0 = 1 \\
f_y(2, 0) &= (xe^y - x \sin(xy))_{(2,0)} = 2e^0 - 2 \cdot 0 = 2.
\end{aligned}
$$

The gradient of f at $(2, 0)$ is

$$
\nabla f|_{(2,0)} = f_x(2, 0)\mathbf{i} + f_y(2,0)\mathbf{j} = \mathbf{i} + 2\mathbf{j}
$$

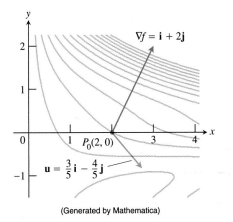

FIGURE 11.28 It is customary to picture ∇f as a vector in the domain of f. In the case of $f(x, y) = xe^y + \cos(xy)$, the domain is the entire plane. The rate at which f changes in the direction $\mathbf{u} = (3/5)\mathbf{i} - (4/5)\mathbf{j}$ is $\nabla f \cdot \mathbf{u} = -1$. (Example 2)

(Figure 11.28). The derivative of f at $(2, 0)$ in the direction of $\mathbf{v}$ is therefore

$$(D_{\mathbf{u}}f)\,|_{(2,0)} = \nabla f|_{(2,0)} \cdot \mathbf{u} \qquad \text{Eq. (4)}$$

$$= (\mathbf{i} + 2\mathbf{j}) \cdot \left(\frac{3}{5}\mathbf{i} - \frac{4}{5}\mathbf{j}\right) = \frac{3}{5} - \frac{8}{5} = -1.$$

Properties of Directional Derivatives

Evaluating the dot product in the formula

$$D_{\mathbf{u}}f = \nabla f \cdot \mathbf{u} = |\nabla f||\mathbf{u}|\cos\theta = |\nabla f|\cos\theta,$$

where θ is the angle between the vectors $\mathbf{u}$ and ∇f, reveals the following properties.

Properties of the Directional Derivative $D_{\mathbf{u}}f = \nabla f \cdot \mathbf{u} = |\nabla f|\cos\theta$

1. The function f increases most rapidly when $\cos\theta = 1$ or when $\mathbf{u}$ is the direction of ∇f. That is, at each point P in its domain, f increases most rapidly in the direction of the gradient vector ∇f at P. The derivative in this direction is

$$D_{\mathbf{u}}f = |\nabla f|\cos(0) = |\nabla f|.$$

2. Similarly, f decreases most rapidly in the direction of $-\nabla f$. The derivative in this direction is $D_{\mathbf{u}}f = |\nabla f|\cos(\pi) = -|\nabla f|$.

3. Any direction $\mathbf{u}$ orthogonal to the gradient is a direction of zero change in f because θ then equals $\pi/2$ and

$$D_{\mathbf{u}}f = |\nabla f|\cos(\pi/2) = |\nabla f| \cdot 0 = 0.$$

As we discuss later, these properties hold in three dimensions as well as two.

Example 3   Finding Directions of Maximal, Minimal, and Zero Change

Find the directions in which $f(x, y) = (x^2/2) + (y^2/2)$

(a) Increases most rapidly at the point $(1, 1)$

(b) Decreases most rapidly at $(1, 1)$.

(c) What are the directions of zero change in f at $(1, 1)$?

Solution

(a) The function increases most rapidly in the direction of ∇f at $(1, 1)$. The gradient there is

$$(\nabla f)_{(1,1)} = (x\mathbf{i} + y\mathbf{j})_{(1,1)} = \mathbf{i} + \mathbf{j}.$$

Its direction is

$$\mathbf{u} = \frac{\mathbf{i} + \mathbf{j}}{|\mathbf{i} + \mathbf{j}|} = \frac{\mathbf{i} + \mathbf{j}}{\sqrt{(1)^2 + (1)^2}} = \frac{1}{\sqrt{2}}\mathbf{i} + \frac{1}{\sqrt{2}}\mathbf{j}.$$

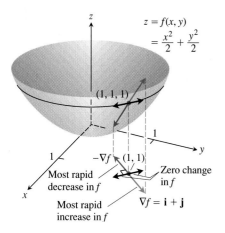

FIGURE 11.29 The direction in which $f(x, y) = (x^2/2) + (y^2/2)$ increases most rapidly at $(1, 1)$ is the direction of $\nabla f|_{(1,1)} = \mathbf{i} + \mathbf{j}$. It corresponds to the direction of steepest ascent on the surface at $(1, 1, 1)$.

(b) The function decreases most rapidly in the direction of $-\nabla f$ at $(1, 1)$, which is

$$-\mathbf{u} = -\frac{1}{\sqrt{2}}\mathbf{i} - \frac{1}{\sqrt{2}}\mathbf{j}.$$

(c) The directions of zero change at $(1, 1)$ are the directions orthogonal to ∇f:

$$\mathbf{n} = -\frac{1}{\sqrt{2}}\mathbf{i} + \frac{1}{\sqrt{2}}\mathbf{j} \quad \text{and} \quad -\mathbf{n} = \frac{1}{\sqrt{2}}\mathbf{i} - \frac{1}{\sqrt{2}}\mathbf{j}.$$

See Figure 11.29. *opposite units*

Gradients and Tangents to Level Curves

If a differentiable function $f(x, y)$ has a constant value c along a smooth curve $\mathbf{r} = g(t)\mathbf{i} + h(t)\mathbf{j}$ (making the curve a level curve of f), then $f(g(t), h(t)) = c$. Differentiating both sides of this equation with respect to t leads to the equations

$$\frac{d}{dt}f(g(t), h(t)) = \frac{d}{dt}(c)$$

$$\frac{\partial f}{\partial x}\frac{dg}{dt} + \frac{\partial f}{\partial y}\frac{dh}{dt} = 0 \qquad \text{Chain Rule}$$

$$\underbrace{\left(\frac{\partial f}{\partial x}\mathbf{i} + \frac{\partial f}{\partial y}\mathbf{j}\right)}_{\nabla f} \cdot \underbrace{\left(\frac{dg}{dt}\mathbf{i} + \frac{dh}{dt}\mathbf{j}\right)}_{\frac{d\mathbf{r}}{dt}} = 0. \qquad (5)$$

Equation (5) says that ∇f is normal to the tangent vector $d\mathbf{r}/dt$, so it is normal to the curve.

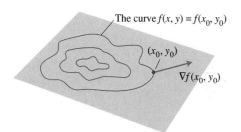

FIGURE 11.30 The gradient of a differentiable function of two variables at a point is always normal to the function's level curve through that point.

At every point (x_0, y_0) in the domain of $f(x, y)$, the gradient of f is normal to the level curve through (x_0, y_0) (Figure 11.30).

Equation (5) validates our observation that streams flow perpendicular to the contours in topographical maps (Figure 11.25). Since the downflowing stream will reach its destination in the fastest way, it must flow in the direction of the negative gradient vectors from Property 2 for the directional derivative. Equation (5) tells us these directions are perpendicular to the level curves.

This observation also enables us to find equations for tangent lines to level curves. They are the lines normal to the gradients. The line through a point $P_0(x_0, y_0)$ normal to a vector $\mathbf{N} = A\mathbf{i} + B\mathbf{j}$ has the equation

$$A(x - x_0) + B(y - y_0) = 0.$$

(Exercise 59). If $\mathbf{N}$ is the gradient $(\nabla f)_{(x_0,y_0)} = f_x(x_0, y_0)\mathbf{i} + f_y(x_0, y_0)\mathbf{j}$, the equation becomes *tangent line*

$$f_x(x_0, y_0)(x - x_0) + f_y(x_0, y_0)(y - y_0) = 0. \qquad (6)$$

Note →

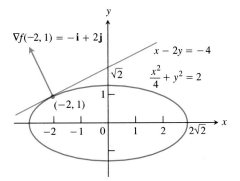

$\nabla f(-2, 1) = -\mathbf{i} + 2\mathbf{j}$

$x - 2y = -4$

$\sqrt{2}$

$\dfrac{x^2}{4} + y^2 = 2$

$(-2, 1)$

$2\sqrt{2}$

FIGURE 11.31 We can find the tangent to the ellipse $(x^2/4) + y^2 = 2$ by treating the ellipse as a level curve of the function $f(x, y) = (x^2/4) + y^2$. (Example 4)

(handwritten)
$f_x(-2,1) = \left(\tfrac{1}{2}x + 0\right)_{(-2,1)} = -1$

$f_y(-2,1) = (0 + 2y)_{(-2,1)} = 2$

These rules have the same form as the corresponding rules for derivatives, as they should (Exercise 63).

Example 4 Finding the Tangent Line to an Ellipse

Find an equation for the tangent to the ellipse

$$\frac{x^2}{4} + y^2 = 2$$

(handwritten) JUSt remember that the given points are usually (x_0, y_0)

(handwritten under point) x_0, y_0

(Figure 11.31) at the point $(-2, 1)$.

Solution   The ellipse is a level curve of the function

$$f(x, y) = \frac{x^2}{4} + y^2.$$

(handwritten) x_0, y_0

The gradient of f at $(-2, 1)$ is

$$\nabla f|_{(-2,1)} = \left(\frac{x}{2}\mathbf{i} + 2y\mathbf{j}\right)_{(-2,1)} = -\mathbf{i} + 2\mathbf{j}.$$

The tangent is the line

$$(-1)(x + 2) + (2)(y - 1) = 0 \qquad \text{Eq. (6)}$$
$$x - 2y = -4.$$

Algebra Rules for Gradients

If we know the gradients of two functions f and g, we automatically know the gradients of their constant multiples, sum, difference, product, and quotient.

Algebra Rules for Gradients

1. *Constant Multiple Rule:* $\qquad \nabla(kf) = k\nabla f \qquad$ (any number k)

2. *Sum Rule:* $\qquad\qquad\quad \nabla(f + g) = \nabla f + \nabla g$

3. *Difference Rule:* $\qquad\quad \nabla(f - g) = \nabla f - \nabla g$

4. *Product Rule:* $\qquad\qquad \nabla(fg) = f\nabla g + g\nabla f$

5. *Quotient Rule:* $\qquad\qquad \nabla\left(\dfrac{f}{g}\right) = \dfrac{g\nabla f - f\nabla g}{g^2}$

Example 5 Illustrating the Gradient Rules

We illustrate the rules with

$$f(x, y) = x - y \qquad g(x, y) = 3y$$
$$\nabla f = \mathbf{i} - \mathbf{j} \qquad\quad \nabla g = 3\mathbf{j}.$$

We have

1. $\nabla(2f) = \nabla(2x - 2y) = 2\mathbf{i} - 2\mathbf{j} = 2\nabla f$

2. $\nabla(f + g) = \nabla(x + 2y) = \mathbf{i} + 2\mathbf{j} = \nabla f + \nabla g$

3. $\nabla(f - g) = \nabla(x - 4y) = \mathbf{i} - 4\mathbf{j} = \nabla f - \nabla g$

4. $\nabla(fg) = \nabla(3xy - 3y^2) = 3y\mathbf{i} + (3x - 6y)\mathbf{j}$

$= 3y(\mathbf{i} - \mathbf{j}) + 3y\mathbf{j} + (3x - 6y)\mathbf{j}$

$= 3y(\mathbf{i} - \mathbf{j}) + (3x - 3y)\mathbf{j}$

$= 3y(\mathbf{i} - \mathbf{j}) + (x - y)3\mathbf{j} = g\nabla f + f\nabla g$

5. $\nabla\left(\dfrac{f}{g}\right) = \nabla\left(\dfrac{x-y}{3y}\right) = \nabla\left(\dfrac{x}{3y} - \dfrac{1}{3}\right)$

$= \dfrac{1}{3y}\mathbf{i} - \dfrac{x}{3y^2}\mathbf{j}$

$= \dfrac{3y\mathbf{i} - 3x\mathbf{j}}{9y^2} = \dfrac{3y(\mathbf{i} - \mathbf{j}) - (3x - 3y)\mathbf{j}}{9y^2}$

$= \dfrac{3y(\mathbf{i} - \mathbf{j}) - (x - y)3\mathbf{j}}{9y^2} = \dfrac{g\nabla f - f\nabla g}{g^2}.$

Increments and Distance

The directional derivative plays the role of an ordinary derivative when we want to estimate how much the value of a function f changes if we move a small distance ds from a point P_0 to another point nearby. If f were a function of a single variable, we would have

$$df = f'(P_0)\, ds. \qquad \text{Ordinary derivative} \times \text{increment}$$

For a function of two or more variables, we use the formula

$$df = (\nabla f|_{P_0} \cdot \mathbf{u})\, ds, \qquad \text{Directional derivative} \times \text{increment}$$

where $\mathbf{u}$ is the direction of the motion away from P_0.

Estimating the Change in f in a Direction u

To estimate the change in the value of a function f when we move a small distance ds from a point P_0 in a particular direction $\mathbf{u}$, use the formula

$$df = \underbrace{(\nabla f|_{P_0} \cdot \mathbf{u})}_{\substack{\text{directional} \\ \text{derivative}}} \quad \cdot \quad \underbrace{ds}_{\substack{\text{distance} \\ \text{increment}}}$$

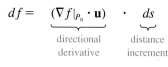

Example 6   Estimating Change in the Value of $f(x, y)$

Estimate how much the value of

$$f(x, y) = xe^y$$

will change if the point $P(x, y)$ moves 0.1 unit from $P_0(2, 0)$ straight toward $P_1(4, 1)$.

Solution   We first find the derivative of f at P_0 in the direction of the vector

$$\overrightarrow{P_0P_1} = 2\mathbf{i} + \mathbf{j}.$$

The direction of this vector is

$$\mathbf{u} = \frac{\overrightarrow{P_0P_1}}{|\overrightarrow{P_0P_1}|} = \frac{\overrightarrow{P_0P_1}}{\sqrt{5}} = \frac{2}{\sqrt{5}}\mathbf{i} + \frac{1}{\sqrt{5}}\mathbf{j}.$$

The gradient of f at P_0 is

$$\nabla f_{(2,0)} = (e^y\mathbf{i} + xe^y\mathbf{j})_{(2,0)} = \mathbf{i} + 2\mathbf{j}.$$

add after multiplying

Therefore,

$$\nabla f|_{P_0} \cdot \mathbf{u} = (\mathbf{i} + 2\mathbf{j}) \cdot \left(\frac{2}{\sqrt{5}}\mathbf{i} + \frac{1}{\sqrt{5}}\mathbf{j}\right) = \frac{2}{\sqrt{5}} + \frac{2}{\sqrt{5}} = \frac{4}{\sqrt{5}}.$$

The change df in f that results from moving $ds = 0.1$ unit away from P_0 in the direction of $\mathbf{u}$ is approximately

$$df = (\nabla f|_{P_0} \cdot \mathbf{u})(ds) = \left(\frac{4}{\sqrt{5}}\right)(0.1) \approx 0.18 \text{ units.}$$

Functions of Three Variables

We obtain three-variable formulas by adding the z-terms to the two-variable formulas. For a differentiable function $f(x, y, z)$ and a unit vector $\mathbf{u} = u_1\mathbf{i} + u_2\mathbf{j} + u_3\mathbf{k}$ in space, we have

$$\nabla f = \frac{\partial f}{\partial x}\mathbf{i} + \frac{\partial f}{\partial y}\mathbf{j} + \frac{\partial f}{\partial z}\mathbf{k}$$

and

$$D_\mathbf{u}f = \nabla f \cdot \mathbf{u} = \frac{\partial f}{\partial x}u_1 + \frac{\partial f}{\partial y}u_2 + \frac{\partial f}{\partial z}u_3.$$

The directional derivative can once again be written in the form

$$D_\mathbf{u}f = \nabla f \cdot \mathbf{u} = |\nabla f||u|\cos\theta = |\nabla f|\cos\theta,$$

so the properties listed earlier for functions of two variables continue to hold. At any given point, f increases most rapidly in the direction of ∇f and decreases most rapidly in the direction of $-\nabla f$. In any direction orthogonal to ∇f, the derivative is zero.

Example 7 Finding Directions of Maximal, Minimal, and Zero Change

(a) Find the derivative of $f(x, y, z) = x^3 - xy^2 - z$ at $P_0(1, 1, 0)$ in the direction of $\mathbf{v} = 2\mathbf{i} - 3\mathbf{j} + 6\mathbf{k}$.

(b) In what directions does f change most rapidly at P_0, and what are the rates of change in these directions?

Solution

Note

(a) The direction of $\mathbf{v}$ is obtained by dividing $\mathbf{v}$ by its length:

$$|\mathbf{v}| = \sqrt{(2)^2 + (-3)^2 + (6)^2} = \sqrt{49} = 7$$

$$\mathbf{u} = \frac{\mathbf{v}}{|\mathbf{v}|} = \frac{2}{7}\mathbf{i} - \frac{3}{7}\mathbf{j} + \frac{6}{7}\mathbf{k}.$$

The partial derivatives of f at P_0 are

$$f_x = (3x^2 - y^2)_{(1,1,0)} = 2,$$

$$f_y = -2xy\,|_{(1,1,0)} = -2, \qquad f_z = -1\,|_{(1,1,0)} = -1.$$

The gradient of f at P_0 is

$$\nabla f|_{(1,1,0)} = 2\mathbf{i} - 2\mathbf{j} - \mathbf{k}.$$

The derivative of f at P_0 in the direction of $\mathbf{v}$ is therefore

$$(D_{\mathbf{u}}f)_{(1,1,0)} = \nabla f|_{(1,1,0)} \cdot \mathbf{u} = (2\mathbf{i} - 2\mathbf{j} - \mathbf{k}) \cdot \left(\frac{2}{7}\mathbf{i} - \frac{3}{7}\mathbf{j} + \frac{6}{7}\mathbf{k}\right)$$

$$= \frac{4}{7} + \frac{6}{7} - \frac{6}{7} = \frac{4}{7}.$$

(b) The function increases most rapidly in the direction of $\nabla f = 2\mathbf{i} - 2\mathbf{j} - \mathbf{k}$ and decreases most rapidly in the direction of $-\nabla f$. The rates of change in the directions are, respectively,

$$|\nabla f| = \sqrt{(2)^2 + (-2)^2 + (-1)^2} = \sqrt{9} = 3 \qquad \text{and} \qquad -|\nabla f| = -3.$$

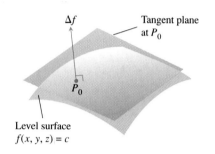

FIGURE 11.32 The gradient of a differentiable function of three variables at a point P_0 is normal to the function's level surface through that point. Thus, the gradient defines the normal to the tangent plane at P_0.

Tangent Planes and Normal Lines

The gradient vector for a differentiable function of three variables $f(x, y, z)$ satisfies all the properties for the gradients of two variables. In particular, just as we established the validity of Equation (5), at every point P_0 in the domain of $f(x, y, z)$, the gradient ∇f is normal to the level surface through P_0 (Figure 11.32). This observation leads to the following definitions.

> **Definitions**   Tangent Plane and Normal Line
> The **tangent plane** at the point $P_0(x_0, y_0, z_0)$ on the level surface $f(x, y, z) = c$ is the plane through P_0 normal to $\nabla f|_{P_0}$.
>
> The **normal line** of the surface at P_0 is the line through P_0 parallel to $\nabla f|_{P_0}$.

Thus, from Section 10.3, the tangent plane and normal line, respectively, have the following equations:

$$f_x(P_0)(x - x_0) + f_y(P_0)(y - y_0) + f_z(P_0)(z - z_0) = 0 \tag{7}$$

$$x = x_0 + f_x(P_0)\,t, \qquad y = y_0 + f_y(P_0)\,t, \qquad z = z_0 + f_z(P_0)\,t. \tag{8}$$

Example 8   Finding the Tangent Plane and Normal Line

Find the tangent plane and normal line of the surface

$$f(x, y, z) = x^2 + y^2 + z - 9 = 0 \qquad \text{A circular paraboloid}$$

at the point $P_0(1, 2, 4)$.

Solution   The surface is shown in Figure 11.33.

The tangent plane is the plane through P_0 perpendicular to the gradient of f at P_0. The gradient is

$$\nabla f|_{P_0} = (2x\mathbf{i} + 2y\mathbf{j} + \mathbf{k})_{(1,2,4)} = 2\mathbf{i} + 4\mathbf{j} + \mathbf{k}.$$

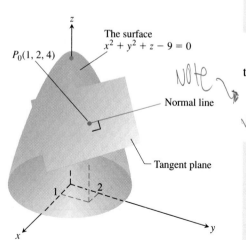

FIGURE 11.33 The tangent plane and normal line to the surface $x^2 + y^2 + z - 9 = 0$ at $P_0(1, 2, 4)$. (Example 8)

The plane is therefore the plane

$$2(x - 1) + 4(y - 2) + (z - 4) = 0, \quad \text{or} \quad 2x + 4y + z = 14.$$

The line normal to the surface at P_0 is

$$x = 1 + 2t, \quad y = 2 + 4t, \quad z = 4 + t.$$

Planes Tangent to a Surface $z = f(x, y)$

To find an equation for the plane tangent to a surface $z = f(x, y)$ at a point $P_0(x_0, y_0, z_0)$ where $z_0 = f(x_0, y_0)$, we first observe that the equation $z = f(x, y)$ is equivalent to $f(x, y) - z = 0$. The surface $z = f(x, y)$ is therefore the zero level surface of the function $F(x, y, z) = f(x, y) - z$. The partial derivatives of F are

$$F_x = \frac{\partial}{\partial x}(f(x, y) - z) = f_x - 0 = f_x$$

$$F_y = \frac{\partial}{\partial y}(f(x, y) - z) = f_y - 0 = f_y$$

$$F_z = \frac{\partial}{\partial z}(f(x, y) - z) = 0 - 1 = -1.$$

The formula

$$F_x(P_0)(x - x_0) + F_y(P_0)(y - y_0) + F_z(P_0)(z - z_0) = 0$$

for the plane tangent to the level surface at P_0 therefore reduces to

Eq. (7) restated for $F(x, y, z)$

$$f_x(x_0, y_0)(x - x_0) + f_y(x_0, y_0)(y - y_0) - (z - z_0) = 0.$$

Plane Tangent to a Surface $z = f(x, y)$ at $(x_0, y_0, f(x_0, y_0))$
The plane tangent to the surface $z = f(x, y)$ at the point $P_0(x_0, y_0, z_0) = (x_0, y_0, f(x_0, y_0))$ is

$$f_x(x_0, y_0)(x - x_0) + f_y(x_0, y_0)(y - y_0) - (z - z_0) = 0. \tag{9}$$

Example 9   Finding a Plane Tangent to a Surface $z = f(x, y)$

Find the plane tangent to the surface $z = x \cos y - ye^x$ at $(0, 0, 0)$.

Solution   We calculate the partial derivatives of $f(x, y) = x \cos y - ye^x$ and use Equation (9):

$$f_x(0, 0) = (\cos y - ye^x)_{(0,0)} = 1 - 0 \cdot 1 = 1$$

$$f_y(0, 0) = (-x \sin y - e^x)_{(0,0)} = 0 - 1 = -1.$$

The tangent plane is therefore

$$1 \cdot (x - 0) - 1 \cdot (y - 0) - (z - 0) = 0, \quad \text{Eq. (9)}$$

or

$$x - y - z = 0.$$

Other Applications

The formula for estimating the change in $f(x, y, z)$ when we move a small distance ds from a point P_0 in a particular direction $\mathbf{u}$ in space holds as well:

$$df = (\nabla f|_{P_0} \cdot \mathbf{u}) \, ds. \tag{10}$$

Example 10   Estimating Change in the Value of $f(x, y, z)$

Estimate how much the value of

$$f(x, y, z) = y \sin x + 2yz$$

will change if the point $P(x, y, z)$ moves 0.1 units from $P_0(0, 1, 0)$ straight toward $P_1(2, 2, -2)$.

Solution   We first find the derivative of f at P_0 in the direction of the vector $\overrightarrow{P_0P_1} = 2\mathbf{i} + \mathbf{j} - 2\mathbf{k}$. The direction of this vector is

$$\mathbf{u} = \frac{\overrightarrow{P_0P_1}}{|\overrightarrow{P_0P_1}|} = \frac{\overrightarrow{P_0P_1}}{3} = \frac{2}{3}\mathbf{i} + \frac{1}{3}\mathbf{j} - \frac{2}{3}\mathbf{k}.$$

The gradient of f at P_0 is

$$\nabla f|_{(0,1,0)} = ((y \cos x)\mathbf{i} + (\sin x + 2z)\mathbf{j} + 2y\mathbf{k}))_{(0,1,0)} = \mathbf{i} + 2\mathbf{k}.$$

Therefore,

$$\nabla f|_{P_0} \cdot \mathbf{u} = (\mathbf{i} + 2\mathbf{k}) \cdot \left(\frac{2}{3}\mathbf{i} + \frac{1}{3}\mathbf{j} - \frac{2}{3}\mathbf{k}\right) = \frac{2}{3} - \frac{4}{3} = -\frac{2}{3}.$$

The change df in f that results from moving $ds = 0.1$ units away from P_0 in the direction of $\mathbf{u}$ is approximately

$$df = (\nabla f|_{P_0} \cdot \mathbf{u})(ds) = \left(-\frac{2}{3}\right)(0.1) \approx -0.067 \text{ units.}$$

Example 11   Finding Parametric Equations for a Line Tangent to a Space Curve

The surfaces

$$f(x, y, z) = x^2 + y^2 - 2 = 0 \qquad \text{A cylinder}$$

and

$$g(x, y, z) = x + z - 4 = 0 \qquad \text{A plane}$$

meet in an ellipse E (Figure 11.34). Find parametric equations for the line tangent to E at the point $P_0(1, 1, 3)$.

Solution   The tangent line is orthogonal to both ∇f and ∇g at P_0 and therefore parallel to $\mathbf{v} = \nabla f \times \nabla g$. The components of $\mathbf{v}$ and the coordinates of P_0 give us equations for the line. We have

$$\nabla f_{(1,1,3)} = (2x\mathbf{i} + 2y\mathbf{j})_{(1,1,3)} = 2\mathbf{i} + 2\mathbf{j}$$

$$\nabla g_{(1,1,3)} = (\mathbf{i} + \mathbf{k})_{(1,1,3)} = \mathbf{i} + \mathbf{k}$$

$$\mathbf{v} = (2\mathbf{i} + 2\mathbf{j}) \times (\mathbf{i} + \mathbf{k}) = \begin{vmatrix} \mathbf{i} & \mathbf{j} & \mathbf{k} \\ 2 & 2 & 0 \\ 1 & 0 & 1 \end{vmatrix} = 2\mathbf{i} - 2\mathbf{j} - 2\mathbf{k}.$$

The line is

$$x = 1 + 2t, \qquad y = 1 - 2t, \qquad z = 3 - 2t.$$

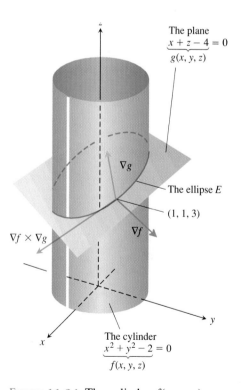

The plane
$\underbrace{x + z - 4 = 0}_{g(x, y, z)}$

The ellipse E

$(1, 1, 3)$

$\nabla f \times \nabla g$

∇g

∇f

The cylinder
$\underbrace{x^2 + y^2 - 2 = 0}_{f(x, y, z)}$

FIGURE 11.34 The cylinder $f(x, y, z) = x^2 + y^2 - 2 = 0$ and the plane $g(x, y, z) = x + z - 4 = 0$ intersect in an ellipse E. (Example 11)

EXERCISES 11.5

Calculating Gradients at Points

In Exercises 1–4, find the gradient of the function at the given point. Then sketch the gradient together with the level curve that passes through the point.

1. $f(x, y) = y - x$, $(2, 1)$

2. $f(x, y) = \ln(x^2 + y^2)$, $(1, 1)$

3. $g(x, y) = y - x^2$, $(-1, 0)$

4. $g(x, y) = \dfrac{x^2}{2} - \dfrac{y^2}{2}$, $(\sqrt{2}, 1)$

In Exercises 5–8, find ∇f at the given point.

5. $f(x, y, z) = x^2 + y^2 - 2z^2 + z \ln x$, $(1, 1, 1)$

6. $f(x, y, z) = 2z^3 - 3(x^2 + y^2)z + \tan^{-1} xz$, $(1, 1, 1)$

7. $f(x, y, z) = (x^2 + y^2 + z^2)^{-1/2} + \ln(xyz)$, $(-1, 2, -2)$

8. $f(x, y, z) = e^{x+y} \cos z + (y + 1) \sin^{-1} x$, $(0, 0, \pi/6)$

Finding Directional Derivatives in the xy-Plane

In Exercises 9–16, find the derivative of the function at P_0 in the direction of $\mathbf{A}$.

9. $f(x, y) = 2xy - 3y^2$, $P_0(5, 5)$, $\mathbf{A} = 4\mathbf{i} + 3\mathbf{j}$

10. $f(x, y) = 2x^2 + y^2$, $P_0(-1, 1)$, $\mathbf{A} = 3\mathbf{i} - 4\mathbf{j}$

11. $g(x, y) = x - (y^2/x) + \sqrt{3} \sec^{-1}(2xy)$, $P_0(1, 1)$, $\mathbf{A} = 12\mathbf{i} + 5\mathbf{j}$

12. $h(x, y) = \tan^{-1}(y/x) + \sqrt{3} \sin^{-1}(xy/2)$, $P_0(1, 1)$, $\mathbf{A} = 3\mathbf{i} - 2\mathbf{j}$

13. $f(x, y, z) = xy + yz + zx$, $P_0(1, -1, 2)$, $\mathbf{A} = 3\mathbf{i} + 6\mathbf{j} - 2\mathbf{k}$

14. $f(x, y, z) = x^2 + 2y^2 - 3z^2$, $P_0(1, 1, 1)$, $\mathbf{A} = \mathbf{i} + \mathbf{j} + \mathbf{k}$

15. $g(x, y, z) = 3e^x \cos yz$, $P_0(0, 0, 0)$, $\mathbf{A} = 2\mathbf{i} + \mathbf{j} - 2\mathbf{k}$

16. $h(x, y, z) = \cos xy + e^{yz} + \ln zx$, $P_0(1, 0, 1/2)$, $\mathbf{A} = \mathbf{i} + 2\mathbf{j} + 2\mathbf{k}$

Directions of Most Rapid Increase and Decrease

In Exercises 17–22, find the directions in which the functions increase and decrease most rapidly at P_0. Then find the derivatives of the functions in these directions.

17. $f(x, y) = x^2 + xy + y^2$, $P_0(-1, 1)$

18. $f(x, y) = x^2 y + e^{xy} \sin y$, $P_0(1, 0)$

19. $f(x, y, z) = (x/y) - yz$, $P_0(4, 1, 1)$

20. $g(x, y, z) = xe^y + z^2$, $P_0(1, \ln 2, 1/2)$

21. $f(x, y, z) = \ln xy + \ln yz + \ln xz$, $P_0(1, 1, 1)$

22. $h(x, y, z) = \ln(x^2 + y^2 - 1) + y + 6z$, $P_0(1, 1, 0)$

Estimating Change

23. By about how much will
$$f(x, y, z) = \ln\sqrt{x^2 + y^2 + z^2}$$
change if the point $P(x, y, z)$ moves from $P_0(3, 4, 12)$ a distance of $ds = 0.1$ units in the direction of $3\mathbf{i} + 6\mathbf{j} - 2\mathbf{k}$?

24. By about how much will
$$f(x, y, z) = e^x \cos yz$$
change as the point $P(x, y, z)$ moves from the origin a distance of $ds = 0.1$ units in the direction of $2\mathbf{i} + 2\mathbf{j} - 2\mathbf{k}$?

25. By about how much will
$$g(x, y, z) = x + x \cos z - y \sin z + y$$
change if the point $P(x, y, z)$ moves from $P_0(2, -1, 0)$ a distance of $ds = 0.2$ units toward the point $P_1(0, 1, 2)$?

26. By about how much will
$$h(x, y, z) = \cos(\pi xy) + xz^2$$
change if the point $P(x, y, z)$ moves from $P_0(-1, -1, -1)$ a distance of $ds = 0.1$ units toward the origin?

Tangent Planes and Normal Lines to Surfaces

In Exercises 27–34, find equations for the
  (a) Tangent plane and
  (b) Normal line at the point P_0 on the given surface.

27. $x^2 + y^2 + z^2 = 3$, $P_0(1, 1, 1)$

28. $x^2 + y^2 - z^2 = 18$, $P_0(3, 5, -4)$

29. $2z - x^2 = 0$, $P_0(2, 0, 2)$

30. $x^2 + 2xy - y^2 + z^2 = 7$, $P_0(1, -1, 3)$

31. $\cos \pi x - x^2 y + e^{yz} + yz = 4$, $P_0(0, 1, 2)$

32. $x^2 - xy - y^2 - z = 0$, $P_0(1, 1, -1)$

33. $x + y + z = 1$, $P_0(0, 1, 0)$

34. $x^2 + y^2 - 2xy - x + 3y - z = -4$, $P_0(2, -3, 18)$

In Exercises 35–38, find an equation for the plane that is tangent to the given surface at the given point.

35. $z = \ln(x^2 + y^2)$, $(1, 0, 0)$

36. $z = e^{-(x^2+y^2)}$, $(0, 0, 1)$

37. $z = \sqrt{y - x}$, $(1, 2, 1)$

38. $z = 4x^2 + y^2$, $(1, 1, 5)$

Tangent Lines to Curves

In Exercises 39–42, sketch the curve $f(x, y) = c$ together with ∇f and the tangent line at the given point. Then write an equation for the tangent line.

39. $x^2 + y^2 = 4$, $(\sqrt{2}, \sqrt{2})$

40. $x^2 - y = 1$, $(\sqrt{2}, 1)$

41. $xy = -4$, $(2, -2)$

42. $x^2 - xy + y^2 = 7$, $(-1, 2)$

In Exercises 43–48, find parametric equations for the line tangent to the curve of intersection of the surfaces at the given point.

43. Surfaces: $x + y^2 + 2z = 4$, $x = 1$

  Point: $(1, 1, 1)$

44. Surfaces: $xyz = 1$, $x^2 + 2y^2 + 3z^2 = 6$

  Point: $(1, 1, 1)$

45. Surfaces: $x^2 + 2y + 2z = 4$, $y = 1$

  Point: $(1, 1, 1/2)$

46. Surfaces: $x + y^2 + z = 2$, $y = 1$

  Point: $(1/2, 1, 1/2)$

47. Surfaces: $x^3 + 3x^2y^2 + y^3 + 4xy - z^2 = 0$, $x^2 + y^2 + z^2 = 11$

  Point: $(1, 1, 3)$

48. Surfaces: $x^2 + y^2 = 4$, $x^2 + y^2 - z = 0$

  Point: $(\sqrt{2}, \sqrt{2}, 4)$

Theory and Examples

49. *Zero directional derivative* In what direction is the derivative of $f(x, y) = xy + y^2$ at $P(3, 2)$ equal to zero?

50. *Zero directional derivative* In what directions is the derivative of $f(x, y) = (x^2 - y^2)/(x^2 + y^2)$ at $P(1, 1)$ equal to zero?

51. *Writing to Learn* Is there a direction $\mathbf{u}$ in which the rate of change of $f(x, y) = x^2 - 3xy + 4y^2$ at $P(1, 2)$ equals 14? Give reasons for your answer.

52. *Changing temperature along a circle* Is there a direction $\mathbf{u}$ in which the rate of change of the temperature function $T(x, y, z) = 2xy - yz$ (temperature in degrees Celsius, distance in feet) at $P(1, -1, 1)$ is $-3°C/\text{ft}$? Give reasons for your answer.

53. *Writing to Learn* The derivative of $f(x, y)$ at $P_0(1, 2)$ in the direction of $\mathbf{i} + \mathbf{j}$ is $2\sqrt{2}$ and in the direction of $-2\mathbf{j}$ is -3. What is the derivative of f in the direction of $-\mathbf{i} - 2\mathbf{j}$? Give reasons for your answer.

54. *Writing to Learn* The derivative of $f(x, y, z)$ at a point P is greatest in the direction of $\mathbf{v} = \mathbf{i} + \mathbf{j} - \mathbf{k}$. In this direction, the value of the derivative is $2\sqrt{3}$.

 (a) What is ∇f at P? Give reasons for your answer.

 (b) What is the derivative of f at P in the direction of $\mathbf{i} + \mathbf{j}$?

55. *Temperature change along a circle* Suppose that the Celsius temperature at the point (x, y) in the xy-plane is $T(x, y) = x \sin 2y$ and that distance in the xy-plane is measured in meters. A particle is moving *clockwise* around the circle of radius 1 m centered at the origin at the constant rate of 2 m/sec.

 (a) How fast is the temperature experienced by the particle changing in degrees Celsius per meter at the point $P(1/2, \sqrt{3}/2)$?

 (b) How fast is the temperature experienced by the particle changing in degrees Celsius per second at P?

56. *Change along the involute of a circle* Find the derivative of $f(x, y) = x^2 + y^2$ in the direction of the unit tangent vector of the curve

$$\mathbf{r}(t) = (\cos t + t \sin t)\mathbf{i} + (\sin t - t \cos t)\mathbf{j}, \qquad t > 0$$

(Figure 11.35).

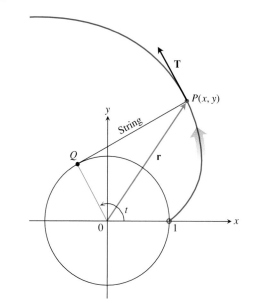

FIGURE 11.35 *The involute of the unit circle.* If you move out along the involute, covering distance along the curve at a constant rate, your distance from the origin will increase at a constant rate as well. (This is how to interpret the result of your calculation in Exercise 56.)

57. *Change along a helix* Find the derivative of $f(x, y, z) = x^2 + y^2 + z^2$ in the direction of the unit tangent vector of the helix

$$\mathbf{r}(t) = (\cos t)\mathbf{i} + (\sin t)\mathbf{j} + t\mathbf{k}$$

at the points where $t = -\pi/4$, 0, and $\pi/4$. The function f gives the square of the distance from a point $P(x, y, z)$ on the helix to the origin. The derivatives calculated here give the rates at which the square of the distance is changing with respect to t as P moves through the points where $t = -\pi/4$, 0, and $\pi/4$.

58. *Changing temperature along a space curve* The Celsius temperature in a region in space is given by $T(x, y, z) = 2x^2 - xyz$. A particle is moving in this region and its position at time t is given by $x = 2t^2$, $y = 3t$, $z = -t^2$, where time is measured in seconds and distance in meters.

(a) How fast is the temperature experienced by the particle changing in degrees Celsius per meter when the particle is at the point $P(8, 6, -4)$?

(b) How fast is the temperature experienced by the particle changing in degrees Celsius per second at P?

59. *Lines in the xy-plane* Show that $A(x - x_0) + B(y - y_0) = 0$ is an equation for the line in the xy-plane through the point (x_0, y_0) normal to the vector $\mathbf{N} = A\mathbf{i} + B\mathbf{j}$.

60. *Normal curves and tangent curves* A smooth curve is *normal* to a surface $f(x, y, z) = c$ at a point of intersection if the curve's velocity vector is a nonzero scalar multiple of ∇f at the point. The curve is *tangent* to the surface at a point of intersection if its velocity vector is orthogonal to ∇f there.

(a) Show that the curve

$$\mathbf{r}(t) = \sqrt{t}\,\mathbf{i} + \sqrt{t}\,\mathbf{j} - \frac{1}{4}(t + 3)\mathbf{k}$$

is normal to the surface $x^2 + y^2 - z = 3$ when $t = 1$.

(b) Show that the curve

$$\mathbf{r}(t) = \sqrt{t}\,\mathbf{i} + \sqrt{t}\,\mathbf{j} + (2t - 1)\mathbf{k}$$

is tangent to the surface $x^2 + y^2 - z = 1$ when $t = 1$.

61. *Writing to Learn: Directional derivatives and scalar components* How is the derivative of a differentiable function $f(x, y, z)$ at a point P_0 in the direction of a unit vector $\mathbf{u}$ related to the scalar component of $(\nabla f)_{P_0}$ in the direction of $\mathbf{u}$? Give reasons for your answer.

62. *Writing to Learn: Directional derivatives and partial derivatives* Assuming that the necessary derivatives of $f(x, y, z)$ are defined, how are $D_\mathbf{i}f$, $D_\mathbf{j}f$, and $D_\mathbf{k}f$ related to f_x, f_y, and f_z? Give reasons for your answer.

63. *The algebra rules for gradients* Given a constant k and the gradients

$$\nabla f = \frac{\partial f}{\partial x}\mathbf{i} + \frac{\partial f}{\partial y}\mathbf{j} + \frac{\partial f}{\partial z}\mathbf{k}$$

and

$$\nabla g = \frac{\partial g}{\partial x}\mathbf{i} + \frac{\partial g}{\partial y}\mathbf{j} + \frac{\partial g}{\partial z}\mathbf{k},$$

use the scalar equations

$$\frac{\partial}{\partial x}(kf) = k\frac{\partial f}{\partial x}, \qquad \frac{\partial}{\partial x}(f \pm g) = \frac{\partial f}{\partial x} \pm \frac{\partial g}{\partial x},$$

$$\frac{\partial}{\partial x}(fg) = f\frac{\partial g}{\partial x} + g\frac{\partial f}{\partial x}, \qquad \frac{\partial}{\partial x}\left(\frac{f}{g}\right) = \frac{g\frac{\partial f}{\partial x} - f\frac{\partial g}{\partial x}}{g^2},$$

and so on, to establish the following rules.

(a) $\nabla(kf) = k\nabla f$

(b) $\nabla(f + g) = \nabla f + \nabla g$

(c) $\nabla(f - g) = \nabla f - \nabla g$

(d) $\nabla(fg) = f\nabla g + g\nabla f$

(e) $\nabla\left(\dfrac{f}{g}\right) = \dfrac{g\nabla f - f\nabla g}{g^2}$

11.6 Linearization and Differentials

Linearization of a Function of Two Variables • Accuracy of the Standard Linear Approximation • Predicting Change with Differentials • Absolute, Relative, and Percentage Change • Functions of More Than Two Variables

In this section, we generalize the concepts of linearization and differentials to functions of two or more variables. We do this in a way similar to the way we find linear approximations for functions of a single variable (Section 3.6). The differential helps us determine the sensitivity of a multivariable function to changes in each of its independent variables. The mathematical results of the section stem from the Increment Theorem (Theorem 3, Section 11.3).

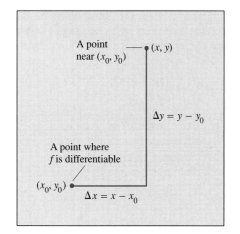

FIGURE 11.36 If f is differentiable at (x_0, y_0), then the value of f at any point (x, y) nearby is approximately $f(x_0, y_0) + f_x(x_0, y_0) \Delta x + f_y(x_0, y_0) \Delta y$.

Linearization of a Function of Two Variables

Suppose we wish to replace the function $z = f(x, y)$ with one that is simpler to work with. We want the replacement to be effective near a point (x_0, y_0) at which we know the values of f, f_x, and f_y and at which f is differentiable. Since f is differentiable, we know from Theorem 3 that the equation

$$\Delta z = f_x(x_0, y_0) \Delta x + f_y(x_0, y_0) \Delta y + \epsilon_1 \Delta x + \epsilon_2 \Delta y. \tag{1}$$

holds for f at (x_0, y_0). Therefore, if we move from (x_0, y_0) to any point (x, y) by increments $\Delta x = x - x_0$ and $\Delta y = y - y_0$ (Figure 11.36), the new value of f will be

$$f(x, y) = f(x_0, y_0) + f_x(x_0, y_0)(x - x_0)$$
$$+ f_y(x_0, y_0)(y - y_0) + \epsilon_1 \Delta x + \epsilon_2 \Delta y,$$

Eq. (1), with
$\Delta x = x - x_0$,
$\Delta y = y - y_0$, and
$\Delta z = f(x, y) - f(x_0, y_0)$

where ϵ_1, $\epsilon_2 \to 0$ as Δx, $\Delta y \to 0$. If the increments Δx and Δy are small, the products $\epsilon_1 \Delta x$ and $\epsilon_2 \Delta y$ will eventually be smaller still and we will have

$$f(x, y) \approx \underbrace{f(x_0, y_0) + f_x(x_0, y_0)(x - x_0) + f_y(x_0, y_0)(y - y_0)}_{L(x, y)}.$$

In other words, as long as Δx and Δy are small, f will have approximately the same value as the linear function L. If f is hard to use and our work can tolerate the error involved, we may safely replace f by L.

Definitions   Linearization, Standard Linear Approximation

The **linearization** of a function $f(x, y)$ at a point (x_0, y_0) where f is differentiable is the function

$$L(x, y) = f(x_0, y_0) + f_x(x_0, y_0)(x - x_0) + f_y(x_0, y_0)(y - y_0).$$

The approximation

$$f(x, y) \approx L(x, y)$$

is the **standard linear approximation** of f at (x_0, y_0).

From Section 11.5, Equation (9), we see that the plane $z = L(x, y)$ is tangent to the surface $z = f(x, y)$ at the point (x_0, y_0). Thus, the linearization of a function of two variables is a tangent-*plane* approximation in the same way that the linearization of a function of a single variable is a tangent-*line* approximation.

Example 1   Finding a Linearization

Find the linearization of

$$f(x, y) = x^2 - xy + \frac{1}{2} y^2 + 3$$

at the point $(3, 2)$.

Solution We first evaluate f, f_x, and f_y at the point $(x_0, y_0) = (3, 2)$:

$$f(3, 2) = \left(x^2 - xy + \frac{1}{2}y^2 + 3\right)_{(3,2)} = 8$$

$$f_x(3, 2) = \frac{\partial}{\partial x}\left(x^2 - xy + \frac{1}{2}y^2 + 3\right)_{(3,2)} = (2x - y)_{(3,2)} = 4$$

$$f_y(3, 2) = \frac{\partial}{\partial y}\left(x^2 - xy + \frac{1}{2}y^2 + 3\right)_{(3,2)} = (-x + y)_{(3,2)} = -1,$$

giving

$$L(x, y) = f(x_0, y_0) + f_x(x_0, y_0)(x - x_0) + f_y(x_0, y_0)(y - y_0)$$
$$= 8 + (4)(x - 3) + (-1)(y - 2) = 4x - y - 2.$$

The linearization of f at $(3, 2)$ is $L(x, y) = 4x - y - 2$.

Accuracy of the Standard Linear Approximation

Suppose that $L(x, y)$ is the linearization of a differentiable function $f(x, y)$ at (x_0, y_0) and we use L to approximate f at points (x, y) close to (x_0, y_0). How accurate can we expect the approximation to be? As you might expect, the closeness of the approximation depends on three things:

1. The closeness of x to x_0

2. The closeness of y to y_0

3. The "curviness" of f near (x_0, y_0), as measured by the magnitude of the second partial derivatives.

In fact, if we can find a common upper bound M for $|f_{xx}|$, $|f_{yy}|$, and $|f_{xy}|$ on a rectangle R centered at (x_0, y_0) (Figure 11.37), then we can bound the error throughout R by using a simple formula (derived in Section 11.10)

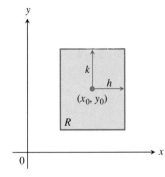

FIGURE 11.37 The rectangular region R: $|x - x_0| \le h$, $|y - y_0| \le k$ in the xy-plane. On this kind of region, we can find useful error bounds for our approximations.

The Error in the Standard Linear Approximation
If f has continuous first and second partial derivatives throughout an open set containing a rectangle R centered at (x_0, y_0) and if M is any upper bound for the values of $|f_{xx}|$, $|f_{yy}|$, and $|f_{xy}|$ on R, then the error $E(x, y)$ incurred in replacing $f(x, y)$ on R by its linearization

$$L(x, y) = f(x_0, y_0) + f_x(x_0, y_0)(x - x_0) + f_y(x_0, y_0)(y - y_0)$$

satisfies the inequality

$$|E(x, y)| \le \frac{1}{2}M(|x - x_0| + |y - y_0|)^2.$$

When we need to make $|E(x, y)|$ small for a given M, we just make $|x - x_0|$ and $|y - y_0|$ small.

Example 2   Bounding the Error in Example 1

In Example 1, we found the linearization of

$$f(x, y) = x^2 - xy + \frac{1}{2}y^2 + 3$$

at $(3, 2)$ to be

$$L(x, y) = 4x - y - 2.$$

Find an upper bound for the error in the approximation $f(x, y) \approx L(x, y)$ over the rectangle

$$R: \quad |x - 3| \le 0.1, \qquad |y - 2| \le 0.1.$$

Express the upper bound as a percentage of $f(3, 2)$, the value of f at the center of the rectangle.

Solution   We use the inequality

$$|E(x, y)| \le \frac{1}{2}M(|x - x_0| + |y - y_0|)^2.$$

To find a suitable value for M, we calculate f_{xx}, f_{xy}, and f_{yy}, finding, after a routine differentiation, that all three derivatives are constant, with values

$$|f_{xx}| = |2| = 2, \qquad |f_{xy}| = |-1| = 1, \qquad |f_{yy}| = |1| = 1.$$

The largest of these is 2, so we may safely take M to be 2. With $(x_0, y_0) = (3, 2)$, we then know that, throughout R,

$$|E(x, y)| \le \frac{1}{2}(2)(|x - 3| + |y - 2|)^2 = (|x - 3| + |y - 2|)^2.$$

Finally, since $|x - 3| \le 0.1$ and $|y - 2| \le 0.1$ on R, we have

$$|E(x, y)| \le (0.1 + 0.1)^2 = 0.04.$$

As a percentage of $f(3, 2) = 8$, the error is no greater than

$$\frac{0.04}{8} \times 100 = 0.5\%.$$

Interpret   As long as (x, y) stays in R, the approximation $f(x, y) \approx L(x, y)$ will be in error by no more than 0.04, which is $1/2\%$ of the value of f at the center of R.

Predicting Change with Differentials

Suppose that we know the values of a differentiable function $f(x, y)$ and its first partial derivatives at a point (x_0, y_0) and we want to predict how much the value of f will change if we move to a point $(x_0 + \Delta x, y_0 + \Delta y)$ nearby. If Δx and Δy are small, f and its linearization at (x_0, y_0) will change by nearly the same amount, so the change in L will give a practical estimate of the change in f.

The change in f is

$$\Delta f = f(x_0 + \Delta x, y_0 + \Delta y) - f(x_0, y_0).$$

A straightforward calculation from the definition of $L(x, y)$, using the notation $x - x_0 = \Delta x$ and $y - y_0 = \Delta y$, shows that the corresponding change in L is

$$\Delta L = L(x_0 + \Delta x, y_0 + \Delta y) - L(x_0, y_0)$$
$$= f_x(x_0, y_0)\, \Delta x + f_y(x_0, y_0)\, \Delta y.$$

The formula for Δf is usually as hard to work with as the formula for f. The change in L, however, is just a known constant times Δx plus a known constant times Δy.

The change ΔL is usually described in the more suggestive notation

$$df = f_x(x_0, y_0)\, dx + f_y(x_0, y_0)\, dy,$$

in which df denotes the change in the linearization that results from the changes dx and dy in x and y. As usual, we call dx and dy differentials of x and y, and call df the corresponding *total* differential of f.

Definition   Total Differential

If we move from (x_0, y_0) to a point $(x_0 + dx, y_0 + dy)$ nearby, the resulting change

$$df = f_x(x_0, y_0)\, dx + f_y(x_0, y_0)\, dy$$

in the linearization of f is called the **total differential of f.**

Absolute Change versus Relative Change

If you measure a 20-volt potential with an error of 10 volts, your reading is probably too crude to be useful. You are off by 50%. If you measure a 200,000-volt potential with an error of 10 volts, however, your reading is within 0.005% of the true value. An absolute error of 10 volts is significant in the first case but of no consequence in the second because the relative error is so small.

In other cases, a small relative error— say, traveling a few meters too far in a journey of hundreds of thousands of meters—can have spectacular consequences.

Example 3   Sensitivity to Change

Your company manufactures right circular cylindrical molasses storage tanks that are 25 ft high with a radius of 5 ft. How sensitive are the tanks' volumes to small variations in height and radius?

Solution   As a function of radius r and height h, the typical tank's volume is

$$V = \pi r^2 h.$$

The change in volume caused by small changes dr and dh in radius and height is approximately

$$dV = V_r(5, 25)\, dr + V_h(5, 25)\, dh \qquad \text{Total differential with}$$
$$= (2\pi r h)_{(5,25)}\, dr + (\pi r^2)_{(5,25)}\, dh \qquad f = V \text{ and } (x_0, y_0) = (5, 25)$$
$$= 250\pi\, dr + 25\pi\, dh.$$

Thus, a 1-unit change in r will change V by about 250π units. A 1-unit change in h will change V by about 25π units. The tank's volume is 10 times more sensitive to a small change in r than it is to a small change of equal size in h. As a quality control engineer concerned with being sure the tanks have the correct volume, you would want to pay special attention to their radii.

In contrast, if the values of r and h are reversed to make $r = 25$ and $h = 5$, then the total differential in V becomes

$$dV = (2\pi r h)_{(25,5)}\, dr + (\pi r^2)_{(25,5)} \quad dh = 250\pi\, dr + 625\pi\, dh.$$

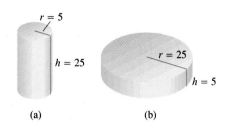

FIGURE 11.38 The volume of cylinder (a) is more sensitive to a small change in r than it is to an equally small change in h. The volume of cylinder (b) is more sensitive to small changes in h than it is to small changes in r.

Now the volume is more sensitive to changes in h than to changes in r (Figure 11.38).

The general rule to be learned from this example is that functions are most sensitive to small changes in the variables that generate the largest partial derivatives.

Absolute, Relative, and Percentage Change

When we move from (x_0, y_0) to a point nearby, we can describe the corresponding change in the value of a function $f(x, y)$ in three different ways.

	True	Estimate
Absolute change:	Δf	df
Relative change:	$\dfrac{\Delta f}{f(x_0, y_0)}$	$\dfrac{df}{f(x_0, y_0)}$
Percentage change:	$\dfrac{\Delta f}{f(x_0, y_0)} \times 100$	$\dfrac{df}{f(x_0, y_0)} \times 100$

Example 4 Estimating Change in Volume

Suppose that a cylindrical can is designed to have a radius of 1 in. and a height of 5 in., but that the radius and height are off by the amounts $dr = +0.03$ and $dh = -0.1$. Estimate the resulting absolute, relative, and percentage changes in the volume of the can.

Solution To estimate the absolute change in V, we evaluate

$$dV = V_r(r_0, h_0)\, dr + V_h(r_0, h_0)\, dh$$

to get

$$dV = 2\pi r_0 h_0\, dr + \pi r_0^2\, dh = 2\pi(1)(5)(0.0) + \pi(1)^2(-0.1)$$
$$= 0.3\pi - 0.1\pi = 0.2\pi \approx 0.63 \text{ in.}^3$$

We divide this by $V(r_0, h_0)$ to estimate the relative change:

$$\frac{dV}{V(r_0, h_0)} = \frac{0.2\pi}{\pi r_0^2 h_0} = \frac{0.2\pi}{\pi(1)^2(5)} = 0.04.$$

We multiply this by 100 to estimate the percentage change:

$$\frac{dV}{V(r_0, h_0)} \times 100 = 0.04 \times 100 = 4\%.$$

Example 5 Predicting Measurement Error

The volume $V = \pi r^2 h$ of a right circular cylinder is to be calculated from measured values of r and h. Suppose that r is measured with an error of no more than 2% and h with an error of no more than 0.5%. Estimate the resulting possible percentage error in the calculation of V.

Solution   We are told that

$$\left| \frac{dr}{r} \times 100 \right| \leq 2 \qquad \text{and} \qquad \left| \frac{dh}{h} \times 100 \right| \leq 0.5.$$

Since

$$\frac{dV}{V} = \frac{2\pi rh\, dr + \pi r^2\, dh}{\pi r^2 h} = \frac{2\, dr}{r} + \frac{dh}{h},$$

we have

$$\left| \frac{dV}{V} \right| = \left| 2\frac{dr}{r} + \frac{dh}{h} \right|$$

$$\leq \left| 2\frac{dr}{r} \right| + \left| \frac{dh}{h} \right|$$

$$\leq 2(0.02) + 0.005 = 0.045.$$

We estimate the error in the volume calculation to be at most 4.5%.

How accurately do we have to measure r and h to have a reasonable chance of calculating $V = \pi r^2 h$ with an error, say, of less than 2%? Questions like this are hard to answer because there is usually no single right answer. Since

$$\frac{dV}{V} = 2\frac{dr}{r} + \frac{dh}{h},$$

we see that dV/V is controlled by a combination of dr/r and dh/h. If we can measure h with great accuracy, we might come out all right even if we are sloppy about measuring r. On the other hand, our measurement of h might have so large a dh that the resulting dV/V would be too crude an estimate of $\Delta V/V$ to be useful even if dr were zero.

What we do in such cases is look for a reasonable square about the measured values (r_0, h_0) in which V will not vary by more than the allowed amount from $V_0 = \pi r_0^2 h_0$.

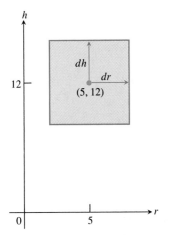

FIGURE 11.39 A small square about the point $(5, 12)$ in the rh-plane. (Example 6)

Example 6   Controlling the Error

Find a reasonable square about the point $(r_0, h_0) = (5, 12)$ in which the value of $V = \pi r^2 h$ will not vary by more than ± 0.1.

Solution   We approximate the variation ΔV by the differential

$$dV = 2\pi r_0 h_0\, dr + \pi r_0^2\, dh = 2\pi(5)(12)\, dr + \pi(5)^2\, dh = 120\pi\, dr + 25\pi\, dh.$$

Since the region to which we are restricting our attention is a square (Figure 11.39), we may set $dh = dr$ to get

$$dV = 120\pi\, dr + 25\pi\, dr = 145\pi\, dr.$$

We then ask, How small must we take dr to be sure that $|dV|$ is no larger than 0.1? To answer, we start with the inequality

$$|dV| \leq 0.1,$$

express dV in terms of dr,

$$|145\pi \, dr| \leq 0.1,$$

and find a corresponding upper bound for dr:

$$|dr| \leq \frac{0.1}{145\pi} \approx 2.1 \times 10^{-4}. \qquad \text{Rounding down to make sure } dr \text{ won't accidentally be too big}$$

With $dh = dr$, then, the square we want is described by the inequalities

$$|r - 5| \leq 2.1 \times 10^{-4}, \qquad |h - 12| \leq 2.1 \times 10^{-4}.$$

As long as (r, h) stays in this square, we may expect $|dV|$ to be less than or equal to 0.1 and we may expect $|\Delta V|$ to be approximately the same size.

Functions of More Than Two Variables

Analogous results hold for differentiable functions of more than two variables.

1. The **linearization** of $f(x, y, z)$ at a point $P_0(x_0, y_0, z_0)$ is

$$L(x, y, z) = f(P_0) + f_x(P_0)(x - x_0) + f_y(P_0)(y - y_0) + f_z(P_0)(z - z_0).$$

2. Suppose that R is a closed rectangular solid centered at P_0 and lying in an open region on which the second partial derivatives of f are continuous. Suppose also that $|f_{xx}|$, $|f_{yy}|$, $|f_{zz}|$, $|f_{xy}|$, $|f_{xz}|$, and $|f_{yz}|$ are all less than or equal to M throughout R. Then the **error** $E(x, y, z) = f(x, y, z) - L(x, y, z)$ in the approximation of f by L is bounded throughout R by the inequality

$$|E| \leq \frac{1}{2} M (|x - x_0| + |y - y_0| + |z - z_0|)^2.$$

3. If the second partial derivatives of f are continuous and if x, y, and z change from x_0, y_0, and z_0 by small amounts dx, dy, and dz, the **total differential**

$$df = f_x(P_0) \, dx + f_y(P_0) \, dy + f_z(P_0) \, dz$$

gives a good approximation of the resulting change in f.

Example 7   Finding a Linear Approximation in 3-Space

Find the linearization $L(x, y, z)$ of

$$f(x, y, z) = x^2 - xy + 3 \sin z$$

at the point $(x_0, y_0, z_0) = (2, 1, 0)$. Find an upper bound for the error incurred in replacing f by L on the rectangle

$$R: \quad |x - 2| \leq 0.01, \qquad |y - 1| \leq 0.02, \qquad |z| \leq 0.01.$$

Solution   A routine evaluation gives

$$f(2, 1, 0) = 2, \qquad f_x(2, 1, 0) = 3, \qquad f_y(2, 1, 0) = -2, \qquad f_z(2, 1, 0) = 3.$$

Thus,

$$L(x, y, z) = 2 + 3(x - 2) + (-2)(y - 1) + 3(z - 0) = 3x - 2y + 3z - 2.$$

Since

$$f_{xx} = 2, \qquad f_{yy} = 0, \qquad f_{zz} = -3 \sin z,$$
$$f_{xy} = -1, \qquad f_{xz} = 0, \qquad f_{yz} = 0,$$

we may safely take M to be max $|-3 \sin z| = 3$. Hence, the error incurred by replacing f by L on R satisfies

$$|E| \le \frac{1}{2}(3)(0.01 + 0.02 + 0.01)^2 = 0.0024.$$

The error will be no greater than 0.0024.

Example 8   Finding the Sag in Uniformly Loaded Beams

A horizontal rectangular beam, supported at both ends, will sag when subjected to a uniform load (constant weight per unit length). The amount S of sag (Figure 11.40) is calculated with the formula

$$S = C \frac{px^4}{wh^3}.$$

In this equation,

p = the load (newtons per meter of beam length)

x = the length between supports (meters)

w = the width of the beam (meters)

h = the height of the beam (meters)

C = a constant that depends on the units of measurement and on the material
  from which the beam is made.

Find dS for a beam 4 m long, 10 cm wide, and 20 cm high that is subjected to a load of 100 N/m (Figure 11.41). What conclusions can be drawn about the beam from the expression for dS?

Solution   Since S is a function of the four independent variables p, x, w, and h, its total differential is defined by

$$dS = S_p \, dp + S_x \, dx + S_w \, dw + S_h \, dh.$$

When we write this out for a particular set of values p_0, x_0, w_0, and h_0 and simplify the result, we find that

$$dS = S_0 \left(\frac{dp}{p_0} + \frac{4 \, dx}{x_0} - \frac{dw}{w_0} - \frac{3 \, dh}{h_0} \right),$$

where $S_0 = S(p_0, x_0, w_0, h_0) = Cp_0 x_0^4 / (w_0 h_0^3)$.

If $p_0 = 100$ N/m, $x_0 = 4$ m, $w_0 = 0.1$ m, and $h_0 = 0.2$ m, then

$$dS = S_0 \left(\frac{dp}{100} + dx - 10 \, dw - 15 \, dh \right).$$

Here is what we can learn from this equation for dS. Since dp and dx appear with positive coefficients, increases in p and x will increase the sag. The coefficients of dw and dh are negative, so increases in w and h will decrease

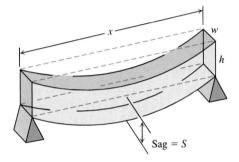

FIGURE 11.40 A beam supported at its two ends before and after loading. Example 8 shows how the sag S is related to the weight of the load and the dimensions of the beam.

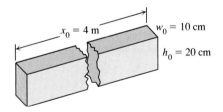

FIGURE 11.41 The dimensions of the beam in Example 8.

the sag (make the beam stiffer). The sag is not very sensitive to changes in load because the coefficient of dp is $1/100$. The magnitude of the coefficient of dh is greater than the magnitude of the coefficient of dw. Making the beam 1 cm higher will therefore decrease the sag more than making the beam 1 cm wider.

EXERCISES 11.6

Finding Linearizations

In Exercises 1–6, find the linearization $L(x, y)$ of the function at each point.

1. $f(x, y) = x^2 + y^2 + 1$ at (a) $(0, 0)$, (b) $(1, 1)$

2. $f(x, y) = (x + y + 2)^2$ at (a) $(0, 0)$, (b) $(1, 2)$

3. $f(x, y) = 3x - 4y + 5$ at (a) $(0, 0)$, (b) $(1, 1)$

4. $f(x, y) = x^3 y^4$ at (a) $(1, 1)$, (b) $(0, 0)$

5. $f(x, y) = e^x \cos y$ at (a) $(0, 0)$, (b) $(0, \pi/2)$

6. $f(x, y) = e^{2y-x}$ at (a) $(0, 0)$, (b) $(1, 2)$

Upper Bounds for Errors in Linear Approximations

In Exercises 7–12, find the linearization $L(x, y)$ of the function $f(x, y)$ at P_0. Then find an upper bound for the magnitude $|E|$ of the error in the approximation $f(x, y) \approx L(x, y)$ over the rectangle R.

7. $f(x, y) = x^2 - 3xy + 5$ at $P_0(2, 1)$,

   R: $|x - 2| \le 0.1$, $|y - 1| \le 0.1$

8. $f(x, y) = (1/2)x^2 + xy + (1/4)y^2 + 3x - 3y + 4$ at $P_0(2, 2)$,

   R: $|x - 2| \le 0.1$, $|y - 2| \le 0.1$

9. $f(x, y) = 1 + y + x \cos y$ at $P_0(0, 0)$,

   R: $|x| \le 0.2$, $|y| \le 0.2$

   (Use $|\cos y| \le 1$ and $|\sin y| \le 1$ in estimating E.)

10. $f(x, y) = xy^2 + y \cos (x - 1)$ at $P_0(1, 2)$,

    R: $|x - 1| \le 0.1$, $|y - 2| \le 0.1$

11. $f(x, y) = e^x \cos y$ at $P_0(0, 0)$,

    R: $|x| \le 0.1$, $|y| \le 0.1$

    (Use $e^x \le 1.11$ and $|\cos y| \le 1$ in estimating E.)

12. $f(x, y) = \ln x + \ln y$ at $P_0(1, 1)$,

    R: $|x - 1| \le 0.2$, $|y - 1| \le 0.2$

Sensitivity to Change: Estimates

13. *Writing to Learn* You plan to calculate the area of a long, thin rectangle from measurements of its length and width. Which dimension should you measure more carefully? Give reasons for your answer.

14. *Writing to Learn*

    (a) Around the point $(1, 0)$, is $f(x, y) = x^2(y + 1)$ more sensitive to changes in x or to changes in y? Give reasons for your answer.

    (b) What ratio of dx to dy will make df equal zero at $(1, 0)$?

15. *Estimating maximum error* Suppose that T is to be found from the formula $T = x (e^y + e^{-y})$, where x and y are found to be 2 and $\ln 2$ with maximum possible errors of $|dx| = 0.1$ and $|dy| = 0.02$. Estimate the maximum possible error in the computed value of T.

16. *Estimating volume of a cylinder* About how accurately may $V = \pi r^2 h$ be calculated from measurements of r and h that are in error by 1%?

17. *Maximum percentage error* If $r = 5.0$ cm and $h = 12.0$ cm to the nearest millimeter, what should we expect the maximum percentage error in calculating $V = \pi r^2 h$ to be?

18. *Estimating volume of a cylinder* To estimate the volume of a cylinder of radius about 2 m and height about 3 m, about how accurately should the radius and height be measured so that the error in the volume estimate will not exceed 0.1 m^3? Assume that the possible error dr in measuring r is equal to the possible error dh in measuring h.

19. *Controlling error within a square* Give a reasonable square centered at $(1, 1)$ over which the value of $f(x, y) = x^3y^4$ will not vary by more than ± 0.1.

20. *Variation in electrical resistance* The resistance R produced by wiring resistors of R_1 and R_2 ohms in parallel (Figure 11.42) can be calculated from the formula

    $$\frac{1}{R} = \frac{1}{R_1} + \frac{1}{R_2}.$$

    (a) Show that

    $$dR = \left(\frac{R}{R_1}\right)^2 dR_1 + \left(\frac{R}{R_2}\right)^2 dR_2.$$

    (b) *Writing to Learn* You have designed a two-resistor circuit like the one in Figure 11.42 to have resistances of $R_1 = 100$ ohms and $R_2 = 400$ ohms, but there is always some variation in manufacturing and the resistors received by your firm will probably not have these exact values. Will the value of R be more sensitive to variation in R_1 or to variation in R_2? Give reasons for your answer.

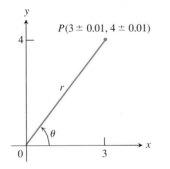

FIGURE 11.42 The circuit in Exercises 20 and 21.

21. (*Continuation of Exercise 20*) In another circuit like the one in Figure 11.42, you plan to change R_1 from 20 to 20.1 ohms and R_2 from 25 to 24.9 ohms. By about what percentage will this change R?

22. *Error carryover in coordinate changes*

y

$P(3 \pm 0.01, 4 \pm 0.01)$

4

r

θ

0   3   x

(a) If $x = 3 \pm 0.01$ and $y = 4 \pm 0.01$, as shown here, with approximately what accuracy can you calculate the polar coordinates r and θ of the point $P(x, y)$ from the formulas $r^2 = x^2 + y^2$ and $\theta = \tan^{-1}(y/x)$? Express your estimates as percentage changes of the values that r and θ have at the point $(x_0, y_0) = (3, 4)$.

(b) *Writing to Learn* At the point $(x_0, y_0) = (3, 4)$, are the values of r and θ more sensitive to changes in x or to changes in y? Give reasons for your answer.

Functions of Three Variables

Find the linearizations $L(x, y, z)$ of the functions in Exercises 23–28 at the given points.

23. $f(x, y, z) = xy + yz + xz$ at

(a) (1, 1, 1)   (b) (1, 0, 0)   (c) (0, 0, 0)

24. $f(x, y, z) = x^2 + y^2 + z^2$ at

(a) (1, 1, 1)   (b) (0, 1, 0)   (c) (1, 0, 0)

25. $f(x, y, z) = \sqrt{x^2 + y^2 + z^2}$ at

(a) (1, 0, 0)   (b) (1, 1, 0)   (c) (1, 2, 2)

26. $f(x, y, z) = (\sin xy)/z$ at

(a) $(\pi/2, 1, 1)$ (b) (2, 0, 1)

27. $f(x, y, z) = e^x + \cos(y + z)$ at

(a) (0, 0, 0)   (b) $\left(0, \frac{\pi}{2}, 0\right)$ (c) $\left(0, \frac{\pi}{4}, \frac{\pi}{4}\right)$

28. $f(x, y, z) = \tan^{-1}(xyz)$ at

(a) (1, 0, 0)   (b) (1, 1, 0)   (c) (1, 1, 1)

In Exercises 29–32, find the linearization $L(x, y, z)$ of the function $f(x, y, z)$ at P_0. Then find an upper bound for the magnitude of the error E in the approximation $f(x, y, z) \approx L(x, y, z)$ over the region R.

29. $f(x, y, z) = xz - 3yz + 2$ at $P_0(1, 1, 2)$

R: $|x - 1| \le 0.01$, $|y - 1| \le 0.01$, $|z - 2| \le 0.02$

30. $f(x, y, z) = x^2 + xy + yz + (1/4) z^2$ at $P_0(1, 1, 2)$

R: $|x - 1| \le 0.01$, $|y - 1| \le 0.01$, $|z - 2| \le 0.08$

31. $f(x, y, z) = xy + 2yz - 3xz$ at $P_0(1, 1, 0)$

R: $|x - 1| \le 0.01$, $|y - 1| \le 0.01$, $|z| \le 0.01$

32. $f(x, y, z) = \sqrt{2} \cos x \sin(y + z)$ at $P_0(0, 0, \pi/4)$

R: $|x| \le 0.01$, $|y| \le 0.01$, $|z - \pi/4| \le 0.01$

Theory and Examples

33. *The sagging beam revisited* The beam of Example 8 is tipped on its side so that $h = 0.1$ m and $w = 0.2$ m.

(a) What is the value of dS now?

(b) Compare the sensitivity of the newly positioned beam to a small change in height with its sensitivity to an equally small change in width.

34. *Designing a soda can* A standard 12 fl oz can of soda is essentially a cylinder of radius $r = 1$ in. and height $h = 5$ in.

(a) At these dimensions, how sensitive is the can's volume to a small change in radius versus a small change in height?

(b) Could you design a soda can that *appears* to hold more soda but in fact holds the same 12 fl oz? What might its dimensions be? (There is more than one correct answer.)

35. *Value of a 2 × 2 determinant* If $|a|$ is much greater than $|b|, |c|$, and $|d|$, to which of a, b, c, and d is the value of the determinant

$$f(a, b, c, d) = \begin{vmatrix} a & b \\ c & d \end{vmatrix}$$

most sensitive? Give reasons for your answer.

36. *Estimating error of a product* Estimate how strongly simultaneous errors of 2% in a, b, and c might affect the calculation of the product

$$p(a, b, c) = abc.$$

37. *Designing a box* Estimate how much wood it takes to make a hollow rectangular box whose inside measurements are 5 ft long by 3 ft wide by 2 ft deep if the box is made of lumber 1/2 in. thick and the box has no top.

38. *Surveying a triangular field* The area of a triangle is $(1/2)ab \sin C$, where a and b are the lengths of two sides of the triangle and C is the measure of the included angle. In surveying a triangular plot, you have measured a, b, and C to be 150 ft, 200 ft, and 60°, respectively. By about how much could your area calculation be in error if your values of a and b are off by half a foot each and your measurement of C is off by 2°? See the figure. Remember to use radians.

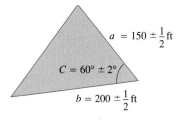

$a = 150 \pm \frac{1}{2}$ ft

$C = 60° \pm 2°$

$b = 200 \pm \frac{1}{2}$ ft

39. *Estimating maximum error* Suppose that $u = xe^y + y \sin z$ and that x, y, and z can be measured with maximum possible errors of ± 0.2, ± 0.6, and $\pm \pi/180$, respectively. Estimate the maximum possible error in calculating u from the measured values $x = 2$, $y = \ln 3$, $z = \pi/2$.

40. *The Wilson lot size formula* The Wilson lot size formula in economics says that the most economical quantity Q of goods (radios, shoes, brooms, whatever) for a store to order is given by the formula $Q = \sqrt{2KM/h}$, where K is the cost of placing the order, M is the number of items sold per week, and h is the weekly holding cost for each item (cost of space, utilities, security, and so on). To which of the variables K, M, and h is Q most sensitive near the point $(K_0, M_0, h_0) = (2, 20, 0.05)$? Give reasons for your answer.

41. *The linearization of f(x, y) is a tangent-plane approximation* Show that the tangent plane at the point $P_0(x_0, y_0, f(x_0, y_0))$ on the surface $z = f(x, y)$ defined by a differentiable function f is the plane

$$f_x(x_0, y_0)(x - x_0) + f_y(x_0, y_0)(y - y_0) - (z - f(x_0, y_0)) = 0$$

or

$$z = f(x_0, y_0) + f_x(x_0, y_0)(x - x_0) + f_y(x_0, y_0)(y - y_0).$$

Thus, the tangent plane at P_0 is the graph of the linearization of f at P_0 (Figure 11.43).

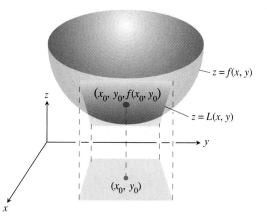

$(x_0, y_0, f(x_0, y_0))$

$z = f(x, y)$

$z = L(x, y)$

(x_0, y_0)

FIGURE 11.43 The graph of a function $z = f(x, y)$ and its linearization at a point (x_0, y_0). The plane defined by L is tangent to the surface at the point above the point (x_0, y_0). This furnishes a geometric explanation of why the values of L lie close to those of f in the immediate neighborhood of (x_0, y_0). (Exercise 41)

11.7 Extreme Values and Saddle Points

Behavior on Closed Bounded Regions • Derivative Tests for Local Extreme Values • Absolute Maxima and Minima on Closed Bounded Regions • Limitations of the First Derivative Test, and Summary

Finding the maximum and minimum values of functions of several variables, and knowing where they occur, is an important application of multivariable differential calculus. For example, what is the highest temperature on a heated metal plate, and where is it taken on? Where does a given surface attain its highest point above a given patch of the xy-plane? As we see in this section, we can often answer questions like these by examining the partial derivatives of some appropriate function.

Behavior on Closed Bounded Regions

As we saw when we were working with functions of a single variable, differentiable functions were just what we wanted for modeling optimization problems. Because these functions are continuous, we knew that on closed intervals they did assume both maximum and minimum values. Because they are differentiable, we knew that they would assume these values only at domain endpoints or at interior domain points where the first derivative vanished. Occasionally, we encountered functions that failed to be differentiable at one or more interior domain points and we had to add these points to the list to be investigated as well.

We also saw that the condition that $f'(c) = 0$ did not always signal the presence of an extreme value. At such a point c, the graph might have an inflection point instead of a local maximum or minimum. The graph might rise as it approached c from the left, level off at c, then rise again as it left c. Or it might fall toward c, level off at c, and then resume falling. That is, the graph might cross its tangent line at $x = c$.

Functions of two variables exhibit similar behavior. As we mentioned in Section 11.2, continuous functions of two variables assume extreme values on closed, bounded domains (see Figures 11.44 and 11.45). In addition, as we see in this section, we can narrow the search for these extreme values by examining the functions' first partial derivatives. A function of two variables can assume extreme values only at domain boundary points or at interior domain points where both first partial derivatives are zero or where one or both of the first partial derivatives fails to exist.

Once again, the vanishing of derivatives at an interior point (a, b) does not always signal the presence of an extreme value. The surface that is the graph of the function might be shaped like a saddle right above (a, b) and cross its tangent plane there.

Derivative Tests for Local Extreme Values

To find the local extreme values of a function of a single variable, we look for points where the graph has a horizontal tangent line. At such points, we then look for local maxima, local minima, and points of inflection. For a function $f(x, y)$ of two variables, we look for points where the surface $z = f(x, y)$ has a horizontal tangent *plane*. At such points, we then look for local maxima, local minima, and saddle points (more about saddle points in a moment).

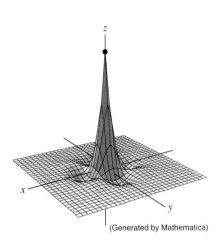

(Generated by Mathematica)

FIGURE 11.44 The function

$$z = (\cos x)(\cos y)e^{-\sqrt{x^2+y^2}}$$

has a maximum value of 1 and a minimum value of about -0.067 on the square region $|x| \leq 3\pi/2, |y| \leq 3\pi/2$.

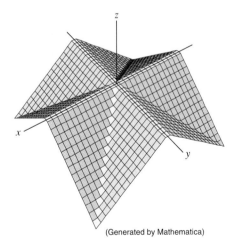

(Generated by Mathematica)

FIGURE 11.45 The "roof surface"

$$z = \frac{1}{2}(||x| - |y|| - |x| - |y|)$$

viewed from the point $(10, 15, 20)$. The defining function has a maximum value of 0 and a minimum value of $-a$ on the square region $|x| \leq a, |y| \leq a$.

Definitions   Local Maximum and Local Minimum

Let $f(x, y)$ be defined on a region R containing the point (a, b). Then

   1. $f(a, b)$ is a **local maximum** value of f if $f(a, b) \geq f(x, y)$ for all domain points (x, y) in an open disk centered at (a, b)

   2. $f(a, b)$ is a **local minimum** value of f if $f(a, b) \leq f(x, y)$ for all domain points (x, y) in an open disk centered at (a, b).

Local maxima correspond to mountain peaks on the surface $z = f(x, y)$ and local minima correspond to valley bottoms (Figure 11.46). At such points, the tangent planes, when they exist, are horizontal. Local extrema are also called **relative extrema.**

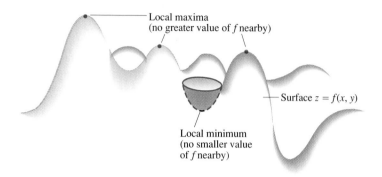

Local maxima
(no greater value of f nearby)

Surface $z = f(x, y)$

Local minimum
(no smaller value
of f nearby)

FIGURE 11.46 A local maximum is a mountain peak and a local minimum is a valley low.

As with functions of a single variable, the key to identifying the local extrema is a first derivative test.

> **Theorem 10**   First Derivative Test for Local Extreme Values
>
> If $f(x, y)$ has a local maximum or minimum value at an interior point (a, b) of its domain and if the first partial derivatives exist there, then $f_x(a, b) = 0$ and $f_y(a, b) = 0$.

Proof   Suppose that f has a local maximum value at an interior point (a, b) of its domain. Then

1. $x = a$ is an interior point of the domain of the curve $z = f(x, b)$ in which the plane $y = b$ cuts the surface $z = f(x, y)$ (Figure 11.47).

2.   The function $z = f(x, b)$ is a differentiable function of x at $x = a$ (the derivative is $f_x(a, b)$).

3.   The function $z = f(x, b)$ has a local maximum value at $x = a$.

4.   The value of the derivative of $z = f(x, b)$ at $x = a$ is therefore zero (Theorem 2, Section 3.1). Since this derivative is $f_x(a, b)$, we conclude that $f_x(a, b) = 0$.

A similar argument with the function $z = f(a, y)$ shows that $f_y(a, b) = 0$.

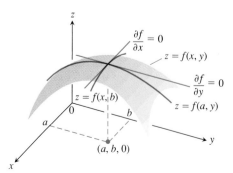

$\dfrac{\partial f}{\partial x} = 0$

$z = f(x, y)$

$\dfrac{\partial f}{\partial y} = 0$

$z = f(x, b)$

$z = f(a, y)$

$(a, b, 0)$

FIGURE 11.47 A local maximum of f occurs at $x = a, y = b$.

This proves the theorem for local maximum values. The proof for local minimum values is left as Exercise 36.   ▬

If we substitute the values $f_x(a, b) = 0$ and $f_y(a, b) = 0$ into the equation

$$f_x(a, b)(x - a) + f_y(a, b)(y - b) - (z - f(a, b)) = 0$$

for the tangent plane to the surface $z = f(x, y)$ at (a, b), the equation reduces to

$$0 \cdot (x - a) + 0 \cdot (y - b) - z + f(a, b) = 0$$

or

$$z = f(a, b).$$

Thus, Theorem 10 says that the surface does indeed have a horizontal tangent plane at a local extremum, provided there is a tangent plane there.

As in the single-variable case, Theorem 10 says that the only places a function $f(x, y)$ can ever have an extreme value are

1. Interior points where $f_x = f_y = 0$

2. Interior points where one or both of f_x and f_y do not exist

3. Boundary points of the function's domain.

> **Definition   Critical Point**
> An interior point of the domain of a function $f(x, y)$ where both f_x and f_y are zero or where one or both of f_x and f_y do not exist is a **critical point** of f.

Thus, the only points where a function $f(x, y)$ can assume extreme values are critical points and boundary points. As with differentiable functions of a single variable, not every critical point gives rise to a local extremum. A differentiable function of a single variable might have a point of inflection. A differentiable function of two variables might have a *saddle point*.

> **Definition   Saddle Point**
> A differentiable function $f(x, y)$ has a **saddle point** at a critical point (a, b) if in every open disk centered at (a, b) there are domain points (x, y) where $f(x, y) > f(a, b)$ and domain points (x, y) where $f(x, y) < f(a, b)$. The corresponding point $(a, b, f(a, b))$ on the surface $z = f(x, y)$ is called a saddle point of the surface (Figure 11.48).

Example 1   Finding Local Extreme Values

Find the local extreme values of $f(x, y) = x^2 + y^2$.

Solution   The domain of f is the entire plane (so there are no boundary points) and the partial derivatives $f_x = 2x$ and $f_y = 2y$ exist everywhere. Therefore, local extreme values can occur only where

$$f_x = 2x = 0 \qquad \text{and} \qquad f_y = 2y = 0.$$

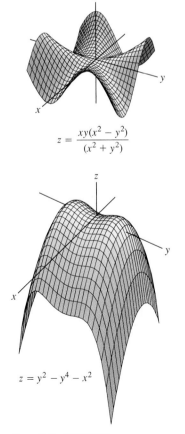

$$z = \frac{xy(x^2 - y^2)}{(x^2 + y^2)}$$

$$z = y^2 - y^4 - x^2$$

(Generated by Mathematica)

FIGURE 11.48 Saddle points at the origin.

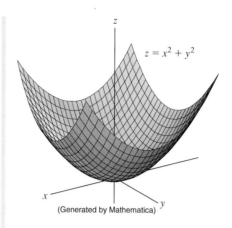

FIGURE 11.49 The graph of the function $f(x, y) = x^2 + y^2$ is the paraboloid $z = x^2 + y^2$. The function has only one critical point, the origin, which gives rise to a local minimum value of 0. (Example 1)

The only possibility is the origin, where the value of f is zero. Since f is never negative, we see that the origin gives a local minimum (Figure 11.49).

Example 2   Identifying a Saddle Point

Find the local extreme values (if any) of $f(x, y) = y^2 - x^2$.

Solution   The domain of f is the entire plane (so there are no boundary points) and the partial derivatives $f_x = -2x$ and $f_y = 2y$ exist everywhere. Therefore, local extrema can occur only at the origin $(0, 0)$. Along the positive x-axis, however, f has the value $f(x, 0) = -x^2 < 0$; along the positive y-axis, f has the value $f(0, y) = y^2 > 0$. Therefore, every open disk in the xy-plane centered at $(0, 0)$ contains points where the function is positive and points where it is negative. The function has a saddle point at the origin (Figure 11.50) instead of a local extreme value. We conclude that the function has no local extreme values.

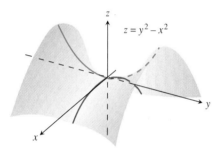

FIGURE 11.50 The origin is a saddle point of the function $f(x, y) = y^2 - x^2$. There are no local extreme values. (Example 2)

That $f_x = f_y = 0$ at an interior point (a, b) of R does not guarantee f has a local extreme value there. If f and its first and second partial derivatives are continuous on R, however, we may be able to learn more from the following theorem, proved in Section 11.10.

Theorem 11   Second Derivative Test for Local Extreme Values

Suppose that $f(x, y)$ and its first and second partial derivatives are continuous throughout a disk centered at (a, b) and that $f_x(a, b) = f_y(a, b) = 0$. Then

i. f has a **local maximum** at (a, b) if $f_{xx} < 0$ and $f_{xx}f_{yy} - f_{xy}^2 > 0$ at (a, b).

ii. f has a **local minimum** at (a, b) if $f_{xx} > 0$ and $f_{xx}f_{yy} - f_{xy}^2 > 0$ at (a, b).

iii. f has a **saddle point** at (a, b) if $f_{xx}f_{yy} - f_{xy}^2 < 0$ at (a, b).

iv. **The test is inconclusive** at (a, b) if $f_{xx}f_{yy} - f_{xy}^2 = 0$ at (a, b). In this case, we must find some other way to determine the behavior of f at (a, b).

The expression $f_{xx}f_{yy} - f_{xy}^2$ is called the **discriminant** or **Hessian** of f. It is sometimes easier to remember it in determinant form,

$$f_{xx}f_{yy} - f_{xy}^2 = \begin{vmatrix} f_{xx} & f_{xy} \\ f_{xy} & f_{yy} \end{vmatrix}.$$

Theorem 11 says that if the discriminant is positive at the point (a, b), then the surface curves the same way in all directions: downwards if $f_{xx} < 0$, giving rise to a local maximum, and upwards if $f_{xx} > 0$, giving a local minimum. On the other hand, if the discriminant is negative at (a, b), then the surface curves up in some directions and down in others, so we have a saddle point.

Example 3 Finding Local Extreme Values

Find the local extreme values of the function

$$f(x, y) = xy - x^2 - y^2 - 2x - 2y + 4.$$

Solution The function is defined and differentiable for all x and y and its domain has no boundary points. The function therefore has extreme values only at the points where f_x and f_y are simultaneously zero. This leads to

$$f_x = y - 2x - 2 = 0, \qquad f_y = x - 2y - 2 = 0,$$

or

$$x = y = -2.$$

Therefore, the point $(-2, -2)$ is the only point where f may take on an extreme value. To see if it does so, we calculate

$$f_{xx} = -2, \qquad f_{yy} = -2, \qquad f_{xy} = 1.$$

The discriminant of f at $(a, b) = (-2, -2)$ is

$$f_{xx}f_{yy} - f_{xy}^2 = (-2)(-2) - (1)^2 = 4 - 1 = 3.$$

The combination

$$f_{xx} < 0 \qquad \text{and} \qquad f_{xx}f_{yy} - f_{xy}^2 > 0$$

tells us that f has a local maximum at $(-2, -2)$. The value of f at this point is $f(-2, -2) = 8$.

Example 4 Searching for Local Extreme Values

Find the local extreme values of $f(x, y) = xy$.

Solution Since f is differentiable everywhere (Figure 11.51), it can assume extreme values only where

$$f_x = y = 0 \qquad \text{and} \qquad f_y = x = 0.$$

Thus, the origin is the only point where f might have an extreme value. To see what happens there, we calculate

$$f_{xx} = 0, \qquad f_{yy} = 0, \qquad f_{xy} = 1.$$

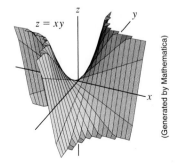

FIGURE 11.51 The surface $z = xy$ has a saddle point at the origin. (Example 4)

(Generated by Mathematica)

The discriminant,

$$f_{xx}f_{yy} - f_{xy}^2 = -1,$$

is negative. Therefore, the function has a saddle point at $(0, 0)$. We conclude that $f(x, y) = xy$ has no local extreme values.

Absolute Maxima and Minima on Closed Bounded Regions

We organize the search for the absolute extrema of a continuous function $f(x, y)$ on a closed and bounded region R into three steps.

Step 1: *List the interior points* of R where f may have local maxima and minima and evaluate f at these points. These are the points where $f_x = f_y = 0$ or where one or both of f_x and f_y fail to exist (the critical points of f).

Step 2: *List the boundary points* of R where f has local maxima and minima and evaluate f at these points. We show how to do this shortly.

Step 3: *Look through the lists* for the maximum and minimum values of f. These will be the absolute maximum and minimum values of f on R. Since absolute maxima and minima are also local maxima and minima, the absolute maximum and minimum values of f already appear somewhere in the lists made in steps 1 and 2. We have only to glance at the lists to see what they are.

Example 5   Finding Absolute Extrema

Find the absolute maximum and minimum values of

$$f(x, y) = 2 + 2x + 2y - x^2 - y^2$$

on the triangular plate in the first quadrant bounded by the lines $x = 0$, $y = 0$, $y = 9 - x$.

Solution   Since f is differentiable, the only places where f can assume these values are points inside the triangle (Figure 11.52) where $f_x = f_y = 0$ and points on the boundary.

Interior Points

For these we have

$$f_x = 2 - 2x = 0, \qquad f_y = 2 - 2y = 0,$$

yielding the single point $(x, y) = (1, 1)$. The value of f there is

$$f(1, 1) = 4.$$

Boundary Points

We take the triangle one side at a time:

1. On the segment OA, $y = 0$. The function

$$f(x, y) = f(x, 0) = 2 + 2x - x^2$$

may now be regarded as a function of x defined on the closed interval $0 \leq x \leq 9$. Its extreme values (we know from Chapter 3) may occur at the endpoints

$$\begin{aligned} x &= 0 & \text{where} & \quad f(0, 0) = 2 \\ x &= 9 & \text{where} & \quad f(9, 0) = 2 + 18 - 81 = -61 \end{aligned}$$

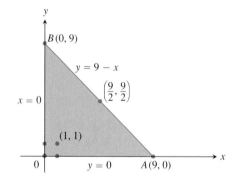

FIGURE 11.52 This triangular plate is the domain of the function in Example 5.

and at the interior points where $f'(x, 0) = 2 - 2x = 0$. The only interior point where $f'(x, 0) = 0$ is $x = 1$, where

$$f(x, 0) = f(1, 0) = 3.$$

2. On the segment OB, $x = 0$ and

$$f(x, y) = f(0, y) = 2 + 2y - y^2.$$

We know from the symmetry of f in x and y and from the analysis we just carried out that the candidates on this segment are

$$f(0, 0) = 2, \qquad f(0, 9) = -61, \qquad f(0, 1) = 3.$$

3. We have already accounted for the values of f at the endpoints of AB, so we need only look at the interior points of AB. With $y = 9 - x$, we have

$$f(x, y) = 2 + 2x + 2(9 - x) - x^2 - (9 - x)^2 = -61 + 18x - 2x^2.$$

Setting $f'(x, 9 - x) = 18 - 4x = 0$ gives

$$x = \frac{18}{4} = \frac{9}{2}.$$

At this value of x,

$$y = 9 - \frac{9}{2} = \frac{9}{2} \qquad \text{and} \qquad f(x, y) = f\left(\frac{9}{2}, \frac{9}{2}\right) = -\frac{41}{2}.$$

Summary

We list all the candidates: $4, 2, -61, 3, -(41/2)$. The maximum is 4, which f assumes at $(1, 1)$. The minimum is -61, which f assumes at $(0, 9)$ and $(9, 0)$.

Solving extreme value problems with algebraic constraints on the variables usually require the method of Lagrange multipliers in the next section. But sometimes we can solve such problems directly, as in the next example.

Example 6   Solving a Volume Problem with a Constraint

A delivery company accepts only rectangular boxes whose length and girth (perimeter of a cross section) do not sum over 108 in. Find the dimensions of an acceptable box of largest volume.

Solution   Let x, y, and z represent the length, width, and height of the rectangular box, respectively. Then the girth is $2y + 2z$. We want to maximize the volume $V = xyz$ of the box (Figure 11.53) satisfying $x + 2y + 2z = 108$ (the largest box accepted by the delivery company). Thus, we can write the volume of the box as a function of two variables.

$$V(y, z) = (108 - 2y - 2z)yz \qquad \begin{array}{l} V = xyz \text{ and} \\ x = 108 - 2y - 2z \end{array}$$
$$= 108yz - 2y^2z - 2yz^2$$

Setting the first partial derivatives equal to zero,

$$V_y(y, z) = 108z - 4yz - 2z^2 = (108 - 4y - 2z)z = 0$$
$$V_z(y, z) = 108y - 2y^2 - 4yz = (108 - 2y - 4z)y = 0,$$

gives the critical points $(0, 0)$, $(0, 54)$, $(54, 0)$, and $(18, 18)$. The volume is zero at $(0, 0)$, $(0, 54)$, $(54, 0)$, which are not maximum values. At the point $(18, 18)$, we apply the second derivative test (Theorem 11):

$$V_{yy} = -4z, \qquad V_{zz} = -4y, \qquad V_{yz} = 108 - 4y - 4z.$$

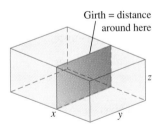

Girth = distance around here

FIGURE 11.53 The box in Example 6.

Then

$$V_{yy}V_{zz} - V_{yz}{}^2 = 16yz - 16(27 - y - z)^2.$$

Thus,

$$V_{yy}(18, 18) = -4(18) < 0$$

and

$$[V_{yy}V_{zz} - V_{yz}{}^2]_{(18,18)} = 16(18)(18) - 16(-9)^2 > 0$$

imply that $(18, 18)$ gives a maximum volume. The dimensions of the package are $x = 108 - 2(18) - 2(18) = 36$ in., $y = 18$ in., and $z = 18$ in. The maximum volume is $V = (36)(18)(18) = 11{,}664$ in.^{3}, or 6.75 ft^3.

Limitations of the First Derivative Test, and Summary

Despite the power of Theorem 10, we urge you to remember its limitations. It does not apply to boundary points of a function's domain, where it is possible for a function to have extreme values along with nonzero derivatives. Also, it does not apply to points where either f_x or f_y fails to exist.

Summary of Max-Min Tests

The extreme values of $f(x, y)$ can occur only at

i. **boundary points** of the domain of f

ii. **critical points** (interior points where $f_x = f_y = 0$ or points where f_x or f_y fail to exist).

If the first- and second-order partial derivatives of f are continuous throughout a disk centered at a point (a, b) and $f_x(a, b) = f_y(a, b) = 0$, you may be able to classify $f(a, b)$ with the **second derivative test**:

i. $f_{xx} < 0$ and $f_{xx}f_{yy} - f_{xy}{}^2 > 0$ at $(a, b) \Rightarrow$ **local maximum**

ii. $f_{xx} > 0$ and $f_{xx}f_{yy} - f_{xy}{}^2 > 0$ at $(a, b) \Rightarrow$ **local minimum**

iii. $f_{xx}f_{yy} - f_{xy}{}^2 < 0$ at $(a, b) \Rightarrow$ **saddle point**

iv. $f_{xx}f_{yy} - f_{xy}{}^2 = 0$ at $(a, b) \Rightarrow$ **test is inconclusive.**

EXERCISES 11.7

Finding Local Extrema

Find all the local maxima, local minima, and saddle points of the functions in Exercises 1–20.

1. $f(x, y) = x^2 + xy + y^2 + 3x - 3y + 4$

2. $f(x, y) = 2xy - 5x^2 - 2y^2 + 4x + 4y - 4$

3. $f(x, y) = x^2 + xy + 3x + 2y + 5$

4. $f(x, y) = 5xy - 7x^2 + 3x - 6y + 2$

5. $f(x, y) = 3x^2 + 6xy + 7y^2 - 2x + 4y$

6. $f(x, y) = 2x^2 + 3xy + 4y^2 - 5x + 2y$

7. $f(x, y) = x^2 - y^2 - 2x + 4y + 6$

8. $f(x, y) = x^2 - 2xy + 2y^2 - 2x + 2y + 1$

9. $f(x, y) = 3 + 2x + 2y - 2x^2 - 2xy - y^2$

10. $f(x, y) = x^3 - y^3 - 2xy + 6$

11. $f(x, y) = x^3 + 3xy + y^3$

12. $f(x, y) = 6x^2 - 2x^3 + 3y^2 + 6xy$

13. $f(x, y) = 9x^3 + y^3/3 - 4xy$

14. $f(x, y) = x^3 + y^3 + 3x^2 - 3y^2 - 8$

15. $f(x, y) = 4xy - x^4 - y^4$

16. $f(x, y) = x^4 + y^4 + 4xy$

17. $f(x, y) = \dfrac{1}{x^2 + y^2 - 1}$

18. $f(x, y) = \dfrac{1}{x} + xy + \dfrac{1}{y}$

19. $f(x, y) = y \sin x$

20. $f(x, y) = e^{2x} \cos y$

Finding Absolute Extrema

In Exercises 21–26, find the absolute maxima and minima of the functions on the given domains.

21. $f(x, y) = 2x^2 - 4x + y^2 - 4y + 1$ on the closed triangular plate bounded by the lines $x = 0$, $y = 2$, $y = 2x$ in the first quadrant

22. $f(x, y) = x^2 + y^2$ on the closed triangular plate bounded by the lines $x = 0$, $y = 0$, $y + 2x = 2$ in the first quadrant

23. $T(x, y) = x^2 + xy + y^2 - 6x + 2$ on the rectangular plate $0 \le x \le 5$, $-3 \le y \le 0$

24. $f(x, y) = 48xy - 32x^3 - 24y^2$ on the rectangular plate $0 \le x \le 1$, $0 \le y \le 1$

25. $f(x, y) = (4x - x^2) \cos y$ on the rectangular plate $1 \le x \le 3$, $-\pi/4 \le y \le \pi/4$

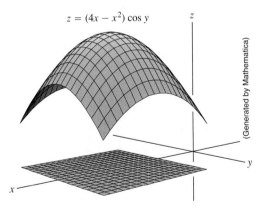

$z = (4x - x^2) \cos y$

The function and domain in Exercise 25.

26. $f(x, y) = 4x - 8xy + 2y + 1$ on the triangular plate bounded by the lines $x = 0$, $y = 0$, $x + y = 1$ in the first quadrant

27. *Maximizing an integral* Find two numbers a and b with $a \le b$ such that

$$\int_a^b (6 - x - x^2) \, dx$$

has its largest value.

28. *Maximizing an integral* Find two numbers a and b with $a \le b$ such that

$$\int_a^b (24 - 2x - x^2)^{1/3} \, dx$$

has its largest value.

29. *Temperature extremes* The flat circular plate in Figure 11.54 has the shape of the region $x^2 + y^2 \le 1$. The plate, including the boundary where $x^2 + y^2 = 1$, is heated so that the temperature at the point (x, y) is

$$T(x, y) = x^2 + 2y^2 - x.$$

Find the temperatures at the hottest and coldest points on the plate.

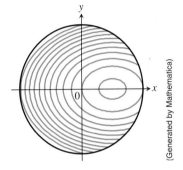

FIGURE 11.54 Curves of constant temperature are called isotherms. The figure shows isotherms of the temperature function $T(x, y) = x^2 + 2y^2 - x$ on the disk $x^2 + y^2 \le 1$ in the xy-plane. Exercise 29 asks you to locate the extreme temperatures.

30. *Identifying critical points* Find the critical point of

$$f(x, y) = xy + 2x - \ln x^2 y$$

in the open first quadrant ($x > 0$, $y > 0$) and show that f takes on a minimum there (Figure 11.55).

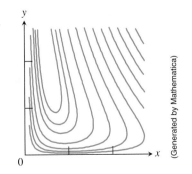

FIGURE 11.55 The function $f(x, y) = xy + 2x - \ln x^2 y$ (selected level curves shown here) takes on a minimum value somewhere in the open first quadrant $x > 0$, $y > 0$. (Exercise 30)

Theory and Examples

31. *Writing to Learn* Find the maxima, minima, and saddle points of $f(x, y)$, if any, given that

(a) $f_x = 2x - 4y$ and $f_y = 2y - 4x$

(b) $f_x = 2x - 2$ and $f_y = 2y - 4$

(c) $f_x = 9x^2 - 9$ and $f_y = 2y + 4$.

Describe your reasoning in each case.

32. *Writing to Learn: When the second derivative is inconclusive* The discriminant $f_{xx}f_{yy} - f_{xy}^2$ is zero at the origin for each of the following functions, so the second derivative test fails there. Determine whether the function has a maximum, a minimum, or neither at the origin by imagining what the surface $z = f(x, y)$ looks like. Describe your reasoning in each case.

(a) $f(x, y) = x^2y^2$

(b) $f(x, y) = 1 - x^2y^2$

(c) $f(x, y) = xy^2$

(d) $f(x, y) = x^3y^2$

(e) $f(x, y) = x^3y^3$

(f) $f(x, y) = x^4y^4$

33. Show that $(0, 0)$ is a critical point of $f(x, y) = x^2 + kxy + y^2$ no matter what value the constant k has. (*Hint:* Consider two cases: $k = 0$ and $k \neq 0$.)

34. *Writing to Learn* For what values of the constant k does the second derivative test guarantee that $f(x, y) = x^2 + kxy + y^2$ will have a saddle point at $(0, 0)$? A local minimum at $(0, 0)$? For what values of k is the second derivative test inconclusive? Give reasons for your answers.

35. (a) *Writing to Learn* If $f_x(a, b) = f_y(a, b) = 0$, must f have a local maximum or minimum value at (a, b)? Give reasons for your answer.

(b) *Writing to Learn* Can you conclude anything about $f(a, b)$ if f and its first and second partial derivatives are continuous throughout a disk centered at (a, b) and $f_{xx}(a, b)$ and $f_{yy}(a, b)$ differ in sign? Give reasons for your answer.

36. *Proving Theorem 10 for a local minimum* Using the proof of Theorem 10 given in the text for the case in which f has a local maximum at (a, b), prove the theorem for the case in which f has a local minimum at (a, b).

37. *Maximum distance from a plane* Among all the points on the graph of $z = 10 - x^2 - y^2$ that lie above the plane $x + 2y + 3z = 0$, find the point farthest from the plane.

38. *Minimum distance to a plane* Find the point on the graph of $z = x^2 + y^2 + 10$ nearest the plane $x + 2y - z = 0$.

39. *Writing to Learn* The function $f(x, y) = x + y$ fails to have an absolute maximum value in the closed first quadrant ($x \geq 0$ and $y \geq 0$). Does this contradict the discussion on finding absolute extrema given in the text? Give reasons for your answer.

40. Consider the function $f(x, y) = x^2 + y^2 + 2xy - x - y + 1$ over the square $0 \leq x \leq 1$ and $0 \leq y \leq 1$.

(a) *Minimum along a line segment* Show that f has an absolute minimum along the line segment $2x + 2y = 1$ in this square. What *is* the absolute minimum value?

(b) *Absolute maximum* Find the absolute maximum value of f over the square.

Extreme Values on Parametrized Curves

To find the extreme values of a function $f(x, y)$ on a curve $x = x(t)$, $y = y(t)$, we treat f as a function of the single variable t and use the Chain Rule to find where df/dt is zero. As in any other single-variable case, the extreme values of f are then found among the values at the

(a) Critical points (points where df/dt is zero or fails to exist)

(b) Endpoints of the parameter domain.

In Exercises 41–44, find the absolute maximum and minimum values of the functions on the curves.

41. Functions:

(a) $f(x, y) = x + y$

(b) $g(x, y) = xy$

(c) $h(x, y) = 2x^2 + y^2$

Curves:

i. The semicircle $x^2 + y^2 = 4$, $y \geq 0$

ii. The quarter circle $x^2 + y^2 = 4$, $x \geq 0$, $y \geq 0$

Use the parametric equations $x = 2 \cos t$, $y = 2 \sin t$.

42. Functions:

(a) $f(x, y) = 2x + 3y$

(b) $g(x, y) = xy$

(c) $h(x, y) = x^2 + 3y^2$

Curves:

i. The semi-ellipse $(x^2/9) + (y^2/4) = 1$, $y \geq 0$

ii. The quarter ellipse $(x^2/9) + (y^2/4) = 1$, $x \geq 0$, $y \geq 0$

Use the parametric equations $x = 3 \cos t$, $y = 2 \sin t$.

43. Function: $f(x, y) = xy$

Curves:

i. The line $x = 2t$, $y = t + 1$

ii. The line segment $x = 2t$, $y = t + 1$, $-1 \leq t \leq 0$

iii. The line segment $x = 2t$, $y = t + 1$, $0 \leq t \leq 1$

44. Functions:

(a) $f(x, y) = x^2 + y^2$

(b) $g(x, y) = 1/(x^2 + y^2)$

Curves:

i. The line $x = t$, $y = 2 - 2t$

ii. The line segment $x = t$, $y = 2 - 2t$, $0 \leq t \leq 1$

45. *Least squares and regression lines* When we try to fit a line $y = mx + b$ to a set of numerical data points $(x_1, y_1), (x_2, y_2), \ldots, (x_n, y_n)$ (Figure 11.56), we usually choose the line that minimizes the sum of the squares of the vertical distances from the points to the line. In theory, this means finding the values of m and b that minimize the value of the function

$$w = (mx_1 + b - y_1)^2 + \cdots + (mx_n + b - y_n)^2.$$

CD-ROM
WEBsite

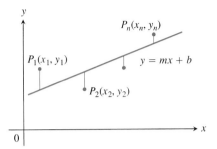

FIGURE 11.56 To fit a line to noncollinear points, we choose the line that minimizes the sum of the squares of the deviations.

Use the first and second derivative tests to show that these values are

$$m = \frac{\left(\sum x_k\right)\left(\sum y_k\right) - n\sum x_k y_k}{\left(\sum x_k\right)^2 - n\sum x_k^2},$$

$$b = \frac{1}{n}\left(\sum y_k - m\sum x_k\right).$$

46. *Craters of Mars* One theory of crater formation suggests that the frequency of large craters should fall off as the square of the diameter (Marcus, *Science*, June 21, 1968, p. 1334). Pictures from *Mariner IV* show the frequencies listed in Table 11.1. Use the results of Exercise 45 to fit a line of the form $F = m(1/D^2) + b$ to the data. Plot the data and draw the line.

Table 11.1 Crater sizes on Mars		
Diameter in km, D	$1/D^2$ (for left value of class interval)	Frequency, F
32–45	0.001	51
45–64	0.0005	22
64–90	0.00024	14
90–128	0.000123	4

COMPUTER EXPLORATIONS

Exploring Local Extrema at Critical Points

In Exercises 47–52, you will explore functions to identify local extrema at critical points. Use a CAS to perform the following steps.

(a) Plot the function over the given rectangle.

(b) Plot some level curves in the rectangle.

(c) Calculate the function's first partial derivatives and use the CAS equation solver to find the critical points. How do the critical points relate to the level curves plotted in part (b)? Which critical points, if any, appear to give a saddle point? Give reasons for your answer.

(d) Calculate the function's second partial derivatives and find the discriminant $f_{xx}f_{yy} - f_{xy}^2$.

(e) Using the max-min tests, classify the critical points found in part (c). Are your findings consistent with your discussion in part (c)?

47. $f(x, y) = x^2 + y^3 - 3xy, \quad -5 \le x \le 5, \quad -5 \le y \le 5$

48. $f(x, y) = x^3 - 3xy^2 + y^2, \quad -2 \le x \le 2, \quad -2 \le y \le 2$

49. $f(x, y) = x^4 + y^2 - 8x^2 - 6y + 16, \quad -3 \le x \le 3, \quad -6 \le y \le 6$

50. $f(x, y) = 2x^4 + y^4 - 2x^2 - 2y^2 + 3, \quad -3/2 \le x \le 3/2, \\ -3/2 \le y \le 3/2$

51. $f(x, y) = 5x^6 + 18x^5 - 30x^4 + 30xy^2 - 120x^3, \quad -4 \le x \le 3, \\ -2 \le y \le 2$

52. $f(x, y) = \begin{cases} x^5 \ln(x^2 + y^2), & (x, y) \ne (0, 0) \\ 0, & (x, y) = (0, 0) \end{cases}$

$-2 \le x \le 2, \quad -2 \le y \le 2$

11.8 Lagrange Multipliers

Constrained Maxima and Minima • The Method of Lagrange Multipliers
• Lagrange Multipliers with Two Constraints

As we saw in Section 11.7, we sometimes need to find the extreme values of a function whose domain is constrained to lie within some particular subset of the plane, such as a disk or a closed triangular region. As we saw in Example 6 of Section 11.7, however, and as Figure 11.57 shows here, a function may be subject to other kinds of constraints as well.

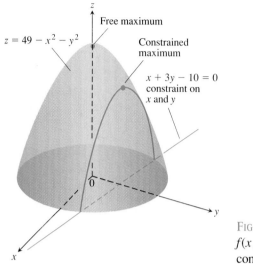

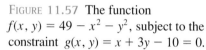

FIGURE 11.57 The function
$f(x, y) = 49 - x^2 - y^2$, subject to the
constraint $g(x, y) = x + 3y - 10 = 0$.

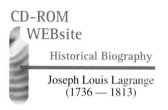

CD–ROM
WEBsite

Historical Biography

Joseph Louis Lagrange
(1736 — 1813)

In this section, we explore a powerful method for finding extreme values of
constrained functions: the method of *Lagrange multipliers*. Lagrange developed the
method in 1755 to solve max-min problems in geometry. Today the method is important in economics, in engineering (where it is used in designing multistage rock-
ets, for example), and in mathematics.

Constrained Maxima and Minima

Example 1   Finding a Minimum with Constraint

Find the point $P(x, y, z)$ closest to the origin on the plane $2x + y - z - 5 = 0$.

Solution   The problem asks us to find the minimum value of the function

$$|\overrightarrow{OP}| = \sqrt{(x - 0)^2 + (y - 0)^2 + (z - 0)^2}$$
$$= \sqrt{x^2 + y^2 + z^2}$$

subject to the constraint that

$$2x + y - z - 5 = 0.$$

Since $|\overrightarrow{OP}|$ has a minimum value wherever the function

$$f(x, y, z) = x^2 + y^2 + z^2$$

has a minimum value, we may solve the problem by finding the minimum value
of $f(x, y, z)$ subject to the constraint $2x + y - z - 5 = 0$ (thus avoiding square
roots). If we regard x and y as the independent variables in this equation and
write z as

$$z = 2x + y - 5,$$

our problem reduces to one of finding the points (x, y) at which the function

$$h(x, y) = f(x, y, 2x + y - 5) = x^2 + y^2 + (2x + y - 5)^2$$

has its minimum value or values. Since the domain of h is the entire xy-plane, the first derivative test of Section 11.7 tells us that any minima that h might have must occur at points where

$$h_x = 2x + 2(2x + y - 5)(2) = 0, \qquad h_y = 2y + 2(2x + y - 5) = 0.$$

This leads to

$$10x + 4y = 20, \qquad 4x + 4y = 10,$$

and the solution

$$x = \frac{5}{3}, \qquad y = \frac{5}{6}.$$

We may apply a geometric argument together with the second derivative test to show that these values minimize h. The z-coordinate of the corresponding point on the plane $z = 2x + y - 5$ is

$$z = 2\left(\frac{5}{3}\right) + \frac{5}{6} - 5 = -\frac{5}{6}.$$

Therefore, the point we seek is

$$\text{Closest point:} \qquad P\left(\frac{5}{3}, \frac{5}{6}, -\frac{5}{6}\right).$$

The distance from P to the origin is $5/\sqrt{6} \approx 2.04$.

Attempts to solve a constrained maximum or minimum problem by substitution, as we might call the method of Example 1, do not always go smoothly. This is one of the reasons for learning the new method of this section.

Example 2   Finding a Minimum with Constraint

Find the points closest to the origin on the hyperbolic cylinder $x^2 - z^2 - 1 = 0$.

Solution 1   The cylinder is shown in Figure 11.58. We seek the points on the cylinder closest to the origin. These are the points whose coordinates minimize the value of the function

$$f(x, y, z) = x^2 + y^2 + z^2 \qquad \text{Square of the distance}$$

subject to the constraint that $x^2 - z^2 - 1 = 0$. If we regard x and y as independent variables in the constraint equation, then

$$z^2 = x^2 - 1$$

and the values of $f(x, y, z) = x^2 + y^2 + z^2$ on the cylinder are given by the function

$$h(x, y) = x^2 + y^2 + (x^2 - 1) = 2x^2 + y^2 - 1.$$

To find the points on the cylinder whose coordinates minimize f, we look for the points in the xy-plane whose coordinates minimize h. The only extreme value of h occurs where

$$h_x = 4x = 0 \qquad \text{and} \qquad h_y = 2y = 0,$$

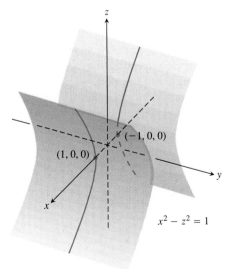

FIGURE 11.58 The hyperbolic cylinder $x^2 - z^2 - 1 = 0$ in Example 2.

The hyperbolic cylinder $x^2 - z^2 = 1$

On this part,
$x = \sqrt{z^2 + 1}$.

On this part,
$x = -\sqrt{z^2 + 1}$.

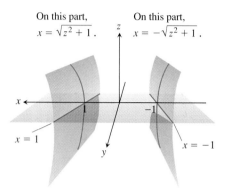

FIGURE 11.59 The region in the xy-plane from which the first two coordinates of the points (x, y, z) on the hyperbolic cylinder $x^2 - z^2 = 1$ are selected excludes the band $-1 < x < 1$ in the xy-plane.

that is, at the point $(0, 0)$. But now we're in trouble: There are no points on the cylinder where both x and y are zero. What went wrong?

What happened was that the first derivative test found (as it should have) the point *in the domain of h* where h has a minimum value. We, on the other hand, want the points *on the cylinder* where h has a minimum value. Although the domain of h is the entire xy-plane, the domain from which we can select the first two coordinates of the points (x, y, z) on the cylinder is restricted to the "shadow" of the cylinder on the xy-plane; it does not include the band between the lines $x = -1$ and $x = 1$ (Figure 11.59).

We can avoid this problem if we treat y and z as independent variables (instead of x and y) and express x in terms of y and z as

$$x^2 = z^2 + 1.$$

With this substitution, $f(x, y, z) = x^2 + y^2 + z^2$ becomes

$$k(y, z) = (z^2 + 1) + y^2 + z^2 = 1 + y^2 + 2z^2$$

and we look for the points where k takes on its smallest value. The domain of k in the yz-plane now matches the domain from which we select the y- and z-coordinates of the points (x, y, z) on the cylinder. Hence, the points that minimize k in the plane will have corresponding points on the cylinder. The smallest values of k occur where

$$k_y = 2y = 0 \qquad \text{and} \qquad k_z = 4z = 0,$$

or where $y = z = 0$. This leads to

$$x^2 = z^2 + 1 = 1, \qquad x = \pm 1.$$

The corresponding points on the cylinder are $(\pm 1, 0, 0)$. We can see from the inequality

$$k(y, z) = 1 + y^2 + 2z^2 \geq 1$$

that the points $(\pm 1, 0, 0)$ give a minimum value for k. We can also see that the minimum distance from the origin to a point on the cylinder is 1 unit.

Solution 2 Another way to find the points on the cylinder closest to the origin is to imagine a small sphere centered at the origin expanding like a soap bubble until it just touches the cylinder (Figure 11.60). At each point of contact, the cylinder and sphere have the same tangent plane and normal line. Therefore, if the sphere and cylinder are represented as the level surfaces obtained by setting

$$f(x, y, z) = x^2 + y^2 + z^2 - a^2 \qquad \text{and} \qquad g(x, y, z) = x^2 - z^2 - 1$$

equal to 0, then the gradients ∇f and ∇g will be parallel where the surfaces touch. At any point of contact, we should therefore be able to find a scalar λ ("lambda") such that

$$\nabla f = \lambda \nabla g,$$

or

$$2x\mathbf{i} + 2y\mathbf{j} + 2z\mathbf{k} = \lambda(2x\mathbf{i} - 2z\mathbf{k}).$$

Thus, the coordinates x, y, and z of any point of tangency will have to satisfy the three scalar equations

$$2x = 2\lambda x, \qquad 2y = 0, \qquad 2z = -2\lambda z. \tag{1}$$

$x^2 - z^2 - 1 = 0$

$x^2 + y^2 + z^2 - a^2 = 0$

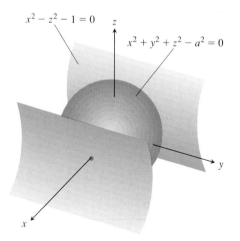

FIGURE 11.60 A sphere expanding like a soap bubble centered at the origin until it just touches the hyperbolic cylinder
$x^2 - z^2 - 1 = 0.$

For what values of λ will a point (x, y, z) whose coordinates satisfy the equations in (1) also lie on the surface $x^2 - z^2 - 1 = 0$? To answer this question, we use our knowledge that no point on the surface has a zero x-coordinate to conclude that $x \neq 0$ in the first of Equations (1). Hence, $2x = 2\lambda x$ only if

$$2 = 2\lambda, \quad \text{or} \quad \lambda = 1.$$

For $\lambda = 1$, the equation $2z = -2\lambda z$ becomes $2z = -2z$. If this equation is to be satisfied as well, z must be zero. Since $y = 0$ also (from the equation $2y = 0$), we conclude that the points we seek all have coordinates of the form

$$(x, 0, 0).$$

What points on the surface $x^2 - z^2 = 1$ have coordinates of this form? The answer is the points $(x, 0, 0)$ for which

$$x^2 - (0)^2 = 1, \quad x^2 = 1, \quad \text{or} \quad x = \pm 1.$$

The points on the cylinder closest to the origin are the points $(\pm 1, 0, 0)$.

CD-ROM
WEBsite

The Method of Lagrange Multipliers

In Solution 2 of Example 2, we solved the problem by the **method of Lagrange multipliers**. In general terms, the method says that the extreme values of a function $f(x, y, z)$ whose variables are subject to a constraint $g(x, y, z) = 0$ are to be found on the surface $g = 0$ at the points where

$$\nabla f = \lambda \nabla g$$

for some scalar λ (called a **Lagrange multiplier**).

To explore the method further and see why it works, we first make the following observation, which we state as a theorem.

Theorem 12 The Orthogonal Gradient Theorem

Suppose that $f(x, y, z)$ is differentiable in a region whose interior contains a smooth curve

$$C: \quad \mathbf{r}(t) = g(t)\mathbf{i} + h(t)\mathbf{j} + k(t)\mathbf{k}.$$

If P_0 is a point on C where f has a local maximum or minimum relative to its values on C, then ∇f is orthogonal to C at P_0.

Proof We show that ∇f is orthogonal to the curve's velocity vector at P_0. The values of f on C are given by the composite $f(g(t), h(t), k(t))$, whose derivative with respect to t is

$$\frac{df}{dt} = \frac{\partial f}{\partial x}\frac{dg}{dt} + \frac{\partial f}{\partial y}\frac{dh}{dt} + \frac{\partial f}{\partial z}\frac{dk}{dt} = \nabla f \cdot \mathbf{v}.$$

At any point P_0 where f has a local maximum or minimum relative to its values on the curve, $df/dt = 0$, so

$$\nabla f \cdot \mathbf{v} = 0.$$

By dropping the z-terms in Theorem 12, we obtain a similar result for functions of two variables.

Corollary of Theorem 12

At the points on a smooth curve $\mathbf{r}(t) = g(t)\mathbf{i} + h(t)\mathbf{j}$ where a differentiable function $f(x, y)$ takes on its local maxima and minima relative to its values on the curve, $\nabla f \cdot \mathbf{v} = 0$.

Theorem 12 is the key to the method of Lagrange multipliers. Suppose that $f(x, y, z)$ and $g(x, y, z)$ are differentiable and that P_0 is a point on the surface $g(x, y, z) = 0$ where f has a local maximum or minimum value relative to its other values on the surface. Then f takes on a local maximum or minimum at P_0 relative to its values on every differentiable curve through P_0 on the surface $g(x, y, z) = 0$. Therefore, ∇f is orthogonal to the velocity vector of every such differentiable curve through P_0. So is ∇g, however (because ∇g is orthogonal to the level surface $g = 0$, as we saw in Section 11.5). Therefore, at P_0, ∇f is some scalar multiple λ of ∇g.

The Method of Lagrange Multipliers

Suppose that $f(x, y, z)$ and $g(x, y, z)$ are differentiable. To find the local maximum and minimum values of f subject to the constraint $g(x, y, z) = 0$, find the values of $x, y, z,$ and λ that simultaneously satisfy the equations

$$\nabla f = \lambda \nabla g \qquad \text{and} \qquad g(x, y, z) = 0.$$

For functions of two independent variables, the appropriate equations are

$$\nabla f = \lambda \nabla g \qquad \text{and} \qquad g(x, y) = 0.$$

Example 3   Using the Method of Lagrange Multipliers

Find the greatest and smallest values that the function

$$f(x, y) = xy$$

takes on the ellipse (Figure 11.61)

$$\frac{x^2}{8} + \frac{y^2}{2} = 1.$$

Solution   We want the extreme values of $f(x, y) = xy$ subject to the constraint

$$g(x, y) = \frac{x^2}{8} + \frac{y^2}{2} - 1 = 0.$$

To do so, we first find the values of $x, y,$ and λ for which

$$\nabla f = \lambda \nabla g \qquad \text{and} \qquad g(x, y) = 0.$$

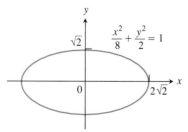

FIGURE 11.61 Example 3 shows how to find the largest and smallest values of the product xy on this ellipse.

The gradient equation gives

$$y\mathbf{i} + x\mathbf{j} = \frac{\lambda}{4}x\mathbf{i} + \lambda y\mathbf{j},$$

from which we find

$$y = \frac{\lambda}{4}x, \qquad x = \lambda y, \qquad \text{and} \qquad y = \frac{\lambda}{4}(\lambda y) = \frac{\lambda^2}{4}y,$$

so that $y = 0$ or $\lambda = \pm 2$. We now consider these two cases.

Case 1: If $y = 0$, then $x = y = 0$. But $(0, 0)$ is not on the ellipse. Hence, $y \neq 0$.

Case 2: If $y \neq 0$, then $\lambda = \pm 2$ and $x = \pm 2y$. Substituting this in the equation $g(x, y) = 0$ gives

$$\frac{(\pm 2y)^2}{8} + \frac{y^2}{2} = 1, \qquad 4y^2 + 4y^2 = 8, \qquad \text{and} \qquad y = \pm 1.$$

The function $f(x, y) = xy$ therefore takes on its extreme values on the ellipse at the four points $(\pm 2, 1)$, $(\pm 2, -1)$. The extreme values are $xy = 2$ and $xy = -2$.

The Geometry of the Solution

The level curves of the function $f(x, y) = xy$ are the hyperbolas $xy = c$ (Figure 11.62). The farther the hyperbolas lie from the origin, the larger the absolute value of f. We want to find the extreme values of $f(x, y)$, given that the point (x, y) also lies on the ellipse $x^2 + 4y^2 = 8$. Which hyperbolas intersecting the ellipse lie farthest from the origin? The hyperbolas that just graze the ellipse, the ones that are tangent to it, are farthest. At these points, any vector normal to the hyperbola is normal to the ellipse, so $\nabla f = y\mathbf{i} + x\mathbf{j}$ is a multiple ($\lambda = \pm 2$) of $\nabla g = (x/4)\mathbf{i} + y\mathbf{j}$. At the point $(2, 1)$, for example,

$$\nabla f = \mathbf{i} + 2\mathbf{j}, \qquad \nabla g = \frac{1}{2}\mathbf{i} + \mathbf{j}, \qquad \text{and} \qquad \nabla f = 2\nabla g.$$

At the point $(-2, 1)$,

$$\nabla f = \mathbf{i} - 2\mathbf{j}, \qquad \nabla g = -\frac{1}{2}\mathbf{i} + \mathbf{j}, \qquad \text{and} \qquad \nabla f = -2\nabla g.$$

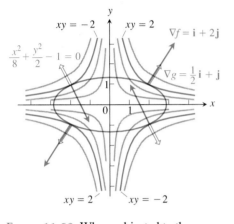

FIGURE 11.62 When subjected to the constraint $g(x, y) = x^2/8 + y^2/2 - 1 = 0$, the function $f(x, y) = xy$ takes on extreme values at the four points $(\pm 2, \pm 1)$. These are the points on the ellipse when ∇f (red) is a scalar multiple of ∇g (blue). (Example 3)

Example 4   Finding Extreme Function Values on a Circle

Find the maximum and minimum values of the function $f(x, y) = 3x + 4y$ on the circle $x^2 + y^2 = 1$.

Solution   We model this as a Lagrange multiplier problem with

$$f(x, y) = 3x + 4y, \qquad g(x, y) = x^2 + y^2 - 1$$

and look for the values of x, y, and λ that satisfy the equations

$$\nabla f = \lambda \nabla g: \quad 3\mathbf{i} + 4\mathbf{j} = 2x\lambda\mathbf{i} + 2y\lambda\mathbf{j}$$
$$g(x, y) = 0: \quad x^2 + y^2 - 1 = 0.$$

The gradient equation implies that $\lambda \neq 0$ and gives

$$x = \frac{3}{2\lambda}, \qquad y = \frac{2}{\lambda}.$$

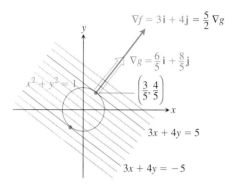

FIGURE 11.63 The function $f(x, y) = 3x + 4y$ takes on its largest value on the unit circle $g(x, y) = x^2 + y^2 - 1 = 0$ at the point $(3/5, 4/5)$ and its smallest value at the point $(-3/5, -4/5)$ (Example 4). At each of these points, ∇f is a scalar multiple of ∇g. The figure shows the gradients at the first point but not the second.

These equations tell us, among other things, that x and y have the same sign. With these values for x and y, the equation $g(x, y) = 0$ gives

$$\left(\frac{3}{2\lambda}\right)^2 + \left(\frac{2}{\lambda}\right)^2 - 1 = 0,$$

so

$$\frac{9}{4\lambda^2} + \frac{4}{\lambda^2} = 1, \qquad 9 + 16 = 4\lambda^2, \qquad 4\lambda^2 = 25, \qquad \text{and} \qquad \lambda = \pm\frac{5}{2}.$$

Thus,

$$x = \frac{3}{2\lambda} = \pm\frac{3}{5}, \qquad y = \frac{2}{\lambda} = \pm\frac{4}{5},$$

and $f(x, y) = 3x + 4y$ has extreme values at $(x, y) = \pm(3/5, 4/5)$.

By calculating the value of $3x + 4y$ at the points $\pm(3/5, 4/5)$, we see that its maximum and minimum values on the circle $x^2 + y^2 = 1$ are

$$3\left(\frac{3}{5}\right) + 4\left(\frac{4}{5}\right) = \frac{25}{5} = 5 \qquad \text{and} \qquad 3\left(-\frac{3}{5}\right) + 4\left(-\frac{4}{5}\right) = -\frac{25}{5} = -5.$$

The Geometry of the Solution

The level curves of $f(x, y) = 3x + 4y$ are the lines $3x + 4y = c$ (Figure 11.63). The farther the lines lie from the origin, the larger the absolute value of f. We want to find the extreme values of $f(x, y)$ given that the point (x, y) also lies on the circle $x^2 + y^2 = 1$. Which lines intersecting the circle lie farthest from the origin? The lines tangent to the circle are farthest. At the points of tangency, any vector normal to the line is normal to the circle, so the gradient $\nabla f = 3\mathbf{i} + 4\mathbf{j}$ is a multiple $(\lambda = \pm 5/2)$ of the gradient $\nabla g = 2x\mathbf{i} + 2y\mathbf{j}$. At the point $(3/5, 4/5)$, for example,

$$\nabla f = 3\mathbf{i} + 4\mathbf{j}, \qquad \nabla g = \frac{6}{5}\mathbf{i} + \frac{8}{5}\mathbf{j}, \qquad \text{and} \qquad \nabla f = \frac{5}{2}\nabla g.$$

Lagrange Multipliers with Two Constraints

Many problems require us to find the extreme values of a differentiable function $f(x, y, z)$ whose variables are subject to two constraints. If the constraints are

$$g_1(x, y, z) = 0 \qquad \text{and} \qquad g_2(x, y, z) = 0$$

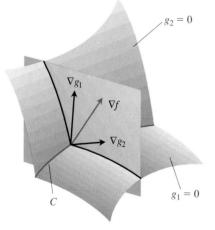

FIGURE 11.64 The vectors ∇g_1 and ∇g_2 lie in a plane perpendicular to the curve C because ∇g_1 is normal to the surface $g_1 = 0$ and ∇g_2 is normal to the surface $g_2 = 0$.

and g_1 and g_2 are differentiable, with ∇g_1 not parallel to ∇g_2, we find the constrained local maxima and minima of f by introducing two Lagrange multipliers λ and μ (mu, pronounced "mew"). That is, we locate the points $P(x, y, z)$ where f takes on its constrained extreme values by finding the values of $x, y, z, \lambda,$ and μ that simultaneously satisfy the equations

$$\nabla f = \lambda \nabla g_1 + \mu \nabla g_2, \qquad g_1(x, y, z) = 0, \qquad g_2(x, y, z) = 0. \qquad (2)$$

Equations (2) have a nice geometric interpretation. The surfaces $g_1 = 0$ and $g_2 = 0$ (usually) intersect in a smooth curve, say C (Figure 11.64). Along this curve we seek the points where f has local maximum and minimum values relative to its other values on the curve. These are the points where ∇f is normal to C, as we saw in Theorem 12. But ∇g_1 and ∇g_2 are also normal to C at these points because C lies in the surfaces $g_1 = 0$ and $g_2 = 0$. Therefore, ∇f lies in the plane determined by ∇g_1 and ∇g_2, which means that $\nabla f = \lambda \nabla g_1 + \mu \nabla g_2$ for some λ and μ. Since the points we seek also lie in both surfaces, their coordinates must satisfy the equations $g_1(x, y, z) = 0$ and $g_2(x, y, z) = 0$, which are the remaining requirements in Equations (2).

Example 5   Finding Extremes of Distance on an Ellipse

The plane $x + y + z = 1$ cuts the cylinder $x^2 + y^2 = 1$ in an ellipse (Figure 11.65). Find the points on the ellipse that lie closest to and farthest from the origin.

Solution   We find the extreme values of

$$f(x, y, z) = x^2 + y^2 + z^2$$

(the square of the distance from (x, y, z) to the origin) subject to the constraints

$$g_1(x, y, z) = x^2 + y^2 - 1 = 0 \tag{3}$$

$$g_2(x, y, z) = x + y + z - 1 = 0. \tag{4}$$

The gradient equation in Equations (2) then gives

$$\nabla f = \lambda \nabla g_1 + \mu \nabla g_2$$
$$2x\mathbf{i} + 2y\mathbf{j} + 2z\mathbf{k} = \lambda(2x\mathbf{i} + 2y\mathbf{j}) + \mu(\mathbf{i} + \mathbf{j} + \mathbf{k})$$
$$2x\mathbf{i} + 2y\mathbf{j} + 2z\mathbf{k} = (2\lambda x + \mu)\mathbf{i} + (2\lambda y + \mu)\mathbf{j} + \mu\mathbf{k}$$

or

$$2x = 2\lambda x + \mu, \qquad 2y = 2\lambda y + \mu, \qquad 2z = \mu. \tag{5}$$

The scalar equations in (5) yield

$$2x = 2\lambda x + 2z \implies (1 - \lambda)x = z,$$
$$2y = 2\lambda y + 2z \implies (1 - \lambda)y = z. \tag{6}$$

Equations (6) are satisfied simultaneously if either $\lambda = 1$ and $z = 0$ or $\lambda \neq 1$ and $x = y = z/(1 - \lambda)$.

If $z = 0$, then solving Equations (3) and (4) simultaneously to find the corresponding points on the ellipse gives the two points $(1, 0, 0)$ and $(0, 1, 0)$. This makes sense when you look at Figure 11.65.

If $x = y$, then Equations (3) and (4) give

$$x^2 + x^2 - 1 = 0 \qquad x + x + z - 1 = 0$$
$$2x^2 = 1 \qquad\qquad z = 1 - 2x$$
$$x = \pm\frac{\sqrt{2}}{2} \qquad\qquad z = 1 \mp \sqrt{2}.$$

The corresponding points on the ellipse are

$$P_1 = \left(\frac{\sqrt{2}}{2}, \frac{\sqrt{2}}{2}, 1 - \sqrt{2}\right) \quad \text{and} \quad P_2 = \left(-\frac{\sqrt{2}}{2}, -\frac{\sqrt{2}}{2}, 1 + \sqrt{2}\right).$$

Here we need to be careful, however. Although P_1 and P_2 both give local maxima of f on the ellipse, P_2 is farther from the origin than P_1.

The points on the ellipse closest to the origin are $(1, 0, 0)$ and $(0, 1, 0)$. The point on the ellipse farthest from the origin is P_2.

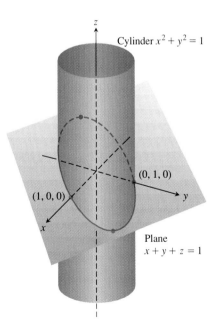

FIGURE 11.65 On the ellipse where the plane and cylinder meet, what are the points closest to and farthest from the origin? (Example 5)

EXERCISES 11.8

Two Independent Variables with One Constraint

1. *Extrema on an ellipse* Find the points on the ellipse $x^2 + 2y^2 = 1$ where $f(x, y) = xy$ has its extreme values.

2. *Extrema on a circle* Find the extreme values of $f(x, y) = xy$ subject to the constraint $g(x, y) = x^2 + y^2 - 10 = 0$.

3. *Maximum on a line* Find the maximum value of $f(x, y) = 49 - x^2 - y^2$ on the line $x + 3y = 10$ (Figure 11.57).

4. *Extrema on a line* Find the local extreme values of $f(x, y) = x^2y$ on the line $x + y = 3$.

5. *Constrained minimum* Find the points on the curve $xy^2 = 54$ nearest the origin.

6. *Constrained minimum* Find the points on the curve $x^2y = 2$ nearest the origin.

7. *Writing to Learn* Use the method of Lagrange multipliers to find

   (a) *Minimum on a hyperbola* The minimum value of $x + y$, subject to the constraints $xy = 16, x > 0, y > 0$

   (b) *Maximum on a line* The maximum value of xy, subject to the constraint $x + y = 16$.

   Comment on the geometry of each solution.

8. *Extrema on a curve* Find the points on the curve $x^2 + xy + y^2 = 1$ in the xy-plane that are nearest to and farthest from the origin.

9. *Minimum surface area with fixed volume* Find the dimensions of the closed right circular cylindrical can of smallest surface area whose volume is 16π cm^3.

10. *Cylinder in a sphere* Find the radius and height of the open right circular cylinder of largest surface area that can be inscribed in a sphere of radius a. What *is* the largest surface area?

11. *Rectangle of greatest area in an ellipse* Use the method of Lagrange multipliers to find the dimensions of the rectangle of greatest area that can be inscribed in the ellipse $x^2/16 + y^2/9 = 1$ with sides parallel to the coordinate axes.

12. *Rectangle of longest perimeter in an ellipse* Find the dimensions of the rectangle of largest perimeter that can be inscribed in the ellipse $x^2/a^2 + y^2/b^2 = 1$ with sides parallel to the coordinate axes. What *is* the largest perimeter?

13. *Extrema on a circle* Find the maximum and minimum values of $x^2 + y^2$ subject to the constraint $x^2 - 2x + y^2 - 4y = 0$.

14. *Extrema on a circle* Find the maximum and minimum values of $3x - y + 6$ subject to the constraint $x^2 + y^2 = 4$.

15. *Ant on a metal plate* The temperature at a point (x, y) on a metal plate is $T(x, y) = 4x^2 - 4xy + y^2$. An ant on the plate walks around the circle of radius 5 centered at the origin. What are the highest and lowest temperatures encountered by the ant?

16. *Cheapest storage tank* Your firm has been asked to design a storage tank for liquid petroleum gas. The customer's specifications

call for a cylindrical tank with hemispherical ends, and the tank is to hold 8000 m^3 of gas. The customer also wants to use the smallest amount of material possible in building the tank. What radius and height do you recommend for the cylindrical portion of the tank?

Three Independent Variables with One Constraint

17. *Minimum distance to a point* Find the point on the plane $x + 2y + 3z = 13$ closest to the point $(1, 1, 1)$.

18. *Maximum distance to a point* Find the point on the sphere $x^2 + y^2 + z^2 = 4$ farthest from the point $(1, -1, 1)$.

19. *Minimum distance to the origin* Find the minimum distance from the surface $x^2 + y^2 - z^2 = 1$ to the origin.

20. *Minimum distance to the origin* Find the point on the surface $z = xy + 1$ nearest the origin.

21. *Minimum distance to the origin* Find the points on the surface $z^2 = xy + 4$ closest to the origin.

22. *Minimum distance to the origin* Find the point(s) on the surface $xyz = 1$ closest to the origin.

23. *Extrema on a sphere* Find the maximum and minimum values of

$$f(x, y, z) = x - 2y + 5z$$

on the sphere $x^2 + y^2 + z^2 = 30$.

24. *Extrema on a sphere* Find the points on the sphere $x^2 + y^2 + z^2 = 25$ where $f(x, y, z) = x + 2y + 3z$ has its maximum and minimum values.

25. *Minimizing a sum of squares* Find three real numbers whose sum is 9 and the sum of whose squares is as small as possible.

26. *Maximizing a product* Find the largest product the positive numbers x, y, and z can have if $x + y + z^2 = 16$.

27. *Rectangular box of longest volume in a sphere* Find the dimensions of the closed rectangular box with maximum volume that can be inscribed in the unit sphere.

28. *Box with vertex on a plane* Find the volume of the largest closed rectangular box in the first octant having three faces in the coordinate planes and a vertex on the plane $x/a + y/b + z/c = 1$, where $a > 0$, $b > 0$, and $c > 0$.

29. *Hottest point on a space probe* A space probe in the shape of the ellipsoid

$$4x^2 + y^2 + 4z^2 = 16$$

enters Earth's atmosphere and its surface begins to heat. After 1 h, the temperature at the point (x, y, z) on the probe's surface is

$$T(x, y, z) = 8x^2 + 4yz - 16z + 600.$$

Find the hottest point on the probe's surface.

30. *Extreme temperatures on a sphere* Suppose that the Celsius temperature at the point (x, y, z) on the sphere $x^2 + y^2 + z^2 = 1$ is $T = 400xyz^2$. Locate the highest and lowest temperatures on the sphere.

31. *Maximizing a utility function: an example from economics* In economics, the usefulness or *utility* of amounts x and y of two capital goods G_1 and G_2 is sometimes measured by a function $U(x, y)$. For example, G_1 and G_2 might be two chemicals a pharmaceutical company needs to have on hand and $U(x, y)$ the gain from manufacturing a product whose synthesis requires different amounts of the chemicals depending on the process used. If G_1 costs a dollars per kilogram, G_2 costs b dollars per kilogram, and the total amount allocated for the purchase of G_1 and G_2 together is c dollars, then the company's managers want to maximize $U(x, y)$ given that $ax + by = c$. Thus, they need to solve a typical Lagrange multiplier problem.

Suppose that

$$U(x, y) = xy + 2x$$

and that the equation $ax + by = c$ simplifies to

$$2x + y = 30.$$

Find the maximum value of U and the corresponding values of x and y subject to this latter constraint.

32. *Locating a radio telescope* You are in charge of erecting a radio telescope on a newly discovered planet. To minimize interference, you want to place it where the magnetic field of the planet is weakest. The planet is spherical, with a radius of 6 units. Based on a coordinate system whose origin is at the center of the planet, the strength of the magnetic field is given by $M(x, y, z) = 6x - y^2 + xz + 60$. Where should you locate the radio telescope?

Extreme Values Subject to Two Constraints

33. Maximize the function $f(x, y, z) = x^2 + 2y - z^2$ subject to the constraints $2x - y = 0$ and $y + z = 0$.

34. Minimize the function $f(x, y, z) = x^2 + y^2 + z^2$ subject to the constraints $x + 2y + 3z = 6$ and $x + 3y + 9z = 9$.

35. *Minimum distance to the origin* Find the point closest to the origin on the line of intersection of the planes $y + 2z = 12$ and $x + y = 6$.

36. *Maximum value on line of intersection* Find the maximum value that $f(x, y, z) = x^2 + 2y - z^2$ can have on the line of intersection of the planes $2x - y = 0$ and $y + z = 0$.

37. *Extrema on a curve of intersection* Find the extreme values of $f(x, y, z) = x^2yz + 1$ on the intersection of the plane $z = 1$ with the sphere $x^2 + y^2 + z^2 = 10$.

38. **(a)** *Maximum on line of intersection* Find the maximum value of $w = xyz$ on the line of intersection of the two planes $x + y + z = 40$ and $x + y - z = 0$.

(b) *Writing to Learn* Give a geometric argument to support your claim that you have found a maximum, and not a minimum, value of w.

39. *Extrema on a circle of intersection* Find the extreme values of the function $f(x, y, z) = xy + z^2$ on the circle in which the plane $y - x = 0$ intersects the sphere $x^2 + y^2 + z^2 = 4$.

40. *Minimum distance to the origin* Find the point closest to the origin on the curve of intersection of the plane $2y + 4z = 5$ and the cone $z^2 = 4x^2 + 4y^2$.

Theory and Examples

41. *The condition $\nabla f = \lambda \nabla g$ is not sufficient* Although $\nabla f = \lambda \nabla g$ is a necessary condition for the occurrence of an extreme value of $f(x, y)$ subject to the condition $g(x, y) = 0$, it does not in itself guarantee that one exists. As a case in point, try using the method of Lagrange multipliers to find a maximum value of $f(x, y) = x + y$ subject to the constraint that $xy = 16$. The method will identify the two points $(4, 4)$ and $(-4, -4)$ as candidates for the location of extreme values. Yet the sum $(x + y)$ has no maximum value on the hyperbola $xy = 16$. The farther you go from the origin on this hyperbola in the first quadrant, the larger the sum $f(x, y) = x + y$ becomes.

42. *A least squares plane* The plane $z = Ax + By + C$ is to be "fitted" to the following points (x_k, y_k, z_k):

$$(0, 0, 0), \quad (0, 1, 1), \quad (1, 1, 1), \quad (1, 0, -1).$$

Find the values of A, B, and C that minimize

$$\sum_{k=1}^{4} (Ax_k + By_k + C - z_k)^2,$$

the sum of the squares of the deviations.

43. **(a)** *Maximum on a sphere* Show that the maximum value of $a^2b^2c^2$ on a sphere of radius r centered at the origin of a Cartesian abc-coordinate system is $(r^2/3)^3$.

(b) *Geometric and arithmetic means* Using part (a), show that for nonnegative numbers a, b, and c,

$$(abc)^{1/3} \leq \frac{a + b + c}{3};$$

that is, the *geometric mean* of three nonnegative numbers is less than or equal to their *arithmetic mean*.

44. *Sum of products* Let $a_1, a_2, \ldots, a_n$ be n positive numbers. Find the maximum of $\sum_{n}^{i=1} a_i x_i$ subject to the constraint $\sum_{n}^{i=1} x_i^2 = 1$.

COMPUTER EXPLORATIONS

Implementing the Method of Lagrange Multipliers

In Exercises 45–50, use a CAS to perform the following steps implementing the method of Lagrange multipliers for finding constrained extrema:

(a) Form the function $h = f - \lambda_1 g_1 - \lambda_2 g_2$, where f is the function to optimize subject to the constraints $g_1 = 0$ and $g_2 = 0$.

(b) Determine all the first partial derivatives of h, including the partials with respect to λ_1 and λ_2, and set them equal to 0.

(c) Solve the system of equations found in part (b) for all the unknowns, including λ_1 and λ_2.

(d) Evaluate f at each of the solution points found in part (c) and select the extreme value subject to the constraints asked for in the exercise.

45. Minimize $f(x, y, z) = xy + yz$ subject to the constraints $x^2 + y^2 - 2 = 0$ and $x^2 + z^2 - 2 = 0$.

46. Minimize $f(x, y, z) = xyz$ subject to the constraints $x^2 + y^2 - 1 = 0$ and $x - z = 0$.

47. Maximize $f(x, y, z) = x^2 + y^2 + z^2$ subject to the constraints $2y + 4z - 5 = 0$ and $4x^2 + 4y^2 - z^2 = 0$.

48. Minimize $f(x, y, z) = x^2 + y^2 + z^2$ subject to the constraints $x^2 - xy + y^2 - z^2 - 1 = 0$ and $x^2 + y^2 - 1 = 0$.

49. Minimize $f(x, y, z, w) = x^2 + y^2 + z^2 + w^2$ subject to the constraints $2x - y + z - w - 1 = 0$ and $x + y - z + w - 1 = 0$.

50. Determine the distance from the line $y = x + 1$ to the parabola $y^2 = x$. (*Hint:* Let (x, y) be a point on the line and (w, z) a point on the parabola. You want to minimize $(x - w)^2 + (y - z)^2$.)

11.9 *Partial Derivatives with Constrained Variables

Decide Which Variables Are Dependent and Which Are Independent •
How to Find $\partial w / \partial x$ When the Variables in $w = f(x, y, z)$ Are Constrained
by Another Equation • Notation • Arrow Diagrams

In finding partial derivatives of functions like $w = f(x, y)$, we have assumed x and y to be independent. In many applications, however, this is not the case. For example, the internal energy U of a gas may be expressed as a function $U = f(P, V, T)$ of pressure P, volume V, and temperature T. If the individual molecules of the gas do not interact, however, P, V, and T obey (and are constrained by) the ideal gas law

$$PV = nRT \qquad (n \text{ and } R \text{ constant}).$$

and fail to be independent. Finding partial derivatives in situations like these can be complicated, but it is better to face the complication now than to meet it for the first time while you are also trying to learn economics, engineering, or physics.

Decide Which Variables Are Dependent and Which Are Independent

If the variables in a function $w = f(x, y, z)$ are constrained by a relation like the one imposed on x, y, and z by the equation $z = x^2 + y^2$, the geometric meanings and the numerical values of the partial derivatives of f will depend on which variables are chosen to be dependent and which are chosen to be independent. To see how this choice can affect the outcome, we consider the calculation of $\partial w / \partial x$ when $w = x^2 + y^2 + z^2$ and $z = x^2 + y^2$.

> **Example 1**   Finding a Partial Derivative with Constrained Independent Variables
>
> Find $\partial w / \partial x$ if $w = x^2 + y^2 + z^2$ and $z = x^2 + y^2$.
>
> **Solution**   We are given two equations in the four unknowns x, y, z, and w. Like many such systems, this one can be solved for two of the unknowns (the dependent variables) in terms of the others (the independent variables). In

---

*This section is based on notes written for MIT by Arthur P. Mattuck.

being asked for $\partial w / \partial x$, we are told that w is to be a dependent variable and x an independent variable. The possible choices for the other variables come down to

Dependent	Independent
w, z	x, y
w, y	x, z

In either case, we can express w explicitly in terms of the selected independent variables. We do this by using the second equation to eliminate the remaining dependent variable in the first equation.

In the first case, the remaining dependent variable is z. We eliminate it from the first equation by replacing it by $x^2 + y^2$. The resulting expression for w is

$$w = x^2 + y^2 + z^2 = x^2 + y^2 + (x^2 + y^2)^2$$
$$= x^2 + y^2 + x^4 + 2x^2y^2 + y^4$$

and

$$\frac{\partial w}{\partial x} = 2x + 4x^3 + 4xy^2. \tag{1}$$

This is the formula for $\partial w / \partial x$ when x and y are the independent variables.

In the second case, where the independent variables are x and z and the remaining dependent variable is y, we eliminate the dependent variable y in the expression for w by replacing y^2 by $z - x^2$. This gives

$$w = x^2 + y^2 + z^2 = x^2 + (z - x^2) + z^2 = z + z^2$$

and

$$\frac{\partial w}{\partial x} = 0. \tag{2}$$

This is the formula for $\partial w / \partial x$ when x and z are the independent variables.

The formulas for $\partial w / \partial x$ in Equations (1) and (2) are genuinely different. We cannot change either formula into the other by using the relation $z = x^2 + y^2$. There is not just one $\partial w / \partial x$, there are two, and we see that the original instruction to find $\partial w / \partial x$ was incomplete. *Which* $\partial w / \partial x$? we ask.

The geometric interpretations of Equations (1) and (2) help to explain why the equations differ. The function $w = x^2 + y^2 + z^2$ measures the square of the distance from the point (x, y, z) to the origin. The condition $z = x^2 + y^2$ says that the point (x, y, z) lies on the paraboloid of revolution shown in Figure 11.66. What does it mean to calculate $\partial w / \partial x$ at a point $P(x, y, z)$ that can move only on this surface? What is the value of $\partial w / \partial x$ when the coordinates of P are, say, $(1, 0, 1)$?

If we take x and y to be independent, then we find $\partial w / \partial x$ by holding y fixed (at $y = 0$ in this case) and letting x vary. Hence, P moves along the parabola $z = x^2$ in the xz-plane. As P moves on this parabola, w, which is the square of the distance from P to the origin, changes. We calculate $\partial w / \partial x$ in this case (our first solution above) to be

$$\frac{\partial w}{\partial x} = 2x + 4x^3 + 4xy^2.$$

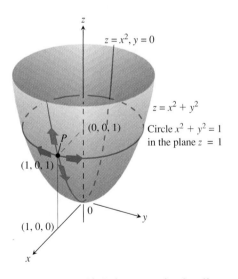

FIGURE 11.66 If P is constrained to lie on the paraboloid $z = x^2 + y^2$, the value of the partial derivative of $w = x^2 + y^2 + z^2$ with respect to x at P depends on the direction of motion (Example 1). (a) As x changes, with $y = 0$, P moves up or down the surface on the parabola $z = x^2$ in the xz-plane with $\partial w / \partial x = 2x + 4x^3 + 4xy^2$. (b) As x changes, with $z = 1$, P moves on the circle $x^2 + y^2 = 1$, $z = 1$, and $\partial w / \partial x = 0$.

At the point $P(1, 0, 1)$, the value of this derivative is

$$\frac{\partial w}{\partial x} = 2 + 4 + 0 = 6.$$

If we take x and z to be independent, then we find $\partial w/\partial x$ by holding z fixed while x varies. Since the z-coordinate of P is 1, varying x moves P along a circle in the plane $z = 1$. As P moves along this circle, its distance from the origin remains constant, and w, being the square of this distance, does not change. That is,

$$\frac{\partial w}{\partial x} = 0,$$

as we found in our second solution.

How to Find $\partial w / \partial x$ When the Variables in $w = f(x, y, z)$ Are Constrained by Another Equation

As we saw in Example 1, a typical routine for finding $\partial w/\partial x$ when the variables in the function $w = f(x, y, z)$ are related by another equation has three steps. These steps apply to finding $\partial w/\partial y$ and $\partial w/\partial z$ as well.

Step 1: *Decide* which variables are to be dependent and which are to be independent. (In practice, the decision is based on the physical or theoretical context of our work. In the exercises at the end of this section, we say which variables are which.)

Step 2: *Eliminate* the other dependent variable(s) in the expression for w.

Step 3: *Differentiate* as usual.

If we cannot carry out step 2 after deciding which variables are dependent, we differentiate the equations as they are and try to solve for $\partial w/\partial x$ afterward. The next example shows how this is done.

Example 2   Finding a Partial Derivative with Identified Constrained Independent Variables

Find $\partial w/\partial x$ at the point $(x, y, z) = (2, -1, 1)$ if

$$w = x^2 + y^2 + z^2, \qquad z^3 - xy + yz + y^3 = 1,$$

and x and y are the independent variables.

Solution   It is not convenient to eliminate z in the expression for w. We therefore differentiate both equations implicitly with respect to x, treating x and y as independent variables and w and z as dependent variables. This gives

$$\frac{\partial w}{\partial x} = 2x + 2z \frac{\partial z}{\partial x} \tag{3}$$

and

$$3z^2 \frac{\partial z}{\partial x} - y + y \frac{\partial z}{\partial x} + 0 = 0. \tag{4}$$

These equations may now be combined to express $\partial w / \partial x$ in terms of x, y, and z. We solve Equation (4) for $\partial z / \partial x$ to get

$$\frac{\partial z}{\partial x} = \frac{y}{y + 3z^2}$$

and substitute into Equation (3) to get

$$\frac{\partial w}{\partial x} = 2x + \frac{2yz}{y + 3z^2}.$$

The value of this derivative at $(x, y, z) = (2, -1, 1)$ is

$$\left(\frac{\partial w}{\partial x} \right)_{(2,-1,1)} = 2(2) + \frac{2(-1)(1)}{-1 + 3(1)^2} = 4 + \frac{-2}{2} = 3.$$

Notation

To show what variables are assumed to be independent in calculating a derivative, we can use the following notation:

$$\left(\frac{\partial w}{\partial x} \right)_{y} \qquad \partial w / \partial x \text{ with } x \text{ and } y \text{ independent}$$

$$\left(\frac{\partial f}{\partial y} \right)_{x,\,t} \qquad \partial f / \partial y \text{ with } y, x \text{ and } t \text{ independent}$$

Example 3 Finding a Partial Derivative with Constrained Variables Notationally Identified

Find $(\partial w / \partial x)_{y,z}$ if $w = x^2 + y - z + \sin t$ and $x + y = t$.

Solution   With x, y, z independent, we have

$$t = x + y, \qquad w = x^2 + y - z + \sin (x + y)$$

$$\left(\frac{\partial w}{\partial x} \right)_{y,\,z} = 2x + 0 - 0 + \cos (x + y) \frac{\partial}{\partial x} (x + y)$$

$$= 2x + \cos (x + y).$$

Arrow Diagrams

In solving problems like the one in Example 3, it often helps to start with an arrow diagram that shows how the variables and functions are related. If

$$w = x^2 + y - z + \sin t \qquad \text{and} \qquad x + y = t$$

and we are asked to find $\partial w / \partial x$ when x, y, and z are independent, the appropriate diagram is one like this:

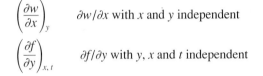

$$\begin{pmatrix} x \\ y \\ z \end{pmatrix} \quad \rightarrow \quad \begin{pmatrix} x \\ y \\ z \\ t \end{pmatrix} \quad \rightarrow \quad w \tag{5}$$

Independent   Intermediate   Dependent
variables   variables   variable

To avoid confusion between the independent and intermediate variables with the same symbolic names in the diagram, it is helpful to rename the intermediate variables (so they are seen as *functions* of the independent variables). Thus, let $u = x$, $v = y$, and $s = z$ denote the renamed intermediate variables. With this notation, the arrow diagram becomes

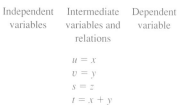

(6)

Independent   Intermediate   Dependent
variables   variables and   variable
               relations

$u = x$
$v = y$
$s = z$
$t = x + y$

The diagram shows the independent variables on the left, the intermediate variables and their relation to the independent variables in the middle, and the dependent variable on the right. The function w now becomes

$$w = u^2 + v - s + \sin t,$$

where

$$u = x, \qquad v = y, \qquad s = z, \qquad \text{and} \qquad t = x + y.$$

To find $\partial w/\partial x$, we apply the four-variable form of the Chain Rule to w, guided by the arrow diagram (6):

$$\frac{\partial w}{\partial x} = \frac{\partial w}{\partial u}\frac{\partial u}{\partial x} + \frac{\partial w}{\partial v}\frac{\partial v}{\partial x} + \frac{\partial w}{\partial s}\frac{\partial s}{\partial x} + \frac{\partial w}{\partial t}\frac{\partial t}{\partial x}.$$

$$= (2u)(1) + (1)(0) + (-1)(0) + (\cos t)(1)$$

$$= 2u + \cos t$$

$$= 2x + \cos (x + y). \qquad \text{Substituting the original independent variables } u = x \text{ and } t = x + y.$$

EXERCISES 11.9

Finding Partial Derivatives with Constrained Variables

In Exercises 1–3, begin by drawing a diagram that shows the relations among the variables.

1. If $w = x^2 + y^2 + z^2$ and $z = x^2 + y^2$, find

(a) $\left(\dfrac{\partial w}{\partial y}\right)_z$ (b) $\left(\dfrac{\partial w}{\partial z}\right)_x$ (c) $\left(\dfrac{\partial w}{\partial z}\right)_y$.

2. If $w = x^2 + y - z + \sin t$ and $x + y = t$, find

(a) $\left(\dfrac{\partial w}{\partial y}\right)_{x,z}$ (b) $\left(\dfrac{\partial w}{\partial y}\right)_{z,t}$ (c) $\left(\dfrac{\partial w}{\partial z}\right)_{x,y}$

(d) $\left(\dfrac{\partial w}{\partial z}\right)_{y,t}$ (e) $\left(\dfrac{\partial w}{\partial t}\right)_{x,z}$ (f) $\left(\dfrac{\partial w}{\partial t}\right)_{y,z}$.

3. Let $U = f(P, V, T)$ be the internal energy of a gas that obeys the ideal gas law $PV = nRT$ (n and R constant). Find

(a) $\left(\dfrac{\partial U}{\partial P}\right)_V$ **(b)** $\left(\dfrac{\partial U}{\partial T}\right)_V$.

4. Find

(a) $\left(\dfrac{\partial w}{\partial x}\right)_y$ **(b)** $\left(\dfrac{\partial w}{\partial z}\right)_y$

at the point $(x, y, z) = (0, 1, \pi)$ if

$$w = x^2 + y^2 + z^2 \quad \text{and} \quad y \sin z + z \sin x = 0.$$

5. Find

(a) $\left(\dfrac{\partial w}{\partial y}\right)_x$ **(b)** $\left(\dfrac{\partial w}{\partial y}\right)_z$

at the point $(w, x, y, z) = (4, 2, 1, -1)$ if

$$w = x^2y^2 + yz - z^3 \quad \text{and} \quad x^2 + y^2 + z^2 = 6.$$

6. Find $(\partial u/\partial y)_x$ at the point $(u, v) = (\sqrt{2}, 1)$, if $x = u^2 + v^2$ and $y = uv$.

7. Suppose that $x^2 + y^2 = r^2$ and $x = r \cos \theta$, as in polar coordinates. Find

$$\left(\dfrac{\partial x}{\partial r}\right)_\theta \quad \text{and} \quad \left(\dfrac{\partial r}{\partial x}\right)_y.$$

8. Suppose that

$$w = x^2 - y^2 + 4z + t \quad \text{and} \quad x + 2z + t = 25.$$

Show that the equations

$$\dfrac{\partial w}{\partial x} = 2x - 1 \quad \text{and} \quad \dfrac{\partial w}{\partial x} = 2x - 2$$

each give $\partial w/\partial x$, depending on which variables are chosen to be dependent and which variables are chosen to be independent. Identify the independent variables in each case.

Partial Derivatives without Specific Formulas

9. Establish the fact, widely used in hydrodynamics, that if $f(x, y, z) = 0$, then

$$\left(\dfrac{\partial x}{\partial y}\right)_z \left(\dfrac{\partial y}{\partial z}\right)_x \left(\dfrac{\partial z}{\partial x}\right)_y = -1.$$

(*Hint:* Express all the derivatives in terms of the formal partial derivatives $\partial f/\partial x$, $\partial f/\partial y$, and $\partial f/\partial z$.)

10. If $z = x + f(u)$, where $u = xy$, show that

$$x\dfrac{\partial z}{\partial x} - y\dfrac{\partial z}{\partial y} = x.$$

11. Suppose that the equation $g(x, y, z) = 0$ determines z as a differentiable function of the independent variables x and y and that $g_z \neq 0$. Show that

$$\left(\dfrac{\partial z}{\partial y}\right)_x = -\dfrac{\partial g/\partial y}{\partial g/\partial z}.$$

12. Suppose that $f(x, y, z, w) = 0$ and $g(x, y, z, w) = 0$ determine z and w as differentiable functions of the independent variables x and y, and suppose that

$$\dfrac{\partial f}{\partial z}\dfrac{\partial g}{\partial w} - \dfrac{\partial f}{\partial w}\dfrac{\partial g}{\partial z} \neq 0.$$

Show that

$$\left(\dfrac{\partial z}{\partial x}\right)_y = -\dfrac{\dfrac{\partial f}{\partial x}\dfrac{\partial g}{\partial w} - \dfrac{\partial f}{\partial w}\dfrac{\partial g}{\partial x}}{\dfrac{\partial f}{\partial z}\dfrac{\partial g}{\partial w} - \dfrac{\partial f}{\partial w}\dfrac{\partial g}{\partial z}}$$

and

$$\left(\dfrac{\partial w}{\partial y}\right)_x = -\dfrac{\dfrac{\partial f}{\partial z}\dfrac{\partial g}{\partial y} - \dfrac{\partial f}{\partial y}\dfrac{\partial g}{\partial z}}{\dfrac{\partial f}{\partial z}\dfrac{\partial g}{\partial w} - \dfrac{\partial f}{\partial w}\dfrac{\partial g}{\partial z}}.$$

11.10 Taylor's Formula for Two Variables

Derivation of the Second Derivative Test • Error Formula for Linear Approximations • Taylor's Formula for Functions of Two Variables

This section uses Taylor's formula (Section 8.7) to derive the second derivative test for local extreme values (Section 11.7) and the error formula for linearizations of functions of two independent variables (Section 11.6). The use of Taylor's formula in these derivations leads to an extension of the formula that provides polynomial approximations of all orders for functions of two independent variables.

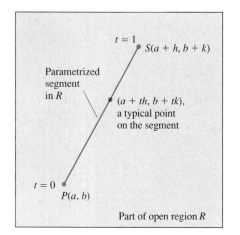

FIGURE 11.67 We begin the derivation of the second derivative test at $P(a, b)$ by parametrizing a typical line segment from P to a point S nearby.

Derivation of the Second Derivative Test

Let $f(x, y)$ have continuous partial derivatives in an open region R containing a point $P(a, b)$ where $f_x = f_y = 0$ (Figure 11.67). Let h and k be increments small enough to put the point $S(a + h, b + k)$ and the line segment joining it to P inside R. We parametrize the segment PS as

$$x = a + th, \qquad y = b + tk, \qquad 0 \le t \le 1.$$

If $F(t) = f(a + th, b + tk)$, the Chain Rule gives

$$F'(t) = f_x \frac{dx}{dt} + f_y \frac{dy}{dt} = hf_x + kf_y.$$

Since f_x and f_y are differentiable (they have continuous partial derivatives), F' is a differentiable function of t and

$$F'' = \frac{\partial F'}{\partial x} \frac{dx}{dt} + \frac{\partial F'}{\partial y} \frac{dy}{dt} = \frac{\partial}{\partial x}(hf_x + kf_y) \cdot h + \frac{\partial}{\partial y}(hf_x + kf_y) \cdot k$$

$$= h^2 f_{xx} + 2hk f_{xy} + k^2 f_{yy}. \qquad {\scriptstyle f_{xy} = f_{yx}}$$

Since F and F' are continuous on $[0, 1]$ and F' is differentiable on $(0, 1)$, we can apply Taylor's formula with $n = 2$ and $a = 0$ to obtain

$$F(1) = F(0) + F'(0)(1 - 0) + F''(c)\frac{(1 - 0)^2}{2}$$

$$F(1) = F(0) + F'(0) + \frac{1}{2}F''(c) \tag{1}$$

for some c between 0 and 1. Writing Equation (1) in terms of f gives

$$f(a + h, b + k) = f(a, b) + hf_x(a, b) + kf_y(a, b)$$
$$+ \frac{1}{2}(h^2 f_{xx} + 2hk f_{xy} + k^2 f_{yy})\Big|_{(a+ch, b+ck)} \tag{2}$$

Since $f_x(a, b) = f_y(a, b) = 0$, this last equation reduces to

$$f(a + h, b + k) - f(a, b) = \frac{1}{2}(h^2 f_{xx} + 2hk f_{xy} + k^2 f_{yy})\Big|_{(a+ch, b+ck)} \tag{3}$$

The presence of an extremum of f at (a, b) is determined by the sign of $f(a + h, b + k) - f(a, b)$. By Equation (3), this is the same as the sign of

$$Q(c) = (h^2 f_{xx} + 2hk f_{xy} + k^2 f_{yy})|_{(a+ch, b+ck)}.$$

Now, if $Q(0) \ne 0$, the sign of $Q(c)$ will be the same as the sign of $Q(0)$ for sufficiently small values of h and k. We can predict the sign of

$$Q(0) = h^2 f_{xx}(a, b) + 2hk f_{xy}(a, b) + k^2 f_{yy}(a, b) \tag{4}$$

from the signs of f_{xx} and $f_{xx}f_{yy} - f_{xy}{}^2$ at (a, b). Multiply both sides of Equation (4) by f_{xx} and rearrange the right-hand side to get

$$f_{xx}Q(0) = (hf_{xx} + kf_{xy})^2 + (f_{xx}f_{yy} - f_{xy}{}^2)k^2 \tag{5}$$

at (a, b). From Equation (5), we see that

1. If $f_{xx} < 0$ and $f_{xx}f_{yy} - f_{xy}{}^2 > 0$ at (a, b), then $Q(0) < 0$ for all sufficiently small nonzero values of h and k, and f has a *local maximum* value at (a, b).

2. If $f_{xx} > 0$ and $f_{xx}f_{yy} - f_{xy}^2 > 0$ at (a, b), then $Q(0) > 0$ for all sufficiently small nonzero values of h and k, and f has a *local minimum* value at (a, b).

3. If $f_{xx}f_{yy} - f_{xy}^2 < 0$ at (a, b), there are combinations of arbitrarily small nonzero values of h and k for which $Q(0) > 0$, and other values for which $Q(0) < 0$. Arbitrarily close to the point $P_0(a, b, f(a, b))$ on the surface $z = f(x, y)$ there are points above P_0 and points below P_0, so f has a *saddle point* at (a, b).

4. If $f_{xx}f_{yy} - f_{xy}^2 = 0$, another test is needed. The possibility that $Q(0)$ equals zero prevents us from drawing conclusions about the sign of $Q(c)$.

Error Formula for Linear Approximations

We want to show that the difference $E(x, y)$ between the values of a function $f(x, y)$ and its linearization $L(x, y)$ at (x_0, y_0) satisfies the inequality

$$|E(x, y)| \leq \frac{1}{2} M(|x - x_0| + |y - y_0|)^2.$$

The function f is assumed to have continuous second partial derivatives throughout an open set containing a closed rectangular region R centered at (x_0, y_0). The number M is the largest value that any of $|f_{xx}|, |f_{yy}|$, and $|f_{xy}|$ take on R.

The inequality we want comes from Equation (2). We substitute x_0 and y_0 for a and b, and $x - x_0$ and $y - y_0$ for h and k, respectively, and rearrange the result as

$$f(x, y) = \underbrace{f(x_0, y_0) + f_x(x_0, y_0)(x - x_0) + f_y(x_0, y_0)(y - y_0)}_{\text{Linearization } L(x, y)}$$

$$\underbrace{+ \frac{1}{2}((x - x_0)^2 f_{xx} + 2(x - x_0)(y - y_0)f_{xy} + (y - y_0)^2 f_{yy})|_{(x_0 + c(x - x_0),\, y_0 + c(y - y_0))}}_{\text{Error } E(x, y)}.$$

This remarkable equation reveals that

$$|E| \leq \frac{1}{2}(|x - x_0|^2 |f_{xx}| + 2|x - x_0||y - y_0||f_{xy}| + |y - y_0|^2 |f_{yy}|).$$

Hence, if M is an upper bound for the values of $|f_{xx}|, |f_{xy}|$, and $|f_{yy}|$ on R,

$$|E| \leq \frac{1}{2}(|x - x_0|^2 M + 2|x - x_0||y - y_0|M + |y - y_0|^2 M)$$

$$\leq \frac{1}{2} M(|x - x_0| + |y - y_0|)^2.$$

Taylor's Formula for Functions of Two Variables

The formulas derived earlier for F' and F'' can be obtained by applying to $f(x, y)$ the operators

$$\left(h\frac{\partial}{\partial x} + k\frac{\partial}{\partial y}\right) \qquad \text{and} \qquad \left(h\frac{\partial}{\partial x} + k\frac{\partial}{\partial y}\right)^2 = h^2\frac{\partial^2}{\partial x^2} + 2hk\frac{\partial^2}{\partial x\,\partial y} + k^2\frac{\partial^2}{\partial y^2}.$$

These are the first two instances of a more general formula,

$$F^{(n)}(t) = \frac{d^n}{dt^n}F(t) = \left(h\frac{\partial}{\partial x} + k\frac{\partial}{\partial y}\right)^n f(x, y), \tag{6}$$

which says that applying d^n/dt^n to $F(t)$ gives the same result as applying the operator

$$\left(h\frac{\partial}{\partial x} + k\frac{\partial}{\partial y} \right)^n$$

to $f(x, y)$ after expanding it by the binomial theorem.

If partial derivatives of f through order $n + 1$ are continuous throughout a rectangular region centered at (a, b), we may extend the Taylor formula for $F(t)$ to

$$F(t) = F(0) + F'(0)t + \frac{F''(0)}{2!}t^2 + \cdots + \frac{F^{(n)}(0)}{n!}t^n + \text{remainder}$$

and take $t = 1$ to obtain

$$F(1) = F(0) + F'(0) + \frac{F''(0)}{2!} + \cdots + \frac{F^{(n)}(0)}{n!} + \text{remainder}.$$

When we replace the first n derivatives on the right of this last series by their equivalent expressions from Equation (6) evaluated at $t = 0$ and add the appropriate remainder term, we arrive at the following formula.

Theorem 13 Taylor's Formula for f(x, y) at the Point (a, b)

Suppose that $f(x, y)$ and its partial derivatives through order $n + 1$ are continuous throughout an open rectangular region R centered at a point (a, b). Then, throughout R,

$$f(a + h, b + k) = f(a, b) + (hf_x + kf_y)|_{(a,b)} + \frac{1}{2!}(h^2f_{xx} + 2hkf_{xy} + k^2f_{yy})|_{(a,b)}$$

$$+ \frac{1}{3!}(h^3f_{xxx} + 3h^2kf_{xxy} + 3hk^2f_{xyy} + k^3f_{yyy})|_{(a,b)} + \cdots + \frac{1}{n!}\left(h\frac{\partial}{\partial x} + k\frac{\partial}{\partial y} \right)^n f\bigg|_{(a,b)}$$

$$+ \frac{1}{(n+1)!}\left(h\frac{\partial}{\partial x} + k\frac{\partial}{\partial y} \right)^{n+1} f\bigg|_{(a+ch,\, b+ck)} \tag{7}$$

The first n derivative terms are evaluated at (a, b). The last term is evaluated at some point $(a + ch, b + ck)$ on the line segment joining (a, b) and $(a + h, b + k)$.

If $(a, b) = (0, 0)$ and we treat h and k as independent variables (denoting them now by x and y), then Equation (7) assumes the following simpler form.

Corollary to Theorem 13 Taylor's Formula for f(x, y) at the Origin

$$f(x, y) = f(0, 0) + xf_x + yf_y + \frac{1}{2!}(x^2f_{xx} + 2xyf_{xy} + y^2f_{yy})$$

$$+ \frac{1}{3!}(x^3f_{xxx} + 3x^2yf_{xxy} + 3xy^2f_{xyy} + y^3f_{yyy}) + \cdots + \frac{1}{n!}\left(x\frac{\partial}{\partial x} + y\frac{\partial}{\partial y} \right)^n f$$

$$+ \frac{1}{(n+1)!}\left(x\frac{\partial}{\partial x} + y\frac{\partial}{\partial y} \right)^{n+1} f\bigg|_{(cx,cy)} \tag{8}$$

The first n derivative terms are evaluated at $(0, 0)$. The last term is evaluated at a point on the line segment joining the origin and (x, y).

Taylor's formula provides polynomial approximations of two-variable functions. The first n derivative terms give the polynomial; the last term gives the approximation error. The first three terms of Taylor's formula give the function's linearization. To improve on the linearization, we add higher power terms.

Example 1 Finding a Quadratic Approximation

Find a quadratic $f(x, y) = \sin x \sin y$ near the origin. How accurate is the approximation if $|x| \le 0.1$ and $|y| \le 0.1$?

Solution We take $n = 2$ in Equation (8):

$$f(x, y) = f(0, 0) + (xf_x + yf_y) + \frac{1}{2}(x^2 f_{xx} + 2xy f_{xy} + y^2 f_{yy})$$

$$+ \frac{1}{6}(x^3 f_{xxx} + 3x^2 y f_{xxy} + 3xy^2 f_{xyy} + y^3 f_{yyy})_{(cx, cy)}$$

with

$$
\begin{aligned}
f(0, 0) &= \sin x \sin y\,|_{(0,0)} = 0, & f_{xx}(0, 0) &= -\sin x \sin y\,|_{(0,0)} = 0, \\
f_x(0, 0) &= \cos x \sin y\,|_{(0,0)} = 0, & f_{xy}(0, 0) &= \cos x \cos y\,|_{(0,0)} = 1, \\
f_y(0, 0) &= \sin x \cos y\,|_{(0,0)} = 0, & f_{yy}(0, 0) &= -\sin x \sin y\,|_{(0,0)} = 0,
\end{aligned}
$$

we have

$$\sin x \sin y \approx 0 + 0 + 0 + \frac{1}{2}(x^2(0) + 2xy(1) + y^2(0))$$

$$\sin x \sin y \approx xy.$$

The error in the approximation is

$$E(x, y) = \frac{1}{6}(x^3 f_{xxx} + 3x^2 y f_{xxy} + 3xy^2 f_{xyy} + y^3 f_{yyy})\,|_{(cx, cy)}.$$

The third derivatives never exceed 1 in absolute value because they are products of sines and cosines. Also, $|x| \le 0.1$ and $|y| \le 0.1$. Hence,

$$|E(x, y)| \le \frac{1}{6}((0.1)^3 + 3(0.1)^3 + 3(0.1)^3 + (0.1)^3) \le \frac{8}{6}(0.1)^3 \le 0.00134$$

(rounded up). The error will not exceed 0.00134 if $|x| \le 0.1$ and $|y| \le 0.1$.

EXERCISES 11.10

Finding Quadratic and Cubic Approximations

In Exercises 1–10, use Taylor's formula for $f(x, y)$ at the origin to find quadratic and cubic approximations of f near the origin.

1. $f(x, y) = xe^y$

2. $f(x, y) = e^x \cos y$

3. $f(x, y) = y \sin x$

4. $f(x, y) = \sin x \cos y$

5. $f(x, y) = e^x \ln (1 + y)$

6. $f(x, y) = \ln (2x + y + 1)$

7. $f(x, y) = \sin (x^2 + y^2)$

8. $f(x, y) = \cos (x^2 + y^2)$

9. $f(x, y) = \dfrac{1}{1 - x - y}$

10. $f(x, y) = \dfrac{1}{1 - x - y + xy}$

11. Use Taylor's formula to find a quadratic approximation of $f(x, y) = \cos x \cos y$ at the origin. Estimate the error in the approximation if $|x| \le 0.1$ and $|y| \le 0.1$.

12. Use Taylor's formula to find a quadratic approximation of $e^x \sin y$ at the origin. Estimate the error in the approximation if $|x| \le 0.1$ and $|y| \le 0.1$.

Questions to Guide Your Review

1. What is a real-valued function of two independent variables? Three independent variables? Give examples.

2. What does it mean for sets in the plane or in space to be open? closed? Give examples. Give examples of sets that are neither open nor closed.

3. How can you display the values of a function $f(x, y)$ of two independent variables graphically? How do you do the same for a function $f(x, y, z)$ of three independent variables?

4. What does it mean for a function $f(x, y)$ to have limit L as $(x, y) \rightarrow (x_0, y_0)$? What are the basic properties of limits of functions of two independent variables?

5. When is a function of two (three) independent variables continuous at a point in its domain? Give examples of functions that are continuous at some points but not others.

6. What can be said about algebraic combinations and composites of continuous functions?

7. Explain the two-path test for nonexistence of limits.

8. How are the partial derivatives $\partial f/\partial x$ and $\partial f/\partial y$ of a function $f(x, y)$ defined? How are they interpreted and calculated?

9. How does the relation between first partial derivatives and continuity of functions of two independent variables differ from the relation between first derivatives and continuity for real-valued functions of a single independent variable? Give an example.

10. What does it mean for a function $f(x, y)$ to be differentiable? What does the Increment Theorem say about differentiability?

11. What is the Mixed Derivative Theorem for mixed second-order partial derivatives? How can it help in calculating partial derivatives of second and higher orders? Give examples.

12. How can you sometimes decide from examining f_x and f_y that a function $f(x, y)$ is differentiable? What is the relation between the differentiability of f and the continuity of f at a point?

13. What is the Chain Rule? What form does it take for functions of two independent variables? Three independent variables? Functions defined on surfaces? How do you diagram these different

forms? Give examples. What pattern enables one to remember all the different forms?

14. What is the derivative of a function $f(x, y)$ at a point P_0 in the direction of a unit vector $\mathbf{u}$? What rate does it describe? What geometric interpretation does it have? Give examples.

15. What is the gradient vector of a function $f(x, y)$? How is it related to the function's directional derivatives? State the analogous results for functions of three independent variables.

16. How do you find the tangent line at a point on a level curve of a differentiable function $f(x, y)$? How do you find the tangent plane and normal line at a point on a level surface of a differentiable function $f(x, y, z)$? Give examples.

17. How can you use directional derivatives to estimate change?

18. How do you linearize a function $f(x, y)$ of two independent variables at a point (x_0, y_0)? Why might you want to do this? How do you linearize a function of three independent variables?

19. What can you say about the accuracy of linear approximations of functions of two (three) independent variables?

20. If (x, y) moves from (x_0, y_0) to a point $(x_0 + dx, y_0 + dy)$ nearby, how can you estimate the resulting change in the value of a differentiable function $f(x, y)$? Give an example.

21. How do you define local maxima, local minima, and saddle points for a differentiable function $f(x, y)$? Give examples.

22. What derivative tests are available for determining the local extreme values of a function $f(x, y)$? How do they enable you to narrow your search for these values? Give examples.

23. How do you find the extrema of a continuous function $f(x, y)$ on a closed bounded region of the xy-plane? Give an example.

24. Describe the method of Lagrange multipliers and give examples.

25. If $w = f(x, y, z)$, where the variables x, y, and z are constrained by an equation $g(x, y, z) = 0$, what is the meaning of the notation $(\partial w/\partial x)_y$? How can an arrow diagram help you calculate this partial derivative with constrained variables? Give examples.

26. How does Taylor's formula for a function $f(x, y)$ generate polynomial approximations and error estimates?

Practice Exercises

Domain, Range, and Level Curves

In Exercises 1–4, find the domain and range of the given function and identify its level curves. Sketch a typical level curve.

1. $f(x, y) = 9x^2 + y^2$

2. $f(x, y) = e^{x+y}$

3. $g(x, y) = 1/xy$

4. $g(x, y) = \sqrt{x^2 - y}$

In Exercises 5–8, find the domain and range of the given function and identify its level surfaces. Sketch a typical level surface.

5. $f(x, y, z) = x^2 + y^2 - z$

6. $g(x, y, z) = x^2 + 4y^2 + 9z^2$

7. $h(x, y, z) = \dfrac{1}{x^2 + y^2 + z^2}$

8. $k(x, y, z) = \dfrac{1}{x^2 + y^2 + z^2 + 1}$

Evaluating Limits

Find the limits in Exercises 9–14.

9. $\displaystyle\lim_{(x,y)\to(\pi,\ln2)} e^y \cos x$

10. $\displaystyle\lim_{(x,y)\to(0,0)} \dfrac{2 + y}{x + \cos y}$

11. $\displaystyle\lim_{(x,y)\to(1,1)} \dfrac{x - y}{x^2 - y^2}$

12. $\displaystyle\lim_{(x,y)\to(1,1)} \dfrac{x^3y^3 - 1}{xy - 1}$

13. $\displaystyle\lim_{P\to(1,-1,e)} \ln |x + y + z|$

14. $\displaystyle\lim_{P\to(1,-1,-1)} \tan^{-1}(x + y + z)$

By considering different paths of approach, show that the limits in Exercises 15 and 16 do not exist.

15. $\displaystyle\lim_{\substack{(x,y)\to(0,0)\\ y\neq x^2}} \dfrac{y}{x^2 - y}$

16. $\displaystyle\lim_{\substack{(x,y)\to(0,0)\\ xy\neq 0}} \dfrac{x^2 + y^2}{xy}$

17. *Continuous extension* Let $f(x, y) = (x^2 - y^2)/(x^2 + y^2)$ for $(x, y) \neq (0, 0)$. Is it possible to define $f(0, 0)$ in a way that makes f continuous at the origin? Why?

18. *Continuous extension* Let

$$f(x, y) = \begin{cases} \dfrac{\sin (x - y)}{|x| + |y|}, & |x| + |y| \neq 0 \\ 0, & (x, y) = (0, 0). \end{cases}$$

Is f continuous at the origin? Why?

Partial Derivatives

In Exercises 19–24, find the partial derivative of the function with respect to each variable.

19. $g(r, \theta) = r \cos \theta + r \sin \theta$

20. $f(x, y) = \dfrac{1}{2} \ln (x^2 + y^2) + \tan^{-1} \dfrac{y}{x}$

21. $f(R_1, R_2, R_3) = \dfrac{1}{R_1} + \dfrac{1}{R_2} + \dfrac{1}{R_3}$

22. $h(x, y, z) = \sin (2\pi x + y - 3z)$

23. $P(n, R, T, V) = \dfrac{nRT}{V}$ (the Ideal Gas Law)

24. $f(r, l, T, w) = \dfrac{1}{2rl} \sqrt{\dfrac{T}{\pi w}}$

Second-Order Partials

Find the second-order partial derivatives of the functions in Exercises 25–28.

25. $g(x, y) = y + \dfrac{x}{y}$

26. $g(x, y) = e^x + y \sin x$

27. $f(x, y) = x + xy - 5x^3 + \ln (x^2 + 1)$

28. $f(x, y) = y^2 - 3xy + \cos y + 7e^y$

Chain Rule Calculations

29. Find dw/dt at $t = 0$ if $w = \sin (xy + \pi), x = e^t$, and $y = \ln (t + 1)$.

30. Find dw/dt at $t = 1$ if $w = xe^y + y \sin z - \cos z$, $x = 2\sqrt{t}$, $y = t - 1 + \ln t$, and $z = \pi t$.

31. Find $\partial w/\partial r$ and $\partial w/\partial s$ when $r = \pi$ and $s = 0$ if $w = \sin (2x - y)$, $x = r + \sin s$, $y = rs$.

32. Find $\partial w/\partial u$ and $\partial w/\partial v$ when $u = v = 0$ if $w = \ln \sqrt{1 + x^2} - \tan^{-1} x$ and $x = 2e^u \cos v$.

33. Find the value of the derivative of $f(x, y, z) = xy + yz + xz$ with respect to t on the curve $x = \cos t$, $y = \sin t$, $z = \cos 2t$ at $t = 1$.

34. Show that if $w = f(s)$ is any differentiable function of s and if $s = y + 5x$, then

$$\dfrac{\partial w}{\partial x} - 5\dfrac{\partial w}{\partial y} = 0.$$

Implicit Differentiation

Assuming that the equations in Exercises 35 and 36 define y as a differentiable function of x, find the value of dy/dx at point P.

35. $1 - x - y^2 - \sin xy = 0$, $P(0, 1)$

36. $2xy + e^{x+y} - 2 = 0$, $P(0, \ln 2)$

Directional Derivatives

In Exercises 37–40, find the directions in which f increases and decreases most rapidly at P_0 and find the derivative of f in each direction. Also, find the derivative of f at P_0 in the direction of the vector $\mathbf{v}$.

37. $f(x, y) = \cos x \cos y$, $P_0(\pi/4, \pi/4)$, $\mathbf{v} = 3\mathbf{i} + 4\mathbf{j}$

38. $f(x, y) = x^2e^{-2y}$, $P_0(1, 0)$, $\mathbf{v} = \mathbf{i} + \mathbf{j}$

39. $f(x, y, z) = \ln (2x + 3y + 6z)$, $P_0(-1, -1, 1)$, $\mathbf{v} = 2\mathbf{i} + 3\mathbf{j} + 6\mathbf{k}$

40. $f(x, y, z) = x^2 + 3xy - z^2 + 2y + z + 4$, $P_0(0, 0, 0)$, $\mathbf{v} = \mathbf{i} + \mathbf{j} + \mathbf{k}$

41. *Derivative in velocity direction* Find the derivative of $f(x, y, z) = xyz$ in the direction of the velocity vector of the helix

$$\mathbf{r}(t) = (\cos 3t)\mathbf{i} + (\sin 3t)\mathbf{j} + 3t\mathbf{k}$$

at $t = \pi/3$.

42. *Maximum directional derivative* What is the largest value that the directional derivative of $f(x, y, z) = xyz$ can have at the point $(1, 1, 1)$?

43. *Directional derivatives with given values* At the point $(1, 2)$, the function $f(x, y)$ has a derivative of 2 in the direction toward $(2, 2)$ and a derivative of -2 in the direction toward $(1, 1)$.

(a) Find $f_x(1, 2)$ and $f_y(1, 2)$.

(b) Find the derivative of f at $(1, 2)$ in the direction toward the point $(4, 6)$.

44. *Writing to Learn* Which of the following statements are true if $f(x, y)$ is differentiable at (x_0, y_0)? Give reasons for your answers.

(a) If $\mathbf{u}$ is a unit vector, the derivative of f at (x_0, y_0) in the direction of $\mathbf{u}$ is $(f_x(x_0, y_0)\mathbf{i} + f_y(x_0, y_0)\mathbf{j}) \cdot \mathbf{u}$.

(b) The derivative of f at (x_0, y_0) in the direction of $\mathbf{u}$ is a vector.

(c) The directional derivative of f at (x_0, y_0) has its greatest value in the direction of ∇f.

(d) At (x_0, y_0), vector ∇f is normal to the curve $f(x, y) = f(x_0, y_0)$.

Gradients, Tangent Planes, and Normal Lines

In Exercises 45 and 46, sketch the surface $f(x, y, z) = c$ together with ∇f at the given points.

45. $x^2 + y + z^2 = 0$; $(0, -1, \pm 1)$, $(0, 0, 0)$

46. $y^2 + z^2 = 4$; $(2, \pm 2, 0)$, $(2, 0, \pm 2)$

In Exercises 47 and 48, find an equation for the plane tangent to the level surface $f(x, y, z) = c$ at the point P_0. Also, find parametric equations for the line that is normal to the surface at P_0.

47. $x^2 - y - 5z = 0$, $P_0(2, -1, 1)$

48. $x^2 + y^2 + z = 4$, $P_0(1, 1, 2)$

In Exercises 49 and 50, find an equation for the plane tangent to the surface $z = f(x, y)$ at the given point.

49. $z = \ln(x^2 + y^2)$, $(0, 1, 0)$

50. $z = 1/(x^2 + y^2)$, $(1, 1, 1/2)$

In Exercises 51 and 52, find equations for the lines that are tangent and normal to the level curve $f(x, y) = c$ at the point P_0. Then sketch the lines and level curve together with ∇f at P_0.

51. $y - \sin x = 1$, $P_0(\pi, 1)$

52. $\dfrac{y^2}{2} - \dfrac{x^2}{2} = \dfrac{3}{2}$, $P_0(1, 2)$

Tangent Lines to Curves

In Exercises 53 and 54, find parametric equations for the line that is tangent to the curve of intersection of the surfaces at the given point.

53. Surfaces: $x^2 + 2y + 2z = 4$, $y = 1$
   Point: $(1, 1, 1/2)$

54. Surfaces: $x + y^2 + z = 2$, $y = 1$
   Point: $(1/2, 1, 1/2)$

Linearizations

In Exercises 55 and 56, find the linearization $L(x, y)$ of the function $f(x, y)$ at the point P_0. Then find an upper bound for the magnitude of the error E in the approximation $f(x, y) \approx L(x, y)$ over the rectangle R.

55. $f(x, y) = \sin x \cos y$, $P_0(\pi/4, \pi/4)$

$R: \quad \left| x - \dfrac{\pi}{4} \right| \le 0.1, \quad \left| y - \dfrac{\pi}{4} \right| \le 0.1$

56. $f(x, y) = xy - 3y^2 + 2$, $P_0(1, 1)$

$R: \quad |x - 1| \le 0.1, \quad |y - 1| \le 0.2$

Find the linearizations of the functions in Exercises 57 and 58 at the given points.

57. $f(x, y, z) = xy + 2yz - 3xz$ at $(1, 0, 0)$ and $(1, 1, 0)$

58. $f(x, y, z) = \sqrt{2} \cos x \sin(y + z)$ at $(0, 0, \pi/4)$ and $(\pi/4, \pi/4, 0)$

Estimates and Sensitivity to Change

59. *Measuring the volume of a pipeline* You plan to calculate the volume inside a stretch of pipeline that is about 36 in. in diameter and 1 mi long. With which measurement should you be more careful, the length or the diameter? Why?

60. *Writing to Learn: Sensitivity to change* Near the point $(1, 2)$, is $f(x, y) = x^2 - xy + y^2 - 3$ more sensitive to changes in x or to changes in y? How do you know?

61. *Change in an electrical circuit* Suppose that the current I (amperes) in an electrical circuit is related to the voltage V (volts) and the resistance R (ohms) by the equation $I = V/R$. If the voltage drops from 24 to 23 volts and the resistance drops from 100 to 80 ohms, will I increase or decrease? By about how much? Is the change in I more sensitive to change in the voltage or to change in the resistance? How do you know?

62. *Maximum error in estimating the area of an ellipse* If $a = 10$ cm and $b = 16$ cm to the nearest millimeter, what should you expect the maximum percentage error to be in the calculated area $A = \pi ab$ of the ellipse $x^2/a^2 + y^2/b^2 = 1$?

63. *Error in estimating a product* Let $y = uv$ and $z = u + v$, where u and v are positive independent variables.

(a) If u is measured with an error of 2% and v with an error of 3%, about what is the percentage error in the calculated value of y?

(b) Show that the percentage error in the calculated value of z is less than the percentage error in the value of y.

64. *Cardiac index* To make different people comparable in studies of cardiac output (Section 2.7, Exercise 25), researchers divide the measured cardiac output by the body surface area to find the *cardiac index* C:

$$C = \frac{\text{cardiac output}}{\text{body surface area}}.$$

The body surface area B of a person with weight w and height h is approximated by the formula

$$B = 71.84 w^{0.425} h^{0.725},$$

which gives B in square centimeters when w is measured in kilograms and h in centimeters. You are about to calculate the cardiac index of a person with the following measurements:

Cardiac output:	7 L/min
Weight:	70 kg
Height:	180 cm

Which will have a greater effect on the calculation, a 1 kg error in measuring the weight or a 1 cm error in measuring the height?

Local Extrema

Test the functions in Exercises 65–70 for local maxima and minima and saddle points. Find each function's value at these points.

65. $f(x, y) = x^2 - xy + y^2 + 2x + 2y - 4$

66. $f(x, y) = 5x^2 + 4xy - 2y^2 + 4x - 4y$

67. $f(x, y) = 2x^3 + 3xy + 2y^3$

68. $f(x, y) = x^3 + y^3 - 3xy + 15$

69. $f(x, y) = x^3 + y^3 + 3x^2 - 3y^2$

70. $f(x, y) = x^4 - 8x^2 + 3y^2 - 6y$

Absolute Extrema

In Exercises 71–78, find the absolute maximum and minimum values of f on the region R.

71. $f(x, y) = x^2 + xy + y^2 - 3x + 3y$

R: The triangular region cut from the first quadrant by the line $x + y = 4$

72. $f(x, y) = x^2 - y^2 - 2x + 4y + 1$

R: The rectangular region in the first quadrant bounded by the coordinate axes and the lines $x = 4$ and $y = 2$

73. $f(x, y) = y^2 - xy - 3y + 2x$

R: The square region enclosed by the lines $x = \pm 2$ and $y = \pm 2$

74. $f(x, y) = 2x + 2y - x^2 - y^2$

R: The square region bounded by the coordinate axes and the lines $x = 2$, $y = 2$ in the first quadrant

75. $f(x, y) = x^2 - y^2 - 2x + 4y$

R: The triangular region bounded below by the x-axis, above by the line $y = x + 2$, and on the right by the line $x = 2$

76. $f(x, y) = 4xy - x^4 - y^4 + 16$

R: The triangular region bounded below by the line $y = -2$, above by the line $y = x$, and on the right by the line $x = 2$

77. $f(x, y) = x^3 + y^3 + 3x^2 - 3y^2$

R: The square region enclosed by the lines $x = \pm 1$ and $y = \pm 1$

78. $f(x, y) = x^3 + 3xy + y^3 + 1$

R: The square region enclosed by the lines $x = \pm 1$ and $y = \pm 1$

Lagrange Multipliers

79. *Extrema on a circle* Find the extreme values of $f(x, y) = x^3 + y^2$ on the circle $x^2 + y^2 = 1$.

80. *Extrema on a circle* Find the extreme values of $f(x, y) = xy$ on the circle $x^2 + y^2 = 1$.

81. *Extrema in a disk* Find the extreme values of $f(x, y) = x^2 + 3y^2 + 2y$ on the unit disk $x^2 + y^2 \le 1$.

82. *Extrema in a disk* Find the extreme values of $f(x, y) = x^2 + y^2 - 3x - xy$ on the disk $x^2 + y^2 \le 9$.

83. *Extrema on a sphere* Find the extreme values of $f(x, y, z) = x - y + z$ on the unit sphere $x^2 + y^2 + z^2 = 1$.

84. *Minimum distance to origin* Find the points on the surface $z^2 - xy = 4$ closest to the origin.

85. *Minimizing cost of a box* A closed rectangular box is to have volume V cm^3. The cost of the material used in the box is a cents/cm^2 for top and bottom, b cents/cm^2 for front and back, and c cents/cm^2 for the remaining sides. What dimensions minimize the total cost of materials?

86. *Least volume* Find the plane $x/a + y/b + z/c = 1$ that passes through the point $(2, 1, 2)$ and cuts off the least volume from the first octant.

87. *Extrema on curve of intersecting surfaces* Find the extreme values of $f(x, y, z) = x(y + z)$ on the curve of intersection of the right circular cylinder $x^2 + y^2 = 1$ and the hyperbolic cylinder $xz = 1$.

88. *Minimum distance to origin on curve of intersecting plane and cone* Find the point closest to the origin on the curve of intersection of the plane $x + y + z = 1$ and the cone $z^2 = 2x^2 + 2y^2$.

Partial Derivatives with Constrained Variables

In Exercises 89 and 90, begin by drawing a diagram that shows the relations among the variables.

89. If $w = x^2 e^{yz}$ and $z = x^2 - y^2$, find

(a) $\left(\dfrac{\partial w}{\partial y}\right)_z$ (b) $\left(\dfrac{\partial w}{\partial z}\right)_x$ (c) $\left(\dfrac{\partial w}{\partial z}\right)_y$.

90. Let $U = f(P, V, T)$ be the internal energy of a gas that obeys the ideal gas law $PV = nRT$ (n and R constant). Find

(a) $\left(\dfrac{\partial U}{\partial T}\right)_P$ (b) $\left(\dfrac{\partial U}{\partial V}\right)_T$.

Theory and Examples

91. *Finding partial derivatives* Let $w = f(r, \theta)$, $r = \sqrt{x^2 + y^2}$, and $\theta = \tan^{-1}(y/x)$. Find $\partial w/\partial x$ and $\partial w/\partial y$ and express your answers in terms of r and θ.

92. *Finding partial derivatives* Let $z = f(u, v)$, $u = ax + by$, and $v = ax - by$. Express z_x and z_y in terms of f_u, f_v, and the constants a and b.

93. *Verifying an equation* If a and b are constants, $w = u^3 + \tanh u + \cos u$, and $u = ax + by$, show that

$$a \frac{\partial w}{\partial y} = b \frac{\partial w}{\partial x}.$$

94. *Using the Chain Rule* If $w = \ln(x^2 + y^2 + 2z)$, $x = r + s$, $y = r - s$, and $z = 2rs$, find w_r and w_s by the Chain Rule. Then check your answer another way.

95. *Angle between vectors* The equations $e^u \cos v - x = 0$ and $e^u \sin v - y = 0$ define u and v as differentiable functions of x and y. Show that the angle between the vectors

$$\frac{\partial u}{\partial x}\mathbf{i} + \frac{\partial u}{\partial y}\mathbf{j} \quad \text{and} \quad \frac{\partial v}{\partial x}\mathbf{i} + \frac{\partial v}{\partial y}\mathbf{j}$$

is constant.

96. *Polar coordinates and second derivatives* Introducing polar coordinates $x = r \cos \theta$ and $y = r \sin \theta$ changes $f(x, y)$ to $g(r, \theta)$. Find the value of $\partial^2 g/\partial \theta^2$ at the point $(r, \theta) = (2, \pi/2)$, given that

$$\frac{\partial f}{\partial x} = \frac{\partial f}{\partial y} = \frac{\partial^2 f}{\partial x^2} = \frac{\partial^2 f}{\partial y^2} = 1$$

at that point.

97. *Normal line parallel to a plane* Find the points on the surface

$$(y + z)^2 + (z - x)^2 = 16$$

where the normal line is parallel to the yz-plane.

98. *Tangent plane parallel to xy-plane* Find the points on the surface

$$xy + yz + zx - x - z^2 = 0$$

where the tangent plane is parallel to the xy-plane.

99. *When gradient is parallel to position vector* Suppose that $\nabla f(x, y, z)$ is always parallel to the position vector $x\mathbf{i} + y\mathbf{j} + z\mathbf{k}$. Show that $f(0, 0, a) = f(0, 0, -a)$ for any a.

100. *Directional derivative in all directions, but no gradient* Show that the directional derivative of

$$f(x, y, z) = \sqrt{x^2 + y^2 + z^2}$$

at the origin equals 1 in any direction but that f has no gradient vector at the origin.

101. *Normal line through origin* Show that the line normal to the surface $xy + z = 2$ at the point $(1, 1, 1)$ passes through the origin.

102. *Tangent plane and normal line*

(a) Sketch the surface $x^2 - y^2 + z^2 = 4$.

(b) Find a vector normal to the surface at $(2, -3, 3)$. Add the vector to your sketch.

(c) Find equations for the tangent plane and normal line at $(2, -3, 3)$.

Additional Exercises: Theory, Examples, Applications

Partial Derivatives

1. *Function with saddle at the origin* If you did Exercise 66 in Section 11.2, you know that the function

$$f(x, y) = \begin{cases} xy\dfrac{x^2 - y^2}{x^2 + y^2}, & (x, y) \neq (0, 0) \\ 0, & (x, y) = (0, 0) \end{cases}$$

(see the accompanying figure) is continuous at $(0, 0)$. Find $f_{xy}(0, 0)$ and $f_{yx}(0, 0)$.

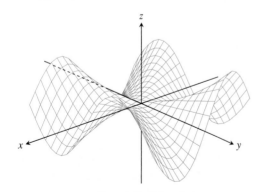

(Generated by Mathematica)

2. *Finding a function from second partials* Find a function $w = f(x, y)$ whose first partial derivatives are $\partial w/\partial x = 1 + e^x \cos y$ and $\partial w/\partial y = 2y - e^x \sin y$, and whose value at the point $(\ln 2, 0)$ is $\ln 2$.

3. *A proof of Leibniz's Rule* Leibniz's Rule says that if f is continuous on $[a, b]$ and if $u(x)$ and $v(x)$ are differentiable functions of x whose values lie in $[a, b]$, then

$$\frac{d}{dx} \int_{u(x)}^{v(x)} f(t) \, dt = f(v(x)) \frac{dv}{dx} - f(u(x)) \frac{du}{dx}.$$

Prove the rule by setting

$$g(u, v) = \int_u^v f(t) \, dt, \qquad u = u(x), \qquad v = v(x)$$

and calculating dg/dx with the Chain Rule.

4. *Finding a function with constrained second partials* Suppose that f is a twice-differentiable function of r, that $r = \sqrt{x^2 + y^2 + z^2}$, and that

$$f_{xx} + f_{yy} + f_{zz} = 0.$$

Show that for some constants a and b,

$$f(r) = \frac{a}{r} + b.$$

5. *Homogeneous functions* A function $f(x, y)$ is *homogeneous of degree n* (n a nonnegative integer) if $f(tx, ty) = t^n f(x, y)$ for all t, x, and y. For such a function (sufficiently differentiable), prove that

(a) $x\dfrac{\partial f}{\partial x} + y\dfrac{\partial f}{\partial y} = nf(x, y)$

(b) $x^2\left(\dfrac{\partial^2 f}{\partial x^2}\right) + 2xy\left(\dfrac{\partial^2 f}{\partial x \partial y}\right) + y^2\left(\dfrac{\partial^2 f}{\partial y^2}\right) = n(n - 1)f.$

6. *Surface in polar coordinates* Let

$$f(r, \theta) = \begin{cases} \dfrac{\sin 6r}{6r}, & r \neq 0 \\ 1, & r = 0, \end{cases}$$

where r and θ are polar coordinates. Find

(a) $\lim_{r \to 0} f(r, \theta)$ **(b)** $f_r(0, 0)$ **(c)** $f_\theta(r, \theta),\ \ r \neq 0.$

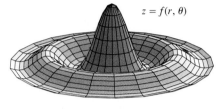

$z = f(r, \theta)$

(Generated by Mathematica)

Gradients and Tangents

7. *Properties of position vectors* Let $\mathbf{r} = x\mathbf{i} + y\mathbf{j} + z\mathbf{k}$ and let $r = |\mathbf{r}|$.

(a) Show that $\nabla r = \mathbf{r}/r$.

(b) Show that $\nabla(r^n) = nr^{n-2}\mathbf{r}$.

(c) Find a function whose gradient equals $\mathbf{r}$.

(d) Show that $\mathbf{r} \cdot d\mathbf{r} = r\, dr$.

(e) Show that $\nabla(\mathbf{A} \cdot \mathbf{r}) = \mathbf{A}$ for any constant vector $\mathbf{A}$.

8. *Gradient orthogonal to tangent* Suppose that a differentiable function $f(x, y)$ has the constant value c along the differentiable curve $x = g(t), y = h(t)$; that is

$$f(g(t), h(t)) = c$$

for all values of t. Differentiate both sides of this equation with respect to t to show that ∇f is orthogonal to the curve's tangent vector at every point on the curve.

9. *Curve tangent to a surface* Show that the curve

$$\mathbf{r}(t) = (\ln t)\mathbf{i} + (t \ln t)\mathbf{j} + t\mathbf{k}$$

is tangent to the surface

$$xz^2 - yz + \cos xy = 1$$

at $(0, 0, 1)$.

10. *Curve tangent to a surface* Show that the curve

$$\mathbf{r}(t) = \left(\frac{t^3}{4} - 2\right)\mathbf{i} + \left(\frac{4}{t} - 3\right)\mathbf{j} + \cos(t - 2)\mathbf{k}$$

is tangent to the surface

$$x^3 + y^3 + z^3 - xyz = 0$$

at $(0, -1, 1)$.

Extreme Values

11. *Extrema on a surface* Show that the only possible maxima and minima of z on the surface $z = x^3 + y^3 - 9xy + 27$ occur at $(0, 0)$ and $(3, 3)$. Show that neither a maximum nor a minimum occurs at $(0, 0)$. Determine whether z has a maximum or a minimum at $(3, 3)$.

12. *Maximum in closed first quadrant* Find the maximum value of $f(x, y) = 6xye^{-(2x+3y)}$ in the closed first quadrant (includes the nonnegative axes).

13. *Minimum volume cut from first octant* Find the minimum volume for a region bounded by the planes $x = 0, y = 0, z = 0$ and a plane tangent to the ellipsoid

$$\frac{x^2}{a^2} + \frac{y^2}{b^2} + \frac{z^2}{c^2} = 1$$

at a point in the first octant.

14. *Minimum distance from line to parabola in xy-plane* By minimizing the function $f(x, y, u, v) = (x - u)^2 + (y - v)^2$ subject to the constraints $y = x + 1$ and $u = v^2$, find the minimum distance in the xy-plane from the line $y = x + 1$ to the parabola $y^2 = x$.

Theory and Examples

15. *Boundedness of first partials implies continuity* Prove the following theorem: If $f(x, y)$ is defined in an open region R of the xy-plane and if f_x and f_y are bounded on R, then $f(x, y)$ is continuous on R. (The assumption of boundedness is essential.)

16. *Writing to Learn* Suppose that $\mathbf{r}(t) = g(t)\mathbf{i} + h(t)\mathbf{j} + k(t)\mathbf{k}$ is a smooth curve in the domain of a differentiable function $f(x, y, z)$. Describe the relation between df/dt, ∇f, and $\mathbf{v} = d\mathbf{r}/dt$. What can be said about ∇f and $\mathbf{v}$ at interior points of the curve where f has extreme values relative to its other values on the curve? Give reasons for your answer.

17. *Finding functions from partial derivatives* Suppose that f and g are functions of x and y such that

$$\frac{\partial f}{\partial y} = \frac{\partial g}{\partial x} \quad \text{and} \quad \frac{\partial f}{\partial x} = \frac{\partial g}{\partial y},$$

and suppose that

$$\frac{\partial f}{\partial x} = 0, \quad f(1, 2) = g(1, 2) = 5 \quad \text{and} \quad f(0, 0) = 4.$$

Find $f(x, y)$ and $g(x, y)$.

18. *Rate of change of the rate of change* We know that if $f(x, y)$ is a function of two variables and if $\mathbf{u} = a\mathbf{i} + b\mathbf{j}$ is a unit vector, then $D_{\mathbf{u}}f(x, y) = f_x(x, y)a + f_y(x, y)b$ is the rate of change of $f(x, y)$ at (x, y) in the direction of $\mathbf{u}$. Give a similar formula for the rate of change *of the rate of change* of $f(x, y)$ at (x, y) in the direction $\mathbf{u}$.

19. *Path of a heat-seeking particle* A heat-seeking particle has the property that at any point (x, y) in the plane it moves in the direction of maximum temperature increase. If the temperature at

(x, y) is $T(x, y) = -e^{-2y} \cos x$, find an equation $y = f(x)$ for the path of a heat-seeking particle at the point $(\pi/4, 0)$.

20. *Velocity after a ricochet* A particle traveling in a straight line with constant velocity $\mathbf{i} + \mathbf{j} - 5\mathbf{k}$ passes through the point $(0, 0, 30)$ and hits the surface $z = 2x^2 + 3y^2$. The particle ricochets off the surface, the angle of reflection being equal to the angle of incidence. Assuming no loss of speed, what is the velocity of the particle after the ricochet? Simplify your answer.

21. *Directional derivatives tangent to a surface* Let S be the surface that is the graph of $f(x, y) = 10 - x^2 - y^2$. Suppose that the temperature in space at each point (x, y, z) is $T(x, y, z) = x^2y + y^2z + 4x + 14y + z$.

    (a) Among all the possible directions tangential to the surface S at the point $(0, 0, 10)$, which direction will make the rate of change of temperature at $(0, 0, 10)$ a maximum?

    (b) Which direction tangential to S at the point $(1, 1, 8)$ will make the rate of change of temperature a maximum?

22. *Drilling another borehole* On a flat surface of land, geologists drilled a borehole straight down and hit a mineral deposit at 1000 ft. They drilled a second borehole 100 ft to the north of the first and hit the mineral deposit at 950 ft. A third borehole 100 ft east of the first borehole struck the mineral deposit at 1025 ft. The geologists have reasons to believe that the mineral deposit is in the shape of a dome, and for the sake of economy, they would like to find where the deposit is closest to the surface. Assuming the surface to be the xy-plane, in what direction from the first borehole would you suggest the geologists drill their fourth borehole?

The One-Dimensional Heat Equation

If $w(x, t)$ represents the temperature at position x at time t in a uniform conducting rod with perfectly insulated sides (see the accompanying figure), then the partial derivatives w_{xx} and w_t satisfy a differential equation of the form

$$w_{xx} = \frac{1}{c^2} w_t.$$

This equation is called the **one-dimensional heat equation.** The value of the positive constant c^2 is determined by the material from which the rod is made. It has been determined experimentally for a

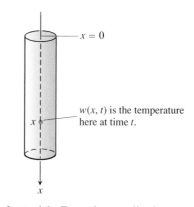

$x = 0$

$w(x, t)$ is the temperature here at time t.

broad range of materials. For a given application, one finds the appropriate value in a table. For dry soil, for example, $c^2 = 0.19\ \text{ft}^2/\text{day}$.

In chemistry and biochemistry, the heat equation is known as the **diffusion equation.** In this context, $w(x, t)$ represents the concentration of a dissolved substance, a salt for instance, diffusing along a tube filled with liquid. The value of $w(x, t)$ is the concentration at point x at time t. In other applications, $w(x, t)$ represents the diffusion of a gas down a long, thin pipe.

In electrical engineering, the heat equation appears in the forms

$$v_{xx} = RCv_t$$

and

$$i_{xx} = RCi_t.$$

These equations describe the voltage v and the flow of current i in a coaxial cable or in any other cable in which leakage and inductance are negligible. The functions and constants in these equations are

$$v(x, t) = \text{voltage at point } x \text{ at time } t$$
$$R = \text{resistance per unit length}$$
$$C = \text{capacitance to ground per unit of cable length}$$
$$i(x, t) = \text{current at point } x \text{ at time } t.$$

23. Find all solutions of the one-dimensional heat equation of the form $w = e^{rt} \sin \pi x$, where r is a constant.

24. Find all solutions of the one-dimensional heat equation that have the form $w = e^{rt} \sin kx$ and satisfy the conditions that $w(0, t) = 0$ and $w(L, t) = 0$. What happens to these solutions as $t \to \infty$?

12 Multiple Integrals

OVERVIEW   The problems we can solve by integrating functions of two and three variables are similar to the problems solved by single-variable integration, but more general. As in the previous chapter, we can perform the necessary calculations by drawing on our experience with functions of a single variable.

12.1 Double Integrals

Double Integrals over Rectangles • Properties of Double Integrals • Double Integrals as Volumes • Fubini's Theorem for Calculating Double Integrals • Double Integrals over Bounded Nonrectangular Regions • Finding Limits of Integration

We now show how to integrate a continuous function $f(x, y)$ over a bounded region in the xy-plane. There are many similarities between the "double" integrals we define here and the "single" integrals we defined in Chapter 4 for functions of a single variable. Every double integral can be evaluated in stages, using the single-integration methods already at our command.

Double Integrals over Rectangles

Suppose that $f(x, y)$ is defined on a rectangular region R given by

$$R: \quad a \leq x \leq b, \quad c \leq y \leq d.$$

We imagine R to be covered by a network of lines parallel to the x- and y-axes (Figure 12.1). These lines divide R into small pieces of area $\Delta A = \Delta x \, \Delta y$. We number these in some order $\Delta A_1, \Delta A_2, \ldots, \Delta A_n$, choose a point (x_k, y_k) in each piece ΔA_k, and form the sum

$$S_n = \sum_{k=1}^{n} f(x_k, y_k) \, \Delta A_k. \tag{1}$$

If f is continuous throughout R, then, as we refine the mesh (or two-dimensional partition) width to make both Δx and Δy go to zero, the sums in Equation (1) approach a limit called the **double integral** of f over R. The notation for it is

$$\iint\limits_{R} f(x, y) \, dA \qquad \text{or} \qquad \iint\limits_{R} f(x, y) \, dx \, dy.$$

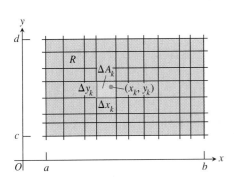

FIGURE 12.1 Rectangular grid partitioning the region R into small rectangles of area $\Delta A_k = \Delta x_k \, \Delta y_k$.

975

Thus,

$$\iint\limits_R f(x, y)\, dA = \lim_{\Delta A \to 0} \sum_{k=1}^{n} f(x_k, y_k)\, \Delta A_k. \qquad (2)$$

As with functions of a single variable, the sums approach this limit no matter how the intervals $[a, b]$ and $[c, d]$ that determine R are partitioned, as long as the norms of the partitions both go to zero. The limit in Equation (2) is also independent of the order in which the areas ΔA_k are numbered and independent of the choice of the point (x_k, y_k) within each ΔA_k. The values of the individual approximating sums S_n depend on these choices, but the sums approach the same limit in the end. The proof of the existence and uniqueness of this limit for a continuous function f is given in more advanced texts. The continuity of f is a sufficient condition for the existence of the double integral, but not a necessary one. The limit in question exists for many discontinuous functions as well.

Properties of Double Integrals

Like single integrals, double integrals of continuous functions have algebraic properties that are useful in computations and applications.

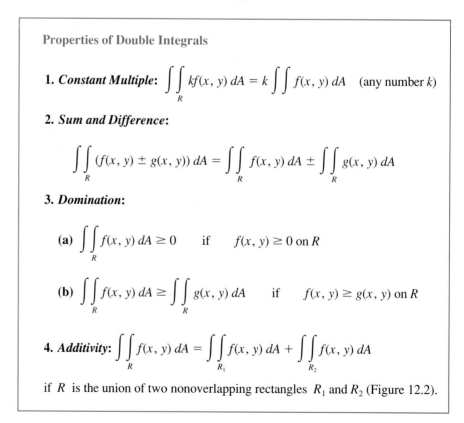

Properties of Double Integrals

1. **Constant Multiple:** $\iint\limits_R kf(x, y)\, dA = k \iint\limits_R f(x, y)\, dA$ (any number k)

2. **Sum and Difference:**

$$\iint\limits_R (f(x, y) \pm g(x, y))\, dA = \iint\limits_R f(x, y)\, dA \pm \iint\limits_R g(x, y)\, dA$$

3. **Domination:**

(a) $\iint\limits_R f(x, y)\, dA \geq 0$ if $f(x, y) \geq 0$ on R

(b) $\iint\limits_R f(x, y)\, dA \geq \iint\limits_R g(x, y)\, dA$ if $f(x, y) \geq g(x, y)$ on R

4. **Additivity:** $\iint\limits_R f(x, y)\, dA = \iint\limits_{R_1} f(x, y)\, dA + \iint\limits_{R_2} f(x, y)\, dA$

if R is the union of two nonoverlapping rectangles R_1 and R_2 (Figure 12.2).

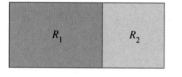

$$\iint\limits_{R_1 \cup R_2} f(x, y)\, dA = \iint\limits_{R_1} f(x, y)\, dA + \iint\limits_{R_2} f(x, y)\, dA$$

FIGURE 12.2 Double integrals have the same kind of domain additivity property that single integrals have.

Double Integrals as Volumes

When $f(x, y)$ is positive, we may interpret the double integral of f over a rectangular region R as the volume of the solid prism bounded below by R and above by

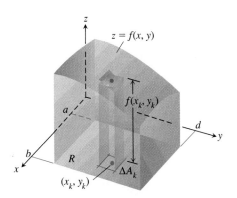

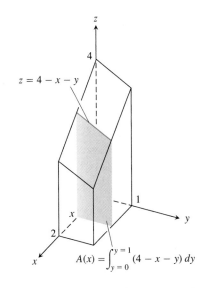

FIGURE 12.3 Approximating solids with rectangular prisms leads us to define the volumes of more general prisms as double integrals. The volume of the prism shown here is the double integral of $f(x, y)$ over the base region R.

FIGURE 12.4 To obtain the cross-section area $A(x)$, we hold x fixed and integrate with respect to y.

the surface $z = f(x, y)$ (Figure 12.3). Each term $f(x_k, y_k)\ \Delta A_k$ in the sum $S_n = \Sigma\ f(x_k, y_k)\ \Delta A_k$ is the volume of a vertical rectangular prism that approximates the volume of the portion of the solid that stands directly above the base ΔA_k. The sum S_n thus approximates what we want to call the total volume of the solid. We *define* this volume to be

$$\text{Volume} = \lim S_n = \iint_R f(x, y)\ dA. \tag{3}$$

As you might expect, this more general method of calculating volume agrees with the methods in Chapter 5, but we do not prove this here.

Fubini's Theorem for Calculating Double Integrals

Suppose that we wish to calculate the volume under the plane $z = 4 - x - y$ over the rectangular region $R: 0 \le x \le 2, 0 \le y \le 1$ in the xy-plane. If we apply the method of slicing from Section 5.1, with slices perpendicular to the x-axis (Figure 12.4), then the volume is

$$\int_{x=0}^{x=2} A(x)\ dx, \tag{4}$$

where $A(x)$ is the cross-section area at x. For each value of x, we may calculate $A(x)$ as the integral

$$A(x) = \int_{y=0}^{y=1} (4 - x - y)\ dy, \tag{5}$$

which is the area under the curve $z = 4 - x - y$ in the plane of the cross section at x. In calculating $A(x)$, x is held fixed and the integration takes place with respect to y. Combining Equations (4) and (5), we see that the volume of the entire solid is

$$\text{Volume} = \int_{x=0}^{x=2} A(x)\ dx = \int_{x=0}^{x=2} \left(\int_{y=0}^{y=1} (4 - x - y)\ dy \right) dx$$

$$= \int_{x=0}^{x=2} \left[4y - xy - \frac{y^2}{2} \right]_{y=0}^{y=1} dx = \int_{x=0}^{x=2} \left(\frac{7}{2} - x \right) dx \tag{6}$$

$$= \left[\frac{7}{2} x - \frac{x^2}{2} \right]_0^2 = 5 \text{ cubic units}.$$

If we had just wanted to write instructions for calculating the volume, without carrying out any of the integrations, we could have written

$$\text{Volume} = \int_0^2 \int_0^1 (4 - x - y)\ dy\ dx.$$

The expression on the right, called an **iterated** or **repeated integral,** says that the volume is obtained by integrating $4 - x - y$ with respect to y from $y = 0$ to $y = 1$, holding x fixed, and then integrating the resulting expression in x with respect to x from $x = 0$ to $x = 2$.

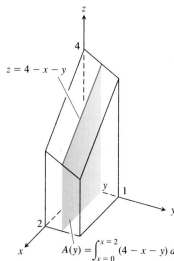

$$A(y) = \int_{x=0}^{x=2} (4 - x - y) \, dx$$

FIGURE 12.5 To obtain the cross-section area $A(y)$, we hold y fixed and integrate with respect to x.

What would have happened if we had calculated the volume by slicing with planes perpendicular to the y-axis (Figure 12.5)? As a function of y, the typical cross-section area is

$$A(y) = \int_{x=0}^{x=2} (4 - x - y) \, dx = \left[4x - \frac{x^2}{2} - xy \right]_{x=0}^{x=2} = 6 - 2y. \qquad (7)$$

The volume of the entire solid is therefore

$$\text{Volume} = \int_{y=0}^{y=1} A(y) \, dy = \int_{y=0}^{y=1} (6 - 2y) \, dy = \left[6y - y^2 \right]_0^1 = 5,$$

in agreement with our earlier calculation.

Again, we may give instructions for calculating the volume as an iterated integral by writing

$$\text{Volume} = \int_0^1 \int_0^2 (4 - x - y) \, dx \, dy.$$

The expression on the right says we can find the volume by integrating $4 - x - y$ with respect to x from $x = 0$ to $x = 2$ as in Equation (7) and integrating the result with respect to y from $y = 0$ to $y = 1$. In this iterated integral, the order of integration is first x and then y, the reverse of the order in Equation (6).

What do these two volume calculations with iterated integrals have to do with the double integral

$$\iint_R (4 - x - y) \, dA$$

over the rectangle $R: 0 \le x \le 2$, $0 \le y \le 1$? The answer is that they both give the value of the double integral. A theorem published in 1907 by Guido Fubini says that the double integral of any continuous function over a rectangle can be calculated as an iterated integral in either order of integration. (Fubini proved his theorem in greater generality, but this is how it translates into what we're doing now.)

Theorem 1 Fubini's Theorem (First Form)

If $f(x, y)$ is continuous throughout the rectangular region $R: a \le x \le b$, $c \le y \le d$, then

$$\iint_R f(x, y) \, dA = \int_c^d \int_a^b f(x, y) \, dx \, dy = \int_a^b \int_c^d f(x, y) \, dy \, dx.$$

Fubini's theorem says that double integrals over rectangles can be calculated as iterated integrals. Thus, we can evaluate a double integral by integrating with respect to one variable at a time.

Fubini's theorem also says that we may calculate the double integral by integrating in *either* order, a genuine convenience, as we see in Example 3. In particular, when we calculate a volume by slicing, we may use either planes perpendicular to the x-axis or planes perpendicular to the y-axis.

Example 1 Evaluating a Double Integral

Calculate $\iint_R f(x, y)\, dA$ for

$$f(x, y) = 1 - 6x^2 y \qquad \text{and} \qquad R: \ 0 \le x \le 2, \quad -1 \le y \le 1.$$

Solution By Fubini's theorem,

$$\iint_R f(x, y)\, dA = \int_{-1}^{1} \int_{0}^{2} (1 - 6x^2 y)\, dx\, dy = \int_{-1}^{1} \left[x - 2x^3 y \right]_{x=0}^{x=2} dy$$

$$= \int_{-1}^{1} (2 - 16y)\, dy = \left[2y - 8y^2 \right]_{-1}^{1} = 4 \text{ units cubed.}$$

Reversing the order of integration gives the same answer:

$$\int_{0}^{2} \int_{-1}^{1} (1 - 6x^2\, y)\, dy\, dx = \int_{0}^{2} \left[y - 3x^2\, y^2 \right]_{y=-1}^{y=1} dx$$

$$= \int_{0}^{2} [(1 - 3x^2) - (-1 - 3x^2)]\, dx$$

$$= \int_{0}^{2} 2\, dx = 4 \text{ units cubed.}$$

> **USING TECHNOLOGY**
>
> *Multiple Integration* Most computer algebra systems can calculate both multiple and iterated integrals. The typical procedure is to apply the CAS integrate command in nested iterations according to the order of integration you specify.

Integral	Typical CAS Formulation
$\iint x^2 y\, dx\, dy$	int(int(x ^ 2 * y, x), y);
$\int_{-\pi/3}^{\pi/4} \int_{0}^{1} x \cos y\, dx\, dy$	int(int(x* cos(y), x = 0 .. 1), y = −Pi/3 .. Pi/4);

If a CAS cannot produce an exact value for a definite integral, it can usually find an approximate value numerically.

Double Integrals over Bounded Nonrectangular Regions

To define the double integral of a function $f(x, y)$ over a bounded nonrectangular region, like the one shown in Figure 12.6, we again imagine R to be covered by a rectangular grid, but we include in the partial sum only the small pieces of area $\Delta A = \Delta x\, \Delta y$ that lie entirely within the region (shaded in the figure). We number the pieces in some order, choose an arbitrary point (x_k, y_k) in each ΔA_k, and form the sum

$$S_n = \sum_{k=1}^{n} f(x_k, y_k)\, \Delta A_k.$$

The only difference between this sum and the one in Equation (1) for rectangular regions is that now the areas ΔA_k may not cover all of R. As the mesh becomes in-

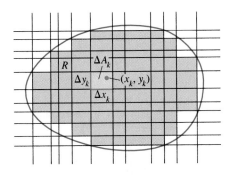

FIGURE 12.6 A rectangular grid partitioning a bounded nonrectangular region into cells.

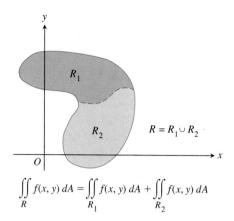

$$\iint\limits_{R} f(x, y)\, dA = \iint\limits_{R_1} f(x, y)\, dA + \iint\limits_{R_2} f(x, y)\, dA$$

FIGURE 12.7 The additivity property for rectangular regions holds for regions bounded by continuous curves.

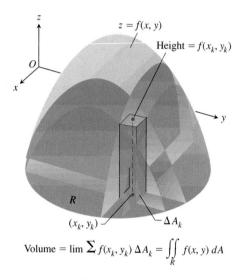

Volume $= \lim \sum f(x_k, y_k)\, \Delta A_k = \iint\limits_{R} f(x, y)\, dA$

FIGURE 12.8 We define the volumes of solids with curved bases the same way we define the volumes of solids with rectangular bases.

creasingly fine and the number of terms in S_n increases, however, more and more of R is included. If f is continuous and the boundary of R is made from the graphs of a finite number of continuous functions of x and/or continuous functions of y joined end to end, then the sums S_n will have a limit as the norms of the partitions that define the rectangular grid independently approach zero. We call the limit the **double integral** of f over R:

$$\iint\limits_{R} f(x, y)\, dA = \lim_{\Delta A \to 0} \sum f(x_k, y_k)\, \Delta A_k.$$

This limit may also exist under less restrictive circumstances.

Double integrals of continuous functions over nonrectangular regions have the same algebraic properties as integrals over rectangular regions. The domain additivity property corresponding to property 5 says that if R is decomposed into nonoverlapping regions R_1 and R_2 with boundaries that are again made of a finite number of line segments or smooth curves (see Figure 12.7 for an example), then

$$\iint\limits_{R} f(x, y)\, dA = \iint\limits_{R_1} f(x, y)\, dA + \iint\limits_{R_2} f(x, y)\, dA.$$

If $f(x, y)$ is positive and continuous over R we define the volume of the solid region between R and the surface $z = f(x, y)$ to be $\iint_R f(x, y)\, dA$, as before (Figure 12.8).

If R is a region like the one shown in the xy-plane in Figure 12.9, bounded "above" and "below" by the curves $y = g_2(x)$ and $y = g_1(x)$ and on the sides by the lines $x = a$, $x = b$, we may again calculate the volume by the method of slicing. We first calculate the cross-section area

$$A(x) = \int_{y=g_1(x)}^{y=g_2(x)} f(x, y)\, dy$$

and then integrate $A(x)$ from $x = a$ to $x = b$ to get the volume as an iterated integral:

$$V = \int_a^b A(x)\, dx = \int_a^b \int_{g_1(x)}^{g_2(x)} f(x, y)\, dy\, dx. \tag{8}$$

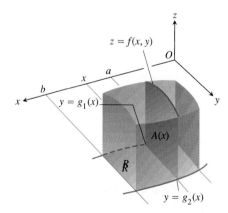

FIGURE 12.9 The area of the vertical slice shown here is

$$A(x) = \int_{g_1(x)}^{g_2(x)} f(x, y)\, dy.$$

To calculate the volume of the solid, we integrate this area from $x = a$ to $x = b$.

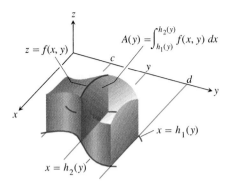

$$z = f(x, y)$$

$$A(y) = \int_{h_1(y)}^{h_2(y)} f(x, y)\, dx$$

$$x = h_1(y)$$

$$x = h_2(y)$$

FIGURE 12.10 The volume of the solid shown here is

$$\int_c^d A(y)\, dy = \int_c^d \int_{h_1(y)}^{h_2(y)} f(x, y)\, dx\, dy.$$

Similarly, if R is a region like the one shown in Figure 12.10, bounded by the curves $x = h_2(y)$ and $x = h_1(y)$ and the lines $y = c$ and $y = d$, then the volume calculated by slicing is given by the iterated integral

$$\text{Volume} = \int_c^d \int_{h_1(y)}^{h_2(y)} f(x, y)\, dx\, dy. \tag{9}$$

That the iterated integrals in Equations (8) and (9) both give the volume that we defined to be the double integral of f over R is a consequence of the following stronger form of Fubini's theorem.

Theorem 2   Fubini's Theorem (Stronger Form)

Let $f(x, y)$ be continuous on a region R.

1. If R is defined by $a \le x \le b$, $g_1(x) \le y \le g_2(x)$, with g_1 and g_2 continuous on $[a, b]$, then

$$\iint_R f(x, y)\, dA = \int_a^b \int_{g_1(x)}^{g_2(x)} f(x, y)\, dy\, dx.$$

2. If R is defined by $c \le y \le d$, $h_1(y) \le x \le h_2(y)$, with h_1 and h_2 continuous on $[c, d]$, then

$$\iint_R f(x, y)\, dA = \int_c^d \int_{h_1(y)}^{h_2(y)} f(x, y)\, dx\, dy.$$

Example 2   Finding Volume

Find the volume of the prism whose base is the triangle in the xy-plane bounded by the x-axis and the lines $y = x$ and $x = 1$ and whose top lies in the plane

$$z = f(x, y) = 3 - x - y.$$

Solution   See Figure 12.11. For any x between 0 and 1, y may vary from $y = 0$ to $y = x$ (Figure 12.11b). Hence,

$$V = \int_0^1 \int_0^x (3 - x - y)\, dy\, dx = \int_0^1 \left[3y - xy - \frac{y^2}{2} \right]_{y=0}^{y=x} dx$$

$$= \int_0^1 \left(3x - \frac{3x^2}{2} \right) dx = \left[\frac{3x^2}{2} - \frac{x^3}{2} \right]_{x=0}^{x=1} = 1 \text{ cubic unit.}$$

When the order of integration is reversed (Figure 12.11c), the integral for the volume is

$$V = \int_0^1 \int_y^1 (3 - x - y)\, dx\, dy = \int_0^1 \left[3x - \frac{x^2}{2} - xy \right]_{x=y}^{x=1} dy$$

$$= \int_0^1 \left(3 - \frac{1}{2} - y - 3y + \frac{y^2}{2} + y^2 \right) dy$$

$$= \int_0^1 \left(\frac{5}{2} - 4y + \frac{3}{2} y^2 \right) dy = \left[\frac{5}{2} y - 2y^2 + \frac{y^3}{2} \right]_{y=0}^{y=1} = 1 \text{ cubic unit.}$$

The two integrals are equal, as they should be.

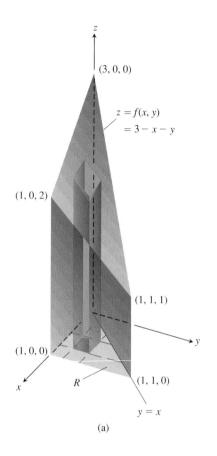

(a)

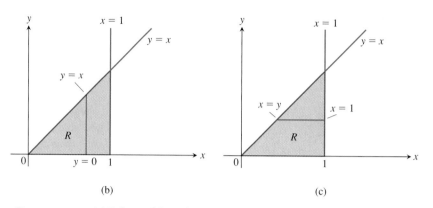

(b)

(c)

FIGURE 12.11 (a) Prism with a triangular base in the xy-plane. The volume of this prism is defined as a double integral over R. To evaluate it as an iterated integral, we may integrate first with respect to y and then with respect to x, or the other way around (Example 2). (b) Integration limits of

$$\int_{x=0}^{x=1} \int_{y=0}^{y=x} f(x, y) \, dy \, dx.$$

If we integrate first with respect to y, we integrate along a vertical line through R and then integrate from left to right to include all the vertical lines in R. (c) Integration limits of

$$\int_{y=0}^{y=1} \int_{x=y}^{x=1} f(x, y) \, dx \, dy.$$

If we integrate first with respect to x, we integrate along a horizontal line through R and then integrate from bottom to top to include all the horizontal lines in R.

Although Fubini's theorem assures us that a double integral may be calculated as an iterated integral in either order of integration, the value of one integral may be easier to find than the value of the other. The next example shows how this can happen.

Example 3   Evaluating a Double Integral

Calculate

$$\iint_R \frac{\sin x}{x} \, dA,$$

where R is the triangle in the xy-plane bounded by the x-axis, the line $y = x$, and the line $x = 1$.

Solution   The region of integration is shown in Figure 12.12. If we integrate first with respect to y and then with respect to x, we find

$$\int_0^1 \left(\int_0^x \frac{\sin x}{x} \, dy \right) dx = \int_0^1 \left(y \frac{\sin x}{x} \right]_{y=0}^{y=x} \right) dx = \int_0^1 \sin x \, dx$$

$$= -\cos (1) + 1 \approx 0.46 \text{ unit cubed.}$$

If we reverse the order of integration and attempt to calculate

$$\int_0^1 \int_y^1 \frac{\sin x}{x} \, dx \, dy,$$

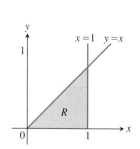

FIGURE 12.12 The region of integration in Example 3.

we are stopped because $\int ((\sin x)/x)\, dx$ cannot be expressed in terms of elementary functions.

There is no general rule for predicting which order of integration will be the good one in circumstances like these, so don't worry about how to start your integrations. Just forge ahead and if the order you first choose doesn't work, try the other.

Finding Limits of Integration

The hardest part of evaluating a double integral can be finding the limits of integration. Fortunately, there is a good procedure to follow.

Procedure for Finding Limits of Integration

A. To evaluate $\iint_R f(x, y)\, dA$ over a region R, integrating first with respect to y and then with respect to x, take the following steps.

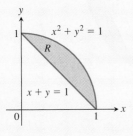 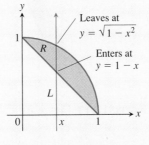 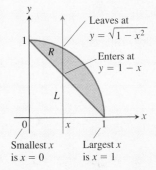

Step 1: *A sketch.* Sketch the region of integration and label the bounding curves.

Step 2: *The y-limits of integration.* Imagine a vertical line L cutting through R in the direction of increasing y. Mark the y-values where L enters and leaves. These are the y-limits of integration and are usually functions of x (instead of constants).

Step 3: *The x-limits of integration.* Choose x-limits that include all the vertical lines through R. The integral is

$$\iint_R f(x, y)\, dA =$$

$$\int_{x=0}^{x=1} \int_{y=1-x}^{y=\sqrt{1-x^2}} f(x, y)\, dy\, dx.$$

B. To evaluate the same double integral as an iterated integral with the order of integration reversed, use horizontal lines instead of vertical lines. The integral is

$$\iint_R f(x, y)\, dA = \int_0^1 \int_{1-y}^{\sqrt{1-y^2}} f(x, y)\, dx\, dy.$$

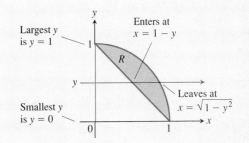

Example 4   Reversing the Order of Integration

Sketch the region of integration for the integral

$$\int_0^2 \int_{x^2}^{2x} (4x + 2) \, dy \, dx$$

and write an equivalent integral with the order of integration reversed.

Solution   The region of integration is given by the inequalities $x^2 \le y \le 2x$ and $0 \le x \le 2$. It is therefore the region bounded by the curves $y = x^2$ and $y = 2x$ between $x = 0$ and $x = 2$ (Figure 12.13a).

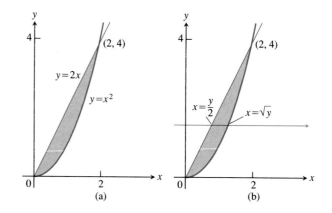

FIGURE 12.13 Figure for Example 4.

To find limits for integrating in the reverse order, we imagine a horizontal line passing from left to right through the region. It enters at $x = y/2$ and leaves at $x = \sqrt{y}$. To include all such lines, we let y run from $y = 0$ to $y = 4$ (Figure 12.13b). The integral is

$$\int_0^4 \int_{y/2}^{\sqrt{y}} (4x + 2) \, dx \, dy.$$

The common value of these integrals is 8.

EXERCISES 12.1

Finding Regions of Integration and Double Integrals

In Exercises 1–10, sketch the region of integration and evaluate the integral.

1. $\int_0^3 \int_0^2 (4 - y^2) \, dy \, dx$

2. $\int_0^3 \int_{-2}^0 (x^2 y - 2xy) \, dy \, dx$

3. $\int_{-1}^0 \int_{-1}^1 (x + y + 1) \, dx \, dy$

4. $\int_{\pi}^{2\pi} \int_0^{\pi} (\sin x + \cos y) \, dx \, dy$

5. $\int_0^{\pi} \int_0^x x \sin y \, dy \, dx$

6. $\int_0^{\pi} \int_0^{\sin x} y \, dy \, dx$

7. $\int_1^{\ln 8}\int_0^{\ln y} e^{x+y}\,dx\,dy$

8. $\int_1^2\int_y^{y^2} dx\,dy$

9. $\int_0^1\int_0^{y^2} 3y^3 e^{xy}\,dx\,dy$

10. $\int_1^4\int_0^{\sqrt{x}} \frac{3}{2} e^{y/\sqrt{x}}\,dy\,dx$

In Exercises 11–16, integrate f over the given region.

11. *Quadrilateral* $f(x, y) = x/y$ over the region in the first quadrant bounded by the lines $y = x$, $y = 2x$, $x = 1$, $x = 2$

12. *Square* $f(x, y) = 1/(xy)$ over the square $1 \le x \le 2$, $1 \le y \le 2$

13. *Triangle* $f(x, y) = x^2 + y^2$ over the triangular region with vertices $(0, 0)$, $(1, 0)$, and $(0, 1)$

14. *Rectangle* $f(x, y) = y \cos xy$ over the rectangle $0 \le x \le \pi$, $0 \le y \le 1$

15. *Triangle* $f(u, v) = v - \sqrt{u}$ over the triangular region cut from the first quadrant of the uv-plane by the line $u + v = 1$

16. *Curved region* $f(s, t) = e^s \ln t$ over the region in the first quadrant of the st-plane that lies above the curve $s = \ln t$ from $t = 1$ to $t = 2$

Each of Exercises 17–20 gives an integral over a region in a Cartesian coordinate plane. Sketch the region and evaluate the integral.

17. $\int_{-2}^0\int_v^{-v} 2\,dp\,dv$ (the pv-plane)

18. $\int_0^1\int_0^{\sqrt{1-s^2}} 8t\,dt\,ds$ (the st-plane)

19. $\int_{-\pi/3}^{\pi/3}\int_0^{\sec t} 3 \cos t\,du\,dt$ (the tu-plane)

20. $\int_0^3\int_1^{4-2u} \frac{4-2u}{v^2}\,dv\,du$ (the uv-plane)

Reversing the Order of Integration

In Exercises 21–30, sketch the region of integration and write an equivalent double integral with the order of integration reversed.

21. $\int_0^1\int_2^{4-2x} dy\,dx$

22. $\int_0^2\int_{y-2}^0 dx\,dy$

23. $\int_0^1\int_y^{\sqrt{y}} dx\,dy$

24. $\int_0^1\int_{1-x}^{1-x^2} dy\,dx$

25. $\int_0^1\int_1^{e^x} dy\,dx$

26. $\int_0^{\ln 2}\int_{e^y}^2 dx\,dy$

27. $\int_0^{3/2}\int_0^{9-4x^2} 16x\,dy\,dx$

28. $\int_0^2\int_0^{4-y^2} y\,dx\,dy$

29. $\int_0^1\int_{-\sqrt{1-y^2}}^{\sqrt{1-y^2}} 3y\,dx\,dy$

30. $\int_0^2\int_{-\sqrt{4-x^2}}^{\sqrt{4-x^2}} 6x\,dy\,dx$

Evaluating Double Integrals

In Exercises 31–40, sketch the region of integration, reverse the order of integration, and evaluate the integral.

31. $\int_0^\pi\int_x^\pi \frac{\sin y}{y}\,dy\,dx$

32. $\int_0^2\int_x^2 2y^2 \sin xy\,dy\,dx$

33. $\int_0^1\int_y^1 x^2 e^{xy}\,dx\,dy$

34. $\int_0^2\int_0^{4-x^2} \frac{xe^{2y}}{4-y}\,dy\,dx$

35. $\int_0^{2\sqrt{\ln 3}}\int_{y/2}^{\sqrt{\ln 3}} e^{x^2}\,dx\,dy$

36. $\int_0^3\int_{\sqrt{x/3}}^1 e^{y^3}\,dy\,dx$

37. $\int_0^{1/16}\int_{y^{1/4}}^{1/2} \cos(16\pi x^5)\,dx\,dy$

38. $\int_0^8\int_{\sqrt[3]{x}}^2 \frac{dy\,dx}{y^4+1}$

39. *Square region* $\iint_R (y - 2x^2)\,dA$ where R is the region bounded by the square $|x| + |y| = 1$

40. *Triangular region* $\iint_R xy\,dA$ where R is the region bounded by the lines $y = x$, $y = 2x$, and $x + y = 2$

Volume Beneath a Surface $z = f(x, y)$

41. Find the volume of the region bounded by the paraboloid $z = x^2 + y^2$ and below by the triangle enclosed by the lines $y = x$, $x = 0$, and $x + y = 2$ in the xy-plane.

42. Find the volume of the solid that is bounded above by the cylinder $z = x^2$ and below by the region enclosed by the parabola $y = 2 - x^2$ and the line $y = x$ in the xy-plane.

43. Find the volume of the solid whose base is the region in the xy-plane that is bounded by the parabola $y = 4 - x^2$ and the line $y = 3x$, while the top of the solid is bounded by the plane $z = x + 4$.

44. Find the volume of the solid in the first octant bounded by the coordinate planes, the cylinder $x^2 + y^2 = 4$, and the plane $z + y = 3$.

45. Find the volume of the solid in the first octant bounded by the coordinate planes, the plane $x = 3$, and the parabolic cylinder $z = 4 - y^2$.

46. Find the volume of the solid cut from the first octant by the surface $z = 4 - x^2 - y$.

47. Find the volume of the wedge cut from the first octant by the cylinder $z = 12 - 3y^2$ and the plane $x + y = 2$.

48. Find the volume of the solid cut from the square column $|x| + |y| \le 1$ by the planes $z = 0$ and $3x + z = 3$.

49. Find the volume of the solid that is bounded on the front and back by the planes $x = 2$ and $x = 1$, on the sides by the cylinders $y = \pm 1/x$, and above and below by the planes $z = x + 1$ and $z = 0$.

50. Find the volume of the solid bounded on the front and back by the planes $x = \pm\pi/3$, on the sides by the cylinders $y = \pm \sec x$, above by the cylinder $z = 1 + y^2$, and below by the xy-plane.

Integrals over Unbounded Regions

Evaluate the improper integrals in Exercises 51–54 as iterated integrals.

51. $\displaystyle\int_1^\infty \int_{e^{-x}}^1 \frac{1}{x^3 y}\, dy\, dx$

52. $\displaystyle\int_{-1}^1 \int_{-1/\sqrt{1-x^2}}^{1/\sqrt{1-x^2}} (2y + 1)\, dy\, dx$

53. $\displaystyle\int_{-\infty}^\infty \int_{-\infty}^\infty \frac{1}{(x^2 + 1)(y^2 + 1)}\, dx\, dy$

54. $\displaystyle\int_0^\infty \int_0^\infty xe^{-(x+2y)}\, dx\, dy$

Approximating Double Integrals

In Exercises 55 and 56, approximate the double integral of $f(x, y)$ over the region R partitioned by the given vertical lines $x = a$ and horizontal lines $y = c$. In each subrectangle, use (x_k, y_k) as indicated for your approximation.

$$\iint_R f(x, y)\, dA \approx \sum_{k=1}^n f(x_k, y_k)\, \Delta A_k$$

55. $f(x, y) = x + y$ over the region R bounded above by the semicircle $y = \sqrt{1 - x^2}$ and below by the x-axis, using the partition $x = -1, -1/2, 0, 1/4, 1/2, 1$ and $y = 0, 1/2, 1$ with (x_k, y_k) the lower left corner in the kth subrectangle (provided the subrectangle lies within R)

56. $f(x, y) = x + 2y$ over the region R inside the circle $(x - 2)^2 + (y - 3)^2 = 1$ using the partition $x = 1, 3/2, 2, 5/2, 3$ and $y = 2, 5/2, 3, 7/2, 4$ with (x_k, y_k) the center (centroid) in the kth subrectangle (provided the subrectangle lies within R)

Theory and Examples

57. *Circular sector* Integrate $f(x, y) = \sqrt{4 - x^2}$ over the smaller sector cut from the disk $x^2 + y^2 \le 4$ by the rays $\theta = \pi/6$ and $\theta = \pi/2$.

58. *Unbounded region* Integrate $f(x, y) = 1/[(x^2 - x)(y - 1)^{2/3}]$ over the infinite rectangle $2 \le x < \infty, 0 \le y \le 2$.

59. *Noncircular cylinder* A solid right (noncircular) cylinder has its base R in the xy-plane and is bounded above by the paraboloid $z = x^2 + y^2$. The cylinder's volume is

$$V = \int_0^1 \int_0^y (x^2 + y^2)\, dx\, dy + \int_1^2 \int_0^{2-y} (x^2 + y^2)\, dx\, dy.$$

Sketch the base region R and express the cylinder's volume as a single iterated integral with the order of integration reversed. Then evaluate the integral to find the volume.

60. *Converting to a double integral* Evaluate the integral

$$\int_0^2 (\tan^{-1} \pi x - \tan^{-1} x)\, dx.$$

(*Hint*: Write the integrand as an integral.)

61. *Maximizing a double integral* What region R in the xy-plane maximizes the value of

$$\iint_R (4 - x^2 - 2y^2)\, dA?$$

Give reasons for your answer.

62. *Minimizing a double integral* What region R in the xy-plane minimizes the value of

$$\iint_R (x^2 + y^2 - 9)\, dA?$$

Give reasons for your answer.

63. *Writing to Learn* Is it all right to evaluate the integral of a continuous function $f(x, y)$ over a rectangular region in the xy-plane and get different answers depending on the order of integration? Give reasons for your answer.

64. *Writing to Learn* How would you evaluate the double integral of a continuous function $f(x, y)$ over the region R in the xy-plane enclosed by the triangle with vertices $(0, 1), (2, 0)$, and $(1, 2)$? Give reasons for your answer.

65. *Unbounded region* Prove that

$$\int_{-\infty}^\infty \int_{-\infty}^\infty e^{-x^2-y^2}\, dx\, dy = \lim_{b\to\infty} \int_{-b}^b \int_{-b}^b e^{-x^2-y^2}\, dx\, dy$$

$$= 4\left(\int_0^\infty e^{-x^2}\, dx\right)^2.$$

66. *Improper double integral* Evaluate the improper integral

$$\int_0^1 \int_0^3 \frac{x^2}{(y - 1)^{2/3}}\, dy\, dx.$$

COMPUTER EXPLORATIONS

Evaluating Double Integrals Numerically

Use a CAS double-integral evaluator to estimate the values of the integrals in Exercises 67–70.

67. $\displaystyle\int_1^3 \int_1^x \frac{1}{xy}\, dy\, dx$

68. $\displaystyle\int_0^1 \int_0^1 e^{-(x^2+y^2)}\, dy\, dx$

69. $\displaystyle\int_0^1 \int_0^1 \tan^{-1} xy\, dy\, dx$

70. $\displaystyle\int_{-1}^1 \int_0^{\sqrt{1-x^2}} 3\sqrt{1 - x^2 - y^2}\, dy\, dx$

Use a CAS double-integral evaluator to find the integrals in Exercises 71–76. Then reverse the order of integration and evaluate, again with a CAS.

71. $\int_0^1 \int_{2y}^4 e^{x^2} \, dx \, dy$

72. $\int_0^3 \int_{x^2}^9 x \cos (y^2) \, dy \, dx$

73. $\int_0^2 \int_{y^3}^{4\sqrt{2y}} \left(x^2 y - xy^2 \right) dx \, dy$

74. $\int_0^2 \int_0^{4-y^2} e^{xy} \, dx \, dy$

75. $\int_1^2 \int_0^{x^2} \frac{1}{x+y} \, dy \, dx$

76. $\int_1^2 \int_{y^3}^8 \frac{1}{\sqrt{x^2 + y^2}} \, dy \, dx$

12.2 Areas, Moments, and Centers of Mass*

Areas of Bounded Regions in the Plane • Average Value • Moments and Centers of Mass • Masses Distributed over a Plane Region • Thin, Flat Plates with Continuous Mass Distributions • Moments of Inertia • Centroids of Geometric Figures

In this section, we show how to use double integrals to calculate the areas of bounded regions in the plane and to find the average value of a function of two variables. Then we study the physical problem of finding the center of mass of a thin plate covering a region in the plane.

Areas of Bounded Regions in the Plane

If we take $f(x, y) = 1$ in the definition of the double integral over a region R in the preceding section, the partial sums reduce to

$$S_n = \sum_{k=1}^{n} f(x_k, y_k) \, \Delta A_k = \sum_{k=1}^{n} \Delta A_k.$$

This approximates what we would like to call the area of R. As Δx and Δy approach zero, the coverage of R by the ΔA_k's (Figure 12.14) becomes increasingly complete, and we define the area of R to be the limit

$$\text{Area} = \lim_{n \to \infty} \sum_{k=1}^{n} \Delta A_k = \iint_R dA.$$

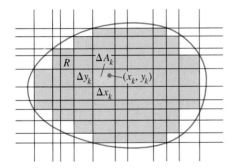

FIGURE 12.14 The first step in defining the area of a region is to partition the interior of the region into cells.

Definition   Area
The **area** of a closed, bounded plane region R is

$$A = \iint_R dA.$$

As with the other definitions in this chapter, the definition here applies to a greater variety of regions than does the earlier single-variable definition of area, but it agrees with the earlier definition on regions to which they both apply.

---

*The material on mass and moments for planar regions presented in this section does not require the coverage from Chapter 5. The essential ideas are all given here, some of which may be a review for students who studied moments in Chapter 5.

To evaluate the integral in the definition of area, we integrate the constant function $f(x, y) = 1$ over R.

Example 1 Finding Area

Find the area of the region R bounded by $y = x$ and $y = x^2$ in the first quadrant.

Solution We sketch the region (Figure 12.15) and calculate the area as

$$A = \int_0^1 \int_{x^2}^x dy\, dx = \int_0^1 \left[y \right]_{x^2}^x dx$$

$$= \int_0^1 (x - x^2)\, dx = \left[\frac{x^2}{2} - \frac{x^3}{3} \right]_0^1 = \frac{1}{6} \text{ square unit}.$$

Notice that the single integral $\int_0^1 (x - x^2)\, dx$, obtained from evaluating the inside iterated integral, is the integral for the area between these two curves using the method of Section 4.6.

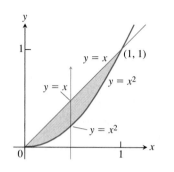

FIGURE 12.15 The region in Example 1

Example 2 Finding Area

Find the area of the region R enclosed by the parabola $y = x^2$ and the line $y = x + 2$.

Solution If we divide R into the regions R_1 and R_2 shown in Figure 12.16a, we may calculate the area as

$$A = \iint_{R_1} dA + \iint_{R_2} dA = \int_0^1 \int_{-\sqrt{y}}^{\sqrt{y}} dx\, dy + \int_1^4 \int_{y-2}^{\sqrt{y}} dx\, dy.$$

On the other hand, reversing the order of integration (Figure 12.16b) gives

$$A = \int_{-1}^2 \int_{x^2}^{x+2} dy\, dx.$$

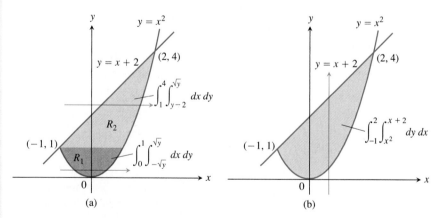

FIGURE 12.16 Calculating this area takes (a) two double integrals if the first integration is with respect to x, but (b) only one if the first integration is with respect to y. (Example 2)

This result is simpler and is the only one we would bother to write down in practice. The area is

$$A = \int_{-1}^{2} \Big[y\Big]_{x^2}^{x+2}\, dx = \int_{-1}^{2} (x + 2 - x^2)\, dx = \left[\frac{x^2}{2} + 2x - \frac{x^3}{3}\right]_{-1}^{2} = \frac{9}{2} \text{ square units}.$$

Average Value

The average value of an integrable function of a single variable on a closed interval is the integral of the function over the interval divided by the length of the interval. For an integrable function of two variables defined on a closed and bounded region that has a measurable area, the average value is the integral over the region divided by the area of the region. If f is the function and R the region, then

$$\textbf{Average value} \text{ of } f \text{ over } R = \frac{1}{\text{area of } R} \iint\limits_{R} f\, dA. \tag{1}$$

If f is the area density of a thin plate covering R, then the double integral of f over R divided by the area of R is the plate's average density in units of mass per unit area. If $f(x, y)$ is the distance from the point (x, y) to a fixed point P, then the average value of f over R is the average distance of points in R from P.

Example 3   Finding Average Value

Find the average value of $f(x, y) = x \cos xy$ over the rectangle $R: 0 \le x \le \pi$, $0 \le y \le 1$.

Solution   The value of the integral of f over R is

$$\int_{0}^{\pi} \int_{0}^{1} x \cos xy\, dy\, dx = \int_{0}^{\pi} \Big[\sin xy\Big]_{y=0}^{y=1}\, dx$$

$$= \int_{0}^{\pi} (\sin x - 0)\, dx = -\cos x\Big]_{0}^{\pi} = 1 + 1 = 2.$$

The area of R is π. The average value of f over R is $2/\pi$.

Moments and Centers of Mass

Many structures and mechanical systems behave as if their masses were concentrated at a single point, called the center of mass. It is important to know how to locate this point, and doing so is basically a mathematical enterprise. We develop our mathematical model in stages. The first stage is to imagine masses m_1, m_2, and m_3 on a rigid x-axis supported by a fulcrum at the origin.

Mass versus weight

Weight is the force that results from gravity pulling on a mass. If an object of mass m is placed in a location where the acceleration of gravity is g, the object's weight there is

$$F = mg$$

(as in Newton's second law).

The resulting system might balance, or it might not. It depends on how large the masses are and how they are arranged.

Each mass m_k exerts a downward force $m_k g$ equal to the magnitude of the mass times the acceleration of gravity. Each of these forces has a tendency to turn the axis about the origin, the way you turn a seesaw. This turning effect, called a **torque,** is measured by multiplying the force $m_k g$ by the signed distance x_k from the point of application to the origin. Masses to the left of the origin exert negative (counterclockwise) torque. Masses to the right of the origin exert positive (clockwise) torque.

The sum of the torques measures the tendency of a system to rotate about the origin. This sum is called the **system torque.**

$$\text{System torque} = \sum m_k g x_k \tag{2}$$

The system will balance if and only if its torque is zero.

If we factor out the g in Equation (2), we see that the system torque is

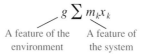

Thus, the torque is the product of the gravitational acceleration g, which is a feature of the environment in which the system happens to reside, and the number $\sum m_k x_k$, which is a feature of the system itself, a constant that stays the same no matter where the system is placed. The constant is called the **moment of the system about the origin.**

$$\text{Moment of system about origin} = \sum m_k x_k \tag{3}$$

We usually want to know where to place the fulcrum to make the system balance, that is, at what point $\bar{x}$ to place it to make the torque zero.

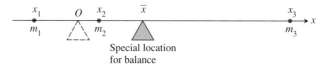

Special location
for balance

The torque of each mass about the fulcrum in this special location is

$$\text{Torque of } m_k \text{ about } \bar{x} = \begin{pmatrix} \text{signed distance} \\ \text{of } m_k \text{ from } \bar{x} \end{pmatrix}\begin{pmatrix} \text{downward} \\ \text{force} \end{pmatrix}$$
$$= (x_k - \bar{x})m_k g.$$

When we write the equation that says that the sum of these torques is zero, we get an equation we can solve for $\bar{x}$:

$$\sum (x_k - \bar{x})m_k g = 0 \qquad \text{Sum of the torques equals zero}$$

$$g \sum (x_k - \bar{x})m_k = 0 \qquad \text{Constant Multiple Rule for Sums}$$

$$\sum (m_k x_k - \bar{x}m_k) = 0 \qquad g \text{ divided out, } m_k \text{ distributed}$$

$$\sum m_k x_k - \sum \bar{x}m_k = 0 \qquad \text{Difference Rule for Sums}$$

$$\sum m_k x_k = \bar{x} \sum m_k \qquad \begin{array}{l}\text{Rearranged, Constant Multiple} \\ \text{Rule again}\end{array}$$

$$\bar{x} = \frac{\sum m_k x_k}{\sum m_k}. \qquad \text{Solved for } \bar{x}$$

This last equation tells us to find $\bar{x}$ by dividing the system's moment about the origin by the system's total mass:

$$\bar{x} = \frac{\sum x_k m_k}{\sum m_k} = \frac{\text{system moment about origin}}{\text{system mass}}.$$

The point $\bar{x}$ is called the system's **center of mass.**

Masses Distributed over a Plane Region

Suppose that we have a finite collection of masses located in the plane, with mass m_k at the point (x_k, y_k) (see Figure 12.17). The mass of the system is

$$\text{System mass:} \qquad M = \sum m_k.$$

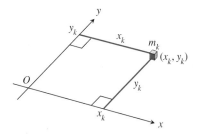

FIGURE 12.17 Each mass m_k has a moment about each axis.

Each mass m_k has a moment about each axis. Its moment about the x-axis is $m_k y_k$, and its moment about the y-axis is $m_k x_k$. The moments of the entire system about the two axes are

$$\text{Moment about } x-\text{axis:} \qquad M_x = \sum m_k y_k,$$
$$\text{Moment about } y-\text{axis:} \qquad M_y = \sum m_k x_k.$$

The x-coordinate of the system's center of mass is defined to be

$$\bar{x} = \frac{M_y}{M} = \frac{\sum m_k x_k}{\sum m_k}. \tag{4}$$

With this choice of $\bar{x}$, as in the one-dimensional case, the system balances about the line $x = \bar{x}$ (Figure 12.18).

The y-coordinate of the system's center of mass is defined to be

$$\bar{y} = \frac{M_x}{M} = \frac{\sum m_k y_k}{\sum m_k}. \tag{5}$$

With this choice of $\bar{y}$, the system balances about the line $y = \bar{y}$ as well. The torques exerted by the masses about the line $y = \bar{y}$ cancel out. Thus, as far as balance is concerned, the system behaves as if all its mass were at the single point $(\bar{x}, \bar{y})$. We call this point the system's *center of mass.*

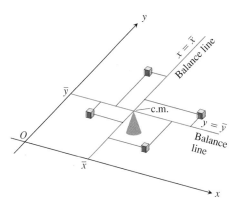

FIGURE 12.18 A two-dimensional array of masses balances on its center of mass.

Thin, Flat Plates with Continuous Mass Distributions

In many applications, we need to find the center of mass of a thin, flat plate: a disk of aluminum, say, or a triangular sheet of steel. In such cases, we assume the distribution of mass to be continuous, and the formulas we use to calculate $\bar{x}$ and $\bar{y}$ contain integrals instead of finite sums. The integrals arise in the following way.

Density

A material's density is its mass per unit volume. In practice, however, we tend to use units we can conveniently measure. For wires, rods, and narrow strips, we use mass per unit length. For flat sheets and plates, we use mass per unit area.

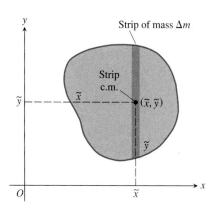

FIGURE 12.19 A plate cut into thin strips parallel to the y-axis. The moment exerted by a typical strip about each axis is the moment its mass Δm would exert if concentrated at the strips's center of mass $(\tilde{x}, \tilde{y})$.

Imagine the plate occupying a region in the xy-plane, cut into thin strips parallel to one of the axes (in Figure 12.19, the y-axis). The center of mass of a typical strip is $(\tilde{x}, \tilde{y})$. We treat the strip's mass Δm as if it were concentrated at $(\tilde{x}, \tilde{y})$. The moment of the strip about the y-axis is then $\tilde{x} \Delta m$. The moment of the strip about the x-axis is $\tilde{y} \Delta m$. Equations (4) and (5) then become

$$\bar{x} = \frac{M_y}{M} = \frac{\sum \tilde{x} \Delta m}{\sum \Delta m}, \qquad \bar{y} = \frac{M_x}{M} = \frac{\sum \tilde{y} \Delta m}{\sum \Delta m}.$$

The sums in these equations are Riemann sums for integrals and approach these integrals as limiting values as the strips into which the plate is cut become narrower and narrower. We can write these as double integrals to accommodate a great variety of shapes and density functions. **Mass** itself is the integral of the continuous density function, denoted here by $\delta(x, y)$. (Some physicists use the symbol $\rho(x, y)$ for density.) The formulas for mass, first moments, and center of mass are given in Table 12.1.

Table 12.1 Mass and first moment formulas for thin plates covering regions in the xy-plane

Density: $\delta(x, y)$

Mass: $M = \displaystyle\iint \delta(x, y)\, dA$

First moments: $M_x = \displaystyle\iint y\delta(x, y)\, dA, \qquad M_y = \displaystyle\iint x\delta(x, y)\, dA$

Center of mass: $\bar{x} = \dfrac{M_y}{M}, \qquad \bar{y} = \dfrac{M_x}{M}$

CD-ROM
WEBsite

Example 4   Finding the Center of Mass of a Thin Plate of Variable Density

A thin plate covers the triangular region bounded by the x-axis and the lines $x = 1$ and $y = 2x$ in the first quadrant. The plate's density at the point (x, y) is $\delta(x, y) = 6x + 6y + 6$. Find the plate's mass, first moments, and center of mass about the coordinate axes.

Solution   We sketch the plate and put in enough detail to determine the limits of integration for the integrals we have to evaluate (Figure 12.20).

The plate's mass is

$$M = \int_0^1 \int_0^{2x} \delta(x, y)\, dy\, dx = \int_0^1 \int_0^{2x} (6x + 6y + 6)\, dy\, dx$$

$$= \int_0^1 \left[6xy + 3y^2 + 6y \right]_{y=0}^{y=2x} dx$$

$$= \int_0^1 (24x^2 + 12x)\, dx = \left[8x^3 + 6x^2 \right]_0^1 = 14.$$

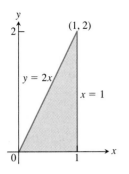

FIGURE 12.20 The triangular region covered by the plate in Example 4.

Notice that we integrate y times the density function to calculate M_x and x times density to find M_y.

The first moment about the x-axis is

$$M_x = \int_0^1 \int_0^{2x} y\delta(x, y) \, dy \, dx = \int_0^1 \int_0^{2x} (6xy + 6y^2 + 6y) \, dy \, dx$$

$$= \int_0^1 \left[3xy^2 + 2y^3 + 3y^2 \right]_{y=0}^{y=2x} dx = \int_0^1 (28x^3 + 12x^2) \, dx$$

$$= \left[7x^4 + 4x^3 \right]_0^1 = 11.$$

A similar calculation gives the moment about the y-axis:

$$M_y \int_0^1 \int_0^{2x} x\delta(x, y) \, dy \, dx = 10.$$

The coordinates of the center of mass are therefore

$$\bar{x} = \frac{M_y}{M} = \frac{10}{14} = \frac{5}{7}, \qquad \bar{y} = \frac{M_x}{M} = \frac{11}{14}.$$

Moments of Inertia

A body's first moments (Table 12.1) tell us about balance and about the torque the body exerts about different axes in a gravitational field. If the body is a rotating shaft, however, we are more likely to be interested in how much energy is stored in the shaft or about how much energy it will take to accelerate the shaft to a particular angular velocity. This is where the second moment or moment of inertia comes in.

Think of partitioning the shaft into small blocks of mass Δm_k and let r_k denote the distance from the kth block's center of mass to the axis of rotation (Figure 12.21). If the shaft rotates at an angular velocity of $\omega = d\theta/dt$ radians per second, the block's center of mass will trace its orbit at a linear speed of

$$v_k = \frac{d}{dt}(r_k\theta) = r_k \frac{d\theta}{dt} = r_k\omega.$$

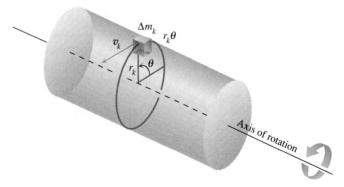

FIGURE 12.21 To find an integral for the amount of energy stored in a rotating shaft, we first imagine the shaft to be partitioned into small blocks. Each block has its own kinetic energy. We add the contributions of the individual blocks to find the kinetic energy of the shaft.

The block's kinetic energy will be approximately

$$\frac{1}{2}\Delta m_k v_k^2 = \frac{1}{2}\Delta m_k (r_k \omega)^2 = \frac{1}{2}\omega^2 r_k^2 \Delta m_k.$$

The kinetic energy of the shaft will be approximately

$$\sum \frac{1}{2}\omega^2 r_k^2 \Delta m_k.$$

The integral approached by these sums as the shaft is partitioned into smaller and smaller blocks gives the shaft's kinetic energy:

$$KE_{shaft} = \int \frac{1}{2}\omega^2 r^2 \, dm = \frac{1}{2}\omega^2 \int r^2 \, dm. \tag{6}$$

The factor

$$I = \int r^2 \, dm \tag{7}$$

is the moment of inertia of the shaft about its axis of rotation, and we see from Equation (6) that the shaft's kinetic energy is

$$KE_{shaft} = \frac{1}{2}I\omega^2. \tag{8}$$

To start a shaft of inertial moment I rotating at an angular velocity ω, we need to provide a kinetic energy of $KE = (1/2)I\omega^2$. To stop the shaft, we have to take this amount of energy back out. To start a locomotive with mass m moving at a linear velocity v, we need to provide a kinetic energy of $KE = (1/2)mv^2$. To stop the locomotive, we have to remove this amount of energy. The shaft's moment of inertia is analogous to the locomotive's mass. What makes the locomotive hard to start or stop is its mass. What makes the shaft hard to start or stop is its moment of inertia. The moment of inertia takes into account not only the mass but also its distribution.

The moment of inertia also plays a role in determining how much a horizontal metal beam will bend under a load. The stiffness of the beam is a constant times I, the moment of inertia of a typical cross section of the beam about the beam's longitudinal axis. The greater the value of I, the stiffer the beam and the less it will bend under a given load. That is why we use I-beams instead of beams whose cross sections are square. The flanges at the top and bottom of the beam hold most of the beam's mass away from the longitudinal axis to maximize the value of I (Figure 12.22).

If you want to see the moment of inertia at work, try the following experiment. Tape two coins to the ends of a pencil and twiddle the pencil about the center of mass. The moment of inertia accounts for the resistance you feel each time you change the direction of motion. Now move the coins an equal distance toward the center of mass and twiddle the pencil again. The system has the same mass and the same center of mass but now offers less resistance to the changes in motion. The moment of inertia has been reduced. The moment of inertia is what gives a baseball bat, golf club, or tennis racket its "feel." Tennis rackets that weigh the same, look the same, and have identical centers of mass will feel different and behave differently if their masses are not distributed the same way.

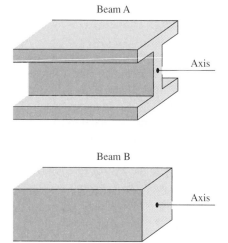

FIGURE 12.22 The greater the polar moment of inertia of the cross section of a beam about the beam's longitudinal axis, the stiffer the beam. Beams A and B have the same cross-section area, but A is stiffer.

First moments are "balancing" moments. Second moments are "turning" moments.

Table 12.2 gives the formulas for moments of inertia (also called second moments), and for radii of gyration.

Table 12.2 Second moment formulas for thin plates in the *xy*-plane

Moments of inertia (second moments):

About the *x*-axis: $I_x = \displaystyle\iint y^2 \delta(x, y)\, dA$ About the origin $I_0 = \displaystyle\iint (x^2 + y^2)\delta(x, y)\, dA = I_x + I_y$
                                                    (polar moment):

About the *y*-axis: $I_y = \displaystyle\iint x^2 \delta(x, y)\, dA$

About a line *L*: $I_L = \displaystyle\iint r^2(x, y)\delta(x, y)\, dA,$ where $r(x, y) = $ distance from (x, y) to L

Radii of gyration: About the *x*-axis: $R_x = \sqrt{I_x/M}$

                            About the *y*-axis: $R_y = \sqrt{I_y/M}$

                            About the origin: $R_0 = \sqrt{I_0/M}$

The mathematical difference between the **first moments** M_x and M_y and the **moments of inertia,** or **second moments,** I_x and I_y is that the second moments use the *squares* of the "lever-arm" distances x and y.

The moments I_0 is also called the **polar moment** of inertia about the origin. It is calculated by integrating the density $\delta(x, y)$ (mass per unit area) times $r^2 = x^2 + y^2$, the square of the distance from a representative point (x, y) to the origin. Notice that $I_0 = I_x + I_y$; once we find two, we get the third automatically. (The moment I_0 is sometimes called I_z, for moment of inertia about the z-axis. The identity $I_z = I_x + I_y$ is then called the **Perpendicular Axis Theorem.**)

The **radius of gyration** R_x is defined by the equation

$$I_x = MR_x^2.$$

It tells how far from the x-axis the entire mass of the plate might be concentrated to give the same I_x. The radius of gyration gives a convenient way to express the moment of inertia in terms of a mass and a length. The radii R_y and R_0 are defined in a similar way, with

$$I_y = MR_y^2 \qquad \text{and} \qquad I_0 = MR_0^2.$$

We take square roots to get the formulas in Table 12.2.

Example 5   Finding Moments of Inertia and Radii of Gyration

For the thin plate in Example 4 (Figure 12.20), find the moments of inertia and radii of gyration about the coordinate axes and the origin.

Notice that we integrate y^2 times density in calculating I_x and x^2 times density to find I_y.

Solution Using the density function $\delta(x, y) = 6x + 6y + 6$ given in Example 4, the moment of inertia about the x-axis is

$$
I_x = \int_0^1 \int_0^{2x} y^2 \delta(x, y) \, dy \, dx = \int_0^1 \int_0^{2x} (6xy^2 + 6y^3 + 6y^2) \, dy \, dx
$$

$$
= \int_0^1 \left[2xy^3 + \frac{3}{2}y^4 + 2y^3 \right]_{y=0}^{y=2x} dx = \int_0^1 (40x^4 + 16x^3) \, dx
$$

$$
= \left[8x^5 + 4x^4 \right]_0^1 = 12.
$$

Similarly, the moment of inertia about the y-axis is

$$
I_y = \int_0^1 \int_0^{2x} x^2 \delta(x, y) \, dy \, dx = \frac{39}{5}.
$$

Since we know I_x and I_y, we do not need to evaluate an integral to find I_0; we can use the equation $I_0 = I_x + I_y$ instead:

$$
I_0 = 12 + \frac{39}{5} = \frac{60 + 39}{5} = \frac{99}{5}.
$$

The three radii of gyration are

$$
R_x = \sqrt{I_x/M} = \sqrt{12/14} = \sqrt{6/7} \approx 0.93
$$

$$
R_y = \sqrt{I_y/M} = \sqrt{\left(\frac{39}{5}\right)/14} = \sqrt{39/70} \approx 0.75
$$

$$
R_0 = \sqrt{I_0/M} = \sqrt{\left(\frac{99}{5}\right)/14} = \sqrt{99/70} \approx 1.19.
$$

Centroids of Geometric Figures

When the density of an object is constant, it cancels out of the numerator and denominator of the formulas for $\bar{x}$ and $\bar{y}$. As far as $\bar{x}$ and $\bar{y}$ are concerned, δ might as well be 1. Thus, when δ is constant, the location of the center of mass becomes a feature of the object's shape and not of the material of which it is made. In such cases, engineers may call the center of mass the **centroid** of the shape. To find a centroid, we set δ equal to 1 and proceed to find $\bar{x}$ and $\bar{y}$ as before, by dividing first moments by masses.

Example 6   Finding the Centroid of a Region

Find the centroid of the region in the first quadrant that is bounded above by the line $y = x$ and below by the parabola $y = x^2$.

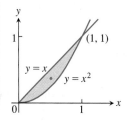

FIGURE 12.23 Example 6 finds the centroid of the region shown here.

Solution We sketch the region and include enough detail to determine the limits of integration (Figure 12.23). We then set δ equal to 1 and evaluate the appropriate formulas from Table 12.1:

$$M = \int_0^1 \int_{x^2}^x 1 \, dy \, dx = \int_0^1 [y]_{y=x^2}^{y=x} \, dx = \int_0^1 (x - x^2) \, dx = \left[\frac{x^2}{2} - \frac{x^3}{3} \right]_0^1 = \frac{1}{6}$$

$$M_x = \int_0^1 \int_{x^2}^x y \, dy \, dx = \int_0^1 \left[\frac{y^2}{2} \right]_{y=x^2}^{y=x} dx$$

$$= \int_0^1 \left(\frac{x^2}{2} - \frac{x^4}{2} \right) dx = \left[\frac{x^3}{6} - \frac{x^5}{10} \right]_0^1 = \frac{1}{15}$$

$$M_y = \int_0^1 \int_{x^2}^x x \, dy \, dx = \int_0^1 [xy]_{y=x^2}^{y=x} \, dx = \int_0^1 (x^2 - x^3) \, dx = \left[\frac{x^3}{3} - \frac{x^4}{4} \right]_0^1 = \frac{1}{12}.$$

From these values of M, M_x, and M_y, we find

$$\bar{x} = \frac{M_y}{M} = \frac{1/12}{1/6} = \frac{1}{2} \quad \text{and} \quad \bar{y} = \frac{M_x}{M} = \frac{1/15}{1/6} = \frac{2}{5}.$$

The centroid is the point $(1/2, \ 2/5)$.

EXERCISES 12.2

Area by Double Integration

In Exercises 1–8, sketch the region bounded by the given lines and curves. Then express the region's area as an iterated double integral and evaluate the integral.

1. The coordinate axes and the line $x + y = 2$
2. The lines $x = 0$, $y = 2x$, and $y = 4$
3. The parabola $x = -y^2$ and the line $y = x + 2$
4. The parabola $x = y - y^2$ and the line $y = -x$
5. The curve $y = e^x$ and the lines $y = 0$, $x = 0$, and $x = \ln 2$
6. The curves $y = \ln x$ and $y = 2 \ln x$ and the line $x = e$, in the first quadrant
7. The parabolas $x = y^2$ and $x = 2y - y^2$
8. The parabolas $x = y^2 - 1$ and $x = 2y^2 - 2$

Identifying the Region of Integration

The integrals and sums of integrals in Exercises 9–14 give the areas of regions in the xy-plane. Sketch each region, label each bounding curve with its equation, and give the coordinates of the points where the curves intersect. Then find the area of the region.

9. $\int_0^6 \int_{y^2/3}^{2y} dx \, dy$

10. $\int_0^3 \int_{-x}^{x(2-x)} dy \, dx$

11. $\int_0^{\pi/4} \int_{\sin x}^{\cos x} dy \, dx$

12. $\int_{-1}^2 \int_{y^2}^{y+2} dx \, dy$

13. $\int_{-1}^0 \int_{-2x}^{1-x} dy \, dx + \int_0^2 \int_{-x/2}^{1-x} dy \, dx$

14. $\int_0^2 \int_{x^2-4}^0 dy \, dx + \int_0^4 \int_0^{\sqrt{x}} dy \, dx$

Average Values

15. Find the average value of $f(x, y) = \sin(x + y)$ over
    (a) the rectangle $0 \le x \le \pi$, $0 \le y \le \pi$
    (b) the rectangle $0 \le x \le \pi$, $0 \le y \le \pi/2$

16. Which do you think will be larger, the average value of $f(x, y) = xy$ over the square $0 \le x \le 1, 0 \le y \le 1$, or the average value of f over the quarter circle $x^2 + y^2 \le 1$ in the first quadrant? Calculate them to find out.

17. Find the average height of the paraboloid $z = x^2 + y^2$ over the square $0 \le x \le 2, 0 \le y \le 2$.

18. Find the average value of $f(x, y) = 1/(xy)$ over the square $\ln 2 \le x \le 2 \ln 2, \ln 2 \le y \le 2 \ln 2$.

Constant Density

19. *Finding center of mass* Find a center of mass of a thin plate of density $\delta = 3$ bounded by the lines $x = 0$, $y = x$, and the parabola $y = 2 - x^2$ in the first quadrant.

20. *Finding moments of inertia and radii of gyration* Find the moments of inertia and radii of gyration about the coordinate axes of a thin rectangular plate of constant density δ bounded by the lines $x = 3$ and $y = 3$ in the first quadrant.

21. *Finding a centroid* Find the centroid of the region in the first quadrant bounded by the x-axis, the parabola $y^2 = 2x$, and the line $x + y = 4$.

22. *Finding a centroid* Find the centroid of the triangular region cut from the first quadrant by the line $x + y = 3$.

23. *Finding a centroid* Find the centroid of the semicircular region bounded by the x-axis and the curve $y = \sqrt{1 - x^2}$.

24. *Finding a centroid* The area of the region in the first quadrant bounded by the parabola $y = 6x - x^2$ and the line $y = x$ is 125/6 square units. Find the centroid.

25. *Finding a centroid* Find the centroid of the region cut from the first quadrant by the circle $x^2 + y^2 = a^2$.

26. *Finding a centroid* Find the centroid of the region between the x-axis and the arch $y = \sin x$, $0 \le x \le \pi$.

27. *Finding moments of inertia* Find the moment of inertia about the x-axis of a thin plate of density $\delta = 1$ bounded by the circle $x^2 + y^2 = 4$. Then use your result to find I_y and I_0 for the plate.

28. *Finding a moment of inertia* Find the moment of inertia with respect to the y-axis of a thin sheet of constant density $\delta = 1$ bounded by the curve $y = (\sin^2 x)/x^2$ and the interval $\pi \le x \le 2\pi$ of the x-axis.

29. *The centroid of an infinite region* Find the centroid of the infinite region in the second quadrant enclosed by the coordinate axes and the curve $y = e^x$. (Use improper integrals in the mass-moment formulas.)

30. *The first moment of an infinite plate* Find the first moment about the y-axis of a thin plate density $\delta(x, y) = 1$ covering the infinite region under the curve $y = e^{-x^2/2}$ in the first quadrant.

Variable Density

31. *Finding a moment of inertia and radius of gyration* Find the moment of inertia and radius of gyration about the x-axis of a thin plate bounded by the parabola $x = y - y^2$ and the line $x + y = 0$ if $\delta(x, y) = x + y$.

32. *Finding mass* Find the mass of a thin plate occupying the smaller region cut from the ellipse $x^2 + 4y^2 = 12$ by the parabola $x = 4y^2$ if $\delta(x, y) = 5x$.

33. *Finding a center of mass* Find the center of mass of a thin triangular plate bounded by the y-axis and the lines $y = x$ and $y = 2 - x$ if $\delta(x, y) = 6x + 3y + 3$.

34. *Finding a center of mass and moment of inertia* Find the center of mass and moment of inertia about the x-axis of a thin plate bounded by the curves $x = y^2$ and $x = 2y - y^2$ if the density at the point (x, y) is $\delta(x, y) = y + 1$.

35. *Center of mass, moment of inertia, and radius of gyration* Find the center of mass and the moment of inertia and radius of gyration about the y-axis of a thin rectangular plate cut from the first quadrant by the lines $x = 6$ and $y = 1$ if $\delta(x, y) = x + y + 1$.

36. *Center of mass, moment of inertia, and radius of gyration* Find the center of mass, moment of inertia and radius of gyration about the y-axis of a thin plate bounded by the line $y = 1$ and the parabola $y = x^2$ if the density is $\delta(x, y) = y + 1$.

37. *Center of mass, moment of inertia, and radius of gyration* Find the center of mass and the moment of inertia and radius of gyration about the y-axis of a thin plate bounded by the x-axis, the lines $x = \pm 1$, and the parabola $y = x^2$ if $\delta(x, y) = 7y + 1$.

38. *Center of mass, moment of inertia, and radius of gyration* Find the center of mass and the moment of inertia and radius of gyration about the x-axis of a thin rectangular plate bounded by the lines $x = 0$, $x = 20$, $y = -1$, and $y = 1$ if $\delta(x, y) = 1 + (x/20)$.

39. *Center of mass, moments of inertia, and radii of gyration* Find the center of mass, the moment of inertia and radii of gyration about the coordinate axes, and the polar moment of inertia and radius of gyration of a thin triangular plate bounded by the lines $y = x$, $y = -x$, and $y = 1$ if $\delta(x, y) = y + 1$.

40. *Center of mass, moments of inertia, and radii of gyration* Repeat Exercise 39 for $\delta(x, y) = 3x^2 + 1$.

Theory and Examples

41. *Bacterium population* If $f(x, y) = (10{,}000e^y)/(1 + |x|/2)$ represents the "population density" of a certain bacterium on the xy-plane, where x and y are measured in centimeters, find the total population of bacteria within the rectangle $-5 \le x \le 5$ and $-2 \le y \le 0$.

42. *Regional population* If $f(x, y) = 100(y + 1)$ represents the population density of a planar region on Earth, where x and y are measured in miles, find the number of people in the region bounded by the curves $x = y^2$ and $x = 2y - y^2$.

43. *Appliance design* When we design an appliance, one of the concerns is how hard the appliance will be to tip over. When tipped, it will right itself as long as its center of mass lies on the correct side of the *fulcrum*, the point on which the appliance is riding as it tips. Suppose that the profile of an appliance of approximately constant density is parabolic, like an old-fashioned radio. It fills the region $0 \le y \le a(1 - x^2)$, $-1 \le x \le 1$, in the xy-plane (see accompanying figure). What values of a will guarantee that the appliance will have to be tipped more than 45° to fall over?

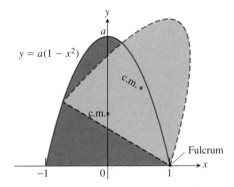

$y = a(1 - x^2)$

c.m.

c.m.

Fulcrum

44. *Minimizing a moment of inertia* A rectangular plate of constant density $\delta(x, y) = 1$ occupies the region bounded by the lines $x = 4$ and $y = 2$ in the first quadrant. The moment of inertia I_a of the rectangle about the line $y = a$ is given by the integral

$$I_a = \int_0^4 \int_0^2 (y - a)^2 \, dy \, dx.$$

Find the value of a that minimizes I_a.

45. *Centroid of unbounded region* Find the centroid of the infinite region in the xy-plane bounded by the curves $y = 1/\sqrt{1 - x^2}$, $y = -1/\sqrt{1 - x^2}$, and the lines $x = 0$, $x = 1$.

46. *Radius of gyration of slender rod* Find the radius of gyration of a slender rod of constant linear density δ gm/cm and length L cm with respect to an axis

(a) Through the rod's center of mass perpendicular to the rod's axis

(b) Perpendicular to the rod's axis at one end of the rod.

47. (*Continuation of Exercise 34*) A thin plate of now constant density δ occupies the region R in the xy-plane bounded by the curves $x = y^2$ and $x = 2y - y^2$.

(a) *Constant density* Find δ such that the plate has the same mass as the plate in Exercise 34.

(b) *Average value* Compare the value of δ found in part (a) with the average value of $\delta(x, y) = y + 1$ over R.

48. *Average temperature in Texas* According to the *Texas Almanac*, Texas has 254 counties and a National Weather Service station in each county. Assume that at time t_0, each of the 254 weather stations recorded the local temperature. Find a formula that would give a reasonable approximation to the average temperature in Texas at time t_0. Your answer should involve information that you would expect to be readily available in the *Texas Almanac*.

The Parallel Axis Theorem

Let $L_{c.m.}$ be a line in the xy-plane that runs through the center of mass of a thin plate of mass m covering a region in the plane. Let L be a line in the plane parallel to and h units away from $L_{c.m.}$. The **Parallel**

Axis Theorem says that under these conditions the moments of inertia I_L and $I_{c.m.}$ of the plate about L and $L_{c.m.}$ satisfy the equation

$$I_L = I_{c.m.} + mh^2.$$

This equation gives a quick way to calculate one moment when the other moment and the mass are known.

49. *Proof of the Parallel Axis Theorem*

(a) Show that the first moment of a thin flat plate about any line in the plane of the plate through the plate's center of mass is zero. (*Hint*: Place the center of mass at the origin with the line along the y-axis. What does the formula $\bar{x} = M_y/M$ then tell you?)

(b) Use the result in part (a) to derive the Parallel Axis Theorem. Assume that the plane is coordinatized in a way that makes $L_{c.m.}$ the y-axis and L the line $x = h$. Then expand the integrand of the integral for I_L to rewrite the integral as the sum of integrals whose values you recognize.

50. *Finding moments of inertia*

(a) Use the Parallel Axis Theorem and the results of Example 4 to find the moments of inertia of the plate in Example 4 about the vertical and horizontal lines through the plate's center of mass.

(b) Use the results in part (a) to find the plate's moments of inertia about the lines $x = 1$ and $y = 2$.

Pappus's Formula

Pappus knew that the centroid of the union of two nonoverlapping plane regions lies on the line segment joining their individual centroids. More specifically, suppose that m_1 and m_2 are the masses of thin plates P_1 and P_2 that cover nonoverlapping regions in the xy-plane. Let $\mathbf{c}_1$ and $\mathbf{c}_2$ be the vectors from the origin to the respective centers of mass of P_1 and P_2. Then the center of mass of the union $P_1 \cup P_2$ of the two plates is determined by the vector

$$\mathbf{c} = \frac{m_1 \mathbf{c}_1 + m_2 \mathbf{c}_2}{m_1 + m_2}. \tag{9}$$

Equation (9) is known as **Pappus's formula**. For more than two nonoverlapping plates, as long as their number is finite, the formula generalizes to

$$\mathbf{c} = \frac{m_1 \mathbf{c}_1 + m_2 \mathbf{c}_2 + \cdots + m_n \mathbf{c}_n}{m_1 + m_2 + \cdots + m_n}. \tag{10}$$

This formula is especially useful for finding the centroid of a plate of irregular shape that is made up of pieces of constant density whose centroids we know from geometry. We find the centroid of each piece and apply Equation (10) to find the centroid of the plate.

51. Derive Pappus's formula (Equation (9)). (*Hint*: Sketch the plates as regions in the first quadrant and label their centers of mass as $(\bar{x}_1, \bar{y}_1)$ and $(\bar{x}_2, \bar{y}_2)$. What are the moments of $P_1 \cup P_2$ about the coordinate axes?)

52. Use Equation (9) and mathematical induction to show that Equation (10) holds for any positive integer $n > 2$.

53. Let A, B, and C be the shapes indicated in Figure 12.24a. Use Pappus's formula to find the centroid of

(a) $A \cup B$ (b) $A \cup C$

(c) $B \cup C$ (d) $A \cup B \cup C$.

54. *Locating center of mass* Locate the center of mass of the carpenter's square in Figure 12.24b.

55. An isosceles triangle T has base $2a$ and altitude h. The base lies along the diameter of a semicircular disk D of radius a so that the two together make a shape resembling an ice cream cone. What relation must hold between a and h to place the centroid of $T \cup D$ on the common boundary of T and D? Inside T?

56. An isosceles triangle T of altitude h has as its base one side of a square Q whose edges have length s. (The square and triangle do not overlap.) What relation must hold between h and s to place the centroid of $T \cup Q$ on the base of the triangle? Compare your answer with the answer to Exercise 55.

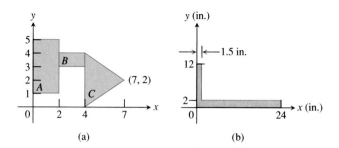

FIGURE 12.24 The figures for Exercises 53 and 54.

 Double Integrals in Polar Form

Integrals in Polar Coordinates   •   Finding Limits of Integration   •   Changing Cartesian Integrals into Polar Integrals

Integrals are sometimes easier to evaluate if we change to polar coordinates. This section shows how to accomplish the change and how to evaluate integrals over regions whose boundaries are given by polar equations.

Integrals in Polar Coordinates

When we defined the double integral of a function over a region R in the xy-plane, we began by cutting R into rectangles whose sides were parallel to the coordinate axes. These were the natural shapes to use because their sides have either constant x-values or constant y-values. In polar coordinates, the natural shape is a "polar rectangle" whose sides have constant r- and θ-values.

Suppose that a function $f(r, \theta)$ is defined over a region R that is bounded by the rays $\theta = \alpha$ and $\theta = \beta$ and by the continuous curves $r = g_1(\theta)$ and $r = g_2(\theta)$. Suppose also that $0 \leq g_1(\theta) \leq g_2(\theta) \leq a$ for every value of θ between α and β. Then R lies in a fan-shaped region Q defined by the inequalities $0 \leq r \leq a$ and $\alpha \leq \theta \leq \beta$. See Figure 12.25.

We cover Q by a grid of circular arcs and rays. The arcs are cut from circles centered at the origin, with radii Δr, $2\Delta r$, ..., $m\Delta r$, where $\Delta r = a/m$. The rays are given by

$$\theta = \alpha, \qquad \theta = \alpha + \Delta\theta, \qquad \theta = \alpha + 2\Delta\theta, \qquad \dots, \qquad \theta = \alpha + m'\Delta\theta = \beta,$$

where $\Delta\theta = (\beta - \alpha)/m'$. The arcs and rays partition Q into small patches called "polar rectangles."

We number the polar rectangles that lie inside R (the order does not matter), calling their areas ΔA_1, ΔA_2, ..., ΔA_n.

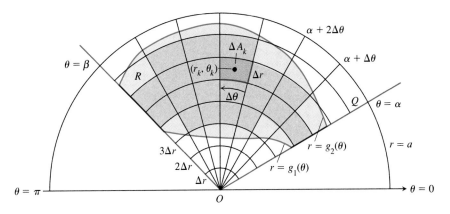

FIGURE 12.25 The region $R: g_1(\theta) \le r \le g_2(\theta)$, $\alpha \le \theta \le \beta$, is contained in the fan-shaped region $Q: 0 \le r \le a$, $\alpha \le \theta \le \beta$. The partition of Q by circular arcs and rays induces a partition of R.

We let (r_k, θ_k) be the center of the polar rectangle whose area is ΔA_k. By "center," we mean the point that lies halfway between the circular arcs on the ray that bisects the arcs. We then form the sum

$$S_n = \sum_{k=1}^{n} f(r_k, \theta_k) \, \Delta A_k. \tag{1}$$

If f is continuous throughout R, this sum will approach a limit as we refine the grid to make Δr and $\Delta \theta$ go to zero. The limit is called the double integral of f over R. In symbols,

$$\lim_{n \to \infty} S_n = \iint\limits_{R} f(r, \theta) \, dA.$$

To evaluate this limit, we first have to write the sum S_n in a way that expresses ΔA_k in terms of Δr and $\Delta \theta$. The radius of the inner arc bounding ΔA_k is $r_k - (\Delta r/2)$ (Figure 12.26). The radius of the outer arc is $r_k + (\Delta r/2)$. The areas of the circular sectors subtended by these arcs at the origin are

Inner radius: $\quad \dfrac{1}{2} \left(r_k - \dfrac{\Delta r}{2} \right)^2 \Delta \theta$

Outer radius: $\quad \dfrac{1}{2} \left(r_k + \dfrac{\Delta r}{2} \right)^2 \Delta \theta.$

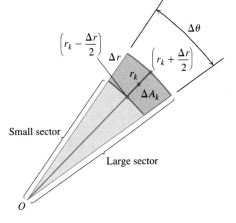

FIGURE 12.26 The observation that

$$\Delta A_k = \begin{pmatrix} \text{area of} \\ \text{large sector} \end{pmatrix} - \begin{pmatrix} \text{area of} \\ \text{small sector} \end{pmatrix}$$

leads to the formula $\Delta A_k = r_k \, \Delta r \, \Delta \theta$. The text explains why.

Therefore,

$\Delta A_k = $ area of large section $-$ area of small section

$$= \frac{\Delta \theta}{2} \left[\left(r_k + \frac{\Delta r}{2} \right)^2 - \left(r_k - \frac{\Delta r}{2} \right)^2 \right] = \frac{\Delta \theta}{2} \, (2r_k \, \Delta r) = r_k \, \Delta r \, \Delta \theta.$$

Combining this result with Equation (1) gives

$$S_n = \sum_{k=1}^{n} f(r_k, \theta_k) r_k \, \Delta r \, \Delta \theta.$$

A version of Fubini's theorem now says that the limit approached by these sums can be evaluated by repeated single integrations with respect to r and θ as

$$\iint\limits_{R} f(r, \theta)\, dA = \int_{\theta=\alpha}^{\theta=\beta} \int_{r=g_1(\theta)}^{r=g_2(\theta)} f(r, \theta)\, r\, dr\, d\theta. \qquad (2)$$

Finding Limits of Integration

The procedure for finding limits of integration in rectangular coordinates also works for polar coordinates.

How to Integrate in Polar Coordinates

To evaluate $\iint_R f(r, \theta)\, dA$ over a region R in polar coordinates, integrating first with respect to r and then with respect to θ, take the following steps.

Step 1: *A sketch.* Sketch the region and label the bounding curves.

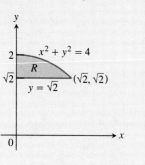

Step 2: *The r-limits of integration.* Imagine a ray L from the origin cutting through R in the direction of increasing r. Mark the r-values where L enters and leaves R. These are the r-limits of integration. They usually depend on the angle θ that L makes with the positive x-axis.

Step 3: *The θ-limits of integration.* Find the smallest and largest θ-values that bound R. These are the θ-limits of integration.

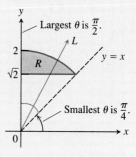

The integral is

$$\iint\limits_{R} f(r, \theta)\, dA = \int_{\theta=\pi/4}^{\theta=\pi/2} \int_{r=\sqrt{2}\csc\theta}^{r=2} f(r, \theta)\, r\, dr\, d\theta.$$

Example 1   Finding Limits of Integration

Find the limits of integration for integrating $f(r, \theta)$ over the region R that lies inside the cardioid $r = 1 + \cos\theta$ and outside the circle $r = 1$.

Solution

Step 1: *A sketch.* We sketch the region and label the bounding curves (Figure 12.27).

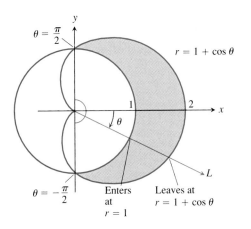

FIGURE 12.27 The sketch for Example 1.

Step 2: *The r-limits of integration.* A typical ray from the origin enters R where $r = 1$ and leaves where $r = 1 + \cos \theta$.

Step 3: *The θ-limits of integration.* The rays from the origin that intersect R run from $\theta = -\pi/2$ to $\theta = \pi/2$. The integral is

$$\int_{-\pi/2}^{\pi/2} \int_1^{1+\cos\theta} f(r, \theta) \, r \, dr \, d\theta.$$

If $f(r, \theta)$ is the constant function whose value is 1, then the integral f over R is the area of R.

Area in Polar Coordinates

The area of a closed and bounded region R in the polar coordinate plane is

$$A = \int \int_R r \, dr \, d\theta. \tag{3}$$

As you might expect, this formula for area is consistent with all earlier formulas, although we do not prove the fact.

Example 2 Finding Area in Polar Coordinates

Find the area enclosed by the lemniscate $r^2 = 4 \cos 2\theta$.

Solution We graph the lemniscate to determine the limits of integration (Figure 12.28) and see that the total area is 4 times the first-quadrant portion.

$$A = 4 \int_0^{\pi/4} \int_0^{\sqrt{4\cos 2\theta}} r \, dr \, d\theta = 4 \int_0^{\pi/4} \left[\frac{r^2}{2} \right]_{r=0}^{r=\sqrt{4\cos 2\theta}} d\theta$$

$$= 4 \int_0^{\pi/4} 2 \cos 2\theta \, d\theta = 4 \sin 2\theta \Big]_0^{\pi/4} = 4.$$

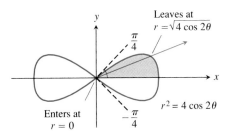

FIGURE 12.28 To integrate over the shaded region, we run r from 0 to $\sqrt{4 \cos 2\theta}$ and θ from 0 to $\pi/4$. (Example 2)

Changing Cartesian Integrals into Polar Integrals

The procedure for changing a Cartesian integral $\int \int_R f(x, y) \, dx \, dy$ into a polar integral has two steps.

Step 1: Substitute $x = r \cos \theta$ and $y = r \sin \theta$, and replace $dx \, dy$ by $r \, dr \, d\theta$ in the Cartesian integral.

Step 2: Supply polar limits of integration for the boundary of R.

The Cartesian integral then becomes

$$\int \int_R f(x, y) \, dx \, dy = \int \int_G f(r \cos \theta, r \sin \theta) r \, dr \, d\theta, \tag{4}$$

where G denotes the region of integration in polar coordinates. This is like the substitution method in Chapter 4 except that there are now two variables to substitute for instead of one. Notice that $dx\, dy$ is not replaced by $dr\, d\theta$ but by $r\, dr\, d\theta$.

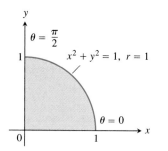

FIGURE 12.29 In polar coordinates, this region is described by simple inequalities:

$$0 \le r \le 1 \qquad \text{and} \qquad 0 \le \theta \le \pi/2.$$

(Example 3)

Example 3   Changing Cartesian Integrals to Polar

Find the polar moment of inertia about the origin of a thin plate of density $\delta(x, y) = 1$ bounded by the quarter circle $x^2 + y^2 = 1$ in the first quadrant.

Solution   We sketch the plate to determine the limits of integration (Figure 12.29).

In Cartesian coordinates, the polar moment is the value of the integral

$$\int_0^1 \int_0^{\sqrt{1-x^2}} (x^2 + y^2)\, dy\, dx.$$

Integration with respect to y gives

$$\int_0^1 \left(x^2\sqrt{1 - x^2} + \frac{(1 - x^2)^{3/2}}{3} \right) dx,$$

an integral difficult to evaluate without tables.

Things go better if we change the original integral to polar coordinates. Substituting $x = r \cos \theta$, $y = r \sin \theta$ and replacing $dx\, dy$ by $r\, dr\, \theta$, we get

$$\int_0^1 \int_0^{\sqrt{1-x^2}} (x^2 + y^2)\, dy\, dx = \int_0^{\pi/2} \int_0^1 (r^2)\, r\, dr\, d\theta$$

$$= \int_0^{\pi/2} \left[\frac{r^4}{4} \right]_{r=0}^{r=1} d\theta = \int_0^{\pi/2} \frac{1}{4}\, d\theta = \frac{\pi}{8}.$$

Why is the polar coordinate transformation so effective here? One reason is that $x^2 + y^2$ simplifies to r^2. Another is that the limits of integration become constants.

Example 4   Evaluating Integrals Using Polar Coordinates

Evaluate

$$\iint\limits_{R} e^{x^2+y^2}\, dy\, dx,$$

where R is the semicircular region bounded by the x-axis and the curve $y = \sqrt{1 - x^2}$ (Figure 12.30).

Solution   In Cartesian coordinates, the integral in question is a nonelementary integral and there is no direct way to integrate $e^{x^2+y^2}$ with respect to either x or y. Yet this integral and others like it are important in mathematics—in statistics, for example—and we need to find a way to evaluate it. Polar coordinates save

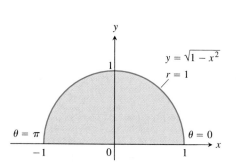

FIGURE 12.30 The semicircular region in Example 4 is the region

$$0 \le r \le 1, \qquad 0 \le \theta \le \pi.$$

the day. Substituting $x = r \cos \theta$, $y = r \sin \theta$ and replacing $dy\, dx$ by $r\, dr\, d\theta$ enables us to evaluate the integral as

$$\iint_R e^{x^2 + y^2}\, dy\, dx = \int_0^\pi \int_0^1 e^{r^2} r\, dr\, d\theta = \int_0^\pi \left[\frac{1}{2} e^{r^2} \right]_0^1 d\theta$$

$$= \int_0^\pi \frac{1}{2}(e - 1)\, d\theta = \frac{\pi}{2}(e - 1).$$

The r in the $r\, dr\, d\theta$ was just what we needed to integrate e^{r^2}. Without it, we would have been stuck, as we were at the beginning.

EXERCISES 12.3

Evaluating Polar Integrals

In Exercises 1–16, change the Cartesian integral into an equivalent polar integral. Then evaluate the polar integral.

1. $\int_{-1}^{1} \int_0^{\sqrt{1-x^2}} dy\, dx$

2. $\int_{-1}^{1} \int_{-\sqrt{1-x^2}}^{\sqrt{1-x^2}} dy\, dx$

3. $\int_0^1 \int_0^{\sqrt{1-y^2}} (x^2 + y^2)\, dx\, dy$

4. $\int_{-1}^{1} \int_{-\sqrt{1-y^2}}^{\sqrt{1-y^2}} (x^2 + y^2)\, dy\, dx$

5. $\int_{-a}^{a} \int_{-\sqrt{a^2-x^2}}^{\sqrt{a^2-x^2}} dy\, dx$

6. $\int_0^2 \int_0^{\sqrt{4-y^2}} (x^2 + y^2)\, dx\, dy$

7. $\int_0^6 \int_0^y x\, dx\, dy$

8. $\int_0^2 \int_0^x y\, dy\, dx$

9. $\int_{-1}^{0} \int_{-\sqrt{1-x^2}}^{0} \dfrac{2}{1 + \sqrt{x^2 + y^2}}\, dy\, dx$

10. $\int_{-1}^{1} \int_{-\sqrt{1-y^2}}^{0} \dfrac{4\sqrt{x^2 + y^2}}{1 + x^2 + y^2}\, dx\, dy$

11. $\int_0^{\ln 2} \int_0^{\sqrt{(\ln 2)^2 - y^2}} e^{\sqrt{x^2 + y^2}}\, dx\, dy$

12. $\int_0^1 \int_0^{\sqrt{1-x^2}} e^{-(x^2 + y^2)}\, dy\, dx$

13. $\int_0^2 \int_0^{\sqrt{1-(x-1)^2}} \dfrac{x + y}{x^2 + y^2}\, dy\, dx$

14. $\int_0^2 \int_{-\sqrt{1-(y-1)^2}}^{0} xy^2\, dx\, dy$

15. $\int_{-1}^{1} \int_{-\sqrt{1-y^2}}^{\sqrt{1-y^2}} \ln (x^2 + y^2 + 1)\, dx\, dy$

16. $\int_{-1}^{1} \int_{-\sqrt{1-x^2}}^{\sqrt{1-x^2}} \dfrac{2}{(1 + x^2 + y^2)^2}\, dy\, dx$

Finding Area in Polar Coordinates

17. Find the area of the region cut from the first quadrant by the curve $r = 2(2 - \sin 2\theta)^{1/2}$.

18. *Cardioid overlapping a circle* Find the area of the region that lies inside the cardioid $r = 1 + \cos \theta$ and outside the circle $r = 1$.

19. *One leaf of a rose* Find the area enclosed by one leaf of the rose $r = 12 \cos 3\theta$.

20. *Snail shell* Find the area of the region enclosed by the positive x-axis and spiral $r = 4\theta/3$, $0 \le \theta \le 2\pi$. The region looks like a snail shell.

21. *Cardioid in the first quadrant* Find the area of the region cut from the first quadrant by the cardioid $r = 1 + \sin \theta$.

22. *Overlapping cardioids* Find the area of the region common to the interiors of the cardioids $r = 1 + \cos \theta$ and $r = 1 - \cos \theta$.

Masses and Moments

23. *First moment of a plate* Find the first moment about the x-axis of a thin plate of constant density $\delta(x, y) = 3$, bounded below by the x-axis and above by the cardioid $r = 1 - \cos \theta$.

24. *Inertial and polar moments of a disk* Find the moment of inertia about the x-axis and the polar moment of inertia about the origin of a thin disk bounded by the circle $x^2 + y^2 = a^2$ if the disk's density at the point (x, y) is $\delta(x, y) = k(x^2 + y^2)$, k a constant.

25. *Mass of a plate* Find the mass of a thin plate covering the region outside the circle $r = 3$ and inside the circle $r = 6 \sin \theta$ if the plate's density function is $\delta(x, y) = 1/r$.

26. *Polar moment of a cardioid overlapping circle* Find the polar moment of inertia about the origin of a thin plate covering the region that lies inside the cardioid $r = 1 - \cos \theta$ and outside the circle $r = 1$ if the plate's density function is $\delta(x, y) = 1/r^2$.

27. *Centroid of a cardioid region* Find the centroid of the region enclosed by the cardioid $r = 1 + \cos \theta$.

28. *Polar moment of a cardioid region* Find the polar moment of inertia about the origin of a thin plate enclosed by the cardioid $r = 1 + \cos \theta$ if the plate's density function is $\delta(x, y) = 1$.

Average Values

29. *Average height of a hemisphere* Find the average height of the hemisphere $z = \sqrt{a^2 - x^2 - y^2}$ above the disk $x^2 + y^2 \le a^2$ in the xy-plane.

30. *Average height of a cone* Find the average height of the (single) cone $z = \sqrt{x^2 + y^2}$ above the disk $x^2 + y^2 \le a^2$ in the xy-plane.

31. *Average distance from interior of disk to center* Find the average distance from a point $P(x, y)$ in the disk $x^2 + y^2 \le a^2$ to the origin.

32. *Average distance squared from a point in a disk to a point in its boundary.* Find the average value of the *square* of the distance from the point $P(x, y)$ in the disk $x^2 + y^2 \le 1$ to the boundary point $A(1, 0)$.

Theory and Examples

33. *Converting to a polar integral* Integrate $f(x, y) = [\ln (x^2 + y^2)]/\sqrt{x^2 + y^2}$ over the region $1 \le x^2 + y^2 \le e$.

34. *Converting to a polar integral* Integrate $f(x, y) = [\ln (x^2 + y^2)]/(x^2 + y^2)$ over the region $1 \le x^2 + y^2 \le e^2$.

35. *Volume of noncircular right cylinder* The region that lies inside the cardioid $r = 1 + \cos \theta$ and outside the circle $r = 1$ is the base of a solid right cylinder. The top of the cylinder lies in the plane $z = x$. Find the cylinder's volume.

36. *Volume of noncircular right cylinder* The region enclosed by the lemniscate $r^2 = 2 \cos 2\theta$ is the base of a solid right cylinder whose top is bounded by the sphere $z = \sqrt{2 - r^2}$. Find the cylinder's volume.

37. *Converting to polar integrals*

(a) The usual way to evaluate the improper integral $I = \int_0^\infty e^{-x^2} dx$ is first to calculate its square:

$$I^2 = \left(\int_0^\infty e^{-x^2} dx \right)\left(\int_0^\infty e^{-y^2} dy \right) = \int_0^\infty \int_0^\infty e^{-(x^2+y^2)} dx\, dy.$$

Evaluate the last integral using polar coordinates and solve the resulting equation for I.

(b) Evaluate

$$\lim_{x \to \infty} \operatorname{erf}(x) = \lim_{x \to \infty} \int_0^x \frac{2e^{-t^2}}{\sqrt{\pi}} dt.$$

38. *Converting to a polar integral* Evaluate the integral

$$\int_0^\infty \int_0^\infty \frac{1}{(1 + x^2 + y^2)^2} dx\, dy.$$

39. *Writing to Learn* Integrate the function $f(x, y) = 1/(1 - x^2 - y^2)$ over the disk $x^2 + y^2 \le 3/4$. Does the integral of $f(x, y)$ over the disk $x^2 + y^2 \le 1$ exist? Give reasons for your answer.

40. *Area formula in polar coordinates* Use the double integral in polar coordinates to derive the formula

$$A = \int_\alpha^\beta \frac{1}{2} r^2\, d\theta$$

for the area of the fan-shaped region between the origin and polar curve $r = f(\theta), \alpha \le \theta \le \beta$.

41. *Average distance to a given point inside a disk* Let P_0 be a point inside a circle of radius a and let h denote the distance from P_0 to the center of the circle. Let d denote the distance from an arbitrary point P to P_0. Find the average value of d^2 over the region enclosed by the circle. (*Hint*: Simplify your work by placing the center of the circle at the origin and P_0 on the x-axis.)

42. *Area* Suppose that the area of a region in the polar coordinate plane is

$$A = \int_{\pi/4}^{3\pi/4} \int_{\csc \theta}^{2 \sin \theta} r\, dr\, d\theta.$$

Sketch the region and find its area.

COMPUTER EXPLORATIONS

Coordinate Conversions

In Exercises 43–46, use a CAS to change the Cartesian integrals into an equivalent polar integral and evaluate the polar integral. Perform the following steps in each exercise.

(a) Plot the Cartesian region of integration in the xy-plane.

(b) Change each boundary curve of the Cartesian region in part (a) to its polar representation by solving its Cartesian equation for r and θ.

(c) Using the results in part (b), plot the polar region of integration in the $r\theta$-plane.

(d) Change the integrand from Cartesian to polar coordinates. Determine the limits of integration from your plot in part (c) and evaluate the polar integral using the CAS integration utility.

43. $\displaystyle\int_0^1 \int_x^1 \frac{y}{x^2 + y^2} dy\, dx$

44. $\displaystyle\int_0^1 \int_0^{x/2} \frac{x}{x^2 + y^2} dy\, dx$

45. $\displaystyle\int_0^1 \int_{-y/3}^{y/3} \frac{y}{\sqrt{x^2 + y^2}} dx\, dy$

46. $\displaystyle\int_0^1 \int_y^{2-y} \sqrt{x + y}\, dx\, dy$

12.4 Triple Integrals in Rectangular Coordinates

Triple Integrals • Properties of Triple Integrals • Volume of a Region in Space • Finding Limits of Integration • Average Value of a Function in Space

We use triple integrals to find the volumes of three-dimensional shapes, the masses and moments of solids, and the average values of functions of three variables. In Chapter 13, we also see how these integrals arise in the studies of vector fields and fluid flow.

Triple Integrals

If $F(x, y, z)$ is a function defined on a closed bounded region D in space—the region occupied by a solid ball, for example, or a lump of clay—then the integral of F over D may be defined in the following way. We partition a rectangular region containing D into rectangular cells by planes parallel to the coordinate planes (Figure 12.31). We number the cells that lie inside D from 1 to n in some order, a typical cell having dimensions Δx_k by Δy_k by Δz_k and volume ΔV_k. We choose a point (x_k, y_k, z_k) in each cell and form the sum

$$S_n = \sum_{k=1}^{n} F(x_k, y_k, z_k) \, \Delta V_k. \tag{1}$$

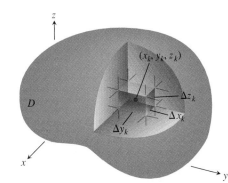

FIGURE 12.31 Partitioning a solid with rectangular cells of volume ΔV_k.

If F is continuous and the bounding surface of D is made of smooth surfaces joined along continuous curves, then as Δx_k, Δy_k, and Δz_k approach zero independently, the sums S_n approach a limit

$$\lim_{n \to \infty} S_n = \iiint_D F(x, y, z) \, dV. \tag{2}$$

We call this limit the **triple integral of F over D.** The limit also exists for some discontinuous functions.

Properties of Triple Integrals

Triple integrals have the same algebraic properties as double and single integrals.

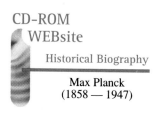

CD-ROM
WEBsite

Historical Biography

Max Planck
(1858 — 1947)

Properties of Triple Integrals
If $F = F(x, y, z)$ and $G = G(x, y, z)$ are continuous, then

1. *Constant Multiple:*
$$\iiint\limits_{D} kF\, dV = k \iiint\limits_{D} F\, dV \qquad \text{(any number } k\text{)}$$

2. *Sum and Difference:*
$$\iiint\limits_{D} (F \pm G)\, dV = \iiint\limits_{D} F\, dV \pm \iiint\limits_{D} G\, dV$$

3. *Domination:*

(a) $\iiint\limits_{D} F\, dV \geq 0 \qquad \text{if } F \geq 0 \text{ on } D$

(b) $\iiint\limits_{D} F\, dV \geq \iiint\limits_{D} G\, dV \qquad \text{if } F \geq G \text{ on } D$

4. *Additivity:*

$$\iiint\limits_{D} F\, dV = \iiint\limits_{D_1} F\, dV + \iiint\limits_{D_2} F\, dV + \cdots + \iiint\limits_{D_n} F\, dV$$

if D is the union of a finite number of nonoverlapping cells.

Volume of a Region in Space

If F is the constant function whose value is 1, then the sums in Equation (1) reduce to

$$S_n = \sum F(x_k, y_k, z_k)\, \Delta V_k = \sum 1 \cdot \Delta V_k = \sum \Delta V_k.$$

As Δx, Δy, and Δz approach zero, the cells ΔV_k become smaller and more numerous and fill up more and more of D. We therefore define the volume of D to be the triple integral

$$\lim_{n \to \infty} \sum_{k=1}^{n} \Delta V_k = \iiint\limits_{D} dV.$$

Definition   Volume
The **volume** of a closed, bounded region D in space is

$$V = \iiint\limits_{D} dV. \tag{3}$$

As we see in a moment, this integral enables us to calculate the volumes of solids enclosed by curved surfaces.

Finding Limits of Integration

We evaluate a triple integral by applying a three-dimensional version of Fubini's Theorem (Section 12.1) to evaluate it by three repeated single integrations. As with double integrals, there is a geometric procedure for finding the limits of integration for these single integrals.

How to Find Limits of Integration in Triple Integrals

To evaluate

$$\iiint_D F(x, y, z)\, dV$$

over a region D, integrating first with respect to z, then with respect to y, finally with x, take the following steps.

Step 1: *A sketch.* Sketch the region D along with its "shadow" R (vertical projection) in the xy-plane. Label the upper and lower bounding surfaces of D and the upper and lower bounding curves of R.

Step 2: *The z-limits of integration.* Draw a line M passing through a typical point (x, y) in R parallel to the z-axis. As z increases, M enters D at $z = f_1(x, y)$ and leaves at $z = f_2(x, y)$. These are the z-limits of integration.

Step 3: *The y-limits of integration.* Draw a line L through (x, y) parallel to the y-axis. As y increases, L enters R at $y = g_1(x)$ and leaves at $y = g_2(x)$. These are the y-limits of integration.

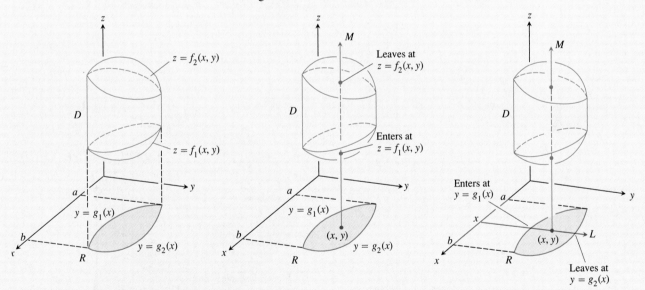

Step 4: *The x-limits of integration.* Choose x-limits that include all lines through R parallel to the y-axis ($x = a$ and $x = b$ in the preceding figure). These are the x-limits of integration. The integral is

$$\int_{x=a}^{x=b} \int_{y=g_1(x)}^{y=g_2(x)} \int_{z=f_1(x, y)}^{z=f_2(x, y)} F(x, y, z)\, dz\, dy\, dx.$$

Follow similar procedures if you change the order of integration. The "shadow" of region D lies in the plane of the last two variables with respect to which the iterated integration takes place.

Example 1   Finding a Volume

Find the volume of the region D enclosed by the surfaces $z = x^2 + 3y^2$ and $z = 8 - x^2 - y^2$.

Solution   The volume is

$$V = \iiint\limits_{D} dz \, dy \, dx,$$

the integral of $F(x, y, z) = 1$ over D. To find the limits of integration for evaluating the integral, we take these steps.

Step 1: *A sketch.* The surfaces (Figure 12.32) intersect on the elliptical cylinder $x^2 + 3y^2 = 8 - x^2 - y^2$ or $x^2 + 2y^2 = 4$. The boundary of the region R, the projection of D onto the xy-plane, is an ellipse with the same equation: $x^2 + 2y^2 = 4$. The "upper" boundary of R is the curve $y = \sqrt{(4 - x^2)/2}$. The lower boundary is the curve $y = -\sqrt{(4 - x^2)/2}$.

Step 2: *The z-limits of integration.* The line M passing through a typical point (x, y) in R parallel to the z-axis enters D at $z = x^2 + 3y^2$ and leaves at $z = 8 - x^2 - y^2$.

Step 3: *The y-limits of integration.* The line L through (x, y) parallel to the y-axis enters R at $y = -\sqrt{(4 - x^2)/2}$ and leaves at $y = \sqrt{(4 - x^2)/2}$.

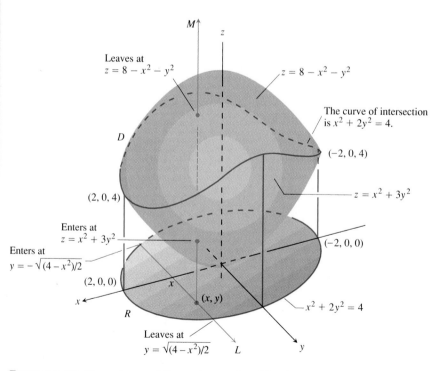

FIGURE 12.32 The volume of the region enclosed by these two paraboloids is calculated in Example 1.

Step 4: *The x-limits of integration.* As L sweeps across R, the value of x varies from $x = -2$ at $(-2, 0, 0)$ to $x = 2$ at $(2, 0, 0)$. The volume of D is

$$V = \iiint_D dz\,dy\,dx$$

$$= \int_{-2}^{2} \int_{-\sqrt{(4-x^2)/2}}^{\sqrt{(4-x^2)/2}} \int_{x^2+3y^2}^{8-x^2-y^2} dz\,dy\,dx$$

$$= \int_{-2}^{2} \int_{-\sqrt{(4-x^2)/2}}^{\sqrt{(4-x^2)/2}} (8 - 2x^2 - 4y^2)\,dy\,dx$$

$$= \int_{-2}^{2} \left[(8 - 2x^2)y - \frac{4}{3}y^3 \right]_{y=-\sqrt{(4-x^2)/2}}^{y=\sqrt{(4-x^2)/2}} dx$$

$$= \int_{-2}^{2} \left(2(8 - 2x^2)\sqrt{\frac{4 - x^2}{2}} - \frac{8}{3}\left(\frac{4 - x^2}{2}\right)^{3/2} \right) dx$$

$$= \int_{-2}^{2} \left[8\left(\frac{4 - x^2}{2}\right)^{3/2} - \frac{8}{3}\left(\frac{4 - x^2}{2}\right)^{3/2} \right] dx = \frac{4\sqrt{2}}{3} \int_{-2}^{2} (4 - x^2)^{3/2}\,dx$$

$$= 8\pi\sqrt{2} \text{ units cubed.} \qquad \text{After integration with the substitution } x = 2\sin u$$

In the next example, we project D onto the xz-plane instead of the xy-plane so you can see how to use a different order of integration.

Example 2 Finding the Limits of Integration in the Order *dy dz dx*

Set up the limits of integration for evaluating the triple integral of a function $F(x, y, z)$ over the tetrahedron D with vertices $(0, 0, 0)$, $(1, 1, 0)$, $(0, 1, 0)$, and $(0, 1, 1)$.

Solution

Step 1: *A sketch.* We sketch D along with its "shadow" R in the xz-plane (Figure 12.33). The upper (right-hand) bounding surface of D lies in the plane $y = 1$. The lower (left-hand) bounding surface lies in the plane $y = x + z$. The upper boundary of R is the line $z = 1 - x$. The lower boundary is the line $z = 0$.

Step 2: *The y-limits of integration.* The line through a typical point (x, z) in R parallel to the y-axis enters D at $y = x + z$ and leaves at $y = 1$.

Step 3: *The z-limits of integration.* The line L through (x, z) parallel to the z-axis enters R at $z = 0$ and leaves at $z = 1 - x$.

Step 4: *The x-limits of integration.* As L sweeps across R, the value of x varies from $x = 0$ to $x = 1$. The integral is

$$\int_0^1 \int_0^{1-x} \int_{x+z}^1 F(x, y, z)\,dy\,dz\,dx.$$

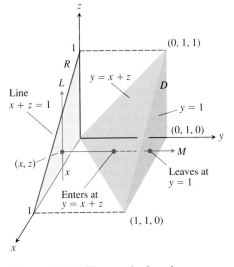

FIGURE 12.33 The tetrahedron in Example 2.

Example 3   Revisiting Example 2 Using the Order *dz dy dx*

To integrate $F(x, y, z)$ over the tetrahedron D in the order *dz dy dx*, we perform steps 2 through 4 in the following way.

Step 2: *The z-limits of integration.* A line parallel to the z-axis through a typical point (x, y) in the xy-plane "shadow" enters the tetrahedron at $z = 0$ and exits through the upper plane where $z = y - x$ (Figure 12.33).

Step 3: *The y-limits of integration.* A line through (x, y) parallel to the y-axis enters the shadow in the xy-plane at $y = x$ and exits at $y = 1$.

Step 4: *The x-limits of integration.* As the line parallel to the y-axis in step 3 sweeps out the shadow, the value of x varies from $x = 0$ to $x = 1$ at the point $(1, 1, 0)$. The integral is

$$\int_0^1 \int_x^1 \int_0^{y-x} F(x, y, z) \, dz \, dy \, dx.$$

For example, if $F(x, y, z) = 1$, we would find the volume of the tetrahedron to be

$$
\begin{aligned}
V &= \int_0^1 \int_x^1 \int_0^{y-x} dz \, dy \, dx \\
&= \int_0^1 \int_x^1 (y - x) \, dy \, dx \\
&= \int_0^1 \left[\frac{1}{2} y^2 - xy \right]_{y=x}^{y=1} dx \\
&= \int_0^1 \left(\frac{1}{2} - x + \frac{1}{2} x^2 \right) dx \\
&= \left[\frac{1}{2} x - \frac{1}{2} x^2 + \frac{1}{6} x^3 \right]_0^1 \\
&= \frac{1}{6} \text{ of a cubic unit.}
\end{aligned}
$$

You will get the same result by integrating

$$V = \int_0^1 \int_0^{1-x} \int_{x+z}^1 dy \, dz \, dx$$

from Example 2. Try it and see!

As we know, there are sometimes (but not always) two different orders in which the single integrations for evaluating a double integral may be worked. For triple integrals, there could be as many as *six*.

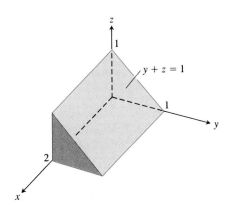

FIGURE 12.34 Example 4 gives six different iterated triple integrals for the volume of this prism.

Example 4   Using Different Orders of Integration

Each of the following integrals gives the volume of the solid shown in Figure 12.34.

(a) $\displaystyle\int_0^1\int_0^{1-z}\int_0^2 dx\,dy\,dz$ **(b)** $\displaystyle\int_0^1\int_0^{1-y}\int_0^2 dx\,dz\,dy$

(c) $\displaystyle\int_0^1\int_0^2\int_0^{1-z} dy\,dx\,dz$ **(d)** $\displaystyle\int_0^2\int_0^1\int_0^{1-z} dy\,dz\,dx$

(e) $\displaystyle\int_0^1\int_0^2\int_0^{1-y} dz\,dx\,dy$ **(f)** $\displaystyle\int_0^2\int_0^1\int_0^{1-y} dz\,dy\,dx$

Let's work out the integrals in parts (b) and (c):

$$V = \int_0^1\int_0^{1-y}\int_0^2 dx\,dz\,dy \qquad \text{Integral in part (b)}$$

$$= \int_0^1\int_0^{1-y} 2\,dz\,dy$$

$$= \int_0^1 \Big[2z\Big]_{z=0}^{z=1-y} dy$$

$$= \int_0^1 2(1-y)\,dy$$

$$= 1 \text{ cubic unit.}$$

Also,

$$V = \int_0^1\int_0^2\int_0^{1-z} dy\,dx\,dz \qquad \text{Integral in part (c)}$$

$$= \int_0^1\int_0^2 (1-z)\,dx\,dz$$

$$= \int_0^1 \Big[x - zx\Big]_{x=0}^{x=2} dz$$

$$= \int_0^1 (2 - 2z)\,dz$$

$$= 1 \text{ cubic unit.}$$

Average Value of a Function in Space

The average value of a function F over a region D in space is defined by the formula

$$\textbf{Average value} \text{ of } F \text{ over } D = \frac{1}{\text{volume of } D}\iiint_D F\,dV. \qquad (4)$$

For example, if $F(x, y, z) = \sqrt{x^2 + y^2 + z^2}$, then the average value of F over D is the average distance of points in D from the origin. If $F(x, y, z)$ is the density of a solid that occupies a region D in space, then the average value of F over D is the average density of the solid in units of mass per unit volume.

Example 5   Finding an Average Value

Find the average value of $F(x, y, z) = xyz$ over the cube bounded by the coordinate planes and the planes $x = 2$, $y = 2$, and $z = 2$ in the first octant.

Solution   We sketch the cube with enough detail to show the limits of integration (Figure 12.35). We then use Equation (4) to calculate the average value of F over the cube.

The volume of the cube is $(2)(2)(2) = 8$. The value of the integral of F over the cube is

$$\int_0^2 \int_0^2 \int_0^2 xyz \, dx \, dy \, dz = \int_0^2 \int_0^2 \left[\frac{x^2}{2} yz \right]_{x=0}^{x=2} dy \, dz = \int_0^2 \int_0^2 2yz \, dy \, dz$$

$$= \int_0^2 \left[y^2 z \right]_{y=0}^{y=2} dz = \int_0^2 4z \, dz = \left[2z^2 \right]_0^2 = 8.$$

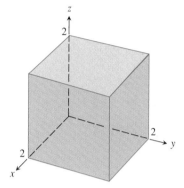

FIGURE 12.35 The region of integration in Example 5.

With these values, Equation (4) gives

$$\text{Average value of} \atop xyz \text{ over the cube} = \frac{1}{\text{volume}} \iiint_{\text{cube}} xyz \, dV = \left(\frac{1}{8} \right)(8) = 1.$$

In evaluating the integral, we chose the order $dx \, dy \, dz$, but any of the other five possible orders would have done as well.

EXERCISES 12.4

Evaluating Triple Integrals in Different Iterations

1. Evaluate the integral in Example 2 taking $F(x, y, z) = 1$ to find the volume of the tetrahedron.

2. *Volume of rectangular solid* Write six different iterated triple integrals for the volume of the rectangular solid in the first octant bounded by the coordinate planes and the planes $x = 1$, $y = 2$, and $z = 3$. Evaluate one of the integrals.

3. *Volume of tetrahedron* Write six different iterated triple integrals for the volume of the tetrahedron cut from the first octant by the plane $6x + 3y + 2z = 6$. Evaluate one of the integrals.

4. *Volume of solid* Write six different iterated triple integrals for the volume of the region in the first octant enclosed by the cylinder $x^2 + z^2 = 4$ and the plane $y = 3$. Evaluate one of the integrals.

5. *Volume enclosed by paraboloids* Let D be the region bounded by the paraboloids $z = 8 - x^2 - y^2$ and $z = x^2 + y^2$. Write six dif-

ferent triple iterated integrals for the volume of D. Evaluate one of the integrals.

6. *Volume inside paraboloid beneath a plane* Let D be the region bounded by the paraboloid $z = x^2 + y^2$ and the plane $z = 2y$. Write triple iterated integrals in the order $dz \, dx \, dy$ and $dz \, dy \, dx$ that give the volume of D. Do not evaluate either integral.

Evaluating Triple Iterated Integrals

Evaluate the integrals in Exercises 7–20.

7. $\int_0^1 \int_0^1 \int_0^1 (x^2 + y^2 + z^2) \, dz \, dy \, dx$

8. $\int_0^{\sqrt{2}} \int_0^{3y} \int_{x^2+3y^2}^{8-x^2-y^2} dz \, dx \, dy$

9. $\int_1^e \int_1^e \int_1^e \frac{1}{xyz} \, dx \, dy \, dz$

10. $\int_0^1 \int_0^{3-3x} \int_0^{3-3x-y} dz \, dy \, dx$

11. $\int_0^1 \int_0^\pi \int_0^\pi y \sin z \, dx \, dy \, dz$

12. $\int_{-1}^{1}\int_{-1}^{1}\int_{-1}^{1} (x + y + z)\, dy\, dx\, dz$

13. $\int_{0}^{3}\int_{0}^{\sqrt{9-x^2}}\int_{0}^{\sqrt{9-x^2}} dz\, dy\, dx$ **14.** $\int_{0}^{2}\int_{-\sqrt{4-y^2}}^{\sqrt{4-y^2}}\int_{0}^{2x+y} dz\, dx\, dy$

15. $\int_{0}^{1}\int_{0}^{2-x}\int_{0}^{2-x-y} dz\, dy\, dx$ **16.** $\int_{0}^{1}\int_{0}^{1-x^2}\int_{3}^{4-x^2-y} x\, dz\, dy\, dx$

17. $\int_{0}^{\pi}\int_{0}^{\pi}\int_{0}^{\pi} \cos(u + v + w)\, du\, dv\, dw$ (*uvw*-space)

18. $\int_{1}^{e}\int_{1}^{e}\int_{1}^{e} \ln r \ln s \ln t\, dt\, dr\, ds$ (*rst*-space)

19. $\int_{0}^{\pi/4}\int_{0}^{\ln \sec v}\int_{-\infty}^{2t} e^x\, dx\, dt\, dv$ (*tvx*-space)

20. $\int_{0}^{7}\int_{0}^{2}\int_{0}^{\sqrt{4-q^2}} \dfrac{q}{r+1}\, dp\, dq\, dr$ (*pqr*-space)

Volumes Using Triple Integrals

21. Here is the region of integration of the integral

$$\int_{-1}^{1}\int_{x^2}^{1}\int_{0}^{1-y} dz\, dy\, dx.$$

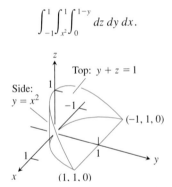

Rewrite the integral as an equivalent iterated integral in the order

(a) *dy dz dx*   **(b)** *dy dx dz*

(c) *dx dy dz*   **(d)** *dx dz dy*

(e) *dz dx dy*.

22. Here is the region of integration of the integral

$$\int_{0}^{1}\int_{-1}^{0}\int_{0}^{y^2} dz\, dy\, dx.$$

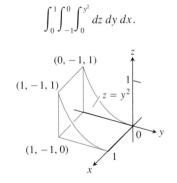

Rewrite the integral as an equivalent iterated integral in the order

(a) *dy dz dx*   **(b)** *dy dx dz*

(c) *dx dy dz*   **(d)** *dx dz dy*

(e) *dz dx dy*.

Find the volumes of the regions in Exercises 23–36.

23. The region between the cylinder $z = y^2$ and the *xy*-plane that is bounded by the planes $x = 0, x = 1, y = -1, y = 1$

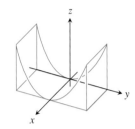

24. The region in the first octant bounded by the coordinate planes and the planes $x + z = 1, y + 2z = 2$

25. The region in the first octant bounded by the coordinate planes, the plane $y + z = 2$, and the cylinder $x = 4 - y^2$

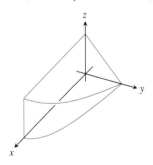

26. The wedge cut from the cylinder $x^2 + y^2 = 1$ by the planes $z = -y$ and $z = 0$

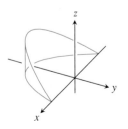

27. The tetrahedron in the first octant bounded by the coordinate planes and the plane $x + y/2 + z/3 = 1$

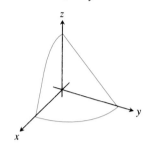

28. The region in the first octant bounded by the coordinate planes, the plane $y = 1 - x$, and the surface $z = \cos(\pi x/2), 0 \le x \le 1$

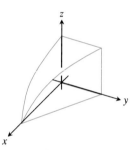

29. The region common to the interiors of the cylinders $x^2 + y^2 = 1$ and $x^2 + z^2 = 1$ (Figure 12.36)

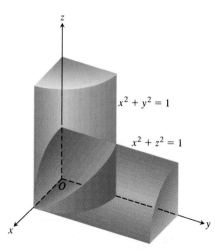

$x^2 + y^2 = 1$

$x^2 + z^2 = 1$

FIGURE 12.36 One-eighth of the region common to the cylinders $x^2 + y^2 = 1$ and $x^2 + z^2 = 1$ in Exercise 29.

30. The region in the first octant bounded by the coordinate planes and the surface $z = 4 - x^2 - y$

31. The region in the first octant bounded by the coordinate planes, the plane $x + y = 4$, and the cylinder $y^2 + 4z^2 = 16$

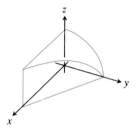

32. The region cut from the cylinder $x^2 + y^2 = 4$ by the plane $z = 0$ and the plane $x + z = 3$

33. The region between the planes $x + y + 2z = 2$ and $2x + 2y + z = 4$ in the first octant

34. The finite region bounded by the planes $z = x$, $x + z = 8$, $z = y$, $y = 8$, and $z = 0$.

35. The region cut from the solid elliptical cylinder $x^2 + 4y^2 \le 4$ by the xy-plane and the plane $z = x + 2$

36. The region bounded in back by the plane $x = 0$, on the front and sides by the parabolic cylinder $x = 1 - y^2$, on the top by the paraboloid $z = x^2 + y^2$, and on the bottom by the xy-plane

Average Values

In Exercises 37–40, find the average value of $F(x, y, z)$ over the given region.

37. $F(x, y, z) = x^2 + 9$ over the cube in the first octant bounded by the coordinate planes and the planes $x = 2$, $y = 2$, and $z = 2$

38. $F(x, y, z) = x + y - z$ over the rectangular solid in the first octant bounded by the coordinate planes and the planes $x = 1$, $y = 1$, and $z = 2$

39. $F(x, y, z) = x^2 + y^2 + z^2$ over the cube in the first octant bounded by the coordinate planes and the planes $x = 1$, $y = 1$, and $z = 1$

40. $F(x, y, z) = xyz$ over the cube in the first octant bounded by the coordinate planes and the planes $x = 2$, $y = 2$, and $z = 2$

Changing the Order of Integration

Evaluate the integrals in Exercises 41–44 by changing the order of integration in an appropriate way.

41. $\int_0^4 \int_0^1 \int_{2y}^2 \frac{4 \cos (x^2)}{2\sqrt{z}} \, dx \, dy \, dz$

42. $\int_0^1 \int_0^1 \int_{x^2}^1 12xze^{zy^2} \, dy \, dx \, dz$

43. $\int_0^1 \int_{\sqrt[3]{z}}^1 \int_0^{\ln 3} \frac{\pi e^{2x} \sin \pi y^2}{y^2} \, dx \, dy \, dz$

44. $\int_0^2 \int_0^{4-x^2} \int_0^x \frac{\sin 2z}{4 - z} \, dy \, dz \, dx$

Theory and Examples

45. *Finding upper limit of iterated integral* Solve for a:

$$\int_0^1 \int_0^{4-a-x^2} \int_a^{4-x^2-y} dz \, dy \, dx = \frac{4}{15}.$$

46. *Ellipsoid* For what value of c is the volume of the ellipsoid $x^2 + (y/2)^2 + (z/c)^2 = 1$ equal to 8π?

47. *Writing to Learn: Minimizing a triple integral* What domain D in space minimizes the value of the integral

$$\iiint_D (4x^2 + 4y^2 + z^2 - 4) \, dV?$$

Give reasons for your answer.

48. *Writing to Learn: Maximizing a triple integral* What domain D in space maximizes the value of the integral

$$\iiint_D (1 - x^2 - y^2 - z^2) \, dV?$$

Give reasons for your answer.

COMPUTER EXPLORATIONS

Numerical Evaluations

In Exercises 49–52, use a CAS integration utility to evaluate the triple integral of the given function over the specified solid region.

49. $F(x, y, z) = x^2 y^2 z$ over the solid cylinder bounded by $x^2 + y^2 = 1$ and the planes $z = 0$ and $z = 1$

50. $F(x, y, z) = |xyz|$ over the solid bounded below by the paraboloid $z = x^2 + y^2$ and above by the plane $z = 1$

51. $F(x, y, z) = \dfrac{z}{(x^2 + y^2 + z^2)^{3/2}}$ over the solid bounded below by the cone $z = \sqrt{x^2 + y^2}$ and above by the plane $z = 1$

52. $F(x, y, z) = x^4 + y^2 + z^2$ over the solid sphere $x^2 + y^2 + z^2 \le 1$

12.5 Masses and Moments in Three Dimensions

Masses and Moments

This section shows how to calculate the masses and moments of three-dimensional objects in Cartesian coordinates. The formulas are similar to those for two-dimensional objects. For calculations in spherical and cylindrical coordinates, see Section 12.6.

Masses and Moments

If $\delta(x, y, z)$ is the density of an object occupying a region D in space (mass per unit volume), the integral of δ over D gives the mass of the object. To see why,

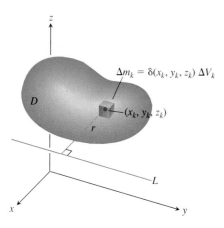

imagine partitioning the object into n mass elements like the one in Figure 12.37. The object's mass is the limit

$$M = \lim_{n \to \infty} \sum_{k=1}^{n} \Delta m_k = \lim_{n \to \infty} \sum_{k=1}^{n} \delta(x_k, y_k, z_k) \, \Delta V_k = \iiint_D \delta(x, y, z) \, dV.$$

To find the **first moments about the coordinate planes**, we use the signed distance from each plane. For example,

$$M_{yz} = \iiint_D x\delta(x, y, z) \, dV$$

gives the first moment about the yz-plane.

Extending the moments of inertia to triple integrals is similar. If $r(x, y, z)$ is the distance from the point (x, y, z) in D to a line L, then the moment of inertia of the mass $\Delta m_k = \delta(x_k, y_k, z_k) \, \Delta V_k$ about the line L (shown in Figure 12.37) is approximately $\Delta I_k = r^2(x_k, y_k, z_k) \, \Delta m_k$. **The moment of inertia about L of the entire object is**

$$I_L = \lim_{n \to \infty} \sum_{k=1}^{n} \Delta I_k = \lim_{n \to \infty} \sum_{k=1}^{n} r^2(x_k, y_k, z_k)\delta(x_k, y_k, z_k) \, \Delta V_k = \iiint_D r^2 \delta \, dV.$$

If L is the x-axis, then $r^2 = y^2 + z^2$ (Figure 12.38) and

$$I_x = \iiint_D (y^2 + z^2)\delta \, dV.$$

Similarly,

$$I_y = \iiint_D (x^2 + z^2)\,\delta\, dV \qquad \text{and} \qquad I_z = \iiint_D (x^2 + z^2)\,\delta\, dV.$$

The mass and moment formulas in space analogous to those discussed for planar regions in Section 12.2 are summarized in Table 12.3.

FIGURE 12.37 To define an object's mass and moment of inertia about a line, we first imagine it to be partitioned into a finite number of mass elements Δm_k.

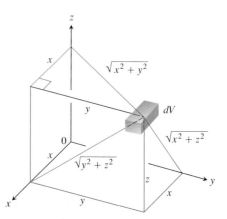

FIGURE 12.38 Distances from dV to the coordinate planes and axes.

Table 12.3 Mass and moment formulas for objects in space

Mass: $\quad M = \iiint_D \delta \, dV \qquad (\delta = \delta(x, y, z) = \text{density})$

First moments about the coordinate planes:

$$M_{yz} = \iiint_D x \, \delta \, dV, \qquad M_{xz} = \iiint_D y \, \delta \, dV, \qquad M_{xy} = \iiint_D z \, \delta \, dV$$

Center of mass:

$$\bar{x} = \frac{M_{yz}}{M}, \qquad \bar{y} = \frac{M_{xz}}{M}, \qquad \bar{z} = \frac{M_{xy}}{M}$$

Moments of inertia (second moments) about the coordinate axes:

$$I_x = \iiint (y^2 + z^2) \, \delta \, dV$$

$$I_y = \iiint (x^2 + z^2) \, \delta \, dV$$

$$I_z = \iiint (x^2 + y^2) \, \delta \, dV$$

Moments of inertia about a line L:

$$I_L = \iiint r^2 \delta \, dV \qquad (r(x, y, z) = \text{distance from the point } (x, y, z) \text{ to line } L)$$

Radius of gyration about a line L:

$$R_L = \sqrt{I_L/M}$$

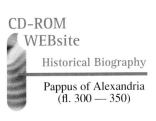

CD-ROM
WEBsite

Historical Biography

Pappus of Alexandria
(fl. 300 — 350)

Example 1   Finding the Center of Mass of a Solid in Space

Find the center of mass of a solid of constant density δ bounded below by the disk $R: x^2 + y^2 \leq 4$ in the plane $z = 0$ and above by the paraboloid $z = 4 - x^2 - y^2$ (Figure 12.39).

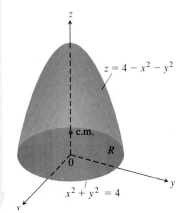

FIGURE 12.39 Example 1 finds the center of mass of this solid.

Solution   By symmetry, $\bar{x} = \bar{y} = 0$. To find $\bar{z}$, we first calculate

$$M_{xy} = \iiint_R \int_{z=0}^{z=4-x^2-y^2} z\,\delta\,dz\,dy\,dx = \iint_R \left[\frac{z^2}{2}\right]_{z=0}^{z=4-x^2-y^2} \delta\,dy\,dx$$

$$= \frac{\delta}{2}\iint_R (4 - x^2 - y^2)^2\,dy\,dx$$

$$= \frac{\delta}{2}\int_0^{2\pi}\int_0^2 (4 - r^2)^2 r\,dr\,d\theta \qquad \text{Polar coordinates}$$

$$= \frac{\delta}{2}\int_0^{2\pi}\left[-\frac{1}{6}(4-r^2)^3\right]_{r=0}^{r=2} d\theta = \frac{16\delta}{3}\int_0^{2\pi} d\theta = \frac{32\pi\delta}{3}.$$

A similar calculation gives

$$M = \iiint_R \int_0^{4-x^2-y^2} \delta\,dz\,dy\,dx = 8\pi\delta.$$

Therefore $\bar{z} = (M_{xy}/M) = 4/3$, and the center of mass is $(\bar{x}, \bar{y}, \bar{z}) = (0, 0, 4/3)$.

When the density of a solid object is constant (as in Example 1), the center of mass is called the **centroid** of the object (as was the case for two-dimensional shapes in Section 12.2).

Example 2   Finding the Moments of Inertia About the Coordinate Planes

Find I_x, I_y, I_z for the rectangular solid of constant density δ shown in Figure 12.40.

Solution   The formula for I_x gives

$$I_x = \int_{-c/2}^{c/2}\int_{-b/2}^{b/2}\int_{-a/2}^{a/2} (y^2 + z^2)\,\delta\,dx\,dy\,dz.$$

We can avoid some of the work of integration by observing that $(y^2 + z^2)\delta$ is an even function of x, y, and z and therefore

$$I_x = 8\int_0^{c/2}\int_0^{b/2}\int_0^{a/2} (y^2 + z^2)\,\delta\,dx\,dy\,dz = 4a\delta\int_0^{c/2}\int_0^{b/2} (y^2 + z^2)\,dy\,dz$$

$$= 4a\delta\int_0^{c/2}\left[\frac{y^3}{3} + z^2 y\right]_{y=0}^{y=b/2} dz$$

$$= 4a\delta\int_0^{c/2}\left(\frac{b^3}{24} + \frac{z^2 b}{2}\right) dz$$

$$= 4a\delta\left(\frac{b^3 c}{48} + \frac{c^3 b}{48}\right) = \frac{abc\delta}{12}(b^2 + c^2) = \frac{M}{12}(b^2 + c^2).$$

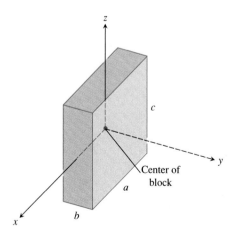

FIGURE 12.40 Example 2 calculates I_x, I_y, and I_z for the block shown here. The origin lies at the center of the block.

Similarly,

$$I_y = \frac{M}{12}(a^2 + c^2) \qquad \text{and} \qquad I_z = \frac{M}{12}(a^2 + b^2).$$

EXERCISES 12.5

Constant Density

The solids in Exercises 1–12 all have constant density $\delta = 1$.

1. *Example 1 Revisited* Evaluate the integral for I_x in Table 12.3 directly to show that the shortcut in Example 2 gives the same answer. Use the results in Example 2 to find the radius of gyration of the rectangular solid about each coordinate axis.

2. *Moments of inertia* The coordinate axes in the figure run through the centroid of a solid wedge parallel to the labeled edges. Find I_x, I_y, and I_z if $a = b = 6$ and $c = 4$.

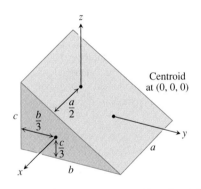

3. *Moments of inertia* Find the moments of inertia of the rectangular solid shown here with respect to its edges by calculating I_x, I_y, and I_z.

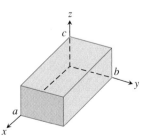

4. (a) *Centroid and moments of inertia* Find the centroid and the moments of inertia I_x, I_y, and I_z of the tetrahedron whose vertices are the points $(0, 0, 0)$, $(1, 0, 0)$, $(0, 1, 0)$, and $(0, 0, 1)$.

   (b) *Radius of gyration* Find the radius of gyration of the tetrahedron about the x-axis. Compare it with the distance from the centroid to the x-axis.

5. *Center of mass and moments of inertia* A solid "trough" of constant density is bounded below by the surface $z = 4y^2$, above by the plane $z = 4$, and on the ends by the planes $x = 1$ and $x = -1$. Find the center of mass and the moments of inertia with respect to the three axes.

6. *Center of mass* A solid of constant density is bounded below by the plane $z = 0$, on the sides by the elliptic cylinder $x^2 + 4y^2 = 4$, and above by the plane $z = 2 - x$ (see the figure).

   (a) Find $\bar{x}$ and $\bar{y}$.

   (b) Evaluate the integral

   $$M_{xy} = \int_{-2}^{2} \int_{-(1/2)\sqrt{4-x^2}}^{(1/2)\sqrt{4-x^2}} \int_{0}^{2-x} z \, dz \, dy \, dx$$

   using integral tables to carry out the final integration with respect to x. Then divide M_{xy} by M to verify that $\bar{z} = 5/4$.

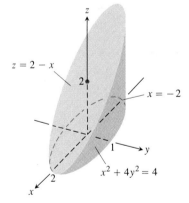

7. (a) *Center of mass* Find the center of mass of a solid of constant density bounded below by the paraboloid $z = x^2 + y^2$ and above by the plane $z = 4$.

   (b) Find the plane $z = c$ that divides the solid into two parts of equal volume. This plane does not pass through the center of mass.

8. *Moments and radii of gyration* A solid cube, 2 units on a side, is bounded by the planes $x = \pm 1$, $z = \pm 1$, $y = 3$, and $y = 5$. Find the center of mass and the moments of inertia and radii of gyration about the coordinate axes.

9. *Moment of inertia and radius of gyration about a line* A wedge like the one in Exercise 2 has $a = 4$, $b = 6$, and $c = 3$. Make a quick sketch to check for yourself that the square of the distance from a typical point (x, y, z) of the wedge to the line $L: z = 0, y = 6$ is $r^2 = (y - 6)^2 + z^2$. Then calculate the moment of inertia and radius of gyration of the wedge about L.

10. *Moment of inertia and radius of gyration about a line* A wedge like the one in Exercise 2 has $a = 4$, $b = 6$, and $c = 3$. Make a quick sketch to check for yourself that the square of the distance from a typical point (x, y, z) of the wedge to the line $L: x = 4, y = 0$ is $r^2 = (x - 4)^2 + y^2$. Then calculate the moment of inertia and radius of gyration of the wedge about L.

11. *Moment of inertia and radius of gyration about a line* A solid like the one in Exercise 3 has $a = 4$, $b = 2$, and $c = 1$. Make a quick sketch to check for yourself that the square of the distance between a typical point (x, y, z) of the solid and the line $L: y = 2, z = 0$ is $r^2 = (y - 2)^2 + z^2$. Then find the moment of inertia and radius of gyration of the solid about L.

12. *Moment of inertia of radius of gyration about a line* A solid like the one in Exercise 3 has $a = 4$, $b = 2$, and $c = 1$. Make a quick sketch to check for yourself that the square of the distance between a typical point (x, y, z) of the solid and the line $L: x = 4, y = 0$ is $r^2 = (x - 4)^2 + y^2$. Then find the moment of inertia and radius of gyration of the solid about L.

Variable Density

In Exercises 13 and 14, find

(a) The mass of the solid

(b) The center of mass.

13. A solid region in the first octant is bounded by the coordinate planes and the plane $x + y + z = 2$. The density of the solid is $\delta(x, y, z) = 2x$.

14. A solid in the first octant is bounded by the planes $y = 0$ and $z = 0$ and by the surfaces $z = 4 - x^2$ and $x = y^2$ (see the figure). Its density function is $\delta(x, y, z) = kxy$, k a constant.

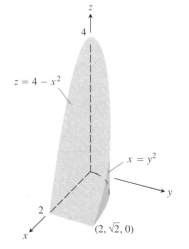

$z = 4 - x^2$

$x = y^2$

$(2, \sqrt{2}, 0)$

In Exercises 15 and 16, find

(a) The mass of the solid

(b) The center of mass

(c) The moments of inertia about the coordinate axes

(d) The radii of gyration about the coordinate axes.

15. A solid cube in the first octant is bounded by the coordinate planes and by the planes $x = 1$, $y = 1$, and $z = 1$. The density of the cube is $\delta(x, y, z) = x + y + z + 1$.

16. A wedge like the one in Exercise 2 has dimensions $a = 2$, $b = 6$, and $c = 3$. The density is $\delta(x, y, z) = x + 1$. Notice that if the density is constant, the center of mass will be $(0, 0, 0)$.

17. *Mass* Find the mass of the solid bounded by the planes $x + z = 1$, $x - z = -1$, $y = 0$ and the surface $y = \sqrt{z}$. The density of the solid is $\delta(x, y, z) = 2y + 5$.

18. *Mass* Find the mass of the solid region bounded by the parabolic surfaces $z = 16 - 2x^2 - 2y^2$ and $z = 2x^2 + 2y^2$ if the density of the solid is $\delta(x, y, z) = \sqrt{x^2 + y^2}$.

Work

In Exercises 19 and 20, calculate the following.

(a) The amount of work done by (constant) gravity g in moving the liquid filling in the container to the xy-plane. (*Hint*: Partition the liquid into small volume elements ΔV_i and find the work done (approximately) by gravity on each element. Summation and passage to the limit gives a triple integral to evaluate.)

(b) The work done by gravity in moving the center of mass down to the xy-plane.

19. The container is a cubical box in the first octant bounded by the coordinate planes and the planes $x = 1$, $y = 1$, and $z = 1$. The density of the liquid filling the box is $\delta(x, y, z) = x + y + z + 1$ (see Exercise 15).

20. The container is in the shape of the region bounded by $y = 0$, $z = 0$, $z = 4 - x^2$, and $x = y^2$. The density of the liquid filling the region is $\delta(x, y, z) = kxy$, k a constant. (see Exercise 14).

The Parallel Axis Theorem

The Parallel Axis Theorem (Exercises 12.2) holds in three dimensions as well as in two. Let $L_{c.m.}$ be a line through the center of mass of a body of mass m and let L be a parallel line h units away from $L_{c.m.}$. The **Parallel Axis Theorem** says that the moments of inertia $I_{c.m.}$ and I_L of the body about $L_{c.m.}$ and L satisfy the equation

$$I_L = I_{c.m.} + mh^2. \qquad (1)$$

As in the two-dimensional case, the theorem gives a quick way to calculate one moment when the other moment and the mass are known.

21. *Proof of the Parallel Axis Theorem*

(a) Show that the first moment of a body in space about any plane through the body's center of mass is zero. (*Hint:* Place the body's center of mass at the origin and let the plane be the yz-plane. What does the formula $\bar{x} = M_{yz}/M$ then tell you?)

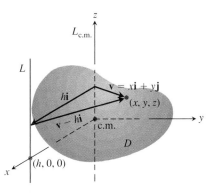

(b) To prove the Parallel Axis Theorem, place the body with its center of mass at the origin, with the line $L_{c.m.}$ along the z-axis and the line L perpendicular to the xy-plane at the point $(h, 0, 0)$. Let D be the region of space occupied by the body. Then, in the notation of the figure,

$$I_L = \iiint_D |\mathbf{v} - h\mathbf{i}|^2 \, dm.\qquad(2)$$

Expand the integrand in this integral and complete the proof.

22. The moment of inertia about a diameter of a solid sphere of constant density and radius a is $(2/5)ma^2$, where m is the mass of the sphere. Find the moment of inertia about a line tangent to the sphere.

23. The moment of inertia of the solid in Exercise 3 about the z-axis is $I_z = abc(a^2 + b^2)/3$.

(a) Use Equation (1) to find the moment of inertia and radius of gyration of the solid about the line parallel to the z-axis through the solid's center of mass.

(b) Use Equation (1) and the result in part (a) to find the moment of inertia and radius of gyration of the solid about the line $x = 0, y = 2b$.

24. If $a = b = 6$ and $c = 4$, the moment of inertia of the solid wedge in Exercise 2 about the x-axis is $I_x = 208$. Find the moment of inertia of the wedge about the line $y = 4, z = -4/3$ (the edge of the wedge's narrow end).

Pappus's Formula

Pappus's formula (Exercises 12.2) holds in three dimensions as well as in two. Suppose that bodies B_1 and B_2 of mass m_1 and m_2, respectively, occupy nonoverlapping regions in space and that $\mathbf{c}_1$ and $\mathbf{c}_2$ are the vectors from the origin to the bodies' respective centers of mass.

Then the center of mass of the union $B_1 \cup B_2$ of the two bodies is determined by the vector

$$\mathbf{c} = \frac{m_1\mathbf{c}_1 + m_2\mathbf{c}_2}{m_1 + m_2}.\qquad(3)$$

As before, this formula is called **Pappus's formula.** As in the two-dimensional case, the formula generalizes to

$$\mathbf{c} = \frac{m_1\mathbf{c}_1 + m_2\mathbf{c}_2 + \cdots + m_n\mathbf{c}_n}{m_1 + m_2 + \cdots + m_n}\qquad(4)$$

for n bodies.

25. Derive Pappus's formula (Equation 3). (*Hint:* Sketch B_1 and B_2 as nonoverlapping regions in the first octant and label their centers of mass $(\bar{x}_1, \bar{y}_1, \bar{z}_1)$ and $(\bar{x}_2, \bar{y}_2, \bar{z}_2)$. Express the moments of $B_1 \cup B_2$ about the coordinate planes in terms of the masses m_1 and m_2 and the coordinates of these centers.)

26. The accompanying figure shows a solid made from three rectangular solids of constant density $\delta = 1$. Use Pappus's formula to find the center of mass of

(a) $A \cup B$

(b) $A \cup C$

(c) $B \cup C$

(d) $A \cup B \cup C$.

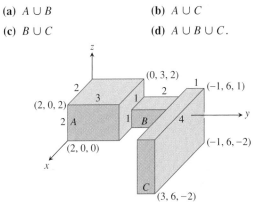

27. (a) Suppose that a solid right circular cone C of base radius a and altitude h is constructed on the circular base of a solid hemisphere S of radius a so that the union of the two solids resembles an ice cream cone. The centroid of a solid cone lies one-fourth of the way from the base toward the vertex. The centroid of a solid hemisphere lies three-eighths of the way from the base to the top. What relation must hold between h and a to place the centroid of $C \cup S$ in the common base of the two solids?

(b) If you have not already done so, answer the analogous question about a triangle and a semicircle (Section 12.2, Exercise 55). The answers are not the same.

28. A solid pyramid P with height h and four congruent sides is built with its base as one face of a solid cube C whose edges have length s. The centroid of a solid pyramid lies one-fourth of the way from the base toward the vertex. What relation must hold between h and s to place the centroid of $P \cup C$ in the base of the pyramid? Compare your answer with the answer to Exercise 27. Also compare it with the answer to Exercise 56 in Section 12.2.

12.6 Triple Integrals in Cylindrical and Spherical Coordinates

Integration in Cylindrical Coordinates • Spherical Coordinates •
Integration in Spherical Coordinates

When a calculation in physics, engineering, or geometry involves a cylinder, cone, or sphere, we can often simplify our work by using cylindrical or spherical coordinates.

Integration in Cylindrical Coordinates

We obtain cylindrical coordinates for space by combining polar coordinates in the xy-plane with the usual z-axis. This assigns to every point in space one or more coordinate triples of the form (r, θ, z), as shown in Figure 12.41.

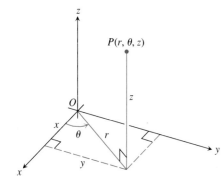

FIGURE 12.41 The cylindrical coordinates of a point in space are r, θ, and z.

> **Definition** Cylindrical Coordinates
> **Cylindrical coordinates** represent a point P in space by ordered triples (r, θ, z) in which
>
> **1.** r and θ are polar coordinates for the vertical projection of P on the xy-plane
>
> **2.** z is the rectangular vertical coordinate.

The values of $x, y, r,$ and θ in rectangular and cylindrical coordinates are related by the usual equations.

Equations Relating Rectangular (x, y, z) and Cylindrical (r, θ, z) Coordinates

$$x = r \cos \theta, \qquad y = r \sin \theta, \qquad z = z,$$
$$r^2 = x^2 + y^2, \qquad \tan \theta = y/x$$

In cylindrical coordinates, the equation $r = a$ describes not just a circle in the xy-plane but an entire cylinder about the z-axis (Figure 12.42). The z-axis is given by $r = 0$. The equation $\theta = \theta_0$ describes the plane that contains the z-axis and makes an angle θ_0 with the positive x-axis. And, just as in rectangular coordinates, the equation $z = z_0$ describes a plane perpendicular to the z-axis.

Cylindrical coordinates are good for describing cylinders whose axes run along the z-axis and planes that either contain the z-axis or lie perpendicular to the z-axis. Surfaces like these have equations of constant coordinate value:

$r = 4$ Cylinder, radius 4, axis the z-axis

$\theta = \dfrac{\pi}{3}$ Plane containing the z-axis

$z = 2.$ Plane perpendicular to the z-axis

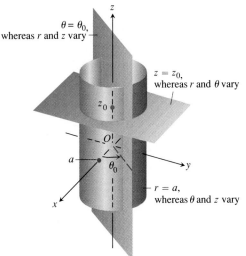

FIGURE 12.42 Constant-coordinate equations in cylindrical coordinates yield cylinders and planes.

The volume element for subdividing a region in space with cylindrical coordinates is

$$dV = dz \, r \, dr \, d\theta \tag{1}$$

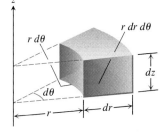

FIGURE 12.43 The volume element in cylindrical coordinates is $dV = dz \, r \, dr \, d\theta$.

(Figure 12.43). Triple integrals in cylindrical coordinates are then evaluated as iterated integrals, as in the following example.

Example 1   Finding Limits of Integration in Cylindrical Coordinates

Find the limits of integration in cylindrical coordinates for integrating a function $f(r, \theta, z)$ over the region D bounded below by the plane $z = 0$, laterally by the circular cylinder $x^2 + (y - 1)^2 = 1$, and above by the paraboloid $z = x^2 + y^2$.

Solution

Step 1: *A sketch* (Figure 12.44). The base of D is also the region's projection R on the xy-plane. The boundary of R is the circle $x^2 + (y - 1)^2 = 1$. Its polar coordinate equation is

$$
\begin{aligned}
x^2 + (y - 1)^2 &= 1 \\
x^2 + y^2 - 2y + 1 &= 1 \\
r^2 - 2r \sin \theta &= 0 \\
r &= 2 \sin \theta.
\end{aligned}
$$

Step 2: *The z-limits of integration.* A line M through a typical point (r, θ) in R parallel to the z-axis enters D at $z = 0$ and leaves at $z = x^2 + y^2 = r^2$.

Step 3: *The r-limits of integration.* A ray L through (r, θ) from the origin enters R at $r = 0$ and leaves at $r = 2 \sin \theta$.

Step 4: *The θ-limits of integration.* As L sweeps across R, the angle θ it makes with the positive x-axis runs from $\theta = 0$ to $\theta = \pi$. The integral is

$$\iiint\limits_{D} f(r, \theta, z) \, dV = \int_0^\pi \int_0^{2 \sin \theta} \int_0^{r^2} f(r, \theta, z) \, dz \, r \, dr \, d\theta.$$

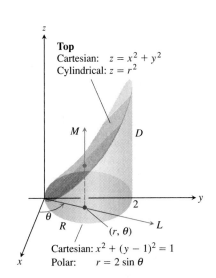

FIGURE 12.44 The figure for Example 1.

Example 1 illustrates a good procedure for finding limits of integration in cylindrical coordinates. The procedure is summarized in the following box.

How to Integrate in Cylindrical Coordinates

To evaluate

$$\iiint_D f(r, \theta, z) \, dV$$

over a region D in space in cylindrical coordinates, integrating first with respect to z, then with respect to r, and finally with respect to θ, take the following steps.

Step 1: *A sketch.* Sketch the region D along with its projection R on the xy-plane. Label the surfaces and curves that bound D and R.

Step 2: *The z-limits of integration.* Draw a line M through a typical point (r, θ) of R parallel to the z-axis. As z increases, M enters D at $z = g_1(r, \theta)$ and leaves at $z = g_2(r, \theta)$. These are the z-limits of integration.

Step 3: *The r-limits of integration.* Draw a ray L through (r, θ) from the origin. The ray enters R at $r = h_1(\theta)$ and leaves at $r = h_2(\theta)$. These are the r-limits of integration.

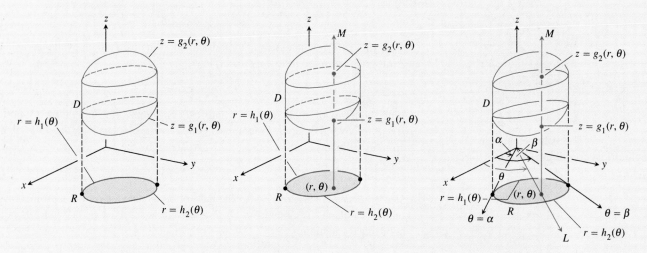

Step 4: *The θ-limits of integration.* As L sweeps across R, the angle θ it makes with the positive x-axis runs from $\theta = \alpha$ to $\theta = \beta$. These are the θ-limits of integration. The integral is

$$\iiint_D f(r, \theta, z) \, dV = \int_{\theta=\alpha}^{\theta=\beta} \int_{r=h_1(\theta)}^{r=h_2(\theta)} \int_{z=g_1(r,\theta)}^{z=g_2(r,\theta)} f(r, \theta, z) \, dz \, r \, dr \, d\theta.$$

Example 2   Finding a Centroid

Find the centroid $(\delta = 1)$ of the solid enclosed by the cylinder $x^2 + y^2 = 4$, bounded above by the paraboloid $z = x^2 + y^2$, and bounded below by the xy-plane.

Solution

Step 1: *A sketch.* We sketch the solid, bounded above by the paraboloid $z = r^2$ and below by the plane $z = 0$ (Figure 12.45). Its base R is the disk $|r| \le 2$ in the xy-plane.

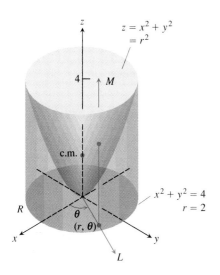

FIGURE 12.45 Example 2 shows how to find the centroid of this solid.

A few books give spherical coordinates in the order (ρ, θ, ϕ), with θ and ϕ reversed. In some cases, you may also find r being used for ρ. Watch out for this when you read elsewhere.

The solid's centroid $(\bar{x}, \bar{y}, \bar{z})$ lies on its axis of symmetry, here the z-axis. This makes $\bar{x} = \bar{y} = 0$. To find $\bar{z}$, we divide the first moment M_{xy} by the mass M.

To find the limits of integration for the mass and moment integrals, we continue with the four basic steps. We completed step 1 with our initial sketch. The remaining steps give the limits of integration.

Step 2: *The z-limits.* A line M through a typical point (r, θ) in the base parallel to the z-axis enters the solid at $z = 0$ and leaves at $z = r^2$.

Step 3: *The r-limits.* A ray L through (r, θ) from the origin enters R at $r = 0$ and leaves at $r = 2$.

Step 4: *The θ-limits.* As L sweeps over the base like a clock hand, the angle θ it makes with the positive x-axis runs from $\theta = 0$ to $\theta = 2\pi$. The value of M_{xy} is

$$M_{xy} = \int_0^{2\pi}\int_0^2\int_0^{r^2} z \, dz \, r \, dr \, d\theta = \int_0^{2\pi}\int_0^2 \left[\frac{z^2}{2}\right]_0^{r^2} r \, dr \, d\theta$$

$$= \int_0^{2\pi}\int_0^2 \frac{r^5}{2} \, dr \, d\theta = \int_0^{2\pi}\left[\frac{r^6}{12}\right]_0^2 d\theta = \int_0^{2\pi}\frac{16}{3} \, d\theta = \frac{32\pi}{3}.$$

The value of M is

$$M = \int_0^{2\pi}\int_0^2\int_0^{r^2} dz \, r \, dr \, d\theta = \int_0^{2\pi}\int_0^2 \Big[z\Big]_0^{r^2} r \, dr \, d\theta$$

$$= \int_0^{2\pi}\int_0^2 r^3 \, dr \, d\theta = \int_0^{2\pi}\left[\frac{r^4}{4}\right]_0^2 d\theta = \int_0^{2\pi} 4 \, d\theta = 8\pi.$$

Therefore,

$$\bar{z} = \frac{M_{xy}}{M} = \frac{32\pi}{3}\frac{1}{8\pi} = \frac{4}{3},$$

and the centroid is $(0, 0, 4/3)$. Notice that the centroid lies outside the solid.

Spherical Coordinates

Spherical coordinates locate points in space with angles and a distance, as shown in Figure 12.46.

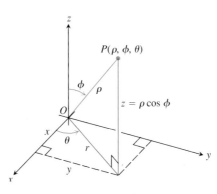

FIGURE 12.46 The spherical coordinates ρ, ϕ, and θ and their relation to x, y, z, and r.

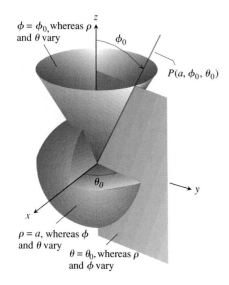

$\phi = \phi_0$, whereas ρ and θ vary

ϕ_0

$P(a, \phi_0, \theta_0)$

θ_0

$\rho = a$, whereas ϕ and θ vary

$\theta = \theta_0$, whereas ρ and ϕ vary

FIGURE 12.47 Constant-coordinate equations in spherical coordinates yield spheres, single cones, and half-planes.

The first coordinate, $\rho = |\overrightarrow{OP}|$, is the point's distance from the origin. Unlike r, *the variable ρ is never negative.* The second coordinate, ϕ, is the angle $\overrightarrow{OP}$ makes with the positive z-axis. It is required to lie in the interval $[0, \pi]$. The third coordinate is the angle θ as measured in cylindrical coordinates.

Definition Spherical Coordinates

Spherical coordinates represent a point P in space by ordered triples (ρ, ϕ, θ) in which

1. ρ is the distance from P to the origin

2. ϕ is the angle $\overrightarrow{OP}$ makes with the positive z-axis $(0 \le \phi \le \pi)$

3. θ is the angle from cylindrical coordinates.

The equation $\rho = a$ describes the sphere of radius a centered at the origin (Figure 12.47). The equation $\phi = \phi_0$ describes a single cone whose vertex lies at the origin and whose axis lies along the z-axis. (We broaden our interpretation to include the xy-plane as the cone $\phi = \pi/2$.) If ϕ_0 is greater than $\pi/2$, the cone $\phi = \phi_0$ opens downward. The equation $\theta = \theta_0$ describes the half-plane that contains the z-axis and makes an angle θ_0 with the positive x-axis.

Equations Relating Spherical Coordinates to Cartesian and Cylindrical Coordinates

$$r = \rho \sin \phi, \qquad x = r \cos \theta = \rho \sin \phi \cos \theta,$$
$$z = \rho \cos \phi, \qquad y = r \sin \theta = \rho \sin \phi \sin \theta, \tag{3}$$
$$\rho = \sqrt{x^2 + y^2 + z^2} = \sqrt{r^2 + z^2}.$$

Example 3 Converting Cartesian to Spherical

Find a spherical coordinate equation for the sphere $x^2 + y^2 + (z - 1)^2 = 1$.

Solution We use Equations (3) to substitute for x, y, and z:

$$x^2 + y^2 + (z - 1)^2 = 1$$
$$\rho^2 \sin^2 \phi \, \cos^2 \theta + \rho^2 \sin^2 \phi \, \sin^2 \theta + (\rho \cos \phi - 1)^2 = 1 \qquad \text{Eqs. (3)}$$
$$\rho^2 \sin^2 \phi \underbrace{(\cos^2 \theta + \sin^2 \theta)}_{1} + \rho^2 \cos^2 \phi - 2\rho \cos \phi + 1 = 1$$

$$\rho^2 \underbrace{(\sin^2 \phi + \cos^2 \phi)}_{1} = 2\rho \cos \phi$$

$$\rho^2 = 2\rho \cos \phi$$
$$\rho = 2 \cos \phi.$$

See Figure 12.48.

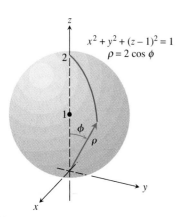

$x^2 + y^2 + (z - 1)^2 = 1$
$\rho = 2 \cos \phi$

ϕ

ρ

FIGURE 12.48 The sphere in Example 3.

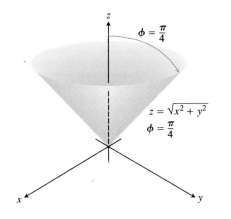

FIGURE 12.49 **The cone in Example 4.**

Example 4 Converting Cartesian to Spherical

Find a spherical coordinate equation for the cone $z = \sqrt{x^2 + y^2}$ (Figure 12.49).

Solution 1 *Use geometry.* The cone is symmetric with respect to the z-axis and cuts the first quadrant of the yz-plane along the line $z = y$. The angle between the cone and the positive z-axis is therefore $\pi/4$ radians. The cone consists of the points whose spherical coordinates have ϕ equal to $\pi/4$, so its equation is $\phi = \pi/4$.

Solution 2 *Use algebra.* If we use Equations (3) to substitute for x, y, and z we obtain the same result:

$$z = \sqrt{x^2 + y^2}$$
$$\rho \cos \phi = \sqrt{\rho^2 \sin^2 \phi} \qquad \text{Example 3}$$
$$\rho \cos \phi = \rho \sin \phi \qquad \rho \geq 0, \sin \phi \geq 0$$
$$\cos \phi = \sin \phi$$
$$\phi = \frac{\pi}{4}. \qquad 0 \leq \phi \leq \pi$$

Integration in Spherical Coordinates

Spherical coordinates are good for describing spheres centered at the origin, half-planes hinged along the z-axis, and single-napped cones whose vertices lie at the origin and whose axes lie along the z-axis. Surfaces like these have equations of constant coordinate value:

$$\rho = 4 \qquad \text{Sphere, radius 4, center at origin}$$

$$\phi = \frac{\pi}{3} \qquad \begin{array}{l}\text{Cone opening up from the origin, making an} \\ \text{angle of } \pi/3 \text{ radians with the positive } z\text{-axis}\end{array}$$

$$\theta = \frac{\pi}{3}. \qquad \begin{array}{l}\text{Half-plane, hinged along the } z\text{-axis, making an} \\ \text{angle of } \pi/3 \text{ radians with the positive } x\text{-axis}\end{array}$$

The volume element in spherical coordinates is the volume of a **spherical wedge** defined by the differentials $d\rho$, $d\phi$, and $d\theta$ (Figure 12.50). The wedge is approx-

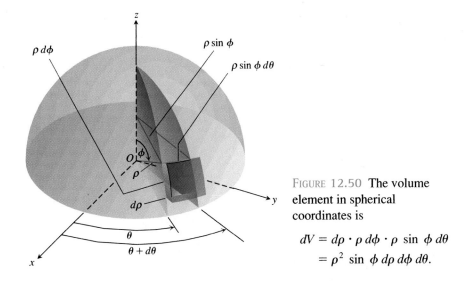

FIGURE 12.50 **The volume element in spherical coordinates is**

$$dV = d\rho \cdot \rho \, d\phi \cdot \rho \sin \phi \, d\theta$$
$$= \rho^2 \sin \phi \, d\rho \, d\phi \, d\theta.$$

imately a rectangular box with one side a circular arc of length $\rho\, d\phi$, another side a circular arc of length $\rho \sin \phi\, d\theta$, and thickness $d\rho$. Therefore, the volume element in spherical coordinates is

$$dV = \rho^2 \sin \phi\, d\rho\, d\phi\, d\theta, \tag{4}$$

and triple integrals take the form

$$\iiint F(\rho, \phi, \theta)\, dV = \iiint F(\rho, \phi, \theta)\rho^2 \sin \phi\, d\rho\, d\phi\, d\theta. \tag{5}$$

To evaluate these integrals, we usually integrate first with respect to ρ. The procedure for finding the limits of integration is shown in the following box. We restrict our attention to integrating over domains that are solids of revolution about the z-axis (or portions thereof) and for which the limits for θ and ϕ are constant.

How to Integrate in Spherical Coordinates

To evaluate

$$\iiint_D f(\rho, \phi, \theta)\, dV$$

over a region D in space in spherical coordinates, integrating first with respect to ρ, then with respect to ϕ, and finally with respect to θ, take the following steps.

Step 1: *A sketch.* Sketch the region D along with its projection R on the xy-plane. Label the surfaces that bound D.

Step 2: *The ρ-limits of integration.* Draw a ray M from the origin through D making an angle ϕ with the positive z-axis. Also draw the projection of M on the xy-plane (call the projection L). The ray L makes an angle θ with the positive x-axis. As ρ increases, M enters D at $\rho = g_1(\phi, \theta)$ and leaves at $\rho = g_2(\phi, \theta)$. These are the ρ-limits of integration.

Step 3: *The ϕ-limits of integration.* For any given θ, the angle ϕ that M makes with the z-axis runs from $\phi = \phi_{\min}$ to $\phi = \phi_{\max}$. These are the ϕ-limits of integration.

Step 4: *The θ-limits of integration.* The ray L sweeps over R as θ runs from α to β. These are the θ-limits of integration. The integral is

$$\iiint_D f(\rho, \phi, \theta)\, dV = \int_{\theta=\alpha}^{\theta=\beta} \int_{\phi=\phi_{\min}}^{\phi=\phi_{\max}} \int_{\rho=g_1(\phi,\theta)}^{\rho=g_2(\phi,\theta)} f(\rho, \phi, \theta)\rho^2 \sin \phi\, d\rho\, d\phi\, d\theta. \tag{6}$$

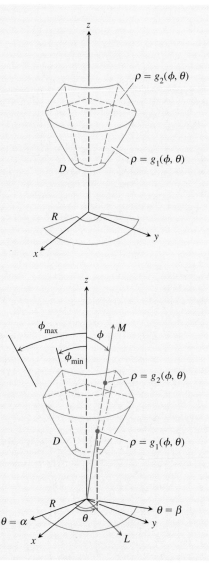

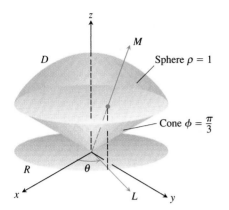

FIGURE 12.51 The ice cream cone in Example 5.

Example 5   Finding a Volume in Spherical Coordinates

Find the volume of the "ice cream cone" D cut from the solid sphere $\rho \leq 1$ by the cone $\phi = \pi/3$.

Solution   The volume is $V = \iiint_D \rho^2 \sin \phi \, d\rho \, d\phi \, d\theta$, the integral of $f(\rho, \phi, \theta) = 1$ over D.

To find the limits of integration for evaluating the integral, we take the following steps.

Step 1: *A sketch.* We sketch D and its projection R on the xy-plane (Figure 12.51).

Step 2: *The ρ-limits of integration.* We draw a ray M from the origin through D making an angle ϕ with the positive z-axis. We also draw L, the projection of M on the xy-plane, along with the angle θ that L makes with the positive x-axis. Ray M enters D at $\rho = 0$ and leaves at $\rho = 1$.

Step 3: *The ϕ-limits of integration.* The cone $\phi = \pi/3$ makes an angle of $\pi/3$ with the positive z-axis. For any given θ, the angle ϕ can run from $\phi = 0$ to $\phi = \pi/3$.

Step 4: *The θ-limits of integration.* The ray L sweeps over R as θ runs from 0 to 2π. The volume is

$$V = \iiint_D \rho^2 \sin \phi \, d\rho \, d\phi \, d\theta = \int_0^{2\pi} \int_0^{\pi/3} \int_0^1 \rho^2 \sin \phi \, d\rho \, d\phi \, d\theta$$

$$= \int_0^{2\pi} \int_0^{\pi/3} \left[\frac{\rho^3}{3} \right]_0^1 \sin \phi \, d\phi \, d\theta = \int_0^{2\pi} \int_0^{\pi/3} \frac{1}{3} \sin \phi \, d\phi \, d\theta$$

$$= \int_0^{2\pi} \left[-\frac{1}{3} \cos \phi \right]_0^{\pi/3} d\theta = \int_0^{2\pi} \left(-\frac{1}{6} + \frac{1}{3} \right) d\theta = \frac{1}{6}(2\pi) = \frac{\pi}{3}.$$

Example 6   Finding a Moment of Inertia

A solid of constant density $\delta = 1$ occupies the region D in Example 5. Find the solid's moment of inertia about the z-axis.

Solution   In rectangular coordinates, the moment is

$$I_z = \iiint (x^2 + y^2) \, dV.$$

In spherical coordinates, $x^2 + y^2 = (\rho \sin \phi \cos \theta)^2 + (\rho \sin \phi \sin \theta)^2 = \rho^2 \sin^2 \phi$. Hence,

$$I_z = \iiint (\rho^2 \sin^2 \phi)\rho^2 \sin \phi \, d\rho \, d\phi \, d\theta = \iiint \rho^4 \sin^3 \phi \, d\rho \, d\phi \, d\theta.$$

For the region in Example 5, this becomes

$$I_z = \int_0^{2\pi} \int_0^{\pi/3} \int_0^1 \rho^4 \sin^3 \phi \, d\rho \, d\phi \, d\theta = \int_0^{2\pi} \int_0^{\pi/3} \left[\frac{\rho^5}{5} \right]_0^1 \sin^3 \phi \, d\phi \, d\theta$$

$$= \frac{1}{5} \int_0^{2\pi} \int_0^{\pi/3} (1 - \cos^2 \phi) \sin \phi \, d\phi \, d\theta = \frac{1}{5} \int_0^{2\pi} \left[-\cos \phi + \frac{\cos^3 \phi}{3} \right]_0^{\pi/3} d\theta$$

$$= \frac{1}{5} \int_0^{2\pi} \left(-\frac{1}{2} + 1 + \frac{1}{24} - \frac{1}{3} \right) d\theta = \frac{1}{5} \int_0^{2\pi} \frac{5}{24} \, d\theta = \frac{1}{24} (2\pi) = \frac{\pi}{12}.$$

Coordinate Conversion Formulas

Cylindrical to Rectangular	Spherical to Rectangular	Spherical to Cylindrical
$x = r \cos \theta$	$x = \rho \sin \phi \cos \theta$	$r = \rho \sin \phi$
$y = r \sin \theta$	$y = \rho \sin \phi \sin \theta$	$z = \rho \cos \phi$
$z = z$	$z = \rho \cos \phi$	$\theta = \theta$

Corresponding volume elements

$$dV = dx \, dy \, dz$$
$$= dz \, r \, dr \, d\theta$$
$$= \rho^2 \sin \phi \, d\rho \, d\phi \, d\theta$$

EXERCISES 12.6

Evaluating Integrals in Cylindrical Coordinates

Evaluate the cylindrical coordinate integrals in Exercises 1–6.

1. $\displaystyle\int_0^{2\pi} \int_0^1 \int_r^{\sqrt{2-r^2}} dz \, r \, dr \, d\theta$

2. $\displaystyle\int_0^{2\pi} \int_0^3 \int_{r^2/3}^{\sqrt{18-r^2}} dz \, r \, dr \, d\theta$

3. $\displaystyle\int_0^{2\pi} \int_0^{\theta/2\pi} \int_0^{3+24r^2} dz \, r \, dr \, d\theta$

4. $\displaystyle\int_0^{\pi} \int_0^{\theta/\pi} \int_{-\sqrt{4-r^2}}^{3\sqrt{4-r^2}} z \, dz \, r \, dr \, d\theta$

5. $\displaystyle\int_0^{2\pi} \int_0^1 \int_r^{1/\sqrt{2-r^2}} 3 \, dz \, r \, dr \, d\theta$

6. $\displaystyle\int_0^{2\pi} \int_0^1 \int_{-1/2}^{1/2} (r^2 \sin^2 \theta + z^2) \, dz \, r \, dr \, d\theta$

Changing Order of Integration in Cylindrical Coordinates

The integrals we have seen so far suggest that there are preferred orders of integration for cylindrical coordinates, but other orders usually work well and are occasionally easier to evaluate. Evaluate the integrals in Exercises 7–10.

7. $\displaystyle\int_0^{2\pi} \int_0^3 \int_0^{z/3} r^3 \, dr \, dz \, d\theta$

8. $\displaystyle\int_{-1}^1 \int_0^{2\pi} \int_0^{1+\cos \theta} 4r \, dr \, d\theta \, dz$

9. $\displaystyle\int_0^1 \int_0^{\sqrt{z}} \int_0^{2\pi} (r^2 \cos^2 \theta + z^2) \, r \, d\theta \, dr \, dz$

10. $\displaystyle\int_0^2 \int_{r-2}^{\sqrt{4-r^2}} \int_0^{2\pi} (r \sin \theta + 1) \, r \, d\theta \, dz \, dr$

11. Let D be the region bounded below by the plane $z = 0$, above by the sphere $x^2 + y^2 + z^2 = 4$, and on the sides by the cylinder $x^2 + y^2 = 1$. Set up the triple integrals in cylindrical coordinates that give the volume of D using the following orders of integration.

(a) $dz\, dr\, d\theta$

(b) $dr\, dz\, d\theta$

(c) $d\theta\, dz\, dr$

12. Let D be the region bounded below by the cone $z = \sqrt{x^2 + y^2}$ and above by the paraboloid $z = 2 - x^2 - y^2$. Set up the triple integrals in cylindrical coordinates that give the volume of D using the following orders of integration.

(a) $dz\, dr\, d\theta$

(b) $dr\, dz\, d\theta$

(c) $d\theta\, dz\, dr$

13. Give the limits of integration for evaluating the integral

$$\int \int \int f(r, \theta, z)\, dz\, r\, dr\, d\theta$$

as an iterated integral over the region that is bounded below by the plane $z = 0$, on the side by the cylinder $r = \cos\theta$, and on top by the paraboloid $z = 3r^2$.

14. Convert the integral

$$\int_{-1}^{1} \int_{0}^{\sqrt{1-y^2}} \int_{0}^{x} (x^2 + y^2)\, dz\, dx\, dy$$

to an equivalent integral in cylindrical coordinates and evaluate the result.

Finding Iterated Integrals in Cylindrical Coordinates

In Exercises 15–20, set up the iterated integral for evaluating $\int\int\int_D f(r, \theta, z)\, dz\, r\, dr\, d\theta$ over the given region D.

15. D is the right circular cylinder whose base is the circle $r = 2\sin\theta$ in the xy-plane and whose top lies in the plane $z = 4 - y$.

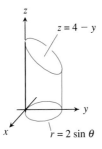

16. D is the right circular cylinder whose base is the circle $r = 3\cos\theta$ and whose top lies in the plane $z = 5 - x$.

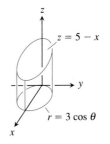

17. D is the solid right cylinder whose base is the region in the xy-plane that lies inside the cardioid $r = 1 + \cos\theta$ and outside the circle $r = 1$ and whose top lies in the plane $z = 4$.

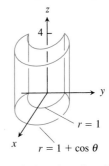

18. D is the solid right cylinder whose base is the region between the circles $r = \cos\theta$ and $r = 2\cos\theta$ and whose top lies in the plane $z = 3 - y$.

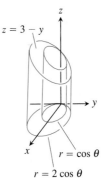

19. D is the prism whose base is the triangle in the xy-plane bounded by the x-axis and the lines $y = x$ and $x = 1$ and whose top lies in the plane $z = 2 - y$.

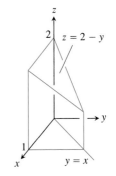

20. D is the prism whose base is the triangle in the xy-plane bounded by the y-axis and the lines $y = x$ and $y = 1$ and whose top lies in the plane $z = 2 - x$.

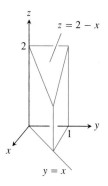

Evaluating Integrals in Spherical Coordinates

Evaluate the spherical coordinate integrals in Exercises 21–26.

21. $\displaystyle\int_0^\pi \int_0^\pi \int_0^{2\sin\phi} \rho^2 \sin\phi \, d\rho \, d\phi \, d\theta$

22. $\displaystyle\int_0^{2\pi} \int_0^{\pi/4} \int_0^2 (\rho\cos\phi)\rho^2 \sin\phi \, d\rho \, d\phi \, d\theta$

23. $\displaystyle\int_0^{2\pi} \int_0^\pi \int_0^{(1-\cos\phi)/2} \rho^2 \sin\phi \, d\rho \, d\phi \, d\theta$

24. $\displaystyle\int_0^{3\pi/2} \int_0^\pi \int_0^1 5\rho^3 \sin^3\phi \, d\rho \, d\phi \, d\theta$

25. $\displaystyle\int_0^{2\pi} \int_0^{\pi/3} \int_{\sec\phi}^2 3\rho^2 \sin\phi \, d\rho \, d\phi \, d\theta$

26. $\displaystyle\int_0^{2\pi} \int_0^{\pi/4} \int_0^{\sec\phi} (\rho\cos\phi)\rho^2 \sin\phi \, d\rho \, d\phi \, d\theta$

Changing Order of Integration in Spherical Coordinates

The previous integrals suggest there are preferred orders of integration for spherical coordinates, but other orders are possible and occasionally easier to evaluate. Evaluate the integrals in Exercises 27–30.

27. $\displaystyle\int_0^2 \int_{-\pi}^0 \int_{\pi/4}^{\pi/2} \rho^3 \sin 2\phi \, d\phi \, d\theta \, d\rho$

28. $\displaystyle\int_{\pi/6}^{\pi/3} \int_{\csc\phi}^{2\csc\phi} \int_0^{2\pi} \rho^2 \sin\phi \, d\theta \, d\rho \, d\phi$

29. $\displaystyle\int_0^1 \int_0^\pi \int_0^{\pi/4} 12\rho \sin^3\phi \, d\phi \, d\theta \, d\rho$

30. $\displaystyle\int_{\pi/6}^{\pi/2} \int_{-\pi/2}^{\pi/2} \int_{\csc\phi}^2 5\rho^4 \sin^3\phi \, d\rho \, d\theta \, d\phi$

31. Let D be the region in Exercise 11. Set up the triple integrals in spherical coordinates that give the volume of D using the following orders of integration.

(a) $d\rho \, d\phi \, d\theta$ \qquad\qquad (b) $d\phi \, d\rho \, d\theta$

32. Let D be the region bounded below by the cone $z = \sqrt{x^2 + y^2}$ and above by the plane $z = 1$. Set up the triple integrals in spherical coordinates that give the volume of D using the following orders of integration.

(a) $d\rho \, d\phi \, d\theta$ \qquad\qquad (b) $d\phi \, d\rho \, d\theta$

Finding Iterated Integrals in Spherical Coordinates

In Exercises 33–38, (a) find the spherical coordinate limits for the integral that calculates the volume of the given solid and (b) then evaluate the integral.

33. The solid between the sphere $\rho = \cos\phi$ and the hemisphere $\rho = 2, z \geq 0$

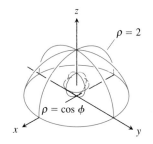

34. The solid bounded below by the hemisphere $\rho = 1, z \geq 0$, and above by the cardioid of revolution $\rho = 1 + \cos\phi$

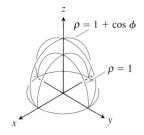

35. The solid enclosed by the cardioid of revolution $\rho = 1 - \cos\phi$

36. The upper portion cut from the solid in Exercise 35 by the xy-plane

37. The solid bounded below by the sphere $\rho = 2\cos\phi$ and above by the cone $z = \sqrt{x^2 + y^2}$

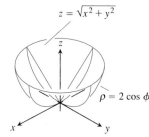

38. The solid bounded below by the *xy*-plane, on the sides by the sphere $\rho = 2$, and above by the cone $\phi = \pi/3$

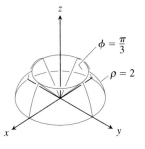

Rectangular, Cylindrical, and Spherical Coordinates

39. Set up triple integrals for the volume of the sphere $\rho = 2$ in (a) spherical, (b) cylindrical, and (c) rectangular coordinates.

40. Let *D* be the region in the first octant that is bounded below by the cone $\phi = \pi/4$ and above by the sphere $\rho = 3$. Express the volume of *D* as an iterated triple integral in (a) cylindrical and (b) spherical coordinates. Then (c) find *V*.

41. Let *D* be the smaller cap cut from a solid ball of radius 2 units by a plane 1 unit from the center of the sphere. Express the volume of *D* as an iterated triple integral in (a) spherical, (b) cylindrical, and (c) rectangular coordinates. Then (d) find the volume by evaluating one of the three triple integrals.

42. Express the moment of inertia I_z of the solid hemisphere $x^2 + y^2 + z^2 \le 1$, $z \ge 0$, as an iterated integral in (a) cylindrical and (b) spherical coordinates. Then (c) find I_z.

Volumes

Find the volumes of the solids in Exercises 43–48.

43.   **44.**

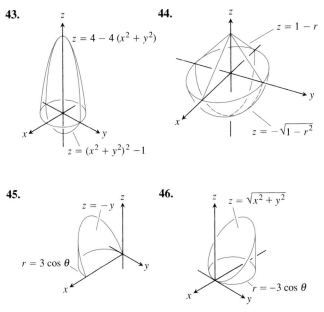

45.   **46.**

47.   **48.**

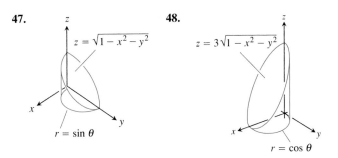

49. *Sphere and cones* Find the volume of the portion of the solid sphere $\rho \le a$ that lies between the cones $\phi = \pi/3$ and $\phi = 2\pi/3$.

50. *Sphere and half-planes* Find the volume of the region cut from the solid sphere $\rho \le a$ by the half-planes $\theta = 0$ and $\theta = \pi/6$ in the first octant.

51. *Sphere and plane* Find the volume of the smaller region cut from the solid sphere $\rho \le 2$ by the plane $z = 1$.

52. *Cone and planes* Find the volume of the solid enclosed by the cone $z = \sqrt{x^2 + y^2}$ between the planes $z = 1$ and $z = 2$.

53. *Cylinder and paraboloid* Find the volume of the region bounded below by the plane $z = 0$, laterally by the cylinder $x^2 + y^2 = 1$, and above by the paraboloid $z = x^2 + y^2$.

54. *Cylinder and paraboloids* Find the volume of the region bounded below by the paraboloid $z = x^2 + y^2$, laterally by the cylinder $x^2 + y^2 = 1$, and above by the paraboloid $z = x^2 + y^2 + 1$.

55. *Cylinder and cones* Find the volume of the solid cut from the thick-walled cylinder $1 \le x^2 + y^2 \le 2$ by the cones $z = \pm\sqrt{x^2 + y^2}$.

56. *Sphere and cylinder* Find the volume of the region that lies inside the sphere $x^2 + y^2 + z^2 = 2$ and outside the cylinder $x^2 + y^2 = 1$.

57. *Cylinder and planes* Find the volume of the region enclosed by the cylinder $x^2 + y^2 = 4$ and the planes $z = 0$ and $y + z = 4$.

58. *Cylinder and planes* Find the volume of the region enclosed by the cylinder $x^2 + y^2 = 4$ and the planes $z = 0$ and $x + y + z = 4$.

59. *Region trapped by paraboloids* Find the volume of the region bounded above by the paraboloid $z = 5 - x^2 - y^2$ and below by the paraboloid $z = 4x^2 + 4y^2$.

60. *Paraboloid and cylinder* Find the volume of the region bounded above by the paraboloid $z = 9 - x^2 - y^2$, below by the *xy*-plane, and lying *outside* the cylinder $x^2 + y^2 = 1$.

61. *Cylinder and sphere* Find the volume of the region cut from the solid cylinder $x^2 + y^2 \le 1$ by the sphere $x^2 + y^2 + z^2 = 4$.

62. *Sphere and paraboloid* Find the volume of the region bounded above by the sphere $x^2 + y^2 + z^2 = 2$ and below by the paraboloid $z = x^2 + y^2$.

Average Values

63. Find the average value of the function $f(r, \theta, z) = r$ over the region bounded by the cylinder $r = 1$ between the planes $z = -1$ and $z = 1$.

64. Find the average value of the function $f(r, \theta, z) = r$ over the solid ball bounded by the sphere $r^2 + z^2 = 1$. (This is the sphere $x^2 + y^2 + z^2 = 1$.)

65. Find the average value of the function $f(\rho, \phi, \theta) = \rho$ over the solid ball $\rho \le 1$.

66. Find the average value of the function $f(\rho, \phi, \theta) = \rho \cos \phi$ over the solid upper ball $\rho \le 1, 0 \le \phi \le \pi/2$.

Masses, Moments, and Centroids

67. *Center of mass* A solid of constant density is bounded below by the plane $z = 0$, above by the cone $z = r$, $r \ge 0$, and on the sides by the cylinder $r = 1$. Find the center of mass.

68. *Centroid* Find the centroid of the region in the first octant that is bounded above by the cone $z = \sqrt{x^2 + y^2}$, below by the plane $z = 0$, and on the sides by the cylinder $x^2 + y^2 = 4$ and the planes $x = 0$ and $y = 0$.

69. *Centroid* Find the centroid of the solid in Exercise 38.

70. *Centroid* Find the centroid of the solid bounded above by the sphere $\rho = a$ and below by the cone $\phi = \pi/4$.

71. *Centroid* Find the centroid of the region that is bounded above by the surface $z = \sqrt{r}$, on the sides by the cylinder $r = 4$, and below by the xy-plane.

72. *Centroid* Find the centroid of the region cut from the solid ball $r^2 + z^2 \le 1$ by the half-planes $\theta = -\pi/3, r \ge 0$, and $\theta = \pi/3$, $r \ge 0$.

73. *Inertia and radius of gyration* Find the moment of inertia and radius of gyration about the z-axis of a thick-walled right circular cylinder bounded on the inside by the cylinder $r = 1$, on the outside by the cylinder $r = 2$, and on the top and bottom by the planes $z = 4$ and $z = 0$. (Take $\delta = 1$.)

74. *Moments of inertia of solid circular cylinder* Find the moment of inertia of a solid circular cylinder of radius 1 and height 2 (a) about the axis of the cylinder and (b) about a line through the centroid perpendicular to the axis of the cylinder. (Take $\delta = 1$.)

75. *Moment of inertia of solid cone* Find the moment of inertia of a right circular cone of base radius 1 and height 1 about an axis through the vertex parallel to the base. (Take $\delta = 1$.)

76. *Moment of inertia of solid sphere* Find the moment of inertia of a solid sphere of radius a about a diameter. (Take $\delta = 1$.)

77. *Moment of inertia of solid cone* Find the moment of inertia of a right circular cone of base radius a and height h about its axis. (*Hint*: Place the cone with its vertex at the origin and its axis along the z-axis.)

78. *Variable density* A solid is bounded on the top by the paraboloid $z = r^2$, on the bottom by the plane $z = 0$, and on the sides by the cylinder $r = 1$. Find the center of mass and the moment of inertia and radius of gyration about the z-axis if the density is

 (a) $\delta(r, \theta, z) = z$

 (b) $\delta(r, \theta, z) = r$.

79. *Variable density* A solid is bounded below by the cone $z = \sqrt{x^2 + y^2}$ and above by the plane $z = 1$. Find the center of mass and the moment of inertia and radius of gyration about the z-axis if the density is

 (a) $\delta(r, \theta, z) = z$

 (b) $\delta(r, \theta, z) = z^2$.

80. *Variable density* A solid ball is bounded by the sphere $\rho = a$. Find the moment of inertia and radius of gyration about the z-axis if the density is

 (a) $\delta(\rho, \phi, \theta) = \rho^2$

 (b) $\delta(\rho, \phi, \theta) = r = \rho \sin \phi$.

81. *Centroid of solid semiellipsoid* Show that the centroid of the solid semiellipsoid of revolution $(r^2/a^2) + (z^2/h^2) \le 1, z \ge 0$, lies on the z-axis three-eighths of the way from the base to the top. The special case $h = a$ gives a solid hemisphere. Thus, the centroid of a solid hemisphere lies on the axis of symmetry three-eighths of the way from the base to the top.

82. *Centroid of solid cone* Show that the centroid of a solid right circular cone is one-fourth of the way from the base to the vertex. (In general, the centroid of a solid cone or pyramid is one-fourth of the way from the centroid of the base to the vertex.)

83. *Variable density* A solid right circular cylinder is bounded by the cylinder $r = a$ and the planes $z = 0$ and $z = h, h > 0$. Find the center of mass and the moment of inertia and radius of gyration about the z-axis if the density is $\delta(r, \theta, z) = z + 1$.

84. *Mass of planet's atmosphere* A spherical planet of radius R has an atmosphere whose density is $\mu = \mu_0 e^{-ch}$, where h is the altitude above the surface of the planet, μ_0 is the density at sea level, and c is a positive constant. Find the mass of the planet's atmosphere.

85. *Density at center of a planet* A planet is in the shape of a sphere of radius R and total mass M with spherically symmetric density distribution that increases linearly as one approaches its center. What is the density at the center of this planet if the density at its edge (surface) is taken to be zero?

Theory and Examples

86. *Vertical circular cylinders in spherical coordinates* Find an equation of the form $\rho = f(\theta)$ for the cylinder $x^2 + y^2 = a^2$.

87. *Vertical planes in cylindrical coordinates*

   (a) Show that planes perpendicular to the *x*-axis have equations of the form $r = a \sec \theta$ in cylindrical coordinates.

   (b) Show that planes perpendicular to the *y*-axis have equations of the form $r = b \csc \theta$.

88. *(Continuation of Exercise 87)* Find an equation of the form $r = f(\theta)$ in cylindrical coordinates for the plane $ax + by = c$, $c \neq 0$.

89. *Writing to Learn: Symmetry* What symmetry will you find in a surface that has an equation of the form $r = f(z)$ in cylindrical coordinates? Give reasons for your answer.

90. *Writing to Learn: Symmetry* What symmetry will you find in a surface that has an equation of the form $\rho = f(\phi)$ in spherical coordinates? Give reasons for your answer.

12.7 Substitutions in Multiple Integrals

Substitutions in Double Integrals • Substitutions in Triple Integrals

This section shows how to evaluate multiple integrals by substitution. As in single integration, the goal of substitution is to replace complicated integrals by ones that are easier to evaluate. Substitutions accomplish this by simplifying the integrand, the limits of integration, or both.

Substitutions in Double Integrals

The polar coordinate substitution of Section 12.3 is a special case of a more general substitution method for double integrals, a method that pictures changes in variables as transformations of regions.

Suppose that a region G in the uv-plane is transformed one-to-one into the region R in the xy-plane by equations of the form

$$x = g(u, v), \qquad y = h(u, v),$$

as suggested in Figure 12.52. We call R the **image** of G under the transformation, and G the **preimage** of R. Any function $f(x, y)$ defined on R can be thought of as a function $f(g(u, v), h(u, v))$ defined on G as well. How is the integral of $f(x, y)$ over R related to the integral of $f(g(u, v), h(u, v))$ over G?

The answer is: If g, h, and f have continuous partial derivatives and $J(u, v)$ (to be discussed in a moment) is zero only at isolated points, if at all, then

$$\iint_R f(x, y) \, dx \, dy = \iint_G f(g(u, v), h(u, v)) \, |J(u, v)| \, du \, dv. \tag{1}$$

Notice the "Reversed" Order

The transforming equations $x = g(u, v)$ and $y = h(u, v)$ go from G to R, but we use them to change an integral over R into an integral over G.

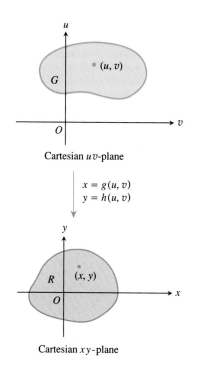

Cartesian uv-plane

$$x = g(u, v)$$
$$y = h(u, v)$$

Cartesian xy-plane

FIGURE 12.52 The equations $x = g(u, v)$ and $y = h(u, v)$ allow us to change an integral over a region R in the xy-plane into an integral over a region G in the uv-plane.

The factor $J(u, v)$, whose absolute value appears in Equation (1), is the *Jacobian* of the coordinate transformation, named after German mathematician Carl Jacobi.

Definition   Jacobian determinant or Jacobian

The **Jacobian determinant** or **Jacobian** of the coordinate transformation $x = g(u, v), y = h(u, v)$ is

$$J(u, v) = \begin{vmatrix} \dfrac{\partial x}{\partial u} & \dfrac{\partial x}{\partial v} \\[2mm] \dfrac{\partial y}{\partial u} & \dfrac{\partial y}{\partial v} \end{vmatrix} = \frac{\partial x}{\partial u}\frac{\partial y}{\partial v} - \frac{\partial y}{\partial u}\frac{\partial x}{\partial v}. \tag{2}$$

The Jacobian is also denoted by

$$J(u, v) = \frac{\partial(x, y)}{\partial(u, v)}$$

to help remember how the determinant in Equation (2) is constructed from the partial derivatives of x and y. The derivation of Equation (1) is intricate and properly belongs to a course in advanced calculus. We do not give the derivation here.

For polar coordinates, we have r and θ in place of u and v. With $x = r \cos \theta$ and $y = r \sin \theta$, the Jacobian is

$$J(r, \theta) = \begin{vmatrix} \dfrac{\partial x}{\partial r} & \dfrac{\partial x}{\partial \theta} \\[2mm] \dfrac{\partial y}{\partial r} & \dfrac{\partial y}{\partial \theta} \end{vmatrix} = \begin{vmatrix} \cos \theta & -r \sin \theta \\ \sin \theta & r \cos \theta \end{vmatrix} = r(\cos^2 \theta + \sin^2 \theta) = r.$$

Hence, Equation (1) becomes

$$\iint\limits_{R} f(x, y) \, dx \, dy = \iint\limits_{G} f(r \cos \theta, r \sin \theta) \, |r| \, dr \, d\theta$$

$$= \iint\limits_{G} f(r \cos \theta, r \sin \theta) \, r \, dr \, d\theta, \qquad \text{If } r \geq 0 \tag{3}$$

which is Equation (4) in Section 12.3.

Figure 12.53 shows how the equations $x = r \cos \theta$, $y = r \sin \theta$ transform the rectangle $G: 0 \leq r \leq 1, \ 0 \leq \theta \leq \pi/2$ into the quarter circle R bounded by $x^2 + y^2 = 1$ in the first quadrant of the xy-plane.

Notice that the integral on the right-hand side of Equation (3) is not the integral of $f(r \cos \theta, r \sin \theta)$ over a region in the polar coordinate plane. It is the integral of the product of $f(r \cos \theta, r \sin \theta)$ and r over a region G in the *Cartesian* $r\theta$-plane.

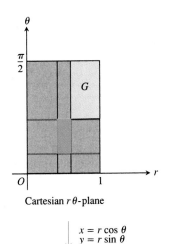

Cartesian $r\theta$-plane

$$x = r\cos\theta$$
$$y = r\sin\theta$$

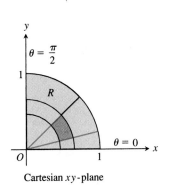

Cartesian xy-plane

FIGURE 12.53 The equations $x = r\cos\theta,\ y = r\sin\theta$ transform G into R.

Here is an example of another substitution.

Example 1   Applying a Transformation to Integrate

Evaluate

$$\int_0^4 \int_{x=y/2}^{x=(y/2)+1} \frac{2x-y}{2}\,dx\,dy$$

by applying the transformation

$$u = \frac{2x-y}{2}, \qquad v = \frac{y}{2} \tag{4}$$

and integrating over an appropriate region in the uv-plane.

Solution   We sketch the region R of integration in the xy-plane and identify its boundaries (Figure 12.54).

To apply Equation (1), we need to find the corresponding uv-region G and the Jacobian of the transformation. To find them, we first solve Equations (4) for x and y in terms of u and v. Routine algebra gives

$$x = u + v \qquad y = 2v. \tag{5}$$

We then find the boundaries of G by substituting these expressions into the equations for the boundaries of R (Figure 12.54).

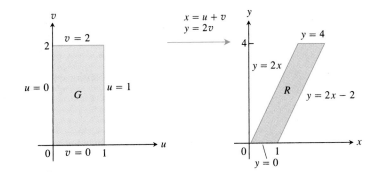

FIGURE 12.54 The equations $x = u + v$ and $y = 2v$ transform G into R. Reversing the transformation by the equations $u = (2x - y)/2$ and $v = y/2$ transforms R into G. See Example 1.

xy-equations for the boundary of R	Corresponding uv-equations for the boundary of G	Simplified uv-equations
$x = y/2$	$u + v = 2v/2 = v$	$u = 0$
$x = (y/2) + 1$	$u + v = (2v/2) + 1 = v + 1$	$u = 1$
$y = 0$	$2v = 0$	$v = 0$
$y = 4$	$2v = 4$	$v = 2$

The Jacobian of the transformation (again from Equations (5)) is

$$J(u, v) = \begin{vmatrix} \dfrac{\partial x}{\partial u} & \dfrac{\partial x}{\partial v} \\ \dfrac{\partial y}{\partial u} & \dfrac{\partial y}{\partial v} \end{vmatrix} = \begin{vmatrix} \dfrac{\partial}{\partial u}(u + v) & \dfrac{\partial}{\partial v}(u + v) \\ \dfrac{\partial}{\partial u}(2v) & \dfrac{\partial}{\partial v}(2v) \end{vmatrix} = \begin{vmatrix} 1 & 1 \\ 0 & 2 \end{vmatrix} = 2.$$

We now have everything we need to apply Equation (1):

$$\int_0^4 \int_{x=y/2}^{x=(y/2)+1} \frac{2x - y}{2}\, dx\, dy = \int_{v=0}^{v=2} \int_{u=0}^{u=1} u|J(u, v)|\, du\, dv$$

$$= \int_0^2 \int_0^1 (u)(2)\, du\, dv = \int_0^2 \left[u^2 \right]_0^1 dv = \int_0^2 dv = 2.$$

Example 2   Applying a Transformation to Integrate

Evaluate

$$\int_0^1 \int_0^{1-x} \sqrt{x + y}\,(y - 2x)^2\, dy\, dx.$$

Solution   We sketch the region R of integration in the xy-plane and identify its boundaries (Figure 12.55). The integrand suggests the transformation $u = x + y$ and $v = y - 2x$. Routine algebra produces x and y as functions of u and v:

$$x = \frac{u}{3} - \frac{v}{3}, \qquad y = \frac{2u}{3} + \frac{v}{3}. \tag{6}$$

From Equations (6), we can find the boundaries of the uv-region G (Figure 12.55).

xy-equations for the boundary of R	Corresponding uv-equations for the boundary of G	Simplified uv-equations
$x + y = 1$	$\left(\dfrac{u}{3} - \dfrac{v}{3}\right) + \left(\dfrac{2u}{3} + \dfrac{v}{3}\right) = 1$	$u = 1$
$x = 0$	$\dfrac{u}{3} - \dfrac{v}{3} = 0$	$v = u$
$y = 0$	$\dfrac{2u}{3} + \dfrac{v}{3} = 0$	$v = -2u$

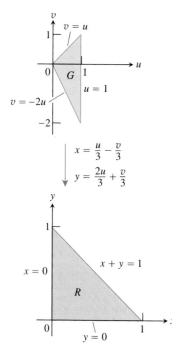

FIGURE 12.55 The equations $x = (u/3) - (v/3)$ and $y = (2u/3) + (v/3)$ transform G into R. Reversing the transformation by the equations $u = x + y$ and $v = y - 2x$ transforms R into G. See Example 2.

The Jacobian of the transformation in Equations (6) is

$$J(u, v) = \begin{vmatrix} \dfrac{\partial x}{\partial u} & \dfrac{\partial x}{\partial v} \\ \dfrac{\partial y}{\partial u} & \dfrac{\partial y}{\partial v} \end{vmatrix} = \begin{vmatrix} \dfrac{1}{3} & -\dfrac{1}{3} \\ \dfrac{2}{3} & \dfrac{1}{3} \end{vmatrix} = \frac{1}{3}.$$

Applying Equation (1), we evaluate the integral:

$$\int_0^1 \int_0^{1-x} \sqrt{x+y}\,(y-2x)^2\,dy\,dx = \int_{u=0}^{u=1} \int_{v=-2u}^{v=u} u^{1/2} v^2\,|J(u,v)|\,dv\,du$$

$$= \int_0^1 \int_{-2u}^{u} u^{1/2} v^2 \left(\frac{1}{3}\right) dv\,du = \frac{1}{3}\int_0^1 u^{1/2} \left[\frac{1}{3}\,v^3\right]_{v=-2u}^{v=u} du$$

$$= \frac{1}{9}\int_0^1 u^{1/2}\,(u^3 + 8u^3)\,du = \int_0^1 u^{7/2}\,du = \frac{2}{9}\,u^{9/2}\Big]_0^1 = \frac{2}{9}.$$

Substitutions in Triple Integrals

The cylindrical and spherical coordinate substitutions in Section 12.6 are special cases of a substitution method that pictures changes of variables in triple integrals as transformations of three-dimensional regions. The method is like the method for double integrals except that now we work in three dimensions instead of two.

Suppose that a region G in uvw-space is transformed one-to-one into the region D in xyz-space by differentiable equations of the form

$$x = g(u, v, w), \qquad y = h(u, v, w), \qquad z = k(u, v, w),$$

as suggested in Figure 12.56. Then any function $F(x, y, z)$ defined on D can be thought of as a function

$$F(g(u, v, w), h(u, v, w), k(u, v, w)) = H(u, v, w)$$

defined on G. If g, h, and k have continuous first partial derivatives, then the integral of $F(x, y, z)$ over D is related to the integral of $H(u, v, w)$ over G by the equation

$$\iiint_D F(x, y, z)\,dx\,dy\,dz = \iiint_G H(u, v, w)\,|J(u, v, w)|\,du\,dv\,dw. \tag{7}$$

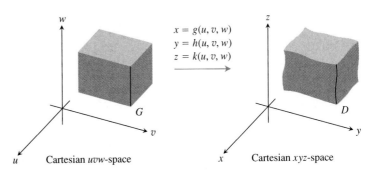

FIGURE 12.56 The equations $x = g(u, v, w)$, $y = h(u, v, w)$, and $z = k(u, v, w)$ allow us to change an integral over a region D in Cartesian xyz-space into an integral over a region G in Cartesian uvw-space.

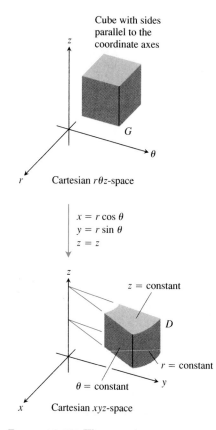

FIGURE 12.57 The equations $x = r \cos \theta$, $y = r \sin \theta$, and $z = z$ transform G into D.

The factor $J(u, v, w)$, whose absolute value appears in this equation, is the **Jacobian determinant**

$$J(u, v, w) = \begin{vmatrix} \dfrac{\partial x}{\partial u} & \dfrac{\partial x}{\partial v} & \dfrac{\partial x}{\partial w} \\[2mm] \dfrac{\partial y}{\partial u} & \dfrac{\partial y}{\partial v} & \dfrac{\partial y}{\partial w} \\[2mm] \dfrac{\partial z}{\partial u} & \dfrac{\partial z}{\partial v} & \dfrac{\partial z}{\partial w} \end{vmatrix} = \frac{\partial(x, y, z)}{\partial(u, v, w)}. \tag{8}$$

As in the two-dimensional case, the derivation of the change-of-variable formula in Equation (7) is complicated and we do not go into it here.

For cylindrical coordinates, r, θ, and z take the place of u, v, and w. The transformation from *Cartesian $r\theta z$-space* to Cartesian xyz-space is given by the equations

$$x = r \cos \theta, \qquad y = r \sin \theta, \qquad z = z$$

(Figure 12.57). The Jacobian of the transformation is

$$J(r, \theta, z) = \begin{vmatrix} \dfrac{\partial x}{\partial r} & \dfrac{\partial x}{\partial \theta} & \dfrac{\partial x}{\partial z} \\[2mm] \dfrac{\partial y}{\partial r} & \dfrac{\partial y}{\partial \theta} & \dfrac{\partial y}{\partial z} \\[2mm] \dfrac{\partial z}{\partial r} & \dfrac{\partial z}{\partial \theta} & \dfrac{\partial z}{\partial z} \end{vmatrix} = \begin{vmatrix} \cos \theta & -r \sin \theta & 0 \\ \sin \theta & r \cos \theta & 0 \\ 0 & 0 & 1 \end{vmatrix}$$

$$= r \cos^2 \theta + r \sin^2 \theta = r.$$

The corresponding version of Equation (7) is

$$\iiint_D F(x, y, z)\, dx\, dy\, dz = \iiint_G H(r, \theta, z)\, |r|\, dr\, d\theta\, dz. \tag{9}$$

We can drop the absolute value signs whenever $r \geq 0$.

For spherical coordinates, ρ, ϕ, and θ take the place of u, v, and w. The transformation from Cartesian $\rho\phi\theta$-space to Cartesian xyz-space is given by

$$x = \rho \sin \phi \cos \theta, \qquad y = \rho \sin \phi \sin \theta, \qquad z = \rho \cos \phi$$

(Figure 12.58). The Jacobian of the transformation is

$$J(\rho, \phi, \theta) = \begin{vmatrix} \dfrac{\partial x}{\partial \rho} & \dfrac{\partial x}{\partial \phi} & \dfrac{\partial x}{\partial \theta} \\[2mm] \dfrac{\partial y}{\partial \rho} & \dfrac{\partial y}{\partial \phi} & \dfrac{\partial y}{\partial \theta} \\[2mm] \dfrac{\partial z}{\partial \rho} & \dfrac{\partial z}{\partial \phi} & \dfrac{\partial z}{\partial \theta} \end{vmatrix} = \rho^2 \sin \phi \tag{10}$$

(Exercise 17). The corresponding version of Equation (7) is

$$\iiint_D F(x, y, z)\, dx\, dy\, dz = \iiint_G H(\rho, \phi, \theta)\, |\rho^2 \sin \phi|\, d\rho\, d\phi\, d\theta. \tag{11}$$

We can drop the absolute value signs because $\sin \phi$ is never negative.

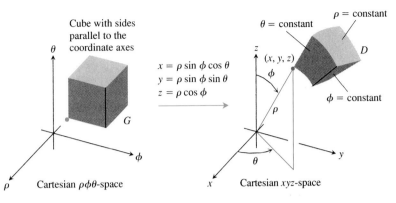

FIGURE 12.58 The equations $x = \rho \sin \phi \cos \theta$, $y = \rho \sin \phi \sin \theta$, and $z = \rho \cos \phi$ transform G into D.

Here is an example of another substitution. Although we could evaluate the integral in this example directly, we have chosen it to illustrate the substitution method in a simple (and fairly intuitive) setting.

Example 3   Applying a Transformation to Integrate

Evaluate

$$\int_0^3 \int_0^4 \int_{x=y/2}^{x=(y/2)+1} \left(\frac{2x - y}{2} + \frac{z}{3} \right) dx \, dy \, dz$$

by applying the transformation

$$u = (2x - y)/2, \qquad v = y/2, \qquad w = z/3 \qquad (12)$$

and integrating over an appropriate region in uvw-space.

Solution   We sketch the region D of integration in xyz-space and identify its boundaries (Figure 12.59). In this case, the bounding surfaces are planes.

To apply Equation (7), we need to find the corresponding uvw-region G and the Jacobian of the transformation. To find them, we first solve Equations (12) for x, y, and z in terms of u, v, and w. Routine algebra gives

$$x = u + v, \qquad y = 2v, \qquad z = 3w. \qquad (13)$$

We then find the boundaries of G by substituting these expressions into the equations for the boundaries of D:

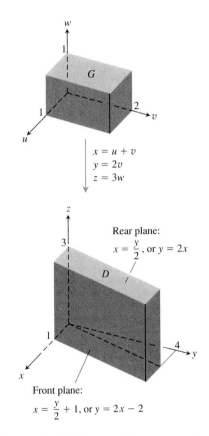

FIGURE 12.59 The equations $x = u + v$, $y = 2v$, and $z = 3w$ transform G into D. Reversing the transformation by the equations $u = (2x - y)/2$, $v = y/2$, and $w = z/3$ transforms D into G. See Example 3.

xyz-equations for the boundary of D	Corresponding uvw-equations for the boundary of G	Simplified uvw-equations
$x = y/2$	$u + v = 2v/2 = v$	$u = 0$
$x = (y/2) + 1$	$u + v = (2v/2) + 1 = v + 1$	$u = 1$
$y = 0$	$2v = 0$	$v = 0$
$y = 4$	$2v = 4$	$v = 2$
$z = 0$	$3w = 0$	$w = 0$
$z = 3$	$3w = 3$	$w = 1$

The Jacobian of the transformation, again from Equations (13), is

$$J(u, v, w) = \begin{vmatrix} \dfrac{\partial x}{\partial u} & \dfrac{\partial x}{\partial v} & \dfrac{\partial x}{\partial w} \\[6pt] \dfrac{\partial y}{\partial u} & \dfrac{\partial y}{\partial v} & \dfrac{\partial y}{\partial w} \\[6pt] \dfrac{\partial z}{\partial u} & \dfrac{\partial z}{\partial v} & \dfrac{\partial z}{\partial w} \end{vmatrix} = \begin{vmatrix} 1 & 1 & 0 \\ 0 & 2 & 0 \\ 0 & 0 & 3 \end{vmatrix} = 6.$$

We now have everything we need to apply Equation (7):

$$\int_0^3 \int_0^4 \int_{x=y/2}^{x=(y/2)+1} \left(\frac{2x - y}{2} + \frac{z}{3} \right) dx \, dy \, dz$$

$$= \int_0^1 \int_0^2 \int_0^1 (u + w) \, |J(u, v, w)| \, du \, dv \, dw$$

$$= \int_0^1 \int_0^2 \int_0^1 (u + w)(6) \, du \, dv \, dw = 6 \int_0^1 \int_0^2 \left[\frac{u^2}{2} + uw \right]_0^1 dv \, dw$$

$$= 6 \int_0^1 \int_0^2 \left(\frac{1}{2} + w \right) dv \, dw = 6 \int_0^1 \left[\frac{v}{2} + vw \right]_0^2 dw = 6 \int_0^1 (1 + 2w) \, dw$$

$$= 6 \left[w + w^2 \right]_0^1 = 6(2) = 12.$$

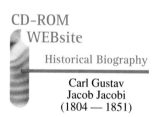

CD-ROM
WEBsite

Historical Biography

Carl Gustav
Jacob Jacobi
(1804 — 1851)

Using the substitution theorem for multiple integrals can lead to computational difficulties when the coordinate transformations are nonlinear. The goal of this section was only to introduce you to the ideas involved. A thorough discussion of transformations, the Jacobian, and the multivariable substitution is best given in an advanced calculus course after you have studied linear algebra.

EXERCISES 12.7

Finding Jacobians and Transformed Regions for Two Variables

1. (a) Solve the system

$$u = x - y, \qquad v = 2x + y$$

for x and y in terms of u and v. Then find the value of the Jacobian $\partial(x, y)/\partial(u, v)$.

(b) Find the image under the transformation $u = x - y$, $v = 2x + y$ of the triangular region with vertices $(0, 0)$, $(1, 1)$, and $(1, -2)$ in the xy-plane. Sketch the transformed region in the uv-plane.

2. (a) Solve the system

$$u = x + 2y, \qquad v = x - y$$

for x and y in terms of u and v. Then find the value of the Jacobian $\partial(x, y)/\partial(u, v)$.

(b) Find the image under the transformation $u = x + 2y$, $v = x - y$ of the triangular region in the xy-plane bounded by the lines $y = 0$, $y = x$, and $x + 2y = 2$. Sketch the transformed region in the uv-plane.

3. (a) Solve the system

$$u = 3x + 2y, \qquad v = x + 4y$$

for x and y in terms of u and v. Then find the value of the Jacobian $\partial(x, y)/\partial(u, v)$.

(b) Find the image under the transformation $u = 3x + 2y$, $v = x + 4y$ of the triangular region in the xy-plane bounded by the x-axis, the y-axis, and the line $x + y = 1$. Sketch the transformed region in the uv-plane.

4. (a) Solve the system

$$u = 2x - 3y, \qquad v = -x + y$$

for x and y in terms of u and v. Then find the value of the Jacobian $\partial(x, y)/\partial(u, v)$.

(b) Find the image under the transformation $u = 2x - 3y$, $v = -x + y$ of the parallelogram R in the xy-plane with boundaries $x = -3$, $x = 0$, $y = x$, and $y = x + 1$. Sketch the transformed region in the uv-plane.

Applying Transformations to Evaluate Double Integrals

5. Evaluate the integral

$$\int_0^4 \int_{x=y/2}^{x=(y/2)+1} \frac{2x - y}{2} \, dx \, dy$$

from Example 1 directly by integration with respect to x and y to confirm that its value is 2.

6. Use the transformation in Exercise 1 to evaluate the integral

$$\iint\limits_R (2x^2 - xy - y^2) \, dx \, dy$$

for the region R in the first quadrant bounded by the lines $y = -2x + 4$, $y = -2x + 7$, $y = x - 2$, and $y = x + 1$.

7. Use the transformation in Exercise 3 to evaluate the integral

$$\iint\limits_R (3x^2 + 14xy + 8y^2) \, dx \, dy$$

for the region R in the first quadrant bounded by the lines $y = -(3/2)x + 1$, $y = -(3/2)x + 3$, $y = -(1/4)x$, and $y = -(1/4)x + 1$.

8. Use the transformation and parallelogram R in Exercise 4 to evaluate the integral

$$\iint\limits_R 2(x - y) \, dx \, dy.$$

9. Let R be the region in the first quadrant of the xy-plane bounded by the hyperbolas $xy = 1$, $xy = 9$ and the lines $y = x$, $y = 4x$. Use the transformation $x = u/v$, $y = uv$ with $u > 0$ and $v > 0$ to rewrite

$$\iint\limits_R \left(\sqrt{\frac{y}{x}} + \sqrt{xy} \right) dx \, dy$$

as an integral over an appropriate region G in the uv-plane. Then evaluate the uv-integral over G.

10. (a) Find the Jacobian of the transformation $x = u$, $y = uv$, and sketch the region G: $1 \le u \le 2$, $1 \le uv \le 2$ in the uv-plane.

(b) Then use Equation (1) to transform the integral

$$\int_1^2 \int_1^2 \frac{y}{x} \, dy \, dx$$

into an integral over G, and evaluate both integrals.

11. *Polar moment of inertia of an elliptical plate* A thin plate of constant density covers the region bounded by the ellipse $x^2/a^2 + y^2/b^2 = 1$, $a > 0$, $b > 0$, in the xy-plane. Find the first moment of the plate about the origin. (*Hint:* Use the transformation $x = ar \cos \theta$, $y = br \sin \theta$.)

12. *Finding area of an ellipse* The area πab of the ellipse $x^2/a^2 + y^2/b^2 = 1$ can be found by integrating the function $f(x, y) = 1$ over the region bounded by the ellipse in the xy-plane. Evaluating the integral directly requires a trigonometric substitution. An easier way to evaluate the integral is to use the transformation $x = au$, $y = bv$ and evaluate the transformed integral over the disk G: $u^2 + v^2 \le 1$ in the uv-plane. Find the area this way.

13. Use the transformation in Exercise 2 to evaluate the integral

$$\int_0^{2/3} \int_y^{2-2y} (x + 2y)e^{(y-x)} \, dx \, dy$$

by first writing it as an integral over a region G in the uv-plane.

14. Use the transformation $x = u + (1/2)v$, $y = v$ to evaluate the integral

$$\int_0^2 \int_{y/2}^{(y+4)/2} y^3(2x - y)e^{(2x-y)^2} \, dx \, dy$$

by first writing it as an integral over a region G in the uv-plane.

Finding Jacobian Determinants

15. Find the Jacobian $\partial(x, y)/\partial(u, v)$ for the transformation

(a) $x = u \cos v$, $y = u \sin v$

(b) $x = u \sin v$, $y = u \cos v$.

16. Find the Jacobian $\partial(x, y, z)/\partial(u, v, w)$ of the transformation

(a) $x = u \cos v$, $y = u \sin v$, $z = w$

(b) $x = 2u - 1$, $y = 3v - 4$, $z = (1/2)(w - 4)$.

17. Evaluate the determinant in Equation (10) to show that the Jacobian of the transformation from Cartesian $\rho\phi\theta$-space to Cartesian xyz-space is $\rho^2 \sin \phi$.

18. *Substitutions in single integrals* How can substitutions in single definite integrals be viewed as transformations of regions? What is the Jacobian in such a case? Illustrate with an example.

Applying Transformations to Evaluate Triple Integrals

19. Evaluate the integral in Example 3 by integrating with respect to x, y, and z.

20. *Volume of an ellipsoid* Find the volume of the ellipsoid

$$\frac{x^2}{a^2} + \frac{y^2}{b^2} + \frac{z^2}{c^2} = 1.$$

(*Hint*: Let $x = au$, $y = bv$, and $z = cw$. Then find the volume of an appropriate region in uvw-space.)

21. Evaluate

$$\iiint |xyz|\, dx\, dy\, dz$$

over the solid ellipsoid

$$\frac{x^2}{a^2} + \frac{y^2}{b^2} + \frac{z^2}{c^2} \leq 1.$$

(*Hint*: Let $x = au$, $y = bv$, and $z = cw$. Then integrate over an appropriate region in uvw-space.)

22. Let D be the region in xyz-space defined by the inequalities

$$1 \leq x \leq 2, \qquad 0 \leq xy \leq 2, \qquad 0 \leq z \leq 1.$$

Evaluate

$$\iiint_D (x^2 y + 3\, xyz)\, dx\, dy\, dz$$

by applying the transformation

$$u = x, \qquad v = xy, \qquad w = 3z$$

and integrating over an appropriate region G in uvw-space.

23. *Centroid of a solid semiellipsoid* Assuming the result that the centroid of a solid hemisphere lies on the axis of symmetry three-eighths of the way from the base toward the top, show, by transforming the appropriate integrals, that the center of mass of a solid semiellipsoid $(x^2/a^2) + (y^2/b^2) + (z^2/c^2) \leq 1$, $z \geq 0$, lies on the z-axis three-eighths of the way from the base toward the top. (You can do this without evaluating any of the integrals.)

24. *Cylindrical shells* In Section 5.2, we learned how to find the volume of a solid of revolution using the shell method; namely, if the region between the curve $y = f(x)$ and the x-axis from a to b $(0 < a < b)$ is revolved about the y-axis, the volume of the resulting solid is $\int_a^b 2\pi x f(x)\, dx$. Prove that finding volumes by using triple integrals gives the same result. (*Hint*: Use cylindrical coordinates with the roles of y and z changed.)

Questions to Guide Your Review

1. Define the double integral of a function of two variables over a bounded region in the coordinate plane.

2. How are double integrals evaluated as iterated integrals? Does the order of integration matter? How are the limits of integration determined? Give examples.

3. How are double integrals used to calculate areas, average values, masses, moments, centers of mass, and radii of gyration? Give examples.

4. How can you change a double integral in rectangular coordinates into a double integral in polar coordinates? Why might it be worthwhile to do so? Give an example.

5. Define the triple integral of a function $f(x, y, z)$ over a bounded region in space.

6. How are triple integrals in rectangular coordinates evaluated? How are the limits of integration determined? Give an example.

7. How are triple integrals in rectangular coordinates used to calculate volumes, average values, masses, moments, centers of mass, and radii of gyration? Give examples.

8. How are triple integrals defined in cylindrical and spherical coordinates? Why might one prefer working in one of these coordinate systems to working in rectangular coordinates?

9. How are triple integrals in cylindrical and spherical coordinates evaluated? How are the limits of integration found? Give examples.

10. How are substitutions in double integrals pictured as transformations of two-dimensional regions? Give a sample calculation.

11. How are substitutions in triple integrals pictured as transformations of three-dimensional regions? Give a sample calculation.

Practice Exercises

Planar Regions of Integration

In Exercises 1–4, sketch the region of integration and evaluate the double integral.

1. $\displaystyle\int_1^{10}\int_0^{1/y} ye^{xy}\,dx\,dy$

2. $\displaystyle\int_0^1\int_0^{x^3} e^{y/x}\,dy\,dx$

3. $\displaystyle\int_0^{3/2}\int_{-\sqrt{9-4t^2}}^{\sqrt{9-4t^2}} t\,ds\,dt$

4. $\displaystyle\int_0^1\int_{\sqrt{y}}^{2-\sqrt{y}} xy\,dx\,dy$

Reversing the Order of Integration

In Exercises 5–8, sketch the region of integration and write an equivalent integral with the order of integration reversed. Then evaluate both integrals.

5. $\displaystyle\int_0^4\int_{-\sqrt{4-y}}^{(y-4)/2} dx\,dy$

6. $\displaystyle\int_0^1\int_{x^2}^x \sqrt{x}\,dy\,dx$

7. $\displaystyle\int_0^{3/2}\int_{-\sqrt{9-4y^2}}^{\sqrt{9-4y^2}} y\,dx\,dy$

8. $\displaystyle\int_0^2\int_0^{4-x} 2x\,dy\,dx$

Evaluating Double Integrals

Evaluate the integrals in Exercises 9–12.

9. $\displaystyle\int_0^1\int_{2y}^2 4\cos(x^2)\,dx\,dy$

10. $\displaystyle\int_0^2\int_{y/2}^1 e^{x^2}\,dx\,dy$

11. $\displaystyle\int_0^8\int_{\sqrt[3]{x}}^2 \frac{dy\,dx}{y^4+1}$

12. $\displaystyle\int_0^1\int_{\sqrt[3]{y}}^1 \frac{2\pi\sin\pi x^2}{x^2}\,dx\,dy$

Areas and Volumes

13. *Area between line and parabola* Find the area of the region enclosed by the line $y = 2x + 4$ and the parabola $y = 4 - x^2$ in the xy-plane.

14. *Area bounded by lines and parabola* Find the area of the "triangular" region in the xy-plane that is bounded on the right by the parabola $y = x^2$, on the left by the line $x + y = 2$, and above by the line $y = 4$.

15. *Volume of the region under a paraboloid* Find the volume under the paraboloid $z = x^2 + y^2$ above the triangle enclosed by the lines $y = x$, $x = 0$, and $x + y = 2$ in the xy-plane.

16. *Volume of the region under parabolic cylinder* Find the volume under the parabolic cylinder $z = x^2$ above the region enclosed by the parabola $y = 6 - x^2$ and the line $y = x$ in the xy-plane.

Average Values

Find the average value of $f(x, y) = xy$ over the regions in Exercises 17 and 18.

17. The square bounded by the lines $x = 1$, $y = 1$ in the first quadrant

18. The quarter circle $x^2 + y^2 \le 1$ in the first quadrant

Masses and Moments

19. *Centroid* Find the centroid of the "triangular" region bounded by the lines $x = 2$, $y = 2$ and the hyperbola $xy = 2$ in the xy-plane.

20. *Centroid* Find the centroid of the region between the parabola $x + y^2 - 2y = 0$ and the line $x + 2y = 0$ in the xy-plane.

21. *Polar moment* Find the polar moment of inertia about the origin of a thin triangular plate of constant density $\delta = 3$ bounded by the y-axis and the lines $y = 2x$ and $y = 4$ in the xy-plane.

22. *Polar moment* Find the polar moment of inertia about the center of a thin rectangular sheet of constant density $\delta = 1$ bounded by the lines

(a) $x = \pm 2$, $y = \pm 1$ in the xy-plane

(b) $x = \pm a$, $y = \pm b$ in the xy-plane.

(*Hint:* Find I_x. Then use the formula for I_x to find I_y and add the two to find I_0.)

23. *Inertial moment and radius of gyration* Find the moment of inertia and radius of gyration about the x-axis of a thin plate of constant density δ covering the triangle with vertices $(0, 0)$, $(3, 0)$, and $(3, 2)$ in the xy-plane.

24. *Plate with variable density* Find the center of mass and the moments of inertia and radii of gyration about the coordinate axes of a thin plate bounded by the line $y = x$ and the parabola $y = x^2$ in the xy-plane if the density is $\delta(x, y) = x + 1$.

25. *Plate with variable density* Find the mass and first moments about the coordinate axes of a thin square plate bounded by the lines $x = \pm 1$, $y = \pm 1$ in the xy-plane if the density is $\delta(x, y) = x^2 + y^2 + 1/3$.

26. *Triangles with same inertial moment and radius of gyration* Find the moment of inertia and radius of gyration about the x-axis of a thin triangular plate of constant density δ whose base lies along the interval $[0, b]$ on the x-axis and whose vertex lies on the line $y = h$ above the x-axis. As you will see, it does not matter where on the line this vertex lies. All such triangles have the same moment of inertia and radius of gyration about the x-axis.

Polar Coordinates

Evaluate the integrals in Exercises 27 and 28 by changing to polar co-ordinates.

27. $\int_{-1}^{1} \int_{-\sqrt{1-x^2}}^{\sqrt{1-x^2}} \frac{2 \, dy \, dx}{(1 + x^2 + y^2)^2}$

28. $\int_{-1}^{1} \int_{-\sqrt{1-y^2}}^{\sqrt{1-y^2}} \ln (x^2 + y^2 + 1) \, dx \, dy$

29. *Centroid* Find the centroid of the region in the polar coordinate plane defined by the inequalities $0 \le r \le 3$, $-\pi/3 \le \theta \le \pi/3$.

30. *Centroid* Find the centroid of the region in the first quadrant bounded by the rays $\theta = 0$ and $\theta = \pi/2$ and the circles $r = 1$ and $r = 3$.

31. (a) *Centroid* Find the centroid of the region in the polar coordinate plane that lies inside the cardioid $r = 1 + \cos\theta$ and outside the circle $r = 1$.

   (b) Sketch the region and show the centroid in your sketch.

32. (a) *Writing to Learn: Centroid* Find the centroid of the plane region defined by the polar coordinate inequalities $0 \le r \le a$, $-\alpha \le \theta \le \alpha$ $(0 < \alpha \le \pi)$. How does the centroid move as $\alpha \to \pi^-$?

   (b) Sketch the region for $\alpha = 5\pi/6$ and show the centroid in your sketch.

33. *Integrating over lemniscate* Integrate the function $f(x, y) = 1/(1 + x^2 + y^2)^2$ over the region enclosed by one loop of the lemniscate $(x^2 + y^2)^2 - (x^2 - y^2) = 0$.

34. Integrate $f(x, y) = 1/(1 + x^2 + y^2)^2$ over

   (a) *Triangular region* The triangle with vertices $(0, 0)$, $(1, 0)$, $(1, \sqrt{3})$

   (b) *First quadrant* The first quadrant of the xy-plane.

Triple Integrals in Cartesian Coordinates

Evaluate the integrals in Exercises 35–38.

35. $\int_{0}^{\pi} \int_{0}^{\pi} \int_{0}^{\pi} \cos (x + y + z) \, dx \, dy \, dz$

36. $\int_{\ln 6}^{\ln 7} \int_{0}^{\ln 2} \int_{\ln 4}^{\ln 5} e^{(x+y+z)} \, dz \, dy \, dx$

37. $\int_{0}^{1} \int_{0}^{x^2} \int_{0}^{x+y} (2x - y - z) \, dz \, dy \, dx$

38. $\int_{1}^{e} \int_{1}^{x} \int_{0}^{z} \frac{2y}{z^3} \, dy \, dz \, dx$

39. *Volume* Find the volume of the wedge-shaped region enclosed on the side by the cylinder $x = -\cos y$, $-\pi/2 \le y \le \pi/2$, on the top by the plane $z = -2x$, and below by the xy-plane.

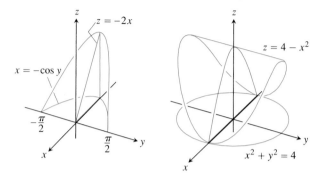

40. *Volume* Find the volume of the solid that is bounded above by the cylinder $z = 4 - x^2$, on the sides by the cylinder $x^2 + y^2 = 4$, and below by the xy-plane.

41. *Average value* Find the average value of $f(x, y, z) = 30xz\sqrt{x^2 + y}$ over the rectangular solid in the first octant bounded by the coordinate planes and the planes $x = 1$, $y = 3$, $z = 1$.

42. *Average value* Find the average value of ρ over the solid sphere $\rho \le a$ (spherical coordinates).

Cylindrical and Spherical Coordinates

43. *Cylindrical to rectangular coordinates* Convert

$$\int_{0}^{2\pi} \int_{0}^{\sqrt{2}} \int_{r}^{\sqrt{4-r^2}} 3 \, dz \, r \, dr \, d\theta, \qquad r \ge 0$$

to **(a)** rectangular coordinates with the order of integration $dz \, dx \, dy$ and **(b)** spherical coordinates. Then **(c)** evaluate one of the integrals.

44. *Rectangular to cylindrical coordinates* **(a)** Convert to cylindrical coordinates. Then **(b)** evaluate the new integral.

$$\int_{0}^{1} \int_{-\sqrt{1-x^2}}^{\sqrt{1-x^2}} \int_{-(x^2+y^2)}^{(x^2+y^2)} 21xy^2 \, dz \, dy \, dx$$

45. *Rectangular to spherical coordinates* **(a)** Convert to spherical coordinates. Then **(b)** evaluate the new integral.

$$\int_{-1}^{1} \int_{-\sqrt{1-x^2}}^{\sqrt{1-x^2}} \int_{\sqrt{x^2+y^2}}^{1} dz \, dy \, dx$$

46. *Rectangular, cylindrical, and spherical coordinates* Write an iterated triple integral for the integral of $f(x, y, z) = 6 + 4y$ over the region in the first octant bounded by the cone $z = \sqrt{x^2 + y^2}$, the cylinder $x^2 + y^2 = 1$, and the coordinate planes in **(a)** rectangular coordinates, **(b)** cylindrical coordinates, and **(c)** spherical coordinates. Then **(d)** find the integral of f by evaluating one of the triple integrals.

47. *Cylindrical to rectangular coordinates* Set up an integral in rectangular coordinates equivalent to the integral

$$\int_0^{\pi/2} \int_1^{\sqrt{3}} \int_1^{\sqrt{4-r^2}} r^3 \, (\sin \theta \, \cos \theta) \, z^2 \, dz \, dr \, d\theta.$$

Arrange the order of integration to be z first, then y, then x.

48. *Rectangular to cylindrical coordinates* The volume of a solid is

$$\int_0^2 \int_0^{\sqrt{2x-x^2}} \int_{-\sqrt{4-x^2-y^2}}^{\sqrt{4-x^2-y^2}} dz \, dy \, dx.$$

(a) Describe the solid by giving equations for the surfaces that form its boundary.

(b) Convert the integral to cylindrical coordinates but do not evaluate the integral.

49. *Spherical versus cylindrical coordinates* Triple integrals involving spherical shapes do not always require spherical coordinates for convenient evaluation. Some calculations may be accomplished more easily with cylindrical coordinates. As a case in point, find the volume of the region bounded above by the sphere $x^2 + y^2 + z^2 = 8$ and below by the plane $z = 2$ by using (a) cylindrical coordinates and (b) spherical coordinates.

50. *Finding* I_z *in spherical coordinates* Find the moment of inertia about the z-axis of a solid of constant density $\delta = 1$ that is bounded above by the sphere $\rho = 2$ and below by the cone $\phi = \pi/3$ (spherical coordinates).

51. *Moment of inertia of a "thick" sphere* Find the moment of inertia of a solid of constant density δ bounded by two concentric spheres of radii a and b ($a < b$) about a diameter.

52. *Moment of inertia of an apple* Find the moment of inertia about the z-axis of a solid of density $\delta = 1$ enclosed by the spherical coordinate surface $\rho = 1 - \cos \phi$.

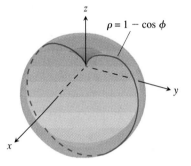

Additional Exercises: Theory, Examples, Applications

Volumes

1. *Sand pile: double and triple integrals* The base of a sand pile covers the region in the xy-plane that is bounded by the parabola $x^2 + y = 6$ and the line $y = x$. The height of the sand above the point (x, y) is x^2. Express the volume of sand as (a) a double integral, (b) a triple integral. Then (c) find the volume.

2. *Water in a hemispherical bowl* A hemispherical bowl of radius 5 cm is filled with water to within a 3 cm of the top. Find the volume of water in the bowl.

3. *Solid Cylindrical Region between Two Planes* Find the volume of the portion of the solid cylinder $x^2 + y^2 \le 1$ that lies between the planes $z = 0$ and $x + y + z = 2$.

4. *Sphere and paraboloid* Find the volume of the region bounded above by the sphere $x^2 + y^2 + z^2 = 2$ and below by the paraboloid $z = x^2 + y^2$.

5. *Two paraboloids* Find the volume of the region bounded above by the paraboloid $z = 3 - x^2 - y^2$ and below by the paraboloid $z = 2x^2 + 2y^2$.

6. *Spherical coordinates* Find the volume of the region enclosed by the spherical coordinate surface $\rho = 2 \sin \phi$ (see accompanying figure).

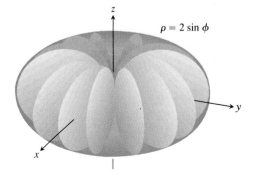

7. *Hole in sphere* A circular cylindrical hole is bored through a solid sphere, the axis of the hole being a diameter of the sphere. The volume of the remaining solid is

$$V = 2 \int_0^{2\pi} \int_0^{\sqrt{3}} \int_1^{\sqrt{4-z^2}} r \, dr \, dz \, d\theta.$$

(a) Find the radius of the hole and the radius of the sphere.

(b) Evaluate the integral.

8. *Sphere and cylinder* Find the volume of material cut from the solid sphere $r^2 + z^2 \leq 9$ by the cylinder $r = 3 \sin \theta$.

9. *Two paraboloids* Find the volume of the region enclosed by the surfaces $z = x^2 + y^2$ and $z = (x^2 + y^2 + 1)/2$.

10. *Cylinder and surface z = xy* Find the volume of the region in the first octant that lies between the cylinders $r = 1$ and $r = 2$ and that is bounded below by the xy-plane and above by the surface $z = xy$.

Changing the Order of Integration

11. Evaluate the integral

$$\int_0^\infty \frac{e^{-ax} - e^{-bx}}{x} \, dx.$$

(*Hint:* Use the relation

$$\frac{e^{-ax} - e^{-bx}}{x} = \int_a^b e^{-xy} \, dy$$

to form a double integral and evaluate the integral by changing the order of integration.)

12. (a) *Polar coordinates* Show, by changing to polar coordinates, that

$$\int_0^{a \sin\beta} \int_{y \cot \beta}^{\sqrt{a^2 - y^2}} \ln (x^2 + y^2) \, dx \, dy = a^2 \beta \left(\ln a - \frac{1}{2} \right),$$

where $a > 0$ and $0 < \beta < \pi/2$.

(b) Rewrite the Cartesian integral with the order of integration reversed.

13. *Reducing a double to a single integral* By changing the order of integration, show that the following double integral can be reduced to a single integral:

$$\int_0^x \int_0^u e^{m(x-t)} f(t) \, dt \, du = \int_0^x (x-t) e^{m(x-t)} f(t) \, dt.$$

Similarly, it can be shown that

$$\int_0^x \int_0^v \int_0^u e^{m(x-t)} f(t) \, dt \, du \, dv = \int_0^x \frac{(x-t)^2}{2} e^{m(x-t)} f(t) \, dt.$$

14. *Transforming a double integral to obtain constant limits* Sometimes a multiple integral with variable limits can be changed into one with constant limits. By changing the order of integration, show that

$$\int_0^1 f(x) \left(\int_0^x g(x - y) f(y) \, dy \right) dx$$

$$= \int_0^1 f(y) \left(\int_y^1 g(x - y) f(x) \, dx \right) dy$$

$$= \frac{1}{2} \int_0^1 \int_0^1 g(|x - y|) f(x) f(y) \, dx \, dy.$$

Masses and Moments

15. *Minimizing polar inertia* A thin plate of constant density is to occupy the triangular region in the first quadrant of the xy-plane having vertices $(0, 0)$, $(a, 0)$, and $(a, 1/a)$. What value of a will minimize the plate's polar moment of inertia about the origin?

16. *Polar inertia of triangular plate* Find the polar moment of inertia about the origin of a thin triangular plate of constant density $\delta = 3$ bounded by the y-axis and the lines $y = 2x$ and $y = 4$ in the xy-plane.

17. *Mass and polar inertia of a counterweight* The counterweight of a flywheel of constant density 1 has the form of the smaller segment cut from a circle of radius a by a chord at a distance b from the center ($b < a$). Find the mass of the counterweight and its polar moment of inertia about the center of the wheel.

18. *Centroid of boomerang* Find the centroid of the boomerang-shaped region between the parabolas $y^2 = -4(x - 1)$ and $y^2 = -2(x - 2)$ in the xy-plane.

Theory and Applications

19. Evaluate

$$\int_0^a \int_0^b e^{\max(b^2 x^2, a^2 y^2)} \, dy \, dx,$$

where a and b are positive numbers and

$$\max(b^2 x^2, a^2 y^2) = \begin{cases} b^2 x^2 & \text{if } b^2 x^2 \geq a^2 y^2 \\ a^2 y^2 & \text{if } b^2 x^2 < a^2 y^2. \end{cases}$$

20. Show that

$$\iint \frac{\partial^2 F(x, y)}{\partial x \, \partial y} \, dx \, dy$$

over the rectangle $x_0 \leq x \leq x_1, y_0 \leq y \leq y_1$, is

$$F(x_1, y_1) - F(x_0, y_1) - F(x_1, y_0) + F(x_0, y_0).$$

21. Suppose that $f(x, y)$ can be written as a product $f(x, y) = F(x)G(y)$ of a function of x and a function of y. Then the integral of f over the rectangle $R: a \le x \le b$, $c \le y \le d$ can be evaluated as a product as well, by the formula

$$\iint\limits_R f(x, y)\, dA = \left(\int_a^b F(x)\, dx\right)\left(\int_c^d G(y)\, dy\right). \qquad (1)$$

The argument is that

$$\iint\limits_R f(x, y)\, dA = \int_c^d \left(\int_a^b F(x)G(y)\, dx\right) dy \qquad (i)$$

$$= \int_c^d \left(G(y) \int_a^b F(x)\, dx\right) dy \qquad (ii)$$

$$= \int_c^d \left(\int_a^b F(x)\, dx\right) G(y)\, dy \qquad (iii)$$

$$= \left(\int_a^b F(x)\, dx\right) \int_c^d G(y)\, dy. \qquad (iv)$$

(a) *Writing to Learn* Give reasons for steps i through iv.

When it applies, Equation (1) can be a time saver. Use it to evaluate the following integrals.

(b) $\displaystyle\int_0^{\ln 2} \int_0^{\pi/2} e^x \cos y\, dy\, dx$

(c) $\displaystyle\int_1^2 \int_{-1}^1 \frac{x}{y^2}\, dx\, dy$

22. Let $D_{\mathbf{u}} f$ denote the derivative of $f(x, y) = (x^2 + y^2)/2$ in the direction of the unit vector $\mathbf{u} = u_1\mathbf{i} + u_2\mathbf{j}$.

(a) *Finding average value* Find the average value of $D_{\mathbf{u}} f$ over the triangular region cut from the first quadrant by the line $x + y = 1$.

(b) *Average value and centroid* Show in general that the average value of $D_{\mathbf{u}} f$ over a region in the xy-plane is the value of $D_{\mathbf{u}} f$ at the centroid of the region.

23. *The value of* Γ $(1/2)$ The gamma function,

$$\Gamma(x) = \int_0^\infty t^{x-1} e^{-t}\, dt,$$

extends the factorial function from the nonnegative integers to other real values. Of particular interest in the theory of differential equations is the number

$$\Gamma\left(\frac{1}{2}\right) = \int_0^\infty t^{(1/2)-1} e^{-t}\, dt = \int_0^\infty \frac{e^{-t}}{\sqrt{t}}\, dt. \qquad (2)$$

(a) If you have not yet done Exercise 37 in Section 12.3, do it now to show that

$$I = \int_0^\infty e^{-y^2}\, dy = \frac{\sqrt{\pi}}{2}.$$

(b) Substitute $y = \sqrt{t}$ in Equation (2) to show that $\Gamma(1/2) = 2I = \sqrt{\pi}$.

24. *Total electrical charge over circular plate* The electrical charge distribution on a circular plate of radius R meters is $\sigma(r, \theta) = kr(1 - \sin \theta)$ coulomb/m^2 (k a constant). Integrate σ over the plate to find the total charge Q.

25. *A parabolic rain gauge* A bowl is in the shape of the graph of $z = x^2 + y^2$ from $z = 0$ to $z = 10$ in. You plan to calibrate the bowl to make it into a rain gauge. What height in the bowl would correspond to 1 in. of rain? 3 in. of rain?

26. *Water in a satellite dish* A parabolic satellite dish is 2 m wide and 1/2 m deep. It axis of symmetry is tilted 30 degrees from the vertical.

(a) Set up, but do not evaluate, a triple integral in rectangular coordinates that gives the amount of water the satellite dish will hold. (*Hint:* Put your coordinate system so that the satellite dish is in "standard position" and the plane of the water level is slanted.) (*Caution:* The limits of integration are not "nice")

(b) What would be the smallest tilt of the satellite dish so that it holds no water?

27. *An infinite half-cylinder* Let D be the interior of the infinite right circular half-cylinder of radius 1 with its single-end face suspended 1 unit above the origin and its axis the ray from $(0, 0, 1)$ to ∞. Use cylindrical coordinates to evaluate

$$\iiint\limits_D z(r^2 + z^2)^{-5/2}\, dV.$$

28. *Hypervolume* We have learned that $\int_a^b 1\, dx$ is the length of the interval $[a, b]$ on the number line (one-dimensional space), $\iint_R 1\, dA$ is the area of region R in the xy-plane (two-dimensional space), and $\iiint_D 1\, dV$ is the volume of the region D in three-dimensional space (xyz-space). We could continue: If Q is a region in 4-space ($xyzw$-space), then $\iiiint_Q 1\, dV$ is the "hypervolume" of Q. Use your generalizing abilities and a Cartesian coordinate system of 4-space to find the hypervolume inside the unit 4-sphere $x^2 + y^2 + z^2 + w^2 = 1$.

13 Integration in Vector Fields

OVERVIEW This chapter treats integration in vector fields. The mathematics in this chapter is the mathematics engineers and physicists use to describe fluid flow, design underwater transmission cables, explain the flow of heat in stars, and calculate the work it takes to put a satellite in orbit.

13.1 Line Integrals

Definitions and Notation • Evaluation for Smooth Curves •
Additivity • Mass and Moment Calculations

When a curve $\mathbf{r}(t) = g(t)\mathbf{i} + h(t)\mathbf{j} + k(t)\mathbf{k}, a \leq t \leq b,$ passes through the domain of a function $f(x, y, z)$ in space, the values of f along the curve are given by the composite function $f(g(t), h(t), k(t))$. If we integrate this composite with respect to arc length from $t = a$ to $t = b$, we calculate the *line integral* of f along the curve. Despite the three-dimensional geometry, the line integral is an ordinary integral of a real-valued function over an interval of real numbers.

The importance of line integrals lies in their application. These are the integrals with which we calculate the work done by variable forces along paths in space and the rates at which fluids flow along curves and across boundaries.

Definitions and Notation

Suppose that $f(x, y, z)$ is a real-valued function whose domain contains the curve $\mathbf{r}(t) = g(t)\mathbf{i} + h(t)\mathbf{j} + k(t)\mathbf{k}, a \leq t \leq b$. We partition the curve into a finite number of subarcs (Figure 13.1). The typical subarc has length Δs_k. In each subarc we choose a point (x_k, y_k, z_k) and form the sum

$$S_n = \sum_{k=1}^{n} f(x_k, y_k, z_k)\,\Delta s_k.$$

If f is continuous and the functions g, h, and k have continuous first derivatives, then these sums approach a limit as n increases and the lengths Δs_k approach zero. We call this limit the **line integral of f over the curve from a to b.** If the curve is denoted by a single letter, C for example, the notation for the integral is

$$\int_C f(x, y, z)\,ds \qquad \text{``The integral of } f \text{ over } C\text{''} \tag{1}$$

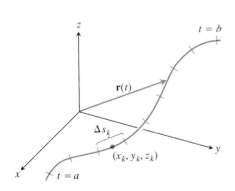

FIGURE 13.1 The curve $\mathbf{r}(t)$ partitioned into small arcs from $t = a$ to $t = b$. The length of a typical subarc is Δs_k.

Evaluation for Smooth Curves

If $\mathbf{r}(t)$ is smooth for $a \le t \le b$ ($\mathbf{v} = d\mathbf{r}/dt$ is continuous and never $\mathbf{0}$), we can use the equation

$$s(t) = \int_a^t |\mathbf{v}(\tau)| \, d\tau \qquad \text{Eq. (3) of Section 10.6 with } t_0 = a$$

to express ds in Equation (1) as $ds = |\mathbf{v}(t)| \, dt$. A theorem from advanced calculus says that we can then evaluate the integral of f over C as

$$\int_C f(x, y, z) \, ds = \int_a^b f(g(t), h(t), k(t)) \, |\mathbf{v}(t)| \, dt.$$

This formula will evaluate the integral correctly no matter what parametrization we use, as long as the parametrization is smooth.

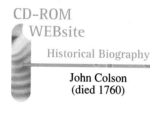

CD-ROM
WEBsite
Historical Biography
John Colson
(died 1760)

> #### How to Evaluate a Line Integral
>
> To integrate a continuous function $f(x, y, z)$ over a curve C:
>
> Step 1. Find a smooth parametrization of C,
>
> $$\mathbf{r}(t) = g(t)\mathbf{i} + h(t)\mathbf{j} + k(t)\mathbf{k}, \qquad a \le t \le b$$
>
> Step 2. Evaluate the integral as
>
> $$\int_C f(x, y, z) \, ds = \int_a^b f(g(t), h(t), k(t)) \, |\mathbf{v}(t)| \, dt. \tag{2}$$

If f has the constant value 1, then the integral of f over C gives the length of C.

Example 1   Evaluating a Line Integral

Integrate $f(x, y, z) = x - 3y^2 + z$ over the line segment C joining the origin and the point $(1, 1, 1)$ (Figure 13.2).

Solution   We choose the simplest parametrization we can think of:

$$\mathbf{r}(t) = t\mathbf{i} + t\mathbf{j} + t\mathbf{k}, \qquad 0 \le t \le 1.$$

The components have continuous first derivatives and $|\mathbf{v}(t)| = |\mathbf{i} + \mathbf{j} + \mathbf{k}| = \sqrt{1^2 + 1^2 + 1^2} = \sqrt{3}$ is never 0, so the parametrization is smooth. The integral of f over C is

$$\int_C f(x, y, z) \, ds = \int_0^1 f(t, t, t) \, (\sqrt{3}) \, dt \qquad \text{Eq. (2)}$$

$$= \int_0^1 (t - 3t^2 + t)\sqrt{3} \, dt$$

$$= \sqrt{3} \int_0^1 (2t - 3t^2) \, dt = \sqrt{3} \left[t^2 - t^3 \right]_0^1 = 0.$$

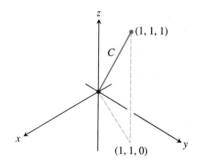

FIGURE 13.2 The integration path in Example 1.

Additivity

Line integrals have the useful property that if a curve C is made by joining a finite number of curves $C_1, C_2, \ldots, C_n$ end to end, then the integral of a function over C is the sum of the integrals over the curves that make it up:

$$\int_C f \, ds = \int_{C_1} f \, ds + \int_{C_2} f \, ds + \cdots + \int_{C_n} f \, ds. \tag{3}$$

Example 2   Line Integral for Two Joined Paths

Figure 13.3 shows another path from the origin to $(1, 1, 1)$, the union of line segments C_1 and C_2. Integrate $f(x, y, z) = x - 3y^2 + z$ over $C_1 \cup C_2$.

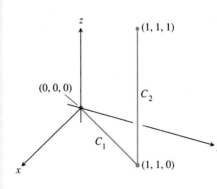

FIGURE 13.3 The path of integration in Example 2.

Solution   We choose the simplest parametrizations for C_1 and C_2 we can think of, checking the lengths of the velocity vectors as we go along:

$$C_1: \quad \mathbf{r}(t) = t\mathbf{i} + t\mathbf{j}, \quad 0 \le t \le 1; \quad |\mathbf{v}| = \sqrt{1^2 + 1^2} = \sqrt{2}$$
$$C_2: \quad \mathbf{r}(t) = \mathbf{i} + \mathbf{j} + t\mathbf{k}, \quad 0 \le t \le 1; \quad |\mathbf{v}| = \sqrt{0^2 + 0^2 + 1^2} = 1.$$

With these parametrizations we find that

$$\int_{C_1 \cup C_2} f(x, y, z) \, ds = \int_{C_1} f(x, y, z) \, ds + \int_{C_2} f(x, y, z) \, ds \qquad \text{Eq. (3)}$$

$$= \int_0^1 f(t, t, 0)\sqrt{2} \, dt + \int_0^1 f(1, 1, t) \, (1) \, dt \qquad \text{Eq. (2)}$$

$$= \int_0^1 (t - 3t^2 + 0)\sqrt{2} \, dt + \int_0^1 (1 - 3 + t)(1) \, dt$$

$$= \sqrt{2}\left[\frac{t^2}{2} - t^3\right]_0^1 + \left[\frac{t^2}{2} - 2t\right]_0^1 = -\frac{\sqrt{2}}{2} - \frac{3}{2}.$$

Notice three things about the integrations in Examples 1 and 2. First, as soon as the components of the appropriate curve were substituted into the formula for f, the integration became a standard integration with respect to t. Second, the integral of

f over $C_1 \cup C_2$ was obtained by integrating f over each section of the path and adding the results. Third, the integrals of f over C and $C_1 \cup C_2$ had different values. For most functions, the value of the integral along a path joining two points changes if you change the path between them. For some functions, however, the value remains the same, as we see in Section 13.3.

Mass and Moment Calculations

We treat coil springs and wires like masses distributed along smooth curves in space. The distribution is described by a continuous density function $\delta(x, y, z)$ (mass per unit length). The spring's or wire's mass, center of mass, and moments are then calculated with the formulas in Table 13.1. The formulas also apply to thin rods.

Table 13.1 Mass and moment formulas for coil springs, thin rods, and wires lying along a smooth curve C in space

Mass: $\qquad M = \int_C \delta(x, y, z) \, ds$

First moments about the coordinate planes:

$$M_{yz} = \int_C x \, \delta \, ds, \qquad M_{xz} = \int_C y \, \delta \, ds, \qquad M_{xy} = \int_C z \, \delta \, ds$$

Coordinates of the center of mass:

$$\bar{x} = M_{yz}/M, \qquad \bar{y} = M_{xz}/M, \qquad \bar{z} = M_{xy}/M$$

Moments of inertia about axes and other lines:

$$I_x = \int_C (y^2 + z^2)\delta \, ds, \qquad I_y = \int_C (x^2 + z^2)\delta \, ds$$

$$I_z = \int_C (x^2 + y^2)\delta \, ds, \qquad I_L = \int_C r^2\delta \, ds$$

$$r(x, y, z) = \text{distance from point } (x, y, z) \text{ to line } L$$

Radius of gyration about a line L: $\qquad R_L = \sqrt{I_L/M}$

Example 3 Finding Mass, Center of Mass, Moment of Inertia, Radius of Gyration

A coil spring lies along the helix

$$\mathbf{r}(t) = (\cos 4t)\mathbf{i} + (\sin 4t)\mathbf{j} + t\mathbf{k}, \qquad 0 \le t \le 2\pi.$$

The spring's density is a constant, $\delta = 1$. Find the spring's mass and center of mass, and its moment of inertia and radius of gyration about the z-axis.

Solution We sketch the spring (Figure 13.4). Because of the symmetries involved, the center of mass lies at the point $(0, 0, \pi)$ on the z-axis.

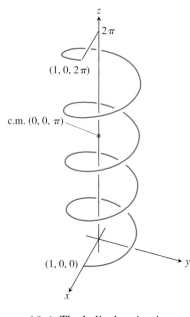

FIGURE 13.4 The helical spring in Example 3.

For the remaining calculations, we first find $|\mathbf{v}(t)|$:

$$|\mathbf{v}(t)| = \sqrt{\left(\frac{dx}{dt}\right)^2 + \left(\frac{dy}{dt}\right)^2 + \left(\frac{dz}{dt}\right)^2}$$

$$= \sqrt{(-4\ \sin\ 4t)^2 + (4\ \cos\ 4t)^2 + 1} = \sqrt{17}.$$

We then evaluate the formulas from Table 13.1 using Equation (2):

$$M = \int_{\text{Helix}} \delta\ ds = \int_0^{2\pi} (1)\sqrt{17}\ dt = 2\pi\sqrt{17}$$

$$I_z = \int_{\text{Helix}} (x^2 + y^2)\delta\ ds = \int_0^{2\pi} (\cos^2\ 4t + \sin^2\ 4t)(1)\sqrt{17}\ dt$$

$$= \int_0^{2\pi} \sqrt{17}\ dt = 2\pi\sqrt{17}$$

$$R_z = \sqrt{I_z/M} = \sqrt{2\pi\sqrt{17}/(2\pi\sqrt{17})} = 1.$$

Notice that the radius of gyration about the z-axis is the radius of the cylinder around which the helix winds.

Example 4   Finding an Arch's Center of Mass

A slender metal arch, denser at the bottom than top, lies along the semicircle $y^2 + z^2 = 1,\ z \geq 0$, in the yz-plane (Figure 13.5). Find the center of the arch's mass if the density at the point (x, y, z) on the arch is $\delta(x, y, z) = 2 - z$.

Solution   We know that $\bar{x} = 0$ and $\bar{y} = 0$ because the arch lies in the yz-plane with its mass distributed symmetrically about the z-axis. To find $\bar{z}$, we parametrize the circle as

$$\mathbf{r}(t) = (\cos t)\mathbf{j} + (\sin t)\mathbf{k}, \qquad 0 \leq t \leq \pi.$$

For this parametrization,

$$|\mathbf{v}(t)| = \sqrt{\left(\frac{dx}{dt}\right)^2 + \left(\frac{dy}{dt}\right)^2 + \left(\frac{dz}{dt}\right)^2} = \sqrt{(0)^2 + (-\sin t)^2 + (\cos t)^2} = 1.$$

The formulas in Table 13.1 then give

$$M = \int_C \delta\ ds = \int_C (2 - z)\ ds = \int_0^\pi (2 - \sin t)\ (1)\ dt = 2\pi - 2$$

$$M_{xy} = \int_C z\delta\ ds = \int_C z(2 - z)\ ds = \int_0^\pi (\sin t)(2 - \sin t)\ dt$$

$$= \int_0^\pi (2\ \sin t - \sin^2 t)\ dt = \frac{8 - \pi}{2}$$

$$\bar{z} = \frac{M_{xy}}{M} = \frac{8 - \pi}{2} \cdot \frac{1}{2\pi - 2} = \frac{8 - \pi}{4\pi - 4} \approx 0.57.$$

With $\bar{z}$ to the nearest hundredth, the center of mass is $(0, 0, 0.57)$.

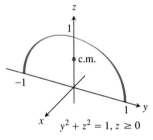

FIGURE 13.5 Example 4 shows how to find the center of mass of a circular arch of variable density.

EXERCISES 13.1

Graphs of Vector Equations

Match the vector equations in Exercises 1–8 with the graphs (a)–(h) given here.

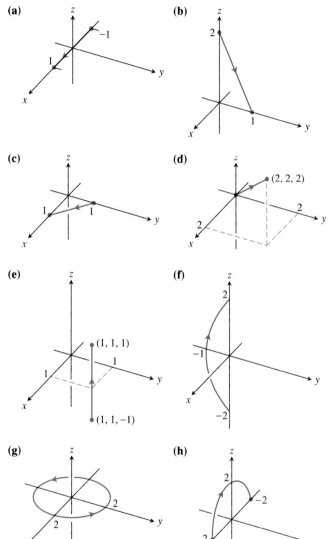

1. $\mathbf{r}(t) = t\mathbf{i} + (1 - t)\mathbf{j}, \quad 0 \le t \le 1$

2. $\mathbf{r}(t) = \mathbf{i} + \mathbf{j} + t\mathbf{k}, \quad -1 \le t \le 1$

3. $\mathbf{r}(t) = (2 \cos t)\mathbf{i} + (2 \sin t)\mathbf{j}, \quad 0 \le t \le 2\pi$

4. $\mathbf{r}(t) = t\mathbf{i}, \quad -1 \le t \le 1$

5. $\mathbf{r}(t) = t\mathbf{i} + t\mathbf{j} + t\mathbf{k}, \quad 0 \le t \le 2$

6. $\mathbf{r}(t) = t\mathbf{j} + (2 - 2t)\mathbf{k}, \quad 0 \le t \le 1$

7. $\mathbf{r}(t) = (t^2 - 1)\mathbf{j} + 2t\mathbf{k}, \quad -1 \le t \le 1$

8. $\mathbf{r}(t) = (2 \cos t)\mathbf{i} + (2 \sin t)\mathbf{k}, \quad 0 \le t \le \pi$

Evaluating Line Integrals over Space Curves

9. Evaluate $\int_C (x + y)\, ds$ where C is the straight-line segment $x = t$, $y = (1 - t)$, $z = 0$, from $(0, 1, 0)$ to $(1, 0, 0)$.

10. Evaluate $\int_C (x - y + z - 2)\, ds$ where C is the straight-line segment $x = t$, $y = (1 - t)$, $z = 1$, from $(0, 1, 1)$ to $(1, 0, 1)$.

11. Evaluate $\int_C (xy + y + z)\, ds$ along the curve $\mathbf{r}(t) = 2t\mathbf{i} + t\mathbf{j} + (2 - 2t)\mathbf{k}, 0 \le t \le 1$.

12. Evaluate $\int_C \sqrt{x^2 + y^2}\, ds$ along the curve $\mathbf{r}(t) = (4 \cos t)\mathbf{i} + (4 \sin t)\mathbf{j} + 3t\mathbf{k}, -2\pi \le t \le 2\pi$.

13. Find the line integral of $f(x, y, z) = x + y + z$ over the straight-line segment from $(1, 2, 3)$ to $(0, -1, 1)$.

14. Find the line integral of $f(x, y, z) = \sqrt{3}/(x^2 + y^2 + z^2)$ over the curve $\mathbf{r}(t) = t\mathbf{i} + t\mathbf{j} + t\mathbf{k}, 1 \le t \le \infty$.

15. Integrate $f(x, y, z) = x + \sqrt{y} - z^2$ over the path from $(0, 0, 0)$ to $(1, 1, 1)$ (Figure 13.6a) given by

C_1: $\mathbf{r}(t) = t\mathbf{i} + t^2\mathbf{j}, \quad 0 \le t \le 1$

C_2: $\mathbf{r}(t) = \mathbf{i} + \mathbf{j} + t\mathbf{k}, \quad 0 \le t \le 1$

16. Integrate $f(x, y, z) = x + \sqrt{y} - z^2$ over the path from $(0, 0, 0)$ to $(1, 1, 1)$ (Figure 13.6b) given by

C_1: $\mathbf{r}(t) = t\mathbf{k}, \quad 0 \le t \le 1$

C_2: $\mathbf{r}(t) = t\mathbf{j} + \mathbf{k}, \quad 0 \le t \le 1$

C_3: $\mathbf{r}(t) = t\mathbf{i} + \mathbf{j} + \mathbf{k}, \quad 0 \le t \le 1$

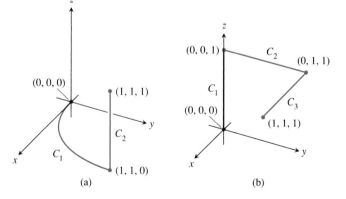

FIGURE 13.6 The paths of integration for Exercises 15 and 16.

17. Integrate $f(x, y, z) = (x + y + z)/(x^2 + y^2 + z^2)$ over the path $\mathbf{r}(t) = t\mathbf{i} + t\mathbf{j} + t\mathbf{k}, 0 < a \le t \le b$.

18. Integrate $f(x, y, z) = -\sqrt{x^2 + z^2}$ over the circle

$$\mathbf{r}(t) = (a \cos t)\mathbf{j} + (a \sin t)\mathbf{k}, \qquad 0 \le t \le 2\pi.$$

Line Integrals over Plane Curves

In Exercises 19–22, integrate f over the given curve.

19. $f(x, y) = x^3/y$, $\quad C: \quad y = x^2/2$, $\quad 0 \le x \le 2$

20. $f(x, y) = (x + y^2)/\sqrt{1 + x^2}$, $\quad C: \quad y = x^2/2$ from $(1, 1/2)$ to $(0, 0)$

21. $f(x, y) = x + y$, $\quad C: \quad x^2 + y^2 = 4$ in the first quadrant from $(2, 0)$ to $(0, 2)$

22. $f(x, y) = x^2 - y$, $\quad C: \quad x^2 + y^2 = 4$ in the first quadrant from $(0, 2)$ to $(\sqrt{2}, \sqrt{2})$

Mass and Moments

23. *Mass of a wire* Find the mass of a wire that lies along the curve $\mathbf{r}(t) = (t^2 - 1)\mathbf{j} + 2t\mathbf{k}, 0 \le t \le 1$, if the density is $\delta = (3/2)t$.

24. *Center of mass of a curved wire* A wire of density $\delta(x, y, z) = 15\sqrt{y + 2}$ lies along the curve $\mathbf{r}(t) = (t^2 - 1)\mathbf{j} + 2t\mathbf{k}, -1 \le t \le 1$. Find its center of mass. Then sketch the curve and center of mass together.

25. *Mass of wire with variable density* Find the mass of a thin wire lying along the curve $\mathbf{r}(t) = \sqrt{2}t\mathbf{i} + \sqrt{2}t\mathbf{j} + (4 - t^2)\mathbf{k}, 0 \le t \le 1$, if the density is (a) $\delta = 3t$ and (b) $\delta = 1$.

26. *Center of mass of wire with variable density* Find the center of mass of a thin wire lying along the curve $\mathbf{r}(t) = t\mathbf{i} + 2t\mathbf{j} + (2/3)t^{3/2}\mathbf{k}$, $0 \le t \le 2$, if the density is $\delta = 3\sqrt{5 + t}$.

27. *Moment of inertia and radius of gyration of wire hoop* A circular wire hoop of constant density δ lies along the circle $x^2 + y^2 = a^2$ in the xy-plane. Find the hoop's moment of inertia and radius of gyration about the z-axis.

28. *Inertia and radii of gyration of slender rod* A slender rod of constant density lies along the line segment $\mathbf{r}(t) = t\mathbf{j} + (2 - 2t)\mathbf{k}, 0 \le t \le 1$, in the yz-plane. Find the moments of inertia and radii of gyration of the rod about the three coordinate axes.

29. *Two springs of constant density* A spring of constant density δ lies along the helix

$$\mathbf{r}(t) = (\cos t)\mathbf{i} + (\sin t)\mathbf{j} + t\mathbf{k}, \quad 0 \le t \le 2\pi.$$

(a) Find I_z and R_z.

(b) Suppose that you have another spring of constant density δ that is twice as long as the spring in part (a) and lies along

the helix for $0 \le t \le 4\pi$. Do you expect I_z and R_z for the longer spring to be the same as those for the shorter one, or should they be different? Check your predictions by calculating I_z and R_z for the longer spring.

30. *Wire of constant density* A wire of constant density $\delta = 1$ lies along the curve

$$\mathbf{r}(t) = (t \cos t)\mathbf{i} + (t \sin t)\mathbf{j} + (2\sqrt{2}/3)t^{3/2}\mathbf{k}, \quad 0 \le t \le 1.$$

Find $\bar{z}, I_z$, and R_z.

31. *The arch in Example 4* Find I_x and R_x for the arch in Example 4.

32. *Center of mass, moments of inertia, and radii of gyration for wire with variable density* Find the center of mass, and the moments of inertia and radii of gyration about the coordinate axes of a thin wire lying along the curve

$$\mathbf{r}(t) = t\mathbf{i} + \frac{2\sqrt{2}}{3}t^{3/2}\mathbf{j} + \frac{t^2}{2}\mathbf{k}, \quad 0 \le t \le 2,$$

if the density is $\delta = 1/(t + 1)$.

COMPUTER EXPLORATIONS

Evaluating Line Integrals Numerically

In Exercises 33–36, use a CAS to perform the following steps to evaluate the line integrals.

(a) Find $ds = |\mathbf{v}(t)| \, dt$ for the path $\mathbf{r}(t) = g(t)\mathbf{i} + h(t)\mathbf{j} + k(t)\mathbf{k}$.

(b) Express the integrand $f(g(t), h(t), k(t))|\mathbf{v}(t)|$ as a function of the parameter t.

(c) Evaluate $\int_C f \, ds$ using Equation (2) in the text.

33. $f(x, y, z) = \sqrt{1 + 30x^2 + 10y}$; $\quad \mathbf{r}(t) = t\mathbf{i} + t^2\mathbf{j} + 3t^2\mathbf{k}$, $0 \le t \le 2$

34. $f(x, y, z) = \sqrt{1 + x^3 + 5y^3}$; $\quad \mathbf{r}(t) = t\mathbf{i} + \frac{1}{3}t^2\mathbf{j} + \sqrt{t}\mathbf{k}$, $0 \le t \le 2$

35. $f(x, y, z) = x\sqrt{y} - 3z^2$; $\quad \mathbf{r}(t) = (\cos 2t)\mathbf{i} + (\sin 2t)\mathbf{j} + 5t\mathbf{k}$, $0 \le t \le 2\pi$

36. $f(x, y, z) = \left(1 + \frac{9}{4}z^{1/3}\right)^{1/4}$; $\quad \mathbf{r}(t) = (\cos 2t)\mathbf{i} + (\sin 2t)\mathbf{j} + t^{5/2}\mathbf{k}$, $0 \le t \le 2\pi$

13.2 Vector Fields, Work, Circulation, and Flux

Vector Fields • Gradient Fields • Work Done by a Force over a
Curve in Space • Notation and Evaluation • Flow Integrals and
Circulation • Flux Across a Plane Curve

When we study physical phenomena that are represented by vectors, we replace integrals over closed intervals by integrals over paths through vector fields. We use such integrals to find the work done in moving an object along a path against a variable force (a vehicle sent into space against Earth's gravitational field) or to find the work done by a vector field in moving an object along a path through the field (the work done by an accelerator in raising the energy of a particle). We also use them to find the rates at which fluids flow along and across curves.

Vector Fields

A **vector field** on a domain in the plane or in space is a function that assigns a vector to each point in the domain. A field of three-dimensional vectors might have a formula like

$$\mathbf{F}(x, y, z) = M(x, y, z)\mathbf{i} + N(x, y, z)\mathbf{j} + P(x, y, z)\mathbf{k}.$$

The field is **continuous** if the **component functions** M, N, and P are continuous, **differentiable** if M, N, and P are differentiable, and so on. A field of two-dimensional vectors might have a formula like

$$\mathbf{F}(x, y) = M(x, y)\mathbf{i} + N(x, y)\mathbf{j}.$$

If we attach a projectile's velocity vector to each point of the projectile's trajectory in the plane of motion, we have a two-dimensional field defined along the trajectory. If we attach the gradient vector of a scalar function to each point of a level surface of the function, we have a three-dimensional field on the surface. If we attach the velocity vector to each point of a flowing fluid, we have a three-dimensional field defined on a region in space. These and other fields are illustrated in Figures 13.7 through 13.15. Some of the illustrations give formulas for the fields as well.

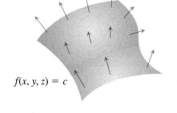

FIGURE 13.7 The velocity vectors $\mathbf{v}(t)$ of a projectile's motion make a vector field along the trajectory.

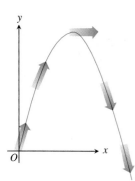

$f(x, y, z) = c$

FIGURE 13.8 The field of gradient vectors ∇f on a surface $f(x, y, z) = c$.

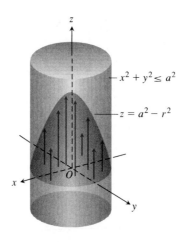

$x^2 + y^2 \le a^2$

$z = a^2 - r^2$

FIGURE 13.9 The flow of fluid in a long cylindrical pipe. The vectors $\mathbf{v} = (a^2 - r^2)\mathbf{k}$ inside the cylinder that have their bases in the xy-plane have their tips on the paraboloid $z = a^2 - r^2$.

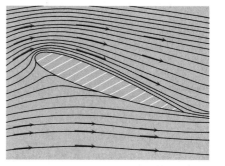

FIGURE 13.10 Velocity vectors of a flow around an airfoil in a wind tunnel. The streamlines were made visible by kerosene smoke. (Adapted from *NCFMF Book of Film Notes*, 1974, MIT Press with Education Development Center, Inc., Newton, Massachusetts.)

FIGURE 13.11 Streamlines in a contracting channel. The water speeds up as the channel narrows and the velocity vectors increase in length. (Adapted from *NCFMF Book of Film Notes*, 1974, MIT Press with Education Development Center, Inc., Newton, Massachusetts.)

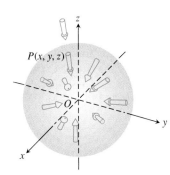

FIGURE 13.12 Vectors in the gravitational field

$$\mathbf{F} = -\frac{GM(x\mathbf{i} + y\mathbf{j} + z\mathbf{k})}{(x^2 + y^2 + z^2)^{3/2}}.$$

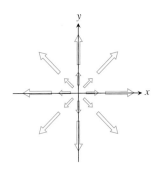

FIGURE 13.13 The radial field $\mathbf{F} = x\mathbf{i} + y\mathbf{j}$ of position vectors of points in the plane. Notice the convention that an arrow is drawn with its tail, not its head, at the point where $\mathbf{F}$ is evaluated.

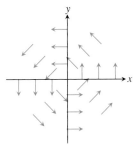

FIGURE 13.14 The circumferential or "spin" field of unit vectors

$$\mathbf{F} = (-y\mathbf{i} + x\mathbf{j})/(x^2 + y^2)^{1/2}$$

in the plane. The field is not defined at the origin.

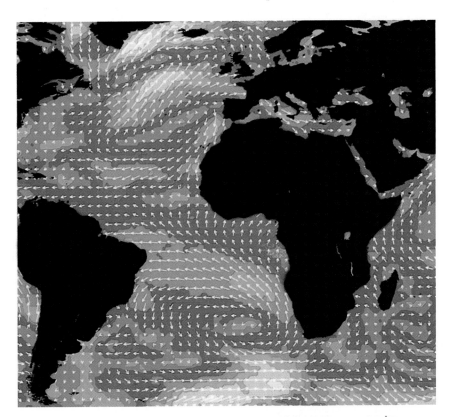

WIND SPEED, M/S

0   2   4   6   8   10   12   14   16+

FIGURE 13.15 NASA's *Seasat* used radar during a 3-day period in September 1978 to take 350,000 wind measurements over the world's oceans. The arrows show wind direction; their length and the color contouring indicate speed. Notice the heavy storm south of Greenland.

To sketch the fields that had formulas, we picked a representative selection of domain points and sketched the vectors attached to them. The arrows representing the vectors are drawn with their tails, not their heads, at the points where the vector functions are evaluated. This is different from the way we draw position vectors of planets and projectiles, with their tails at the origin and their heads at the planet's and projectile's locations.

Gradient Fields

Definition   Gradient Field
The **gradient field** of a differentiable function $f(x, y, z)$ is the field of gradient vectors

$$\nabla f = \frac{\partial f}{\partial x}\mathbf{i} + \frac{\partial f}{\partial y}\mathbf{j} + \frac{\partial f}{\partial z}\mathbf{k}.$$

Example 1   Finding a Gradient Field

Find the gradient field of $f(x, y, z) = xyz$.

Solution   The gradient field of f is the field $\mathbf{F} = \nabla f = yz\mathbf{i} + xz\mathbf{j} + xy\mathbf{k}.$

As we see in Section 13.3, gradient fields are of special importance in engineering, mathematics, and physics.

Work Done by a Force over a Curve in Space

Suppose that the vector field $\mathbf{F} = M(x, y, z)\mathbf{i} + N(x, y, z)\mathbf{j} + P(x, y, z)\mathbf{k}$ represents a force throughout a region in space (it might be the force of gravity or an electromagnetic force of some kind) and that

$$\mathbf{r}(t) = g(t)\mathbf{i} + h(t)\mathbf{j} + k(t)\mathbf{k}, \qquad a \leq t \leq b,$$

is a smooth curve in the region. Then the integral of $\mathbf{F} \cdot \mathbf{T}$, the scalar component of $\mathbf{F}$ in the direction of the curve's unit tangent vector, over the curve is called the work done by $\mathbf{F}$ over the curve from a to b (Figure 13.16).

$B \, t = b$

T

$\mathbf{F}$

$A \, t = a$

FIGURE 13.16 Figure for the definition of work.

Definition   Work Over a Smooth Curve
The **work** done by a force $\mathbf{F} = M\mathbf{i} + N\mathbf{j} + P\mathbf{k}$ over a smooth curve $\mathbf{r}(t)$ from $t = a$ to $t = b$ is

$$W = \int_{t=a}^{t=b} \mathbf{F} \cdot \mathbf{T} \, ds. \tag{1}$$

We motivate Equation (1) with the same kind of reasoning we used in Chapter 5 to derive the formula $W = \int_a^b F(x) \, dx$ for the work done by a continuous force of magnitude $F(x)$ directed along an interval of the x-axis. We divide the curve into short segments, apply the constant-force-times-distance formula for work to approximate the work over each curved segment, add the results to approximate the work over the entire curve, and calculate the work as the limit of the approximating sums as the segments become shorter and more numerous. To find exactly what the limiting integral should be, we partition the parameter interval $[a, b]$ in the usual way and choose a point c_k in each subinterval $[t_k, t_{k+1}]$. The partition of $[a, b]$ determines ("induces," we say) a partition of the curve, with the point P_k being the tip of the position vector $\mathbf{r}(t_k)$ and Δs_k being the length of the curve segment $P_k P_{k+1}$ (Figure 13.17).

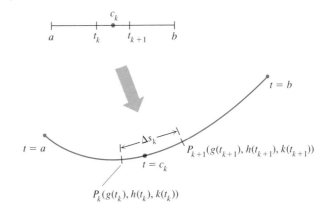

FIGURE 13.17 Each partition of $[a, b]$ induces a partition of the curve $\mathbf{r}(t) = g(t)\mathbf{i} + h(t)\mathbf{j} + k(t)\mathbf{k}.$

If $\mathbf{F}_k$ denotes the value of $\mathbf{F}$ at the point on the curve corresponding to $t = c_k$ and $\mathbf{T}_k$ denotes the curve's unit tangent vector at this point, then $\mathbf{F}_k \cdot \mathbf{T}_k$ is the scalar component of $\mathbf{F}$ in the direction of $\mathbf{T}$ at $t = c_k$ (Figure 13.18). The work done by $\mathbf{F}$ along the curve segment $P_k P_{k+1}$ is approximately

$$\begin{pmatrix} \text{Force component in} \\ \text{direction of motion} \end{pmatrix} \times \begin{pmatrix} \text{distance} \\ \text{applied} \end{pmatrix} = \mathbf{F}_k \cdot \mathbf{T}_k \, \Delta s_k.$$

The work done by $\mathbf{F}$ along the curve from $t = a$ to $t = b$ is approximately

$$\sum_{k=1}^{n} \mathbf{F}_k \cdot \mathbf{T}_k \, \Delta s_k.$$

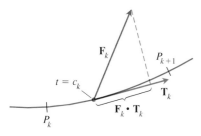

FIGURE 13.18 An enlarged view of the curve segment $P_k P_{k+1}$ in Figure 13.17, showing the force and unit tangent vectors at the point on the curve where $t = c_k$.

As the norm of the partition of $[a, b]$ approaches zero, the norm of the induced partition of the curve approaches zero and these sums approach the line integral

$$\int_{t=a}^{t=b} \mathbf{F} \cdot \mathbf{T} \, ds.$$

The sign of the number we calculate with this integral depends on the direction in which the curve is traversed as t increases. If we reverse the direction of motion, we reverse the direction of $\mathbf{T}$ and change the sign of $\mathbf{F} \cdot \mathbf{T}$ and its integral.

Notation and Evaluation

Table 13.2 shows six ways to write the work integral in Equation (1). Despite their variety, the formulas in Table 13.2 are all evaluated the same way.

Table 13.2 Different ways to write the work integral

$$\mathbf{W} = \int_{t=a}^{t=b} \mathbf{F} \cdot \mathbf{T}\, ds$$ The definition

$$= \int_{t=a}^{t=b} \mathbf{F} \cdot d\mathbf{r}$$ Compact differential form

$$= \int_{a}^{b} \mathbf{F} \cdot \frac{d\mathbf{r}}{dt}\, dt$$ Expanded to include dt; emphasizes the parameter t and velocity vector $d\mathbf{r}/dt$

$$= \int_{a}^{b} \left(M\frac{dg}{dt} + N\frac{dh}{dt} + P\frac{dk}{dt} \right) dt$$ Emphasizes the component functions

$$= \int_{a}^{b} \left(M\frac{dx}{dt} + N\frac{dy}{dt} + P\frac{dz}{dt} \right) dt$$ Abbreviates the components of $\mathbf{r}$

$$= \int_{a}^{b} M\, dx + N\, dy + P\, dz$$ dt's canceled; the most common form

How to Evaluate a Work Integral

To evaluate the work integral, take these steps.

Step 1. Evaluate $\mathbf{F}$ on the curve as a function of the parameter t.

Step 2. Find $d\mathbf{r}/dt$.

Step 3. Dot $\mathbf{F}$ with $d\mathbf{r}/dt$.

Step 4. Integrate from $t = a$ to $t = b$.

Example 2   Finding Work Done by a Variable Force Over a Space Curve

Find the work done by $\mathbf{F} = (y - x^2)\mathbf{i} + (z - y^2)\mathbf{j} + (x - z^2)\mathbf{k}$ over the curve $\mathbf{r}(t) = t\mathbf{i} + t^2\mathbf{j} + t^3\mathbf{k}, 0 \le t \le 1,$ from $(0, 0, 0)$ to $(1, 1, 1)$ (Figure 13.19).

Solution

Step 1: *Evaluate* $\mathbf{F}$ *on the curve.*

$$\mathbf{F} = (y - x^2)\mathbf{i} + (z - y^2)\mathbf{j} + (x - z^2)\mathbf{k}$$
$$= \underbrace{(t^2 - t^2)}_{0}\mathbf{i} + (t^3 - t^4)\mathbf{j} + (t - t^6)\mathbf{k}$$

Step 2: *Find* $d\mathbf{r}/dt$.

$$\frac{d\mathbf{r}}{dt} = \frac{d}{dt}(t\mathbf{i} + t^2\mathbf{j} + t^3\mathbf{k}) = \mathbf{i} + 2t\mathbf{j} + 3t^2\mathbf{k}$$

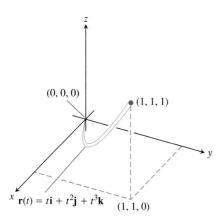

FIGURE 13.19 The curve in Example 2.

Step 3: *Dot* **F** *with* d**r**/dt.

$$\mathbf{F} \cdot \frac{d\mathbf{r}}{dt} = [(t^3 - t^4)\mathbf{j} + (t - t^6)\mathbf{k}] \cdot (\mathbf{i} + 2t\mathbf{j} + 3t^2\mathbf{k})$$

$$= (t^3 - t^4)(2t) + (t - t^6)(3t^2) = 2t^4 - 2t^5 + 3t^3 - 3t^8$$

Step 4: *Integrate from* $t = 0$ *to* $t = 1$.

$$\text{Work} = \int_0^1 (2t^4 - 2t^5 + 3t^3 - 3t^8)\, dt$$

$$= \left[\frac{2}{5}t^5 - \frac{2}{6}t^6 + \frac{3}{4}t^4 - \frac{3}{9}t^9 \right]_0^1 = \frac{29}{60}$$

Flow Integrals and Circulation

Instead of being a force field, suppose that **F** represents the velocity field of a fluid flowing through a region in space (a tidal basin or the turbine chamber of a hydroelectric generator, for example). Under these circumstances, the integral of **F** · **T** along a curve in the region gives the fluid's flow along the curve.

Definitions   Flow, Flow Integral, and Circulation

If **r**(t) is a smooth curve in the domain of a continuous velocity field **F**, the **flow** along the curve from $t = a$ to $t = b$ is

$$\text{Flow} = \int_a^b \mathbf{F} \cdot \mathbf{T}\, ds. \tag{2}$$

The integral in this case is called a **flow integral.** If the curve is a closed loop, the flow is called the **circulation** around the curve.

We evaluate flow integrals the same way we evaluate work integrals.

Example 3   Finding Flow Along a Helix

A fluid's velocity field is **F** = $x\mathbf{i} + z\mathbf{j} + y\mathbf{k}$. Find the flow along the helix **r**(t) = $(\cos t)\mathbf{i} + (\sin t)\mathbf{j} + t\mathbf{k}, 0 \le t \le \pi/2$.

Solution

Step 1: *Evaluate* **F** *on the curve*.

$$\mathbf{F} = x\mathbf{i} + z\mathbf{j} + y\mathbf{k} = (\cos t)\mathbf{i} + t\mathbf{j} + (\sin t)\mathbf{k}$$

Step 2: *Find* d**r**/dt.

$$\frac{d\mathbf{r}}{dt} = (-\sin t)\mathbf{i} + (\cos t)\mathbf{j} + \mathbf{k}$$

Step 3: *Find* $\mathbf{F} \cdot (d\mathbf{r}/dt)$.

$$\mathbf{F} \cdot \frac{d\mathbf{r}}{dt} = (\cos t)(-\sin t) + (t)(\cos t) + (\sin t)(1)$$

$$= -\sin t \cos t + t \cos t + \sin t$$

Step 4: *Integrate from* $t = a$ *to* $t = b$.

$$\text{Flow} = \int_{t=a}^{t=b} \mathbf{F} \cdot \frac{d\mathbf{r}}{dt}\, dt = \int_0^{\pi/2} (-\sin t \cos t + t \cos t + \sin t)\, dt$$

$$= \left[\frac{\cos^2 t}{2} + t \sin t\right]_0^{\pi/2} = \left(0 + \frac{\pi}{2}\right) - \left(\frac{1}{2} + 0\right) = \frac{\pi}{2} - \frac{1}{2}$$

Example 4   Finding Circulation Around a Circle

Find the circulation of the field $\mathbf{F} = (x - y)\mathbf{i} + x\mathbf{j}$ around the circle $\mathbf{r}(t) = (\cos t)\mathbf{i} + (\sin t)\mathbf{j}, 0 \leq t \leq 2\pi$.

Solution

1. On the circle, $\mathbf{F} = (x - y)\mathbf{i} + x\mathbf{j} = (\cos t - \sin t)\mathbf{i} + (\cos t)\mathbf{j}$.

2. $\dfrac{d\mathbf{r}}{dt} = (-\sin t)\mathbf{i} + (\cos t)\mathbf{j}$

3. $\mathbf{F} \cdot \dfrac{d\mathbf{r}}{dt} = -\sin t \cos t + \underbrace{\sin^2 t + \cos^2 t}_{1}$

4. $\text{Circulation} = \displaystyle\int_0^{2\pi} \mathbf{F} \cdot \frac{d\mathbf{r}}{dt}\, dt = \int_0^{2\pi} (1 - \sin t \cos t)\, dt$

$$= \left[t - \frac{\sin^2 t}{2}\right]_0^{2\pi} = 2\pi$$

Flux Across a Plane Curve

To find the rate at which a fluid is entering or leaving a region enclosed by a smooth curve C in the xy-plane, we calculate the line integral over C of $\mathbf{F} \cdot \mathbf{n}$, the scalar component of the fluid's velocity field in the direction of the curve's outward-pointing normal vector. The value of this integral is the *flux* of $\mathbf{F}$ across C. *Flux* is Latin for *flow*, but many flux calculations involve no motion at all. If $\mathbf{F}$ were an electric field or a magnetic field, for instance, the integral of $\mathbf{F} \cdot \mathbf{n}$ would still be called the flux of the field across C.

Definition   Flux Across a Closed Curve in the Plane

If C is a smooth closed curve in the domain of a continuous vector field $\mathbf{F} = M(x, y)\mathbf{i} + N(x, y)\mathbf{j}$ in the plane and if $\mathbf{n}$ is the outward-pointing unit normal vector on C, the **flux** of $\mathbf{F}$ across C is

$$\text{Flux of } \mathbf{F} \text{ across } C = \int_C \mathbf{F} \cdot \mathbf{n}\, ds. \tag{3}$$

Notice the difference between flux and circulation. The flux of $\mathbf{F}$ across C is the line integral with respect to arc length of $\mathbf{F} \cdot \mathbf{n}$, the scalar component of $\mathbf{F}$ in the direction of the outward normal. The circulation of $\mathbf{F}$ around C is the line integral with respect to arc length of $\mathbf{F} \cdot \mathbf{T}$, the scalar component of $\mathbf{F}$ in the direction of the unit tangent vector. Flux is the integral of the normal component of $\mathbf{F}$; circulation is the integral of the tangential component of $\mathbf{F}$.

To evaluate the integral in Equation (3), we begin with a smooth parametrization

$$x = g(t), \qquad y = h(t), \qquad a \le t \le b,$$

that traces the curve C exactly once as t increases from a to b. We can find the outward unit normal vector $\mathbf{n}$ by crossing the curve's unit tangent vector $\mathbf{T}$ with the vector $\mathbf{k}$. But which order do we choose, $\mathbf{T} \times \mathbf{k}$ or $\mathbf{k} \times \mathbf{T}$? Which one points outward? It depends on which way C is traversed as t increases. If the motion is clockwise, $\mathbf{k} \times \mathbf{T}$ points outward; if the motion is counterclockwise, $\mathbf{T} \times \mathbf{k}$ points outward (Figure 13.20). The usual choice is $\mathbf{n} = \mathbf{T} \times \mathbf{k}$, the choice that assumes counterclockwise motion. Thus, although the value of the arc length integral in the definition of flux in Equation (3) does not depend on which way C is traversed, the formulas we are about to derive for evaluating the integral in Equation (3) will assume counterclockwise motion.

In terms of components,

$$\mathbf{n} = \mathbf{T} \times \mathbf{k} = \left(\frac{dx}{ds} \mathbf{i} + \frac{dy}{ds} \mathbf{j} \right) \times \mathbf{k} = \frac{dy}{ds} \mathbf{i} - \frac{dx}{ds} \mathbf{j}.$$

If $\mathbf{F} = M(x, y)\mathbf{i} + N(x, y)\mathbf{j}$, then

$$\mathbf{F} \cdot \mathbf{n} = M(x, y) \frac{dy}{ds} - N(x, y) \frac{dx}{ds}.$$

Hence,

$$\int_C \mathbf{F} \cdot \mathbf{n}\, ds = \int_C \left(M \frac{dy}{ds} - N \frac{dx}{ds} \right) ds = \oint_C M\, dy - N\, dx.$$

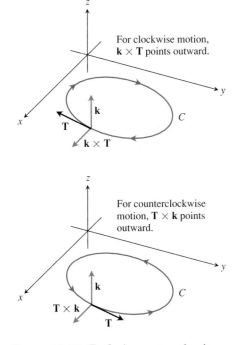

FIGURE 13.20 To find an outward unit normal vector for a smooth curve C in the xy-plane that is traversed counterclockwise as t increases, we take $\mathbf{n} = \mathbf{T} \times \mathbf{k}$.

For clockwise motion, $\mathbf{k} \times \mathbf{T}$ points outward.

For counterclockwise motion, $\mathbf{T} \times \mathbf{k}$ points outward.

We put a directed circle $\circlearrowleft$ on the last integral as a reminder that the integration around the closed curve C is to be in the counterclockwise direction. To evaluate this integral, we express M, dy, N, and dx in terms of t and integrate from $t = a$ to $t = b$. We do not need to know either $\mathbf{n}$ or ds to find the flux.

Formula for Calculating Flux Across a Smooth Closed Plane Curve

$$(\text{Flux of } \mathbf{F} = M\mathbf{i} + N\mathbf{j} \text{ across } C) = \oint_C M\, dy - N\, dx \qquad (4)$$

The integral can be evaluated from any smooth parametrization $x = g(t)$, $y = h(t), a \le t \le b$, that traces C counterclockwise exactly once.

Example 5   Finding Flux Across a Circle

Find the flux of $\mathbf{F} = (x - y)\mathbf{i} + x\mathbf{j}$ across the circle $x^2 + y^2 = 1$ in the xy-plane.

Solution   The parametrization $\mathbf{r}(t) = (\cos t)\mathbf{i} + (\sin t)\mathbf{j}, 0 \le t \le 2\pi$, traces the circle counterclockwise exactly once. We can therefore use this parametrization in Equation (4). With

$$M = x - y = \cos t - \sin t, \qquad dy = d(\sin t) = \cos t \, dt$$
$$N = x = \cos t, \qquad dx = d(\cos t) = -\sin t \, dt,$$

We find

$$\text{Flux} = \int_C M \, dy - N \, dx = \int_0^{2\pi} (\cos^2 t - \sin t \cos t + \cos t \sin t) \, dt \qquad \text{Eq. (4)}$$

$$= \int_0^{2\pi} \cos^2 t \, dt = \int_0^{2\pi} \frac{1 + \cos 2t}{2} \, dt = \left[\frac{t}{2} + \frac{\sin 2t}{4} \right]_0^{2\pi} = \pi.$$

The flux of $\mathbf{F}$ across the circle is π. Since the answer is positive, the net flow across the curve is outward. A net inward flow would have given a negative flux.

EXERCISES 13.2

Vector and Gradient Fields

Find the gradient fields of the functions in Exercises 1–4.

1. $f(x, y, z) = (x^2 + y^2 + z^2)^{-1/2}$

2. $f(x, y, z) = \ln \sqrt{x^2 + y^2 + z^2}$

3. $g(x, y, z) = e^z - \ln (x^2 + y^2)$

4. $g(x, y, z) = xy + yz + xz$

5. Give a formula $\mathbf{F} = M(x, y)\mathbf{i} + N(x, y)\mathbf{j}$ for the vector field in the plane that has the property that $\mathbf{F}$ points toward the origin with magnitude inversely proportional to the square of the distance from (x, y) to the origin. (The field is not defined at $(0, 0)$.)

6. Give a formula $\mathbf{F} = M(x, y)\mathbf{i} + N(x, y)\mathbf{j}$ for the vector field in the plane that has the properties that $\mathbf{F} = \mathbf{0}$ at $(0, 0)$ and that at any other point (a, b), $\mathbf{F}$ is tangent to the circle $x^2 + y^2 = a^2 + b^2$ and points in the clockwise direction with magnitude $|\mathbf{F}| = \sqrt{a^2 + b^2}$.

Work

In Exercises 7–12, find the work done by force $\mathbf{F}$ from $(0, 0, 0)$ to $(1, 1, 1)$ over each of the following paths (Figure 13.21):

(a) The straight-line path C_1: $\mathbf{r}(t) = t\mathbf{i} + t\mathbf{j} + t\mathbf{k}, \ 0 \le t \le 1$

(b) The curved path C_2: $\mathbf{r}(t) = t\mathbf{i} + t^2\mathbf{j} + t^4\mathbf{k}, \ 0 \le t \le 1$

(c) The path $C_3 \cup C_4$ consisting of the line segment from $(0, 0, 0)$ to $(1, 1, 0)$ followed by the segment from $(1, 1, 0)$ to $(1, 1, 1)$

7. $\mathbf{F} = 3y\mathbf{i} + 2x\mathbf{j} + 4z\mathbf{k}$

8. $\mathbf{F} = [1/(x^2 + 1)]\mathbf{j}$

9. $\mathbf{F} = \sqrt{z}\mathbf{i} - 2x\mathbf{j} + \sqrt{y}\mathbf{k}$

10. $\mathbf{F} = xy\mathbf{i} + yz\mathbf{j} + xz\mathbf{k}$

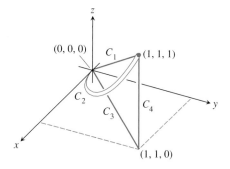

FIGURE 13.21 The paths from $(0, 0, 0)$ to $(1, 1, 1)$.

11. $\mathbf{F} = (3x^2 - 3x)\mathbf{i} + 3z\mathbf{j} + \mathbf{k}$

12. $\mathbf{F} = (y + z)\mathbf{i} + (z + x)\mathbf{j} + (x + y)\mathbf{k}$

In Exercises 13–16, find the work done by $\mathbf{F}$ over the curve in the direction of increasing t.

13. $\mathbf{F} = xy\mathbf{i} + y\mathbf{j} - yz\mathbf{k}$

$\mathbf{r}(t) = t\mathbf{i} + t^2\mathbf{j} + t\mathbf{k}, \ 0 \le t \le 1$

14. $\mathbf{F} = 2y\mathbf{i} + 3x\mathbf{j} + (x + y)\mathbf{k}$

$\mathbf{r}(t) = (\cos t)\mathbf{i} + (\sin t)\mathbf{j} + (t/6)\mathbf{k}, \ 0 \le t \le 2\pi$

15. $\mathbf{F} = z\mathbf{i} + x\mathbf{j} + y\mathbf{k}$

$\mathbf{r}(t) = (\sin t)\mathbf{i} + (\cos t)\mathbf{j} + t\mathbf{k}, \ 0 \le t \le 2\pi$

16. $\mathbf{F} = 6z\mathbf{i} + y^2\mathbf{j} + 12x\mathbf{k}$

$\mathbf{r}(t) = (\sin t)\mathbf{i} + (\cos t)\mathbf{j} + (t/6)\mathbf{k}, \ 0 \le t \le 2\pi$

Line Integrals and Vector Fields in the Plane

17. Evaluate $\int_C xy\,dx + (x + y)\,dy$ along the curve $y = x^2$ from $(-1, 1)$ to $(2, 4)$.

18. Evaluate $\int_C (x - y)\,dx + (x + y)\,dy$ counterclockwise around the triangle with vertices $(0, 0)$, $(1, 0)$, and $(0, 1)$.

19. Evaluate $\int_C \mathbf{F} \cdot \mathbf{T}\,ds$ for the vector field $\mathbf{F} = x^2\mathbf{i} - y\mathbf{j}$ along the curve $x = y^2$ from $(4, 2)$ to $(1, -1)$.

20. Evaluate $\int_C \mathbf{F} \cdot d\mathbf{r}$ for the vector field $\mathbf{F} = y\mathbf{i} - x\mathbf{j}$ counterclockwise along the unit circle $x^2 + y^2 = 1$ from $(1, 0)$ to $(0, 1)$.

21. *Work* Find the work done by the force $\mathbf{F} = xy\mathbf{i} + (y - x)\mathbf{j}$ over the straight line from $(1, 1)$ to $(2, 3)$.

22. *Work* Find the work done by the gradient of $f(x, y) = (x + y)^2$ counterclockwise around the circle $x^2 + y^2 = 4$ from $(2, 0)$ to itself.

23. *Circulation and flux* Find the circulation and flux of the fields
$$\mathbf{F}_1 = x\mathbf{i} + y\mathbf{j} \quad\text{and}\quad \mathbf{F}_2 = -y\mathbf{i} + x\mathbf{j}$$
around and across each of the following curves.

(a) The circle $\mathbf{r}(t) = (\cos t)\mathbf{i} + (\sin t)\mathbf{j}, \quad 0 \le t \le 2\pi$

(b) The ellipse $\mathbf{r}(t) = (\cos t)\mathbf{i} + (4 \sin t)\mathbf{j}, \quad 0 \le t \le 2\pi$

24. *Flux across a circle* Find the flux of the fields
$$\mathbf{F}_1 = 2x\mathbf{i} - 3y\mathbf{j} \quad\text{and}\quad \mathbf{F}_2 = 2x\mathbf{i} + (x - y)\mathbf{j}$$
across the circle
$$\mathbf{r}(t) = (a \cos t)\mathbf{i} + (a \sin t)\mathbf{j}, \quad 0 \le t \le 2\pi.$$

Circulation and Flux

In Exercises 25–28, find the circulation and flux of the field $\mathbf{F}$ around and across the closed semicircular path that consists of the semicircular arch $\mathbf{r}_1(t) = (a \cos t)\mathbf{i} + (a \sin t)\mathbf{j}, 0 \le t \le \pi$, followed by the line segment $\mathbf{r}_2(t) = t\mathbf{i}, -a \le t \le a$.

25. $\mathbf{F} = x\mathbf{i} + y\mathbf{j}$

26. $\mathbf{F} = x^2\mathbf{i} + y^2\mathbf{j}$

27. $\mathbf{F} = -y\mathbf{i} + x\mathbf{j}$

28. $\mathbf{F} = -y^2\mathbf{i} + x^2\mathbf{j}$

29. *Flow integrals* Find the flow of the velocity field $\mathbf{F} = (x + y)\mathbf{i} - (x^2 + y^2)\mathbf{j}$ along each of the following paths from $(1, 0)$ to $(-1, 0)$ in the xy-plane.

(a) The upper half of the circle $x^2 + y^2 = 1$

(b) The line segment from $(1, 0)$ to $(-1, 0)$

(c) The line segment from $(1, 0)$ to $(0, -1)$ followed by the line segment from $(0, -1)$ to $(-1, 0)$.

30. *Flux across a triangle* Find the flux of the field $\mathbf{F}$ in Exercise 29 outward across the triangle with vertices $(1, 0)$, $(0, 1)$, $(-1, 0)$.

Sketching and Finding Fields in the Plane

31. *Spin field* Draw the spin field
$$\mathbf{F} = -\frac{y}{\sqrt{x^2 + y^2}}\mathbf{i} + \frac{x}{\sqrt{x^2 + y^2}}\mathbf{j}$$

(see Figure 13.14) along with its horizontal and vertical components at a representative assortment of points on the circle $x^2 + y^2 = 4$.

32. *Radial field* Draw the radial field
$$\mathbf{F} = x\mathbf{i} + y\mathbf{j}$$

(see Figure 13.13) along with its horizontal and vertical components at a representative assortment of points on the circle $x^2 + y^2 = 1$.

33. *A field of tangent vectors* Find a field $\mathbf{G} = P(x, y)\mathbf{i} + Q(x, y)\mathbf{j}$ in the xy-plane with the property that at any point $(a, b) \ne (0, 0)$, $\mathbf{G}$ is a vector of magnitude $\sqrt{a^2 + b^2}$ tangent to the circle $x^2 + y^2 = a^2 + b^2$ and pointing in the counterclockwise direction. (The field is undefined at $(0, 0)$.)

(b) *Writing to Learn* How is $\mathbf{G}$ related to the spin field $\mathbf{F}$ in Figure 13.14?

34. *A field of tangent vectors*

(a) Find a field $\mathbf{G} = P(x, y)\mathbf{i} + Q(x, y)\mathbf{j}$ in the xy-plane with the property that at any point $(a, b) \ne (0, 0)$, $\mathbf{G}$ is a unit vector tangent to the circle $x^2 + y^2 = a^2 + b^2$ and pointing in the clockwise direction.

(b) *Writing to Learn* How is $\mathbf{G}$ related to the spin field $\mathbf{F}$ in Figure 13.14?

35. *Unit vectors pointing toward the origin* Find a field $\mathbf{F} = M(x, y)\mathbf{i} + N(x, y)\mathbf{j}$ in the xy-plane with the property that at each point $(x, y) \ne (0, 0)$, $\mathbf{F}$ is a unit vector pointing toward the origin. (The field is undefined at $(0, 0)$.)

36. *Two "central" fields* Find a field $\mathbf{F} = M(x, y)\mathbf{i} + N(x, y)\mathbf{j}$ in the xy-plane with the property that at each point $(x, y) \ne (0, 0)$, $\mathbf{F}$ points toward the origin and $|\mathbf{F}|$ is (a) the distance from (x, y) to the origin, (b) inversely proportional to the distance from (x, y) to the origin. (The field is undefined at $(0, 0)$.)

Flow Integrals in Space

In Exercises 37–40, $\mathbf{F}$ is the velocity field of a fluid flowing through a region in space. Find the flow along the given curve in the direction of increasing t.

37. $\mathbf{F} = -4xy\mathbf{i} + 8y\mathbf{j} + 2\mathbf{k}$
$$\mathbf{r}(t) = t\mathbf{i} + t^2\mathbf{j} + \mathbf{k}, \quad 0 \le t \le 2$$

38. $\mathbf{F} = x^2\mathbf{i} + yz\mathbf{j} + y^2\mathbf{k}$
$$\mathbf{r}(t) = 3t\mathbf{j} + 4t\mathbf{k}, \quad 0 \le t \le 1$$

39. $\mathbf{F} = (x - z)\mathbf{i} + x\mathbf{k}$
$$\mathbf{r}(t) = (\cos t)\mathbf{i} + (\sin t)\mathbf{k}, \quad 0 \le t \le \pi$$

40. $\mathbf{F} = -y\mathbf{i} + x\mathbf{j} + 2\mathbf{k}$
$$\mathbf{r}(t) = (-2 \cos t)\mathbf{i} + (2 \sin t)\mathbf{j} + 2t\mathbf{k}, \quad 0 \le t \le 2\pi$$

41. *Circulation* Find the circulation of $\mathbf{F} = 2x\mathbf{i} + 2z\mathbf{j} + 2y\mathbf{k}$ around the closed path consisting of the following three curves traversed in the direction of increasing t:

C_1: $\mathbf{r}(t) = (\cos t)\mathbf{i} + (\sin t)\mathbf{j} + t\mathbf{k}$, $\quad 0 \le t \le \pi/2$

C_2: $\mathbf{r}(t) = \mathbf{j} + (\pi/2)(1 - t)\mathbf{k}$, $\quad 0 \le t \le 1$

C_3: $\mathbf{r}(t) = t\mathbf{i} + (1 - t)\mathbf{j}$, $\quad 0 \le t \le 1$

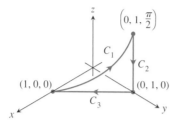

42. *Zero circulation* Let C be the ellipse in which the plane $2x + 3y - z = 0$ meets the cylinder $x^2 + y^2 = 12$. Show, without evaluating either line integral directly, that the circulation of the field $\mathbf{F} = x\mathbf{i} + y\mathbf{j} + z\mathbf{k}$ around C in either direction is zero.

43. *Flow along a curve* The field $\mathbf{F} = xy\mathbf{i} + y\mathbf{j} - yz\mathbf{k}$ is the velocity field of a flow in space. Find the flow from $(0, 0, 0)$ to $(1, 1, 1)$ along the curve of intersection of the cylinder $y = x^2$ and the plane $z = x$. (*Hint:* Use $t = x$ as the parameter.)

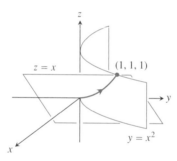

44. *Flow of a gradient field* Find the flow of the field $\mathbf{F} = \nabla(xy^2z^3)$:

(a) Once around the curve C in Exercise 42, clockwise as viewed from above

(b) Along the line segment from $(1, 1, 1)$ to $(2, 1, -1)$.

Theory and Examples

45. *Writing to Learn: Work and area* Suppose that $f(t)$ is differentiable and positive for $a \le t \le b$. Let C be the path $\mathbf{r}(t) = t\mathbf{i} + f(t)\mathbf{j}$,

$a \le t \le b$, and $\mathbf{F} = y\mathbf{i}$. Is there any relation between the value of the work integral

$$\int_C \mathbf{F} \cdot d\mathbf{r}$$

and the area of the region bounded by the t-axis, the graph of f, and the lines $t = a$ and $t = b$? Give reasons for your answer.

46. *Work done by a radial force with constant magnitude* A particle moves along the smooth curve $y = f(x)$ from $(a, f(a))$ to $(b, f(b))$. The force moving the particle has constant magnitude k and always points away from the origin. Show that the work done by the force is

$$\int_C \mathbf{F} \cdot \mathbf{T} \, ds = k[(b^2 + (f(b))^2)^{1/2} - (a^2 + (f(a))^2)^{1/2}].$$

COMPUTER EXPLORATIONS

Finding Work Numerically

In Exercises 47–52, use a CAS to perform the following steps for finding the work done by force $\mathbf{F}$ over the given path:

(a) Find $d\mathbf{r}$ for the path $\mathbf{r}(t) = g(t)\mathbf{i} + h(t)\mathbf{j} + k(t)\mathbf{k}$.

(b) Evaluate the force $\mathbf{F}$ along the path.

(c) Evaluate $\displaystyle\int_C \mathbf{F} \cdot d\mathbf{r}$.

47. $\mathbf{F} = xy^6\mathbf{i} + 3x(xy^5 + 2)\mathbf{j}$; $\quad \mathbf{r}(t) = (2 \cos t)\mathbf{i} + (\sin t)\mathbf{j}$, $0 \le t \le 2\pi$

48. $\mathbf{F} = \dfrac{3}{1 + x^2}\mathbf{i} + \dfrac{2}{1 + y^2}\mathbf{j}$; $\quad \mathbf{r}(t) = (\cos t)\mathbf{i} + (\sin t)\mathbf{j}$, $\quad 0 \le t \le \pi$

49. $\mathbf{F} = (y + yz \cos xyz)\mathbf{i} + (x^2 + xz \cos xyz)\mathbf{j} + (z + xy \cos xyz)\mathbf{k}$; $\mathbf{r}(t) = 2 \cos t\mathbf{i} + 3 \sin t\mathbf{j} + \mathbf{k}$, $\quad 0 \le t \le 2\pi$

50. $\mathbf{F} = 2xy\mathbf{i} - y^2\mathbf{j} + ze^x\mathbf{k}$; $\quad \mathbf{r}(t) = -t\mathbf{i} + \sqrt{t}\mathbf{j} + 3t\mathbf{k}$, $\quad 1 \le t \le 4$

51. $\mathbf{F} = (2y + \sin x)\mathbf{i} + (z^2 + (1/3) \cos y)\mathbf{j} + x^4\mathbf{k}$; $\mathbf{r}(t) = (\sin t)\mathbf{i} + (\cos t)\mathbf{j} + (\sin 2t)\mathbf{k}$, $\quad -\pi/2 \le t \le \pi/2$

52. $\mathbf{F} = (x^2y)\mathbf{i} + \dfrac{1}{3}x^3\mathbf{j} + xy\mathbf{k}$; $\quad \mathbf{r}(t) = (\cos t)\mathbf{i} + (\sin t)\mathbf{j} + (2 \sin^2 (t) - 1)\mathbf{k}$, $\quad 0 \le t \le 2\pi$

Path Independence, Potential Functions, and Conservative Fields

Path Independence • Assumptions in Effect From Now On: Connectivity • Line Integrals in Conservative Fields • Finding Potentials for Conservative Fields • Exact Differential Forms

In gravitational and electric fields, the amount of work it takes to move a mass or a charge from one point to another depends only on the object's initial and final positions and not on the path taken in between. This section discusses the notion of path independence of work integrals and describes the remarkable properties of fields in which work integrals are path independent.

Path Independence

If A and B are two points in an open region D in space, the work $\int \mathbf{F} \cdot d\mathbf{r}$ done in moving a particle from A to B by a field $\mathbf{F}$ defined on D usually depends on the path taken. For some special fields, however, the integral's value is the same for all paths from A to B. If this is true for all points A and B in D, we say that the integral $\int \mathbf{F} \cdot d\mathbf{r}$ is path independent in D and that $\mathbf{F}$ is conservative on D.

CD-ROM
WEBsite

> **Definitions**   Path Independence and Conservative Field
>
> Let $\mathbf{F}$ be a field defined on an open region D in space and suppose that for any two points A and B in D the work $\int_B^A \mathbf{F} \cdot d\mathbf{r}$ done in moving from A to B is the same over all paths from A to B. Then the integral $\int \mathbf{F} \cdot d\mathbf{r}$ is **path independent in D** and the field $\mathbf{F}$ is **conservative on D.**

The word *conservative* comes from physics, where it refers to fields in which the principle of conservation of energy holds (it does, in conservative fields).

Under conditions normally met in practice, a field $\mathbf{F}$ is conservative if and only if it is the gradient field of a scalar function f; that is, if and only if $\mathbf{F} = \nabla f$ for some f. The function f is then called a potential function for $\mathbf{F}$.

> **Definition**   Potential Function
>
> If $\mathbf{F}$ is a field defined on D and $\mathbf{F} = \nabla f$ for some scalar function f on an open region D in space, then f is called a **potential function for $\mathbf{F}$ on D.**

An electric potential is a scalar function whose gradient field is an electric field. A gravitational potential is a scalar function whose gradient field is a gravitational field, and so on. As we will see, once we have found a potential function f for a field $\mathbf{F}$, we can evaluate all the work integrals in the domain of $\mathbf{F}$ with the formula

$$\int_A^B \mathbf{F} \cdot d\mathbf{r} = \int_A^B \nabla f \cdot d\mathbf{r} = f(B) - f(A). \tag{1}$$

If you think of ∇F for functions of several variables as being something like the derivative f' for functions of a single variable, then you see that Equation (1) is the vector calculus analogue of the Fundamental Theorem of Calculus formula

$$\int_a^b f'(x) \, dx = f(b) - f(a).$$

Conservative fields have other remarkable properties we study as we go along. For example, saying that $\mathbf{F}$ is conservative on D is equivalent to saying that the integral of $\mathbf{F}$ around every closed path in D is zero. Naturally, we need to impose conditions on the curves, fields, and domains to make Equation (1) and its implications hold.

Assumptions in Effect from Now On: Connectivity

We assume that all curves are **piecewise smooth,** that is, made up of finitely many smooth pieces connected end to end, as discussed in Section 10.5. We also assume that the components of **F** have continuous first partial derivatives. When $\mathbf{F} = \nabla f$, this continuity requirement guarantees that the mixed second derivatives of the potential function f are equal, a result we will find revealing in studying conservative fields **F.**

We assume D to be an *open* region in space. This means that every point in D is the center of a ball that lies entirely in D. We also assume D to be **connected,** which in an open region means that every point can be connected to every other point by a smooth curve that lies entirely in the region.

CD-ROM
WEBsite

Historical Biography

Gustav Robert Kirchoff
(1824 — 1887)

Line Integrals in Conservative Fields

The following result provides a convenient way to evaluate a line integral in a conservative field. The result establishes that the value of the integral depends only on the endpoints and not on the specific path joining them.

Theorem 1   The Fundamental Theorem of Line Integrals

1. Let $\mathbf{F} = M\mathbf{i} + N\mathbf{j} + P\mathbf{k}$ be a vector field whose components are continuous throughout an open connected region D in space. Then there exists a differentiable function f such that

$$\mathbf{F} = \nabla f = \frac{\partial f}{\partial x}\mathbf{i} + \frac{\partial f}{\partial y}\mathbf{j} + \frac{\partial f}{\partial z}\mathbf{k}$$

if and only if for all points A and B in D the value of $\int_A^B \mathbf{F} \cdot d\mathbf{r}$ is independent of the path joining A to B in D.

2. If the integral is independent of the path from A to B, its value is

$$\int_A^B \mathbf{F} \cdot d\mathbf{r} = f(B) - f(A).$$

Proof that F = ∇f Implies Path Independence of the Integral   Suppose that A and B are two points in D and that $C: \mathbf{r}(t) = g(t)\mathbf{i} + h(t)\mathbf{j} + k(t)\mathbf{k}, a \le t \le b$, is a smooth curve in D joining A and B. Along the curve, f is a differentiable function of t and

$$\frac{df}{dt} = \frac{\partial f}{\partial x}\frac{dx}{dt} + \frac{\partial f}{\partial y}\frac{dy}{dt} + \frac{\partial f}{\partial z}\frac{dz}{dt} \qquad \text{Chain Rule}$$

$$= \nabla f \cdot \left(\frac{dx}{dt}\mathbf{i} + \frac{dy}{dt}\mathbf{j} + \frac{dz}{dt}\mathbf{k}\right) = \nabla f \cdot \frac{d\mathbf{r}}{dt} = \mathbf{F} \cdot \frac{d\mathbf{r}}{dt}. \qquad \begin{array}{l}\text{Because}\\ \mathbf{F} = \nabla f\end{array}$$

Therefore,

$$\int_C \mathbf{F} \cdot d\mathbf{r} = \int_{t=a}^{t=b} \mathbf{F} \cdot \frac{d\mathbf{r}}{dt}\, dt = \int_a^b \frac{df}{dt}\, dt$$

$$= f(g(t), h(t), k(t)) \Big]_a^b = f(B) - f(A).$$

Thus, the value of the work integral depends only on the values of f at A and B and not on the path in between. This proves part 2 as well as the forward implication in part 1. We omit the more technical proof of the reverse implication. ▬

Example 1   Finding Work Done by a Conservative Field

Find the work done by the conservative field

$$\mathbf{F} = yz\mathbf{i} + xz\mathbf{j} + xy\mathbf{k} = \nabla(xyz)$$

along any smooth curve C joining the point $(-1, 3, 9)$ to $(1, 6, -4)$.

Solution   With $f(x, y, z) = xyz$, we have

$$\int_A^B \mathbf{F} \cdot d\mathbf{r} = \int_A^B \nabla f \cdot d\mathbf{r} \qquad \mathbf{F} = \nabla f$$

$$= f(B) - f(A) \qquad \text{Fundamental Theorem, Part 2}$$

$$= xyz \big|_{(1,6,-4)} - xyz \big|_{(-1,3,9)}$$

$$= (1)(6)(-4) - (-1)(3)(9)$$

$$= -24 + 27 = 3.$$

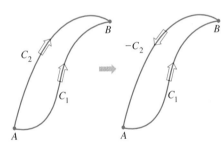

FIGURE 13.22 If we have two paths from A to B, one of them can be reversed to make a loop.

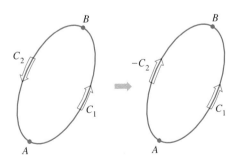

FIGURE 13.23 If A and B lie on a loop, we can reverse part of the loop to make two paths from A to B.

Theorem 2   Closed-Loop Property of Conservative Fields

The following statements are equivalent.

1. $\int \mathbf{F} \cdot d\mathbf{r} = 0$ around every closed loop in D.

2. The field $\mathbf{F}$ is conservative on D.

Proof that (1) $\Rightarrow$ (2)   We want to show that for any two points A and B in D, the integral of $\mathbf{F} \cdot d\mathbf{r}$ has the same value over any two paths C_1 and C_2 from A to B. We reverse the direction on C_2 to make a path $-C_2$ from B to A (Figure 13.22). Together, C_1 and $-C_2$ make a closed loop C, and

$$\int_{C_1} \mathbf{F} \cdot d\mathbf{r} - \int_{C_2} \mathbf{F} \cdot d\mathbf{r} = \int_{C_1} \mathbf{F} \cdot d\mathbf{r} + \int_{-C_2} \mathbf{F} \cdot d\mathbf{r} = \int_C \mathbf{F} \cdot d\mathbf{r} = 0.$$

Thus, the integrals over C_1 and C_2 give the same value. ▬

Proof that (2) $\Rightarrow$ (1)   We want to show that the integral of $\mathbf{F} \cdot d\mathbf{r}$ is zero over any closed loop C. We pick two points A and B on C and use them to break C into two pieces: C_1 from A and B followed by C_2 from B back to A (Figure 13.23). Then

$$\oint_C \mathbf{F} \cdot d\mathbf{r} = \int_{C_1} \mathbf{F} \cdot d\mathbf{r} + \int_{C_2} \mathbf{F} \cdot d\mathbf{r} = \int_A^B \mathbf{F} \cdot d\mathbf{r} - \int_A^B \mathbf{F} \cdot d\mathbf{r} = 0.$$ ▬

The following diagram summarizes the results of Theorems 1 and 2.

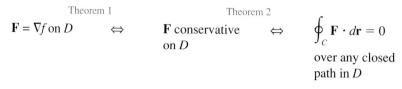

Now that we see how convenient it is to evaluate line integrals in conservative fields, two questions remain.

1. How do we know when a given field $\mathbf{F}$ is conservative?

2. If $\mathbf{F}$ is in fact conservative, how do we find a potential function f (so that $\mathbf{F} = \nabla f$)?

Finding Potentials for Conservative Fields

The test for being conservative is the following.

Component Test for Conservative Fields

Let $\mathbf{F} = M(x, y, z)\mathbf{i} + N(x, y, z)\mathbf{j} + P(x, y, z)\mathbf{k}$ be a field whose component functions have continuous first partial derivatives. Then, $\mathbf{F}$ is conservative if and only if

$$\frac{\partial P}{\partial y} = \frac{\partial N}{\partial z}, \qquad \frac{\partial M}{\partial z} = \frac{\partial P}{\partial x}, \qquad \text{and} \qquad \frac{\partial N}{\partial x} = \frac{\partial M}{\partial y}. \qquad (2)$$

Proof that Equations (2) hold if $\mathbf{F}$ is conservative There is a potential function f such that

$$\mathbf{F} = M\mathbf{i} + N\mathbf{j} + P\mathbf{k} = \frac{\partial f}{\partial x}\mathbf{i} + \frac{\partial f}{\partial y}\mathbf{j} + \frac{\partial f}{\partial z}\mathbf{k}.$$

Hence,

$$\frac{\partial P}{\partial y} = \frac{\partial}{\partial y}\left(\frac{\partial f}{\partial z}\right) = \frac{\partial^2 f}{\partial y\,\partial z}$$

$$= \frac{\partial^2 f}{\partial z\,\partial y} \qquad \text{Continuity implies that the mixed partial derivatives are equal.}$$

$$= \frac{\partial}{\partial z}\left(\frac{\partial f}{\partial y}\right) = \frac{\partial N}{\partial z}.$$

The others in Equations (2) are proved similarly.

The second half of the proof, that Equations (2) imply that $\mathbf{F}$ is conservative, is a consequence of Stokes' Theorem, taken up in Section 13.7.

Once we know $\mathbf{F}$ is conservative, we usually want to find a potential function for $\mathbf{F}$. This requires solving the equation $\nabla f = \mathbf{F}$ or

$$\frac{\partial f}{\partial x}\mathbf{i} + \frac{\partial f}{\partial y}\mathbf{j} + \frac{\partial f}{\partial z}\mathbf{k} = M\mathbf{i} + N\mathbf{j} + P\mathbf{k}$$

CD-ROM
WEBsite

for f. We accomplish this by integrating the three equations

$$\frac{\partial f}{\partial x} = M, \qquad \frac{\partial f}{\partial y} = N, \qquad \frac{\partial f}{\partial z} = P,$$

as illustrated in the next example.

Example 2   Finding a Potential Function

Show that $\mathbf{F} = (e^x \cos y + yz)\mathbf{i} + (xz - e^x \sin y)\mathbf{j} + (xy + z)\mathbf{k}$ is conservative and find a potential function for it.

Solution   We apply the test in Equations (2) to

$$M = e^x \cos y + yz, \qquad N = xz - e^x \sin y, \qquad P = xy + z$$

and calculate

$$\frac{\partial P}{\partial y} = x = \frac{\partial N}{\partial z}, \qquad \frac{\partial M}{\partial z} = y = \frac{\partial P}{\partial x}, \qquad \frac{\partial N}{\partial x} = -e^x \sin y + z = \frac{\partial M}{\partial y}.$$

Together, these equalities tell us that there is a function f with $\nabla f = \mathbf{F}.$
    We find f by integrating the equations

$$\frac{\partial f}{\partial x} = e^x \cos y + yz, \qquad \frac{\partial f}{\partial y} = xz - e^x \sin y, \qquad \frac{\partial f}{\partial z} = xy + z. \tag{3}$$

We integrate the first equation with respect to x, holding y and z fixed, to get

$$f(x, y, z) = e^x \cos y + xyz + g(y, z).$$

We write the constant of integration as a function of y and z because its value may change if y and z change. We then calculate $\partial f / \partial y$ from this equation and match it with the expression for $\partial f / \partial y$ in Equations (3). This gives

$$-e^x \sin y + xz + \frac{\partial g}{\partial y} = xz - e^x \sin y,$$

so $\partial g / \partial y = 0$. Therefore, g is a function of z alone, and

$$f(x, y, z) = e^x \cos y + xyz + h(z).$$

We now calculate $\partial f / \partial z$ from this equation and match it to the formula for $\partial f / \partial z$ in Equations (3). This gives

$$xy + \frac{dh}{dz} = xy + z, \qquad \text{or} \qquad \frac{dh}{dz} = z,$$

so

$$h(z) = \frac{z^2}{2} + C.$$

Hence,

$$f(x, y, z) = e^x \cos y + xyz + \frac{z^2}{2} + C.$$

We have infinitely many potential functions for $\mathbf{F}$, one for each value of C.

Example 3   Showing That a Field Is Not Conservative

Show that $\mathbf{F} = (2x - 3)\mathbf{i} - z\mathbf{j} + (\cos z)\mathbf{k}$ is not conservative.

Solution   We apply the component test in Equations (2) and find right away that

$$\frac{\partial P}{\partial y} = \frac{\partial}{\partial y}(\cos z) = 0, \qquad \frac{\partial N}{\partial z} = \frac{\partial}{\partial z}(-z) = -1.$$

The two are unequal, so $\mathbf{F}$ is not conservative. No further testing is required.

CD-ROM
WEBsite

Historical Biography

Ernst Mach
(1838 — 1916)

Exact Differential Forms

As we see in the next section and again later on, it is often convenient to express work and circulation integrals in the "differential" form

$$\int_A^B M\,dx + N\,dy + P\,dz$$

mentioned in Section 13.2. Such integrals are relatively easy to evaluate if $M\,dx + N\,dy + P\,dz$ is the total differential of a function f. For then

$$\int_A^B M\,dx + N\,dy + P\,dz = \int_A^B \frac{\partial f}{\partial x}\,dx + \frac{\partial f}{\partial y}\,dy + \frac{\partial f}{\partial z}\,dz$$

$$= \int_A^B \nabla f \cdot d\mathbf{r}$$

$$= f(B) - f(A). \qquad \text{Theorem 1}$$

Thus,

$$\int_A^B df = f(B) - f(A),$$

just as with differentiable functions of a single variable.

Definitions   Differential Form and Exact Differential Form
Any form $M(x, y, z)\,dx + N(x, y, z)\,dy + P(x, y, z)\,dz$ is a **differential form**. A differential form is **exact** on a domain D in space if

$$M\,dx + N\,dy + P\,dz = \frac{\partial f}{\partial x}\,dx + \frac{\partial f}{\partial y}\,dy + \frac{\partial f}{\partial z}\,dz = df$$

for some scalar function f throughout D.

Notice that if $M\,dx + N\,dy + P\,dz = df$ on D, then $\mathbf{F} = M\mathbf{i} + N\mathbf{j} + P\mathbf{k}$ is the gradient field of f on D. Conversely, if $\mathbf{F} = \nabla f$, then the form $M\,dx + N\,dy + P\,dz$ is exact. The test for the form's being exact is therefore the same as the test for $\mathbf{F}$'s being conservative.

Component Test for Exactness of $M\,dx + N\,dy + P\,dz$

The differential form $M\,dx + N\,dy + P\,dz$ is exact if and only if

$$\frac{\partial P}{\partial y} = \frac{\partial N}{\partial z}, \qquad \frac{\partial M}{\partial z} = \frac{\partial P}{\partial x}, \qquad \text{and} \qquad \frac{\partial N}{\partial x} = \frac{\partial M}{\partial y}.$$

This is equivalent to saying that the field $\mathbf{F} = M\mathbf{i} + N\mathbf{j} + P\mathbf{k}$ is conservative.

Example 4   Showing That a Differential Form Is Exact

Show that $y\,dx + x\,dy + 4\,dz$ is exact and evaluate the integral

$$\int_{(1,1,1)}^{(2,3,-1)} y\,dx + x\,dy + 4\,dz$$

over the line segment from $(1, 1, 1)$ to $(2, 3, -1)$.

Solution   We let $M = y$, $N = x$, $P = 4$ and apply the Test for Exactness:

$$\frac{\partial P}{\partial y} = 0 = \frac{\partial N}{\partial z}, \qquad \frac{\partial M}{\partial z} = 0 = \frac{\partial P}{\partial x}, \qquad \frac{\partial N}{\partial x} = 1 = \frac{\partial M}{\partial y}.$$

These equalities tell us that $y\,dx + x\,dy + 4\,dz$ is exact, so

$$y\,dx + x\,dy + 4\,dz = df$$

for some function f, and the integral's value is $f(2, 3, -1) - f(1, 1, 1)$.

We find f up to a constant by integrating the equations

$$\frac{\partial f}{\partial x} = y, \qquad \frac{\partial f}{\partial y} = x, \qquad \frac{\partial f}{\partial z} = 4. \tag{4}$$

From the first equation we get

$$f(x, y, z) = xy + g(y, z).$$

The second equation tells us that

$$\frac{\partial f}{\partial y} = x + \frac{\partial g}{\partial y} = x, \qquad \text{or} \qquad \frac{\partial g}{\partial y} = 0.$$

Hence, g is a function of z alone, and

$$f(x, y, z) = xy + h(z).$$

The third of Equations (4) tells us that

$$\frac{\partial f}{\partial z} = 0 + \frac{dh}{dz} = 4, \qquad \text{or} \qquad h(z) = 4z + C.$$

Therefore,

$$f(x, y, z) = xy + 4z + C.$$

The value of the integral is

$$f(2, 3, -1) - f(1, 1, 1) = 2 + C - (5 + C) = -3.$$

EXERCISES 13.3

Testing for Conservative Fields

CD-ROM WEBsite Which fields in Exercises 1–6 are conservative and which are not?

1. $\mathbf{F} = yz\mathbf{i} + xz\mathbf{j} + xy\mathbf{k}$

2. $\mathbf{F} = (y \sin z)\mathbf{i} + (x \sin z)\mathbf{j} + (xy \cos z)\mathbf{k}$

3. $\mathbf{F} = y\mathbf{i} + (x + z)\mathbf{j} - y\mathbf{k}$

4. $\mathbf{F} = -y\mathbf{i} + x\mathbf{j}$

5. $\mathbf{F} = (z + y)\mathbf{i} + z\mathbf{j} + (y + x)\mathbf{k}$

6. $\mathbf{F} = (e^x \cos y)\mathbf{i} - (e^x \sin y)\mathbf{j} + z\mathbf{k}$

Finding Potential Functions

In Exercises 7–12, find a potential function f for the field $\mathbf{F}$.

7. $\mathbf{F} = 2x\mathbf{i} + 3y\mathbf{j} + 4z\mathbf{k}$

8. $\mathbf{F} = (y + z)\mathbf{i} + (x + z)\mathbf{j} + (x + y)\mathbf{k}$

9. $\mathbf{F} = e^{y+2z}(\mathbf{i} + x\mathbf{j} + 2x\mathbf{k})$

10. $\mathbf{F} = (y \sin z)\mathbf{i} + (x \sin z)\mathbf{j} + (xy \cos z)\mathbf{k}$

11. $\mathbf{F} = (\ln x + \sec^2 (x + y))\mathbf{i}$

$$+ \left(\sec^2 (x + y) + \frac{y}{y^2 + z^2} \right)\mathbf{j} + \frac{z}{y^2 + z^2}\mathbf{k}$$

12. $\mathbf{F} = \dfrac{y}{1 + x^2y^2}\mathbf{i} + \left(\dfrac{x}{1 + x^2y^2} + \dfrac{z}{\sqrt{1 - y^2z^2}} \right)\mathbf{j}$

$$+ \left(\dfrac{y}{\sqrt{1 - y^2z^2}} + \dfrac{1}{z} \right)\mathbf{k}$$

Evaluating Integrals of Exact Differential Forms

In Exercises 13–22, show that the differential forms in the integrals are exact. Then evaluate the integrals.

13. $\displaystyle\int_{(0,0,0)}^{(2,3,-6)} 2x \, dx + 2y \, dy + 2z \, dz$

14. $\displaystyle\int_{(1,1,2)}^{(3,5,0)} yz \, dx + xz \, dy + xy \, dz$

15. $\displaystyle\int_{(0,0,0)}^{(1,2,3)} 2xy \, dx + (x^2 - z^2) \, dy - 2yz \, dz$

16. $\displaystyle\int_{(0,0,0)}^{(3,3,1)} 2x \, dx - y^2 \, dy - \frac{4}{1 + z^2} \, dz$

17. $\displaystyle\int_{(1,0,0)}^{(0,1,1)} \sin y \cos x \, dx + \cos y \sin x \, dy + dz$

18. $\displaystyle\int_{(0,2,1)}^{(1,\pi/2,2)} 2 \cos y \, dx + \left(\frac{1}{y} - 2x \sin y \right) dy + \frac{1}{z} \, dz$

19. $\displaystyle\int_{(1,1,1)}^{(1,2,3)} 3x^2 \, dx + \frac{z^2}{y} \, dy + 2z \ln y \, dz$

20. $\displaystyle\int_{(1,2,1)}^{(2,1,1)} (2x \ln y - yz) \, dx + \left(\frac{x^2}{y} - xz \right) dy - xy \, dz$

21. $\displaystyle\int_{(1,1,1)}^{(2,2,2)} \frac{1}{y} \, dx + \left(\frac{1}{z} - \frac{x}{y^2} \right) dy - \frac{y}{z^2} \, dz$

22. $\displaystyle\int_{(-1,-1,-1)}^{(2,2,2)} \frac{2x \, dx + 2y \, dy + 2z \, dz}{x^2 + y^2 + z^2}$

23. *Revisiting Example 4* Evaluate the integral

$$\int_{(1,1,1)}^{(2,3,-1)} y \, dx + x \, dy + 4 \, dz$$

from Example 4 by finding parametric equations for the line segment from $(1, 1, 1)$ to $(2, 3, -1)$ and evaluating the line integral of $\mathbf{F} = y\mathbf{i} + x\mathbf{j} + 4\mathbf{k}$ along the segment. Since $\mathbf{F}$ is conservative, the integral is independent of the path.

24. Evaluate

$$\int_C x^2 \, dx + yz \, dy + (y^2/2) \, dz$$

along the line segment C joining $(0, 0, 0)$ to $(0, 3, 4)$.

Theory, Applications, and Examples

Independence of path Show that the values of the integrals in Exercises 25 and 26 do not depend on the path taken from A to B.

25. $\displaystyle\int_A^B z^2 \, dx + 2y \, dy + 2xz \, dz$

26. $\displaystyle\int_A^B \frac{x \, dx + y \, dy + z \, dz}{\sqrt{x^2 + y^2 + z^2}}$

In Exercises 27 and 28, find a potential function for $\mathbf{F}$.

27. $\mathbf{F} = \dfrac{2x}{y}\mathbf{i} + \left(\dfrac{1 - x^2}{y^2} \right)\mathbf{j}$

28. $\mathbf{F} = (e^x \ln y)\mathbf{i} + \left(\dfrac{e^x}{y} + \sin z \right)\mathbf{j} + (y \cos z)\mathbf{k}$

29. *Work along different paths* Find the work done by $\mathbf{F} = (x^2 + y)\mathbf{i} + (y^2 + x)\mathbf{j} + ze^z\mathbf{k}$ over the following paths from $(1, 0, 0)$ to $(1, 0, 1)$.

(a) The line segment $x = 1, y = 0, 0 \le z \le 1$

(b) The helix $\mathbf{r}(t) = (\cos t)\mathbf{i} + (\sin t)\mathbf{j} + (t/2\pi)\mathbf{k}, 0 \leq t \leq 2\pi$

(c) The x-axis from $(1, 0, 0)$ to $(0, 0, 0)$ followed by the parabola $z = x^2, y = 0$ from $(0, 0, 0)$ to $(1, 0, 1)$

30. *Work along different paths* Find the work done by $\mathbf{F} = e^{yz}\mathbf{i} + (xze^{yz} + z \cos y)\mathbf{j} + (xye^{yz} + \sin y)\mathbf{k}$ over the following paths from $(1, 0, 1)$ to $(1, \pi/2, 0)$.

CD-ROM
WEBsite

(a) The line segment $x = 1, y = \pi t/2, z = 1 - t, 0 \leq t \leq 1$

(b) The line segment from $(1, 0, 1)$ to the origin followed by the line segment from the origin to $(1, \pi/2, 0)$

(c) The line segment from $(1, 0, 1)$ to $(1, 0, 0)$, followed by the x-axis from $(1, 0, 0)$ to the origin, followed by the parabola $y = \pi x^2/2, z = 0$ from there to $(1, \pi/2, 0)$

31. *Evaluating a work integral two ways* Let $\mathbf{F} = \nabla(x^3 y^2)$ and let C be the path in the xy-plane from $(-1, 1)$ to $(1, 1)$ that consists of the line segment from $(-1, 1)$ to $(0, 0)$ followed by the line segment from $(0, 0)$ to $(1, 1)$. Evaluate $\int_C \mathbf{F} \cdot d\mathbf{r}$ in two ways.

(a) Find parametrizations for the segments that make up C and evaluate the integral.

(b) Using $f(x, y) = x^3 y^2$ as a potential function for $\mathbf{F}$.

32. *Integral along different paths* Evaluate $\int_C 2x \cos y \, dx - x^2 \sin y \, dy$ along the following paths C in the xy-plane.

(a) The parabola $y = (x - 1)^2$ from $(1, 0)$ to $(0, 1)$

(b) The line segment from $(-1, \pi)$ to $(1, 0)$

(c) The x-axis from $(-1, 0)$ to $(1, 0)$

(d) The astroid $\mathbf{r}(t) = (\cos^3 t)\mathbf{i} + (\sin^3 t)\mathbf{j}, 0 \leq t \leq 2\pi$, counterclockwise from $(1, 0)$ back to $(1, 0)$

33. (a) *Exact differential form* How are the constants a, b, and c related if the following differential form is exact?

$$(ay^2 + 2czx) \, dx + y(bx + cz) \, dy + (ay^2 + cx^2) \, dz$$

(b) *Gradient field* For what values of b and c will

$$\mathbf{F} = (y^2 + 2czx)\mathbf{i} + y(bx + cz)\mathbf{j} + (y^2 + cx^2)\mathbf{k}$$

be a gradient field?

34. *Gradient of a line integral* Suppose that $\mathbf{F} = \nabla f$ is a conservative vector field and

$$g(x, y, z) = \int_{(0,0,0)}^{(x,y,z)} \mathbf{F} \cdot d\mathbf{r}.$$

Show that $\nabla g = \mathbf{F}$.

35. *Writing to Learn: Path of least work* You have been asked to find the path along which a force field $\mathbf{F}$ will perform the least work in moving a particle between two locations. A quick calculation on your part shows $\mathbf{F}$ to be conservative. How should you respond? Give reasons for your answer.

36. *Writing to Learn: A revealing experiment* By experiment, you find that a force field $\mathbf{F}$ performs only half as much work in moving an object along path C_1 from A to B as it does in moving the object along path C_2 from A to B. What can you conclude about $\mathbf{F}$? Give reasons for your answer.

37. *Work by a constant force* Show that the work done by a constant force field $\mathbf{F} = a\mathbf{i} + b\mathbf{j} + c\mathbf{k}$ in moving a particle along any path from A to B is $W = \mathbf{F} \cdot \overrightarrow{AB}$.

38. *Gravitational field*

(a) Find a potential function for the gravitational field

$$\mathbf{F} = -GmM \frac{x\mathbf{i} + y\mathbf{j} + z\mathbf{k}}{(x^2 + y^2 + z^2)^{3/2}} \quad (G, m, \text{ and } M \text{ are constants}).$$

(b) Let P_1 and P_2 be points at distance b. s_1 and s_2 from the origin. Show that the work done by the gravitational field in a. in moving a particle from P_1 to P_2 is

$$GmM\left(\frac{1}{s_2} - \frac{1}{s_1}\right).$$

13.4 Green's Theorem in the Plane

Flux Density at a Point: Divergence • Circulation Density at a Point: The **k**-Component of Curl • Two Forms for Green's Theorem • Mathematical Assumptions • Using Green's Theorem to Evaluate Line Integrals • Proof of Green's Theorem for Special Regions • Extending the Proof to Other Regions

In the preceding section, we learned how to evaluate flow integrals for conservative fields. We found a potential function for the field, evaluated it at the path endpoints, and calculated the integral as the appropriate difference of those values.

In this section, we see how to evaluate flow and flux integrals across closed plane curves when the vector field is not conservative. The means for doing so is a theorem known as Green's Theorem which converts line integrals to double integrals.

Green's Theorem is one of the great theorems of calculus. It is deep and surprising, and has far-reaching consequences. In pure mathematics, it ranks in importance with the Fundamental Theorem of Calculus. In applied mathematics, the generalizations of Green's Theorem to three dimensions provide the foundation for theorems about electricity, magnetism, and fluid flow.

We talk in terms of velocity fields of fluid flows because fluid flows are easy to picture. Be aware, however, that Green's Theorem applies to any vector field satisfying certain mathematical conditions. It does not depend for its validity on the field's having a particular physical interpretation.

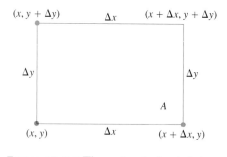

FIGURE 13.24 The rectangle for defining the flux density (divergence) of a vector field at a point (x, y).

Flux Density at a Point: Divergence

We need two new ideas for Green's Theorem. The first is the idea of the flux density of a vector field at a point, which in mathematics is called the *divergence* of the vector field. We obtain it in the following way.

Suppose that $\mathbf{F}(x, y) = M(x, y)\mathbf{i} + N(x, y)\mathbf{j}$ is the velocity field of a fluid flow in the plane and that the first partial derivatives of M and N are continuous at each point of a region R. Let (x, y) be a point in R and let A be a small rectangle with one corner at (x, y) that, along with its interior, lies entirely in R (Figure 13.24). The sides of the rectangle, parallel to the coordinate axes, have lengths of Δx and Δy. The rate at which fluid leaves the rectangle across the bottom edge is approximately

$$\mathbf{F}(x, y) \cdot (-\mathbf{j}) \, \Delta x = -N(x, y) \, \Delta x.$$

This is the scalar component of the velocity at (x, y) in the direction of the outward normal times the length of the segment. If the velocity is in meters per second, for example, the exit rate will be in meters per second times meters or square meters per second. The rates at which the fluid crosses the other three sides in the directions of their outward normals can be estimated in a similar way. All told, we have

Exit Rates:

Top: $\quad \mathbf{F}(x, y + \Delta y) \cdot \mathbf{j} \, \Delta x = N(x, y + \Delta y) \, \Delta x$

Bottom: $\quad \mathbf{F}(x, y) \cdot (-\mathbf{j}) \, \Delta x = -N(x, y) \, \Delta x$

Right: $\quad \mathbf{F}(x + \Delta x, y) \cdot \mathbf{i} \, \Delta y = M(x + \Delta x, y) \, \Delta y$

Left: $\quad \mathbf{F}(x, y) \cdot (-\mathbf{i}) \, \Delta y = -M(x, y) \, \Delta y.$

Combining opposite pairs gives

Top and bottom: $(N(x, y + \Delta y) - N(x, y)) \Delta x \approx \left(\dfrac{\partial N}{\partial y} \Delta y \right) \Delta x$

Right and left: $(M(x + \Delta x, y) - M(x, y)) \Delta y \approx \left(\dfrac{\partial M}{\partial x} \Delta x \right) \Delta y.$

Adding these last two equations gives

Flux across rectangle boundary $\approx \left(\dfrac{\partial M}{\partial x} + \dfrac{\partial N}{\partial y} \right) \Delta x \, \Delta y.$

We now divide by $\Delta x \, \Delta y$ to estimate the total flux per unit area or flux density for the rectangle:

$$\frac{\text{Flux across rectangle boundary}}{\text{rectangle area}} \approx \left(\frac{\partial M}{\partial x} + \frac{\partial N}{\partial y} \right).$$

Finally, we let Δx and Δy approach zero to define what we call the *flux density* of **F** at the point (x, y).

In mathematics, we call the flux density the *divergence* of **F**. The symbol for it is div **F**, pronounced "divergence of **F**" or "div **F**."

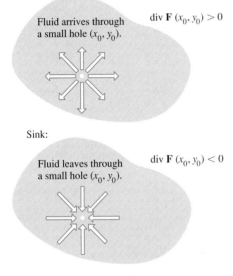

Source:

Fluid arrives through a small hole (x_0, y_0).

div **F** $(x_0, y_0) > 0$

Sink:

Fluid leaves through a small hole (x_0, y_0).

div **F** $(x_0, y_0) < 0$

Definition Flux Density or Divergence

The **flux density** or **divergence** of a vector field $\mathbf{F} = M\mathbf{i} + N\mathbf{j}$ at the point (x, y) is

$$\text{div } \mathbf{F} = \frac{\partial M}{\partial x} + \frac{\partial N}{\partial y}. \tag{1}$$

FIGURE 13.25 In the flow of fluid across a plane region, the divergence is positive at a "source," a point where fluid enters the system, and negative at a "sink," a point where the fluid leaves the system.

Intuitively, if water were flowing into a region through a small hole at the point (x_0, y_0), the lines of flow would diverge there (hence the name) and, since water would be flowing out of a small rectangle about (x_0, y_0), the divergence of **F** at (x_0, y_0) would be positive. If the water were draining out of the hole instead of flowing in, the divergence would be negative. See Figure 13.25.

Example 1 Finding Divergence

Find the divergence of $\mathbf{F}(x, y) = (x^2 - y)\mathbf{i} + (xy - y^2)\mathbf{j}$.

Solution We use the formula in Equation (1):

$$\text{div } \mathbf{F} = \frac{\partial M}{\partial x} + \frac{\partial N}{\partial y} = \frac{\partial}{\partial x}(x^2 - y) + \frac{\partial}{\partial y}(xy - y^2)$$

$$= 2x + x - 2y = 3x - 2y.$$

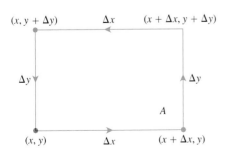

$(x, y + \Delta y)$ Δx $(x + \Delta x, y + \Delta y)$

Δy Δy

A

(x, y) Δx $(x + \Delta x, y)$

FIGURE 13.26 The rectangle for defining the circulation density (curl) of a vector field at a point (x, y).

Circulation Density at a Point: The k-Component of Curl

The second of the two new ideas we need for Green's Theorem is the idea of circulation density of a vector field **F** at a point. To obtain it, we return to the velocity field

$$\mathbf{F}(x, y) = M(x, y)\mathbf{i} + N(x, y)\,\mathbf{j}$$

and the rectangle A. The rectangle is redrawn here as Figure 13.26.

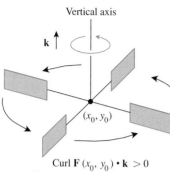

Curl $\mathbf{F}\,(x_0,\,y_0)\cdot\mathbf{k}>0$
Counterclockwise circulation

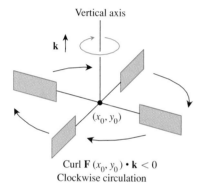

Curl $\mathbf{F}\,(x_0,\,y_0)\cdot\mathbf{k}<0$
Clockwise circulation

FIGURE 13.27 In the flow of an incompressible fluid over a plane region, the **k**-component of the curl measures the rate of the fluid's rotation at a point. The **k**-component of the curl is positive at points where the rotation is counterclockwise and negative where the rotation is clockwise.

The counterclockwise circulation of $\mathbf{F}$ around the boundary of A is the sum of flow rates along the sides. For the bottom edge, the flow rate is approximately

$$\mathbf{F}(x,\,y)\cdot\mathbf{i}\,\Delta x=M(x,\,y)\,\Delta x.$$

This is the scalar component of the velocity $\mathbf{F}(x,\,y)$ in the direction of the tangent vector $\mathbf{i}$ times the length of the segment. The rates of flow along the other sides in the counterclockwise direction are expressed in a similar way. In all, we have

Top: $\mathbf{F}(x,\,y+\Delta y)\cdot(-\mathbf{i})\,\Delta x=-M(x,\,y+\Delta y)\,\Delta x$

Bottom: $\mathbf{F}(x,\,y)\cdot\mathbf{i}\,\Delta x=M(x,\,y)\,\Delta x$

Right: $\mathbf{F}(x+\Delta x,\,y)\cdot\mathbf{j}\,\Delta y=N(x+\Delta x,\,y)\,\Delta y$

Left: $\mathbf{F}(x,\,y)\cdot(-\mathbf{j})\,\Delta y=-N(x,\,y)\,\Delta y.$

We add opposite pairs to get

Top and bottom:

$$-(M(x,\,y+\Delta y)-M(x,\,y))\,\Delta x\approx-\left(\frac{\partial M}{\partial y}\,\Delta y\right)\Delta x$$

Right and left:

$$(N(x+\Delta x,\,y)-N(x,\,y))\,\Delta y\approx\left(\frac{\partial N}{\partial x}\,\Delta x\right)\Delta y.$$

Adding these last two equations and dividing by $\Delta x\,\Delta y$ gives an estimate of the circulation density for the rectangle:

$$\frac{\text{Circulation around rectangle}}{\text{rectangle area}}\approx\frac{\partial N}{\partial x}-\frac{\partial M}{\partial y}.$$

We let Δx and Δy approach zero to define what we call the *circulation density* of $\mathbf{F}$ at the point $(x,\,y)$.

The positive orientation of the circulation density for the plane is the *counterclockwise* rotation around the vertical axis, looking downward on the xy-plane from the tip of the (vertical) unit vector $\mathbf{k}$ (Figure 13.27). The circulation value is actually the **k**-component of a more general circulation vector we define in Section 13.7, called the *curl* of the vector field $\mathbf{F}$. For Green's Theorem, we need only this **k**-component.

Definition   k-Component of Circulation Density or Curl
The k-component of the circulation density or curl of a vector field $\mathbf{F}=M\mathbf{i}+N\mathbf{j}$ at the point $(x,\,y)$ is the scalar

$$(\text{curl }\mathbf{F})\cdot\mathbf{k}=\frac{\partial N}{\partial x}-\frac{\partial M}{\partial y}. \tag{2}$$

If water is moving about a region in the xy-plane in a thin layer, then the **k**-component of the circulation, or curl, at a point $(x_0,\,y_0)$ gives a way to measure how fast and in what direction a small paddle wheel will spin if it is put into the water at $(x_0,\,y_0)$ with its axis perpendicular to the plane, parallel to $\mathbf{k}$ (Figure 13.27).

Example 2   Finding the k-Component of the Curl

Find the **k**-component of the curl for the vector field

$$\mathbf{F}(x, y) = (x^2 - y)\,\mathbf{i} + (xy - y^2)\,\mathbf{j}.$$

Solution   We use the formula in Equation (2):

$$(\text{curl } \mathbf{F}) \cdot \mathbf{k} = \frac{\partial N}{\partial x} - \frac{\partial M}{\partial y} = \frac{\partial}{\partial x}(xy - y^2) - \frac{\partial}{\partial y}(x^2 - y) = y + 1.$$

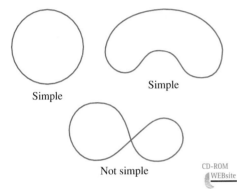

Simple

Simple

Not simple

CD-ROM
WEBsite

FIGURE 13.28 In proving Green's Theorem, we distinguish between two kinds of closed curves, simple and not simple. Simple curves do not cross themselves. A circle is simple but a figure 8 is not.

Two Forms for Green's Theorem

In one form, Green's Theorem says that under suitable conditions the outward flux of a vector field across a simple closed curve in the plane (Figure 13.28) equals the double integral of the divergence of the field over the region enclosed by the curve. Recall the formulas for flux in Equations (3) and (4) in Section 13.2.

Theorem 3   Green's Theorem (Flux-Divergence or Normal Form)
The outward flux of a field $\mathbf{F} = M\mathbf{i} + N\mathbf{j}$ across a simple closed curve C equals the double integral of div $\mathbf{F}$ over the region R enclosed by C.

$$\underbrace{\oint_C \mathbf{F} \cdot \mathbf{n}\,ds = \oint_C M\,dy - N\,dx}_{\text{Outward flux}} = \underbrace{\iint_R \left(\frac{\partial M}{\partial x} + \frac{\partial N}{\partial y}\right) dx\,dy}_{\text{Divergence integral}} \qquad (3)$$

In another form, Green's Theorem says that the counterclockwise circulation of a vector field around a simple closed curve is the double integral of the **k**-component of the curl of the field over the region enclosed by the curve.

CD-ROM
WEBsite

Theorem 4   Green's Theorem (Circulation-Curl or Tangential Form)
The counterclockwise circulation of a field $\mathbf{F} = M\mathbf{i} + N\mathbf{j}$ around a simple closed curve C in the plane equals the double integral of $(\text{curl } \mathbf{F}) \cdot \mathbf{k}$ over the region R enclosed by C.

$$\underbrace{\oint_C \mathbf{F} \cdot \mathbf{T}\,ds = \oint_C M\,dx + N\,dy}_{\text{Counterclockwise circulation}} = \underbrace{\iint_R \left(\frac{\partial N}{\partial x} - \frac{\partial M}{\partial y}\right) dx\,dy}_{\text{Curl integral}} \qquad (4)$$

The two forms of Green's Theorem are equivalent. Applying Equation (3) to the field $\mathbf{G}_1 = N\mathbf{i} - M\mathbf{j}$ gives Equation (4), and applying Equation (4) to $\mathbf{G}_2 = -N\mathbf{i} + M\mathbf{j}$ gives Equation (3).

Mathematical Assumptions

We need two kinds of assumptions for Green's Theorem to hold. First, we need conditions on M and N to ensure the existence of the integrals. The usual assumptions are that M, N, and their first partial derivatives are continuous at every point of some open region containing C and R. Second, we need geometric conditions on the curve C. It must be simple, closed, and made up of pieces along which we can integrate M and N. The usual assumptions are that C is piecewise smooth. The proof we give for Green's Theorem, however, assumes things about the shape of R as well. You can find proofs that are less restrictive in more advanced texts. First let's look at examples.

Example 3   Supporting Green's Theorem

Verify both forms of Green's Theorem for the field

$$\mathbf{F}(x, y) = (x - y)\,\mathbf{i} + x\mathbf{j}$$

and the region R bounded by the unit circle

$$C: \quad \mathbf{r}(t) = (\cos t)\,\mathbf{i} + (\sin t)\,\mathbf{j}, \qquad 0 \le t \le 2\pi.$$

Solution   We have

$$M = \cos t - \sin t, \qquad dx = d(\cos t) = -\sin t\,dt,$$
$$N = \cos t, \qquad dy = d(\sin t) = \cos t\,dt,$$
$$\frac{\partial M}{\partial x} = 1, \qquad \frac{\partial M}{\partial y} = -1, \qquad \frac{\partial N}{\partial x} = 1, \qquad \frac{\partial N}{\partial y} = 0.$$

The two sides of Equation (3) are

$$\oint_C M\,dy - N\,dx = \int_{t=0}^{t=2\pi} (\cos t - \sin t)(\cos t\,dt) - (\cos t)(-\sin t\,dt)$$

$$= \int_0^{2\pi} \cos^2 t\,dt = \pi$$

$$\iint_R \left(\frac{\partial M}{\partial x} + \frac{\partial N}{\partial y}\right) dx\,dy = \iint_R (1 + 0)\,dx\,dy$$

$$= \iint_R dx\,dy = \text{area of unit circle} = \pi.$$

The two sides of Equation (4) are

$$\oint_C M\,dx + N\,dy = \int_{t=0}^{t=2\pi} (\cos t - \sin t)(-\sin t\,dt) + (\cos t)(\cos t\,dt)$$

$$= \int_0^{2\pi} (-\sin t \cos t + 1)\,dt = 2\pi$$

$$\iint_R \left(\frac{\partial N}{\partial x} - \frac{\partial M}{\partial y}\right) dx\,dy = \iint_R (1 - (-1))\,dx\,dy = 2\iint_R dx\,dy = 2\pi.$$

Using Green's Theorem to Evaluate Line Integrals

If we construct a closed curve C by piecing a number of different curves end to end, the process of evaluating a line integral over C can be lengthy because there are so many different integrals to evaluate. If C bounds a region R to which

Green's Theorem applies, however, we can use Green's Theorem to change the line integral around C into one double integral over R.

Example 4   Evaluating a Line Integral Using Green's Theorem

Evaluate the integral

$$\oint_C xy\, dy - y^2\, dx,$$

where C is the square cut from the first quadrant by the lines $x = 1$ and $y = 1$.

Solution   We can use either form of Green's Theorem to change the line integral into a double integral over the square.

1. *With the Normal Form Equation* (3): Taking $M = xy$, $N = y^2$, and C and R as the square's boundary and interior gives

$$\oint_C xy\, dy - y^2\, dx = \iint_R (y + 2y)\, dx\, dy = \int_0^1 \int_0^1 3y\, dx\, dy$$

$$= \int_0^1 [3xy]_{x=0}^{x=1}\, dy = \int_0^1 3y\, dy = \frac{3}{2}y^2 \Big]_0^1 = \frac{3}{2}.$$

2. *With the Tangential Form Equation* (4): Taking $M = -y^2$ and $N = xy$ gives the same result:

$$\oint_C - y^2\, dx + xy\, dy = \iint_R (y - (-2y))\, dx\, dy = \frac{3}{2}.$$

Example 5   Finding Outward Flux

Calculate the outward flux of the field $\mathbf{F}(x, y) = x\mathbf{i} + y^2\mathbf{j}$ across the square bounded by the lines $x = \pm 1$ and $y = \pm 1$.

Solution   Calculating the flux with a line integral would take four integrations, one for each side of the square. With Green's Theorem, we can change the line integral to one double integral. With $M = x$, $N = y^2$, C the square, and R the square's interior, we have

$$\text{Flux} = \oint_C \mathbf{F} \cdot \mathbf{n}\, ds = \oint_C M\, dy - N\, dx$$

$$= \iint_R \left(\frac{\partial M}{\partial x} + \frac{\partial N}{\partial y} \right) dx\, dy \qquad \text{Green's Theorem}$$

$$= \int_{-1}^1 \int_{-1}^1 (1 + 2y)\, dx\, dy = \int_{-1}^1 [x + 2xy]_{x=-1}^{x=1}\, dy$$

$$= \int_{-1}^1 (2 + 4y)\, dy = [2y + 2y^2]_{-1}^1 = 4.$$

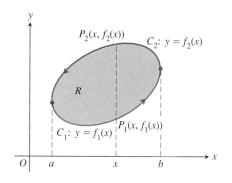

FIGURE 13.29 The boundary curve C is made up of C_1, the graph of $y = f_1(x)$, and C_2, the graph of $y = f_2(x)$.

Proof of Green's Theorem for Special Regions

Let C be a smooth simple closed curve in the xy-plane with the property that lines parallel to the axes cut it in no more than two points. Let R be the region enclosed by C and suppose that $M, N,$ and their first partial derivatives are continuous at every point of some open region containing C and R. We want to prove the circulation-curl form of Green's Theorem,

$$\oint_C M \, dx + N \, dy = \iint_R \left(\frac{\partial N}{\partial x} - \frac{\partial M}{\partial y} \right) dx \, dy. \tag{5}$$

Figure 13.29 shows C made up of two directed parts:

$$C_1: \quad y = f_1(x), \quad a \le x \le b, \qquad C_2: \quad y = f_2(x), \quad b \ge x \ge a.$$

For any x between a and b, we can integrate $\partial M / \partial y$ with respect to y from $y = f_1(x)$ to $y = f_2(x)$ and obtain

$$\int_{f_1(x)}^{f_2(x)} \frac{\partial M}{\partial y} \, dy = M(x, y) \Big]_{y=f_1(x)}^{y=f_2(x)} = M(x, f_2(x)) - M(x, f_1(x)).$$

We can then integrate this with respect to x from a to b:

$$\int_a^b \int_{f_1(x)}^{f_2(x)} \frac{\partial M}{\partial y} \, dy \, dx = \int_a^b [M(x, f_2(x)) - M(x, f_1(x))] \, dx$$

$$= -\int_b^a M(x, f_2(x)) \, dx - \int_a^b M(x, f_1(x)) \, dx$$

$$= -\int_{C_2} M \, dx - \int_{C_1} M \, dx$$

$$= -\oint_C M \, dx.$$

Therefore

$$\oint_C M \, dx = \iint_R \left(-\frac{\partial M}{\partial y} \right) dx \, dy. \tag{6}$$

Equation (6) is half the result we need for Equation (5). We derive the other half by integrating $\partial N / \partial x$ first with respect to x and then with respect to y, as suggested by Figure 13.30. This shows the curve C of Figure 13.29 decomposed into the two directed parts $C_1': x = g_1(y), d \ge y \ge c$ and $C_2': x = g_2(y), c \le y \le d$. The result of this double integration is

$$\oint_C N \, dy = \iint_R \frac{\partial N}{\partial x} \, dx \, dy. \tag{7}$$

Combining Equations (6) and (7) gives Equation (5). This concludes the proof.

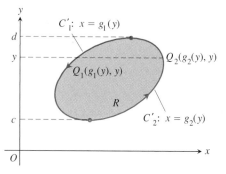

FIGURE 13.30 The boundary curve C is made up of C_1', the graph of $x = g_1(y)$, and C_2', the graph of $x = g_2(y)$.

Extending the Proof to Other Regions

The argument we just gave does not apply directly to the rectangular region in Figure 13.31 because the lines $x = a$, $x = b$, $y = c$, and $y = d$ meet the region's boundary in more than two points. If we divide the boundary C into four directed line segments, however,

$$C_1: \quad y = c, \quad a \leq x \leq b, \qquad C_2: \quad x = b, \quad c \leq y \leq d$$
$$C_3: \quad y = d, \quad b \geq x \geq a, \qquad C_4: \quad x = a, \quad d \geq y \geq c,$$

we can modify the argument in the following way.

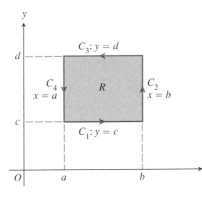

FIGURE 13.31 To prove Green's Theorem for a rectangle, we divide the boundary into four directed line segments.

Proceeding as in the proof of Equation (7), we have

$$\int_c^d \int_a^b \frac{\partial N}{\partial x} \, dx \, dy = \int_c^d \left(N(b, y) - N(a, y) \right) dy$$

$$= \int_c^d N(b, y) \, dy + \int_d^c N(a, y) \, dy \qquad (8)$$

$$= \int_{C_2} N \, dy + \int_{C_4} N \, dy.$$

Because y is constant along C_1 and C_3, $\int_{C_1} N \, dy = \int_{C_3} N \, dy = 0$, so we can add $\int_{C_1} N \, dy + \int_{C_3} N \, dy$ to the right-hand side of Equation (8) without changing the equality. Doing so, we have

$$\int_c^d \int_a^b \frac{\partial N}{\partial x} \, dx \, dy = \oint_C N \, dy. \qquad (9)$$

Similarly, we can show that

$$\int_a^b \int_c^d \frac{\partial M}{\partial y} \, dy \, dx = -\oint_C M \, dx. \qquad (10)$$

Subtracting Equation (10) from Equation (9), we again arrive at

$$\oint_C M \, dx + N \, dy = \iint_R \left(\frac{\partial N}{\partial x} - \frac{\partial M}{\partial y} \right) dx \, dy.$$

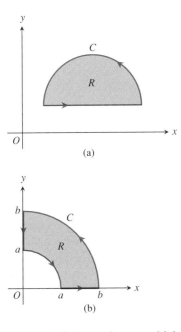

FIGURE 13.32 Other regions to which Green's Theorem applies.

Regions like those in Figure 13.32 can be handled with no greater difficulty. Equation (5) still applies. It also applies to the horseshoe-shaped region R shown in Figure 13.33, as we see by putting together the regions R_1 and R_2 and their boundaries. Green's Theorem applies to C_1, R_1 and to $C_2, R_2,$ yielding

$$\int_{C_1} M\, dx + N\, dy = \int\int_{R_1} \left(\frac{\partial N}{\partial x} - \frac{\partial M}{\partial y} \right) dx\, dy$$

$$\int_{C_2} M\, dx + N\, dy = \int\int_{R_2} \left(\frac{\partial N}{\partial x} - \frac{\partial M}{\partial y} \right) dx\, dy.$$

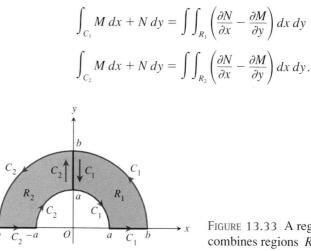

FIGURE 13.33 A region R that combines regions R_1 and R_2.

When we add these two equations, the line integral along the y-axis from b to a for C_1 cancels the integral over the same segment but in the opposite direction for C_2. Hence,

$$\oint_C M\, dx + N\, dy = \int\int_R \left(\frac{\partial N}{\partial x} - \frac{\partial M}{\partial y} \right) dx\, dy,$$

where C consists of the two segments of the x-axis from $-b$ to $-a$ and from a to b and of the two semicircles, and where R is the region inside C.

The device of adding line integrals over separate boundaries to build up an integral over a single boundary can be extended to any finite number of subregions. In Figure 13.34a, let C_1 be the boundary, oriented counterclockwise, of the region R_1 in the first quadrant. Similarly, for the other three quadrants, C_i is the boundary of the region R_i, $i = 2, 3, 4.$ By Green's Theorem,

$$\oint_{C_i} M\, dx + N\, dy = \int\int_{R_i} \left(\frac{\partial N}{\partial x} - \frac{\partial M}{\partial y} \right) dx\, dy. \tag{11}$$

We add Equations (11) for $i = 1, 2, 3, 4,$ and get (Figure 13.34b):

$$\oint_{r=b} (M\, dx + N\, dy) + \oint_{r=a} (M\, dx + N\, dy) = \int\int_{a \le r \le b} \left(\frac{\partial N}{\partial x} - \frac{\partial M}{\partial y} \right) dx\, dy. \tag{12}$$

Equation (12) says that the double integral of $(\partial N / \partial x) - (\partial M / \partial y)$ over the annular ring R equals the line integral of $M\, dx + N\, dy$ over the complete boundary of R in the direction that keeps R on our left as we progress (Figure 13.34b).

Example 6 Verifying Green's Theorem for an Annular Ring

Verify the circulation form of Green's Theorem (Equation (4)) on the annular ring $R: h^2 \le x^2 + y^2 \le 1, 0 < h < 1$ (Figure 13.35), if

$$M = \frac{-y}{x^2 + y^2}, \qquad N = \frac{x}{x^2 + y^2}.$$

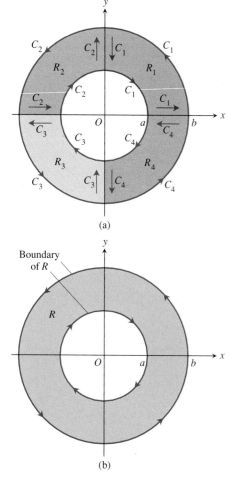

FIGURE 13.34 The annular region R combines four smaller regions. In polar coordinates, $r = a$ for the inner circle, $r = b$ for the outer circle, and $a \le r \le b$ for the region itself.

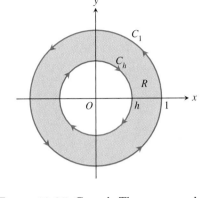

FIGURE 13.35 Green's Theorem may be applied to the annular region R by integrating along the boundaries as shown. (Example 6)

Solution   The boundary of R consists of the circle

$$C_1: \quad x = \cos t, \quad y = \sin t, \quad 0 \le t \le 2\pi,$$

traversed counterclockwise as t increases, and the circle

$$C_h: \quad x = h \cos \theta, \quad y = -h \sin \theta, \quad 0 \le \theta \le 2\pi,$$

traversed clockwise as θ increases. The functions M and N and their partial derivatives are continuous throughout R. Moreover,

$$\frac{\partial M}{\partial y} = \frac{(x^2 + y^2)(-1) + y(2y)}{(x^2 + y^2)^2}$$

$$= \frac{y^2 - x^2}{(x^2 + y^2)^2} = \frac{\partial N}{\partial x},$$

so

$$\iint_R \left(\frac{\partial N}{\partial x} - \frac{\partial M}{\partial y} \right) dx \, dy = \iint_R 0 \, dx \, dy = 0.$$

The integral of $M \, dx + N \, dy$ over the boundary of R is

$$\int_C M \, dx + N \, dy = \oint_{C_1} \frac{x \, dy - y \, dx}{x^2 + y^2} + \oint_{C_h} \frac{x \, dy - y \, dx}{x^2 + y^2}$$

$$= \int_0^{2\pi} (\cos^2 t + \sin^2 t) \, dt - \int_0^{2\pi} \frac{h^2(\cos^2 \theta + \sin^2 \theta)}{h^2} \, d\theta$$

$$= 2\pi - 2\pi = 0.$$

The functions M and N in Example 6 are discontinuous at $(0, 0)$, so we cannot apply Green's Theorem to the circle C_1 and the region inside it. We must exclude the origin. We do so by excluding the points inside C_h.

We could replace the circle C_1 in Example 6 by an ellipse or any other simple closed curve K surrounding C_h (Figure 13.36). The result would still be

$$\oint_K (M \, dx + N \, dy) + \oint_{C_h} (M \, dx + N \, dy) = \iint_R \left(\frac{\partial N}{\partial x} - \frac{\partial M}{\partial y} \right) dy \, dx = 0,$$

which leads to the surprising conclusion that

$$\oint_K (M \, dx + N \, dy) = 2\pi$$

for any such curve K. We can explain this result by changing to polar coordinates. With

$$x = r \cos \theta, \qquad\qquad y = r \sin \theta,$$
$$dx = -r \sin \theta \, d\theta + \cos \theta \, dr, \qquad dy = r \cos \theta \, d\theta + \sin \theta \, dr,$$

we have

$$\frac{x \, dy - y \, dx}{x^2 + y^2} = \frac{r^2(\cos^2 \theta + \sin^2 \theta) \, d\theta}{r^2} = d\theta,$$

and θ increases by 2π as we traverse K once counterclockwise.

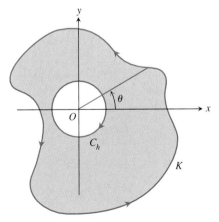

FIGURE 13.36 The region bounded by the circle C_h and the curve K.

EXERCISES 13.4

Verifying Green's Theorem

In Exercises 1–4, verify the conclusion of Green's Theorem by evaluating both sides of Equations (3) and (4) for the field $\mathbf{F} = M\mathbf{i} + N\mathbf{j}$. Take the domains of integration in each case to be the disk $R: x^2 + y^2 \leq a^2$ and its bounding circle $C: \mathbf{r} = (a \cos t)\mathbf{i} + (a \sin t)\mathbf{j}, 0 \leq t \leq 2\pi$.

1. $\mathbf{F} = -y\mathbf{i} + x\mathbf{j}$ **2.** $\mathbf{F} = y\mathbf{i}$

3. $\mathbf{F} = 2x\mathbf{i} - 3y\mathbf{j}$ **4.** $\mathbf{F} = -x^2 y\mathbf{i} + xy^2\mathbf{j}$

Counterclockwise Circulation and Outward Flux

In Exercises 5–10, use Green's Theorem to find the counterclockwise circulation and outward flux for the field $\mathbf{F}$ and curve C.

5. $\mathbf{F} = (x - y)\mathbf{i} + (y - x)\mathbf{j}$

  $C:$ The square bounded by $x = 0, x = 1, y = 0, y = 1$

6. $\mathbf{F} = (x^2 + 4y)\mathbf{i} + (x + y^2)\mathbf{j}$

  $C:$ The square bounded by $x = 0, x = 1, y = 0, y = 1$

7. $\mathbf{F} = (y^2 - x^2)\mathbf{i} + (x^2 + y^2)\mathbf{j}$

  $C:$ The triangle bounded by $y = 0, x = 3$, and $y = x$

8. $\mathbf{F} = (x + y)\mathbf{i} - (x^2 + y^2)\mathbf{j}$

  $C:$ The triangle bounded by $y = 0, x = 1$, and $y = x$

9. $\mathbf{F} = (x + e^x \sin y)\mathbf{i} + (x + e^x \cos y)\mathbf{j}$

  $C:$ The right-hand loop of the lemniscate $r^2 = \cos 2\theta$

10. $\mathbf{F} = \left(\tan^{-1}\dfrac{y}{x}\right)\mathbf{i} + \ln(x^2 + y^2)\mathbf{j}$

  $C:$ The boundary of the region defined by the polar coordinate inequalities $1 \leq r \leq 2, 0 \leq \theta \leq \pi$

11. Find the counterclockwise circulation and outward flux of the field $\mathbf{F} = xy\mathbf{i} + y^2\mathbf{j}$ around and over the boundary of the region enclosed by the curves $y = x^2$ and $y = x$ in the first quadrant.

12. Find the counterclockwise circulation and the outward flux of the field $\mathbf{F} = (-\sin y)\mathbf{i} + (x \cos y)\mathbf{j}$ around and over the square cut from the first quadrant by the lines $x = \pi/2$ and $y = \pi/2$.

13. Find the outward flux of the field

$$\mathbf{F} = \left(3xy - \frac{x}{1 + y^2}\right)\mathbf{i} + (e^x + \tan^{-1} y)\mathbf{j}$$

across the cardioid $r = a(1 + \cos \theta), a > 0$.

14. Find the counterclockwise circulation of $\mathbf{F} = (y + e^x \ln y)\mathbf{i} + (e^x/y)\mathbf{j}$ around the boundary of the region that is bounded above by the curve $y = 3 - x^2$ and below by the curve $y = x^4 + 1$.

Work

In Exercises 15 and 16, find the work done by $\mathbf{F}$ in moving a particle once counterclockwise around the given curve.

15. $\mathbf{F} = 2xy^3\mathbf{i} + 4x^2 y^2\mathbf{j}$

  $C:$ The boundary of the "triangular" region in the first quadrant enclosed by the x-axis, the line $x = 1$, and the curve $y = x^3$

16. $\mathbf{F} = (4x - 2y)\mathbf{i} + (2x - 4y)\mathbf{j}$

  $C:$ The circle $(x - 2)^2 + (y - 2)^2 = 4$

Evaluating Line Integrals in the Plane

Apply Green's Theorem to evaluate the integrals in Exercises 17–20.

17. $\displaystyle\oint_C (y^2\, dx + x^2\, dy)$

  $C:$ The triangle bounded by $x = 0, x + y = 1, y = 0$

18. $\displaystyle\oint_C (3y\, dx + 2x\, dy)$

  $C:$ The boundary of $0 \leq x \leq \pi, 0 \leq y \leq \sin x$

19. $\displaystyle\oint_C (6y + x)\, dx + (y + 2x)\, dy$

  $C:$ The circle $(x - 2)^2 + (y - 3)^2 = 4$

20. $\displaystyle\oint_C (2x + y^2)\, dx + (2xy + 3y)\, dy$

  $C:$ Any simple closed curve in the plane for which Green's theorem holds

Calculating Area with Green's Theorem

If a simple closed curve C in the plane and the region R it encloses satisfy the hypotheses of Green's Theorem, the area of R is given by

---

Green's Theorem Area Formula

$$\text{Area of } R = \frac{1}{2}\oint_C x\, dy - y\, dx \qquad (13)$$

The reason is that by Equation (3), run backward,

$$\text{Area of } R = \iint_R dy\, dx = \iint_R \left(\frac{1}{2} + \frac{1}{2}\right) dy\, dx$$

$$= \oint_C \frac{1}{2} x\, dy - \frac{1}{2} y\, dx.$$

Use the Green's Theorem area formula (Equation (13)) to find the areas of the regions enclosed by the curves in Exercises 21–24.

21. The circle $\mathbf{r}(t) = (a \cos t)\mathbf{i} + (a \sin t)\mathbf{j}, \quad 0 \leq t \leq 2\pi$

22. The ellipse $\mathbf{r}(t) = (a \cos t)\mathbf{i} + (b \sin t)\mathbf{j}, \quad 0 \leq t \leq 2\pi$

23. The astroid (Figure 5.30) $\mathbf{r}(t) = (\cos^3 t)\mathbf{i} + (\sin^3 t)\mathbf{j}, \quad 0 \leq t \leq 2\pi$

24. The curve $\mathbf{r}(t) = t^2\mathbf{i} + ((t^3/3) - t)\mathbf{j}$, $-\sqrt{3} \le t \le \sqrt{3}$ (see accompanying figure).

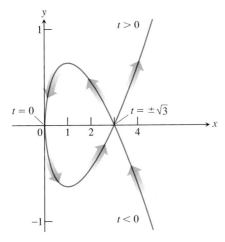

Theory and Examples

25. Let C be the boundary of a region on which Green's Theorem holds. Use Green's Theorem to calculate

(a) $\oint_C f(x)\, dx + g(y)\, dy$

(b) $\oint_C ky\, dx + hx\, dy$ (k and h constants).

26. *Integral dependent only on area* Show that the value of

$$\oint_C xy^2\, dx + (x^2y + 2x)\, dy$$

around any square depends only on the area of the square and not on its location in the plane.

27. *Writing to Learn* What is special about the integral

$$\oint_C 4x^3y\, dx + x^4\, dy?$$

Give reasons for your answer.

28. *Writing to Learn* What is special about the integral

$$\oint_C -y^3\, dx + x^3\, dy?$$

Give reasons for your answer.

29. *Area as a line integral* Show that if R is a region in the plane bounded by a piecewise smooth simple closed curve C, then

$$\text{Area of } R = \oint_C x\, dy = -\oint_C y\, dx.$$

30. *Definite integral as a line integral* Suppose that a nonnegative function $y = f(x)$ has a continuous first derivative on $[a, b]$. Let C be the boundary of the region in the xy-plane that is bounded below by the x-axis, above by the graph of f, and on the sides by the lines $x = a$ and $x = b$. Show that

$$\int_a^b f(x)\, dx = -\oint_C y\, dx.$$

31. *Area and the centroid* Let A be the area and $\bar{x}$ the x-coordinate of the centroid of a region R that is bounded by a piecewise smooth simple closed curve C in the xy-plane. Show that

$$\frac{1}{2}\oint_C x^2\, dy = -\oint_C xy\, dx = \frac{1}{3}\oint_C x^2\, dy - xy\, dx = A\bar{x}.$$

32. *Moment of inertia* Let I_y be the moment of inertia about the y-axis of the region in Exercise 31. Show that

$$\frac{1}{3}\oint_C x^3\, dy = -\oint_C x^2y\, dx = \frac{1}{4}\oint_C x^3\, dy - x^2y\, dx = I_y.$$

33. *Green's Theorem and Laplace's equation* Assuming that all the necessary derivatives exist and are continuous, show that if $f(x, y)$ satisfies the Laplace equation

$$\frac{\partial^2 f}{\partial x^2} + \frac{\partial^2 f}{\partial y^2} = 0,$$

then

$$\oint_C \frac{\partial f}{\partial y}\, dx - \frac{\partial f}{\partial x}\, dy = 0$$

for all closed curves C to which Green's Theorem applies. (The converse is also true: If the line integral is always zero, then f satisfies the Laplace equation.)

34. *Maximizing work* Among all smooth simple closed curves in the plane, oriented counterclockwise, find the one along which the work done by

CD-ROM
WEBsite

$$\mathbf{F} = \left(\frac{1}{4}x^2y + \frac{1}{3}y^3\right)\mathbf{i} + x\mathbf{j}$$

is greatest. (*Hint:* Where is (curl $\mathbf{F}$) $\cdot$ $\mathbf{k}$ positive?)

35. *Regions with many holes* Green's Theorem holds for a region R with any finite number of holes as long as the bounding curves are smooth, simple, and closed and we integrate over each component of the boundary in the direction that keeps R on our immediate left as we go along (Figure 13.37 on the next page).

(a) Let $f(x, y) = \ln (x^2 + y^2)$ and let C be the circle $x^2 + y^2 = a^2$. Evaluate the flux integral

$$\oint_C \nabla f \cdot \mathbf{n}\, ds.$$

(b) Let K be an arbitrary smooth simple closed curve in the plane that does not pass through $(0, 0)$. Use Green's Theorem to show that

$$\oint_K \nabla f \cdot \mathbf{n} \, ds$$

has two possible values, depending on whether $(0, 0)$ lies inside K or outside K.

FIGURE 13.37 Green's Theorem holds for regions with more than one hole. (Exercise 35)

36. *Bendixson's criterion* The **streamlines** of a planar fluid flow are the smooth curves traced by the fluid's individual particles. The vectors $\mathbf{F} = M(x, y)\mathbf{i} + N(x, y)\mathbf{j}$ of the flow's velocity field are the tangent vectors of the streamlines. Show that if the flow takes place over a *simply connected* region R (no holes or missing points) and that if $M_x + N_y \neq 0$ throughout R, then none of the streamlines in R is closed. In other words, no particle of fluid ever has a closed trajectory in R. The criterion $M_x + N_y \neq 0$ is called **Bendixson's criterion** for the nonexistence of closed trajectories.

37. Establish Equation (7) to finish the proof of the special case of Green's Theorem.

38. Establish Equation (10) to complete the argument for the extension of Green's Theorem.

39. *Writing to Learn: Curl component of conservative fields* Can anything be said about the curl component of a conservative two-dimensional vector field? Give reasons for your answer.

40. *Writing to Learn: Circulation of conservative fields* Does Green's Theorem give any information about the circulation of a conservative field? Does this agree with anything else you know? Give reasons for your answer.

COMPUTER EXPLORATIONS

Finding Circulation

In Exercises 41–44, use a CAS and Green's Theorem to find the counterclockwise circulation of the field $\mathbf{F}$ around the simple closed curve C. Perform the following CAS steps.

(a) Plot C in the xy-plane.

(b) Determine the integrand $(\partial N / \partial x) - (\partial M / \partial y)$ for the curl form of Green's Theorem.

(c) Determine the (double integral) limits of integration from your plot in part (a) and evaluate the curl integral for the circulation.

41. $\mathbf{F} = (2x - y)\mathbf{i} + (x + 3y)\mathbf{j}$, C: The ellipse $x^2 + 4y^2 = 4$

42. $\mathbf{F} = (2x^3 - y^3)\mathbf{i} + (x^3 + y^3)\mathbf{j}$, C: The ellipse $\dfrac{x^2}{4} + \dfrac{y^2}{9} = 1$

43. $\mathbf{F} = x^{-1}e^y\mathbf{i} + (e^y \ln x + 2x)\mathbf{j}$,

C: The boundary of the region defined by $y = 1 + x^4$ (below) and $y = 2$ (above)

44. $\mathbf{F} = xe^y\mathbf{i} + 4x^2 \ln y\mathbf{j}$, C: The triangle with vertices $(0, 0)$, $(2, 0)$, and $(0, 4)$

13.5   Surface Area and Surface Integrals

Surface Area   •   A Practical Formula   •   Surface Integrals   •
Algebraic Properties; The Surface Area Differential   •   Orientation   •
Surface Integral for Flux   •   Moments and Masses of Thin Shells

We know how to integrate a function over a flat region in a plane, but what if the function is defined over a curved surface? How do we calculate its integral then? The trick to evaluating one of these so-called surface integrals is to rewrite it as a double integral over a region in a coordinate plane beneath the surface

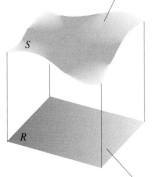

Surface $f(x, y, z) = c$

S

R

The vertical projection or "shadow" of S on a coordinate plane

FIGURE 13.38 As we soon see, the integral of a function $g(x, y, z)$ over a surface S in space can be calculated by evaluating a related double integral over the vertical projection or "shadow" of S on a coordinate plane.

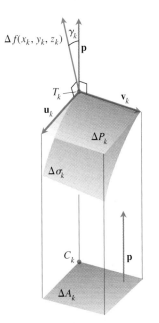

$\Delta f(x_k, y_k, z_k)$ γ_k **p**

T_k $\mathbf{v}_k$

$\mathbf{u}_k$

ΔP_k

$\Delta \sigma_k$

C_k **p**

ΔA_k

FIGURE 13.40 Magnified view from the preceding figure. The vector $\mathbf{u}_k \times \mathbf{v}_k$ (not shown) is parallel to the vector ∇f because both vectors are normal to the plane of ΔP_k.

(Figure 13.38). In Sections 13.7 and 13.8, we see how surface integrals provide just what we need to generalize the two forms of Green's Theorem to three dimensions.

Surface Area

Figure 13.39 shows a surface S lying above its "shadow" region R in a plane beneath it. The surface is defined by the equation $f(x, y, z) = c$. If the surface is **smooth** (∇f is continuous and never vanishes on S), we can define and calculate its area as a double integral over R.

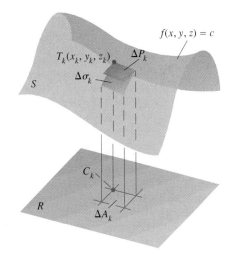

$f(x, y, z) = c$

$T_k(x_k, y_k, z_k)$ ΔP_k

$\Delta \sigma_k$

S

C_k

R ΔA_k

FIGURE 13.39 A surface S and its vertical projection onto a plane beneath it. You can think of R as the shadow of S on the plane. The tangent plate ΔP_k approximates the surface patch $\Delta \sigma_k$ above ΔA_k.

The first step in defining the area of S is to partition the region R into small rectangles ΔA_k of the kind we would use if we were defining an integral over R. Directly above each ΔA_k lies a patch of surface $\Delta \sigma_k$ that we may approximate with a portion ΔP_k of a tangent plane. To be specific, we suppose that ΔP_k is a portion of the plane that is tangent to the surface at the point $T_k(x_k, y_k, z_k)$ directly above the back corner C_k of ΔA_k. If the tangent plane is parallel to R, then ΔP_k will be congruent to ΔA_k. Otherwise, it will be a parallelogram whose area is somewhat larger than the area of ΔA_k.

Figure 13.40 gives a magnified view of $\Delta \sigma_k$ and ΔP_k, showing the gradient vector $\nabla f(x_k, y_k, z_k)$ at T_k and a unit vector **p** that is normal to R. The figure also shows the angle γ_k between ∇f and **p**. The other vectors in the picture, $\mathbf{u}_k$ and $\mathbf{v}_k$, lie along the edges of the patch ΔP_k in the tangent plane. Thus, both $\mathbf{u}_k \times \mathbf{v}_k$ and ∇f are normal to the tangent plane.

We now need to know from advanced vector geometry that $|(\mathbf{u}_k \times \mathbf{v}_k) \cdot \mathbf{p}|$ is the area of the projection of the parallelogram determined by $\mathbf{u}_k$ and $\mathbf{v}_k$ onto any plane whose normal is **p**. (A proof is given in Appendix 12.) In our case, this translates into the statement

$$|(\mathbf{u}_k \times \mathbf{v}_k) \cdot \mathbf{p}| = \Delta A_k.$$

Now, $|\mathbf{u}_k \times \mathbf{v}_k|$ itself is the area ΔP_k (standard fact about cross products) so this last equation becomes

$$\underbrace{|\mathbf{u}_k \times \mathbf{v}_k|}_{\Delta P_k} \quad \underbrace{|\mathbf{p}|}_{1} \quad \underbrace{|\cos (\text{angle between } \mathbf{u}_k \times \mathbf{v}_k \text{ and } \mathbf{p})|}_{\substack{\text{Same as } |\cos \gamma_k| \text{ because } \nabla f \text{ and } \mathbf{u}_k \times \mathbf{v}_k \\ \text{are both normal to the tangent plane}}} = \Delta A_k$$

or

$$\Delta P_k |\cos \gamma_k| = \Delta A_k$$

or

$$\Delta P_k = \frac{\Delta A_k}{|\cos \gamma_k|},$$

provided $\cos \gamma_k \neq 0$. We will have $\cos \gamma_k \neq 0$ as long as ∇f is not parallel to the ground plane and $\nabla f \cdot \mathbf{p} \neq 0$.

Since the patches ΔP_k approximate the surface patches $\Delta \sigma_k$ that fit together to make S, the sum

$$\sum \Delta P_k = \sum \frac{\Delta A_k}{|\cos \gamma_k|} \tag{1}$$

looks like an approximation of what we might like to call the surface area of S. It also looks as if the approximation would improve if we refined the partition of R. In fact, the sums on the right-hand side of Equation (1) are approximating sums for the double integral

$$\iint_R \frac{1}{|\cos \gamma|} \, dA. \tag{2}$$

We therefore define the **area** of S to be the value of this integral whenever it exists.

A Practical Formula

For any surface $f(x, y, z) = c$, we have $|\nabla f \cdot \mathbf{p}| = |\nabla f| |\mathbf{p}| |\cos \gamma|$, so

$$\frac{1}{|\cos \gamma|} = \frac{|\nabla f|}{|\nabla f \cdot \mathbf{p}|}.$$

This combines with Equation (2) to give a practical formula for area.

Formula for Surface Area

The area of the surface $f(x, y, z) = c$ over a closed and bounded plane region R is

$$\text{Surface area} = \iint_R \frac{|\nabla f|}{|\nabla f \cdot \mathbf{p}|} \, dA, \tag{3}$$

where $\mathbf{p}$ is a unit vector normal to R and $\nabla f \cdot \mathbf{p} \neq 0$.

Thus, the area is the double integral over R of the magnitude of ∇f divided by the magnitude of the scalar component of ∇f normal to R.

We reached Equation (3) under the assumption that $\nabla f \cdot \mathbf{p} \neq 0$ throughout R and that ∇f is continuous. Whenever the integral exists, however, we define its value to be the area of the portion of the surface $f(x, y, z) = c$ that lies over R.

In the exercises, we show how Equation (3) simplifies if the surface is defined by $z = f(x, y)$.

Example 1 Finding Surface Area

Find the area of the surface cut from the bottom of the paraboloid $x^2 + y^2 - z = 0$ by the plane $z = 4$.

Solution We sketch the surface S and the region R below it in the xy-plane (Figure 13.41). The surface S is part of the level surface $f(x, y, z) = x^2 + y^2 - z = 0$, and R is the disk $x^2 + y^2 \leq 4$ in the xy-plane. To get a unit vector normal to the plane of R, we can take $\mathbf{p} = \mathbf{k}$.

At any point (x, y, z) on the surface, we have

$$f(x, y, z) = x^2 + y^2 - z$$
$$\nabla f = 2x\mathbf{i} + 2y\mathbf{j} - \mathbf{k}$$
$$|\nabla f| = \sqrt{(2x)^2 + (2y)^2 + (-1)^2}$$
$$= \sqrt{4x^2 + 4y^2 + 1}$$
$$|\nabla f \cdot \mathbf{p}| = |\nabla f \cdot \mathbf{k}| = |-1| = 1.$$

In the region R, $dA = dx\,dy$. Therefore,

$$\text{Surface area} = \iint_R \frac{|\nabla f|}{|\nabla f \cdot \mathbf{p}|}\,dA \qquad \text{Eq. (3)}$$

$$= \iint_{x^2+y^2\leq4} \sqrt{4x^2 + 4y^2 + 1}\,dx\,dy$$

$$= \int_0^{2\pi}\int_0^2 \sqrt{4r^2 + 1}\,r\,dr\,d\theta \qquad \text{Polar coordinates}$$

$$= \int_0^{2\pi} \left[\frac{1}{12}(4r^2 + 1)^{3/2}\right]_0^2 d\theta$$

$$= \int_0^{2\pi} \frac{1}{12}(17^{3/2} - 1)\,d\theta = \frac{\pi}{6}(17\sqrt{17} - 1).$$

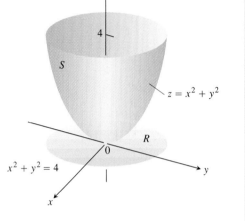

FIGURE 13.41 The area of this parabolic surface in Example 1.

Example 2 Finding Surface Area

Find the area of the cap cut from the hemisphere $x^2 + y^2 + z^2 = 2, z \geq 0$, by the cylinder $x^2 + y^2 = 1$ (Figure 13.42).

Solution The cap S is part of the level surface $f(x, y, z) = x^2 + y^2 + z^2 = 2$. It projects one-to-one onto the disk $R: x^2 + y^2 \leq 1$ in the xy-plane. The vector $\mathbf{p} = \mathbf{k}$ is normal to the plane of R.

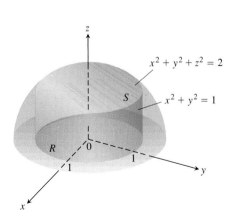

FIGURE 13.42 The cap cut from the hemisphere by the cylinder in Example 2

At any point on the surface,

$$f(x, y, z) = x^2 + y^2 + z^2$$

$$\nabla f = 2x\mathbf{i} + 2y\mathbf{j} + 2z\mathbf{k}$$

$$|\nabla f| = 2\sqrt{x^2 + y^2 + z^2} = 2\sqrt{2} \qquad \text{Because } x^2 + y^2 +$$
$$\qquad\qquad\qquad z^2 = 2 \text{ at points of } S$$

$$|\nabla f \cdot \mathbf{p}| = |\nabla f \cdot \mathbf{k}| = |2z| = 2z.$$

Therefore,

$$\text{Surface area} = \iint_R \frac{|\nabla f|}{|\nabla f \cdot \mathbf{p}|}\, dA = \iint_R \frac{2\sqrt{2}}{2z}\, dA = \sqrt{2} \iint_R \frac{dA}{z}. \qquad (4)$$

What do we do about the z?

Since z is the z-coordinate of a point on the sphere, we can express it in terms of x and y as

$$z = \sqrt{2 - x^2 - y^2}.$$

We continue the work of Equation (4) with this substitution:

$$\text{Surface area} = \sqrt{2} \iint_R \frac{dA}{z} = \sqrt{2} \iint_{x^2+y^2 \le 1} \frac{dA}{\sqrt{2 - x^2 - y^2}}$$

$$= \sqrt{2} \int_0^{2\pi} \int_0^1 \frac{r\, dr\, d\theta}{\sqrt{2 - r^2}} \qquad \text{Polar coordinates}$$

$$= \sqrt{2} \int_0^{2\pi} \left[-(2 - r^2)^{1/2} \right]_{r=0}^{r=1} d\theta$$

$$= \sqrt{2} \int_0^{2\pi} (\sqrt{2} - 1)\, d\theta = 2\pi(2 - \sqrt{2}).$$

Surface Integrals

We now show how to integrate a function over a surface, using the ideas just developed for calculating surface area.

Suppose, for example, that we have an electrical charge distributed over a surface $f(x, y, z) = c$ like the one shown in Figure 13.43 and that the function $g(x, y, z)$ gives the charge per unit area (charge density) at each point on S. Then we may calculate the total charge on S as an integral in the following way.

We partition the shadow region R on the ground plane beneath the surface into small rectangles of the kind we would use if we were defining the surface area of S. Then directly above each ΔA_k lies a patch of surface $\Delta\sigma_k$ that we approximate with a parallelogram-shaped portion of tangent plane, ΔP_k.

Up to this point the construction proceeds as in the definition of surface area, but now we take an additional step: We evaluate g at (x_k, y_k, z_k) and approximate the total charge on the surface patch $\Delta\sigma_k$ by the product $g(x_k, y_k, z_k)\, \Delta P_k$. The rationale is that when the partition of R is sufficiently fine, the value of g throughout $\Delta\sigma_k$ is nearly constant and ΔP_k is nearly the same as $\Delta\sigma_k$. The total charge over S is then approximated by the sum

$$\text{Total charge} \approx \sum g(x_k, y_k, z_k)\, \Delta P_k = \sum g(x_k, y_k, z_k) \frac{\Delta A_k}{|\cos \gamma_k|}.$$

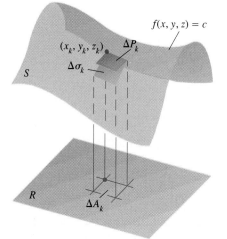

FIGURE 13.43 If we know how an electrical charge is distributed over a surface, we can find the total charge with a suitably modified surface integral.

If f, the function defining the surface S, and its first partial derivatives are continuous, and if g is continuous over S, then the sums on the right-hand side of the last equation approach the limit

$$\iint\limits_R g(x, y, z) \frac{dA}{|\cos \gamma|} = \iint\limits_R g(x, y, z) \frac{|\nabla f|}{|\nabla f \cdot \mathbf{p}|} dA \tag{5}$$

as the partition of R is refined in the usual way. This limit is called the integral of g over the surface S and is calculated as a double integral over R. The value of the integral is the total charge on the surface S.

As you might expect, the formula in Equation (5) defines the integral of *any* function g over the surface S as long as the integral exists.

Definitions Integral of g over S and Surface Integral

If R is the shadow region of a surface S defined by the equation $f(x, y, z) = c$, and g is a continuous function defined at the points of S, then the **integral of g over S** is the integral

$$\iint\limits_R g(x, y, z) \frac{|\nabla f|}{|\nabla f \cdot \mathbf{p}|} dA, \tag{6}$$

where $\mathbf{p}$ is a unit vector normal to R and $\nabla f \cdot \mathbf{p} \neq 0$. The integral itself is called a **surface integral.**

The integral in Equation (6) takes on different meanings in different applications. If g has the constant value 1, the integral gives the area of S. If g gives the mass density of a thin shell of material modeled by S, the integral gives the mass of the shell.

Algebraic Properties; The Surface Area Differential

We can abbreviate the integral in Equation (6) by writing $d\sigma$ for $(|\nabla f|/|\nabla f \cdot \mathbf{p}|) dA$.

The Surface Area Differential and the Differential Form for Surface Integrals

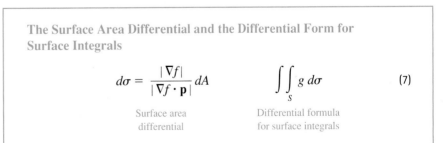

$$d\sigma = \frac{|\nabla f|}{|\nabla f \cdot \mathbf{p}|} dA \qquad\qquad \iint\limits_S g\, d\sigma \tag{7}$$

Surface area differential

Differential formula for surface integrals

Surface integrals behave like other double integrals, the integral of the sum of two functions being the sum of their integrals and so on. The domain additivity property takes the form

$$\iint\limits_S g\, d\sigma = \iint\limits_{S_1} g\, d\sigma + \iint\limits_{S_2} g\, d\sigma + \cdots + \iint\limits_{S_n} g\, d\sigma.$$

The idea is that if S is partitioned by smooth curves into a finite number of nonoverlapping smooth patches (i.e., if S is **piecewise smooth**), then the integral over S is the sum of the integrals over the patches. Thus, the integral of a function over the surface of a cube is the sum of the integrals over the faces of the cube. We integrate over a turtle shell of welded plates by integrating one plate at a time and adding the results.

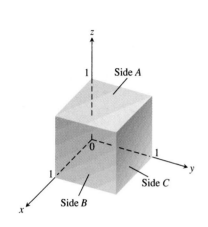

FIGURE 13.44 **The cube in Example 3**

Example 3   Integrating Over a Surface

Integrate $g(x, y, z) = xyz$ over the surface of the cube cut from the first octant by the planes $x = 1, y = 1$, and $z = 1$ (Figure 13.44).

Solution   We integrate xyz over each of the six sides and add the results. Since $xyz = 0$ on the sides that lie in the coordinate planes, the integral over the surface of the cube reduces to

$$\iint\limits_{\substack{\text{Cube} \\ \text{surface}}} xyz \, d\sigma = \iint\limits_{\text{Side } A} xyz \, d\sigma + \iint\limits_{\text{Side } B} xyz \, d\sigma + \iint\limits_{\text{Side } C} xyz \, d\sigma.$$

Side A is the surface $f(x, y, z) = z = 1$ over the square region $R_{xy} : 0 \le x \le 1$, $0 \le y \le 1$, in the xy-plane. For this surface and region,

$$\mathbf{p} = \mathbf{k}, \qquad \nabla f = \mathbf{k}, \qquad |\nabla f| = 1, \qquad |\nabla f \cdot \mathbf{p}| = |\mathbf{k} \cdot \mathbf{k}| = 1$$

$$d\sigma = \frac{|\nabla f|}{|\nabla f \cdot \mathbf{p}|} dA = \frac{1}{1} dx \, dy = dx \, dy$$

$$xyz = xy(1) = xy$$

and

$$\iint\limits_{\text{Side } A} xyz \, d\sigma = \iint\limits_{R_{xy}} xy \, dx \, dy = \int_0^1 \int_0^1 xy \, dx \, dy = \int_0^1 \frac{y}{2} \, dy = \frac{1}{4}.$$

Symmetry tells us that the integrals of xyz over sides B and C are also $1/4$. Hence,

$$\iint\limits_{\substack{\text{Cube} \\ \text{surface}}} xyz \, d\sigma = \frac{1}{4} + \frac{1}{4} + \frac{1}{4} = \frac{3}{4}.$$

Orientation

We call a smooth surface S **orientable** or **two-sided** if it is possible to define a field $\mathbf{n}$ of unit normal vectors on S that varies continuously with position. Any patch or subportion of an orientable surface is orientable. Spheres and other smooth closed surfaces in space (smooth surfaces that enclose solids) are orientable. By convention, we choose $\mathbf{n}$ on a closed surface to point outward.

Once $\mathbf{n}$ has been chosen, we say that we have **oriented** the surface, and we call the surface together with its normal field an **oriented surface.** The vector $\mathbf{n}$ at any point is called the **positive direction** at that point (Figure 13.45).

The Möbius band in Figure 13.46 is not orientable. No matter where you start to construct a continuous unit normal field (shown as the shaft of a thumbtack in the

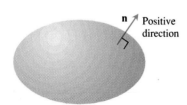

FIGURE 13.45 **Smooth closed surfaces in space are orientable. The outward unit normal vector defines the positive direction at each point.**

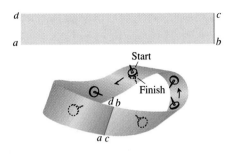

FIGURE 13.46 To make a Möbius band, take a rectangular strip of paper *abcd*, give the end *bc* a single twist, and paste the ends of the strip together to match *a* with *c* and *b* with *d*. The Möbius band is a nonorientable or one-sided surface.

figure), moving the vector continuously around the surface in the manner shown will return it to the starting point with a direction opposite to the one it had when it started out. The vector at that point cannot point both ways and yet it must if the field is to be continuous. We conclude that no such field exists.

Surface Integral for Flux

Suppose that **F** is a continuous vector field defined over an oriented surface S and that **n** is the chosen unit normal field on the surface. We call the integral of **F** · **n** over S the flux of **F** across S in the positive direction. Thus, the flux is the integral over S of the scalar component of **F** in the direction of **n**.

> **Definition**   Flux
>
> The **flux** of a three-dimensional vector field **F** across an oriented surface S in the direction of **n** is
>
> $$\text{Flux} = \iint_S \mathbf{F} \cdot \mathbf{n} \, d\sigma. \tag{8}$$

The definition is analogous to the flux of a two-dimensional field **F** across a plane curve C. In the plane (Section 13.2), the flux is

$$\int_C \mathbf{F} \cdot \mathbf{n} \, ds,$$

the integral of the scalar component of **F** normal to the curve.

If **F** is the velocity field of a three-dimensional fluid flow, the flux of **F** across S is the net rate at which fluid is crossing S in the chosen positive direction. We discuss such flows in more detail in Section 13.7.

If **S** is part of a level surface $g(x, y, z) = c$, then **n** may be taken to be one of the two fields

$$\mathbf{n} = \pm \frac{\nabla g}{|\nabla g|}, \tag{9}$$

depending on which one gives the preferred direction. The corresponding flux is

$$\text{Flux} = \iint_S \mathbf{F} \cdot \mathbf{n} \, d\sigma$$

$$= \iint_R \left(\mathbf{F} \cdot \frac{\pm \nabla g}{|\nabla g|} \right) \frac{|\nabla g|}{|\nabla g \cdot \mathbf{p}|} \, dA \qquad \text{(9) and (7)} \tag{8}$$

$$= \iint_R \mathbf{F} \cdot \frac{\pm \nabla g}{|\nabla g \cdot \mathbf{p}|} \, dA. \tag{10}$$

Example 4   Finding Flux

Find the flux of **F** $= yz\mathbf{j} + z^2\mathbf{k}$ outward through the surface S cut from the cylinder $y^2 + z^2 = 1, z \geq 0$, by the planes $x = 0$ and $x = 1$.

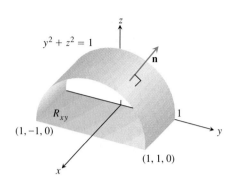

FIGURE 13.47 Example 4 calculates the flux of a vector field outward through this surface. The area of the shadow region R_{xy} is 2.

Solution   The outward normal field on S (Figure 13.47) may be calculated from the gradient of $g(x, y, z) = y^2 + z^2$ to be

$$\mathbf{n} = +\frac{\nabla g}{|\nabla g|} = \frac{2y\mathbf{j} + 2z\mathbf{k}}{\sqrt{4y^2 + 4z^2}} = \frac{2y\mathbf{j} + 2z\mathbf{k}}{2\sqrt{1}} = y\mathbf{j} + z\mathbf{k}.$$

With $\mathbf{p} = \mathbf{k}$, we also have

$$d\sigma = \frac{|\nabla g|}{|\nabla g \cdot \mathbf{k}|} dA = \frac{2}{|2z|} dA = \frac{1}{z} dA.$$

We can drop the absolute value bars because $z \geq 0$ on S.
The value of $\mathbf{F} \cdot \mathbf{n}$ on the surface is

$$\begin{aligned}\mathbf{F} \cdot \mathbf{n} &= (yz\mathbf{j} + z^2\mathbf{k}) \cdot (y\mathbf{j} + z\mathbf{k}) \\ &= y^2z + z^3 = z(y^2 + z^2) \\ &= z. \qquad\qquad {\scriptstyle y^2 + z^2 = 1 \text{ on } S}\end{aligned}$$

Therefore, the flux of $\mathbf{F}$ outward through S is

$$\iint_S \mathbf{F} \cdot \mathbf{n}\, d\sigma = \iint_S (z)\left(\frac{1}{z}\, dA\right) = \iint_{R_{xy}} dA = \text{area}(R_{xy}) = 2.$$

Moments and Masses of Thin Shells

Thin shells of material like bowls, metal drums, and domes are modeled with surfaces. Their moments and masses are calculated with the formulas in Table 13.3.

Table 13.3 Mass and moment formulas for very thin shells

Mass: $M = \iint_S \delta(x, y, z)\, d\sigma$ ($\delta(x, y, z) = $ density at (x, y, z), mass per unit area)

First moments about the coordinate planes:

$$M_{yz} = \iint_S x\delta\, d\sigma, \qquad M_{xz} = \iint_S y\delta\, d\sigma, \qquad M_{xy} = \iint_S z\delta\, d\sigma$$

Coordinates of center of mass:

$$\bar{x} = M_{yz}/M, \qquad \bar{y} = M_{xz}/M, \qquad \bar{z} = M_{xy}/M$$

Moments of inertia about coordinate axes:

$$I_x = \iint_S (y^2 + z^2)\delta\, d\sigma, \qquad I_y = \iint_S (x^2 + z^2)\delta\, d\sigma,$$

$$I_z = \iint_S (x^2 + Y^2)\delta\, d\sigma, \qquad I_L = \iint_S r^2\delta\, d\sigma,$$

$r(x, y, z) = $ distance from point (x, y, z) to line L

Radius of gyration about a line L: $R_L = \sqrt{I_L/M}$

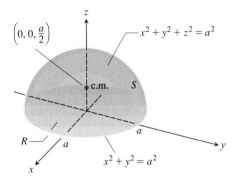

FIGURE 13.48 The center of mass of a thin hemispherical shell of constant density lies on the axis of symmetry halfway from the base to the top. (Example 5)

Example 5 Finding Center of Mass

Find the center of mass of a thin hemispherical shell of radius a and constant density δ.

Solution We model the shell with the hemisphere

$$f(x, y, z) = x^2 + y^2 + z^2 = a^2, \qquad z \geq 0$$

(Figure 13.48). The symmetry of the surface about the z-axis tells us that $\bar{x} = \bar{y} = 0$. It remains only to find $\bar{z}$ from the formula $\bar{z} = M_{xy}/M$.
The mass of the shell is

$$M = \iint_S \delta \, d\sigma = \delta \iint_S d\sigma = (\delta)(\text{area of } S) = 2\pi a^2 \delta.$$

To evaluate the integral for M_{xy}, we take $\mathbf{p} = \mathbf{k}$ and calculate

$$|\nabla f| = |2x\mathbf{i} + 2y\mathbf{j} + 2z\mathbf{k}| = 2\sqrt{x^2 + y^2 + z^2} = 2a$$

$$|\nabla f \cdot \mathbf{p}| = |\nabla f \cdot \mathbf{k}| = |2z| = 2z$$

$$d\sigma = \frac{|\nabla f|}{|\nabla f \cdot \mathbf{p}|} \, dA = \frac{a}{z} \, dA.$$

Then

$$M_{xy} = \iint_S z\delta \, d\sigma = \delta \iint_R z \frac{a}{z} \, dA = \delta a \iint_R dA = \delta a(\pi a^2) = \delta \pi a^3$$

$$\bar{z} = \frac{M_{xy}}{M} = \frac{\pi a^3 \delta}{2\pi a^2 \delta} = \frac{a}{2}.$$

The shell's center of mass is the point $(0, 0, a/2)$.

EXERCISES 13.5

Surface Area

1. Find the area of the surface cut from the paraboloid $x^2 + y^2 - z = 0$ by the plane $z = 2$.

2. Find the area of the band cut from the paraboloid $x^2 + y^2 - z = 0$ by the planes $z = 2$ and $z = 6$.

3. Find the area of the region cut from the plane $x + 2y + 2z = 5$ by the cylinder whose walls are $x = y^2$ and $x = 2 - y^2$.

4. Find the area of the portion of the surface $x^2 - 2z = 0$ that lies above the triangle bounded by the lines $x = \sqrt{3}$, $y = 0$, and $y = x$ in the xy-plane.

5. Find the area of the surface $x^2 - 2y - 2z = 0$ that lies above the triangle bounded by the lines $x = 2$, $y = 0$, and $y = 3x$ in the xy-plane.

6. Find the area of the cap cut from the sphere $x^2 + y^2 + z^2 = 2$ by the cone $z = \sqrt{x^2 + y^2}$.

7. Find the area of the ellipse cut from the plane $z = cx$ (c a constant) by the cylinder $x^2 + y^2 = 1$.

8. Find the area of the upper portion of the cylinder $x^2 + z^2 = 1$ that lies between the planes $x = \pm 1/2$ and $y = \pm 1/2$.

9. Find the area of the portion of the paraboloid $x = 4 - y^2 - z^2$ that lies above the ring $1 \leq y^2 + z^2 \leq 4$ in the yz-plane.

10. Find the area of the surface cut from the paraboloid $x^2 + y + z^2 = 2$ by the plane $y = 0$.

11. Find the area of the surface $x^2 - 2 \ln x + \sqrt{15}y - z = 0$ above the square $R: 1 \leq x \leq 2, 0 \leq y \leq 1$, in the xy-plane.

12. Find the area of the surface $2x^{3/2} + 2y^{3/2} - 3z = 0$ above the square $R: 0 \leq x \leq 1, 0 \leq y \leq 1$, in the xy-plane.

Surface Integrals

13. Integrate $g(x, y, z) = x + y + z$ over the surface of the cube cut from the first octant by the planes $x = a$, $y = a$, $z = a$.

14. Integrate $g(x, y, z) = y + z$ over the surface of the wedge in the first octant bounded by the coordinate planes and the planes $x = 2$ and $y + z = 1$.

15. Integrate $g(x, y, z) = xyz$ over the surface of the rectangular solid cut from the first octant by the planes $x = a$, $y = b$, and $z = c$.

16. Integrate $g(x, y, z) = xyz$ over the surface of the rectangular solid bounded by the planes $x = \pm a$, $y = \pm b$, and $z = \pm c$.

17. Integrate $g(x, y, z) = x + y + z$ over the portion of the plane $2x + 2y + z = 2$ that lies in the first octant.

18. Integrate $g(x, y, z) = x\sqrt{y^2 + 4}$ over the surface cut from the parabolic cylinder $y^2 + 4z = 16$ by the planes $x = 0$, $x = 1$, and $z = 0$.

Flux Across a Surface

In Exercises 19 and 20, find the flux of the field **F** across the portion of the given surface in the specified direction.

19. $\mathbf{F}(x, y, z) = -\mathbf{i} + 2\mathbf{j} + 3\mathbf{k}$

S: rectangular surface $z = 0$, $0 \le x \le 2$, $0 \le y \le 3$, direction **k**

20. $\mathbf{F}(x, y, z) = yx^2\mathbf{i} - 2\mathbf{j} + xz\mathbf{k}$

S: rectangular surface $y = 0$, $-1 \le x \le 2$, $2 \le z \le 7$, direction $-\mathbf{j}$

In Exercises 21–26, find the flux of the field **F** across the portion of the sphere $x^2 + y^2 + z^2 = a^2$ in the first octant in the direction away from the origin.

21. $\mathbf{F}(x, y, z) = z\mathbf{k}$ **22.** $\mathbf{F}(x, y, z) = -y\mathbf{i} + x\mathbf{j}$

23. $\mathbf{F}(x, y, z) = y\mathbf{i} - x\mathbf{j} + \mathbf{k}$ **24.** $\mathbf{F}(x, y, z) = zx\mathbf{i} + zy\mathbf{j} + z^2\mathbf{k}$

25. $\mathbf{F}(x, y, z) = x\mathbf{i} + y\mathbf{j} + z\mathbf{k}$

26. $\mathbf{F}(x, y, z) = \dfrac{x\mathbf{i} + y\mathbf{j} + z\mathbf{k}}{\sqrt{x^2 + y^2 + z^2}}$

27. Find the flux of the field $\mathbf{F}(x, y, z) = z^2\mathbf{i} + x\mathbf{j} - 3z\mathbf{k}$ outward through the surface cut from the parabolic cylinder $z = 4 - y^2$ by the planes $x = 0$, $x = 1$, and $z = 0$.

28. Find the flux of the field $\mathbf{F}(x, y, z) = 4x\mathbf{i} + 4y\mathbf{j} + 2\mathbf{k}$ outward (away from the z-axis) through the surface cut from the bottom of the paraboloid $z = x^2 + y^2$ by the plane $z = 1$.

29. Let S be the portion of the cylinder $y = e^x$ in the first octant that projects parallel to the x-axis onto the rectangle R_{yz}: $1 \le y \le 2$, $0 \le z \le 1$ in the yz-plane (see the accompanying figure). Let **n** be the unit vector normal to S that points away from the yz-plane. Find the flux of the field $\mathbf{F}(x, y, z) = -2\mathbf{i} + 2y\mathbf{j} + z\mathbf{k}$ across S in the direction of **n**.

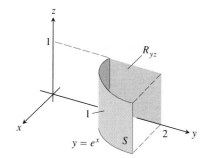

30. Let S be the portion of the cylinder $y = \ln x$ in the first octant whose projection parallel to the y-axis onto the xz-plane is the rectangle R_{xz}: $1 \le x \le e$, $0 \le z \le 1$. Let **n** be the unit vector normal to S that points away from the xz-plane. Find the flux of $\mathbf{F} = 2y\mathbf{j} + z\mathbf{k}$ through S in the direction of **n**.

31. Find the outward flux of the field $\mathbf{F} = 2xy\mathbf{i} + 2yz\mathbf{j} + 2xz\mathbf{k}$ across the surface of the cube cut from the first octant by the planes $x = a$, $y = a$, $z = a$.

32. Find the outward flux of the field $\mathbf{F} = xz\mathbf{i} + yz\mathbf{j} + \mathbf{k}$ across the surface of the upper cap cut from the solid sphere $x^2 + y^2 + z^2 \le 25$ by the plane $z = 3$.

Moments and Masses

33. *Centroid* Find the centroid of the portion of the sphere $x^2 + y^2 + z^2 = a^2$ that lies in the first octant.

34. *Centroid* Find the centroid of the surface cut from the cylinder $y^2 + z^2 = 9$, $z \ge 0$, by the planes $x = 0$ and $x = 3$ (resembles the surface in Example 4).

35. *Thin shell of constant density* Find the center of mass and the moment of inertia and radius of gyration about the z-axis of a thin shell of constant density δ cut from the cone $x^2 + y^2 - z^2 = 0$ by the planes $z = 1$ and $z = 2$.

36. *Conical surface of constant density* Find the moment of inertia about the z-axis of a thin shell of constant density δ cut from the cone $4x^2 + 4y^2 - z^2 = 0$, $z \ge 0$, by the circular cylinder $x^2 + y^2 = 2x$ (see the accompanying figure).

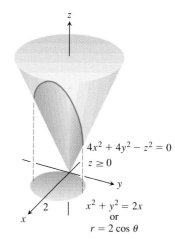

37. *Spherical shells*

  (a) Find the moment of inertia about a diameter of a thin spherical shell of radius a and constant density δ. (Work with a hemispherical shell and double the result.)

  (b) Use the Parallel Axis Theorem (Exercises 12.5) and the result in part (a) to find the moment of inertia about a line tangent to the shell.

38. (a) *Cones with and without ice cream* Find the centroid of the lateral surface of a solid cone of base radius a and height h (cone surface minus the base).

(b) Use Pappus's formula (Exercises 12.5) and the result in part (a) to find the centroid of the complete surface of a solid cone (side plus base).

(c) *Writing to Learn* A cone of radius a and height h is joined to a hemisphere of radius a to make a surface S that resembles an ice cream cone. Use Pappus's formula and the results in part (a) and Example 5 to find the centroid of S. How high does the cone have to be to place the centroid in the plane shared by the bases of the hemisphere and cone?

Special Formulas for Surface Area

If S is the surface defined by a function $z = f(x, y)$ that has continuous first partial derivatives throughout a region R_{xy} in the xy-plane (Figure 13.49), then S is also the level surface $F(x, y, z) = 0$ of the function $F(x, y, z) = f(x, y) - z$. Taking the unit normal to R_{xy} to be $\mathbf{p} = \mathbf{k}$ then gives

$$|\nabla F| = |f_x \mathbf{i} + f_y \mathbf{j} - \mathbf{k}| - \sqrt{f_x^2 + f_y^2 + 1}$$

$$|\nabla F \cdot \mathbf{p}| = |(f_x \mathbf{i} + f_y \mathbf{j} - \mathbf{k}) \cdot \mathbf{k}| = |-1| = 1$$

and

$$\iint\limits_{R_{xy}} \frac{|\nabla F|}{|\nabla F \cdot \mathbf{p}|}\, dA = \iint\limits_{R_{xy}} \sqrt{f_y^2 + f_y^2 + 1}\, dx\, dy, \qquad (11)$$

Similarly, the area of a smooth surface $x = f(y, z)$ over a region R_{yz} in the yz-plane is

$$A = \iint\limits_{R_{yz}} \sqrt{f_y^2 + f_z^2 + 1}\, dy\, dz, \qquad (12)$$

and the area of a smooth $y = f(x, z)$ over a region R_{xz} in the xz-plane is

$$A = \iint\limits_{R_{xz}} \sqrt{f_x^2 + f_z^2 + 1}\, dx\, dz. \qquad (13)$$

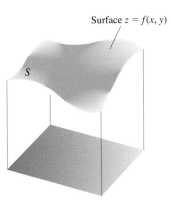

Surface $z = f(x, y)$

FIGURE 13.49 For a surface $z = f(x, y)$, the surface area formula in Equation (3) takes the form

$$A = \iint\limits_{R_{xy}} \sqrt{f_x^2 + f_y^2 + 1}\, dx\, dy.$$

Use Equations (11)–(13) to find the area of the surfaces in Exercises 39–44.

39. The surface cut from the bottom of the paraboloid $z = x^2 + y^2$ by the plane $z = 3$

40. The surface cut from the "nose" of the paraboloid $x = 1 - y^2 - z^2$ by the yz-plane

41. The portion of the cone $z = \sqrt{x^2 + y^2}$ that lies over the region between the circle $x^2 + y^2 = 1$ and the ellipse $9x^2 + 4y^2 = 36$ in the xy-plane. (*Hint:* Use formulas from geometry to find the area of the region.)

42. The triangle cut from the plane $2x + 6y + 3z = 6$ by the bounding planes of the first octant. Calculate the area three ways, once with each area formula

43. The surface in the first octant cut from the cylinder $y = (2/3)z^{3/2}$ by the planes $x = 1$ and $y = 16/3$

44. The portion of the plane $y + z = 4$ that lies above the region cut from the first quadrant of the xz-plane by the parabola $x = 4 - z^2$

13.6

Parametrized Surfaces

Parametrizations of Surfaces • Surface Area • Surface Integrals

We have defined curves in the plane in three different ways:

Explicit form:	$y = f(x)$
Implicit form:	$F(x, y) = 0$
Parametric vector form:	$\mathbf{r}(t) = f(t)\mathbf{i} + g(t)\mathbf{j}, \qquad a \le t \le b.$

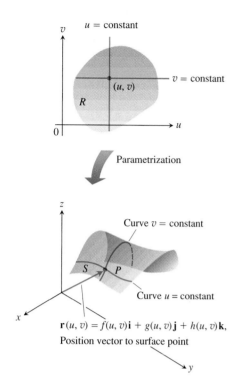

FIGURE 13.50 A parametrized surface.

We have analogous definitions of surfaces in space:

Explicit form: $z = f(x, y)$

Implicit form: $F(x, y, z) = 0.$

There is also a parametric form that gives the position of a point on the surface as a vector function of two variables. The present section extends the investigation of surface area and surface integrals to surfaces described parametrically.

Parametrizations of Surfaces

Let

$$\mathbf{r}(u, v) = f(u, v)\mathbf{i} + g(u, v)\mathbf{j} + h(u, v)\mathbf{k} \tag{1}$$

be a continuous vector function that is defined on a region R in the uv-plane and one-to-one on the interior of R (Figure 13.50). We call the range of $\mathbf{r}$ the **surface** S defined or traced by $\mathbf{r}$. Equation (1) together with the domain R constitute a **parametrization** of the surface. The variables u and v are the **parameters**, and R is the **parameter domain.** To simplify our discussion, we take R to be a rectangle defined by inequalities of the form $a \leq u \leq b, c \leq v \leq d$. The requirement that $\mathbf{r}$ be one-to-one on the interior of R ensures that S does not cross itself. Notice that Equation (1) is the vector equivalent of *three* parametric equations:

$$x = f(u, v), \qquad y = g(u, v), \qquad z = h(u, v).$$

Example 1   Parametrizing a Cone

Find a parametrization of the cone

$$z = \sqrt{x^2 + y^2}, \qquad 0 \leq z \leq 1.$$

Solution   Here, cylindrical coordinates provide everything we need. A typical point (x, y, z) on the cone (Figure 13.51) has $x = r \cos \theta$, $y = r \sin \theta$, and $z = \sqrt{x^2 + y^2} = r$, with $0 \leq r \leq 1$ and $0 \leq \theta \leq 2\pi$. Taking $u = r$ and $v = \theta$ in Equation (1) gives the parametrization

$$\mathbf{r}(r, \theta) = (r \cos \theta)\mathbf{i} + (r \sin \theta)\mathbf{j} + r\mathbf{k}, \qquad 0 \leq r \leq 1, \quad 0 \leq \theta \leq 2\pi.$$

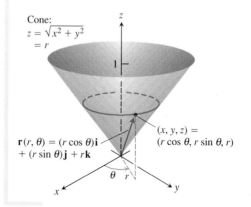

FIGURE 13.51 The cone in Example 1.

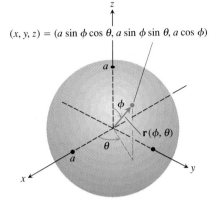

$(x, y, z) = (a \sin \phi \cos \theta, a \sin \phi \sin \theta, a \cos \phi)$

FIGURE 13.52 The sphere in Example 2.

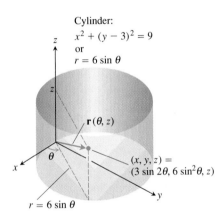

FIGURE 13.53 The cylinder in Example 3.

Example 2 Parametrizing a Sphere

Find a parametrization of the sphere $x^2 + y^2 + z^2 = a^2$.

Solution Spherical coordinates provide what we need. A typical point (x, y, z) on the sphere (Figure 13.52) has $x = a \sin \phi \cos \theta$, $y = a \sin \phi \sin \theta$, and $z = a \cos \phi$, $0 \le \phi \le \pi$, $0 \le \theta \le 2\pi$. Taking $u = \phi$ and $v = \theta$ in Equation (1) gives the parametrization

$$\mathbf{r}(\phi, \theta) = (a \sin \phi \cos \theta)\mathbf{i} + (a \sin \phi \sin \theta)\mathbf{j} + (a \cos \phi)\mathbf{k},$$
$$0 \le \phi \le \pi, \quad 0 \le \theta \le 2\pi.$$

Example 3 Parametrizing a Cylinder

Find a parametrization of the cylinder

$$x^2 + (y - 3)^2 = 9, \qquad 0 \le z \le 5.$$

Solution In cylindrical coordinates, a point (x, y, z) has $x = r \cos \theta$, $y = r \sin \theta$, and $z = z$. For points on the cylinder $x^2 + (y - 3)^2 = 9$ (Figure 13.53), the equation is the same as the polar equation for the cylinder's base in the xy-plane:

$$x^2 + (y^2 - 6y + 9) = 9$$
$$r^2 - 6r \sin \theta = 0$$

or

$$r = 6 \sin \theta, \qquad 0 \le \theta \le \pi.$$

A typical point on the cylinder therefore has

$$x = r \cos \theta = 6 \sin \theta \cos \theta = 3 \sin 2\theta$$
$$y = r \sin \theta = 6 \sin^2 \theta$$
$$z = z.$$

Taking $u = \theta$ and $v = z$ in Equation (1) gives the parametrization

$$\mathbf{r}(\theta, z) = (3 \sin 2\theta)\mathbf{i} + (6 \sin^2 \theta)\mathbf{j} + z\,\mathbf{k}, \qquad 0 \le \theta \le \pi, \quad 0 \le z \le 5.$$

Surface Area

Our goal is to find a double integral for calculating the area of a curved surface S based on the parametrization

$$\mathbf{r}(u, v) = f(u, v)\mathbf{i} + g(u, v)\mathbf{j} + h(u, v)\mathbf{k}, \qquad a \le u \le b, \quad c \le v \le d.$$

We need S to be smooth for the construction we are about to carry out. The definition of smoothness involves the partial derivatives of $\mathbf{r}$ with respect to u and v:

$$\mathbf{r}_u = \frac{\partial \mathbf{r}}{\partial u} = \frac{\partial f}{\partial u}\mathbf{i} + \frac{\partial g}{\partial u}\mathbf{j} + \frac{\partial h}{\partial u}\mathbf{k}$$

$$\mathbf{r}_v = \frac{\partial \mathbf{r}}{\partial v} = \frac{\partial f}{\partial v}\mathbf{i} + \frac{\partial g}{\partial v}\mathbf{j} + \frac{\partial h}{\partial v}\mathbf{k}.$$

> **Definition** Smooth Parametrized Surface
>
> A parametrized surface $\mathbf{r}(u, v) = f(u, v)\mathbf{i} + g(u, v)\mathbf{j} + h(u, v)\mathbf{k}$ is **smooth** if $\mathbf{r}_u$ and $\mathbf{r}_v$ are continuous and $\mathbf{r}_u \times \mathbf{r}_v$ is never zero on the parameter domain.

Now consider a small rectangle ΔA_{uv} in R with sides on the lines $u = u_0$, $u = u_0 + \Delta u$, $v = v_0$, and $v = v_0 + \Delta v$ (Figure 13.54). Each side of ΔA_{uv} maps to a curve on the surface S, and together these four curves bound a "curved area element" $\Delta \sigma_{uv}$. In the notation of the figure, the side $v = v_0$ maps to curve C_1, the side $u = u_0$ maps to C_2, and their common vertex (u_0, v_0) maps to P_0.

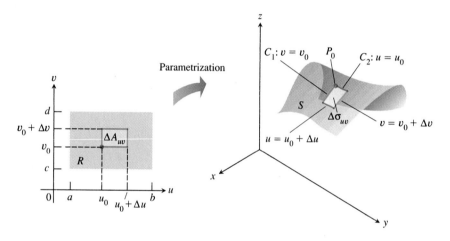

FIGURE 13.54 A rectangular area element ΔA_{uv} in the uv-plane maps onto a curved area element $\Delta \sigma_{uv}$ on S.

Figure 13.55 shows an enlarged view of $\Delta \sigma_{uv}$. The vector $\mathbf{r}_u(u_0, v_0)$ is tangent to C_1 at P_0. Likewise, $\mathbf{r}_v(u_0, v_0)$ is tangent to C_2 at P_0. The cross product $\mathbf{r}_u \times \mathbf{r}_v$ is normal to the surface at P_0. (Here is where we begin to use the assumption that S is smooth. We want to be sure that $\mathbf{r}_u \times \mathbf{r}_v \neq \mathbf{0}$.)

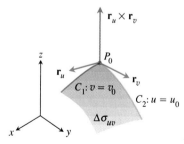

FIGURE 13.55 A magnified view of a surface area element $\Delta \sigma_{uv}$.

We next approximate the surface element $\Delta \sigma_{uv}$ by the parallelogram on the tangent plane whose sides are determined by the vectors $\Delta u \mathbf{r}_u$ and $\Delta v \mathbf{r}_v$ (Figure 13.56). The area of this parallelogram is

$$|\Delta u \mathbf{r}_u \times \Delta v \mathbf{r}_v| = |\mathbf{r}_u \times \mathbf{r}_v| \, \Delta u \, \Delta v. \tag{2}$$

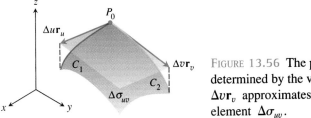

FIGURE 13.56 The parallelogram determined by the vectors $\Delta u \mathbf{r}_u$ and $\Delta v \mathbf{r}_v$ approximates the surface area element $\Delta \sigma_{uv}$.

A partition of the region R in the uv-plane by rectangular regions ΔA_{uv} generates a partition of the surface S into surface area elements $\Delta \sigma_{uv}$. We approximate the area of each surface element $\Delta \sigma_{uv}$ by the parallelogram area in Equation (2) and sum these areas together to obtain an approximation of the area of S:

$$\sum_u \sum_v |\mathbf{r}_u \times \mathbf{r}_v| \, \Delta u \, \Delta v. \tag{3}$$

As Δu and Δv approach zero independently, the continuity of $\mathbf{r}_u$ and $\mathbf{r}_v$ guarantees that the sum in Equation (3) approaches the double integral $\int_c^d \int_a^b |\mathbf{r}_u \times \mathbf{r}_v| \, du \, dv$. This double integral gives the area of the surface S.

Parametric Formula for the Area of a Smooth Surface
The **area** of the smooth surface

$$\mathbf{r}(u, v) = f(u, v)\mathbf{i} + g(u, v)\mathbf{j} + h(u, v)\mathbf{k}, \qquad a \le u \le b, \quad c \le v \le d$$

is

$$A = \int_c^d \int_a^b |\mathbf{r}_u \times \mathbf{r}_v| \, du \, dv. \tag{4}$$

As in Section 13.5, we can abbreviate the integral in Equation (4) by writing $d\sigma$ for $|\mathbf{r}_u \times \mathbf{r}_v| \, du \, dv$.

Surface Area Differential and the Differential Formula for Surface Area

$$d\sigma = |\mathbf{r}_u \times \mathbf{r}_v| \, du \, dv \qquad \iint_S d\sigma \tag{5}$$

Surface area differential

Differential formula for surface area

Example 4   Finding Surface Area (Cone)

Find the surface area of the cone in Example 1 (Figure 13.51).

Solution   In Example 1, we found the parametrization

$$\mathbf{r}(r, \theta) = (r \cos \theta)\mathbf{i} + (r \sin \theta)\mathbf{j} + r\mathbf{k}, \qquad 0 \le r \le 1, \quad 0 \le \theta \le 2\pi.$$

To apply Equation (4), we first find $\mathbf{r}_r \times \mathbf{r}_\theta$:

$$\mathbf{r}_r \times \mathbf{r}_\theta = \begin{vmatrix} \mathbf{i} & \mathbf{j} & \mathbf{k} \\ \cos\theta & \sin\theta & 1 \\ -r\sin\theta & r\cos\theta & 0 \end{vmatrix}$$

$$= -(r\cos\theta)\mathbf{i} - (r\sin\theta)\mathbf{j} + \underbrace{(r\cos^2\theta + r\sin^2\theta)}_{r}\mathbf{k}.$$

Thus, $|\mathbf{r}_r \times \mathbf{r}_\theta| = \sqrt{r^2\cos^2\theta + r^2\sin^2\theta + r^2} = \sqrt{2r^2} = \sqrt{2}\,r$. The area of the cone is

$$A = \int_0^{2\pi}\int_0^1 |\mathbf{r}_r \times \mathbf{r}_\theta|\,dr\,d\theta \qquad \text{Eq. (4) with } u = r, v = \theta$$

$$= \int_0^{2\pi}\int_0^1 \sqrt{2}\,r\,dr\,d\theta = \int_0^{2\pi} \frac{\sqrt{2}}{2}\,d\theta = \frac{\sqrt{2}}{2}(2\pi) = \pi\sqrt{2} \text{ units squared.}$$

Example 5 Finding Surface Area (Sphere)

Find the surface area of a sphere of radius a.

Solution We use the parametrization from Example 2:

$$\mathbf{r}(\phi, \theta) = (a\sin\phi\cos\theta)\mathbf{i} + (a\sin\phi\sin\theta)\mathbf{j} + (a\cos\phi)\mathbf{k},$$

$$0 \le \phi \le \pi, \quad 0 \le \theta \le 2\pi.$$

For $\mathbf{r}_\phi \times \mathbf{r}_\theta$, we get

$$\mathbf{r}_\phi \times \mathbf{r}_\theta = \begin{vmatrix} \mathbf{i} & \mathbf{j} & \mathbf{k} \\ a\cos\phi\cos\theta & a\cos\phi\sin\theta & -a\sin\phi \\ -a\sin\phi\sin\theta & a\sin\phi\cos\theta & 0 \end{vmatrix}$$

$$= (a^2\sin^2\phi\cos\theta)\mathbf{i} + (a^2\sin^2\phi\sin\theta)\mathbf{j} + (a^2\sin\phi\cos\phi)\mathbf{k}.$$

Thus,

$$|\mathbf{r}_\phi \times \mathbf{r}_\theta| = \sqrt{a^4\sin^4\phi\cos^2\theta + a^4\sin^4\phi\sin^2\theta + a^4\sin^2\phi\cos^2\phi}$$

$$= \sqrt{a^4\sin^4\phi + a^4\sin^2\phi\cos^2\phi} = \sqrt{a^4\sin^2\phi(\sin^2\phi + \cos^2\phi)}$$

$$= a^2\sqrt{\sin^2\phi} = a^2\sin\phi,$$

since $\sin\phi \ge 0$ for $0 \le \phi \le \pi$. Therefore, the area of the sphere is

$$A = \int_0^{2\pi}\int_0^{\pi} a^2\sin\phi\,d\phi\,d\theta$$

$$= \int_0^{2\pi} \left[-a^2\cos\phi\right]_0^{\pi}\,d\theta = \int_0^{2\pi} 2a^2\,d\theta = 4\pi a^2 \text{ units squared.}$$

Surface Integrals

Having found a formula for calculating the area of a parametrized surface, we can now integrate a function over the surface using the parametrized form.

Definition   Integral Over a Smooth Parametrized Surface

If S is a smooth surface defined parametrically as $\mathbf{r}(u, v) = f(u, v)\mathbf{i} + g(u, v)\mathbf{j} + h(u, v)\mathbf{k}, a \le u \le b, c \le v \le d$, and $G(x, y, z)$ is a continuous function defined on S, then the **integral of G over S** is

$$\iint\limits_{S} G(x, y, z) \, d\sigma = \int_{c}^{d} \int_{a}^{b} G(f(u, v), g(u, v), h(u, v)) |\mathbf{r}_u \times \mathbf{r}_v| \, du \, dv.$$

Example 6   Integrating Over a Surface Defined Parametrically

Integrate $G(x, y, z) = x^2$ over the cone $z = \sqrt{x^2 + y^2}, 0 \le z \le 1$.

Solution   Continuing the work in Examples 1 and 4, we have $|\mathbf{r}_r \times \mathbf{r}_\theta| = \sqrt{2}\, r$ and

$$\iint\limits_{S} x^2 \, d\sigma = \int_{0}^{2\pi} \int_{0}^{1} (r^2 \cos^2 \theta)(\sqrt{2}r) \, dr \, d\theta \qquad x = r \cos \theta$$

$$= \sqrt{2} \int_{0}^{2\pi} \int_{0}^{1} r^3 \cos^2 \theta \, dr \, d\theta$$

$$= \frac{\sqrt{2}}{4} \int_{0}^{2\pi} \cos^2 \theta \, d\theta = \frac{\sqrt{2}}{4} \left[\frac{\theta}{2} + \frac{1}{4} \sin 2\theta \right]_{0}^{2\pi} = \frac{\pi\sqrt{2}}{4}.$$

Example 7   Finding Flux

Find the flux of $\mathbf{F} = yz\mathbf{i} + x\mathbf{j} - z^2\mathbf{k}$ outward through the parabolic cylinder $y = x^2, 0 \le x \le 1, 0 \le z \le 4$ (Figure 13.57).

Solution   On the surface we have $x = x$, $y = x^2$, and $z = z$, so we automatically have the parametrization $\mathbf{r}(x, z) = x\mathbf{i} + x^2\mathbf{j} + z\mathbf{k}, 0 \le x \le 1, 0 \le z \le 4$. The cross product of tangent vectors is

$$\mathbf{r}_x \times \mathbf{r}_z = \begin{vmatrix} \mathbf{i} & \mathbf{j} & \mathbf{k} \\ 1 & 2x & 0 \\ 0 & 0 & 1 \end{vmatrix} = 2x\mathbf{i} - \mathbf{j}.$$

The unit normal pointing outward from the surface is

$$\mathbf{n} = \frac{\mathbf{r}_x \times \mathbf{r}_z}{|\mathbf{r}_x \times \mathbf{r}_z|} = \frac{2x\mathbf{i} - \mathbf{j}}{\sqrt{4x^2 + 1}}.$$

On the surface, $y = x^2$, so the vector field there is

$$\mathbf{F} = yz\mathbf{i} + x\mathbf{j} - z^2\mathbf{k} = x^2z\mathbf{i} + x\mathbf{j} - z^2\mathbf{k}.$$

Thus,

$$\mathbf{F} \cdot \mathbf{n} = \frac{1}{\sqrt{4x^2 + 1}} ((x^2z)(2x) + (x)(-1) + (-z^2)(0))$$

$$= \frac{2x^3z - x}{\sqrt{4x^2 + 1}}.$$

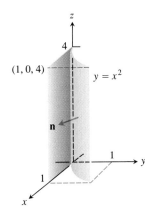

FIGURE 13.57 The parabolic surface in Example 7.

The flux of $\mathbf{F}$ outward through the surface is

$$\iint_S \mathbf{F} \cdot \mathbf{n} \, d\sigma = \int_0^4 \int_0^1 \frac{2x^3 z - x}{\sqrt{4x^2 + 1}} |\mathbf{r}_x \times \mathbf{r}_z| \, dx \, dz$$

$$= \int_0^4 \int_0^1 \frac{2x^3 z - x}{\sqrt{4x^2 + 1}} \sqrt{4x^2 + 1} \, dx \, dz$$

$$= \int_0^4 \int_0^1 (2x^3 z - x) \, dx \, dz = \int_0^4 \left[\frac{1}{2} x^4 z - \frac{1}{2} x^2 \right]_{x=0}^{x=1} dz$$

$$= \int_0^4 \frac{1}{2} (z - 1) \, dz = \frac{1}{4} (z - 1)^2 \Big]_0^4$$

$$= \frac{1}{4} (9) - \frac{1}{4} (1) = 2.$$

Example 8   Finding a Center of Mass

Find the center of mass of a thin shell of constant density δ cut from the cone $z = \sqrt{x^2 + y^2}$ by the planes $z = 1$ and $z = 2$ (Figure 13.58).

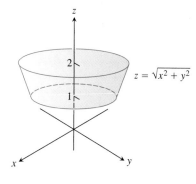

Solution   The symmetry of the surface about the z-axis tells us that $\bar{x} = \bar{y} = 0$. We find $\bar{z} = M_{xy}/M$. Working as in Examples 1 and 4, we have

$$\mathbf{r}(r, \theta) = r \cos \theta \mathbf{i} + r \sin \theta \mathbf{j} + r \mathbf{k}, \qquad 1 \le r \le 2, \quad 0 \le \theta \le 2\pi,$$

and

$$|\mathbf{r}_r \times \mathbf{r}_\theta| = \sqrt{2} \, r.$$

Therefore,

$$M = \iint_S \delta \, d\sigma = \int_0^{2\pi} \int_1^2 \delta \sqrt{2} \, r \, dr \, d\theta$$

$$= \delta\sqrt{2} \int_0^{2\pi} \left[\frac{r^2}{2} \right]_1^2 d\theta = \delta\sqrt{2} \int_0^{2\pi} \left(2 - \frac{1}{2} \right) d\theta$$

$$= \delta\sqrt{2} \left[\frac{3\theta}{2} \right]_0^{2\pi} = 3\pi\delta\sqrt{2}$$

$$M_{xy} = \iint_S \delta z \, d\sigma = \int_0^{2\pi} \int_1^2 \delta r \sqrt{2} r \, dr \, d\theta$$

$$= \delta\sqrt{2} \int_0^{2\pi} \int_1^2 r^2 \, dr \, d\theta = \delta\sqrt{2} \int_0^{2\pi} \left[\frac{r^3}{3} \right]_1^2 d\theta$$

$$= \delta\sqrt{2} \int_0^{2\pi} \frac{7}{3} \, d\theta = \frac{14}{3} \pi\delta\sqrt{2}$$

$$\bar{z} = \frac{M_{xy}}{M} = \frac{14\pi\delta\sqrt{2}}{3(3\pi\delta\sqrt{2})} = \frac{14}{9}.$$

The shell's center of mass is the point $(0, 0, 14/9)$.

FIGURE 13.58 The cone frustum formed when the cone $z = \sqrt{x^2 + y^2}$ is cut by the planes $z = 1$ and $z = 2$. (Example 8)

EXERCISES 13.6

Finding Parametrizations for Surfaces

In Exercises 1–16, find a parametrization of the surface. (There are many correct ways to do these, so your answers may not be the same as those in the back of the book.)

1. The paraboloid $z = x^2 + y^2$, $z \leq 4$

2. The paraboloid $z = 9 - x^2 - y^2$, $z \geq 0$

3. *Cone frustrum* The first-octant portion of the cone $z = \sqrt{x^2 + y^2}/2$ between the planes $z = 0$ and $z = 3$

4. *Cone frustrum* The portion of the cone $z = 2\sqrt{x^2 + y^2}$ between the planes $z = 2$ and $z = 4$

5. *Spherical cap* The cap cut from the sphere $x^2 + y^2 + z^2 = 9$ by the cone $z = \sqrt{x^2 + y^2}$

6. *Spherical cap* The portion of the sphere $x^2 + y^2 + z^2 = 4$ in the first octant between the xy-plane and the cone $z = \sqrt{x^2 + y^2}$

7. *Spherical band* The portion of the sphere $x^2 + y^2 + z^2 = 3$ between the planes $z = \sqrt{3}/2$ and $z = -\sqrt{3}/2$

8. *Spherical cap* The upper portion cut from the sphere $x^2 + y^2 + z^2 = 8$ by the plane $z = -2$

9. *Parabolic cylinder between planes* The surface cut from the parabolic cylinder $z = 4 - y^2$ by the planes $x = 0$, $x = 2$, and $z = 0$

10. *Parabolic cylinder between planes* The surface cut from the parabolic cylinder $y = x^2$ by the planes $z = 0$, $z = 3$, and $y = 2$

11. *Circular cylinder band* The portion of the cylinder $y^2 + z^2 = 9$ between the planes $x = 0$ and $x = 3$

12. *Circular cylinder band* The portion of the cylinder $x^2 + z^2 = 4$ above the xy-plane between the planes $y = -2$ and $y = 2$

13. *Tilted plane inside cylinder* The portion of the plane $x + y + z = 1$
    (a) Inside the cylinder $x^2 + y^2 = 9$
    (b) Inside the cylinder $y^2 + z^2 = 9$

14. *Tilted plane inside cylinder* The portion of the plane $x - y + 2z = 2$
    (a) Inside the cylinder $x^2 + z^2 = 3$
    (b) Inside the cylinder $y^2 + z^2 = 2$

15. *Circular cylinder band* The portion of the cylinder $(x - 2)^2 + z^2 = 4$ between the planes $y = 0$ and $y = 3$

16. *Circular cylinder band* The portion of the cylinder $y^2 + (z - 5)^2 = 25$ between the planes $x = 0$ and $x = 10$

Areas of Parametrized Surfaces

In Exercises 17–26, use a parametrization to express the area of the surface as a double integral. Then evaluate the integral. (There are many correct ways to set up the integrals, so your integrals may not be the same as those in the back of the book. They should have the same values, however.)

17. *Tilted plane inside cylinder* The portion of the plane $y + 2z = 2$ inside the cylinder $x^2 + y^2 = 1$

18. *Plane inside cylinder* The portion of the plane $z = -x$ inside the cylinder $x^2 + y^2 = 4$

19. *Cone frustrum* The portion of the cone $z = 2\sqrt{x^2 + y^2}$ between the planes $z = 2$ and $z = 6$

20. *Cone frustrum* The portion of the cone $z = \sqrt{x^2 + y^2}/3$ between the planes $z = 1$ and $z = 4/3$

21. *Circular cylinder band* The portion of the cylinder $x^2 + y^2 = 1$ between the planes $z = 1$ and $z = 4$

22. *Circular cylinder band* The portion of the cylinder $x^2 + z^2 = 10$ between the planes $y = -1$ and $y = 1$

23. *Parabolic cap* The cap cut from the paraboloid $z = 2 - x^2 - y^2$ by the cone $z = \sqrt{x^2 + y^2}$

24. *Parabolic band* The portion of the paraboloid $z = x^2 + y^2$ between the planes $z = 1$ and $z = 4$

25. *Sawed-off sphere* The lower portion cut from the sphere $x^2 + y^2 + z^2 = 2$ by the cone $z = \sqrt{x^2 + y^2}$

26. *Spherical band* The portion of the sphere $x^2 + y^2 + z^2 = 4$ between the planes $z = -1$ and $z = \sqrt{3}$

Integrals Over Parametrized Surfaces

In Exercises 27–34, integrate the given function over the given surface.

27. *Parabolic cylinder* $G(x, y, z) = x$, over the parabolic cylinder $y = x^2$, $0 \leq x \leq 2$, $0 \leq z \leq 3$

28. *Circular cylinder* $G(x, y, z) = z$, over the cylindrical surface $y^2 + z^2 = 4$, $z \geq 0$, $1 \leq x \leq 4$

29. *Sphere* $G(x, y, z) = x^2$, over the unit sphere $x^2 + y^2 + z^2 = 1$

30. *Hemisphere* $G(x, y, z) = z^2$, over the hemisphere $x^2 + y^2 + z^2 = a^2$, $z \geq 0$

31. *Portion of plane* $F(x, y, z) = z$, over the portion of the plane $x + y + z = 4$ that lies above the square $0 \leq x \leq 1$, $0 \leq y \leq 1$, in the xy-plane

32. *Cone* $F(x, y, z) = z - x$, over the cone $z = \sqrt{x^2 + y^2}$, $0 \leq z \leq 1$

33. *Parabolic dome* $H(x, y, z) = x^2\sqrt{5 - 4z}$, over the parabolic dome $z = 1 - x^2 - y^2$, $z \geq 0$

34. *Spherical cap* $H(x, y, z) = yz$, over the part of the sphere $x^2 + y^2 + z^2 = 4$ that lies above the cone $z = \sqrt{x^2 + y^2}$

Flux Across Parametrized Surfaces

In Exercises 35–44, use a parametrization to find the flux $\iint_S \mathbf{F} \cdot \mathbf{n} \, d\sigma$ across the surface in the given direction.

35. *Parabolic cylinder* $\mathbf{F} = z^2\mathbf{i} + x\mathbf{j} - 3z\mathbf{k}$ outward (normal away from the x-axis) through the surface cut from the parabolic cylinder $z = 4 - y^2$ by the planes $x = 0$, $x = 1$, and $z = 0$

36. *Parabolic cylinder* $\mathbf{F} = x^2 \mathbf{j} - xz\mathbf{k}$ outward (normal away from the yz-plane) through the surface cut from the parabolic cylinder $y = x^2$, $-1 \le x \le 1$, by the planes $z = 0$ and $z = 2$

37. *Sphere* $\mathbf{F} = z\mathbf{k}$ across the portion of the sphere $x^2 + y^2 + z^2 = a^2$ in the first octant in the direction away from the origin

38. *Sphere* $\mathbf{F} = x\mathbf{i} + y\mathbf{j} + z\mathbf{k}$ across the sphere $x^2 + y^2 + z^2 = a^2$ in the direction away from the origin

39. *Plane* $\mathbf{F} = 2xy\mathbf{i} + 2yz\mathbf{j} + 2xz\mathbf{k}$ upward across the portion of the plane $x + y + z = 2a$ that lies above the square $0 \le x \le a$, $0 \le y \le a$, in the xy-plane

40. *Cylinder* $\mathbf{F} = x\mathbf{i} + y\mathbf{j} + z\mathbf{k}$ outward through the portion of the cylinder $x^2 + y^2 = 1$ cut by the planes $z = 0$ and $z = a$

41. *Cone* $\mathbf{F} = xy\mathbf{i} - z\mathbf{k}$ outward (normal away from the z-axis) through the cone $z = \sqrt{x^2 + y^2}$, $0 \le z \le 1$

42. *Cone* $\mathbf{F} = y^2 \mathbf{i} + xz\mathbf{j} - \mathbf{k}$ outward (normal away from the z-axis) through the cone $z = 2\sqrt{x^2 + y^2}$, $0 \le z \le 2$

43. *Cone frustrum* $\mathbf{F} = -x\mathbf{i} - y\mathbf{j} + z^2\mathbf{k}$ outward (normal away from the z-axis) through the portion of the cone $z = \sqrt{x^2 + y^2}$ between the planes $z = 1$ and $z = 2$

44. *Paraboloid* $\mathbf{F} = 4x\mathbf{i} + 4y\mathbf{j} + 2\mathbf{k}$ outward (normal way from the z-axis) through the surface cut from the bottom of the paraboloid $z = x^2 + y^2$ by the plane $z = 1$

Moments and Masses

45. *Center of mass, inertia, radius of gyration* Find the center of mass and the moment of inertia and radius of gyration about the z-axis of a thin shell of constant density δ cut from the cone $x^2 + y^2 - z^2 = 0$ by the planes $z = 1$ and $z = 2$.

46. *Inertia of conical shell* Find the moment of inertia about the z-axis of a thin conical shell $z = \sqrt{x^2 + y^2}$, $0 \le z \le 1$, of constant density δ.

Planes Tangent to Parametrized Surfaces

The tangent plane at a point $P_0(f(u_0, v_0), g(u_0, v_0), h(u_0, v_0))$ on a parametrized surface $\mathbf{r}(u, v) = f(u, v)\mathbf{i} + g(u, v)\mathbf{j} + h(u, v)\mathbf{k}$ is the plane through P_0 normal to the vector $\mathbf{r}_u(u_0, v_0) \times \mathbf{r}_v(u_0, v_0)$, the cross product of the tangent vectors $\mathbf{r}_u(u_0, v_0)$ and $\mathbf{r}_v(u_0, v_0)$ at P_0. In Exercises 47–50, find an equation for the plane tangent to the surface at P_0. Then find a Cartesian equation for the surface and sketch the surface and tangent plane together.

47. *Cone* The cone $\mathbf{r}(r, \theta) = (r \cos \theta)\mathbf{i} + (r \sin \theta)\mathbf{j} + r\mathbf{k}$, $r \ge 0$, $0 \le \theta \le 2\pi$ at the point $P_0(\sqrt{2}, \sqrt{2}, 2)$ corresponding to $(r, \theta) = (2, \pi/4)$

48. *Hemisphere* The hemisphere surface $\mathbf{r}(\phi, \theta) = (4 \sin \phi \cos \theta)\mathbf{i} + (4 \sin \phi \sin \theta)\mathbf{j} + (4 \cos \phi)\mathbf{k}$, $0 \le \phi \le \pi/2$, $0 \le \theta \le 2\pi$, at the point $P_0(\sqrt{2}, \sqrt{2}, 2\sqrt{3})$ corresponding to $(\phi, \theta) = (\pi/6, \pi/4)$

49. *Circular cylinder* The circular cylinder $\mathbf{r}(\theta, z) = (3 \sin 2\theta)\mathbf{i} + (6 \sin^2 \theta)\mathbf{j} + z\mathbf{k}$, $0 \le \theta \le \pi$, at the point $P_0(3\sqrt{3}/2, 9/2, 0)$ corresponding to $(\theta, z) = (\pi/3, 0)$ (See Example 3.)

50. *Parabolic cylinder* The parabolic cylinder surface $\mathbf{r}(x, y) = x\mathbf{i} + y\mathbf{j} - x^2\mathbf{k}$, $-\infty < x < \infty$, $-\infty < y < \infty$, at the point $P_0(1, 2, -1)$ corresponding to $(x, y) = (1, 2)$

Further Examples of Parametrizations

51. (a) A *torus of revolution* (doughnut) is obtained by rotating a circle C in the xz-plane about the z-axis in space. (See the accompanying figure.) If C has radius $r > 0$ and center $(R, 0, 0)$, show that a parametrization of the torus is

$$\mathbf{r}(u, v) = ((R + r \cos u)\cos v)\mathbf{i} + ((R + r \cos u)\sin v)\mathbf{j} + (r \sin u)\mathbf{k},$$

where $0 \le u \le 2\pi$ and $0 \le v \le 2\pi$ are the angles in the figure.

(b) Show that the surface area of the torus is $A = 4\pi^2 Rr$.

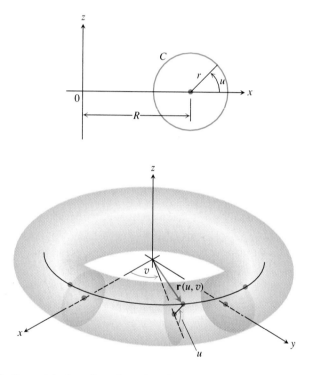

52. *Parametrization of a surface of revolution* Suppose that the parametrized curve C: $(f(u), g(u))$ is revolved about the x-axis, where $g(u) > 0$ for $a \le u \le b$.

(a) Show that

$$\mathbf{r}(u, v) = f(u)\mathbf{i} + (g(u)\cos v)\mathbf{j} + (g(u)\sin v)\mathbf{k}$$

is a parametrization of the resulting surface of revolution, where $0 \le v \le 2\pi$ is the angle from the xy-plane to the point $\mathbf{r}(u, v)$ on the surface. (See the accompanying figure.) Notice that $f(u)$ measures distance *along* the axis of revolution and $g(u)$ measures distance *from* the axis of revolution.

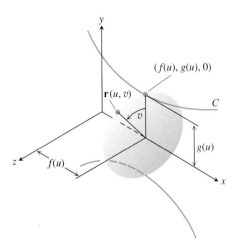

(*f*(*u*), *g*(*u*), 0)

r(*u*, *v*)

v

C

g(*u*)

f(*u*)

53. **(a)** *Parametrization of an ellipsoid* Recall the parametrization $x = a \cos \theta$, $y = b \sin \theta$, $0 \le \theta \le 2\pi$ for the ellipse $(x^2/a^2) + (y^2/b^2) = 1$ (Section P.6, Example 6). Using the angles θ and ϕ in spherical coordinates, show that

$$\mathbf{r}(\theta, \phi) = (a \cos \theta \cos \phi)\mathbf{i} + (b \sin \theta \cos \phi)\mathbf{j} + (c \sin \phi)\mathbf{k}$$

is a parametrization of the ellipsoid $(x^2/a^2) + (y^2/b^2) + (z^2/c^2) = 1$.

(b) Write an integral for the surface area of the ellipsoid, but do not evaluate the integral.

(b) Find a parametrization for the surface obtained by revolving the curve $x = y^2$, $y \ge 0$, about the *x*-axis.

13.7 Stokes' Theorem

Circulation Density: Curl • Stokes' Theorem • Paddle Wheel Interpretation of $\nabla \times \mathbf{F}$ • Proof of Stokes' Theorem for Polyhedral Surfaces • Stokes' Theorem for Surfaces with Holes • An Important Identity • Conservative Fields and Stokes' Theorem

In this section, we generalize the circulation-curl form of Green's Theorem to velocity fields in space.

Circulation Density: Curl

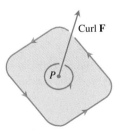

Curl **F**

P

FIGURE 13.59 The circulation vector at a point *P* in a plane in a three-dimensional fluid flow. Notice its right-hand relation to the circulation line.

As we saw in Section 13.4, the **k**-component of the circulation density or curl of a two-dimensional field $\mathbf{F} = M\mathbf{i} + N\mathbf{j}$ at a point (x, y) is the scalar quantity $(\partial N/\partial x - \partial M/\partial y)$. In three dimensions, the circulation around a point P in a plane is described with a vector. This vector is normal to the plane of the circulation (Figure 13.59) and points in the direction that gives it a right-hand relation to the circulation line. The length of the vector gives the rate of the fluid's rotation, which usually varies as the circulation plane is tilted about P. It turns out that the vector of greatest circulation in a flow with velocity field $\mathbf{F} = M\mathbf{i} + N\mathbf{j} + P\mathbf{k}$ is

$$\text{curl } \mathbf{F} = \left(\frac{\partial P}{\partial y} - \frac{\partial N}{\partial z}\right)\mathbf{i} + \left(\frac{\partial M}{\partial z} - \frac{\partial P}{\partial x}\right)\mathbf{j} + \left(\frac{\partial N}{\partial x} - \frac{\partial M}{\partial y}\right)\mathbf{k}. \tag{1}$$

Notice that $(\text{curl } \mathbf{F}) \cdot \mathbf{k} = (\partial N / \partial x - \partial M / \partial y)$, consistent with our definition in Section 13.4 for $\mathbf{F} = M\mathbf{i} + N\mathbf{j}$. The formula for curl $\mathbf{F}$ in Equation (1) is usually written using the symbolic operator

$$\nabla = \mathbf{i}\frac{\partial}{\partial x} + \mathbf{j}\frac{\partial}{\partial y} + \mathbf{k}\frac{\partial}{\partial z}. \tag{2}$$

(The symbol ∇ is pronounced "del.") The curl of $\mathbf{F}$ is $\nabla \times \mathbf{F}$:

$$\nabla \times \mathbf{F} = \begin{vmatrix} \mathbf{i} & \mathbf{j} & \mathbf{k} \\ \dfrac{\partial}{\partial x} & \dfrac{\partial}{\partial y} & \dfrac{\partial}{\partial z} \\ M & N & P \end{vmatrix}$$

$$= \left(\frac{\partial P}{\partial y} - \frac{\partial N}{\partial z}\right)\mathbf{i} + \left(\frac{\partial M}{\partial z} - \frac{\partial P}{\partial x}\right)\mathbf{j} + \left(\frac{\partial N}{\partial x} - \frac{\partial M}{\partial y}\right)\mathbf{k}$$

$$= \text{curl } \mathbf{F}.$$

$$\boxed{\text{curl } \mathbf{F} = \nabla \times \mathbf{F}} \tag{3}$$

Example 1 Finding Curl F

Find the curl of $\mathbf{F} = (x^2 - y)\mathbf{i} + 4z\mathbf{j} + x^2\mathbf{k}$.

Solution

$$\text{curl } \mathbf{F} = \nabla \times \mathbf{F}$$

$$= \begin{vmatrix} \mathbf{i} & \mathbf{j} & \mathbf{k} \\ \dfrac{\partial}{\partial x} & \dfrac{\partial}{\partial y} & \dfrac{\partial}{\partial z} \\ x^2 - y & 4z & x^2 \end{vmatrix} \quad \text{Eq. (3)}$$

$$= \left(\frac{\partial}{\partial y}(x^2) - \frac{\partial}{\partial z}(4z)\right)\mathbf{i} - \left(\frac{\partial}{\partial x}(x^2) - \frac{\partial}{\partial z}(x^2 - y)\right)\mathbf{j}$$

$$+ \left(\frac{\partial}{\partial x}(4z) - \frac{\partial}{\partial y}(x^2 - y)\right)\mathbf{k}$$

$$= (0 - 4)\mathbf{i} - (2x - 0)\mathbf{j} + (0 + 1)\mathbf{k}$$

$$= -4\mathbf{i} - 2x\mathbf{j} + \mathbf{k}$$

As we will see, the operator ∇ has a number of other applications. For instance, when applied to a scalar function $f(x, y, z)$, it gives the gradient of f:

$$\nabla f = \frac{\partial f}{\partial x}\mathbf{i} + \frac{\partial f}{\partial y}\mathbf{j} + \frac{\partial f}{\partial z}\mathbf{k}.$$

This may now be read as "del f" as well as "grad f."

Stokes' Theorem

Stokes' Theorem says that, under conditions normally met in practice, the circulation of a vector field around the boundary of an oriented surface in space in the direction counterclockwise with respect to the surface's unit normal vector field **n** (Figure 13.60) equals the integral of the normal component of the curl of the field over the surface.

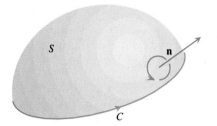

FIGURE 13.60 The orientation of the bounding curve C gives it a right-handed relation to the normal field **n**.

Theorem 5   Stokes' Theorem

The circulation of a vector field $\mathbf{F} = M\mathbf{i} + N\mathbf{j} + P\mathbf{k}$ around the boundary C of an oriented surface S in the direction counterclockwise with respect to the surface's unit normal vector **n** equals the integral of $\nabla \times \mathbf{F} \cdot \mathbf{n}$ over S.

$$\oint_C \mathbf{F} \cdot d\mathbf{r} = \iint_S \nabla \times \mathbf{F} \cdot \mathbf{n} \, d\sigma \qquad (4)$$

Counterclockwise   Curl integral
circulation

Notice from Equation (4) that if two different oriented surfaces S_1 and S_2 have the same boundary C, their curl integrals are equal:

$$\iint_{S_1} \nabla \times \mathbf{F} \cdot \mathbf{n}_1 \, d\sigma = \iint_{S_2} \nabla \times \mathbf{F} \cdot \mathbf{n}_2 \, d\sigma.$$

Both curl integrals equal the counterclockwise circulation integral on the left side of Equation (4) as long as the unit normal vectors $\mathbf{n}_1$ and $\mathbf{n}_2$ correctly orient the surfaces.

Naturally, we need some mathematical restrictions on $\mathbf{F}$, C, and S to ensure the existence of the integrals in Stokes' equation. The usual restrictions are that all the functions and derivatives involved be continuous.

If C is a curve in the xy-plane, oriented counterclockwise, and R is the region in the xy-plane bounded by C, then $d\sigma = dx \, dy$ and

$$(\nabla \times \mathbf{F}) \cdot \mathbf{n} = (\nabla \times \mathbf{F}) \cdot \mathbf{k} = \left(\frac{\partial N}{\partial x} - \frac{\partial M}{\partial y} \right).$$

Under these conditions, Stokes' equation becomes

$$\oint_C \mathbf{F} \cdot d\mathbf{r} = \iint_R \left(\frac{\partial N}{\partial x} - \frac{\partial M}{\partial y} \right) dx \, dy,$$

Green:

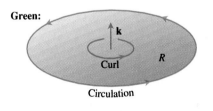

Stokes:

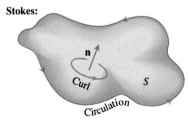

FIGURE 13.61 Green's Theorem versus Stokes' Theorem.

which is the circulation-curl form of the equation in Green's Theorem. Conversely, by reversing these steps we can rewrite the circulation-curl form of Green's Theorem for two-dimensional fields in del notation as

$$\oint_C \mathbf{F} \cdot d\mathbf{r} = \iint_R \nabla \times \mathbf{F} \cdot \mathbf{k} \, dA. \qquad (5)$$

See Figure 13.61.

Example 2   Verifying Stokes' Equation for a Hemisphere

Evaluate Equation (4) for the hemisphere $S: x^2 + y^2 + z^2 = 9, z \geq 0$, its bounding circle $C: x^2 + y^2 = 9, z = 0$, and the field $\mathbf{F} = y\mathbf{i} - x\mathbf{j}$.

Solution   We calculate the counterclockwise circulation around C (as viewed from above) using the parametrization $\mathbf{r}(\theta) = (3 \cos \theta)\mathbf{i} + (3 \sin \theta)\mathbf{j}$, $0 \leq \theta \leq 2\pi$:

$$d\mathbf{r} = (-3 \sin \theta \, d\theta)\mathbf{i} + (3 \cos \theta \, d\theta)\mathbf{j}$$

$$\mathbf{F} = y\mathbf{i} - x\mathbf{j} = (3 \sin \theta)\mathbf{i} - (3 \cos \theta)\mathbf{j}$$

$$\mathbf{F} \cdot d\mathbf{r} = -9 \sin^2 \theta \, d\theta - 9 \cos^2 \theta \, d\theta = -9 \, d\theta$$

$$\oint_C \mathbf{F} \cdot d\mathbf{r} = \int_0^{2\pi} -9 \, d\theta = -18\pi.$$

For the curl integral of $\mathbf{F}$, we have

$$\nabla \times \mathbf{F} = \left(\frac{\partial P}{\partial y} - \frac{\partial N}{\partial z}\right)\mathbf{i} + \left(\frac{\partial M}{\partial z} - \frac{\partial P}{\partial x}\right)\mathbf{j} + \left(\frac{\partial N}{\partial x} - \frac{\partial M}{\partial y}\right)\mathbf{k}$$

$$= (0 - 0)\mathbf{i} + (0 - 0)\mathbf{j} + (-1 - 1)\mathbf{k} = -2\mathbf{k}$$

$$\mathbf{n} = \frac{x\mathbf{i} + y\mathbf{j} + z\mathbf{k}}{\sqrt{x^2 + y^2 + z^2}} = \frac{x\mathbf{i} + y\mathbf{j} + z\mathbf{k}}{3} \qquad \text{Outer unit normal}$$

$$d\sigma = \frac{3}{z} \, dA \qquad\qquad \text{Section 13.5, Example}$$
$$\qquad\qquad\qquad\qquad\qquad\qquad \text{5, with } a = 3$$

$$\nabla \times \mathbf{F} \cdot \mathbf{n} \, d\sigma = -\frac{2z}{3} \frac{3}{z} \, dA = -2 \, dA$$

and

$$\iint_S \nabla \times \mathbf{F} \cdot \mathbf{n} \, d\sigma = \iint_{x^2+y^2\leq 9} -2 \, dA = -18\pi.$$

The circulation around the circle equals the integral of the curl over the hemisphere, as it should.

Example 3   Finding Circulation

Find the circulation of the field $\mathbf{F} = (x^2 - y)\mathbf{i} + 4z\mathbf{j} + x^2\mathbf{k}$ around the curve C in which the plane $z = 2$ meets the cone $z = \sqrt{x^2 + y^2}$, counterclockwise as viewed from above (Figure 13.62).

Solution   Stokes' Theorem enables us to find the circulation by integrating over the surface of the cone. Traversing C in the counterclockwise direction viewed from above corresponds to taking the *inner* normal $\mathbf{n}$ to the cone, the normal with a positive z-component).

We parametrize the cone as

$$\mathbf{r}(r, \theta) = (r \cos \theta)\mathbf{i} + (r \sin \theta)\mathbf{j} + r\mathbf{k}, \qquad 0 \leq r \leq 2, \quad 0 \leq \theta \leq 2\pi.$$

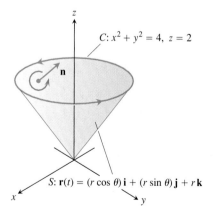

$C: x^2 + y^2 = 4, \; z = 2$

$S: \mathbf{r}(t) = (r \cos \theta)\,\mathbf{i} + (r \sin \theta)\,\mathbf{j} + r\,\mathbf{k}$

FIGURE 13.62 The curve C and cone S in Example 3.

We then have

$$\mathbf{n} = \frac{\mathbf{r}_r \times \mathbf{r}_\theta}{|\mathbf{r}_r \times \mathbf{r}_\theta|} = \frac{-(r \cos \theta)\mathbf{i} - (r \sin \theta)\mathbf{j} + r\mathbf{k}}{r\sqrt{2}} \qquad \text{Section 13.6, Example 4}$$

$$= \frac{1}{\sqrt{2}}(-(\cos \theta)\mathbf{i} - (\sin \theta)\mathbf{j} + \mathbf{k})$$

$$d\sigma = r\sqrt{2}\, dr\, d\theta \qquad \text{Section 13.6, Example 4}$$

$$\nabla \times \mathbf{F} = -4\mathbf{i} - 2x\mathbf{j} + \mathbf{k} \qquad \text{Example 1}$$

$$= -4\mathbf{i} - 2r \cos \theta \mathbf{j} + \mathbf{k}. \qquad x = r \cos \theta$$

Accordingly,

$$\nabla \times \mathbf{F} \cdot \mathbf{n} = \frac{1}{\sqrt{2}}(4 \cos \theta + 2r \cos \theta \sin \theta + 1)$$

$$= \frac{1}{\sqrt{2}}(4 \cos \theta + r \sin 2\theta + 1)$$

and the circulation is

$$\oint_C \mathbf{F} \cdot d\mathbf{r} = \iint_S \nabla \times \mathbf{F} \cdot \mathbf{n}\, d\sigma \qquad \text{Stokes' Theorem, Eq. (4)}$$

$$= \int_0^{2\pi} \int_0^2 \frac{1}{\sqrt{2}}(4 \cos \theta + r \sin 2\theta + 1)(r\sqrt{2}\, dr\, d\theta) = 4\pi.$$

Paddle Wheel Interpretation of $\nabla \times \mathbf{F}$

Suppose that $\mathbf{v}(x, y, z)$ is the velocity of a moving fluid whose density at (x, y, z) is $\delta(x, y, z)$ and let $\mathbf{F} = \delta\mathbf{v}$. Then

$$\oint_C \mathbf{F} \cdot d\mathbf{r}$$

is the circulation of the fluid around the closed curve C. By Stokes' Theorem, the circulation is equal to the flux of $\nabla \times \mathbf{F}$ through a surface S spanning C:

$$\oint_C \mathbf{F} \cdot d\mathbf{r} = \iint_S \nabla \times \mathbf{F} \cdot \mathbf{n}\, d\sigma.$$

Suppose we fix a point Q in the domain of $\mathbf{F}$ and a direction $\mathbf{u}$ at Q. Let C be a circle of radius ρ, with center at Q, whose plane is normal to $\mathbf{u}$. If $\nabla \times \mathbf{F}$ is continuous at Q, the average value of the $\mathbf{u}$-component of $\nabla \times \mathbf{F}$ over the circular disk S bounded by C approaches the $\mathbf{u}$-component of $\nabla \times \mathbf{F}$ at Q as $\rho \to 0$:

$$(\nabla \times \mathbf{F} \cdot \mathbf{u})_Q = \lim_{\rho \to 0} \frac{1}{\pi\rho^2} \iint_S \nabla \times \mathbf{F} \cdot \mathbf{u}\, d\sigma.$$

If we replace the double integral in this last equation by the circulation, we get

$$(\nabla \times \mathbf{F} \cdot \mathbf{u})_Q = \lim_{\rho \to 0} \frac{1}{\pi\rho^2} \oint_C \mathbf{F} \cdot d\mathbf{r}. \qquad (6)$$

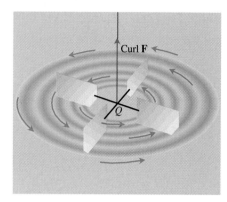

FIGURE 13.63 The paddle wheel interpretation of curl **F**.

The left-hand side of Equation (6) has its maximum value when **u** is the direction of $\nabla \times \mathbf{F}$. When ρ is small, the limit on the right-hand side of Equation (6) is approximately

$$\frac{1}{\pi\rho^2} \oint_C \mathbf{F} \cdot d\mathbf{r},$$

which is the circulation around C divided by the area of the disk (circulation density). Suppose that a small paddle wheel of radius ρ is introduced into the fluid at Q, with its axle directed along **u**. The circulation of the fluid around C will affect the rate of spin of the paddle wheel. The wheel will spin fastest when the circulation integral is maximized; therefore it will spin fastest when the axle of the paddle wheel points in the direction of $\nabla \times \mathbf{F}$ (Figure 13.63).

Example 4 Relating $\nabla \times \mathbf{F}$ to Circulation Density

A fluid of constant density rotates around the z-axis with velocity $\mathbf{v} = \omega(-y\mathbf{i} + x\mathbf{j})$, where ω is a positive constant called the *angular velocity* of the rotation (Figure 13.64). If $\mathbf{F} = \mathbf{v}$, find $\nabla \times \mathbf{F}$ and relate it to the circulation density.

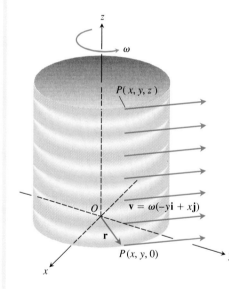

FIGURE 13.64 A steady rotational flow parallel to the xy-plane, with constant angular velocity ω in the positive (counterclockwise) direction.

Solution With $\mathbf{F} = \mathbf{v} = -\omega y\mathbf{i} + \omega x\mathbf{j}$,

$$\nabla \times \mathbf{F} = \left(\frac{\partial P}{\partial y} - \frac{\partial N}{\partial z}\right)\mathbf{i} + \left(\frac{\partial M}{\partial z} - \frac{\partial P}{\partial x}\right)\mathbf{j} + \left(\frac{\partial N}{\partial x} - \frac{\partial M}{\partial y}\right)\mathbf{k}$$

$$= (0 - 0)\mathbf{i} + (0 - 0)\mathbf{j} + (\omega - (-\omega))\mathbf{k} = 2\omega\mathbf{k}.$$

By Stokes' Theorem, the circulation of **F** around a circle C of radius ρ bounding a disk S in a plane normal to $\nabla \times \mathbf{F}$, say the xy-plane, is

$$\oint_C \mathbf{F} \cdot d\mathbf{r} = \int\int_S \nabla \times \mathbf{F} \cdot \mathbf{n} \, d\sigma = \int\int_S 2\omega\mathbf{k} \cdot \mathbf{k} \, dx \, dy = (2\omega)(\pi\rho^2).$$

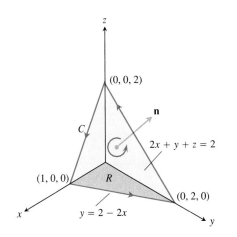

FIGURE 13.65 The planar surface in Example 5.

Thus,

$$(\nabla \times \mathbf{F}) \cdot \mathbf{k} = 2\omega = \frac{1}{\pi\rho^2}\oint_C \mathbf{F} \cdot d\mathbf{r},$$

in agreement with Equation (6) with $\mathbf{u} = \mathbf{k}$.

Example 5   Applying Stokes' Theorem

Use Stokes' Theorem to evaluate $\int_C \mathbf{F} \cdot d\mathbf{r}$, if $\mathbf{F} = xz\mathbf{i} + xy\mathbf{j} + 3xz\mathbf{k}$ and C is the boundary of the portion of the plane $2x + y + z = 2$ in the first octant, traversed counterclockwise as viewed from above (Figure 13.65).

Solution   The plane is the level surface $f(x, y, z) = 2$ of the function $f(x, y, z) = 2x + y + z$. The unit normal vector

$$\mathbf{n} = \frac{\nabla f}{|\nabla f|} = \frac{(2\mathbf{i} + \mathbf{j} + \mathbf{k})}{|2\mathbf{i} + \mathbf{j} + \mathbf{k}|} = \frac{1}{\sqrt{6}}(2\mathbf{i} + \mathbf{j} + \mathbf{k})$$

is consistent with the counterclockwise motion around C. To apply Stokes' Theorem, we find

$$\text{curl } \mathbf{F} = \nabla \times \mathbf{F} = \begin{vmatrix} \mathbf{i} & \mathbf{j} & \mathbf{k} \\ \frac{\partial}{\partial x} & \frac{\partial}{\partial y} & \frac{\partial}{\partial z} \\ xz & xy & 3xz \end{vmatrix} = (x - 3z)\mathbf{j} + y\mathbf{k}.$$

On the plane, z equals $2 - 2x - y$, so

$$\nabla \times \mathbf{F} = (x - 3(2 - 2x - y))\mathbf{j} + y\mathbf{k} = (7x + 3y - 6)\mathbf{j} + y\mathbf{k}$$

and

$$\nabla \times \mathbf{F} \cdot \mathbf{n} = \frac{1}{\sqrt{6}}(7x + 3y - 6 + y) = \frac{1}{\sqrt{6}}(7x + 4y - 6).$$

The surface area element is

$$d\sigma = \frac{|\nabla f|}{|\nabla f \cdot \mathbf{k}|} dA = \frac{\sqrt{6}}{1} dx\,dy.$$

The circulation is

$$\oint_C \mathbf{F} \cdot d\mathbf{r} = \iint_S \nabla \times \mathbf{F} \cdot \mathbf{n}\, d\sigma \qquad \text{Stokes' Theorem, Eq. (4)}$$

$$= \int_0^1 \int_0^{2-2x} \frac{1}{\sqrt{6}}(7x + 4y - 6)\sqrt{6}\, dy\, dx$$

$$= \int_0^1 \int_0^{2-2x} (7x + 4y - 6)\, dy\, dx = -1.$$

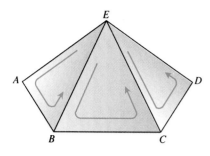

FIGURE 13.66 **Part of a polyhedral surface.**

Proof of Stokes' Theorem for Polyhedral Surfaces

Let S be a polyhedral surface consisting of a finite number of plane regions. (Think of one of Buckminster Fuller's geodesic domes.) We apply Green's Theorem to each separate panel of S. There are two types of panels:

1. Those that are surrounded on all sides by other panels

2. Those that have one or more edges that are not adjacent to other panels.

The boundary Δ of S consists of those edges of the type 2 panels that are not adjacent to other panels. In Figure 13.66, the triangles EAB, BCE, and CDE represent a part of S, with $ABCD$ part of the boundary Δ. Applying Green's Theorem to the three triangles in turn and adding the results, we get

$$\left(\oint_{EAB} + \oint_{BCE} + \oint_{CDE} \right) \mathbf{F} \cdot d\mathbf{r} = \left(\iint_{EAB} + \iint_{BCE} + \iint_{CDE} \right) \nabla \times \mathbf{F} \cdot \mathbf{n} \, d\sigma. \quad (7)$$

The three line integrals on the left-hand side of Equation (7) combine into a single line integral taken around the periphery $ABCDE$ because the integrals along interior segments cancel in pairs. For example, the integral along segment BE in triangle ABE is opposite in sign to the integral along the same segment in triangle EBC. The same holds for segment CE. Hence, Equation (7) reduces to

$$\oint_{ABCDE} \mathbf{F} \cdot d\mathbf{r} = \int\!\!\int_{ABCDE} \nabla \times \mathbf{F} \cdot \mathbf{n} \, d\sigma.$$

When we apply Green's Theorem to all the panels and add the results, we get

$$\oint_{\Delta} \mathbf{F} \cdot d\mathbf{r} = \iint_{S} \nabla \times \mathbf{F} \cdot \mathbf{n} \, d\sigma.$$

This is Stokes' Theorem for a polyhedral surface S. You can find proofs for more general surfaces in advanced calculus texts.

Stokes' Theorem for Surfaces with Holes

Stokes' Theorem can be extended to an oriented surface S that has one or more holes (Figure 13.67), in a way analogous to the extension of Green's Theorem: The surface integral over S of the normal component of $\nabla \times \mathbf{F}$ equals the sum of the line integrals around all the boundary curves of the tangential component of $\mathbf{F}$, where the curves are to be traced in the direction induced by the orientation of S.

An Important Identity

The following identity arises frequently in mathematics and the physical sciences.

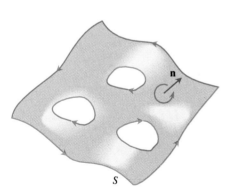

FIGURE 13.67 **Stokes' Theorem also holds for oriented surfaces with holes.**

$$\operatorname{curl} \operatorname{grad} f = \mathbf{0} \qquad \text{or} \qquad \nabla \times \nabla f = \mathbf{0} \qquad (8)$$

Connected and simply connected.

Connected and simply connected.

Connected but not simply connected.

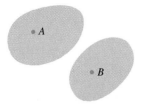

Simply connected but not connected.
No path from A to B lies entirely in the region.

FIGURE 13.68 Connectivity and simple connectivity are not the same. Neither implies the other, as these pictures of plane regions illustrate. To make three-dimensional regions with these properties, thicken the plane regions into cylinders.

This identity holds for any function $f(x, y, z)$ whose second partial derivatives are continuous. The proof goes like this:

$$\nabla \times \nabla f = \begin{vmatrix} \mathbf{i} & \mathbf{j} & \mathbf{k} \\ \dfrac{\partial}{\partial x} & \dfrac{\partial}{\partial y} & \dfrac{\partial}{\partial z} \\ \dfrac{\partial f}{\partial x} & \dfrac{\partial f}{\partial y} & \dfrac{\partial f}{\partial z} \end{vmatrix} = (f_{zy} - f_{yz})\mathbf{i} - (f_{zx} - f_{xz})\mathbf{j} + (f_{yx} - f_{xy})\mathbf{k}.$$

If the second partial derivatives are continuous, the mixed second derivatives in parentheses are equal (Theorem 4, Section 11.3) and the vector is zero.

Conservative Fields and Stokes' Theorem

In Section 13.3, we found that saying that a field $\mathbf{F}$ is conservative in an open region D in space is equivalent to saying that the integral of $\mathbf{F}$ around every closed loop in D is zero. This, in turn, is equivalent in *simply connected* open regions to saying that $\nabla \times \mathbf{F} = \mathbf{0}$. A region D is **simply connected** if every closed path in D can be contracted to a point in D without ever leaving D. If D consisted of space with a line removed, for example, D would not be simply connected. There would be no way to contract a loop around the line to a point without leaving D. On the other hand, space itself *is* simply connected (Figure 13.68).

Theorem 6   Relation of Curl F = 0 to the Closed-Loop Property
If $\nabla \times \mathbf{F} = \mathbf{0}$ at every point of a simply connected open region D in space, then on any piecewise smooth closed path C in D,

$$\oint_C \mathbf{F} \cdot d\mathbf{r} = 0.$$

Sketch of a Proof   Theorem 6 is usually proved in two steps. The first step is for simple closed curves. A theorem from topology, a branch of advanced mathematics, states that every differentiable simple closed curve C in a simply connected open region D is the boundary of a smooth two-sided surface S that also lies in D. Hence, by Stokes' Theorem,

$$\oint_C \mathbf{F} \cdot d\mathbf{r} = \iint_S \nabla \times \mathbf{F} \cdot \mathbf{n} \, d\sigma = 0.$$

The second step is for curves that cross themselves, like the one in Figure 13.69. The idea is to break these into simple loops spanned by orientable surfaces, apply Stokes' Theorem one loop at a time, and add the results.

FIGURE 13.69 In a simply connected open region in space, differentiable curves that cross themselves can be divided into loops to which Stokes' Theorem applies.

The following diagram summarizes the results for conservative fields defined on connected, simply connected open regions.

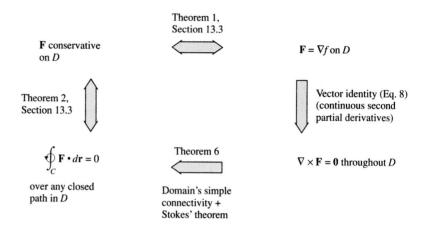

EXERCISES 13.7

Using Stokes' Theorem to Calculate Circulation

In Exercises 1–6, use the surface integral in Stokes' Theorem to calculate the circulation of the field **F** around the curve *C* in the indicated direction.

1. $\mathbf{F} = x^2\mathbf{i} + 2x\mathbf{j} + z^2\mathbf{k}$

    C: The ellipse $4x^2 + y^2 = 4$ in the *xy*-plane, counterclockwise when viewed from above

2. $\mathbf{F} = 2y\mathbf{i} + 3x\mathbf{j} - z^2\mathbf{k}$

    C: The circle $x^2 + y^2 = 9$ in the *xy*-plane, counterclockwise when viewed from above

3. $\mathbf{F} = y\mathbf{i} + xz\mathbf{j} + z^2\mathbf{k}$

    C: The boundary of the triangle cut from the plane $x + y + z = 1$ by the first octant, counterclockwise when viewed from above

4. $\mathbf{F} = (y^2 + z^2)\mathbf{i} + (x^2 + z^2)\mathbf{j} + (x^2 + y^2)\mathbf{k}$

    C: The boundary of the triangle cut from the plane $x + y + z = 1$ by the first octant, counterclockwise when viewed from above

5. $\mathbf{F} = (y^2 + z^2)\mathbf{i} + (x^2 + y^2)\mathbf{j} + (x^2 + y^2)\mathbf{k}$

    C: The square bounded by the lines $x = \pm 1$ and $y = \pm 1$ in the *xy*-plane, counterclockwise when viewed from above

6. $\mathbf{F} = x^2y^3\mathbf{i} + \mathbf{j} + z\mathbf{k}$

    C: The intersection of the cylinder $x^2 + y^2 = 4$ and the hemisphere $x^2 + y^2 + z^2 = 16, z \geq 0$

Flux of the Curl

7. Let **n** be the outer unit normal of the elliptical shell

    $$S: \quad 4x^2 + 9y^2 + 36z^2 = 36, \qquad z \geq 0,$$

    and let

    $$\mathbf{F} = y\mathbf{i} + x^2\mathbf{j} + (x^2 + y^4)^{3/2} \sin e^{\sqrt{xyz}}\,\mathbf{k}.$$

    Find the value of

    $$\iint_S \nabla \times \mathbf{F} \cdot \mathbf{n}\, d\sigma.$$

    (*Hint:* One parametrization of the ellipse at the base of the shell is $x = 3 \cos t$, $y = 2 \sin t$, $0 \leq t \leq 2\pi$.)

8. Let **n** be the outer unit normal (normal away from the origin) of the parabolic shell

    $$S: \quad 4x^2 + y + z^2 = 4, \qquad y \geq 0,$$

    and let

    $$\mathbf{F} = \left(-z + \frac{1}{2 + x}\right)\mathbf{i} + (\tan^{-1} y)\mathbf{j} + \left(x + \frac{1}{4 + z}\right)\mathbf{k}.$$

    Find the value of

    $$\iint_S \nabla \times \mathbf{F} \cdot \mathbf{n}\, d\sigma.$$

9. Let S be the cylinder $x^2 + y^2 = a^2$, $0 \le z \le h$, together with its top, $x^2 + y^2 \le a^2$, $z = h$. Let $\mathbf{F} = -y\mathbf{i} + x\mathbf{j} + x^2\mathbf{k}$. Use Stokes' Theorem to find the flux of $\nabla \times \mathbf{F}$ outward through S.

10. Evaluate

$$\iint_S \nabla \times (y\mathbf{i}) \cdot \mathbf{n} \, d\sigma,$$

where S is the hemisphere $x^2 + y^2 + z^2 = 1$, $z \ge 0$.

11. *Flux of* curl F Show that

$$\iint_S \nabla \times \mathbf{F} \cdot \mathbf{n} \, d\sigma$$

has the same value for all oriented surfaces S that span C and that induce the same positive direction on C.

12. *Writing to Learn* Let $\mathbf{F}$ be a differentiable vector field defined on a region containing a smooth closed oriented surface S and its interior. Let $\mathbf{n}$ be the unit normal vector field on S. Suppose that S is the union of two surfaces S_1 and S_2 joined along a smooth simple closed curve C. Can anything be said about

$$\iint_S \nabla \times \mathbf{F} \cdot \mathbf{n} \, d\sigma?$$

Give reasons for your answer.

Stokes' Theorem for Parametrized Surfaces

In Exercises 13–18, use the surface integral in Stokes' Theorem to calculate the flux of the curl of the field $\mathbf{F}$ across the surface S in the direction of the outward unit normal $\mathbf{n}$.

13. $\mathbf{F} = 2z\mathbf{i} + 3x\mathbf{j} + 5y\mathbf{k}$

S: $\mathbf{r}(r, \theta) = (r \cos \theta)\mathbf{i} + (r \sin \theta)\mathbf{j} + (4 - r^2)\mathbf{k}$, $0 \le r \le 2$, $0 \le \theta \le 2\pi$

14. $\mathbf{F} = (y - z)\mathbf{i} + (z - x)\mathbf{j} + (x + z)\mathbf{k}$

S: $\mathbf{r}(r, \theta) = (r \cos \theta)\mathbf{i} + (r \sin \theta)\mathbf{j} + (9 - r^2)\mathbf{k}$, $0 \le r \le 3$, $0 \le \theta \le 2\pi$

15. $\mathbf{F} = x^2y\mathbf{i} + 2y^3z\mathbf{j} + 3z\mathbf{k}$

S: $\mathbf{r}(r, \theta) = (r \cos \theta)\mathbf{i} + (r \sin \theta)\mathbf{j} + r\mathbf{k}$, $0 \le r \le 1$, $0 \le \theta \le 2\pi$

16. $\mathbf{F} = (x - y)\mathbf{i} + (y - z)\mathbf{j} + (z - x)\mathbf{k}$

S: $\mathbf{r}(r, \theta) = (r \cos \theta)\mathbf{i} + (r \sin \theta)\mathbf{j} + (5 - r)\mathbf{k}$, $0 \le r \le 5$, $0 \le \theta \le 2\pi$

17. $\mathbf{F} = 3y\mathbf{i} + (5 - 2x)\mathbf{j} + (z^2 - 2)\mathbf{k}$

S: $\mathbf{r}(\phi, \theta) = (\sqrt{3} \sin \phi \cos \theta)\mathbf{i} + (\sqrt{3} \sin \phi \sin \theta)\mathbf{j} + (\sqrt{3} \cos \phi)\mathbf{k}$, $0 \le \phi \le \pi/2$, $0 \le \theta \le 2\pi$

18. $\mathbf{F} = y^2\mathbf{i} + z^2\mathbf{j} + x\mathbf{k}$

S: $\mathbf{r}(\phi, \theta) = (2 \sin \phi \cos \theta)\mathbf{i} + (2 \sin \phi \sin \theta)\mathbf{j} + (2 \cos \phi)\mathbf{k}$, $0 \le \phi \le \pi/2$, $0 \le \theta \le 2\pi$

Theory and Examples

19. *Zero circulation* Use the identity $\nabla \times \nabla f = \mathbf{0}$ (Equation (8) in the text) and Stokes' Theorem to show that the circulations of the following fields around the boundary of any smooth orientable surface in space are zero.

(a) $\mathbf{F} = 2x\mathbf{i} + 2y\mathbf{j} + 2z\mathbf{k}$

(b) $\mathbf{F} = \nabla(xy^2z^3)$

(c) $\mathbf{F} = \nabla \times (x\mathbf{i} + y\mathbf{j} + z\mathbf{k})$

(d) $\mathbf{F} = \nabla f$

20. *Zero circulation* Let $f(x, y, z) = (x^2 + y^2 + z^2)^{-1/2}$. Show that the clockwise circulation of the field $\mathbf{F} = \nabla f$ around the circle $x^2 + y^2 = a^2$ in the xy-plane is zero

(a) By taking $\mathbf{r} = (a \cos t)\mathbf{i} + (a \sin t)\mathbf{j}$, $0 \le t \le 2\pi$, and integrating $\mathbf{F} \cdot d\mathbf{r}$ over the circle

(b) By applying Stokes' Theorem.

21. Let C be a simple closed smooth curve in the plane $2x + 2y + z = 2$, oriented as shown here. Show that

$$\oint_C 2y \, dx + 3z \, dy - x \, dz$$

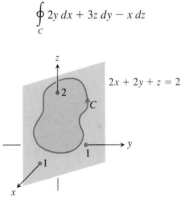

depends only on the area of the region enclosed by C and not on the position or shape of C.

22. Show that if $\mathbf{F} = x\mathbf{i} + y\mathbf{j} + z\mathbf{k}$, then $\nabla \times \mathbf{F} = \mathbf{0}$.

23. Find a vector field with twice-differentiable components whose curl is $x\mathbf{i} + y\mathbf{j} + z\mathbf{k}$ or prove that no such field exists.

24. *Writing to Learn* Does Stokes' Theorem say anything special about circulation in a field whose curl is zero? Give reasons for your answer.

25. Let R be a region in the xy-plane that is bounded by a piecewise smooth simple closed curve C and suppose that the moments of inertia of R about the x- and y-axes are known to be I_x and I_y. Evaluate the integral

$$\oint_C \nabla(r^4) \cdot \mathbf{n} \, ds,$$

where $r = \sqrt{x^2 + y^2}$, in terms of I_x and I_y.

26. *Zero curl, yet not conservative* Show that the curl of

$$\mathbf{F} = \frac{-y}{x^2 + y^2}\mathbf{i} + \frac{x}{x^2 + y^2}\mathbf{j} + z\mathbf{k}$$

is zero but that

$$\oint_C \mathbf{F} \cdot d\mathbf{r}$$

is not zero if C is the circle $x^2 + y^2 = 1$ in the xy-plane. (Theorem 6 does not apply here because the domain of $\mathbf{F}$ is not simply connected. The field $\mathbf{F}$ is not defined along the z-axis so there is no way to contract C to a point without leaving the domain of $\mathbf{F}$.)

13.8   Divergence Theorem and a Unified Theory

Divergence in Three Dimensions • Divergence Theorem • Proof of the Divergence Theorem for Special Regions • Divergence Theorem for Other Regions • Gauss's Law: One of the Four Great Laws of Electromagnetic Theory • Continuity Equation of Hydrodynamics • Unifying the Integral Theorems

The divergence form of Green's Theorem in the plane states that the net outward flux of a vector field across a simple closed curve can be calculated by integrating the divergence of the field over the region enclosed by the curve. The corresponding theorem in three dimensions, called the Divergence Theorem, states that the net outward flux of a vector field across a closed surface in space can be calculated by integrating the divergence of the field over the region enclosed by the surface. In this section, we prove the Divergence Theorem and show how it simplifies the calculation of flux. We also derive Gauss's law for flux in an electric field and the continuity equation of hydrodynamics. Finally, we unify the chapter's vector integral theorems into a single fundamental theorem.

Divergence in Three Dimensions

The **divergence** of a vector field $\mathbf{F} = M(x, y, z)\mathbf{i} + N(x, y, z)\mathbf{j} + P(x, y, z)\mathbf{k}$ is the scalar function

$$\text{div } \mathbf{F} = \nabla \cdot \mathbf{F} = \frac{\partial M}{\partial x} + \frac{\partial N}{\partial y} + \frac{\partial P}{\partial z}. \tag{1}$$

The symbol "div $\mathbf{F}$" is read as "divergence of $\mathbf{F}$" or "div $\mathbf{F}$." The notation $\nabla \cdot \mathbf{F}$ is read "del dot $\mathbf{F}$."

Div $\mathbf{F}$ has the same physical interpretation in three dimensions that it does in two. If $\mathbf{F}$ is the velocity field of a fluid flow, the value of div $\mathbf{F}$ at a point (x, y, z) is the rate at which fluid is being piped in or drained away at (x, y, z). The divergence is the flux per unit volume or flux density at the point.

Example 1   Finding Divergence

Find the divergence of $\mathbf{F} = 2xz\mathbf{i} - xy\mathbf{j} - z\mathbf{k}$.

Solution   The divergence of $\mathbf{F}$ is

$$\nabla \cdot \mathbf{F} = \frac{\partial}{\partial x}(2xz) + \frac{\partial}{\partial y}(-xy) + \frac{\partial}{\partial z}(-z) = 2z - x - 1.$$

Historical Biography

Mikhail Vasilievich Ostrogradsky
(1801 — 1862)

CD-ROM
WEBsite

Divergence Theorem

The Divergence Theorem says that under suitable conditions, the outward flux of a vector field across a closed surface (oriented outward) equals the triple integral of the divergence of the field over the region enclosed by the surface.

Theorem 7 Divergence Theorem

The flux of a vector field $\mathbf{F}$ across a closed oriented surface S in the direction of the surface's outward unit normal field $\mathbf{n}$ equals the integral of $\nabla \cdot \mathbf{F}$ over the region D enclosed by the surface:

$$\underset{S}{\iint} \mathbf{F} \cdot \mathbf{n}\, d\sigma = \underset{D}{\iiint} \nabla \cdot \mathbf{F}\, dV. \qquad (2)$$

Outward   Divergence
flux   integral

Example 2 Supporting the Divergence Theorem

Evaluate both sides of Equation (2) for the field $\mathbf{F} = x\mathbf{i} + y\mathbf{j} + z\mathbf{k}$ over the sphere $x^2 + y^2 + z^2 = a^2$.

Solution The outer unit normal to S, calculated from the gradient of $f(x, y, z) = x^2 + y^2 + z^2 - a^2$, is

$$\mathbf{n} = \frac{2(x\mathbf{i} + y\mathbf{j} + z\mathbf{k})}{\sqrt{4(x^2 + y^2 + z^2)}} = \frac{x\mathbf{i} + y\mathbf{j} + z\mathbf{k}}{a}.$$

Hence,

$$\mathbf{F} \cdot \mathbf{n}\, d\sigma = \frac{x^2 + y^2 + z^2}{a}\, d\sigma = \frac{a^2}{a}\, d\sigma = a\, d\sigma$$

because $x^2 + y^2 + z^2 = a^2$ on the surface. Therefore,

$$\underset{S}{\iint} \mathbf{F} \cdot \mathbf{n}\, d\sigma = \underset{S}{\iint} a\, d\sigma = a \underset{S}{\iint} d\sigma = a(4\pi a^2) = 4\pi a^3.$$

The divergence of $\mathbf{F}$ is

$$\nabla \cdot \mathbf{F} = \frac{\partial}{\partial x}(x) + \frac{\partial}{\partial y}(y) + \frac{\partial}{\partial z}(z) = 3,$$

so

$$\underset{D}{\iiint} \nabla \cdot \mathbf{F}\, dV = \underset{D}{\iiint} 3\, dV = 3\left(\frac{4}{3}\pi a^3\right) = 4\pi a^3.$$

Example 3 Finding Flux

Find the flux of $\mathbf{F} = xy\mathbf{i} + yz\mathbf{j} + xz\mathbf{k}$ outward through the surface of the cube cut from the first octant by the planes $x = 1$, $y = 1$, and $z = 1$.

Solution   Instead of calculating the flux as a sum of six separate integrals, one for each face of the cube, we can calculate the flux by integrating the divergence

$$\nabla \cdot \mathbf{F} = \frac{\partial}{\partial x}(xy) + \frac{\partial}{\partial y}(yz) + \frac{\partial}{\partial z}(xz) = y + z + x$$

over the cube's interior:

$$\text{Flux} = \iint\limits_{\substack{\text{Cube} \\ \text{surface}}} \mathbf{F} \cdot \mathbf{n}\, d\sigma = \iiint\limits_{\substack{\text{Cube} \\ \text{interior}}} \nabla \cdot \mathbf{F}\, dV \qquad \text{The Divergence}\\ \text{Theorem}$$

$$= \int_0^1 \int_0^1 \int_0^1 (x + y + z)\, dx\, dy\, dz = \frac{3}{2}. \qquad \text{Routine integration}$$

Proof of the Divergence Theorem for Special Regions

To prove the Divergence Theorem, we assume that the components of $\mathbf{F}$ have continuous first partial derivatives. We also assume that D is a convex region with no holes or bubbles, such as a solid sphere, cube, or ellipsoid, and that S is a piecewise smooth surface. In addition, we assume that any line perpendicular to the xy-plane at an interior point of the region R_{xy} that is the projection of D on the xy-plane intersects the surface S in exactly two points, producing surfaces

$$S_1: \quad z = f_1(x, y), \quad (x, y) \text{ in } R_{xy}$$
$$S_2: \quad z = f_2(x, y), \quad (x, y) \text{ in } R_{xy},$$

with $f_1 \leq f_2$. We make similar assumptions about the projection of D onto the other coordinate planes. See Figure 13.70.

The components of the unit normal vector $\mathbf{n} = n_1\mathbf{i} + n_2\mathbf{j} + n_3\mathbf{k}$ are the cosines of the angles α, β, and γ that $\mathbf{n}$ makes with $\mathbf{i}$, $\mathbf{j}$, and $\mathbf{k}$ (Figure 13.71). This is true because all the vectors involved are unit vectors. We have

$$n_1 = \mathbf{n} \cdot \mathbf{i} = |\mathbf{n}||\mathbf{i}| \cos \alpha = \cos \alpha$$
$$n_2 = \mathbf{n} \cdot \mathbf{j} = |\mathbf{n}||\mathbf{j}| \cos \beta = \cos \beta$$
$$n_3 = \mathbf{n} \cdot \mathbf{k} = |\mathbf{n}||\mathbf{k}| \cos \gamma = \cos \gamma.$$

Thus,

$$\mathbf{n} = (\cos \alpha)\mathbf{i} + (\cos \beta)\mathbf{j} + (\cos \gamma)\mathbf{k}$$

and

$$\mathbf{F} \cdot \mathbf{n} = M \cos \alpha + N \cos \beta + P \cos \gamma.$$

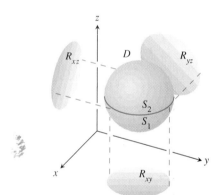

FIGURE 13.70 We first prove the Divergence Theorem for the kind of three-dimensional region shown here. We then extend the theorem to other regions.

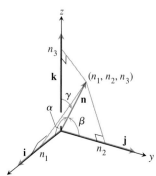

FIGURE 13.71 The scalar components of the unit normal vector $\mathbf{n}$ are the cosines of the angles α, β, and γ that it makes with $\mathbf{i}$, $\mathbf{j}$, and $\mathbf{k}$.

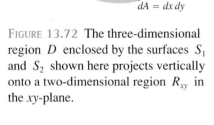

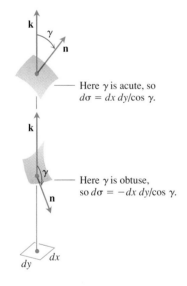

FIGURE 13.72 The three-dimensional region D enclosed by the surfaces S_1 and S_2 shown here projects vertically onto a two-dimensional region R_{xy} in the xy-plane.

FIGURE 13.73 An enlarged view of the area patches in Figure 13.72. The relations $d\sigma = \pm dx\, dy/\cos\gamma$ are derived in Section 13.5.

In component form, the Divergence Theorem states that

$$\iint_S (M\cos\alpha + N\cos\beta + P\cos\gamma)\,d\sigma = \iiint_D \left(\frac{\partial M}{\partial x} + \frac{\partial N}{\partial y} + \frac{\partial P}{\partial z}\right) dx\, dy\, dz.$$

We prove the theorem by proving the three following equalities:

$$\iint_S M\cos\alpha\, d\sigma = \iiint_D \frac{\partial M}{\partial x}\, dx\, dy\, dz \qquad (3)$$

$$\iint_S N\cos\beta\, d\sigma = \iiint_D \frac{\partial N}{\partial y}\, dx\, dy\, dz \qquad (4)$$

$$\iint_S P\cos\gamma\, d\sigma = \iiint_D \frac{\partial P}{\partial z}\, dx\, dy\, dz \qquad (5)$$

We prove Equation (5) by converting the surface integral on the left to a double integral over the projection R_{xy} of D on the xy-plane (Figure 13.72). The surface S consists of an upper part S_2 whose equation is $z = f_2(x, y)$ and a lower part S_1 whose equation is $z = f_1(x, y)$. On S_2, the outer normal $\mathbf{n}$ has a positive $\mathbf{k}$-component and

$$\cos\gamma\, d\sigma = dx\, dy \qquad \text{because} \qquad d\sigma = \frac{dA}{|\cos\gamma|} = \frac{dx\, dy}{\cos\gamma}.$$

See Figure 13.73. On S_1, the outer normal $\mathbf{n}$ has a negative $\mathbf{k}$-component and

$$\cos\gamma\, d\sigma = -dx\, dy.$$

Therefore,

$$\iint_S P\cos\gamma\, d\sigma = \iint_{S_2} P\cos\gamma\, d\sigma + \iint_{S_1} P\cos\gamma\, d\sigma$$

$$= \iint_{R_{xy}} P(x, y, f_2(x, y))\, dx\, dy - \iint_{R_{xy}} P(x, y, f_1(x, y))\, dx\, dy$$

$$= \iint_{R_{xy}} [P(x, y, f_2(x, y)) - P(x, y, f_1(x, y))]\, dx\, dy$$

$$= \iint_{R_{xy}} \left[\int_{f_1(x,y)}^{f_2(x,y)} \frac{\partial P}{\partial z}\, dz\right] dx\, dy = \iiint_D \frac{\partial P}{\partial z}\, dz\, dx\, dy.$$

This proves Equation (5).

The proofs for Equations (3) and (4) follow the same pattern; or just permute x, y, z; M, N, P; α, β, γ, in order, and get those results from Equation (5).

Divergence Theorem for Other Regions

The Divergence Theorem can be extended to regions that can be partitioned into a finite number of simple regions of the type just discussed and to regions that can be defined as limits of simpler regions in certain ways. For example, suppose that D is the region between two concentric spheres and the $\mathbf{F}$ has continuously differen-

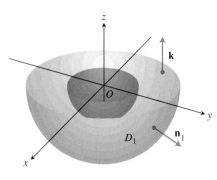

FIGURE 13.74 The lower half of the solid region between two concentric spheres.

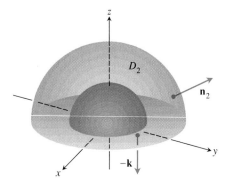

FIGURE 13.75 The upper half of the solid region between two concentric spheres.

tiable components throughout D and on the bounding surfaces. Split D by an equatorial plane and apply the Divergence Theorem to each half separately. The bottom half, D_1, is shown in Figure 13.74. The surface S_1 that bounds D_1 consists of an outer hemisphere, a plane washer-shaped base, and an inner hemisphere. The Divergence Theorem says that

$$\iint_{S_1} \mathbf{F} \cdot \mathbf{n}_1 \, d\sigma_1 = \iiint_{D_1} \nabla \cdot \mathbf{F} \, dV_1. \tag{6}$$

The unit normal $\mathbf{n}_1$ that points outward from D_1 points away from the origin along the outer surface, equals $\mathbf{k}$ along the flat base, and points toward the origin along the inner surface. Next apply the Divergence Theorem to D_2, and its surface S_2 (Figure 13.75):

$$\iint_{S_2} \mathbf{F} \cdot \mathbf{n}_2 \, d\sigma_2 = \iiint_{D_2} \nabla \cdot \mathbf{F} \, dV_2. \tag{7}$$

As we follow $\mathbf{n}_2$ over S_2, pointing outward from D_2, we see that $\mathbf{n}_2$ equals $-\mathbf{k}$ along the washer-shaped base in the xy-plane, points away from the origin on the outer sphere, and points toward the origin on the inner sphere. When we add Equations (6) and (7), the integrals over the flat base cancel because of the opposite signs of $\mathbf{n}_1$ and $\mathbf{n}_2$. We thus arrive at the result

$$\iint_{S} \mathbf{F} \cdot \mathbf{n} \, d\sigma = \iiint_{D} \nabla \cdot \mathbf{F} \, dV,$$

with D the region between the spheres, S the boundary of D consisting of two spheres, and $\mathbf{n}$ the unit normal to S directed outward from D.

Example 4   Finding Outward Flux

Find the net outward flux of the field

$$\mathbf{F} = \frac{x\mathbf{i} + y\mathbf{j} + z\mathbf{k}}{\rho^3}, \qquad \rho = \sqrt{x^2 + y^2 + z^2}$$

across the boundary of the region $D: 0 < a^2 \le x^2 + y^2 + z^2 \le b^2$.

Solution   The flux can be calculated by integrating $\nabla \cdot \mathbf{F}$ over D. We have

$$\frac{\partial \rho}{\partial x} = \frac{1}{2}(x^2 + y^2 + z^2)^{-1/2}(2x) = \frac{x}{\rho}$$

and

$$\frac{\partial M}{\partial x} = \frac{\partial}{\partial x}(x\rho^{-3}) = \rho^{-3} - 3x\rho^{-4}\frac{\partial \rho}{\partial x} = \frac{1}{\rho^3} - \frac{3x^2}{\rho^5}.$$

Similarly,

$$\frac{\partial N}{\partial y} = \frac{1}{\rho^3} - \frac{3y^2}{\rho^5} \qquad \text{and} \qquad \frac{\partial P}{\partial z} = \frac{1}{\rho^3} - \frac{3z^2}{\rho^5}.$$

Hence,

$$\text{div } \mathbf{F} = \frac{3}{\rho^3} - \frac{3}{\rho^5}(x^2 + y^2 + z^2) = \frac{3}{\rho^3} - \frac{3\rho^2}{\rho^5} = 0$$

and

$$\iiint\limits_{D} \nabla \cdot \mathbf{F} \, dV = 0.$$

So the integral of $\nabla \cdot \mathbf{F}$ over D is zero and the net outward flux across the boundary of D is zero. There is more to learn from this example, though. The flux leaving D across the inner sphere S_a is the negative of the flux leaving D across the outer sphere S_b (because the sum of these fluxes is zero). Hence, the flux of $\mathbf{F}$ across S_a in the direction away from the origin equals the flux of $\mathbf{F}$ across S_b in the direction away from the origin. Thus, the flux of $\mathbf{F}$ across a sphere centered at the origin is independent of the radius of the sphere. What is this flux?

To find it, we evaluate the flux integral directly. The outward unit normal on the sphere of radius a is

$$\mathbf{n} = \frac{x\mathbf{i} + y\mathbf{j} + z\mathbf{k}}{\sqrt{x^2 + y^2 + z^2}} = \frac{x\mathbf{i} + y\mathbf{j} + z\mathbf{k}}{a}.$$

Hence, on the sphere,

$$\mathbf{F} \cdot \mathbf{n} = \frac{x\mathbf{i} + y\mathbf{j} + z\mathbf{k}}{a^3} \cdot \frac{x\mathbf{i} + y\mathbf{j} + z\mathbf{k}}{a} = \frac{x^2 + y^2 + z^2}{a^4} = \frac{a^2}{a^4} = \frac{1}{a^2}$$

and

$$\iint\limits_{S_a} \mathbf{F} \cdot \mathbf{n} \, d\sigma = \frac{1}{a^2} \iint\limits_{S_a} d\sigma = \frac{1}{a^2} (4\pi a^2) = 4\pi.$$

The outward flux of $\mathbf{F}$ across any sphere centered at the origin is 4π.

Gauss's Law: One of the Four Great Laws of Electromagnetic Theory

There is still more to be learned from Example 4. In electromagnetic theory, the electric field created by a point charge q located at the origin is

$$\mathbf{E}(x, y, z) = \frac{1}{4\pi\epsilon_0} \frac{q}{|\mathbf{r}|^2} \left(\frac{\mathbf{r}}{|\mathbf{r}|} \right) = \frac{q}{4\pi\epsilon_0} \frac{\mathbf{r}}{|\mathbf{r}|^3} = \frac{q}{4\pi\epsilon_0} \frac{x\mathbf{i} + y\mathbf{j} + z\mathbf{k}}{\rho^3},$$

where ϵ_0 is a physical constant, $\mathbf{r}$ is the position vector of the point (x, y, z), and $\rho = |\mathbf{r}| = \sqrt{x^2 + y^2 + z^2}$. In the notation of Example 4,

$$\mathbf{E} = \frac{q}{4\pi\epsilon_0} \mathbf{F}.$$

The calculations in Example 4 show that the outward flux of $\mathbf{E}$ across any sphere centered at the origin is q/ϵ_0, but this result is not confined to spheres. The outward flux of $\mathbf{E}$ across any closed surface S that encloses the origin (and to which the Divergence Theorem applies) is also q/ϵ_0. To see why, we have only to imagine a large sphere S_a centered at the origin and enclosing the surface S. Since

$$\nabla \cdot \mathbf{E} = \nabla \cdot \frac{q}{4\pi\epsilon_0} \mathbf{F} = \frac{q}{4\pi\epsilon_0} \nabla \cdot \mathbf{F} = 0$$

when $\rho > 0$, the integral of $\nabla \cdot \mathbf{E}$ over the region D between S and S_a is zero. Hence, by the Divergence Theorem,

$$\iint\limits_{\substack{\text{Boundary} \\ \text{of } D}} \mathbf{E} \cdot \mathbf{n}\, d\sigma = 0,$$

and the flux of $\mathbf{E}$ across S in the direction away from the origin must be the same as the flux of $\mathbf{E}$ across S_a in the direction away from the origin, which is q/ϵ_0. This statement, called *Gauss's law*, also applies to charge distributions that are more general than the one assumed here, as you will see in nearly any physics text.

$$\text{Gauss's law:} \qquad \iint\limits_{S} \mathbf{E} \cdot \mathbf{n}\, d\sigma = \frac{q}{\epsilon_0}$$

Continuity Equation of Hydrodynamics

Let D be a region in space bounded by a closed oriented surface S. If $\mathbf{v}(x, y, z)$ is the velocity field of a fluid flowing smoothly through D, $\delta = \delta(t, x, y, z)$ is the fluid's density at (x, y, z) at time t, and $\mathbf{F} = \delta\mathbf{v}$, then the **continuity equation** of hydrodynamics states that

$$\nabla \cdot \mathbf{F} + \frac{\partial \delta}{\partial t} = 0.$$

If the functions involved have continuous first partial derivatives, the equation evolves naturally from the Divergence Theorem, as we now see.

First, the integral

$$\iint\limits_{S} \mathbf{F} \cdot \mathbf{n}\, d\sigma$$

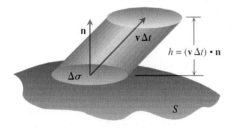

FIGURE 13.76 The fluid that flows upward through the patch $\Delta\sigma$ in a short time Δt fills a "cylinder" whose volume is approximately base × height = $\mathbf{v} \cdot \mathbf{n}\, \Delta\sigma\, \Delta t$.

is the rate at which mass leaves D across S (leaves because $\mathbf{n}$ is the outer normal). To see why, consider a patch of area $\Delta\sigma$ on the surface (Figure 13.76). In a short time interval Δt, the volume ΔV of fluid that flows across the patch is approximately equal to the volume of a cylinder with base area $\Delta\sigma$ and height $(\mathbf{v}\,\Delta t) \cdot \mathbf{n}$, where $\mathbf{v}$ is a velocity vector rooted at a point of the patch:

$$\Delta V \approx \mathbf{v} \cdot \mathbf{n}\, \Delta\sigma\, \Delta t.$$

The mass of this volume of fluid is about

$$\Delta m \approx \delta\mathbf{v} \cdot \mathbf{n}\, \Delta\sigma\, \Delta t,$$

so the rate at which mass is flowing out of D across the patch is about

$$\frac{\Delta m}{\Delta t} \approx \delta\mathbf{v} \cdot \mathbf{n}\, \Delta\sigma.$$

This leads to the approximation

$$\frac{\Sigma\, \Delta m}{\Delta t} \approx \Sigma\, \delta\mathbf{v} \cdot \mathbf{n}\, \Delta\sigma$$

as an estimate of the average rate at which mass flows across S. Finally, letting $\Delta\sigma \to 0$ and $\Delta t \to 0$ gives the instantaneous rate at which mass leaves D across S as

$$\frac{dm}{dt} = \iint_S \delta\mathbf{v} \cdot \mathbf{n} \, d\sigma,$$

which for our particular flow is

$$\frac{dm}{dt} = \iint_S \mathbf{F} \cdot \mathbf{n} \, d\sigma,$$

Now let B be a solid sphere centered at a point Q in the flow. The average value of $\nabla \cdot \mathbf{F}$ over B is

$$\frac{1}{\text{volume of } B} \iiint_B \nabla \cdot \mathbf{F} \, dV.$$

It is a consequence of the continuity of the divergence that $\nabla \cdot \mathbf{F}$ actually takes on this value at some point P in B. Thus,

$$(\nabla \cdot \mathbf{F})_P = \frac{1}{\text{volume of } B} \iiint_B \nabla \cdot \mathbf{F} \, dV = \frac{\iint_S \mathbf{F} \cdot \mathbf{n} \, d\sigma}{\text{volume of } B}$$

$$= \frac{\text{rate at which mass leaves } B \text{ across its surface } S}{\text{volume of } B}. \tag{8}$$

The fraction on the right describes decrease in mass per unit volume.

Now let the radius of B approach zero while the center Q stays fixed. The left side of Equation (8) converges to $(\nabla \cdot \mathbf{F})_Q$, the right side to $(-\partial\delta/\partial t)_Q$. The equality of these two limits is the continuity equation

$$\nabla \cdot \mathbf{F} = -\frac{\partial\delta}{\partial t}.$$

The continuity equation "explains" $\nabla \cdot \mathbf{F}$: The divergence of $\mathbf{F}$ at a point is the rate at which the density of the fluid is decreasing there.

The Divergence Theorem

$$\iint_S \mathbf{F} \cdot \mathbf{n} \, d\sigma = \iiint_D \nabla \cdot \mathbf{F} \, dV$$

now says that the net decrease in density of the fluid in region D is accounted for by the mass transported across the surface S. So, the theorem is a statement about conservation of mass (Exercise 31).

Unifying the Integral Theorems

If we think of a two-dimensional field $\mathbf{F} = M(x, y)\mathbf{i} + N(x, y)\mathbf{j}$ as a three-dimensional field whose $\mathbf{k}$-component is zero, then $\nabla \cdot \mathbf{F} = (\partial M/\partial x) + (\partial N/\partial y)$ and the normal form of Green's Theorem can be written as

$$\oint_C \mathbf{F} \cdot \mathbf{n} \, ds = \iint_R \left(\frac{\partial M}{\partial x} + \frac{\partial N}{\partial y} \right) dx \, dy = \iint_R \nabla \cdot \mathbf{F} \, dA.$$

Similarly, $\nabla \times \mathbf{F} \cdot \mathbf{k} = (\partial N / \partial x) - (\partial M / \partial y)$, so the tangential form of Green's Theorem can be written as

$$\oint_C \mathbf{F} \cdot d\mathbf{r} = \iint_R \left(\frac{\partial N}{\partial x} - \frac{\partial M}{\partial y} \right) dx\, dy = \iint_R \nabla \times \mathbf{F} \cdot \mathbf{k}\, dA.$$

With the equations of Green's Theorem now in del notation, we can see their relationships to the equations in Stokes' Theorem and the Divergence Theorem.

Green's Theorem and Its Generalization to Three Dimensions

Normal form of Green's Theorem:
$$\oint_C \mathbf{F} \cdot \mathbf{n}\, ds = \iint_R \nabla \cdot \mathbf{F}\, dA$$

Divergence Theorem:
$$\iint_S \mathbf{F} \cdot \mathbf{n}\, d\sigma = \iiint_D \nabla \cdot \mathbf{F}\, dV$$

Tangential form of Green's Theorem:
$$\oint_C \mathbf{F} \cdot d\mathbf{r} = \iint_R \nabla \times \mathbf{F} \cdot \mathbf{k}\, dA$$

Stokes' Theorem:
$$\oint_C \mathbf{F} \cdot d\mathbf{r} = \iint_S \nabla \times \mathbf{F} \cdot \mathbf{n}\, d\sigma$$

Notice how Stokes' Theorem generalizes the tangential (curl) form of Green's Theorem from a flat surface in the plane to a surface in three-dimensional space. In each case, the integral of the normal component of curl $\mathbf{F}$ over the interior of the surface equals the circulation of $\mathbf{F}$ around the boundary.

Likewise, the Divergence Theorem generalizes the normal (flux) form of Green's Theorem from a two-dimensional region in the plane to a three-dimensional region in space. In each case, the integral of $\nabla \cdot \mathbf{F}$ over the interior of the region equals the total flux of the field across the boundary.

There is still more to be learned here. All these results can be thought of as forms of a *single fundamental theorem*. Think back to the Fundamental Theorem of Calculus in Section 4.5. It says that if $f(x)$ is differentiable on $[a, b]$, then

$$\int_a^b \frac{df}{dx}\, dx = f(b) - f(a).$$

If we let $\mathbf{F} = f(x)\mathbf{i}$ throughout $[a, b]$, then $(df/dx) = \nabla \cdot \mathbf{F}$. If we define the unit vector field $\mathbf{n}$ normal to the boundary of $[a, b]$ to be $\mathbf{i}$ at b and $-\mathbf{i}$ at a (Figure 13.77), then

$$f(b) - f(a) = f(b)\mathbf{i} \cdot (\mathbf{i}) + f(a)\mathbf{i} \cdot (-\mathbf{i})$$
$$= \mathbf{F}(b) \cdot \mathbf{n} + \mathbf{F}(a) \cdot \mathbf{n}$$
$$= \text{total outward flux of } \mathbf{F} \text{ across the boundary of } [a, b].$$

$\mathbf{n} = -\mathbf{i}$ $\mathbf{n} = \mathbf{i}$

FIGURE 13.77 The outward unit normals at the boundary of $[a, b]$ in one-dimensional space.

The Fundamental Theorem now says that

$$\mathbf{F}(b) \cdot \mathbf{n} + \mathbf{F}(a) \cdot \mathbf{n} = \int_{[a,b]} \nabla \cdot \mathbf{F} \, dx$$

The Fundamental Theorem of Calculus, the flux form of Green's Theorem, and the Divergence Theorem all say that the integral of the differential operator $\nabla \cdot$ operating on a field $\mathbf{F}$ over a region equals the sum of the normal field components over the boundary of the region. (Here we are interpreting the line integral in Green's Theorem and the surface integral in the Divergence Theorem as "sums" over the boundary.)

Stokes' Theorem and the circulation form of Green's Theorem say that, when things are properly oriented, the integral of the normal component of the curl operating on a field equals the sum of the tangential field components on the boundary of the surface.

The beauty of these interpretations is the observance of a marvelous underlying principle, which we might state as follows.

> The integral of a differential operator acting on a field over a region equals the sum of the field components appropriate to the operator over the boundary of the region.

EXERCISES 13.8

Calculating Divergence

In Exercises 1–4, find the divergence of the field.

1. The spin field in Figure 13.14.

2. The radial field in Figure 13.13

3. The gravitational field in Figure 13.12

4. The velocity field in Figure 13.9

Using the Divergence Theorem to Calculate Outward Flux

In Exercises 5–16, use the Divergence Theorem to find the outward flux of $\mathbf{F}$ across the boundary of the region D.

5. *Cube* $\mathbf{F} = (y - x)\mathbf{i} + (z - y)\mathbf{j} + (y - x)\mathbf{k}$

  D: The cube bounded by the planes $x = \pm 1$, $y = \pm 1$, and $z = \pm 1$

6. $\mathbf{F} = x^2\mathbf{i} + y^2\mathbf{j} + z^2\mathbf{k}$

  (a) *Cube* D: The cube cut from the first octant by the planes $x = 1$, $y = 1$, and $z = 1$

  (b) *Cube* D: The cube bounded by the planes $x = \pm 1$, $y = \pm 1$, and $z = \pm 1$

  (c) *Cylindrical can* D: The region cut from the solid cylinder $x^2 + y^2 \le 4$ by the planes $z = 0$ and $z = 1$

7. *Cylinder and paraboloid* $\mathbf{F} = y\mathbf{i} + xy\mathbf{j} - z\mathbf{k}$

  D: The region inside the solid cylinder $x^2 + y^2 \le 4$ between the plane $z = 0$ and the paraboloid $z = x^2 + y^2$

8. *Sphere* $\mathbf{F} = x^2\mathbf{i} + xz\mathbf{j} + 3z\mathbf{k}$

  D: The solid sphere $x^2 + y^2 + z^2 \le 4$

9. *Portion of sphere* $\mathbf{F} = x^2\mathbf{i} - 2xy\mathbf{j} + 3xz\mathbf{k}$

  D: The region cut from the first octant by the sphere $x^2 + y^2 + z^2 = 4$

10. *Cylindrical can* $\mathbf{F} = (6x^2 + 2xy)\mathbf{i} + (2y + x^2z)\mathbf{j} + 4x^2y^3\mathbf{k}$

  D: The region cut from the first octant by the cylinder $x^2 + y^2 = 4$ and the plane $z = 3$

11. *Wedge* $\mathbf{F} = 2xz\mathbf{i} - xy\mathbf{j} - z^2\mathbf{k}$

  D: The wedge cut from the first octant by the plane $y + z = 4$ and the elliptical cylinder $4x^2 + y^2 = 16$

12. *Sphere* $\mathbf{F} = x^3\mathbf{i} + y^3\mathbf{j} + z^3\mathbf{k}$

  D: The solid sphere $x^2 + y^2 + z^2 \le a^2$

13. *Thick sphere* $\mathbf{F} = \sqrt{x^2 + y^2 + z^2} \, (x\mathbf{i} + y\mathbf{j} + z\mathbf{k})$

  D: The region $1 \le x^2 + y^2 + z^2 \le 2$

14. *Thick sphere* $\mathbf{F} = (x\mathbf{i} + y\mathbf{j} + z\mathbf{k})/\sqrt{x^2 + y^2 + z^2}$

  D: The region $1 \le x^2 + y^2 + z^2 \le 4$

15. *Thick sphere* $\mathbf{F} = (5x^3 + 12xy^2)\mathbf{i} + (y^3 + e^y \sin z)\mathbf{j} + (5z^3 + e^y \cos z)\mathbf{k}$

D: The solid region between the spheres $x^2 + y^2 + z^2 = 1$ and $x^2 + y^2 + z^2 = 2$

16. *Thick cylinder* $\mathbf{F} = \ln(x^2 + y^2)\mathbf{i} - \left(\dfrac{2z}{x}\tan^{-1}\dfrac{y}{x}\right)\mathbf{j} + z\sqrt{x^2 + y^2}\,\mathbf{k}$

D: The thick-walled cylinder $1 \le x^2 + y^2 \le 2$, $-1 \le z \le 2$

Properties of Curl and Divergence

17. *div (curl G) = 0*

(a) Show that if the necessary partial derivatives of the components of the field $\mathbf{G} = M\mathbf{i} + N\mathbf{j} + P\mathbf{k}$ are continuous, then $\nabla \cdot \nabla \times \mathbf{G} = 0$.

(b) *Writing to Learn* What, if anything, can you conclude about the flux of the field $\nabla \times \mathbf{G}$ across a closed surface? Give reasons for your answer.

18. *Identities* Let $\mathbf{F}_1$ and $\mathbf{F}_2$ be differentiable vector fields and let a and b be arbitrary real constants. Verify the following identities.

(a) $\nabla \cdot (a\mathbf{F}_1 + b\mathbf{F}_2) = a\nabla \cdot \mathbf{F}_1 + b\,\nabla \cdot \mathbf{F}_2$

(b) $\nabla \times (a\mathbf{F}_1 + b\mathbf{F}_2) = a\nabla \times \mathbf{F}_1 + b\,\nabla \times \mathbf{F}_2$

(c) $\nabla \cdot (\mathbf{F}_1 \times \mathbf{F}_2) = \mathbf{F}_2 \cdot \nabla \times \mathbf{F}_1 - \mathbf{F}_1 \cdot \nabla \times \mathbf{F}_2$

19. *Identities* Let $\mathbf{F}$ be a differentiable vector field and let $g(x, y, z)$ be a differentiable scalar function. Verify the following identities.

(a) $\nabla \cdot (g\mathbf{F}) = g\nabla \cdot \mathbf{F} + \nabla g \cdot \mathbf{F}$

(b) $\nabla \times (g\mathbf{F}) = g\nabla \times \mathbf{F} + \nabla g \times \mathbf{F}$

20. *Identities* If $\mathbf{F} = M\mathbf{i} + N\mathbf{j} + P\mathbf{k}$ is a differentiable vector field, we define the notation $\mathbf{F} \cdot \nabla$ to mean

$$M\frac{\partial}{\partial x} + N\frac{\partial}{\partial y} + P\frac{\partial}{\partial z}.$$

For differentiable vector fields $\mathbf{F}_1$ and $\mathbf{F}_2$, verify the following identities.

(a) $\nabla \times (\mathbf{F}_1 \times \mathbf{F}_2) = (\mathbf{F}_2 \cdot \nabla)\mathbf{F}_1 - (\mathbf{F}_1 \cdot \nabla)\mathbf{F}_2 + (\nabla \cdot \mathbf{F}_2)\mathbf{F}_1 - (\nabla \cdot \mathbf{F}_1)\mathbf{F}_2$

(b) $\nabla(\mathbf{F}_1 \cdot \mathbf{F}_2) = (\mathbf{F}_1 \cdot \nabla)\mathbf{F}_2 + (\mathbf{F}_2 \cdot \nabla)\mathbf{F}_1 + \mathbf{F}_1 \times (\nabla \times \mathbf{F}_2) + \mathbf{F}_2 \times (\nabla \times \mathbf{F}_1)$

Theory and Examples

21. *Writing to Learn: Bounding divergence* Let $\mathbf{F}$ be a field whose components have continuous first partial derivatives throughout a portion of space containing a region D bounded by a smooth closed surface S. If $|\mathbf{F}| \le 1$, can any bound be placed on the size of

$$\iiint_D \nabla \cdot \mathbf{F}\, dV?$$

Give reasons for your answer.

22. *Writing to Learn: Flux of a position vector* The base of the closed cubelike surface shown here is the unit square in the *xy*-plane. The four sides lie in the planes $x = 0$, $x = 1$, $y = 0$, and $y = 1$. The top is an arbitrary smooth surface whose identity is unknown. Let $\mathbf{F} = x\mathbf{i} - 2y\mathbf{j} + (z + 3)\mathbf{k}$ and suppose the outward flux of $\mathbf{F}$ through side A is 1 and through side B is -3. Can you conclude anything about the outward flux through the top? Give reasons for your answer.

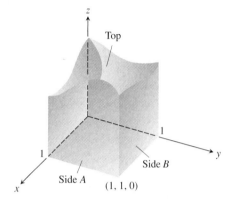

23. (a) *Flux of position vector* Show that the flux of the position vector field $\mathbf{F} = x\mathbf{i} + y\mathbf{j} + z\mathbf{k}$ outward through a smooth closed surface S is three times the volume of the region enclosed by the surface.

(b) Let $\mathbf{n}$ be the outward unit normal vector field on S. Show that it is not possible for $\mathbf{F}$ to be orthogonal to $\mathbf{n}$ at every point of S.

24. *Maximum flux* Among all rectangular solids defined by the inequalities $0 \le x \le a$, $0 \le y \le b$, $0 \le z \le 1$, find the one for which the total flux of $\mathbf{F} = (-x^2 - 4xy)\mathbf{i} - 6yz\mathbf{j} + 12z\mathbf{k}$ outward through the six sides is greatest. What *is* the greatest flux?

25. *Volume of a solid region* Let $\mathbf{F} = x\mathbf{i} + y\mathbf{j} + z\mathbf{k}$ and suppose that the surface S and region D satisfy the hypotheses of the Divergence Theorem. Show that the volume of D is given by the formula

$$\text{Volume of } D = \frac{1}{3}\iint_S \mathbf{F} \cdot \mathbf{n}\, d\sigma.$$

26. *Flux of a constant field* Show that the outward flux of a constant vector field $\mathbf{F} = \mathbf{C}$ across any closed surface to which the Divergence Theorem applies is zero.

27. *Harmonic functions* A function $f(x, y, z)$ is said to be **harmonic** in a region D in space if it satisfies the Laplace equation

$$\nabla^2 f = \nabla \cdot \nabla f = \frac{\partial^2 f}{\partial x^2} + \frac{\partial^2 f}{\partial y^2} + \frac{\partial^2 f}{\partial z^2} = 0$$

throughout D.

(a) Suppose that f is harmonic throughout a bounded region D enclosed by a smooth surface S and that $\mathbf{n}$ is the chosen unit normal vector on S. Show that the integral over S of $\nabla f \cdot \mathbf{n}$, the derivative of f in the direction of $\mathbf{n}$, is zero.

(b) Show that if f is harmonic on D, then

$$\iint_S f \, \nabla f \cdot \mathbf{n} \, d\sigma = \iiint_D |\nabla f|^2 \, dV.$$

28. *Flux of a gradient field* Let S be the surface of the portion of the solid sphere $x^2 + y^2 + z^2 \leq a^2$ that lies in the first octant and let $f(x, y, z) = \ln \sqrt{x^2 + y^2 + z^2}$. Calculate

$$\iint_S \nabla f \cdot \mathbf{n} \, d\sigma.$$

($\nabla f \cdot \mathbf{n}$ is the derivative of f in the direction of $\mathbf{n}$.)

29. *Green's first formula* Suppose that f and g are scalar functions with continuous first- and second-order partial derivatives throughout a region D that is bounded by a closed piecewise smooth surface S. Show that

$$\iint_S f \, \nabla g \cdot \mathbf{n} \, d\sigma = \iiint_D (f \, \nabla^2 g + \nabla f \cdot \nabla g) \, dV. \tag{9}$$

Equation (9) is **Green's first formula.** (*Hint:* Apply the Divergence Theorem to the field $\mathbf{F} = f \, \nabla g$.)

30. *Green's second formula* (*Continuation of Exercise 29*) Interchange f and g in Equation (9) to obtain a similar formula. Then subtract this formula from Equation (9) to show that

$$\iint_S (f \, \nabla g - g \, \nabla f) \cdot \mathbf{n} \, d\sigma = \iiint_D (f \, \nabla^2 g - g \, \nabla^2 f) \, dV. \tag{10}$$

This equation is **Green's second formula.**

31. *Conservation of mass* Let $\mathbf{v}(t, x, y, z)$ be a continuously differentiable vector field over the region D in space and let $p(t, x, y, z)$ be a continuously differentiable scalar function. The variable t represents the time domain. The Law of Conservation of Mass asserts that

$$\frac{d}{dt} \iiint_D p(t, x, y, z) \, dV = -\iint_S p\mathbf{v} \cdot \mathbf{n} \, d\sigma,$$

where S is the surface enclosing D.

(a) Give a physical interpretation of the conservation of mass law if $\mathbf{v}$ is a velocity flow field and p represents the density of the fluid at point (x, y, z) at time t.

(b) Use the Divergence Theorem and Leibniz's Rule,

$$\frac{d}{dt} \iiint_D p(t, x, y, z) \, dV = \iiint_D \frac{\partial p}{\partial t} \, dV,$$

to show that the Law of Conservation of Mass is equivalent to the continuity equation,

$$\nabla \cdot p\mathbf{v} + \frac{\partial p}{\partial t} = 0.$$

(In the first term $\nabla \cdot p\mathbf{v}$, the variable t is held fixed, and in the second term $\partial p / \partial t$, it is assumed that the point (x, y, z) in D is held fixed.)

32. *The heat diffusion equation* Let $T(t, x, y, z)$ be a function with continuous second derivatives giving the temperature at time t at the point (x, y, z) of a solid occupying a region D in space. If the solid's heat capacity and mass density are denoted by the constants c and ρ, respectively, the quantity $c\rho T$ is called the solid's **heat energy per unit volume.**

(a) Explain why $-\nabla T$ points in the direction of heat flow.

(b) Let $-k\nabla T$ denote the **energy flux vector.** (Here the constant k is called the **conductivity.**) Assuming the Law of Conservation of Mass with $-k\nabla T = \mathbf{v}$ and $c\rho T = p$ in Exercise 31, derive the diffusion (heat) equation

$$\frac{\partial T}{\partial t} = K \nabla^2 T,$$

where $K = k/(c\rho) > 0$ is the *diffusivity* constant. (Notice that if $T(t, x)$ represents the temperature at time t at position x in a uniform conducting rod with perfectly insulated sides, then $\nabla^2 T = \partial^2 T / \partial x^2$ and the diffusion equation reduces to the one-dimensional heat equation in Chapter 11's Additional Exercises.)

Questions to Guide Your Review

1. What are line integrals? How are they evaluated? Give examples.

2. How can you use line integrals to find the centers of mass of springs? Explain.

3. What is a vector field? A gradient field? Give examples.

4. How do you calculate the work done by a force in moving a particle along a curve? Give an example.

5. What are flow, circulation, and flux?

6. What is special about path independent fields?

7. How can you tell when a field is conservative? How do you find the work done by a conservative field?

8. What is a potential function? Show by example how to find a potential function for a conservative field.

9. What is a differential form? What does it mean for such a form to be exact? How do you test for exactness? Give examples.

10. What is the divergence of a vector field? How can you interpret it?

11. What is the curl of a vector field? How can you interpret it?

12. What are the two forms of Green's Theorem? How can you interpret them?

13. How do you calculate the area of a curved surface in space? Give an example.

14. What is an oriented surface? How do you calculate the flux of a three-dimensional vector field across an oriented surface? Give an example.

15. What are surface integrals? What can you calculate with them? Give an example.

16. What is a parametrized surface? How do you find the area of such a surface? Give examples.

17. How do you integrate a function over a parametrized surface? Give an example.

18. What is Stokes' Theorem? How can you interpret it?

19. Summarize the chapter's results on conservative fields.

20. What is the Divergence Theorem? How can you interpret it?

21. How does the Divergence Theorem generalize Green's Theorem?

22. How does Stokes' Theorem generalize Green's Theorem?

23. How can Green's Theorem, Stokes' Theorem, and the Divergence Theorem be regarded as forms of a single fundamental theorem?

Practice Exercises

Evaluating Line Integrals

1. The accompanying figure shows two polygonal paths in space joining the origin to the point $(1, 1, 1)$. Integrate $f(x, y, z) = 2x - 3y^2 - 2z + 3$ over each path.

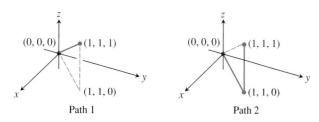

Path 1   Path 2

2. The accompanying figure shows three polygonal paths joining the origin to the point $(1, 1, 1)$. Integrate $f(x, y, z) = x^2 + y - z$ over each path.

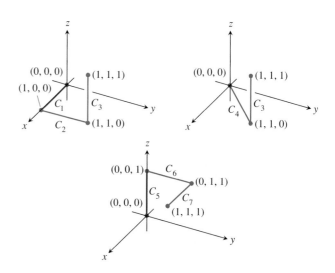

3. Integrate $f(x, y, z) = \sqrt{x^2 + z^2}$ over the circle

$$\mathbf{r}(t) = (a \cos t)\mathbf{j} + (a \sin t)\mathbf{k}, \qquad 0 \le t \le 2\pi.$$

4. Integrate $f(x, y, z) = \sqrt{x^2 + z^2}$ over the involute curve

$$\mathbf{r}(t) = (\cos t + t \sin t)\mathbf{i} + (\sin t - t \cos t)\mathbf{j}, \qquad 0 \le t \le \sqrt{3}.$$

Evaluate the integrals in Exercises 5 and 6.

5. $\displaystyle\int_{(-1,1,1)}^{(4,-3,0)} \frac{dx + dy + dz}{\sqrt{x + y + z}}$

6. $\displaystyle\int_{(1,1,1)}^{(10,3,3)} dx - \sqrt{\frac{z}{y}}\, dy - \sqrt{\frac{y}{z}}\, dz$

7. Integrate $\mathbf{F} = -(y \sin z)\mathbf{i} + (x \sin z)\mathbf{j} + (xy \cos z)\mathbf{k}$ around the circle cut from the sphere $x^2 + y^2 + z^2 = 5$ by the plane $z = -1$, clockwise as viewed from above.

8. Integrate $\mathbf{F} = 3x^2 y\mathbf{i} + (x^3 + 1)\mathbf{j} + 9z^2\mathbf{k}$ around the circle cut from the sphere $x^2 + y^2 + z^2 = 9$ by the plane $x = 2$.

Evaluate the integrals in Exercises 9 and 10.

9. $\displaystyle\int_C 8x \sin y\, dx - 8y \cos x\, dy$

C is the square cut from the first quadrant by the lines $x = \pi/2$ and $y = \pi/2$.

10. $\displaystyle\int_C y^2\, dx + x^2\, dy$

C is the circle $x^2 + y^2 = 4$.

Evaluating Surface Integrals

11. *Area of an elliptical region* Find the area of the elliptical region cut from the plane $x + y + z = 1$ by the cylinder $x^2 + y^2 = 1$.

12. *Area of a parabolic cap* Find the area of the cap cut from the paraboloid $y^2 + z^2 = 3x$ by the plane $x = 1$.

13. *Area of a spherical cap* Find the area of the cap cut from the top of the sphere $x^2 + y^2 + z^2 = 1$ by the plane $z = \sqrt{2}/2$.

14. **(a)** *Hemisphere cut by cylinder* Find the area of the surface cut from the hemisphere $x^2 + y^2 + z^2 = 4$, $z \ge 0$, by the cylinder $x^2 + y^2 = 2x$.

(b) Find the area of the portion of the cylinder that lies inside the hemisphere. (*Hint:* Project onto the xz-plane. Or evaluate the integral $\int h\, ds$, where h is the altitude of the cylinder and ds is the element of arc length on the circle $x^2 + y^2 = 2x$ in the xy-plane.)

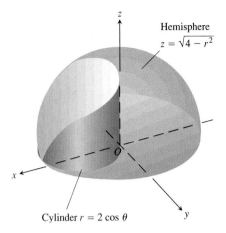

Hemisphere
$z = \sqrt{4 - r^2}$

Cylinder $r = 2 \cos \theta$

15. *Area of a triangle* Find the area of the triangle in which the plane $(x/a) + (y/b) + (z/c) = 1$ ($a, b, c > 0$) intersects the first octant. Check your answer with an appropriate vector calculation.

16. *Parabolic cylinder cut by planes* Integrate

(a) $g(x, y, z) = \dfrac{yz}{\sqrt{4y^2 + 1}}$ **(b)** $g(x, y, z) = \dfrac{z}{\sqrt{4y^2 + 1}}$

over the surface cut from the parabolic cylinder $y^2 - z = 1$ by the planes $x = 0$, $x = 3$, and $z = 0$.

17. *Circular cylinder cut by planes* Integrate $g(x, y, z) = x^4 y(y^2 + z^2)$ over the portion of the cylinder $y^2 + z^2 = 25$ that lies in the first octant between the planes $x = 0$ and $x = 1$ and above the plane $z = 3$.

18. *Area of Wyoming* The state of Wyoming is bounded by the meridians $111° \ 3'$ and $104° \ 3'$ west longitude and by the circles $41°$ and $45°$ north latitude. Assuming that Earth is a sphere of radius $R = 3959$ mi, find the area of Wyoming.

Parametrized Surfaces

Find the parametrizations for the surfaces in Exercises 19–24. (There are many ways to do these, so your answers may not be the same as those in the back of the book.)

19. *Spherical band* The portion of the sphere $x^2 + y^2 + z^2 = 36$ between the planes $z = -3$ and $z = 3\sqrt{3}$

20. *Parabolic cap* The portion of the paraboloid $z = -(x^2 + y^2)/2$ above the plane $z = -2$

21. *Cone* The cone $z = 1 + \sqrt{x^2 + y^2}$, $z \le 3$

22. *Plane above square* The portion of the plane $4x + 2y + 4z = 12$ that lies above the square $0 \le x \le 2$, $0 \le y \le 2$ in the first quadrant

23. *Portion of paraboloid* The portion of the paraboloid $y = 2(x^2 + z^2)$, $y \le 2$, that lies above the xy-plane

24. *Portion of hemisphere* The portion of the hemisphere $x^2 + y^2 + z^2 = 10$, $y \ge 0$, in the first octant

25. *Surface area* Find the area of the surface

$$\mathbf{r}(u, v) = (u + v)\mathbf{i} + (u - v)\mathbf{j} + v\mathbf{k}, \qquad 0 \le u \le 1, \quad 0 \le v \le 1.$$

26. *Surface integral* Integrate $f(x, y, z) = xy - z^2$ over the surface in Exercise 25.

27. *Area of a helicoid* Find the surface area of the helicoid

$$\mathbf{r}(r, \theta) = r \cos \theta \mathbf{i} + r \sin \theta \mathbf{j} + \theta \mathbf{k}, \qquad 0 \le \theta \le 2\pi, \quad 0 \le r \le 1,$$

in the accompanying figure.

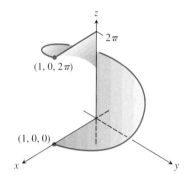

28. *Surface integral* Evaluate the integral $\iint_S \sqrt{x^2 + y^2 + 1} \; d\sigma$, where S is the helicoid in Exercise 27.

Conservative Fields

Which of the fields in Exercises 29–32 are conservative, and which are not?

29. $\mathbf{F} = x\mathbf{i} + y\mathbf{j} + z\mathbf{k}$

30. $\mathbf{F} = (x\mathbf{i} + y\mathbf{j} + z\mathbf{k})/(x^2 + y^2 + z^2)^{3/2}$

31. $\mathbf{F} = xe^y\mathbf{i} + ye^z\mathbf{j} + ze^x\mathbf{k}$

32. $\mathbf{F} = (\mathbf{i} + z\mathbf{j} + y\mathbf{k})/(x + yz)$

Find potential functions for the fields in Exercises 33 and 34.

33. $\mathbf{F} = 2\mathbf{i} + (2y + z)\mathbf{j} + (y + 1)\mathbf{k}$

34. $\mathbf{F} = (z \cos xz)\mathbf{i} + e^y\mathbf{j} + (x \cos xz)\mathbf{k}$

Work and Circulation

In Exercises 35 and 36, find the work done by each field along the paths from $(0, 0, 0)$ to $(1, 1, 1)$ in Exercise 1.

35. $\mathbf{F} = 2xy\mathbf{i} + \mathbf{j} + x^2\mathbf{k}$ **36.** $\mathbf{F} = 2xy\mathbf{i} + x^2\mathbf{j} + \mathbf{k}$

37. *Finding work in two ways* Find the work done by

$$\mathbf{F} = \frac{x\mathbf{i} + y\mathbf{j}}{(x^2 + y^2)^{3/2}}$$

over the plane curve $\mathbf{r}(t) = (e^t \cos t)\mathbf{i} + (e^t \sin t)\mathbf{j}$ from the point $(1, 0)$ to the point $(e^{2\pi}, 0)$ in two ways:

(a) By using the parametrization of the curve to evaluate the work integral

(b) By evaluating a potential function for $\mathbf{F}$.

38. *Flow along different paths* Find the flow of the field $\mathbf{F} = \nabla(x^2ze^y)$

(a) Once around the ellipse C in which the plane $x + y + z = 1$ intersects the cylinder $x^2 + z^2 = 25$, clockwise as viewed from the positive y-axis

(b) Along the curved boundary of the helicoid in Exercise 27 from $(1, 0, 0)$ to $(1, 0, 2\pi)$.

In Exercises 39 and 40, use the surface integral in Stokes' Theorem to find the circulation of the field $\mathbf{F}$ around the curve C in the indicated direction.

39. *Circulation around an ellipse* $\mathbf{F} = y^2\mathbf{i} - y\mathbf{j} + 3z^2\mathbf{k}$

C: The ellipse in which the plane $2x + 6y - 3z = 6$ meets the cylinder $x^2 + y^2 = 1$, counterclockwise as viewed from above

40. *Circulation around a circle* $\mathbf{F} = (x^2 + y)\mathbf{i} + (x + y)\mathbf{j} + (4y^2 - z)\mathbf{k}$

C: The circle in which the plane $z = -y$ meets the sphere $x^2 + y^2 + z^2 = 4$, counterclockwise as viewed from above

Mass and Moments

41. *Wire with different densities* Find the mass of a thin wire lying along the curve $\mathbf{r}(t) = \sqrt{2}t\mathbf{i} + \sqrt{2}t\mathbf{j} + (4 - t^2)\mathbf{k}, 0 \le t \le 1$, if the density at t is (a) $\delta = 3t$ and (b) $\delta = 1$.

42. *Wire with variable density* Find the center of mass of a thin wire lying along the curve $\mathbf{r}(t) = t\mathbf{i} + 2t\mathbf{j} + (2/3)t^{2/3}\mathbf{k}, 0 \le t \le 2$, if the density at t is $\delta = 3\sqrt{5 + t}$.

43. *Wire with variable density* Find the center of mass and the moments of inertia and radii of gyration about the coordinate axes of a thin wire lying along the curve

$$\mathbf{r}(t) = t\mathbf{i} + \frac{2\sqrt{2}}{3}t^{3/2}\mathbf{j} + \frac{t^2}{2}\mathbf{k}, \qquad 0 \le t \le 2,$$

if the density at t is $\delta = 1/(t + 1)$.

44. *Center of mass of an arch* A slender metal arch lies along the semicircle $y = \sqrt{a^2 - x^2}$ in the xy-plane. The density at the point (x, y) on the arch is $\delta(x, y) = 2a - y$. Find the center of mass.

45. *Wire with constant density* A wire of constant density $\delta = 1$ lies along the curve $\mathbf{r}(t) = (e^t \cos t)\mathbf{i} + (e^t \sin t)\mathbf{j} + e^t\mathbf{k}, 0 \le t \le \ln 2$. Find $\bar{z}, I_z$, and R_z.

46. *Helical wire with constant density* Find the mass and center of mass of a wire of constant density δ that lies along the helix $\mathbf{r}(t) = (2 \sin t)\mathbf{i} + (2 \cos t)\mathbf{j} + 3t\mathbf{k}, 0 \le t \le 2\pi$.

47. *Inertia, radius of gyration, center of mass of a shell* Find I_z, R_z, and the center of mass of a thin shell of density $\delta(x, y, z) = z$ cut from the upper portion of the sphere $x^2 + y^2 + z^2 = 25$ by the plane $z = 3$.

48. *Moment of inertia of a cube* Find the moment of inertia about the z-axis of the surface of the cube cut from the first octant by the planes $x = 1, y = 1$, and $z = 1$ if the density is $\delta = 1$.

Flux Across a Plane Curve or Surface

Use Green's Theorem to find the counterclockwise circulation and outward flux for the fields and curves in Exercises 49 and 50.

49. *Square* $\mathbf{F} = (2xy + x)\mathbf{i} + (xy - y)\mathbf{j}$

   C: The square bounded by $x = 0, x = 1, y = 0, y = 1$

50. *Triangle* $\mathbf{F} = (y - 6x^2)\mathbf{i} + (x + y^2)\mathbf{j}$

   C: The triangle made by the lines $y = 0, y = x$, and $x = 1$

51. *Zero line integral* Show that

$$\oint_C \ln x \, \sin y \, dy - \frac{\cos y}{x} \, dx = 0$$

for any closed curve C to which Green's Theorem applies.

52. (a) *Outward flux and area* Show that the outward flux of the position vector field $\mathbf{F} = x\mathbf{i} + y\mathbf{j}$ across any closed curve to which Green's Theorem applies is twice the area of the region enclosed by the curve.

   (b) Let $\mathbf{n}$ be the outward unit normal vector to a closed curve to which Green's Theorem applies. Show that it is not possible for $\mathbf{F} = x\mathbf{i} + y\mathbf{j}$ to be orthogonal to $\mathbf{n}$ at every point of C.

In Exercises 53–56, find the outward flux of $\mathbf{F}$ across the boundary of D.

53. *Cube* $\mathbf{F} = 2xy\mathbf{i} + 2yz\mathbf{j} + 2xz\mathbf{k}$

   D: The cube cut from the first octant by the planes $x = 1$, $y = 1, z = 1$

54. *Spherical cap* $\mathbf{F} = xz\mathbf{i} + yz\mathbf{j} + \mathbf{k}$

   D: The entire surface of the upper cap cut from the solid sphere $x^2 + y^2 + z^2 \leq 25$ by the plane $z = 3$

55. *Spherical cap* $\mathbf{F} = -2x\mathbf{i} - 3y\mathbf{j} + z\mathbf{k}$

   D: The upper region cut from the solid sphere $x^2 + y^2 + z^2 \leq 2$ by the paraboloid $z = x^2 + y^2$

56. *Cone and cylinder* $\mathbf{F} = (6x + y)\mathbf{i} - (x + z)\mathbf{j} + 4yz\mathbf{k}$

   D: The region in the first octant bounded by the cone $z = \sqrt{x^2 + y^2}$, the cylinder $x^2 + y^2 = 1$, and the coordinate planes

57. *Hemisphere, cylinder, and plane* Let S be the surface that is bounded on the left by the hemisphere $x^2 + y^2 + z^2 = a^2, y \leq 0$, in the middle by the cylinder $x^2 + z^2 = a^2, 0 \leq y \leq a$, and on the right by the plane $y = a$. Find the flux of $\mathbf{F} = y\mathbf{i} + z\mathbf{j} + x\mathbf{k}$ outward across S.

58. *Cylinder and Planes* Find the outward flux of the field $\mathbf{F} = 3xz^2\mathbf{i} + y\mathbf{j} - z^3\mathbf{k}$ across the surface of the solid in the first octant that is bounded by the cylinder $x^2 + 4y^2 = 16$ and the planes $y = 2z$, $x = 0$, and $z = 0$.

59. *Cylindrical can* Use the Divergence Theorem to find the flux of $\mathbf{F} = xy^2\mathbf{i} + x^2y\mathbf{j} + y\mathbf{k}$ outward through the surface of the region enclosed by the cylinder $x^2 + y^2 = 1$ and the planes $z = 1$ and $z = -1$.

60. *Hemisphere* Find the flux of $\mathbf{F} = (3z + 1)\mathbf{k}$ upward across the hemisphere $x^2 + y^2 + z^2 = a^2, z \geq 0$ (a) with the Divergence Theorem and (b) by evaluating the flux integral directly.

Additional Exercises: Theory, Examples, Applications

Finding Areas with Green's Theorem

Use the Green's Theorem area formula, Equation (22) in Exercises 13.4, to find the areas of the regions enclosed by the curves in Exercises 1–4.

1. The limaçon $x = 2 \cos t - \cos 2t, y = 2 \sin t - \sin 2t, 0 \leq t \leq 2\pi$

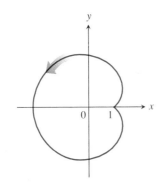

2. The deltoid $x = 2 \cos t + \cos 2t, y = 2 \sin t - \sin 2t, 0 \leq t \leq 2\pi$

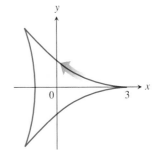

3. The eight curve $x = (1/2)\sin 2t$, $y = \sin t$, $0 \le t \le \pi$ (one loop)

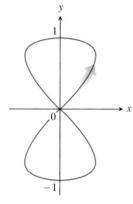

4. The teardrop $x = 2a\cos t - a\sin 2t$, $y = b\sin t$, $0 \le t \le 2\pi$

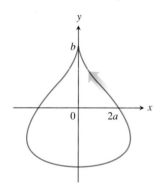

Theory and Applications

5. *Fields with nonzero curl*

(a) Give an example of a vector field $\mathbf{F}(x, y, z)$ that has value **0** at only one point and such that curl $\mathbf{F}$ is nonzero everywhere. Be sure to identify the point and compute the curl.

(b) Give an example of a vector field $\mathbf{F}(x, y, z)$ that has value **0** on precisely one line and such that curl $\mathbf{F}$ is nonzero everywhere. Be sure to identify the line and compute the curl.

(c) Give an example of a vector field $\mathbf{F}(x, y, z)$ that has value **0** on a surface and such that curl $\mathbf{F}$ is nonzero everywhere. Be sure to identify the surface and compute the curl.

6. *Field normal to a sphere* Find all points (a, b, c) on the sphere $x^2 + y^2 + z^2 = R^2$ where the vector field $\mathbf{F} = yz^2\mathbf{i} + xz^2\mathbf{j} + 2xyz\mathbf{k}$ is normal to the surface and $\mathbf{F}(a, b, c) \ne \mathbf{0}$.

7. *Minimal flux* Among all rectangular regions $0 \le x \le a$, $0 \le y \le b$, find the one for which the total outward flux of $\mathbf{F} = (x^2 + 4xy)\mathbf{i} - 6y\mathbf{j}$ across the four sides is least. What *is* the least flux?

8. *Maximum circulation* Find an equation for the plane through the origin such that the circulation of the flow field $\mathbf{F} = z\mathbf{i} + x\mathbf{j} + $ $y\mathbf{k}$ around the circle of intersection of the plane with the sphere $x^2 + y^2 + z^2 = 4$ is a maximum.

9. *Work on a string* A string lies along the circle $x^2 + y^2 = 4$ from $(2, 0)$ to $(0, 2)$ in the first quadrant. The density of the string is $\rho(x, y) = xy$.

(a) Partition the string into a finite number of subarcs to show that the work done by gravity to move the string straight down to the *x*-axis is given by

$$\text{Work} = \lim_{n \to \infty} \sum_{k=1}^{n} gx_k y_k^2 \,\Delta s_k = \int_C gxy^2 \,ds,$$

where g is the gravitational constant.

(b) Find the total work done by evaluating the line integral in part (a).

(c) *Moving the center of mass* Show that the total work done equals the work required to move the string's center of mass $(\bar{x}, \bar{y})$ straight down to the *x*-axis.

10. *Work on a thin sheet* A thin sheet lies along the portion of the plane $x + y + z = 1$ in the first octant. The density of the sheet is $\delta(x, y, z) = xy$.

(a) Partition the sheet into a finite number of subpieces to show that the work done by gravity to move the sheet straight down to the *xy*-plane is given by

$$\text{Work} = \lim_{n \to \infty} \sum_{k=1}^{n} gx_k y_k z_k \,\Delta\sigma_k = \iint_S gxyz \,d\sigma,$$

where g is the gravitational constant.

(b) Find the total work done by evaluating the surface integral in part (a).

(c) *Moving the center of mass* Show that the total work done equals the work required to move the sheet's center of mass $(\bar{x}, \bar{y}, \bar{z})$ straight down to the *xy*-plane.

11. *Archimedes' principle* If an object such as a ball is placed in a liquid, it will either sink to the bottom, float, or sink a certain distance and remain suspended in the liquid. Suppose that a fluid has constant weight density w and that the fluid's surface coincides with the plane $z = 4$. A spherical ball remains suspended in the fluid and occupies the region $x^2 + y^2 + (z - 2)^2 \le 1$.

(a) Show that the surface integral giving the magnitude of the total force on the ball due to the fluid's pressure is

$$\text{Force} = \lim_{n \to \infty} \sum_{k=1}^{n} w(4 - z_k) \,\Delta\sigma_k = \iint_S w(4 - z) \,d\sigma.$$

(b) *Buoyant force integral* Since the ball is not moving, it is being held up by the buoyant force of the liquid. Show that the magnitude of the buoyant force on the sphere is

$$\text{Buoyant force} = \iint_S w(z - 4)\mathbf{k} \cdot \mathbf{n} \,d\sigma,$$

where **n** is the outer unit normal at (x, y, z). This illustrates Archimedes' principle that the magnitude of the buoyant force on a submerged solid equals the weight of the displaced fluid.

(c) Use the Divergence Theorem to find the magnitude of the buoyant force in part (b).

12. *A gravitational field is not a curl* Let

$$\mathbf{F} = -\frac{GmM}{|\mathbf{r}|^3}\,\mathbf{r}$$

be the gravitational force field defined for $\mathbf{r} \neq \mathbf{0}$. Use Gauss's law in Section 13.8 to show that there is no continuously differentiable vector field **H** satisfying $\mathbf{F} = \nabla \times \mathbf{H}$.

13. *Equal line and surface integrals* If $f(x, y, z)$ and $g(x, y, z)$ are continuously differentiable scalar functions defined over the oriented surface S with boundary curve C, prove that

$$\iint_S (\nabla f \times \nabla g) \cdot \mathbf{n}\, d\sigma = \oint_C f\, \nabla g \cdot d\mathbf{r}.$$

14. *Fields with equal divergence and equal curls* Suppose that $\nabla \cdot \mathbf{F}_1 = \nabla \cdot \mathbf{F}_2$ and $\nabla \times \mathbf{F}_1 = \nabla \times \mathbf{F}_2$ over a region D enclosed by the oriented surface S with outward unit normal **n** and that $\mathbf{F}_1 \cdot \mathbf{n} = \mathbf{F}_2 \cdot \mathbf{n}$ on S. Prove that $\mathbf{F}_1 = \mathbf{F}_2$ throughout D.

15. *Zero vector field?* Prove or disprove that if $\nabla \cdot \mathbf{F} = 0$ and $\nabla \times \mathbf{F} = \mathbf{0}$, then $\mathbf{F} = \mathbf{0}$.

16. *Volume as the flux of the position vector field* Show that the volume V of a region D in space enclosed by the oriented surface S with outward normal **n** satisfies the identity

$$V = \frac{1}{3} \iint_S \mathbf{r} \cdot \mathbf{n}\, d\sigma,$$

where **r** is the position vector of the point (x, y, z) in D.

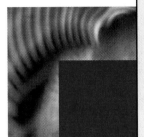

Appendices

A.1 Mathematical Induction

Many formulas, like

$$1 + 2 + \cdots + n = \frac{n(n + 1)}{2},$$

can be shown to hold for every positive integer n by applying an axiom called the *mathematical induction principle*. A proof that uses this axiom is called a *proof by mathematical induction* or a *proof by induction*.

The steps in proving a formula by induction are the following.

Step 1: Check that the formula holds for $n = 1$.

Step 2: Prove that if the formula holds for any positive integer $n = k$, then it also holds for the next integer, $n = k + 1$.

Once these steps are completed (the axiom says), we know that the formula holds for all positive integers n. By step 1, it holds for $n = 1$. By step 2, it holds for $n = 2$, and therefore by step 2 also for $n = 3$, and by step 2 again for $n = 4$, and so on. If the first domino falls, and the kth domino always knocks over the $(k + 1)$st when it falls, all the dominoes fall.

From another point of view, suppose we have a sequence of statements S_1, S_2, $\ldots, S_n, \ldots$, one for each positive integer. Suppose we can also show that assuming any one of the statements to be true implies the next statement in line is true. Finally, suppose we can show that S_1 is true. Then we may conclude that the statements are true from S_1 on.

Example 1   Sum of the First n Positive Integers

Prove that for every positive integer n,

$$1 + 2 + \cdots + n = \frac{n(n + 1)}{2}.$$

Solution   We accomplish the proof by carrying out the two steps above.

Step 1: The formula holds for $n = 1$ because

$$1 = \frac{1(1 + 1)}{2}.$$

1143

Step 2: If the formula holds for $n = k$, does it also hold for $n = k + 1$? The answer is yes, and here's why: If

$$1 + 2 + \cdots + k = \frac{k(k + 1)}{2},$$

then

$$1 + 2 + \cdots + k + (k + 1) = \frac{k(k + 1)}{2} + (k + 1) = \frac{k^2 + k + 2k + 2}{2}$$

$$= \frac{(k + 1)(k + 2)}{2} = \frac{(k + 1)((k + 1) + 1)}{2}.$$

The last expression in this string of equalities is the expression $n(n + 1)/2$ for $n = (k + 1)$.

The mathematical induction principle now guarantees the original formula for all positive integers n. Notice that all *we* have to do is carry out steps 1 and 2. The mathematical induction principle does the rest.

Example 2   Sum of Powers of 1/2

Prove that for all positive integers n,

$$\frac{1}{2^1} + \frac{1}{2^2} + \cdots + \frac{1}{2^n} = 1 - \frac{1}{2^n}.$$

Solution   We accomplish the proof by carrying out the two steps of mathematical induction.

Step 1: The formula holds for $n = 1$ because

$$\frac{1}{2^1} = 1 - \frac{1}{2^1}.$$

Step 2: If

$$\frac{1}{2^1} + \frac{1}{2^2} + \cdots + \frac{1}{2^k} = 1 - \frac{1}{2^k},$$

then

$$\frac{1}{2^1} + \frac{1}{2^2} + \cdots + \frac{1}{2^k} + \frac{1}{2^{k+1}} = 1 - \frac{1}{2^k} + \frac{1}{2^{k+1}} = 1 - \frac{1 \cdot 2}{2^k \cdot 2} + \frac{1}{2^{k+1}}$$

$$= 1 - \frac{2}{2^{k+1}} + \frac{1}{2^{k+1}} = 1 - \frac{1}{2^{k+1}}.$$

Thus, the original formula holds for $n = (k + 1)$ whenever it holds for $n = k$.

With these steps verified, the mathematical induction principle now guarantees the formula for every positive integer n.

Other Starting Integers

Instead of starting at $n = 1$, some induction arguments start at another integer. The steps for such an argument are as follows.

Step 1: Check that the formula holds for $n = n_1$ (the first appropriate integer).

Step 2: Prove that if the formula holds for any integer $n = k \geq n_1$, then it also holds for $n = (k + 1)$.

Once these steps are completed, the mathematical induction principle guarantees the formula for all $n \geq n_1$.

Example 3   Factorial Exceeding Exponential

Show that $n! > 3^n$ if n is large enough.

Solution   How large is large enough? We experiment:

n	1	2	3	4	5	6	7
$n!$	1	2	6	24	120	720	5040
3^n	3	9	27	81	243	729	2187

It looks as if $n! > 3^n$ for $n \geq 7$. To be sure, we apply mathematical induction. We take $n_1 = 7$ in step 1 and try for step 2.

Suppose that $k! > 3^k$ for some $k \geq 7$. Then

$$(k + 1)! = (k + 1)(k!) > (k + 1)\, 3^k > 7 \cdot 3^k > 3^{k+1}.$$

Thus, for $k \geq 7$,

$$k! > 3^k \quad \Rightarrow \quad (k + 1)! > 3^{k+1}.$$

The mathematical induction principle now guarantees $n! \geq 3^n$ for all $n \geq 7$.

EXERCISES A.1

1. *General triangle inequality* Assuming that the triangle inequality $|a + b| \leq |a| + |b|$ holds for any two numbers a and b, show that

$$|x_1 + x_2 + \cdots + x_n| \leq |x_1| + |x_2| + \cdots + |x_n|$$

for any n numbers.

2. *Geometric sum* Show that if $r \neq 1$, then

$$1 + r + r^2 + \cdots + r^n = \frac{1 - r^{n+1}}{1 - r}$$

for every positive integer n.

3. *Positive integer power rule* Use the Product Rule,

$$\frac{d}{dx}(uv) = u\frac{dv}{dx} + v\frac{du}{dx},$$

and the equation

$$\frac{d}{dx}(x) = 1$$

to show that

$$\frac{d}{dx}(x^n) = nx^{n-1}$$

for every positive integer n.

4. *Products into sums* Suppose a function $f(x)$ has the property that $f(x_1 x_2) = f(x_1) + f(x_2)$ for any two positive numbers x_1 and x_2. Show that

$$f(x_1 x_2 \cdots x_n) = f(x_1) + f(x_2) + \cdots + f(x_n)$$

for the product of any n positive numbers $x_1, x_2 \ldots, x_n$.

5. *Geometric sum* Show that

$$\frac{2}{3^1} + \frac{2}{3^2} + \cdots + \frac{2}{3^n} = 1 - \frac{1}{3^n}$$

for all positive integers n.

6. Show that $n! > n^3$ if n is large enough.

7. Show that $2^n > n^2$ if n is large enough.

8. Show that $2^n \geq 1/8$ for $n \geq -3$.

9. *Sums of squares* Show that the sum of the squares of the first n positive integers is

$$\frac{n\left(n + \dfrac{1}{2}\right)(n + 1)}{3}.$$

10. *Sums of cubes* Show that the sum of the cubes of the first n positive integers is $(n(n + 1)/2)^2$.

11. *Rules for finite sums* Show that the following finite sum rules hold for every positive integer n.

(a) $\displaystyle\sum_{k=1}^{n} (a_k + b_k) = \sum_{k=1}^{n} a_k + \sum_{k=1}^{n} b_k$

(b) $\displaystyle\sum_{k=1}^{n} (a_k - b_k) = \sum_{k=1}^{n} a_k - \sum_{k=1}^{n} b_k$

(c) $\displaystyle\sum_{k=1}^{n} ca_k = c \cdot \sum_{k=1}^{n} a_k$ (any number c)

(d) $\displaystyle\sum_{k=1}^{n} a_k = n \cdot c$ (if a_k has the constant value c)

12. *Integer powers and absolute value* Show that $|x^n| = |x|^n$ for every positive integer n and every real number x.

A.2 Proofs of Limit Theorems in Section 1.2

This appendix proves Theorem 1 and Theorem 4 from Section 1.2.

Theorem 1   Properties of Limits

The following rules hold if $\lim_{x \to c} f(x) = L$ and $\lim_{x \to c} g(x) = M$ (L and M real numbers).

1. *Sum Rule:* $\qquad\qquad\qquad\qquad$ $\displaystyle\lim_{x \to c} [f(x) + g(x)] = L + M$

2. *Difference Rule:* $\qquad\qquad\quad$ $\displaystyle\lim_{x \to c} [f(x) - g(x)] = L - M$

3. *Product Rule:* $\qquad\qquad\qquad$ $\displaystyle\lim_{x \to c} f(x) \cdot g(x) = L \cdot M$

4. *Constant Multiple Rule:* $\qquad$ $\displaystyle\lim_{x \to c} k f(x) = kL$ (any number k)

5. *Quotient Rule:* $\qquad\qquad\qquad$ $\displaystyle\lim_{x \to c} \frac{f(x)}{g(x)} = \frac{L}{M},$ if $M \neq 0$

6. *Power Rule:* $\qquad\qquad\qquad\quad$ If m and n are integers, then

$$\lim_{x \to c} [f(x)]^{m/n} = L^{m/n}$$

provided $L^{m/n}$ is a real number.

Proof of the Sum Rule   Let $\epsilon > 0$ be given. We want to find a positive number δ such that for all x

$$0 < |x - c| < \delta \implies |f(x) + g(x) - (L + M)| < \epsilon.$$

Regrouping terms, we get

$$|f(x) + g(x) - (L + M)| = |(f(x) - L) + (g(x) - M)|$$

$$\leq |f(x) - L| + |g(x) - M|. \qquad \text{Triangle Inequality:}$$
$$\qquad\qquad\qquad\qquad\qquad\qquad\qquad\qquad |a + b| \leq |a| + |b|$$

Since $\lim_{x \to c} f(x) = L$, there exists a number $\delta_1 > 0$ such that for all x

$$0 < |x - c| < \delta_1 \Rightarrow |f(x) - L| < \epsilon/2.$$

Similarly, since $\lim_{x \to c} g(x) = M$, there exists a number $\delta_2 > 0$ such that for all x

$$0 < |x - c| < \delta_2 \Rightarrow |g(x) - M| < \epsilon/2.$$

Let $\delta = \min\{\delta_1, \delta_2\}$, the smaller of δ_1 and δ_2. If $0 < |x - c| < \delta$ then $|x - c| < \delta_1$, so $|f(x) - L| < \epsilon/2$, and $|x - c| < \delta_2$, so $|g(x) - M| < \epsilon/2$. Therefore,

$$|f(x) + g(x) - (L + M)| < \frac{\epsilon}{2} + \frac{\epsilon}{2} = \epsilon,$$

which shows that $\lim_{x \to c} (f(x) + g(x)) = L + M$. ▬

CD-ROM
WEBsite

Historical Biography

John Wallis
(1616 — 1703)

The Difference Rule is obtained by replacing $g(x)$ by $-g(x)$ and M by $-M$ in the Sum Rule. The Constant Multiple Rule is the special case $g(x) = k$ of the Product Rule. The Power Rule is proved in more advanced texts, but we prove here the Product and Quotient Rules.

Proof of the Limit Product Rule   We show that for any $\epsilon > 0$ there exists a $\delta > 0$ such that for all x in the intersection D of the domains of f and g,

$$0 < |x - c| < \delta \Rightarrow |f(x)\, g(x) - LM| < \epsilon.$$

Suppose then that ϵ is a positive number and write $f(x)$ and $g(x)$ as

$$f(x) = L + (f(x) - L), \qquad g(x) = M + (g(x) - M).$$

Multiply these expressions together and subtract LM:

$$
\begin{aligned}
f(x) \cdot g(x) - LM &= (L + (f(x) - L))(M + (g(x) - M)) - LM \\
&= LM + L(g(x) - M) + M(f(x) - L) + \\
&\quad (f(x) - L)(g(x) - M) - LM \\
&= L(g(x) - M) + M(f(x) - L) + (f(x) - L)(g(x) - M).
\end{aligned}
\tag{1}
$$

Since f and g have limits L and M as $x \to c$, there exist positive numbers δ_1, δ_2, δ_3, and δ_4 such that for all x in D

$$
\begin{aligned}
0 < |x - c| < \delta_1 &\Rightarrow |f(x) - L| < \sqrt{\epsilon/3} \\
0 < |x - c| < \delta_2 &\Rightarrow |g(x) - M| < \sqrt{\epsilon/3} \\
0 < |x - c| < \delta_3 &\Rightarrow |f(x) - L| < \epsilon/(3(1 + |M|)) \\
0 < |x - c| < \delta_4 &\Rightarrow |g(x) - M| < \epsilon/(3(1 + |L|)).
\end{aligned}
\tag{2}
$$

If we take δ to be the smallest of the numbers δ_1 through δ_4, the inequalities on the right-hand side of (2) will hold simultaneously for $0 < |x - c| < \delta$. Therefore, for all x in D, $0 < |x - c| < \delta$ implies

$$
\begin{aligned}
&|f(x) \cdot g(x) - LM| \\
&\leq |L||g(x) - M| + |M||f(x) - L| + |f(x) - L||g(x) - M| \\
&\leq (1 + |L|)|g(x) - M| + (1 + |M|)|f(x) - L| + |f(x) - L||g(x) - M| \\
&\leq \frac{\epsilon}{3} + \frac{\epsilon}{3} + \sqrt{\frac{\epsilon}{3}}\sqrt{\frac{\epsilon}{3}} = \epsilon.
\end{aligned}
$$

Triangle inequality applied to Eq. (1)

Values from Eq. (2)

This completes the proof of the Limit Product Rule. ▬

Proof of the Limit Quotient Rule   We show that $\lim_{x \to c} (1/g(x)) = 1/M$. We can then conclude from the Limit Product Rule that

$$\lim_{x \to c} \frac{f(x)}{g(x)} = \lim_{x \to c} \left(f(x) \cdot \frac{1}{g(x)} \right) = \lim_{x \to c} f(x) \cdot \lim_{x \to c} g(x) = L \cdot \frac{1}{M} = \frac{L}{M}.$$

Let $\epsilon > 0$ be given. To show that $\lim_{x \to c} (1/g(x)) = 1/M$, we need to show that there exists a $\delta > 0$ such that for all x

$$0 < |x - c| < \delta \;\Rightarrow\; \left| \frac{1}{g(x)} - \frac{1}{M} \right| < \epsilon.$$

Since $|M| > 0$, there exists a positive number δ_1 such that for all x

$$0 < |x - c| < \delta_1 \;\Rightarrow\; |g(x) - M| < \left| \frac{M}{2} \right|. \tag{3}$$

CD–ROM
WEBsite

Historical Biography

Gilles Personne
de Roberval
(1602 — 1675)

For any numbers A and B it can be shown that $|A| - |B| \le |A - B|$ and $|B| - |A| \le |A - B|$, from which it follows that $||A| - |B|| \le |A - B|$. With $A = g(x)$ and $B = M$, this becomes

$$||g(x)| - |M|| \le |g(x) - M|,$$

which can be combined with the inequality on the right in Eq. (3) to get, in turn,

$$||g(x)| - |M|| < \frac{|M|}{2}$$

$$-\frac{|M|}{2} < |g(x)| - |M| < \frac{|M|}{2}$$

$$\frac{|M|}{2} < |g(x)| < \frac{3|M|}{2} \tag{4}$$

$$|M| < 2|g(x)| < 3|M|$$

$$\frac{1}{|g(x)|} < \frac{2}{|M|} < \frac{3}{|g(x)|}.$$

Therefore, $0 < |x - c| < \delta_1$ implies that

$$\left| \frac{1}{g(x)} - \frac{1}{M} \right| = \left| \frac{M - g(x)}{Mg(x)} \right| \le \frac{1}{|M|} \cdot \frac{1}{|g(x)|} \cdot |M - g(x)|$$

$$< \frac{1}{|M|} \cdot \frac{2}{|M|} \cdot |M - g(x)|. \qquad \text{Inequality (4)} \tag{5}$$

Since $(1/2)|M|^2 \epsilon > 0$, there exists a number $\delta_2 > 0$ such that for all x

$$0 < |x - c| < \delta_2 \;\Rightarrow\; |M - g(x)| < \frac{\epsilon}{2} |M|^2. \tag{6}$$

If we take δ to be the smaller of δ_1 and δ_2, the conclusions in Eqs. (5) and (6) both hold for all x such that $0 < |x - c| < \delta$. Combining these conclusions gives

$$0 < |x - c| < \delta \;\Rightarrow\; \left| \frac{1}{g(x)} - \frac{1}{M} \right| < \epsilon.$$

This concludes the proof of the Limit Quotient Rule.

> **Theorem 4** The Sandwich Theorem
>
> Suppose that $g(x) \leq f(x) \leq h(x)$ for all x in some open interval containing c, except possibly at $x = c$ itself. Suppose also that $\lim_{x \to c} g(x) = \lim_{x \to c} h(x) = L$. Then $\lim_{x \to c} f(x) = L$.

Proof for Right-hand Limits Suppose that $\lim_{x \to c^+} g(x) = \lim_{x \to c^+} h(x) = L$. Then for any $\epsilon > 0$ there exists a $\delta > 0$ such that for all x the inequality $c < x < c + \delta$ implies

$$L - \epsilon < g(x) < L + \epsilon \quad \text{and} \quad L - \epsilon < h(x) < L + \epsilon.$$

These inequalities combine with $g(x) \leq f(x) \leq h(x)$ to give

$$L - \epsilon < g(x) \leq f(x) \leq h(x) < L + \epsilon,$$

$$L - \epsilon < f(x) < L + \epsilon,$$

$$-\epsilon < f(x) - L < \epsilon.$$

Therefore, for all x, the inequality $c < x < c + \delta$ implies $|f(x) - L| < \epsilon$.   ━

Proof for Left-hand Limits Suppose that $\lim_{x \to c^-} g(x) = \lim_{x \to c^-} h(x) = L$. Then for any $\epsilon > 0$ there exists a $\delta > 0$ such that for all x the inequality $c - \delta < x < c$ implies

$$L - \epsilon < g(x) < L + \epsilon \quad \text{and} \quad L - \epsilon < h(x) < L + \epsilon.$$

We conclude as before that for all x, $c - \delta < x < c$ implies $|f(x) - L| < \epsilon$.   ━

Proof for Two-sided Limits If $\lim_{x \to c} g(x) = \lim_{x \to c} h(x) = L$, then $g(x)$ and $h(x)$ both approach L as $x \to c^+$ and as $x \to c^-$; so $\lim_{x \to c^+} f(x) = L$ and $\lim_{x \to c^-} f(x) = L$. Hence, $\lim_{x \to c} f(x)$ exists and equals L.   ━

EXERCISES A.2

1. *Generalized limit sum rule* Suppose that functions $f_1(x), f_2(x)$, and $f_3(x)$ have limits L_1, L_2, and L_3, respectively, as $x \to c$. Show that their sum has limit $L_1 + L_2 + L_3$. Use mathematical induction (Appendix 1) to generalize this result to the sum of any finite number of functions.

2. *Generalized limit product rule* Use mathematical induction and the Limit Product Rule in Theorem 1 to show that if functions $f_1(x)$, $f_2(x), \ldots, f_n(x)$ have limits L_1, L_2, $\ldots$, L_n as $x \to c$, then

$$\lim_{x \to c} f_1(x) f_2(x) \cdot \cdots \cdot f_n(x) = L_1 \cdot L_2 \cdot \cdots \cdot L_n.$$

3. *Positive integer power rule* Use the fact that $\lim_{x \to c} x = c$ and the result of Exercise 2 to show that $\lim_{x \to c} x^n = c^n$ for any integer $n > 1$.

4. *Limits of polynomials* Use the fact that $\lim_{x \to c} (k) = k$ for any number k together with the results of Exercises 1 and 3 to show that $\lim_{x \to c} f(x) = f(c)$ for any polynomial function

$$f(x) = a_n x^n + a_{n-1} x^{n-1} + \cdots + a_1 x + a_0.$$

5. *Limits of rational functions* Use Theorem 1 and the result of Exercise 4 to show that if $f(x)$ and $g(x)$ are polynomial functions and $g(c) \neq 0$, then

$$\lim_{x \to c} \frac{f(x)}{g(x)} = \frac{f(c)}{g(c)}.$$

6. *Composites of continuous functions* Figure A.1 gives the diagram for a proof that the composite of two continuous functions is continuous. Reconstruct the proof from the diagram. The statement to be proved is this: If f is continuous at $x = c$ and g is continuous at $f(c)$, then $g \circ f$ is continuous at c.

Assume that c is an interior point of the domain of f and that $f(c)$ is an interior point of the domain of g. This will make the limits involved two-sided. (The arguments for the cases that involve one-sided limits are similar.)

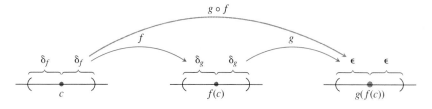

FIGURE A.1 A diagram for a proof that the composite of two continuous functions is continuous. The continuity of composites holds for any finite number of functions. The only requirement is that each function be continuous where it is applied. In the figure, f is to be continuous at c and g at $f(c)$.

A.3 Proof of the Chain Rule

This appendix proves the Chain Rule in Section 2.5 using ideas from Section 3.6.

> **Theorem 4** The Chain Rule
>
> If $f(u)$ is differentiable at the point $u = g(x)$, and $g(x)$ is differentiable at x, then the composite function $(f \circ g)(x) = f(g(x))$ is differentiable at x, and
>
> $$(f \circ g)'(x) = f'(g(x)) \cdot g'(x).$$
>
> In Leibniz's notation, if $y = f(u)$ and $u = g(x)$, then
>
> $$\frac{dy}{dx} = \frac{dy}{du} \cdot \frac{du}{dx},$$
>
> where dy/du is evaluated at $u = g(x)$.

Proof To be more precise, we show that if g is differentiable at x_0 and f is differentiable at $g(x_0)$, then the composite is differentiable at x_0 and

$$\left. \frac{dy}{dx} \right|_{x=x_0} = f'(g(x_0)) \cdot g'(x_0).$$

Let Δx be an increment in x and let Δu and Δy be the corresponding increments in u and y. As you can see in Figure A.2,

$$\left. \frac{dy}{dx} \right|_{x=x_0} = \lim_{\Delta x \to 0} \frac{\Delta y}{\Delta x},$$

so our goal is to show that this limit is $f'(g(x_0)) \cdot g'(x_0)$.

By Equation (3) in Section 3.6,

$$\Delta u = g'(x_0)\,\Delta x + \epsilon_1\,\Delta x = (g'(x_0) + \epsilon_1)\,\Delta x,$$

where $\epsilon_1 \to 0$ as $\Delta x \to 0$. Similarly,

$$\Delta y = f'(u_0)\,\Delta u + \epsilon_2\,\Delta u = (f'(u_0) + \epsilon_2)\,\Delta u,$$

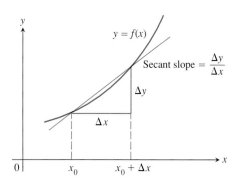

FIGURE A.2 The graph of y as a function of x. The derivative of y with respect to x at $x = x_0$ is $\lim_{\Delta x \to 0} \Delta y / \Delta x$.

where $\epsilon_2 \to 0$ as $\Delta u \to 0$. Notice also that $\Delta u \to 0$ as $\Delta x \to 0$. Combining the equations for Δu and Δy gives

$$\Delta y = (f'(u_0) + \epsilon_2)(g'(x_0) + \epsilon_1) \, \Delta x,$$

so

$$\frac{\Delta y}{\Delta x} = f'(u_0) \, g'(x_0) + \epsilon_2 \, g'(x_0) + f'(u_0) \, \epsilon_1 + \epsilon_2 \epsilon_1.$$

Since ϵ_1 and ϵ_2 go to zero as Δx goes to zero, three of the four terms on the right vanish in the limit, leaving

$$\lim_{\Delta x \to 0} \frac{\Delta y}{\Delta x} = f'(u_0) \, g'(x_0) = f'(g(x_0)) \cdot g'(x_0).$$

This concludes the proof.

Complex Numbers

The Development of the Real Numbers • The Complex Number System • Argand Diagrams • Euler's Formula • Products • Quotients • Powers and De Moivre's Theorem • Roots • The Fundamental Theorem of Algebra

Complex numbers are expressions of the form $a + ib$, where a and b are real numbers and i is a symbol for $\sqrt{-1}$. Unfortunately, "real" and "imaginary" have connotations that somehow place $\sqrt{-1}$ in a less favorable position in our minds than $\sqrt{2}$. As a matter of fact, a good deal of imagination, in the sense of *inventiveness,* has been required to construct the *real* number system, which forms the basis of the calculus. In this appendix, we review the various stages of this invention. The further invention of a complex number system will then not seem so strange.

The Development of the Real Numbers

The earliest stage of number development was the recognition of the **counting numbers** $1, 2, 3, \ldots$, which we now call the **natural numbers** or the **positive integers.** These numbers can be added or multiplied together without getting outside the system. That is, the system of positive integers is **closed** under the operations of addition and multiplication. If m and n are any positive integers, then

$$m + n = p \qquad \text{and} \qquad mn = q \tag{1}$$

are also positive integers.

Given the two positive integers on the left-hand side of either equation in Equations (1), we can find the corresponding positive integer on the right. More than this, we can sometimes specify the positive integers m and p and find a positive integer n such that $m + n = p$. For instance, $3 + n = 7$ can be solved when the only numbers we know are the positive integers. The equation $7 + n = 3$, however, cannot be solved unless the number system is enlarged.

The number zero and the negative integers were invented to solve equations like $7 + n = 3$. In a civilization that recognizes all the **integers**

$$\ldots, -3, -2, -1, 0, 1, 2, 3, \ldots, \tag{2}$$

an educated person can always find the missing integer that solves the equation $m + n = p$ when given the other two integers in the equation.

Suppose that our educated people also know how to multiply any two of the integers in Equation (2). If, in Equations (1), they are given m and q, they discover that sometimes they can find n and sometimes they cannot. If their imagination is still in good working order, they may be inspired to invent still more numbers and introduce fractions as ordered pairs m/n of integers m and n. The number zero has special properties that may bother them for a while, but they ultimately discover that it is handy to have all ratios of integers m/n, excluding only those having zero in the denominator. This system, called the set of **rational numbers,** is now rich enough for them to perform the so-called **rational operations** of arithmetic:

1. (a) addition   **2.** (a) multiplication

    (b) subtraction   (b) division

on any two numbers in the system, *except that they cannot divide by zero.*

The geometry of the unit square (Figure A.3) and the Pythagorean Theorem showed that they could construct a geometric line segment that, in terms of some basic unit of length, has length equal to $\sqrt{2}$. Thus, they could solve the equation

$$x^2 = 2$$

by a geometric construction. Then they discovered, however, that the line segment representing $\sqrt{2}$ and the line segment representing the unit of length 1 were incommensurable quantities. This means that the ratio $\sqrt{2}/1$ cannot be expressed as the ratio of two *integer* multiples of some other, presumably more fundamental, unit of length. That is, our educated people could not find a rational number solution of the equation $x^2 = 2$.

They could not find it because there *is* no rational number whose square is 2. To see why, suppose that there were such a rational number. Then we could find integers p and q with no common factor other than 1 and such that

$$\left(\frac{p}{q}\right)^2 = 2$$

or

$$p^2 = 2q^2. \tag{3}$$

Since p and q are integers, p must be even; otherwise, its product with itself would be odd. In symbols, $p = 2p_1$, where p_1 is an integer. This step leads to $2p_1^2 = q^2$, which says q must be even, say $q = 2q_1$, where q_1 is an integer. This makes 2 a factor of both p and q, contrary to our choice of p and q as integers with no common factor other than 1. Hence, there is no rational number whose square is 2.

Although our educated people could not find a rational solution of the equation $x^2 = 2$, they could get a sequence of rational numbers

$$\frac{1}{1}, \quad \frac{7}{5}, \quad \frac{41}{29}, \quad \frac{239}{169}, \quad \cdots, \tag{4}$$

whose squares form a sequence

$$\frac{1}{1}, \quad \frac{49}{25}, \quad \frac{1681}{841}, \quad \frac{57,121}{28,561}, \quad \cdots \tag{5}$$

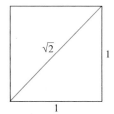

Figure A.3 With a straightedge and compass, it is possible to construct a line segment of irrational length.

that converges to 2 as its limit. This time their imagination suggested that they needed a concept of a limit of a sequence of rational numbers. If we accept that an increasing sequence that is bounded from above always approaches a limit and observe that the sequence in Equation (4) has these properties, then we want it to have a limit L. This assumption would also mean, from Equation (5), that $L^2 = 2$, and hence L is *not* one of our rational numbers. If to the rational numbers we further add the limits of all bounded increasing sequences of rational numbers, we arrive at the system of all "real" numbers. The word *real* is placed in quotes because there is nothing that is either "more real" or "less real" about this system than there is about any other mathematical system.

The Complex Number System

Imagination was called upon at many stages during the development of the real number system. In fact, the art of invention was needed at least three times in constructing the systems we have discussed so far:

1. The *first invented* system: the set of *all integers* as constructed from the counting numbers

2. The *second invented* system: the set of *rational numbers* m/n as constructed from the integers

3. The *third invented* system: the set of all *real numbers* x as constructed from the rational numbers.

These invented systems form a hierarchy in which each system contains the previous system. Each system is also richer than its predecessor in that it permits additional operations to be performed without going outside the system:

1. In the system of all integers, we can solve all equations of the form

$$x + a = 0, \tag{6}$$

where a can be any integer.

2. In the system of all rational numbers, we can solve all equations of the form

$$ax + b = 0, \tag{7}$$

provided a and b are rational numbers and $a \neq 0$.

3. In the system of all real numbers, we can solve all the equations in Equations (6) and (7) and, in addition, all quadratic equations

$$ax^2 + bx + c = 0 \quad \text{having} \quad a \neq 0 \quad \text{and} \quad b^2 - 4ac \geq 0. \tag{8}$$

You are probably familiar with the formula that gives the solutions of Equation (8), namely,

$$x = \frac{-b \pm \sqrt{b^2 - 4ac}}{2a}, \tag{9}$$

and also know that when the discriminant, $d = b^2 - 4ac$, is negative, the solutions in Equation (9) do *not* belong to any of the systems discussed above. In fact, the very simple quadratic equation

$$x^2 + 1 = 0$$

is impossible to solve if the only number systems that can be used are the three invented systems mentioned so far.

Thus, we come to the *fourth invented* system, the set of all complex numbers $a + ib$. We could dispense entirely with the symbol i and use a notation like (a, b). We would then speak simply of a pair of real numbers a and b. Since, under algebraic operations, the numbers a and b are treated somewhat differently, it is essential to keep the *order* straight. We therefore might say that the **complex number system** consists of the set of all ordered pairs of real numbers (a, b), together with the rules by which they are to be equated, added, multiplied, and so on, listed below. We use both the (a, b) notation and the notation $a + ib$ in the discussion that follows. We call a the **real part** and b the **imaginary part** of the complex number (a, b).

We make the following definitions.

Equality

$$a + ib = c + id$$
if and only if
$$a = c \quad \text{and} \quad b = d$$

Two complex numbers (a, b) and (c, d) are *equal* if and only if $a = c$ and $b = d$.

Addition

$$(a + ib) + (c + id)$$
$$= (a + c) + i(b + d)$$

The sum of the two complex numbers (a, b) and (c, d) is the complex number $(a + c, b + d)$.

Multiplication

$$(a + ib)(c + id)$$
$$= (ac - bd) + i(ad + bc)$$

The product of two complex numbers (a, b) and (c, d) is the complex number $(ac - bd, ad + bc)$.

$$c(a + ib) = ac + i(bc)$$

The product of a real number c and the complex number (a, b) is the complex number (ac, bc).

The set of all complex numbers (a, b) in which the second number b is zero has all the properties of the set of real numbers a. For example, addition and multiplication of $(a, 0)$ and $(c, 0)$ give

$$(a, 0) + (c, 0) = (a + c, 0)$$
$$(a, 0) \cdot (c, 0) = (ac, 0),$$

which are numbers of the same type with imaginary part equal to zero. Also, if we multiply a "real number" $(a, 0)$ and the complex number (c, d), we get

$$(a, 0) \cdot (c, d) = (ac, ad) = a(c, d).$$

In particular, the complex number $(0, 0)$ plays the role of zero in the complex number system, and the complex number $(1, 0)$ plays the role of unity.

The number pair $(0, 1)$, which has real part equal to zero and imaginary part equal to one, has the property that its square,

$$(0, 1)(0, 1) = (-1, 0),$$

has real part equal to minus one and imaginary part equal to zero. Therefore, in the system of complex numbers (a, b), there is a number $x = (0, 1)$ whose square can be added to unity $= (1, 0)$ to produce zero $= (0, 0)$; that is,

$$(0, 1)^2 + (1, 0) = (0, 0).$$

The equation

$$x^2 + 1 = 0$$

therefore has a solution $x = (0, 1)$ in this new number system.

You are probably more familiar with the $a + ib$ notation than you are with the notation (a, b). And since the laws of algebra for the ordered pairs enable us to write

$$(a, b) = (a, 0) + (0, b) = a(1, 0) + b(0, 1),$$

whereas $(1, 0)$ behaves like unity and $(0, 1)$ behaves like a square root of minus one, we need not hesitate to write $a + ib$ in place of (a, b). The i associated with b is like a tracer element that tags the imaginary part of $a + ib$. We can pass at will from the realm of ordered pairs (a, b) to the realm of expressions $a + ib$, and conversely. Yet there is nothing less "real" about the symbol $(0, 1) = i$ than there is about the symbol $(1, 0) = 1$, once we have learned the laws of algebra in the complex number system (a, b).

To reduce any rational combination of complex numbers to a single complex number, we apply the laws of elementary algebra, replacing i^2 wherever it appears by -1. Of course, we cannot divide by the complex number $(0, 0) = 0 + i0$. If $a + ib \neq 0$, however, we may carry out a division as follows:

$$\frac{c + id}{a + ib} = \frac{(c + id)(a - ib)}{(a + ib)(a - ib)} = \frac{(ac + bd) + i(ad - bc)}{a^2 + b^2}.$$

The result is a complex number $x + iy$ with

$$x = \frac{ac + bd}{a^2 + b^2}, \qquad y = \frac{ad - bc}{a^2 + b^2},$$

and $a^2 + b^2 \neq 0$, since $a + ib = (a, b) \neq (0, 0)$.

The number $a - ib$ that is used as multiplier to clear the i from the denominator is called the **complex conjugate** of $a + ib$. It is customary to use $\bar{z}$ (read "z bar") to denote the complex conjugate of z; thus,

$$z = a + ib, \qquad \bar{z} = a - ib.$$

Multiplying the numerator and denominator of the fraction $(c + id)/(a + ib)$ by the complex conjugate of the denominator will always replace the denominator by a real number.

Example 1   Operations with Complex Numbers

(a) $(2 + 3i) + (6 - 2i) = (2 + 6) + (3 - 2)i = 8 + i$

(b) $(2 + 3i) - (6 - 2i) = (2 - 6) + (3 - (-2))i = -4 + 5i$

(c) $(2 + 3i)(6 - 2i) = (2)(6) + (2)(-2i) + (3i)(6) + (3i)(-2i)$

$$= 12 - 4i + 18i - 6i^2 = 12 + 14i + 6 = 18 + 14i$$

(d) $\dfrac{2 + 3i}{6 - 2i} = \dfrac{2 + 3i}{6 - 2i}\dfrac{6 + 2i}{6 + 2i}$

$$= \frac{12 + 4i + 18i + 6i^2}{36 + 12i - 12i - 4i^2}$$

$$= \frac{6 + 22i}{40} = \frac{3}{20} + \frac{11}{20}i$$

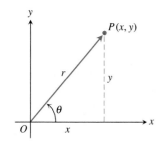

FIGURE A.4 This Argand diagram represents $z = x + iy$ both as a point $P(x, y)$ and as a vector $\overrightarrow{OP}$.

Argand Diagrams

There are two geometric representations of the complex number $z = x + iy$:

1. as the point $P(x, y)$ in the xy-plane

2. as the vector $\overrightarrow{OP}$ from the origin to P.

In each representation, the x-axis is called the **real axis** and the y-axis is the **imaginary axis**. Both representations are **Argand diagrams** for $x + iy$ (Figure A.4).

In terms of the polar coordinates of x and y, we have

$$x = r \cos \theta, \qquad y = r \sin \theta,$$

and

$$z = x + iy = r(\cos \theta + i \sin \theta). \tag{10}$$

We define the **absolute value** of a complex number $x + iy$ to be the length r of a vector $\overrightarrow{OP}$ from the origin to $P(x, y)$. We denote the absolute value by vertical bars; thus,

$$|x + iy| = \sqrt{x^2 + y^2}.$$

If we always choose the polar coordinates r and θ so that r is nonnegative, then

$$r = |x + iy|.$$

The polar angle θ is called the **argument** of z and is written $\theta = \arg z$. Of course, any integer multiple of 2π may be added to θ to produce another appropriate angle.

The following equation gives a useful formula connecting a complex number z, its conjugate $\bar{z}$, and its absolute value $|z|$, namely,

$$z \cdot \bar{z} = |z|^2.$$

Euler's Formula

The identity

$$e^{i\theta} = \cos \theta + i \sin \theta,$$

called **Euler's formula,** enables us to rewrite Equation (10) as

$$z = re^{i\theta}.$$

This formula, in turn, leads to the following rules for calculating products, quotients, powers, and roots of complex numbers. It also leads to Argand diagrams for $e^{i\theta}$. Since $\cos \theta + i \sin \theta$ is what we get from Equation (10) by taking $r = 1$, we can say that $e^{i\theta}$ is represented by a unit vector that makes an angle θ with the positive x-axis, as shown in Figure A.5.

Products

To multiply two complex numbers, we multiply their absolute values and add their angles. Let

$$z_1 = r_1 e^{i\theta_1}, \qquad z_2 = r_2 e^{i\theta_2}, \tag{11}$$

so that

$$|z_1| = r_1, \qquad \arg z_1 = \theta_1; \qquad |z_2| = r_2, \qquad \arg z_2 = \theta_2.$$

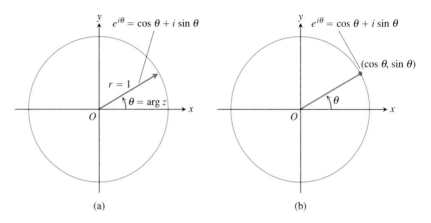

FIGURE A.5 Argand diagrams for $e^{i\theta} = \cos\theta + i\sin\theta$ (a) as a vector and (b) as a point.

Then

$$z_1 z_2 = r_1 e^{i\theta_1} \cdot r_2 e^{i\theta_2} = r_1 r_2 e^{i(\theta_1 + \theta_2)}$$

and hence

$$|z_1 z_2| = r_1 r_2 = |z_1| \cdot |z_2|$$
$$\arg(z_1 z_2) = \theta_1 + \theta_2 = \arg z_1 + \arg z_2. \tag{12}$$

Thus, the product of two complex numbers is represented by a vector whose length is the product of the lengths of the two factors and whose argument is the sum of their arguments (Figure A.6). In particular, a vector may be rotated counterclockwise through an angle θ by multiplying it by $e^{i\theta}$. Multiplication by i rotates 90°, by -1 rotates 180°, by $-i$ rotates 270°, and so on.

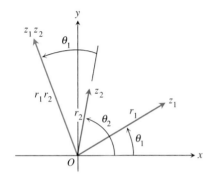

FIGURE A.6 When z_1 and z_2 are multiplied, $|z_1 z_2| = r_1 \cdot r_2$ and $\arg(z_1 z_2) = \theta_1 + \theta_2$.

Example 2   Finding a Product of Complex Numbers

Let $z_1 = 1 + i$, $z_2 = \sqrt{3} - i$. We plot these complex numbers in an Argand diagram (Figure A.7) from which we read off the polar representations

$$z_1 = \sqrt{2}e^{i\pi/4}, \qquad z_2 = 2e^{-i\pi/6}.$$

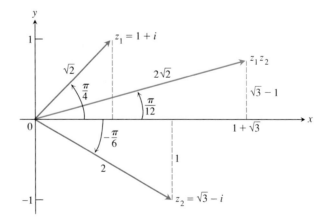

FIGURE A.7 To multiply two complex numbers, multiply their absolute values and add their arguments.

exp (A) stands for e^A.

Then

$$z_1 z_2 = 2\sqrt{2} \exp\left(\frac{i\pi}{4} - \frac{i\pi}{6}\right) = 2\sqrt{2} \exp\left(\frac{i\pi}{12}\right)$$

$$= 2\sqrt{2}\left(\cos\frac{\pi}{12} + i\sin\frac{\pi}{12}\right) \approx 2.73 + 0.73i.$$

Quotients

Suppose that $r_2 \neq 0$ in Equation (11). Then

$$\frac{z_1}{z_2} = \frac{r_1 e^{i\theta_1}}{r_2 e^{i\theta_2}} = \frac{r_1}{r_2} e^{i(\theta_1 - \theta_2)}.$$

Hence,

$$\left|\frac{z_1}{z_2}\right| = \frac{r_1}{r_2} = \frac{|z_1|}{|z_2|} \qquad \text{and} \qquad \arg\left(\frac{z_1}{z_2}\right) = \theta_1 - \theta_2 = \arg z_1 - \arg z_2.$$

That is, we divide lengths and subtract angles.

Example 3   Finding a Quotient of Complex Numbers

Let $z_1 = 1 + i$ and $z_2 = \sqrt{3} - i$, as in Example 2. Then

$$\frac{1+i}{\sqrt{3}-i} = \frac{\sqrt{2}e^{i\pi/4}}{2e^{-i\pi/6}} = \frac{\sqrt{2}}{2} e^{5\pi i/12} \approx 0.707\left(\cos\frac{5\pi}{12} + i\sin\frac{5\pi}{12}\right)$$

$$\approx 0.183 + 0.683i.$$

Powers and De Moivre's Theorem

If n is a positive integer, we may apply the product formulas in Equations (12) to find

$$z^n = z \cdot z \cdot \cdots \cdot z. \qquad n \text{ factors}$$

With $z = re^{i\theta}$, we obtain

$$z^n = (re^{i\theta})^n = r^n e^{i(\theta+\theta+\cdots+\theta)} \qquad n \text{ summands}$$

$$= r^n e^{in\theta}. \tag{13}$$

The length $r = |z|$ is raised to the nth power and the angle $\theta = \arg z$ is multiplied by n.

If we take $r = 1$ in Equation (13), we obtain De Moivre's Theorem.

> **De Moivre's Theorem**
> $$(\cos\theta + i\sin\theta)^n = \cos n\theta + i\sin n\theta. \tag{14}$$

If we expand the left-hand side of De Moivre's equation (Equation 14) by the Binomial Theorem and reduce it to the form $a + ib$, we obtain formulas for $\cos n\theta$ and $\sin n\theta$ as polynomials of degree n in $\cos\theta$ and $\sin\theta$.

Example 4 Obtaining Formulas for cos 3θ and sin 3θ

Express cos 3θ and sin 3θ in terms of cos θ and sin θ.

Solution Taking $n = 3$ in De Moivre's Equation (Equation (14)), we have

$$(\cos \theta + i \sin \theta)^3 = \cos 3\theta + i \sin 3\theta.$$

The left-hand side of this equation is

$$\cos^3 \theta + 3i \cos^2 \theta \sin \theta - 3 \cos \theta \sin^2 \theta - i \sin^3 \theta.$$

The real part of this must equal cos 3θ and the imaginary part must equal sin 3θ. Therefore,

$$\cos 3\theta = \cos^3 \theta - 3 \cos \theta \sin^2 \theta,$$
$$\sin 3\theta = 3 \cos^2 \theta \sin \theta - \sin^3 \theta.$$

Roots

If $z = re^{i\theta}$ is a complex number different from zero and n is a positive integer, then there are precisely n different complex numbers $w_0, w_1, \ldots, w_{n-1}$, that are nth roots of z. To see why, let $w = \rho e^{i\alpha}$ be an nth root of $z = re^{i\theta}$, so that

$$w^n = z$$

or

$$\rho^n e^{in\alpha} = re^{i\theta}.$$

Then

$$\rho = \sqrt[n]{r}$$

is the real, positive nth root of r. As regards the angle, although we cannot say that $n\alpha$ and θ must be equal, we can say that they may differ only by an integer multiple of 2π. That is,

$$n\alpha = \theta + 2k\pi, \qquad k = 0, \pm 1, \pm 2, \ldots.$$

Therefore,

$$\alpha = \frac{\theta}{n} + k \frac{2\pi}{n}.$$

Hence, all the nth roots of $z = re^{i\theta}$ are given by

$$\sqrt[n]{re^{i\theta}} = \sqrt[n]{r} \exp i\left(\frac{\theta}{n} + k \frac{2\pi}{n}\right), \qquad k = 0, \pm 1, \pm 2, \ldots. \qquad (15)$$

There might appear to be infinitely many different answers corresponding to the infinitely many possible values of k, but $k = n + m$ gives the same answer as $k = m$ in Equation (15). Thus, we need only take n consecutive values for k to obtain all the different nth roots of z. For convenience, we take

$$k = 0, 1, 2, \ldots, n - 1.$$

All the nth roots of $re^{i\theta}$ lie on a circle centered at the origin and having radius equal to the real, positive nth root of r. One of them has argument $\alpha = \theta/n$. The others are uniformly spaced around the circle, each being separated from its neighbors by an angle equal to $2\pi/n$. Figure A.8 illustrates the placement of the three cube roots, w_0, w_1, w_2, of the complex number $z = re^{i\theta}$.

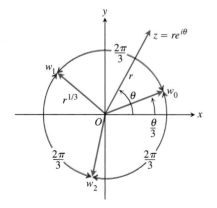

FIGURE A.8 **The three cube roots of** $z = re^{i\theta}$.

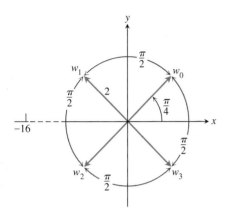

FIGURE A.9 The four fourth roots of -16.

Example 5   Finding Fourth Roots

Find the four fourth roots of -16.

Solution   As our first step, we plot the number -16 in an Argand diagram (Figure A.9) and determine its polar representation $re^{i\theta}$. Here, $z = -16$, $r = +16$, and $\theta = \pi$. One of the fourth roots of $16e^{i\pi}$ is $2e^{i\pi/4}$. We obtain others by successive additions of $2\pi/4 = \pi/2$ to the argument of this first one. Hence,

$$\sqrt[4]{16 \exp i\pi} = 2 \exp i\left(\frac{\pi}{4}, \frac{3\pi}{4}, \frac{5\pi}{4}, \frac{7\pi}{4}\right),$$

and the four roots are

$$w_0 = 2\left[\cos\frac{\pi}{4} + i\sin\frac{\pi}{4}\right] = \sqrt{2}\,(1 + i)$$

$$w_1 = 2\left[\cos\frac{3\pi}{4} + i\sin\frac{3\pi}{4}\right] = \sqrt{2}\,(-1 + i)$$

$$w_2 = 2\left[\cos\frac{5\pi}{4} + i\sin\frac{5\pi}{4}\right] = \sqrt{2}\,(-1 - i)$$

$$w_3 = 2\left[\cos\frac{7\pi}{4} + i\sin\frac{7\pi}{4}\right] = \sqrt{2}\,(1 - i).$$

The Fundamental Theorem of Algebra

One may well say that the invention of $\sqrt{-1}$ is all well and good and leads to a number system that is richer than the real number system alone, but where will this process end? Are we also going to invent still more systems so as to obtain $\sqrt[4]{-1}$, $\sqrt[6]{-1}$, and so on? By now it should be clear that is not necessary. These numbers are already expressible in terms of the complex number system $a + ib$. In fact, the Fundamental Theorem of Algebra says that with the introduction of the complex numbers, we have enough numbers to factor every polynomial into a product of linear factors and hence enough numbers to solve every possible polynomial equation.

The Fundamental Theorem of Algebra
Every polynomial equation of the form

$$a_n z^n + a_{n-1} z^{n-1} + a_{n-2} z^{n-2} + \cdots + a_1 z + a_0 = 0,$$

in which the coefficients $a_0, a_1, \ldots, a_n$ are any complex numbers, whose degree n is greater than or equal to one, and whose leading coefficient a_0 is not zero, has exactly n roots in the complex number system, provided each multiple root of multiplicity m is counted as m roots.

A proof of this theorem can be found in almost any text on the theory of functions of a complex variable.

EXERCISES A.4

Operations with Complex Numbers

1. *How computers multiply complex numbers* Find $(a, b) \cdot (c, d) = (ac - bd, ad + bc)$.

(a) $(2, 3) \cdot (4, -2)$ (b) $(2, -1) \cdot (-2, 3)$

(c) $(-1, -2) \cdot (2, 1)$

(This is how complex numbers are multiplied by computers.)

2. Solve the following equations for the real numbers, x and y.

(a) $(3 + 4i)^2 - 2(x - iy) = x + iy$

(b) $\left(\dfrac{1 + i}{1 - i}\right)^2 + \dfrac{1}{x + iy} = 1 + i$

(c) $(3 - 2i)(x + iy) = 2(x - 2iy) + 2i - 1$

Graphing and Geometry

3. How may the following complex numbers be obtained from $z = x + iy$ geometrically? Sketch.

(a) $\bar{z}$ (b) $\overline{(-z)}$

(c) $-z$ (d) $1/z$

4. Show that the distance between the two points z_1 and z_2 in an Argand diagram is $|z_1 - z_2|$.

In Exercises 5–10, graph the points $z = x + iy$ that satisfy the given conditions.

5. (a) $|z| = 2$ (b) $|z| < 2$ (c) $|z| > 2$

6. $|z - 1| = 2$ **7.** $|z + 1| = 1$

8. $|z + 1| = |z - 1|$ **9.** $|z + i| = |z - 1|$

10. $|z + 1| \geq |z|$

Express the complex numbers in Exercises 11–14 in the form $re^{i\theta}$, with $r \geq 0$ and $-\pi < \theta \leq \pi$. Draw an Argand diagram for each calculation.

11. $(1 + \sqrt{-3})^2$ **12.** $\dfrac{1 + i}{1 - i}$

13. $\dfrac{1 + i\sqrt{3}}{1 - i\sqrt{3}}$ **14.** $(2 + 3i)(1 - 2i)$

Powers and Roots

Use De Moivre's Theorem to express the trigonometric functions in Exercises 15 and 16 in terms of $\cos \theta$ and $\sin \theta$.

15. $\cos 4\theta$

16. $\sin 4\theta$

17. Find the three cube roots of 1.

18. Find the two square roots of i.

19. Find the three cube roots of $-8i$.

20. Find the six sixth roots of 64.

21. Find the four solutions of the equation $z^4 - 2z^2 + 4 = 0$.

22. Find the six solutions of the equation $z^6 + 2z^3 + 2 = 0$.

23. Find all solutions of the equation $x^4 + 4x^2 + 16 = 0$.

24. Solve the equation $x^4 + 1 = 0$.

Theory and Examples

25. *Complex numbers and vectors in the plane* Show with an Argand diagram that the law for adding complex numbers is the same as the parallelogram law for adding vectors.

26. *Complex arithmetic with conjugates* Show that the conjugate of the sum (product, or quotient) of two complex numbers, z_1 and z_2 is the same as the sum (product, or quotient) of their conjugates.

27. *Complex roots of polynomials with real coefficients come in complex-conjugate pairs*

(a) Extend the results of Exercise 26 to show that $f(\bar{z}) = \overline{f(z)}$ if

$$f(z) = a_n z^n + a_{n-1} z^{n-1} + \cdots + a_1 z + a_0$$

is a polynomial with real coefficients $a_0, \ldots, a_n$.

(b) If z is a root of the equation $f(z) = 0$, where $f(z)$ is a polynomial with real coefficients as in part (a), show that the conjugate $\bar{z}$ is also a root of the equation. (*Hint:* Let $f(z) = u + iv = 0$; then both u and v are zero. Use the fact that $f(\bar{z}) = \overline{f(z)} = u - iv$.)

28. *Absolute value of a conjugate* Show that $|\bar{z}| = |z|$.

29. *When $z = \bar{z}$* If z and $\bar{z}$ are equal, what can you say about the location of the point z in the complex plane?

30. *Real and imaginary parts* Let $Re(z)$ denote the real part of z and $Im(z)$ the imaginary part. Show that the following relations hold for any complex numbers z, z_1, and z_2.

(a) $z + \bar{z} = 2Re(z)$ (b) $z - \bar{z} = 2i Im(z)$

(c) $|Re(z)| \leq |z|$

(d) $|z_1 + z_2|^2 = |z_1|^2 + |z_2|^2 + 2 Re(z_1 \bar{z}_2)$

(e) $|z_1 + z_2| \leq |z_1| + |z_2|$

A.5   Simpson's One-Third Rule

Simpson's rule for approximating $\int_a^b f(x)\,dx$ is based on approximating the graph of f with parabolic arcs.

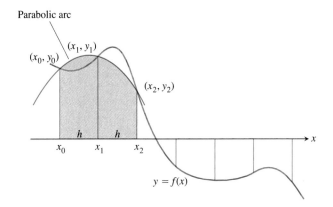

FIGURE A.10 Simpson's Rule approximates short stretches of curve with parabolic arcs.

The area of the shaded region under the parabola in Figure A.11 is

$$\text{Area} = \frac{h}{3}(y_0 + 4y_1 + y_2).$$

This formula is known as Simpson's One-Third Rule.

    We can derive the formula as follows. To simplify the algebra, we use the coordinate system in Figure A.11. The area under the parabola is the same no matter where the y-axis is, as long as we preserve the vertical scale. The parabola has an equation of the form $y = Ax^2 + Bx + C$, so the area under it from $x = -h$ to $x = h$ is

$$\text{Area} = \int_{-h}^{h}(Ax^2 + Bx + C)\,dx = \left[\frac{Ax^3}{3} + \frac{Bx^2}{2} + Cx\right]_{-h}^{h}$$

$$= \frac{2Ah^3}{3} + 2Ch$$

$$= \frac{h}{3}(2Ah^2 + 6C).$$

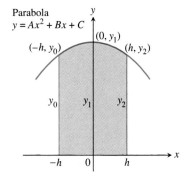

FIGURE A.11 By integrating from $-h$ to h, the shaded area is found to be
$$\frac{h}{3}(y_0 + 4y_1 + y_2).$$

Since the curve passes through $(-h, y_0)$, $(0, y_1)$, and (h, y_2), we also have

$$y_0 = Ah^2 - Bh + C, \qquad y_1 = C, \qquad y_2 = Ah^2 + Bh + C.$$

From these equations we obtain

$$C = y_1$$
$$Ah^2 - Bh = y_0 - y_1$$
$$Ah^2 + Bh = y_2 - y_1$$
$$2Ah^2 = y_0 + y_2 - 2y_1.$$

These substitutions for C and $2Ah^2$ give

$$\text{Area} = \frac{h}{3}(2Ah^2 + 6C) = \frac{h}{3}((y_0 + y_2 - 2y_1) + 6y_1) = \frac{h}{3}(y_0 + 4y_1 + y_2).$$

 A.6 Cauchy's Mean Value Theorem and the Stronger Form of l'Hôpital's Rule

This appendix proves the finite-limit case of the stronger form of l'Hôpital's Rule (Section 7.6, Theorem 2) as stated here.

L'Hôpital's Rule (Stronger Form)

Suppose that

$$f(x_0) = g(x_0) = 0$$

and that the functions f and g are both differentiable on an open interval (a, b) that contains the point x_0. Suppose also that $g'(x) \neq 0$ at every point in (a, b) except possibly x_0. Then

$$\lim_{x \to x_0} \frac{f(x)}{g(x)} = \lim_{x \to x_0} \frac{f'(x)}{g'(x)}, \tag{1}$$

assuming the limit on the right exists.

The proof of the stronger form of l'Hôpital's Rule is based on Cauchy's Mean Value Theorem, a Mean Value Theorem that involves two functions instead of one. We prove Cauchy's Theorem first and then show how it leads to l'Hôpital's Rule.

Cauchy's Mean Value Theorem

Suppose functions f and g are continuous on $[a, b]$ and differentiable throughout (a, b) and also suppose $g'(x) \neq 0$ throughout (a, b). Then there exists a number c in (a, b) at which

$$\frac{f'(c)}{g'(c)} = \frac{f(b) - f(a)}{g(b) - g(a)}. \tag{2}$$

The ordinary Mean Value Theorem (Section 3.2, Theorem 4) is the case $g(x) = x$.

Proof of Cauchy's Mean Value Theorem We apply the Mean Value Theorem of Section 3.2 twice. First we use it to show that $g(a) \neq g(b)$. For if $g(b)$ did equal $g(a)$, then the Mean Value Theorem would give

$$g'(c) = \frac{g(b) - g(a)}{b - a} = 0$$

for some c between a and b, which cannot happen because $g'(x) \neq 0$ in (a, b).

We next apply the Mean Value Theorem to the function

$$F(x) = f(x) - f(a) - \frac{f(b) - f(a)}{g(b) - g(a)} [g(x) - g(a)].$$

This function is continuous and differentiable where f and g are, and $F(b) = F(a) = 0$. Therefore, there is a number c between a and b for which $F'(c) = 0$. When expressed in terms of f and g, this equation becomes

$$F'(c) = f'(c) - \frac{f(b) - f(a)}{g(b) - g(a)} [g'(c)] = 0$$

or

$$\frac{f'(c)}{g'(c)} = \frac{f(b) - f(a)}{g(b) - g(a)},$$

which is Equation (2).   ▬

Proof of the Stronger Form of l'Hôpital's Rule   We first establish Equation (1) for the case $x \to x_0{}^+$. The method needs almost no change to apply to $x \to x_0{}^-$, and the combination of these two cases establishes the result.

Suppose that x lies to the right of x_0. Then $g'(x) \neq 0$, and we can apply Cauchy's Mean Value Theorem to the closed interval from x_0 to x. This step produces a number c between x_0 and x such that

$$\frac{f'(c)}{g'(c)} = \frac{f(x) - f(x_0)}{g(x) - g(x_0)}.$$

But $f(x_0) = g(x_0) = 0$, so

$$\frac{f'(c)}{g'(c)} = \frac{f(x)}{g(x)}.$$

As x approaches x_0, c approaches x_0 because it lies between x and x_0. Therefore,

$$\lim_{x \to x_0{}^+} \frac{f(x)}{g(x)} = \lim_{c \to x_0{}^+} \frac{f'(c)}{g'(c)} = \lim_{x \to x_0{}^+} \frac{f'(x)}{g'(x)},$$

which establishes l'Hôpital's Rule for the case where x approaches x_0 from above. The case where x approaches x_0 from below is proved by applying Cauchy's Mean Value Theorem to the closed interval $[x, x_0]$, $x < x_0$.   ▬

A.7   Limits That Arise Frequently

This appendix verifies limits (4) through (6) in Section 8.1, Table 8.1.

Limit 4: If $|x| < 1$, $\lim_{n \to \infty} x^n = 0$ We need to show that to each $\epsilon > 0$ there corresponds an integer N so large that $|x^n| < \epsilon$ for all n greater than N. Since $\epsilon^{1/n} \to 1$, while $|x| < 1$, there exists an integer N for which $\epsilon^{1/N} > |x|$. In other words,

$$|x^N| = |x|^N < \epsilon. \tag{1}$$

This integer is the one we seek because, if $|x| < 1$, then

$$|x^n| < |x^N| \qquad \text{for all } n > N. \tag{2}$$

Combining Equations (1) and (2) produces $|x^n| < \epsilon$ for all $n > N$, concluding the proof.

Limit 5: For any number x, $\displaystyle\lim_{n\to\infty} \left(1 + \frac{x}{n}\right)^n = e^x$ Let

$$a_n = \left(1 + \frac{x}{n}\right)^n.$$

Then

$$\ln a_n = \ln \left(1 + \frac{x}{n}\right)^n = n \ln \left(1 + \frac{x}{n}\right) \to x,$$

as we can see by the following application of l'Hôpital's Rule, in which we differentiate with respect to n:

$$\lim_{n\to\infty} n \ln \left(1 + \frac{x}{n}\right) = \lim_{n\to\infty} \frac{\ln (1 + x/n)}{1/n}$$

$$= \lim_{n\to\infty} \frac{\left(\dfrac{1}{1 + x/n}\right) \cdot \left(-\dfrac{x}{n^2}\right)}{-1/n^2} = \lim_{n\to\infty} \frac{x}{1 + x/n} = x.$$

Apply Theorem 3, Section 8.1, with $f(x) = e^x$ to conclude that

$$\left(1 + \frac{x}{n}\right)^n = a_n = e^{\ln a_n} \to e^x.$$

Limit 6: For any number x, $\displaystyle\lim_{n\to\infty} \frac{x^n}{n!} = 0$ Since

$$-\frac{|x|^n}{n!} \le \frac{x^n}{n!} \le \frac{|x|^n}{n!},$$

all we need to show is that $|x|^n/n! \to 0$. We can then apply the Sandwich Theorem for Sequences (Section 8.1, Theorem 2) to conclude that $x^n/n! \to 0$.

The first step in showing that $|x|^n/n! \to 0$ is to choose an integer $M > |x|$, so that $(|x|/M) < 1$. By Limit 4, just proved, we then have $(|x|/M)^n \to 0$. We then restrict our attention to values of $n > M$. For these values of n, we can write

$$\frac{|x|^n}{n!} = \frac{|x|^n}{1 \cdot 2 \cdot \cdots \cdot M \cdot \underbrace{(M + 1)(M + 2) \cdot \cdots \cdot n}_{(n-M) \text{ factors}}}$$

$$\le \frac{|x|^n}{M! M^{n-M}} = \frac{|x|^n M^M}{M! M^n} = \frac{M^M}{M!} \left(\frac{|x|}{M}\right)^n.$$

Thus,

$$0 \le \frac{|x|^n}{n!} \le \frac{M^M}{M!} \left(\frac{|x|}{M}\right)^n.$$

Now, the constant $M^M/M!$ does not change as n increases. Thus, the Sandwich Theorem tells us that $|x|^n/n! \to 0$ because $(|x|/M)^n \to 0$.

 A.8 ## Proof of Taylor's Theorem

This appendix proves Taylor's Theorem (Section 8.7, Theorem 16) in the following form.

> **Theorem 16**   Taylor's Theorem
> If f and its first n derivatives $f', f'', \ldots, f^{(n)}$ are continuous on $[a, b]$ or on $[b, a]$, and $f^{(n)}$ is differentiable on (a, b) or on (b, a), then there exists a number c between a and b such that
>
> $$f(b) = f(a) + f'(a)(b - a) + \frac{f''(a)}{2!}(b - a)^2 + \cdots$$
>
> where
>
> $$+ \frac{f^{(n)}(a)}{n!}(b - a)^n + \frac{f^{(n+1)}(c)}{(n + 1)!}(b - a)^{n+1}.$$

Proof   We prove Taylor's Theorem assuming $a < b$. The proof for $a > b$ is nearly the same.

Then for any x in the interval $[a, b]$, the Taylor polynomial

$$P_n(x) = f(a) + f'(a)(x - a) + \frac{f''(a)}{2!}(x - a)^2 + \cdots + \frac{f^{(n)}(a)}{n!}(x - a)^n$$

and its first n derivatives match the function f and its first n derivatives at $x = a$. We do not disturb that matching if we add another term of the form $K(x - a)^{n+1}$, where K is any constant, because such a term and its first n derivatives are all equal to zero at $x = a$. The new function

$$\phi_n(x) = P_n(x) + K(x - a)^{n+1}$$

and its first n derivatives still agree with f and its first n derivatives at $x = a$.

We now choose the particular value of K that makes the curve $y = \phi_n(x)$ agree with the original curve $y = f(x)$ at $x = b$. In symbols,

$$f(b) = P_n(b) + K(b - a)^{n+1} \qquad \text{or} \qquad K = \frac{f(b) - P_n(b)}{(b - a)^{n+1}}. \tag{1}$$

With K defined by the last equation, the function

$$F(x) = f(x) - \phi_n(x)$$

measures the difference between the original function f and the approximating function ϕ_n for each x in $[a, b]$.

We now use Rolle's Theorem (Section 3.2). First, because $F(a) = F(b) = 0$ and both F and F' are continuous on $[a, b]$, we know that

$$F'(c_1) = 0 \qquad \text{for some } c_1 \text{ in } (a, b).$$

Next, because $F'(a) = F'(c_1) = 0$ and both F' and F'' are continuous on $[a, c_1]$, we know that

$$F''(c_2) = 0 \qquad \text{for some } c_2 \text{ in } (a, c_1).$$

Rolle's Theorem, applied successively to F'', F''', ..., $F^{(n-1)}$, implies the existence of

$$c_3 \text{ in } (a, c_2) \qquad \text{such that } F'''(c_3) = 0$$
$$c_4 \text{ in } (a, c_3) \qquad \text{such that } F^{(4)}(c_4) = 0$$
$$\vdots$$
$$c_n \text{ in } (a, c_{n-1}) \qquad \text{such that } F^{(n)}(c_n) = 0.$$

Finally, because $F^{(n)}$ is continuous on $[a, c_n]$ and differentiable on (a, c_n), and $F^{(n)}(a) = F^{(n)}(c_n) = 0$, Rolle's Theorem implies that there is a number c_{n+1} in (a, c_n) such that

$$F^{(n+1)}(c_{n+1}) = 0. \tag{2}$$

If we differentiate $F(x) = f(x) - P_n(x) - K(x - a)^{n+1}$ a total of $n + 1$ times, we get

$$F^{(n+1)}(x) = f^{(n+1)}(x) - 0 - (n + 1)!K. \tag{3}$$

Equations (2) and (3) together give

$$K = \frac{f^{(n+1)}(c)}{(n + 1)!} \qquad \text{for some number } c = c_{n+1} \text{ in } (a, b). \tag{4}$$

Equations (1) and (4) give

$$f(b) = P_n(b) + \frac{f^{(n+1)}(c)}{(n + 1)!} (b - a)^{n+1}. \tag{5}$$

This concludes the proof. ▬

The Distributive Law for Vector Cross Products

In this appendix, we prove the distributive law

$$\mathbf{u} \times (\mathbf{v} + \mathbf{w}) = \mathbf{u} \times \mathbf{v} + \mathbf{u} \times \mathbf{w}$$

from Property 2 in Section 10.2.

Proof To derive the distributive law, we construct $\mathbf{u} \times \mathbf{v}$ a new way. We draw $\mathbf{u}$ and $\mathbf{v}$ from the common point O and construct a plane M perpendicular to $\mathbf{u}$ at O (Figure A.12). We then project $\mathbf{v}$ orthogonally onto M, yielding a vector $\mathbf{v}'$ with length $|\mathbf{v}| \sin \theta$. We rotate $\mathbf{v}'$ 90° about $\mathbf{u}$ in the positive sense to produce a vector $\mathbf{v}''$. Finally, we multiply $\mathbf{v}''$ by the length of $\mathbf{u}$. The resulting vector $|\mathbf{u}|\mathbf{v}''$

is equal to $\mathbf{u} \times \mathbf{v}$ since $\mathbf{v}''$ has the same direction as $\mathbf{u} \times \mathbf{v}$ by its construction (Figure A.12) and

$$|\mathbf{u}||\mathbf{v}''| = |\mathbf{u}||\mathbf{v}'| = |\mathbf{u}||\mathbf{v}| \sin \theta = |\mathbf{u} \times \mathbf{v}|.$$

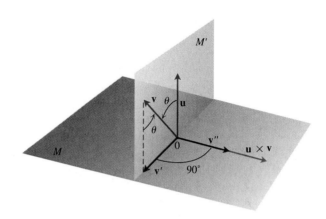

FIGURE A.12 As explained in the text, $\mathbf{u} \times \mathbf{v} = |\mathbf{u}|\mathbf{v}''$.

Now each of these three operations, namely,

1. projection onto M

2. rotation about $\mathbf{u}$ through $90°$

3. multiplication by the scalar $|\mathbf{u}|$

when applied to a triangle whose plane is not parallel to $\mathbf{u}$, will produce another triangle. If we start with the triangle whose sides are $\mathbf{v}$, $\mathbf{w}$, and $\mathbf{v} + \mathbf{w}$ (Figure A.13) and apply these three steps, we successively obtain the following:

1. A triangle whose sides are $\mathbf{v}'$, $\mathbf{w}'$, and $(\mathbf{v} + \mathbf{w})'$ satisfying the vector equation

$$\mathbf{v}' + \mathbf{w}' = (\mathbf{v} + \mathbf{w})'$$

2. A triangle whose sides are $\mathbf{v}''$, $\mathbf{w}''$, and $(\mathbf{v} + \mathbf{w})''$ satisfying the vector equation

$$\mathbf{v}'' + \mathbf{w}'' = (\mathbf{v} + \mathbf{w})''$$

(the double prime on each vector has the same meaning as in Figure A.12)

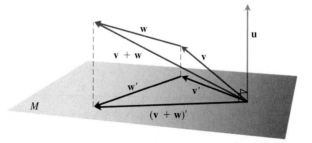

FIGURE A.13 The vectors, $\mathbf{v}, \mathbf{w}, \mathbf{v} + \mathbf{w}$, and their projections onto a plane perpendicular to $\mathbf{u}$.

3. A triangle whose sides are $|\mathbf{u}|\mathbf{v}''$, $|\mathbf{u}|\mathbf{w}''$, and $|\mathbf{u}|(\mathbf{v}+\mathbf{w})''$ satisfying the vector equation

$$|\mathbf{u}|\mathbf{v}'' + |\mathbf{u}|\mathbf{w}'' = |\mathbf{u}|(\mathbf{v}+\mathbf{w})''.$$

Substituting $|\mathbf{u}|\mathbf{v}'' = \mathbf{u} \times \mathbf{v}$, $|\mathbf{u}|\mathbf{w}'' = \mathbf{u} \times \mathbf{w}$, and $|\mathbf{u}|(\mathbf{v}+\mathbf{w})'' = \mathbf{u} \times (\mathbf{v}+\mathbf{w})$ from our discussion above into this last equation gives

$$\mathbf{u} \times \mathbf{v} + \mathbf{u} \times \mathbf{w} = \mathbf{u} \times (\mathbf{v}+\mathbf{w}),$$

which is the law we wanted to establish.

A.10 Determinants and Cramer's Rule

A rectangular array of numbers such as

$$A = \begin{bmatrix} 2 & 1 & 3 \\ 1 & 0 & -2 \end{bmatrix}$$

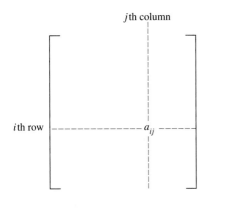

is called a **matrix.** We call A a 2 by 3 matrix because it has two rows and three columns. An m by n matrix has m rows and n columns, and the **entry** or **element** (number) in the ith row and jth column is denoted by a_{ij}. The matrix

$$A = \begin{bmatrix} 2 & 1 & 3 \\ 1 & 0 & -2 \end{bmatrix}$$

has

$$a_{11} = 2, \qquad a_{12} = 1, \qquad a_{13} = 3,$$
$$a_{21} = 1, \qquad a_{22} = 0, \qquad a_{23} = -2.$$

A matrix with the same number of rows as columns is a **square matrix.** It is a **square matrix of order** n if the number of rows and columns is n.

With each square matrix A we associate a number $\det A$ or $|a_{ij}|$, called the **determinant** of A, calculated from the entries of A in the following way. For $n = 1$ and $n = 2$, we define

$$\det [a] = a \tag{1}$$

$$\det \begin{bmatrix} a_{11} & a_{12} \\ a_{21} & a_{22} \end{bmatrix} = a_{11}a_{22} - a_{21}a_{12}. \tag{2}$$

For a matrix of order 3, we write

$$\det A = \det \begin{bmatrix} a_{11} & a_{12} & a_{13} \\ a_{21} & a_{22} & a_{23} \\ a_{31} & a_{32} & a_{33} \end{bmatrix} = \begin{array}{l} \text{sum of all signed products} \\ \text{of the form } \pm\, a_{1i}a_{2j}a_{3k}, \end{array} \tag{3}$$

where i, j, k is a permutation of 1, 2, 3 in some order. There are $3! = 6$ such permutations, so there are six terms in the sum. The sign is positive when the index of the permutation is even and negative when the index is odd.

The vertical bars in the notation $|a_{ij}|$ do not mean absolute value.

Definition Index of a Permutation

Given any permutation of the numbers $1, 2, 3, \ldots, n,$ denote the permutation by $i_1, i_2, i_3, \ldots, i_n.$ In this arrangement, some of the numbers following i_1 may be less than $i_1,$ and the number of these is called the **number of inversions** in the arrangement pertaining to $i_1.$ Likewise, there are a number of inversions pertaining to each of the other i's; it is the number of indices that come after that particular i in the arrangement and are less than it. The **index** of the permutation is the sum of all the numbers of inversions pertaining to the separate indices.

Example 1 Finding the Index of a Permutation

For $n = 5,$ the permutation

$$5 \quad 3 \quad 1 \quad 2 \quad 4$$

has four inversions pertaining to the first element, 5, two inversions pertaining to the second element, 3, and no further inversions, so the index is $4 + 2 = 6.$

The following table shows the permutations of 1, 2, 3, the index of each permutation, and the signed product in the determinant of Equation (3).

Permutation	Index	Signed product
1 2 3	0	$+a_{11}a_{22}a_{33}$
1 3 2	1	$-a_{11}a_{23}a_{32}$
2 1 3	1	$-a_{12}a_{21}a_{33}$
2 3 1	2	$+a_{12}a_{23}a_{31}$
3 1 2	2	$+a_{13}a_{21}a_{32}$
3 2 1	3	$-a_{13}a_{22}a_{31}$

The sum of the six signed products is

$$a_{11}(a_{22}a_{33} - a_{23}a_{32}) - a_{12}(a_{21}a_{33} - a_{23}a_{31}) + a_{13}(a_{21}a_{32} - a_{22}a_{31})$$

$$= a_{11}\begin{vmatrix} a_{22} & a_{23} \\ a_{32} & a_{33} \end{vmatrix} - a_{12}\begin{vmatrix} a_{21} & a_{23} \\ a_{31} & a_{33} \end{vmatrix} + a_{13}\begin{vmatrix} a_{21} & a_{22} \\ a_{31} & a_{32} \end{vmatrix} = \begin{vmatrix} a_{11} & a_{12} & a_{13} \\ a_{21} & a_{22} & a_{23} \\ a_{31} & a_{32} & a_{33} \end{vmatrix}.$$

The formula

$$\begin{vmatrix} a_{11} & a_{12} & a_{13} \\ a_{21} & a_{22} & a_{23} \\ a_{31} & a_{32} & a_{33} \end{vmatrix} = a_{11}\begin{vmatrix} a_{22} & a_{23} \\ a_{32} & a_{33} \end{vmatrix} - a_{12}\begin{vmatrix} a_{21} & a_{23} \\ a_{31} & a_{33} \end{vmatrix} + a_{13}\begin{vmatrix} a_{21} & a_{22} \\ a_{31} & a_{32} \end{vmatrix} \qquad (4)$$

reduces the calculation of a 3 by 3 determinant to the calculation of three 2 by 2 determinants.

Many people prefer to remember the following scheme for calculating the six signed products in the determinant of a 3 by 3 matrix:

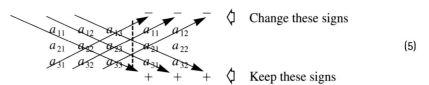

$$(5)$$

Minors and Cofactors

The second-order determinants on the right-hand side of Equation (4) are called the **minors** (short for "minor determinants") of the entries they multiply. Thus,

$$\begin{vmatrix} a_{22} & a_{23} \\ a_{32} & a_{33} \end{vmatrix} \text{ is the minor of } a_{11}, \qquad \begin{vmatrix} a_{21} & a_{23} \\ a_{31} & a_{33} \end{vmatrix} \text{ is the minor of } a_{12},$$

and so on. The minor of the element a_{ij} in a matrix A is the determinant of the matrix that remains after we delete the row and column containing a_{ij}.

$$\begin{vmatrix} a_{11} & a_{12} & a_{13} \\ a_{21} & a_{22} & a_{23} \\ a_{31} & a_{32} & a_{33} \end{vmatrix}; \qquad \text{the minor of } a_{22} \text{ is } \begin{vmatrix} a_{11} & a_{13} \\ a_{31} & a_{33} \end{vmatrix}$$

$$\begin{vmatrix} a_{11} & a_{12} & a_{13} \\ a_{21} & a_{22} & a_{23} \\ a_{31} & a_{32} & a_{33} \end{vmatrix}; \qquad \text{the minor of } a_{23} \text{ is } \begin{vmatrix} a_{11} & a_{12} \\ a_{31} & a_{32} \end{vmatrix}$$

The **cofactor** A_{ij} of a_{ij} is $(-1)^{i+j}$ times the minor of a_{ij}. Thus,

$$A_{22} = (-1)^{2+2} \begin{vmatrix} a_{11} & a_{13} \\ a_{31} & a_{33} \end{vmatrix} = \begin{vmatrix} a_{11} & a_{13} \\ a_{31} & a_{33} \end{vmatrix}$$

$$A_{23} = (-1)^{2+3} \begin{vmatrix} a_{11} & a_{12} \\ a_{31} & a_{32} \end{vmatrix} = - \begin{vmatrix} a_{11} & a_{12} \\ a_{31} & a_{32} \end{vmatrix}.$$

The factor $(-1)^{i+j}$ changes the sign of the minor when $i + j$ is odd. There is a checkerboard pattern for remembering these changes:

$$\begin{array}{ccc} + & - & + \\ - & + & - \\ + & - & +. \end{array}$$

In the upper left corner, $i = 1$, $j = 1$ and $(-1)^{1+1} = +1$. In going from any cell to an adjacent cell in the same row or column, we change i by 1 or j by 1, but not both, so we change the exponent from even to odd or from odd to even, which changes the sign from + to − or from − to +.

When we rewrite Equation (4) in terms of cofactors we get

$$\det A = a_{11}A_{11} + a_{12}A_{12} + a_{13}A_{13}. \tag{6}$$

Example 2   Finding a Determinant Two Ways

Find the determinant of

$$A = \begin{bmatrix} 2 & 1 & 3 \\ 3 & -1 & -2 \\ 2 & 3 & 1 \end{bmatrix}.$$

Solution 1

Using Equation (6)

The cofactors are

$$A_{11} = (-1)^{1+1} \begin{vmatrix} -1 & -2 \\ 3 & 1 \end{vmatrix}, \qquad A_{12} = (-1)^{1+2} \begin{vmatrix} 3 & -2 \\ 2 & 1 \end{vmatrix},$$

$$A_{13} = (-1)^{1+3} \begin{vmatrix} 3 & -1 \\ 2 & 3 \end{vmatrix}.$$

To find det A, we multiply each element of the first row of A by its cofactor and add:

$$\det A = 2 \begin{vmatrix} -1 & -2 \\ 3 & 1 \end{vmatrix} + (-1) \begin{vmatrix} 3 & -2 \\ 2 & 1 \end{vmatrix} + 3 \begin{vmatrix} 3 & -1 \\ 2 & 3 \end{vmatrix}$$

$$= 2(-1 + 6) - 1(3 + 4) + 3(9 + 2) = 10 - 7 + 33 = 36.$$

Solution 2

Using the Scheme (5)

We find

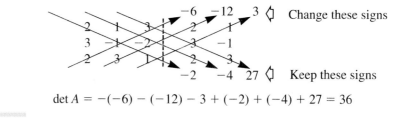

$$\det A = -(-6) - (-12) - 3 + (-2) + (-4) + 27 = 36$$

Expanding by Columns or by Other Rows

The determinant of a square matrix can be calculated from the cofactors of any row or any column.

If we were to expand the determinant in Example 2 by cofactors according to elements of its third column, say, we would get

$$+3 \begin{vmatrix} 3 & -1 \\ 2 & 3 \end{vmatrix} - (-2) \begin{vmatrix} 2 & 1 \\ 2 & 3 \end{vmatrix} + 1 \begin{vmatrix} 2 & 1 \\ 3 & -1 \end{vmatrix}$$

$$= 3(9 + 2) + 2(6 - 2) + 1(-2 - 3) = 33 + 8 - 5 = 36.$$

Useful Facts About Determinants

Fact 1: If two rows (or columns) are identical, the determinant is zero.

Fact 2: Interchanging two rows (or columns) changes the sign of the determinant.

Fact 3: The determinant is the sum of the products of the elements of the ith row (or column) by their cofactors, for any i.

Fact 4: The determinant of the transpose of a matrix is the same as the determinant of the original matrix. (The **transpose** of a matrix is obtained by writing the rows as columns.)

Fact 5: Multiplying each element of some row (or column) by a constant c multiplies the determinant by c.

Fact 6: If all elements above the main diagonal (or all below it) are zero, the determinant is the product of the elements on the main diagonal. (The **main diagonal** is the diagonal from upper left to lower right.)

Example 3   Illustrating Fact 6

$$\begin{vmatrix} 3 & 4 & 7 \\ 0 & -2 & 5 \\ 0 & 0 & 5 \end{vmatrix} = (3)(-2)(5) = -30$$

Fact 7: If the elements of any row are multiplied by the cofactors of the corresponding elements of a different row and these products are summed, then the sum is zero.

Example 4   Illustrating Fact 7

If A_{11}, A_{12}, A_{13} are the cofactors of the elements of the first row of $A = (a_{ij})$, then the sums

$$a_{21}A_{11} + a_{22}A_{12} + a_{23}A_{13}$$

(elements of second row times cofactors of elements of first row) and

$$a_{31}A_{11} + a_{32}A_{12} + a_{33}A_{13}$$

are both zero.

Fact 8: If the elements of any column are multiplied by the cofactors of the corresponding elements of a different column and these products are summed, then the sum is zero.

Fact 9: If each element of a row is multiplied by a constant c and the results added to a different row, then the determinant is not changed. A similar result holds for columns.

Example 5   Adding a Multiple of One Row to Another Row

If we start with

$$A = \begin{bmatrix} 2 & 1 & 3 \\ 3 & -1 & -2 \\ 2 & 3 & 1 \end{bmatrix}$$

and add -2 times row 1 to row 2 (subtract 2 times row 1 from row 2), we get

$$B = \begin{bmatrix} 2 & 1 & 3 \\ -1 & -3 & -8 \\ 2 & 3 & 1 \end{bmatrix}.$$

Since $\det A = 36$ (Example 2), we should find that $\det B = 36$ as well. Indeed we do, as the following calculation shows:

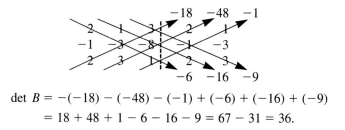

$$\det B = -(-18) - (-48) - (-1) + (-6) + (-16) + (-9)$$
$$= 18 + 48 + 1 - 6 - 16 - 9 = 67 - 31 = 36.$$

Example 6   Evaluating a Fourth-Order Determinant by Applying Fact 9

Evaluate the fourth order determinant

$$D = \begin{vmatrix} 1 & -2 & 3 & 1 \\ 2 & 1 & 0 & 2 \\ -1 & 2 & 1 & -2 \\ 0 & 1 & 2 & 1 \end{vmatrix}.$$

Solution   We subtract 2 times row 1 from row 2 and add row 1 to row 3 to get

$$D = \begin{vmatrix} 1 & -2 & 3 & 1 \\ 0 & 5 & -6 & 0 \\ 0 & 0 & 4 & -1 \\ 0 & 1 & 2 & 1 \end{vmatrix}.$$

We then multiply the elements of the first column by their cofactors to get

$$D = \begin{vmatrix} 5 & -6 & 0 \\ 0 & 4 & -1 \\ 1 & 2 & 1 \end{vmatrix} = 5(4 + 2) - (-6)(0 + 1) + 0 = 36.$$

Cramer's Rule

If the determinant $D = \det A = \begin{vmatrix} a_{11} & a_{12} \\ a_{21} & a_{22} \end{vmatrix} = 0$, then the system

$$a_{11}x + a_{12}y = b_1$$
$$a_{21}x + a_{22}y = b_2 \tag{7}$$

has either infinitely many solutions or no solution at all. The system

$$x + y = 0$$
$$2x + 2y = 0$$

whose determinant is

$$D = \begin{vmatrix} 1 & 1 \\ 2 & 2 \end{vmatrix} = 2 - 2 = 0$$

has infinitely many solutions. We can find an x to match any given y. The system

$$x + y = 0$$
$$2x + 2y = 2$$

has no solution. If $x + y = 0$, then $2x + 2y = 2(x + y)$ cannot be 2.

If $D \neq 0$, then the system (7) has a unique solution, and Cramer's Rule states that it may be found from the formulas

$$x = \frac{\begin{vmatrix} b_1 & a_{12} \\ b_2 & a_{22} \end{vmatrix}}{D}, \qquad y = \frac{\begin{vmatrix} a_{11} & b_1 \\ a_{21} & b_2 \end{vmatrix}}{D}. \tag{8}$$

The numerator in the formula for x comes from replacing the first column in A (the x-column) by the column of constants b_1 and b_2 (the b-column). Replacing the y-column by the b-column gives the numerator of the y-solution.

Example 7   Using Cramer's Rule

Solve the system

$$3x - y = 9$$
$$x + 2y = -4.$$

Solution   We use Equations (8). The determinant of the coefficient matrix is

$$D = \begin{vmatrix} 3 & -1 \\ 1 & 2 \end{vmatrix} = 6 + 1 = 7.$$

Hence,

$$x = \frac{\begin{vmatrix} 9 & -1 \\ -4 & 2 \end{vmatrix}}{D} = \frac{18 - 4}{7} = \frac{14}{7} = 2$$

$$y = \frac{\begin{vmatrix} 3 & 9 \\ 1 & -4 \end{vmatrix}}{D} = \frac{-12 - 9}{7} = \frac{-21}{7} = -3.$$

Systems of three equations in three unknowns work the same way. If

$$D = \det A = \begin{vmatrix} a_{11} & a_{12} & a_{13} \\ a_{21} & a_{22} & a_{23} \\ a_{31} & a_{32} & a_{33} \end{vmatrix} = 0,$$

then the system

$$a_{11}x + a_{12}y + a_{13}z = b_1$$
$$a_{21}x + a_{22}y + a_{23}z = b_2$$
$$a_{31}x + a_{32}y + a_{33}z = b_3$$

has either infinitely many solutions or no solution at all. If $D \neq 0$, then the system has a unique solution, given by Cramer's Rule:

$$x = \frac{1}{D}\begin{vmatrix} b_1 & a_{12} & a_{13} \\ b_2 & a_{22} & a_{23} \\ b_3 & a_{32} & a_{33} \end{vmatrix}, \qquad y = \frac{1}{D}\begin{vmatrix} a_{11} & b_1 & a_{13} \\ a_{21} & b_2 & a_{23} \\ a_{31} & b_3 & a_{33} \end{vmatrix}, \qquad z = \frac{1}{D}\begin{vmatrix} a_{11} & a_{12} & b_1 \\ a_{21} & a_{22} & b_2 \\ a_{31} & a_{32} & b_3 \end{vmatrix}.$$

The pattern continues in higher dimensions.

EXERCISES A.10

Evaluting Determinants

Evaluate the following determinants.

1. $\begin{vmatrix} 2 & 3 & 1 \\ 4 & 5 & 2 \\ 1 & 2 & 3 \end{vmatrix}$

2. $\begin{vmatrix} 2 & -1 & -2 \\ -1 & 2 & 1 \\ 3 & 0 & -3 \end{vmatrix}$

3. $\begin{vmatrix} 1 & 2 & 3 & 4 \\ 0 & 1 & 2 & 3 \\ 0 & 0 & 2 & 1 \\ 0 & 0 & 3 & 2 \end{vmatrix}$

4. $\begin{vmatrix} 1 & -1 & 2 & 3 \\ 2 & 1 & 2 & 6 \\ 1 & 0 & 2 & 3 \\ -2 & 2 & 0 & -5 \end{vmatrix}$

Evaluate the following determinants by expanding according to the cofactors of (a) the third row and (b) the second column.

5. $\begin{vmatrix} 2 & -1 & 2 \\ 1 & 0 & 3 \\ 0 & 2 & 1 \end{vmatrix}$

6. $\begin{vmatrix} 1 & 0 & -1 \\ 0 & 2 & -2 \\ 2 & 0 & 1 \end{vmatrix}$

7. $\begin{vmatrix} 1 & 1 & 0 & 0 \\ 0 & 0 & -2 & 1 \\ 0 & -1 & 0 & 7 \\ 3 & 0 & 2 & 1 \end{vmatrix}$

8. $\begin{vmatrix} 0 & 1 & 0 & 0 \\ 0 & 1 & 1 & 0 \\ 1 & 1 & 1 & 1 \\ 1 & 1 & 0 & 0 \end{vmatrix}$

Systems of Equations

Solve the following systems of equations by Cramer's Rule.

9. $x + 8y = 4$
$3x - y = -13$

10. $2x + 3y = 5$
$3x - y = 2$

11. $4x - 3y = 6$
$3x - 2y = 5$

12. $x + y + z = 2$
$2x - y + z = 0$
$x + 2y - z = 4$

13. $2x + y - z = 2$
$x - y + z = 7$
$2x + 2y + z = 4$

14. $2x - 4y = 6$
$x + y + z = 1$
$5y + 7z = 10$

15. $x - z = 3$
$2y - 2z = 2$
$2x + z = 3$

16. $x_1 + x_2 - x_3 + x_4 = 2$
$x_1 - x_2 + x_3 + x_4 = -1$
$x_1 + x_2 + x_3 - x_4 = 2$
$x_1 + x_3 + x_4 = -1$

Theory and Examples

17. *Infinitely many or no solutions* Find values of h and k for which the system

$$2x + hy = 8$$
$$x + 3y = k$$

has (a) infinitely many solutions and (b) no solution at all.

18. *A zero determinant* For what value of x will

$$\begin{vmatrix} x & x & 1 \\ 2 & 0 & 5 \\ 6 & 7 & 1 \end{vmatrix} = 0?$$

19. *A zero determinant* Suppose u, v, and w are twice-differentiable functions of x that satisfy the relation $au + bv + cw = 0$, where a, b, and c are constants, not all zero. Show that

$$\begin{vmatrix} u & v & w \\ u' & v' & w' \\ u'' & v'' & w'' \end{vmatrix} = 0.$$

20. *Partial fractions* Expanding the quotient

$$\frac{ax + b}{(x - r_1)(x - r_2)}$$

by partial fractions calls for finding the values of C and D that make the equation

$$\frac{ax + b}{(x - r_1)(x - r_2)} = \frac{C}{x - r_1} + \frac{D}{x - r_2}$$

hold for all x.

(a) Find a system of linear equations that determines C and D.

(b) *Writing to Learn* Under what circumstances does the system of equations in part (a) have a unique solution? That is, when is the determinant of the coefficient matrix of the system different from zero?

The Mixed Derivative Theorem and the Increment Theorem

This appendix derives the Mixed Derivative Theorem (Theorem 2, Section 11.3) and the Increment Theorem for Functions of Two Variables (Theorem 3, Section 11.3). Euler first published his theorem in 1734, in a series of papers he wrote on hydrodynamics.

> **Theorem 2**   The Mixed Derivative Theorem
>
> If $f(x, y)$ and its partial derivatives f_x, f_y, f_{xy}, and f_{yx} are defined throughout an open region containing a point (a, b) and are all continuous at (a, b), then $f_{xy}(a, b) = f_{yx}(a, b)$.

Proof   The equality of $f_{xy}(a, b)$ and $f_{yx}(a, b)$ can be established by four applications of the Mean Value Theorem (Theorem 4, Section 3.2). By hypothesis, the point (a, b) lies in the interior of a rectangle R in the xy-plane on which f, f_x, f_y, f_{xy}, and f_{yx} are all defined. We let h and k be the numbers such that the point $(a + h, b + k)$ also lies in R, and we consider the difference

$$\Delta = F(a + h) - F(a), \tag{1}$$

where

$$F(x) = f(x, b + k) - f(x, b). \tag{2}$$

We apply the Mean Value Theorem to F, which is continuous because it is differentiable, and Equation (1) becomes

$$\Delta = hF'(c_1), \tag{3}$$

where c_1 lies between a and $a + h$. From Equation (2),

$$F'(x) = f_x(x, b + k) - f_x(x, b),$$

so Equation (3) becomes

$$\Delta = h[f_x(c_1, b + k) - f_x(c_1, b)]. \tag{4}$$

Now we apply the Mean Value Theorem to the function $g(y) = f_x(c_1, y)$ and have

$$g(b + k) - g(b) = kg'(d_1),$$

or

$$f_x(c_1, b + k) - f_x(c_1, b) = kf_{xy}(c_1, d_1)$$

for some d_1 between b and $b + k$. By substituting this into Equation (4), we get

$$\Delta = hkf_{xy}(c_1, d_1) \tag{5}$$

for some point (c_1, d_1) in the rectangle R' whose vertices are the four points (a, b), $(a + h, b)$, $(a + h, b + k)$, and $(a, b + k)$. (See Figure A.14.)

By substituting from Equation (2) into Equation (1), we may also write

$$\begin{aligned} \Delta &= f(a + h, b + k) - f(a + h, b) - f(a, b + k) + f(a, b) \\ &= [f(a + h, b + k) - f(a, b + k)] - [f(a + h, b) - f(a, b)] \tag{6} \\ &= \phi(b + k) - \phi(b), \end{aligned}$$

where

$$\phi(y) = f(a + h, y) - f(a, y). \tag{7}$$

The Mean Value Theorem applied to Equation (6) now gives

$$\Delta = k\phi'(d_2) \tag{8}$$

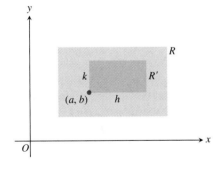

FIGURE A.14   The key to proving $f_{xy}(a, b) = f_{yx}(a, b)$ is that no matter how small R' is, f_{xy} and f_{yx} take on equal values somewhere inside R' (although not necessarily at the same point).

for some d_2 between b and $b + k$. By Equation (7),

$$\phi'(y) = f_y(a + h, y) - f_y(a, y). \tag{9}$$

Substituting from Equation (9) into Equation (8) gives

$$\Delta = k[f_y(a + h, d_2) - f_y(a, d_2)].$$

Finally, we apply the Mean Value Theorem to the expression in brackets and get

$$\Delta = khf_{yx}(c_2, d_2) \tag{10}$$

for some c_2 between a and $a + h$.

Together, Equations (5) and (10) show that

$$f_{xy}(c_1, d_1) = f_{yx}(c_2, d_2), \tag{11}$$

where (c_1, d_1) and (c_2, d_2) both lie in the rectangle R' (Figure A.14). Equation (11) is not quite the result we want, since it says only that f_{xy} has the same value at (c_1, d_1) that f_{yx} has at (c_2, d_2). The numbers h and k in our discussion, however, may be made as small as we wish. The hypothesis that f_{xy} and f_{yx} are both continuous at (a, b) means that $f_{xy}(c_1, d_1) = f_{xy}(a, b) + \epsilon_1$ and $f_{yx}(c_2, d_2) = f_{yx}(a, b) + \epsilon_2$, where $\epsilon_1, \epsilon_2 \to 0$ as $h, k \to 0$. Hence, if we let h and $k \to 0$, we have $f_{xy}(a, b) = f_{yx}(a, b)$.

The equality of $f_{xy}(a, b)$ and $f_{yx}(a, b)$ can be proved with hypotheses weaker than the ones we assumed. For example, it is enough for f, f_x, and f_y to exist in R and for f_{xy} to be continuous at (a, b). Then f_{yx} will exist at (a, b) and will equal f_{xy} at that point.

The Increment Theorem for Functions of Two Variables

Suppose that the first partial derivatives of $z = f(x, y)$ are defined throughout an open region R containing the point (x_0, y_0) and that f_x and f_y are continuous at (x_0, y_0). Then the change $\Delta z = f(x_0 + \Delta x, y_0 + \Delta y) - f(x_0, y_0)$ in the value of f that results from moving from (x_0, y_0) to another point $(x_0 + \Delta x, y_0 + \Delta y)$ in R satisfies an equation of the form

$$\Delta z = f_x(x_0, y_0) \Delta x + f_y(x_0, y_0) \Delta y + \epsilon_1 \Delta x + \epsilon_2 \Delta y,$$

in which $\epsilon_1, \epsilon_2 \to 0$ as $\Delta x, \Delta y \to 0$.

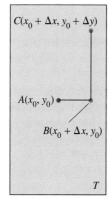

FIGURE A.15 The rectangular region T in the proof of the Increment Theorem. The figure is drawn for Δx and Δy positive, but either increment might be zero or negative.

Proof We work within a rectangle T centered at $A(x_0, y_0)$ and lying within R, and we assume that Δx and Δy are already so small that the line segment joining A to $B(x_0 + \Delta x, y_0)$ and the line segment joining B to $C(x_0 + \Delta x, y_0 + \Delta y)$ lie in the interior of T (Figure A.15).

We may think of Δz as the sum $\Delta z = \Delta z_1 + \Delta z_2$ of two increments, where

$$\Delta z_1 = f(x_0 + \Delta x, y_0) - f(x_0, y_0)$$

is the change in the value of f from A to B and

$$\Delta z_2 = f(x_0 + \Delta x, y_0 + \Delta y) - f(x_0 + \Delta x, y_0)$$

is the change in the value of f from B to C (Figure A.16).

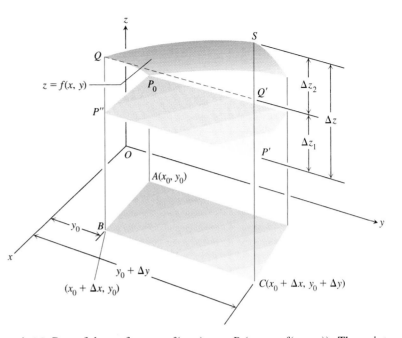

FIGURE A.16 Part of the surface $z = f(x, y)$ near $P_0(x_0, y_0, f(x_0, y_0))$. The points P_0, P', and P'' have the same height $z_0 = f(x_0, y_0)$ above the xy-plane. The change in z is $\Delta z = P'S$. The change

$$\Delta z_1 = f(x_0 + \Delta x, y_0) - f(x_0, y_0),$$

shown as $P''Q = P'Q'$, is caused by changing x from x_0 to $x_0 + \Delta x$ while holding y equal to y_0. Then, with x held equal to $x_0 + \Delta x$,

$$\Delta z_2 = f(x_0 + \Delta x, y_0 + \Delta y) - f(x_0 + \Delta x, y_0)$$

is the change in z caused by changing y from y_0 to $y_0 + \Delta y$, which is represented by $Q'S$. The total change in z is the sum of Δz_1 and Δz_2.

On the closed interval of x-values joining x_0 to $x_0 + \Delta x$, the function $F(x) = f(x, y_0)$ is a differentiable (and hence continuous) function of x, with derivative

$$F'(x) = f_x(x, y_0).$$

By the Mean Value Theorem (Theorem 4, Section 3.2), there is an x-value c between x_0 and $x_0 + \Delta x$ at which

$$F(x_0 + \Delta x) - F(x_0) = F'(c) \, \Delta x$$

or

$$f(x_0 + \Delta x, y_0) - f(x_0, y_0) = f_x(c, y_0) \, \Delta x$$

or

$$\Delta z_1 = f_x(c, y_0) \, \Delta x. \tag{12}$$

Similarly, $G(y) = f(x_0 + \Delta x, y)$ is a differentiable (and hence continuous) function of y on the closed y-interval joining y_0 and $y_0 + \Delta y$, with derivative

$$G'(y) = f_y(x_0 + \Delta x, y).$$

Hence, there is a y-value d between y_0 and $y_0 + \Delta y$ at which

$$G(y_0 + \Delta y) - G(y_0) = G'(d)\, \Delta y$$

or

$$f(x_0 + \Delta x, y_0 + \Delta y) - f(x_0 + \Delta x, y) = f_y(x_0 + \Delta x, d)\, \Delta y$$

or

$$\Delta z_2 = f_y(x_0 + \Delta x, d)\, \Delta y. \tag{13}$$

Now, as Δx and $\Delta y \to 0$, we know that $c \to x_0$ and $d \to y_0$. Therefore, since f_x and f_y are continuous at (x_0, y_0), the quantities

$$\epsilon_1 = f_x(c, y_0) - f_x(x_0, y_0),$$

$$\epsilon_2 = f_y(x_0 + \Delta x, d) - f_y(x_0, y_0) \tag{14}$$

both approach zero as Δx and $\Delta y \to 0$.

Finally,

$$\begin{aligned}
\Delta z &= \Delta z_1 + \Delta z_2 \\
&= f_x(c, y_0)\, \Delta x + f_y(x_0 + \Delta x, d)\, \Delta y && \text{From (12) and (13)} \\
&= [f_x(x_0, y_0) + \epsilon_1]\, \Delta x + [f_y(x_0, y_0) + \epsilon_2]\, \Delta y && \text{From (14)} \\
&= f_x(x_0, y_0)\, \Delta x + f_y(x_0, y_0)\, \Delta y + \epsilon_1\, \Delta x + \epsilon_2\, \Delta y,
\end{aligned}$$

where ϵ_1 and $\epsilon_2 \to 0$ as Δx and $\Delta y \to 0$, which is what we set out to prove. ▬

Analogous results hold for functions of any finite number of independent variables. Suppose that the first partial derivatives of $w = f(x, y, z)$ are defined throughout an open region containing the point (x_0, y_0, z_0) and that f_x, f_y, and f_z are continuous at (x_0, y_0, z_0). Then

$$\begin{aligned}
\Delta w &= f(x_0 + \Delta x, y_0 + \Delta y, z_0 + \Delta z) - f(x_0, y_0, z_0) \\
&= f_x\, \Delta x + f_y\, \Delta y + f_z\, \Delta z + \epsilon_1\, \Delta x + \epsilon_2\, \Delta y + \epsilon_3\, \Delta z, \tag{15}
\end{aligned}$$

where ϵ_1, ϵ_2, $\epsilon_3 \to 0$ as Δx, Δy, and $\Delta z \to 0$.

The partial derivatives f_x, f_y, f_z in Equation (15) are to be evaluated at the point (x_0, y_0, z_0).

Equation (15) can be proved by treating Δw as the sum of three increments,

$$\Delta w_1 = f(x_0 + \Delta x, y_0, z_0) - f(x_0, y_0, z_0) \tag{16}$$

$$\Delta w_2 = f(x_0 + \Delta x, y_0 + \Delta y, z_0) - f(x_0 + \Delta x, y_0, z_0) \tag{17}$$

$$\Delta w_3 = f(x_0 + \Delta x, y_0 + \Delta y, z_0 + \Delta z) - f(x_0 + \Delta x, y_0 + \Delta y, z_0), \tag{18}$$

and applying the Mean Value Theorem to each of these separately. Two coordinates remain constant and only one varies in each of these partial increments Δw_1, Δw_2, Δw_3. In Equation (17), for example, only y varies, since x is held equal to $x_0 + \Delta x$ and z is held equal to z_0. Since $f(x_0 + \Delta x, y, z_0)$ is a continuous function of y with a derivative f_y, it is subject to the Mean Value Theorem, and we have

$$\Delta w_2 = f_y(x_0 + \Delta x, y_1, z_0)\, \Delta y$$

for some y_1 between y_0 and $y_0 + \Delta y$.

A.12 The Area of a Parallelogram's Projection on a Plane

This appendix proves the result needed in Section 13.5 that $|(\mathbf{u} \times \mathbf{v}) \cdot \mathbf{p}|$ is the area of the projection of the parallelogram with sides determined by $\mathbf{u}$ and $\mathbf{v}$ onto any plane whose normal is $\mathbf{p}$. (See Figure A.17.)

Theorem

The area of the orthogonal projection of the parallelogram determined by two vectors $\mathbf{u}$ and $\mathbf{v}$ in space onto a plane with unit normal vector $\mathbf{p}$ is

$$\text{Area} = |(\mathbf{u} \times \mathbf{v}) \cdot \mathbf{p}|.$$

Proof In the notation of Figure A.17, which shows a typical parallelogram determined by vectors $\mathbf{u}$ and $\mathbf{v}$ and its orthogonal projection onto a plane with unit normal vector $\mathbf{p}$,

$$
\begin{aligned}
\mathbf{u} &= \overrightarrow{PP'} + \mathbf{u}' + \overrightarrow{Q'Q} \\
&= \mathbf{u}' + \overrightarrow{PP'} - \overrightarrow{QQ'} \quad (\overrightarrow{Q'Q} = -\overrightarrow{QQ'}) \\
&= \mathbf{u}' + s\mathbf{p}. \quad \text{\small(For some scalar s because}\\
&\qquad\qquad\qquad\qquad\text{\small $\overrightarrow{PP'} - \overrightarrow{QQ'}$) is parallel to $\mathbf{p}$)}
\end{aligned}
$$

Similarly,

$$\mathbf{v} = \mathbf{v}' + t\mathbf{p}$$

for some scalar t. Hence,

$$
\begin{aligned}
\mathbf{u} \times \mathbf{v} &= (\mathbf{u}' + s\mathbf{p}) \times (\mathbf{v}' + t\mathbf{p}) \\
&= (\mathbf{u}' \times \mathbf{v}') + s(\mathbf{p} \times \mathbf{v}') + t(\mathbf{u}' \times \mathbf{p}) + \underbrace{st(\mathbf{p} \times \mathbf{p})}_{0}. \quad (1)
\end{aligned}
$$

The vectors $\mathbf{p} \times \mathbf{v}'$ and $\mathbf{u}' \times \mathbf{p}$ are both orthogonal to $\mathbf{p}$. Hence, when we dot both sides of Equation (1) with $\mathbf{p}$, the only surviving term on the right is $(\mathbf{u}' \times \mathbf{v}') \cdot \mathbf{p}$. We are left with

$$(\mathbf{u} \times \mathbf{v}) \cdot \mathbf{p} = (\mathbf{u}' \times \mathbf{v}') \cdot \mathbf{p}.$$

In particular,

$$|(\mathbf{u} \times \mathbf{v}) \cdot \mathbf{p}| = |(\mathbf{u}' \times \mathbf{v}') \cdot \mathbf{p}|. \quad (2)$$

The absolute value on the right is the volume of the box determined by $\mathbf{u}'$, $\mathbf{v}'$, and $\mathbf{p}$. The height of this particular box is $|\mathbf{p}| = 1$, so the box's volume is numerically the same as its base area, the area of parallelogram $P'Q'R'S'$. Combining this observation with Equation (2) gives

$$\text{Area of } P'Q'R'S' = |(\mathbf{u}' \times \mathbf{v}') \cdot \mathbf{p}| = |(\mathbf{u} \times \mathbf{v}) \cdot \mathbf{p}|,$$

which says that the area of the orthogonal projection of the parallelogram determined by $\mathbf{u}$ and $\mathbf{v}$ onto a plane with unit normal vector $\mathbf{p}$ is $|(\mathbf{u} \times \mathbf{v}) \cdot \mathbf{p}|$, what we set out to prove.

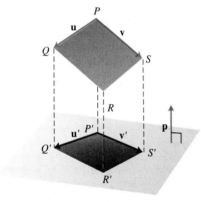

FIGURE A.17 The parallelogram determined by two vectors $\mathbf{u}$ and $\mathbf{v}$ in space and the orthogonal projection of the parallelogram onto a plane. The projection lines, orthogonal to the plane, lie parallel to the unit normal vector $\mathbf{p}$.

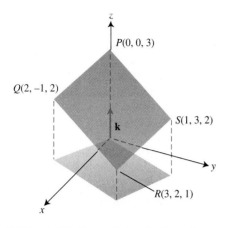

FIGURE A.18 Example 1 calculates the area of the orthogonal projection of parallelogram *PQRS* on the *xy*-plane.

Example 1   Finding the Area of a Projection

Find the area of the orthogonal projection onto the *xy*-plane of the parallelogram determined by the points $P(0, 0, 3)$, $Q(2, -1, 2)$, $R(3, 2, 1)$, and $S(1, 3, 2)$ (Figure A.18)

Solution   With

$$\mathbf{u} = \overrightarrow{PQ} = 2\mathbf{i} - \mathbf{j} - \mathbf{k}, \qquad \mathbf{v} = \overrightarrow{PS} = \mathbf{i} + 3\mathbf{j} - \mathbf{k}, \qquad \text{and} \qquad \mathbf{p} = \mathbf{k},$$

the area is

$$\text{Area} = (\mathbf{u} \times \mathbf{v}) \cdot \mathbf{p} = \begin{vmatrix} 2 & -1 & -1 \\ 1 & 3 & -1 \\ 0 & 0 & 1 \end{vmatrix} = \begin{vmatrix} 2 & -1 \\ 1 & 3 \end{vmatrix} = 7.$$

Answers

ANSWERS BEGIN ON THE NEXT PAGE

73. $\frac{1}{6} \ln \left| \frac{x+3}{x-3} \right| + C$

75. $\frac{2x^{3/2}}{3} - x + 2\sqrt{x} - 2 \ln (\sqrt{x} + 1) + C$

77. $2 \sin \sqrt{x} + C$

79. $\ln |u + \sqrt{1 + u^2}| + C$

81. $\frac{1}{12} \ln \left| \frac{3+v}{3-v} \right| + \frac{1}{6} \tan^{-1} \frac{v}{3} + C$

83. $\frac{x^2}{2} + 2x + 3 \ln |x - 1| - \frac{1}{x-1} + C$

85. $-\cos (2\sqrt{x}) + C$

87. $\frac{\sqrt{3}}{3} \tan^{-1} \left(\frac{\theta - 1}{\sqrt{3}} \right) + C$

89. $\frac{1}{4} \sec^2 \theta + C$

91. $-\frac{2}{3}(x + 4) \sqrt{2 - x} + C$

93. $\frac{1}{2} [x \ln |x - 1| - x - \ln |x - 1|] + C$

95. $\frac{1}{4} \ln |z| - \frac{1}{4z} - \frac{1}{4} \left[\frac{1}{2} \ln (z^2 + 4) + \frac{1}{2} \tan^{-1} \left(\frac{z}{2} \right) \right] + C$

97. $-\frac{\tan^{-1} x}{x} + \ln |x| - \ln \sqrt{1 + x^2} + C$

99. $\tan x - x + C$

101. $\ln |\csc (2x) + \cot (2x)| + C$ **103.** $\frac{1}{4}$

105. $\sec^{-1} |2x - 1| + C$ **107.** $\frac{1}{6}(3 + 4e^\theta)^{3/2} + C$

109. $\frac{1}{3} \left(\frac{27^{3\theta+1}}{\ln 27} \right) + C$

111. $2\sqrt{r} - 2 \ln (1 + \sqrt{r}) + C$

113. $4 \sec^{-1} \left| \frac{7m}{2} \right| + C$ **115.** The limit does not exist.

117. 2   **119.** 1

121. 0   **123.** $-\frac{1}{2}$

125. 1   **127.** ∞

129. $\frac{\pi}{2}$ **131.** 6

133. $\ln 3$ **135.** 2

137. $\frac{\pi}{6}$ **139.** Diverges

141. Diverges   **143.** Converges

145. $\ln |y - 1| - \ln |y| = e^x - 1 - \ln 2$

147. $y = \ln |x - 2| - \ln |x - 1| + \ln 2$

Chapter 7 Additional Exercises, pp. 603–606

1. $x(\sin^{-1} x)^2 + 2(\sin^{-1} x) \sqrt{1 - x^2} - 2x + C$

3. $\frac{x^2 \sin^{-1} x}{2} + \frac{x\sqrt{1 - x^2} - \sin^{-1} x}{4} + C$

5. $\frac{\ln |\sec 2\theta + \tan 2\theta| + 2\theta}{4} + C$

7. $\frac{1}{2} [\ln |t - \sqrt{1 - t^2}| - \sin^{-1} t] + C$

9. $\frac{1}{16} \ln \left| \frac{x^2 + 2x + 2}{x^2 - 2x + 2} \right| + \frac{1}{8}[\tan^{-1} (x + 1) + \tan^{-1} (x - 1)] + C$

11. $\frac{\pi}{2}$ **13.** $\frac{1}{\sqrt{e}}$

15. 0   **17.** 1

19. $\frac{32\pi}{35}$ **21.** 2π

23. (a) π (b) $\pi(2e - 5)$

25. (b) $\pi \left[\frac{8(\ln 2)^2}{3} - \frac{16(\ln 2)}{9} + \frac{16}{27} \right]$

27. $\frac{1}{2}$ **31.** $\frac{\pi}{2}(3b - a) + 2$

33. 6   **35.** $P(x) = -3x^2 + 1$

37. $\frac{1}{2} < p \le 1$ **39.** (b) 1

41. $\frac{e^{2x}}{13}(3 \sin 3x + 2 \cos 3x) + C$

43. $\frac{\cos x \sin 3x - 3 \sin x \cos 3x}{8} + C$

45. $\frac{e^{ax}}{a^2 + b^2}(a \sin bx - b \cos bx) + C$

47. $x \ln (ax) - x + C$

CHAPTER 8

Section 8.1, pp. 617–619

1. $a_1 = 0, a_2 = -\frac{1}{4}, a_3 = -\frac{2}{9}, a_4 = -\frac{3}{16}$

3. $a_1 = 1, a_2 = -\frac{1}{3}, a_3 = \frac{1}{5}, a_4 = -\frac{1}{7}$

5. $a_n = (-1)^{n+1}, n \ge 1$ **7.** $a_n = n^2 - 1, n \ge 1$

9. $a_n = 4n - 3, n \ge 1$ **11.** $a_n = \frac{1 + (-1)^{n+1}}{2}, n \ge 1$

13. Converges, 2   **15.** Converges, -1

17. Diverges   **19.** Diverges

21. Converges, $\frac{1}{2}$ **23.** Converges, $\sqrt{2}$

25. Converges, 0   **27.** Converges, 0

29. Diverges   **31.** Converges, e^7

33. Converges, 1   **35.** Converges, 1

37. Converges, 4   **39.** Converges, 0

41. Diverges   **43.** Converges, e^{-1}

45. Converges, $e^{2/3}$ **47.** Converges, x $(x > 0)$

49. Converges, 0   **51.** Converges, $\frac{\pi}{2}$

53. Converges, 0   **55.** Converges, 0

57. $N = 692, a_n = \sqrt[n]{0.5}, L = 1$ **59.** $N = 65, a_n = (0.9)^n, L = 0$

61. (b) $\sqrt{2}$ **63.** (b) 1

Section 8.2, pp. 625–627

1. $1, \dfrac{3}{2}, \dfrac{7}{4}, \dfrac{15}{8}, \dfrac{31}{16}, \dfrac{63}{32}, \dfrac{127}{64}, \dfrac{255}{128}, \dfrac{511}{256}, \dfrac{1023}{512}$

3. $2, 1, -\dfrac{1}{2}, -\dfrac{1}{4}, \dfrac{1}{8}, \dfrac{1}{16}, -\dfrac{1}{32}, -\dfrac{1}{64}, \dfrac{1}{128}, \dfrac{1}{256}$

5. 1, 1, 2, 3, 5, 8, 13, 21, 34, 55

7. (b) $\sqrt{3}$

9. (a) $f(x) = x^2 - 2$, $1.414213562 \approx \sqrt{2}$

    (b) $f(x) = \tan(x) - 1$, $0.7853981635 \approx \dfrac{\pi}{4}$

    (c) $f(x) = e^x$, diverges

11. Nondecreasing, bounded

13. Not nondecreasing, bounded

15. Converges, monotonic sequence theorem

17. Converges, monotonic sequence theorem

19. Diverges, definition of divergence

21. Converges, monotonic sequence theorem

23. Diverges, definition of divergence

27. 1   **29.** -0.73908513

31. 0.85375017

Section 8.3, pp. 637–639

1. $s_n = \dfrac{2\left[1 - \left(\dfrac{1}{3}\right)^n\right]}{1 - \left(\dfrac{1}{3}\right)}, 3$

3. $s_n = \dfrac{1 - \left(-\dfrac{1}{2}\right)^n}{1 - \left(-\dfrac{1}{2}\right)}, \dfrac{2}{3}$

5. $s_n = \dfrac{1}{2} - \dfrac{1}{n+2}, \dfrac{1}{2}$

7. $1 - \dfrac{1}{4} + \dfrac{1}{16} - \dfrac{1}{64} + \cdots, \dfrac{4}{5}$

9. $(5+1) + \left(\dfrac{5}{2} + \dfrac{1}{3}\right) + \left(\dfrac{5}{4} + \dfrac{1}{9}\right) + \left(\dfrac{5}{8} + \dfrac{1}{27}\right) + \cdots, \dfrac{23}{2}$

11. $(1+1) + \left(\dfrac{1}{2} - \dfrac{1}{6}\right) + \left(\dfrac{1}{4} + \dfrac{1}{25}\right) + \left(\dfrac{1}{8} - \dfrac{1}{125}\right) + \cdots, \dfrac{17}{6}$

13. 1   **15.** 5

17. 1   **19.** Converges, $2 + \sqrt{2}$

21. Converges, 1   **23.** Converges, $\dfrac{e^2}{e^2 - 1}$

25. Converges, $\dfrac{x}{x-1}$ **27.** Diverges

29. Diverges   **31.** Diverges

33. $a = 1, r = -x$; converges to $\dfrac{1}{1+x}$ for $|x| < 1$

35. $a = 3, r = \dfrac{x-1}{2}$, converges to $\dfrac{6}{3-x}$ for x in $(-1, 3)$

37. $|x| < \dfrac{1}{2}, \dfrac{1}{1-2x}$ **39.** $1 < x < 5, \dfrac{2}{x-1}$

41. $\dfrac{23}{99}$ **43.** $\dfrac{7}{9}$

45. $\dfrac{41{,}333}{33{,}300}$ **47.** 28 m

49. 8 m^2

51. (a) $3\left(\dfrac{4}{3}\right)^{n-1}$

    (b) $A_n = A + \dfrac{1}{3}A + \dfrac{1}{3}\left(\dfrac{4}{9}\right)A + \cdots + \dfrac{1}{3}\left(\dfrac{4}{9}\right)^{n-2}A, \ \lim\limits_{n\to\infty} A_n = \dfrac{2\sqrt{3}}{5}$

53. (a) $\displaystyle\sum_{n=-2}^{\infty} \dfrac{1}{(n+4)(n+5)}$

    (b) $\displaystyle\sum_{n=0}^{\infty} \dfrac{1}{(n+2)(n+3)}$

    (c) $\displaystyle\sum_{n=5}^{\infty} \dfrac{1}{(n-3)(n-2)}$

55. $\ln\left(\dfrac{8}{9}\right)$ **61.** It diverges.

Section 8.4, pp. 649–651

1. Diverges   **3.** Diverges

5. Converges   **7.** Converges

9. Diverges; $\dfrac{1}{2\sqrt{n} + \sqrt[3]{n}} \geq \dfrac{1}{2n + n} = \dfrac{1}{3n}$

11. Converges; $\dfrac{\sin^2 n}{2^n} \leq \dfrac{1}{2^n}$

13. Converges; $\left(\dfrac{n}{3n+1}\right)^n < \left(\dfrac{n}{3n}\right)^n = \left(\dfrac{1}{3}\right)^n$

15. Diverges; limit comparison with $\sum \dfrac{1}{n}$

17. Converges; limit comparison with $\sum \dfrac{1}{n^2}$

19. Converges; limit comparison with $\sum \dfrac{1}{n^{5/4}}$

21. Converges, $\rho = 1/2$ **23.** Diverges, $\rho = \infty$

25. Converges, $\rho = 1/10$ **27.** Converges, $\rho = 0$

29. Converges, $\rho = 0$ **31.** Converges, $\rho = 0$

33. Diverges, $\rho = \infty$

35. Converges; geometric series, $r = \dfrac{1}{e} < 1$

37. Diverges; p-series, $p < 1$

39. Diverges; limit comparison with $\sum \dfrac{1}{n}$

41. Converges; limit comparison with $\sum \dfrac{1}{n^{3/2}}$

43. Converges; Ratio Test   **45.** Converges; Ratio Test

47. Converges; Integral Test **49.** Converges; Integral Test

51. Converges; compare with $\sum \dfrac{3}{(1.25)^n}$

53. Converges; compare with $\sum \dfrac{1}{n^2}$

55. Converges; compare with $\sum \dfrac{1}{n^2}$

57. Converges; $\dfrac{\tan^{-1} n}{n^{1.1}} < \dfrac{\left(\dfrac{\pi}{2}\right)}{n^{1.1}}$

59. Diverges; nth-Term Test

61. Converges; Ratio Test   **63.** Diverges; Ratio Test

65. Diverges; $a_n = \left(\dfrac{1}{3}\right)^{(1/n!)} \to 1$ **71.** $a = 1$

Section 8.5, pp. 658–660

1. Converges by Theorem 8   **3.** Diverges; $a_n \nrightarrow 0$

5. Converges by Theorem 8   **7.** Diverges; $a_n \to \dfrac{1}{2} \neq 0$

9. Converges by Theorem 8

11. Converges absolutely. Series of absolute values is a convergent geometric series.

13. Converges conditionally. $\dfrac{1}{\sqrt{n+1}} \to 0$ but $\displaystyle\sum_{n=1}^{n} \dfrac{1}{\sqrt{n+1}}$ diverges.

15. Converges absolutely. Compare with $\displaystyle\sum_{n=1}^{\infty} \dfrac{1}{n^2}$.

17. Converges conditionally. $\dfrac{1}{n+3} \to 0$ but $\displaystyle\sum_{n=1}^{\infty} \dfrac{1}{n+3}$ diverges. Compare with $\displaystyle\sum_{n=1}^{\infty} \dfrac{1}{n}$.

19. Diverges; $\dfrac{3+n}{5+n} \to 1$

21. Converges conditionally; $\left(\dfrac{1}{n^2} + \dfrac{1}{n}\right) \to 0$ but $\dfrac{1+n}{n^2} > \dfrac{1}{n}$.

23. Converges absolutely; Ratio Test

25. Converges absolutely by Integral Test

27. Diverges; $a_n \nrightarrow 0$

29. Converges absolutely by the Ratio Test

31. Converges absolutely; $\dfrac{1}{n^2 + 2n + 1} < \dfrac{1}{n^2}$

33. Converges absolutely since $\left|\dfrac{\cos n\pi}{n\sqrt{n}}\right| = \left|\dfrac{(-1)^{n+1}}{n^{3/2}}\right| = \dfrac{1}{n^{3/2}}$ (convergent p-series).

35. Converges absolutely n^{th} by Root Test

37. Diverges; $a_n \to \infty$

39. Converges conditionally; $\sqrt{n+1} - \sqrt{n} = \dfrac{1}{\sqrt{n} + \sqrt{n+1}} \to 0$, but series of absolute values diverges. Compare with $\Sigma \dfrac{1}{\sqrt{n}}$.

41. Diverges; $a_n \to \dfrac{1}{2} \neq 0$

43. Converges absolutely; $\text{sech } n = \dfrac{2}{e^n + e^{-n}} = \dfrac{2e^n}{e^{2n} + 1} < \dfrac{2e^n}{e^{2n}} = \dfrac{2}{e^n}$, a term from a convergent geometric series.

45. $|\text{Error}| < 0.2$ **47.** $|\text{Error}| < 2 \times 10^{-11}$

49. 0.54030

51. (a) $a_n \geq a_{n+1}$ fails

   (b) $-\dfrac{1}{2}$

Section 8.6, pp. 668–669

1. (a) 1, $-1 < x < 1$ (b) $-1 < x < 1$ (c) None

3. (a) $\dfrac{1}{4}$, $-\dfrac{1}{2} < x < 0$ (b) $-\dfrac{1}{2} < x < 0$ (c) None

5. (a) 10, $-8 < x < 12$ (b) $-8 < x < 12$ (c) None

7. (a) 1, $-1 < x < 1$ (b) $-1 < x < 1$ (c) None

9. (a) 3, $[-3, 3]$ (b) $[-3, 3]$ (c) None

11. (a) ∞, for all x (b) For all x (c) None

13. (a) ∞, for all x (b) For all x (c) None

15. (a) 1, $-1 \leq x < 1$ (b) $-1 < x < 1$ (c) $x = -1$

17. (a) 5, $-8 < x < 2$ (b) $-8 < x < 2$ (c) None

19. (a) 3, $-3 < x < 3$ (b) $-3 < x < 3$ (c) None

21. (a) 1, $-1 < x < 1$ (b) $-1 < x < 1$ (c) None

23. (a) 0, $x = 0$ (b) $x = 0$ (c) None

25. (a) 2, $-4 < x \leq 0$ (b) $-4 < x < 0$ (c) $x = 0$

27. (a) 1, $-1 \leq x \leq 1$ (b) $-1 \leq x \leq 1$ (c) None

29. (a) $\dfrac{1}{4}$, $1 \leq x \leq \dfrac{3}{2}$ (b) $1 \leq x \leq \dfrac{3}{2}$ (c) None

31. (a) 1, $(-1 - \pi) \leq x < (1 - \pi)$
   (b) $(-1 - \pi) < x < (1 - \pi)$
   (c) $x = -1 - \pi$

33. $-1 < x < 3$, $\dfrac{4}{3 + 2x - x^2}$

35. $0 < x < 16$, $\dfrac{2}{4 - \sqrt{x}}$

37. $-\sqrt{2} < x < \sqrt{2}$, $\dfrac{3}{2 - x^2}$

39. $1 < x < 5$, $\dfrac{2}{x - 1}$, $1 < x < 5$, $\dfrac{-2}{(x - 1)^2}$

41. (a) $\cos x = 1 - \dfrac{x^2}{2!} + \dfrac{x^4}{4!} - \dfrac{x^6}{6!} + \dfrac{x^8}{8!} - \dfrac{x^{10}}{10!} + \cdots$; converges for all x

   (b) and (c) $2x - \dfrac{2^3 x^3}{3!} + \dfrac{2^5 x^5}{5!} - \dfrac{2^7 x^7}{7!} + \dfrac{2^9 x^9}{9!} - \dfrac{2^{11} x^{11}}{11!} + \cdots$

43. (a) $\dfrac{x^2}{2} + \dfrac{x^4}{12} + \dfrac{x^6}{45} + \dfrac{17x^8}{2520} + \dfrac{31x^{10}}{14,175}$, $-\dfrac{\pi}{2} < x < \dfrac{\pi}{2}$

   (b) $1 + x^2 + \dfrac{2x^4}{3} + \dfrac{17x^6}{45} + \dfrac{62x^8}{315} + \cdots$, $-\dfrac{\pi}{2} < x < \dfrac{\pi}{2}$

Section 8.7, pp. 681–683

1. $P_0(x) = 0$, $P_1(x) = x - 1$, $P_2(x) = (x - 1) - \dfrac{1}{2}(x - 1)^2$,

   $P_3(x) = (x - 1) - \dfrac{1}{2}(x - 1)^2 + \dfrac{1}{3}(x - 1)^3$

3. $P_0(x) = \dfrac{1}{2}$, $P_1(x) = \dfrac{1}{2} - \dfrac{x}{4}$, $P_2(x) = \dfrac{1}{2} - \dfrac{x}{4} + \dfrac{x^2}{8}$,

   $P_3(x) = \dfrac{1}{2} - \dfrac{x}{4} + \dfrac{x^2}{8} - \dfrac{x^3}{16}$

5. $P_0(x) = \dfrac{1}{\sqrt{2}}, \ P_1(x) = \dfrac{1}{\sqrt{2}} - \dfrac{1}{\sqrt{2}}\left(x - \dfrac{\pi}{4}\right),$

$P_2(x) = \dfrac{1}{\sqrt{2}} - \dfrac{1}{\sqrt{2}}\left(x - \dfrac{\pi}{4}\right) - \dfrac{1}{2\sqrt{2}}\left(x - \dfrac{\pi}{4}\right)^2, \ P_3(x) =$

$\dfrac{1}{\sqrt{2}} - \dfrac{1}{\sqrt{2}}\left(x - \dfrac{\pi}{4}\right) - \dfrac{1}{2\sqrt{2}}\left(x - \dfrac{\pi}{4}\right)^2 + \dfrac{1}{6\sqrt{2}}\left(x - \dfrac{\pi}{4}\right)^3$

7. $\displaystyle\sum_{n=0}^{\infty} \dfrac{(-x)^n}{n!} = 1 - x + \dfrac{x^2}{2!} - \dfrac{x^3}{3!} + \dfrac{x^4}{4!} - \cdots$

9. $\displaystyle\sum_{n=0}^{\infty} \dfrac{(-1)^n 3^{2n+1} x^{2n+1}}{(2n+1)!}$ **11.** $\displaystyle\sum_{n=0}^{\infty} \dfrac{x^{2n}}{(2n)!}$

13. $x^4 - 2x^3 - 5x + 4$

15. $8 + 10(x - 2) + 6(x - 2)^2 + (x - 2)^3$

17. $\displaystyle\sum_{n=0}^{\infty} (-1)^n (n + 1)(x - 1)^n$ **19.** $\displaystyle\sum_{n=0}^{\infty} \dfrac{e^2}{n!}(x - 2)^n$

21. $\displaystyle\sum_{n=0}^{\infty} \dfrac{(-5x)^n}{n!} = 1 - 5x + \dfrac{5^2 x^2}{2!} - \dfrac{5^3 x^3}{3!} + \cdots$

23. $\displaystyle\sum_{n=0}^{\infty} \dfrac{(-1)^n \left(\dfrac{\pi x}{2}\right)^{2n+1}}{(2n+1)!} = \dfrac{\pi x}{2} - \dfrac{\pi^3 x^3}{2^3 \cdot 3!} + \dfrac{\pi^5 x^5}{2^5 \cdot 5!} - \dfrac{\pi^7 x^7}{2^7 \cdot 7!} + \cdots$

25. $\displaystyle\sum_{n=0}^{\infty} \dfrac{x^{n+1}}{n!} = x + x^2 + \dfrac{x^3}{2!} + \dfrac{x^4}{3!} + \dfrac{x^5}{4!} + \cdots$

27. $\displaystyle\sum_{n=2}^{\infty} \dfrac{(-1)^n x^{2n}}{(2n)!} = \dfrac{x^4}{4!} - \dfrac{x^6}{6!} + \dfrac{x^8}{8!} - \dfrac{x^{10}}{10!} + \cdots$

29. $x - \dfrac{\pi^2 x^3}{2!} + \dfrac{\pi^4 x^5}{4!} - \dfrac{\pi^6 x^7}{6!} + \cdots = \displaystyle\sum_{n=0}^{\infty} \dfrac{(-1)^n \pi^{2n} x^{2n+1}}{(2n)!}$

31. $\displaystyle\sum_{n=1}^{\infty} \dfrac{(-1)^{n+1}(2x)^{2n}}{2 \cdot (2n)!} = \dfrac{(2x)^2}{2 \cdot 2!} - \dfrac{(2x)^4}{2 \cdot 4!} + \dfrac{(2x)^6}{2 \cdot 6!} - \dfrac{(2x)^8}{2 \cdot 8!} + \cdots$

33. $\displaystyle\sum_{n=1}^{\infty} \dfrac{(-1)^{n-1} 2^n x^{n+1}}{n} = 2x^2 - \dfrac{2^2 x^3}{2} + \dfrac{2^3 x^4}{3} - \dfrac{2^4 x^5}{4} + \cdots$

35. $|x| < (0.06)^{1/5} < 0.56968$

37. $|\,\text{Error}\,| < \dfrac{(10^{-3})^3}{6} < 1.67 \times 10^{-10}, \ -10^{-3} < x < 0$

39. **(a)** $|\,\text{Error}\,| < \dfrac{(3^{0.1})(0.1)^3}{6} < 1.87 \times 10^{-4}$

(b) $|\,\text{Error}\,| < \dfrac{(0.1)^3}{6} < 1.67 \times 10^{-4}$

45. **(a)** $L(x) = 0$ **(b)** $Q(x) = -\dfrac{x^2}{2}$

47. **(a)** $L(x) = 1$ **(b)** $Q(x) = 1 + \dfrac{x^2}{2}$

Section 8.8, pp. 690–691

1. $1 + \dfrac{x}{2} - \dfrac{x^2}{8} + \dfrac{x^3}{16}$

3. $1 + \dfrac{1}{2}x - \dfrac{3}{8}x^2 + \dfrac{5}{16}x^3 + \cdots$ **5.** $1 - x + \dfrac{3x^2}{4} - \dfrac{x^3}{2}$

7. $1 - \dfrac{x^3}{2} + \dfrac{3x^6}{8} - \dfrac{5x^9}{16}$ **9.** $1 + \dfrac{1}{2x} - \dfrac{1}{8x^2} + \dfrac{1}{16x^3}$

11. $(1 + x)^4 = 1 + 4x + 6x^2 + 4x^3 + x^4$

13. $(1 - 2x)^3 = 1 - 6x + 12x^2 - 8x^3$

15. $y = \displaystyle\sum_{n=0}^{\infty} \dfrac{(-1)^n}{n!} x^n = e^{-x}$ **17.** $y = \displaystyle\sum_{n=1}^{\infty} \dfrac{x^n}{n!} = e^x - 1$

19. $y = \displaystyle\sum_{n=2}^{\infty} \dfrac{x^n}{n!} = e^x - x - 1$ **21.** $y = \displaystyle\sum_{n=0}^{\infty} \dfrac{x^{2n}}{2^n n!} = e^{x^2/2}$

23. $y = \displaystyle\sum_{n=0}^{\infty} 2x^n = \dfrac{2}{1 - x}$ **25.** $y = \displaystyle\sum_{n=0}^{\infty} \dfrac{x^{2n+1}}{(2n+1)!} = \sinh x$

27. $y = 2 + x - 2\displaystyle\sum_{n=1}^{\infty} \dfrac{(-1)^{n+1} x^{2n}}{(2n)!}$

29. $y = -2(x - 2) - \displaystyle\sum_{n=1}^{\infty} \left[\dfrac{2(x - 2)^{2n}}{(2n)!} + \dfrac{3(x - 2)^{2n+1}}{(2n+1)!}\right]$

31. $y = a + bx + \dfrac{1}{6}x^3 - \dfrac{ax^4}{3 \cdot 4} - \dfrac{bx^5}{4 \cdot 5} - \dfrac{x^7}{6 \cdot 6 \cdot 7} + \dfrac{ax^8}{3 \cdot 4 \cdot 7 \cdot 8} +$

$\dfrac{bx^9}{4 \cdot 5 \cdot 8 \cdot 9} + \cdots. \ \text{For } n \geq 6, \ a_n = \dfrac{a_{n-4}}{n(n-1)}$

33. $\dfrac{x^3}{3} - \dfrac{x^7}{7 \cdot 3!} + \dfrac{x^{11}}{11 \cdot 5!}$

35. **(a)** $\dfrac{x^2}{2} - \dfrac{x^4}{12}$

(b) $\dfrac{x^2}{2} - \dfrac{x^4}{3 \cdot 4} + \dfrac{x^6}{5 \cdot 6} - \dfrac{x^8}{7 \cdot 8} + \cdots + (-1)^{15}\dfrac{x^{32}}{31 \cdot 32}$

37. $\dfrac{1}{2}$ **39.** -1

41. $2!$ **45.** 500 terms

47. **(a)** $x + \dfrac{x^3}{6} + \dfrac{3x^5}{40} + \dfrac{5x^7}{112}$, radius of convergence $= 1$

(b) $\dfrac{\pi}{2} - x - \dfrac{x^3}{6} - \dfrac{3x^5}{40} - \dfrac{5x^7}{112}$

Section 8.9, pp. 697–698

1. $f(x) = 1$ **3.** $f(x) = \displaystyle\sum_{n=1}^{\infty} \dfrac{2(-1)^{n+1}}{n} \sin nx$

5. $f(x) = \dfrac{\pi^2}{12} + \displaystyle\sum_{n=1}^{\infty} \dfrac{(-1)^n}{n^2} \cos nx$

7. $f(x) = \dfrac{2 \sinh \pi}{\pi}\left[\dfrac{1}{2} + \displaystyle\sum_{n=1}^{\infty} \dfrac{(-1)^n}{n^2 + 1}(\cos nx - n \sin nx)\right]$

9. $f(x) = \dfrac{1}{2}\cos x + \dfrac{1}{\pi}\displaystyle\sum_{n=2}^{\infty} \dfrac{n(1 + (-1)^n)}{n^2 - 1} \sin nx$

11. $f(x) = \dfrac{1}{2} + \dfrac{2}{\pi}\displaystyle\sum_{k=0}^{\infty} \dfrac{(-1)^k}{2k + 1} \cos(2k + 1)x$

13. $f(x) = \dfrac{5}{4} + \dfrac{4}{\pi^2}\displaystyle\sum_{n=1}^{\infty} \dfrac{1}{n^2}\left[(-1)^n - \cos\dfrac{n\pi}{2}\right](\cos(n\pi x) +$

$\dfrac{2}{\pi}\displaystyle\sum_{n=1}^{\infty} \dfrac{1}{n}\left[(-1)^n - \dfrac{2}{n\pi}\sin\dfrac{n\pi}{2}\right]\sin(n\pi x)$

15. Set $x = \pi, \ \dfrac{\pi^2}{4} = \dfrac{\pi^2}{12} + \displaystyle\sum_{n=1}^{\infty} \dfrac{(-1)^n}{n^2} \cos n\pi, \ \text{or} \ \dfrac{\pi^2}{6} = \displaystyle\sum_{n=1}^{\infty} \dfrac{1}{n^2} =$

$1 + \dfrac{1}{4} + \dfrac{1}{9} + \dfrac{1}{16} + \cdots + \dfrac{1}{n^2} + \cdots.$

17. 0

19. 0 if $m \neq n$; L if $m = n$

21. 0 if $m \neq n$; 0 if $m = n$

Section 8.10, pp. 705–706

1. $f(x) = \dfrac{\pi}{2} + \dfrac{2}{\pi} \displaystyle\sum_{n=1}^{\infty} \dfrac{[(-1)^n - 1]}{n^2} \cos nx$

3. $f(x) = (e - 1) + 2 \displaystyle\sum_{n=1}^{\infty} \dfrac{[e(-1)^n - 1]}{1 + n^2\pi^2} \cos n\pi x$

5. $f(x) = -\dfrac{1}{4} + \dfrac{4}{\pi} \displaystyle\sum_{n=1}^{\infty} \left[\dfrac{1}{n} \sin \dfrac{n\pi}{2} + \dfrac{1}{\pi n^2}\left((-1)^{n+1} + \cos \dfrac{n\pi}{2} \right) \right]$
$\cos \dfrac{n\pi x}{2}$

7. $f(x) = \dfrac{1}{2} + \displaystyle\sum_{n=1}^{\infty} \dfrac{4}{n^2\pi^2} \left[1 + (-1)^n - 2\cos \dfrac{n\pi}{2} \right] \cos n\pi x$

9. $f(x) = 2 \displaystyle\sum_{n=1}^{\infty} \dfrac{(-1)^n}{n\pi} \sin n\pi x$

11. $f(x) = \dfrac{8}{\pi} \displaystyle\sum_{k=1}^{\infty} \dfrac{k}{4k^2 - 1} \sin 2kx$

13. $f(x) = \sin x$

15. $f(x) = \dfrac{2}{\pi} \displaystyle\sum_{n=1}^{\infty} \left[\dfrac{1}{n} - \dfrac{2}{n^2\pi} \sin \dfrac{n\pi}{2} \right] \sin \dfrac{n\pi x}{2}$

17. (a) $f(x) = \dfrac{4}{\pi} \left[\sin x + \dfrac{\sin 3x}{3} + \dfrac{\sin 5x}{5} + \dfrac{\sin 7x}{7} + \cdots \right]$

(b) Evaluate $f(x)$ at $x = \dfrac{\pi}{2} \Rightarrow \dfrac{\pi}{4} = 1 - \dfrac{1}{3} + \dfrac{1}{5} - \dfrac{1}{7} + \cdots.$

19. $\displaystyle\sum_{n=1}^{\infty} \dfrac{(-1)^n}{4n^2 - 1} = \dfrac{1}{2} - \dfrac{\pi}{4}$

Practice 8 Practice Exercises, pp. 708–711

1. Converges to 1

3. Converges to -1

5. Diverges

7. Converges to 0

9. Converges to 1

11. Converges to e^{-5}

13. Converges to 3

15. Converges to ln 2

17. Diverges

19. $\dfrac{1}{6}$

21. $\dfrac{3}{2}$

23. $\dfrac{e}{e - 1}$

25. Diverges

27. Converges conditionally

29. Converges conditionally

31. Converges absolutely

33. Converges absolutely

35. Converges absolutely

37. Converges absolutely

39. Converges absolutely

41. (a) 3, $-7 \leq x < -1$

(b) $-7 < x < -1$

(c) $x = -7$

43. (a) $\dfrac{1}{3}$, $0 \leq x \leq \dfrac{2}{3}$ (b) $0 \leq x \leq \dfrac{2}{3}$ (c) None

45. (a) ∞, for all x (b) For all x (c) None

47. (a) $\sqrt{3}$, $-\sqrt{3} < x < \sqrt{3}$

(b) $-\sqrt{3} < x < \sqrt{3}$

(c) None

49. (a) e, $(-e, e)$ (b) $(-e, e)$ (c) { }

51. $\dfrac{1}{1 + x}$, $\dfrac{1}{4}$, $\dfrac{4}{5}$

53. $\sin x$, π, 0

55. e^x, ln 2, 2

57. $\displaystyle\sum_{n=0}^{\infty} 2^n x^n$

59. $\displaystyle\sum_{n=0}^{\infty} \dfrac{(-1)^n \pi^{2n+1} x^{2n+1}}{(2n + 1)!}$

61. $\displaystyle\sum_{n=0}^{\infty} \dfrac{(-1)^n x^{5n}}{(2n)!}$

63. $\displaystyle\sum_{n=0}^{\infty} \dfrac{\left(\dfrac{\pi x}{2}\right)^n}{n!}$

65. $2 - \dfrac{(x + 1)}{2 \cdot 1!} + \dfrac{3(x + 1)^2}{2^3 \cdot 2!} + \dfrac{9(x + 1)^3}{2^5 \cdot 3!} + \cdots$

67. $\dfrac{1}{4} - \dfrac{1}{4^2}(x - 3) + \dfrac{1}{4^3}(x - 3)^2 - \dfrac{1}{4^4}(x - 3)^3 + \cdots$

69. $y = \displaystyle\sum_{n=0}^{\infty} \dfrac{(-1)^{n+1}}{n!} x^n = -e^{-x}$

71. $y = 3 \displaystyle\sum_{n=0}^{\infty} \dfrac{(-1)^n 2^n}{n!} x^n = 3e^{-2x}$

73. $y = -1 - x + 2 \displaystyle\sum_{n=2}^{\infty} \dfrac{x^n}{n!} = 2e^x - 3x - 3$

75. $y = -1 - x + 2 \displaystyle\sum_{n=0}^{\infty} \dfrac{x^n}{n!} = 2e^x - 1 - x$

77. (a) $\dfrac{7}{2}$

79. (a) $\dfrac{1}{12}$

81. (a) -2

83. $r = -3$, $s = \dfrac{9}{2}$

85. $f(x) = \dfrac{1}{2} + \dfrac{6}{\pi} \displaystyle\sum_{n=1}^{\infty} \dfrac{1}{2n - 1} \sin [(2n - 1)x]$

87. $f(x) = \pi - 2 \displaystyle\sum_{n=1}^{\infty} \dfrac{(-1)^n}{n} \sin nx$

89. $f(x) = \dfrac{3}{2} + \dfrac{2}{\pi^2} \displaystyle\sum_{n=1}^{\infty} \dfrac{(-1)^n - 1}{n^2} \cos \dfrac{n\pi x}{2} - \dfrac{2}{\pi} \displaystyle\sum_{n=1}^{\infty} \dfrac{(-1)^n}{n} \sin \dfrac{n\pi x}{2}$

91. (a) $f(x) = \dfrac{1}{2} + \dfrac{2}{\pi} \displaystyle\sum_{n=1}^{\infty} \dfrac{\sin\left(\dfrac{n\pi}{2}\right)}{n} \cos n\pi x$

(b) $f(x) = \dfrac{2}{\pi} \displaystyle\sum_{n=1}^{\infty} \dfrac{1}{n}\left(1 - \cos \dfrac{n\pi}{2}\right) \sin n\pi x$

93. (a) $f(x) = \dfrac{2}{\pi} + \dfrac{1}{\pi} \displaystyle\sum_{n=1}^{\infty} \left[\dfrac{1}{n + 1} - \dfrac{1}{n - 1} + \dfrac{\cos [(n - 1)\pi]}{n - 1} - \dfrac{\cos [(n + 1)\pi]}{n + 1} \right] \cos n\pi x$

(b) $f(x) = \sin \pi x$

95. (a) $f(x) = 6 + \dfrac{12}{\pi^2} \displaystyle\sum_{n=1}^{\infty} \dfrac{4(-1)^n - 1}{n^2} \cos \dfrac{n\pi x}{3}$

(b) $f(x) = \dfrac{6}{\pi^3} \displaystyle\sum_{n=1}^{\infty} \dfrac{(6 - 5n^2\pi^2)(-1)^n - 6}{n^3} \sin \dfrac{n\pi x}{3}$

97. (b) $|\,\text{Error}\,| < \sin\left(\dfrac{1}{42}\right) < 0.02381$; an underestimate because the remainder is positive

99. $\dfrac{2}{3}$

101. $\ln\left(\dfrac{n+1}{2n}\right)$; the series converges to $\ln\left(\dfrac{1}{2}\right)$.

103. (a) ∞ (b) $a = 1, b = 0$

105. It converges.

113. (a) -3 is the fixed point.   (b) 0.2 is the fixed point.

Chapter 8 Additional Exercises, pp. 711–715

1. Converges; Direct Comparison Test
3. Diverges; nth-Term Test
5. Converges; Direct Comparison Test
7. Diverges; nth-Term Test

9. With $a = \dfrac{\pi}{3}$, $\cos x = \dfrac{1}{2} - \dfrac{\sqrt{3}}{2}\left(x - \dfrac{\pi}{3}\right) - \dfrac{1}{4}\left(x - \dfrac{\pi}{3}\right)^2 + \dfrac{\sqrt{3}}{12}\left(x - \dfrac{\pi}{3}\right)^3 + \cdots$.

11. With $a = 0$, $e^x = 1 + x + \dfrac{x^2}{2!} + \dfrac{x^3}{3!} + \cdots$.

13. With $a = 22\pi$, $\cos x = 1 - \dfrac{1}{2}(x - 22\pi)^2 + \dfrac{1}{4!}(x - 22\pi)^4 - \dfrac{1}{6!}(x - 22\pi)^6 + \cdots$.

15. Converges, limit $= b$ **17.** $\dfrac{\pi}{2}$

21. (a) $\dfrac{b^2\sqrt{3}}{4}\displaystyle\sum_{n=0}^{\infty}\dfrac{3^n}{4^n}$ (b) $\sqrt{3}b^2$

    (c) No. For example, the three vertices of the original triangle are not removed. The set of points not removed has area 0.

23. (a) No, the limit does not appear to depend on the value of a.
    (b) Yes, the limit depends on the value of b.

    (c) $\displaystyle\lim_{n\to\infty}\left(1 - \dfrac{\cos\left(\dfrac{a}{n}\right)}{bn}\right)^n = e^{-1/b}$

25. $b = \pm\dfrac{1}{5}$ **29.** (b) Yes

35. (a) $\displaystyle\sum_{n=1}^{\infty} nx^{n-1}$ (b) 6 (c) $\dfrac{1}{q}$

37. (a) $R_n = \dfrac{C_0 e^{-kt_0}(1 - e^{-nkt_0})}{1 - e^{-kt_0}}$, $R = \dfrac{C_0(e^{-kt_0})}{1 - e^{-kt_0}} = \dfrac{C_0}{e^{kt_0} - 1}$

    (b) $R_1 = \dfrac{1}{e} \approx 0.368$, $R_{10} = R(1 - e^{-10}) \approx R(0.9999546) \approx 0.58195$; $R \approx 0.58198$; $0 < \dfrac{R - R_{10}}{R} < 0.0001$

    (c) 7

CHAPTER 9

Section 9.1, pp. 726–728

1. (a) $\langle 9, -6\rangle$ (b) $3\sqrt{13}$
3. (a) $\langle 1, 3\rangle$ (b) $\sqrt{10}$
5. (a) $\langle 12, -19\rangle$ (b) $\sqrt{505}$
7. (a) $\left\langle \dfrac{1}{5}, \dfrac{14}{5}\right\rangle$ (b) $\dfrac{\sqrt{197}}{5}$
9. $\langle 1, -4\rangle$ **11.** $\langle -2, -3\rangle$
13. $\left\langle -\dfrac{1}{2}, \dfrac{\sqrt{3}}{2}\right\rangle$ **15.** $\left\langle -\dfrac{\sqrt{3}}{2}, \dfrac{1}{2}\right\rangle$

17. The vector $\mathbf{v}$ is horizontal and 1 in. long. The vectors $\mathbf{u}$ and $\mathbf{w}$ are $\dfrac{11}{16}$ in. long. $\mathbf{w}$ is vertical and $\mathbf{u}$ makes a 45° angle with the horizontal. All vectors must be drawn to scale.

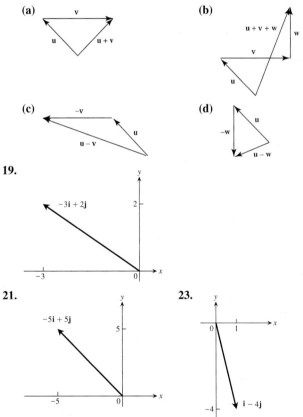

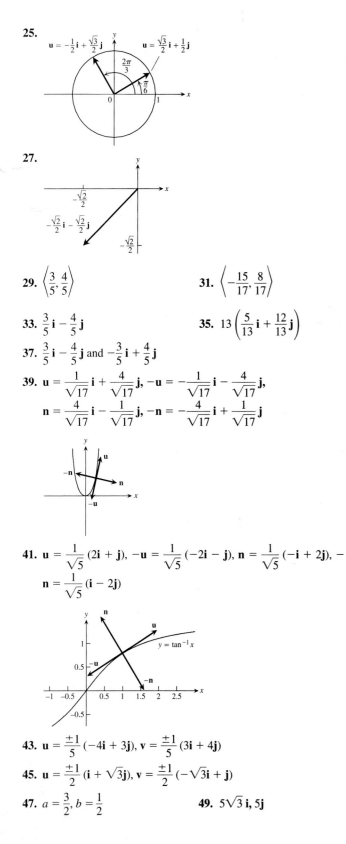

25.

$\mathbf{u} = -\frac{1}{2}\mathbf{i} + \frac{\sqrt{3}}{2}\mathbf{j}$ $\mathbf{u} = \frac{\sqrt{3}}{2}\mathbf{i} + \frac{1}{2}\mathbf{j}$

27.

$-\frac{\sqrt{2}}{2}\mathbf{i} - \frac{\sqrt{2}}{2}\mathbf{j}$

29. $\left\langle \frac{3}{5}, \frac{4}{5} \right\rangle$

31. $\left\langle -\frac{15}{17}, \frac{8}{17} \right\rangle$

33. $\frac{3}{5}\mathbf{i} - \frac{4}{5}\mathbf{j}$

35. $13\left(\frac{5}{13}\mathbf{i} + \frac{12}{13}\mathbf{j}\right)$

37. $\frac{3}{5}\mathbf{i} - \frac{4}{5}\mathbf{j}$ and $-\frac{3}{5}\mathbf{i} + \frac{4}{5}\mathbf{j}$

39. $\mathbf{u} = \frac{1}{\sqrt{17}}\mathbf{i} + \frac{4}{\sqrt{17}}\mathbf{j}, \ -\mathbf{u} = -\frac{1}{\sqrt{17}}\mathbf{i} - \frac{4}{\sqrt{17}}\mathbf{j},$

$\mathbf{n} = \frac{4}{\sqrt{17}}\mathbf{i} - \frac{1}{\sqrt{17}}\mathbf{j}, \ -\mathbf{n} = -\frac{4}{\sqrt{17}}\mathbf{i} + \frac{1}{\sqrt{17}}\mathbf{j}$

41. $\mathbf{u} = \frac{1}{\sqrt{5}}(2\mathbf{i} + \mathbf{j}), \ -\mathbf{u} = \frac{1}{\sqrt{5}}(-2\mathbf{i} - \mathbf{j}), \ \mathbf{n} = \frac{1}{\sqrt{5}}(-\mathbf{i} + 2\mathbf{j}), \ -$

$\mathbf{n} = \frac{1}{\sqrt{5}}(\mathbf{i} - 2\mathbf{j})$

43. $\mathbf{u} = \frac{\pm 1}{5}(-4\mathbf{i} + 3\mathbf{j}), \ \mathbf{v} = \frac{\pm 1}{5}(3\mathbf{i} + 4\mathbf{j})$

45. $\mathbf{u} = \frac{\pm 1}{2}(\mathbf{i} + \sqrt{3}\mathbf{j}), \ \mathbf{v} = \frac{\pm 1}{2}(-\sqrt{3}\mathbf{i} + \mathbf{j})$

47. $a = \frac{3}{2}, b = \frac{1}{2}$

49. $5\sqrt{3}\,\mathbf{i}, 5\mathbf{j}$

51. $\approx \langle -338.095, 725.046 \rangle$

53. **(a)** $(5\cos 60°, 5\sin 60°) = \left(\frac{5}{2}, \frac{5\sqrt{3}}{2}\right)$

(b) $(5\cos 60° + 10\cos 315°, 5\sin 60° + 10\sin 315°) =$

$\left(\frac{5 + \sqrt{2}}{2}, \frac{5\sqrt{3} - 10\sqrt{2}}{2}\right)$

Section 9.2, pp. 735–737

$\mathbf{v} \cdot \mathbf{u}$	$|\mathbf{v}|$	$|\mathbf{u}|$
1. -20	$2\sqrt{5}$	$2\sqrt{5}$

$\cos\theta$	$|\mathbf{u}|\cos\theta$	$\text{proj}_\mathbf{v}\,\mathbf{u}$
-1	$-2\sqrt{5}$	$-2\mathbf{i} + 4\mathbf{j}$

$\mathbf{v} \cdot \mathbf{u}$	$|\mathbf{v}|$	$|\mathbf{u}|$
3. $\sqrt{3} - \sqrt{2}$	$\sqrt{2}$	$\sqrt{5}$

$\cos\theta$	$|\mathbf{u}|\cos\theta$	$\text{proj}_\mathbf{v}\,\mathbf{u}$
$\dfrac{\sqrt{30} - \sqrt{20}}{10}$	$\dfrac{\sqrt{6} - 2}{2}$	$\dfrac{\sqrt{3} - \sqrt{2}}{2}(-\mathbf{i} + \mathbf{j})$

$\mathbf{v} \cdot \mathbf{u}$	$|\mathbf{v}|$	$|\mathbf{u}|$
5. $\dfrac{1}{6}$	$\dfrac{\sqrt{30}}{6}$	$\dfrac{\sqrt{30}}{6}$

$\cos\theta$	$|\mathbf{u}|\cos\theta$	$\text{proj}_\mathbf{v}\,\mathbf{u}$
$\dfrac{1}{5}$	$\dfrac{1}{\sqrt{30}}$	$\dfrac{1}{5}\left\langle \dfrac{1}{\sqrt{2}}, \dfrac{1}{\sqrt{3}} \right\rangle$

7. ≈ 0.64 rad　　　　**9.** ≈ 1.85

11. Angle at $A = \cos^{-1}\left(\dfrac{1}{\sqrt{5}}\right) \approx 63.435$ degrees, angle at $B = \cos^{-1}\left(\dfrac{3}{5}\right) \approx 53.130$ degrees, angle at $C = \cos^{-1}\left(\dfrac{1}{\sqrt{5}}\right) \approx$ 63.435 degrees.

13. The sum of two vectors of equal length is *always* orthogonal to their difference, as we can see from the equation $(\mathbf{v}_1 + \mathbf{v}_2) \cdot (\mathbf{v}_1 - \mathbf{v}_2) = \mathbf{v}_1 \cdot \mathbf{v}_1 + \mathbf{v}_2 \cdot \mathbf{v}_1 - \mathbf{v}_1 \cdot \mathbf{v}_2 - \mathbf{v}_2 \cdot \mathbf{v}_2 = |\mathbf{v}_1|^2 - |\mathbf{v}_2|^2 = 0.$

19. Horizontal component: ≈ 1188 ft/sec, vertical component: ≈ 167 ft/sec

21. **(a)** Since $|\cos\theta| \le 1$, we have $|\mathbf{u} \cdot \mathbf{v}| = |\mathbf{u}||\mathbf{v}||\cos\theta| \le |\mathbf{u}||\mathbf{v}|(1) = |\mathbf{u}||\mathbf{v}|.$

(b) We have equality precisely when $|\cos\theta| = 1$ or when one or both of $\mathbf{u}$ and $\mathbf{v}$ are $\mathbf{0}$. In the case of nonzero vectors, we have equality when $\theta = 0$ or π, that is, when the vectors are parallel.

23.

27. $x + 2y = 4$

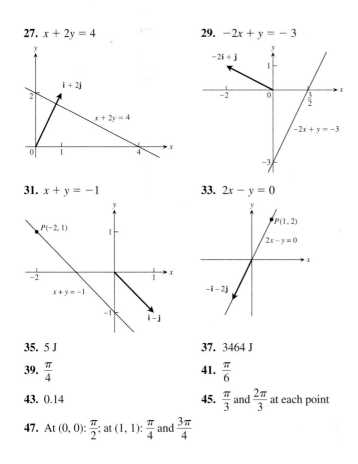

29. $-2x + y = -3$

31. $x + y = -1$

33. $2x - y = 0$

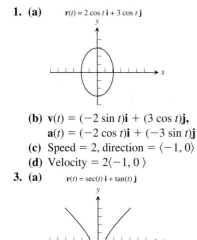

35. 5 J

37. 3464 J

39. $\dfrac{\pi}{4}$

41. $\dfrac{\pi}{6}$

43. 0.14

45. $\dfrac{\pi}{3}$ and $\dfrac{2\pi}{3}$ at each point

47. At $(0, 0)$: $\dfrac{\pi}{2}$; at $(1, 1)$: $\dfrac{\pi}{4}$ and $\dfrac{3\pi}{4}$

Section 9.3, pp. 746–749

1. (a) $r(t) = 2 \cos t\,\mathbf{i} + 3 \cos t\,\mathbf{j}$

(b) $\mathbf{v}(t) = (-2 \sin t)\mathbf{i} + (3 \cos t)\mathbf{j}$,
$\mathbf{a}(t) = (-2 \cos t)\mathbf{i} + (-3 \sin t)\mathbf{j}$
(c) Speed $= 2$, direction $= \langle -1, 0 \rangle$
(d) Velocity $= 2\langle -1, 0 \rangle$

3. (a) $r(t) = \sec(t)\,\mathbf{i} + \tan(t)\,\mathbf{j}$

(b) $\mathbf{v} = (\sec t \tan t)\mathbf{i} + (\sec^2 t)\mathbf{j}$, $\mathbf{a}(t) = (\sec t \tan^2 t + \sec^3 t)\mathbf{i} + (2 \sec^2 t \tan t)\mathbf{j}$
(c) Speed $= \dfrac{2\sqrt{5}}{3}$, direction $= \left\langle \dfrac{1}{\sqrt{5}}, \dfrac{2}{\sqrt{5}} \right\rangle$
(d) Velocity $= \left(\dfrac{2\sqrt{5}}{3} \right) \left\langle \dfrac{1}{\sqrt{5}}, \dfrac{2}{\sqrt{5}} \right\rangle$

5. $t = 0, \pi, 2\pi$

7. $t =$ all nonnegative integer multiples of $\dfrac{\pi}{2}$

9. $\cos^{-1}\left(\dfrac{3}{5} \right) \approx 53.130$ degrees

11. (a) $3\mathbf{i}$ **(b)** $t \neq 0, -3$ **(c)** $t = 0, -3$

13. (a) $y = -1$ **(b)** $x = 0$

15. $-3\mathbf{i} + (4\sqrt{2} - 2)\mathbf{j}$

17. $(\sec t)\mathbf{i} + (\ln | \sec t |)\mathbf{j} + \mathbf{C}$

19. $\mathbf{r}(t) = ((t + 1)^{3/2} - 1)\mathbf{i} - (e^{-t} - 1)\mathbf{j}$

21. $\mathbf{r}(t) = (8t + 100)\mathbf{i} + (-16t^2 + 8t)\mathbf{j}$

23. 2

25. (a) $\mathbf{v}(t) = (\cos t)\mathbf{i} - (2 \sin 2t)\mathbf{j}$

(b) $t = \dfrac{\pi}{2}, \dfrac{3\pi}{2}$
(c) $y = 1 - 2x^2$, $-1 \leq x \leq 1$. The particle starts at $(0, 1)$, goes to $(1, -1)$, then goes to $(-1, -1)$, and then goes to $(0, 1)$, tracing the curve twice.

27. $\mathbf{r}(t) = \left(\dfrac{3}{2}t^2 + \dfrac{3\sqrt{10}}{5}t + 1 \right)\mathbf{i} + \left(-\dfrac{1}{2}t^2 - \dfrac{\sqrt{10}}{5}t + 2 \right)\mathbf{j}$

29. (a) **i.** Constant speed
    ii. Yes, orthogonal
    iii. Counterclockwise movement
    iv. Yes
(b) **i.** Constant speed
    ii. Yes, orthogonal
    iii. Counterclockwise movement
    iv. Yes
(c) **i.** Constant speed
    ii. Yes, orthogonal
    iii. Counterclockwise movement
    iv. No
(d) **i.** Constant speed
    ii. Yes, orthogonal
    iii. Clockwise movement
    iv. Yes
(e) **i.** Variable speed
    ii. Not orthogonal in general
    iii. Counterclockwise movement
    iv. Yes

31. (a) 160 sec   **(b)** 225 m   **(c)** $\dfrac{15}{4}$ m/sec

33. (a) Referring to the figure, look at the circular arc from the point where $t = 0$ to the point "m". On one hand, this arc has length given by ($r_0\theta$), but it also has length given by (vt). Setting those two quantities equal gives the result.

(b) $\mathbf{a}(t) = -\dfrac{v^2}{r_0}\left[\left(\cos\dfrac{vt}{r_0}\right)\mathbf{i} + \left(\sin\dfrac{vt}{r_0}\right)\mathbf{j}\right]$

(c) From part (b), $\mathbf{a}(t) = -\left(\dfrac{v}{r_0}\right)^2\mathbf{r}(t)$. So, by Newton's second law, $\mathbf{F} = -m\left(\dfrac{v}{r_0}\right)^2\mathbf{r}$. Substituting for $\mathbf{F}$ in the law of gravitation gives the result.

(d) Set $\dfrac{vT}{r_0} = 2\pi$ and solve for vT.

(e) Substitute $\dfrac{2\pi r_0}{T}$ for v in $v^2 = \dfrac{GM}{r_0}$ and solve for T^2.

35. (a) Apply the corollary to each component separately.

(b) Follows immediately from part (a) since any two antiderivatives of $\mathbf{r}(t)$ must have identical derivatives, namely $\mathbf{r}(t)$.

37. Let $\mathbf{C} = \langle C_1, C_2\rangle$, $\dfrac{d\mathbf{C}}{dt} = \left\langle\dfrac{dC_1}{dt}, \dfrac{dC_2}{dt}\right\rangle = \langle 0, 0\rangle$.

39. $\mathbf{u} = \langle u_1, u_2\rangle$, $\mathbf{v} = \langle v_1, v_2\rangle$

(a) $\dfrac{d}{dt}(\mathbf{u} + \mathbf{v}) = \dfrac{d}{dt}(\langle u_1 + v_1, u_2 + v_2\rangle)$

$= \left\langle\dfrac{d}{dt}(u_1 + v_1), \dfrac{d}{dt}(u_2 + v_2)\right\rangle$

$= \langle u'_1 + v'_1, u'_2 + v'_2\rangle$

$= \langle u'_1, u'_2\rangle + \langle v'_1, v'_2\rangle = \dfrac{d\mathbf{u}}{dt} + \dfrac{d\mathbf{v}}{dt}$

(b) $\dfrac{d}{dt}(\mathbf{u} - \mathbf{v}) = \dfrac{d}{dt}(\langle u_1 - v_1, u_2 - v_2\rangle)$

$= \left\langle\dfrac{d}{dt}(u_1 - v_1), \dfrac{d}{dt}(u_2 - v_2)\right\rangle$

$= \langle u'_1 - v'_1, u'_2 - v'_2\rangle$

$= \langle u'_1, u'_2\rangle - \langle v'_1, v'_2\rangle = \dfrac{d\mathbf{u}}{dt} - \dfrac{d\mathbf{v}}{dt}$

41. $f(t)$ and $g(t)$ differentiable at $c \Rightarrow f(t)$ and $g(t)$ continuous at $c \Rightarrow$ $\mathbf{r}(t) = f(t)\mathbf{i} + g(t)\mathbf{j}$ is continuous at c.

43. (a) Let $\mathbf{r}(t) = f(t)\mathbf{i} + g(t)\mathbf{j}$. Then $\dfrac{d}{dt}\displaystyle\int_a^t \mathbf{r}(q)\,dq = \dfrac{d}{dt}\displaystyle\int_a^t [f(q)\mathbf{i} +$

$g(q)\mathbf{j}]\,dq = \dfrac{d}{dt}\left[\left(\displaystyle\int_a^t f(q)\,dq\right)\mathbf{i} + \left(\displaystyle\int_a^t g(q)\,dq\right)\mathbf{j}\right] = \left(\dfrac{d}{dt}\displaystyle\int_a^t f(q)\,dq\right)\mathbf{i}$

$+ \left(\dfrac{d}{dt}\displaystyle\int_a^t g(q)\,dq\right)\mathbf{j} = f(t)\mathbf{i} + g(t)\mathbf{j} = \mathbf{r}(t)$.

(b) Let $\mathbf{S}(t) = \displaystyle\int_a^t \mathbf{r}(q)\,dq$. Then part (a) shows that $\mathbf{S}(t)$ is an antiderivative of $\mathbf{r}(t)$. Let $\mathbf{R}(t)$ be any antiderivative of $\mathbf{r}(t)$. Then, according to Exercise 35, part (b), $\mathbf{S}(t) = \mathbf{R}(t) + \mathbf{C}$. Letting $t = a$, we have $\mathbf{0} = \mathbf{S}(a) = \mathbf{R}(a) + \mathbf{C}$. Therefore,

$\mathbf{C} = -\mathbf{R}(a)$ and $\mathbf{S}(t) = \mathbf{R}(t) - \mathbf{R}(a)$. The result follows by letting $t = b$.

Section 9.4, pp. 757–760

1. 50 sec
3. (a) 72.2 sec, 25,510 m   **(b)** 4020 m   **(c)** 6378 m
5. $t \approx 2.135$ sec, $x \approx 66.42$ ft
7. (a) $v_0 \approx 9.9$ m/sec
   (b) $\alpha \approx 18.4°$ or $71.6°$
9. 190 mph
11. The golf ball will clip the leaves at the top.
13. 149 ft/sec, 2.25 sec   **15.** $39.3°$ or $50.7°$
17. 46.6 ft/sec   **21.** 1.92 sec, 73.7 ft (approx.)
23. 4.00 ft, 7.80 ft/sec
25. (b) $\mathbf{v}_0$ would bisect $\angle AOR$
27. (a) (Assuming that "x" is zero at the point of impact.) $\mathbf{r}(t) = (x(t))\mathbf{i} + (y(t))\mathbf{j}$, where $x(t) = (35\cos 27°)t$ and $y(t) = 4 + (35\sin 27°)t - 16t^2$.
   (b) At $t \approx 0.497$ sec, it reaches its maximum height of about 7.945 ft.
   (c) Range $\approx 37,45$ ft, flight time ≈ 1.201 sec
   (d) At $t \approx 0.254$ and $t \approx 0.740$ sec, when it is ≈ 29.554 and ≈ 14.396 ft from where it will land.
   (e) Yes. It changes things because the ball won't clear the net.
31. (a) $\mathbf{r}(t) = (x(t))\mathbf{i} + (y(t))\mathbf{j}$, where $x(t) = \left(\dfrac{1}{0.08}\right)(1 - e^{-0.08t})$

$(152\cos 20° - 7.6)$ and $y(t) = 3 + \left(\dfrac{152}{0.08}\right)(1 - e^{-0.08t})$

$(\sin 20°) + \left(\dfrac{32}{0.08^2}\right)(1 - 0.08t - e^{-0.08t})$

   (b) At $t \approx 1.527$ sec, it reaches its maximum height of about 41.893 ft.
   (c) Range ≈ 351.734 ft, flight time ≈ 3.181 sec.
   (d) At $t \approx 0.877$ and $t \approx 2.190$ sec, when it is about 106.028 and 251.530 ft from home plate.
   (e) No. The wind gust would need to be greater than 12.846 ft/sec in the direction of the hit for the ball to clear the fence for a home run.

Section 9.5, pp. 768–770

1. (a) and (e) are the same.
   (b) and (g) are the same.
   (c) and (h) are the same.
   (d) and (f) are the same.
3. (a) $(1, 1)$ **(b)** $(1, 0)$ **(c)** $(0, 0)$ **(d)** $(-1, -1)$

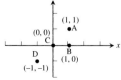

5. (a) $\left(\sqrt{2}, \dfrac{3\pi}{4}\right)$ or $\left(\sqrt{2}, -\dfrac{5\pi}{4}\right)$

(b) $\left(2, -\dfrac{\pi}{3}\right)$ or $\left(-2, \dfrac{2\pi}{3}\right)$

(c) $\left(3, \dfrac{\pi}{2}\right)$ or $\left(3, \dfrac{5\pi}{2}\right)$

(d) $(1, \pi)$ or $(-1, 0)$

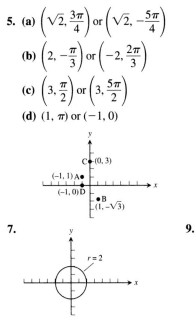

7.

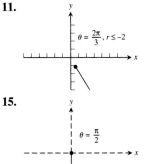

9.

11.

13.

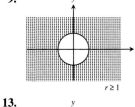

15.

17.

19. $y = 0$, the x-axis
21. $y = 4$, a horizontal line
23. $x + y = 1$, a line (slope $= -1$, y-intercept $= 1$)
25. $x^2 + (y - 2)^2 = 4$, a circle (center $= (0, 2)$, radius $= 2$)

27. $xy = 1 \left(\text{or } y = \dfrac{1}{x}\right)$, a hyperbola

29. $y = e^x$, the exponential curve
31. $y = \ln x$, the logarithmic curve
33. $(x + 2)^2 + y^2 = 4$, a circle (center $= (-2, 0)$, radius $= 2$)
35. $(x - 1)^2 + (y - 1)^2 = 2$, a circle (center $= (1, 1)$, radius $= \sqrt{2}$)
37. $r \cos \theta = 7$

39. $\theta = \dfrac{\pi}{4}$

41. $r^2 = 4$ or $r = 2$
43. $r^2(4 \cos^2 \theta + 9 \sin^2 \theta) = 36$
45. $r \sin^2 \theta = 4 \cos \theta$
47. $r = 4 \sin \theta$

49. (a)

(b) Length of interval $= 2\pi$
51. (a)

(b) Length of interval $= \dfrac{\pi}{2}$
53. (a)

(b) Length of interval $= 2\pi$
55. (a)

(b) Required interval $= (-\infty, \infty)$
57. (a)

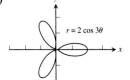

(b) Length of interval $= \pi$
59. x-axis, y-axis, origin   **61.** y-axis
63. (a) Because $r = a \sec \theta$ is equivalent to $r \cos \theta = a$, which is equivalent to the Cartesian equation $x = a$
(b) $r = a \csc \theta$ is equivalent to $y = a$.

67. $(0, 0), \left(1, \dfrac{\pi}{2}\right), \left(1, \dfrac{3\pi}{2}\right)$ **69.** $(0, 0), \left(\dfrac{1}{2}, \pm\dfrac{\pi}{3}\right)$

71. $(0, 0), \left(\pm\dfrac{1}{\sqrt[4]{2}}, \dfrac{\pi}{8}\right)$

73. $\left(1, \dfrac{\pi}{12}\right), \left(1, \dfrac{5\pi}{12}\right), \left(1, \dfrac{7\pi}{12}\right), \left(1, \dfrac{11\pi}{12}\right), \left(1, \dfrac{13\pi}{12}\right), \left(1, \dfrac{17\pi}{12}\right),$
$\left(1, \dfrac{19\pi}{12}\right), \left(1, \dfrac{23\pi}{12}\right)$

75. Part (a)
81. $d = [(x_2 - x_1)^2 + (y_2 - y_1)^2]^{1/2} = [(r_2 \cos \theta_2 - r_1 \cos \theta_1)^2 + (r_2 \sin \theta_2 - r_1 \sin \theta_1)^2]^{1/2}$, and then simplify using trigonometric identities.

1236   Answers

Section 9.6, pp. 777–779

1. At $\theta = 0$: -1; at $\theta = \pi$: 1

3. At $(2, 0)$: $-\frac{2}{3}$; at $\left(-1, \frac{\pi}{2}\right)$: 0; at $(2, \pi)$: $\frac{2}{3}$; at $\left(5, \frac{3\pi}{2}\right)$: 0

5. $\theta = \frac{\pi}{2}$ $[x = 0]$

7. $\theta = 0$ $[y = 0]$, $\theta = \frac{\pi}{5}\left[y = \left(\tan\frac{\pi}{5}\right)x\right]$, $\theta = \frac{2\pi}{5}\left[y = \left(\tan\frac{2\pi}{5}\right)x\right]$,

$\theta = \frac{3\pi}{5}\left[y = \left(\tan\frac{3\pi}{5}\right)x\right]$, $\theta = \frac{4\pi}{5}\left[y = \left(\tan\frac{4\pi}{5}\right)x\right]$

9. Horizontal at $\left(-\frac{1}{2}, \frac{\pi}{6}\right)\left[y = -\frac{1}{4}\right]$, $\left(-\frac{1}{2}, \frac{5\pi}{6}\right)\left[y = -\frac{1}{4}\right]$,

$\left(-2, \frac{3\pi}{2}\right)$ $[y = 2]$;

vertical at $\left(0, \frac{\pi}{2}\right)$ $[x = 0]$, $\left(-\frac{3}{2}, \frac{7\pi}{6}\right)\left[x = \frac{3\sqrt{3}}{4}\right]$, $\left(-1.5, \frac{11\pi}{6}\right)$

$\left[x = -\frac{3\sqrt{3}}{4}\right]$

11. Horizontal at $(0, 0)$ $[y = 0]$, $\left(2, \frac{\pi}{2}\right)$ $[y = 2]$, $(0, \pi)$ $[y = 0]$;

vertical at $\left(\sqrt{2}, \frac{\pi}{4}\right)$ $[x = 1]$, $\left(\sqrt{2}, \frac{3\pi}{4}\right)$ $[x = -1]$

13. 18π **15.** $\frac{\pi}{8}$

17. 2   **19.** $\frac{\pi}{2} - 1$

21. $5\pi - 8$ **23.** $3\sqrt{3} - \pi$

25. $\frac{\pi}{3} + \frac{\sqrt{3}}{2}$ **27.** $12\pi - 9\sqrt{3}$

29. (a) $\frac{3}{2} - \frac{\pi}{4}$ **31.** $\frac{19}{3}$

33. 8   **35.** $3(\sqrt{2} + \ln(1 + \sqrt{2}))$

37. $\frac{\pi}{8} + \frac{3}{8}$ **39.** 2π

45. (a) Let $r = 1.75 + \frac{0.06\theta}{2\pi}$, $0 \le \theta \le 12\pi$.

(b) Since $\frac{dr}{d\theta} = \frac{b}{2\pi}$, this is just Equation (4) for the length of the curve.

(c) ≈ 741.420 cm, or ≈ 7.414 m

(d) $\left(r^2 + \left(\frac{b}{2\pi}\right)^2\right)^{1/2} = r\left(1 + \left(\frac{b}{2\pi r}\right)^2\right)^{1/2} \approx r$ since $\left(\frac{b}{2\pi r}\right)^2$ is a very small quantity squared

(e) $L \approx 741.420$ cm (from part (c)), $L_a \approx 741.416$ cm

Chapter 9 Practice Exercises, pp. 780–784

1. (a) $\langle -17, 32 \rangle$ (b) $\sqrt{1313}$

3. (a) $\langle 6, -8 \rangle$ (b) 10

5. $\left\langle -\frac{\sqrt{3}}{2}, -\frac{1}{2} \right\rangle$ [assuming counterclockwise]

7. $\left\langle \frac{8}{\sqrt{17}}, -\frac{2}{\sqrt{17}} \right\rangle$

9. Length = 2, direction is $\frac{1}{\sqrt{2}}\mathbf{i} + \frac{1}{\sqrt{2}}\mathbf{j}$.

11. $\left.\frac{d\mathbf{r}}{dt}\right|_{t=\pi/2} = 2(-\mathbf{i})$

13. Unit tangents $\pm\left(\frac{1}{\sqrt{5}}\mathbf{i} + \frac{2}{\sqrt{5}}\mathbf{j}\right)$, unit normals $\pm$

$\left(-\frac{2}{\sqrt{5}}\mathbf{i} + \frac{1}{\sqrt{5}}\mathbf{j}\right)$

15.

17. $|\mathbf{v}| = \sqrt{2}$, $|\mathbf{u}| = \sqrt{5}$, $\mathbf{u} \cdot \mathbf{v} = \mathbf{v} \cdot \mathbf{u} = 3$, $\theta = \cos^{-1}\left(\frac{3}{\sqrt{10}}\right) \approx$

0.32 rad, $|\mathbf{u}| \cos\theta = \frac{3\sqrt{2}}{2}$, $\text{proj}_{\mathbf{v}}\, \mathbf{u} = \frac{3}{2}(\mathbf{i} + \mathbf{j})$

19. $\mathbf{u} = \left(\frac{2}{5}\mathbf{i} - \frac{1}{5}\mathbf{j}\right) + \left(\frac{3}{5}\mathbf{i} + \frac{6}{5}\mathbf{j}\right)$

21. (a) $\mathbf{v}(t) = (-4\sin t)\mathbf{i} + (\sqrt{2}\cos t)\mathbf{j}$,

$\mathbf{a}(t) = (-4\cos t)\mathbf{i} + (-\sqrt{2}\sin t)\mathbf{j}$

(b) 3

(c) $\cos^{-1}\frac{7}{9} \approx 38.942$ degrees

23. 1   **25.** $6\mathbf{i}$

27. $\mathbf{r}(t) = (\cos t - 1)\mathbf{i} + (\sin t + 1)\mathbf{j}$

29. $\mathbf{r}(t) = \mathbf{i} + t^2\mathbf{j}$

31.

33. (d)   **35.** (l)

37. (k)   **39.** (i)

41. (a)

(b) 2π

43. (a)

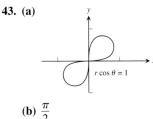

$r \cos \theta = 1$

(b) $\dfrac{\pi}{2}$

45. Tangent lines at $\theta = \dfrac{\pi}{4}, \dfrac{3\pi}{4}, \dfrac{5\pi}{4},$ and $\dfrac{7\pi}{4}$; Cartesian equations are $y = \pm x.$

47. Horizontal: $y = 0,\ y \approx \pm 0.443,\ y \approx \pm 1.739;$
vertical: $x = 2,\ x \approx 0.067,\ x \approx -1.104$

49. $y = \pm x + \sqrt{2}$ and $y = \pm x - \sqrt{2}$

51. $x = y,$ a line

53. $x^2 = 4y,$ a parabola

55. $x = 2,$ a vertical line

57. $r = -5 \sin \theta$

59. $r^2 \cos^2 \theta + 4r^2 \sin^2 \theta = 16,$ or $r^2 = \dfrac{16}{\cos^2 \theta + 4 \sin^2 \theta}$

61. $\dfrac{9\pi}{2}$

63. $2 + \dfrac{\pi}{4}$

65. 8

67. $\pi - 3$

69. Speed ≈ 591.982 mph, direction ≈ 8.179 degrees north of east

71. It hits the ground ≈ 2.135 sec later, approximately 66.421 ft from where it left the thrower's hand. Assuming it does not bounce or roll, it will still be there 3 sec after it was thrown.

73. (a)

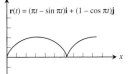

$r(t) = (\pi t - \sin \pi t)\mathbf{i} + (1 - \cos \pi t)\mathbf{j}$

(b) $\mathbf{v}(0) = \langle 0, 0 \rangle$ $\quad \mathbf{v}(1) = \langle 2\pi, 0 \rangle$
$\mathbf{a}(0) = \langle 0, \pi^2 \rangle$ $\quad \mathbf{a}(1) = \langle 0, -\pi^2 \rangle$
$\mathbf{v}(2) = \langle 0, 0 \rangle$ $\quad \mathbf{v}(3) = \langle 2\pi, 0 \rangle$
$\mathbf{a}(2) = \langle 0, \pi^2 \rangle$ $\quad \mathbf{a}(3) = \langle 0, -\pi^2 \rangle$

(c) Topmost point: 2π ft/sec; center of wheel: π ft/sec. Reasons: Since the wheel rolls half a circumference, or π feet every second, the center of the wheel will move π feet every second. Since the rim of the wheel is turning at a rate of π ft/sec about the center, the velocity of the topmost point relative to the center is π ft/sec, giving it a total velocity of 2π ft/sec.

75. (a) ≈ 59.195 ft/sec

(b) ≈ 74.584 ft/sec

77. We have $x = (v_0 t) \cos \alpha$ and $y + \dfrac{gt^2}{2} = (v_0 t) \sin \alpha.$ Squaring and adding gives $x^2 + \left(y + \dfrac{gt^2}{2}\right)^2 = (v_0 t)^2 (\cos^2 \alpha + \sin^2 \alpha) = v_0^2 t^2.$

79. (a) $\mathbf{r}(t) = \left[(155 \cos 18° - 11.7)\left(\dfrac{1}{0.09}\right)(1 - e^{-0.09t})\right]\mathbf{i} +$
$\left[4 + \left(\dfrac{155 \sin 18°}{0.09}\right)(1 - e^{-0.09t}) + \dfrac{32}{0.09^2}(1 - 0.09t - e^{-0.09t})\right]\mathbf{j}$

$x(t) = (155 \cos 18° - 11.7)\left(\dfrac{1}{0.09}\right)(1 - e^{-0.09t})$

$y(t) = 4 + \left(\dfrac{155 \sin 18°}{0.09}\right)(1 - e^{-0.09t}) + \dfrac{32}{0.09^2}(1 - 0.09t - e^{-0.09t})$

(b) At ≈ 1.404 sec, it reaches a maximum height of ≈ 36.921 ft.

(c) Range ≈ 352.52 ft, flight time ≈ 2.959 sec

(d) At times $t \approx 0.753$ and $t \approx 2.068$ sec, when it is ≈ 98.799 and ≈ 256.138 ft from home plate

(e) No, the batter has not hit a home run. If the drag coefficient k is less than $\approx 0.011,$ the hit will be a home run.

81. The widths between the successive turns are constant and are given by $2\pi a.$

Chapter 9 Additional Exercises, pp. 784–785

1. (a) $\mathbf{v} = 4\mathbf{i} + 2\mathbf{j}$

(b) $\mathbf{r}(t) = 4t\mathbf{i} + \left(2t + \dfrac{16t^3}{100} - \dfrac{120t^2}{100}\right)\mathbf{j},$ where $0 \le t \le 5$

(c)

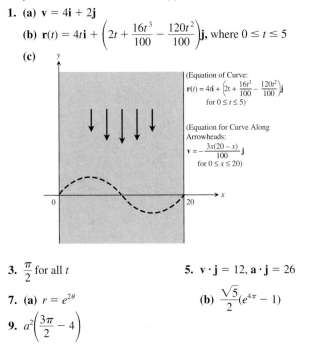

3. $\dfrac{\pi}{2}$ for all t

5. $\mathbf{v} \cdot \mathbf{j} = 12,\ \mathbf{a} \cdot \mathbf{j} = 26$

7. (a) $r = e^{2\theta}$

(b) $\dfrac{\sqrt{5}}{2}(e^{4\pi} - 1)$

9. $a^2\left(\dfrac{3\pi}{2} - 4\right)$

CHAPTER 10

Section 10.1, pp. 794–796

1. The line through the point $(2, 3, 0)$ parallel to the z-axis
3. The x-axis
5. The circle $x^2 + y^2 = 4$ in the plane $z = -2$
7. The circle $y^2 + z^2 = 1$ in the yz-plane
9. The circle $x^2 + y^2 = 16$ in the xy-plane
11. (a) The first quadrant of the xy-plane
    (b) The fourth quadrant of the xy-plane
13. (a) The ball of radius 1 centered at the origin
    (b) All points greater than 1 unit from the origin
15. (a) The upper hemisphere of radius 1 centered at the origin
    (b) The solid upper hemisphere of radius 1 centered at the origin
17. (a) $x = 3$ (b) $y = -1$ (c) $z = -2$
19. (a) $z = 1$ (b) $x = 3$ (c) $y = -1$
21. (a) $x^2 + (y - 2)^2 = 4, z = 0$
    (b) $(y - 2)^2 + z^2 = 4, x = 0$
    (c) $x^2 + z^2 = 4, y = 2$
23. (a) $y = 3, z = -1$ (b) $x = 1, z = -1$ (c) $x = 1, y = 3$
25. $x^2 + y^2 + z^2 = 25, z = 3$
27. $0 \le z \le 1$ 29. $z \le 0$
31. (a) $(x - 1)^2 + (y - 1)^2 + (z - 1)^2 < 1$
    (b) $(x - 1)^2 + (y - 1)^2 + (z - 1)^2 > 1$
33. $3\left(\frac{2}{3}\mathbf{i} + \frac{1}{3}\mathbf{j} - \frac{2}{3}\mathbf{k}\right)$
35. $5(\mathbf{k})$
37. $\sqrt{\frac{1}{2}}\left(\frac{1}{\sqrt{3}}\mathbf{i} - \frac{1}{\sqrt{3}}\mathbf{j} - \frac{1}{\sqrt{3}}\mathbf{k}\right)$
39. (a) $2\mathbf{i}$ (b) $-\sqrt{3}\mathbf{k}$
    (c) $\frac{3}{10}\mathbf{j} + \frac{2}{5}\mathbf{k}$ (d) $6\mathbf{i} - 2\mathbf{j} + 3\mathbf{k}$
41. $\frac{7}{13}(12\mathbf{i} - 5\mathbf{k})$
43. (a) $5\sqrt{2}$
    (b) $\frac{3}{5\sqrt{2}}\mathbf{i} + \frac{4}{5\sqrt{2}}\mathbf{j} - \frac{1}{\sqrt{2}}\mathbf{k}$
    (c) $(1/2, 3, 5/2)$
45. (a) $\sqrt{3}$
    (b) $-\frac{1}{\sqrt{3}}\mathbf{i} - \frac{1}{\sqrt{3}}\mathbf{j} - \frac{1}{\sqrt{3}}\mathbf{k}$
    (c) $\left(\frac{5}{2}, \frac{7}{2}, \frac{9}{2}\right)$
47. $A(4, -3, 5)$
49. $(x - 1)^2 + (y - 2)^2 + (z - 3)^2 = 14$
51. $C(-2, 0, 2), a = 2\sqrt{2}$ 53. $C(-2, 0, 2), a = 2\sqrt{2}$
55. $C\left(-\frac{1}{4}, -\frac{1}{4}, -\frac{1}{4}\right), a = \frac{5\sqrt{3}}{4}$
57. (a) $\sqrt{y^2 + z^2}$ (b) $\sqrt{x^2 + z^2}$ (c) $\sqrt{x^2 + y^2}$
59. (a) $\frac{3}{2}\mathbf{i} + \frac{3}{2}\mathbf{j} - 3\mathbf{k}$ (b) $\mathbf{i} + \mathbf{j} - 2\mathbf{k}$ (c) $(2, 2, 1)$

Section 10.2, pp. 805–807

1. (a) $-25, 5, 5$ (b) -1
   (c) -5 (d) $-2\mathbf{i} + 4\mathbf{j} - \sqrt{5}\mathbf{k}$
3. (a) $25, 15, 5$ (b) $\frac{1}{3}$
   (c) $\frac{5}{3}$ (d) $\frac{1}{9}(10\mathbf{i} + 11\mathbf{j} - 2\mathbf{k})$
5. (a) $2, \sqrt{34}, \sqrt{3}$ (b) $\frac{2}{\sqrt{3}\sqrt{34}}$
   (c) $\frac{2}{\sqrt{34}}$ (d) $\frac{1}{17}(5\mathbf{j} - 3\mathbf{k})$
7. $\left(\frac{3}{2}\mathbf{i} + \frac{3}{2}\mathbf{j}\right) + \left(-\frac{3}{2}\mathbf{i} + \frac{3}{2}\mathbf{j} + 4\mathbf{k}\right)$
9. $\left(\frac{14}{3}\mathbf{i} + \frac{28}{3}\mathbf{j} - \frac{14}{3}\mathbf{k}\right) + \left(\frac{10}{3}\mathbf{i} - \frac{16}{3}\mathbf{j} - \frac{22}{3}\mathbf{k}\right)$
11. 0.75 rad   13. 1.77 rad
17. $|\mathbf{u} \times \mathbf{v}| = 3$, direction is $\frac{2}{3}\mathbf{i} + \frac{1}{3}\mathbf{j} + \frac{2}{3}\mathbf{k}$; $|\mathbf{v} \times \mathbf{u}| = 3$, direction is $-\frac{2}{3}\mathbf{i} - \frac{1}{3}\mathbf{j} - \frac{2}{3}\mathbf{k}$
19. $|\mathbf{u} \times \mathbf{v}| = 0$, no direction; $|\mathbf{v} \times \mathbf{u}| = 0$, no direction
21. $|\mathbf{u} \times \mathbf{v}| = 6$, direction is $-\mathbf{k}$; $|\mathbf{v} \times \mathbf{u}| = 6$, direction is $\mathbf{k}$
23. $|\mathbf{u} \times \mathbf{v}| = 6\sqrt{5}$, direction is $\frac{1}{\sqrt{5}}\mathbf{i} - \frac{2}{\sqrt{5}}\mathbf{k}$; $|\mathbf{v} \times \mathbf{u}| = 6\sqrt{5}$, direction is $-\frac{1}{\sqrt{5}}\mathbf{i} + \frac{2}{\sqrt{5}}\mathbf{k}$
25. $\mathbf{u} \times \mathbf{v} = \mathbf{i} + \mathbf{k}$ 27. $\mathbf{u} \times \mathbf{v} = -2\mathbf{k}$

29. (a) $2\sqrt{6}$ (b) $\pm\frac{1}{\sqrt{6}}(2\mathbf{i} + \mathbf{j} + \mathbf{k})$
31. (a) $\frac{\sqrt{2}}{2}$ (b) $\pm\frac{1}{\sqrt{2}}(\mathbf{i} - \mathbf{j})$
33. 8   35. 7
37. (a) None   (b) $\mathbf{u}$ and $\mathbf{w}$
39. $10\sqrt{3}$ ft · lb
41. (a) True   (b) Not always true
    (c) True   (d) True
    (e) Not always true   (f) True
    (g) True   (h) True
43. (a) $\text{proj}_\mathbf{v}\, \mathbf{u} = \frac{\mathbf{u} \cdot \mathbf{v}}{\mathbf{v} \cdot \mathbf{v}}\mathbf{v}$ (b) $\pm\mathbf{u} \times \mathbf{v}$
    (c) $\pm(\mathbf{u} \times \mathbf{v}) \times \mathbf{w}$ (d) $|(\mathbf{u} \times \mathbf{v}) \cdot \mathbf{w}|$
45. (a) Yes   (b) No   (c) Yes   (d) No
47. No, $\mathbf{v}$ need not equal $\mathbf{w}$. For example, $\mathbf{i} + \mathbf{j} \ne -\mathbf{i} + \mathbf{j}$, but $\mathbf{i} \times (\mathbf{i} + \mathbf{j}) = \mathbf{i} \times \mathbf{i} + \mathbf{i} \times \mathbf{j} = 0 + \mathbf{k} = \mathbf{k}$ and $\mathbf{i} \times (-\mathbf{i} + \mathbf{j}) = -\mathbf{i} \times \mathbf{i} + \mathbf{i} \times \mathbf{j} = 0 + \mathbf{k} = \mathbf{k}$.

49. 2

51. 13

53. $\dfrac{11}{2}$

55. $\dfrac{25}{2}$

57. If $\mathbf{u} = a_1\mathbf{i} + a_2\mathbf{j}$ and $\mathbf{v} = b_1\mathbf{i} + b_2\mathbf{j}$, then $\mathbf{u} \times \mathbf{v} = \begin{vmatrix} \mathbf{i} & \mathbf{j} & \mathbf{k} \\ a_1 & a_2 & 0 \\ b_1 & b_2 & 0 \end{vmatrix} =$

$\begin{vmatrix} a_1 & a_2 \\ b_1 & b_2 \end{vmatrix} \mathbf{k}$ and the triangle's area is $\dfrac{1}{2}|\mathbf{u} \times \mathbf{v}| = \pm\dfrac{1}{2}\begin{vmatrix} a_1 & a_2 \\ b_1 & b_2 \end{vmatrix}$.

The applicable sign is $(+)$ if the acute angle from $\mathbf{u}$ to $\mathbf{v}$ runs counterclockwise in the xy-plane and $(-)$ if it runs clockwise.

45. $x = 1 - t, y = 1 + t, z = -1$

47. $x = 4, y = 3 + 6t, z = 1 + 3t$

49. $L1$ intersects $L2$; $L2$ is parallel to $L3$; $L1$ and $L3$ are skew.

51. $x = 2 + 2t, y = -4 - t, z = 7 + 3t; x = -2 - t, y = -2 + (1/2)t, z = 1 - (3/2)t$

53. $(0, -1/2, -3/2), (-1, 0, -3), (1, -1, 0)$

55. The line and plane are not parallel.

57. Many answers are possible. One possibility is $x + y = 3$ and $2y + z = 7$.

59. $\dfrac{x}{a} + \dfrac{y}{b} + \dfrac{z}{c} = 1$ describes all planes *except* those through the origin or parallel to a coordinate axis.

Section 10.3, pp. 813–815

1. Vector form: $\mathbf{r}(t) = (3 + t)\mathbf{i} + (t - 4)\mathbf{j} + (t - 1)\mathbf{k}$
Parametric form: $x = 3 + t, y = -4 + t, z = -1 + t$

3. Vector form: $\mathbf{r}(t) = (5t - 2)\mathbf{i} + (5t)\mathbf{j} + (3 - 5t)\mathbf{k}$
Parametric form: $x = -2 + 5t, y = 5t, z = 3 - 5t$

5. Vector form: $\mathbf{r}(t) = (2t + 3)\mathbf{i} - (t + 2)\mathbf{j} + (3t + 1)\mathbf{k}$
Parametric form: $x = 3 + 2t, y = -2 - t, z = 1 + 3t$

7. Vector form: $\mathbf{r}(t) = (3t + 2)\mathbf{i} + (7t + 4)\mathbf{j} + (5 - 5t)\mathbf{k}$
Parametric form: $x = 2 + 3t, y = 4 + 7t, z = 5 - 5t$

9. Vector form: $\mathbf{r}(t) = (2 - 2t)\mathbf{i} + (4t + 3)\mathbf{j} - (2t)\mathbf{k}$
Parametric form: $x = 2 - 2t, y = 3 + 4t, z = -2t$

11. $x = t, y = t, z = \dfrac{3}{2}t, 0 \le t \le 1$

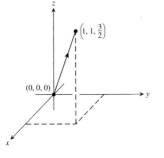

13. $x = 0, y = 1 - 2t, z = 1, 0 \le t \le 1$

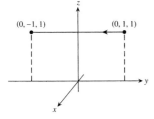

15. $3x - 2y - z = -3$

17. $7x - 5y - 4z = 6$

19. $x + 3y + 4z = 34$

21. $(1, 2, 3), -20x + 12y + z = 7$

23. $y + z = 3$

25. $x - y + z = 0$

29. 0

33. 19/5

35. $9/\sqrt{41}$

39. 0.82 rad

41. $(3/2, -3/2, 1/2)$

43. $(1, 1, 0)$

Section 10.4, pp. 824–825

1. Graph (d), ellipsoid

3. Graph (a), cylinder

5. Graph (l), hyperbolic paraboloid

7. Graph (b), cylinder

9. Graph (k), hyperbolic paraboloid

11. Graph (h), cone

13. (a) $\dfrac{2\pi(9 - c^2)}{9}$ (b) 8π (c) $\dfrac{4\pi abc}{3}$

Section 10.5, pp. 835–838

1. $\mathbf{v} = \mathbf{i} + 2t\mathbf{j} + 2\mathbf{k}; \mathbf{a} = 2\mathbf{j};$ speed: 3; direction: $\dfrac{1}{3}\mathbf{i} + \dfrac{2}{3}\mathbf{j} + \dfrac{2}{3}\mathbf{k};$
$\mathbf{v}(1) = 3\left(\dfrac{1}{3}\mathbf{i} + \dfrac{2}{3}\mathbf{j} + \dfrac{2}{3}\mathbf{k}\right)$

3. $\mathbf{v} = (-2\sin t)\mathbf{i} + (3\cos t)\mathbf{j} + 4\mathbf{k}; \mathbf{a} = (-2\cos t)\mathbf{i} - (3\sin t)\mathbf{j};$
speed: $2\sqrt{5}$; direction: $\left(-\dfrac{1}{\sqrt{5}}\right)\mathbf{i} + \left(\dfrac{2}{\sqrt{5}}\right)\mathbf{k};$
$\mathbf{v}\left(\dfrac{\pi}{2}\right) = 2\sqrt{5}\left[\left(-\dfrac{1}{\sqrt{5}}\right)\mathbf{i} + \left(\dfrac{2}{\sqrt{5}}\right)\mathbf{k}\right]$

5. $\mathbf{v} = \left(\dfrac{2}{t + 1}\right)\mathbf{i} + 2t\mathbf{j} + t\mathbf{k}; \mathbf{a} = \left(\dfrac{-2}{(t + 1)^2}\right)\mathbf{i} + 2\mathbf{j} + \mathbf{k};$
speed: $\sqrt{6}$; direction: $\dfrac{1}{\sqrt{6}}\mathbf{i} + \dfrac{2}{\sqrt{6}}\mathbf{j} + \dfrac{1}{\sqrt{6}}\mathbf{k}; \mathbf{v}(1) =$
$\sqrt{6}\left(\dfrac{1}{\sqrt{6}}\mathbf{i} + \dfrac{2}{\sqrt{6}}\mathbf{j} + \dfrac{1}{\sqrt{6}}\mathbf{k}\right)$

7. $\pi/2$

9. $\pi/2$

11. $t = 0, \pi, 2\pi$

13. $\left(\dfrac{1}{4}\right)\mathbf{i} + 7\mathbf{j} + \left(\dfrac{3}{2}\right)\mathbf{k}$

15. $\left(\dfrac{\pi + 2\sqrt{2}}{2}\right)\mathbf{j} + 2\mathbf{k}$

17. $(\ln 4)\mathbf{i} + (\ln 4)\mathbf{j} + (\ln 2)\mathbf{k}$

19. $\mathbf{r}(t) = \left(\dfrac{-t^2}{2} + 1\right)\mathbf{i} + \left(\dfrac{-t^2}{2} + 2\right)\mathbf{j} + \left(\dfrac{-t^2}{2} + 3\right)\mathbf{k}$

21. $\mathbf{r}(t) = ((t + 1)^{3/2} - 1)\mathbf{i} + (-e^{-t} + 1)\mathbf{j} + (\ln (t + 1) + 1)\mathbf{k}$

23. $\mathbf{r}(t) = 8t\mathbf{i} + 8t\mathbf{j} + (-16t^2 + 100)\mathbf{k}$

25. $x = t, y = -1, z = 1 + t$

27. $x = at, y = a, z = 2\pi b + bt$

29. $\mathbf{r}(t) = \left(\frac{3}{2}t^2 + \frac{6}{\sqrt{11}}t + 1\right)\mathbf{i} - \left(\frac{1}{2}t^2 + \frac{2}{\sqrt{11}}t - 2\right)\mathbf{j} +$

$\left(\frac{1}{2}t^2 + \frac{2}{\sqrt{11}}t + 3\right)\mathbf{k} = \left(\frac{1}{2}t^2 + \frac{2t}{\sqrt{11}}\right)(3\mathbf{i} - \mathbf{j} + \mathbf{k}) +$

$(\mathbf{i} + 2\mathbf{j} + 3\mathbf{k})$

31. Max $|\mathbf{v}| = 2$, min $|\mathbf{v}| = 0$, max $|\mathbf{a}| = $ min $|\mathbf{a}| = 1$

33. Max $|\mathbf{v}| = 3$, min $|\mathbf{v}| = 2$, max $|\mathbf{a}| = 3$, min $|\mathbf{a}| = 2$

Section 10.6, pp. 846–847

1. $\mathbf{T} = \left(-\frac{2}{3} \sin t\right)\mathbf{i} + \left(\frac{2}{3} \cos t\right)\mathbf{j} + \frac{\sqrt{5}}{3}\mathbf{k}, 3\pi$

3. $\mathbf{T} = \frac{1}{\sqrt{1 + t}}\mathbf{i} + \frac{\sqrt{t}}{\sqrt{1 + t}}\mathbf{k}, \frac{52}{3}$

5. $\mathbf{T} = (-\cos t)\mathbf{j} + (\sin t)\mathbf{k}, \frac{3}{2}$

7. $\mathbf{T} = \left(\frac{\cos t - t \sin t}{t + 1}\right)\mathbf{i} + \left(\frac{\sin t + t \cos t}{t + 1}\right)\mathbf{j} + \left(\frac{\sqrt{2}t^{1/2}}{t + 1}\right)\mathbf{k},$

$\frac{\pi^2}{2} + \pi$

9. $(0, 5, 24\pi)$ **11.** $s(t) = 5t, L = \frac{5\pi}{2}$

13. $s(t) = \sqrt{3}\, e^t - \sqrt{3}, L = \frac{3\sqrt{3}}{4}$

15. $\mathbf{T} = (\cos t)\mathbf{i} - (\sin t)\mathbf{j}, \mathbf{N} = (-\sin t)\mathbf{i} - (\cos t)\mathbf{j}, \kappa = \cos t$

17. $\mathbf{T} = \frac{1}{\sqrt{1 + t^2}}\mathbf{i} - \frac{t}{\sqrt{1 + t^2}}\mathbf{j}, \mathbf{N} = \frac{-t}{\sqrt{1 + t^2}}\mathbf{i} - \frac{1}{\sqrt{1 + t^2}}\mathbf{j},$

$\kappa = \frac{1}{2(\sqrt{1 + t^2})^3}$

19. $\sqrt{2} + \ln (1 + \sqrt{2})$

21. (a) Cylinder is $x^2 + y^2 = 1$, plane is $x + z = 1$.

(b) and **(c)**

(d) $L = \int_0^{2\pi} \sqrt{1 + \sin^2 t}\, dt$ **(e)** $L \approx 7.64$

23. $\left(x - \frac{\pi}{2}\right)^2 + y^2 = 1$

Section 10.7, pp. 854–856

1. $\mathbf{T} = \frac{3 \cos t}{5}\mathbf{i} - \frac{3 \sin t}{5}\mathbf{j} + \frac{4}{5}\mathbf{k}, \mathbf{N} = (-\sin t)\mathbf{i} - (\cos t)\mathbf{j},$

$\mathbf{B} = \left(\frac{4}{5} \cos t\right)\mathbf{i} - \left(\frac{4}{5} \sin t\right)\mathbf{j} - \frac{3}{5}\mathbf{k}, \kappa = \frac{3}{25}, \tau = -\frac{4}{25}$

3. $\mathbf{T} = \left(\frac{\cos t - \sin t}{\sqrt{2}}\right)\mathbf{i} + \left(\frac{\cos t + \sin t}{\sqrt{2}}\right)\mathbf{j},$

$\mathbf{N} = \left(\frac{-\cos t - \sin t}{\sqrt{2}}\right)\mathbf{i} + \left(\frac{-\sin t + \cos t}{\sqrt{2}}\right)\mathbf{j}, \mathbf{B} = \mathbf{k},$

$\kappa = \frac{1}{e^t\sqrt{2}}, \tau = 0$

5. $\mathbf{T} = \frac{t}{\sqrt{t^2 + 1}}\mathbf{i} + \frac{1}{\sqrt{t^2 + 1}}\mathbf{j}, \mathbf{N} = \frac{\mathbf{i}}{\sqrt{t^2 + 1}} - \frac{t\mathbf{j}}{\sqrt{t^2 + 1}},$

$\mathbf{B} = -\mathbf{k}, \kappa = \frac{1}{t(t^2 + 1)^{3/2}}, \tau = 0$

7. $\mathbf{T} = \left(\text{sech}\frac{t}{a}\right)\mathbf{i} + \left(\tanh\frac{t}{a}\right)\mathbf{j}, \mathbf{N} = \left(-\tanh\frac{t}{a}\right)\mathbf{i} + \left(\text{sech}\frac{t}{a}\right)\mathbf{j},$

$\mathbf{B} = \mathbf{k}, \kappa = \frac{1}{a} \text{sech}^2\frac{t}{a}, \tau = 0$ **9.** $\mathbf{a} = |a|\mathbf{N}$

11. $\mathbf{a}(1) = \frac{4}{3}\mathbf{T} + \frac{2\sqrt{5}}{3}\mathbf{N}$ **13.** $\mathbf{a}(0) = 2\mathbf{N}$

15. $\mathbf{r}\left(\frac{\pi}{4}\right) = \frac{\sqrt{2}}{2}\mathbf{i} + \frac{\sqrt{2}}{2}\mathbf{j} - \mathbf{k}, \mathbf{T}\left(\frac{\pi}{4}\right) = -\frac{\sqrt{2}}{2}\mathbf{i} + \frac{\sqrt{2}}{2}\mathbf{j},$

$\mathbf{N}\left(\frac{\pi}{4}\right) = -\frac{\sqrt{2}}{2}\mathbf{i} - \frac{\sqrt{2}}{2}\mathbf{j}, \mathbf{B}\left(\frac{\pi}{4}\right) = \mathbf{k}$; osculating plane: $z = -1$;

normal plane: $-x + y = 0$; rectifying plane: $x + y = \sqrt{2}$

17. Yes. If the car is moving on a curved path ($\kappa \neq 0$), then $a_N = \kappa |\mathbf{v}|^2 \neq 0$ and $\mathbf{a} \neq \mathbf{0}$.

21. $|\mathbf{F}| = \kappa\left[m\left(\frac{ds}{dt}\right)^2\right]$ **23. (b)** $\cos x$

25. (b) $\mathbf{N} = \frac{-2e^{2t}}{\sqrt{1 + 4e^{4t}}}\mathbf{i} + \frac{1}{\sqrt{1 + 4e^{4t}}}\mathbf{j}$

(c) $\mathbf{N} = -\frac{1}{2}\left(\sqrt{4 - t^2}\mathbf{i} + t\mathbf{j}\right)$

29. $\frac{1}{2b}$

33. (a) $b - a$ **(b)** π

37. $\kappa = \frac{2}{(1 + 4x^2)^{3/2}}$ **39.** $\kappa = \frac{|\sin x|}{(1 + \cos^2 x)^{3/2}}$

Section 10.8, pp. 865–866

1. $T = 93.2$ min   **3.** $a = 6763$ km

5. $D = 6480$ km

7. (a) 42,167 km   **(b)** 35,788 km

(c) *Syncom 3, GOES 4*, and *Intelsat 5*

9. $a = 383,200$ km from the center of Earth, or about 376,821 km from the surface

Chapter 10 Practice Exercises, pp. 867–869

1. Length = 7, direction is $\frac{2}{7}\mathbf{i} - \frac{3}{7}\mathbf{j} + \frac{6}{7}\mathbf{k}$.

3. $\frac{8}{\sqrt{33}}\mathbf{i} - \frac{2}{\sqrt{33}}\mathbf{j} + \frac{8}{\sqrt{33}}\mathbf{k}$

5. $|\mathbf{v}| = \sqrt{2}, |\mathbf{u}| = 3, \mathbf{v} \cdot \mathbf{u} = \mathbf{u} \cdot \mathbf{v} = 3, \mathbf{v} \times \mathbf{u} = -2\mathbf{i} + 2\mathbf{j} - \mathbf{k},$

$\mathbf{u} \times \mathbf{v} = 2\mathbf{i} - 2\mathbf{j} + \mathbf{k}, |\mathbf{v} \times \mathbf{u}| = 3, \theta = \cos^{-1}\left(\frac{1}{\sqrt{2}}\right) = \frac{\pi}{4},$

$|\mathbf{u}| \cos \theta = \frac{3}{\sqrt{2}}, \text{proj}_\mathbf{v}\, \mathbf{u} = \frac{3}{2}(\mathbf{i} + \mathbf{j})$

7. $\frac{4}{3}(2\mathbf{i} + \mathbf{j} - \mathbf{k}) - \frac{1}{3}(5\mathbf{i} + \mathbf{j} + 11\mathbf{k})$

9. $\mathbf{u} \times \mathbf{v} = \mathbf{k}$

11. $2\sqrt{7}$

13. (a) $\sqrt{14}$ (b) 1

17. $x = 1 - 3t, y = 2, z = 3 + 7t$ **19.** $2x + y + z = 5$

21. $-9x + y + 7z = 4$

23. $(0, -1/2, -3/2), (-1, 0, -3), (1, -1, 0)$

25. $\frac{\pi}{3}$ **29.** $7x - 3y - 5z = -14$

31. $\frac{1}{\sqrt{14}}(-2\mathbf{i} - 3\mathbf{j} + \mathbf{k})$ **33.** $(4/3, -2/3, -2/3)$

35. (a) No   (b) No   (c) No

      (d) No   (e) Yes

37. $\sqrt{78}/3$ **39.** $\sqrt{2}$

41. 3   **43.** $11/\sqrt{107}$

45. $x^2 + y^2 + z^2 = 4$ **47.** $z = -(x^2 + y^2)$

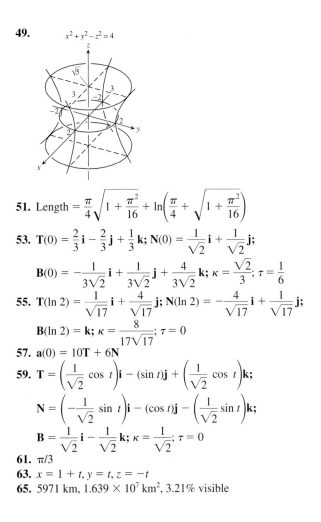

49. $x^2 + y^2 - z^2 = 4$

51. Length = $\frac{\pi}{4}\sqrt{1 + \frac{\pi^2}{16}} + \ln\left(\frac{\pi}{4} + \sqrt{1 + \frac{\pi^2}{16}}\right)$

53. $\mathbf{T}(0) = \frac{2}{3}\mathbf{i} - \frac{2}{3}\mathbf{j} + \frac{1}{3}\mathbf{k}; \mathbf{N}(0) = \frac{1}{\sqrt{2}}\mathbf{i} + \frac{1}{\sqrt{2}}\mathbf{j};$

$\mathbf{B}(0) = -\frac{1}{3\sqrt{2}}\mathbf{i} + \frac{1}{3\sqrt{2}}\mathbf{j} + \frac{4}{3\sqrt{2}}\mathbf{k}; \kappa = \frac{\sqrt{2}}{3}; \tau = \frac{1}{6}$

55. $\mathbf{T}(\ln 2) = \frac{1}{\sqrt{17}}\mathbf{i} + \frac{4}{\sqrt{17}}\mathbf{j}; \mathbf{N}(\ln 2) = -\frac{4}{\sqrt{17}}\mathbf{i} + \frac{1}{\sqrt{17}}\mathbf{j};$

$\mathbf{B}(\ln 2) = \mathbf{k}; \kappa = \frac{8}{17\sqrt{17}}; \tau = 0$

57. $\mathbf{a}(0) = 10\mathbf{T} + 6\mathbf{N}$

59. $\mathbf{T} = \left(\frac{1}{\sqrt{2}}\cos t\right)\mathbf{i} - (\sin t)\mathbf{j} + \left(\frac{1}{\sqrt{2}}\cos t\right)\mathbf{k};$

$\mathbf{N} = \left(-\frac{1}{\sqrt{2}}\sin t\right)\mathbf{i} - (\cos t)\mathbf{j} - \left(\frac{1}{\sqrt{2}}\sin t\right)\mathbf{k};$

$\mathbf{B} = \frac{1}{\sqrt{2}}\mathbf{i} - \frac{1}{\sqrt{2}}\mathbf{k}; \kappa = \frac{1}{\sqrt{2}}; \tau = 0$

61. $\pi/3$

63. $x = 1 + t, y = t, z = -t$

65. 5971 km, 1.639×10^7 km², 3.21% visible

Chapter 10 Additional Exercises, pp. 870–872

1. $(26, 23, -1/3)$ **3.** $|\mathbf{F}| = 20$ lb

9. (b) $6/\sqrt{14}$

15. $\frac{32}{41}\mathbf{i} + \frac{23}{41}\mathbf{j} - \frac{13}{41}\mathbf{k}$

17. (a) $|\mathbf{F}| = \frac{GMm}{d^2}\left(1 + \sum_{i=1}^{n} \frac{2}{(i^2 + 1)^{3/2}}\right)$

      (b) Yes

21. (a) $\frac{dx}{dt} = \dot{r}\cos\theta - r\dot{\theta}\sin\theta, \frac{dy}{dt} = \dot{r}\sin\theta + r\dot{\theta}\cos\theta$

      (b) $\frac{dr}{dt} = \dot{x}\cos\theta + \dot{y}\sin\theta, r\frac{d\theta}{dt} = -\dot{x}\sin\theta + \dot{y}\cos\theta$

23. (a) $\mathbf{v}(1) = -\mathbf{u}_r + 3\mathbf{u}_\theta, \mathbf{a}(1) = -9\mathbf{u}_r - 6\mathbf{u}_\theta$

      (b) 6.5 in.

CHAPTER 11

Section 11.1, pp. 880–882

1. (a) All points in the xy-plane   (b) All reals
   (c) The lines $y - x = c$ (d) No boundary points
   (e) Both open and closed   (f) Unbounded
3. (a) All points in the xy-plane   (b) $z \geq 0$
   (c) For $f(x, y) = 0$, the origin; for $f(x, y) \neq 0$, ellipses with the center $(0, 0)$ and major and minor axes along the x- and y-axes, respectively
   (d) No boundary points   (e) Both open and closed
   (f) Unbounded
5. (a) All points in the xy-plane   (b) All reals
   (c) For $f(x, y) = 0$, the x- and y-axes; for $f(x, y) \neq 0$, hyperbolas with the x- and y-axes as asymptotes
   (d) No boundary points   (e) Both open and closed
   (f) Unbounded
7. (a) All (x, y) satisfying $x^2 + y^2 < 16$ (b) $z \geq \frac{1}{4}$
   (c) Circles centered at the origin with radii $r < 4$
   (d) Boundary is the circle $x^2 + y^2 = 16$
   (e) Open   (f) Bounded
9. (a) $(x, y) \neq (0, 0)$ (b) All reals
   (c) The circles with center $(0, 0)$ and radii $r > 0$
   (d) Boundary is the single point $(0, 0)$.
   (e) Open   (f) Unbounded
11. (a) All (x, y) satisfying $-1 \leq y - x \leq 1$
    (b) $-\pi/2 \leq z \leq \pi/2$
    (c) Straight lines of the form $y - x = c$, where $-1 \leq c \leq 1$
    (d) Boundary is two straight lines $y = 1 + x$ and $y = -1 + x$.
    (e) Closed   (f) Unbounded
13. Graph (f)   15. Graph (a)   17. Graph (d)
19. (a)   (b)

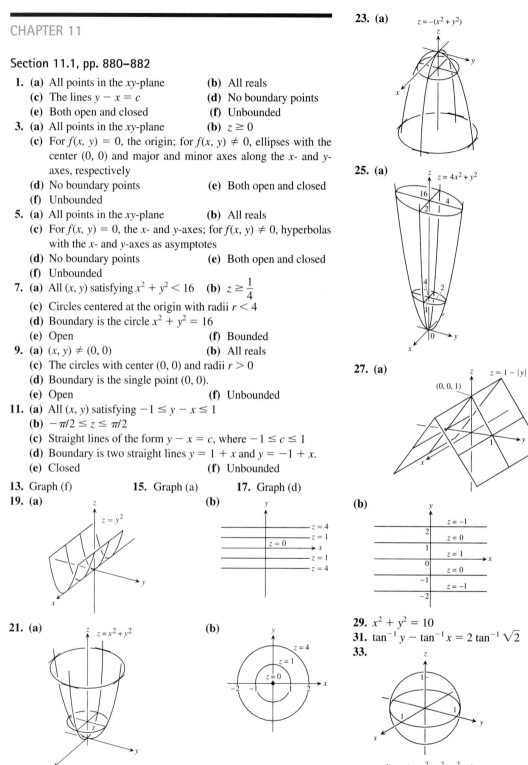

21. (a)   (b)

23. (a) $z = -(x^2 + y^2)$ (b)

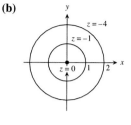

25. (a) $z = 4x^2 + y^2$ (b)

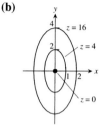

27. (a) $z = 1 - |y|$

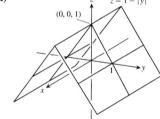

(b)

29. $x^2 + y^2 = 10$
31. $\tan^{-1} y - \tan^{-1} x = 2 \tan^{-1} \sqrt{2}$
33.   35.

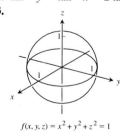

$f(x, y, z) = x^2 + y^2 + z^2 = 1$

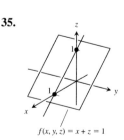

$f(x, y, z) = x + z = 1$

37.

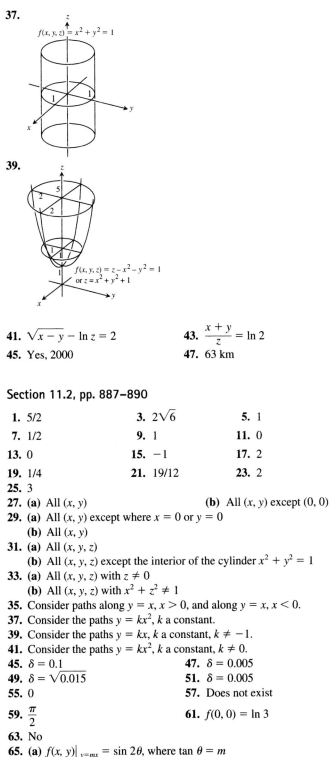

$f(x, y, z) = x^2 + y^2 = 1$

39.

$f(x, y, z) = z - x^2 - y^2 = 1$
or $z = x^2 + y^2 + 1$

41. $\sqrt{x - y} - \ln z = 2$

43. $\dfrac{x + y}{z} = \ln 2$

45. Yes, 2000

47. 63 km

Section 11.2, pp. 887–890

1. $5/2$

3. $2\sqrt{6}$

5. 1

7. $1/2$

9. 1

11. 0

13. 0

15. -1

17. 2

19. $1/4$

21. $19/12$

23. 2

25. 3

27. (a) All (x, y) **(b)** All (x, y) except $(0, 0)$

29. (a) All (x, y) except where $x = 0$ or $y = 0$
(b) All (x, y)

31. (a) All (x, y, z)
(b) All (x, y, z) except the interior of the cylinder $x^2 + y^2 = 1$

33. (a) All (x, y, z) with $z \neq 0$
(b) All (x, y, z) with $x^2 + z^2 \neq 1$

35. Consider paths along $y = x$, $x > 0$, and along $y = x$, $x < 0$.

37. Consider the paths $y = kx^2$, k a constant.

39. Consider the paths $y = kx$, k a constant, $k \neq -1$.

41. Consider the paths $y = kx^2$, k a constant, $k \neq 0$.

45. $\delta = 0.1$

47. $\delta = 0.005$

49. $\delta = \sqrt{0.015}$

51. $\delta = 0.005$

55. 0

57. Does not exist

59. $\dfrac{\pi}{2}$

61. $f(0, 0) = \ln 3$

63. No

65. (a) $f(x, y)\big|_{y=mx} = \sin 2\theta$, where $\tan \theta = m$

67. The limit is 1.

69. The limit is 0.

Section 11.3, pp. 899–901

1. $\dfrac{\partial f}{\partial x} = 4x$, $\dfrac{\partial f}{\partial y} = -3$

3. $\dfrac{\partial f}{\partial x} = 2x(y + 2)$, $\dfrac{\partial f}{\partial y} = x^2 - 1$

5. $\dfrac{\partial f}{\partial x} = 2y(xy - 1)$, $\dfrac{\partial f}{\partial y} = 2x(xy - 1)$

7. $\dfrac{\partial f}{\partial x} = \dfrac{x}{\sqrt{x^2 + y^2}}$, $\dfrac{\partial f}{\partial y} = \dfrac{y}{\sqrt{x^2 + y^2}}$

9. $\dfrac{\partial f}{\partial x} = \dfrac{-1}{(x + y)^2}$, $\dfrac{\partial f}{\partial y} = \dfrac{-1}{(x + y)^2}$

11. $\dfrac{\partial f}{\partial x} = \dfrac{-y^2 - 1}{(xy - 1)^2}$, $\dfrac{\partial f}{\partial y} = \dfrac{-x^2 - 1}{(xy - 1)^2}$

13. $\dfrac{\partial f}{\partial x} = e^{x+y+1}$, $\dfrac{\partial f}{\partial y} = e^{x+y+1}$

15. $\dfrac{\partial f}{\partial x} = \dfrac{1}{x + y}$, $\dfrac{\partial f}{\partial y} = \dfrac{1}{x + y}$

17. $\dfrac{\partial f}{\partial x} = 2 \sin (x - 3y) \cos (x - 3y)$, $\dfrac{\partial f}{\partial y} = -6 \sin (x - 3y) \cos (x - 3y)$

19. $\dfrac{\partial f}{\partial x} = yx^{y-1}$, $\dfrac{\partial f}{\partial y} = x^y \ln x$

21. $\dfrac{\partial f}{\partial x} = -g(x)$, $\dfrac{\partial f}{\partial y} = g(y)$

23. $f_x = y^2$, $f_y = 2xy$, $f_z = -4z$

25. $f_x = 1$, $f_y = -y(y^2 + z^2)^{-1/2}$, $f_z = -z(y^2 + z^2)^{-1/2}$

27. $f_x = \dfrac{yz}{\sqrt{1 - x^2y^2z^2}}$, $f_y = \dfrac{xz}{\sqrt{1 - x^2y^2z^2}}$, $f_z = \dfrac{xy}{\sqrt{1 - x^2y^2z^2}}$

29. $f_x = \dfrac{1}{x + 2y + 3z}$, $f_y = \dfrac{2}{x + 2y + 3z}$, $f_z = \dfrac{3}{x + 2y + 3z}$

31. $f_x = -2xe^{-(x^2+y^2+z^2)}$, $f_y = -2ye^{-(x^2+y^2+z^2)}$, $f_z = -2ze^{-(x^2+y^2+z^2)}$

33. $f_x = \text{sech}^2 (x + 2y + 3z)$, $f_y = 2 \text{ sech}^2 (x + 2y + 3z)$, $f_z = 3 \text{ sech}^2 (x + 2y + 3z)$

35. $\dfrac{\partial f}{\partial t} = -2\pi \sin (2\pi t - \alpha)$, $\dfrac{\partial f}{\partial \alpha} = \sin (2\pi t - \alpha)$

37. $\dfrac{\partial h}{\partial \rho} = \sin \phi \cos \theta$, $\dfrac{\partial h}{\partial \phi} = \rho \cos \phi \cos \theta$, $= \dfrac{\partial h}{\partial \theta} = -\rho \sin \phi \sin \theta$

39. $W_P(P, V, \delta, v, g) = V$, $W_V(P, V, \delta, v, g) = P + \dfrac{\delta v^2}{2g}$,

$W_\delta(P, V, \delta, v, g) = \dfrac{Vv^2}{2g}$, $W_v(P, V, \delta, v, g) = \dfrac{V\delta v}{g}$,

$W_g(P, V, \delta, v, g) = -\dfrac{V\delta v^2}{2g^2}$

41. $\dfrac{\partial f}{\partial x} = 1 + y$, $\dfrac{\partial f}{\partial y} = 1 + x$, $\dfrac{\partial^2 f}{\partial x^2} = 0$, $\dfrac{\partial^2 f}{\partial y^2} = 0$, $\dfrac{\partial^2 f}{\partial y \partial x} = \dfrac{\partial^2 f}{\partial x \partial y} = 1$

43. $\dfrac{\partial g}{\partial x} = 2xy + y \cos x$, $\dfrac{\partial g}{\partial y} = x^2 - \sin y + \sin x$, $\dfrac{\partial^2 g}{\partial x^2} = 2y - y \sin x$,

$\dfrac{\partial^2 g}{\partial y^2} = -\cos y$, $\dfrac{\partial^2 g}{\partial y \partial x} = \dfrac{\partial^2 g}{\partial x \partial y} = 2x + \cos x$

45. $\dfrac{\partial r}{\partial x} = \dfrac{1}{x + y}$, $\dfrac{\partial r}{\partial y} = \dfrac{1}{x + y}$, $\dfrac{\partial^2 r}{\partial x^2} = \dfrac{-1}{(x + y)^2}$, $\dfrac{\partial^2 r}{\partial y^2} = \dfrac{-1}{(x + y)^2}$,

$\dfrac{\partial^2 r}{\partial y \partial x} = \dfrac{\partial^2 r}{\partial x \partial y} = \dfrac{-1}{(x + y)^2}$

47. $\dfrac{\partial w}{\partial x} = \dfrac{2}{2x + 3y}$, $\dfrac{\partial w}{\partial y} = \dfrac{3}{2x + 3y}$, $\dfrac{\partial^2 w}{\partial y \partial x} = \dfrac{\partial^2 w}{\partial x \partial y} = \dfrac{-6}{(2x + 3y)^2}$

49. $\dfrac{\partial w}{\partial x} = y^2 + 2xy^3 + 3x^2y^4, \dfrac{\partial w}{\partial y} = 2xy + 3x^2y^2 + 4x^3y^3,$

$\dfrac{\partial^2 w}{\partial y\, \partial x} = \dfrac{\partial^2 w}{\partial x\, \partial y} = 2y + 6xy^2 + 12x^2y^3$

51. **(a)** x first   **(b)** y first   **(c)** x first

    (d) x first   **(e)** y first   **(f)** y first

53. $f_x(1, 2) = -13, f_y(1, 2) = -2$

55. 12   **57.** -2

59. $\dfrac{\partial A}{\partial a} = \dfrac{a}{bc \sin A}, \dfrac{\partial A}{\partial a} = \dfrac{c \cos A - b}{bc \sin A}$

61. $v_x = \dfrac{\ln v}{(\ln u)(\ln v) - 1}$ **77.** Yes

Section 11.4, pp. 908–910

1. $\dfrac{dw}{dt} = 0, \dfrac{dw}{dt}(\pi) = 0$

3. **(a)** $\dfrac{dw}{dt} = 1,$ **(b)** $\dfrac{dw}{dt}(3) = 1$

5. **(a)** $\dfrac{dw}{dt} = 4t \tan^{-1} t + 1,$ **(b)** $\dfrac{dw}{dt}(1) = \pi + 1$

7. **(a)** $\dfrac{\partial z}{\partial u} = 4 \cos v \ln (u \sin v) + 4 \cos v, \dfrac{\partial z}{\partial v} =$

    $-4u \sin v \ln (u \sin v) + \dfrac{4u \cos^2 v}{\sin v}$

    (b) $\dfrac{\partial z}{\partial u} = \sqrt{2}\, (\ln 2 + 2), \dfrac{\partial z}{\partial v} = -2\sqrt{2}\, (\ln 2 - 2)$

9. **(a)** $\dfrac{\partial w}{\partial u} = 2u + 4uv, \dfrac{\partial w}{\partial v} = -2v + 2u^2$

    (b) $\dfrac{\partial w}{\partial u} = 3, \dfrac{\partial w}{\partial v} = -\dfrac{3}{2}$

11. **(a)** $\dfrac{\partial u}{\partial x} = 0, \dfrac{\partial u}{\partial y} = \dfrac{z}{(z - y)^2}, \dfrac{\partial u}{\partial z} = \dfrac{-y}{(z - y)^2}$

    (b) $\dfrac{\partial u}{\partial x} = 0, \dfrac{\partial u}{\partial y} = 1, \dfrac{\partial u}{\partial z} = -2$

13. $\dfrac{dz}{dt} = \dfrac{\partial z}{\partial x}\dfrac{dx}{dt} + \dfrac{\partial z}{\partial y}\dfrac{dy}{dt}$

15. $\dfrac{\partial w}{\partial u} = \dfrac{\partial w}{\partial x}\dfrac{\partial x}{\partial u} + \dfrac{\partial w}{\partial y}\dfrac{\partial y}{\partial u} + \dfrac{\partial w}{\partial z}\dfrac{\partial z}{\partial u}, \dfrac{\partial w}{\partial v} = \dfrac{\partial w}{\partial x}\dfrac{\partial x}{\partial v} + \dfrac{\partial w}{\partial y}\dfrac{\partial y}{\partial v} + \dfrac{\partial w}{\partial z}\dfrac{\partial z}{\partial v}$

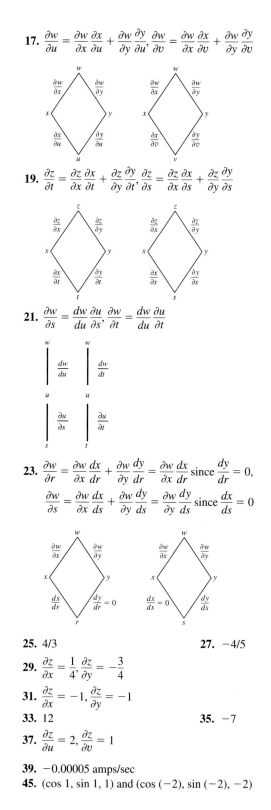

17. $\dfrac{\partial w}{\partial u} = \dfrac{\partial w}{\partial x}\dfrac{\partial x}{\partial u} + \dfrac{\partial w}{\partial y}\dfrac{\partial y}{\partial u}, \dfrac{\partial w}{\partial v} = \dfrac{\partial w}{\partial x}\dfrac{\partial x}{\partial v} + \dfrac{\partial w}{\partial y}\dfrac{\partial y}{\partial v}$

19. $\dfrac{\partial z}{\partial t} = \dfrac{\partial z}{\partial x}\dfrac{\partial x}{\partial t} + \dfrac{\partial z}{\partial y}\dfrac{\partial y}{\partial t}, \dfrac{\partial z}{\partial s} = \dfrac{\partial z}{\partial x}\dfrac{\partial x}{\partial s} + \dfrac{\partial z}{\partial y}\dfrac{\partial y}{\partial s}$

21. $\dfrac{\partial w}{\partial s} = \dfrac{dw}{du}\dfrac{\partial u}{\partial s}, \dfrac{\partial w}{\partial t} = \dfrac{dw}{du}\dfrac{\partial u}{\partial t}$

23. $\dfrac{\partial w}{\partial r} = \dfrac{\partial w}{\partial x}\dfrac{dx}{dr} + \dfrac{\partial w}{\partial y}\dfrac{dy}{dr} = \dfrac{\partial w}{\partial x}\dfrac{dx}{dr}$ since $\dfrac{dy}{dr} = 0,$

$\dfrac{\partial w}{\partial s} = \dfrac{\partial w}{\partial x}\dfrac{dx}{ds} + \dfrac{\partial w}{\partial y}\dfrac{dy}{ds} = \dfrac{\partial w}{\partial y}\dfrac{dy}{ds}$ since $\dfrac{dx}{ds} = 0$

25. 4/3   **27.** $-4/5$

29. $\dfrac{\partial z}{\partial x} = \dfrac{1}{4}, \dfrac{\partial z}{\partial y} = -\dfrac{3}{4}$

31. $\dfrac{\partial z}{\partial x} = -1, \dfrac{\partial z}{\partial y} = -1$

33. 12   **35.** -7

37. $\dfrac{\partial z}{\partial u} = 2, \dfrac{\partial z}{\partial v} = 1$

39. -0.00005 amps/sec

45. $(\cos 1, \sin 1, 1)$ and $(\cos (-2), \sin (-2), -2)$

47. (a) Maximum at $\left(-\dfrac{\sqrt{2}}{2}, \dfrac{\sqrt{2}}{2}\right)$ and $\left(\dfrac{\sqrt{2}}{2}, -\dfrac{\sqrt{2}}{2}\right)$; minimum at

$\left(\dfrac{\sqrt{2}}{2}, \dfrac{\sqrt{2}}{2}\right)$ and $\left(-\dfrac{\sqrt{2}}{2}, -\dfrac{\sqrt{2}}{2}\right)$

(b) Max = 6, min = 2

49. $2x\sqrt{x^8 + x^3} + \displaystyle\int_0^{x^2} \dfrac{3x^2}{2\sqrt{t^4 + x^3}}\, dt$

Section 11.5, pp. 923–925

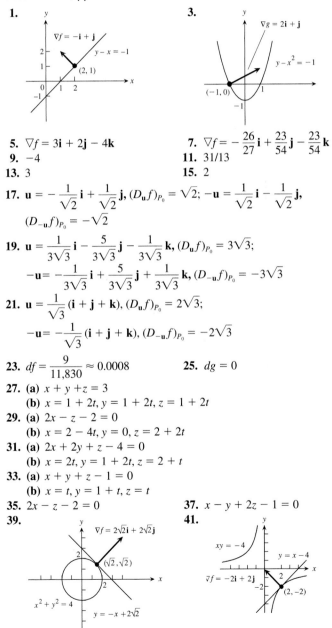

1. $\nabla f = -\mathbf{i} + \mathbf{j}$, $y - x = -1$, $(2, 1)$

3. $\nabla g = 2\mathbf{i} + \mathbf{j}$, $y - x^2 = -1$, $(-1, 0)$

5. $\nabla f = 3\mathbf{i} + 2\mathbf{j} - 4\mathbf{k}$

7. $\nabla f = -\dfrac{26}{27}\mathbf{i} + \dfrac{23}{54}\mathbf{j} - \dfrac{23}{54}\mathbf{k}$

9. -4

11. $31/13$

13. 3

15. 2

17. $\mathbf{u} = -\dfrac{1}{\sqrt{2}}\mathbf{i} + \dfrac{1}{\sqrt{2}}\mathbf{j}$, $(D_{\mathbf{u}}f)_{P_0} = \sqrt{2}$; $-\mathbf{u} = \dfrac{1}{\sqrt{2}}\mathbf{i} - \dfrac{1}{\sqrt{2}}\mathbf{j}$,

$(D_{-\mathbf{u}}f)_{P_0} = -\sqrt{2}$

19. $\mathbf{u} = \dfrac{1}{3\sqrt{3}}\mathbf{i} - \dfrac{5}{3\sqrt{3}}\mathbf{j} - \dfrac{1}{3\sqrt{3}}\mathbf{k}$, $(D_{\mathbf{u}}f)_{P_0} = 3\sqrt{3}$;

$-\mathbf{u} = -\dfrac{1}{3\sqrt{3}}\mathbf{i} + \dfrac{5}{3\sqrt{3}}\mathbf{j} + \dfrac{1}{3\sqrt{3}}\mathbf{k}$, $(D_{-\mathbf{u}}f)_{P_0} = -3\sqrt{3}$

21. $\mathbf{u} = \dfrac{1}{\sqrt{3}}(\mathbf{i} + \mathbf{j} + \mathbf{k})$, $(D_{\mathbf{u}}f)_{P_0} = 2\sqrt{3}$;

$-\mathbf{u} = -\dfrac{1}{\sqrt{3}}(\mathbf{i} + \mathbf{j} + \mathbf{k})$, $(D_{-\mathbf{u}}f)_{P_0} = -2\sqrt{3}$

23. $df = \dfrac{9}{11,830} \approx 0.0008$ **25.** $dg = 0$

27. (a) $x + y + z = 3$

(b) $x = 1 + 2t, y = 1 + 2t, z = 1 + 2t$

29. (a) $2x - z - 2 = 0$

(b) $x = 2 - 4t, y = 0, z = 2 + 2t$

31. (a) $2x + 2y + z - 4 = 0$

(b) $x = 2t, y = 1 + 2t, z = 2 + t$

33. (a) $x + y + z - 1 = 0$

(b) $x = t, y = 1 + t, z = t$

35. $2x - z - 2 = 0$ **37.** $x - y + 2z - 1 = 0$

39. $\nabla f = 2\sqrt{2}\mathbf{i} + 2\sqrt{2}\mathbf{j}$, $(\sqrt{2}, \sqrt{2})$, $x^2 + y^2 = 4$, $y = -x + 2\sqrt{2}$

41. $xy = -4$, $y = x - 4$, $\nabla f = -2\mathbf{i} + 2\mathbf{j}$, $(2, -2)$

43. $x = 1, y = 1 + 2t, z = 1 - 2t$

45. $x = 1 - 2t, y = 1, z = \dfrac{1}{2} + 2t$

47. $x = 1 + 90t, y = 1 - 90t, z = 3$

49. $\mathbf{u} = \dfrac{7}{\sqrt{53}}\mathbf{i} - \dfrac{2}{\sqrt{53}}\mathbf{j}$, $-\mathbf{u} = -\dfrac{7}{\sqrt{53}}\mathbf{i} + \dfrac{2}{\sqrt{53}}\mathbf{j}$

51. No, the maximum rate of change is $\sqrt{185} < 14$.

53. $-\dfrac{7}{\sqrt{5}}$

55. (a) $\dfrac{\sqrt{3}}{2}\sin\sqrt{3} - \dfrac{1}{2}\cos\sqrt{3} \approx 0.935°C/ft$

(b) $\sqrt{3}\sin\sqrt{3} - \cos\sqrt{3} \approx 1.87°C/sec$

57. At $-\dfrac{\pi}{4}, -\dfrac{\pi}{2\sqrt{2}}$; at $0, 0$; at $\dfrac{\pi}{4}, \dfrac{\pi}{2\sqrt{2}}$

Section 11.6, pp. 934–936

1. (a) $L(x, y) = 1$ **(b)** $L(x, y) = 2x + 2y - 1$

3. (a) $L(x, y) = 3x - 4y + 5$ **(b)** $L(x, y) = 3x - 4y + 5$

5. (a) $L(x, y) = 1 + x$ **(b)** $L(x, y) = -y + \dfrac{\pi}{2}$

7. $L(x, y) = 7 + x - 6y$; 0.06 **9.** $L(x, y) = x + y + 1$; 0.08

11. $L(x, y) = 1 + x$; 0.0222

13. Pay more attention to the smaller of the two dimensions. It will generate the larger partial derivative.

15. Maximum error (estimate) ≤ 0.31 in magnitude

17. Maximum percentage error $= \pm 4.83\%$

19. Let $|x - 1| \leq 0.014$, $|y - 1| \leq 0.014$

21. $\approx 0.1\%$

23. (a) $L(x, y, z) = 2x + 2y + 2z - 3$

(b) $L(x, y, z) = y + z$

(c) $L(x, y, z) = 0$

25. (a) $L(x, y, z) = x$

(b) $L(x, y, z) = \dfrac{1}{\sqrt{2}}x + \dfrac{1}{\sqrt{2}}y$

(c) $L(x, y, z) = \dfrac{1}{3}x + \dfrac{2}{3}y + \dfrac{2}{3}z$

27. (a) $L(x, y, z) = 2 + x$

(b) $L(x, y, z) = x - y - z + \dfrac{\pi}{2} + 1$

(c) $L(x, y, z) = x - y - z + \dfrac{\pi}{2} + 1$

29. $L(x, y, z) = 2x - 6y - 2z + 6$, 0.0024

31. $L(x, y, z) = x + y - z - 1$, 0.00135

33. (a) $S_0\left(\dfrac{1}{100}\, dp + dx - 5\, dw - 30\, dh\right)$

(b) More sensitive to a change in height

35. f is most sensitive to a change in d

37. $\dfrac{47}{24}\text{ ft}^3$

39. Magnitude of possible error ≤ 4.8

Section 11.7, pp. 944–947

1. $f(-3, 3) = -5$, local minimum   **3.** $f(-2, 1)$, saddle point

5. $f\left(\dfrac{13}{12}, -\dfrac{3}{4}\right) = -\dfrac{31}{12}$, local minimum

7. $f(1, 2)$, saddle point   **9.** $f(0, 1) = 4$, local maximum

11. $f(0, 0)$, saddle point; $f(-1, -1) = 1$, local maximum

13. $f(0, 0)$, saddle point; $f\left(\dfrac{4}{9}, \dfrac{4}{3}\right) = -\dfrac{64}{81}$, local minimum

15. $f(0, 0)$, saddle point; $f(1, 1) = 2, f(-1, -1) = 2$, local maxima

17. $f(0, 0) = -1$, local maximum

19. $f(n\pi, 0)$, saddle point; $f(n\pi, 0) = 0$ for every n

21. Absolute maximum: 1 at $(0, 0)$; absolute minimum: -5 at $(1, 2)$

23. Absolute maximum: 11 at $(0, -3)$; absolute minimum: -10 at $(4, -2)$

25. Absolute maximum: 4 at $(2, 0)$; absolute minimum: $\dfrac{3\sqrt{2}}{2}$ at $\left(3, -\dfrac{\pi}{4}\right), \left(3, \dfrac{\pi}{4}\right), \left(1, -\dfrac{\pi}{4}\right)$, and $\left(1, \dfrac{\pi}{4}\right)$

27. $a = -3, b = 2$

29. Hottest: $2\dfrac{1°}{4}$ at $\left(-\dfrac{1}{2}, \dfrac{\sqrt{3}}{2}\right)$ and $\left(-\dfrac{1}{2}, -\dfrac{\sqrt{3}}{2}\right)$; coldest: $-\dfrac{1°}{4}$ at $\left(\dfrac{1}{2}, 0\right)$

31. **(a)** $f(0, 0)$, saddle point
   (b) $f(1, 2)$, local minimum
   (c) $f(1, -2)$, local minimum; $f(-1, -2)$, saddle point

37. $(1/6, 1/3, 355/36)$

41. **(a)** On the semicircle, max $f = 2\sqrt{2}$ at $t = \dfrac{\pi}{4}$, min $f = -2$ at $t = \pi$; on the quarter circle, max $f = 2\sqrt{2}$ at $t = \dfrac{\pi}{4}$, min $f = 2$ at $t = 0, \dfrac{\pi}{2}$
   (b) On the semicircle, max $g = 2$ at $t = \dfrac{\pi}{4}$, min $g = -2$ at $t = \dfrac{3\pi}{4}$; on the quarter circle, max $g = 2$ at $t = \dfrac{\pi}{4}$, min $g = 0$ at $t = 0, \dfrac{\pi}{2}$
   (c) On the semicircle, max $h = 8$ at $t = 0, \pi$; min $h = 4$ at $t = \dfrac{\pi}{2}$; on the quarter circle, max $h = 8$ at $t = 0$, min $h = 4$ at $t = \dfrac{\pi}{2}$

43. **(i)** min $f = -\dfrac{1}{2}$ at $t = -\dfrac{1}{2}$; no max
   (ii) max $f = 0$ at $t = -1, 0$; min $f = -\dfrac{1}{4}$ at $t = -\dfrac{1}{2}$
   (iii) max $f = 4$ at $t = 1$; min $f = 0$ at $t = 0$

Section 11.8, pp. 956–958

1. $\left(\pm\dfrac{1}{\sqrt{2}}, \dfrac{1}{2}\right), \left(\pm\dfrac{1}{\sqrt{2}}, -\dfrac{1}{2}\right)$

3. 39   **5.** $(3, \pm3\sqrt{2})$

7. **(a)** 8   **(b)** 64

9. $r = 2$ cm, $h = 4$ cm   **11.** $\ell = 4\sqrt{2}, w = 3\sqrt{2}$

13. $f(0, 0) = 0$ is minimum, $f(2, 4) = 20$ is maximum

15. Lowest $= 0°$, highest $= 125°$ **17.** $\left(\dfrac{3}{2}, 2, \dfrac{5}{2}\right)$

19. 1   **21.** $(0, 0, 2), (0, 0, -2)$

23. $f(1, -2, 5) = 30$ is maximum, $f(-1, 2, -5) = -30$ is minimum.

25. 3, 3, 3   **27.** $\dfrac{2}{\sqrt{3}}$ by $\dfrac{2}{\sqrt{3}}$ by $\dfrac{2}{\sqrt{3}}$ units

29. $(\pm4/3, -4/3, -4/3)$ **31.** $U(8, 14) = \$128$

33. $f(2/3, 4/3, -4/3) = \dfrac{4}{3}$ **35.** $(2, 4, 4)$

37. Maximum is $1 + 6\sqrt{3}$ at $(\pm\sqrt{6}, \sqrt{3}, 1)$, minimum is $1 - 6\sqrt{3}$ at $(\pm\sqrt{6}, -\sqrt{3}, 1)$.

39. Maximum is 4 at $(0, 0, \pm2)$, minimum is 2 at $(\pm\sqrt{2}, \pm\sqrt{2}, 0)$

Section 11.9, pp. 962–963

1. **(a)** 0   **(b)** $1 + 2z$ **(c)** $1 + 2z$

3. **(a)** $\dfrac{\partial U}{\partial P} + \dfrac{\partial U}{\partial T}\left(\dfrac{V}{nR}\right)$ **(b)** $\dfrac{\partial U}{\partial P}\left(\dfrac{nR}{V}\right) + \dfrac{\partial U}{\partial T}$

5. **(a)** 5   **(b)** 5

7. $\left(\dfrac{\partial x}{\partial r}\right)_\theta = \cos\theta$
   $\left(\dfrac{\partial r}{\partial x}\right)_y = \dfrac{x}{\sqrt{x^2 + y^2}}$

Section 11.10, p. 967

1. Quadratic: $x + xy$; cubic: $x + xy + \dfrac{1}{2}xy^2$

3. Quadratic: xy; cubic: xy

5. Quadratic: $y + \dfrac{1}{2}(2xy - y^2)$;
   cubic: $y + \dfrac{1}{2}(2xy - y^2) + \dfrac{1}{6}(3x^2y - 3xy^2 + 2y^3)$

7. Quadratic: $\dfrac{1}{2}(2x^2 + 2y^2) = x^2 + y^2$; cubic: $x^2 + y^2$

9. Quadratic: $1 + (x + y) + (x + y)^2$;
   cubic: $1 + (x + y) + (x + y)^2 + (x + y)^3$

11. Quadratic: $1 - \dfrac{1}{2}x^2 - \dfrac{1}{2}y^2$; $E(x, y) \leq 0.00134$

Chapter 11 Practice Exercises, pp. 968–972

1. Domain: all points in the xy-plane; range: $z \geq 0$. Level curves are ellipses with major axis along the y-axis and minor axis along the x-axis.

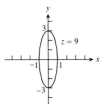

3. Domain: all (x, y) such that $x \neq 0$ and $y \neq 0$; range: $z \neq 0$. Level curves are hyperbolas with the x- and y-axes as asymptotes.

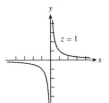

5. Domain: all points in xyz-space; range: all real numbers. Level surfaces are paraboloids of revolution with the z-axis as axis.

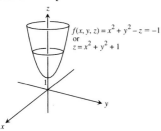

7. Domain: all (x, y, z) such that $(x, y, z) \neq (0, 0, 0)$; range: positive real numbers. Level surfaces are spheres with center $(0, 0, 0)$ and radius $r > 0$.

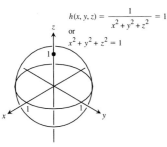

9. -2 **11.** $1/2$

13. 1 **15.** Let $y = kx^2$, $k \neq 1$

17. No; $\lim\limits_{(x,y) \to (0,0)} f(x, y)$ does not exist.

19. $\dfrac{\partial g}{\partial r} = \cos\theta + \sin\theta$, $\dfrac{\partial g}{\partial \theta} = -r\sin\theta + r\cos\theta$

21. $\dfrac{\partial f}{\partial R_1} = -\dfrac{1}{R_1^2}$, $\dfrac{\partial f}{\partial R_2} = -\dfrac{1}{R_2^2}$, $\dfrac{\partial f}{\partial R_3} = -\dfrac{1}{R_3^2}$

23. $\dfrac{\partial P}{\partial n} = \dfrac{RT}{V}$, $\dfrac{\partial P}{\partial R} = \dfrac{nT}{V}$, $\dfrac{\partial P}{\partial T} = \dfrac{nR}{V}$, $\dfrac{\partial P}{\partial V} = -\dfrac{nRT}{V^2}$

25. $\dfrac{\partial^2 g}{\partial x^2} = 0$, $\dfrac{\partial^2 g}{\partial y^2} = \dfrac{2x}{y^3}$, $\dfrac{\partial^2 g}{\partial y\, \partial x} = \dfrac{\partial^2 g}{\partial x\, \partial y} = -\dfrac{1}{y^2}$

27. $\dfrac{\partial^2 f}{\partial x^2} = -30x + \dfrac{2 - 2x^2}{(x^2 + 1)^2}$, $\dfrac{\partial^2 f}{\partial y^2} = 0$, $\dfrac{\partial^2 f}{\partial y\, \partial x} = \dfrac{\partial^2 f}{\partial x\, \partial y} = 1$

29. $\dfrac{dw}{dt}\Big|_{t=0} = -1$

31. $\dfrac{\partial w}{\partial r}\Big|_{(r,s)=(\pi,0)} = 2$, $\dfrac{\partial w}{\partial s}\Big|_{(r,s)=(\pi,0)} = 2 - \pi$

33. $\dfrac{df}{dt}\Big|_{t=1} = -(\sin 1 + \cos 2)(\sin 1) + (\cos 1 + \cos 2)(\cos 1) - 2(\sin 1 + \cos 1)(\sin 2)$

35. $\dfrac{dy}{dx}\Big|_{(x,y)=(0,1)} = -1$

37. Increases most rapidly in the direction $\mathbf{u} = -\dfrac{\sqrt{2}}{2}\mathbf{i} - \dfrac{\sqrt{2}}{2}\mathbf{j}$; decreases most rapidly in the direction $-\mathbf{u} = \dfrac{\sqrt{2}}{2}\mathbf{i} + \dfrac{\sqrt{2}}{2}\mathbf{j}$; $D_{\mathbf{u}}f = \dfrac{\sqrt{2}}{2}$; $D_{-\mathbf{u}}f = -\dfrac{\sqrt{2}}{2}$; $D_{\mathbf{u}_1}f = -\dfrac{7}{10}$ where $\mathbf{u}_1 = \dfrac{\mathbf{v}}{|\mathbf{v}|}$

39. Increases most rapidly in the direction $\mathbf{u} = \dfrac{2}{7}\mathbf{i} + \dfrac{3}{7}\mathbf{j} + \dfrac{6}{7}\mathbf{k}$; decreases most rapidly in the direction $-\mathbf{u} = -\dfrac{2}{7}\mathbf{i} - \dfrac{3}{7}\mathbf{j} - \dfrac{6}{7}\mathbf{k}$; $D_{\mathbf{u}}f = 7$; $D_{-\mathbf{u}}f = -7$; $D_{\mathbf{u}_1}f = 7$ where $\mathbf{u}_1 = \dfrac{\mathbf{v}}{|\mathbf{v}|}$

41. $\pi/\sqrt{2}$

43. (a) $f_x(1, 2) = f_y(1, 2) = 2$ (b) $14/5$

45.

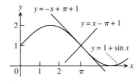

47. Tangent: $4x - y - 5z = 4$; normal line: $x = 2 + 4t$, $y = -1 - t$, $z = 1 - 5t$

49. $2y - z - 2 = 0$

51. Tangent: $x + y = \pi + 1$; normal line: $y = x - \pi + 1$

53. $x = 1 - 2t$, $y = 1$, $z = 1/2 + 2t$

55. Answers will depend on the upper bound used for $|f_{xx}|$, $|f_{xy}|$, $|f_{yy}|$. With $M = \sqrt{2}/2$, $|E| \leq 0.0142$. With $M = 1$, $|E| \leq 0.02$.

57. $L(x, y, z) = y - 3z$, $L(x, y, z) = x + y - z - 1$

59. Be more careful with the diameter.

61. $dI = 0.038$, % change in $I = 15.83\%$, more sensitive to voltage change

63. (a) 5%

65. Local minimum of -8 at $(-2, -2)$

67. Saddle point at $(0, 0)$, $f(0, 0) = 0$; local maximum of $1/4$ at $(-1/2, -1/2)$

69. Saddle point at $(0, 0)$, $f(0, 0) = 0$; local minimum of -4 at $(0, 2)$; local maximum of 4 at $(-2, 0)$; saddle point at $(-2, 2)$, $f(-2, 2) = 0$

71. Absolute maximum: 28 at $(0, 4)$; absolute minimum: $-9/4$ at $(3/2, 0)$

73. Absolute maximum: 18 at $(2, -2)$; absolute minimum: $-17/4$ at $(-2, 1/2)$

75. Absolute maximum: 8 at $(-2, 0)$; absolute minimum: -1 at $(1, 0)$

77. Absolute maximum: 4 at $(1, 0)$; absolute minimum: -4 at $(0, -1)$

79. Absolute maximum: 1 at $(0, \pm 1)$ and $(1, 0)$; absolute minimum: -1 at $(-1, 0)$

81. Maximum: 5 at $(0, 1)$; minimum: $-1/3$ at $(0, -1/3)$

83. Maximum: $\sqrt{3}$ at $\left(\dfrac{1}{\sqrt{3}}, -\dfrac{1}{\sqrt{3}}, \dfrac{1}{\sqrt{3}}\right)$;

minimum: $-\sqrt{3}$ at $\left(-\dfrac{1}{\sqrt{3}}, \dfrac{1}{\sqrt{3}}, -\dfrac{1}{\sqrt{3}}\right)$

85. Width $= \left(\dfrac{c^2 V}{ab}\right)^{1/3}$, depth $= \left(\dfrac{b^2 V}{ac}\right)^{1/3}$, height $= \left(\dfrac{a^2 V}{bc}\right)^{1/3}$

87. Maximum: $\dfrac{3}{2}$ at $\left(\dfrac{1}{\sqrt{2}}, \dfrac{1}{\sqrt{2}}, \sqrt{2}\right)$ and $\left(-\dfrac{1}{\sqrt{2}}, -\dfrac{1}{\sqrt{2}}, -\sqrt{2}\right)$;

minimum: $\dfrac{1}{2}$ at $\left(-\dfrac{1}{\sqrt{2}}, \dfrac{1}{\sqrt{2}}, -\sqrt{2}\right)$ and $\left(\dfrac{1}{\sqrt{2}}, -\dfrac{1}{\sqrt{2}}, \sqrt{2}\right)$

89. (a) $(2y + x^2 z)e^{yz}$

(b) $x^2 e^{yz}\left(y - \dfrac{z}{2y}\right)$

(c) $(1 + x^2 y)e^{yz}$

91. $\dfrac{\partial w}{\partial x} = \cos\theta \dfrac{\partial w}{\partial r} - \dfrac{\sin\theta}{r}\dfrac{\partial w}{\partial\theta}$, $\dfrac{\partial w}{\partial y} = \sin\theta \dfrac{\partial w}{\partial r} + \dfrac{\cos\theta}{r}\dfrac{\partial w}{\partial\theta}$

97. $(t, -t \pm 4, t)$, t a real number

Chapter 11 Additional Exercises, pp. 972–974

1. $f_{xy}(0, 0) = -1$, $f_{yx}(0, 0) = 1$

7. (c) $\dfrac{r^2}{2} = \dfrac{1}{2}(x^2 + y^2 + z^2)$ **13.** $V = \dfrac{\sqrt{3}abc}{2}$

17. $f(x, y) = \dfrac{y}{2} + 4$, $g(x, y) = \dfrac{x}{2} + \dfrac{9}{2}$

19. $y = 2 \ln|\sin x| + \ln 2$

21. (a) $\dfrac{1}{\sqrt{53}}(2\mathbf{i} + 7\mathbf{j})$

(b) $\dfrac{-1}{\sqrt{29{,}097}}(98\mathbf{i} - 127\mathbf{j} + 58\mathbf{k})$

23. $w = e^{-c^2\pi^2 t}\sin\pi x$

Section 12.1, pp. 984–987

1. 16

3. 1

5. $\dfrac{\pi^2}{2} + 2$

7. $8\ln 8 - 16 + e$

9. $e - 2$

11. $\dfrac{3}{2}\ln 2$

13. 1/6

15. $-1/10$

17. 8

19. 2π

21. $\displaystyle\int_2^4 \int_0^{(4-y)/2} dx\, dy$

23. $\displaystyle\int_0^1 \int_{x^2}^x dy\, dx$

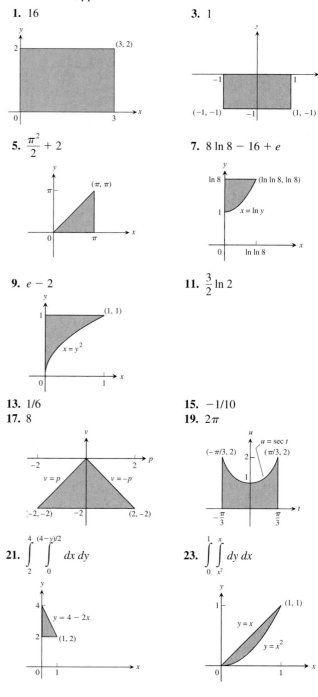

25. $\displaystyle\int_1^e \int_{\ln y}^1 dx\, dy$

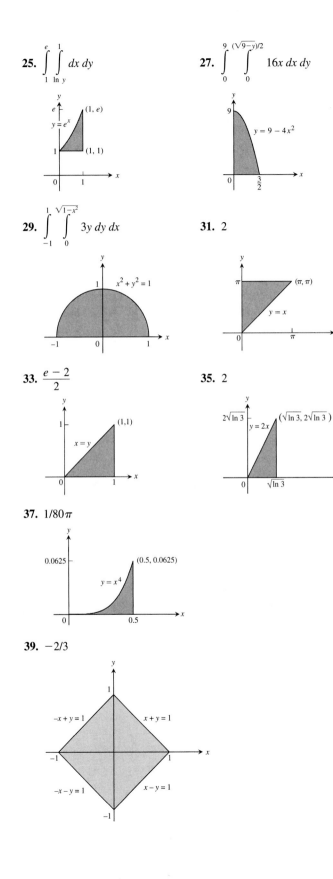

27. $\displaystyle\int_0^9 \int_0^{(\sqrt{9-y})/2} 16x\, dx\, dy$

29. $\displaystyle\int_{-1}^1 \int_0^{\sqrt{1-x^2}} 3y\, dy\, dx$

31. 2

33. $\dfrac{e-2}{2}$

35. 2

37. $1/80\pi$

39. $-2/3$

41. 4/3

43. 625/12

45. 16

47. 20

49. $2(1 + \ln 2)$

51. 1

53. π^2

55. $-\dfrac{3}{32}$

57. $\dfrac{20\sqrt{3}}{9}$

59. $\displaystyle\int_0^1 \int_x^{2-x} (x^2 + y^2)\, dy\, dx = \dfrac{4}{3}$

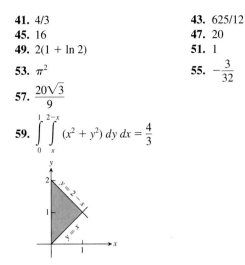

63. No, by Fubini's theorem, the two orders of integration must give the same result.

67. 0.603

69. 0.233

Section 12.2, pp. 997–1000

1. $\displaystyle\int_0^2 \int_0^{2-x} dy\, dx = 2$ or $\displaystyle\int_0^2 \int_0^{2-y} dx\, dy = 2$

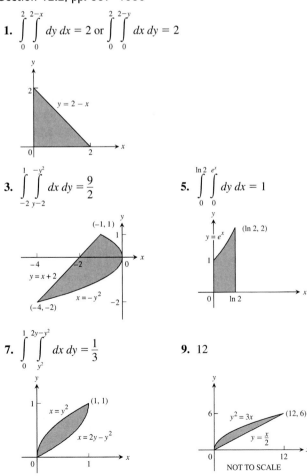

3. $\displaystyle\int_{-2}^1 \int_{y-2}^{-y^2} dx\, dy = \dfrac{9}{2}$

5. $\displaystyle\int_0^{\ln 2} \int_0^{e^x} dy\, dx = 1$

7. $\displaystyle\int_0^1 \int_{y^2}^{2y-y^2} dx\, dy = \dfrac{1}{3}$

9. 12

11. $\sqrt{2} - 1$

13. $\dfrac{3}{2}$

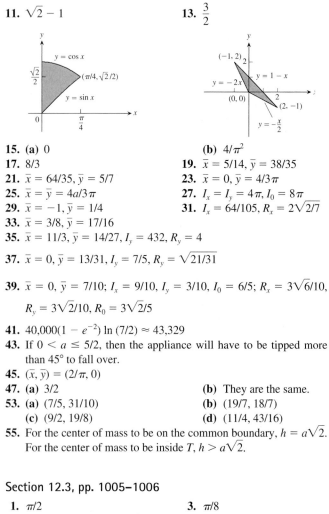

15. (a) 0 **(b)** $4/\pi^2$

17. 8/3

19. $\bar{x} = 5/14, \bar{y} = 38/35$

21. $\bar{x} = 64/35, \bar{y} = 5/7$

23. $\bar{x} = 0, \bar{y} = 4/3\pi$

25. $\bar{x} = \bar{y} = 4a/3\pi$

27. $I_x = I_y = 4\pi, I_0 = 8\pi$

29. $\bar{x} = -1, \bar{y} = 1/4$

31. $I_x = 64/105, R_x = 2\sqrt{2/7}$

33. $\bar{x} = 3/8, \bar{y} = 17/16$

35. $\bar{x} = 11/3, \bar{y} = 14/27, I_y = 432, R_y = 4$

37. $\bar{x} = 0, \bar{y} = 13/31, I_y = 7/5, R_y = \sqrt{21/31}$

39. $\bar{x} = 0, \bar{y} = 7/10; I_x = 9/10, I_y = 3/10, I_0 = 6/5; R_x = 3\sqrt{6}/10,$

$R_y = 3\sqrt{2}/10, R_0 = 3\sqrt{2}/5$

41. $40{,}000(1 - e^{-2}) \ln (7/2) \approx 43{,}329$

43. If $0 < a \le 5/2$, then the appliance will have to be tipped more than 45° to fall over.

45. $(\bar{x}, \bar{y}) = (2/\pi, 0)$

47. (a) 3/2 **(b)** They are the same.

53. (a) (7/5, 31/10) **(b)** (19/7, 18/7)

  (c) (9/2, 19/8) **(d)** (11/4, 43/16)

55. For the center of mass to be on the common boundary, $h = a\sqrt{2}$. For the center of mass to be inside $T, h > a\sqrt{2}$.

Section 12.3, pp. 1005–1006

1. $\pi/2$

3. $\pi/8$

5. πa^2

7. 36

9. $(1 - \ln 2)\pi$

11. $(2 \ln 2 - 1)(\pi/2)$

13. $\pi/2 + 1$

15. $\pi(\ln 4 - 1)$

17. $2(\pi - 1)$

19. 12π

21. $3\pi/8 + 1$

23. 4

25. $6\sqrt{3} - 2\pi$

27. $\bar{x} = 5/6, \bar{y} = 0$

29. $\dfrac{2a}{3}$

31. $\dfrac{2a}{3}$

33. $2\pi(2 - \sqrt{e})$

35. $\dfrac{4}{3} + \dfrac{5\pi}{8}$

37. (a) $\dfrac{\sqrt{\pi}}{2}$ **(b)** 1

39. $\pi \ln 4$, no

41. $\dfrac{1}{2}(a^2 + 2h^2)$

Section 12.4, pp. 1014–1017

1. 1/6

3.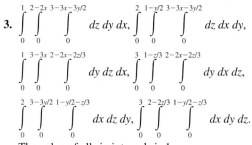

The value of all six integrals is 1.

5.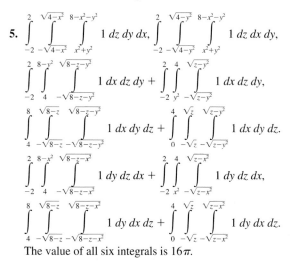

The value of all six integrals is 16π.

7. 1

9. 1

11. $\dfrac{\pi^3}{2} (1 - \cos 1)$

13. 18

15. 7/6

17. 0

19. $\dfrac{1}{2} - \dfrac{\pi}{8}$

21. (a) $\displaystyle\int_{-1}^{1} \int_{0}^{1-x^2} \int_{x^2}^{1-z} dy \, dz \, dx$ **(b)** $\displaystyle\int_{0}^{1} \int_{-\sqrt{1-z}}^{\sqrt{1-z}} \int_{x^2}^{1-z} dy \, dx \, dz$

  (c) $\displaystyle\int_{0}^{1} \int_{0}^{1-z} \int_{-\sqrt{y}}^{\sqrt{y}} dx \, dy \, dz$ **(d)** $\displaystyle\int_{0}^{1} \int_{0}^{1-y} \int_{-\sqrt{y}}^{\sqrt{y}} dx \, dz \, dy$

  (e)

23. 2/3

25. 20/3

27. 1

29. 16/3

31. $8\pi - \dfrac{32}{3}$

33. 2

35. 4π

37. 31/3

39. 1

41. $2 \sin 4$

43. 4

45. $a = 3$ or $a = 13/3$

47. The domain is the set of all point (x, y, z) such that $4x^2 + 4y^2 + z^2 \leq 4$.

Section 12.5, pp. 1021–1023

1. $R_x = \sqrt{\dfrac{b^2 + c^2}{12}},\ R_y = \sqrt{\dfrac{a^2 + c^2}{12}},\ R_z = \sqrt{\dfrac{a^2 + b^2}{12}}$

3. $I_x = \dfrac{M}{3}(b^2 + c^2),\ I_y = \dfrac{M}{3}(a^2 + c^2),\ I_z = \dfrac{M}{3}(a^2 + b^2)$

5. $\bar{x} = \bar{y} = 0,\ \bar{z} = \dfrac{12}{5},\ I_x = 7904/105 \approx 75.28,\ I_y = 4832/63 \approx 76.70,\ I_z = 256/45 \approx 5.69$

7. (a) $\bar{x} = \bar{y} = 0, \bar{z} = 8/3$ (b) $c = 2\sqrt{2}$

9. $I_L = 1386,\ R_L = \sqrt{\dfrac{77}{2}}$ **11.** $I_L = \dfrac{40}{3},\ R_L = \sqrt{\dfrac{5}{3}}$

13. (a) $4/3$ (b) $\bar{x} = 4/5, \bar{y} = \bar{z} = 2/5$

15. (a) $5/2$ (b) $\bar{x} = \bar{y} = \bar{z} = 8/15$

   (c) $I_x = I_y = I_z = 11/6$ (d) $R_x = R_y = R_z = \sqrt{\dfrac{11}{15}}$

17. 3

19. (a) $\dfrac{4}{3}g$ (b) $\dfrac{4}{3}g$

23. (a) $I_{\text{c.m.}} = \dfrac{abc(a^2 + b^2)}{12},\ R_{\text{c.m.}} = \sqrt{\dfrac{a^2 + b^2}{12}}$

   (b) $I_L = \dfrac{abc(a^2 + 7b^2)}{3},\ R_L = \sqrt{\dfrac{a^2 + 7b^2}{3}}$

27. (a) $h = a\sqrt{3}$ (b) $h = a\sqrt{2}$

Section 12.6, pp. 1032–1037

1. $\dfrac{4\pi(\sqrt{2} - 1)}{3}$ **3.** $\dfrac{17\pi}{5}$

5. $\pi(6\sqrt{2} - 8)$ **7.** $\dfrac{3\pi}{10}$

9. $\pi/3$

11. (a) $\displaystyle\int_0^{2\pi}\int_0^1\int_0^{\sqrt{4-r^2}} r\, dz\, dr\, d\theta$

   (b) $\displaystyle\int_0^{2\pi}\int_0^{\sqrt{3}}\int_0^1 r\, dr\, dz\, d\theta + \int_0^{2\pi}\int_{\sqrt{3}}^2\int_0^{\sqrt{4-z^2}} r\, dr\, dz\, d\theta$

   (c) $\displaystyle\int_0^1\int_0^{\sqrt{4-r^2}}\int_0^{2\pi} r\, d\theta\, dz\, dr$

13. $\displaystyle\int_{-\pi/2}^{\pi/2}\int_0^{\cos\theta}\int_0^{3r^2} f(r, \theta, z)\, dz\, r\, dr\, d\theta$

15. $\displaystyle\int_0^\pi\int_0^{2\sin\theta}\int_0^{4-r\sin\theta} f(r, \theta, z)\, dz\, r\, dr\, d\theta$

17. $\displaystyle\int_{-\pi/2}^{\pi/2}\int_1^{1+\cos\theta}\int_0^4 f(r, \theta, z)\, dz\, r\, dr\, d\theta$

19. $\displaystyle\int_0^{\pi/4}\int_0^{\sec\theta}\int_0^{2-r\sin\theta} f(r, \theta, z)\, dz\, r\, dr\, d\theta$

21. π^2 **23.** $\pi/3$

25. 5π **27.** 2π

29. $\left(\dfrac{8 - 5\sqrt{2}}{2}\right)\pi$

31. (a) $\displaystyle\int_0^{2\pi}\int_0^{\pi/6}\int_0^2 \rho^2 \sin\phi\, d\rho\, d\phi\, d\theta + \int_0^{2\pi}\int_{\pi/6}^{\pi/2}\int_0^{\csc\phi} \rho^2 \sin\phi\, d\rho\, d\phi\, d\theta$

   (b) $\displaystyle\int_0^{2\pi}\int_1^2\int_{\pi/6}^{\sin^{-1}(1/\rho)} \rho^2 \sin\phi\, d\phi\, d\rho\, d\theta + \int_0^{2\pi}\int_0^2\int_0^{\pi/6} \rho^2 \sin\phi\, d\phi\, d\rho\, d\theta$

33. $\displaystyle\int_0^{2\pi}\int_0^{\pi/2}\int_{\cos\phi}^2 \rho^2 \sin\phi\, d\rho\, d\phi\, d\theta = \dfrac{31\pi}{6}$

35. $\displaystyle\int_0^{2\pi}\int_0^\pi\int_0^{1-\cos\phi} \rho^2 \sin\phi\, d\rho\, d\phi\, d\theta = \dfrac{8\pi}{3}$

37. $\displaystyle\int_0^{2\pi}\int_{\pi/4}^{\pi/2}\int_0^{2\cos\phi} \rho^2 \sin\phi\, d\rho\, d\phi\, d\theta = \dfrac{\pi}{3}$

39. (a) $\displaystyle 8\int_0^{\pi/2}\int_0^{\pi/2}\int_0^2 \rho^2 \sin\phi\, d\rho\, d\phi\, d\theta$

   (b) $\displaystyle 8\int_0^{\pi/2}\int_0^2\int_0^{\sqrt{4-r^2}} r\, dz\, dr\, d\theta$

   (c) $\displaystyle 8\int_0^2\int_0^{\sqrt{4-x^2}}\int_0^{\sqrt{4-x^2-y^2}} dz\, dy\, dx$

41. (a) $\displaystyle\int_0^{2\pi}\int_0^{\pi/3}\int_{\sec\phi}^2 \rho^2 \sin\phi\, d\rho\, d\phi\, d\theta$

   (b) $\displaystyle\int_0^{2\pi}\int_0^{\sqrt{3}}\int_1^{\sqrt{4-r^2}} r\, dz\, dr\, d\theta$

   (c) $\displaystyle 8\int_{-\sqrt{3}}^{\sqrt{3}}\int_{-\sqrt{3-x^2}}^{\sqrt{3-x^2}}\int_1^{\sqrt{4-x^2-y^2}} dz\, dy\, dx$

   (d) $5\pi/3$

43. $8\pi/3$ **45.** $9/4$

47. $\dfrac{3\pi - 4}{18}$ **49.** $\dfrac{2\pi a^3}{3}$

51. $5\pi/3$ **53.** $\pi/2$

55. $\dfrac{4(2\sqrt{2} - 1)\pi}{3}$ **57.** 16π

59. $5\pi/2$ **61.** $\dfrac{4\pi(8 - 3\sqrt{3})}{3}$

63. 2/3

65. 3/4

67. $\bar{x} = \bar{y} = 0, \bar{z} = 3/8$

69. $(\bar{x}, \bar{y}, \bar{z}) = (0, 0, 3/8)$

71. $\bar{x} = \bar{y} = 0, \bar{z} = 5/6$

73. $I_z = 30\pi, R_z = \sqrt{\dfrac{5}{2}}$

75. $I_x = \pi/4$

77. $\dfrac{a^4 h \pi}{10}$

79. (a) $(\bar{x}, \bar{y}, \bar{z}) = \left(0, 0, \dfrac{4}{5}\right), I_z = \dfrac{\pi}{12}, R_z = \sqrt{\dfrac{1}{3}}$

    (b) $(\bar{x}, \bar{y}, \bar{z}) = \left(0, 0, \dfrac{5}{6}\right), I_z = \dfrac{\pi}{14}, R_z = \sqrt{\dfrac{5}{14}}$

83. $(\bar{x}, \bar{y}, \bar{z}) = \left(0, 0, \dfrac{2h^2 + 3h}{3h + 6}\right), I_z = \dfrac{\pi a^4(h^2 + 2h)}{4}, R_z = \dfrac{a}{\sqrt{2}}$

85. $\dfrac{3M}{\pi R^3}$

89. The surface's equation $r = f(z)$ tells us that the point $(r, \theta, z) = (f(z), \theta, z)$ will lie on the surface for all θ. In particular, $(f(z), \theta + \pi, z)$ lies on the surface whenever $(f(z), \theta, z)$ lies on the surface, so the surface is symmetric with respect to the z-axis.

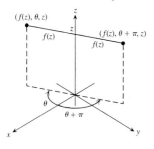

Section 12.7, pp. 1044–1046

1. (a) $x = \dfrac{u + v}{3}, y = \dfrac{v - 2u}{3}; \dfrac{1}{3}$

    (b) Triangular region with boundaries $u = 0, v = 0$, and $u + v = 3$

3. (a) $x = \dfrac{1}{5}(2u - v), y = \dfrac{1}{10}(3v - u); \dfrac{1}{10}$

    (b) Triangular region with boundaries $3v = u, v = 2u$, and $3u + v = 10$

7. 64/5

9. $\displaystyle\int_1^2 \int_1^3 (u + v)\dfrac{2u}{v} \, du \, dv = 8 + \dfrac{52}{3}\ln 2$

11. $\dfrac{\pi a b(a^2 + b^2)}{4}$

13. $\dfrac{1}{3}\left(1 + \dfrac{3}{e^2}\right) \approx 0.4687$

15. (a) $\begin{vmatrix} \cos v & -u \sin v \\ \sin v & u \cos v \end{vmatrix} = u \cos^2 v + u \sin^2 v = u$

    (b) $\begin{vmatrix} \sin v & u \cos v \\ \cos v & -u \sin v \end{vmatrix} = -u \sin^2 v - u \cos^2 v = -u$

19. 12

21. $\dfrac{a^2 b^2 c^2}{6}$

Chapter 12 Practice Exercises, pp. 1047–1049

1. $9e - 9$

3. 9/2

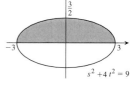

5. $\displaystyle\int_{-2}^0 \int_{2x+4}^{4-x^2} dy \, dx = \dfrac{4}{3}$

7. $\displaystyle\int_{-3}^3 \int_0^{(1/2)\sqrt{9-x^2}} y \, dy \, dx = \dfrac{9}{2}$

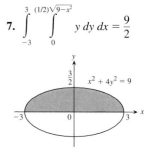

9. $\sin 4$

11. $\dfrac{\ln 17}{4}$

13. 4/3

15. 4/3

17. 1/4

19. $\bar{x} = \bar{y} = \dfrac{1}{2 - \ln 4}$

21. $I_0 = 104$

23. $I_x = 2\delta, R_x = \sqrt{\dfrac{2}{3}}$

25. $M = 4, M_x = 0, M_y = 0$

27. π

29. $\bar{x} = \dfrac{3\sqrt{3}}{\pi}, \bar{y} = 0$

31. (a) $\bar{x} = \dfrac{15\pi + 32}{6\pi + 48}, \bar{y} = 0$

    (b)

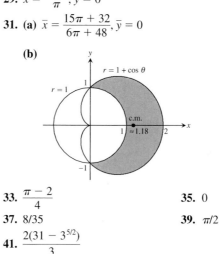

33. $\dfrac{\pi - 2}{4}$

35. 0

37. 8/35

39. $\pi/2$

41. $\dfrac{2(31 - 3^{5/2})}{3}$

43. (a) $\displaystyle\int_{-\sqrt{2}}^{\sqrt{2}}\int_{-\sqrt{2-y^2}}^{\sqrt{2-y^2}}\int_{\sqrt{x^2+y^2}}^{\sqrt{4-x^2-y^2}} 3\, dz\, dx\, dy$

(b) $\displaystyle\int_{0}^{2\pi}\int_{0}^{\pi/4}\int_{0}^{2} 3\rho^2 \sin\phi\, d\rho\, d\phi\, d\theta$

(c) $2\pi(8 - 4\sqrt{2})$

45. $\displaystyle\int_{0}^{2\pi}\int_{0}^{\pi/4}\int_{0}^{\sec\phi} \rho^2 \sin\phi\, d\rho\, d\phi\, d\theta = \frac{\pi}{3}$

47. $\displaystyle\int_{0}^{1}\int_{\sqrt{1-x^2}}^{\sqrt{3-x^2}}\int_{1}^{\sqrt{4-x^2-y^2}} z^2xy\, dz\, dy\, dx + \int_{1}^{\sqrt{3}}\int_{0}^{\sqrt{3-x^2}}\int_{1}^{\sqrt{4-x^2-y^2}} z^2xy\, dz\, dy\, dx$

49. (a) $\dfrac{8\pi(4\sqrt{2} - 5)}{3}$ **(b)** $\dfrac{8\pi(4\sqrt{2} - 5)}{3}$

51. $I_z = \dfrac{8\pi\delta(b^5 - a^5)}{15}$

Chapter 12 Additional Exercises, pp. 1049–1051

1. (a) $\displaystyle\int_{-3}^{2}\int_{x}^{6-x^2} x^2\, dy\, dx$

(b) $\displaystyle\int_{-3}^{2}\int_{x}^{6-x^2}\int_{0}^{x^2} dz\, dy\, dx$

(c) $125/4$

3. 2π **5.** $3\pi/2$

7. (a) Hole radius $= 1$, sphere radius $= 2$

(b) $4\sqrt{3}\pi$

9. $\pi/4$

11. $\ln\left(\dfrac{b}{a}\right)$ **15.** $1/\sqrt[4]{3}$

17. Mass $= a^2 \cos^{-1}\left(\dfrac{b}{a}\right) - b\sqrt{a^2 - b^2}$, $I_0 =$
$$\frac{a^4}{2}\cos^{-1}\left(\frac{b}{a}\right) - \frac{b^3}{2}\sqrt{a^2 - b^2} - \frac{b}{6}(a^2 - b^2)^{3/2}$$

19. $\dfrac{1}{ab}(e^{a^2b^2} - 1)$

21. (b) 1 **(c)** 0

25. $h = \sqrt{20}$ in., $h = \sqrt{60}$ in.   **27.** $2\pi\left[\dfrac{1}{3} - \left(\dfrac{1}{3}\right)\dfrac{\sqrt{2}}{2}\right]$

CHAPTER 13

Section 13.1, pp. 1058–1059

1. Graph (c)   **3.** Graph (g)

5. Graph (d)   **7.** Graph (f)

9. $\sqrt{2}$ **11.** $\dfrac{13}{2}$

13. $3\sqrt{14}$ **15.** $\dfrac{1}{6}(5\sqrt{5} + 9)$

17. $\sqrt{3}\ln\left(\dfrac{b}{a}\right)$ **19.** $\dfrac{10\sqrt{5} - 2}{3}$

21. 8 **23.** $2\sqrt{2} - 1$

25. (a) $4\sqrt{2} - 2$ **(b)** $\sqrt{2} + \ln(1 + \sqrt{2})$

27. $I_z = 2\pi\delta a^3$, $R_z = a$

29. (a) $I_z = 2\pi\sqrt{2}\delta$, $R_z = 1$ **(b)** $I_z = 4\pi\sqrt{2}\delta$, $R_z = 1$

31. $I_x = 2\pi - 2$, $R_x = 1$

Section 13.2, pp. 1068–1070

1. $\nabla f = -(x\mathbf{i} + y\mathbf{j} + z\mathbf{k})(x^2 + y^2 + z^2)^{-3/2}$

3. $\nabla g = -\left(\dfrac{2x}{x^2 + y^2}\right)\mathbf{i} - \left(\dfrac{2y}{x^2 + y^2}\right)\mathbf{j} + e^z\mathbf{k}$

5. $\mathbf{F} = -\dfrac{kx}{(x^2 + y^2)^{3/2}}\mathbf{i} - \dfrac{ky}{(x^2 + y^2)^{3/2}}\mathbf{j}$, any $k > 0$

7. (a) 9/2　　**(b)** 13/3　　**(c)** 9/2

9. (a) 1/3　　**(b)** $-1/5$　　**(c)** 0

11. (a) 2　　**(b)** 3/2　　**(c)** 1/2

13. 1/2　　　　　　　**15.** $-\pi$

17. 69/4　　　　　　**19.** $-39/2$

21. 25/6

23. (a) $\text{Circ}_1 = 0$, $\text{circ}_2 = 2\pi$, $\text{flux}_1 = 2\pi$, $\text{flux}_2 = 0$

(b) $\text{Circ}_1 = 0$, $\text{circ}_2 = 8\pi$, $\text{flux}_1 = 8\pi$, $\text{flux}_2 = 0$

25. $\text{Circ} = 0$, $\text{flux} = a^2\pi$　　**27.** $\text{Circ} = a^2\pi$, $\text{flux} = 0$

29. (a) $-\dfrac{\pi}{2}$　　**(b)** 0　　**(c)** 1

31.

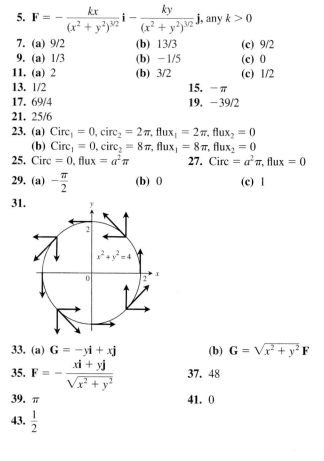

33. (a) $\mathbf{G} = -y\mathbf{i} + x\mathbf{j}$　　**(b)** $\mathbf{G} = \sqrt{x^2 + y^2}\,\mathbf{F}$

35. $\mathbf{F} = -\dfrac{x\mathbf{i} + y\mathbf{j}}{\sqrt{x^2 + y^2}}$　　**37.** 48

39. π　　　　　　　**41.** 0

43. $\dfrac{1}{2}$

Section 13.3, pp. 1078–1079

1. Conservative　　**3.** Not conservative

5. Not conversative

7. $f(x, y, z) = x^2 + \dfrac{3y^2}{2} + 2z^2 + C$

9. $f(x, y, z) = xe^{y+2z} + C$

11. $f(x, y, z) = x \ln x - x + \tan(x + y) + \dfrac{1}{2}\ln(y^2 + z^2) + C$

13. 49　　　　　　　**15.** -16

17. 1　　　　　　　**19.** $9 \ln 2$

21. 0　　　　　　　**23.** -3

27. $\mathbf{F} = \nabla\left(\dfrac{x^2 - 1}{y}\right)$

29. (a) 1　　**(b)** 1　　**(c)** 1

31. (a) 2　　**(b)** 2

33. $f(x, y, z) = \dfrac{GmM}{(x^2 + y^2 + z^2)^{1/2}}$

35. (a) $c = b = 2a$

(b) $c = b = 2$

37. It does not matter what path you use. The work will be the same on any path because the field is conservative.

39. The force $\mathbf{F}$ is conservative because all partial derivatives of M, N, and P are zero. $f(x, y, z) = ax + by + cz + C$; $A = (x_a, y_a, z_a)$ and $B = (x_b, y_b, z_b)$. Therefore, $BF \cdot \mathbf{dr} = f(B) - f(A) = a(x_b - x_a) + b(y_b - y_a) + c(z_b - z_a) = \mathbf{F} \cdot \overrightarrow{AB}$.

Section 13.4, pp. 1090–1092

1. $\text{Flux} = 0$, $\text{circ} = 2\pi a^2$　　**3.** $\text{Flux} = -\pi a^2$, $\text{circ} = 0$

5. $\text{Flux} = 2$, $\text{circ} = 0$　　**7.** $\text{Flux} = -9$, $\text{circ} = 9$

9. $\text{Flux} = 1/2$, $\text{circ} = 1/2$　　**11.** $\text{Flux} = 1/5$, $\text{circ} = -1/12$

13. 0　　　　　　　**15.** 2/33

17. 0　　　　　　　**19.** $\dfrac{-16\pi}{3}$

21. πa^2　　　　　**23.** $\dfrac{3}{8}\pi$

25. (a) 0

(b) $(h - k)(\text{area of the region})$

35. (a) 0

Section 13.5, pp. 1101–1103

1. $\dfrac{13}{3}\pi$　　　　　　**3.** 4

5. $6\sqrt{6} - 2\sqrt{2}$　　**7.** $\pi\sqrt{c^2 + 1}$

9. $\dfrac{\pi}{6}(17\sqrt{17} - 5\sqrt{5})$　　**11.** $3 + 2\ln 2$

13. $9a^3$　　　　　**15.** $\dfrac{abc}{4}(ab + ac + bc)$

17. 2　　　　　　　**19.** 18

21. $\dfrac{\pi a^3}{6}$　　　　　**23.** $\dfrac{\pi a^2}{4}$

25. $\dfrac{\pi a^3}{2}$　　　　　**27.** -32

29. -4　　　　　　**31.** $3a^4$

33. $\left(\dfrac{a}{2}, \dfrac{a}{2}, \dfrac{a}{2}\right)$

35. $(\bar{x}, \bar{y}, \bar{z}) = \left(0, 0, \dfrac{14}{9}\right)$, $I_z = \dfrac{15\pi\sqrt{2}}{2}\delta$, $R_z = \dfrac{\sqrt{10}}{2}$

37. (a) $\dfrac{8\pi}{3}a^4\delta$　　**(b)** $\dfrac{20\pi}{3}a^4\delta$

39. $\dfrac{\pi}{6}(13\sqrt{13} - 1)$　　**41.** $5\pi\sqrt{2}$

43. $\dfrac{2}{3}(5\sqrt{5} - 1)$

Section 13.6, pp. 1111–1113

1. $\mathbf{r}(r, \theta) = (r\cos\theta)\mathbf{i} + (r\sin\theta)\mathbf{j} + r^2\mathbf{k}$, $0 \le r \le 2$, $0 \le \theta \le 2\pi$

3. $\mathbf{r}(r, \theta) = (r\cos\theta)\mathbf{i} + (r\sin\theta)\mathbf{j} + (r/2)\mathbf{k}$, $0 \le r \le 6$, $0 \le \theta \le \pi/2$

5. $\mathbf{r}(r, \theta) = (r\cos\theta)\mathbf{i} + (r\sin\theta)\mathbf{j} + \sqrt{9 - r^2}\,\mathbf{k}$,

$0 \le r \le \dfrac{3\sqrt{2}}{2}$, $0 \le \theta \le 2\pi$;

also $\mathbf{r}(\phi, \theta) = (3\sin\phi\cos\theta)\mathbf{i} + (3\sin\phi\sin\theta)\mathbf{j} + (3\cos\phi)\mathbf{k}$,

$0 \le \phi \le \dfrac{\pi}{4}$, $0 \le \theta \le 2\pi$

7. $\mathbf{r}(\phi, \theta) = (\sqrt{3} \sin \phi \cos \theta)\mathbf{i} + (\sqrt{3} \sin \phi \sin \theta)\mathbf{j} + (\sqrt{3} \cos \phi)\mathbf{k},$
$\dfrac{\pi}{3} \leq \phi \leq \dfrac{2\pi}{3}, 0 \leq \theta \leq 2\pi$

9. $\mathbf{r}(x, y) = x\mathbf{i} + y\mathbf{j} + (4 - y^2)\mathbf{k}, 0 \leq x \leq 2, -2 \leq y \leq 2$

11. $\mathbf{r}(u, v) = u\mathbf{i} + (3 \cos v)\mathbf{j} + (3 \sin v)\mathbf{k}, 0 \leq u \leq 3, 0 \leq v \leq 2\pi$

13. (a) $\mathbf{r}(r, \theta) = (r \cos \theta)\mathbf{i} + (r \sin \theta)\mathbf{j} + (1 - r \cos \theta - r \sin \theta)\mathbf{k},$
$0 \leq r \leq 3, 0 \leq \theta \leq 2\pi$
(b) $\mathbf{r}(u, v) = (1 - u \cos v - u \sin v)\mathbf{i} + (u \cos v)\mathbf{j} + (u \sin v)\mathbf{k},$
$0 \leq u \leq 3, 0 \leq v \leq 2\pi$

15. $\mathbf{r}(u, v) = (4 \cos^2 v)\mathbf{i} + u\mathbf{j} + (4 \cos v \sin v)\mathbf{k},$
$0 \leq u \leq 3, -\pi/2 \leq v \leq \pi/2;$
another way: $\mathbf{r}(u, v) = (2 + 2 \cos v)\mathbf{i} + u\mathbf{j} + (2 \sin v)\mathbf{k},$
$0 \leq u \leq 3, 0 \leq v \leq 2\pi$

17. $\displaystyle\int_0^{2\pi}\int_0^1 \dfrac{\sqrt{5}}{2} r \, dr \, d\theta = \dfrac{\pi\sqrt{5}}{2}$ **19.** $\displaystyle\int_0^{2\pi}\int_1^3 r\sqrt{5} \, dr \, d\theta = 8\pi\sqrt{5}$

21. $\displaystyle\int_0^{2\pi}\int_1^4 1 \, du \, dv = 6\pi$

23. $\displaystyle\int_0^{2\pi}\int_0^1 u\sqrt{4u^2 + 1} \, du \, dv = \dfrac{(5\sqrt{5} - 1)}{6}\pi$

25. $\displaystyle\int_0^{2\pi}\int_{\pi/4}^{\pi} 2 \sin \phi \, d\phi \, d\theta = (4 + 2\sqrt{2})\pi$

27. $\displaystyle\iint_S x \, d\sigma = \int_0^3\int_0^2 u\sqrt{4u^2 + 1} \, du \, dv = \dfrac{17\sqrt{17} - 1}{4}$

29. $\displaystyle\iint_S x^2 \, d\sigma = \int_0^{2\pi}\int_0^{\pi} \sin^3 \phi \cos^2 \theta \, d\phi \, d\theta = \dfrac{4\pi}{3}$

31. $\displaystyle\iint_S z \, d\sigma = \int_0^1\int_0^1 (4 - u - v)\sqrt{3} \, dv \, du = 3\sqrt{3} \text{ (for } x = u, y = v)$

33. $\displaystyle\iint_S x^2\sqrt{5 - 4z} \, d\sigma =$
$\displaystyle\int_0^1\int_0^{2\pi} u^2 \cos^2 v \cdot \sqrt{4u^2 + 1} \cdot u \sqrt{4u^2 + 1} \, dv \, du =$
$\displaystyle\int_0^1\int_0^{2\pi} u^3(4u^2 + 1) \cos^2 v \, dv \, du = \dfrac{11\pi}{12}$

35. -32 **37.** $\dfrac{\pi a^3}{6}$

39. $\dfrac{13a^4}{6}$ **41.** $\dfrac{2\pi}{3}$

43. $-\dfrac{73}{6}\pi$

45. $(\bar{x}, \bar{y}, \bar{z}) = (0, 0, 14/9),$
$I_z = \dfrac{(15\sqrt{2})\pi\delta}{2}$
$R_z = \sqrt{5/2}$

47.

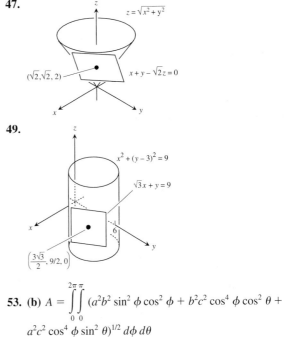

49.

53. (b) $A = \displaystyle\int_0^{2\pi}\int_0^{\pi} (a^2b^2 \sin^2 \phi \cos^2 \phi + b^2c^2 \cos^4 \phi \cos^2 \theta +$
$a^2c^2 \cos^4 \phi \sin^2 \theta)^{1/2} \, d\phi \, d\theta$

Section 13.7, pp. 1122–1124

1. 4π **3.** $-5/6$
5. 0 **7.** -6π
9. $2\pi a^2$ **13.** 12π
15. $-\pi/4$ **17.** -15π
25. $16I_y + 16I_x$

Section 13.8, pp. 1133–1135

1. 0 **3.** 0
5. -16 **7.** -8π
9. 3π **11.** $-40/3$
13. 12π **15.** $12\pi(4\sqrt{2} - 1)$
21. The integral's value never exceeds the surface area of S.

Chapter 13 Practice Exercises, pp. 1136–1139

1. Path 1: $2\sqrt{3}$; path 2: $1 + 3\sqrt{2}$
3. $4a^2$ **5.** 0
7. $8\pi \sin(1)$ **9.** 0
11. $\pi\sqrt{3}$ **13.** $2\pi\left(1 - \dfrac{1}{\sqrt{2}}\right)$
15. $\dfrac{abc}{2}\sqrt{\dfrac{1}{a^2} + \dfrac{1}{b^2} + \dfrac{1}{c^2}}$ **17.** 50

19. $\mathbf{r}(\phi, \theta) = (6 \sin \phi \cos \theta)\mathbf{i} + (6 \sin \phi \sin \theta)\mathbf{j} + (6 \cos \phi)\mathbf{k},$
$\dfrac{\pi}{6} \leq \phi \leq \dfrac{2\pi}{3}, 0 \leq \theta \leq 2\pi$

21. $\mathbf{r}(r, \theta) = (r \cos \theta)\mathbf{i} + (r \sin \theta)\mathbf{j} + (1 + r)\mathbf{k},$
$0 \le r \le 2, 0 \le \theta \le 2\pi$

23. $\mathbf{r}(u, v) = (u \cos v)\mathbf{i} + 2u^2\mathbf{j} + (u \sin v)\mathbf{k}, 0 \le u \le 1, 0 \le v \le \pi$

25. $\sqrt{6}$

27. $\pi[\sqrt{2} + \ln(1 + \sqrt{2})]$

29. Conservative

31. Not conservative

33. $f(x, y, z) = y^2 + yz + 2x + z$

35. Path 1: 2; path 2: 8/3

37. (a) $1 - e^{-2\pi}$ **(b)** $1 - e^{-2\pi}$

39. 0

41. (a) $4\sqrt{2} - 2$ **(b)** $\sqrt{2} + \ln(1 + \sqrt{2})$

43. $(\bar{x}, \bar{y}, \bar{z}) = \left(1, \dfrac{16}{15}, \dfrac{2}{3}\right);\ I_x = \dfrac{232}{45},\ I_y = \dfrac{64}{15},\ I_z = \dfrac{56}{9};\ R_x = \dfrac{2\sqrt{29}}{3\sqrt{5}},$
$R_y = \dfrac{4\sqrt{2}}{\sqrt{15}},\ R_z = \dfrac{2\sqrt{7}}{3}$

45. $\bar{z} = \dfrac{3}{2},\ I_z = \dfrac{7\sqrt{3}}{3},\ R_z = \sqrt{\dfrac{7}{3}}$

47. $(\bar{x}, \bar{y}, \bar{z}) = (0, 0, 49/12),\ I_z = 640\pi,\ R_z = 2\sqrt{2}$

49. Flux: 3/2; circ: $-1/2$

53. 3

55. $\dfrac{2\pi}{3}(7 - 8\sqrt{2})$

57. 0

59. π

Chapter 13 Additional Exercises, pp. 1139–1141

1. 6π

3. 2/3

5. (a) $\mathbf{F}(x, y, z) = z\mathbf{i} + x\mathbf{j} + y\mathbf{k}$
(b) $\mathbf{F}(x, y, z) = z\mathbf{i} + y\mathbf{k}$
(c) $\mathbf{F}(x, y, z) = z\mathbf{i}$

7. $a = 2, b = 1$; the minimum flux is -4.

9. (b) $\dfrac{16}{3}g$

(c) $\text{Work} = \left(\displaystyle\int_C gxy\, ds\right)\bar{y} = g\displaystyle\int_C xy^2\, ds$

11. (c) $\dfrac{4}{3}\pi w$

15. False if $\mathbf{F} = y\mathbf{i} + x\mathbf{j}$

APPENDICES

Appendix A.4

1. (a) $(14, 8)$ **(b)** $(-1, 8)$ **(c)** $(0, -5)$

3. (a) By reflecting z across the real axis
(b) By reflecting z across the imaginary axis
(c) By reflecting z in the real axis and then multiplying the length of the vector by $1/|z|^2$

5. (a) Points on the circle $x^2 + y^2 = 4$
(b) points inside the circle $x^2 + y^2 = 4$
(c) points outside the circle $x^2 + y^2 = 4$

7. Points on a circle of radius 1, center $(-1, 0)$

9. Points on the line $y = -x$

11. $4e^{2\pi i/3}$

13. $1e^{2\pi i/3}$

21. $\cos^4\theta - 6\cos^2\theta \sin^2\theta + \sin^4\theta$

23. $1, -\dfrac{1}{2} \pm \dfrac{\sqrt{3}}{2}i$

25. $2i, -\sqrt{3} - i, \sqrt{3} - i$

27. $\dfrac{\sqrt{6}}{2} \pm \dfrac{\sqrt{2}}{2}i, -\dfrac{\sqrt{6}}{2} \pm \dfrac{\sqrt{2}}{2}i$

29. $1 \pm \sqrt{3}i, -1, \pm \sqrt{3}i$

Appendix A.10

1. -5

3. 1

5. -7

7. 38

9. $x = -4, y = 1$

11. $x = 3, y = 2$

13. $x = 3, y = -2, z = 2$

15. $x = 2, y = 0, z = -1$

17. (a) $h = 6, k = 4$ **(b)** $h = 6, k \ne 4$

Index

A Brief Table of Integrals

1. $\displaystyle\int u\, dv = uv - \int v\, du$

2. $\displaystyle\int a^u\, du = \frac{a^u}{\ln a} + C, \quad a \neq 1, \quad a > 0$

3. $\displaystyle\int \cos u\, du = \sin u + C$

4. $\displaystyle\int \sin u\, du = -\cos u + C$

5. $\displaystyle\int (ax + b)^n\, dx = \frac{(ax+b)^{n+1}}{a(n+1)} + C, \quad n \neq -1$

6. $\displaystyle\int (ax + b)^{-1}\, dx = \frac{1}{a}\ln|ax+b| + C$

7. $\displaystyle\int x(ax + b)^n\, dx = \frac{(ax+b)^{n+1}}{a^2}\left[\frac{ax+b}{n+2} - \frac{b}{n+1}\right] + C, \quad n \neq -1, -2$

8. $\displaystyle\int x(ax + b)^{-1}\, dx = \frac{x}{a} - \frac{b}{a^2}\ln|ax+b| + C$

9. $\displaystyle\int x(ax + b)^{-2}\, dx = \frac{1}{a^2}\left[\ln|ax+b| + \frac{b}{ax+b}\right] + C$

10. $\displaystyle\int \frac{dx}{x(ax+b)} = \frac{1}{b}\ln\left|\frac{x}{ax+b}\right| + C$

11. $\displaystyle\int (\sqrt{ax+b})^n\, dx = \frac{2}{a}\frac{(\sqrt{ax+b})^{n+2}}{n+2} + C, \quad n \neq -2$

12. $\displaystyle\int \frac{\sqrt{ax+b}}{x}\, dx = 2\sqrt{ax+b} + b\int \frac{dx}{x\sqrt{ax+b}}$

13. (a) $\displaystyle\int \frac{dx}{x\sqrt{ax-b}} = \frac{2}{\sqrt{b}}\tan^{-1}\sqrt{\frac{ax-b}{b}} + C$

    (b) $\displaystyle\int \frac{dx}{x\sqrt{ax+b}} = \frac{1}{\sqrt{b}}\ln\left|\frac{\sqrt{ax+b}-\sqrt{b}}{\sqrt{ax+b}+\sqrt{b}}\right| + C$

14. $\displaystyle\int \frac{\sqrt{ax+b}}{x^2}\, dx = -\frac{\sqrt{ax+b}}{x} + \frac{a}{2}\int \frac{dx}{x\sqrt{ax+b}} + C$

15. $\displaystyle\int \frac{dx}{x^2\sqrt{ax+b}} = -\frac{\sqrt{ax+b}}{bx} - \frac{a}{2b}\int \frac{dx}{x\sqrt{ax+b}} + C$

16. $\displaystyle\int \frac{dx}{a^2+x^2} = \frac{1}{a}\tan^{-1}\frac{x}{a} + C$

17. $\displaystyle\int \frac{dx}{(a^2+x^2)^2} = \frac{x}{2a^2(a^2+x^2)} + \frac{1}{2a^3}\tan^{-1}\frac{x}{a} + C$

18. $\displaystyle\int \frac{dx}{a^2-x^2} = \frac{1}{2a}\ln\left|\frac{x+a}{x-a}\right| + C$

19. $\displaystyle\int \frac{dx}{(a^2-x^2)^2} = \frac{x}{2a^2(a^2-x^2)} + \frac{1}{4a^3}\ln\left|\frac{x+a}{x-a}\right| + C$

20. $\displaystyle\int \frac{dx}{\sqrt{a^2+x^2}} = \sinh^{-1}\frac{x}{a} + C = \ln(x + \sqrt{a^2+x^2}) + C$

21. $\displaystyle\int \sqrt{a^2+x^2}\, dx = \frac{x}{2}\sqrt{a^2+x^2} + \frac{a^2}{2}\ln(x+\sqrt{a^2+x^2}) + C$

22. $\displaystyle\int x^2\sqrt{a^2+x^2}\, dx = \frac{x}{8}(a^2+2x^2)\sqrt{a^2+x^2} - \frac{a^4}{8}\ln(x+\sqrt{a^2+x^2}) + C$

23. $\displaystyle\int \frac{\sqrt{a^2+x^2}}{x}\, dx = \sqrt{a^2+x^2} - a\ln\left|\frac{a+\sqrt{a^2+x^2}}{x}\right| + C$

24. $\displaystyle\int \frac{\sqrt{a^2+x^2}}{x^2}\, dx = \ln(x+\sqrt{a^2+x^2}) - \frac{\sqrt{a^2+x^2}}{x} + C$

25. $\displaystyle\int \frac{x^2}{\sqrt{a^2+x^2}}\, dx = -\frac{a^2}{2}\ln(x+\sqrt{a^2+x^2}) + \frac{x\sqrt{a^2+x^2}}{2} + C$

26. $\displaystyle\int \frac{dx}{x\sqrt{a^2+x^2}} = -\frac{1}{a}\ln\left|\frac{a+\sqrt{a^2+x^2}}{x}\right| + C$

27. $\displaystyle\int \frac{dx}{x^2\sqrt{a^2+x^2}} = -\frac{\sqrt{a^2+x^2}}{a^2x} + C$

28. $\displaystyle\int \frac{dx}{\sqrt{a^2-x^2}} = \sin^{-1}\frac{x}{a} + C$

29. $\displaystyle\int \sqrt{a^2-x^2}\, dx = \frac{x}{2}\sqrt{a^2-x^2} + \frac{a^2}{2}\sin^{-1}\frac{x}{a} + C$

30. $\displaystyle\int x^2\sqrt{a^2-x^2}\, dx = \frac{a^4}{8}\sin^{-1}\frac{x}{a} - \frac{1}{8}x\sqrt{a^2-x^2}(a^2-2x^2) + C$

31. $\displaystyle\int \frac{\sqrt{a^2-x^2}}{x}\, dx = \sqrt{a^2-x^2} - a\ln\left|\frac{a+\sqrt{a^2-x^2}}{x}\right| + C$

32. $\displaystyle\int \frac{\sqrt{a^2-x^2}}{x^2}\, dx = -\sin^{-1}\frac{x}{a} - \frac{\sqrt{a^2-x^2}}{x} + C$

33. $\displaystyle\int \frac{x^2}{\sqrt{a^2-x^2}}\, dx = \frac{a^2}{2}\sin^{-1}\frac{x}{a} - \frac{1}{2}x\sqrt{a^2-x^2} + C$

34. $\displaystyle\int \frac{dx}{x\sqrt{a^2-x^2}} = -\frac{1}{a}\ln\left|\frac{a+\sqrt{a^2-x^2}}{x}\right| + C$

35. $\displaystyle\int \frac{dx}{x^2\sqrt{a^2-x^2}} = -\frac{\sqrt{a^2-x^2}}{a^2x} + C$

36. $\displaystyle\int \frac{dx}{\sqrt{x^2-a^2}} = \cosh^{-1}\frac{x}{a} + C = \ln\left|x + \sqrt{x^2-a^2}\right| + C$

37. $\displaystyle\int \sqrt{x^2-a^2}\, dx = \frac{x}{2}\sqrt{x^2-a^2} - \frac{a^2}{2}\ln\left|x + \sqrt{x^2-a^2}\right| + C$

38. $\displaystyle\int (\sqrt{x^2-a^2})^n\, dx = \frac{x(\sqrt{x^2-a^2})^n}{n+1} - \frac{na^2}{n+1}\int (\sqrt{x^2-a^2})^{n-2}\, dx, \qquad n \neq -1$

39. $\displaystyle\int \frac{dx}{(\sqrt{x^2-a^2})^n} = \frac{x(\sqrt{x^2-a^2})^{2-n}}{(2-n)a^2} - \frac{n-3}{(n-2)a^2}\int \frac{dx}{(\sqrt{x^2-a^2})^{n-2}}, \qquad n \neq 2$

40. $\displaystyle\int x(\sqrt{x^2-a^2})^n\, dx = \frac{(\sqrt{x^2-a^2})^{n+2}}{n+2} + C, \qquad n \neq -2$

41. $\displaystyle\int x^2\sqrt{x^2-a^2}\, dx = \frac{x}{8}(2x^2-a^2)\sqrt{x^2-a^2} - \frac{a^4}{8}\ln\left|x + \sqrt{x^2-a^2}\right| + C$

42. $\displaystyle\int \frac{\sqrt{x^2-a^2}}{x}\, dx = \sqrt{x^2-a^2} - a\sec^{-1}\left|\frac{x}{a}\right| + C$

43. $\displaystyle\int \frac{\sqrt{x^2-a^2}}{x^2}\, dx = \ln\left|x + \sqrt{x^2-a^2}\right| - \frac{\sqrt{x^2-a^2}}{x} + C$

44. $\displaystyle\int \frac{x^2}{\sqrt{x^2-a^2}}\, dx = \frac{a^2}{2}\ln\left|x + \sqrt{x^2-a^2}\right| + \frac{x}{2}\sqrt{x^2-a^2} + C$

45. $\displaystyle\int \frac{dx}{x\sqrt{x^2-a^2}} = \frac{1}{a}\sec^{-1}\left|\frac{x}{a}\right| + C = \frac{1}{a}\cos^{-1}\left|\frac{a}{x}\right| + C$

46. $\displaystyle\int \frac{dx}{x^2\sqrt{x^2-a^2}} = \frac{\sqrt{x^2-a^2}}{a^2x} + C$

47. $\displaystyle\int \frac{dx}{\sqrt{2ax-x^2}} = \sin^{-1}\left(\frac{x-a}{a}\right) + C$

48. $\displaystyle\int \sqrt{2ax-x^2}\, dx = \frac{x-a}{2}\sqrt{2ax-x^2} + \frac{a^2}{2}\sin^{-1}\left(\frac{x-a}{a}\right) + C$

49. $\displaystyle\int (\sqrt{2ax-x^2})^n\, dx = \frac{(x-a)(\sqrt{2ax-x^2})^n}{n+1} + \frac{na^2}{n+1}\int (\sqrt{2ax-x^2})^{n-2}\, dx$

50. $\displaystyle\int \frac{dx}{(\sqrt{2ax-x^2})^n} = \frac{(x-a)(\sqrt{2ax-x^2})^{2-n}}{(n-2)a^2} + \frac{n-3}{(n-2)a^2}\int \frac{dx}{(\sqrt{2ax-x^2})^{n-2}}$

51. $\displaystyle\int x\sqrt{2ax-x^2}\, dx = \frac{(x+a)(2x-3a)\sqrt{2ax-x^2}}{6} + \frac{a^3}{2}\sin^{-1}\left(\frac{x-a}{a}\right) + C$

52. $\displaystyle\int \frac{\sqrt{2ax-x^2}}{x}\, dx = \sqrt{2ax-x^2} + a\sin^{-1}\left(\frac{x-a}{a}\right) + C$

53. $\displaystyle\int \frac{\sqrt{2ax-x^2}}{x^2}\, dx = -2\sqrt{\frac{2a-x}{x}} - \sin^{-1}\left(\frac{x-a}{a}\right) + C$

54. $\displaystyle\int \frac{x\, dx}{\sqrt{2ax-x^2}} = a\sin^{-1}\left(\frac{x-a}{a}\right) - \sqrt{2ax-x^2} + C$

55. $\displaystyle\int \frac{dx}{x\sqrt{2ax-x^2}} = -\frac{1}{a}\sqrt{\frac{2a-x}{x}} + C$

56. $\displaystyle\int \sin ax\, dx = -\frac{1}{a}\cos ax + C$

57. $\displaystyle\int \cos ax\, dx = \frac{1}{a}\sin ax + C$

58. $\displaystyle\int \sin^2 ax\, dx = \frac{x}{2} - \frac{\sin 2ax}{4a} + C$

59. $\displaystyle\int \cos^2 ax\, dx = \frac{x}{2} + \frac{\sin 2ax}{4a} + C$

60. $\displaystyle\int \sin^n ax \, dx = -\frac{\sin^{n-1} ax \cos ax}{na} + \frac{n-1}{n}\int \sin^{n-2} ax \, dx$

61. $\displaystyle\int \cos^n ax \, dx = \frac{\cos^{n-1} ax \sin ax}{na} + \frac{n-1}{n}\int \cos^{n-2} ax \, dx$

62. (a) $\displaystyle\int \sin ax \cos bx \, dx = -\frac{\cos (a+b)x}{2(a+b)} - \frac{\cos (a-b)x}{2(a-b)} + C, \qquad a^2 \neq b^2$

(b) $\displaystyle\int \sin ax \sin bx \, dx = \frac{\sin (a-b)x}{2(a-b)} - \frac{\sin (a+b)x}{2(a+b)} + C, \qquad a^2 \neq b^2$

(c) $\displaystyle\int \cos ax \cos bx \, dx = \frac{\sin (a-b)x}{2(a-b)} + \frac{\sin (a+b)x}{2(a+b)} + C, \qquad a^2 \neq b^2$

63. $\displaystyle\int \sin ax \cos ax \, dx = -\frac{\cos 2ax}{4a} + C$

64. $\displaystyle\int \sin^n ax \cos ax \, dx = \frac{\sin^{n+1} ax}{(n+1)a} + C, \qquad n \neq -1$

65. $\displaystyle\int \frac{\cos ax}{\sin ax} \, dx = \frac{1}{a}\ln|\sin ax| + C$

66. $\displaystyle\int \cos^n ax \sin ax \, dx = -\frac{\cos^{n+1} ax}{(n+1)a} + C, \qquad n \neq -1$

67. $\displaystyle\int \frac{\sin ax}{\cos ax} \, dx = -\frac{1}{a}\ln|\cos ax| + C$

68. $\displaystyle\int \sin^n ax \cos^m ax \, dx = -\frac{\sin^{n-1} ax \cos^{m+1} ax}{a(m+n)} + \frac{n-1}{m+n}\int \sin^{n-2} ax \cos^m ax \, dx, \qquad n \neq -m \qquad \text{(reduces } \sin^n ax\text{)}$

69. $\displaystyle\int \sin^n ax \cos^m ax \, dx = \frac{\sin^{n+1} ax \cos^{m-1} ax}{a(m+n)} + \frac{m-1}{m+n}\int \sin^n ax \cos^{m-2} ax \, dx, \qquad m \neq -n \qquad \text{(reduces } \cos^m ax\text{)}$

70. $\displaystyle\int \frac{dx}{b + c \sin ax} = \frac{-2}{a\sqrt{b^2 - c^2}}\tan^{-1}\left[\sqrt{\frac{b-c}{b+c}}\tan\left(\frac{\pi}{4} - \frac{ax}{2}\right)\right] + C, \qquad b^2 > c^2$

71. $\displaystyle\int \frac{dx}{b + c \sin ax} = \frac{-1}{a\sqrt{c^2 - b^2}}\ln\left|\frac{c + b \sin ax + \sqrt{c^2 - b^2} \cos ax}{b + c \sin ax}\right| + C, \qquad b^2 < c^2$

72. $\displaystyle\int \frac{dx}{1 + \sin ax} = -\frac{1}{a}\tan\left(\frac{\pi}{4} - \frac{ax}{2}\right) + C$

73. $\displaystyle\int \frac{dx}{1 - \sin ax} = \frac{1}{a}\tan\left(\frac{\pi}{4} + \frac{ax}{2}\right) + C$

74. $\displaystyle\int \frac{dx}{b + c \cos ax} = \frac{2}{a\sqrt{b^2 - c^2}}\tan^{-1}\left[\sqrt{\frac{b-c}{b+c}}\tan\frac{ax}{2}\right] + C, \qquad b^2 > c^2$

75. $\displaystyle\int \frac{dx}{b + c \cos ax} = \frac{1}{a\sqrt{c^2 - b^2}}\ln\left|\frac{c + b \cos ax + \sqrt{c^2 - b^2} \sin ax}{b + c \cos ax}\right| + C, \qquad b^2 < c^2$

76. $\displaystyle\int \frac{dx}{1 + \cos ax} = \frac{1}{a}\tan\frac{ax}{2} + C$

77. $\displaystyle\int \frac{dx}{1 - \cos ax} = -\frac{1}{a}\cot\frac{ax}{2} + C$

78. $\displaystyle\int x \sin ax \, dx = \frac{1}{a^2}\sin ax - \frac{x}{a}\cos ax + C$

79. $\displaystyle\int x \cos ax \, dx = \frac{1}{a^2}\cos ax + \frac{x}{a}\sin ax + C$

80. $\displaystyle\int x^n \sin ax \, dx = -\frac{x^n}{a}\cos ax + \frac{n}{a}\int x^{n-1}\cos ax \, dx$

81. $\displaystyle\int x^n \cos ax \, dx = \frac{x^n}{a}\sin ax - \frac{n}{a}\int x^{n-1}\sin ax \, dx$

82. $\displaystyle\int \tan ax \, dx = \frac{1}{a}\ln|\sec ax| + C$

83. $\displaystyle\int \cot ax \, dx = \frac{1}{a}\ln|\sin ax| + C$

84. $\displaystyle\int \tan^2 ax \, dx = \frac{1}{a}\tan ax - x + C$

85. $\displaystyle\int \cot^2 ax \, dx = -\frac{1}{a}\cot ax - x + C$

86. $\displaystyle\int \tan^n ax \, dx = \frac{\tan^{n-1} ax}{a(n-1)} - \int \tan^{n-2} ax \, dx, \qquad n \neq 1$

87. $\displaystyle\int \cot^n ax \, dx = -\frac{\cot^{n-1} ax}{a(n-1)} - \int \cot^{n-2} ax \, dx, \qquad n \neq 1$

88. $\displaystyle\int \sec ax \, dx = \frac{1}{a}\ln|\sec ax + \tan ax| + C$

89. $\displaystyle\int \csc ax \, dx = -\frac{1}{a}\ln|\csc ax + \cot ax| + C$

90. $\displaystyle\int \sec^2 ax \, dx = \frac{1}{a}\tan ax + C$

91. $\displaystyle\int \csc^2 ax \, dx = -\frac{1}{a}\cot ax + C$

92. $\displaystyle\int \sec^n ax \, dx = \frac{\sec^{n-2} ax \tan ax}{a(n-1)} + \frac{n-2}{n-1}\int \sec^{n-2} ax \, dx, \qquad n \neq 1$

93. $\displaystyle\int \csc^n ax\, dx = -\frac{\csc^{n-2} ax\, \cot ax}{a(n-1)} + \frac{n-2}{n-1}\int \csc^{n-2} ax\, dx, \qquad n \neq 1$

94. $\displaystyle\int \sec^n ax\, \tan ax\, dx = \frac{\sec^n ax}{na} + C, \qquad n \neq 0$

95. $\displaystyle\int \csc^n ax\, \cot ax\, dx = -\frac{\csc^n ax}{na} + C, \qquad n \neq 0$

96. $\displaystyle\int \sin^{-1} ax\, dx = x \sin^{-1} ax + \frac{1}{a}\sqrt{1-a^2x^2} + C$

97. $\displaystyle\int \cos^{-1} ax\, dx = x \cos^{-1} ax - \frac{1}{a}\sqrt{1-a^2x^2} + C$

98. $\displaystyle\int \tan^{-1} ax\, dx = x \tan^{-1} ax - \frac{1}{2a}\ln(1+a^2x^2) + C$

99. $\displaystyle\int x^n \sin^{-1} ax\, dx = \frac{x^{n+1}}{n+1}\sin^{-1} ax - \frac{a}{n+1}\int \frac{x^{n+1}\, dx}{\sqrt{1-a^2x^2}}, \qquad n \neq -1$

100. $\displaystyle\int x^n \cos^{-1} ax\, dx = \frac{x^{n+1}}{n+1}\cos^{-1} ax + \frac{a}{n+1}\int \frac{x^{n+1}\, dx}{\sqrt{1-a^2x^2}}, \qquad n \neq -1$

101. $\displaystyle\int x^n \tan^{-1} ax\, dx = \frac{x^{n+1}}{n+1}\tan^{-1} ax - \frac{a}{n+1}\int \frac{x^{n+1}\, dx}{\sqrt{1+a^2x^2}}, \qquad n \neq -1$

102. $\displaystyle\int e^{ax}\, dx = \frac{1}{a}e^{ax} + C$

103. $\displaystyle\int b^{ax}\, dx = \frac{1}{a}\frac{b^{ax}}{\ln b} + C, \qquad b > 0, \qquad b \neq 1$

104. $\displaystyle\int xe^{ax}\, dx = \frac{e^{ax}}{a^2}(ax - 1) + C$

105. $\displaystyle\int x^n e^{ax}\, dx = \frac{1}{a}x^n e^{ax} - \frac{n}{a}\int x^{n-1} e^{ax}\, dx$

106. $\displaystyle\int x^n b^{ax}\, dx = \frac{x^n b^{ax}}{a \ln b} - \frac{n}{a \ln b}\int x^{n-1} b^{ax}\, dx, \qquad b > 0, \qquad b \neq 1$

107. $\displaystyle\int e^{ax} \sin bx\, dx = \frac{e^{ax}}{a^2 + b^2}(a \sin bx - b \cos bx) + C$

108. $\displaystyle\int e^{ax} \cos bx\, dx = \frac{e^{ax}}{a^2 + b^2}(a \cos bx + b \sin bx) + C$

109. $\displaystyle\int \ln ax\, dx = x \ln ax - x + C$

110. $\displaystyle\int x^n (\ln ax)^m\, dx = \frac{x^{n+1}(\ln ax)^m}{n+1} - \frac{m}{n+1}\int x^n (\ln ax)^{m-1}\, dx, \qquad n \neq -1$

111. $\displaystyle\int x^{-1}(\ln ax)^m\, dx = \frac{(\ln ax)^{m+1}}{m+1} + C, \qquad m \neq -1$

112. $\displaystyle\int \frac{dx}{x \ln ax} = \ln|\ln ax| + C$

113. $\displaystyle\int \sinh ax\, dx = \frac{1}{a}\cosh ax + C$

114. $\displaystyle\int \cosh ax\, dx = \frac{1}{a}\sinh ax + C$

115. $\displaystyle\int \sinh^2 ax\, dx = \frac{\sinh 2ax}{4a} - \frac{x}{2} + C$

116. $\displaystyle\int \cosh^2 ax\, dx = \frac{\sinh 2ax}{4a} + \frac{x}{2} + C$

117. $\displaystyle\int \sinh^n ax\, dx = \frac{\sinh^{n-1} ax\, \cosh ax}{na} - \frac{n-1}{n}\int \sinh^{n-2} ax\, dx, \qquad n \neq 0$

118. $\displaystyle\int \cosh^n ax\, dx = \frac{\cosh^{n-1} ax\, \sinh ax}{na} + \frac{n-1}{n}\int \cosh^{n-2} ax\, dx, \qquad n \neq 0$

119. $\displaystyle\int x \sinh ax\, dx = \frac{x}{a}\cosh ax - \frac{1}{a^2}\sinh ax + C$

120. $\displaystyle\int x \cosh ax\, dx = \frac{x}{a}\sinh ax - \frac{1}{a^2}\cosh ax + C$

121. $\displaystyle\int x^n \sinh ax\, dx = \frac{x^n}{a}\cosh ax - \frac{n}{a}\int x^{n-1} \cosh ax\, dx$

122. $\displaystyle\int x^n \cosh ax\, dx = \frac{x^n}{a}\sinh ax - \frac{n}{a}\int x^{n-1} \sinh ax\, dx$

123. $\displaystyle\int \tanh ax\, dx = \frac{1}{a}\ln(\cosh ax) + C$

124. $\displaystyle\int \coth ax\, dx = \frac{1}{a}\ln|\sinh ax| + C$

125. $\displaystyle\int \tanh^2 ax\, dx = x - \frac{1}{a}\tanh ax + C$

126. $\displaystyle\int \coth^2 ax\, dx = x - \frac{1}{a}\coth ax + C$

127. $\displaystyle\int \tanh^n ax\, dx = -\frac{\tanh^{n-1} ax}{(n-1)a} + \int \tanh^{n-2} ax\, dx, \qquad n \neq 1$

128. $\displaystyle\int \coth^n ax\, dx = -\frac{\coth^{n-1} ax}{(n-1)a} + \int \coth^{n-2} ax\, dx, \qquad n \neq 1$

129. $\displaystyle\int \operatorname{sech} ax\, dx = \frac{1}{a}\sin^{-1}(\tanh ax) + C$

130. $\displaystyle\int \operatorname{csch} ax\, dx = \frac{1}{a}\ln\left|\tanh \frac{ax}{2}\right| + C$

131. $\displaystyle\int \text{sech}^2\, ax\, dx = \frac{1}{a}\tanh ax + C$

132. $\displaystyle\int \text{csch}^2\, ax\, dx = -\frac{1}{a}\coth ax + C$

133. $\displaystyle\int \text{sech}^n\, ax\, dx = \frac{\text{sech}^{n-2} ax \tanh ax}{(n-1)a} + \frac{n-2}{n-1}\int \text{sech}^{n-2}\, ax\, dx, \qquad n \neq 1$

134. $\displaystyle\int \text{csch}^n\, ax\, dx = -\frac{\text{csch}^{n-2} ax \coth ax}{(n-1)a} - \frac{n-2}{n-1}\int \text{csch}^{n-2}\, ax\, dx, \qquad n \neq 1$

135. $\displaystyle\int \text{sech}^n\, ax \tanh ax\, dx = -\frac{\text{sech}^n ax}{na} + C, \qquad n \neq 0$

136. $\displaystyle\int \text{csch}^n\, ax \coth ax\, dx = -\frac{\text{csch}^n ax}{na} + C, \qquad n \neq 0$

137. $\displaystyle\int e^{ax} \sinh bx\, dx = \frac{e^{ax}}{2}\left[\frac{e^{bx}}{a+b} - \frac{e^{-bx}}{a-b}\right] + C, \qquad a^2 \neq b^2$

138. $\displaystyle\int e^{ax} \cosh bx\, dx = \frac{e^{ax}}{2}\left[\frac{e^{bx}}{a+b} + \frac{e^{-bx}}{a-b}\right] + C, \qquad a^2 \neq b^2$

139. $\displaystyle\int_0^\infty x^{n-1} e^{-x}\, dx = \Gamma(n) = (n-1)!, \qquad n > 0$

140. $\displaystyle\int_0^\infty e^{-ax^2}\, dx = \frac{1}{2}\sqrt{\frac{\pi}{a}}, \qquad a > 0$

141. $\displaystyle\int_0^{\pi/2} \sin^n x\, dx = \int_0^{\pi/2} \cos^n x\, dx = \begin{cases} \dfrac{1 \cdot 3 \cdot 5 \cdots (n-1)}{2 \cdot 4 \cdot 6 \cdots n} \cdot \dfrac{\pi}{2}, & \text{if } n \text{ is an even integer} \geq 2 \\[2mm] \dfrac{2 \cdot 4 \cdot 6 \cdots (n-1)}{3 \cdot 5 \cdot 7 \cdots n}, & \text{if } n \text{ is an odd integer} \geq 3 \end{cases}$

Conic Sections

A **circle** is the set of points in a plane whose distance from a fixed point in the plane is constant. The fixed point is the **center** of the circle; the constant distance is the **radius**. An **ellipse** is the set of points in a plane whose distances from two fixed points in the plane have a constant sum. A **hyperbola** is the set of points in a plane whose distances from two fixed points in the plane have a constant difference. In each case, the fixed points are the **foci** of the conic section. A **parabola** is the set of points in a plane equidistant from a given fixed point and a given fixed line in the plane. The fixed point is the **focus** of the parabola; the line is the **directrix.**

Ellipses and Circle in Standard Position

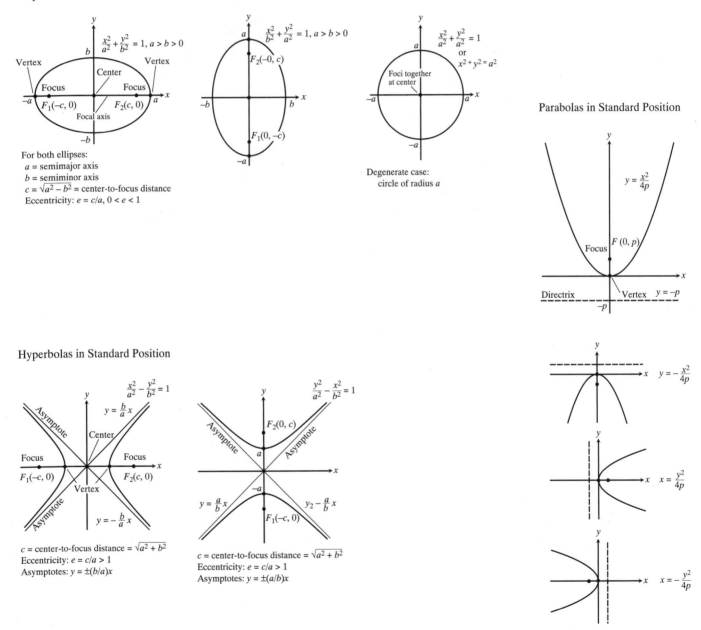

For both ellipses:
a = semimajor axis
b = semiminor axis
$c = \sqrt{a^2 - b^2}$ = center-to-focus distance
Eccentricity: $e = c/a$, $0 < e < 1$

Degenerate case:
circle of radius a

Parabolas in Standard Position

$y = \frac{x^2}{4p}$

$y = -\frac{x^2}{4p}$

$x = \frac{y^2}{4p}$

$x = -\frac{y^2}{4p}$

All parabolas have eccentricity $e = 1$

Hyperbolas in Standard Position

$\frac{x^2}{a^2} - \frac{y^2}{b^2} = 1$

c = center-to-focus distance = $\sqrt{a^2 + b^2}$
Eccentricity: $e = c/a > 1$
Asymptotes: $y = \pm(b/a)x$

$\frac{y^2}{a^2} - \frac{x^2}{b^2} = 1$

c = center-to-focus distance = $\sqrt{a^2 + b^2}$
Eccentricity: $e = c/a > 1$
Asymptotes: $y = \pm(a/b)x$

Vector Operator Formulas in Cartesian, Cylindrical, and Spherical Coordinates; Vector Identities

Formulas for Grad, Div, Curl, and the Laplacian

	Cartesian (x, y, z) $\mathbf{i}$, $\mathbf{j}$, and $\mathbf{k}$ are unit vectors in the directions of increasing x, y, and z. F_x, F_y, and F_z are the scalar components of $\mathbf{F}(x, y, z)$ in these directions.	Cylindrical (r, θ, z) $\mathbf{u}_r$, $\mathbf{u}_\theta$, and $\mathbf{k}$ are unit vectors in the directions of increasing r, θ, and z. F_r, F_θ, and F_z are the scalar components of $\mathbf{F}(r, \theta, z)$ in these directions.	Spherical (ρ, ϕ, θ) $\mathbf{u}_\rho$, $\mathbf{u}_\phi$, and $\mathbf{u}_\theta$ are unit vectors in the directions of increasing ρ, ϕ, and θ. F_ρ, F_ϕ, and F_θ are the scalar components of $\mathbf{F}(\rho, \phi, \theta)$ in these directions.
Gradient	$\nabla f = \dfrac{\partial f}{\partial x}\mathbf{i} + \dfrac{\partial f}{\partial y}\mathbf{j} + \dfrac{\partial f}{\partial z}\mathbf{k}$	$\nabla f = \dfrac{\partial f}{\partial r}\mathbf{u}_r + \dfrac{1}{r}\dfrac{\partial f}{\partial \theta}\mathbf{u}_\theta + \dfrac{\partial f}{\partial z}\mathbf{k}$	$\nabla f = \dfrac{\partial f}{\partial \rho}\mathbf{u}_\rho + \dfrac{1}{\rho}\dfrac{\partial f}{\partial \phi}\mathbf{u}_\phi + \dfrac{1}{\rho \sin \phi}\dfrac{\partial f}{\partial \theta}\mathbf{u}_\theta$
Divergence	$\nabla \cdot \mathbf{F} = \dfrac{\partial F_x}{\partial x} + \dfrac{\partial F_y}{\partial y} + \dfrac{\partial F_z}{\partial z}$	$\nabla \cdot \mathbf{F} = \dfrac{1}{r}\dfrac{\partial}{\partial r}(rF_r) + \dfrac{1}{r}\dfrac{\partial F_\theta}{\partial \theta} + \dfrac{\partial F_z}{\partial z}$	$\nabla \cdot \mathbf{F} = \dfrac{1}{\rho^2}\dfrac{\partial}{\partial \rho}(\rho^2 F_\rho)$ $+ \dfrac{1}{\rho \sin \phi}\dfrac{\partial}{\partial \phi}(F_\phi \sin \phi) + \dfrac{1}{\rho \sin \phi}\dfrac{\partial F_\theta}{\partial \theta}$
Curl	$\nabla \times \mathbf{F} = \begin{vmatrix} \mathbf{i} & \mathbf{j} & \mathbf{k} \\ \dfrac{\partial}{\partial x} & \dfrac{\partial}{\partial y} & \dfrac{\partial}{\partial z} \\ F_x & F_y & F_z \end{vmatrix}$	$\nabla \times \mathbf{F} = \begin{vmatrix} \dfrac{1}{r}\mathbf{u}_r & \mathbf{u}_\theta & \dfrac{1}{r}\mathbf{k} \\ \dfrac{\partial}{\partial r} & \dfrac{\partial}{\partial \theta} & \dfrac{\partial}{\partial z} \\ F_r & F_\theta & F_z \end{vmatrix}$	$\nabla \times \mathbf{F} = \begin{vmatrix} \dfrac{\mathbf{u}_\rho}{\rho^2 \sin \phi} & \dfrac{\mathbf{u}_\phi}{\rho \sin \phi} & \dfrac{\mathbf{u}_\theta}{\rho} \\ \dfrac{\partial}{\partial \rho} & \dfrac{\partial}{\partial \phi} & \dfrac{\partial}{\partial \theta} \\ F_\rho & \rho F_\phi & \rho \sin \phi\, F_\theta \end{vmatrix}$
Laplacian	$\nabla^2 f = \dfrac{\partial^2 f}{\partial x^2} + \dfrac{\partial^2 f}{\partial y^2} + \dfrac{\partial^2 f}{\partial z^2}$	$\nabla^2 f = \dfrac{1}{r}\dfrac{\partial}{\partial r}\left(r\dfrac{\partial f}{\partial r}\right) + \dfrac{1}{r^2}\dfrac{\partial^2 f}{\partial \theta^2} + \dfrac{\partial^2 f}{\partial z^2}$	$\nabla^2 f = \dfrac{1}{\rho^2}\dfrac{\partial}{\partial \rho}\left(\rho^2 \dfrac{\partial f}{\partial \rho}\right)$ $+ \dfrac{1}{\rho^2 \sin \phi}\dfrac{\partial}{\partial \phi}\left(\sin \phi \dfrac{\partial f}{\partial \rho}\right) + \dfrac{1}{\rho^2 \sin^2 \phi}\dfrac{\partial^2 f}{\partial \theta^2}$

Vector Triple Products

$(\mathbf{u} \times \mathbf{v}) \cdot \mathbf{w} = (\mathbf{v} \times \mathbf{w}) \cdot \mathbf{u} = (\mathbf{w} \times \mathbf{u}) \cdot \mathbf{v}$

$\mathbf{u} \times (\mathbf{v} \times \mathbf{w}) = (\mathbf{u} \cdot \mathbf{w})\mathbf{v} - (\mathbf{u} \cdot \mathbf{v})\mathbf{w}$

Vector Identities for the Cartesian Form of the Operator ∇

In the identities listed here, $f(x, y, z)$ and $g(x, y, z)$ are differentiable scalar functions and $\mathbf{u}(x, y, z)$ and $\mathbf{v}(x, y, z)$ are differentiable vector functions.

$\nabla \cdot f\mathbf{v} = f\nabla \cdot \mathbf{v} + \mathbf{v} \cdot \nabla f = f\nabla \cdot \mathbf{v} + (\mathbf{v} \cdot \nabla) f$

$\nabla \times f\mathbf{v} - f\nabla \times \mathbf{v} + \nabla f \times \mathbf{v}$

$\nabla \cdot (\nabla \times \mathbf{v}) = 0$

$\nabla \times (\nabla f) = \mathbf{0}$

$\nabla(fg) = f\nabla g + g\nabla f$

$\nabla(\mathbf{u} \cdot \mathbf{v}) = (\mathbf{u} \cdot \nabla)\mathbf{v} + (\mathbf{v} \cdot \nabla)\mathbf{u} + \mathbf{u} \times (\nabla \times \mathbf{v}) + \mathbf{v} \times (\nabla \times \mathbf{u})$

$\nabla \cdot (\mathbf{u} \times \mathbf{v}) = \mathbf{v} \cdot (\nabla \times \mathbf{u}) - \mathbf{u} \cdot (\nabla \times \mathbf{v})$

$\nabla \times (\mathbf{u} \times \mathbf{v}) = (\mathbf{v} \cdot \nabla)\mathbf{u} - (\mathbf{u} \cdot \nabla)\mathbf{v} + \mathbf{u}(\nabla \cdot \mathbf{v}) - \mathbf{v}(\nabla \cdot \mathbf{u})$

$\nabla \times (\nabla \times \mathbf{v}) = \nabla(\nabla \cdot \mathbf{v}) - (\nabla \cdot \nabla)\mathbf{v} = \nabla(\nabla \cdot \mathbf{v}) - \nabla^2\mathbf{v}$

$(\nabla \times \mathbf{v}) \times \mathbf{v} = (\mathbf{v} \cdot \nabla)\mathbf{v} - \dfrac{1}{2}\nabla(\mathbf{v} \cdot \mathbf{v})$